HOW TO FIND THE RIGHT PAGE

ILLUSTRATED GUIDE TO BRITAIN'S COAST divides the coastline into 145 sections, each of which is indicated by a box on the key maps on these end-papers (showing Southern England and Wales) or on the end-papers at the back of the book (showing Northern England and Scotland). The number in each box is the number of the page on which the description of each section of coastline begins. The numbering starts at the Severn Bridge, near Bristol, and the guide proceeds anti-clockwise round the entire coast of Britain and main offshore islands.

AA

ILLUSTRATED GUIDE
TO BRITAIN'S COAST

ILLUSTRATED GUIDE TO BRITAIN'S COAST
was edited and designed by
The Reader's Digest Association Limited
for Drive Publications Limited
Berkeley Square House, London W1X 5PD

First Edition Copyright © 1984
Drive Publications Limited
Reprinted with amendments 1987

Printed in Great Britain

Front cover: Bat's Head from Durdle Door, Dorset.
Back cover: Bayard's Cove, Dartmouth, Devon.
This page: The beach at Hastings, East Sussex.
Pages 4-5: Compton Bay, Isle of Wight.
Pages 6-7: The harbour at Portree, Island of Skye.

ILLUSTRATED GUIDE TO BRITAIN'S COAST

PUBLISHED BY
DRIVE PUBLICATIONS LIMITED
FOR THE AUTOMOBILE ASSOCIATION
FANUM HOUSE, BASINGSTOKE,
HAMPSHIRE RG21 2EA

The publishers would like to thank the following
people for major contributions to this book:

WRITERS
Peter Argyle
John Kington, MSc
Andrew Lawson
Philip Llewellin
John Man
David Owen
Franklyn Perring,
    MA, PhD, FLS, FI Biol
Robert Sackville-West
Tom Sanders
Keith Spence
Ann Tweedy
David W. Williams, LlM, PhD

PHOTOGRAPHERS
Martyn Adelman
Neil Holmes
Ian Howes
Andrew Lawson
Colin Molyneux

John Sims
Patrick Thurston
Trevor Wood
Jon Wyand

ARTISTS
David Baird
Colin Emberson
The Garden Studio:
    Owain Bell
    Josephine Martin
    Liz Peperall
    Gillian Platt
    Andrew Riley
    Adrian Williams
Tony Graham
Hayward & Martin
Norman Lacey
Linden Artists:
    Trevor Boyer
    John Francis

We would also like to thank the Chief Coastguard and
Officers of Her Majesty's Coastguard for checking
information about foreshore safety and hazards; the
Nature Conservancy Council, the Royal Society for
Nature Conservation and the Royal Society for the
Protection of Birds for checking information about
nature reserves; and local authorities, Tourist Boards
and Tourist Information Centres round Britain's coast
for their co-operation.

CONTENTS

MILE-BY-MILE ROUND BRITAIN'S COAST

An illustrated survey, starting at the Severn Estuary, near Bristol, and continuing round our entire coastline

8 - 349

SPECIAL FEATURES

EXPLORING THE LIVING WORLD
OF OUR SEASHORE

How to recognise the plants and animals of sandy shores and rock pools, shingle beaches and estuaries

350 - 369

COAST OF CONTRASTS

Boats roll gently at their moorings in the tranquil harbour at Portree, in the Island of Skye, as dawn light floods up behind the 1,300 ft peak of Ben Tianavaig. It is a very different coastal scene from the flat green pastures flanking the swift waters of the Severn Estuary, where our journey of discovery on the following pages begins.

The journey follows the entire coastline of England, Scotland and Wales, a zigzagging 6,000 mile route packed with contrasts. First it moves southwards along the South-West Peninsula towards the promontory of Land's End, where huge granite cliffs brave the onslaught of the Atlantic rollers. The face of the land changes as the route runs eastwards past sheltered fishing coves and holiday beaches fronting the English Channel to reach the white cliffs of Dover, on a tip of England that has been a target for invaders over the centuries. The journey then follows the North Sea coast, past the slumbering creeks and salt-marshes of East Anglia to the high cliffs and deep-cut bays of Yorkshire and the silvery beaches of Northumbria that stretch to the Scottish border.

In eastern Scotland the route lies beside great firths and past golf links and fishing ports on the way to the northernmost shores of Britain, where sea-birds wheel over towering cliffs and light-housemen keep lonely vigil. From Cape Wrath, at Scotland's north-west tip, the route sweeps southwards once more, in and out along the sea lochs of the Western Highlands through some of Britain's most dramatic scenery, then down the Clyde coast and round the Mull of Galloway back towards England. After following the fringe of Lakeland and Lancashire, the journey leads at last through Wales, with its broad bays and jutting headlands, back to the starting point beside the Severn.

The journey takes in, too, our main offshore islands, from the Channel Islands, which are nearer to France than to Britain, to Orkney and Shetland, which are closer to the Arctic Circle than to London. The guide can be read page by page as a continuous journey; but the key maps on the end-papers, showing the way the coastline has been divided, enable you to arrive instantly at any section of the coast you choose.

Resorts and a seafaring city on the Severn estuary

Abnormal tides sweep up and down the lower reaches of the River Severn's broad estuary, racing over acres of soft, glistening mud which gives way to sandy beaches near Weston-super-Mare. The tide can rise and fall more than 50 ft under the Severn Bridge. Bristol, though no longer a great port, retains many links with the days when it was one of Britain's main 'gateways' to Africa and the Americas.

① WESTON-SUPER-MARE

Reaching the sea at low tide involves a walk of more than 1 mile, but Weston-super-Mare's sandy beach more than compensates for the mud-and-shingle shoreline which runs up the coast to the Severn Bridge. Flanked by Brean Down and the wooded ridge of Worlebury Hill, which was fortified during the Iron Age, Weston Bay also provides safe swimming at high water, except at its southern edge, where there are strong currents at the mouth of the River Axe.

Like many other resorts, Weston was little more than a fishing village until the seaside was 'discovered' at the end of the 18th century. It expanded rapidly after 1841, when the railway arrived, and emphasised its holiday-town status by building two piers between 1867 and 1904. Both have survived, adding a dash of Victorian and Edwardian character to the atmosphere of a lively, modern resort.

As well as the pier and a full range of seaside attractions, Weston has a museum, an art gallery, and an aquarium. There are two markets on Sunday, a fair in June and a carnival in July or August. There are riding stables, boat trips and motor boats for hire, fishing trips and fishing from the shore, and facilities for water-skiing and sailing.

TWO ISLAND NATURE RESERVES

Nature reserves occupy two islands in the Bristol Channel. Steep Holm, once a refuge of Viking raiders, belongs to a trust set up in memory of the author and naturalist Kenneth Allsop. It can be visited on Saturdays and Bank Holiday Mondays in summer by boat from Weston-super-Mare. A 2 mile nature trail takes in the sights of the island, including the only wild clumps in Britain of the Mediterranean peony, introduced by monks in the 12th or 13th century. Flat Holm can be visited only by arrangement with South Glamorgan County Council.

Wild peony
Paeonia mascula
Apr.-May

② SAND BAY

A long, low, shrub-covered bank, backed by caravan sites and a holiday camp, overlooks this popular beach where the tide retreats for more than 1 mile. Most of the shore is sandy, but there are patches of mud and expanses of sea-washed turf at the northern end. There are good views from Middle Hope, a headland owned by the National Trust.

At the southern end of the bay, a wooded toll road skirts Worlebury Hill and leads to Weston-super-Mare.

③ WOODSPRING PRIORY

The medieval priory church had been used as a farmhouse for more than 400 years when it was bought as a joint venture by the Landmark Trust and National Trust in 1969. The restored building, together with other parts of the priory that are not open to visitors, stands in tranquil surroundings at the end of a narrow lane. It is seen at its best in late spring and early summer, when the apple trees are heavy with blossom.

The priory was founded in 1210 by William de Courtenay, whose grandfather was one of the assassins of Thomas Becket in 1170.

④ CLEVEDON

Georgian, Regency and many Victorian buildings illustrate some of the stages by which Clevedon developed from a fishing village to a small, fashionable resort during the 19th century. Its gradual expansion owed much to the Elton family of Clevedon Court, a manor house built by Sir John de Clevedon in the 14th century and now owned by the National Trust. Sir Abraham Elton, a wealthy Bristol merchant, acquired the Court estate in 1709. Open to the public on certain days in summer, Clevedon Court has a collection of Nailsea glass and Elton-ware, and there are rare shrubs in the terraced gardens. At Moor Lane, not far from Clevedon Court, there is a craft centre.

Clevedon is proud of its sedate, Victorian atmosphere – typified by the town's famous bowling greens – and of links with such literary figures as the novelist William Thackeray and the poets Samuel Taylor

CLEVEDON PIER *Wrought-iron rails form the graceful Victorian pier, awaiting restoration, which flanks the town's main beach.*

Coleridge and Lord Tennyson, whose poem *In Memoriam* refers to St Andrew's Church. A pier built in 1869 flanks the main beach, where mud mingles with shingle and expanses of flat rock. A footpath known as Lovers' Walk starts at the top of Marine Parade, passes Ladye Bay, where steps lead down to a shore of shingle and seaweed-draped rocks, and follows the coast to Portishead.

There are seaside entertainments, a museum, rowing boats for hire on a marine lake, sea fishing, boat trips and sailing.

Clevedon Court

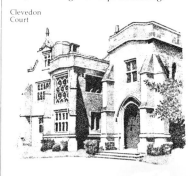

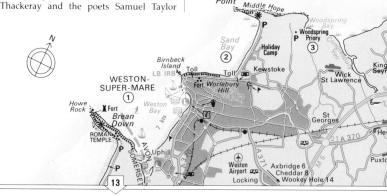

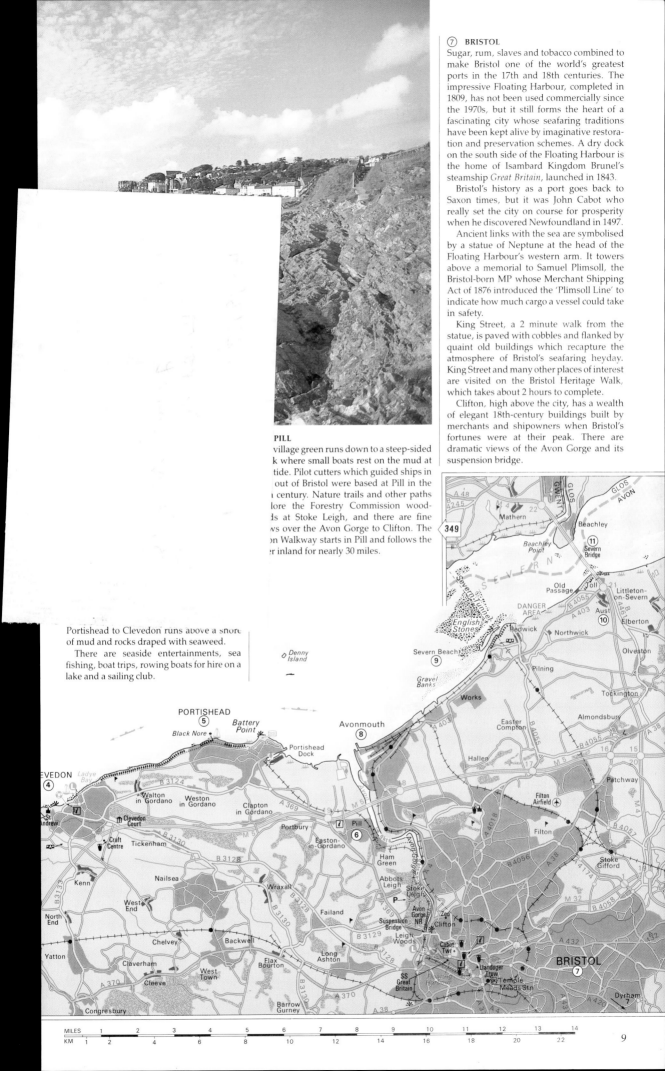

⑦ BRISTOL

Sugar, rum, slaves and tobacco combined to make Bristol one of the world's greatest ports in the 17th and 18th centuries. The impressive Floating Harbour, completed in 1809, has not been used commercially since the 1970s, but it still forms the heart of a fascinating city whose seafaring traditions have been kept alive by imaginative restoration and preservation schemes. A dry dock on the south side of the Floating Harbour is the home of Isambard Kingdom Brunel's steamship *Great Britain*, launched in 1843.

Bristol's history as a port goes back to Saxon times, but it was John Cabot who really set the city on course for prosperity when he discovered Newfoundland in 1497.

Ancient links with the sea are symbolised by a statue of Neptune at the head of the Floating Harbour's western arm. It towers above a memorial to Samuel Plimsoll, the Bristol-born MP whose Merchant Shipping Act of 1876 introduced the 'Plimsoll Line' to indicate how much cargo a vessel could take in safety.

King Street, a 2 minute walk from the statue, is paved with cobbles and flanked by quaint old buildings which recapture the atmosphere of Bristol's seafaring heyday. King Street and many other places of interest are visited on the Bristol Heritage Walk, which takes about 2 hours to complete.

Clifton, high above the city, has a wealth of elegant 18th-century buildings built by merchants and shipowners when Bristol's fortunes were at their peak. There are dramatic views of the Avon Gorge and its suspension bridge.

PILL

village green runs down to a steep-sided k where small boats rest on the mud at tide. Pilot cutters which guided ships in out of Bristol were based at Pill in the century. Nature trails and other paths lore the Forestry Commission wood-ls at Stoke Leigh, and there are fine ws over the Avon Gorge to Clifton. The on Walkway starts in Pill and follows the r inland for nearly 30 miles.

Portishead to Clevedon runs above a shore of mud and rocks draped with seaweed.

There are seaside entertainments, sea fishing, boat trips, rowing boats for hire on a lake and a sailing club.

Bristol has five museums, and an art gallery and arts centre. Markets include a fish market every weekday except Monday, and an antiques and craft market on Thursday and Friday.

⑧ AVONMOUTH

Docks opened in 1877 have enabled Avonmouth to replace Bristol, 6 miles inland up the spectacular Avon Gorge, as one of Britain's busiest ports. Backed by extensive industrial estates, the docks can take ships of up to 70,000 tons and handle cargoes ranging from cocoa beans to chemicals. On the opposite side of the river mouth is the Royal Portbury Dock, opened in 1977.

During the summer, Avonmouth is a base for cruises by *Waverley*, the world's last seagoing paddle-steamer. She visits such places as Penarth, Ilfracombe and Minehead.

⑨ SEVERN BEACH

Walkers and cyclists make the most of the sea-wall which protects Severn Beach and looks out over mud and shingle to the coast of South Wales. Low tide reveals the English Stones reef, where a party of Roundheads were drowned during the Civil War; after being told by a Royalist ferryman that they had reached Wales, they left their boat and were caught by the tide. Britain's longest railway tunnel runs under the reef. Just over 4 miles from end to end, it was built between 1873 and 1886, and lined with more than 76 million bricks.

⑩ AUST

Now a sleepy little place, bright with flowers in summer, Aust was a major landmark for travellers until the Severn Bridge was opened in 1966. As many as 25,000 cars passed through the village every month on their way to and from Old Passage, where three ferries operated. Reeds now spring up through the derelict jetty, but a footpath provides impressive views of the bridge.

⑪ SEVERN BRIDGE

A main span of 3,240 ft, slung between towers 443 ft high, makes this Britain's third longest suspension bridge, after those spanning the Humber and the Firth of Forth. It was opened by the Queen in 1966.

The tides which send water the colour of drinking chocolate foaming under the bridge are exceeded only by those of the Bay of Fundy in Nova Scotia, Canada. Spring tides have an average rise and fall of almost 41 ft – nearly three times greater than the average figure for the British Isles – and have been known to exceed 50 ft.

The bridge's graceful lines and majestic scale can be appreciated from a viewpoint at the Aust service area on the M4.

LOCAL SERVICES

Tourist information Bristol 293891; Weston-super-Mare 26838

HM Coastguard Swansea 66534 or 67761 for information. 999 in emergency (ask for coastguard).

Weather Bristol 8091

Local radio BBC Bristol, 194/227 m, 1548/1323 kHz, 95.5 MHz; IBA West, 238 m, 1260 kHz, 96.3 MHz.

PLACES TO SEE INLAND

Cheddar, 10 miles SE of Weston-super-Mare. Gorge and caves, daily. Museum of Prehistoric Man, daily in summer.

Dyrham Park (NT), 10 miles E of Bristol, via A46. Late 17th-century house and deer park. Park daily, house and garden most afternoons in summer.

King John's Hunting Lodge (NT), Axbridge, 8 miles SE of Weston-super-Mare. Early Tudor, with local history museum. Afternoons in summer.

Wookey Hole, 16 miles SE of Weston-super-Mare. Caves and underground river, fairground collection, Madame Tussaud's store-room. Daily.

BRISTOL, SEAFARING CITY THAT PAVED NEW WAYS TO THE NEW WORLD

Though 6 miles from the sea, Bristol was England's busiest west coast port for hundreds of years. Before the Normans came, Saxons were trading from *Bricgstoc*, 'the place of the bridge', and in the Middle Ages it became a major cloth-exporting port, with wine the principal import. In the 15th century John Cabot and his son Sebastian sailed west from Bristol to seek new lands, and they and other explorers opened up new markets which were exploited by the Society of Merchant Venturers of Bristol, which was granted a royal charter in 1552. Bristol flourished in its trade with the newly discovered lands, and the tidal Avon became a busy waterway with ships sailing through the twisting Avon Gorge to the docks tucked away inland. The Bristol-based ships became known for their smartness and efficiency – hence the saying 'shipshape and Bristol fashion'.

Bristol thrived on the slave trade, and in the first half of the 18th century thousands of black slaves were transported to America, in vile conditions, to be exchanged for cargoes of rum, sugar and tobacco to meet the needs of the city's expanding industries. War with America in 1775-81 and the abolition of the slave trade in 1833 were serious setbacks for the port, but it also faced a threat from the port of Liverpool whose hinterland provided the stage for the Industrial Revolution. Liverpool had docks unaffected by the tides, and although the Avon had been diverted and a 'floating harbour' created in 1809, Bristol could not handle the same amount of traffic as its competitor. The Bristol Dock Company, in 1832, engaged Isambard Kingdom Brunel to improve the docks. In 1837 Brunel's steamship *Great Western*, at 236 ft long the largest steamship built up to that time, left Bristol to become the world's first transatlantic liner, but the crippling dock charges imposed by the Bristol Dock Company forced the Great Western Steamship Company to operate from the port's rival – Liverpool.

THE BUSY AVON *In the late 19th century quays extended into the heart of Bristol. The area beyond the bridge is now part of the city centre, still overlooked by the classical portico of St Mary's on the Quay and the 15th-century St Stephen's Church tower.*

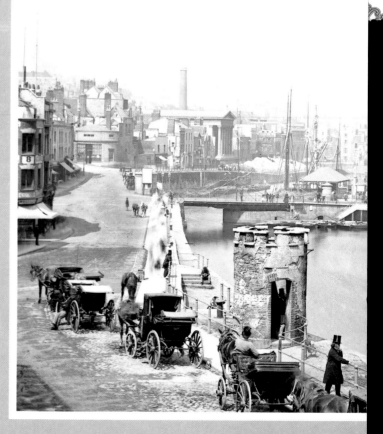

NEW FOUND LAND *A Venetian navigator named John Cabot came to Bristol in the 15th century in search of adventure, an ambition soon realised with the help of Bristol merchants who equipped him for a voyage to discover new lands. About May 20, 1497, Cabot sailed in the* Matthew, *and 35 days later he raised the English flag on an unknown soil, claiming this 'New Found Land' for Henry VII. Bristol remembers him by the Cabot Tower erected on Brandon Hill in 1898.*

MEMORIAL OF SHAME *This tombstone of a negro servant in Henbury churchyard is a reminder of Bristol's days as a slave-trading port. It is said that the Earl of Suffolk released Scipio from slavery and treated him like a son.*

BRUNEL – THE 'LITTLE GIANT' OF VICTORIAN ENGINEERING

In 1831 the 25-year-old engineer Isambard Kingdom Brunel won a competition for the design of a bridge to span the Avon Gorge – the first of many projects that were to make the name Brunel synonymous with Bristol. In 1833 Brunel was appointed Engineer of the newly formed Great Western Railway Company, which proposed to build a line from London to Bristol. He gave them a railway that became renowned for its speed, efficiency and safety. Before the first rail had been laid he was making plans for a steamship that would effectively extend the line to New York. The *Great Western*, a paddle-steamer of 1,340 tons, was launched in 1837, and six years later it was joined by the SS *Great Britain*, the world's first ocean-going ship to be built of iron and the first large ship to be driven by a screw propeller.

Brunel had an enormous capacity for work, and during the building of the Great Western Railway would often roll up his sleeves and wield pick and shovel alongside his navvies, who affectionately nicknamed him the 'little giant'. He was truly a giant in his ideas, most of which have survived. The most spectacular of them is the Clifton Suspension Bridge, beset by financial troubles during Brunel's lifetime and completed five years after his death as a memorial to him.

Isambard Kingdom Brunel, a year before his death in 1859

The SS Great Britain, *salvaged from the Falkland Islands in 1970, is back in the dock in which she was built and is being restored to her former glory by the SS* Great Britain *Project. In restoring her, modern plastics have been used for such features as her figurehead, the Royal Coat of Arms, and the flanking trailboards depicting the arts, industry and sciences.*

With a span of more than 702 ft and soaring 245 ft above the Avon Gorge, the Clifton Suspension Bridge was opened in 1864. Its designer, Isambard Brunel, called it 'my first child, my darling'.

PAYING ON THE NAIL *Before Bristol's Corn Exchange was built, business was conducted in the street, and merchants completed their money transactions on four flat-topped bronze pillars called 'nails'. From this tradition arose the expression 'paying on the nail head', or more commonly, 'paying on the nail', meaning to pay cash at the moment a deal is made. The pillars, the earliest dating from the late 16th century, still stand in Corn Street, outside the 18th-century Corn Exchange which was built by John Wood the Elder, the architect of Bath.*

PIRATES' INN *The handsome, half-timbered Llandoger Trow in King Street was renowned as a meeting place for pirates and smugglers in the 18th century, and it is probable that the old inn was the 'Spyglass Inn' of Robert Louis Stevenson's* Treasure Island, *and that the* Hispaniola *of the story set sail from the quayside only a few yards away. The Llandoger Trow may also have been where Daniel Defoe met Alexander Selkirk, the desert-island castaway whose true adventures were the basis of Robinson Crusoe. Built in 1664, originally as three houses, the inn takes its name from a type of Welsh coastal vessel often seen in Bristol.*

Beaches and mud-flats below the Quantock Hills

The steep-sided Mendip and Quantock Hills frame a coastline where the sea retreats well over 2 miles in some places. Low tide exposes huge areas of sand to the north of the River Parrett's estuary and, to the south-west, vast mud-flats where sea-birds congregate. Further west are small bays between reefs of rock. Inland, an intricate network of canalised rivers, streams and ditches drains areas reclaimed from the sea.

① EAST QUANTOXHEAD
Set in a tranquil patchwork of fields between the A39 and Bridgwater Bay, this beautiful hamlet has belonged to the Luttrell family since shortly after the Norman Conquest. Their home, Court House, is not open to visitors. Quaint, stone-built cottages – some thatched, others with ruddy pantiles – stand near the duckpond. A 10 minute walk from the pond leads to a beach of rocks and smooth shingle.

To the east, a lane runs from Kilve to a small parking area from which a similar beach with many long, low-tide rock pools can be reached in a couple of minutes. Low cliffs are vantage points for views of aircraft attacking targets moored offshore. Red flags fly when the range is in use. The lane passes the ivy-clad ruins of a chapel that was burned out in the 19th century. The blaze was thought to have been fuelled by a consignment of smuggled liquor.

EAST QUANTOXHEAD *Low, crumbling cliffs above the beach half a mile from East Quantoxhead stretch westwards towards Blue Ben.*

② LILSTOCK
Narrow lanes wander northwards from the Bridgwater road to a small, scattered hamlet from whose car park a 2 minute walk leads to the sea. There is a broad band of smooth shingle, but the falling tide uncovers a large area of sand. Eastward views along the low, turf-topped cliffs are dominated by the pale grey buildings of the nuclear power station at Hinkley Point.

③ STOLFORD
The sea deserts this tiny, isolated hamlet at low tide, slipping away to leave a vast expanse of treacherous, glistening mud deposited by the River Parrett. From the sea-wall, local fishermen can be seen traversing the shore with contraptions known as 'mud horses' which prevent them sinking as they race against the returning tide. Thanks to the mud horse – a device unique to Stolford – the hostile conditions yield a harvest of shrimps, prawns and the occasional salmon. There is room to park by the sea-wall, where the mud-flats are backed by shingle and slabs of seaweed-covered rock.

Stolford adjoins Bridgwater Bay National Nature Reserve, which includes Stert Island and extends up the Parrett estuary as far as Combwich. Embracing just over 6,000 acres of mud-flats, saltings and farmland, it is an important feeding and roosting ground for many wildfowl and waders which flock there in the autumn and winter. Birds likely to be seen include shelducks – which visit the bay to moult in summer – wigeon and white-fronted geese. Most of the reserve is 'open', but nobody is allowed on Stert Island from November to March, and a permit obtainable from the Warden is needed at other times of the year. Fenning Island can only be visited at high tides at weekends. Though the mud-flats appear safe to walk on, they can be treacherous.

④ COMBWICH
High tides sometimes flood the village streets, but at low water the River Parrett is reduced to a narrow channel flowing between high banks of dark mud. A few boats moor in a creek which flows into the river.

⑤ BRIDGWATER
Abandoned quays and derelict landing stages are reminders that up to the 18th century this was a busy little port, in the days when the River Parrett was one of Somerset's main commercial arteries. The town still flourishes, but the coasters have gone, just as the building of the M5 has removed the traffic jams for which Bridgwater was once notorious.

The town's most famous son, Admiral Sir Robert Blake, is commemorated by a statue in the Cornhill, and the house where he was born in 1599 is now a museum. Blake became Member of Parliament for Bridgwater in 1625, and as a Parliamentarian was one of Cromwell's outstanding commanders during the Civil War. He successfully defended Bristol, Lyme Regis and Taunton against the Royalists, and in 1649 destroyed most of Prince Rupert's fleet off Spain.

There are livestock and produce markets, both on Wednesday.

⑥ BURNHAM-ON-SEA
Burnham's roots delve back to Saxon times, but the most significant figure in the small town's history is the enterprising Rev. David Davies. At the start of the 19th century he was granted Parliamentary permission to build a lighthouse and levy tolls on ships using the port of Bridgwater. Hoping to turn Burnham into a fashionable spa, he sank wells · on the shore. Opinions about the waters varied considerably – one disgruntled visitor said they smelled like a cesspool blended with bad horseradish – but the venture established the town as a seaside resort.

Most of the beach is sandy, but areas of mud are exposed in some places at low water, when swift currents make it unsafe to bathe. There are views across the mouth of the River Parrett to the Stert Island bird sanctuary. As well as the usual seaside attractions, a regatta is held in August and a carnival in November. There is fishing from the shore for skate, codling, whiting and conger eels. Activities include water-skiing and sailing.

SENTINEL ON STILTS *The lighthouse on the beach at Burnham-on-Sea was built in the 1800s to warn ships of sandbanks, but is no longer used.*

⑦ BERROW
A small holiday village which merges with Burnham-on-Sea, Berrow nestles behind sand-dunes and a golf course which lead to the sandy 'desert' of Berrow Flats that sweeps from Brean Down to the mouth of the River Parrett. Views inland are dominated by the grassy cone of Brent Knoll, once islanded by marshes, on whose summit the outlines of an Iron Age fort are clearly visible. The isolated hill was also used as a place of refuge when Vikings raided the coast in the 8th century.

ASHORE BY MUD HORSE
Some fishermen at Stolford use a unique wooden-framed vehicle called a 'mud horse' to reach their shrimp nets far out on the mud at low tide. The task of emptying the shrimp nets of the catch and repairing torn nets is a race against time. Without his mud horse to support him and his catch the fisherman could not reach the shore before being engulfed by the incoming tide.

The mud horses can be seen in use in the Parrett estuary from April to December, and shrimps are sold at some cottages in Stolford during the summer.

A shrimp fisherman and his mud horse

used by an anti-aircraft unit during the Second World War.

A bird sanctuary was established on Brean Down in 1912. Among the many birds which may be seen are the skylark, jackdaw, rock pipit, peregrine falcon, various gulls and many autumn migrants. Pollock, cod, bass and conger eels are among the fish likely to be caught from the rocks.

BERROW FLATS *Brean Down, a mile-long limestone finger jutting out into the Bristol Channel, gives a grandstand view of sand-flats 100 yds wide extending as far as Burnham-on-Sea.*

⑧ BREAN

A world apart from Brean's holiday camp and caravan sites is the nearby St Bridget's Church, which is believed to have been founded by Irish monks in the 6th century. The present building dates from the 13th century.

A long, low ridge which broadens out into extensive dunes towards Berrow overlooks an immense sandy beach where bathing is safe at high tide. Set back from the northern end of the beach, sheltered by Brean Down, is a tropical bird garden.

St Bridget's Church, Brean

⑨ BREAN DOWN

A steep, stepped path leads walkers to the crest of Brean Down, a bold, limestone headland whose 159 acres have been owned by the National Trust since 1954. It was the site of a Roman temple, excavated in 1957, and retains traces of a field system believed to date from the Iron Age.

At the seaward end of the headland are the ruins of a fort built in 1867 when there were fears of a French invasion. It housed 50 men and was armed with seven muzzle-loaded cannon. The fort was abandoned after the magazine exploded in 1900, but was

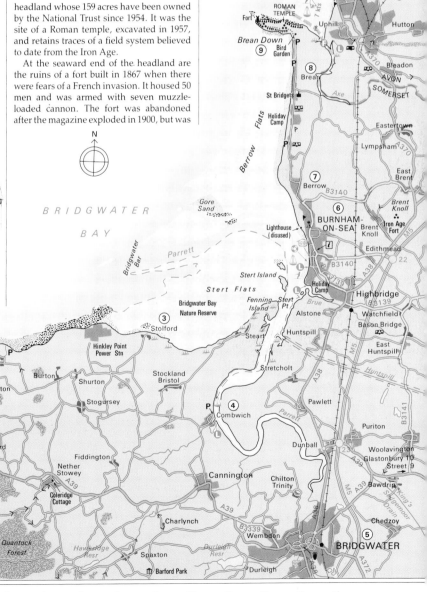

Steep, wooded slopes flanking Minehead's flat sands

Tiny hamlets nestle among wooded hills rising steeply from the Somerset coast. From vantage points such as Selworthy Beacon there are views northwards across the Bristol Channel and southwards on to Exmoor, with its wild ponies, open moors and bubbling streams. The coast changes its character at Minehead, where clean flat sands begin and sweep eastwards, with some shingle and smooth rock, towards the quiet port of Watchet.

① CULBONE

A 2 mile woodland walk from Porlock Weir, following a track etched into steep slopes above the sea, leads to the remarkable church at Culbone. Hidden away in a lonely combe, the medieval building is only 34 ft long by 12 ft wide and is the smallest completed church in regular use anywhere in England. Seats for about 30 people include a family-sized box pew.

The walk can be reduced to a round trip of 3 miles by parking at the foot of the narrow toll road which climbs Ashley Combe and joins the A39 on Culbone Hill, more than 1,000 ft above the broad waters of Porlock Bay.

② PORLOCK WEIR

A sturdy arm of shingle enclosing a tidal inlet enabled Porlock Weir to become a small port when Porlock's harbour was left high and dry by the fickle sea during the Middle Ages. Reached by a narrow channel between banks of sea-smoothed stones, the dock has gates which enable small craft to remain afloat when the tide ebbs.

Attractive old buildings, some colour-washed and roofed with thatch, look out over the 2 mile crescent of Porlock Bay to Hurlstone Point and the steep, green slopes of Bossington Hill. They provided food and shelter for sailors in the days when Porlock Weir's coasters traded across the Bristol Channel, taking timber to South Wales and returning with coal. Boat trips are available.

③ PORLOCK

Set in a natural bowl, flanked by hills whose gradients and acute corners were feared and respected by pioneering motorists, this old, mellow village looks out over fields to the sea that edged northwards centuries ago. The most convenient route to the shore is by way of the lovely little village of Bossington, at the foot of Bossington Hill. A track leads on to a point where the shingle bank is breached by a stream, and there is a small parking area. Strong currents make swimming dangerous anywhere in the bay, but there are good views and the shingle is smooth enough to allow comfortable sunbathing.

④ SELWORTHY

Almost too good to be true, this magical little cluster of thatched, white-walled cottages climbs a tree-clad hillside and looks southwards to the high, rolling heart of the Exmoor National Park. It is watched over by the 14th-century tower of a lovely church whose elaborate roof is a triumph of the woodcarver's art. The pulpit has a 17th-century hour glass used to time sermons, and the iron-bound parish chest dates from the same period. Allerford, 1 mile west, is another picture-postcard village whose ancient packhorse bridge is paved with cobbles.

Selworthy is the starting point for a memorable walk which climbs through woodlands to the gorse-gold summit of Selworthy Beacon, which can also be reached by road from Minehead. It is a superb vantage point, 1,013 ft above sea level, and views inland embrace Dunkery Hill, at 1,705 ft the highest point in Somerset.

⑤ MINEHEAD

Minehead's small, snug harbour is at the end of Quay Street, where several 17th-century cottages with colour-washed walls and thatched roofs recall the history of a town whose records go back to Saxon times. The stone quay was built in 1616, when ships traded as far afield as Portugal, Africa and North America. Like other ports in Somerset, notably Porlock, Minehead's fortunes ebbed as the level of the sea dropped – but the quay was extended to create what the novelist Daniel Defoe described as the safest harbour on this side of the Bristol Channel.

The old part of the town climbs the slopes of North Hill and is dominated by a 15th-century church from whose tower a lantern

OLD MINEHEAD *The cottages facing Minehead's harbour date back to the 17th century, when Minehead ships traded with the New World. Today pleasure craft are the main visitors.*

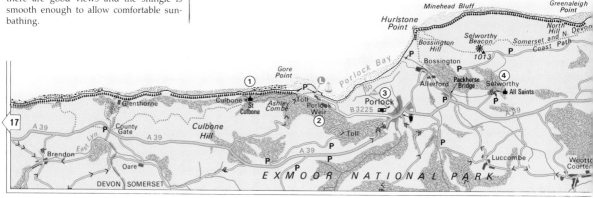

used to guide mariners home. There are walks along Culvercliff, and a nature trail explores North Hill.

Minehead is now a popular holiday resort and touring centre whose mile-long seafront frames a beach where a huge expanse of sand, lightly scattered with pebbles, is revealed at low water. The tide goes out for well over half a mile and sometimes exposes the blackened stumps of a long-lost forest. Strong tidal currents sweep the outer part of the bay, but bathing is safe at high water in the shelter of the harbour. There is a large holiday camp at the eastern end of the beach, where Warren Road ends at a golf course.

Seaside attractions include a miniature railway, and there are fishing trips, boat trips and horses for hire.

Minehead is the western terminus of the privately owned West Somerset Railway, which runs steam-hauled trains between the resort and Bishop's Lydeard during the holiday season. Diesel trains carry passengers throughout the year on the 23 mile route. The company ran its first train in 1976, five years after British Rail closed the line.

STEAM REVIVAL *The independent West Somerset Railway runs from Minehead along the coast to Watchet and then inland to Bishop's Lydeard.*

⑥ DUNSTER
Walking through Dunster is like taking a time-machine journey back through more than 900 years of English history. The setting is beautiful, and few villages can boast such a fascinating collection of mellow, well-preserved buildings, some of which date from the 13th century. The broad High Street

The Yarn Market, Dunster

DUNSTER CASTLE *Dominating the village's skyline is the Norman castle which belonged to the Luttrell family for 600 years.*

runs down to the foot of a steep, isolated hill where the towers and turrets of Dunster Castle rise above the trees. It dates from Norman times and remained in the same family from 1376 until 1976, when it was presented to the National Trust. In 1645-6, during the Civil War, the Royalist garrison withstood a six-month siege before surrendering to a Parliamentary army. One shot fired during the battle hit the picturesque Yarn Market at the opposite end of High Street, and the damage can still be seen.

Dunster's rich heritage includes the Old Nunnery, a tithe barn and a dovecot – all built in the 13th century – a 17th-century watermill which still grinds flour, and a medieval packhorse bridge which spans the River Avill.

To the north, beyond the A39, Dunster Beach is a long stretch of stream-crossed sand and shingle where the tide retreats for more than half a mile. The shore is overlooked by Conygar Hill, whose wooded summit is crowned with a folly tower.

⑦ BLUE ANCHOR
A caravan site overlooks a sandy beach, backed by a narrow strip of shingle, which runs westwards all the way to Minehead. At the eastern end of the beach, where the B3191 swings inland, there are flat rocks where pools are left by the falling tide.

⑧ WATCHET
Somerset's seafaring traditions live on in Watchet, an old-established port whose small harbour is used by ships of up to 2,500 tons. They enter at high water, then rest on the mud while cargoes ranging from timber, cork and steel to wine, cars, farm machinery

and chemicals are loaded or unloaded. Destinations range from Portugal and Spain to the Azores and Pakistan. The present harbour was built after its predecessor was destroyed in the winter of 1900, when a ferocious storm coincided with an abnormally high tide. The old wooden piers had been used to load iron ore, mined in the Brendon Hills, which was shipped to South Wales during the Industrial Revolution.

The port's history is illustrated in the museum in Market Street. During the Civil War a Royalist ship stranded by the falling tide was captured by a troop of enemy soldiers on horseback. Watchet is almost certainly the place where Samuel Taylor Coleridge met the old sailor whose seafaring tales inspired the poet's best known work, *The Rime of the Ancient Mariner.*

⑨ ST AUDRIE'S BAY
In the 19th century, Lord St Audrie built a private gasworks to supply his estate. Traces of the harbour where coal from South Wales was landed have survived, and so has the sunken track used by the fuel-laden packhorses. It runs down to an extensive beach of shingle, sand and long, low tables of tilted rock. Parts of the wall built by Lord St Audrie support a small stretch of the bay's high, crumbling, multi-coloured cliffs. A waterfall cascades on to the shingle a few yards away. The car park above the beach is reached by a toll road which runs down through trees to a small holiday camp.

LOCAL INFORMATION

Tourist information Minehead 2624; Watchet 31824 (summer).

HM Coastguard Hartland 641 for information, 999 in emergency (ask for coastguard).

Weather Bristol 8091.

Local radio BBC Bristol, 194/227 m, 1548/1323 kHz, 95.5/104.4 MHz.

PLACES TO SEE INLAND

Cleeve Abbey, Washford, 2 miles SW of Watchet. 13th-century Cistercian abbey ruins. Daily.

Combe Sydenham Hall, Monksilver, 4 miles S of Watchet. Tudor house, once home of Sir Francis Drake's wife. Most afternoons in summer.

Gaulden Manor, Tolland, 7 miles S of Watchet. 12th-century manor, with gardens. Some afternoons in summer.

Tarr Steps, 13 miles SW of Dunster. Stone clapper bridge across the River Barle near Winsford. Daily.

Taunton, 15 miles SE of Watchet. Somerset County Museum, in medieval castle, incorporates Somerset Light Infantry Museum, most days.

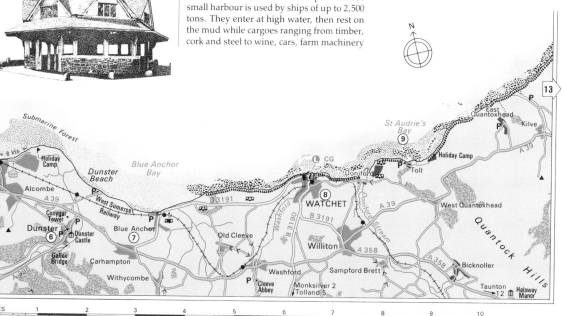

Tall cliffs and deep combes where Exmoor drops to the sea

Exmoor's hills reach the Bristol Channel in a sequence of lofty cliffs and headlands which form one of the most memorable coastlines in England. A few roads wriggle seawards down deep, wooded combes, but the best of the scenery is reserved for walkers. Lynmouth has a sheltered harbour, but elsewhere strong tides and the scarcity of anchorages make this an unsuitable coast for small-boat sailors without expert local knowledge.

① COMBE MARTIN

Men from Derbyshire and Wales were employed in Con.oe Martin's prosperous silver mines during the Middle Ages, but the last workings were closed in the 19th century and all but a few traces have vanished. Strung out along a deep valley, with Exmoor's western flanks rising steeply on one side, the unusually long main street leads to a rock-flanked, shingle-scattered beach with low-tide sands.

Secluded coves, such as Wild Pear Beach, are only a short walk away, and there are many rock pools to be explored. More ambitious walkers can climb the 716 ft Little Hangman and follow the coastal path to its neighbour, the Great Hangman, which towers 1,043 ft above the sea.

The collection of motor cycles on display in Cross Street includes a Brough Superior once owned by T. E. Lawrence – 'Lawrence of Arabia' – while tame monkeys from South America roam the grounds of Higher Leigh Manor on the outskirts. Fishing trips, boat trips and horse riding are available, and a carnival is held in July or August.

② HEDDON'S MOUTH

A 20 minute walk from Hunter's Inn follows the clear waters of the River Heddon down a steep, wooded valley to a secluded cove of pale, sea-smoothed shingle and low-tide sand. Just above the high-water mark are the ruins of a kiln, built in the 18th century, where limestone from South Wales was burned to 'sweeten' Exmoor's acidic soil. Paths on both sides of the river make the

walk a delightful circuit. The path that follows the cliffs eastwards to Woody Bay passes the site of a small fort used by the Romans in the 1st century to keep watch for hostile Welsh tribesmen.

The narrow lane from Hunter's Inn to Combe Martin skirts the summit of Holdstone Down, a heather-clad viewpoint 1,146 ft above sea level. Its neighbour, Trentishoe Down, is part of an extensive tract of beautiful National Trust land that includes the cliffs above Elwill Bay, the lower valley of the River Heddon, and Heddon's Mouth.

③ WOODY BAY

Named after the oak woods which sweep majestically down to the sea, Woody Bay is reached after a 25 minute walk down from the narrow coast road. High cliffs shelter a beach of rocks, shingle and sand. The cliffs are a breeding ground for many sea-birds, including auks, guillemots, kittiwakes, fulmars, shags, razorbills and various gulls. The colonies are seen at their best between March and the end of July.

④ LEE BAY

The most accessible beach between Combe Martin and Lynmouth is sheltered by high, tree-clad slopes and has a broad triangle of low-tide sand framed by smooth expanses of rock. Signs warn that fast-flowing tides can trap walkers exploring the foreshore. Strong currents sweeping past the twin headlands make the bay unsuitable for small boats, but bathing is safe close to the shore in calm weather. Mink have been seen near the

VALLEY OF ROCKS *The limestone mass of Castle Rock, which drops 800 ft to the Bristol Channel, is one of the highest sea cliffs in Britain.*

stream that runs into the bay, and it is also the haunt of dippers, wagtails and the infrequent heron.

A toll road climbs eastwards past Lee Abbey – built as a private house, despite its name – and passes through the Valley of Rocks on its way to Lynton. The valley is remarkable for its jagged pinnacles of eroded limestone known by such names as the Devil's Cheesewring, Ragged Jack and Castle Rock. Mother Meldrum's Cave recalls an old woman who lived in the valley in the 19th century, on whom the novelist R. D. Blackmore based the character of the witch consulted by the heroine of *Lorna Doone.*

⑤ LYNTON AND LYNMOUTH

Although its roots go back to before the Norman Conquest, Lynmouth was not 'discovered' until 1812 when it became a temporary refuge for Percy Bysshe Shelley and his 16-year-old bride, Mary Wollstonecraft. They spent nine weeks in the picturesque little village, avoiding the wrath of the girl's outraged parents. Lyn-

HAVEN BELOW THE HILLS *Lynmouth's peaceful harbour has been carefully restored since the tragedy of 1952, when floodwaters swept down the East and West Lyn after a cloudburst over Exmoor.*

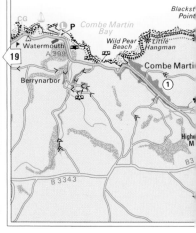

even steeper cliff railway whose 'gravity power' is provided by the 700 gallon water tank fitted to each car. The 862 ft long track, which climbs about 500 ft, was opened in 1890 after most of the money had been provided by the publisher Sir George Newnes, who also built Lynton's Town Hall to commemorate his son's 21st birthday. The Lyn and Exmoor Museum has exhibits which tell the story of the area. There are fishing trips, boat trips and horses for hire.

⑥ WATERS MEET

The rushing East Lyn River meets the Hoaroak Water in a wooded gorge 2 miles east of Lynton. There are beautiful riverside walks, and the National Trust has turned a quaint Victorian fishing lodge into a tea room. The scenery is at its best in the early summer and when autumn turns the leaves to gold, brown and orange.

⑦ COUNTISBURY COMMON

The gorse-clad cliffs on the western edge of the common rise 991 ft above the sea and are said to be the highest in England. There are superb views over the Bristol Channel, and a secluded beach awaits walkers who venture down the long, steep path to Sillery Sand. Footpaths and a narrow lane, closed to cars, run northwards to Foreland Point whose lighthouse is open on weekday afternoons.

County Gate, on the A39 east of Countisbury Common, is the start of a 3 mile nature trail which takes walkers to Glenthorne, where trees shelter the beach. There is a car park at County Gate, where the road crosses the Devon-Somerset boundary.

CLIFF RAILWAY *Cars operated by the weight of water in their tanks climb and descend the steep cliff face between Lynmouth and Lynton.*

mouth's praises were soon being sung by other poets, including Wordsworth, Coleridge and Southey, and it became one of Devon's most popular beauty spots.

Lynmouth became front-page news in August 1952 when weeks of heavy rain culminated in a cloudburst over Exmoor. An estimated 90 million gallons of water fell on the catchment areas of the East and West Lyn rivers in a single night, creating a flood which raged down the gorge-like valleys, swept many buildings into the sea and claimed 34 lives. The 'new' village retains much of the charm of the original. Civil engineers have tamed the rivers which meet near the shore and flow to the sea past a harbour wall whose Rhenish tower was rebuilt in 1954. Its 19th-century predecessor was built by a colonel to supply his home with salt water for the bath. The shore is a mixture of rocks and shingle, but there is a tide-filled swimming pool.

Lynton is reached by a 1-in-4 road or an

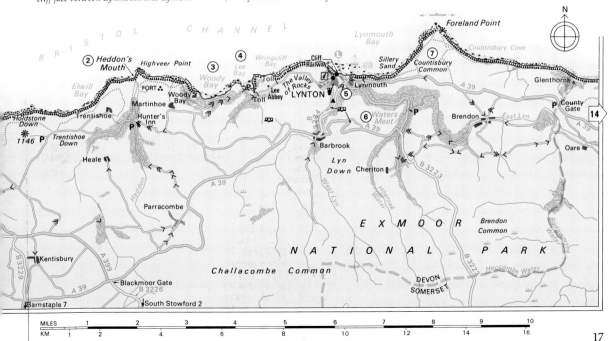

Long beaches for surfers, and a snug harbour at Ilfracombe

Three of Devon's finest surfing beaches at Saunton Sands, Croyde Bay and Woolacombe Sand also attract sunbathers and sandcastle-builders. At Morte Point the long beaches give way to cliffs and a series of rocky coves washed by the Bristol Channel. The broad estuary of the River Taw runs inland to the ancient town of Barnstaple, its tidal waters swirling past embankments and muddy creeks more typical of East Anglia than of Devon.

① BARNSTAPLE

North Devon's bustling 'capital' is one of the oldest boroughs in England, probably dating back to Saxon times and appearing as one of four Devon boroughs mentioned in Domesday Book in 1086. Sheltered moorings on the tidal River Taw encouraged the town's development as a port which reached its peak in the 17th century when there were strong trading links with the colonies in North America.

Shipping went into decline with the coming of the railways, but a few vessels loaded with sand and gravel still visit the quay at high water. There are many interesting old buildings. The parish church, partly 14th century, has a timber-framed leaded broach spire and a fine collection of 17th-century wall monuments. The almshouses in Church Lane were founded in the 17th century. Queen Anne's Walk, built in 1609, was the meeting place of merchants and ship-owners. Like Bideford, Barnstaple has a bridge which dates from the Middle Ages.

The town is at its liveliest on Fridays, when shoppers flock to the Pannier Market for cream, butter and other local produce. The four-day fair in September has been the highlight of Barnstaple's calendar for many years. The town also has a museum, and a craft market and workshop.

② BRAUNTON

South of the large village, a narrow toll road skirts the northern edge of Braunton Marsh, where the atmosphere recalls East Anglia's fenlands. Fields as flat as bowling greens are drained by reedy ditches, grassy embankments keep the sea at bay, and small boats moor in muddy, tide-scoured creeks. North of the toll road lies Braunton Great Field, one of the few surviving relics in England of the open field system, by which, in the Middle Ages, land was communally farmed in long narrow strips. The field is today fine beef-fattening land.

The toll road leads to Braunton Burrows, where emerald-green pastures give way to a wilderness of sand-dunes, 100 ft high in places. The area is a national nature reserve noted for such rare plants as sand toadflax and sea stock. Marsh orchids grow in damp hollows or 'slacks' amid the marram-clad sandhills.

Warning flags fly when parts of the 'desert' are being used by the armed forces, and low-flying aircraft from the nearby RAF base at Chivenor are frequent visitors. A bumpy track runs northwards from White House to join Sandy Lane, a minor road leading into Braunton. The track is known as the American Road, because this area was used by American forces training for the Normandy landings in 1944.

The village of Braunton is notable for its church of St Brannock, the Celtic saint who founded a chapel on the site. The church has a Norman tower, 16th-century bench-ends and a Jacobean pulpit, reading-desk and gallery. The Braunton and District Museum in Church Street has exhibits concerning the farming and seafaring history of the area, and its crafts and domestic life over the centuries. The museum is open at Easter, and Tuesdays to Saturdays in summer.

③ SAUNTON SANDS

Backed by Braunton Burrows, this huge expanse of sand is reached from the B3231 near Saunton and runs southwards for more than 3 miles to Crow Point, off which the waters of the Taw and Torridge meet the Atlantic. Westerly winds create ideal conditions for surfing, but strong currents swirling round Bideford Bar make the southern end of the beach unsafe for swimmers. They should also avoid the rocks below Saunton Down. There are volunteer lifeguard patrols on Sundays in summer.

④ CROYDE

The village's thatched, colour-washed cottages are sheltered by dunes which stand between it and Croyde Bay's sandy beach. Crossed by streams and framed by grassy headlands, the bay is popular with surfers, but bathing is unsafe at low tide. Signs also warn swimmers to keep away from the rocks.

Croyde has a fascinating gem-rock and shell museum, whose exhibits include giant clams from the South Pacific. Visitors can see semi-precious stones being cut, polished and fashioned into jewellery. At the village of Georgeham, 1½ miles north-east, St George's Church stands at the centre of a cluster of thatched and slate-roofed cottages.

A coastal footpath takes walkers to Baggy Point, where National Trust land offers splendid views, with Lundy, 15 miles offshore, visible on a clear day. Baggy Hole, a large cave burrowed into the headland, can be reached by boat at low tide.

⑤ PUTSBOROUGH SAND

This attractive corner of Morte Bay has a sandy, sheltered beach with safe bathing, very good surfing, except where water swirls round the rocks. The beach is reached by a narrow lane from Putsborough, and there is a short walk to the shore.

⑥ WOOLACOMBE

The gorse-clad whaleback of Woolacombe Down climbs steeply above the sandy, surf-pounded beach that sweeps southwards for 2 miles from Woolacombe. A car park runs along the hill's lower slopes, and paths run down through dunes to the shore. On the other side of Woolacombe – where there are almost as many hotels as private houses – the sands give way to rocks where explorers can find many sheltered sun-traps.

Barricane Beach is a rock-framed cove noted for sea-shells swept ashore by the incoming tide. The sands attract many visitors during the holiday season, but paths running over Morte Point and Woolacombe Down are 'escape routes' for walkers. Surfboards can be hired.

⑦ MORTEHOE

Set on a steep hill above Woolacombe, the village has a 13th-century church said to have been founded by a priest named William de Tracey, and is a good base for walkers. Paths go westwards over National Trust land to Morte Point, a headland that claimed many victims in the age of sailing ships. Five vessels were wrecked on the treacherous Morte Stone reef during the winter of 1852. The headland is also reputed to have been a haunt of wreckers in the 18th century.

North of the village, a walk of just over 1 mile leads to Bull Point, where the automatically operated lighthouse is an important landmark for ships in the Bristol Channel.

UNDER THE LANTERN *The cliffs of the North Devon coast form a dramatic backdrop to Ilfracombe's harbour. A light in the chapel on Lantern Hill, above the pier, still guides mariners into port.*

LIFE ON LUNDY ISLAND

Lundy means 'puffin island' in Norse; today the puffin is less common, but more than 400 other species of birds have been recorded there. Grey seals, sika deer, wild goats and Soay sheep also inhabit the island. For years Lundy was the haunt of Vikings, Normans, pirates and outlaws; now the island belongs to the National Trust and is administered by the Landmark Trust.

All around the island there are 400 ft cliffs with superb views of England, Wales and the Atlantic. There are two lighthouses, both erected in 1897, and above Lametry Bay stands Marisco Castle, probably built in 1243 by Henry III. The island's own boat *Oldenburg* sails from Bideford with visitors staying on Lundy. The paddle-steamer *Waverley* makes occasional trips from Ilfracombe in summer.

May is the likeliest time to see Lundy's puffins, when they breed on the clifftops.

⑧ LEE BAY

A deep, wooded valley leads down to this sheltered cove, with its tiny village and large hotel. Clumps of fuchsias and hydrangeas contribute dashes of rich colour. Seaweed-draped rocks are all that is left of the beach at high water, but low tide reveals some sand.

⑨ ILFRACOMBE

Elegant 19th-century buildings are a reminder that North Devon's largest holiday resort developed during the Victorian era, when the new-fangled railway brought tourists flocking to the town. Ilfracombe had, however, already been a busy little harbour for many generations, providing one of the few refuges on a coast whose formidable cliffs and surf-pounded beaches offered few safe havens.

Now bright with private craft and flanked on three sides by attractive old colour-washed buildings, the harbour is occasionally visited by ships which take trippers across the Bristol Channel to resorts in South Wales. The harbour nestles at the foot of Lantern Hill, a crag where the Chapel of St Nicholas has burned a guiding light for sailors ever since it was built about 650 years ago. There is a slipway, but heavy swells and the Bristol Channel's exceptional tides – the rise and fall is the second greatest in the world – make this stretch of coast unsuitable for trailer-borne boats.

Cliffs break the seafront up into a series of small beaches, from White Pebble Bay in the west to Broadstrand in the east, where there are rock pools and expanses of low-tide shale-sand. Capstone Hill rises steeply above the promenade and is ideal for short strolls. The Torrs Walk climbs to 451 ft on the town's western outskirts and is a popular viewpoint from which walkers can continue along the cliffs to Lee Bay.

Chambercombe Manor, 1 mile from the seafront, dates from just after the Norman Conquest. Its attractions include Tudor and Jacobean furniture, Civil War armour and a private chapel built in the 15th century. Bicclescombe Park contains an 18th-century watermill, a children's boating lake and a pets' corner.

There are fishing trips and seaside amusements, a sub-aqua club and yacht club, and a museum and art gallery.

⑩ HELE BAY

Reached by road or by footpath from Ilfracombe, the cliff-clasped bay has a beach of shingle and shingle-scattered sand flanked by rocks. The shore is washed by a stream which flows past a small, tide-filled paddling pool. In the village of Hele, a watermill dating back to 1525, with a wheel 18 ft in diameter, has been restored and produces wholemeal flour for sale to visitors. There are seaside amusements.

⑪ WATER MOUTH

The castellated Watermouth Castle, built in 1825, overlooks a long, narrow inlet, bright with boats, where streams flow seawards over a beach of sand and fine shingle. The castle has a great hall and smugglers' dungeons, and the rooms house various exhibitions.

The small holiday camp provides access to snug little sand-patched coves. During the

CASTLE MUSEUM *Relics of the days of smuggling are among the exhibits of the museum housed in the neo-Gothic Watermouth Castle.*

Second World War, Water Mouth was used to test *Pluto*, the 'pipeline under the ocean' that supplied the Allies with fuel after the D-Day invasion of Normandy. There is a yacht club.

LOCAL INFORMATION

Tourist information Ilfracombe 63001, Woolacombe 870553 (summer), Barnstaple 72742.

HM Coastguard Hartland 641 for information, 999 in emergency (ask for coastguard).

Weather Exeter 8091.

Local radio BBC Devon, 375 m, 801 kHz, 94.8 MHz.

PLACES TO SEE INLAND

Chapel Wood (RSPB), 3 miles N of Braunton. Woodland valley. Permits from warden.

Cobbaton Combat Vehicles Museum, Chittlehampton, off B3227. Second World War vehicles and equipment, and rural bygones. Daily, Easter to mid-Oct.

Marwood Hill, 3 miles N of Barnstaple. Gardens with lake, rare shrubs and exotic trees. Daily.

South Molton. Museum of local history and bygones, most days; Quince Honey Farm, daily.

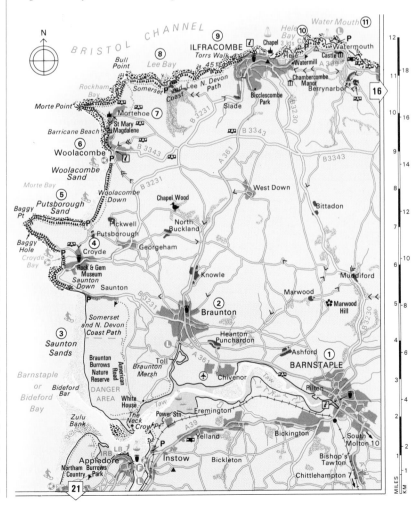

Cobbled streets in Clovelly near the 'Promontory of Hercules'

There are only a few bucket-and-spade beaches on this stretch of Devon's northern coast, but lofty cliffs and headlands provide rich compensation for lovers of wild, wave-sculpted scenery. East of Hartland Point, nature's grandeur contrasts with the picture-postcard charms of Clovelly. In Elizabethan days the Torridge estuary was the starting point of many voyages of adventure for ships crewed by the 'Men of Bideford'.

① SPEKE'S MILL MOUTH

Paths from Milford and Hartland Quay take walkers to this attractive little bay where a waterfall cascades down to a beach of pebbles and tilted tables of sea-smoothed rock. The shore is reached down a steep, zigzag path and sheltered by crumbling cliffs. A footpath runs through a tranquil valley inland towards the village of Milford.

② HARTLAND QUAY

Three of England's most famous sailors – Sir Francis Drake, Sir Walter Raleigh and Sir John Hawkins – financed the building of a small harbour here in the 16th century, providing a welcome refuge on this formidably inhospitable part of the Devon coast. It has not been used commercially since the end of the 19th century, but old coastguard cottages and other buildings now form a hotel. There is also a small museum, open in summer, devoted to local seafaring history. The little bay is backed by impressive cliffs whose layers of rock go from horizontal to vertical in the space of a few yards.

The road to Hartland Quay passes through Stoke, a village with a 14th-century church whose tower, almost 130 ft high and worthy of a cathedral, was built as a landmark for ships. The church's memorials include one to Sir Allen Lane, the publisher who was responsible for founding Penguin Books.

③ HARTLAND POINT

The 'Promontory of Hercules', as it was known to the Romans, 325 ft high, is seen at its awe-inspiring best when pounded by gale-lashed Atlantic waves. The pressure they exert on the crumpled cliffs has been estimated to be as much as 4 tons per square foot. The highest point of the headland has a coastguard lookout station and commands views of Lundy and the broad, tide-ripped mouth of the Bristol Channel. Far below, reached by a footpath, is a lighthouse now operated by remote control and closed to visitors.

Shipload Bay, 1 mile east, is backed by cliffs and has a pebble beach with a little low-tide sand. The cliffs are part of a 120 acre tract of National Trust land which includes East Titchberry, an ancient farm that is not open to visitors. The shore is reached by a long, steep path.

WARNING LIGHT *One of the strongest lighthouse beams on Britain's coast shines out from halfway down the cliffs at Hartland Point.*

④ CLOVELLY

Exploring this enchanting little village is like stepping back into the 19th century. Quaint old whitewashed cottages, bright with flowers, flank the steep, narrow, cobbled streets where traffic amounts to nothing more modern than donkeys and sledges. Although old enough to have been recorded in Domesday Book, 900 years ago, Clovelly could almost be an extravagant film set created to depict the perfect seaside village. It owes a great deal to Christine Hamlyn who owned the estate from 1884 until her death in 1936. She devoted her life to restoring Clovelly's buildings and preserving the village's unique beauty. Many cottages, some of which date from the Tudor period, bear her initials.

The High Street – also known as 'Up-a-long' and 'Down-a-long' – is paved with pebbles from the beach set on edge. It plunges down to a small harbour, where the boats of holidaymakers and lobster fishermen bob at anchor. The quay was lengthened in 1826 to give adequate protection to Clovelly's large fishing fleet, which prospered during the 18th and 19th centuries on huge catches of herring.

There is a beach of shingle and pebbles, with a little sand revealed at low tide. The harbour is overlooked by the Red Lion Hotel, which operates a Land Rover service to carry non-walkers up and down the hill by a private road during the holiday season. The rocky foreshore is tempting, but walkers must beware of the incoming tide. Clifftop paths run west to Mouth Mill and east to Buck's Mills.

The most attractive way to reach Clovelly is along the 3 mile Hobby Drive, which runs through woodlands from Hobby Lodge on the A39 and may be used on payment of a toll. It was built as a hobby by Sir James Hamlyn Williams and helped to alleviate unemployment after the Napoleonic Wars. There are boat trips from Clovelly when the tide is in.

⑤ BUCK'S MILLS

Nestling in a wooded valley, Buck's Mills amounts to little more than one narrow street, hemmed in by whitewashed cottages, which runs for half a mile from a small car park to the sea. Tree-clad cliffs rise up behind a pebbled, sand-patched beach where the ebbing tide leaves many rock pools.

The shore is overlooked by the ivy-covered ruins of a 19th-century lime-kiln big enough to be mistaken for a small fort. Limestone shipped over from South Wales was burned in the kiln and then carted inland by farmers to neutralise acids in the

WELCOMING BEACH *Sheltered by Hartland Point from the force of the Atlantic gales, Shipload Bay offers safe bathing to those who brave the long steep path down to the beach and back.*

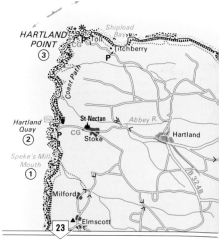

soil. Small boats may be launched, but the presence of a sand-bar creates hazards for sailors without local knowledge.

⑥ WESTWARD HO!

Founded in 1863 and named after Charles Kingsley's adventure story about Elizabethan seafarers, Westward Ho! is the brash newcomer in a county of old-established towns and villages. Its caravan sites, holiday camps and hotels look northwards over 3 miles of sands backed by a huge bank of shingle. The smooth stones shelter Northam Burrows, an expanse of dunes and saltings which includes the Royal North Devon Golf Club and a country park.

A path to the west of the village climbs Kipling's Tor, a gorse-gold hill named after Rudyard Kipling. The author was a pupil at the United Services College in Westward Ho! from 1878 until 1882, and recalled his time there in *Stalky and Co*. The buildings which housed the college are now known as Kipling Terrace. There are surfboards for hire, and other seaside attractions include an open-air swimming pool.

⑦ APPLEDORE

Colour-washed buildings and streets only a few paces wide in places contribute to the rich character of a large fishing village whose seafaring traditions go back more than 1,000 years. It has been a base for fishermen since Anglo-Saxon times, and is said to have been granted 'free port' status by Elizabeth I in gratitude for the part played by Appledore ships and sailors in the defeat of the Spanish Armada in 1588.

Modern vessels are built in a covered yard – the largest in Europe when it was opened in 1970. At Hinks's Yard local craftsmen have built full-sized replicas of a Roman galley, a Viking longship and Sir Francis Drake's *Golden Hinde*, the first English ship to sail round the world. Many aspects of the town's seafaring history are illustrated in the North Devon Maritime Museum in Odun Road. One room is devoted to Appledore's links with Canada's Prince Edward Island in the 19th century when, faced with a timber shortage in Europe, local shipbuilders built ships on the island and then sailed them back to Appledore to be given the finishing touches by craftsmen in Richmond Dock.

The quay beside the River Torridge was completed in 1846 and used by a considerable number of sailing ships until the 1930s. It overlooks a muddy estuary where strong currents make bathing unsafe. A passenger ferry plies between Appledore and Instow, on the opposite side of the Torridge, during the holiday season. There are boats for hire, and a regatta is held in July or August.

CLOVELLY HARBOUR *An 18th-century stone quay and the slipway of a disused lifeboat house frame Clovelly's tiny harbour. The streets of the fishing village climb steeply up the wooded 400 ft cliffs.*

⑧ BIDEFORD

A few small coasters still moor at Bideford's long, tree-lined quay, recalling the days when this was one of the busiest ports in England with ships trading as far afield as North America, the West Indies and Spain. The quay was built in the 17th century when wool was being imported from Spain to meet the demands of the textile mills.

Sir Richard Grenville, the swashbuckling sea captain who helped to found colonies on the far side of the Atlantic, is commemorated in the parish church. A brass plate in the family chapel records how he died of wounds in 1591 after his ship had fought with 15 Spanish galleons off the Azores. A somewhat romanticised version of the battle is given in Tennyson's poem *The Revenge*.

Bideford's most famous landmark is its bridge, the 24 arches have spanned the Torridge since the Middle Ages. It has been widened and strengthened several times, most recently in 1969, but can still be recognised from 16th-century descriptions. Old Ford House has displays of traditional West Country crafts. There are river trips, and a regatta is held in August.

⑨ INSTOW

The ebbing tide reveals a broad expanse of sand, backed by dunes at the northern end of the beach, but tidal currents make it unwise to bathe at low tide. However, the sheltered waters of the Torridge and Taw provide good conditions for water-skiing

and sailing, and Instow has schools and clubs for both sports. In summer, a passenger ferry runs to Appledore from the village's small, stone-built quay.

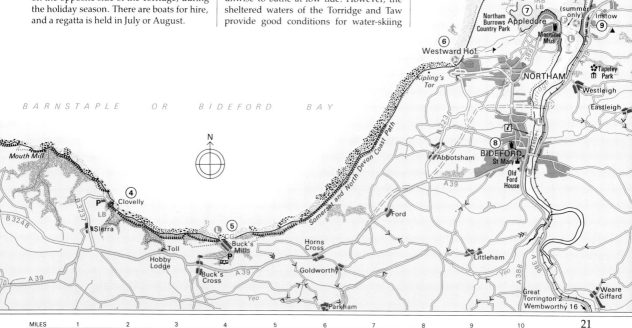

Rocky ramparts between the beaches facing Bude Bay

Narrow, high-banked lanes, some with gradients as steep as 1 in 3, wriggle down from the main coast road to a series of sandy beaches backed by lofty, crumbling cliffs. At low tide many of the beaches merge into one another to create continuous stretches of sand, providing enjoyable beach walking when swift currents make bathing unsafe. Bude, popular with surfers, has a 19th-century canal linked to the Atlantic by a sea lock.

CANAL BY THE SEA *Inside Bude Canal's sea lock, visiting vessels tie up where coastal traders once loaded oats and slate brought down the canal from inland farms and quarries.*

① CRACKINGTON HAVEN
Graves in St Gennys's churchyard, on a hill above Crackington Haven, are reminders that this spectacular part of the Cornish coast has claimed many ships and seafarers. They commemorate seven men who were lost when the Swedish brigantine *William* was wrecked off Crackington Haven in 1894, and seven others who were drowned six years later when storms claimed the steamer *City of Vienna* and the barque *Capricorna*.

The cliffs of Pencannow Point rise to more than 400 ft above Crackington Haven's beach, where stream-washed shingle gives way to low-tide sand flanked by rocks. Swimmers should keep to the middle of the beach, avoiding the southern side at all times.

Walkers who follow the clifftop path from Crackington Haven to Cambeak and on southwards to Rusey Cliff are rewarded by views of some of the most majestic coastal scenery in Britain. The strip of land, 3 miles long, was given to the National Trust in 1959 by Wing Commander A. G. Parnall to commemorate his brother and other airmen who died during the Battle of Britain in 1940.

② MILLOOK HAVEN
Cliffs with strata forced into astonishingly acute angles tower above this small cove. The atmosphere is peaceful, but the shingle beach shelves steeply and is not safe for swimmers. A stream flows down a deep, secluded valley whose sides are climbed by narrow lanes with very steep gradients.

The cliffs between Millook Haven and Chipman Strand are clad with England's westernmost wood of dwarf oaks. Some 140 acres of clifftop land between Dizzard Point and Chipman Strand were given to the National Trust by the Duchy of Cornwall when the Enterprise Neptune campaign for the preservation of Britain's coast was launched in 1965.

③ WIDEMOUTH SAND
The 'hotline' which spans the Atlantic, linking Downing Street to the White House, runs beneath this popular surfing beach whose sands are overlooked from the south by Penhalt Cliff. Widemouth's first cable across the Atlantic was laid in 1963 and extended for 3,517 nautical miles to New Jersey. The second provided a link with Nova Scotia, 2,800 nautical miles away in Canada, laid ten years later.

There are surfboards for hire, but bathing is unsafe at low tide, and swimmers must beware of currents which sweep round rocks flanking the sands. A small car park on Penhalt Cliff, high above the beach, offers memorable views up the rugged coast towards Hartland Point.

④ BUDE
Extensive sands and white-topped waves surging majestically in from the Atlantic make Bude a surfers' paradise. Summerleaze Beach, nearest to the town, has a wide expanse of firm sand, backed by grassy downs. At the north end of the beach is a large seawater swimming pool, an acre in extent, which is refilled by the tides every day. Crooklets Beach, further north, offers particularly fine surfing. Lifeguards patrol both beaches during the summer. Bathing can be hazardous, particularly at low tide, because of the heavy surf and strong undertow.

Surfers operating from beaches in the North Cornwall District Council's area must register with the council if their boards are more than 5 ft long. They must also have third-party insurance. A fee has to be paid to the harbourmaster before a boat may be launched.

Bude's most interesting links with the past are Ebbingford Manor, which dates from the 12th century, and the broad canal whose waters mingle with the sea on Summerleaze Beach. The canal is overlooked by a former blacksmith's shop where barge-hauling horses were shod. It now houses the Bude-Stratton Historical and Folk Exhibition which illustrates local life over the years. Exhibits include a model of the *Ceres*, a smack built at Salcombe in 1811. She was the oldest ship on Lloyd's Register for many years, but went down off Baggy Point, between Appledore and Ilfracombe, while sailing to Bude in 1936.

Bude Castle, which overlooks Summerleaze Beach, was built by Sir Goldsworthy Gurney in 1830 and is now used as offices by the local council. A notable scientist and inventor, Sir Goldsworthy proved that it was possible to build on shifting sands. His castle stands on a 'raft' of concrete and has remained perfectly stable. In 1831, steam carriages designed by Gurney operated the world's first town-to-town service by self-propelled road vehicles. They had a cruising speed of about 12 mph.

A carnival is held in August. Surfboards may be hired, and there are boat trips, rowing boats for hire on the canal, fishing trips for sharks and other species, coarse fishing in the canal, with a permit, and fishing from the shore. Other attractions include a museum, a nature trail in the grounds of Ebbingford Manor, and inland sailing on Tamar Lakes.

THE JOVIAL POET-PRIEST
The Reverend Robert Stephen Hawker, vicar of Morwenstow from 1834 to 1875, is best known for his poem *Song of the Western Men*, but he also made a lasting contribution to the Church by originating the Harvest Festival. He was a colourful character, both in dress and manner, and once hoaxed the superstitious villagers by dressing up as a mermaid. Seated on a rock by the seashore he eventually revealed his identity by standing up and singing the National Anthem.

In Morwenstow Church, Hawker vigorously condemned the plundering of wrecked ships.

Hawker in typical un-priestly garb

a disused watermill dating from 1842. The water wheel and the machinery inside the building are intact.

The land which climbs the valley's southern slope passes Stowe Barton, a house built by the Grenvilles in the 17th century. Their most famous ancestor, whose home was near by, was Sir Richard Grenville. His last battle with the Spaniards, in 1591, was later immortalised by Tennyson in *The Revenge*. Separated from the main British fleet near the Azores, the *Revenge* took on 15 Spanish warships in a battle that raged for hours. Only 20 of the *Revenge's* crew survived, and Grenville was mortally wounded.

⑩ STANBURY MOUTH

A grassy parking area is the starting point for the 15 minute walk which leads to this secluded beach where a stream filters through shingle to a stretch of low-tide sand. The last few yards of the walk involve a

SANDY MOUTH *Jagged pinnacles of rock, shaped by the sea and the winds, rise starkly above the sands like the gaunt ruins of an ancient abbey. The rocky beach makes surfing dangerous at high tide.*

⑤ BUDE CANAL

At the seaward end of Breakwater Road in Bude a sea lock marks the entrance to Bude Canal. It is the only lock on this remarkable waterway which ran 35 miles from Bude to Launceston and rose to a height of 350 ft in 6 miles. The change in levels was achieved by inclined planes, or ramps, between each different level and wheeled tub-boats which were pulled up the ramps on metal rails.

Two methods were used to haul the tubs, both employing water power. On all but one gradient the tubs were hooked on to an endless chain which was driven by a waterwheel, but at Hobbacott they were hauled by a water-filled bucket descending into a pit. The bucket held 15 tons of water and was attached to a chain wound round a drum; as the bucket was lowered into the 225 ft deep pit the drum operated a chain wheel which pulled the tubs up the steep incline.

Opened in 1823, Bude Canal was the longest tub-boat canal ever built. It carried sea sand for the fertilisation of inland farms, and on the return trips brought oats and slate to the trading vessels in Bude harbour. The coming of the railway ended the canal's days, and by the end of the 19th century it had fallen into disuse. Today the waterway runs only as far as Helebridge, but traces of the old inclines can be seen at Marhamchurch and Hobbacott.

⑥ STRATTON

Little more than 1 mile inland from Bude, Stratton was the scene of a Civil War battle in 1643. A plaque and an obelisk on Stamford Hill mark the ground where the Parliamentarians were defeated by Royalist troops commanded by Sir Bevil Grenville, a descendant of the Elizabethan sea captain Sir Richard Grenville. His servant and bodyguard, Anthony Payne, was 7 ft 4 in. tall, weighed 532 lb and is commemorated by a portrait in the Tree Inn, Sir Bevil's headquarters. Payne is buried in the local churchyard, where an inscribed tombstone marks his grave. Members of the Sealed Knot organisation re-enact the Battle of Stamford Hill every May.

⑦ NORTHCOTT MOUTH

There is a car park at Northcott Mouth, but the beach is also within easy walking distance of Bude. The path along the clifftop, which belongs to the National Trust, provides fine views, but tide times should be

checked before setting out along the shore. The sandy beach is punctuated by rocks, and bathing is unsafe for two hours on either side of low water.

⑧ SANDY MOUTH

A 2 minute walk, ending in a short flight of steps, leads from the National Trust's car park to a sandy beach backed by high and remarkably folded cliffs. At low water, when currents make swimming unsafe, the sands run southwards all the way to Bude. Walkers must check the state of the tide before setting out, because the unstable cliffs offer very few escape routes.

⑨ DUCKPOOL

An inscribed stone records that William IV contributed £20 towards the bridge under which a stream flows from the beautiful Coombe Valley to Duckpool. A National Trust car park at the foot of Steeple Point overlooks a sandy, shingle-backed beach flanked by impressive but unstable cliffs. It is always unsafe to swim on the north side of Duckpool, and conditions are especially dangerous for two hours on each side of low water.

The tranquil woodlands of Coombe Valley support a rich variety of plants, birds and small mammals, and are explored by nature trails. At the tiny hamlet of Coombe there is

23

GRIM BEAUTY CARVED BY THE SEA

Crumbling cliffs and rock-strewn coves present a stern face to the Atlantic southwards from Higher Sharpnose Point, near Morwenstow. The ridges of harder rock running out to sea show that Cornwall's rugged northern coast is very gradually losing ground to the relentless pounding of the rollers built up over 3,000 miles of ocean.

scramble over rocks. The beach's isolation makes it unsuitable for swimming at the best of times, and swift currents make conditions particularly dangerous at low water. The path to Stanbury Mouth is overlooked from the south by the white 'dishes' of a Ministry of Defence station where communications satellites are tracked.

⑪ MORWENSTOW
Narrow lanes run westwards from the coast road to this tiny, isolated village whose name recalls Morwenna, a 9th-century Celtic saint. The ancient church, sheltered by wind-bent trees, is a 10 minute walk from the cliffs where Morwenstow's most famous vicar, the eccentric Robert Stephen Hawker,

built a driftwood hut in which to write his poems. Hawker also built the vicarage whose chimneys are scaled-down replicas of church towers. The land between the church and the cliffs is National Trust property dedicated to Hawker's memory.

⑫ WELCOMBE MOUTH
Reached by a narrow, bumpy track which leads to a small car park, the beach at Welcombe Mouth is a mixture of pebbles, rocks and a little low-tide sand. The valley behind the shore, carved by a stream, is a nature reserve. This was the haunt of 'Cruel'

Coppinger, an 18th-century smuggler and wrecker whose exploits are recalled in the maritime museum at Appledore. David Coppinger was a Dane who landed on the Cornish coast during a storm. He became a smuggler, and he and his gang terrorised the district for many years, until the revenue men made a determined effort to capture him. Coppinger escaped to a waiting ship, and was never seen again.

A steep footpath runs southwards to a secluded rock-and-pebble beach at Marsland Mouth, where a stream marks the boundary between Devon and Cornwall.

Fishing harbours at the foot of King Arthur's Tintagel

Legends of King Arthur enrich the natural magic of a spectacularly wild, wave-lashed coast. Among its most dramatic spectacles is Cornwall's highest cliff, aptly called High Cliff. There are many sandy beaches, but most involve walks over fields or through deep, wooded valleys carved by streams. The little harbour at Boscastle and the old fishing village of Port Isaac are two of the few places where buildings run right down to the sea.

① PORT ISAAC

The little harbour with its boats, nets and lobster-pots nestles at the foot of steep slopes lined with whitewashed cottages. The streets are so narrow in some places that there is only just enough room for a car to thread between the buildings. One passage, Squeezibelly Alley, even poses problems for stout pedestrians.

At low tide, cars park on a stretch of fine shingle at the head of the harbour, and areas of sand are uncovered. The harbour is sheltered from the west by Lobber Point, where a clifftop path leads to Pine Haven, a secluded rock-and-shingle cove.

Boats may be launched at Port Isaac, but permission must be obtained from the harbourmaster in advance, and a fee is charged. There are riding stables and fishing trips for mackerel.

② PORTGAVERNE

In the 19th century, a period notable for huge shoals of pilchards, Portgaverne was a natural haven for fishermen. The stone-built 'cellars' where they stored their nets and processed the catch still stand behind the pebbled beach at the head of a narrow, cliff-framed inlet from which slate was also shipped in Victorian times. The road over the headland to Port Isaac passes a car park with superb views north-eastwards to Tintagel. There is a very small parking area in Portgaverne.

③ TREGARDOCK BEACH

Paths cross the fields from Tregardock and the tiny village of Treligga to a secluded beach reached by zigzagging steps. The ebbing tide reveals an expanse of sand with scattered rocks, but currents, undertows and other hazards make conditions unsafe for all but the strongest and most cautious of swimmers.

The clifftop path towards Portgaverne passes Barrett's Zawn, a collapsed tunnel through which slate was hauled.

④ TREBARWITH STRAND

The cliff-backed beach which runs northwards towards Penhallic Point makes Trebarwith a popular place for surfers, but the sands are submerged at high water. The crumbling cliffs were once quarried for slate that was lowered down by windlasses to sailing ships which crept inshore on the rising tide. Coal brought by boat from South Wales was dumped into the sea, then loaded into carts when the waves retreated. The road down to the beach was made in the early 19th century to enable carts to carry shell-sand to farms inland for use as a fertiliser.

Seaward views are dominated by Gull Rock, which looks like a smaller version of Ailsa Craig in the Firth of Clyde. Surfboards may be hired.

⑤ TINTAGEL

Spread out along a clifftop, set back from the sea and more than 300 ft above it, Tintagel has been one of Cornwall's most powerful magnets since the 19th century, when Tennyson's *The Idylls of the King* publicised the village's legendary links with King Arthur and his Knights of the Round Table. His poems were inspired by other works, the earliest of which was written by Geoffrey of Monmouth in the 12th century. There are no facts to support the romantic stories about Tintagel being the Celtic hero's birthplace and seat of power, but dramatic coastal scenery and the ruins on Tintagel Head combine to create an atmosphere which accords well with the Arthurian myths.

A broad footpath runs from the village to what remains of Tintagel Castle, the earliest parts of which were built in about 1145 by Henry III's brother Reginald, Earl of Cornwall. In the 14th century the stronghold was given to Edward the Black Prince, the first Duke of Cornwall. The mainland part of the castle was then joined to The Island by a natural bridge which the relentless waves eventually destroyed.

Nearly 300 steps, some of which are treacherous when wet, take walkers to the top of The Island, where the remains of a Celtic monastery have survived since the Dark Ages. There are breathtaking views of a coast against whose wild beauty stands, incongruously, a huge Victorian hotel between Tintagel and the sea. This has been described as 'an elephantine monument to the directors of the London and South Western Railway', who were among the first to exploit the Arthurian legends. There is a beach of sand and pebbles below Tintagel Head, and another small beach south of The Island. This is reached through Merlin's Cave – the spot where Arthur is said to have

met Merlin, the wizard who promised to make the boy a wise and gallant ruler.

Tintagel's main street is made memorable by the Old Post Office, an enchanting manor-in-miniature dating from the 14th century. It was first used as a post office during Queen Victoria's reign, and is now owned by the National Trust. King Arthur's Hall, on the opposite side of the street, illustrates the legends that have made Tintagel famous. A feature of the building is the 73 stained-glass windows portraying the story of Arthur and his knights.

The path over Glebe Cliff passes Dunderhole Point, where slate was lowered into the holds of sailing ships during the 19th century.

PLANTAGENET MANOR *Tintagel's weather-beaten Old Post Office dates back to the time when the Black Prince owned Tintagel Castle.*

⑥ BOSSINEY HAVEN

A 10 minute walk from Bossiney across fields and down steps cut into the cliff leads to a popular surfing beach whose sands are covered at high tide.

The beach, known locally as Bossiney Cove, is crossed by a small stream which runs down a high wall of vertical rock clad with glistening, dark green moss. Lye Rock, on the bay's western headland, is a breeding ground for puffins, fulmars, cormorants, razorbills and other cliff-nesting sea-birds.

Bossiney Castle, a grassy mound northeast of the village, is said to be the burial place of King Arthur's Round Table. According to legend, the Round Table rises from the ground on Midsummer's Eve.

⑦ ROCKY VALLEY

Starting near a small car park on the B3263, a footpath runs towards the sea down a deep, wooded valley sunk between crags entwined with ivy. The path passes a rock, sheltered by a ruined mill, bearing intricate carvings believed to date from the Bronze Age. The 10 minute walk ends where the valley's stream foams seawards through a miniature gorge cut deep into smooth rocks.

BOSCASTLE HARBOUR *The tiny River Valency winds down through a gentle valley to Boscastle's inner jetty, where small craft tie up at a quayside once busy with sailing ships loading slate.*

A KING AND HIS CASTLE

The legend of King Arthur is a fascinating blend of fact and fiction. According to the 12th-century writer Geoffrey of Monmouth, Arthur was crowned King of the Britons at the age of 15 and won many battles against the invading Anglo-Saxons. Many historians believe that the real King Arthur was a 6th-century British chieftain and was probably born in the West Country. The deeds of chivalry and heroism associated with the king and his Knights of the Round Table stem from the works of later writers, notably Sir Thomas Malory's *Le Morte D'Arthur* and Tennyson's *The Idylls of the King*.

A 14th-century stone carving of King Arthur. It is now in the National Museum, Nuremburg, Germany

Tintagel Castle was, according to legend, the seat of King Arthur and his Knights.

⑧ BOSCASTLE

Boscastle's deep, narrow, fiord-like harbour wriggles inland to a picturesque cluster of buildings restored and preserved by the National Trust. Although difficult to enter unless the sea is millpond-calm, the harbour provides one of the very few havens on a long stretch of coast that can be formidably hostile in bad weather. Its reputation in the days of sail is recalled by a local saying:

'From Padstow Bar to Lundy Light
Is a sailor's grave by day or night.'

The inner jetty embraces a small area of low-tide sand and was rebuilt in 1584 by Sir Richard Grenville, the Elizabethan hero and captain of the *Revenge*, who died fighting the Spanish. The outer breakwater dates from early in the 19th century, when slate was shipped from Boscastle, but it was shattered by a drifting sea-mine in 1941. National Trust masons restored it 21 years later.

One of the old harbour buildings houses the Museum of Witchcraft. Exhibits include what are said to be the remains of Ursula Hemp, a 'witch' executed in 1589.

The road to Boscastle village, set on a hill above the harbour, skirts Forrabury Common, where a Celtic system of land tenure known as 'stitchmeal' has survived for more than 1,000 years. Individuals raise crops on their 'stitches' – long, rectangular plots – during the summer months, but the land becomes common grazing in the winter.

⑨ PENTARGON

This small, rocky cove, hemmed in by dark cliffs, is notable for a stream which cascades down a 120 ft precipice to meet the sea. The cove can be reached by following a footpath from the B3263, but there is no car park on the road.

⑩ THE STRANGLES

Just south of Trevigue, an isolated farmhouse high above the sea, a footpath crosses the gorse-gold clifftop before descending steeply to The Strangles. As its sinister name implies, the beach claimed many storm-tossed victims in the age of sail. More than 20 vessels were wrecked during a single year in the 1820s. The ebbing tide reveals broad expanses of sand between the rocks, but swift currents and strong undertows make the beach unsafe for swimmers.

The clifftop path runs southwards to climb High Cliff, a superb viewpoint owned by the National Trust from which Lundy island, more than 30 miles away, can be seen on a clear day. Towering 731 ft above the sea, it is the highest cliff in Cornwall and one of the highest anywhere on England's coastline.

The cliffs inspired a scene in Thomas Hardy's novel *A Pair of Blue Eyes*. Hardy, then a young architect, visited Cornwall in 1870 to work on the restoration of St Juliot's Church near Boscastle. It was there that he met his future wife, Emma Gifford.

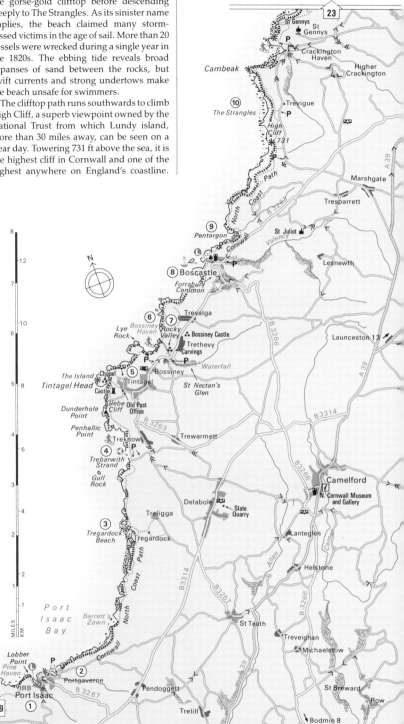

LOCAL INFORMATION

Tourist information Bude 3781 (summer).

HM Coastguard Hartland 641 (north of Tintagel), Falmouth 317575 (south of Tintagel) for information, 999 in emergency (ask for coastguard).

Weather Newquay 2224, Plymouth 8091.

Local radio BBC Cornwall, 457/476 m, 657/630 kHz, 95.2/96.4 MHz.

PLACES TO SEE INLAND

Delabole Slate Quarry, 3 miles SE of Tintagel. Exhibition of the various uses of slate. Open during office hours throughout the year.

Jamaica Inn. On A30 between Launceston and Bodmin. Slate-hung 18th-century coaching inn on Bodmin moor, immortalised in Daphne du Maurier's novel.

North Cornwall Museum and Gallery, Camelford. Late 19th and early 20th-century life. Weekdays in summer.

St Nectan's Glen, 1½ miles NE of Tintagel. Waterfall and 6th-century hermit's chapel.

Wesley's Cottage and Methodist Shrine, Trewint, near Altarnun, 7 miles W of Launceston, off A30. Testaments and period furniture. Daily.

Headlands and wide bays near the quiet Camel estuary

North Cornwall's awe-inspiring cliffs are carved by many small streams, but the River Camel is the only 'gateway' through which tidal waters can flow far inland. Although huge sandbanks are uncovered at low tide, the broad and sheltered estuary is bright with boats during the holiday season. Near its mouth, broad sands provide fine surfing. West of the Camel stretch reefs of rock, while east of Pentire Point there are high cliffs with breezy footpaths.

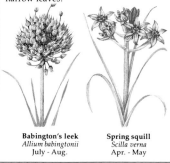
① TREYARNON
Low cliffs sprinkled with a few houses shelter sands washed by a stream. Swimmers should keep to the centre of the beach, and conditions are particularly dangerous near the rocks opposite the car park. A natural swimming pool in the rocks provides safe bathing at low tide. Surfboards may be hired.

② CONSTANTINE BAY
Fences and marram grass, erected and planted to prevent erosion, pattern the dunes overlooking this sandy, surf-washed beach. Contrary currents make swimming dangerous at all times, but signs indicate the safer areas. Rocky reefs make the adjacent Booby's Bay hazardous when the sea is rough, and at high water. Dozens of rock pools are exposed at low tide.

③ TREVOSE HEAD
A toll road climbs from near Harlyn to a car park at the top of Trevose Head, nearly 250 ft above the sea. On a clear day there are splendid views north-eastwards towards Hartland Point and southwards beyond Newquay. The lighthouse is open to visitors.

Padstow's lifeboat is based on the sheltered eastern side of the headland where the North Cornwall Coast Path skirts Mother Ivey's Bay. The bay – a mixture of rocks and low-tide sand – is said to take its name from a formidable old woman who claimed any wreckage found on the shore.

HEADLIGHT *The gleaming lighthouse on Trevose Head, built in 1847, has a beam that is visible 27 miles out to sea.*

④ HARLYN BAY
The discovery of a large Iron Age cemetery in 1900 made Harlyn Bay famous in the archaeological world, but the museum built on the site was demolished in the 1970s to make way for houses. Most of the relics may now be seen in Truro's museum. The horseshoe-shaped bay, half a mile across, faces north and the sandy beach, washed on its eastern flank by a stream, is often pounded by surf. A volunteer rescue service, equipped with a high-speed inflatable rescue craft, is stationed on the beach in summer.

⑤ TREVONE
The village street slopes gently down to a sandy beach, crossed by a stream, with low cliffs and scattered outcrops of rock. The surf can be impressive, but swimmers should keep to the centre of the beach because strong currents sweep round the northern headland. The path over the headland passes Round Hole, which appeared when the roof of a sea-carved cave collapsed. Another path leads to Newtrain Bay, where rocks give way to sand at low tide. Surfboards may be hired.

⑥ PADSTOW
The roots of this little fishing port go back to the 6th century, when St Petroc sailed down from Wales and founded a monastery. It was sacked by Viking raiders in AD 981. The role of the saint in founding the town was later recognised when the Guild of St Petroc was founded by local merchants and ship-owners.

A 15th-century church dedicated to the saint stands on high ground, framed by trees, and looks down on the town's network of narrow streets and old, colour-washed buildings which lead to the harbour. Fishing boats and pleasure craft are watched over by the Court House, used by Sir Walter Raleigh in the 16th century when he was Warden of the Stannaries of Cornwall.

Despite the dreaded Doom Bar sandbank at the mouth of the estuary, Padstow was the most thriving port on Cornwall's northern coast in the days when virtually all trade went by sea. The harbour handled cargoes ranging from fish and wine to slate and ores from local mines. Some ships unloaded timber from North America and sailed back with Cornish emigrants seeking a new life in the New World.

Trade declined as ships became bigger and shifting sands made the River Camel increasingly difficult to navigate. The long-awaited arrival of the railway in 1899 was an even greater blow to the port's trade, although on the brighter side it did enable fish to be sped to London and other important markets.

An extraordinary incident took place during the First World War when a small fleet of Padstow boats were fishing off Pentire Point. A German submarine surfaced near by and ordered the fishermen to make for the shore in their dinghies. The submarine then sank all their boats.

A pleasant walk with fine views of the estuary runs from the harbour to the sandy beaches of Harbour Cove and Hawker's Cove. Padstow's lifeboat used to be based at Hawker's Cove, but the silting up of the Doom Bar prevented easy launching at low water and the lifeboat station was moved to Trevose Head.

The little town is seen at its most lively and traditional on May Day, when the 'Obby 'Oss festivities take place. This ceremony, like the Flora Dance at Helston, is believed to have its origin in a pagan fertility festival celebrating the coming of summer. The 'Oss is represented by a man wearing a black cape which hangs down from a wide circular frame. He wears a fierce mask, suggesting a heathen god, and a plume and tail of horsehair. As the townspeople sing a May Day song, the 'Oss prances through the streets, preceded by a 'Teaser' and followed by dancers dressed in white and wearing spring flowers. At the end of the day the 'Oss is ritually 'done to death', symbolising the passing of the old year – to be resurrected the following May Day.

A carnival and regatta are held in July, and a lifeboat day in August. Attractions include a tropical bird garden, a museum and an aquarium. Boat trips are available, as are water-skiing, sailing and windsurfing lessons, and fishing trips for sharks, bass and mackerel.

⑦ WADEBRIDGE
Sand, silt and the opening of a railway to Padstow in 1899 combined to end Wadebridge's long history as a port. The old days are recalled by quays which flank the Camel below a bridge that dates from the 15th century. It replaced a dangerous ford overlooked by chapels where travellers could pray before crossing. The bridge's piers are said to be built on woolpacks which provided solid foundations on the river's muddy bed.

The Camel is seen at its best from a path which follows the abandoned railway line to Padstow and is never more than a stone's throw from the estuary. The walk takes 2-3 hours and skirts Dennis Hill, where a

The Padstow 'Obby 'Oss

HAYLE BAY *This wedge of golden sand at Polzeath, in a bay sheltered from coastal currents, is one of the safer beaches on this stretch of coast. A lifeguard is on duty there in the summer.*

⑪ LUNDY BAY

The 10 minute walk from the road to Lundy Bay passes a spectacular natural arch created when the roof of a sea-carved cave collapsed many years ago. The path swings down to a beach where tables of smooth rock give way to sand at low water. Walkers on the shore must beware of getting trapped by the incoming tide. From the path which follows the cliffs westwards towards Rumps Point there are wide-ranging views up the coast to Tintagel.

⑫ PORT QUIN

Headlands patchworked with fields sweep down to an attractive inlet where low cliffs embrace a beach of shingle and low-tide sand. The tiny hamlet, whose cottages are dashed with spray during north-westerly gales, was uninhabited for many years in the 19th century. Local tradition maintains that the women and children moved out after Port Quin's fishing boats and crews were lost in a storm. In fact, most of the families emigrated to Canada when the antimony mines near Doyden Point were closed. On Doyden Point stands a 19th-century folly, Doyden Castle. It was built in 1839 by Samuel Symons of Wadebridge as a clifftop retreat where he could drink and gamble with his friends.

monument commemorates Queen Victoria. The Royal Cornwall Show is held in Wadebridge in June.

⑧ ROCK

The old quay at Rock is the main centre for sailing and water-skiing on the Camel. Its small, stone-built warehouse, originally used to store grain, is the headquarters of the Rock Sailing Club, where visiting ski-boats must be registered. The narrow road beyond the quay ends in a car park sheltered by dunes which run down to a beach with wide expanses of sand at low tide – and not a rock in sight. The beach is the departure point for a ferry service that has linked Rock and Padstow since the 14th century.

There are pleasant walks northwards over low cliffs, and a golf course extending to Daymer Bay and Trebetherick. Fishing trips are available, and sailing boats can be hired. There are sailing and water-ski schools.

⑨ TREBETHERICK

A narrow, leafy lane runs down from the village to Daymer Bay where the sandy beach, backed by dunes, is framed by low cliffs. Bathing is safest at high water because of currents in the Camel's tide-scoured channel. Offshore is the Doom Bar, a

sandbank which claimed many ships when the estuary was an important commercial waterway.

Surfboards and speedboats are banned from the beach.

⑩ POLZEATH

Polzeath and New Polzeath overlook the extensive sands of Hayle Bay, where westerly winds provide perfect conditions for surfers. The Greenaway, a short walk from Polzeath, is a pleasant expanse of springy turf above a rocky shore where the ebbing tide leaves many pools. Views across the mouth of the Camel estuary are dominated by Stepper Point, a lofty headland crowned with a 'day mark' tower built as a landmark for seafarers.

North of New Polzeath, where steps lead to the beach, paths to Rumps Point cross the banks and ditches of an Iron Age fort.

LOCAL INFORMATION
Tourist information (Polzeath) Trebetherick 2488 (summer); Wadebridge 3725 (summer); Padstow 532296.
HM Coastguard Falmouth 317575 for information, 999 in emergency (ask for coastguard).
Weather Newquay 2224, Plymouth 8091.
Local radio BBC Cornwall 476 m, 630 kHz, 96.4 MHz.

PLACES TO SEE INLAND
Bodmin Duke of Cornwall's Light Infantry Regimental Museum. Weekdays throughout the year.
Bodmin Farm Park, Fletcher's Bridge, near Bodmin. Animals, old farm implements. Most days in summer.
Lanhydrock (NT), near Bodmin. 17th-century house. Gardens daily, house daily in summer.
Pencarrow House and Gardens, near Bodmin. Georgian mansion. House most days in summer, gardens daily in summer.

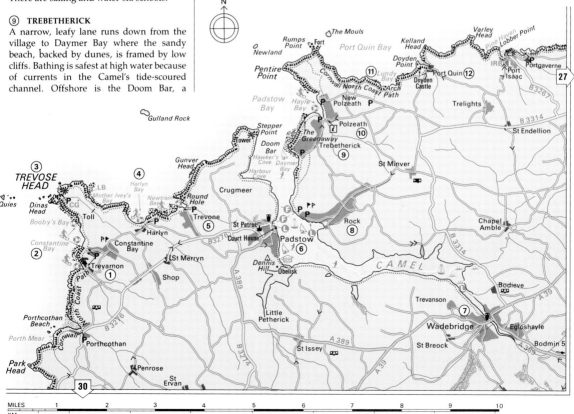

Miles of sands that make Newquay the surfers' capital

Superb surfing beaches, punctuated by craggy headlands, sweep northwards from Perranporth to way beyond Newquay. They are seen at their most dramatic when huge waves, driven by stiff westerly winds, thunder ashore and send their salty spray far inland. But there are also bays and inlets where gentle streams tumbling down from the inland hills wash the sands and the booming surf is just a whisper around a headland.

SANDY HAVEN *Newquay's old harbour, still used by small craft, dries out at low tide, leaving a sandy beach for sheltered bathing.*

① GEAR SANDS

According to Cornish legends, this hummocky wilderness of sand and marram grass covers the city of Langarroc that was buried because its inhabitants became lazy, greedy and immoral. Similar stories are told in other parts of Britain where drifting sand has undoubtedly buried farms, villages and even small towns since medieval times.

A large holiday camp nestles in the dunes close to a cross which guides walkers to the site of St Piran's Oratory. Piran was a Celtic monk who is said to have sailed from Ireland on a millstone and became the patron saint of tinners, and of Cornwall. The tiny oratory, built in the 7th century, vanished beneath the sands for many years and was uncovered by a storm in 1835. It was later protected by an outer shell of concrete, but attracted vandals and now lies beneath a great mound of sand. The spot is marked with a stone bearing St Piran's name.

② HOLYWELL BAY

Holywell village's holiday homes and caravans are hidden from the delightful bay by high dunes. A broad but shallow river meanders seawards past the southern end of the sand-hills and is punctuated by stepping-stones in two places. Immediately south of the beach, Penhale Sands are part of the 'desert' which runs for almost 3 miles to the outskirts of Perranporth. The dunes are part of a military training area, but the clifftop path may be walked unless red flags are flying.

Holywell lies 2 miles to the west of Cubert, a village whose tall church spire can be seen for miles around and serves as a landmark for those heading for the bay.

FISHERMEN'S WATCH TOWER

Until the late 19th century the huer was an important man in Newquay. From his house above Newquay Bay he would watch for the reddening of the sea which indicated that pilchard shoals were in the bay. His name comes from his call, 'Heva! Heva!' ('Found! found!'), which sent the fishermen running to their boats.

The Huer's House, Newquay

③ PORTH JOKE

This attractive little bay, known locally as Polly Joke, amply rewards the 10 minute walk from the car park at West Pentire. The sandy, stream-washed beach, owned by the National Trust, nestles between low cliffs whose rocks give way to gently sloping headlands patchworked with fields. Seals breed on The Chick, a rocky islet off Kelsey Head.

The sands of Porth Joke and neighbouring beaches are rich in minerals which act as a natural fertiliser. Their value was officially acknowledged as long ago as James II's time, when an Act of Parliament gave local farmers permission to take sand from the foreshore.

④ CRANTOCK BEACH

Sheltered from the prevailing winds by Pentire Point West, this beach at the seaward end of the River Gannel's estuary offers a broad expanse of low-tide sand backed by high and extensive dunes. Swimming is safest at high water, but bathers should avoid the Gannel at all times. A small boat ferries walkers across the river to Newquay. The car park behind the dunes is reached by a lane from Crantock, a village whose old-established charms have not been completely submerged by more recent developments.

⑤ NEWQUAY

The town that is now Cornwall's biggest resort and Britain's foremost surfing centre grew up around a 'new quay' whose

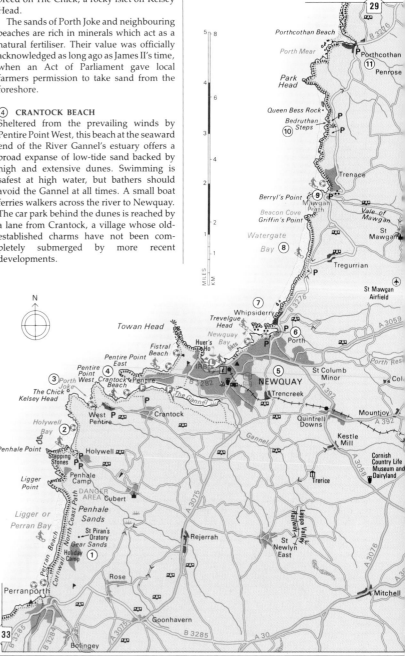

building was sanctioned by the Bishop of Exeter in 1439. Fishing and smuggling became important sources of income, but local ships also traded with ports as far afield as North America. Gigs powered by teams of oarsmen raced out to pilot vessels safely into the harbour – and gig races held during the summer months still rank high among Newquay's many holiday attractions. One of the craft, named after the town, was built in 1812 while two of her rivals also date from the 19th century.

Another link with the past is provided by the small, quaint, whitewashed Huer's House which stands on a cliff above the harbour. In the 18th and 19th centuries, when the sea often seethed with immense shoals of pilchards, a lookout was posted to keep watch for the fish and to guide boats to them by shouting instructions through a horn 1 yd long. One memorable catch in the 1860s is said to have been worth £20,000 – a fortune in those days – and there were enough fish to load 1,000 carts.

The arrival of the railway in 1875 was the most important event in Newquay's history. Although built to carry minerals and clay to the thriving harbour, the line also brought the town within easy reach of Victorian travellers at a time when seaside holidays were becoming increasingly popular. Large hotels were built on the high cliffs above the series of beaches whose sands, surf and safe bathing are the main reasons for Newquay's enduring popularity.

The town's other great natural asset is the fact that its beaches face in every direction other than east, making it easy to find shelter on blustery days. Towan Beach, Great Western Beach, Tolcarne Beach and Lusty Glaze are washed by the waters of Newquay Bay and reached by steps or ramps cut into the cliffs. By contrast, Fistral Beach faces due west and is backed by low dunes which lead to a golf course. Another change of mood is provided by the low-tide sands which fringe the River Gannel's estuary on the town's southern outskirts.

Surfers wishing to use Malibu boards, defined as being more than 5 ft long, must register them at the Municipal Offices at the junction of Manor Road and Marcus Hill, or on beaches with areas specially designated for the boards.

Riding the surf at Newquay

Seaside attractions include indoor and outdoor swimming pools, a museum, a zoo and an aquarium. There are boats for hire on a boating lake, fishing trips for shark, bass, pollock and mackerel, and fishing from the beaches for bass. Surfboards may be hired and there are sub-aqua and sailing clubs.

⑥ **PORTH**
An old lime-kiln beside the beach is a reminder that this was a thriving little port until railways captured much of the coastal trade in the 19th century. Limestone was shipped in from South Wales, burned and carted inland to 'sweeten' Cornwall's acidic soil.

Swimmers should avoid the north side of the sands, where a river runs to the sea past Trevelgue Head. Strong westerly winds

BEDRUTHAN STEPS *Below towering cliffs the Atlantic rollers pound a rock-strewn beach. A local legend says that the huge granite rocks were stepping-stones used by the Cornish giant Bedruthan.*

force waves and spray up through a 'blow hole' in the headland.

⑦ **WHIPSIDERRY**
Steps run steeply down from Whipsiderry to a sandy cove, sheltered by high, vertical cliffs, where the beach is completely submerged at high tide.

A path to Trevelgue Head can be walked in less than 10 minutes. It passes Bronze Age burial mounds, then crosses an impressive series of banks and ditches which made the headland a fortress during the Iron Age.

⑧ **WATERGATE BAY**
Low-flying aircraft from the St Mawgan RAF base roar over the surfers who flock to this long, sandy beach with its backdrop of crumbling cliffs. At low tide the beach runs for more than 2 miles from Trevelgue Head to Griffin's Point, but there is only one access point for cars. The beach witnessed a miniature 'civil war' in 1869 when 'rescuers' intent on loot unsuccessfully tried to prevent a beached ship being towed to safety by a steam tug. Surfboards may be hired.

⑨ **MAWGAN PORTH**
The remains of a settlement believed to date from the 5th century AD are hidden away behind Mawgan Porth's beach. The sands are washed by a stream which flows down from St Columb Major through the wooded Vale of Mawgan. A clifftop path takes walkers past Berryl's Point before dropping steeply down to the secluded sands of Beacon Cove. Surfboards may be hired, and there is fishing from the beach.

A reminder of the hazards of this part of the coast appears in the churchyard in St Mawgan, a village 2 miles inland hidden at the head of a deep wooded valley. A simple wooden tablet shaped like the stern of a boat commemorates nine men and a boy who froze to death in a lifeboat after their ship sank in 1846. Headstones in the churchyard show a wide range of variations on the Celtic cross introduced by the saints who came to the West Country in the 5th century.

⑩ **BEDRUTHAN STEPS**
A long flight of slippery and extremely steep steps plunges down from the grassy clifftop to a dramatic beach where low-tide sands are punctuated by immense rocks. Legend has it that the rocks were stepping-stones used by the giant Bedruthan; more prosaically, they

are granite stacks left isolated on the beach by the erosion of softer rocks around them. One rock is known as Queen Bess Rock after its resemblance to Queen Elizabeth I, when viewed from the right angle. This is one of the most memorable stretches of coast in Britain, but explorers must keep away from the crumbling cliffs and take care not to be trapped by the rising sea. Swimmers venture out at their peril after passing an inscribed stone at the top of the steps. It commemorates a man from Derby who was drowned off Bedruthan in 1903, and it was placed there as a warning to others by his friends 'whose lives were mercifully saved'.

In 1846 the 220 ton *Samaritan*, outward bound from Liverpool with a cargo of fine silks and cottons, was driven ashore near Queen Bess Rock by an October gale. Only two of her crew survived, but there were rich pickings for local beachcombers.

The steps (open in summer) down to the beach were closed after becoming unsafe, but were rebuilt by the National Trust, which has an information centre near by.

⑪ **PORTHCOTHAN**
A stream flows into the sea at the head of this long, narrow inlet, where shingle-speckled sand is backed by a small area of low dunes. Swimming is safest from the middle of the beach, and currents sweeping past the headlands make it dangerous to bathe at low water. A path over the low southern headland leads to Porth Mear, a secluded cove of rock and low-tide shingle.

Clifftop paths between resorts that once were mining villages

Tall chimneys of undressed stone, perched on cliffs or tucked away in sheltered valleys, are reminders of the days when tin and copper were among the mainstays of Cornwall's economy. The cliffs between St Ives Bay and Perranporth are best seen from the long strip of National Trust land which links Godrevy Point and Portreath. The great walls of rock are punctuated by sandy, stream-washed coves reached by narrow lanes.

① GODREVY POINT

Low cliffs rise above the flat rocks, dappled with low-tide pools, which flank the dangerous channel between Godrevy Point and Godrevy Island. The island and its neighbouring rocks claimed many victims before the lighthouse was built in 1859. They included a ship which went down in 1649, laden with Charles I's wardrobe and other personal possessions. Virginia Woolf knew this part of Cornwall well, and her novel *To the Lighthouse* refers to Godrevy.

The narrow road to Godrevy Point's car park skirts the northern end of St Ives Bay where it is crossed by the Red River. As its name implies, this river is stained a deep red by waste from old tin mines. A short walk leads to Navax Point, where grey seals breed and caves reached only from the sea run far into the headland. Gannets, shearwaters, fulmars and other sea-birds may be seen in summer and autumn.

② BASSET'S COVE

This rocky cove, nestling below a clifftop car park, is a main feature of the long strip of National Trust land which runs almost unbroken from Godrevy Point across Hudder Down, Reskajeage Downs and Carvannel Downs to Portreath. The flat-topped cliffs are ideal for bracing walks, and a few steep paths zigzag down to secluded coves.

The path skirts Ralph's Cupboard, a deep, sunless cleft formed by the collapse of a sea-scoured cave. Its name recalls a smuggler who used the cave as a store for contraband. It is also said to have been the home of Wrath, one of Cornwall's legendary giants who waded out to capture passing ships and devour their crews. From the cliffs there are fine views up the coast past St Agnes Head to the Bawden Rocks.

③ PORTREATH

Francis Basset, a member of one of Cornwall's wealthiest mining families, leased land for the building of a pier at Portreath in 1760. It evolved into a thriving little harbour, serving the local tin and copper mines, and in 1809 became the terminus of a horse-powered tramroad that was the county's first railway. Ships laden with ore sailed to Swansea and returned with Welsh coal to fuel the engine-houses whose pumps fought a constant battle to prevent flooding in the mines. Coasters visited the harbour until the 1960s, but when trade ceased the nearby land was turned into an estate of cottages.

The sandy beach is popular with surfers, and surfboards can be hired. There are lifeguard patrols in summer, but swimmers should keep away from the old harbour, where a stream flows into the sea.

④ PORTHTOWAN

Extensive low-tide sands have encouraged Porthtowan's development as a holiday village. Caravans, shops and chalets overlook the beach, and the tall, slim engine-house of a 19th-century copper mine has been turned into a cafe. Walkers who explore the beach at low water should keep an eye on the incoming tide, because the cliffs are too high and unstable to be climbed. There are lifeguard patrols in summer, and surfboards for hire.

The clifftop path between Porthtowan and Portreath crosses Nancekuke Common, where it skirts a large tract of fenced-off land used for many years by the Ministry of Defence.

⑤ CHAPEL PORTH

Reached by a narrow lane from St Agnes, this delightful little cove takes its name from an ancient chapel which once stood in a secluded valley near the sea. The lane ends in a National Trust car park at the head of a sandy, shingle-backed beach flanked by rocks which provide many suntraps. Swimmers and surfers should beware of currents and undertows.

The beach runs southwards to Porthtowan at low water, but walkers should check tide times to avoid being trapped between the incoming sea and the lofty cliffs.

The Chapel Porth nature trail, which takes about 2 hours, blends natural history and industrial archaeology with splendid views. It passes the ruined Charlotte United mine, where copper workings extended out under the sea, and runs northwards as far as the Wheal Coates mine below St Agnes Beacon. Buzzards, jackdaws, ravens, wrens and many sea-birds are likely to be seen on the walk. There are lifeguard patrols in summer, surfboards for hire, and riding stables.

Wheal Coates mine, St Agnes

⑥ ST AGNES BEACON

Paths flanked by gorse and heather take walkers to the 629 ft summit of a hill from which beacon fires blazed to warn of the approach of the Spanish Armada in 1588 and, more recently, to celebrate the Queen's Silver Jubilee in 1977. Nearly 30 miles of coast can be seen on a clear day. The land belongs to the National Trust, which also owns the remains of the nearby Wheal

GODREVY POINT *Savage rocks check the path of the racing tide and churn the sea to flying spume between the point and Godrevy Island.*

Coates mine where tin and copper were worked in the 19th century. The mine's Towanroath shaft reached a depth of more than 600 ft before Wheal Coates closed in 1889. Fountains of spray rise from the mine shafts when gale-driven waves pour into the connecting tunnels at the foot of the cliff.

Grey seals can sometimes be seen swimming off St Agnes Head. The cliffs are a breeding ground for kittiwakes, fulmars, guillemots and herring gulls.

⑦ TREVAUNANCE COVE

Trevaunance Cove, where cliffs tower above a beach of shingle-backed sand, is one of Cornwall's 'lost' ports. Generation after generation of men from St Agnes built harbours for the tin and copper trade, but the relentless sea invariably destroyed them. One, built in 1699, survived for only six years. Cargoes were unloaded by horse-powered windlasses, mounted on the cliffs, while ore went thundering down a series of chutes. Tumbled blocks of granite are all that remain of the last harbour, built early in the 19th century; it finally fell into decay in 1920. The cove is now a popular beach for surfers.

St Agnes, set on high ground to the south, was one of the mining industry's most important centres. Its Polberro mine alone employed nearly 500 people in the 1830s and was at one time the county's greatest producer of tin; it added 'Royal' to its name after being visited by Queen Victoria in 1846. Slate and granite houses, some dating from the early 18th century, line the main street, and old miners' cottages stand in a stepped terrace known as 'Stippy Stappy'.

Lifeguards patrol the beaches in summer, when there are surfboards for hire.

⑧ TREVELLAS PORTH

A steep lane, at one point only just wide enough for a car, runs from Trevellas village to this cliff-clasped cove of greyish sand, where strong currents make bathing unsafe. It lies at the mouth of Trevellas Coombe, a

resort, Perranporth was originally a mining village where tin and copper were worked in the Middle Ages. Later ventures included driving a horizontal shaft from a cove on Cligga Head right into the heart of Perranporth. One of its three pumping engines stood near what are now the tennis courts off Perran Coombe Road. Old mine shafts still pit Cligga Head, sharing a viewpoint with ruined coastal defences and a gliding club.

There are lifeguard patrols along the beach in summer, and surfboards for hire. A carnival is held in July, and sand yachting takes place in winter. Riding stables are available, and there is fishing from the shore for bass.

LOCAL INFORMATION

Tourist information Newquay 71345/6/7; (St Ives) Penzance 796297.

HM Coastguard Falmouth 317575 for information, 999 in emergency (ask for coastguard).

Weather Newquay 2224, Plymouth 8091.

Local radio BBC Cornwall, 476 m, 630 kHz, 96.4 MHz.

PLACES TO SEE INLAND

Camborne Museum. In the public library. Local archaeological, mining and mineral interest.

Camborne School of Mines, Pool, near Redruth. Museum of minerals. Mon.-Fri.

Cornish Engines (NT), East Pool Mine. Beam engines of late 19th century. Daily in summer.

Foster's Pottery Co., Redruth. Guided tours of pottery, Mon.-Fri. in summer; showroom, Mon.-Fri. all year.

deep valley where two tall, stone-built chimneys and the shell of a derelict engine-house are all that remain of the old Blue Hills tin mine. It was opened in the 1830s and closed in 1897. The whole of the valley throbbed with mining activity in the 19th century, but gradually returned to nature.

⑨ PERRANPORTH

'Piran's Port' recalls the legend of St Piran, who is said to have sailed from Ireland on a millstone in the Celtic 'Age of Saints' about 1,300 years ago. Gear Sands, where he built his first church, is now a huge expanse of dunes which conceal extensive holiday camps.

Topped with turf in places, the dunes run down to a superb sandy beach which sweeps northwards for more than 2 miles to Ligger Point and is at least half a mile wide at low tide. Swimmers and surfers should avoid the southern end of the beach, where streams run into the sea by Chapel Rock and create dangerous currents.

Now a popular and compact little holiday

PERRAN BEACH *Sunbathers take to the sands at Perranporth when the tide has retreated and the booming surf is just a distant murmur.*

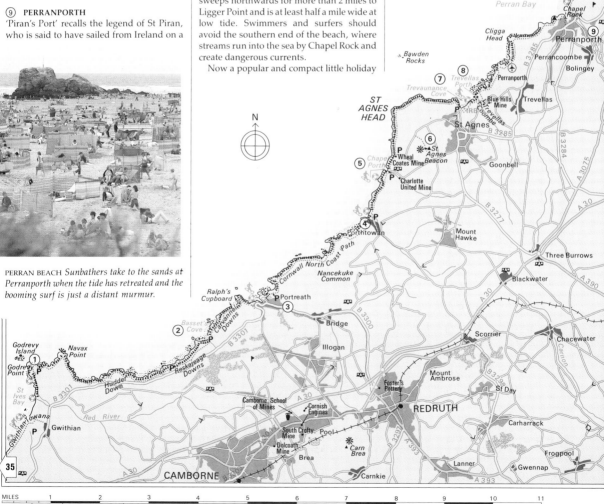

Holiday haven and artists' retreat on a wide, sandy bay

The dune-backed beaches of St Ives Bay attract holidaymaking crowds, but the coast between the town and Cape Cornwall provides a striking contrast. Granite cliffs are topped with a patchwork of small, stone-walled fields overlooked by steep slopes clad in gorse and rich in prehistoric remains. Only at Cape Cornwall and Pendeen Watch may cars be driven close to the sea, and Portheras Cove is the only place suitable for bathing.

① CAPE CORNWALL

A much quieter spot than its well-publicised neighbour Land's End, Cape Cornwall misses by only 1,000 yds the distinction of being the westernmost point in mainland England. The headland – the only one in England or Wales bearing the name of 'Cape' – is crowned with a tall chimney, standing in isolation, which marks the site of the 19th-century Cape Cornwall tin mine. Its long-abandoned workings extended north-westwards under the sea. From the modest summit there are good views of Land's End and the Longships lighthouse.

Cape Cornwall is reached by a narrow, twisting lane from St Just, England's westernmost town and a centre of the tin-mining industry during the Victorian era. From the car park at the end of the road a path leads down to Priest's Cove, a sheltered inlet with a small stretch of sand.

On the clifftops north of Cape Cornwall, more derelict engine-houses, heaps of shale and closed-down mine shafts mark the site of what used to be one of Cornwall's busiest mining communities. The mine on Botallack Head, which ceased working in 1895, was very close to the shore, and miners deep underground could hear the pebbles being scraped along above their heads as the tide ebbed and flowed.

② TREWELLARD

Opened in 1977, the village's Tin Mining Museum vividly illustrates the history of the hazardous industry that played such a major role in Cornwall's life during the 19th century. The museum is on the site of the Geevor Mine, one of the few mines still in working order in the county. Visitors can see the machinery with which tin is extracted when the mine is operating.

Founded in 1911, the company's early interests included the ill-fated Levant mine whose main shaft was more than 2,000 ft deep. In 1919 the 'man-engine' broke and claimed 31 lives. The device was essentially a rod, powered by a steam-engine, which rose and fell 12 ft with every stroke. A miner on his way to work stepped on to one of the rod's many platforms, went down to the end of the stroke, stepped off on to another platform in the shaft, and repeated the process until he reached the appropriate level. It took about 30 minutes to descend the 130 platforms of Levant mine's deepest shaft, from which levels went out more than a mile beneath the Atlantic.

③ PENDEEN WATCH

Ore deposits stain the sea a rich, dark red as it batters the rocky headland from which a lighthouse has guided ships since 1900. From the car park by the lighthouse a cliff path leads down to a tiny cove where a sandy beach is exposed at low tide.

About half a mile east, reached by a path, lies Portheras Cove, a larger but still beautiful and secluded bay with a sandy, shingle-backed beach. Walkers who follow the clifftop path for 6 miles to Zennor can enjoy some of England's finest coastal scenery. Near Rosemergy the path crosses 50 acres of National Trust land, where bracken and boulders lead to cliffs that delight expert climbers. They were used as a training area for commandos in the Second World War and, in 1963, were climbed by Lord Hunt and Sherpa Tensing to celebrate the tenth anniversary of the conquest of Mount Everest.

LANYON QUOIT *The stones of this ancient grave were originally the heart of a huge mound, about 90 ft by 40 ft, erected around 2500 BC.*

One mile inland, in the village of Pendeen, a Mineral and Mining Museum is open daily. An organised cliff walk takes in sites connected with Cornish mining. Two miles further inland, a lane from Trevowhan to Penzance passes Lanyon Quoit, one of the Penwith peninsula's many 'gallery' graves.

④ ZENNOR

This tiny village, built of gale-defying granite, stands 300 ft above the sea in a landscape of wild beauty, and is watched over by the church of St Senara, dating from the 12th century. A memorial by the porch commemorates John Davey (1812-91), said to have been the last person to speak the ancient Cornish language as his native tongue – though this distinction is more generally claimed for Dolly Pentreath, who died at Mousehole in 1777. Postcards with the Lord's Prayer in Cornish are on sale.

The church's best-known feature is the Mermaid Chair, whose medieval carving depicts a mermaid with a mirror in one hand and a comb in the other. She is said to have been enchanted by the singing of a chorister, Matthew Trewhella, who eventually followed her down to the sea at Pendour Cove, beneath the spectacular cliffs of Zennor Head. The couple were never seen again, but legends relate that their sweet singing is sometimes heard at night.

Carving on the Mermaid Chair in Zennor church

D. H. Lawrence and his German-born wife Frieda lived at Zennor from 1915 until 1917, while the novelist worked on *Women in Love*. Rumours that the couple were spies, signalling from the cliffs to German submarines, were fuelled by the fact that Frieda was a cousin to Manfred von Richthofen, the 'Red Baron'. The stories were untrue, but the Lawrences were eventually ordered to leave Cornwall within three days and report to the police when they found another place to live. The unhappy episode was later recalled in 'The Nightmare' chapter of *Kangaroo*, Lawrence's semi-autobiographical novel.

Zennor's Wayside Museum, in the garden of a cottage, has exhibits relating to tin mining and other aspects of local life. They include implements used to cut turf and gorse for fuel.

GUIDING LIGHT *Pendeen Watch lighthouse guides shipping off the coast between Cape Cornwall and Gurnard's Head. Its beam can be seen 20 miles away.*

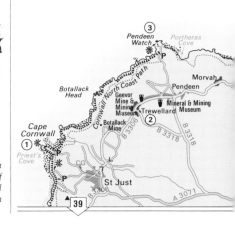

⑤ ST IVES

A sculpture called 'Dual Form', presented to St Ives by Dame Barbara Hepworth, stands outside the Guildhall and symbolises the town's reputation as a haven for artists. Visitors flood in during the holiday season, but the oldest part of St Ives – between the harbour and Porthmeor Beach – retains its old-world character. It is a compact and enchanting maze of narrow streets, and even narrower lanes, paved with granite and squeezed between picturesque buildings. There is much to delight the stroller with an eye for detail.

Porthmeor Beach is ideal for surfing, while Porthgwidden and Porthminster are sheltered by St Ives Head. The harbour also dries out to form a sandy beach at low tide, and is protected by a stone pier built in 1770. It was the work of John Smeaton, the civil engineer who had pioneered bold new techniques when he designed the third Eddystone lighthouse in 1759. John Smeaton's harbour helped St Ives to become Cornwall's biggest pilchard port in the 19th century, when the fish were exported to markets as far afield as Italy.

St Leonard's, a tiny building at the landward end of the pier, dates from the Middle Ages and was a chapel for fishermen. It stands on the site where St Ia, after whom St Ives is named, is said to have arrived by coracle from Ireland, in the 6th century. The building now houses a wall-to-wall photograph of the harbour in the days of sail, together with models of fishing boats.

The harbour is one of the few places between Land's End and Newquay where trailer-borne boats can be launched; but a fee is charged and permission must be obtained from the harbourmaster. St Ives has seaside amusements, museums and art galleries. Lifeguards patrol Porthmeor Beach in summer, surfboards can be hired, and boat and fishing trips are available.

⑥ CARBIS BAY

Steep slopes, sprinkled with houses and hotels, plunge down to the sheltered, sandy beach at Carbis Bay. The rocks near by are popular with fishermen, who catch pollack, plaice and mackerel. At low tide there are walks along the shore to Porth Kidney Sands and on to the old church at Lelant.

⑦ LELANT

Motorists wishing to avoid the narrow streets of St Ives can take advantage of a

SHELTERED WATERS *Modern buildings rub shoulders with the old behind the peaceful harbour at St Ives. Fishing boats and pleasure boats moor at a 200-year-old granite quay.*

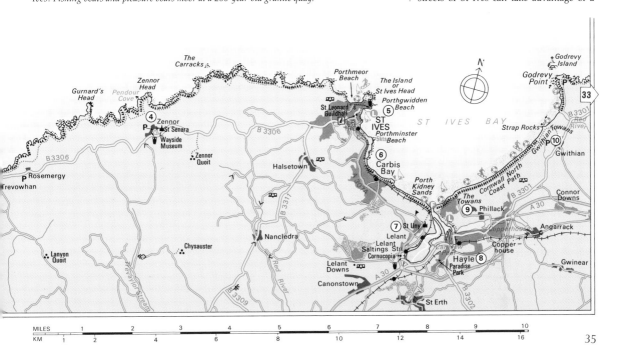

special park-and-ride ticket from Lelant Saltings railway station. Lelant itself is a pretty village that prospered as a port until gale-driven sands started choking the River Hayle's estuary in the 15th century. A *Survey of Cornwall*, published in 1584, described it as 'somtyme a haven town of late decayed by reason of the sands which hath choaked the harbour and buried much of the land and houses'.

The 15th-century church, dedicated to St Uny, stands on the edge of the dunes in a graveyard notable for four lichen-covered Celtic crosses. A path crosses the dunes to Porth Kidney Sands, where lifeguards patrol in summer; swimmers should avoid the estuary where the River Hayle joins the sea, causing cross-currents. Walkers following the long-distance coastal path cross the estuary by ferry.

⑧ **HAYLE**
Copper, tin and a foundry established by John Harvey in 1779 made Hayle the busiest port on Cornwall's western coast for more than 100 years. By the 1830s it had a packet steamer service to Bristol and was linked to the mines of Camborne and Redruth by a railway. A notable cargo, shipped out by the foundry in 1844, was an immense steam-engine built to drain the Haarlem Lake in Holland; the cylinder weighed 25 tons.

The foundry's closure in 1904 started Hayle's decline as a port. Its harbour, built at the estuary of the River Hayle, is still used by private craft, but coal piled high on the riverside wharves is brought in by road. Paradise Park includes a bird garden, rare breeds of animals and a steam railway. At the head of the Hayle estuary an area called the Saltings is a breeding ground for a variety of birds, including kingfishers, cormorants, terns and herons.

⑨ **THE TOWANS**
Low cliffs and a huge expanse of turf-topped dunes – *towan* is Cornish for 'sand-dune' – overlook 3 miles of sands which sweep up the coast from the Hayle estuary towards Godrevy Point. There are caravans and holiday homes among the dunes.

Swimmers should avoid the mouth of the estuary, where they risk encountering swift currents and deep channels. There are lifeguard patrols in summer, and surfboards for hire. Windsurfing beginners are advised to take advantage of the gentler conditions in the estuary, or on Copperhouse or Carnsew pools in Hayle.

⑩ **GWITHIAN TOWANS**
Reached by road, or on foot from Gwithian village, this is part of the 3 mile beach which runs south-westwards from Godrevy Point. Dunes sprinkled with chalets lead to low, unstable cliffs battered by the sea at high tide. North of Strap Rocks, patches of sea are stained by the Red River, which bears waste from old tin mines.

CORNWALL'S MINES: AN UNDERWORLD WHERE FORTUNES WERE MADE

On granite headlands, in boulder-strewn valleys and perched on cliffs high above the sea, the gaunt chimneys and engine-houses of Cornwall's derelict mines are stark relics of the days when fortunes were made in copper and tin mining. Phoenician merchants from North Africa came to Cornwall for tin as long ago as the 5th century BC, and the Romans also extracted ore from near the surface by means of opencast mines. For centuries, deep mines were impossible because of the flooding that occurred when a shaft sank below the water-table. It was the invention of Thomas Newcomen's steam-engine early in the 18th century that first provided a means of pumping water from the workings, and launched the boom years of Cornish mining. Newcomen's engine was developed by Richard Trevithick to become the Cornish beam engine, which enabled mines to go down to great depths. Dolcoath, near Camborne, reached 3,300 ft, the deepest metal mine in Britain. After 1750, copper became the county's most important mineral. By 1800 more than three-quarters of the world's copper was mined in Cornwall, and copper mines outnumbered tin mines until the 1860s. Then the industry declined, due to competition from cheaper imported metal. Many mines were worked into the 20th century, but only a handful weathered the slump of the 1920s.

THEN AND NOW *The largest concentration of mining was in the Camborne-Redruth area, with about 100 mines in 6 square miles. South Crofty, north-east of Camborne, is kept ready for production when the price of tin is right, in conjunction with nearby Pendarves. So is Wheal Jane, east of Redruth. Along the coast derelict mines can be seen from Newquay to St Just, where Geevor near Pendeen is kept in working order.*

THE BEAM ENGINE *The tall engine-houses of the Cornish mines were built to hold Trevithick's beam engines. The beam in the early engines was made of timber – later cast iron was used – and pivoted on the front wall of the engine-house. A rod from the piston mounted vertically in the house was attached to one end of the beam, and at the outer end a series of rods descended into the mine shaft. The pumps were simply plungers attached to the rods, and as the rods moved up and down the plungers lifted the water to a drainage level where it ran away through a boring and into a convenient valley. Some of the largest engines had a cylinder 100 in. in diameter and operated a 450 ton beam. Such an engine could pump more than 400 gallons per minute from a shaft more than 1,000 ft deep.*

In some mines, men descended and climbed the shaft by near-vertical ladders. In others there was a 'man-engine' – a rod fitted with steps to raise and lower miners – alongside the pump. To reach the surface the miner would step on to the device at the bottom of the shaft, ride up until the rod started to descend again, step off and then on to the next step and so on until he reached the top.

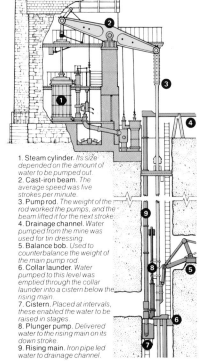

1. **Steam cylinder.** *Its size depended on the amount of water to be pumped out.*
2. **Cast-iron beam.** *The average speed was five strokes per minute.*
3. **Pump rod.** *The weight of the rod worked the pumps, and the beam lifted it for the next stroke.*
4. **Drainage channel.** *Water pumped from the mine was used for tin dressing.*
5. **Balance bob.** *Used to counterbalance the weight of the main pump rod.*
6. **Collar launder.** *Water pumped to this level was emptied through the collar launder into a cistern below the rising main.*
7. **Cistern.** *Placed at intervals, these enabled the water to be raised in stages.*
8. **Plunger pump.** *Delivered water to the rising main on its down stroke.*
9. **Rising main.** *Iron pipe led water to drainage channel.*

BRINK OF SUCCESS *Perched precariously on a cliff edge, the Botallack Mine was in 1816 one of Cornwall's richest tin mines. Its workings ran some* 600 yds beneath the sea and at one time it employed 500 miners and had 11 engine houses. The mine was in operation until 1914.

MINES THAT CAN BE VISITED

Some idea of how tin was mined a century ago can be gained at Poldark Mining, near Helston, where a section of the old underground workings is open to the public. At Geevor Mine, visitors are taken down workings 2,000 ft deep, some extending under the sea. There are guided tours of the processing plant and a museum. Tolgus Mill at Portreath (closed for renovation in 1986) shows another age-old technique of extracting tin – by 'streaming'. Though modern equipment is used, the basic technique is similar to the way in which early gold prospectors panned for gold. A number of engine-houses have been preserved and still have their pumping and winding engines, as at East Pool, Camborne. The Camborne School of Mines Geological Museum has a wide range of rocks and minerals on display.

The Geevor Mine
at Trewellard
near Pendeen

MINERS' WORLD *Cornish miners toiled in a dark and dangerous world of rough-hewn caverns, such as this one at the East Pool Mine, north-east of Camborne. Baulks of timber shored the cavern walls and wooden ladders linked the various levels. At the turn of the century, when this picture was taken, the mine's deepest level was 1,200 ft. It was still producing tin during the Second World War, and closed only in 1949.*

UNDERGROUND TOILER *This typical miner of the 19th century has a coiled fuse at his waist, candles hanging from his neck and a candle stuck to his hard felt hat with clay.*

TIN 'STREAMING' *The earliest method of extracting tin was to wash it out of the ground, using a mixture of fine sand and water, and then skim it off into a mould.*

Land's End, where granite cliffs meet the Atlantic breakers

The seas that wash the Penwith peninsula are so clear that basking sharks, huge but harmless, can sometimes be seen from the high granite cliffs. Land's End attracts a throng of summer visitors, but short walks along the cliffs soon leave the crowds behind, and a few sandy coves can be reached only on foot. Salt-laden Atlantic gales explain the lack of trees on the western side of the peninsula, but woods flank lanes to the east.

① PORTH NANVEN

A narrow, unsignposted lane with few passing places and limited parking twists down from St Just to this cove of sea-smoothed rocks and low-tide sand. The 1¼ mile walk northwards to Cape Cornwall climbs Carn Gloose, a lofty headland where the chimney of a 19th-century tin mine overlooks the impressive Ballowall Barrow, an elaborate burial chamber from the late Bronze Age. From the nearby clifftop there are excellent views of Cape Cornwall and Land's End.

② SENNEN COVE

Steep slopes plunge down to this attractive little harbour with its huddle of thatched, whitewashed cottages. A plaque set into the harbour's granite breakwater was given by Sennen's fishermen to express thanks to Colonel H. W. Williams, who when MP for St Ives in 1908 raised funds for the building of the breakwater. In the lifeboat house a telegram from the Prime Minister pays tribute to the crew's heroic work in August, 1979, when they were at sea for more than 9 hours, to help survivors of the ill-fated Fastnet yacht race. Competitors in the race ran into exceptionally bad weather off the Cornish coast, and several yachts and their crews were lost.

The harbour looks out across Whitesand Bay, a superb surfing beach. Swimming is safest at high water, because strong tidal streams run up and down the coast. Lifeguards patrol the beach during the summer months. Fishing trips are available.

③ LAND'S END

Some 1 million people a year visit this great fist of wave-lashed granite which marks the south-western tip of the British mainland. Rocks mottled with lichen stud the clifftop whose turf has been scoured away by innumerable pairs of feet, and coin-operated telescopes look out over the Atlantic.

The ownership of Land's End changed in 1982, and visitors now pay a charge to enter the area and visit craft workshops and maritime exhibitions. Walkers along the coastal path can by-pass the property.

LAST RESORT *Shuttered against the west winds, the last house in England – or the first – stands four-square on Land's End.*

Just over 1 mile offshore, waves pound the Longships reef and its lighthouse. The original tower was built at Sennen Cove at the end of the 18th century. Every stone was marked before the lighthouse was dismantled and taken block by block to the Longships. The present tower dates from 1873, and its helicopter pad was added 101 years later. It is said that one keeper was kidnapped by wreckers, but the light was kept shining by his young daughter. She was very small, but reached the lamps by standing on the family Bible.

④ MILL BAY

Majestic cliffs rise on either side of this secluded little beach where smooth boulders lead to a small area of low-tide sand. The scanty remains of a mill survive by a stream near the shore. Mill Bay is reached from the B3315 by a toll road, signposted for Nanjizal, which deteriorates into a rough track beyond Bosistow Farm. Cars are parked in a field, and the walk down to the beach takes about 3 minutes.

⑤ PORTHGWARRA

A long, steep slipway up which small boats are winched runs down to Porthgwarra's beach of huge, seaweed-draped boulders and low-tide sand. The cliff on the eastern side of the cove is pierced by a short tunnel. This enchanting spot, at the end of a valley with just a few scattered cottages, is reached by a narrow lane which wriggles between high, grassy banks bright with wild flowers in summer. A 10 minute walk from the car park leads to Gwennap Head and a coast-guard lookout perched high above the sea. The sheer cliffs are a challenge for commandos and other expert climbers who tackle routes with such names as Seal Slab, Pendulum Chimney and Commando Crawl.

⑥ ST LEVAN

The medieval church next to the car park is dedicated to St Levan, who is said to have landed at the nearby beach in the 6th or 7th century, possibly after a voyage from Wales. The church is notable for a fine collection of carved pews, while outside, near the porch, is a tall Celtic cross considerably older than the church itself. There is also a cleft rock on which the saint is said to have rested after fishing trips. He split it with a blow from his staff, and prophesied that the world would come to an end when a pannier-laden packhorse could walk through the cleft.

Opposite the church, a half-mile path ending in a steep scramble leads to Porth Chapel, a beautiful, cliff-flanked cove with smooth rocks and a sandy beach. Swimmers are advised not to venture out in rough seas.

⑦ PORTHCURNO

The high, granite cliffs which shelter Porthcurno's sands from the west are the home of the remarkable and romantic Minack Theatre, where plays are staged in an open-air setting worthy of ancient Greece. The theatre was opened in 1932, when local actors performed *The Tempest*.

On the opposite side of the bay, reached by a 15 minute walk from Treen, is Treryn Dinas, a high, jagged headland fortified during the Iron Age and now owned by the National Trust. Also reached by a short walk from Treen is the Logan Rock, a huge boulder estimated to weigh 66 tons. It can be made to wobble by nothing more than a hefty push, and has been a well-known attraction since the 18th century.

In 1824 the rock was dislodged by a Lieutenant Goldsmith – a nephew of the playwright Oliver Goldsmith – aided by a party of sailors. There was such an outcry that the Admiralty ordered the young officer

ATLANTIC RAMPART *The battered granite cliffs at Land's End, 200 ft high, are the roots of a mountain chain which once extended from the Isles of Scilly through Cornwall to Brittany and beyond.*

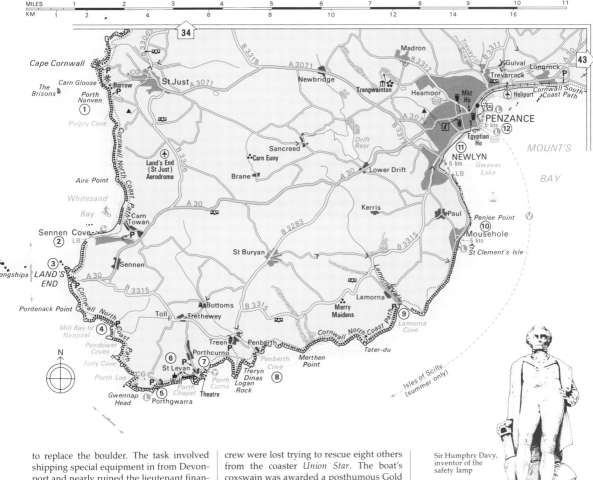

Sir Humphry Davy, inventor of the safety lamp

to replace the boulder. The task involved shipping special equipment in from Devonport and nearly ruined the lieutenant financially. Logan is derived from the Cornish verb *log*, meaning to heave or move.

⑧ PENBERTH COVE
The National Trust has owned Penberth since 1957 and describes it as 'the most perfect of Cornish fishing coves'. It is a beautiful and tranquil place, popular with artists, with a stream, a few cottages, and small fishing boats beached above the rocky shore. Larger craft used to be hauled from the sea by an unusual capstan that resembles a great cartwheel laid on its side.

Penberth never becomes crowded, because there is space for no more than about ten cars to park in the lane, a 2 minute walk from the sea.

⑨ LAMORNA COVE
A leafy lane runs down to Lamorna's tiny harbour, where ships loaded granite in the 19th century. The steep, bracken-clad slopes above the bay are still studded with huge blocks of rock from the quarries. Low tide reveals a small, sandy beach inside the harbour. A walk westwards along the cliffs leads to Tater-du, Britain's first fully automatic lighthouse, which became operational in 1965. Fishing trips are available.

⑩ MOUSEHOLE
The narrow streets and stone-built cottages of 'Mouzel', as it is pronounced, crowd right down to the village's snug little harbour, where the ebbing tide reveals a sandy beach. It was Cornwall's main fishing port for many years, but lost most of its trade when Newlyn was developed in the 19th century. The most dramatic event in Mousehole's history happened in 1595 when the village was sacked by troops from three Spanish ships.

The road to Newlyn passes the Penlee Point lifeboat house from which the *Solomon Browne* set sail during a ferocious storm in December, 1981. She and her eight-man

crew were lost trying to rescue eight others from the coaster *Union Star*. The boat's coxswain was awarded a posthumous Gold Medal, the RNLI's equivalent of the VC.

Mousehole has an art gallery, and fishing trips are available.

⑪ NEWLYN
The fishing industry is little more than a memory in many Cornish ports, but Newlyn's harbour is still packed with trawlers and overlooked by a busy fish market. A new fish quay was opened in 1981. The harbour's oldest pier dates from the Middle Ages, but the main breakwaters were built between 1866 and 1888. In 1896 local fishermen rioted, because they objected to East Coast trawlers fishing on Sundays, and the militia had to be called in.

Beyond the harbour, public gardens overlook a beach where shingle leads to sand and scattered outcrops of low rock. There is an art gallery, and shark-fishing trips are available.

⑫ PENZANCE
Though it has long ceased to be a major West Country port, Penzance still has a harbour for private craft, a small dry dock and a quay from which the *Scillonia* ferry plies between the mainland and the Isles of Scilly. A beach of fine shingle patchworked with low rock runs towards Newlyn, while on the other side of the harbour a huge crescent of sand sweeps eastwards to St Michael's Mount, more than 3 miles away.

Penzance itself is full of interest, and a town trail passes its main features. Market Jew Street is dominated by the lofty Ionic columns of the Market House, completed in 1838. At their feet stands a statue of Penzance's most famous son, Sir Humphry Davy, who was born near by in 1778 and invented the safety lamp for miners. The Morrab Gardens, near the seafront, contain a display of subtropical plants.

Trengwainton, just outside Penzance, was built in 1814 and is now owned by the National Trust. Its gardens include a series

EGYPTIAN HOUSE *This fanciful building in Chapel Street, Penzance, was built in the 1820s and is now a National Trust information centre.*

of walled enclosures containing fine magnolias and camellias, and rhododendrons from the east Himalayas, Assam and Burma. A scenic drive runs alongside a stream.

Seaside attractions include an aquarium, indoor and outdoor swimming pools, boat trips, fishing trips for ling, coalfish, conger eels and sharks, and diving trips. There are museums and an art gallery.

Palm trees and sandy beaches on Arthur's legendary Lyonnesse

According to legend, the Isles of Scilly are all that remain of Lyonnesse, a lovely land ruled over by King Arthur before it vanished beneath the Atlantic. About 28 miles south-west of Land's End, the archipelago consists of well over 100 islands and islets whose climate is so mild that flowers cultivated in small fields are the backbone of the economy in winter. There are delightful walks and miles of sandy beaches washed by the clearest of seas.

TWIN BEACHES *Hugh Town, in St Mary's, straddles a narrow isthmus between Porth Cressa Beach and Town Beach.*

① ST MARY'S

All but about 350 of Scilly's population of 1,600 live on St Mary's, the largest island with 1,554 acres. Gently undulating fields and low, bracken-clad headlands are surrounded by a fascinating, beautiful and easily explored coastline with several sandy beaches and many rocky coves. Bathing is safe in most places, but Pelistry Bay becomes dangerous at high tide when currents sweep over the sand-bar between St Mary's and Toll's Island.

The 'capital' of Scilly, Hugh Town, stands on a narrow strip of land between the sands of Town Beach and Porth Cressa Beach. Its main street, flanked by buildings of gale-defying granite, leads to a harbour where British and French trawlers mingle with private craft, and the sturdy passenger launches which take about 20 minutes to reach St Agnes, Bryher, Tresco or St Martin's. The launches also provide opportunities to take a close look at grey seals and a great variety of sea-birds. Several of the uninhabited islands must not be visited when birds are breeding. Notices with details of the restrictions are posted on The Quay.

Hugh Town developed under the protection of Star Castle, an eight-pointed fortress completed in 1593 and now a hotel. It forms part of The Garrison, the headland which shelters the town from the west and was surrounded by stone ramparts in the first half of the 18th century. The well-preserved fortifications, complete with gun batteries, enhance a popular walk that is particularly delightful towards sunset. The beams of eight lighthouses – the Bishop Rock, Round Island, Peninnis, Wolf Rock, Longships, Pendeen, Tater-du and Lizard – are visible from The Garrison on a clear night.

The history and natural history of the islands are illustrated in Hugh Town's museum by exhibits spanning more than 2,000 years. Its outstanding features include the pilot gig *Klondyke*, built in 1873, and a magnificent bronze gun recovered from the wreck of the 90-gun *Association*, the flagship of Rear-Admiral Sir Cloudesley Shovell,

which sank after striking the Gilstone reef in thick fog in 1707.

Old Town, an attractive cluster of stone cottages, was the main centre of population in St Mary's until Hugh Town took its place. Its sandy, rock-studded bay curves round to a little church, shaded by palm trees, with the date 1662 carved above its door. Many victims of the *Schiller* disaster of 1875 are buried in the graveyard: the German liner was on a passage from New York to Germany when she encountered fog, struck a reef and went down with all but 37 of her 372 passengers and crew.

Porth Hellick, a very sheltered bay of sand framed by seaweed-draped rocks, is the starting point for one of two waymarked nature trails. The other runs from Old Town Bay to the A3111 road near Sandy Banks Farm. A small pillar of rough stone at Porth Hellick marks the spot where Sir Cloudesley Shovell was washed ashore after the *Association* went down. It is said that he survived the wreck and was lying exhausted on the beach when a woman murdered him for his jewel-encrusted rings.

The turf-topped burial chamber on Porth Hellick Down dates from the Bronze Age, and is one of the islands' many tangible links with prehistory. Another burial place, Bant's Carn, is on the north-western rim of St Mary's and overlooks the granite hut circles of a Romano-British village that was inhabited almost 2,000 years ago. Fishing trips and boat trips are available.

Bant's Carn on St Mary's

GRAVEYARD OF SHIPPING

All around the Isles of Scilly, scattered reefs and rocky islets have for centuries taken a grim toll of shipping. Sailing ships blown off course or running for shelter from Atlantic gales and steamships lost in fog have had their hulls ripped open, often with huge loss of life.

Modern navigational aids have lessened the threat in recent years. In 1967, however, the oil tanker *Torrey Canyon* went aground on Seven Stones, north-east of Scilly, and was eventually bombed to burn off the flow of leaking oil that was polluting the beaches of Cornwall and Devon.

The barque Maipu *aground off Bryher in 1879.*

② GUGH

The Old Man of Gugh, a standing stone 9 ft tall, was erected by Gugh's Bronze Age inhabitants. The little island – its name is pronounced to rhyme with 'Hugh' – now has only two houses and is linked to St Agnes by a sand-bar that is covered at high tide. The sandy beaches on either side of the bar provide safe bathing at low water, but the incoming tide creates dangerous currents as it sweeps over the barrier.

③ ST AGNES

A patchwork of tiny fields, sheltered by lofty hedges, is overlooked by the disused St Agnes lighthouse whose portly white tower dominates the little island. The lamp was lit for the first time in 1680 and remained in operation for 231 years.

A road just wide enough for a single vehicle runs from the quay at Porth Conger to the sand-and-shingle beach at Lower Town, on the opposite side of the island. The east window of the hamlet's church is dedicated to crews who manned the lifeboat based near by from 1891 to 1920.

A plaque in the church records the loss of the American schooner *Thomas W. Lawson* in 1907. The only seven-masted schooner ever built, she got into difficulties off Annet, west of St Agnes, and a member of the lifeboat's crew went aboard to act as a pilot. He and 15 members of the crew were lost when the schooner sank, but the captain and engineer were saved from the Hellweathers rocks when the pilot's son, Frederick Hicks, swam to them from the gig *Slippen*. He was awarded an RNLI silver medal and received a gold watch from the US Government. The US authorities also gave gold medals to the other seven members of the gig's crew.

④ BISHOP ROCK

Britain's tallest lighthouse rises 175 ft above the sea and stands sentinel over the south-west tip of the Isles of Scilly. Its 2.6 million candlepower light has a range of nearly 30 miles.

The first tower, a cast-iron structure, vanished during a storm in 1850. Work on its granite-block replacement started two years later, but it vibrated too much and its lantern was often shrouded in spray despite being more than 100 ft up. A survey conducted for

created the subtropical gardens that deserve to be ranked among the wonders of Britain. It is the only place in Europe where New Zealand ironwoods and Mexican yuccas flourish in the open. Other species grow naturally nowhere else in the whole of the Northern Hemisphere. Tresco's beauty is additionally enhanced by two lakes, Great Pool and Abbey Pool, where coots, moorhens, mute swans and other birds nest amid the reeds.

Piper's Hole, on the island's north-eastern tip, is a long, narrow cave which burrows about 80 yds into the island and has a small freshwater pool. The cave is said to have been used by smugglers, and local legends also name it as the home of mermaids.

The Isles of Scilly were a Royalist stronghold in the Civil War and did not capitulate until 1651, when Admiral Blake captured Tresco and mounted guns on Crow Point where they could attack any ships trying to use Hugh Town's harbour. A fort now

TROPICAL TRESCO *Exotic plants flourish in Tresco's Abbey Gardens. Many grow nowhere else in the Northern Hemisphere.*

Trinity House in 1881 resulted in the tower being encased in an outer shell and raised by two storeys. A helicopter pad was added in 1976.

⑤ SAMSON
This small, humpbacked island has been uninhabited since 1855 and is now a breeding ground for lesser black-backed gulls. Its population never recovered from a tragedy which claimed the lives of most of the young islanders during the Napoleonic Wars. They captured a French ship and were sailing her to the mainland when all were lost on the Wolf Rock off Land's End.

In 1798 the leaking, 74-gun *Colossus* tried to ride out a storm off Samson, but her anchor broke and she foundered near Southward Well Point. The warship had helped defeat the French at the Battle of the Nile and was homeward bound with a cargo of art treasures belonging to Sir William Hamilton, the husband of Nelson's mistress. The wreck was located by local divers in 1975.

⑥ BRYHER
Bryher's western coast, battered into weird shapes by the awesome power of Atlantic storms, contrasts with the sheltered beach which faces Tresco and the tranquillity of Rushy Bay, where sands are overlooked by Bronze Age cairns on Samson Hill. The island's population of just over 50 is Scilly's smallest.

⑦ TRESCO
Unlike the rest of the inhabited islands, Tresco is a private estate which the Duchy of Cornwall has leased to the Dorrien Smith family since 1834. The first of the line, Augustus Smith, was an energetic and far-sighted squire who became Lord Proprietor of all the islands. He built Tresco Abbey near the site of the island's medieval priory and

known as Cromwell's Castle was immediately built to control the narrow channel between Tresco and Bryher. It is only a short walk from King Charles' Castle which, despite its name, was built 100 years earlier.

Tresco has much to offer the walker, and the island's superb beaches cater for visitors seeking nothing more than relaxation in the most peaceful and magical of atmospheres.

⑧ ST MARTIN'S
A population of 80 and an area of more than 500 acres make St Martin's the third biggest island in Scilly after St Mary's and Tresco. Its 'capital', Higher Town, has a sailing centre and is overlooked from the east by a steep little hill whose striped tower has been a landmark for sailors since the 17th century. Like Tresco, the island has several beautiful beaches within easy reach of the quay below Higher Town. The sands at Porth Morran on White Island, which is linked to St Martin's by a natural, tide-covered causeway, lead to pits where seaweed was once burned to produce an alkali that was used in the making of soap and glass. It was an important source of income in the islands during the 17th and 18th centuries.

LOCAL INFORMATION
Tourist information Scillonia 22536.
HM Coastguard Scillonia 22651 or 22873, or Falmouth 317575 for information, 999 in emergency (ask for coastguard).
Weather Plymouth 8091.
Local radio BBC Radio Cornwall 97.3 MHz.

HOW TO GET THERE
By sea. RMV *Scillonian III* from Penzance: sailings daily, except Sundays, in summer; less frequently in winter; Penzance 222009.
By air. British Airways helicopter service from Penzance heliport daily except Sundays to St Mary's throughout the year, and to Tresco Mar.-Oct.; Penzance 3871 for information and reservations. Brymon Airways Ltd: flights from Exeter, Newquay and Plymouth; information and reservations Scillonia 22665; Plymouth 707023; (Newquay services only) St Mawgan 860551.

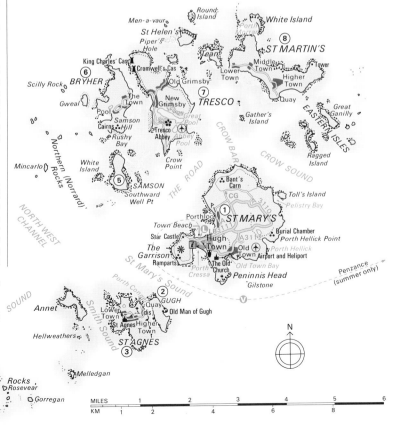

An island castle on a bay of beaches and rocky coves

The rocky shore of Mount's Bay is broken by a succession of coves, linked like beads on a chain by the switchback course of the coastal path. A complete change of mood is provided by The Loe, a tranquil lake surrounded by footpaths, which probes inland towards Helston. There are plenty of places to surf and swim. On many beaches east of St Michael's Mount, however, the shore shelves steeply and bathing is dangerous at low water.

① ST MICHAEL'S MOUNT

Like a giant sandcastle, the granite island rises 300 ft from the waters of Mount's Bay. A real 14th-century castle caps it. Possibly the Romans shipped tin from the island, then called Ictis; certainly in 1135 a Benedictine priory was built on the summit.

The island was later fortified, and in the 14th century a new church with a battlemented tower was built. Since 1679 St Michael's Mount has been the home of the St Aubyn family, but it now belongs to the National Trust and is open to the public.

A causeway, revealed at low tide, or a ferry links St Michael's Mount to the mainland village of Marazion. There is safe swimming from the gently shelving sandy beach west of the causeway. To the east stretches a string of rocky bays, best seen from a path which runs along the clifftop through an avenue of tamarisk and sweet-smelling alexanders.

SAINT'S ISLE *The priory on St Michael's Mount is dedicated to the Archangel who is said to have appeared to local fishermen in AD 495.*

② PERRANUTHNOE

Colour-washed cottages descend the slopes towards the half-mile strip of Perran Sands. To the south-east, gorse blazes on the cliffs above Stackhouse Cove; the long headland cutting off the view is Cudden Point, on whose rocks many ships have foundered.

③ PRUSSIA COVE

This jagged cleft in the coast has an eerie black opening leading right back into the slaty cliffs. There is a slipway used by a few small fishing boats. A lane signposted from Rosudgeon on the A394 leads to a car park, from which the cove can be reached in about 10 minutes' walking.

The cove gets its name from a smuggler, John Carter, who was known as the 'King of Prussia'. Carter is said to have borne a likeness to Frederick the Great, but another explanation of his nickname is that the king was Carter's hero in boyhood games. An inn, also called 'King of Prussia', which stood at the head of the cove in the 18th century, was owned by Carter, who used his job as a cover for smuggling on a grand scale. His activities included the mounting of a battery of guns on the cliffs around his inn – ostensibly to ward off French privateers but also, it is said, to frighten off Revenue men.

More recently, in 1947, the rocks of Prussia Cove claimed the latest victim of many ships wrecked on the Cornish coast over the centuries when the 30,000 ton *Warspite* was blown inshore while being towed to a breaker's yard. The ship was pulled off the rocks – only to go aground again at Marazion, where she eventually broke up.

④ PRAA SANDS

The popular holiday village overlooks a sandy strip 1 mile long, with a backing of high dunes. The western end of the beach is sheltered from westerly winds by the cliffs of Hoe Point; but there are prominent warnings against bathing at low tide.

At the eastern end of Praa Sands there is an easy escape from the crowds by a path up to Lesceave Cliff – 13 gorse-covered acres owned by the National Trust.

⑤ RINSEY HEAD

The engine-house and chimney of Wheal Prosper, an old copper mine partially restored by the National Trust in 1970, stand on this granite headland as a memorial to Cornwall's mining days, from about 1750 to 1870. A car park 100 yds above the mine is reached by a signposted road off the A394.

Half a mile further east along the coast path are the ruins of another copper mine, Wheal Trewavas, perched on the steep granite face of Trewavas Head. The miners tore the metal ore from lodes running out under the sea, until the water broke into the workings and closed the mine in 1850.

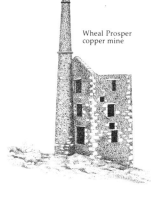

Wheal Prosper copper mine

⑥ PORTHLEVEN

The little town, set between steeply enclosing banks, stands on an attractive section of the coastal path, and has an unexpectedly big harbour. Built in 1811 to import mining machinery and export copper and tin, this now gives haven to small boats with brightly coloured sails. Trailer-borne craft can be launched at high tide; the harbour dries out at low tide.

Despite the calm of Porthleven's inner harbour, this is a tricky section of the coast even for experienced sailors. A memorial on the cliffs just west of the town honours 22 Porthleven fishermen drowned at sea between 1871 and 1948, and also the many unknown mariners whose bodies have been cast up on this part of the coast.

⑦ THE LOE

A freshwater lake more than a mile long is the centrepiece of the 1,600 acre Penrose Estate, owned by the National Trust. Miles of paths wind beside The Loe and its offshoot Carminowe Creek, through woods carpeted with bluebells in spring.

The Loe was formed in the 13th century when a natural sand-bar dammed the River Cober, and gradually a long bank of shingle – today's Loe Bar – was formed. In olden days locals had periodically to dig a channel through Loe Bar to prevent the pent-up waters of the Cober from flooding Helston; today the flow is controlled by a culvert.

Many ships have come to grief on Loe Bar. They include the frigate *Anson* which in 1807 was driven on to the sands; 100 men died within a stone's throw of the shore. Among the crowd who watched the vessel being dashed to pieces was Henry Trengrouse, who the following year invented the rocket apparatus for throwing a line to a ship in distress – a device which, with some improvements, is still used today. The original can be seen in Helston Folk Museum. On the cliffs east of Loe Bar is a memorial to the victims of the 1807 disaster.

⑧ HELSTON

The traditions of this song-famed 'quaint old Cornish town' are kept alive by the annual Flora Day held usually on May 8 to celebrate the coming of summer. Church bells ring, houses are decorated with greenery and hundreds of local dancers follow the town band through the streets to the tune of the Flora, or Furry, Dance.

Helston was granted its first charter by

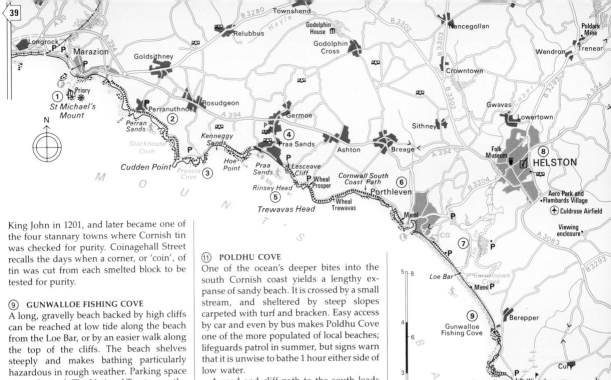

King John in 1201, and later became one of the four stannary towns where Cornish tin was checked for purity. Coinagehall Street recalls the days when a corner, or 'coin', of tin was cut from each smelted block to be tested for purity.

⑨ GUNWALLOE FISHING COVE

A long, gravelly beach backed by high cliffs can be reached at low tide along the beach from the Loe Bar, or by an easier walk along the top of the cliffs. The beach shelves steeply and makes bathing particularly hazardous in rough weather. Parking space is very limited. The National Trust owns the foreshore for 4½ miles from Porthleven to Poldhu Cove.

⑩ CHURCH COVE

This sandy cove, crossed by a stream and less hemmed in by high cliffs than many of its neighbours, was the site chosen for a church by St Winwaloe in the 6th century. The present building dates mainly from the 15th century, and part of its woodwork comes from the *Saint Anthony*, a Portuguese treasure ship wrecked at Church Cove in 1526.

The name of Dollar Cove, a 2 minute walk away, recalls a Spanish galleon that went down laden with 2½ tons of gold coins in 1785. Gold doubloons and other coins have been found on the beach. Dollar Cove's sands are backed by low, soft cliffs where erosion is threatening to let the sea break through and turn the church's site into a tiny, tidal island.

Volunteer lifeguards patrol Church Cove at summer weekends, but bathing in both coves is unsafe at low tide, when strong currents sweep past the headlands. There are surfboards for hire.

⑪ POLDHU COVE

One of the ocean's deeper bites into the south Cornish coast yields a lengthy expanse of sandy beach. It is crossed by a small stream, and sheltered by steep slopes carpeted with turf and bracken. Easy access by car and even by bus makes Poldhu Cove one of the more populated of local beaches; lifeguards patrol in summer, but signs warn that it is unwise to bathe 1 hour either side of low water.

A road and cliff path to the south leads round the gardens of Poldhu Hotel to the Marconi Memorial. This stands near the spot from which the first radio message – a repetition of the Morse letter 'S' – was sent across the Atlantic, on December 12, 1901. The man responsible for the experiment, the Italian Guglielmo Marconi, received it at his base outside St John's, Newfoundland, almost 3,000 miles away.

⑫ POLURRIAN COVE

High cliffs frame a quiet sandy bay in which a stream runs out of a grassy valley and across a delta of hard sand. Winds from the south-west favour surfing, but tidal currents make conditions unsafe at low water.

The cove is reached by a three-quarter-mile footpath from Mullion (starting opposite St Melan's Church), or by a road turning off the Mullion-Mullion Cove road, but there is no car park close to the beach. A path runs southwards over the cliffs to Mullion Cove.

⑬ MULLION COVE

Blocks of greenstone, a hard basaltic rock, form the enclosing breakwaters of the little harbour whose old-world character has enchanted generations of visitors. It is now owned by the National Trust. The need for shelter on this exposed coast was emphasised in 1839, when most of the cove's fishing boats, anchored offshore, were wrecked by a sudden gale. The harbour was built in 1895 and had a lifeboat until 1909.

A natural tunnel through the rocks leads at low tide to a small sandy beach on the south side. Offshore is Mullion Island, closed to the public and a sanctuary for many sea-birds, including kittiwakes.

There is a splendid walk southwards over Mullion Cliff to Predannack Head, which rises some 260 ft above the sea and commands a view embracing the whole of Mount's Bay. The walk passes through part of the Lizard National Nature Reserve; there is a wide range of heathland and clifftop plants, and birds to be seen include kittiwakes, guillemots, razorbills and shags.

CHURCH ON THE BEACH *The tiny 15th-century church of St Winwaloe, at the edge of Church Cove, has a separate belfry some 200 years older, built into the cliffs 14 ft away from the chancel.*

45

LOCAL INFORMATION

Tourist information Penzance 2207/2341; Camborne 712941.

HM Coastguard Falmouth 317575 for information, 999 in emergency (ask for coastguard).

Weather Newquay 2224; Plymouth 8091.

Local radio BBC Cornwall, 476 m, 630 kHz, 96.4 MHz.

PLACES TO SEE INLAND

Aero Park and Flambards Village, SE of Helston. Historic aircraft, old village. Daily in summer.

Culdrose Royal Naval Air Station, SE of Helston. Helicopter base with viewing enclosure. Daily.

Godolphin House, 5 miles NW of Helston. Tudor mansion. Some afternoons in summer.

Poldark Mine, Wendron, 3 miles N of Helston. Daily in summer.

Fishing villages and tales of smugglers round the Lizard

A maze of narrow lanes sunk between high, grassy banks sprawls away to the east of the road between Helston and Lizard Point, the southernmost point on the British mainland. Explorers are rewarded by beautiful little coves, several of which are overlooked by clusters of picture-postcard cottages with thatched roofs and white-washed walls. By contrast, the Lizard's western coast is lined by cliffs and almost uninhabited.

① KYNANCE COVE
Cliffs 200 ft high rise on either side of this spectacular cove whose sandy beach is completely covered at high tide. The Lizard peninsula's complex geology, with its juxtaposition of hard and soft rocks, has enabled the sea to carve the cliffs into caves, arches and tidal islets where sea-birds nest.

The most dramatic feature, known locally as the Devil's Bellows, is a fissure through which the sea roars and spurts like a vast steam-engine. From the nearest car park, which is privately owned, the beach can be reached in about 5 minutes, down flights of steps set into the turf. The beach can only be used for a few hours at low tide, and its many caves can only be explored then.

② LIZARD
A narrow lane runs out of the village to a tongue of wave-washed rocks marking the southern tip of mainland Britain. They form a natural breakwater for Polpeor Cove, where a few small fishing boats rest on a sand-and-shingle beach on which a lifeboat was stationed from 1914 to 1959.

Lizard Point, the landfall for countless homecoming sailors, is also the site of a lighthouse whose 5¼ million candlepower beam can be seen from a distance of 21 miles. The original lighthouse, Cornwall's first, was built on the headland by Sir John Killigrew of Falmouth in 1619. The project was bitterly opposed by the locals: 'They have been so long used to reap profit by the calamity of the ruin of shipping that they claim it as hereditary', Sir John noted.

East of the lighthouse, Housel Bay's small, sandy beach nestles below Pen Olver, the cliff from which the Spanish Armada was first sighted in 1588. It was also used by Marconi in 1901 when he made radio contact with the Isle of Wight a few months before

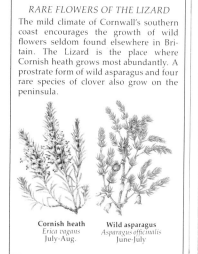

QUEEN'S CHOICE *The polished serpentine stone admired by Queen Victoria is so called because of its snakeskin-like markings.*

the first transmission across the Atlantic.

Lizard village, on a windy plateau, is a centre for the making of ornaments from serpentine, the local rock whose delicate shades and patterns are highlighted by careful polishing. It became fashionable in 1846, when Queen Victoria visited Cornwall and ordered a serpentine table. A museum housed in a threshing barn displays exhibits concerned with Cornish history.

③ CHURCH COVE
Thatched and whitewashed cottages, their walls bright with roses in summer, are passed during the 5 minute walk from the church of St Wynwallow to a small, rocky inlet used by crab and lobster boats. The steep slipway is overlooked by a lifeboat

house built at the end of the 19th century, but the boat is now based at Kilcobben, a short walk to the south.

There is limited parking near the church, where the last sermon in the Cornish language is said to have been preached at the end of the 17th century. One of the church's memorials commemorates the 11 members of the crew of the MV *Polperro* who were lost when she was sunk by German E-boats in Mount's Bay in 1944.

④ CADGWITH
Squeezed into a narrow valley with thatched cottages lining the cliffs around, Cadgwith has been a favourite subject for artists for more than a century. The quaint old buildings run down to a shingle cove with low-tide sand where small boats that fish for crab, lobster and mackerel are beached.

A few yards to the north is another cove of big, sea-smoothed boulders where sands are revealed by the ebbing tide. The steep slopes above the beach are notable for England's only wood of dwarf elms. A short walk southwards along the cliffs leads to the Devil's Frying-pan, a 200 ft deep hole caused by the collapse of a cave.

Cars are parked on the outskirts of the village, a 2 minute walk from the sea.

⑤ RUAN MINOR
Set back from the sea, and watched over by its ivy-clad church tower, Ruan Minor is the starting point for a 3 mile nature trail which visits Poltesco, Carleon Cove, Cadgwith and St Ruan. The walk takes in a fascinating variety of scenery, from wooded valleys to clifftop paths, and illustrates many aspects of the area's natural history.

⑥ CARLEON COVE
This peaceful little cove, a 10 minute walk from Poltesco, was the home of the Lizard Serpentine Company which flourished in the 19th century. It employed nearly 100 people and produced mantlepieces, shop fronts and ornamental urns from the dark green mottled stone quarried near by. Many of the highly polished shop fronts were made for businesses in London and Paris. Two small buildings still stand near the water's edge. The stream which forms a small pool in the shingle at the top of the beach used to turn the wheel which provided power for the factory.

CADGWITH HARBOUR *Crab and lobster boats rest above the tide, and every villager appears to have a vessel on the beach. Many of the houses are built of dark green serpentine stone.*

RARE FLOWERS OF THE LIZARD
The mild climate of Cornwall's southern coast encourages the growth of wild flowers seldom found elsewhere in Britain. The Lizard is the place where Cornish heath grows most abundantly. A prostrate form of wild asparagus and four rare species of clover also grow on the peninsula.

Cornish heath
Erica vagans
July-Aug.

Wild asparagus
Asparagus officinalis
June-July

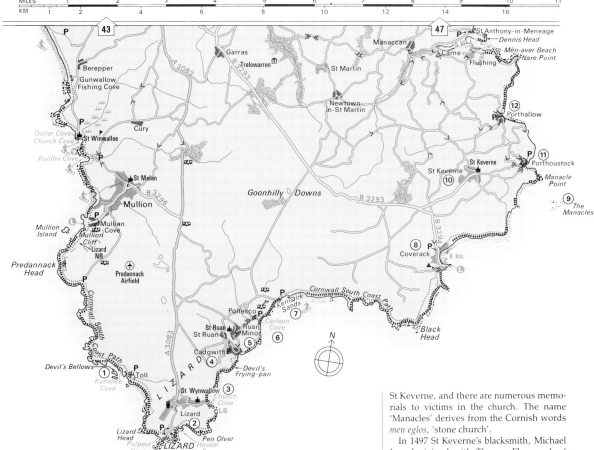

⑦ KENNACK SANDS

Two beaches, joined at low tide, combine to make this one of the longest stretches of sand on the eastern side of the Lizard peninsula. It is a popular place for bucket-and-spade families, and the clear waters offshore attract divers. There are surfboards for hire.

⑧ COVERACK

One of the Lizard peninsula's most memorable villages, Coverack overlooks a sand-and-shingle bay where the sea is remarkably clear. Diving is not allowed, but boats may use the quaint little fishing harbour on payment of a fee to the harbourmaster.

Coverack is one of the many Cornish villages where smuggling once supplemented the fishing industry. One local smuggler is said to have worked in league with his wife who pegged a bright red shirt to the clothes line when it was safe for him to come ashore with contraband. The Paris Hotel by the harbour takes its name from an American ship which ran aground at the turn of the century. Her passengers and crew, more than 700 people in all, were brought safely to shore, and the ship was eventually refloated. One of the village's gift shops used to be a store for salt that was packed into barrels to preserve pilchards.

⑨ THE MANACLES

Deadly rocks lying a mile offshore have wrecked hundreds of ships and claimed thousands of lives over the centuries. They include 106 passengers and crew from the liner *Mohegan* which went down in 1898. Forty-three years earlier the rocks claimed 196 lives when the *John*, an emigrant ship sailing from Plymouth for Canada, was lost.

In 1809 two vessels came to grief on The Manacles within hours of each other. One was the *Despatch*, homeward bound with troops from the Peninsular War with Spain, the other was the 18-gun brig *Primrose*. More

MEMORIAL WINDOW *This testimony in stained glass to the shipwreck victims of the SS Mohegan is in St Keverne's Church.*

than 200 men were drowned in the double tragedy.

The reef can be seen from Manacle Point, a short walk from Porthoustock.

In calm weather it is a popular area for fishing from boats.

⑩ ST KEVERNE

Cottages of cob and local stone are grouped around a large square in this village on the high plateau of the Lizard. Dominating the village is the octagonal spire of St Keverne's Church, which has been a landmark for sailors for 300 years. The spire was rebuilt in 1770 after the original one was struck by lightning.

More than 400 victims of shipwrecks on The Manacles are buried in the graveyard at St Keverne, and there are numerous memorials to victims in the church. The name 'Manacles' derives from the Cornish words *men eglos*, 'stone church'.

In 1497 St Keverne's blacksmith, Michael Joseph, joined with Thomas Flammock of Bodmin to lead a rebellious army of 15,000 men to London in protest against heavy taxes imposed by Henry VII. Their venture ended at Blackheath, where they were defeated by 25,000 men of the king's army. Joseph and Flammock were captured and executed.

⑪ PORTHOUSTOCK

The former quarrying village of Porthoustock is a base for divers who explore The Manacles reef for wrecks. The seas off the Lizard peninsula have much to offer marine archaeologists, but strong currents and other hazards demand a great deal of experience and local knowledge.

Abandoned quarry buildings stand sentinel on either side of the bay, where small fishing boats are beached on a broad bank of shingle that is also used as a car park. A sandy beach is revealed at low tide.

⑫ PORTHALLOW

From Porthallow's small beach, where storm-tossed shingle leads to low-tide sand, there are splendid views across Falmouth Bay to St Mawes, the gleaming white lighthouse on St Anthony Head and the distant bulk of Dodman Point, some 16 miles away. The beach is overlooked by an attractive group of whitewashed cottages.

In the village pub, The Five Pilchards, are relics from the four-masted *Bay of Panama* which was hurled against the cliffs of Nare Point during a violent storm in 1891.

LOCAL INFORMATION

Tourist information Camborne 712941.

HM Coastguard Falmouth 317575 for information, 999 in emergency (ask for coastguard).

Weather Newquay 2224, Plymouth 8091.

Radio BBC Cornwall, 476 m, 630 kHz, 96.4 MHz.

PLACE TO SEE INLAND

Trelowarren, 6 miles NW of Coverack. Mansion of the Restoration period (late 17th century). Some days in summer.

45

Peace on the wooded inlets of the Helford River

The estuary of the Helford River is a tranquil wonderland of narrow creeks which probe far inland between trees and colourful clumps of hydrangeas. Small boats are the ideal way to explore the estuary, but there are many footpaths along the creeks and over the low headlands which separate them. It is worth facing the problems of narrow lanes and limited parking to find a peaceful spot beside the estuary when the beaches are crowded.

INDUSTRIOUS BACKWATER *Beneath the still waters at Porth Navas lives* Ostrea edulis, *the common oyster, in beds that supply the tables of expensive restaurants from September to April.*

① SWANPOOL BEACH
The rock-flanked sands of this popular beach are little more than a stone's throw from a reedy pool on which there is boating in rowing boats and pedal boats. There is safe swimming from the beach, and there are rock pools at low tide. Floats and surf skis can be hired.

② MAENPORTH
Maenporth's sheltered sands become crowded during the holiday season, but there is a pleasant walk southwards over High Cliff and The Hutches to Rosemullion Head. Owned by the National Trust, the headland offers fine views over Falmouth Bay. The white lighthouse on St Anthony Head is a prominent landmark. There are floats for hire, and volunteer lifeguards patrol regularly in summer.

③ MAWNAN
A lane from Mawnan Smith leads to this tiny hamlet, whose 13th-century church overlooks the mouth of the Helford River. The church tower has been a landmark for sailors for centuries, and in recent years trees obscuring the tower have been cut down. In times of war lookouts have been placed there to watch out for the coming of invaders.

One path from the church zigzags down through trees to Parson's Beach with its shore of smooth rocks. Another walk crosses fields to reach sandy coves between Toll Point and Durgan. There is limited parking space by the church.

④ DURGAN
The cottages of this picturesque hamlet, half of which is owned by the National Trust, are clustered behind a sand-and-shingle beach backed by wooded slopes. Small boats moor in sheltered waters where traders from as far afield as the eastern Mediterranean anchored in pre-Roman times. The walk down from the car park takes about 10 minutes.

The beautiful gardens of Glendurgan, covering 40 acres, lie on both sides of a steep valley running down to the water's edge. They were given to the National Trust in 1962 and include a laurel maze planted in 1833. In the sheltered setting exotic plants such as tulip trees, bamboos, tree ferns and mimosa flourish among the primroses, bluebells and hydrangeas. The house itself is not open to visitors.

⑤ HELFORD PASSAGE
Overlooked by a golf course, Helford Passage is one of the Helford River's many popular anchorages for small craft. Its sand-and-shingle beach faces due south across the estuary to a rolling landscape of fields and woodlands.

The passenger ferry to Helford has operated since the Middle Ages, and provides walkers on the coastal path with an alternative to the 8 mile detour through Gweek. There is virtually no parking in the village, but cars may be left in the lane, about a 10 minute walk from the shore.

Sailing boats, rowing boats and motor boats can be hired.

⑥ PORTH NAVAS
This pretty little village of stone cottages on a narrow, tree-lined creek is the headquarters of the Duchy of Cornwall's oyster fisheries in the Helford River, which are said to date back to Roman times. Marked by thin stakes, known as withies, the beds produce nearly a quarter of Britain's oysters. They are gathered by rowing boat, to avoid disturbing or polluting the oyster-beds.

The oyster was not always so highly esteemed as a table delicacy as it is today. In the 19th century oysters were regarded as food only for the poor, who gathered them from the muddy banks of the creeks. As Sam Weller says in Charles Dickens' *Pickwick Papers*: 'It's a wery remarkable circumstance that poverty and oysters always seem to go together.'

⑦ GWEEK
At low tide, when the Helford River flows seawards between acres of glistening mud, it is difficult to believe that Gweek was a busy little port for many hundreds of years. Old quays provide the clue. From the Middle Ages until the 19th century they bustled with activity, because Gweek became Helston's main link with the outside world after the mouth of the River Cober was blocked by a spit of sand and shingle, today's Loe Bar. Timber, coal, lime and other cargoes were exchanged for tin and produce from local farms. Gweek's isolation also provided ideal conditions for smugglers, despite the village having a Customs House.

The woods and creeks around Gweek were well known to the writer Charles Kingsley, who went to school at Helston. He set the scene of part of his novel *Hereward the Wake* in the district, calling Gweek 'Alef's Town'.

A sanctuary for seals was moved to Gweek from St Agnes in 1972, and is open to visitors throughout the summer. Baby seals

SEAL SANCTUARY *Many of the seals stranded on Cornwall's shores end up in the sanctuary at Gweek, where they sometimes breed.*

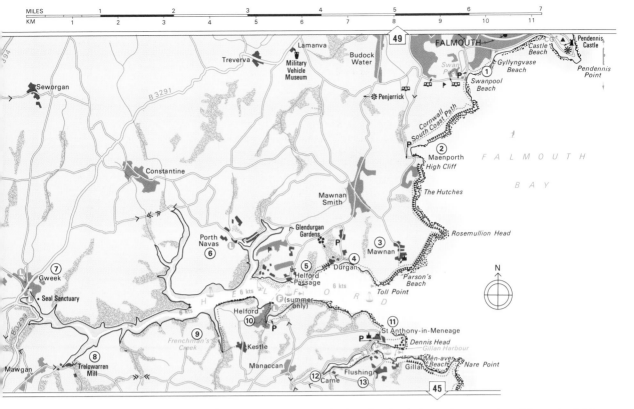

that have lost their parents, together with sick or injured adults found on the beaches, are raised and tended in pools before being returned to the sea. Some seals have been born in the sanctuary. Leading from the sanctuary is a nature trail which follows the river and passes through woodland.

⑧ TRELOWARREN MILL
An old stone bridge spans this attractive little creek where boats moor at a private quay. Trees bow down to meet the tide as it flows in over mud-flats draped with seaweed.

⑨ FRENCHMAN'S CREEK
Immortalised by Daphne du Maurier's novel of the same name, Frenchman's Creek is an idyllic stretch of water whose romantic atmosphere has been preserved by the National Trust. Sheltered by trees whose branches form a leafy tunnel, it is reserved for walkers and small-boat sailors.

One path follows the creek inland from its junction with the Helford River. Another, flanked by ferns and ivy-clad trees, reaches the creek after a 10 minute walk from Kestle. It is a place to find peace even on a sunny August day when Cornwall's beaches are thronged with holidaymakers.

⑩ HELFORD
Thatched roofs, whitewashed walls and little gardens bright with flowers contribute much to the picture-postcard beauty of this creek-side village on the Helford River's southern shore. Visitors' cars are banned from the village from June to September, but it is only a 2 minute walk from the car park to the creek, with its ford and wooden footbridge, where swans and ducks may be seen.

The ferry which links Helford to Helford Passage during the holiday season has operated since the Middle Ages, when the village was a haven for fishermen and coasters which loaded Cornish tin.

There are motor boats for hire, and there is a sailing club.

⑪ ST ANTHONY-IN-MENEAGE
This tiny village clusters round a church said to have been founded in the 12th century by

shipwrecked Normans. The legend maintains that they vowed to build a church dedicated to St Anthony if their lives were spared. There may be some truth in the legend, as the fine-grained granite used in the building of the tower is found only in Normandy. The tower overlooks a shingle beach where muddy sands draped with seaweed are uncovered at low tide. The description of Meneage applied to the surrounding district means 'monks' land', and dates from the time when Celtic monks settled in the area and built the earliest churches.

Gillan Harbour, the creek on which St Anthony-in-Meneage stands, is a sheltered anchorage whose waters are bright with small boats during the summer. The creek can be waded for 1 hour either side of low water.

A short walk eastwards leads to Dennis Head, a fine viewpoint with the remains of an Iron Age fortress. The ancient earthworks were fortified by Royalists during the Civil War, but fell to the Parliamentarians in 1646 after holding out for longer than any place in Cornwall apart from St Michael's Mount and Falmouth's Pendennis Castle.

Motor boats, rowing boats, sailing boats and sailboards can be hired, and there are sailing and sailboard schools.

⑫ CARNE
A small, secluded and attractive hamlet at the head of Gillan Harbour, Carne is seen at its best when high tide laps the tree-lined

shore. A narrow lane follows the inlet seawards to St Anthony.

⑬ FLUSHING
There are very few places to park a car on the southern shores of Gillan Harbour, but footpaths enable walkers to explore the unspoiled coast between Flushing and Porthallow. Flushing itself is a small, scattered community through which a narrow lane runs down to a low-tide beach of shingle, sand and rocks.

The 20 minute walk along the coastal path to Nare Point – a low headland with views across Falmouth Bay – passes similar beaches at Gillan and Mên-aver.

LOCAL INFORMATION

Tourist information Camborne 712941, Falmouth 312300.

HM Coastguard Falmouth 317575 for information, 999 in emergency (ask for coastguard).

Weather Newquay 2224, Plymouth 8091.

Local radio BBC Cornwall, 476 m, 630 kHz, 96.4 MHz.

PLACES TO SEE INLAND

Military Vehicle Museum, Lamanva, 3 miles W of Falmouth. Daily.

Penjerrick, Budock Water, 2½ miles W of Falmouth. Valley garden. Some afternoons in summer.

St Anthony, with its Norman church

A maze of quiet creeks off Falmouth's broad harbour

The ancient port of Falmouth is the gateway to a fascinating maze of creeks and tidal rivers, sheltered by rolling farmland. The tranquil waterways are deep enough for big ships to moor as far inland as King Harry Ferry, and for small coasters to venture up to the old quays at Truro. Motorists who pick their way through the tangled web of narrow lanes discover such delights as the medieval churches at St Clement and St Just.

① FALMOUTH

Blessed with one of the world's finest natural harbours, Falmouth flourished for more than 200 years as a port for Atlantic shipping – the first port of call, from the 17th to the 19th century, for many ships homeward bound and the last stopping place for those sailing west.

The deep, sheltered waters of Carrick Roads were a safe refuge from storms and a convenient anchorage for vessels awaiting orders or replenishing their stores. The town's importance as a link with the outside world is emphasised by the fact that it was the first place in Britain to learn of Nelson's victory at Trafalgar in 1805.

Falmouth's Maritime Museum has a wealth of exhibits dealing with the sailing packets that brought prosperity to the town between 1688 and 1852. The 'Falmouth packets' were fast, lightly armed ships built to carry mail overseas, to ports in Europe and as far away as the West Indies. As the model of the *Crane* in the museum shows, the packets were usually two-masted sloops, square-rigged and with long bowsprits, up to 200 tons in weight. Most were built locally and privately owned, under charter to the Post Office. Their mission involved them in numerous gun battles during the Napoleonic Wars, the mail being jettisoned overboard if capture was inevitable. By the early 19th century as many as 40 packets were operating out of Falmouth; but in 1852 the Post Office switched to a steamboat service from Southampton. A monument in the centre of The Moor in Falmouth commemorates the 150 years of the Packet Service.

Custom House Quay was built more than 300 years ago, but the present Custom House dates from 1815 and is in the Regency Classical style. Also of the Regency period is the 'Queen's Pipe', originally called the 'King's Pipe', an incinerator in which seized contraband tobacco was burned.

The road to Pendennis Point provides fine views of the town, with its docks and shipyards in the foreground and Carrick Roads – a forest of slender masts in summer – stretching away to the north. The headland itself is dominated by Pendennis Castle, one of a chain of coastal fortresses built when Henry VIII feared an invasion from Europe.

Castle Beach and Gyllyngvase Beach, overlooked by steep slopes clad with hotels, form Falmouth's southern boundary. They offer long stretches of sand punctuated by rocks where the ebbing tide leaves many pools to be explored.

As well as seaside amusements, Falmouth has an art gallery and, south of the town on the road to Maenporth, a model village. A regatta is held in August, and boat trips, river cruises and fishing trips are available. Motor boats may be hired, and there is a sailing club.

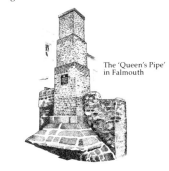

The 'Queen's Pipe' in Falmouth

② PENRYN

Four hundred years older than Falmouth, Penryn was granted its first charter in 1256.

Grass-topped quays and an old warehouse recall its days as a port exporting tin and granite from local mines and quarries. The creek is now used by private craft and a few small fishing boats, which anchor within a stone's throw of fields where hay is harvested in the summer.

③ FLUSHING

This colourful little village was named by Dutch engineers who were employed to build its quays and sea-walls in the 17th century. It developed into a thriving port whose ships traded with the West Indies and North America, and has elegant Queen Anne houses built by naval officers and captains of Falmouth packet ships. Many of the buildings which flank the narrow main street have flights of stone steps leading down to the water, where private craft mingle with fishing boats and the ferry to Falmouth.

A short walk leads to Trefusis Point, where the transport ship *Queen* was wrecked in 1814 after a voyage from Spain. The 200 victims of the disaster are commemorated in the churchyard of the nearby church of St Mylor. A regatta is held in August, and river trips are available.

④ MYLOR CHURCHTOWN

St Mylor's Church, set in grounds where hydrangeas bloom, overlooks a sheltered creek that has become one of Cornwall's most popular bases for yachtsmen. Their craft use quays and jetties where warships were built when the village had a small naval dockyard. The medieval church stands on the site where St Mylor is said to have been martyred in AD 411, and is notable for a fine Celtic cross near the south porch. Inside are many memorials to ill-fated seafarers, such as the commander of a Falmouth packet who died 'bravely defending his ship against the enemy' in 1803, during the Napoleonic Wars.

There are sailing clubs, and sailing boats, rowing boats and motor boats are available for hire.

⑤ MYLOR BRIDGE

This village at the head of Mylor Creek, a haven for small boats, is at its most attractive when high tide laps the small quays. A lane runs northwards to Restronguet Creek and The Pandora, an inn which dates from the 13th century and is said to be the oldest in Cornwall. It was given its present name by the commander of HMS *Pandora*, the ship which went to the Pacific to capture the *Bounty* mutineers after they set their commander, Lt William Bligh, adrift in an open boat in 1789.

⑥ LOE BEACH

Reached by a steep, narrow lane from the village of Feock, the beach of sand and shingle is a launching site for small boats and commands good views down Carrick Roads towards Falmouth. Another lane goes southwards to Restronguet Point and a creek which runs inland to Point and Devoran. Both villages were outlets for Cornish tin in the 19th century.

⑦ TRELISSICK

This beautifully wooded estate, almost islanded by the River Fal and two of its many creeks, was given to the National Trust in 1955 and has a large garden which is open to visitors. Much of the landscaping was done early in the 19th century by a man whose wealth – derived from tin and copper mines – earned him the nickname of 'Guinea-a-Minute' Gilbert.

The garden is notable for more than 130 species and varieties of hydrangea.

SAFETY FAST *Falmouth's lifeboat is a 52 ft Arun-class boat, one of the latest and most powerful. It can travel at 18 knots, and has a range of more than 100 miles.*

⑧ TRURO

Cornwall's administrative centre and unofficial capital is dominated by the lofty spires of a cathedral built between 1880 and 1910. In the Middle Ages Truro became one of the 'stannary' towns which controlled the county's thriving tin industry, and it developed as a port despite being more than 10 miles from the open sea.

Coasters still visit the wharves opposite Boscawen Park, but Truro's role as a major outlet for tin dwindled rapidly in the 17th century as Falmouth was developed. The area controlled by its port authority was greatly reduced during the same period, possibly because Charles II felt that Truro had given his ill-fated father insufficient support during the Civil War.

There is an indoor swimming pool, and river cruises are available. Two indoor markets are held every weekday, and a cattle market every Wednesday.

⑨ MALPAS

Spread out along a headland where the Tresillian River mingles with the Truro, Malpas is a haven for small boats. A ferry helps walkers on their way to the isolated hamlet of Old Kea or the little village of St Michael Penkevil.

⑩ ST CLEMENT

This sleepy little hamlet lies on a wooded stretch of the Tresillian River, about 2 miles east of Truro. Its quaint church dates from the 13th century and has an unusual lych-gate whose upper storey is said to have once served as the local school. In the church porch are preserved stocks with spaces for three victims. A cross in the churchyard dates from Saxon times.

ST JUST'S CHURCH *Bathed in the warmth of the midday sun, the ancient grey stones of the church tower look down on the still-waters of St Just Pool, a tiny creek off Carrick Roads.*

Among those commemorated inside the church is Rear Admiral Robert Carthew Reynolds who was lost, together with all his officers and men, when the 98-gun warship *St George* went down off Jutland in 1811.

⑪ KING HARRY FERRY

The ferry across the River Fal departs from a slipway a few hundred yards south of a thatched cottage which marks the crossing favoured by the old road between London and Penzance. The cottage, which now serves teas, was visited by General Eisenhower during the build-up to the D-Day invasion of Normandy in 1944. The concrete road to the river was built during the same period for the embarkation of American troops. Big ships are often seen riding at anchor in the deep channel, awaiting anything from sailing orders to a final cruise to the breakers' yard.

⑫ TURNAWARE POINT

This peaceful headland has fine views of the River Fal and Carrick Roads, and is an ideal area for strolls and picnics. Owned by the National Trust, it is also a vantage point from which oyster boats may be seen at work during the winter months. Parking is very limited at the end of the concrete-slab road beyond Commerrans Farm.

⑬ ST JUST IN ROSELAND

At high tide the creek below St Just mirrors a 13th-century church whose setting ranks among the most memorable anywhere in Britain. It nestles beneath slopes where bamboo, camellias, Chilean fire bushes, rhododendrons and many subtropical plants flourish in colourful profusion. The path down to the church is flanked by granite tablets carved with verses. The enchanting setting makes it easy to believe the legend that Christ visited St Just as a boy when travelling with Joseph of Arimathea, a tin merchant.

The narrow road from St Just Lane ends on a shingle shore with a small boatyard.

LOCAL INFORMATION
Tourist information Falmouth 312300, Truro 74555.
HM Coastguard Falmouth 317575 for information, 999 in emergency (ask for coastguard).
Weather Newquay 2224, Plymouth 8091.
Local radio BBC Cornwall 476 m, 630 kHz, 96.4 MHz.
PLACE TO SEE INLAND
Truro. County Museum and Art Gallery. Weekdays except Bank Hols.

49

Sheltered bays and green fields along the Cornish Riviera

Lofty headlands, broad bays and cliffs punctuated by delightful coves line the Cornish coast as it runs north-eastwards from Zone Point to the abandoned port of Pentewan. Mevagissey has the narrow streets and boat-packed harbour of a traditional Cornish fishing village. There are miles of clifftop paths, while sailing enthusiasts can cruise the sheltered waters of Carrick Roads and creeks where woods reach down to the water.

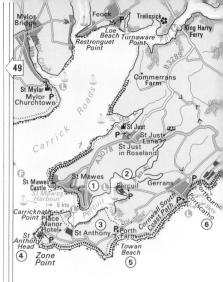

① ST MAWES

Built on steep slopes at the end of a peninsula flanked by Carrick Roads and the Percuil River, St Mawes is a popular but dignified little holiday resort whose delightful setting and mild climate, which have earned this part of the coast the description of the Cornish Riviera, attract many retired people. Its sheltered harbour becomes a floating forest of masts during the holiday season, and low tide reveals several small, sandy beaches.

The main road which forms a triangle round the town passes St Mawes Castle. Built between 1540 and 1543 to guard the eastern approach to Carrick Roads, the castle has three bastions which form a clover-leaf around the low central tower. Though apparently impregnable, the castle capitulated to Cromwell's forces in 1646 without a shot being fired – because its guns faced seaward.

There is a sailing club, and boat trips and fishing trips are available.

St Mawes Castle

② PERCUIL

Although it no longer has a ferry link with St Mawes, this hamlet on the Percuil River is a popular base for small-boat sailors. The lane which runs down to the river from Gerrans passes a National Trust parking area where views of the river's upper reaches are framed by cornfields and woodlands. It is a delightful spot for a picnic.

There is a sailing club, and a regatta is held in August.

③ ST ANTHONY

The grounds of the Place Manor Hotel sweep down to a sheltered little bay at the mouth of the Percuil River. The ebbing tide reveals a beach of fine shingle. It is a pleasant spot, but parking space is very limited.

④ ST ANTHONY HEAD

A lighthouse completed in 1835 and marking the entrance to Carrick Roads is reached by a 3 minute walk from the National Trust car park on the headland. There are superb views across Falmouth Bay. Black Rock, a navigational hazard in the days of sail, is an eye-catching feature in the sea between the headland and Pendennis Point. The rock used to be marked by a tall mast with a red

HIGH LIGHT *Poised 65 ft above the sea, the 225,000 candlepower light on St Anthony Head guides shipping entering Falmouth harbour.*

banner, but it was topped with a conical, granite-based beacon early in the 19th century.

The path from the lighthouse to Carricknath Point passes an attractive little beach with low-tide sands.

⑤ TOWAN BEACH

A 2 minute walk from the National Trust car park at Porth Farm leads to a beach of coarse sand and fine shingle, punctuated by low rocks where many pools are left by the falling tide.

The car park is also a good starting point for a 4 mile coastal walk. The route passes the beautiful Froe Creek, whose northern bank is shaded by a beech wood where herons nest.

⑥ PORTSCATHO

Narrow streets typical of Cornwall's fishing villages run down to Portscatho's tiny harbour, which dries out at low tide. The beach faces due east and has patches of sand between outcrops of rock. To the north, steps lead down from a clifftop car park to more extensive sands at Porthcurnick.

⑦ PENDOWER BEACH

This beautiful beach, backed by low cliffs, was presented to the National Trust in 1961 after funds had been raised by local people to save it from commercial development. The sands, patchworked with areas of rock, are crossed at their western end by a stream which flows down from the wooded Pendower Valley. Its waters meet the sea near a derelict kiln where, in the 19th century, limestone was burned to make fertiliser.

There is a clifftop car park near Pendower House and another, on the far side of the stream, which is approached by a narrow lane from Veryan. The beach is sheltered by the impressive bulk of Nare Head, whose highest point is more than 300 ft above sea level.

⑧ NARE HEAD

An excellent viewpoint in fine weather, the headland's summit is a 15 minute walk from the National Trust car park above rocky Kiberick Cove. It can also be reached by car, but the track is very rough. Carne Beacon, between the headland and Veryan, is an impressive Bronze Age mound. Legend pinpoints it as the grave of a Cornish king who was buried with a golden ship.

Gull Rock, half a mile from Nare Head, is a nesting place for cormorants, shags, guillemots, razorbills and other sea-birds. It is the most prominent part of a reef which claimed many sailing ships. They included the *Hera* which went down in 1914 with a loss of 19 lives.

⑨ PORTLOE

The rocky harbour, overlooked by the 17th-century Lugger Hotel, is almost as narrow as the streets of this pretty little village. The cove has a slipway and is still used by a few small fishing boats. There are memorable walks along the cliffs to Nare Head and Portholland.

⑩ PORTHOLLAND

Cottages whose double doors defy winter storms raging in from the south-west overlook East Portholland's beach of shingle and low-tide sand. A narrow lane runs over the cliffs to West Portholland, where an old lime-kiln stands on the rocky shore.

⑪ PORTHLUNEY COVE

This safe, sandy beach, sheltered by wooded cliffs, is watched over by the towers of Caerhays Castle, which stands on the site of a medieval manor house. The castle dates from 1808 and is the work of the architect John Nash, whose most notable works included London's Marble Arch and Brighton's Royal Pavilion.

The building ruined the Trevanion family, who had owned the Caerhays estate since the 14th century. The last of the line is said to have gained belated revenge for his financial plight by shooting at his ancestors' portraits. The castle is private, but its grounds are occasionally opened in aid of local charities.

⑫ HEMMICK BEACH

A narrow, sunken lane with a 1 in 5 gradient plunges down to this small, sandy beach on

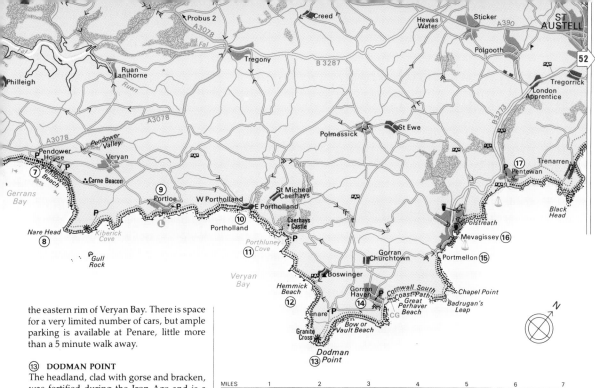

the eastern rim of Veryan Bay. There is space for a very limited number of cars, but ample parking is available at Penare, little more than a 5 minute walk away.

⑬ DODMAN POINT

The headland, clad with gorse and bracken, was fortified during the Iron Age and is a major landmark on Cornwall's southern coast. A 15 minute walk over National Trust land with superb views leads to a granite cross erected by a local clergyman in 1896, 'In the firm hope of the second coming of our Lord Jesus Christ and for the encouragement of those who strive to serve Him'. The path passes the ruin of a small stone building where coastguards sheltered in the 19th century.

Dodman Point was the graveyard of many ships which missed Falmouth in the days before radar. The rector who set up the granite cross spent the night of its dedication on Dodman Point, praying for shipwrecked souls.

The walk along the cliffs to Gorran Haven passes Bow or Vault Beach, whose sand-and-shingle shore is reached by scrambling down a steep path.

⑭ GORRAN HAVEN

The narrow village streets lead to a sandy beach whose southern end is sheltered by a small breakwater and overlooked by 'cellars' once used by fishermen.

The clifftop path to Chapel Point gives access to Great Perhaver Beach and passes Bodrugan's Leap. This is said to be the place where Sir Henry Treworth of Bodrugan spurred his horse over the cliff to escape from his enemies in 1485, after supporting Richard III's ill-fated cause at the Battle of Bosworth.

Fishing trips and boat trips are available.

⑮ PORTMELLON

Signs on the lanes which run steeply down to this rock-clasped cove of sand and shingle warn that the road is sometimes washed by high-tide waves. Buildings facing the beach are fronted by walls 3 ft thick and have gateways with slots into which boards are fitted to keep the sea out. There is a boatyard, with a slipway running down to the beach. The road northwards climbs a headland which provides splendid views of Mevagissey. There are sailing boats for hire.

⑯ MEVAGISSEY

Picturesque old buildings flank the steep and extremely narrow streets of this ancient fishing port, which seethes with visitors during the holiday season. Established in the Middle Ages, Mevagissey developed in the 18th and 19th centuries when its inner and outer harbours provided shelter for a large fleet of boats whose main catch was pilchards. Many were cured and exported to Italy. Another important customer was the Royal Navy who called the fish 'Mevagissey Duck'. Smuggling was a popular and profitable sideline for many years, and the men of Mevagissey once boarded a Customs' cutter to rescue captured colleagues.

Shops selling everything from fish-and-chips to souvenirs and antiques now account for much of the village's trade, but fishing boats still share the sheltered harbours with fleets of pleasure craft.

There are museums and an aquarium. The Mevagissey Museum is in an old boatyard, dating from 1745, and has roof supports made of ships' masts. Boat trips and fishing trips for sharks and other fish can be arranged.

⑰ PENTEWAN

The village of Pentewan nestles at the foot of a steep hill and looks southwards over a broad, sandy beach backed by tents and caravans. Ducks patrol the abandoned harbour built by a local landowner in the 1820s. The dock closed shortly after the First World War, choked with silt swept down from the clay workings near St Austell, the very workings it was built to serve. Its gates remain, together with rusty winches, bollards and mooring chains, and other relics of the venture.

BAY BELOW THE CLIFFS *Away from the bustle of Mevagissey, Polstreath is tucked away in a sheltered cove north of the town. It is reached by steep steps leading down from a clifftop path.*

LOCAL INFORMATION

Tourist information Falmouth 312300.

HM Coastguard Falmouth 317575 for information, 999 in emergency (ask for coastguard).

Weather Newquay 2224, Plymouth 8091.

Local radio BBC Cornwall, 476 m, 630 kHz, 96.4 MHz.

PLACES TO SEE INLAND

Probus, 16 miles NE of St Mawes. Trewithen, early 18th-century house and gardens, house some afternoons in summer, gardens weekday afternoons in summer; Probus Gardens, gardening and landscaping displays, most days.

Beaches on a sandy bay and busy china-clay ports

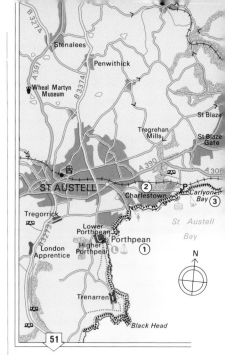

East of Gribbin Head, the sandy sweeps of St Austell Bay give way to a series of delightful little beaches backed by cliffs which rise to more than 300 ft. Behind the cliffs, a patchwork of green and gold fields rolls inland, contrasting with the lunar landscape of china-clay workings north of St Austell. Fowey, Polperro and Looe are quaint old ports with narrow streets, old buildings and harbours bright with boats.

① PORTHPEAN

A narrow, rock-flanked lane whose trees form a leafy tunnel in summer drops steeply down from Higher Porthpean to a sandy beach with fine views across St Austell Bay to Gribbin Head. Its sheltered waters provide safe conditions for bathing, although the beach shelves quite quickly. The ebbing tide reveals patches of rock dappled with pools where prawns can be netted. The village was once a pilchard-fishing community, and the old fish cellars are now used by the local sailing club.

② CHARLESTOWN

This fascinating little port dates from the end of the 18th century and takes its name from Charles Rashleigh, the local mine-owner who financed the venture. The port was designed by John Smeaton, builder of the Eddystone lighthouse.

Copper was the main export for several years, but Charlestown soon became an important outlet for china clay from the huge workings north of St Austell. The white dust of the china clay mingled on the harbourside with black clouds swirling up from coasters discharging coal.

The narrow dock is still used, and in 1971 the gates were widened from 27 ft to 35 ft and the maximum depth of water retained by them was increased to 17 ft 6 in. The outer harbour is flanked by low-tide beaches of sand and shingle.

Behind the dock, old anchors and naval guns stand outside a visitors' centre whose exhibits concentrate on shipwrecks and scenes from Charlestown's history.

③ CARLYON BAY

Overlooked by a private estate with hotels and a golf course, this long, sandy beach is dominated by a leisure complex which offers a range of attractions from an open-air swimming pool to hamburgers. Sailboards and boats may be hired.

④ PAR SANDS

Sands which shelve very gently and run out for half a mile at low tide make this an excellent beach for children. It is overlooked by dunes which shelter a caravan site with a reedy pool. To the west are the tall chimneys and long, low buildings of a works where china clay is processed and loaded into ships at a private harbour built in the 1820s. There are seaside amusements.

⑤ POLKERRIS

'Cellars' where pilchards were salted are a reminder that Polkerris was once numbered among Cornwall's many small fishing ports. Its 'seine house', where fish were processed for oil, was once the largest in Cornwall. The sandy beach, flanked by rocks and cliffs, has a breakwater built by the Rashleighs of Menabilly, a house near Gribbin Head. A cafe now occupies the building where a lifeboat was based from 1859 until 1914. Floats and surfboards may be hired.

MARINERS' MARK *The striped beacon on Gribbin Head was built in the days of sail to signpost the eastern tip of St Austell Bay.*

⑥ GRIBBIN HEAD

An 84 ft high 'daymark' for mariners, built by Trinity House in 1832, crowns this craggy headland, reached by a 20 minute walk over fields from the car park near Menabilly Barton. Walkers skirt the private grounds of Menabilly, Daphne du Maurier's home for many years and the 'Manderley' of her novel *Rebecca*. The path passes Polridmouth Cove where trees, shrubs and low cliffs overlook a

51

TRANQUIL COVE *The curving harbour wall at Polkerris, built to embrace a fishing fleet, calms the waters of St Austell Bay and provides safe bathing from the sandy beach.*

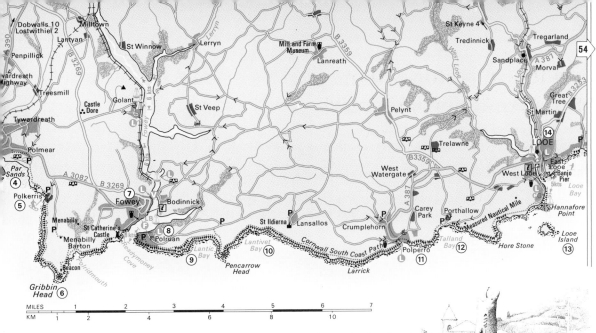

sandy beach which the headland shelters from south-westerly winds.

⑦ FOWEY

Ocean-going ships loading china clay mingle with scores of small craft in the natural harbour whose sheltered waters have made Fowey a busy port since the Middle Ages. Its daring sailors, known as 'Fowey Gallants', featured in many medieval campaigns and were at the Siege of Calais in 1346. They also built up a reputation as fearless smugglers and pirates who harried shipping in the English Channel. The little town's narrow streets run steeply down to quays from which ships of up to 15,000 tons can be seen heading for the wharves where clay is loaded, upstream from the ferry to Bodinnick.

The Haven, a house on the Esplanade, was the home from 1892 until his death in 1944 of the author Sir Arthur Quiller-Couch, who wrote under the pseudonym of 'Q'. In his novels he wrote about Fowey under the name of 'Troy Town'. He was once Mayor of Fowey, and there is a memorial to him on Hall Walk.

Readymoney Cove, south-west of the town centre, has a small, sandy beach framed by cliffs. A wooded path leads to the ruins of St Catherine's Castle, a fortress built by order of Henry VIII to supplement blockhouses which date from the end of the 14th century. The two blockhouses stood one on each side of the harbour mouth, and a chain was stretched between them to seal off the harbour. Grooves worn in the rocks by the chain can still be seen.

There is a museum and an aquarium, and a regatta and carnival are held in August. Boat trips, river cruises and fishing trips can be arranged.

⑧ POLRUAN

The narrow street which plunges down to this village at the entrance to the River Fowey is closed to visitors' cars during the holiday season. Tourists are diverted to a car park with splendid views of Fowey. In the past, many wooden ships were built at Polruan, and there is still a busy boatyard. A passenger ferry runs to Fowey.

⑨ LANTIC BAY

A superb beach of low-tide sand, backed by cliffs, is reached after a 10 minute walk across fields from the National Trust car park east of Polruan. Gorse, bracken and blackberry bushes border the path, which loops round Pencarrow Head whose highest point

is nearly 450 ft above the sea. On clear days the views embrace more than 80 miles of coast, from the southern tip of Cornwall to Bolt Tail in Devon.

⑩ LANTIVET BAY

Exceptionally clear seas wash this secluded bay which faces due south and has several small, low-tide beaches divided by outcrops of rock. The shore is a 15 minute walk from Lansallos, an isolated hamlet with a fascinating 14th-century church. Its features include a medieval bell broken by drunken villagers in the 19th century, and a pulpit, the base of which is part of a pinnacle brought down by lightning in 1923. One gravestone, near the gate, commemorates John Perry, a mariner killed in 1779:

I, by a shot, which rapid flew
Was instantly struck dead.
Lord pardon the offender who
My precious blood did shed.

⑪ POLPERRO

Old, whitewashed cottages, crammed together like sardines in a can, combine with a picturesque little fishing harbour to make Polperro one of England's most memorable villages. It has long been a powerful magnet for tourists who throng the astonishingly narrow streets during the holiday season. Non-resident traffic is banned, however, and it takes about 10 minutes to reach the harbour on foot from the car park.

Smuggling and fishing were Polperro's main sources of income until the 19th century, but the village's future was threatened by a great storm in 1824. It destroyed several buildings, demolished the breakwaters and wrecked almost 50 boats.

⑫ TALLAND BAY

Steep, narrow lanes run down from the A387 to a beach of sand, shingle and rocks flanked by headlands more than 300 ft high. The cliff path to Looe passes landmarks which measure out 1 nautical mile and are used by ships undergoing speed trials.

⑬ LOOE ISLAND

Half a mile off Hannafore Point, and reached by launches from Looe, this is the largest island within easy reach of the Cornish coast. It is privately owned, and a haven for sea-birds. During the Second World War the island was bombed by an enemy aircraft whose pilot mistook it for a British warship.

⑭ LOOE

East Looe and West Looe were both granted

The Shark-fishing Club of Great Britain is based at Looe.

charters in the 14th century and remained independent communities, each with their own members of Parliament, for the next 500 years. Linked by an old, multi-arched bridge, they stand on either side of a narrow estuary whose tide-washed tributaries flow seawards down deep, wooded valleys.

East Looe's web of narrow streets is choked with visitors in the holiday season. It is closed to non-resident traffic, but there are ample parking facilities to cater for all but the busiest of days. Fishing boats land their catches at the town's eastern quay, where sharks are also hauled ashore, weighed and photographed.

A sandy beach at the mouth of the river is sheltered by a jetty known as the Banjo Pier because of its shape. As well as seaside amusements, Looe has a museum, an aquarium and a sub-aqua club.

LOCAL INFORMATION

Tourist information Fowey 3308, Looe 2072 (summer).

HM Coastguard Brixham 58292/3 for information, 999 in emergency (ask for coastguard).

Weather Newquay 2224, Plymouth 8091.

Local radio BBC Cornwall, 457/476 m, 657/630 kHz, 95.2/96.4 MHz.

PLACES TO SEE INLAND

Castle Dore, 2½ miles NE of Fowey. Iron Age earthworks.

Dobwalls, 18 miles NE of St Austell. Forest Railroad Park; Thorburn Museum. Daily in summer.

Lanreath Mill and Farm Museum, 5 miles NW of Looe. Daily in summer.

Paul Corin Music Collection, St Keyne, 6 miles N of Looe. Fairground, cinema and barrel organs. Daily in summer.

Restormel Castle, near Lostwithiel, 9 miles NE of St Austell. Medieval remains. Daily.

Wheal Martyn Museum, 2 miles N of St Austell. History of china-clay industry. Daily in summer.

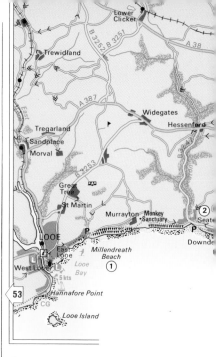

Plymouth, historic home port of the sea-dogs of Devon

The great naval base of Plymouth is a city whose history is laced with memories of such famous seafarers as Sir Francis Drake and the Pilgrim Fathers. Its docks and harbours, where warships mingle with ferries, fishing boats and yachts, seem a world away from the muddy creeks and tree-lined rivers on the Cornish side of the River Tamar, and the sands and cliffs along the coast sweeping westwards towards Looe.

① MILLENDREATH BEACH
This rock-flanked beach is backed by holiday chalets and a dinghy park. There is some sand at low tide, and an artificial pool, filled by the tide, is an attraction for children.

② SEATON
The B3247 from Hessenford runs seawards down a deep, wooded and beautiful valley carved by the River Seaton. At the mouth of the river a sandy beach backed by fine shingle is overlooked by a holiday camp.

A narrow lane runs westwards to Murrayton, notable for the Monkey Sanctuary founded there in 1964 by Leonard Williams, a writer on zoology. Visitors can see Amazon woolly monkeys roaming free, and learn about their habits and the structure of their breeding colony. The sanctuary is open daily in summer, except on Saturdays.

③ DOWNDERRY
Squeezed into a long, narrow strip between steep slopes and the sea, the village has a beach where fine shingle leads to extensive low-tide grey sands. The slopes shelter the south-facing beach from northerly winds, allowing palm trees to grow, and there is an inn right on the beach.

④ PORTWRINKLE
A tiny harbour, tucked away in a rocky cove at the western end of the village, recalls the days when Portwrinkle was a haven for fishermen who sailed out to net pilchards. Paths lead down to a sandy beach overlooked by a golf course. The beam of the Lizard lighthouse, 50 miles away, can be seen from the nearby village of Crafthole on a clear night. Fishing trips and boat trips are available.

⑤ WHITSAND BAY
A granite cross beside the road at Tregonhawke emphasises the fact that Whitsand is not safe for swimmers. It commemorates Edmund Spender and his two sons, all of whom were drowned near by in 1878. Strong cross-currents and deep, tide-carved gullies are the main hazards, but the beach itself offers 4 miles of sands reached by paths which zigzag down cliffs more than 250 ft high in places.

The area around Tregantle Barracks – built as a national monument after the Napoleonic Wars – is used by the army. Red flags fly and access is prohibited when the firing ranges are in use.

The bay looks delightful on a calm, sunny day, but is pounded by surf when strong winds sweep in from the south-west. In the days of sail it was a graveyard for many ships which were driven ashore after struggling to round Rame Head and reach the sheltered waters of Plymouth Sound.

⑥ RAME HEAD
A ruined chapel, built at the end of the 14th century and dedicated to St Michael, crowns this lofty viewpoint and is reached by walking for 10 minutes from the car park near the coastguard lookout. The chapel originally had a beacon which blazed to guide ships safely to Plymouth. Its more recent counterpart, the Eddystone lighthouse, can be seen 8 miles offshore.

The lane to the headland passes St Germanus Church in the hamlet of Rame. The building, parts of which date from the 13th century, is still lit by candles.

⑦ CAWSAND BAY
Narrow streets and old, colour-washed buildings make the twin villages of Cawsand and Kingsand every bit as attractive as their commercialised counterparts elsewhere in Cornwall. Their sand-and-shingle beaches are sheltered from the prevailing winds by Rame Head and offer fine views of ships sailing in and out of Plymouth.

The bay was a great centre for smuggling in the 18th century when bladders of brandy, concealed beneath women's skirts, were taken to Plymouth. It was also an important anchorage before Plymouth breakwater was built. In 1815 the bay was visited by the warship taking Napoleon to exile on St Helena, after his defeat at Waterloo. Patriotic locals foiled a plot to rescue him by towing his ship out to sea.

FINAL DEPARTURE FOR A JOURNEY TO THE NEW WORLD

Plymouth is famous as the port from which the Pilgrim Fathers sailed for the New World – the decisive step in a voyage that had begun from Southampton a month earlier. Two ships, *Mayflower* and *Speedwell*, had set out on this perilous venture, but the *Speedwell* was old and entirely unsuited for the 3,000 mile journey. When she sprang a leak, both ships sailed into Plymouth, and when the journey was continued on September 6, 1620, the *Mayflower* was alone. The point in Sutton Harbour from which 102 Pilgrim Fathers finally set out is today marked by a memorial. Two months later the *Mayflower* dropped anchor off Cape Cod. The Pilgrims endured many hardships before the new 'Plymouth Plantation' began to flourish.

The Mayflower Memorial

The Departure of the Pilgrim Fathers from Plymouth, 1620, *by B. F. Gribble (1873 - 1962).*

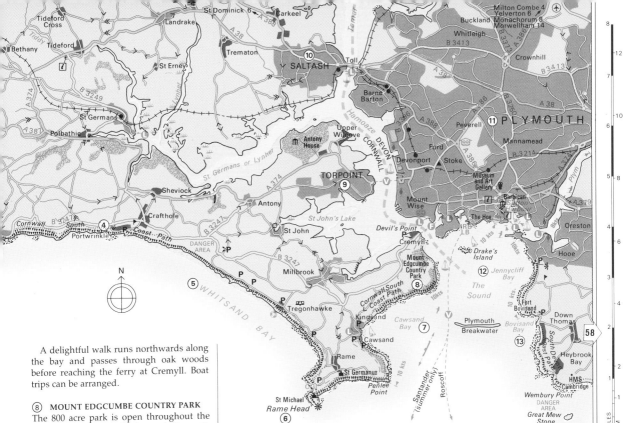

A delightful walk runs northwards along the bay and passes through oak woods before reaching the ferry at Cremyll. Boat trips can be arranged.

⑧ MOUNT EDGCUMBE COUNTRY PARK

The 800 acre park is open throughout the year and offers superb views of Plymouth Sound. Its focal point is Mount Edgcumbe House, a Tudor mansion that was rebuilt after being destroyed by bombs in 1941. The main entrance is at Cremyll, where a ferry takes pedestrians across to Plymouth.

⑨ TORPOINT

Torpoint is a busy little town with two Royal Navy shore bases and a ferry which provides excellent views of the naval dockyards at Devonport. To the south is St John's Lake, a deep inlet of tidal marshes and saltings. At Upper Wilcove, to the north, a small creek is crossed by a road washed by high tides.

Grounds landscaped by Thomas Repton surround Antony House, a mansion built between 1712 and 1721. It now belongs to the National Trust and is open to the public in summer, though descendants of the Carew Pole family, owners of the estate for 500 years, still live there.

⑩ SALTASH

Travellers who pause to explore Saltash discover an interesting little town of narrow streets, attractive old buildings and riverside walks with spectacular views of the River Tamar's two great bridges. The Royal Albert Bridge which carries the railway was designed by Isambard Kingdom Brunel and

ADVENTURERS' POINT *The name of Sutton Harbour commemorates the fishing village that became Plymouth in 1231. From here began the voyages of Drake, Hawkins, Raleigh and Frobisher.*

RAIL LINK *When Prince Albert opened the bridge at Saltash it paved the way for the Great Western Railway's line into Cornwall.*

completed in 1859. It runs alongside the slender suspension bridge that was opened 102 years later. A plaque near The Boatman pub in Old Ferry Road is a reminder that the road bridge replaced a ferry service dating from the 13th century.

⑪ PLYMOUTH

The heart of Plymouth was rebuilt after being devastated by air raids during the Second World War, but the Barbican area around Sutton Harbour has retained many links with the history of the city. Narrow streets pass such gems as the Elizabethan House, furnished as it would have been in Sir Francis Drake's time, and the Island House where the Pilgrim Fathers are believed to have lodged before sailing to North America in 1620. Their voyage is commemorated by the Mayflower Stone and Steps in

Sutton Harbour, where fishing boats now mingle with private craft.

Other famous people who sailed from Plymouth include Captain James Cook and Charles Darwin. It was also the port where four of the six Tolpuddle Martyrs landed in 1838 on their return from transportation to Australia.

Sutton Harbour is watched over by the Citadel, a fortress completed in the 1670s to guard Plymouth Sound. In Plymouth's rebuilt centre, Armada Way is a broad thoroughfare that sweeps gently up to Hoe Park. The Hoe, where Drake finished his game of bowls before sailing out to attack the Spanish Armada in 1588, is dominated by the red and white Smeaton's Tower. Built by John Smeaton, it was the third Eddystone lighthouse, dismantled and shipped back to Plymouth after the rock on which it stood

THE CIRCUMNAVIGATOR *A statue of Sir Francis Drake, one hand resting on the globe, looks out across Plymouth Sound.*

had been eroded by the relentless sea. The Hoe commands panoramic views of Plymouth Sound and its mile-long breakwater. Designed by John Rennie and made of limestone and dovetailed granite blocks, the breakwater took 28 years to build and was completed in 1840. Drake's Island, once a fortress and prison, can be visited by boat from Mayflower Steps.

Devonport, on the western side of the city, was established as a naval base in 1691 and endorsed Plymouth's long-standing role as one of the bastions of British sea power.

Plymouth's attractions include a theatre, a museum, art gallery, aquarium, and indoor and open-air swimming pools. There are fishing and river trips, sailing and windsurfing schools and many sailing clubs. Navy Days are held at the end of August.

⑫ **JENNYCLIFF BAY**
The clifftop car park above Jennycliff Bay provides splendid views of Plymouth and Plymouth Sound. Steps cut into the cliff lead to a small beach of shingle and rocks where the ebbing tide leaves many pools.

⑬ **BOVISAND BAY**
This sandy bay, flanked by low rocks, is overlooked from the north by Fort Bovisand, the regional headquarters of the British Sub-Aqua Club. It was one of many coastal defences built during the 19th century. To the south, Wembury Point comes under the guns of HMS *Cambridge*, the Royal Navy's shore-based gunnery school. Red flags fly when the range is in use.

LOCAL INFORMATION

Tourist information Looe 2072 (summer); Plymouth 264849/264851.

HM Coastguard Brixham 58292/3 for information, 999 in emergency (ask for coastguard).

Weather Plymouth 8091.

Local radio BBC Cornwall, 457/476 m, 657/630 kHz, 95.2/96.4 MHz; BBC Radio Devon, 351 m, 855 kHz, 97.5 MHz; IBA Plymouth Sound, 261 m, 1152 kHz, 96 MHz.

PLACES TO SEE INLAND

Buckland Abbey (NT), near Milton Combe. Sir Francis Drake's home, now a folk and naval museum. Daily in summer, some afternoons in winter.

Cotehele (NT), 9 miles NW of Plymouth. St Dominick. Medieval house with watermill and ship museum. Garden daily, house summer only.

The Garden House, Buckland Monachorum, 9 miles N of Plymouth. Terraced gardens. Some afternoons in summer.

Morwellham Quay Open-Air Museum, Morwellham, 12 miles N of Plymouth, via A390. Village history and old copper mine. Daily.

BEAMS THAT FLASH A WARNING TO SHIPPING ROUND OUR SHORES

On wave-lashed rocks, lofty headlands and rocky outcrops, Britain's lighthouses have been flashing their warning signals to shipping for almost 300 years. Some warn of a nearby hazard, such as a submerged reef, others indicate the approach to a navigation channel while lighthouses like Eddystone and Bishop Rock warn against the perilous rocks on which they stand.

The traditional lighthouse shape evolved through the need for a broad, solid base to withstand the pounding of the sea, and for a round tower to minimise the buffeting of the winds. The earliest structures were built of wood and were usually square or octagonal in shape. Most either fell down or caught fire within a few years. It was not until 1759 that John Smeaton, a London clockmaker, devised a solid, fireproof design using interlocking granite blocks for the construction of the third Eddystone lighthouse. In doing so he introduced a new era of lighthouse building, and many lighthouses built to his basic design are still in operation after more than 100 years.

As efficient as the lighthouses are the men that run them. On duty on some remote lighthouses for four weeks at a time, with four weeks off, they must be good-humoured types able to get on well together in lonely isolation. But they are a dying breed, for one by one Britain's lighthouses are being converted to automatic operation.

THE LIGHTHOUSE ORGANISATIONS *In the 13th century the Archbishop of Canterbury founded a guild of seamen composed of 'Godly disposed men who do bind themselves together in the love of Lord Christ in the name of the Masters and Fellows of Trinity Guild'. One of its functions was 'to build and light proper beacons for the guidance of mariners', though no lighthouses were in fact built until three centuries later. The Guild eventually became known as Trinity House, and today it controls almost 100 lighthouses around the coast of England and Wales. Lighthouses in Scotland and the Isle of Man are run by the Northern Lighthouse Board, created in 1786, which operates some 90 lighthouses.*

GUIDING LIGHTS *The intensity of a lighthouse beam is measured in candlepower, or candela. The most powerful Trinity House light, with 5¼ million candela and a range of 26 miles, is at St Catherine's Point on the Isle of Wight. Power for the light is supplied by diesel-driven generators. Each light has its own characteristic sequence of flashes, which distinguishes it from others. The flashes are governed by blackened sections of the lantern window which interrupt the beam as the lantern rotates.*

OPEN TO VIEW *Many land-based manned lighthouses are open to the public, free of charge, each afternoon except Sundays or during fog, at the discretion of the keeper. Some of the remoter Scottish lighthouses have no set times for visits.*

NORTHERN LIGHT *In the lantern room of the Mull of Kintyre lighthouse the Principal Lightkeeper stands by his charge – the giant reflector and lamp assembly that sends out a beam visible more than 30 miles away. The light from a 2,500 watt lamp is magnified many times by the reflector and* *a lens to produce 1½ million candela, and huge prisms of optical glass concentrate it into a narrow beam. The assembly weighs about 1½ tons, but is so delicately balanced on a bed of mercury that it can be set in motion with one finger.*

Winstanley's first light of 1698

Winstanley's light of 1699

John Rudyard's lighthouse of 1709

Smeaton's granite lighthouse of 1759

The 1882 light, fitted with a helicopter pad in 1982

THE LIGHTS OF EDDYSTONE

The Eddystone rocks, 14 miles off Plymouth, have ripped open many a ship approaching the Devon port. The first lighthouse built there was erected by a ship-owner, Henry Winstanley, who had lost two vessels on the treacherous reef. His flimsy structure of 1698 was strengthened in 1699, but was washed away in 1703, taking its designer with it. Six years later a London silk merchant, John Rudyard, erected a wooden lighthouse which lasted for 47 years and was destroyed by fire on the night of December 2, 1755.

John Smeaton's granite lighthouse, which had 24 candles and could be seen 5 miles away, went into action in 1759 and lasted for 120 years. Even then it was the appearance of cracks in the rock on which it was built, rather than any fault in the lighthouse itself, which caused it to be replaced. It was dismantled and re-erected on Plymouth Hoe as a memorial to Smeaton, and its successor built in 1882 is well on its way to equalling its longevity.

Deep estuaries among the South Hams farmlands

The low, rolling hills of southern Devon are criss-crossed by a maze of narrow lanes which twist and turn down to a coast whose mood changes almost by the mile. Majestic cliffs whose grassy summits stand more than 400 ft above the sea between Bolt Head and Bolt Tail contrast with the softer beauty of tidal estuaries which run far inland between fields and woodlands. Offshore currents make it essential for bathers to heed warning notices.

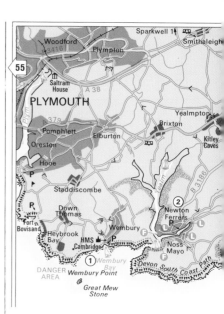

① WEMBURY BAY
This bay is a marine conservation area with a rich variety of plants, birds and creatures which inhabit the tidal strip with its fine shingle, patches of sand and innumerable rock pools. Two waymarked walks, 1 mile and 3 miles in length, start and finish from the National Trust car park by the old watermill near Wembury church. Views across the mouth of Plymouth Sound are dominated by the Great Mew Stone, a steep-sided islet which forms part of the HMS *Cambridge* gunnery school on Wembury Point. Red flags fly when the range is in use and the coastal footpath is closed to walkers.

② NEWTON FERRERS
Wooded slopes rising steeply from the River Yealm's sheltered waters give Newton Ferrers a setting of great beauty and character. A narrow street with several eye-catching old buildings runs down to the estuary where many small boats are beached and moored.

The creek which forms the southern boundary of Newton Ferrers dries out at low tide. It is overlooked by Noss Mayo, another attractive village flanked by National Trust woodland. From the mouth of the Yealm estuary there is a fine walk eastwards over the cliffs to Erme Mouth. There are fishing trips and motor boats for hire. A regatta is held in August.

③ MOTHECOMBE
A 10 minute walk from the car park in this isolated hamlet leads to sandy beaches at the mouth of the River Erme. The river is backed by low, shrub-covered cliffs and runs inland between wooded banks to the A379. It can be crossed on foot within 1 hour of low tide. Bathing is safe only on the incoming tide.

A PLANT WITH NO LEAVES
The unusual plant called butcher's-broom has no true leaves; instead it has leaf-like structures called cladodes which are really flattened stems that bear flowers and berries. Branches are said to have been used by butchers for sweeping their meat-cutting blocks. Butcher's-broom is a woodland plant, but in Devon it also grows on rocky cliffs. It is related to asparagus, and the young shoots are edible.

Butcher's-broom
Ruscus aculeatus
32 in. (80 cm)
Jan.-Apr.

---

④ WONWELL BEACH
A lane that is narrow even by local standards wriggles down to this sandy beach near the mouth of the River Erme. Low cliffs clad with dwarf oaks rise above the shore, overlooking sheltered waters where small craft ride at anchor. A disused kiln on the far bank recalls the days when small coasters landed lime which was burned to make fertiliser. There is very limited parking at the end of the lane.

⑤ BIGBURY-ON-SEA
This bustling little holiday hamlet stands on low cliffs overlooking a sandy beach which curls round to the mouth of the River Avon. Burgh Island, which is linked to the mainland at low tide, has a 14th-century inn, said to have been a base for smugglers, and a ruined hut where watchers once scanned Bigbury Bay for shoals of pilchards.

At low tide, walkers can follow a fascinating 'tidal lane' for 4 miles along the western bank of the Avon from Bigbury to Aveton Gifford. Edged with tall black-and-white poles, the lane crosses creeks where swans cruise past small boats.

HIGH RIDE *Burgh Island is linked to the mainland at low tide, but at high water the gap is spanned by an ungainly looking sea tractor.*

⑥ BANTHAM
Thatched and whitewashed cottages are picturesque links with the days when small coasters sailed to Bantham to unload fish, lime, coal and other cargoes which were then ferried up the River Avon to Aveton Gifford. The tiny port flourished in the shelter of a sandy promontory, clad with bracken and marram grass, where cars now park. A short walk leads to a sandy beach with pool-dappled rocks at its southern end. A line of pink buoys marks the area where strong currents make bathing unsafe.

⑦ THURLESTONE
The thatched cottages of this expanding village overlook a fine bay, and above it is a clifftop golf course edged by sandy coves. The nearby South Milton Sands are dominated by Thurlestone Rock, an isolated pinnacle holed or 'thirled' by the waves,

DEVON THATCH *These cottages at Ringmore, near Bigbury-on-Sea, are typical of many that give the area a distinctive old-world charm.*

which can be reached at low tide. A clifftop path leads to Hope Cove, and there are fine views of Thurlestone Rock and, on a clear day, Eddystone, Rame Head and Bigbury.

⑧ HOPE COVE
The wooded cliffs of Bolt Tail tower above this sandy, rock-flanked cove, which has a small harbour at its northern end. Inner Hope, one of the cove's two hamlets, has retained the character of an old fishing community, with a narrow main street and quaint old buildings.

⑨ BOLBERRY DOWN
More than 400 ft above sea level, this expanse of turf, gorse and bracken is part of a strip of National Trust land which runs all the way from Bolt Tail to Bolt Head and on towards Salcombe. It is a perfect spot for a picnic, and commands superb views along the coast to the mouth of the English Channel. Signposted clifftop walks lead westwards to Hope Cove and eastwards to Soar Mill Cove.

Bolt Tail, a headland that was fortified during the Iron Age, has witnessed many shipwrecks. In 1588, during the rout of the Spanish Armada, the *San Pedro el Major* went down near by with the loss of 40 lives. In 1760, 700 men died when the warship *Ramillies* was driven on to the rocks in a storm.

⑩ SOAR MILL COVE
A 10 minute walk down a steep-sided valley from the car park in Soar leads to a delightful cove with stream-crossed sands, rock pools and low cliffs with many sun traps. The Ham Stone, a few hundred yards offshore, claimed the Finnish barque *Herzogen Cecilie* in 1936. She was one of the last sailing ships to be wrecked on Britain's coast.

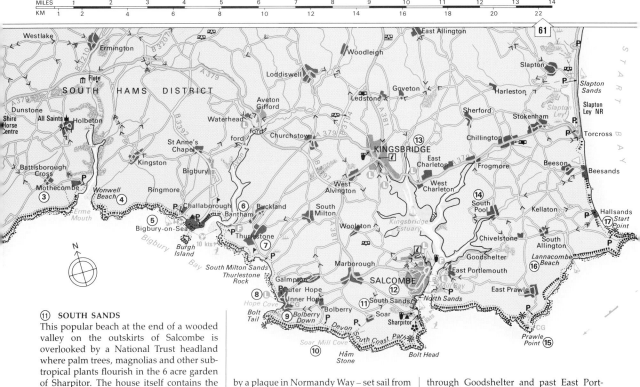

⑪ SOUTH SANDS

This popular beach at the end of a wooded valley on the outskirts of Salcombe is overlooked by a National Trust headland where palm trees, magnolias and other sub-tropical plants flourish in the 6 acre garden of Sharpitor. The house itself contains the Overbeck Museum, where exhibits illustrate Salcombe's history.

The lane from South Sands to Salcombe passes North Sands, another popular beach framed by wooded cliffs.

⑫ SALCOMBE

Long established as a favourite haven for yachtsmen, Salcombe has one of the West Country's finest natural harbours and is the gateway to nearly 2,000 acres of tidal creeks. Small boats can explore the tranquil water-ways as far inland as Kingsbridge.

Salcombe's old-world streets are packed with visitors in the summer months, when the estuary becomes a forest of slender masts and billowing sails set against a backcloth of tree-clad slopes. A regatta first held in 1857 is the highlight of the little town's calendar and embraces such activities as a fishing competition, a contest for sandcastle builders and a 'water' treasure hunt.

All this is a far cry from June 4, 1944, when thousands of Americans – commemorated by a plaque in Normandy Way – set sail from Salcombe to take part in the D-Day landings.

Salcombe has a museum, an art gallery and an indoor swimming pool. Sailing boats, rowing boats and motor boats can be hired, and there are diving trips, fishing trips and boat trips.

⑬ KINGSBRIDGE

The 'capital' of the South Hams district of Devon, Kingsbridge is an interesting old town whose roots go back to a 13th-century charter. It is seen at its best when high tide covers the creek's mudbanks and small boats ride at anchor by the quays. Coasters moored at these quays when Kingsbridge was a thriving inland port. There is a museum, and surfboards and canoes can be hired.

⑭ SOUTH POOL

Tucked away down a tangled skein of narrow lanes, South Pool is a quaint cluster of colour-washed cottages, some nestling beneath thatched roofs, at the head of a narrow creek. A lane can be followed through Goodshelter and past East Port-lemouth to Mill Bay where trees shelter a sandy beach with fine views across the estuary to Salcombe.

⑮ PRAWLE POINT

A sunken lane zigzags down from East Prawle to a car park, from which Prawle Point is reached after a 10 minute walk. Immediately east of the headland is an excellent example of a raised beach, where small fields overlook the rocky shore.

Prawle is derived from the Old English word for a lookout, and Prawle Point remains a rewarding viewpoint for ship-spotters.

⑯ LANNACOMBE BEACH

Brambles flank the very narrow lane which follows a stream down to Lannacombe's rock-flanked, shingle-backed sands. There are no places to park in the lane, but it ends in a bumpy track leading to a space with room for about a dozen cars.

⑰ START POINT

The lighthouse at the end of this bracken-clad, rock-spined headland watches over rocks where five ships were wrecked during a single night in 1891. The lighthouse is a 15 minute walk from a lofty clifftop car park, with a superb view over the sweep of Start Bay.

KINGSBRIDGE ESTUARY *Pleasure craft of all kinds crowd the estuary in summer. Some come and go, others never leave it – for the sheltered waters are ideal for small-boat sailing.*

LOCAL INFORMATION

Tourist information Plymouth 264849/264850, Kingsbridge 3195 (summer).

HM Coastguard Brixham 58292/3 for information, 999 in emergency (ask for coastguard).

Weather Plymouth 8091.

Local radio BBC Radio Devon, 351 m, 855 kHz, 97.5 MHz; IBA Plymouth Sound, 261 m, 1152 kHz, 96 MHz.

PLACES TO SEE INLAND

Dartmoor Wildlife Park, Sparkwell, 4 miles NE of Plymouth. Daily.

Flete, 6 miles NE of Newton Ferrers. Elizabethan house. Some afternoons in summer.

Kitley Caves, Yealmpton. Daily in summer.

National Shire Horse Farm Centre, Dunstone. Farm worked with shire horses. Daily.

Saltram House (NT), near Plymouth. Georgian mansion. Most days in summer. Garden all year.

A golden beach on Start Bay, and a historic port on the Dart

The panoramic sweep of Start Bay, with its shingle banks and sandy coves, contrasts with the more subtle beauty of the River Dart's estuary which curls inland through rolling farmland. To the north, cliffs more than 400 ft high in places lead to Berry Head with its superb views over Tor Bay. There are memories of the Pilgrim Fathers and of a Dartmouth man, Thomas Newcomen, whose steam-engine made him a giant of the Industrial Revolution.

① HALLSANDS

Ruined cottages, perched on a narrow shelf of rock at the foot of a low cliff, are poignant reminders that this was once a small but thriving fishing village, the home of more than 100 people. At the end of the 19th century, 650,000 tons of shingle were taken away to make concrete for new docks at Devonport. The operation removed the village's natural defences and left Hallsands exposed to the ever-hungry sea. Disaster struck on January 26, 1917, when an abnormally high tide coincided with an easterly gale. Villagers watched from the cliff as all but one of the 30 cottages were destroyed. Hallsands can still be an eerie place on a misty, out-of-season day when the foghorn on Start Point booms like the voice of doom.

A short walk over the crumbling cliff leads to North Hallsands, where a small hotel overlooks a beach of smooth, pale pink shingle. It was here that some of the villagers were rehoused in 1924. The area is popular with scuba divers, but there are dangerous currents off Start Point. There are boat trips, and a water-ski school.

② BEESANDS

Steep, narrow lanes run down to this old fishing village, which survived the disaster that overtook neighbouring Hallsands. To-day the single row of cottages of Beesands is protected from storm-driven waves by a barrier of huge boulders. The beach is shingle and shelves steeply in places.

There is a large caravan site at the northern end of the village. Motor boats can be hired, and fishing trips are available.

③ TORCROSS

The great bank of shingle on which part of Torcross stands encloses Slapton Ley, a 270 acre freshwater lake leased to the Field Studies Council as part of a nature reserve. It is an important winter roost for wildfowl, and its placid waters are the haunt of coots, mallards and great crested grebes, which now breed there. Water-lilies and yellow irises bloom during the summer, and permit-holding anglers can fish for pike and perch. The lake is designated as a site of special scientific interest, and residential courses are held at the field studies centre in Slapton village.

Torcross's shingle beach is backed by a sea-wall completed in 1980 after the village's defences had been badly damaged by a storm in the winter of 1978-9.

④ SLAPTON SANDS

The shingle beach is overlooked by a granite monument presented by the United States Army to local people who 'generously left their homes and their lands to provide a battle practice area for the successful assault on Normandy in June 1944'. The inscription adds that training in the Start Bay area saved many lives during 'Operation Overlord', as the D-Day operation was code-named, 'and contributed in no small measure' to its success.

⑤ BLACKPOOL SANDS

Unlike the southern part of Start Bay, Blackpool is a sandy cove sheltered by high, wooded cliffs. Rhododendrons bloom near the beach in the summer months. Dogs are banned from the shore, which is part

of a private estate. A force of Bretons, intent on attacking Dartmouth, was defeated at Blackpool in 1404.

There is a windsurfing school, and skiffs and floats can be hired.

⑥ DARTMOUTH CASTLE

Begun in 1481 and completed 12 years later, the castle was one of the first built to take cannon. Its battery of seven guns covered a 750 ft long chain, resting on six barges, which protected the approach to Dartmouth. The chain's anchorage points on the far cliff are clearly visible. Records reveal that the castle was garrisoned by a captain, 11 musketeers and 28 gunners. Inside are displays of armour, naval pikes and other weapons, and there are fine views up the estuary from the tower.

The castle shares its headland with St Petrox Church, most of which dates from the 17th century. A wooded walk runs southwards to Compass Cove, a secluded spot with a shingle beach.

RIVERSIDE SENTINEL *Built to deter Breton raiders, Dartmouth Castle changed hands twice during the Civil War.*

⑦ DARTMOUTH

Dartmouth's deep-rooted seafaring traditions are epitomised by the Britannia Royal Naval College where George V, George VI and other kings-to-be served as cadets. Prince Charles was a cadet there in 1971. Built in 1905 to replace the *Britannia* training ship which had been moored in the River Dart since 1863, the college dominates the hill above the town.

Crusaders sailed from Dartmouth in the 12th century; in Elizabethan times it was associated with such sea captains as Sir Walter Raleigh, and sent nine ships to fight the Spanish Armada. In 1620 the Pilgrim Fathers' ships *Mayflower* and *Speedwell* put in at Dartmouth for repairs; and on June 4, 1944, more than 400 craft sailed to take part in the D-Day landings.

Fine old buildings which provide tangible links with the town's history include the 17th-century Butterwalk, part of which houses one of Dartmouth's two museums. It was originally a row of merchants' houses, with the first floors supported on columns to form a covered trading area below.

The cobbled quay at Bayard's Cove, where the Pilgrim Fathers' visit is commemorated, has featured in the *Onedin Line* television series, and ends by Bearscove Castle, a small fort built in 1537 as part of Henry VIII's coastal defences.

A colourful collection of yachts, cabin cruisers, ferries and bigger, seagoing ships throngs the Dart in summer, while stately swans mingle with gulls in the Boatfloat, a

BLACKPOOL SANDS *Pine-clad cliffs sweep down to a crescent of fine golden shingle between high rocky headlands. Bathing is safe in calm weather, but the beach shelves steeply.*

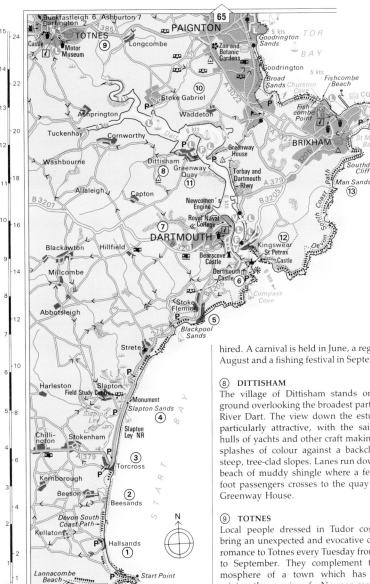

waterway with private craft and boats from Dartmouth, packed with sightseers. Spanning the river is a three-arched bridge built in 1828. The foundations of the original 13th-century bridge can be seen at low water.

An old riverside warehouse on Steamer Quay, on the eastern bank, is the home of the Totnes Motor Museum, whose collection includes vintage Alfa Romeos, an Aston Martin DB3S which raced at Le Mans in 1954, and a 1965 Amphicar, which was equally at home on the road or in the water. There is also a motor-cycle gallery. There are markets every Tuesday and Friday. River trips are available, and motor boats can be hired.

Riley Lynx Sprite 1937

Aston Martin DB3S 1954

small inner harbour between The Quay and the river.

A small building in Royal Avenue Gardens shelters what is believed to be the oldest working steam-engine in the world. It was built in 1711 by Thomas Newcomen, a Dartmouth ironmonger whose inventions made him one of the power-providing pioneers of the Industrial Revolution. The engine worked in the Midlands for 200 years before being taken to Dartmouth in 1963 to mark the 300th anniversary of Newcomen's birth. There is a plaque on the site of his house in Lower Street.

Fishing trips and sea and river cruises are available, and sailing and motor boats can be

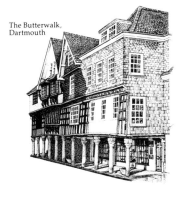

The Butterwalk, Dartmouth

hired. A carnival is held in June, a regatta in August and a fishing festival in September.

⑧ DITTISHAM

The village of Dittisham stands on high ground overlooking the broadest part of the River Dart. The view down the estuary is particularly attractive, with the sails and hulls of yachts and other craft making bold splashes of colour against a backcloth of steep, tree-clad slopes. Lanes run down to a beach of muddy shingle where a ferry for foot passengers crosses to the quay below Greenway House.

⑨ TOTNES

Local people dressed in Tudor costumes bring an unexpected and evocative dash of romance to Totnes every Tuesday from June to September. They complement the atmosphere of a town which has Saxon origins, the remains of a Norman castle and a wealth of architectural treasures. Many buildings date from the Middle Ages, when exports of tin and wool made Totnes one of the most flourishing ports in England. Ships laden with timber from Russia and Scandinavia still sail up the River Dart at high tide to unload at St Peter's Quay. They share the

⑩ STOKE GABRIEL

Lanes from Stoke Gabriel lead to an attractive creek whose upper reach has been dammed to form a tranquil mill pool partly framed by trees. Low tide reveals a muddy shore, carved by deep channels, but it is a popular spot among boating enthusiasts.

⑪ GREENWAY QUAY

Herons and kingfishers dabble and dive for fish near this quay, where the wooded grounds of Greenway House slope down to a thatched cottage and a small jetty. From the jetty a ferry for foot passengers sails to Dittisham on the far side of the River Dart.

Greenway House, hidden from view and not open to visitors, was the birthplace in 1539 of Sir Humphrey Gilbert, the seafarer who claimed Newfoundland for Queen Elizabeth in 1583. It is also believed to be the place where Gilbert's half-brother, Sir Walter Raleigh, was drenched with a bucket of water by a servant while he was enjoying a pipe of tobacco; the man thought his master's guest was on fire. The house was the home of the novelist Agatha Christie from just before the Second World War until her death in 1976.

Motor boats may be hired at the quay.

SUNNY SIDE *Facing south across the River Dart, Kingswear claims to be the sunny side of Dartmouth. Houses and hotels climb the hill above the estuary, taking full advantage of the aspect.*

UNCHANGING ELEGANCE AT BAYARD'S COVE

Dartmouth's unspoiled stretch of waterfront retains all the charm and atmosphere of bygone days. In the 17th century tall-masted ships, including the vessels that carried the Pilgrim Fathers to America, moored at the quay, while merchants, sea-captains and ship-owners bargained in the doorways, and the cobbles echoed to the clatter of carriage wheels.

⑫ KINGSWEAR

Ferries which take foot passengers and cars across the river to Dartmouth make Kingswear a busy place in the holiday season. The ferries share the estuary with private craft and a fleet of small boats which land crabs worth more than £1 million a year. Kingswear Castle, now privately owned, could once be linked to Dartmouth Castle across the river by an iron chain to deter invaders.

Kingswear is also the southern terminus of the Dart Valley Railway Company's steam-hauled Torbay and Dartmouth Line. The line was originally opened in 1864 as part of the Great Western Railway.

⑬ MAN SANDS

A rough track, signposted as unsuitable for cars, leads to this secluded beach of shingle and low-tide sand. It is flanked by the lofty face of Southdown Cliff, whose crest towers nearly 430 ft above the sea.

⑭ ST MARY'S BAY

An unsignposted footpath to the left of the entrance to Pontin's holiday village leads to a beach of sand and shingle enclosed by steep, bracken-clad slopes. The path is narrow, with steps in places, and the walk from the road takes about 5 minutes.

⑮ BERRY HEAD

Huge fortifications built in the 19th century, when Britain was at war with France, cross this high headland, a country park with commanding views of Tor Bay. About 800 sq. miles of sea are visible from the tip of the promontory, 190 ft above sea level, and the Bill of Portland, 46 miles away, can be seen on a clear day.

The lighthouse is said to be the highest and lowest in Britain. It is only 15 ft tall, but the light is 200 ft above sea level. Leaflets detailing the headland's nature trail are sold at the cafe in the main fort.

LOCAL INFORMATION

Tourist information Dartmouth 4224/4154; Totnes 863168 (summer); Brixham 2861.

HM Coastguard Brixham 58292/3 for information, 999 in emergency (ask for coastguard).

Weather Torquay 8091.

Local radio BBC Radio Devon, 351/206 m, 855/1458 kHz, 97.5/97 MHz. IBA Devon Air Radio, 314 m, 954 kHz, 95.1 MHz.

PLACES TO SEE INLAND

Buckfastleigh, 6 miles NW of Totnes. Buckfast Abbey, Benedictine abbey, built 1906-32 on foundations of medieval monastery, daily; Museum of Shellcraft, objects dating back to 1770s and displays of techniques, daily in summer.

Dart Valley Railway. Two restored steam railways, with trains daily in summer from Buckfastleigh to Totnes and between Paignton and Kingswear. Museum and visitor centre at Buckfastleigh.

Dartington 3 miles NW of Totnes. Cider Press Centre, riverside, farm and woodland trails and craft shops, weekdays; Dartington Hall Tweeds, shop open Mon.-Sat.

River Dart Country Park, Holne Park, Ashburton, 10 miles NW of Totnes, off B3357. Nature trails, bathing lake, pony riding. Daily in summer.

A hint of the Mediterranean on the shores of Tor Bay

Torquay, Paignton and the old fishing port of Brixham combine to make Tor Bay one of Britain's most popular areas for seaside holidays. The huge sand-rimmed bay began to attract well-to-do visitors at the end of the 18th century, when wars made the fashionable Grand Tour of Europe impossible. Today its pleasures range from sleek speedboats to salt-caked trawlers, from funfairs and nightclubs to secluded coves accessible only on foot.

① WATCOMBE BEACH
A 5 minute walk from the car park, down a steep but well-surfaced lane, leads to this cliff-flanked cove of coarse sand and fine shingle. The beach is overlooked by a small shop and a miniature promenade.

There are opportunities for many types of seaside recreation. Self-drive powerboats, floats and pedalos may be hired, and there is good fishing from the shore.

② PETIT TOR BEACH
The most 'secret' beach in the Tor Bay area is a shingle cove below cliffs of red, creeper-covered sandstone. The 10 minute walk from Petit Tor Road, where there is limited parking space, includes a steep woodland path. There are no facilities on the beach.

③ BABBACOMBE BEACH
Babbacombe was a popular little resort, patronised by royalty, when Torquay was nothing more than a sleepy fishing village. It was also a haunt of smugglers, where during a raid in 1853 the excisemen found 153 casks of contraband spirits. A 1 in 3 hill corkscrews down from the clifftop to a crescent of sand, which is sheltered by a stone breakwater, and completely covered at high tide.

Across the bay, Oddicombe Beach is lined by cliffs where dark red sandstone contrasts with pale limestone. The sandy shore, backed by a row of neat huts, is served by a cliff railway. Rowing boats, motor boats, floats and canoes may be hired.

④ ANSTEY'S COVE
A short but steep walk from Anstey's Cove Road plunges down to this rock-and-shingle beach which the sea covers at high tide. Redgate Beach, no more than 100 yds away, has sand and shingle between flat rocks, and

is sheltered from the north by a spectacular cliff. Motor boats and floats may be hired there.

Kent's Cavern, within easy walking distance of the car park, was inhabited in prehistoric times and has many beautiful rock formations.

⑤ HOPE'S NOSE
Grassy slopes sweep steeply down from the beautiful Ilsham Marine Drive to the low, rocky headland which marks the northern end of Tor Bay. Shingle coves nestle between expanses of flat rock, which are ideal for anglers. The headland has Devon's biggest kittiwake colony, and is a resting place for migratory birds. The walk down from the road takes about 5 minutes.

⑥ MEADFOOT BEACH
A stone sea-wall and steep slopes clad with shrubs shelter this beach, whose sand vanishes beneath the sea at high tide. It is overlooked by Daddyhole Plain, a clifftop plateau with a car park and panoramic views of Tor Bay.

⑦ TORQUAY
The coming of the Great Western Railway in 1848 enabled Torquay to exploit its natural assets and develop into one of England's best-known seaside resorts. Devotees included the poet Lord Tennyson, who hailed Torquay as 'the loveliest sea village in England'.

Palm trees and other subtropical plants flourish in the mild climate, enhancing the almost Mediterranean atmosphere of the spacious harbour. Hundreds of yachts and cabin cruisers are moored there, together with day-trip boats offering cruises as far afield as the Channel Islands. East of the

TREND-SETTING TRAWLER
One of the most powerful sailing vessels for its size ever built, the Brixham trawler was developed in Brixham late in the 18th century. It proved so· successful that Brixham became the premier fishing port of Britain. When the rich fishing grounds of the North Sea were discovered early in the 19th century the Brixham trawler was the prototype for the huge fleets of trawlers that became established at Hull, Grimsby, Fleetwood and Lowestoft. To-day, only a few of these 75 ft vessels remain, used as yachts.

Brixham trawler

harbour, Beacon Cove and Peaked Tor Cove have shingle beaches and clear water ideal for divers. To the west and south are the town's main beaches – Torre Abbey Sands, Corbyn Beach and Livermead Sands, where a marked lane is set aside for water-skiers.

Torre Abbey was founded as a monastery for the Premonstratensian Order of Canons in 1196. The buildings later fell into ruin, but parts of them were converted into a Georgian mansion in the 18th century. The house was bought by the town in 1930, and is now an art gallery. Near by is the Spanish Barn, a medieval tithe barn where prisoners from the Spanish Armada were held in 1588. Cockington, on the western edge of the town, is a picture-postcard collection of traditional cottages. Many have thatched roofs and some date from the Middle Ages.

There is a wide range of seaside attractions. Sea and river cruises and fishing trips are available. There are indoor and outdoor swimming pools, an aquarium and clubs for sailing, para-gliding, sub-aqua diving, water-skiing and windsurfing. Rowing boats, sailing boats and motor boats may be hired. A carnival is held in July, and there are regattas and powerboat races.

⑧ PAIGNTON
Paignton's snug little harbour, packed with pleasure craft during the holiday season, is a colourful reminder that this busy resort was just a fishing village until well into the 19th century. Its early patrons included Isaac Singer, the sewing-machine millionaire who built Oldway Mansion in the 1870s. It has rooms inspired by the Palace of Versailles, and is now a civic centre set in attractive grounds. Parts of St John's Church are Norman, and Kirkham House in Mill Lane dates from the 14th century.

The beach of reddish sand is backed by a low sea-wall and crossed by one of the West Country's few piers. Space is at a premium at high tide, but the beach shelves gently and is safe for young swimmers and paddlers. The sands stretch northwards for 1 mile from the harbour to Hollicombe Head.

Paignton is the northern terminus of the Dart Valley Railway Company's Torbay and Dartmouth Line, which runs steam-hauled trains to Goodrington, Churston and Kingswear. The town's large zoological and botanical gardens cover 75 acres.

WATCOMBE BEACH *Devon's red-sandstone cliffs tumble down to the sea in a series of small coves round Babbacombe Bay and Tor Bay.*

Seaside attractions include boat trips and fishing. There is an aquarium, a sailing club, a windsurfing school and an indoor swimming pool. A carnival is held in July.

⑨ GOODRINGTON SANDS

One of Tor Bay's most popular beaches, Goodrington has half a mile of sand, bounded to the north by a stone-faced sea-wall. From the car park the beach is approached through a small park with a boating lake.

⑩ BROAD SANDS

A long, concrete sea-wall curves round this beach of shingle-scattered sand reached by a road that passes beneath a Dart Valley Railway viaduct. A 5 minute walk over the cliffs from the car park leads to Elberry Cove, one of the two Tor Bay beaches where water-skiing is permitted from the shore.

⑪ FISHCOMBE BEACH

On the outskirts of Brixham, this small, shingle cove is tucked in at the feet of steep, tree-clad slopes and cliffs of dark red sandstone. Its neighbour, Churston Cove, also has a shingle shore.

BRIXHAM HARBOUR *Brightly painted houses climb the slopes behind the harbour, where a replica of Drake's Golden Hinde looks little larger than the pleasure boats moored alongside it.*

⑫ BRIXHAM

Narrow streets squeezed between attractive old buildings run steeply down to the harbour that has been Brixham's focal point since the Middle Ages. The town was England's major fishing port for 300 years, and trawlers still mingle with scores of private craft. The harbour's most eye-catching feature is a full-size replica of the *Golden Hinde*, the surprisingly small ship in which Sir Francis Drake sailed round the world in 1577-80. This replica was converted from a 1940s fishing trawler; it is moored by the old Market House, built in 1800, which now houses the British Fisheries Museum, devoted to the history of the industry.

Near by, a statue on the quay commemorates the landing of Prince William of Orange, the future King William III, on November 5, 1688, and recalls his vow: 'The liberties of England and the Protestant religion I will maintain.' The museum at Bolton Cross, in the centre of the town, has a section illustrating the history of the Coastguards.

Seaside attractions include an aquarium and an indoor swimming pool. Boat and fishing trips can be arranged, and motor boats can be hired. There is a regular ferry service across the bay to Torquay.

⑬ SHOALSTONE BEACH

There are good views across Tor Bay from this shingle beach, which lies on the north side of Brixham's breakwater. Low tide exposes pools between angled tablets of rock.

There is an open-air swimming pool at the eastern end of the beach.

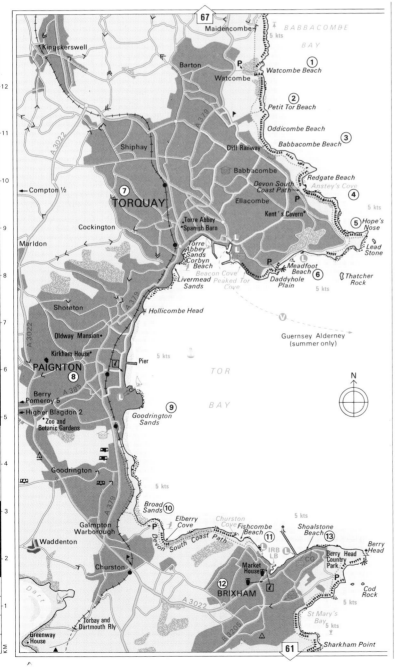

Holiday havens between the Teign and Exe estuaries

The ancient city of Exeter makes an excellent base for exploring a coast whose character has as many facets as a diamond. High cliffs of soft rock, the colour of mellow brick, march northwards from Maidencombe and contrast with the reedy, bird-haunted estuaries where boats ride at anchor. Shaldon, Teignmouth and Dawlish are busy little resorts, while Topsham and Lympstone are picturesque villages tucked away off the main road.

SEASIDE LINE *The railway line built by Brunel to carry the Great Western Railway westwards to Penzance provides passengers with glorious coastal views, and Dawlish with an unusual seafront.*

① MAIDENCOMBE
A short but steep walk from the car park off the A379 leads to this small, sheltered cove. Creeper-clad sandstone cliffs frame a sandy, rock-flanked beach below a small shop. The road to Shaldon passes a clifftop car park with views over Babbacombe Bay. Rowing boats and floats may be hired.

② SHALDON
A network of narrow streets is overlooked from the east by The Ness, a wooded headland at the mouth of the River Teign. The headland is pierced by a well-lit tunnel, about 100 yds long, which leads walkers to Ness Cove where there are sands and seaweed-draped rocks at the foot of a high cliff. A well-preserved lime-kiln, in which limestone from Oddicombe was burned, stands at the landward end of the tunnel, which has several flights of steps. Lime from the kiln was used as builders' mortar and as a fertiliser. Immediately above the tunnel's entrance is the Shaldon Wildlife Collection, whose exhibits range from owls and parrots to monkeys and Indian pythons.

The beach facing Teignmouth is a mixture of fine shingle and coarse sand, but bathing is dangerous at the mouth of the river because of fast currents.

③ ARCH BROOK
At this peaceful spot a stream flows under a small bridge and into the River Teign. The muddy creek, where abandoned boats are patrolled by gulls, is patched with reeds, and trees overhang the water at low tide.

④ COOMBE CELLARS
Hidden away at the end of a narrow lane, the inn at Coombe Cellars was once a haunt of smugglers and had spacious cellars where contraband was concealed. The inn now shares its lonely riverside location with a yacht club.

⑤ TEIGNMOUTH
The town's roots go back to Saxon times, but it was not until the first half of the 19th century that the town really developed as a port and holiday resort. Its sheltered harbour faces up-river and has a quay built in the 1830s. From this quay Dartmoor granite was shipped out to build London Bridge, which was later sold to the United States and now straddles a man-made waterway in Lake Havasu City, Arizona.

The quay is still visited by small, sea-going ships which have to negotiate swift currents in the estuary's narrow mouth. On the seaward side of Teignmouth, tall Victorian buildings overlook a pier and a beach of dark red sand. Bathers should avoid the southern end of the beach where it shelves quickly and is swept by the estuary's currents. To the north, the Parson and Clerk headland is a landmark, while the railway tunnel between Teignmouth and Dawlish is one of several which made the building of this section of the Great Western Railway a considerable feat of engineering.

A plaque in Northumberland Place marks the house where John Keats lived in 1818 while finishing his epic poem *Endymion*. As well as a full range of seaside attractions, including an outdoor swimming pool, there are fishing trips and sea and river cruises.

⑥ DAWLISH
Black swans, East Indian game ducks, South African shelducks, Chinese swan geese and other birds inhabit The Lawn, a delightful little park through which the Dawlish Water flows seawards over a series of small weirs. Right in the heart of Dawlish, it is the town's most memorable feature and looks particularly attractive when illuminated at night.

A bridge under the railway track leads to a long beach where a strip of fine shingle leads to sands whose dark red hue is typical of this part of Devon. At the southern end of the beach, high cliffs shelter a cove where small boats are pulled ashore. Dawlish was popular with the novelist Charles Dickens, who set part of *Nicholas Nickleby* in the town.

Dawlish has the usual attractions of a seaside resort, including an indoor swimming pool. There are fishing trips, and rowing and motor boats for hire.

⑦ DAWLISH WARREN
Chalets, shops, a go-kart track and an amusement arcade make the landward end of Dawlish Warren a lively place during the holiday season – but walkers who stroll out along the dunes, which extend for 1 mile, can enjoy a much more peaceful atmosphere. Fast-flowing currents make bathing dangerous at the point, but there are extensive views up the River Exe. The view to the south is dominated by Langstone Rock, a huge block of sandstone with a natural, wave-carved arch.

Most of Dawlish Warren is a 500 acre nature reserve, where 180 species of birds are recorded every year. They include waders such as black-tailed godwits, greenshanks, curlews and sandpipers. In winter the flocks are enlarged by migrants from the far north, including Brent geese, and from a hide overlooking the main roost as many as 20,000 birds may be visible at once, when the rising waters push the resting birds up towards the high-tide mark.

⑧ STARCROSS
Old, bow-fronted cottages share the village's narrow main street with a tall sandstone building of great interest to industrial archaeologists. It is one of the pump houses built in the 1840s to serve the 'atmospheric' section of Isambard Kingdom Brunel's Great Western Railway between Exeter and Newton Abbot. Pumps evacuated air from a tube between the rails, creating a vacuum which 'pulled' a piston attached to the train. The system proved swift and remarkably quiet, but was abandoned in 1848. One of the main problems was that rats devoured the grease-soaked leather flaps intended to keep the tube air-tight. The building is now a museum devoted to the story of the system – Brunel's one great failure. It overlooks a boat basin and the point from which a ferry for foot passengers sails to Exmouth.

Boat trips, fishing trips, and diving trips and lessons are available, and there is a water-ski school.

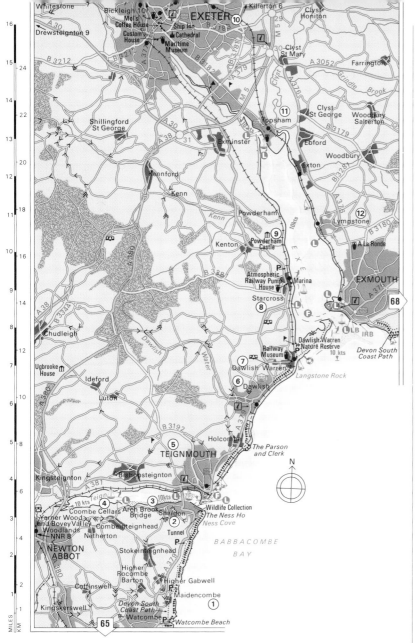

St Canute,
a Danish steam
tug built in 1931

Reed boat from Lake Titicaca in South America

Exeter Maritime Museum, the world's largest collection of working boats. Opened in 1968, it has breathed new life into the port area which was the hub of the city's commercial life for hundreds of years. Vessels from all over the world are on display, including Arabian dhows, coracles from Wales, an elaborate ceremonial canoe from the Ellice Islands and a Chinese sampan. One of the most notable exhibits is *Bertha*, a dredger designed by Brunel in 1844 and used at Bridgwater until 1964; she is the oldest working steam ship in the world.

The museum is at the head of a canal opened in 1566 and the oldest pound-lock waterway in the country. Its construction was forced upon the city when the Countess of Devon, determined to attract trade to her port of Topsham, built a weir down the river from Exeter, blocking access to the city. Her action resulted in a legal battle which dragged on for 300 years.

⑪ TOPSHAM

Built on a peninsula between the tidal rivers Exe and Clyst, Topsham is an enchanting village often bypassed by visitors to the Exeter area. It used to be a bustling port whose fortunes were at their height in the 17th century. Many of the buildings date from that period and have Dutch gables, bow windows and walls hung with wisteria. Sea-birds share the river with swans and yachts. There is a museum, and an open-air swimming pool.

⑫ LYMPSTONE

Narrow streets, colour-washed cottages and cobbled walks leading to the pebbled shore make Lympstone one of the River Exe's delights. It is also a vantage point for observing the estuary's abundant bird life.

⑨ POWDERHAM CASTLE

Set in a deer park beside the River Exe, the home of the Earl and Countess of Devon dates from the end of the 14th century. Parts of the original building have survived, but the castle was extensively altered after being damaged during the Civil War. Its interior has some fine 18th-century plasterwork and a Marble Hall decorated with a 17th-century tapestry woven in Brussels. Portraits and coats of arms trace the history of the family.

⑩ EXETER

Exeter was founded by the Romans as Isca Dumnoniorum, and lengths of Roman wall still stand after nearly 2,000 years. They surround the heart of a fascinating city where new buildings, many of them built to replace those destroyed during air raids in 1942, stand shoulder to shoulder with others dating back to medieval times. Old-world gems include Mol's Coffee House, built in 1596, and the Ship Inn, in Martin's Lane, which is said to have been Sir Francis Drake's favourite tavern.

Exeter Cathedral dates from the 12th century when work was started by Bishop William, the nephew of William the Conqueror. It is a beautiful building with a wealth of carved woodwork and stone, and a remarkable clock believed to have been made at the end of the 15th century. The

nave's rib-vaulted roof, 300 ft long, is decorated with carved and colourful bosses, one of which depicts the murder of Thomas Becket. Despite its age, St Peter's is not Exeter's first cathedral. Its predecessor, a church built by King Canute in 1019, became a cathedral 31 years later when Edward the Confessor enthroned the city's first bishop.

Down by the river, the 17th-century Custom House shares The Quay with the

MEDIEVAL SURVIVOR *Many of Exeter's ancient sites, such as the medieval Stepcote Hill, survived heavy bombing in 1942.*

LOCAL INFORMATION

Tourist information Torquay 27428; Teignmouth 6271; Dawlish 863589; Exeter 72434

HM Coastguard Brixham 58292/3 for information, 999 in emergency (ask for coastguard).

Weather Torquay 8091; Exeter 8091.

Local radio BBC Radio Devon, 206/303 m, 1458/990 kHz, 97 MHz; IBA Devon Air Radio, 314/450 m, 954/666 kHz, 95.1/95.8 MHz.

PLACES TO SEE INLAND

Bickleigh Castle, 10 miles N of Exeter. Medieval fortress. Most afternoons in summer.

Bickleigh Mill Craft Centre and farm, 11 miles N of Exeter. Restored watermill and craft shop. Farm with working oxen and shire horses. Daily in summer, weekends in winter.

Killerton (NT), 6 miles NE of Exeter. 18th-century house and gardens. House daily in summer, gardens all year.

Ugbrooke House, 6 miles N of Newton Abbot. 18th-century house by Robert Adam. Most afternoons in summer.

Yarner Wood and Bovey Valley Woodlands National Nature Reserve, 8 miles NW of Newton Abbot.

Sidmouth, elegant Regency town on a coast of red cliffs

Mile after mile of cliffs tower above the waves to the east of Exmouth, making this a rewarding part of the Devon coast for walkers. Care must be taken, however, because the cliffs are mainly composed of soft, crumbling sandstone. At their feet, sandy beaches alternate with steep shingle banks where strong undertows create dangers in rough seas. Towards Beer, the dark red ramparts give way to chalk cliffs of a startling whiteness.

① EXMOUTH

The waters of the River Exe meet the open sea at Exmouth, a town whose popularity as a holiday resort goes back to the 18th century. A terrace of elegant Georgian houses called the Beacon is a survivor from the town's early days. The long, sandy shore still attracts many visitors, and files of neat, white-painted beach huts crowd its eastern end. Red flags and signs warn that it is dangerous to bathe at the western end of the beach, where powerful currents swirl in and out of the estuary. Swimmers should also avoid the marked area which extends for 300 yds to the east of the lifeboat house.

Ferry passengers from Starcross, on the far bank of the Exe, land near a small dock which is still used by a few coasters. It is a link with Exmouth's heyday as a port in the 16th century, when the town became one of Devon's most important maritime centres and was used as a base by Sir Walter Raleigh, the Elizabethan explorer.

At the eastern end of Queen's Drive, where the beach becomes rocky, 126 acres of National Trust land extend to Sandy Bay. As well as a wide range of seaside attractions, there are boat trips, fishing trips and river cruises, an outdoor swimming pool, a sports centre and a model railway. A carnival is held in July.

② SANDY BAY

The huge Devon Cliffs holiday camp spreads inland behind this sandy beach, which is walled in by high cliffs of crumbling, dark red sandstone. Day visitors are welcome, and there is a large car park above the beach. The headland which towers above the eastern end of the bay is a rifle-range used by the Royal Marines, and red flags fly when it is in use.

Beyond the rifle-range are Otter Cove and Littleham Cove, known locally as Budleigh Bay. Steep paths lead down from the holiday camp to the beaches, where there are banks of dull pink shingle above low-tide sand, many pools and a small, tide-scoured cave. Shire horses are on show at the Country Life Museum, by the holiday camp entrance.

THE BOYHOOD OF RALEIGH *Sir John Millais set the scene for his painting at Budleigh Salterton, using his two sons and a ferryman as models.*

③ BUDLEIGH SALTERTON

Sir John Millais' painting *The Boyhood of Raleigh* was created at Budleigh Salterton. The sea-wall which featured in the picture and the house where Millais lived still stand in a resort which has retained an air of Victorian gentility. Small boats are winched up a beach of smooth, pinkish shingle which shelves steeply and sweeps westwards below high, crumbling cliffs known as The Floors.

There are pleasant walks beside the River Otter, where ships loaded wool and salt before the waterway became choked with silt in the 15th century. At East Budleigh, one of the pews in All Saints' Church bears the coat of arms of the Raleigh family. Sir Walter was born in 1552 at nearby Hayes Barton, the family's thatched farmhouse home. The house is not open to visitors. Bicton Park, up the valley from East Budleigh, has a narrow-gauge railway, a countryside museum and other attractions.

④ OTTERTON

The tranquil little village was referred to as a 'pretty fisher town' in Tudor times, but its atmosphere is now completely rural. Near the river stands a mill, mentioned in the Domesday Book, where water-power is still used to produce wholemeal flour.

⑤ LADRAM BAY

A short walk through a caravan site leads to Ladram Bay's beach, where pale grey shingle contrasts with the deep, rich red of the cliffs. Secluded coves can be reached at low water, but explorers who wander too far risk being trapped by the incoming tide. The sea has carved the cliffs into spectacular shapes, and isolated several huge blocks of sandstone from the mainland.

Motor boats, rowing boats, floats and canoes can be hired.

⑥ SIDMOUTH

Soaring cliffs, their pink-to-red faces patch-worked with greenery, rise on either side of a resort rich in Georgian and Regency architecture. Gothic and bow windows, elegant porches, elaborate wrought-iron balconies and stately columns decorate the house-fronts along the Esplanade between the foot of Peak Hill and the mouth of the River Sid.

The Duke and Duchess of Kent moved to the town in 1819 with their daughter, the future Queen Victoria, to escape their creditors. Their home is now the Royal Glen Hotel. In 1867 the queen presented a window commemorating her father to the church of St Nicholas and St Giles.

Sidmouth's days as a port ended when silt and shingle made the Sid unsuitable for navigation, but small fishing boats still use the beach near the river mouth and are hauled ashore with winches. The shingle beach, which shelves steeply, gives way to

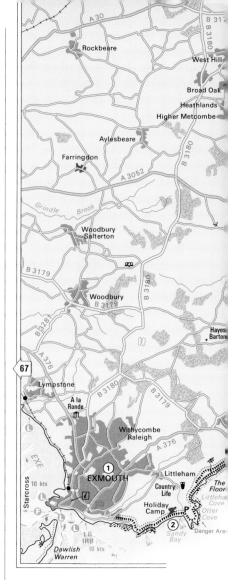

some sand as the tide falls. Attractions for the holidaymaker include a museum, boat trips, a sports centre and a sailing club.

⑦ WESTON MOUTH

A 15 minute walk from the hamlet of Weston, where there is a small parking area, leads through trees and over fields to this secluded beach. A stream races down the

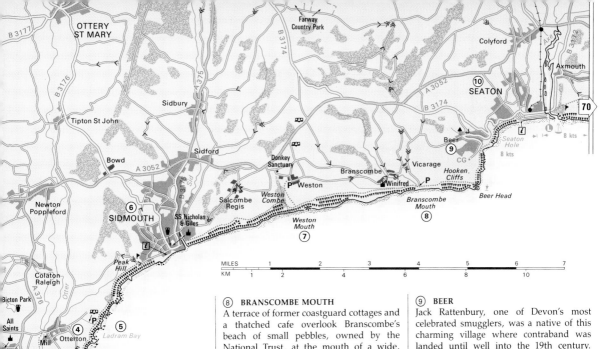

⑧ BRANSCOMBE MOUTH

A terrace of former coastguard cottages and a thatched cafe overlook Branscombe's beach of small pebbles, owned by the National Trust, at the mouth of a wide, picturesque valley. The clifftop walk to Beer Head – the most southerly chalk headland in England – runs along Hooken Cliffs, the scene of a huge landslide in 1790. Ten acres of land slipped about 250 ft during a March night.

Branscombe itself is an attractive village, with a thatched smithy dating from Norman times. Its church, dedicated to St Winifred, dates from the 12th century and has a three-decker pulpit – one of only two in Devon – and the remains of a 15th-century mural depicting a devil spearing adulterers. The road leading from the village square to the beach passes Great Seaside Farm, which dates back to the 14th century.

Thatched smithy
at Branscombe

⑨ BEER

Jack Rattenbury, one of Devon's most celebrated smugglers, was a native of this charming village where contraband was landed until well into the 19th century. Rattenbury defied the excisemen for nearly 50 years, later publishing his *Memoirs of a Smuggler* in 1837 after 'retiring' to become a law-abiding fisherman.

Beer's main street, alongside a trickling stream, slopes down to a shingle beach sheltered by high cliffs of crumbling chalk which sweep southwards to Beer Head. It is still a fishing village, despite lacking a harbour, and small boats land crabs and lobsters. Lace-making used to be another Beer industry; in 1839 Beer supplied lace trimmings worth £1,000 for Queen Victoria's wedding dress.

Attractions include a model railway exhibition and miniature railway. Rowing boats and motor boats can be hired, and a regatta is held in August.

⑩ SEATON

Seaton's beach of shingle and pebbles is bordered by a long sea-wall built in 1980 after an exceptionally violent storm caused serious flooding. The town, mostly Victorian and Edwardian in character, lies at the mouth of the River Axe, where there are dangerous currents. It is flanked to the west by pale chalk cliffs, sheltering a beach of sand and shingle at Seaton Hole, and to the east by darker sandstone heights. There is a small harbour at the mouth of the river, below the point where it is crossed by a concrete bridge, built in 1877 and one of the first of its type in Britain.

An electric tramway runs inland from Seaton to Colyford and Colyton. It is said to be the only one in the world where tramcars with open upper decks are still used on a regular commercial basis. Other attractions of Seaton include a boating pool and a sailing club. Volunteer lifeguards patrol the beach on most weekends in summer.

grassy ravine of Weston Combe before filtering into the sea through a long beach of smooth shingle. The shore is overlooked by high cliffs where bramble thickets alternate with expanses of naked rock.

This part of the coast is pitted with caves, many of which were once used by smugglers to hide brandy, tobacco and other contraband. Slade House Farm, between Weston and the A3052, is a donkey sanctuary which the public can visit. It provides a link with the days when donkeys carried farm produce from clifftop fields to local markets.

THE GIRLHOOD OF VICTORIA *The Regency elegance of Sidmouth, in its valley between the hills, has changed little since Princess Victoria, later Britain's queen, lived there with her parents.*

LOCAL INFORMATION

Tourist information Exmouth 263744 (summer); Budleigh Salterton 5275 (summer); Sidmouth 6441 (summer); Seaton 21660 (summer); Exeter 72434.

HM Coastguard Brixham 58292/3, Portland 820441 for information, 999 in emergency (ask for coastguard).

Weather Exeter 8091.

Local radio BBC Radio Devon, 303 m, 990 kHz, 97.5 MHz. IBA Devon Air Radio, 450 m, 666 kHz, 95.8 MHz.

PLACES TO SEE INLAND

Cadhay, Ottery St Mary. Tudor house. Some afternoons in summer.

Farway Countryside Park, 7 miles NW of Seaton, off B3174. Rare farm breeds. Most days in summer.

Golden sandstone heights that stretch eastwards from Lyme Regis

Dowlands Cliffs, between Seaton and Lyme Regis, are the scene of Britain's biggest recorded landslide, which in 1839 sent 20 acres of land slithering seawards. As if in compensation, a huge bank of shingle has built up over thousands of years between the seaside village of West Bay, near Bridport, and the Isle of Portland. Splendid cliffs dominate Lyme Bay and reach 626 ft at Golden Cap, the highest point on England's southern coast.

① AXMOUTH

This village of thatched and colour-washed cottages was one of the busiest ports in Britain in Roman times, before landslides choked the mouth of the River Axe. Ships sailed out laden with West Country wool and iron, while cargoes from Europe were taken inland along the Foss Way. The village is now 1 mile from the sea, and the muddy river, flanked by saltings, is a feeding ground for sea-birds and wildfowl.

② DOWLANDS CLIFFS

Eight million tons of waterlogged chalk are estimated to have been involved in the great landslide on Christmas Day, 1839. No lives were lost, because cottages on the cliffs had been evacuated during the previous 48 hours. But witnesses later related how the beach had bucked and heaved like the deck of a small boat in rough seas.

The area is now a national nature reserve, rich in plants, wildlife and fossils, but the only access points for walkers are from a lane south of Axmouth, where there is very limited parking space, and from Ware, on the outskirts of Lyme. The waymarked coastal path passes along the landslip. The western end of the landslip is about 15 minutes' walk from the Axmouth end of the path. Beyond this point, it is impossible to leave the path until it reaches the outskirts of Lyme Regis, some 4 miles further east.

③ LYME REGIS

A harbour bright with boats, narrow streets elegant with colour-washed buildings, lofty cliffs and a great sweep of sea combine with a backcloth of high, steep hills to make Lyme Regis one of the most memorable small towns on England's southern coast. Its roots go back to AD 774 when Cynewulf, King of the West Saxons, gave monks permission to produce salt from seawater. The 'Regis' dates from 1284, when Edward I granted the town a charter and used the port as a base for his wars against the French.

Five local ships helped to defeat the Spanish Armada in 1588, but the most notable event in Lyme Regis' history was the Duke of Monmouth's landing in 1685. He stepped ashore on sandy, shingle-backed Monmouth Beach, west of the harbour, raised his standard and declared his intention to wrest the throne from his uncle, James II. Monmouth and his men were defeated at the Battle of Sedgemoor, and 12 of his supporters were hanged on the spot where their leader's ill-fated attempt had started.

Lyme Regis is no longer a commercial port, but its attractive harbour, sheltered by the stone breakwater known as The Cobb and dating from the 14th century, is still used by fishing boats and private craft. In 1980 the town was swept back to its Victorian past during the filming of *The French Lieutenant's Woman*. The novel from which the film was adapted was written by John Fowles, who lives in Lyme Regis.

The town has a museum of local history, prominently featuring the fossils which can be found in the nearby cliffs. Motor boats can be hired, and there are fishing trips, a sailing school and club, and a windsurfing school.

Ever since Mary Anning, a carpenter's daughter, found the complete skeleton of an ichthyosaurus in a cliff near Lyme Regis in 1811, the area has been a happy hunting ground for amateur fossil collectors. Climbing the cliffs is dangerous, but among the fallen rocks at their foot can often be found the remains of animals that lived some 200 million years ago, when the area was under the sea. Descendants of many of the fossilised creatures survive today.

AMMONITE *The fossil most commonly found is that of the spiral-shaped ammonite, an extinct mollusc which is a distant ancestor of today's octopus and squid.*

BRITTLE STAR *This thin-armed starfish, its mouth at the centre of its body (right), appears in rocks at Golden Cap. Its descendants today (left), are little altered in appearance.*

NAUTILUS *Less coiled and smoother than the ammonite, the nautilus shell (right) is largely hollow. The nautilus still lives (left) on Atlantic and Mediterranean sea-beds.*

④ CHARMOUTH

Swans and ducks patrol the deep pool, held back by banked shingle, where the River Char trickles into the sea over a beach which is sandy at low tide. In 1811 the cliffs of Black Ven, now part of a 161 acre nature reserve, yielded the first complete fossil of an ichthyosaurus, a prehistoric marine reptile resembling a giant porpoise. Discovered by

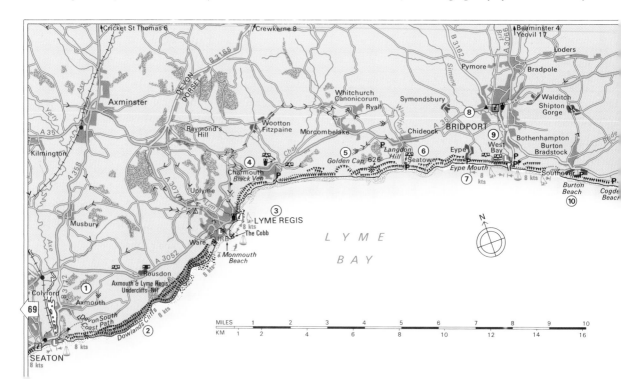

DORSET'S CHANGING FACE *Though rugged in appearance, the soft sandstone cliffs west of Eype Mouth are constantly being eroded by the gales and tides sweeping in from Lyme Bay.*

a local girl, 12-year-old Mary Anning, the fossilised skeleton was 21 ft long.

When Charles II was forced into hiding in 1651 after his defeat by Cromwell at the Battle of Worcester, he took refuge for a time at the Queen's Arms Inn in Charmouth. His plan was to escape to France by sea with the help of Stephen Limbry, a local boatman. But news of his presence leaked out to Roundhead sympathisers, and the king had to flee the town on horseback instead.

⑤ GOLDEN CAP

Clumps of bright yellow gorse and an expanse of golden sandstone near its summit explain the name of the highest cliff in southern England. Golden Cap, 626 ft high, is part of a 2,000 acre National Trust estate embracing most of the coastal land between Charmouth and Seatown. The cliff, a breathtaking viewpoint, can be approached from Seatown or from the National Trust's small, woodland car park on Langdon Hill.

⑥ SEATOWN

Reached by a lane from Chideock, this village with thatched cottages of honey-coloured stone has a beach of golden shingle which shelves steeply above low-tide sand. Like other beaches in the area it is popular with fishermen who cast for bass and mackerel. The coast between Seatown and Charmouth was a favourite landing place for contraband when smuggling was rife in Dorset.

⑦ EYPE MOUTH

A narrow lane from the A35 wriggles down to Eype Mouth's beach of smooth, steeply shelving shingle at the foot of unstable cliffs. There are fine views westwards over Lyme Bay to the chalk cliffs of Beer Head.

⑧ BRIDPORT

This ancient town was so famous for its rope-making industry during the age of sailing ships that being 'stabbed by a Bridport dagger' was another way of saying that a person had been hanged. The hemp used for making ropes flourished locally, together with flax, and is believed to have been introduced by the Romans. Records of the industry in Bridport go back to 1211. Nets are still made in the town, although the last of the old-fashioned ropewalks, where the lengths of hemp were twisted to make rope, was abandoned in 1970. The amount of space needed to make rope is said to explain Bridport's exceptionally broad streets. Bridport is the 'Port Bredy' of several novels by Thomas Hardy.

Bridport has a museum and an art gallery. A street market is held every Wednesday and Saturday morning.

⑨ WEST BAY

Bridport Harbour, as it used to be known, was built in 1740 and visited by as many as 500 ships a year during the 19th century. Sluice gates, added in 1823, enable a torrent of river water to be released to scour sand and shingle from the entrance channel. Schooners and other ships, including naval vessels, were built at West Bay until 1879.

The River Brit flows to the sea between huge 'waves' of fine shingle which slope steeply down to patches of low-tide sand. The shingle runs south-eastwards for several miles, merging eventually with the sweep of Chesil Beach. Cliffs in which bands of hard and soft rock alternate have been eroded to resemble huge, battered shelves.

Rowing boats can be hired, and fishing trips are available.

⑩ BURTON BEACH

From the low cliffs above this beach of shingle and low-tide sand there are wide views which range from Beer Head to the Bill of Portland. The grassy area at the end of the lane from Burton Bradstock is ideal for picnics and forms part of more than 80 acres of National Trust land.

There is a car park in Beach Road. A steep and rather rough track from the B3157 east of Burton Bradstock runs down to a parking area behind the shingle bank of Cogden Beach.

⑪ WEST BEXINGTON

A car park and a few beach huts overlook the shingle shore, which shelves very steeply.

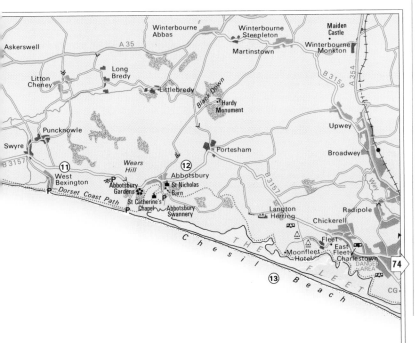

71

LAGOON BEHIND A SWEEP OF SHINGLE

One of Britain's most remarkable wonders of nature, the 10 mile long Chesil Beach which stretches from Abbotsbury to the Isle of Portland is a bank of shingle – 40 ft high in places – piled up on a blue clay reef. The brackish lagoon behind the beach is called the Fleet; it is rich in eel-grass, which provides food for the Abbotsbury swans.

Notices warn of the hazards to swimmers. It is, however, a popular beach for sea fishermen. From the top of Wears Hill, on the road to Abbotsbury, there are views of Chesil Beach and the Isle of Portland.

⑫ **ABBOTSBURY**

St Catherine's Chapel, built in the 14th century and now used to store thatchers' reeds, looks down from a steep hill over the roofs of one of England's most enchanting villages. It has many picture-postcard cottages, a thatched, 15th-century tithe barn and a church with a pulpit that is pock-marked from shots fired during the Civil

War when the village fell to the Parliamentarians. The abbey that gave the village its name was founded in the 11th century, and some idea of its former wealth can be had from the size of the tithe barn, which measures 272 ft by 31 ft and is one of the largest buildings of its kind in Britain. The Church of St Nicholas contains a 13th-century statue of one of the abbots.

The village still celebrates an ancient custom, Garland Day, on May 13 each year. In what is thought to be a survival of sea-god worship, two garlands are carried through the village, and one is sometimes cast into the sea.

South of the village, a 5 minute walk from the car park leads to a unique swannery, where 400-500 mute swans may be seen in summer. The number increases to nearly 1,000 in winter. It is the only nesting colony of mute swans in Britain, and dates from the 11th century, when the Benedictine monks of Abbotsbury reared the birds for meat.

The breezy, gorse-gold summit of Black Down, 3 miles north-east of the village, is

The tithe barn,
Abbotsbury

topped by an octagonal tower built in memory of Vice-Admiral Sir Thomas Masterman Hardy, commander of HMS *Victory*, Nelson's flagship at the Battle of Trafalgar in 1805. He lived in Portesham, at the foot of the hill.

⑬ CHESIL BEACH

Generations of experts on coastal geology have failed to work out how the billions of pebbles which form this immense bank of shingle are automatically graded from west to east, and become bigger and bigger towards the Isle of Portland. The beach is more than 40 ft high in places and has been the graveyard of many a sailing ship when gales swept across Lyme Regis Bay.

In one violent storm in 1795, seven ships of the line were lost and 200 men and women died. The ships were part of a fleet commanded by Rear Admiral Sir Hugh Christian, who was on his way to the West Indies to take up the post of Commander-in-Chief. In 1824 the beach was swamped by a gale-driven tide which swept the 95 ton sloop *Ebenezer* into the Fleet, the 7 mile long lagoon behind the beach. In the same storm the West Indiamen *Carvalho* and *Colville* were less fortunate, both being destroyed with all hands lost.

The storm of 1824 destroyed much of East Fleet village. Fleet House, dating from 1603 and now the Moonfleet Hotel, features in *Moonfleet*, a stirring tale about smugglers written by J. Meade Faulkner and published in 1898. Chesil Beach's shingle absorbs and retains enough of the sun's heat to create a very mild 'mini-climate', which accounts for the subtropical Abbotsbury Gardens where exotic trees, shrubs and flowers flourish. The gardens were part of an estate given by Henry VIII to Sir Guy Strangways in 1543.

LOCAL INFORMATION

Tourist information Seaton 21660 (summer), Lyme Regis 2138, Bridport 24901 (summer).

HM Coastguard Portland 820441 for information, 999 in emergency (ask for coastguard).

Weather Exeter 8091, Bournemouth 8091.

Local radio BBC Radio Devon, 303 m, 990 kHz, 97 MHz.

PLACES TO SEE INLAND

Clapton Court, near Crewkerne. Gardens. Most days.

Mapperton Gardens, Beaminster. Most afternoons in summer.

Montacute House (NT), Yeovil, on A3088. Elizabethan mansion of Ham Hill stone. Most afternoons in summer.

West Country Wildlife Park, Cricket St Thomas, on A30. Daily.

Sculptures in rock where chalk downs meet the sea

The two 'islands' of Portland and Purbeck, where hard rocks have resisted erosion, frame a stretch of coast where Dorset's chalk downs meet the English Channel in a series of high, white cliffs. The sea's constant assault has cut these softer rocks into such magnificent natural sculptures as the great arch of Durdle Door and the almost circular Lulworth Cove. Clifftop paths provide superb views out to sea and over the heathlands to the north.

① ISLE OF PORTLAND

Joined to the mainland by the south-eastern tip of Chesil Beach, the 'Isle of Slingers' of Thomas Hardy's novels is a huge, tilted table of limestone from which quarries have produced pale Portland stone for such buildings as Buckingham Palace and St Paul's Cathedral. The only road link with the mainland is along a causeway running parallel with Chesil Beach.

Links with the Royal Navy dating back to the Crimean War were strengthened in the 1890s when facilities to make and test torpedoes were established. The original harbour was built in 1847 by prisoners awaiting transportation to Australia; the prison built to accommodate them is now a Borstal Institution.

There are fine views over the harbour from the hilltop above Fortuneswell. Portland Castle, on the northern shore, was built by Henry VIII in 1520 as part of his chain of forts along the south coast.

The 'island' slopes gently southwards to the Bill of Portland where a lighthouse and a white-painted Trinity House tower, erected in 1844, overlook dangerous waters with tidal currents racing at up to 7 knots. Swift currents also occur near the point where the Fleet – the lagoon enclosed by Chesil Beach – flows into Portland Harbour.

② WEYMOUTH

A promenade and a long, sandy beach are overlooked by a wonderfully ornate statue of George III, erected in 1810 to commemorate his golden jubilee. The king visited the town in 1789, and established Weymouth as a fashionable resort by becoming the first monarch to use a bathing machine. A band played *God Save the King* as the royal visitor took the plunge.

Wealthy Georgians who followed the King's example have left an elegant legacy of porticoed houses. The Gloucester Hotel was formerly Gloucester Lodge, George III's summer home between 1789 and 1805. The promenade's 19th-century atmosphere is

Statue of George III on Weymouth seafront

epitomised by an equally elaborate clock tower, painted in red, blue and gold, which was built in 1887 to mark the 50th year of Queen Victoria's reign.

In the harbour at the mouth of the River Wey, small boats mingle with ferries which run services across the Channel. South of the river mouth, and within Portland Harbour, are the remains of Sandsfoot Castle. It dates from 1539 and was one of a series of forts built by Henry VIII to guard the southern coasts of England.

As well as the usual seaside attractions, there is a museum and an indoor swimming pool. Fishing trips and boat trips are available and rowing boats and floats can be hired. An RSPB bird reserve at Radipole Lake has an information centre, and nature trails from which grebes, swans, warblers and many other birds can be seen.

③ BOWLEAZE COVE

The cove has a beach of sand, shingle and small, seaweed-covered rocks. Above it, the broad expanse of turf on Furzy Cliff is ideal for picnics, and has views over Weymouth Bay to the Isle of Portland.

Boat trips are available, and there are rowing boats and floats for hire.

④ OSMINGTON MILLS

The Smugglers Inn, built in the 13th century and roofed with thatch, stands beside the path down to this cove of shingle and seaweed-draped rocks. A huge figure of George III on horseback, 280 ft long and 323 ft high, is cut into the chalk slope above Sutton Poyntz, and can be seen from the clifftop path between Osmington Mills and Bowleaze Cove. Curiously, it depicts the king riding away from Weymouth.

DURDLE DOOR *This natural arch of Portland limestone is one of many curious rock formations sculpted by the sea. Durdle is derived from the Anglo-Saxon word* thirl, *meaning 'to pierce'.*

DORSET'S RARE 'SKIPPER'

The dancing flight of the brown and black Lulworth skipper may be seen along a stretch of coast from Sidmouth to Swanage, and particularly on grassland slopes around Lulworth Cove, during July and August. The butterfly was first recorded more than a century ago, and is rare outside Dorset and east Devon.

Lulworth skipper
Thymelicus acteon   Wing underside

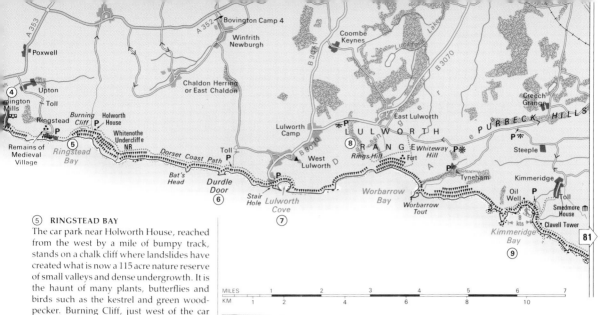

5 RINGSTEAD BAY

The car park near Holworth House, reached from the west by a mile of bumpy track, stands on a chalk cliff where landslides have created what is now a 115 acre nature reserve of small valleys and dense undergrowth. It is the haunt of many plants, butterflies and birds such as the kestrel and green woodpecker. Burning Cliff, just west of the car park, is so called because, in 1826, chemical reactions in the rock ignited oil-rich shales, which smouldered for several years.

Ringstead Bay's steeply shelving shingle beach is reached down a toll road from the village of Upton. To the west of the road, the outlines of Ringstead, a village abandoned during the Middle Ages, can still be seen. One theory is that the population was forced to flee by pirates or French raiders. Others suggest that the people were killed by the Black Death, or that the village's fishermen died in a storm.

6 DURDLE DOOR

This spectacular natural arch ranks high among Britain's coastal wonders. Reached after a 5 minute walk down from the nearest car park, it was formed by the sea eating away relatively soft rocks and leaving an arch of harder Portland stone.

The final approach to the arch is flanked by steep flights of steps which run down to shingle coves whose crystal-clear water makes them ideal for sub-aqua enthusiasts. At Bat's Head, to the west, there is a wave-carved 'mousehole' – the humble start of another arch.

7 LULWORTH COVE

High cliffs of crumbling chalk form a natural amphitheatre around an oyster-shaped cove that is featured in many geography books to illustrate the constant battle between land and sea. The beautiful little bay was formed by waves attacking joints in the Portland stone, creating arches and finally breaking right through to attack and excavate the softer clays behind the rock.

Cliffs on the eastern side of the cove, which has a shingle beach, mark the boundary of the Royal Armoured Corps gunnery range, which covers more than 7,000 acres. Parts of the range, open when the tanks are not firing, are crossed by a series of marked paths. Leaflets detailing the routes and their wide variety of attractions, including the fossilised remains of a forest, are available locally. There are boat trips, and rowing boats for hire.

8 LULWORTH RANGE

A small parking area on the B3070 between West Lulworth and East Lulworth provides dramatic views of tanks and armoured cars firing at moving targets on the Royal Armoured Corps range. The range has been used by the army since 1916 and now covers more than 7,000 acres; about 70,000 shells are fired each year.

The range includes the deserted village of Tyneham, evacuated by its inhabitants in

LULWORTH COVE *Arms of rock embrace a lake-like cove flooded by the sea. The waves breaking into Stair Hole, in the foreground, are gradually carving out a second cove from the softer clays.*

1943 when the range was extended. Tyneham Church houses an exhibition which tells the story of the valley over the centuries. An Iron Age hill-fort stands on Rings Hill and there is a shingle beach at Worbarrow Bay. At the eastern end of the bay is Worbarrow Tout, a stubby promontory with splendid views of the coast; *tout* is an Old English word meaning 'look out'.

From the parking and picnic area on Whiteway Hill there are superb views northwards over heathlands and Wareham Forest.

Full information about access to the range is posted around its perimeter. The range is generally open at most weekends, for a week at Easter and during the Spring Bank Holiday; from the last week in July until the second week in September, and for two weeks at Christmas.

9 KIMMERIDGE BAY

Clavell Tower, a 19th-century folly, overlooks this sweep of shingle which is broken by wide rock ledges rich in marine life. The tower was built in 1820 by the Reverend John Clavell of Smedmore, and is a mixture of classical motifs and Tuscan columns. Although generally said to be a folly, its parapet may have been built to support an astronomical telescope, as Clavell was a keen amateur astronomer.

On the low, unstable cliffs is a 'nodding donkey' oil pump. It bobs at the head of a well which produces about 4.6 million gallons of oil a year. The oil was discovered

in 1958 at a depth of 1,800 ft.

Smedmore House, near the pretty village of Kimmeridge, was built in the 1630s by Sir William Clavell, probably the first man to realise that the area's shales were a source of fuel. He used Kimmeridge shale as a fuel for boiling seawater to extract the salt. He also established an alum factory, and later tried unsuccessfully to turn Kimmeridge into a port by building a stone jetty.

Islands that William held before he conquered England

Lying some 14 miles off the French coast, the Channel Islands are much nearer to France than they are to Britain. Yet the islands were never owned by France. They once belonged to William, Duke of Normandy, and as it was he who conquered England the islanders claim that England is part of the Channel Islands, not the other way round. A mere 30 miles separates Jersey, to the south, from Alderney, to the north. Yet they seem poles apart.

GOREY BAY *At night, Mont Orgueil Castle takes on a fairyland appearance, the soft shadows of the floodlighting contrasting with the bright neon lights of the bars and cafes lining the harbour.*

① ST HELIER

The Royal Square of Jersey's capital, lined with chestnut trees and paved with granite, could be in any small French town; in the adjoining streets there are pavement cafes, perfumeries and bars that stay open all day. But there are reminders that Jersey's nearest mainland neighbour was not always friendly. Looming above the harbour is Fort Regent, built between 1806 and 1814 when Napoleonic France seemed poised to invade. It was a rather belated fortification, since the French had tried to capture the island in 1781, and were soundly defeated by the local militia in the Battle of Jersey. The fort now contains a leisure complex and its towering ramparts are topped by a modern domed and scalloped roof.

On a rocky islet in the bay stands an earlier fortress, the 16th-century Elizabeth Castle. It was named after Elizabeth I by Sir Walter Raleigh, who was Governor of Jersey from 1600 to 1603. The castle was held against Cromwell by Sir George Carteret until it was overwhelmed in 1651. After his restoration to the throne, Charles II remembered Carteret's loyalty and gave him a province in America. Carteret called it New Jersey.

Elizabeth Castle can be visited by means of a causeway at low tide. It contains the Jersey Militia Museum and relics of the German occupation during the Second World War.

② ST AUBIN

Linked to St Helier by a seafront road, lined with houses and hotels all the way, St Aubin was Jersey's original port. It has a small harbour built in 1675, and in the narrow streets above are some of the houses built by merchants who used the port. The harbour faces east across the wide St Aubin's Bay.

③ PORTELET BAY

The beauty of this rocky little bay can best be appreciated from Noirmont Point, a bluff headland on the eastern side. Wooded hills rise steeply from the foreshore, where a sandy beach is exposed at low tide. Just off the shore is an islet, Ile au Guerdain, crowned by an 18th-century Martello tower, one of many in the Channel Islands built as defences during the Napoleonic Wars. This one is sometimes called Janvrin's Tomb, after a Jersey sea captain who was buried there in 1721 when a plague on his ship killed all on board. Above the bay there is a car park, and steep steps lead down to the beach.

FIGS AND FERNS

The Hottentot-fig, introduced from South Africa, grows in the Channel Islands but does not produce ripe seeds. Its flowers range from magenta to yellow. Jersey fern is the only annual fern in Britain, and its golden-green fronds are seen only in Guernsey and Jersey on damp, south-west facing hedgebanks.

Hottentot-fig
Carpobrotus edulis
May – July

Jersey fern
Anogramma leptophylla
Mar – May

Noirmont Point is owned by the States of Jersey, and is preserved as a memorial of the Second World War. The German command bunker can be visited on certain days during the summer. Near by there is a gun platform with a German coastal artillery gun.

④ ST BRELADE'S BAY

This is one of Jersey's most popular beaches and has many of the usual seaside attractions. At low tide there is a mile of firm, golden sand, bathing is safe, and water sports include windsurfing and water-skiing. Boats can be hired. The beach is backed by an attractive promenade with palm-fringed gardens and fountains.

⑤ CORBIÈRE POINT

The jagged, needle-sharp rocks exposed at low tide are frighteningly impressive on this barren peninsula jutting out from Jersey's western corner. On its tip stands Britain's first concrete lighthouse, built in 1874; it can be reached by a causeway at low tide, but cannot be visited.

The tide comes in fast at Corbière, and a siren is sounded when the causeway is about to be covered. A concrete track leads down from the coast road, and there is a car park at the head of the causeway.

⑥ ST OUEN'S BAY

Jersey's finest beach, a shimmering plain of sand, stretches for almost the full length of the island's western coast. When the tide is out the water's edge almost disappears from view; when the tide is coming in it often does so in spectacular fashion, thundering across the beach in great curling arcs of green and white water.

Surf boards can be hired and surfing competitions are held during the summer. Bathing is safe only for strong swimmers, and the beach is patrolled by lifeguards. Behind the beach there are car parks, some of them among the sand-dunes that stretch inland for almost a mile. Also among the dunes are putting greens, a golf course and a golf driving range.

⑦ PLÉMONT POINT

A holiday camp sprawls across this northern headland, but a track near the camp entrance leads down to a sandy beach with rocks and caves. The track, however, is very rough, with few passing places, and in the car park there is room for only a dozen or so cars.

⑧ GRÈVE DE LECQ

The B40 road to this attractive beach runs through the wooded Grève de Lecq valley, passing on its way Le Moulin de Lecq, a watermill which is now an inn, though the wheel is still in place and still turning. The sandy beach has expanses of flat rocks at low tide and is sheltered by grassy cliffs. There are car parks and several cafes.

⑨ THE DEVIL'S HOLE

Between Plémont Point and Sorel Point, rugged rock faces climb sheer from the water, in some places pierced by the waves to leave natural formations such as The Devil's Hole. The C103 road leads to the spot, which is signposted from the B33.

Alongside the footpath leading down from a car park stands a giant effigy of the Evil One, in the middle of a pond, as if to convince visitors they are about to see a work of the Devil. But the hole is a natural phenomenon, where the sea has cut through a huge rock and at high tide boils and booms in a rocky cauldron. At other times the stiff walk down and steep climb back to the car park are hardly worth the effort.

PEACEFUL INVASION *The Garden Rocks, off the south-west cliffs of Alderney, are the home of hundreds of gannets, which settled there during the German occupation of the island.*

⑮ ALDERNEY

Once upon a time, so the story goes, the fairies on Guernsey decided to tow Alderney away. They tied a rope to the cliffs, but succeeded only in bending the rock outwards. Hanging Rock is still there, jutting out like a giant hat peg, and Alderney is still there, only 8 miles from the French coast.

The island's north and north-eastern coasts were fortified with a chain of 12 forts in the mid-19th century, with the intention of blockading Cherbourg. The forts now compete with German blockhouses as landmarks along Alderney's rugged coast.

There are few roads on the island, but rough tracks lead to some magnificent headland views, such as those from Essex Hill, the Giffoine and Telegraph Bay. The best bathing beaches are at Corblets Bay and Arch Bay on the north-east coast, and Braye Bay and Saye Bay on the north coast. There is also a harbour at Braye, the island's only safe anchorage, which is close to St Anne.

Alderney's only town, St Anne, has all the old-world charm of a Normandy village with tiny squares, pastel-shaded cottages and shops and granite-cobbled streets that hammer the remaining shreds of life out of the old cars that abound on the island. Cars can be hired, but a better way to explore the island is on foot or by bicycle. There are boat trips around the island from Braye Harbour.

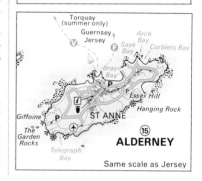

LOCAL INFORMATION

Tourist information Jersey 78000; Alderney 2994

Weather Jersey 23660.

Local radio BBC Radio Jersey, 292 m, 1026 kHz; BBC Radio Guernsey 269 m, 1116 kHz.

ALDERNEY

Same scale as Jersey

⑩ BONNE NUIT BAY

This is another of Jersey's north-coast bays, small and sandy with a fishing harbour at the foot of high cliffs. Anglers may catch mullet or bream from the harbour jetty. Outside the bay is Cheval Rock, and an ancient superstition says that rowing round the rock will avert bad luck for the season.

Just around the headland of Fremont Point are Wolf Caves. A sign near the cliff edge warns that the footpath down should not be attempted by the faint-hearted – it is very steep and rough, and the caves cannot be entered at high tide.

⑪ BOULEY BAY

The bay is mostly shingle, and bathing is not safe except for strong swimmers. There is a small pier from which lobster fishermen operate. Professional skin divers give lessons at the Underwater Centre, and equipment is available for hire. The road out from Bouley Bay, with its twisting hairpin bends, is a venue for the National Motor Hill-climbing Championship.

⑫ ROZEL BAY

Sandier than Bouley Bay, this little fishing harbour is more popular with boat owners than with motorists, who find parking difficult. The eastward approach to the bay is along a wooded valley, and picturesque fishermen's cottages line the street down to the harbour.

⑬ GOREY

Jersey's eastern side has three bays – Fliquet, St Catherine's and the Royal Bay of Grouville which sweeps southwards from the town and harbour of Gorey. Above the harbour stands Mont Orgueil Castle, with its magnificent 13th-century keep, Elizabethan tower and rambling outworks, gates and sally ports. From its ramparts there are views all along the coast – northwards to the mile-long breakwater at St Catherine, southwards down to La Rocque Point.

Cars can be parked on the jetty at Gorey for a limited period, and near by there are restaurants, inns and cafes. The beach is bordered by gardens and a golf course.

⑭ ST CLEMENT'S BAY

This bay on Jersey's south-eastern tip has a 1½ mile long sandy beach and is easily reached from St Helier, 2 miles to the west. A few hundred yards from the shore is Green Island, the southernmost point in the British Isles. It can be reached at low tide and has a small, sheltered beach.

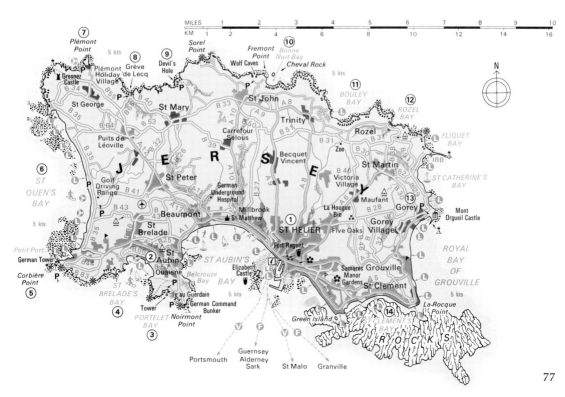

Quiet bays and early flowers near the coast of France

Although Guernsey, Sark and Herm are no more than 8 miles one from another, each has its own traditions and way of life. Guernsey is a bustling commercial community with tourism its main industry, though flowers and tomatoes are nurtured in acres of greenhouses. Herm and Sark, while welcoming visitors, are content to farm the land and let the rest of the world go its own way. There are no private cars on either island, and no airports.

① ST PETER PORT

Guernsey's capital is a town of narrow, cobbled streets and solid grey-granite buildings clambering up a steep hillside above the harbour. French street names give it a Continental flavour, but the architecture is predominantly English, from the Georgian, Victorian and Edwardian periods. In the 18th-century Royal Court sits Guernsey's parliament, the States of Deliberation, for though the islands are Crown Possessions they are not part of the United Kingdom, and Guernsey's laws of government date back to Norman times.

For all St Peter Port's old-world charm, it is the harbour that dominates the town. Its 70 acres include two marinas, docks for car and passenger ferries and three piers from which launches and hydrofoils skim like water insects across to Herm and Sark. At the harbour entrance stands the 13th-century Castle Cornet, which contains three military museums and an art gallery within its massive walls. South of the harbour is the town beach, in Havelet Bay. The foreshore is shingle, with sand at low tide, and bathing there is safe. Havelet Bay is popular with water-skiers, and is also the occasional venue for powerboat racing.

The house in which the French novelist Victor Hugo lived from 1855 until 1870 is now a museum, open on weekdays in summer.

② FERMAIN BAY

The easiest way to approach this small, sheltered bay is by motor launch from St Peter Port. The 15 minute journey ends with a superb view of one of Guernsey's prettiest bays, with trees cloaking the steep cliffs and tumbling almost to the water's edge. The beach has stretches of firm sand at low tide, and there is safe bathing. Alternative approaches to Fermain are by the cliff path from St Peter Port, joined at La Valette just south of the town, or by a narrow lane leading from the main road at St Martin's.

③ MOULIN HUET BAY

There are three beaches within this bay in the south-east corner of Guernsey: Petit Port, Moulin Huet and Saint's Bay. All three are sandy and sheltered.

Moulin Huet beach is approached by a lane, ending at a small car park. Rocks are exposed at low tide, and there are caves in the cliff face. Petit Port is harder to reach, the final approach being down a flight of 365 steps. Saint's Bay is reached by a lane which runs through a wooded vale, then divides just above the beach – about 200 yds down a gentle path. The right fork leads to a slipway.

④ ICART POINT

The whole of Guernsey's south coast is punctuated by tiny coves – many inaccessible except from the sea – rugged bays and rocky headlands. Icart Point is one such

headland, with perhaps the finest views in the island. Westward lie La Bette Bay, Le Jaonnet Bay, Petit Bot Bay and Portelet Bay, with La Moye Point a craggy finger on the skyline.

Petit Bot is one of the few bays on the south coast that can be reached by road, and is also served by the local bus. There is a car park and cafe close to the beach, which has a pebbly foreshore with sand and rocks at half tide.

A cliff path runs the entire length of the south coast, and it can be joined at several headland points – Icart Point is one, La Moye Point is another – where there are car parks and sometimes a cafe.

About 2 miles to the north, at Les Vauxbelets, stands the Little Chapel. This tiny church was built by a monk, Brother Déodat, who based it on the grotto at Lourdes in France. It is open daily.

THE LITTLE CHAPEL *Built by a monk in 1923, this tiny chapel at Les Vauxbelets is decorated with shells and pieces of broken glass and china.*

⑤ ROCQUAINE BAY

Guernsey's coastal scenery changes dramatically on the western coast, from the high cliffs on the south to wide, flat bays of rock, sand and shingle. The cliffs have their last fling at Pleinmont Point, the south-westerly tip of the island. Below the point, Rocquaine Bay curves around a sandy beach – Guernsey's largest – which is never more than an arm's length from the coast road.

A small peninsula of rocks, Pezeries Point, juts into the bay at the southern end, with a view across to Hanois lighthouse about a mile offshore. Within the bay is the tiny fishing harbour of Portelet (one of two places so named on the island), and Fort Grey. The 18th-century fort, reached by a causeway, is a maritime museum devoted mainly to the remains and records of ships wrecked on this treacherous coast.

Cars can be parked at Pezeries Point and at Portelet along the coast road. There is a slipway at Portelet, which also has a small, sandy beach where bathing is safe except at low tide.

⑥ PERELLE BAY

A German lookout tower of the Second World War dominates this small and rocky bay. There are many such fortifications in the Channel Islands, grim reminders that Nazi Germany gained a tiny toehold on British soil. Below the tower a causeway leads to Lihou Island, 18 acres of rock crowned by the ruined walls of a 12th-century priory. The island is accessible only at low tide.

Behind Perelle Bay is one of Guernsey's many megalithic tombs. This one, Le Trepied, is linked with legends of witchcraft and devil worship. In a 17th-century witch trial it was said that the Devil sat on the capstone while witches and warlocks danced around him.

⑦ VAZON BAY

This wide beach of sand and shingle is popular with surfers; they are, however, restricted to the centre of the bay, which is unsuitable for bathing at certain states of the tide. Flags mark the area when surfing is in progress. Beach anglers may catch bass in the turbulent waters.

⑧ COBO BAY

Rust-coloured rocks are exposed at low tide on this sand-and-shingle beach. Signs indicate that bathing is dangerous. Neighbouring Port Soif is almost a lagoon, with high rocks pincering a sandy cove. The tide hurtles in fast and furious, but longboard surfing is prohibited.

The Guernsey Folk Museum is about half a mile south-east of Cobo Bay, on Cobo Road, or the Route de Cobo.

⑨ GRAND HAVRE

Still clinging to the seashore, the coast road heads north from Cobo, skirts the sand-and-pebble beaches of Portinfer and Pequeries and then turns eastward to Grand Havre. This fishing harbour is set in a wide, irregular bay, where there are boat moorings and three slipways.

A sandy beach stretches for about a quarter of a mile in Les Amarreurs and Ladies Bay on the northern shore.

WHEN THE NAZIS RULED

On June 28, 1940, the streets of the Channel Islands echoed to the chilling sound of steel-shod jackboots as the German Army occupied the islands. During the next four years the islands were turned into fortresses, bristling with towers and burrowed with underground bunkers and hospitals. Many still remain, sombre reminders of the days when part of Britain was under Nazi rule. A German Occupation Museum at Forest is open daily in summer.

German lookout tower at Perelle Bay

IDYLLIC ISLE *Peace and solitude are there for the taking on Herm; by crystal-clear waters on The Bears Beach and Fishermans Beach, or along flower-fringed footpaths in the gentle hills.*

⑩ L'ANCRESSE BAY

On Guernsey's northern coast, L'Ancresse Bay takes a deep bite into the land and leaves a broad horseshoe of jagged rocks and shimmering golden sands. There is a wind-surfing school near by, and golf on L'Ancresse Common. L'Ancresse Bay has one of Guernsey's best bathing beaches, with safe swimming at any state of the tide. Half a mile east of the bay is Beaucette Marina, a tiny haven surrounded by high rocks.

⑪ ST SAMPSON

Tall cranes nod and bow at the dockside of this small commercial port, and near the harbour is a central depot for grading and packing tomatoes. By contrast, 1 mile north of the docks, the fishing village of Bordeaux sits prettily by its harbour. The road south from St Sampson is lined with warehouses and oil storage tanks, but soon the road borders the wide beaches of Belle Greve Bay and the harbour walls of St Peter Port come into view.

⑫ HERM

The island of Herm is 1½ miles long, half a mile wide and covers 600 acres. Within that compact space lie towering cliffs, wooded valleys, sandy beaches and enough pasture-land to support 100 Guernsey cows. The island is leased from Guernsey by the Tenant, Major Peter Wood, who lives in the 15th-century granite-built Manor House.

By the small harbour are a few pastel-coloured cottages, a hotel, a pub and a Mediterranean-style shopping piazza. There are no cars, or roads to drive them on, and visitors arriving after a 20 minute boat trip from Guernsey are greeted by a signpost which points the way to the bays and beaches and also states the times it takes to walk to them.

A 12 minute walk northwards skirts Fishermans Beach and The Bears Beach, then the path cuts across heathland to the island's showpiece – Shell Beach. On a golden strand, millions of tiny shells have been washed up, some from as far away as the Gulf of Mexico. About 10 minutes' walk away is Belvoir Bay, small and secluded, and then the going gets tough as the path climbs and dips along the cliffs and valleys of Herm's southern half.

Another walk, from Belvoir or from the harbour, leads to the tiny St Tugual Chapel which dates from Norman times. The identity of St Tugual is surrounded by mystery.

⑬ JETHOU

In AD 700 a great storm divided Jethou from Herm, and now it stands desolate and seawashed, a rocky cone about half a mile off Herm's southern tip. Jethou is privately occupied and cannot be visited.

⑭ SARK

The island of Sark is Europe's last feudal country, governed by the seigneur whose feudal rights date back to 1565, when they were granted by Elizabeth I. The present seigneur, J. M. Beaumont, inherited the title in 1974 on the death of his grandmother – Dame Sibyl Hathaway, the famous Dame of Sark. The gardens of his residence, La Seigneurie, are open to the public on some days in summer.

There are only three forms of transport on the island. Tractor-drawn carriages take visitors up the steep hill from the harbour; horse-drawn carriages can be hired for a leisurely drive around the island; and bicycles can be hired. But to explore the island thoroughly it is best to go on foot – there are places where the carriages cannot go, and a bicycle can be an encumbrance on the steep paths down to bays and beaches.

The island is about 3 miles long and 1½ miles across, and at the southern end is almost cut in two. The southern section, called Little Sark, is reached by a natural causeway of rock, called La Coupée, which rises 250 ft above the sea.

Though some of Sark's bays can be reached without too much effort – Dixcart Bay and Greve de la Ville, for example – the island's glory is in its views from the headlands. From Havre Gosselin the view extends across to the lonely, privately owned Brechou Island. Below the cliffs the sea licks hungrily around jagged rocks and probes the dark caverns of the Gouliot caves. At Banquette almost half of Sark's eastern side can be seen, with the lighthouse at Point Robert away to the south. On a clear day the distant coast of France may appear, a pale grey thread on the horizon.

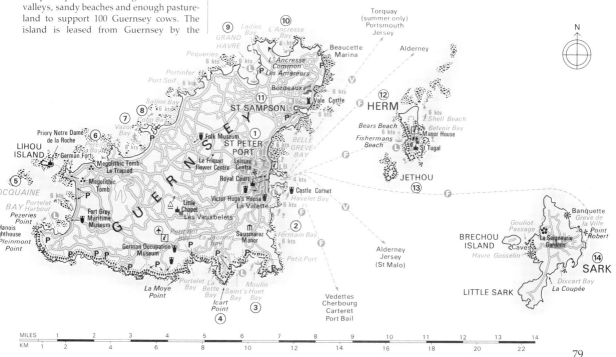

Warm waters on white beaches round the shore of Poole Bay

Breathtaking cliffs and isolated caves where smugglers once landed their contraband bring the Dorset Coast Path to a dramatic end. Eastwards the character of the coast changes abruptly, with the busy natural harbour of Poole and the seaside resort of Bournemouth. In the bays of Poole, Studland and Swanage, some of the warmest seawaters in Britain wash over sandy beaches, while seafaring traditions are maintained by small-boat sailors.

PURBECK BYWAY *Kingston is a typical Purbeck village, with cottages and a church of the local stone and walls splashed with scarlet ivy.*

① WORTH MATRAVERS

The beautiful Norman church of St Nicholas of Myra, patron saint of sailors, cottages of grey Purbeck stone and a central village pond give Worth Matravers an atmosphere of tranquillity. One cottage is named after Isaac Gulliver, an 18th-century smuggler who was revered as a hero by the people of his locality who shared in his spoils.

The village is a good starting point for an excellent 4 mile walk along a fine stretch of the coastal path. A signposted footpath from the village leads to coves at Winspit. From there, a walk along the coastal path to the west leads past the fine viewpoint of St Alban's Head. It is possible to return to Worth Matravers by another signposted footpath from Chapman's Pool but landslips make the path hazardous and the pool is closed to the public. The path often runs close to the cliff edge and is hazardous in windy conditions.

② DURLSTON COUNTRY PARK

Sea-bird colonies along the cliffs are the most notable feature of the varied wildlife of this 260 acre country park. An interesting man-made feature of the park is the Great Globe, a sphere of Portland stone 10 ft in diameter and weighing 40 tons, which has the features of the Earth's surface carved upon it. It was placed there in 1887 by John Mowlem, Swanage-born founder of the building contractors firm. Near by is the 19th-century Durlston Head Castle, built in 1890 as a restaurant and still used as a cafeteria. Further westwards along the coastal path is Anvil Point lighthouse.

③ SWANAGE

Swanage Bay was the scene of a great naval victory by King Alfred over the Danes in 877. Eleven hundred years later, the features of the bay are its safe bathing and sailing, except for the south side where the tidal race over Peveril Ledge is dangerous to small craft. Swimmers should not, however, venture too far north of the bay, for the sea close to Ballard Cliff is treacherous.

At the pier, boats can be hired and deep-sea fishing expeditions organised. There is also fishing from the pier itself and the shore, the catches including flounder, plaice, sole, bass and mackerel. Windsurfing can be arranged there, and the pier's diving school is one of the oldest in the country.

The nearby Wellington Clock Tower once adorned the southern approach to London Bridge, but having been declared an 'unwarrantable obstruction' by the Metropolitan Police, it was moved to Swanage in 1867. Swanage Town Hall, built in 1883, also originated in London – its carved stone façade was once the front of the Mercers' Hall in Cheapside and is reputed to have been designed by Sir Christopher Wren. The oldest building in Swanage is the 13th-century parish church of St Mary the Virgin, in a picturesque setting next to the Millpond. Almost next door to the church is The Old Tithe Barn Museum, housing many relics of the town's past.

④ STUDLAND

The village of Studland is close to woods, sea and downs, and its quiet unspoiled character is exemplified by the unrestored Norman church of St Nicholas of Myra. Many winding lanes and footpaths lead to the excellent sandy beach, owned by the National Trust, and fine bathing area of Studland Bay, where warm shallow waters are protected from all but strong easterly winds. The bay is deep enough only for small craft, but there is a good anchorage for larger vessels in the small bay towards The Foreland. There, too, stand the isolated stacks of chalk, the Old Harry Rocks.

North of the village, Studland Heath National Nature Reserve contains wildlife ranging from wildfowl to lizards. The heathland is the home of the rare and harmless smooth snake; the adder is also found there, so walkers should wear strong shoes and keep to the marked footpaths.

There is a good 1 mile walk from Studland to the Agglestone, a 17 ft high triangular mass of natural ironstone. According to legend, it was carried from the Isle of Wight by the Devil, who planned to drop its 400 tons on Salisbury Cathedral. The burden proved too great, and the task was abandoned.

The Agglestone – a missile miscarried

⑤ WAREHAM

A settlement of the early Britons and then a Roman town, Wareham achieved importance during Saxon times because of its situation at the head of the River Frome. The Danes made the town their headquarters in 866, but after a treaty in 876 they agreed to leave, having reduced the town to ruins. Wareham was then sacked four times in 100 years by the returning conquerors. Later, the town had barely recovered from the strife of the Middle Ages when it was taken by the Roundheads during the Civil War. A section of the Town Walls is known as Bloody Bank, the scene of executions by order of Judge Jeffries after the failure of the Monmouth Rebellion in 1685.

The Saxon church of St Martin houses an effigy of T. E. Lawrence ('Lawrence of Arabia'), who spent his last years at Clouds Hill Cottage, 6 miles to the north-west. In the Town Museum in St Johns Hill there is a pictorial record of Lawrence's life, as well as many items relating to the town's history.

DEVIL'S STACKS *Chalk pillars off The Foreland include Old Harry and the slender Old Harry's Wife, both being gradually eroded by the waves. Old Harry is a synonym for the Devil.*

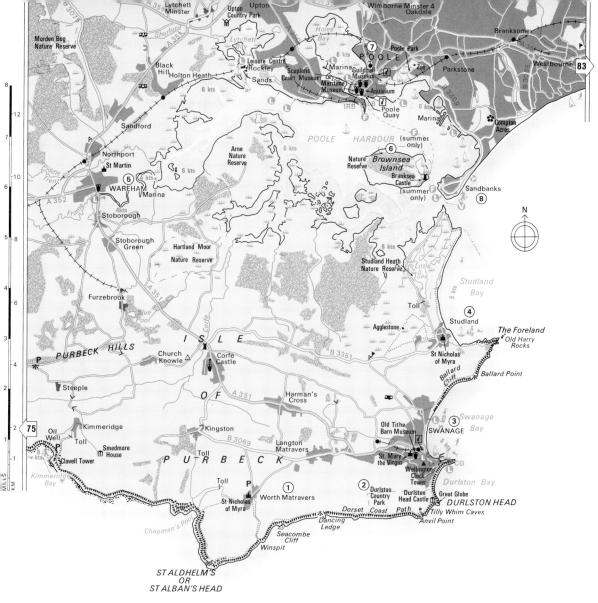

⑥ BROWNSEA ISLAND

Reached by passenger ferry from Sandbanks or Poole Quay, the 500 acres of heath and woodland on Brownsea Island are open every day from Easter to September. Visitors, for a fee, may land their own boats at the western end of the island; dogs are not allowed. The island is owned by the National Trust, and elaborate steps are taken to maintain the nature reserve and bird sanctuary on the north-east side. Its splendid April daffodils, lush rhododendron avenue and rare colony of red squirrels make the island a haven for nature lovers.

Brownsea Island is best known as the birthplace of the Scouting movement – Lord Baden Powell held an experimental camp there in 1907. Branksea Castle was built on the island by Henry VIII as a military fort to defend Poole Harbour.

⑦ POOLE

The natural harbour of Poole might have been specially designed for the yachtsman, fisherman and watersports enthusiast. With a double high tide – a characteristic of this stretch of coast – the harbour has about 14 hours of high water each day. Marinas, sailing clubs and yacht clubs abound on the north-west shores, though small craft should steer clear of the larger vessels using the harbour's main channel.

For the more conventional seaside holiday there are 3 miles of golden beaches extending from Sandbanks to Branksome Dene Chine and on towards Bournemouth, and

bathing spots in the harbourside parks. The Poole Arts Centre – a multi-entertainments complex – and a full range of amusements contribute to the town's growing reputation as a holiday resort.

At Poole Quay, small craft and fishing boats contrast with the activities of a modern port. Poole Aquarium, on the quay, includes a collection of tropical fish, two sharks, piranhas and a reptile house that includes crocodiles and venomous snakes. A craft centre and National Model Museum also form part of the aquarium complex. At Poole Pottery, visitors can buy its products in the adjoining showroom.

Buildings of interest on the quay include the Georgian-style Custom House, old warehouses, and the old harbour offices and three museums. The Maritime Museum reflects the town's seafaring history; the old Guildhall in Market Street houses local history exhibits; and Scaplen's Court Museum features local archaeology.

Behind the lively quay waterfront is the old town, now a conservation area, whose well-preserved Georgian character evokes the days when Poole was a principal port for trade to the New World, particularly Newfoundland. Poole's High Street has shops and daily markets, and the Arndale Centre provides undercover shopping, restaurants and cafes and a sports centre. Poole Park provides a variety of amusements, including a zoo and miniature railway. Upton Country Park is a good setting for a quiet picnic or a leisurely stroll, and includes a nature trail.

⑧ SANDBANKS

This beach area at the entrance to Poole Harbour is one of the best bathing spots on the south coast. The peninsula has sailing facilities and a windsurfing area on its harbour side. Swimmers and surfers should keep away from the harbour entrance, since strong currents make the waters hazardous.

A car ferry from Sandbanks to Studland and the Isle of Purbeck operates all year round.

LOCAL INFORMATION

Tourist information Swanage 422885; Poole 673322.

HM Coastguard Portland 820441 for information, 999 in emergency (ask for coastguard).

Weather Bournemouth 8091.

Local radio BBC Radio Solent, 300/221 m, 999/1359 kHz, 96.1 MHz; IBA Two Counties Radio, 362 m, 828 kHz, 97.2 MHz.

PLACES TO SEE INLAND

Badbury Rings, near Wimborne Minster. Iron Age hill-fort. Daily.

The Blue Pool, 3 miles S of Wareham. Lake in disused clay-pit. Daily in summer.

Compton Acres, Canford Cliffs, Poole. Gardens in English and foreign styles. Daily in summer.

Corfe Castle, 4 miles SE of Wareham. Daily in summer, weekend afternoons in winter.

Merley Bird Gardens, 5 miles N of Poole town centre. Daily.

Priest's House Museum, Wimborne Minster, 7 miles N of Poole. Local history and archaeology. Weekdays in summer.

Holiday bays at Bournemouth, and headlands steeped in history

Beaches as popular as any in the south of England line the broad arcs of Poole Bay and Christchurch Bay, and between them extends the dramatic promontory of Hengistbury Head. Seaside jollity dominates Poole Bay, but at the eastern end of Christchurch Bay, beyond Milford on Sea, there is a complete contrast: a desolate spit thrusting into the Solent and tipped by the gaunt remains of Henry VIII's Hurst Castle.

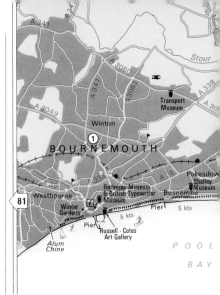

① BOURNEMOUTH

Until the railway came in 1870, Bournemouth was mainly a residential resort where the rich built their villas on the pine-clad slopes of the Bourne valley. The town had little to offer in the way of entertainment until the vogue for sea-bathing in Victorian times gave it the opportunity for development.

The first Winter Gardens Theatre was built in 1876, and in the following years more and more seaside entertainments took their place on or near Bournemouth's seafront, giving it an ever-increasing reputation as a holiday centre. With its neighbouring town of Boscombe to the east and Alum Chine to the west it offers today two piers, a wide range of seaside amusements and 7 miles of sandy beach washed by warm waters; there are lifeguards at the beach offices, and volunteer lifeguards patrol the stretch between Alum Chine and Bournemouth Pier at weekends in summer.

The steep cliffs that shelter the beach are cut by valleys – the 'chines' – which provide shady groves away from the shore. Each of these chines has a public garden and marked paths leading to the beach. The Lower Gardens and Central Gardens provide a lush green contrast to the beach; in summer, brass bands or orchestras play on the bandstand, and picture exhibitions often line the paths.

The original Winter Gardens Theatre was dismantled in 1935 and replaced by an indoor bowling green. After the Second World War the hall was discovered to have good acoustic properties and became the home of the Bournemouth Symphony Orchestra.

Another centre of entertainment, the Pavilion, built in 1929, has a 1,500 seat theatre, a ballroom and a restaurant with terraces overlooking the Lower Gardens and the Bourne stream. The Bournemouth International Centre, opened in 1984, hosts exhibitions and conferences. It has a restaurant, and an indoor swimming pool with a wave-making machine.

Bournemouth is well endowed with museums. The Russell-Cotes Art Gallery houses, amongst other exhibits, the town's last-remaining Bath chair. The Transport Museum is open during high season only, while the Shelley Museum is the only one in the world specifically devoted to the poet Percy Bysshe Shelley, whose son, Percy Florence Shelley, lived in Bournemouth from 1849 to 1889.

② CHRISTCHURCH

Originally, Christchurch was a Saxon town named Twynham, meaning 'the town between two waters', a reference to its two rivers, the Stour and Avon. It was a walled town, one of Alfred the Great's strongholds against the Danes, and still retains its Saxon street plan.

The town, now largely Edwardian in atmosphere, takes its modern name from its priory church. Begun in the 11th century, this took four centuries to complete and, at just over 300 ft, is Britain's longest parish church. Its 120 ft tower holds the country's two oldest bells, cast in 1370.

In the car park of the priory church is Christchurch Tricycle Museum. On display are adults' and children's pedal tricycles dating from Victorian times to the present day. There are Victorian street scenes, models in period costume, and wall displays.

At the quay there are motor boats for hire and harbour trips. The harbour offers safe mooring, but at low tide becomes mud-flats.

It attracts a wide range of birds, and Stanpit Marsh on the harbour's northern shore is a local nature reserve. There is fishing in the harbour by means of permits issued by the local angling club; flatfish, mullet and eel are common catches.

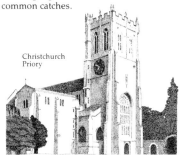

Christchurch Priory

③ HENGISTBURY HEAD

The southern flank of Christchurch Harbour is a 2 mile spit of land, with a spine of low hills between mud-flats and sand-and-pebble beaches. It is at once an important archaeological site, a wildlife conservation area and a leisure centre.

The Head was occupied continuously from the Stone Age to Roman times, and in the Iron Age included one of the country's busiest ports. Though there is nothing on view locally, archaeologists have unearthed coins from the Iron Age and Roman period, pottery and bronze objects.

The combination of shallow harbour, hills and pounding seas has created a patchwork of different habitats – heath, woodland, meadow, salt-marsh, freshwater marsh, dunes, rocky shore and shingle shore. At a headquarters, near the car park, wardens can provide expert guidance on local insects and birds.

The Head has changed considerably in the last century and a half. Originally, the seas ate away slowly at the southern shore, where the coast was reinforced with ironstone. But in 1848 a coal merchant began quarrying the ironstone. Deprived of its natural defences, the sandy coast was eroded fast. Its soil was swept eastwards and dumped on the Head's northern spit, squeezing the harbour tides into a 30 yd wide channel, the Avon Run. A groyne built in 1938 checked the erosion.

A land-train – a mock railway engine with rubber-tyred carriages – takes passengers to the Head's tip, where there are lines of beach huts and a windsurfing school with boards for hire. Swimming is safe except in and near the Avon Run.

The 118 ft summit of Warren Hill offers dramatic views of Christchurch Bay and Bournemouth Bay, and across the Solent to

HEAD LINES *Anglers' lines await a catch from the shore on Hengistbury Head's western side, where a long beach has built up from the sandstone of the cliffs over millions of years.*

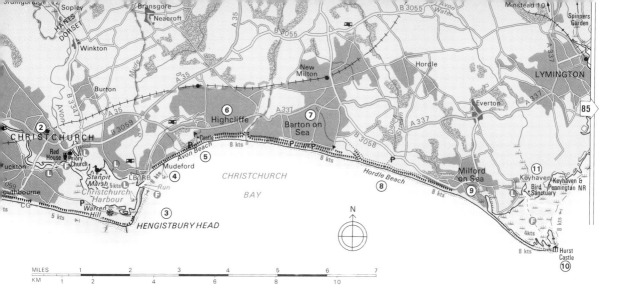

DOWN TO THE SEA *Summer crowds flock to Bournemouth, attracted by its long sandy beaches backed by wide promenades, and tree-clad cliffs which are descended by zigzag paths.*

the Isle of Wight. A nature trail follows the lower eastern slopes through grasslands and woods and past a lilypond. The Head is visited by more than 1 million people a year, posing an increasing threat to land, wildlife and archaeological sites, and visitors are restricted to certain routes.

④ MUDEFORD

The tiny village on the eastern tip of Christchurch Harbour, opposite Hengistbury Head, has fine views up the coast and across to The Needles of the Isle of Wight. Lobster and whelk pots are often piled up on the quayside. There is a ferry across the fast-flowing Avon Run, and several boats that offer trips to catch mackerel and deep-sea fish. Boats can be launched on the harbour side of the quay. Access to the quay is by a road from the village, and there is ample car-parking space.

⑤ AVON BEACH

Extensive sands even at high tide draw holidaymakers to Avon Beach. There are several car parks and a beach cafe. Swimming is safe most of the time, but red flags are hoisted when the undertow is dangerous.

⑥ HIGHCLIFFE

A dilapidated Gothic-style castle, built in the 1830s for Lord Stuart, guards a shady parking area, from which visitors can descend by steps to a fine sandy beach. Further along the coast a stream called Chewton Bunny runs into the sea. From a car park on top of the cliff a path leads down to a groyne-ribbed shingle beach which has sand at low tide.

⑦ BARTON ON SEA

An unpaved road runs along this broad deserted undercliff area, but the road is not open to visitors' cars. Instead, park at the top of the cliff. The cliffs contain a fossil-bearing layer where bones of prehistoric reptiles have been found. There are good, open walks along the mounds formed by earth that has slipped from the cliffs, above a pebbly beach with a scattering of beach huts. On-shore winds can make swimming dangerous.

⑧ HORDLE BEACH

A footpath leads for a third of a mile from a parking area to a small shingly beach overlooked by a ragged line of tank traps, remnants of the last war. The beach is

secluded, but the spot's most charming feature is the clifftop walk through fields towards Milford on Sea, 2 miles away.

⑨ MILFORD ON SEA

The extensive beach is mostly shingle with some low-tide sand. The town itself is modern and predominantly residential, offering little beside the usual beach amenities.

⑩ HURST CASTLE

The castle is set at the end of a 1½ mile spit of pebbles, and was built by Henry VIII in 1544 as part of his south coast defences. Together with forts on the Isle of Wight, it could effectively close the Solent. It is reached either by a 20 minute slog along the pebble causeway, or by ferry from Keyhaven.

The fort was abandoned and re-used many times – King Charles was briefly there in 1648 when he was taken from the Isle of Wight to face trial at Westminster. It was much modified in the 19th century but it is still a solid blockhouse of a place, its ancient shape overlaid with a façade of Victorian brickwork. It has a 12-sided central tower surrounded by a curtain wall with three semi-circular bastions. Troops were billeted there during the Second World War, and the Ministry of Defence still uses the two Victorian wings. The castle is open to the public.

⑪ KEYHAVEN

This tiny tidal inlet, which turns to salt-marsh and mud at low tide, is the terminal for the Hurst Castle ferry and offers safe moorings to a few dozen small boats. It is also in part a nature reserve.

LOCAL INFORMATION
Tourist information Bournemouth 291715; Christchurch 471780.
HM Coastguard Freshwater 752265 for information, 999 in emergency (ask for coastguard).
Weather Bournemouth 8091.
Local radio BBC Radio Solent 300/221 m, 999/1359 kHz, 96.1 MHz. IBA Two Counties Radio, 362 m, 828 kHz, 97.2 MHz.

PLACES TO SEE INLAND
Breamore House, Fordingbridge, 18 miles N of Christchurch. Elizabethan manor house. Most afternoons in summer.
Furzey Gardens, Minstead, 12 miles N of Lymington. Daily.
Macpenny's, Bransgore, 4 miles NE of Christchurch. Woodland garden. Daily.
Rockbourne Roman Villa, Fordingbridge, 15 miles N of Christchurch. Daily in summer.
Spinners Garden, Boldre, 1½ miles N of Lymington. Most afternoons in summer.

A wooded estuary where Nelson's ships were launched

From Lymington to Southampton Water few roads lead down to the coast, which is broken only by the lovely Beaulieu River estuary. The western side of the estuary, part of the Beaulieu estate, is a nature reserve and – despite the river's popularity – remains a peaceful rural retreat, with a delightful riverside footpath between Bucklers Hard and Beaulieu. Along Southampton Water, miles of docks and oil refineries line the waterside.

EIGHTEENTH-CENTURY VIEW *Only the modern craft anchored in the Beaulieu River bring the 20th century to Bucklers Hard, where Georgian cottages face the green where ships' timbers once lay.*

① LYMINGTON
The River Lymington flows down from the high plains of the New Forest, and at its estuary is this pretty town with steep streets leading past Georgian shops to a harbour that is a mass of small boats. The harbour is also a main terminal for the Isle of Wight car and passenger ferries. The ferry itself offers particularly good views of the saltings, the grass-covered mud-flats that fringe this section of the coast.

② PARK SHORE
About 2½ miles south of Bucklers Hard, a signposted gravel road leads for 1 mile down to a gate where a few cars can park. From here, a walk of a third of a mile through fields leads to a long shingle-and-sand beach backed by a rough cement wall and a bank of grass and stones.

From this part of the coast, which is part of the Beaulieu estate, there is a fine view across the Solent to the Isle of Wight.

③ NEEDS ORE POINT
This nose of flat land at the mouth of the Beaulieu River, with its tidal inlets and sweeping views of coast and estuary, has a yacht club and a bird sanctuary, part of the 1,600 acre North Solent National Nature Reserve that covers the whole western shoreline of the Beaulieu River estuary.

The reserve has Britain's largest colony of black-headed gulls – 14,000 pairs, many of which are on Gull Island set in the river's mouth and can be seen only from the river.

Needs Ore Point is approached down a private gravel road which starts 2 miles south of Bucklers Hard near the ruins of

St Leonard's, a grange that once served Beaulieu Abbey. The road is not marked, and entry to the bird sanctuary is by permit, for a small charge from the estate office.

Entrance to the foreshore of pebbles and saltmarsh is forbidden between March 1 and July 31, the height of the breeding season.

④ BUCKLERS HARD
This shipbuilding village, part of the Beaulieu estate, is being restored to its 18th-century appearance. Bucklers Hard was

---

FLEET FIGUREHEAD
A replica of the figurehead from HMS *Gladiator*, launched in 1782, is among the exhibits in the Maritime Museum at Bucklers Hard. The *Gladiator* never saw action, but served as a home for convalescent seamen at Portsmouth until she was broken up in 1817. The museum includes models of many of the ships built for Nelson's fleet.

Roman gladiator for a British ship

---

originally planned by the 2nd Duke of Montagu as a base – 'Montagu Town' – for the import of sugar from the islands of St Vincent and St Lucia in the West Indies. In the event, the French seized the islands and the village became a shipbuilding community. It was ideally suited for that role, for the river is deep, well-sheltered and secure from coastal attack, with a firm, gently sloping beach. It was also encircled with extensive woodlands – a vital resource, since it took 60 acres of timber to build a man-o'-war.

The village consists of two lines of cottages leading down to the beach where, from 1698 to 1827, the wooden-walled ships were built. For almost a century, work was under the control of the family and descendants of master-builder Henry Adams. Among the ships they supervised were the *Euryalus* and *Agamemnon* for Nelson's fleet.

The house in which Adams lived is now a hotel, but one room containing a tableau featuring Adams can be seen from the village street. Next door is the tiny chapel of St Mary, measuring only 25 by 15 ft. A Maritime Museum, open daily, recalls the past achievements of Bucklers Hard, and two reconstructed cottage interiors and an inn scene depict village life in the late 18th century.

There is a charge to enter the village and its displays, and there is a large car park outside the village. A delightful footpath starts near the boatyard and leads north, through woodland and along the Beaulieu River bank, with views of woods and fields opposite, to Beaulieu, 2 miles away. River cruises are available from the jetty.

⑤ BEAULIEU
This sheltered and wooded spot at the head of the Beaulieu River estuary was originally named Bellus Locus, 'beautiful place'. When monks founded an abbey there in the 13th century they changed the Latin name to its Norman French equivalent, Beau Lieu. The abbey was destroyed when Henry VIII dissolved the monasteries, its stones being used to reinforce the king's coastal defences at Cowes, Hurst Castle and Calshot. But it remains a 'beautiful place', for the estate is a masterpiece of conservation and restoration.

The village itself, of mellow red-brick buildings, is set around an old mill at the head of the estuary, which is a favourite mooring for small yachts. Palace House, the home of Lord Montagu, and the remains of Beaulieu Abbey, with a display of monastic life, are open to the public daily. On the same site is the National Motor Museum, a modernistic building of glass and angular brickwork housing more than 200 historic vehicles, also open daily. There are large car parks and tree-studded picnic areas, while a monorail provides an overhead view of the grounds.

⑥ EXBURY GARDENS
These 250 acres, comprising one of Europe's classic gardens, are the creation of Lionel de Rothschild and an expression of his life-long passion for trees and shrubs, especially rhododendrons. Rothschild imported more than 1,000 species of rhododendron from Asia and by patient crossing created 452 new varieties. From this wealth of colours, Lord Rothschild and his 150 gardeners built an ever-changing mosaic of rhododendrons providing blooms the year round.

⑦ LEPE
This small country park has picnic spots among the trees, and beautiful views across the Solent to the Isle of Wight. Bathing is possible, though the sand-and-shingle beach gives way to mud at low tide.

⑧ CALSHOT

A pebbly beach lined with bathing huts leads to a spit of land that was once an RAF flying-boat base. Its four huge hangars and residential buildings now form a large centre for educational and sporting activities.

Calshot's history as an airbase began in 1913, and by the 1920s it was the centre of almost all maritime air training. The Schneider Trophy international air races for seaplanes were held there in 1929 and in 1931, the year in which the trophy was won permanently for Britain.

The airbase closed in 1961 and now Hampshire Education Authority uses it to provide courses for some 100,000 people a year in sailing, canoeing, environmental studies and other activities.

Volunteer lifeguards patrol Calshot beach on Sundays in summer.

⑨ HYTHE

At this industrial and residential suburb of Southampton, flying boats were designed and built in the 1930s and 1940s. The town has a pier 700 yds long, along which a little blue-and-white electric railway takes passengers to the Southampton ferry that runs from the end.

⑩ SOUTHAMPTON

At the head of Southampton Water lie the sprawling docks that made Southampton Britain's major passenger port and the home of the Atlantic liners of the Cunard Company. But its history goes back more than 1,000 years; it was the site of the Roman port of *Clausentum*, it was William the Conqueror's port for his ships coming from Normandy; and it was from Southampton that the Pilgrim Fathers set sail in 1620 – though they called at Dartmouth and Plymouth before crossing the Atlantic.

The 6 miles of quay include the Ocean Dock, where the *Mauretania, Queen Elizabeth* and *Queen Mary* once towered above the warehouses. In Mayflower Park on the Western Esplanade a memorial marks the spot from which the *Mayflower* sailed. Close by, near the old entrance to Royal Pier, there are regular ferry and hydrofoil services to the Isle of Wight.

Despite heavy bombing during the Second World War, Southampton still retains many of its old buildings, including the 16th-century Tudor House, the Norman Bargate and the towers of the old town walls. Wool House in Bugle Street, a medieval warehouse in which French prisoners of war were housed during the 18th and 19th centuries, is now a Maritime Museum, whose exhibits include a large model of the *Queen Mary*. The 15th-century God's House Tower is an archaeological museum.

Another museum in the town is the Southampton Hall of Aviation. R. J. Mitchell, designer of the Spitfire fighter plane, was chief designer of the Supermarine Aviation Works at Woolston, now part of Southampton. The museum contains one of the last Spitfires built, and a Supermarine S6 seaplane from which the fighter was developed.

⑪ NETLEY

A pebbly shore, where swimming in the polluted water is not recommended, leads to the 220 acre Royal Victoria Country Park. At its centre stand the remains of the massive Royal Victoria Military Hospital, founded in 1856 for the victims of the Crimean War. It was largely demolished in 1956, but its chapel has an exhibition showing the hospital's history. The park was taken over by the Hampshire County Council and is open for picnics, sports and nature walks.

Near by are the 12th-century ruins of Netley Abbey, its floors grassed over, its many stone-walled rooms open to the sky.

⑫ HAMBLE

The village of Hamble is one of the most concentrated yachting centres in Britain. It has five yacht marinas, boats for hire and a passenger ferry across the River Hamble to Warsash.

CARS AT BEAULIEU *Two veteran cars from a collection of more than 200 historic vehicles in the National Motor Museum stand before Palace House, formerly the gatehouse of Beaulieu Abbey.*

Yachtsmen's 'capital' near Queen Victoria's island home

Every year thousands of visitors spend their holidays on the Isle of Wight. Yet the island, though it is only 23 miles long by 13 miles wide, has space to absorb and entertain them all. The visitor who wants to escape the crowds can stroll beside peaceful estuaries, walk through the shady grounds of Queen Victoria's favourite home, or stride across breezy clifftops that seem a world away from the busy commercial centres just across the Solent.

MORE THAN MEETS THE EYE *Below the white-tipped Needles lie jagged rocks that have collapsed into the sea. The last fall was in 1810, when a rock arch joining The Needles to the cliffs gave way.*

① THE NEEDLES
The three 100 ft pinnacles of chalk standing in the sea are the remnants of a ridge which once joined the Isle of Wight to the mainland, and are still being eroded. Until the 18th century, a fourth rock, a 120 ft pinnacle known as Lot's Wife, stood in the chain's largest gap; it collapsed in 1764. The lighthouse at the tip of the rocks was built in 1859 to replace one on the clifftop.

A fort, Old Needles Battery, built in 1863 overlooking The Needles, has been restored by the National Trust and contains an exhibition of the fort's history.

② ALUM BAY
The bay, named after the alum mined there as early as the 16th century, is backed by steep but insecure cliffs renowned for their coloured sands. White quartz, red iron oxide, yellow limonite and other minerals combine to create the mixture of colours.

A chair-lift and flights of steps provide access to the pebbly beach. The bay is a favourite mooring spot, and there are boat trips to view The Needles.

A leisure park (open in summer) at the top of the cliff includes a car park, shops and a model railway layout. Half a mile away along the B3322 is a clock museum. A walk along the clifftop to Headon Warren, covered with gorse, heather and ling, gives a panoramic view of The Needles.

③ TOTLAND
A sea-wall 1 mile long fringes a beach of steeply sloping shingle, with sands at low tide, that offers safe bathing. Totland is backed by hills and crumbling clay cliffs that show few signs of habitation. Boat trips run to Alum Bay and The Needles from the pier, where fishing tackle can also be hired.

④ COLWELL BAY
A short walk northwards along the sea-wall from Totland lies Colwell Bay, where holiday houses fringe the beach, low-tide sands offer safe swimming and there are sail-boards for hire.

The bay's northern end is dominated by the massive brick cube of Fort Albert, now converted into flats. The fort was built in 1856 as part of a series of fortifications against a possible French invasion.

⑤ FORT VICTORIA
The fort, which stands on Sconce Point, is the remains of a structure built in 1853 to guard the Solent. It is part of a 50 acre country park which has a large car park and picnic sites.

From the fort's remaining 21 arches there is a fine view across the Solent at its narrowest point. Bathing is prohibited because of rapid currents, but there is good fishing off the shore for many species including bass, plaice, sole and conger-eel.

⑥ YARMOUTH
This neat little town lies beside a large, snug harbour set in the estuary of the River Yar, with wooded banks to the water's edge. The town's beach is pebbly, but the adjoining Norton Beach is sandy and suitable for bathing. The 200 yd wooden pier is popular with fishermen, and the Royal Solent Yacht Club has offshore moorings.

Overlooking the harbour is a castle completed in 1547 as part of the coastal defences built by Henry VIII after his break with Rome. The castle is open to the public, and the original gun platform overlooking the Solent now forms a grassy terrace.

A bridge across the Yar estuary leads to a safe, sandy beach.

⑦ NEWTOWN
This tiny hamlet was, in the 17th century, a thriving port, but the only sign of its past glory is its town hall. Built in 1699, it fell into disrepair in the 19th century as Newtown declined, but it has now been restored and is owned by the National Trust.

The National Trust also preserves the entire estuary of the Newtown River and more than 4 miles of the adjacent Solent shore. From Newtown, a signposted path leads down to the estuary and along a wall that for 300 years enclosed reclaimed pastureland, until in 1954 the sea broke through and flooded the area again. The estuary is a maze of low-lying marshes and narrow creeks where boats moor. An 800 acre nature reserve embraces five different types of habitat – salt-marsh, shingle, sand, woodland and pasture – and some 300 species of plants and 180 species of birds have been recorded there.

⑧ COWES
Narrow streets lead down to the mouth of the River Medina and to the harbour, crammed with the shipwrights' yards and yacht clubs of the world's greatest yachting centre. The Royal Yacht Squadron commands the entrance to the harbour with a row of 21 little brass cannons. It is widely, though not universally, believed that the town owes its name to the grey stone building which now houses the Royal Yacht Squadron – a 'cow', or fortress, built by Henry VIII to defend the Solent. Though the Royal Yacht Squadron was formed in 1815, the town did not become fashionable until the 1890s when Edward, Prince of Wales, raced yachts there.

The Parade, which runs in front of the Royal Yacht Squadron and continues westward as the Prince's Esplanade, is an ideal viewpoint from which to watch the races, especially the numerous regattas held during the nine days of Cowes Week in August. Other major events include the Round the

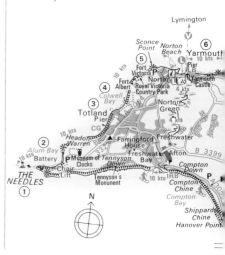

SEA RACERS *Brightly coloured spinnakers thrust racing yachts towards the finishing line during Cowes Week.*

Island Race in June, which attracts some 1,000 entries. A maritime museum in Cowes Library displays relics of the local shipbuilding industry over the last century. To the west of Prince's Esplanade is Gurnard Bay, with two small shingle beaches, weed-covered rocks and a stream running down to the sea.

Cowes is also the island's main port, and car and passenger ferries and hydrofoils run regular services to and from the mainland.

⑨ OSBORNE HOUSE

Queen Victoria called Osborne her 'little paradise', after having it built for herself and her family as a country retreat in 1845-6. The house was built by Thomas Cubitt, to designs by Prince Albert. Around the Italianate villa are extensive gardens with a collection of rare trees, and a full-size Swiss chalet in which the royal children played.

ROYAL DESKS *Queen Victoria and Prince Albert worked side by side at these writing desks in the Queen's sitting-room at Osborne House.*

Visitors can see the state and private apartments, preserved almost exactly as the Queen left them when she died there in 1901. Her son, Edward VII, did not share her enthusiasm for the house, and gave it to the nation in 1902.

The beach along the seaward side of the Osborne estate is private, but in summer the public can visit two other features of the estate. One is Norris Castle, where Queen Victoria stayed as a child. It was built in mock-medieval style in 1795 by James Wyatt for Lord Henry Seymour, and has wide views over the Solent. The other is Barton Manor, 20 acres of gardens including 5 acres of vineyards.

⑩ WOOTTON CREEK

The creek is dammed in the summer season to create a bathing lake, surrounded by mellow woodlands. There is a sailing school at the mouth of the creek on the northern side. Opposite lies Fishbourne, a terminal for the Portsmouth car ferry. There are sandy beaches round the point to the west, but there is no access for cars except through the holiday camps.

⑪ RYDE

The building of a half-mile long pier in 1814 began the transformation of Ryde from a tiny coastal settlement to the major holiday centre it has become today. It has a wealth of Regency and Victorian buildings, but its main attraction to holidaymakers is its broad sweep of gently shelving sands, ideal for swimming, which at low tide extend for nearly a mile out to sea. Care should be taken at the eastern end of the beach, known as Appley Sands, where the tide comes in very fast, covering deep holes.

The pier spans the sands, and trains run right to the end of it, where regular ferry services from Portsmouth berth. Londoners arriving by ferry will feel at home, because the electric trains once ran on the Piccadilly line. There is good fishing from the deeper, western, side of the pier, where plaice and flounder can be taken close inshore.

At Appley Park, at the eastern end of Ryde, the grounds of a former private estate have been neatly landscaped to create public gardens, with trees close to the beach and a golf course. Bathing huts and a cement wall line the shore, and a Victorian Gothic folly houses a shell collection.

⑫ SEAVIEW

The sandy beach of this little village provides safe swimming. A quarter of a mile inland, between the sea and the B3330, lies the 10 acre Flamingo Park, with waterfowl and water gardens. The park has 2,000 birds of 70 different species; most of them are waterfowl, but there are also macaws, a toucan and other tropical species.

⑬ BEMBRIDGE

Bembridge Harbour, often called Brading Harbour, is a bay that provides good anchorage. On its northern side is the Duver, a spit of land leading from the ruined tower of St Helen's Church and backed by a National Trust area of gorse and open grassland where 260 species of plants have been identified. Across the harbour are the remains of a tidal mill. Bembridge also has the island's only remaining windmill, which dates from 1700 and contains much of its original machinery.

Bathing is good all round Bembridge, but yachtsmen must beware of a rock shelf to the south which appears at low tide. The town has a small nautical museum.

Offshore, the strip of sea known as St Helen's Roads was favoured by Nelson as a mooring for the Navy because of the shelter it gave against westerly and south-westerly winds. The four rocky offshore bastions that look like islands are in fact massive granite fortresses built in the 1860s on the order of the Prime Minister, Lord Palmerston, at a time when French invasion was feared. They were never used and are known as 'Palmerston's Follies'.

LOCAL INFORMATION

Tourist information Newport 524343; Ryde 62905 (summer); Yarmouth 760015 (summer).

HM Coastguard Freshwater 752265 for information, 999 in emergency (ask for coastguard).

Weather Portsmouth 8091.

Local radio BBC Radio Solent, 300/221 m, 999/1359 kHz, 96.1 MHz; IBA Radio Victory, 257 m, 1170 kHz, 95 MHz.

PLACES TO SEE INLAND

Brading. Lilliput Museum of Dolls and Toys, daily in summer; Morton Manor, 17th-century house and gardens, most days in summer; Osborn-Smith's Wax Museum, daily; Roman Villa, daily in summer.

Calbourne Watermill. 17th-century working water-mill. Daily in summer.

Carisbrooke Castle. Norman and later, Isle of Wight Museum. Daily.

Robin Hill Country Park. Daily in summer.

Roman Villa, Newport. Daily in summer.

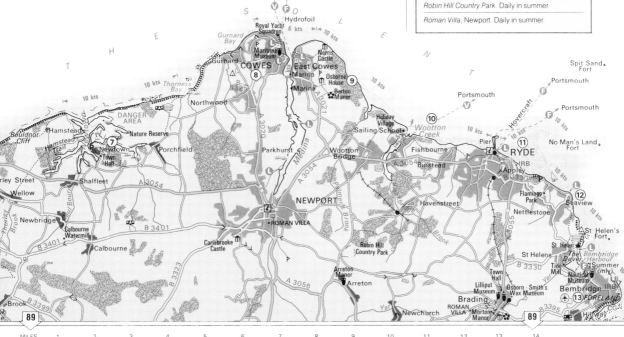

Bays and chines along the Isle of Wight's sunshine coast

Safe sandy beaches sheltered from the prevailing west winds are for many the main attractions of the south coast of the Isle of Wight. But the coastline includes more dramatic landscapes – isolated bays, narrow ravines or 'chines' and, on the more exposed south-west coast, precipitous cliffs revealing chalk beds that are the thickest in the country. All these features are linked by the coastal footpath which runs round the entire island.

① FRESHWATER BAY

The horseshoe-shaped cove has a steep pebbly beach and a short promenade, rimmed by low cliffs of white chalk. A few hundred yards inland is the source of the River Yar, which flows north to Yarmouth and almost divides western Wight from the remainder of the island.

To the west of the bay rises Tennyson Down, a grassy, whale-backed ridge of chalk which rises to 480 ft above the sea. The view embraces Portland Bill to the west and, to the east, the Solent up to Southampton Water, a sweep of 50 miles.

Tennyson Down is named after the poet Lord Tennyson who lived at nearby Farringford House for nearly 40 years. The poet used to walk on the down almost every day, saying that the air was worth 'sixpence a pint'. There is a monument to Tennyson on the summit of the down. Plants growing on the down include cowslips, hairy violets, betony, ragworts and several species of orchids. Cormorants, shags, guillemots and other sea-birds nest in the cliffs.

② BROOK

From the tiny hamlet, a 3 minute walk down Brook Chine leads to a sandy beach, with some pebbles. This is one of several 'chines', or ravines, which cut through the cliffs along the south coast of the Isle of Wight. The word derives from the Anglo-Saxon *cinan*, meaning 'to crack'; others that lead to the sandy foreshore around Compton Bay are Compton Chine and Shippards Chine.

Brook is also the southern starting point of the Hamstead Trail, one of the Isle of Wight's marked cross-country walking routes. At nearby Hanover Point, the Pine Raft – the fossilised remains of a forest – forms rock flats visible at low tide. Behind the 200 ft chalk cliffs facing Compton Bay soars Compton Down, popular with hang-gliders.

To the south-east of Brook Chine more chines lead down to extensive sands, with safe bathing in calm weather around Brighstone Bay. The soft clay cliffs are, however, constantly being eroded, and there are many landslides and cliff falls.

③ WHALE CHINE

This ravine, which is easily missed, leads down from a small car park beside the A3055, 1 mile west of Chale. Descent to the beach is by some 126 wooden steps, and as a result of this descending approach the beach – all 2 miles of it – is refreshingly uncrowded even at the height of summer. There are no facilities on the beach, which is free of rocks and consists of shingle and low-tide sand. Fishing is good, particularly for mackerel.

The cliffs are clearly stratified and some of the strata – the Wealden Beds, formed in a lake about 100 million years ago – are famous for their fossilised oysters, ammonites and lobsters.

④ BLACKGANG CHINE

This chine, supposedly named after a local band of smugglers, has now been overlaid with a large Fantasy Theme Park, which includes a maze, models of Isle of Wight houses, an Indian camp and a series of model dinosaurs, most of them full size.

In the entrance hall hangs a 75 ft whale skeleton – the largest and best preserved in Britain. The 80 ton animal was washed up near by in 1842 and for almost a century its skeleton was preserved, encased in cement, beside the road.

From the chine's top, 400 ft above the sea, there is a superb view of the cliffs leading north-west past Whale Chine. The rocks along the base of these cliffs have claimed 180 ships since 1750. At the base of the cliffs can be seen the Gault Clay – known locally as 'blue slipper' – which by acting as a lubricant to the overlying layers causes continual cliff falls along this coast. Blackgang Chine shows many signs of the slippage, which in recent years has taken away the original coast road and many houses. Until 1913, there were steps to the shore at this point; now there is no access.

⑤ REETH BAY

Just east of St Catherine's lighthouse and its treacherous Rocken End rocks lies perhaps the most secluded beach on the island. A road declared to be unfit for cars drops down for about a mile to a bay some 300 yds across which is otherwise completely cut off by sheer cliffs. There is safe bathing and fishing from a tiny dock.

St Catherine's lighthouse is open to the

public at the discretion of the keeper. Bathing is dangerous near the headland, but the walks in the National Trust's Knowles Farm area offer breathtaking views. Paths cross the landslip area below the cliff, and the main coastal path passes along the clifftop.

Just inland off the coastal path, on the 780 ft summit of St Catherine's Hill, stands an unusual octagonal tower known as the 'Pepper Pot'. It is the relic of a lighthouse built in about 1323 by a local landowner, Walter de Godeston, as an act of penance for having received casks of wine looted from a wrecked ship. A second circular lighthouse was begun near the tower in 1785, but never completed; its base still stands today. The new lighthouse, on the coast near St Catherine's Point, was built in 1838.

⑥ ST LAWRENCE

Close together lie three of the Isle of Wight's gems: a tiny, ancient church, a bird park and a secluded little bay.

St Lawrence Old Church is just 45 by 15 ft – one of the smallest churches in Britain. A Norman building dating from the 12th century, it lies 100 yds up a footpath and is

HILLSIDE RESORT *Set on a series of rocky terraces which zigzag down to the sea, Ventnor has a continental appearance, and the high crest of St Boniface Down shelters its beach from cold winds.*

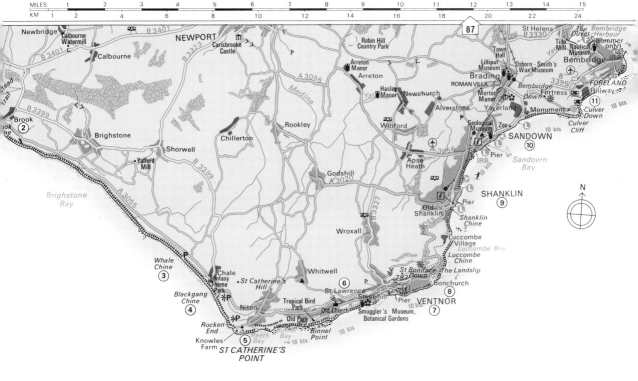

set about with gravestones and shaded by mature yews.

The bird park, occupying part of the Old Park estate, is for tropical birds. Most are in cages, but visitors can walk through most of the cages. The birds include a pair of erectus parrots, male and female bearing such different colours that they were once classified as separate species. The same complex of buildings includes a hotel and a glass works.

The bay at Binnel Point, rocky and with some low-tide sand, is accessible from the main road by a footpath west of St Lawrence, or along the cliffs from Ventnor. It was once a harbour, and the ruins of the old walls still guard it.

⑦ VENTNOR

The resort, developed in Victorian times, descends like an amphitheatre below the slope of the highest point in the Isle of Wight, the 787 ft St Boniface Down. The town has good bathing and a wide range of seaside amusements, though the pier-head was closed in the early 1980s. The Botanic Gardens are extensive and a Museum of Smuggling commemorates a way of life that was once common on the island. A smugglers' pageant is held every June.

One mile west of Ventnor is a small secluded beach – Steephill – that can be reached only by footpath, either from the shore or from the main road above. It is ringed with cliffs and hemmed in by cottages.

The gorse-and-grass summit of St Boniface Down is marred by a large radar and telecommunications site, but there are all-round views over the coast and rolling inland hills.

⑧ BONCHURCH

This tiny village – the 'bon' is a contraction of St Boniface – has an equally tiny and charming beach, with good bathing.

Adjoining the village to the north-east is an area called The Landslip, where the effects of the underlying 'blue slipper' are obvious. Two major 'slips' in the surface strata have occurred in the last two centuries – in 1810 and 1928 – leaving the landscape a mass of contorted blocks which are now overgrown and crossed by paths.

SHADY DELL *Ferns and mosses cling to the rock walls and tall trees form a leafy sunshade above the deep cleft of Shanklin Chine.*

⑨ SHANKLIN

A long, safe, sandy beach is Shanklin's principal attraction for holidaymakers. It has in addition a fairground and pier entertainments. A lift carries passengers from the Esplanade up to Keats Green, from which there is a fine view of the coastline.

At the southern end of the green the cliffs have been sliced by a stream to form a chine. To follow the nature trail through Shanklin Chine is to enter a different world, a grove enclosed by trees that follows the stream from a waterfall at the top to a thatched fisherman's cottage, now a pub and restaurant, at the bottom.

The chine contains a relic of the Second World War: a section of the Pipeline Under The Ocean (PLUTO) that was used to pump fuel across the floor of the Channel during the Normandy landings.

The main part of the town is Victorian and Edwardian, but from the top of Shanklin Chine walkers can continue through Old Shanklin, with its thatched houses, and along the coastal path to Luccombe Village, less than 1 mile away. Walkers who can face

the long return climb can descend Luccombe Chine – 300 rough steps leading to an unspoiled beach.

⑩ SANDOWN

The safe bathing beach of Shanklin continues unbroken along the foreshore of Sandown, which has a pier, pavilion and every beach amusement. The Battery Gardens, once a fortress, offer spectacular cliff-top views. A small zoo set in the granite ruins of Sandown Fort contains Bengal tigers and a reptile house. The town also has a small geological museum.

⑪ CULVER DOWN

The down, rising to more than 300 ft, is topped by a giant stone needle raised in 1849 to the memory of Charles Pelham, Earl of Yarborough, first commodore of the Royal Yacht Squadron. At its seaward end it terminates in the dramatic Culver Cliff, a nesting site for many sea-birds.

The adjoining Bembridge Down is crowned by a fortress built in Lord Palmerston's time and used until after the Second World War. Though now overgrown, it is used by an industrial company.

Culver Down and Bembridge Down together form a saddle from which there are superb views to Bembridge and across Sandown Bay.

LOCAL INFORMATION

Tourist information Sandown 403886, Shanklin 2942, Ventnor 853625 (summer).

HM Coastguard Freshwater 752265 for information, 999 in emergency (ask for coastguard).

Weather Portsmouth 8091.

Local radio BBC Radio Solent, 300/221 m, 999/1359 kHz, 96.1 MHz; IBA Radio Victory, 257 m, 1170 kHz, 95 MHz.

OTHER PLACES TO SEE

Arreton Manor, 4 miles W of Sandown. 17th-century house, National Wireless Museum, folk museum. Daily in summer.

Haseley Manor, 3 miles W of Sandown. Agricultural museum and pottery. Daily most of year.

Longshoreman's Museum, Ventnor. Models, photographs, items of local interest. Daily in summer, winter by appointment.

Yafford Mill, 2 miles E of Brighstone. 18th-century working watermill. Daily in summer.

Stone ramparts that command Portsmouth's historic harbour

This stretch of coast is made up of a series of low-lying islands and peninsulas between which lie marshy harbours crossed by creeks and channels. Its outline has altered over the centuries because of silting, while its closeness to Europe has involved it time and again in Britain's history. The sheltered waters make the area popular with yachtsmen, while the towns and villages that flank the harbours suit most holiday-making tastes.

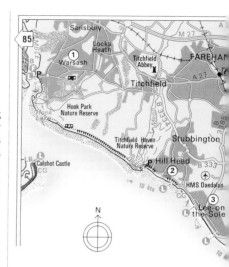

① WARSASH
This small port overlooking the lower Hamble, is an important yachting centre. The river is muddy, and unsuitable for swimming because of strong currents. A ferry crosses the estuary to Hamble; at very low tides cannon and musket balls – the relics of past sea battles – and the remains of several ships are often revealed.

From the car park, which stands on a former lobster pound, there is a pleasant 4 mile walk along the coast past the nature reserve of Hook Park and the silted up mouth of the River Meon to the village of Hill Head. The nature reserve runs down to the foreshore and includes Hook Lake, a silted up inlet from the sea, and old salt workings.

② HILL HEAD
In the 18th century this small village resting on low cliffs was a centre of the smuggling trade, and quantities of brandy were more than once seized there by customs men. There is good swimming from a shingle beach which shelves steeply to a flat sandy bottom, and at low tide it is possible to walk out over the sands and collect cockles.

There is fishing from the shore, mainly for bass and mullet, while at the west end of the village the Titchfield Haven Nature Reserve is frequented by large numbers of ducks, particularly wigeon.

③ LEE-ON-THE-SOLENT
Situated on the outskirts of Gosport, Lee is the site of the HMS *Daedalus* Fleet Air Arm base, where helicopters are kept in readiness to answer calls for assistance from coastguards and police along the south coast.

There is a public slipway for launching boats at the eastern end of the beach. The beach is shingle, with sand at low tide; it is safe for bathing, and there is water-skiing.

④ GOSPORT
The Ferry Gardens, near the passenger ferry to Portsmouth, are an ideal place from which to observe the movements of naval and civilian ships in Portsmouth Harbour. To the south of the ferry, near the big submarine training base of HMS *Dolphin* at Fort Blockhouse, is a fascinating submarine museum. Its exhibits include *Holland I*, the Royal Navy's first submarine, launched in 1901. She sank in 1913 while being towed to a breaker's yard and was salvaged in 1982. Beside the museum the visitors can board a real submarine, HMS *Alliance*, one of the last of the Second World War A-class submarines. She has been restored to her active service condition and looks as she did when last at sea. To the north of the ferry terminal lies the 'wooden-waller' *Foudroyant*, built in 1817 as a 46-gun frigate but now used as a training ship.

There is fishing for pout, bass and pollock by the pier near the ferry, and good bathing at Stokes Bay, the point from which Queen Victoria used to embark for Osborne House on the Isle of Wight.

⑤ PORTCHESTER CASTLE
The castle, visible from the land only at close quarters, stands on the site of a Roman fort thought to have been built in the latter part of the 3rd century AD. The remaining Roman outer walls, 18 ft high and up to 10 ft thick, are the best preserved in northern Europe. They enclose a 12th-century castle, reached by a bridge over a moat, and priory church.

The impressive keep, the walls of which are 12 ft thick at ground level, was built by Henry I. It originally comprised of only a basement with one storey above, but two further floors were later added and the top of the keep today offers a fine view over the castle and its walls, and of Portsmouth Harbour beyond them.

After visiting the buildings, it is worth passing through the Water Gate to walk

VICTORS OF TRAFALGAR

A figurehead of Lord Nelson stands near his flagship HMS *Victory* in Portsmouth – two memorials in wood to the great Battle of Trafalgar which ended Napoleon's dream of commanding the seas. Nelson's battle plan, using a method of attack never tried before, became known as 'the Nelson touch'. It relied heavily on the ability of the *Victory's* gunners to fire a broadside every 80 seconds – a rate unmatched by any other ship in the world. HMS *Victory* first put to sea in 1778, and stayed afloat until 1921. She was then restored to her condition when Nelson and his crew of 850 triumphed at Trafalgar.

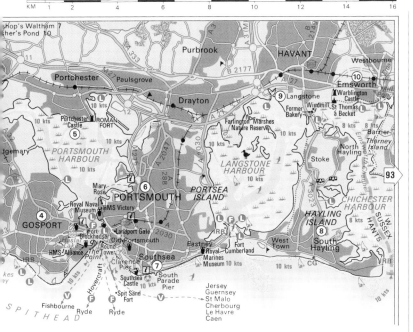

of Eastney barracks. From the peninsula beyond Fort Cumberland, a ferry runs to Hayling Island. A hovercraft service to Ryde, on the Isle of Wight, runs from a terminal near Clarence Pier.

⑧ HAYLING ISLAND

Reached by a bridge much frequented by fishermen, the island is shaped like an inverted T, with marshlands to east and west and 4 miles of sand along its south shore, safe for swimming except at each end. An inlet of Chichester Harbour divides the island almost in two.

Hayling Island's popularity with day trippers and its abundance of seaside entertainments have still left large areas of unspoilt beaches covered with grassy dunes. A delightful walk follows the path of the old railway line from West Town northwards along the west shore, where the wildlife of Langstone Harbour, a nature reserve, can be appreciated. Water sports include sailing, water-skiing from the western tip of the island near the ferry to Portsmouth, and windsurfing. Boats can be hired, and a carnival is held in August.

⑨ LANGSTONE

Not the least of this village's attractions are the splendid views it offers across the marshes of Chichester Harbour, officially designated as an Area of Outstanding Natural Beauty. Langstone's former fishing fleet has long gone, but several old buildings survive, including a former bakery (now a public house) and a windmill. Langstone was the site of a Roman crossing point to Hayling Island, and the remains of a causeway can be seen, while in 1926 the site of a Roman villa was discovered.

A path running eastwards near the shore leads in about 1 mile to the ruins of Warblington Castle, a 16th-century castle destroyed during the Civil War, and to Warblington's attractive church, which has Saxon archways, a 13th-century nave and a 14th-century wooden porch.

⑩ EMSWORTH

A walk down South Street from the village square leads past rows of old houses to the harbour, with fishing boats and a public slipway. Behind the old mill, which now houses a sailing club, is the mill-pond, a large picturesque expanse of water where swans glide and canoeing is possible. A delightful walk follows the edge of the mill-pond, down to the open sea, then leads back to the bridge over the River Ems.

Emsworth was a landing place for smugglers until well into the present century. It once had a substantial oyster fleet, but the pollution of the beds, which led to several deaths from food poisoning, caused its decline from 1902.

Portchester Castle

beside the shore. From there the impressive workmanship of the castle's flint walls can be clearly appreciated.

⑥ PORTSMOUTH

Granted a charter by Richard I in 1194, and established as a naval dockyard during the reign of Henry VII, 'Pompey' retains much of the flavour of the past despite severe damage during the Second World War. What survives of the original town is in the area now known as Old Portsmouth, around the ferry terminal for Gosport and the Isle of Wight. The town was once surrounded by walls and approached through gateways, but only the Landport Gate in St George's

SAFETY ASSURED *Henry V ordered the building of Portsmouth's Round Tower so that 'the safety of the king's ships might be assured'.*

Road still survives in its original position. In Old Commercial Road is the house in which Charles Dickens was born in 1812. It has been restored to show the style of middle-class living in the mid-19th century.

From The Point, a small peninsula jutting out into the harbour and once known as Spice Island, there are fine views. It has impressive sea defences, including the Round Tower of Henry V from which a chain boom used to be stretched across the harbour to a tower on the opposite bank.

From the ferry point there are boat trips around the harbour giving an ideal opportunity to observe naval ships at close range. In the dockyard itself are the Royal Naval Museum, HMS *Victory*, the flagship of Nelson on which he died at the Battle of Trafalgar in 1805, and the hull of the *Mary Rose*, Henry VIII's warship, raised from the Solent sea-bed in 1982. There are Navy Days in August, when the public can visit the Royal Naval base.

Portsmouth is an important ferry port for continental and Isle of Wight traffic. It has a small but thriving commercial port, and several thousand yachts are moored in the harbour. Consequently there is plenty of activity on the water to watch, while anyone sailing should exercise great care.

⑦ SOUTHSEA

Though part of the City of Portsmouth, Southsea has a character of its own as a resort in the traditional sense. Its attractions include two piers, a seaside common and a long shingle beach that is safe for swimming and has patches of sand at low tide. Volunteer lifeguards patrol the beach at weekends in summer. From the shore and pier, cod and bass may be caught and there are fishing trips to deeper waters where mackerel and occasionally shark can be found. On the beach, between Clarence Pier and the Royal Navy War Memorial, is the original anchor of HMS *Victory*.

In Southsea Castle, built by Henry VIII in 1545, is the D-Day Museum. On view there is the Overlord Tapestry, 272 ft long and five years in the weaving, that commemorates the D-Day invasion.

From the castle, three sea forts are visible. Between the two eastern forts lay the wreck of the *Mary Rose* until she was raised in 1982. From the piers there are boat trips around Portsmouth Harbour, and there is water-skiing beyond the half-mile limit. At Eastney the Royal Marines Museum is housed in part

Tidal creeks where yachts sail and sea-birds flock

The narrow entrance to Chichester Harbour opens out into a landlocked lagoon, where peninsulas split the main channel into a multitude of tidal creeks. Until the 19th century many of the waterside villages were busy commercial harbours, and in recent years they have sprung to life again as boating centres. Beyond the harbour there are dangerous currents round Selsey Bill, which separates the Witterings from Bognor Regis.

Market cross, Chichester

① THORNEY ISLAND
The westernmost of the three peninsulas that divide Chichester Harbour, Thorney Island is flat and featureless, and is mainly the property of the Ministry of Defence. The road across the island to the village of West Thorney is closed by a manned barrier at the point where it crosses the channel known as the Great Deep. Though the public cannot set foot on the island, there is a footpath right round its foreshore.

② PRINSTED
At the head of Thorney Channel, Prinsted is a pretty village of old cottages, with a cul-de-sac ending above the tidal flats. There is a small car park, from which a walk along the river-wall gives views down Thorney Channel. South of the village, the road becomes a rough lane leading to boatyards. Small boats can be launched near high water.

③ BOSHAM
One of the beauty spots of the south coast, Bosham (pronounced 'Bozzam') stands on its own little peninsula, looking out over an unspoiled riverscape of reeds, water, mudflats and small boats. The best view of Bosham – and one of the most photographed views in England – is from the south side of the creek, along the Old Bosham Road.

In 1064, Harold, Earl of Wessex, embarked on a voyage to Normandy from Quay Meadow, near Bosham's Saxon church. The meadow remains a green acre of ground, owned today by the National Trust and an ideal spot for a picnic.

In summer a ferry, for foot passengers only, runs from a point 1 mile west of Bosham Hoe across Chichester Channel to West Itchenor.

④ CHICHESTER
The centre of Chichester still has the simple logic of its Roman plan – four main streets (North, South, East and West) meeting at a central point, and surrounded by a roughly circular wall. The Romans called the city Noviomagus. Today Chichester is the administrative capital of West Sussex, with a cathedral dating back to Norman times, a largely traffic-free town centre, streets of superb Georgian houses, and a graceful market cross, built in 1501, at the focal point.

Chichester is well known for its annual summer theatre season, which is held in the Festival Theatre, opened in 1962. On the south-east outskirts of the city is the Southern Leisure Centre, which covers 200 acres of grass, trees and lakes and offers windsurfing tuition, sailing, water-skiing, and fishing for coarse fish and trout.

⑤ DELL QUAY
It is hard to envisage this quiet little sailing village as a bustling port; yet in the 18th century Dell Quay became the main harbour for Chichester, after Chichester Channel had become too silted for ships to reach higher upstream to the city. Near the village are several boatyards, and boats can be launched from the shingle foreshore within 3 hours of high water. Parking is very limited.

⑥ BIRDHAM
Though Birdham is still a village in its own right, it has lost much of its identity to the two major sailing centres that lie near it. The Chichester Yacht Basin is one of the biggest yacht harbours on the south coast, with 1,000 boats moored along its jetties.

Beside the basin is a bustling conglomeration of boatyards, sailing clubs, chandlers and yacht brokers. There are two slipways which visitors can use, for a fee. The disused Chichester Canal, just to the south of the yacht basin, is lined with houseboats and covered with water lilies.

Birdham Pool, just north of the village, is smaller than the yacht basin but more picturesque. Like the basin, it is connected to Chichester Channel by a lock gate.

⑦ WEST ITCHENOR
Like Dell Quay, West Itchenor has changed down the years from commercial harbour to picturesque sailing village. The road runs down to a beach of hard shingle, from which boats can be launched at any state of the tide; parking is very limited near the foreshore. A ferry for foot passengers runs across Chichester Channel between West Itchenor and the Bosham bank in summer.

⑧ WEST WITTERING
Smart estates of substantial houses, many of them on private roads, have grown up behind the old village, centred on the parish church. West Wittering's sandy beach, more than 1 mile long, is reached down a narrow road from the village; the road ends at a large car park below the dunes.

At its western end, opposite Hayling Island, the beach curves round to form a sickle-shaped area of dunes, sheltering a tidal lagoon on its inner side, and with a

INDOMITABLE WATERS *The placid creek at Bosham is said to be the place where King Canute commanded the tide to retreat, as a lesson to his courtiers who believed him to be all-powerful.*

HISTORIC CHURCH
The Saxon church at Bosham features in one of the earliest panels of the Bayeux Tapestry, which depicts the events of the Norman Conquest. It was from Bosham, an important harbour in Saxon times, that Harold, the powerful Earl of Wessex who was soon to become King of England, set out on his fateful voyage to Normandy in 1064. By swearing an oath of loyalty to Duke William, he set in motion the events that led to William invading and conquering England.

Harold in prayer at Bosham church.

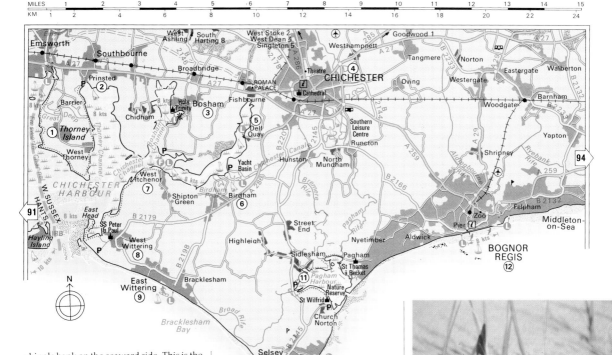

shingle bank on the seaward side. This is the 76 acre East Head, a fragile natural environment, under constant attack both from the sea and from the pressure of visitors walking round from West Wittering beach. Owned by the National Trust, the dunes have been fenced off to enable marram grass to establish itself and stabilise the sand with its roots.

Swimming is safe from West Wittering beach, where volunteer lifeguards patrol at weekends and bank holidays in summer, but is forbidden in the entrance to Chichester Harbour because of dangerous currents.

⑨ EAST WITTERING

From West Wittering beach, East Wittering's caravan parks and estates of small houses stretch for some 2 miles, linking up with those of Bracklesham to form a continuous ribbon of beachside development. There is easy access to the sea at only two points: in East Wittering down Shore Road, where the only parking is some way from the beach, and in Bracklesham down a road which ends at a seaside car park, with a concrete slipway beyond.

⑩ SELSEY BILL

This low-lying headland jutting into the Channel attracts many holidaymakers, and the village of Selsey is expanding rapidly. Fast currents sweeping round the point make it dangerous to swim near it, and so the bathing beaches are half a mile along the coast on either side; even there, bathers are warned at low tide to be careful of currents and hidden pools.

East Beach is the resort's main centre. Protected by a strong sea-wall and many groynes, it has a car park and boat park, with a wooden ramp down to the beach. East Beach still keeps much of the seafaring flavour of old Selsey, with fishing boats offshore, lobster pots in heaps along the sea-wall, and stalls selling locally caught crabs, whelks, cockles and fish.

⑪ PAGHAM HARBOUR

This beautiful and unspoiled stretch of tidal mud-flats and shingle beach is now a nature reserve, covering more than 1,000 acres. The easiest approach is from the car park beside the B2145, 1 mile south of Sidlesham; an information centre there is open at weekends.

Pagham Harbour is a refuge for dozens of species of birds and plants. Among the birds

are little terns, shelducks, curlews, redshanks and oystercatchers. The salt-marsh plants include spartina grass, sea purslane and glasswort, while the hedgerows support a large variety of butterflies, including red admirals.

At the southern end of the harbour is the hamlet of Church Norton, where the tiny chapel of St Wilfrid looks out over the lonely saltings. Wilfrid was a 7th-century missionary who preached Christianity to the heathen inhabitants of Selsey – the South Saxons, whose name was later given to their homeland of 'Sussex'. The name 'Selsey' means *Seal Island* in Old English, and in those days Selsey was a real island, cut off from the mainland by the channel of which Pagham Harbour formed part.

Sidlesham now sprawls along the main road, but its old centre is at the head of a creek opening off Pagham Harbour. Until the mid-19th century Sidlesham was a working harbour, but it is now just a pretty backwater.

Pagham village is the westernmost part of Bognor; but it retains its own flavour, best sampled by walking down the lane from the church and on to the sea-wall round Pagham Harbour. From there a path runs all the way from the harbour to Church Norton, on the opposite side of the harbour mouth.

⑫ BOGNOR REGIS

The centrepiece of a continuous seaside resort that stretches for more than 7 miles from Pagham to Middleton-on-Sea, Bognor

SUMMER VISITORS *From the warm shores of West Africa, little terns come back to Pagham Harbour every summer to breed.*

itself still seems small and unpretentious. The seafront has not a single high-rise building, and even the elegant new civic centre and theatre complex is no taller than the average two-storey hotel. The beach consists of sand backed by shingle, with frequent groynes. Bognor's pier has amusements and cafes at the landward end; the seaward end is derelict, but gradually being restored.

Bognor was founded as a resort in the late 18th century by Sir Richard Hotham, a wealthy London hatter, who wanted to call it 'Hothampton'. Queen Victoria referred to it as her 'dear little Bognor', while her grandson, King George V, gave it the title 'Regis' in 1928 after recovering there from a serious illness. Aldwick, where the king went to recuperate, is today the prosperous western offshoot of Bognor, with private roads serving estates of half-timbered houses with green tiles or thatch.

Felpham, at the eastern end, still keeps something of the atmosphere of a traditional Sussex village, with narrow winding streets and flint-walled cottages.

LOCAL INFORMATION

Tourist information Chichester 775888, Bognor Regis 823140.

HM Coastguard Freshwater 752265 for information, 999 in emergency (ask for coastguard).

Weather Brighton 8091.

Local radio BBC Radio Solent, 300/221 m, 999/1359 kHz, 96.1 MHz; IBA Radio Victory, 257 m, 1170 kHz, 95 MHz; IBA Southern Sound, 225 m, 1332 kHz, 103.4 MHz.

PLACES TO SEE INLAND

Fishbourne, 1 mile W of Chichester. Roman palace. Daily Mar.-Nov.; Sun. Dec.-Feb.

Goodwood House, 3½ miles NE of Chichester, via A285. 18th-century mansion. Some afternoons in summer.

Kingley Vale National Nature Reserve, West Stoke, 3 miles NW of Chichester, off A286.

Uppark (NT), near South Harting, 10 miles NW of Chichester via B2146. 17th-18th-century house. Some afternoons in summer.

Weald and Downland Open Air Museum, Singleton, 5 miles N of Chichester. Re-erected historic buildings. Daily in summer, Sun. and Wed. in winter.

West Dean Gardens, 6 miles N of Chichester. Daily in summer.

Golden beaches within sight of the South Downs

The only breathing-spaces in the relentless march of buildings along 17 miles of coastline are a gap of 2½ miles west of Littlehampton, and a smaller one at Ferring. Towards the east the green ridge of the South Downs not far inland becomes more and more apparent. Two winding rivers, the Arun and the Adur, cut into the coast, providing Littlehampton and Shoreham with harbours that are now favourites with small-boat sailors.

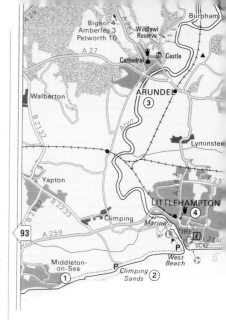

① MIDDLETON-ON-SEA

Now joined to Felpham, Middleton is the easternmost satellite of Bognor Regis, a residential area of largely private estates. The gardens of its houses lead down to the sea-wall, and there is safe bathing from the sand-and-shingle beach. The single road through Middleton ends at a holiday village. During the First World War, Middleton was the site of a seaplane base, and the village developed largely between the wars.

② CLIMPING SANDS

South of the village of Climping, a narrow country lane runs past cottages and farm buildings to the beach, ending at a large car park behind the sea-wall.

The National Trust protects almost 1,000 acres, including 2½ miles of coastline, and so this reminder of what the entire West Sussex coast was once like will be preserved for future generations. Swimming is safe, though the sandy beach is scattered with patches of weed-covered stones. There are good walks along the foreshore in both directions – to Middleton, and to the mouth of the Arun opposite Littlehampton. The medieval church and houses of the village of Atherington now lie under the sea, somewhere off Climping Sands.

③ ARUNDEL

Above the gentle windings of the Arun looms the battlemented grandeur of Arundel Castle, the ancestral home of the Dukes of Norfolk, formerly Earls of Arundel, who have lived there since the 16th century. Though the bulk of the castle dates only from Victorian times, its 11th-century keep and gatehouse and its magnificent setting give it an authentic medieval flavour. Inside are family portraits of the Norfolks, the earliest painted as far back as the 15th-century Wars of the Roses.

ANCESTRAL HOME *For 700 years Arundel Castle has been the seat of the Dukes of Norfolk, hereditary Earl Marshals of England.*

Arundel also has a Roman Catholic cathedral, a 14th-century Gothic parish church and a museum of local history. Down the lane that skirts the castle park are the ponds, hides and interpretation centre of the Arundel Wildfowl Trust, where wildfowl from all over the world, including a colony of black swans, can be seen in idyllic surroundings.

④ LITTLEHAMPTON

With its busy harbour at the mouth of the Arun and its seafront of red-brick Victorian and Edwardian houses and hotels, Little-hampton manages to cram plenty of variety into a small space. The road crossing over the Arun is a good mile upstream. Foot passengers can cross by ferry in summer, or use the cycle and footbridge downstream from the road bridge.

Littlehampton's boatyards and marina are on the west bank of the Arun, down Ferry Road. The road ends at West Beach, a wide sandy beach, backed by high dunes and safe for swimming except near the harbour mouth. The river is fast-running, reaching 7 knots during the spring tides.

The built-up side of Littlehampton is on the east bank of the Arun, where the area beside the harbour mouth is devoted to seaside amusements, car parks and a fun-fair. Between the seafront houses and the sea is a wide green, with gardens and a miniature golf course; bathing huts line the promenade.

Littlehampton's harbour was already flourishing in the Middle Ages, when stone from Caen in Normandy was landed there to build the great Sussex churches and castles. The town's later seafaring history is displayed in a small museum in River Road, which has a fine collection of maritime paintings and ship models.

⑤ RUSTINGTON

East of Littlehampton the coast road runs along the sea-wall before turning inland to the old village centre of Rustington, which still has a few flint-walled cottages and a medieval church. It was in Rustington that Sir Hubert Parry, who lived in the village during the First World War, wrote his setting of Blake's *Jerusalem.*

Rustington has no proper seafront; but the sea can be reached down various lanes. Parking is very limited.

⑥ ANGMERING-ON-SEA

A maze of narrow roads leads from East Preston down to Angmering-on-Sea, 2 miles from its inland parent at Angmering. The houses, largely grouped in private estates, are shaded by mature conifers and ever-greens, which give the village a more permanent look than many resorts. The shingle-and-sand beach can be reached only along paths between the houses.

⑦ FERRING

Reached across a level crossing, Ferring consists of an old village engulfed by later housing. It is still separated from the western suburbs of Worthing by an open expanse of fields and greenery, backing directly on to the beach, with a magnificent plantation of conifers along the Worthing side.

Fishing boats are drawn up on the shingle above the beach, which is pebble-scattered and sandy, and which gives a good view round the coast as far as Worthing pier. There is room to park beside the road.

⑧ GORING-BY-SEA

Laid out with plenty of open space, Goring feels quite distinct from Worthing, though it is in fact its western suburb. Swimming is safe from the shingle-and-sand beach, which is separated from the road by a low grass rise, topped with a row of bathing huts. South of the road is a large car park, with a slope leading to a wide wooden ramp over the shingle. There is a buoyed power-boat channel from the end of the ramp, and sail-boards can be hired.

⑨ WORTHING

The biggest resort in West Sussex, Worthing is a seaside town with plenty of style. It has fine gardens, 5 miles of seafront and a pier that is still fully functioning. There is an open-air swimming pool on the wide promenade, and in summer open-topped buses run along the front.

Worthing became a resort towards the end of the 18th century. Before that, it had been nothing but a few fishing cottages down by the shore, below the old village of Broad-water. Perhaps its atmosphere of peace and quiet compared with the fast pace of Brighton had something to do with the differing characters of the people who put the two places on the map: at Brighton it was the larger-than-life Prince Regent, while at Worthing it was his delicate younger sister, Princess Amelia.

Swimming is safe from nearly all the beach, which consists of sand below shingle; however, there are warnings of submerged sea defences at both ends of the beach, which can be hazardous for swimmers and small boats. East of the pier there is a magnificent view round the coast, past the chimneys of Brighton power station at Portslade and the high-rise towers of Brighton, to the chalk ramparts of Seaford Head and the Seven Sisters.

Worthing's museum and art gallery has an excellent and varied collection, including

MILES | 1 | 2 | 3 | 4 | 5 | 6 | 7
KM | 1 | 2 | 4 | 6 | 8 | 10

displays of costume in period settings. The Archaeology Gallery contains outstanding Anglo-Saxon jewellery and glass from the Saxon cemetery at Highdown Hill.

Two miles inland, at the hamlet of Sompting Abbotts, is the Saxon church of St Mary's, whose tower, built about AD 1000, has a 'Rhenish helm' roof – the only one in Britain. It consists of four diamond-shaped surfaces, rising between four gables and meeting at a central point.

⑩ SOUTH LANCING

For much of its length the coast road has houses along both sides, and the beach, of sand backed with shingle, can be reached only down paths between them. Towards Worthing, an open space of grass is edged by white beach huts. Inland is Lancing College, whose chapel, completed in 1978 after more than a century, is a landmark along this part of the coast and an impressive monument to the survival of the Gothic architectural spirit.

⑪ SHOREHAM-BY-SEA

Only a few hundred yards from the sea, the River Adur makes a right-angled turn to the east, forming a natural harbour 1 mile long and running parallel to the shore line. In recent years the resort of Shoreham Beach

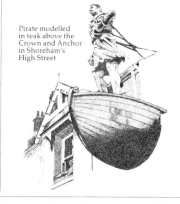

Pirate modelled in teak above the Crown and Anchor in Shoreham's High Street

has sprung up on the shingle bank between the river and the sea; it can be reached either by road from west of the Adur, or by footbridge across the river from the town centre.

The road through Shoreham Beach ends at the coastguard station by the harbour entrance, where there is plenty of parking space. The harbour wall is a favourite place for fishermen, and there are fine views down the coast to Brighton and beyond. At the foot of the coastguard tower is the base of

MUSEUM PIECE *The Marlipins Museum in Shoreham dates from the early 12th century, and is older than most of its exhibits.*

a Victorian fort, built in 1857 at the time of a French invasion scare.

The footbridge across the Adur gives a magnificent view of Shoreham, crowned by the Norman church tower of St Mary de Haura. Known as New Shoreham church, though it dates from 1130, it was the successor to Old Shoreham church, which still stands half a mile upstream. Near by, in the High Street, is the fascinating little Marlipins Museum, housed in an early 12th-century building which is said to be one of the oldest secular buildings in Europe still in active use.

The harbour's commercial centre has shifted eastwards, to the canal that runs parallel with the sea almost to Hove. The shingle bar on the southern side of the canal is dominated by the twin chimneys of Brighton power station.

THE IMPORTANCE OF BEING WORTHING *Oscar Wilde wrote his play*, The Importance of Being Earnest, *at Worthing and named the chief character – found 'in a handbag' – after the town.*

LOCAL INFORMATION
Tourist information Arundel 882268, Littlehampton 3480 (summer), Worthing 39999.
HM Coastguard Shoreham-by-Sea 2226 for information, 999 in emergency (ask for coastguard).
Weather Brighton 8091.
Local radio BBC Radio Solent, 300/221 m, 999/1359 kHz, 96.1 MHz; BBC Radio Sussex, 202 m, 1485 kHz, 95.3 MHz; IBA Southern Sound, 225 m, 1332 kHz, 103.4 MHz.

PLACES TO SEE INLAND
Bignor Roman Villa, 10 miles NE of Littlehampton, via A29. Most days in summer.
Chalk Pits Museum, Amberley, via B2139. Open-air industrial museum. Most days in summer.
Highdown Gardens, 3 miles W of Worthing. Daily in summer, Mon.-Fri. in winter.
Parham, near Storrington, 9 miles NW of Worthing. Elizabethan house and gardens, most afternoons in summer.
Petworth House (NT), 15 miles NW of Littlehampton, via A283. 17th-century mansion. Most afternoons in summer; park daily.
Woods Mill, Henfield, 7 miles N of Shoreham-by-Sea, via A2037. 18th-century mill. Most afternoons in summer.

Channel breezes and holiday fun in 'Sussex by the Sea'

A commercial harbour at the mouth of the River Adur and a cross-Channel port on the River Ouse lie at opposite ends of one of the busiest and most heavily populated stretches of the South Coast. At its heart lies Brighton, the very epitome of the 'Sussex by the Sea' of the music-hall song: a resort which with its piers, promenades, long beaches and huge marina has set the pace in seaside entertainment ever since the time of the Prince Regent.

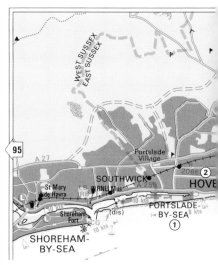

HOVE BEACH *'A wonderful place for setting people up', was how John Constable described the coast near Brighton when he visited it with his sick wife Maria in 1824 and painted this picture.*

① PORTSLADE-BY-SEA

The commercial, eastern arm of Shoreham Harbour is entered by locks not far from the harbour mouth. On the north bank, at Southwick, is a disused lighthouse built in 1846; and near by is the Shoreham lifeboat station, with a small museum on the ground floor. The large expanse of shingle beside the lighthouse, a good spot from which to watch the shipping in Shoreham Harbour, has been designated a village green – though it is completely without grass – and parking is forbidden there.

The Portslade side of the harbour entrance can be reached either on foot across the locks, or by car down Wharf Road, from near the Hove boating lagoon.

② HOVE

Though from the holidaymaker's point of view Hove is part of Brighton, it is in fact a separate borough, with its own modern town hall of aluminium, concrete and brown glass, opened in 1974. The boundary between the two lies just east of Hove's monumental Brunswick Square, which opens on to the seafront and was built in the 1820s.

Hove is a good deal quieter and more sedate than its sister resort, but it has attractions of its own. These include the Sussex county cricket ground; a boating lagoon where windsurfing is taught; a museum of art, with collections of ceramics, ship models and pictures of Sussex; and the British Engineerium. Restored in 1976, a century after it was built, the Engineerium was formerly the pumping station which supplied Brighton and Hove with fresh water, and is now a museum devoted to the history of engineering. The massive beam-engine is 'in steam' on Sundays and Bank Holidays.

Hove is no longer summed up by the stern-faced statue of Queen Victoria at the foot of Grand Avenue. A good many of the large houses built in the 19th century along the seafront are giving way to new flats, overlooking the wide grass lawns that add greatly to the open feeling of the town, while the King Alfred Leisure Centre on the front was one of the first such complexes to be built on the South Coast.

③ BRIGHTON

For two centuries Brighton has been the queen of British seaside resorts. Indeed, it is often claimed that the seaside holiday was invented there, since it was at Brighton that the virtues of seawater were first publicised and promoted on a large scale. Its 19th-century hotels, the Grand and the Metropole, were the ancestors of the seaside palaces that have sprung up from the Costa Brava to Florida, and from Acapulco to the Seychelles.

Brighton today provides all the amenities of a major town: fine parks and houses, a university, an art college, a theatre, a racecourse, excellent restaurants, and good communications by road and rail. It has its own unique attractions as well, foremost of which is the Royal Pavilion, that oriental fantasy near the seafront, built in the early years of the 19th century by George III's flamboyant eldest son, the Prince Regent, later George IV.

George first visited Brighton in 1783, and down the years became more and more attached to the place, using it as an informal retreat from the stifling atmosphere of the court in London. His contribution to the town is summed up by a delightful painting by Rex Whistler in the Royal Pavilion. Called *The Prince Regent Awakening the Spirit of Brighton*, it shows the almost-naked prince, with leering countenance, lifting the veil from a sleeping girl. Brighton has never lost the air of raffishness conveyed so well by this picture.

The most spectacular of recent innovations is the giant marina, below the cliffs at the eastern end of Brighton. Opened in 1978, it is Europe's largest man-made yacht harbour, with moorings for more than 2,000 boats. The marina is a centre for sea angling, either from the breakwaters or from charter boats. There are plans for a health and sports centre with a water theme park, a hotel, apartments, restaurants, shops and a supermarket.

The ideal way to visit the marina is by Volk's Electric Railway, which rattles along the front from a terminus near the Palace Pier. Magnus Volk drove his first car on the line in 1883, making it the oldest electric seafront railway in Britain.

Volk's railway runs beside the elegant cast-iron columns of Madeira Drive, the finishing line of Brighton's best-known annual contests, all of which start from London – the Historic Commercial Vehicle Run in May, the Stock Exchange Walk in June, and the Veteran Car Run in November. In Madeira Drive are the Aquarium and

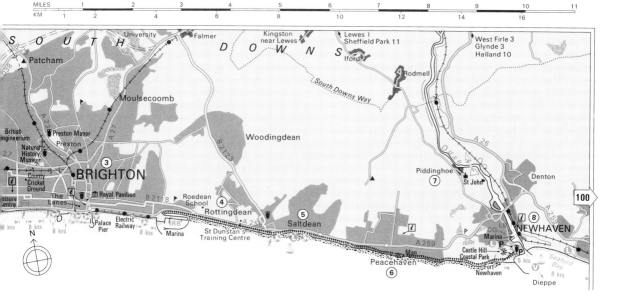

Dolphinarium, together with the 'Pirates' Deep' children's adventure playground.

Brighton's other attractions include the Palace Pier, the shops of The Lanes, Art Gallery and Museum, near the Pavilion; the Booth Museum of Natural History; and Preston Manor, whose furniture and decorations have remained unchanged since before the First World War.

The beach at both Brighton and Hove

THE LANES *Brighton's narrow maze of twisting alleyways is a shoppers' paradise, particularly for collectors of antiques.*

consists of a broad shingle bank, leading down to sand. Swimming is safe, and lifeguards patrol every day during summer. There are no slipways, but boats small enough to be manhandled can be launched over the beach.

④ ROTTINGDEAN

Between the eastern end of Brighton and Rottingdean is an open stretch of downland, where the coast road skirts the cliff edge, giving wide views over the Channel. On the hill above the road are the massive buildings of two schools – Roedean girls' school, built mainly in the 1890s, and St Dunstan's Training Centre for the Blind, a yellow-brick building of the 1930s.

Rottingdean has a small seafront, with a sea-wall promenade leading to Brighton in one direction and to Saltdean in the other. The beach is rocky and uninviting. Old Rottingdean runs inland, along a downland valley. Its narrow street of old flint-built houses opens out into a green beside a large village pond.

In the later years of the 19th century Rottingdean had famous artistic and literary associations. The Pre-Raphaelite artist Sir Edward Burne-Jones lived there towards the end of his life, and Rudyard Kipling spent

PALACE OF FUN *Since 1901, Brighton's Palace Pier has carried every type of seaside amusement on its iron legs. It still has many of the mechanical slot machines that delighted the Edwardians.*

FLOWERS OF THE CLIFFTOP

A plant that originally escaped from gardens, hoary stock is now well established on the south coast. Its flowers smell of cloves and attract butterflies. Round-headed rampion is also common in places along the chalky coastal grasslands between Seaford and Beachy Head.

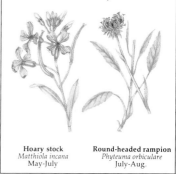

Hoary stock	**Round-headed rampion**
Matthiola incana	*Phyteuma orbiculare*
May-July	July-Aug.

five years there. The Downs round Rottingdean inspired Kipling's poem *Sussex*, which sums up their special qualities in a single line – 'Our blunt, bow-headed, whale-backed Downs.' Kipling relics are on view at Rottingdean's small museum, The Grange, which also has a collection of antique toys. The house was built as a vicarage in the 18th century and was remodelled by Sir Edwin Lutyens in 1919.

⑤ SALTDEAN

Residential estates, mainly built between the wars, are grouped round Saltdean's oval recreation ground on the north side of the coast road. From the car park by the recreation ground a subway leads under the road to a broad concrete promenade. Below the promenade, the beach is mainly rocky but has patches of sand. Powerboats are prohibited, but there is a ramp for small boats, which have to be manhandled through the subway.

⑥ PEACEHAVEN

In 1915 Charles Neville, a wealthy businessman, bought 650 acres on top of the cliffs and planned to build a town there, to be called Anzac-on-Sea, probably because Australian and New Zealand troops were stationed near by. Plots were offered at £50, £75 or £100, depending on their nearness to the sea. Building began immediately the war was over, and the occasion was commemorated by altering the proposed name of Anzac-on-Sea to Peacehaven. The grid pattern of streets designed by Charles

97

'DOCTOR BRIGHTON' – WHERE ROYALTY MADE THE SEASIDE FASHIONABLE

The English invented seaside holidays in the late 17th century, when 'taking the waters' was extended to include bathing in and drinking seawater. In 1750 a Dr Russel published a book extolling the benefits of sea-bathing at Brighthelmstone, as Brighton was then called; he claimed it was an excellent treatment for glandular diseases, so earning the town its contemporary nickname of 'Doctor Brighton'.

Dr Russel's treatment proved immensely popular, but it was not until 1783 that it attracted the attention of royalty – in the handsome shape of the young Prince of Wales, later Prince Regent and George IV, who was suffering from a glandular swelling in the neck. He liked the place so much that he decided to live there, first in a small rented farmhouse but later in the Royal Pavilion, built by Henry Holland and then turned into a fantastic extravaganza by John Nash.

George IV's successors did not share his enthusiasm for the Royal Pavilion, and in 1850 Queen Victoria sold it to the town. It was a 'white elephant' purchase and stood empty until after the Second World War, when it was restored to its former glory. But by 1850 Brighton no longer needed royal patronage, for the coming of the railway in 1841 had made the town a favourite spot for day trippers and quickly earned it the nickname 'London-by-the-Sea'. And before the 20th century was a few years old, intrepid motorists were clanking down the Brighton road.

DOCTOR OF ENTERPRISE *Dr Richard Russel was living in Lewes when he recommended seawater as a cure for many ills. This proved so profitable that he was able to build a house in Brighton, on the site where the Royal Albion Hotel stands today.*

PRINCE OF FASHION *Society idolised the Prince Regent, who entertained lavishly at the Royal Pavilion and was noted for his extravagance. But after becoming George IV he was criticised and ridiculed even by his friends, and died an unloved king.*

BRIGHTON BELLES *As fashion took to the seaside, photographers helped bathing belles to show off their latest daring costumes – many of which never got wet.*

LEGACY IN STONE *Regency Square is among the many elegant terraces that rose in Brighton as wealthy aristocrats, following the example set by the Prince Regent, moved to the seaside for their health and recreation and gave the town its distinctive seafront.*

FANTASY PALACE *The Royal Pavilion began as a modest mansion designed by Henry Holland, but the Prince's later obsession with oriental art led to the ornate building which John Nash completed in 1822.*

DADDY-LONG-LEGS *The Brighton and Rottingdean Seashore Railway was built by Magnus Volk in 1896, and became known as 'Daddy-long-legs'. The double-decker car, powered by an overhead electric cable, was mounted on stilts 24 ft high and ran on an underwater track. The railway was subject to frequent breakdowns and never became popular. It was discontinued after four years.*

HOLIDAY SOUVENIR *Victorian souvenirs of a seaside holiday, such as this plate of 1910, are now much sought after by collectors.*

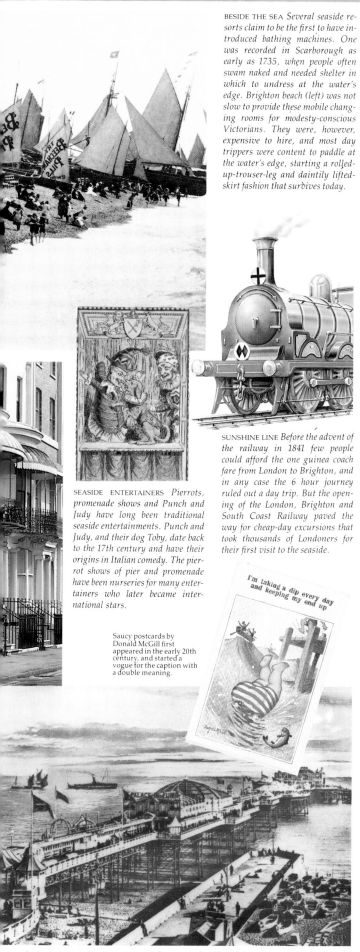

BESIDE THE SEA *Several seaside resorts claim to be the first to have introduced bathing machines. One was recorded in Scarborough as early as 1735, when people often swam naked and needed shelter in which to undress at the water's edge. Brighton beach (left) was not slow to provide these mobile changing rooms for modesty-conscious Victorians. They were, however, expensive to hire, and most day trippers were content to paddle at the water's edge, starting a rolled-up-trouser-leg and daintily lifted-skirt fashion that survives today.*

SEASIDE ENTERTAINERS *Pierrots, promenade shows and Punch and Judy have long been traditional seaside entertainments. Punch and Judy, and their dog Toby, date back to the 17th century and have their origins in Italian comedy. The pierrot shows of pier and promenade have been nurseries for many entertainers who later became international stars.*

SUNSHINE LINE *Before the advent of the railway in 1841 few people could afford the one guinea coach fare from London to Brighton, and in any case the 6 hour journey ruled out a day trip. But the opening of the London, Brighton and South Coast Railway paved the way for cheap-day excursions that took thousands of Londoners for their first visit to the seaside.*

Saucy postcards by Donald McGill first appeared in the early 20th century, and started a vogue for the caption with a double meaning.

I'm taking a dip every day and keeping my end up

'THE FINEST PIER IN THE WORLD' *Few argued with Brighton's proud boast when its Palace Pier was opened in 1899. It offered everything its Victorian visitors desired, on 1,760 ft of promenade deck, with ornate domes and glass-covered sun verandas.*

Neville was preserved in the bungalow development that is seen today.

Peacehaven's promenade is still largely an unmade-up road, running along the top of the cliffs. Halfway along it is a monument to George V, built on the Greenwich Meridian and inscribed with the distances to the major towns of the British Empire. There are steps leading down the cliffs to the beach at two points along the promenade, but it is a long climb.

⑦ PIDDINGHOE

This little village tucked away on the banks of the Sussex Ouse is a refreshing survival so near the sprawling estates of Saltdean and Peacehaven. St John's Church, perched up above the river, has a round Norman tower, topped by a glittering weather-vane in the form of a fish; Rudyard Kipling called it a 'begilded dolphin', but knowledgeable local anglers insist it is a sea trout. Flint-walled cottages and small boats aground in the mud complete the illusion of a country village miles from anywhere.

⑧ NEWHAVEN

For some reason, Newhaven has never expanded like Southampton, Dover and other cross-Channel ports. Ships still berth in the Ouse, rather than in the harbour basin, though in recent years there has been an increase in commercial traffic. The Newhaven-Dieppe service started with paddle-steamers in 1847, and has been going ever since. Until the 16th century there was no harbour at Newhaven, because the Ouse reached the sea at Seaford; but a great storm in 1579 diverted the river, and the 'New Haven' was the result.

Newhaven's commercial activities take place mainly along the east bank of the river; the marina, and the small sandy beach protected by the harbour breakwater, are on the western bank. The road on the western side leads up to Fort Newhaven. The fort was built in the 1860s, as one of 72 coastal forts built by Lord Palmerston as a defence against attacks by the French, and was garrisoned until 1956. It is sited on a headland that gave an excellent field of fire across Newhaven harbour and Seaford Bay. The fort consists of earthworks and artillery emplacements protecting, on the seaward side, old magazines, barrack rooms and a central parade ground.

A bridge leads across the moat to the 40 acre Castle Hill Coastal Park. The hill rises 190 ft above the mouth of the River Ouse and provides panoramic views across Seaford Bay, the Ouse Valley and the South Downs.

Breezy chalk clifftops that sweep towards Beachy Head

Between Brighton and Eastbourne the South Downs of Sussex meet the sea in a series of spectacular coastal features. Chalk cliffs rising east of Brighton lead to the bastion of Seaford Head, beyond which the scalloped white wall of the Seven Sisters culminates in the colossal rampart of Beachy Head. Two rivers – the Ouse, with its busy harbour of Newhaven, and the meandering Cuckmere – cut deeply into the chalk escarpment.

① SEAFORD
Now a popular resort, Seaford was the port of Lewes before a storm in 1579 diverted the course of the Ouse to Newhaven. Its seafront still has large undeveloped open spaces – not surprisingly, perhaps, in view of the tons of water and shingle that are hurled over the sea-wall by westerly gales, and which make repairing the town's sea defences an endless task.

The beach consists of shingle, protected by massive wooden groynes. Because it shelves quite steeply, at high tide it is a beach for strong swimmers only. Volunteer lifeguards patrol the beach at weekends during the summer. There is no proper ramp, but boats can be manhandled over the shingle and launched at any state of the tide.

On the front is Martello tower No. 74, the westernmost of a chain that extends round England's south-east and east coasts. It houses a small local-history museum.

② SEAFORD HEAD NATURE RESERVE
Though only half the height of Beachy Head, Seaford Head is nevertheless a formidable chalk bastion, towering 282 ft above sea level. Its outer edge, extending round to Cuckmere Haven and including part of the Cuckmere Valley, is a nature reserve covering more than 300 acres. The reserve can be reached either on foot from Seaford, or by car from Chyngton Road along the north side of the golf course; the road ends at a large car park on top of the headland, with fine views.

From the car park, paths radiate out into different parts of the reserve. The classic view of the Seven Sisters is from the path that leads to Hope Gap: the names of the Sisters (there are, in fact, eight) are, from west to east: Haven Brow (at 253 ft, the highest), Short Brow, Rough Brow, Brass Point, Flagstaff Point, Flat Hill, Baily's Hill, and Went Hill Brow (the lowest, at 146 ft). In autumn, Hope Gap is noisy with the cries of migrant birds, which land to rest and feed on the berries of shrubs before continuing their southward journey. Willow warblers, blackcaps and redstarts are common visitors; rarer species include hoopoes and ortolan buntings.

It is possible to walk along the foreshore below the cliffs, but there are dangers of rockfalls, and of being cut off by the incoming tide. The rock pools are rich in seaweed, and fulmars can sometimes be seen gliding by the cliffs.

③ CUCKMERE HAVEN
An important 'gap' used by 18th-century smugglers for their cargoes of brandy, lace and other contraband, Cuckmere Haven is now an oasis of tranquillity. The main road is 1 mile inland, and the only way to the beach is by a footpath along the valley.

The Cuckmere river makes a series of enormous loops through water-meadows before reaching the stone-scattered foreshore. The large car park near Exceat Bridge also serves the Seven Sisters Country Park.

④ SEVEN SISTERS COUNTRY PARK
Owned by the East Sussex County Council, this beautiful stretch of countryside covers almost 700 acres of the Cuckmere Valley and the Seven Sisters cliffs, and forms part of the Sussex Heritage Coast, which runs from Seaford to Eastbourne. On its western edge it adjoins the Seaford Head Nature Reserve, along the line of the Cuckmere; its north side is bounded by the main coast road; and to the south it takes in about half of the Seven Sisters cliffs.

The park's varied landscapes include bare chalk, shingle, salt-marsh, downland and scrub, with a variety of plant and animal life. On the north side of the road at Exceat a magnificent group of flint-walled Sussex barns, with sweeping tiled roofs, has been turned into an interpretative centre and administrative buildings. A permanent exhibition, 'The Living World', includes a wide selection of native and foreign insects, and a display of seashore life.

Canoes and small dinghies are allowed on the Cuckmere – there is access from the car

BARRING THE DOOR AGAINST 'OLD BONEY'

When Europe shuddered under the attack by Napoleon Bonaparte in the early 19th century the ripples spread across the English Channel. For the first time in eight centuries England faced the threat of invasion. Hastily a string of fortress towers was built along the east and south-east coasts; looking like upturned buckets, the towers were simple and robust, being based on the design of a fort at Mortella in Corsica which had stood up to heavy bombardment from a British force. Napoleon's invasion never materialised, and the towers had little military significance until 1940, when some were used as observation posts. Originally 103 Martello towers, as they became known, stretched from Seaford in Sussex to Aldeburgh in Suffolk. Some 45 still stand; many are in ruins, but some have been restored as museums, such as the Wish Tower at Eastbourne, or as houses.

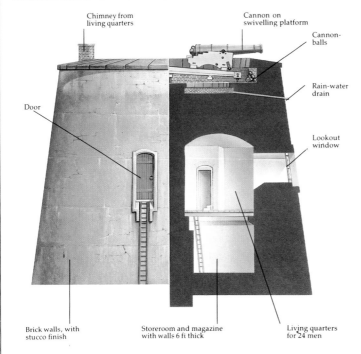

Chimney from living quarters

Cannon on swivelling platform

Cannonballs

Rain-water drain

Door

Lookout window

Brick walls, with stucco finish

Storeroom and magazine with walls 6 ft thick

Living quarters for 24 men

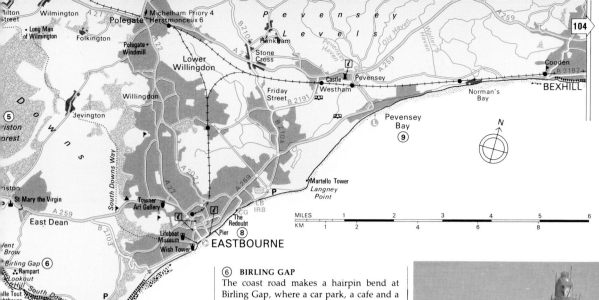

⑦ BEACHY HEAD

park – and coarse fishing is available free of charge. There are two park trails from the park centre, one 3 miles, the other 1½ miles long.

The 80 mile long-distance footpath known as the South Downs Way runs down the Cuckmere Valley, then turns east along the cliffs to end at Eastbourne.

⑤ FRISTON FOREST

For 2 miles between the River Cuckmere and the village of Friston the coast road runs between rolling downland to the south and the shadowy gloom of Friston Forest to the north. Occupying nearly 2,000 acres, the forest is leased to the Forestry Commission, whose aim is to provide a cover of beech and other broadleaved trees.

A waymarked forest walk of 2¾ miles leads from the car park through mixed conifers and beech trees, with fine views opening northwards along the valley called Charleston Bottom. At the eastern end of the forest, Friston's church of St Mary looks out over a reed-fringed pond. A lane beside the church leads down towards Crowlink, where the National Trust owns 632 acres of land, linked at its southern end with the Seven Sisters Country Park. The car park commands wide downland views.

⑥ BIRLING GAP

The coast road makes a hairpin bend at Birling Gap, where a car park, a cafe and a row of cottages perch on the edge of a 30 ft cliff. Fishing boats are winched up the near-vertical cliff from the shingle beach below, which is reached down steep wooden steps. Erosion is a problem, and the line of cottages is steadily shortening as the cliffs beneath them fall away.

Much of the land west and east of Birling Gap belongs to the National Trust. On the side of Lookout Hill, to the east, there is an Iron Age earth rampart.

A mile inland, the village of Eastdean nestles in a fold of the downs, its flint-walled cottages and ancient Tiger Inn overlooking a broad triangular green. The village was once a centre for smugglers, who landed their contraband at the secluded Birling Gap and used the inn as a meeting place. The 3 ft thick walls of the church's Norman tower gave refuge to villagers in earlier times.

⑦ BEACHY HEAD

Rising sheer from the rocky foreshore to a height of 534 ft, Beachy Head is indeed a 'beautiful headland' – the meaning of the Norman French *Beau Chef* from which the name is derived. The greensward on the clifftop is broad enough not to seem crowded even in summer, when the car parks are full. On a clear day the view takes in Dungeness in the east and the Isle of Wight in the west.

A small natural history centre, open during weekend afternoons in summer, in a cottage near the bus park, sells a guide to a

HEADY HEIGHTS *At Beachy Head the South Downs end dramatically with a 534 ft sheer drop, dwarfing the 142 ft lighthouse below.*

clifftop nature trail of about a mile; but this is a walk only for those with a head for heights, since much of the cliff edge is unfenced. Sea-lavender and samphire grow beside the trail, while herring gulls, jackdaws and rock pipits nest and breed on the ledges of the cliffs.

The red-and-white lighthouse at the foot of the headland is 142 ft high and throws its light for 16 miles. The base of an earlier lighthouse, built in 1834 and known as the Belle Tout, stands on the clifftop 1½ miles to the west.

⑧ EASTBOURNE

Striking an agreeable compromise between brashness and gentility, Eastbourne has a fine, long seafront, 3 miles from end to end; a lively pier with a cheerful turquoise-roofed bandstand near by, and plenty of quietly dignified Victorian houses, hotels and public buildings. The town owes its rise to prominence to the 7th Duke of Devonshire, who developed the coastal area from about 1850 onwards.

The beach is mainly shingle, leading down to sand at low tide, and divided by frequent wooden groynes. The main bathing beach, patrolled by lifeguards in summer, is between the bandstand and the Wish Tower gardens, named after the Martello tower which stands above them. The tower (No. 73) houses a museum telling the story of Napoleon's threats of invasion and the measures taken against them; its unusual name comes from the Saxon *wisc*, meaning a 'marshy place'.

Beside the Wish Tower is a lifeboat museum in the former lifeboat house, which was built in 1898 in memory of William Terriss, an actor who was murdered outside a London theatre.

Though there are no ramps along the seafront, Eastbourne is a sailing centre, with

SEVEN SISTERS *The white-faced daughters of the South Downs rise to more than 500 ft in places, and are divided by dells that were ancient river valleys when the downs extended further seaward.*

MARTIAL MUSIC FOR A DAY BY THE SEA

The bandstand clock stands at three, and holidaymakers relax to the music of a military band on Eastbourne's Grand Parade. The arena seats 3,500 people, and bands play daily in spring, summer and early autumn on the bandstand which is part of a wide, three-tiered promenade stretching for 3 miles along the seafront. Each Monday the 'band of the week' marches through the town.

its three sailing clubs and facilities concentrated at the eastern end, past the Napoleonic fortress known as The Redoubt. A rough road leads from the roundabout at the end of Royal Parade towards Langney Point, where a hand-operated public winch can be used to drag boats up the shingle. At Langney Point there is extensive parking along the shingle bank above the beach. This is the informal end of Eastbourne, with old

boats drawn up above tide level, and yet another Martello tower, used as a coast-guard lookout.

Inland, Eastbourne spreads for 5 miles along the eastern edge of the downs as far as Polegate. Most of the town's fine public gardens lie in this direction, as does the Towner Art Gallery, housed in an 18th-century manor house, which has a good collection of maritime pictures.

⑨ **PEVENSEY BAY**
When William the Conqueror landed in England in 1066, he came ashore somewhere near Pevensey. But the exact site will never be known, for the coastline has altered down the centuries and in William's time it was probably a good deal further inland than it is today.

At Pevensey Bay a modern development of chalets and small houses has sprung up, running 2 miles east to Norman's Bay along a partly surfaced road. Small boats can be manhandled over the beach anywhere that the sea can be reached between the houses, and there is direct access to the beach from the car park in the village.

A mile inland is old Pevensey, a picturesque village built in the shadow of its magnificent castle and a place that evokes two vanished ages. The outer castle walls are those of the Roman fortress of Anderida, one of the Forts of the Saxon Shore built at the end of the 3rd century to keep out Saxon invaders. Inside the castle are the moat, towers and keep of a medieval castle, begun soon after the Conquest by Robert of Mortain, William's half-brother, and garrisoned until the 14th century. When the castle was built the sea surrounded it on three sides, and it commanded the entrance to a harbour. The castle is open daily in summer; the Roman fort is open at all times.

LOCAL INFORMATION

Tourist information Seaford 897426; Eastbourne 27474; (Pevensey) Eastbourne 761444 (summer).

HM Coastguard Shoreham-by-Sea 2226, Dover 210008 for information, 999 in emergency (ask for coastguard).

Weather Brighton 8091.

Local radio BBC Radio Sussex, 202 m, 1485 kHz; 95.3 MHz; IBA Southern Sound, 225 m, 1332 kHz; 103.4 MHz.

PLACES TO SEE INLAND

Alfriston, 4 miles NE of Seaford. Clergy House (NT), medieval thatched priest's house, daily in summer;

Drusillas Zoo Park, wildlife, craft workshops, wine cellars and cider museum, miniature railway, daily March to November, winter weekends only.

Long Man of Wilmington, 6 miles NE of Seaford. Chalk figure.

Michelham Priory, 9 miles NW of Eastbourne. 13th-century moated Augustinian priory with Tudor additions, forge and wheelwright's shop. Daily in summer.

Polegate Windmill, 5 miles NW of Eastbourne. Tower mill and windmill museum. Some afternoons in summer.

Royal Greenwich Observatory, near Herstmonceux, 12 miles N of Eastbourne, on A271, via A295. Daily Easter to end September.

The pebbly shore from which William turned inland to conquer

At the centre of this stretch of coast is Hastings, where William the Conqueror turned inland to defeat Harold and his Saxon army, and which in later centuries was one of the most powerful of the Cinque Ports. Reminders of the town's history exist happily along with the dignified residential squares of Victorian times and the holiday amusements of the present day. Only a few miles away are quieter pleasures at Bexhill and Winchelsea.

① BEXHILL

Bexhill's career as a resort began later than most when, in the 1880s, Lord De La Warr built Victorian terrace houses on land he owned between old Bexhill and the sea. Its chief feature is the spectacular De La Warr Pavilion, built in 1935, Bexhill's answer to the usual seaside pier. Its long, low lines and glassed-in staircase dominate the seafront area, and it caters for all kinds of functions, from plays and concerts to exhibitions and conferences.

Old Bexhill is a short way inland, north of the railway at the top of Upper Sea Road. St Peter's Church has a sturdy Norman tower, and is surrounded by weather-boarded houses. Near by are the Manor Gardens, where open-air productions of Shakespeare are presented.

② GALLEY HILL

At its eastern end, Bexhill's seafront road ends at this clifftop viewpoint, with limited parking, giving superb views, straight out to sea, west towards the Bexhill seafront, and east towards the white bulk of the Marine Court flats in St Leonards. From the car park it is only a short walk down the hill to a secluded shingle beach at Glyne Gap.

③ BULVERHYTHE

Bulverhythe's long shingle beach, old fishing boats and rows of beach huts can be reached from the A259, either down Bridge Way and across a railway footbridge, where parking is very limited, or down Cinque Ports Way, where the road swings under the railway, and parking is easier.

The Bo-Peep public house by the main road owes its name to the nursery rhyme which is said to have been written for the landlord's daughter in the 18th century. Bulverhythe was a favourite place for smugglers to land their contraband – the 'sheep' of the rhyme are the smugglers, and the 'tails' their casks of French brandy.

At very low tides, the outline of the Dutch merchantman *Amsterdam*, wrecked in 1748, can sometimes be made out.

④ ST LEONARDS

Though it is now joined to Hastings, St Leonards began life as a separate resort. It was laid out in 1828 by the architect James Burton and his son Decimus round a little valley which ran down to the seashore. Burton's scheme included such strangely named places as Mercatoria (the market area) and Lavatoria Square (where the washerwomen lived). The valley is now a superb public garden, and a good deal of the Burtons' building survives, including the Royal Victoria Hotel.

The most prominent feature of St Leonards is the huge white bulk of Marine Court, built in the 1930s to look like an ocean liner, with balcony sun-decks.

⑤ HASTINGS

Though Hastings gave its name to the battle of October 14, 1066, the Normans and Saxons in fact met in combat at Battle, 6 miles inland. William the Conqueror landed at Pevensey Bay along the coast to the west, marched to Hastings and then turned inland along the ridge that Harold was defending. Hastings ancient and modern meet at the 'Conqueror's Stone', a large rock by the entrance to the pier, on which according to legend William ate after landing in England.

When William landed, Hastings was already an important port, with its harbour at the east end of modern Hastings, where the fishermen still winch their boats ashore on the shingle, below the tall, black-painted net sheds. In the Middle Ages it was one of the most powerful towns of the federation known as the Cinque Ports, linked with Dover, Hythe, Romney and Sandwich, which provided most of the ships and men needed to defend the coast from attacks by the French.

Old Hastings lives on in the narrow, picturesque High Street, which runs up from the fishermen's harbour and looks as though it has hardly changed in 200 years or more. The Old Town is hemmed in on both sides by steep cliffs, each with a lift up to the top. On one side are the open spaces of East Hill, and opposite is West Hill, where William the Conqueror built a massive castle, of which fragments still survive. The soft sandstone is honeycombed with caves, including St Clement's Caves, said to have been used by smugglers in the 18th century for storing contraband.

The RNLI lifeboat house, near the net sheds by the ruined harbour arm, is open every day during the summer. There are still more than 40 fishing boats working out of Hastings, and a Victorian chapel among the net sheds and stalls selling fresh fish is now the Fishermen's Museum. The Old Town Hall, in High Street, has been turned into a well-laid-out local history museum.

The bustle of modern Hastings lies west of the castle, with its twin centres at the pier and the White Rock Pavilion. The joint beach of Hastings and St Leonards is about 3 miles long, and consists of shingle above high-water mark, leading down to sand scattered at low tide with rocks, sheltering rock pools

Net-drying huts at Hastings

FISHERMEN'S BEACH *Sturdy, high-sterned fishing boats rest on The Stade at Hastings, where for centuries fishermen have hauled their boats on to the shingle to unload their catches.*

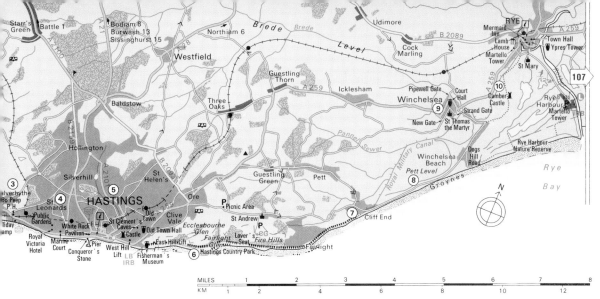

MILES 1 2 3 4 5 6 7 8
KM 1 2 4 6 8 10 12

full of marine life. Volunteer lifeguards patrol the beach at weekends and Bank Holidays in summer.

⑥ HASTINGS COUNTRY PARK

East of Hastings a 520 acre country park covers a stretch of magnificent sandstone cliff, deeply gouged by glens where streams lead down to the sea, with gorse-covered hillsides, woodlands and open grassland.

The park's main landmark is the Victorian church at Fairlight, below which is the main car park, with a visitors' centre. Leaflets describe five separate nature trails, the most picturesque of which runs for 2 miles through Fairlight Glen. The path runs through woodland, past huge boulders, down to Lovers' Seat, named in memory of a girl who waited for her sweetheart to be rowed ashore from his ship. Among the birds to be seen are woodpeckers, linnets, greenfinches and redpolls.

⑦ CLIFF END

From Fairlight the narrow road twists down to sea level at the eastern end of the sandstone cliffs. A road and a footpath lead to a shingle beach, with rows of wooden stakes to prevent erosion. Hundreds of wartime 'dragons' teeth' – angled concrete blocks to deter invaders from landing – are still ranged along the foreshore.

CASTLE ON THE MARSH *When it was built, Camber Castle stood by the sea. But land has been reclaimed and now it is a mile inland.*

⑧ PETT LEVEL

This flat expanse of water-meadows between the sea-wall and the Royal Military Canal is criss-crossed by watercourses and dotted with grazing sheep. Two ponds known as the Colonel Body Memorial Lakes are a popular spot for birdwatchers. The canal, which begins at Pett Level and runs northwards to Hythe, was dug in the early 1800s as part of the defensive system against Napoleon. The 'front line' of the system was the series of Martello towers along the coast.

The road runs below the concrete sea-wall, with frequent steps leading down to the beach, but no proper parking except beside the road. The beach is shingle, leading down to muddy sand.

⑨ WINCHELSEA

This pretty little town, perched up on a ridge overlooking Pett Level, always looks half asleep and three-quarters empty. Yet Winchelsea was once one of the chief ports of the south coast, ranking, along with Rye, as an 'Ancient Town' equal in status to the original five Cinque Ports. Old Winchelsea now lies under the waters of the Channel, somewhere out in Rye Bay. Its last remnants were finally engulfed in a great storm in 1287, and the town was rebuilt on a new site, which was then on the sea but is now more than a mile inland.

Throughout the Middle Ages Winchelsea was constantly attacked by the French, with results that can still be seen in the beautiful parish church of St Thomas the Martyr, which was largely destroyed in a French raid during the 15th century. The build-up of shingle along the shore gradually cut

Winchelsea off from the sea, and it declined into its present picturesque torpor.

Three of the medieval gateways still survive, as does the ancient Court Hall, now a small museum. Winchelsea Beach is a village of chalets, caravans and camp sites above a shingle foreshore.

⑩ CAMBER CASTLE

Accessible only on foot, this impressive ruin crouches low among the fields a mile from the sea. It was built during the 1530s, at a time when Henry VIII feared an invasion by the Roman Catholic powers, and is constructed to the plan of a Tudor rose, with rounded walls to deflect cannon-balls. It is being restored, and is not open to the public.

┌─────────────────────────────────┐
│   LOCAL INFORMATION   │

Tourist information Bexhill-on-Sea 212023; Hastings 424242; Rye 222293.

HM Coastguard Dover 210008 for information, 999 in emergency (ask for coastguard).

Weather Hastings 8091.

PLACES TO SEE INLAND

Bateman's House (NT), Burwash, 11 miles NW of Hastings, via A265. 17th-century house, home of Rudyard Kipling. Most days in summer.

Battle, 6 miles NW of Hastings. Abbey ruins, daily; local history museum, daily in summer.

Bodiam Castle (NT), 11 miles N of Hastings. Medieval castle. Daily in summer, weekdays in winter.

Great Dixter, Northiam, 11 miles N of Hastings. 15th-century house and gardens. Most afternoons in summer.

Sissinghurst Castle Garden (NT), 19 miles N of Hastings, via A229. Most afternoons and all day at weekends in summer.

Misty marshes, giant dunes and a shingle head where gulls breed

Strong currents sweep shingle eastwards to the promontory of Dungeness, where lighthouses, fishing boats, shanty huts and a pair of nuclear power stations form a striking blend of old and new. Behind is the mysterious flatland of Romney Marsh, which has been gradually reclaimed from the sea since Roman times. Today the marsh is a land of tiny villages set among water-meadows where the Romney Marsh sheep graze.

GATEWAY TO RYE *In the 14th century Rye was a walled town. One of its four medieval gates survives – the Landgate, or North Gate, which used to be defended by a portcullis.*

① RYE

Rye is everybody's idea of what a medieval town should be like. It is entered through a powerful stone gateway, and has narrow streets, many of them still cobbled, which rise to a fine old church on the summit of the ridge on which the town is built. With Winchelsea it was one of the two 'Ancient Towns' that in the Middle Ages were given equal status with the Cinque Ports. Rye never suffered Winchelsea's fate of complete decline, and nowadays is full of the tourist bustle that has passed Winchelsea by.

Originally the sea flowed right up to the south side of Rye, and though the sea is now 2 miles away, the town is still surro.nded by water on three of its sides – the River Rother to the east, the Tillingham to the west, and the Royal Military Canal to the south. During the Middle Ages Rye contributed five ships to the royal fleet, so earning the right to supply fish direct to the king's table. It still has a small fishing fleet, and there are usually several fishing boats moored in the Rother, downstream from the road to Folkestone.

Like the Cinque Ports, Rye was constantly under attack by the French, and in 1377 it was almost completely destroyed. A reminder of those early days still exists in the Gun Garden, where a battery of cannons once guarded the approaches to Rye. The three cannons that now point menacingly towards the distant sea were made as recently as 1980, to commemorate the 80th birthday of Queen Elizabeth the Queen Mother.

St Mary's Church still has much of its original Norman stonework, but it is visited mainly for its gilded 'quarterboys' – cherubs which strike the bells on the tower clock at the quarters. Inside the tower the mechanism of the clock, made in 1560, can be seen, and from the top of the tower there are wide views across Romney Marsh and out to sea.

Near the church is Lamb House, named after a former mayor of Rye, where the American author Henry James lived from 1897 to 1914. It is owned by the National Trust and open to the public. There is a small museum in the medieval Ypres Tower.

In the 18th century Rye was a great smuggling centre. The town's most famous pub, the Mermaid Inn, was one of the smugglers' favourite haunts. Many of the houses still have interconnecting attics, through which the smugglers could dodge from house to house to escape the excisemen.

② RYE HARBOUR

A mile and a half from Rye, and quite distinct from it, Rye Harbour is a small cluster of cottages at the mouth of the Rother. The river dries out almost completely at low water. There is a concrete slipway, but the tidal rise and fall is so great that at low tide there is a drop of 4 ft or more from the end of the slipway to the river level.

Most of the triangle bounded by the Rother, the sea, and the Rye-Winchelsea road has been designated a site of special scientific interest, covering 1,800 acres. An 880 acre strip inland from the foreshore is a local nature reserve, with hides from which visitors can watch the rich variety of birds, including terns, which flock to the water of a series of disused gravel pits. Footpaths lead across the reserve and along the coast to Winchelsea Beach.

③ CAMBER

The coast road zigzags past gravel pits and across golf links to this seaside village, which consists of chalets, caravan parks, and a large holiday camp. The vast sand dunes that loom over Camber have been so badly eroded in recent years that they are largely fenced off for replanting with marram grass and shrubs.

There are several car parks, from which footpaths lead across the dunes to the expanse of Camber Sands, where the sea goes out for half a mile at low tide. Swimming is safe, but bathers should beware of the danger of being cut off by the incoming tide.

④ BROOMHILL SANDS

East of Camber the road runs along the foreshore, where the dunes of Camber give way to the shingle of Dungeness. At Jury's Gut Sewer the road turns inland, skirting the Ministry of Defence firing range; red flags mean that firing is in progress, and access to the foreshore is then forbidden. Swimming gets progressively more dangerous towards Dungeness, since the currents grow stronger and the beach more steeply shelving.

⑤ LYDD

Lydd's magnificent church of All Saints is known as the 'Cathedral of Romney Marsh' because of its size and splendour. Its west tower, built in the 1440s, is 132 ft high, and the building is nearly 200 ft long – far too big for the village that clusters round it today, but a reminder of the medieval importance of Lydd.

From Lydd two roads, Galloways and Dengemarsh Road, lead to the Dungeness foreshore. Galloways is closed to traffic when firing is in progress, but Dengemarsh Road is outside the danger area. It runs for 3 miles across the shingle wasteland, ending at a beach popular with fishermen, and passing a windsurfing school on a disused gravel pit.

⑥ DUNGENESS

There has been a lighthouse on Dungeness since 1615, when it was stated that '1,000 persons perished there from want of light every year'. This windswept promontory, where the fog can fall in a thick blanket within minutes, where the shingle foreshore is constantly changing, and where even the toughest sea plants find it hard to survive, now has no fewer than three lighthouses, or what is left of them. Oldest is the base of Samuel Wyatt's lighthouse of 1792, now used as lighthouse-keepers' homes; and near by is the tall brick tower of 1904 which visitors can clamber up in summer to enjoy the spectacular views in every direction. A short distance away is the graceful modern structure, opened in 1961, which in clear weather throws its beam for 17 miles.

Looming in the background are the square blocks of the nuclear power stations, Dungeness 'A' and 'B'. The 'A' station is open to the public on Wednesdays; but visitors are advised to telephone in advance. Children under the age of 12 are not admitted.

Apart from lighthouses and power stations, Dungeness has a lifeboat, the terminus of the Romney, Hythe and Dymchurch Railway, and an assortment of hutments scattered about the shingle, some of them made from old railway carriages. Fish swim in shoals round Dungeness, and freshly caught fish are sold locally.

The Dungeness bird reserve, administered by the RSPB, covers about 1,200 acres of shingle between the Lydd firing ranges and the power station. It is reached down a gravel track which starts at Boulderwall

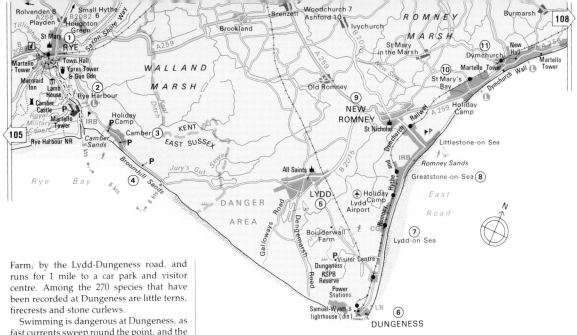

Farm, by the Lydd-Dungeness road, and runs for 1 mile to a car park and visitor centre. Among the 270 species that have been recorded at Dungeness are little terns, firecrests and stone curlews.

Swimming is dangerous at Dungeness, as fast currents sweep round the point, and the shingle slopes very steeply.

COMMON GULL *Despite its name, the common gull is in fact quite rare and Dungeness is its only regular breeding place in England.*

⑦ LYDD-ON-SEA
A single ribbon of bungalows, huts and seaside cottages lies between the Romney, Hythe and Dymchurch Railway on one side and, on the other, the shingle and sea. The beach is wide and sandy below the shingle, with the tide running out for half a mile.

⑧ GREATSTONE-ON-SEA
Even the local inhabitants are hard put to it to tell you where Greatstone-on-Sea ends and Littlestone-on-Sea begins. The two resorts form a straggling development which continues without a break from Lydd-on-Sea to Littlestone, where a row of tall Victorian houses faces a stretch of grass above the sea.

The names of Greatstone and Littlestone recall the days when New Romney had a harbour, which vessels entered between two different-sized spits of shingle. Today the shingle bank is continuous, and below it is the wide expanse of Romney Sands, where swimming is good and safe. Low tide exposes a sunken section of Mulberry Harbour – the harbour of concrete pontoons built for the invasion of Normandy in 1944 and towed across to France. There are a few car parks along the coast road, but elsewhere parking by the narrow road is difficult. There is a footpath along the sea-wall to St Mary's Bay.

⑨ NEW ROMNEY
The 'capital' of Romney Marsh, and one of the five original Cinque Ports, New Romney is a quiet little town with a superb church, originally Norman but greatly enlarged in the 14th century. Until the great storms at the end of the 13th century, the Rother

flowed into the sea at New Romney, and boats could moor below the churchyard wall. But the storms diverted the river mouth to Rye, and New Romney was cut off from the sea.

⑩ ST MARY'S BAY
Holiday cottages, amusements and a holiday camp occupy much of this village. At the south end the beach is shingle, leading down to pebbly sand; further north it is sandier, protected by many groynes.

⑪ DYMCHURCH
During the summer, this old Romney Marsh township is engulfed by amusement arcades and funfairs, which form a lively holiday contrast with the dignified main street and warlike Martello towers. One of these (No. 24, in the centre of Dymchurch) has been restored, with displays illustrating England's Napoleonic defences. The massively strong sea-wall, known as Dymchurch Wall, may date back to Roman times, and is highly necessary, as Dymchurch lies 7½ ft below high-tide level.

In past centuries the complex drainage system of Romney Marsh was run by the romantically named 'Lords of the Level', who operated from Dymchurch; their Court Room, in New Hall at the northern end of Dymchurch, can be visited. New Hall is now the office of the Romney Marsh Level Internal Drainage Board.

The beach is sand reached across shingle and swimming is safe except at the south end, where notices warn of a deep outfall.

LOCAL INFORMATION

Tourist information Rye 222293; Folkestone 58594.

HM Coastguard Dover 210008 for information, 999 in emergency (ask for coastguard).

Weather (Sussex) Hastings 8091; (Kent) Canterbury 8091.

PLACES TO SEE INLAND

Godington Park, Ashford, 14 miles N of New Romney, via A20. Jacobean house. Some afternoons in summer.

Hole Park, Rolvenden, 10 miles NW of Rye, via A28. Gardens. Occasional afternoons.

Smallhythe Place (NT), Small Hythe, 8 miles N of Rye. Timbered 15th-century house, home of Ellen Terry. Most afternoons in summer.

Woodchurch Windmill, 10 miles NW of New Romney, via B2067. Sun. afternoons in summer.

FACING THE FOE *A Martello tower at Dymchurch has been restored, complete with swivelling gun platform, to show how these sturdy 19th-century defences stood ready to repel Napoleon.*

Twin gateways to the Continent in England's walls of chalk

Almost 2,000 years ago the Romans chose Dover as the headquarters of their British fleet, and ever since the famous 'white cliffs' have been a landmark for ships sailing from the Continent. While Dover is a port which also has holiday facilities, Folkestone is primarily a prosperous resort, which also handles cross-Channel ferries. Between the two towns the cliffs form an unbroken wall of chalk, which continues east of Dover.

① HYTHE

One of the original Cinque Ports, Hythe can trace its history back to AD 732, when it was granted a charter by the Saxon King Ethelred. It was originally right on the sea, but down the centuries the shingle has built up, and the town centre is now half a mile or so inland. Hythe's chief feature is the Royal Military Canal, which separates old Hythe from the seaside resort part of the town. Tree-lined and quiet, it was constructed in the early 19th century as part of the sea defences against invasion from France; nowadays it is an ideal stretch of water in which to splash about in a small boat. At the west end of the town is the eastern terminus of the Romney, Hythe and Dymchurch Railway, a miniature railway using replicas of historic steam locomotives.

From the canal, streets of mainly 18th-century houses run up to the big medieval church of St Leonard, notable for its ambulatory or crypt stacked with some 2,000 skulls and 8,000 thigh-bones of people who lived between about 1200 and 1400. The bones were probably placed in the crypt when the graveyard was periodically cleared to make way for fresh burials. One grave in the churchyard is that of Lionel Lukin, who in 1786 converted a Northumberland fishing boat into the first shore-based lifeboat.

Across the canal is seaside Hythe, which lies between the Hythe military firing ranges at one end and the Imperial Hotel's golf course at the other. Steps lead down from the long, straight promenade to a shingle-and-sand beach, protected by massive groynes of concrete and timber. There are generally a few fishing boats drawn up on the shingle towards the Martello tower which marks the end of the rifle-ranges.

② SANDGATE

At Sandgate the low hills of East Kent crowd down to the sea, hardly leaving room for the main road and the rows of attractive old fishermen's and coastguards' cottages squeezed between the road and the sea.

The small esplanade is dominated by the battered remains of Sandgate Castle, one of the chain of castles built by Henry VIII in the 1530s against the threat of invasion. Visits to the castle can be arranged at the Sandgate Castle Gallery antique shop near by. A Martello tower stands inside the castle; and beside it is a reminder of more modern warfare – a Bofors gun, still used for training by the local Sea Cadets.

From Sandgate the main road to Folkestone turns inland, but a better alternative is to take the pretty undercliff toll road, which runs through pinewoods and shrubs, with grassy banks that overlook the sea and are a favourite place for picnics. The lodge at the Folkestone end still proclaims the tolls of half a century ago: '1d. for horse, mule or ass. Hand trucks, barrows, bicycles, 1d.'

③ FOLKESTONE

Folkestone is unusual among seaside resorts in having no proper seafront. What it has instead are the superb clifftop gardens known as The Leas, which run for more than a mile from central Folkestone almost to Sandgate. With wide lawns, luxuriant shrubs and colourful flower beds, they bring a Riviera touch to the Kentish coast.

Folkestone began to develop as a resort with the coming of the railways in the 1840s; before that it was hardly more than a fishing village clustered round the harbour. The old High Street, lined with ancient houses, is now pedestrianised, and runs steeply down to the harbour, where at low tide fishing boats lie at all angles stranded on the mud-flats. Cross-Channel ferries to Ostend, Boulogne and Calais load and unload from the stone pier, as the harbour proper is too small for modern vessels.

East of the harbour is Folkestone's main bathing beach, East Cliff Sands, crammed to bursting on fine summer afternoons. Swimming is safe, and lifeguards patrol throughout the summer. At high tide it is often necessary to leave the sand and take refuge on the concrete terrace above it. The sands are reached from the Stade, the narrow fish-market area by the harbour, which has very limited parking.

Near the centre of The Leas is a statue to Folkestone's most famous figure – William Harvey, discoverer of the circulation of the blood, who was born in Folkestone in 1578, and is shown holding a human heart.

At the opposite end of Folkestone from The Leas a huge stretch of open grassland, above East Cliff Sands, gives magnificent views out to sea. There stand three of the long line of more than 100 Martello towers built along the south-east and east coasts against the threat of French invasion in the early 19th century.

④ THE WARREN

This wilderness of chalk terraces covered with grass and undergrowth took its present shape as recently as 1915, when the latest in a series of landslips cascaded thousands of tons of chalk downhill for 300 yds, burying the railway line and hurling blocks of chalk far into the sea. It is now a favourite place for walkers, or for those who want to sun themselves in peace and quiet. The upper region of small combes is known as 'Little Switzerland'. The easiest access is from the car park above East Cliff Sands.

The beach below The Warren consists of shingle, with sand at low tide, protected by groynes, and can be reached only on foot, either from above or from East Cliff Sands.

⑤ CAPEL-LE-FERNE

At this point the Old Dover Road offers a quiet alternative to the crowded A20, running for 1 mile close to the cliff edge, and giving wide-ranging views of the crowded Channel shipping lanes. A steep footpath leads down from the garden of a cafe, over a footbridge across the railway and on to the beach, where a wide concrete 'apron' has

CHANNEL PORT *The causeway crossing Folkestone Harbour takes rail passengers to the cross-Channel ferries. After Dover, Folkestone is the busiest cross-Channel port on the south coast.*

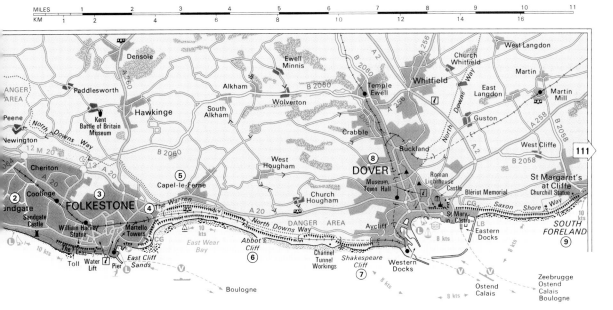

SYMBOLS IN CHALK *The white cliffs of Dover, facing the shortest Channel crossing, have long stirred the hearts of homecoming Englishmen.*

been constructed above the shingle. Allow half an hour to get down and 40 minutes to return to the top.

The walk along the clifftop forms part of the North Downs Way, the long-distance footpath running from Farnham in Surrey to Dover.

⑥ ABBOT'S CLIFF

A rough unmade road leads from the A20 to a clifftop on the edge of the army rifle-range, which occupies part of the heights towards Dover. Visitors are warned to keep out of the range area when red flags are flying. The views out to sea are breathtaking. On returning, beware the turn-out on to the A20, which is very narrow at this point.

⑦ SHAKESPEARE CLIFF

The most monumental of all Dover's 'white cliffs', this massive chalk headland, 300 ft high, towers over the western fringes of Dover. It was this cliff that Edgar described to his blind father Gloucester in Shakespeare's *King Lear*:

> '...how fearful
> And dizzy 'tis to cast one's eyes so low
> The crows and choughs that wing the
> midway air
> Show scarce so gross as beetles....'

The top of the cliff can be reached from Dover, along Snargate Street, past the foot of

the cliff and inland past the Aycliff housing estate. The road soon narrows to a lane, which ends after about a mile at the army's clifftop firing range.

Alternatively, motorists can park just before reaching the foot of the cliff and walk up it by a footpath, part of the North Downs Way. From the same starting point a path over a railway footbridge leads to the foreshore. The abandoned workings of the Channel Tunnel – a project begun in 1880 and revived at intervals – can be reached along the foreshore. This walk should be attempted only when the tide is ebbing, for when the tide comes in there is a danger of being cut off at the foot of the cliffs.

⑧ DOVER

For nearly 2,000 years Dover has been England's main cross-Channel port. The Romans made it the headquarters of their northern fleet, the Classis Britannica; in the Middle Ages it became a Cinque Port, and one of the most powerful castles in the country was built to guard the 'Gateway to England'; during two world wars it was shelled and bombed from across the Channel; and nowadays hardly 5 minutes goes by without a cross-Channel ferry leaving with its load of passengers and container lorries, or a hovercraft roaring out to sea.

Dover has moved with the times in the way it caters for leisure enjoyment as well as commercial interests. The huge outer harbour, which was built at the beginning of the century to take the battleships and cruisers of the Grand Fleet, is now given over in summer to windsurfers and dinghies, while swimmers splash about in the shallows.

The town runs inland up the valley of the Dour, the river from which Dover gets its name. From whichever direction Dover is approached, the castle looms over the town, foursquare and forbidding. It is full of weapons and historic relics, and beside the steep road that leads up to the castle's car park is the ornate gun nicknamed 'Queen Elizabeth's Pocket Pistol', which was given to Elizabeth I by the Dutch. On top of the green mound beside the castle, and adjoining the Saxon church of St Mary-in-Castro, is Dover's most fascinating ruin, the octagonal lower stage of the Roman *pharos*, or lighthouse, built soon after the Roman conquest in the 1st century AD. Its height of 40 ft makes it the tallest surviving Roman structure in Britain.

Swimming from the harbour's sand-and-shingle beach is safe close inshore, but lifeguards patrol regularly only on Sundays. On the promenade are statues of Capt.

Matthew Webb, who in 1875 became the first man to swim the Channel, and of Charles Stewart Rolls, of Rolls-Royce fame, who in 1910 flew the Channel both ways in a single flight. Louis Blériot, who the previous year had been the first man to fly the Channel in any direction, has his own memorial at Dover – a granite outline of an aircraft, in a clearing behind the castle, cut in the turf on the spot where he landed.

CENTURIES APART *About nine centuries separate Dover's St Mary-in-Castro Church from the nearby Roman lighthouse.*

⑨ SOUTH FORELAND

The squat white pepper-pot of the South Foreland lighthouse, operated automatically and not open to the public, can be reached from St Margaret's at Cliffe, down Lighthouse Road. The clifftop walk from Dover forms part of the long-distance Saxon Shore Way, the course of which is marked by a depiction of a horned Viking helmet.

LOCAL INFORMATION

Tourist information Folkestone 58594. Dover 205108.

HM Coastguard Dover 210008 for information. 999 in emergency (ask for coastguard).

Weather Canterbury 8091.

Local radio BBC Radio Kent, 290 m, 1035 KHz, 96.7 MHz; IBA Invicta Sound, 97 0 MHz.

PLACES TO SEE INLAND

Kent Battle of Britain Museum, Hawkinge. 2½ miles N of Folkestone. Sun. and Bank Holidays in summer, some other afternoons July and Aug.

Lympne. 3 miles W of Hythe. Medieval castle, daily in summer. Port Lympne Wildlife Zoo Park. Mansion and Gardens, daily.

Sandling Park, near Hythe. Gardens. Sun. in May and June

Wye and Crundale Downs National Nature Reserve, Wye. 12 miles NW of Hythe

---

Bays where Roman and Viking invaders stormed ashore

When Julius Caesar landed on the coast near Deal in 55 BC, he came, he saw, but he did not conquer, as the Britons drove him off. Conquest was left to the Emperor Claudius, who invaded in AD 43, and almost certainly assembled his troops at Richborough, where the walls of a Roman fort still stand in monumental splendour. In today's more peaceful times, holidaymakers are the new invaders of this historic stretch of coast.

① RAMSGATE

The third member of the trio of Thanet coast resorts, Ramsgate achieves a middle way between the bright lights of Margate and the quiet of Broadstairs. Geographically, it is better placed than either, since it faces due south and gets all the sun that is going. The town is built symmetrically round the harbour, with graceful early 19th-century terraces on either side. In 1981, the harbour took on a new lease of life with the introduction of cross-Channel ferries to Dunkirk.

The harbour is one of the busiest on the south coast, and is especially attractive at night when lights twinkle from the rows of moored yachts in the inner marina. An obelisk on the East Pier commemorates George IV's landing at Ramsgate in 1822, since when the harbour has had the title of 'Royal Harbour'. The local council has marked out a Historic Harbour Trail, with no fewer than 36 points to look out for, from the modern lifeboat to the dry-dock of 1791, now being restored. Ramsgate Harbour's best known historical moment came in 1940, when 82,000 men evacuated from Dunkirk were landed there. A stained-glass window in the church of St George commemorates the event.

The main bathing beach is at Ramsgate Sands, north-east of the harbour. Swimming is safe except by the harbour wall, where the tide can produce dangerous currents. Lifeguards patrol every day throughout the summer. Boats can be launched from a ramp at the western end of the beach, reached by a narrow road from the end of the Royal Esplanade.

A small local museum in the public library, a model village on the clifftop promenade and a collection of historic cars in West Cliff Hall are open daily in summer. There is also a covered swimming pool.

② PEGWELL BAY

Seagoing craft ancient and modern meet in this sandy bay, which is fringed on the north side by low chalk cliffs leading round to Ramsgate. The world's first international hoverport was built there in 1968, and although flights to Calais have now been discontinued, there is still a maintenance department for hovercraft.

On a grassy slope above the hovercraft depot is the *Hugin*, a replica of a dragon-prowed Viking longship. In 1949 she was sailed across the Channel by a Danish crew to mark the 1,500th anniversary of the landing in Kent of Hengist and Horsa, the warrior leaders from Jutland. The traditional site of their landing was at Ebbsfleet, and they were followed 150 years later, in AD 597, by St Augustine, who landed there on his mission to convert the pagans of Kent to Christianity. St Augustine's Cross, put up in 1884, is just outside the village of Cliffs End, down Foads Lane off the main road.

③ RICHBOROUGH PORT

The three huge cooling towers of the Richborough power station are the chief landmark of the flat countryside between Sandwich and Thanet. There are guided tours of the power station on certain days in summer.

Across the road is Richborough Port, built during the First World War to ship men and munitions to France, and used again in the Second World War to construct part of the prefabricated Mulberry Harbour, towed across to Normandy after the D-Day landings.

④ RICHBOROUGH CASTLE

When the Romans conquered Britain in the 1st century AD, the Isle of Thanet, on which Margate, Broadstairs and Ramsgate now stand, was a real island, separated from the mainland by the mile-wide Wantsum Channel. To guard this important waterway the Romans built two forts – Rutupiae (Richborough) at the south-east end, and Regulbium (Reculver) to the north-west.

The last and most powerful castle was built in about AD 285 as one of the chain of fortresses – the Forts of the Saxon Shore – built to deter sea-raiders from across the North Sea. Of the huge square outer wall, almost two complete sides and part of a third survive, together with the base of turrets and bastions. Also visible are the foundations of an enormous triumphal arch built about 200 years earlier. This would have served as a constant reminder to the British of the distant might of Rome, and also been visible for miles out to sea as a landmark for mariners. The museum on the site contains a collection of pottery, building materials, coins, lamps and ornaments.

⑤ SANDWICH

The northernmost of the Cinque Ports, Sandwich is a delightful old town with a baffling medieval street plan of constant twists and turns, medieval gateways, and no fewer than three medieval churches. Though Sandwich is now almost 2 miles inland, the Stour is still navigable along a channel which winds for 5 miles or so to the open sea. In the Middle Ages Sandwich was as much a gateway to England as Dover, and kings, princes and merchants landed at its harbour. But its prosperity declined as the river silted up and ships became larger.

The entrance to the town is guarded by the twin-turreted Barbican Gate, built in 1539, which faces north across a narrow swing bridge over the Stour. Far older is the stone Fisher Gate, overlooking the Quay, built in 1384 at a time of savage raids on Sandwich by the French. In the bloodiest of these, which took place in 1457, 4,000 Frenchmen killed the Mayor and other leading citizens, and since then mayors of Sandwich have worn a black robe in memory of the slaughter.

Many Cinque Port treasures and other exhibits connected with the history of Sandwich are on show in the Guildhall Museum, in the town centre, which is open by appointment. On view in the Council Chamber and Court Room are the 16th-century Mayor's chair, an old jury box which can be folded away when not in use, portraits of notable people connected with Sandwich, and processional maces and halberds, and the 'Common Horn' used to announce royal

---

CABBAGE ON THE CLIFFS

Wild cabbage, the ancestor of garden cabbage, grows on chalk and limestone cliffs. Though it has fleshy leaves and no heart it was once sold as a vegetable in Dover market, but its bitter leaves needed boiling for a long time before they could be eaten.

Wild cabbage
Brassica oleracea
May-August

ST MARGARET'S BAY *From this sheltered cove, cross-Channel swimmers set out every year in the wake of Captain Webb who, in 1875, became the first man to swim the English Channel.*

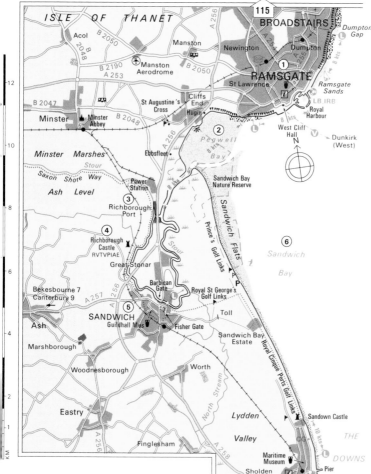

FAMOUS FIVE *A coat of arms at Deal Castle incorporates the lion-and-ship emblem of the privileged 13th-century Cinque Ports.*

tory. They include several examples of the tough Deal 'beach boats' which were designed for launching off the shingle beach to carry pilots, passengers and stores to vessels anchored in The Downs – the stretch of water between Deal and the Goodwins where sailing ships awaited favourable winds to take them down the Channel or up to the Thames Estuary. The Maritime Museum is open every afternoon in summer.

Deal Castle, built by Henry VIII in 1540 and shaped like a Tudor rose, was in former times the residence of the Captain of the Cinque Ports, and is still a powerful-looking fortress. It is open to the public daily. Near by is the old Time Ball Tower, from which ships at anchor in The Downs can check their chronometers. At 1 p.m. Greenwich Mean Time each day the black ball on top of the tower, connected electrically to Greenwich, drops down the central shaft. The tower is a museum of naval communication, telling the story of the building and of the naval signalling system.

At Deal's northern end are the ruins of Sandown Castle, of which only a buttress or two has survived 450 years of pounding by the sea.

POISED FOR ACTION *The Walmer lifeboat sits on its ramp ready to go to sea at a moment's notice to help any ship caught on the Goodwin Sands.*

⑧ WALMER CASTLE

This is the southernmost of three castles – the others are at Deal and Sandown – built in the 1530s by Henry VIII at a time of threatened invasion by the Roman Catholic powers. It is now the official residence of the Lord Warden of the Cinque Ports. When it was built the sea came right up to the walls of the castle; but the shingle built up and the castle is now some way back from the sea, almost hidden behind trees and a thick growth of ivy on the walls.

Walmer Castle saw no action until the Civil War in 1642, when it fell easily to the Parliamentarians. It was recaptured briefly in 1648 when a Kentish army rebelled against the rule of Parliament.

The castle and its gardens are open to the public daily except on Mondays. Inside, the stern military appearance gives way to an elegant 18th-century panelled interior, which has remained much as it was when

---

proclamations. History of another sort is in the dolls' houses and Noah's Arks of the Precinct Toy Collection in Harnet Street.

Sandwich added a word to the English language in the 18th century, when John Montagu, Earl of Sandwich, unwilling to drag himself away from the gambling table for long enough to eat a proper meal, asked for a slice of beef between pieces of bread.

⑥ SANDWICH BAY

North of Deal the shingle gives way to sand dunes, which provide the setting for three championship golf links: Royal Cinque Ports, Royal St George's, and Prince's. A toll road from Sandwich leads to a large car park by the Prince's clubhouse. From there it is possible to walk along the shingle foreshore to the Sandwich Bay Nature Reserve, administered by the Kent Trust for Nature Conservation, in conjunction with the National Trust and the RSPB.

The 700 acre reserve is the last untouched complex of beach and foreshore, together with a hinterland of dunes and salt-marsh, left in Kent. Plants that grow there include sea holly and marsh-orchids; and waders and wildfowl roost and feed in the estuary where the River Stour runs into Sandwich Bay.

There is safe swimming from the wide sands of Sandwich Flats.

⑦ DEAL

A plaque in Marine Road, just south of Deal Castle, proclaims that this was the point where Julius Caesar landed in Britain on August 25, 55 BC. As the line of the coast was very different 2,000 years ago, the information cannot be taken literally, but certainly the galleys would have grounded on sloping shingle similar to the present-day beach.

It was the shingle that saved Deal from becoming a bucket-and-spade resort in Vic-

torian times, as there is no sand to attract the holidaymaker with children. So Deal has remained much as it was in the 18th century, with hardly any Victorian seafront development.

The beach is steeply sloping, and is safe for swimmers close inshore, though children should always have an adult with them. A rescue boat patrols every day in summer, and red flags are flown from the pier when it is too rough to swim. The 1,000 ft long pier, which was opened in 1957, is popular with anglers. They catch a great variety of fish including cod, codling, whiting and flatfish.

In St George's Road is a small museum full of exhibits concerning Deal's maritime his-

---

William Pitt, who became Prime Minister in 1783, was Lord Warden in the 1790s. There are numerous portraits and relics of the Duke of Wellington, who was Lord Warden at the time of his death in the castle in 1852.

Walmer merges into Deal a short way south of Deal Castle; the two places now form a single continuous built-up area.

⑨ **KINGSDOWN**

Reached down a steep hill from Ringwould, the centre of this village consists of a cluster of old fishermen's cottages above a shingle beach, dotted here and there with boats and small huts. The celebrated 'white cliffs' begin at Kingsdown, at the end of Undercliffe Road. There are footpaths along the foreshore and up on to the cliffs; a notice board gives the firing times of the Marines rifle-range, and red flags fly when firing is in progress.

⑩ **ST MARGARET'S BAY**

Below the village of St Margaret's at Cliffe, a narrow road zigzags sharply down to the sea, past the holiday homes of St Margaret's Bay which are built on terraced lanes one above the other. The little cove of shingle and rocks, with towering chalk cliffs on either side, is the nearest point to France, about 21 miles away, and so it has become the traditional starting or finishing point for cross-Channel swimmers.

The beach is protected with groynes made of massive iron girders; swimming is safe close to the beach, except at high tide. At either end of the beach notices warn that the cliff face is unstable, and the foreshore below them should be avoided. There is a car park behind the beach, but the road is so twisting and narrow that in summer it is better to leave the car at the top of the hill and walk down.

The mild climate produces some spectacular near-tropical gardens, full of brilliant fuchsias and other shrubs and plants. One public garden, The Pines, contains a powerful bronze statue, 9 ft tall, of Sir Winston Churchill, made in 1972 by the sculptor Oscar Nemon.

Above the cliffs and reached down Granville Road north-east of the village is the tall granite obelisk of the Dover Patrol Memorial, commemorating men of the Dover Patrol who died in the two world wars while patrolling the Channel and watching out for enemy warships. The rolling heathland on top of the cliffs, known as The Leas, belongs to the National Trust.

There are good clifftop walks to Dover in one direction and Kingsdown in the other, though in the Kingsdown direction walkers have to cross the Royal Marines rifle-range, where access is forbidden when red flags are flying.

LOCAL INFORMATION

Tourist information Deal 361161; (Ramsgate) Thanet 591086.

HM Coastguard Dover 210008 for information, 999 in emergency (ask for coastguard).

Weather Hastings 8091, Canterbury 8091.

Local radio BBC Radio Kent, 290 m, 1035 kHz, 96.7 MHz.

PLACES TO SEE INLAND

Canterbury, 13 miles W of Sandwich. Cathedral, site of Becket's murder in 1170, daily; Museum of Canterbury's Heritage, in medieval poor priests' hospital, weekdays; Roman Pavement, mosaic floors in remains of Roman town house, weekdays; Royal Museum and Art Gallery, with Buffs Regimental Museum, weekdays; Westgate Museum of Arms and Armoury, in 14th-century gatehouse, weekdays.

Howletts Zoo Park, Bekesbourne, 10 miles W of Sandwich, off A257. Tigers, gorillas and other animals. Daily.

112

THE GOODWIN SANDS: EVER-HUNGRY DEVOURER OF SHIPS AND MEN

Four miles off Deal lies one of the world's greatest hazards to shipping – a sand-bar measuring 12 miles long and 5 miles wide at its widest point. Countless vessels have foundered on the treacherous shifting sands and been sucked down, never to be seen again, giving the Goodwin Sands the gruesome nickname of 'The Ship Swallower'.

The name Goodwin is thought to be derived from the Saxon Earl Godwin, father of King Harold. According to one account the sands are the remains of a strip of land called Lomea and owned by Earl Godwin, which was buried under the waves after a storm. There is no evidence, however, that such a land existed, for the Goodwins are all sand, 80 ft deep and resting on a chalk bed.

The hazard is made more difficult by the fact that the sands are constantly moving and changing their shape. Despite the presence of three Trinity House lightships and ten warning buoys, ships still run aground when the sands are covered at high tide, and break their backs as the tide falls. At low tide the Goodwins reveal part of their grim haul: the masts of two American ships, the *North Eastern Victory* and *Luray Victory*, which foundered in 1946, jut from the sand like the bones of a sea monster's victims. The crews of both vessels were rescued.

Between the Goodwin Sands and the shore is a safe channel called The Downs. It was once an anchorage, particularly for sailing ships waiting to move into the Thames. But the channel is narrowing; slowly the sands are shifting west, and may eventually join the mainland.

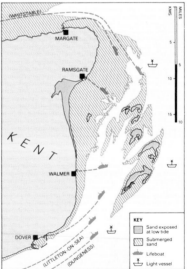

HELP AT HAND Despite modern aids such as radar and echo sounders, ships still founder on the Goodwins with frightening regularity, and no fewer then seven lifeboat stations are on call to go to their aid. Nowhere in the world is there such extensive lifeboat coverage for a single area. Each station is located so that any part of the sands can be reached as quickly as possible, for a ship on the Goodwins may sink and disappear within hours.

The first lifeboat to be stationed in the Goodwins area was sited at Ramsgate in 1852, followed by the Walmer lifeboat in 1857. By 1865 there were four lifeboats concentrated on 11 miles of coast, and more were added before the end of the century. The first of three lightships took station in 1795 at North Sand Head.

A LIGHT THAT FAILED *In November 1954 the South Goodwin lightship was driven from her moorings in a gale and capsized with the loss of her crew of seven. A bird-watcher aboard was saved by helicopter. By next morning the ship was half buried in the sand.*

THE GREAT STORM *In November 1703 the east coast of England was hit by the worst storm the country had ever known – and in The Downs channel a fleet of English men-o'-war caught the full force. Four ships were driven on to the Goodwins and 1,500 seamen died, including Admiral Beaumont. Along the rest of the coast the havoc continued, wrecking ships and harbours and carrying away the first Eddystone lighthouse.*

CALAMITY CORNER *When the French ship* **Agen**, *laden with mahogany, broke in two on the eastern edge of the Goodwins in 1952 she followed two earlier victims at the spot, which became known as 'Calamity Corner'.*

BACK FROM THE GRAVE *Sometimes the Goodwins give up their victims, but only for a short time. This German submarine, U-48, was sunk in 1917 and reappeared in 1921 and again in 1973.*

CRICKET MATCHES AND GHOST SHIPS

TIDE STOPS PLAY *In 1854 a Mr Thompson and a Mr Hammond hit on the bizarre idea of holding a cricket match on the Goodwin Sands. The two teams played on a stretch of flat sand at low tide, returning at sunset. Since then several cricket matches have been played on the sands, often between teams of the Royal Navy dressed in 19th-century costume.*

THE FIFTY-YEAR SHIP *On February 13, 1748 the three-masted schooner* Lady Lovibond *went aground on the sands, steered there deliberately, it is said, by the mate who had been a rival for the captain's wife. Exactly 50 years later the 'ghost ship' was seen by two other vessels, and she has been reported as appearing every 50 years since.*

Holiday playground on a coast that was once an island

In Roman times the Isle of Thanet was a real island, separated from the mainland by a mile-wide stretch of water, the Wantsum Channel. This channel silted up over the centuries, and today Thanet is an island only in name. Along its coastline the resorts of Margate, Broadstairs and Ramsgate unite to form a continuous holiday playground, providing bays and beaches that differ widely in character and amusements that cater for many tastes.

① HERNE BAY

Originally a fishing village, this quiet seaside town was laid out as a resort in the 1830s and has preserved its Victorian atmosphere. The main feature of the seafront is the 80 ft tall clock tower which dates from 1837. Herne Bay's pier was once the second longest in the country after Southend's, before it was severely damaged by storms in 1978 and demolished in 1979. The Pier Pavilion Leisure Centre, built in 1976 at the pier's landward end, is the focus of the town's holiday attractions. It replaced the Grand Pier Pavilion, built in 1910 but destroyed by fire in 1970.

Herne Bay's long straight foreshore is exposed to the full force of wind and tide, and the approaches to the beach from the promenade can be sealed by floodgates in severe storms. The best swimming is at the western end, between the Pier Pavilion and the stone jetty known as Hampton Pier, where the shingle leads down to sand with some mud holes. East of the pavilion the beach becomes more stony. Volunteer lifeguards sometimes patrol the beach. A stone slipway opposite William Street can be used for 2 hours either side of high water.

West of Hampton Pier the foreshore turns sharply south, forming a bay used by powerboats, which are launched from a slipway at the bottom of Swalecliff Avenue, within 3 hours of high water. Offshore is a water-ski channel, but elsewhere there is a speed limit of 8 knots within 500 yds of the high-water mark.

At the eastern end of the town the ground rises, with gently sloping grass banks giving way to steep muddy cliffs, and a pedestrian parade below.

② BISHOPSTONE GLEN

A small, overgrown ravine leads through yellow-brown clay cliffs to a shingle beach. The walk from Herne Bay to the glen along the foreshore is a muddy one; to avoid this, the glen can also be reached from Beltinge or Bishopstone by a footpath, which leads down to some wooden steps on to the beach.

③ RECULVER

Sharply etched against the sky, the twin towers of Reculver's ruined St Mary's Church are the principal landmark of the 10 mile stretch of coast between Herne Bay and Margate. In the 3rd century AD the Romans built the fortress of Regulbium to guard the northern end of the Wantsum Channel, which then separated the mainland of Kent from the Isle of Thanet. In AD 669 King Egbert of Kent founded a monastery and church inside the fort; the present towers date from a rebuilding in the 12th century.

By the early 19th century the sea had washed away half the Roman fort and threatened to undermine the church. Most of it was demolished, but the towers,

nicknamed the Two Sisters, had become so important as a landmark for sailors that they were restored by Trinity House, though without the spires that once made them even more conspicuous.

A small resort of caravan parks and amusement arcades has developed round the ancient ruins. Swimming is possible from the shingle beach round the sea-wall. Shellfish gathered from the foreshore must be boiled thoroughly before consumption.

From Reculver there are good walks westwards to Herne Bay, 3 miles along a clifftop footpath, and eastwards to Margate along the sea-wall.

SISTERS ON THE SHORE *For eight centuries the Two Sisters towers at Reculver have guided sailors in the Thames Estuary.*

④ BIRCHINGTON

Although it now forms the westernmost part of Margate, Birchington still has a recognisable identity as a separate village, grouped around its medieval parish church of All Saints. The Victorian artist Dante Gabriel Rossetti died at Birchington in 1882, and is buried in the churchyard.

At Birchington the shoreline takes on the pattern typical of the Isle of Thanet: low chalk cliffs, protected by a massive sea-wall and buttresses, lead down to seaweed-covered rocks separated by small sandy bays. Birchington has four of these bays, where swimming is safe provided the rocks are avoided. The largest and most popular is Minnis Bay, which has a small grassy area covered with beached sailing dinghies, and a slipway that can be used for 2½ hours either side of high water.

At Grenham Bay there are warnings of cliff falls; there is access at either end of the bay, and a launching ramp at the eastern end. Beresford Gap is reserved for powerboats and water-skiing, and bathing and fishing are forbidden. Epple Bay is the prettiest of the four bays; backed by a small field and golf course, it is a deeply indented

sandy cove, surrounded by steep chalk cliffs and reached either by steps or a ramp.

In the grounds of Quex Park, about a mile south of the Canterbury Road, the Powell-Cotton Museum displays the dozens of animals shot by Major Percy Powell-Cotton (1866-1940) in a lifetime of big-game hunting. The exhibits are arranged in dioramas showing their natural habitats.

⑤ WESTGATE ON SEA

A resort of red-brick Victorian and Edwardian houses, Westgate is the sedate western suburb of Margate. It has plenty of green open spaces, and two bays separated by a promontory laid out with landscaped gardens. At Westgate Bay the cliffs dip sharply, forming a gentle beach with a launching ramp at the western end. St Mildred's Bay is a lively bathing beach, with beach huts and a launching ramp at its eastern end.

In the middle of the wide, grass-covered promontory that divides Westgate from Margate is a delightful sunken garden, which in spring and autumn provides a resting-point for migrant birds.

⑥ MARGATE

For more than 200 years Margate has attracted Londoners to its superb crescent of sand – ever since Benjamin Beale, a Margate Quaker and glovemaker, invented the covered bathing machine in 1753. Before the arrival of the railway, visitors came to Margate from London by sea, in special boats, the 'Margate Hoys'. Passengers came ashore at the stone jetty known as Margate Pier, which was built by John Rennie and curves protectingly round the harbour. It was completed in 1815, one month before the arrival of the first steamboat. Confusingly, Margate's traditional seaside pier was known as the Jetty, but this was almost entirely destroyed by a storm in 1978; only the skeleton of the seaward end still juts forlornly from the sea.

Margate's amusement arcades run along the main seafront of Marine Terrace in a procession of flashing lights and blaring pop music. At their centre is the vast funfair, founded in 1920 and known for 60 years as Dreamland but now renamed the Bembom Brothers Theme Park. Open daily in summer, it includes a big wheel climbing to 140 ft, a scenic railway, a water chute and picnic gardens.

Two other attractions of Margate are both underground. On Grotto Hill is the Shell Grotto, open daily in summer and decorated from floor to ceiling with intricate shell designs. Discovered last century, it is believed to be a temple of ancient but unknown origin. Margate Caves in Northdown Road were hewn out of chalk more than 1,000 years ago and have served as dungeon, church and smugglers' hideout. The caves are open daily in summer.

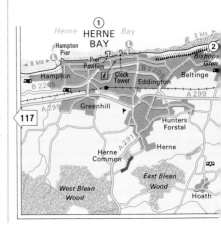

Dickens memorial plaque at Broadstairs

BROADSTAIRS BEACH *The fort-like Bleak House, where Charles Dickens wrote* David Copperfield, *looks down on the sands of Viking Bay, sheltered by the curving arm of a 16th-century pier.*

Swimming is safe, and the gently sloping sands are ideal for children learning to swim. Lifeguards patrol every day throughout the summer. There are two slipways – one into the harbour, which dries out at low tide, the other on the seaward side of the pier.

On the outskirts of Margate, off College Road, stands Draper's Windmill, the survivor of three mills built on the site about 1850 and restored to full working order by the Draper's Mill Trust. It is open to visitors on Sunday afternoons all summer, and also on Thursday evenings in July and August.

⑦ CLIFTONVILLE
At the eastern end of Margate, Cliftonville is built on a clifftop plateau set well back behind a broad expanse of grass. Its centre is a wide rectangular garden, known as The Oval. Cliftonville's main beach is at Palm Bay, where a promenade runs along the foreshore above the beach. From Palm Bay Avenue a ramp leads under the clifftop Princes Walk down to the beach. Opposite the end of Palm Bay Avenue is a powerboat ramp leading to a water-ski channel.

The wide Princes Walk leads into other footpaths, making it possible to walk round Foreness Point to Kingsgate; motorists have to drive almost a mile inland.

⑧ KINGSGATE
On the cliff edge between the road and the sea stands Kingsgate Castle. Battlemented and vast, it was built around 1860 and at one time belonged to Lord Avebury, the Victorian politician who introduced Bank Holidays in 1871.

Botany Bay, at the end of Kingsgate Avenue, is reached by steps down to the beach. Kingsgate Bay, below the castle, has a sheltered sandy beach reached by steps. The nearest car park is at Joss Bay, below North Foreland lighthouse. Joss Bay is a centre for canoeing and surfboarding; there is also good swimming there.

⑨ NORTH FORELAND LIGHTHOUSE
There is said to have been a light of some sort at this point since 1505, to warn ships away from the treacherous Goodwin Sands, 7 miles off the coast. The present lighthouse is 85 ft high, and its beam is visible at night for 20 miles. It is open to the public at weekends and on most weekday afternoons.

⑩ BROADSTAIRS
There are reminders of the novelist Charles Dickens at almost every corner of the narrow, twisting streets of Broadstairs. Bleak House, where he wrote *David Copperfield*, stands high on the north side of the town, looking down on the sands of Viking Bay. Known in Dickens' time as Fort House, it is now the Dickens and Maritime Centre, and is open daily except in winter. Near by is the Dickens House Museum, open daily in summer, which once belonged to Miss Mary Strong, the model for the character of Betsey Trotwood in *David Copperfield*. Every year in June there is a week-long Dickens festival, when local people dress in Dickensian costume.

Swimming is safe from the 'rare good sands', as Dickens called them, since the little harbour is partly protected by a small pier, the successor to one built in the time of Henry VIII. A portcullis arch, known as York Gate, also dates from this period. A slipway can be reached from the car park beside the pier.

From Broadstairs, a road along the coast turns inland at Dumpton Gap, where a steep tarmac track leads down to a concrete ramp on to the sand. Except near high tide, it is possible to walk south along the foreshore to Ramsgate.

LOCAL INFORMATION

Tourist information (Broadstairs) Thanet 68399; (Margate) Thanet 20241; Herne Bay 66031.

HM Coastguard Dover 210008 for information, 999 in emergency (ask for coastguard).

Weather Canterbury 8091.

Local radio BBC Radio Kent, 290 m, 1035 kHz, 96.7 MHz.

PLACES TO SEE INLAND

Fordwich, 10 miles SW of Birchington, off A28. Old-world village on Stour, once port for Canterbury. 16th-century town hall with museum, partly Norman church.

Minster Abbey, 5 miles W of Ramsgate, off B2048. 11th-century abbey, now nunnery. Grounds, cloisters and parts of building. Weekdays, mornings only in winter.

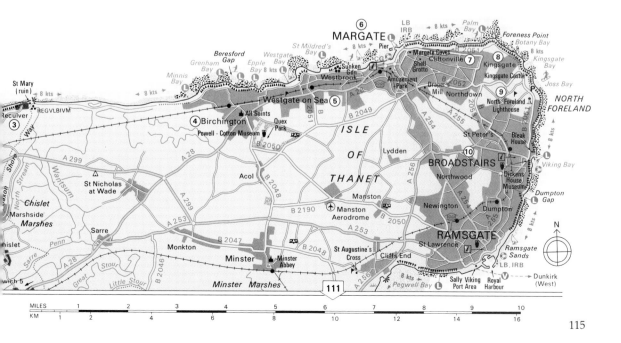

An island of sheep by Kent's apple-blossom shore

In spite of the industrial spread of Sittingbourne, this is still very much the coast of the Garden of England, where the Kentish orchards become a sea of blossom in spring. Across the muddy channel of the Swale is the Isle of Sheppey, whose name means 'Sheep Island' in Anglo-Saxon, and which is still rich farmland, with plentiful bird life, despite the busy container-ship and car-ferry port of Sheerness at its north-west tip.

Best known for his rumbustious diary of life in Restoration London, Samuel Pepys (1633-1703) held office as Charles II's Secretary of the Admiralty. He carried out naval reforms and initiated new ship building; a superior referred to him as 'the right hand of the navy'. One of Pepys's duties was to supervise the construction of the first Sheerness Dockyard in 1665, at the time of the second Anglo-Dutch war. He described the site as 'a most proper place for the purpose'. Most of the present dockyard, however, dates from the early 19th century.

Samuel Pepys, architect of the first Sheerness dockyard

① LOWER HALSTOW
A tiny church built on a low mound above flood level looks down on a small, round-ended dock where sailing dinghies moor. The Romans gathered oysters in Halstow Creek, and in the Middle Ages monks from Canterbury bred the ancestors of today's Romney Marsh sheep.

Deadmans Island provides a link with a sinister past. After the Great Plague of 1665, ships coming to London from foreign ports had to put plague suspects aboard quarantine vessels, called lazarettos, anchored off the island. Those who died on board were buried on the island.

② QUEENBOROUGH
The Isle of Sheppey, on which Queenborough stands, is separated from the Kentish mainland by a channel called the Swale, and linked to it by the impressive Kingsferry Bridge, opened in 1960. The bridge has four corner towers, which house mechanism that lifts the whole centre section vertically when a coaster needs to pass beneath.

Queenborough is now by-passed by the juggernauts and cars making for the harbour at Sheerness, but it still has traces of its former status as an important harbour town, notably in the 18th-century Guildhall which juts into the High Street. The town was named after Queen Philippa, wife of Edward III, who built a castle on the site to guard the northern end of the Swale – an important sea passage in the days when ships stayed as close to the land as possible. The High Street ends at a small esplanade, with a long causeway from which boats can be launched at most states of the tide.

③ SHEERNESS
The north-west tip of Sheppey is largely hidden behind the high wall of Sheerness dockyard, laid out in the time of Charles II and now a flourishing container and car-ferry port. Much of the town consists of Victorian housing for dockyard workers.

In 1797 Sheerness was the scene of the notorious Nore mutiny, when sailors of the Nore Command rebelled against the inhuman conditions in which they lived. Though the mutiny was quelled, it focused attention on the sailors' plight, and led to a general improvement in their conditions.

The sea defences of Sheerness have been strengthened by a massive sea-wall, built above the shingle beach, giving wide views across the Thames Estuary. Volunteer lifeguards patrol at weekends in summer.

④ MINSTER
Below Minster village the land slopes down to a wide beach of sand and mud scattered with stones. To the east the beach is backed by steep clay cliffs, and the coast as far as Leysdown is noted for the fossils which can be found on the beach. Volunteer lifeguards patrol the beach at weekends and Bank Holidays in summer.

Rows of small holiday houses on unmade roads adjoin the village centre, clustered round the ancient parish church of St Mary and St Sexburga, one of the oldest places of Christian worship in England. In the Middle Ages the nuns of Minster Abbey – founded in the 7th century by Sexburga, widow of a Saxon king – used the north half of the church, while the parishioners worshipped in the southern section.

In the church is the tomb of Sir Robert de Shurland, who was Baron of Sheppey and

TRADESMEN'S ENTRANCE *The Kingsferry Bridge rises for coasters plying the narrow Swale Channel between the sea and the Medway.*

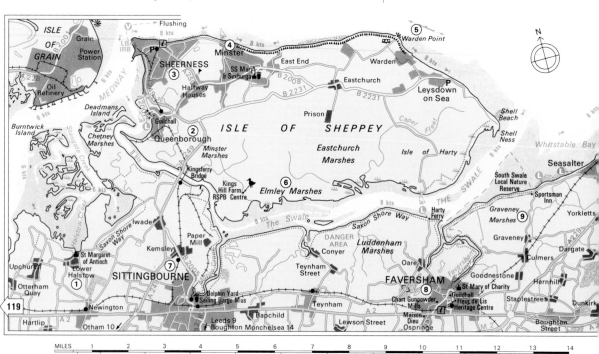

Lord Warden of the Cinque Ports during the 14th century. The carving on the tomb, showing a horse's head rising from the waves, was used by R. H. Barham, author of the *Ingoldsby Legends*, as the basis for one of his narrative poems. According to the legend, a local witch prophesied that the horse would bring about de Shurland's death. To prevent this, he cut off its head; but some months later he stubbed his foot on the skeleton, developed gangrene and died, so fulfilling the prophecy.

The abbey gatehouse, next to the church, houses a museum of Sheppey history.

(5) **WARDEN POINT**
The name 'Warden' means 'watch-hill' in Old English, and this north-east corner of Sheppey is an ideal spot from which to see ships approaching the Thames Estuary. The cliffs are subject to severe landslips, and the houses near the cliff edge are under constant threat. A rough road runs from the Point to the chalets and holiday homes of Warden and Leysdown on Sea.

From Leysdown a road, which soon becomes a track, leads to Shell Ness at the south-east corner of Sheppey. It was at Shell Beach, near Leysdown, that in November 1909 J. T. C. Moore-Brabazon (later Lord Brabazon) became the first British pilot to achieve a circular flight of 1 mile. Brabazon and other aviation pioneers are commemorated by a monument at Eastchurch, 3 miles west of Leysdown.

(6) **ELMLEY MARSHES**
Grazing marshes, shallow pools and salt-marsh beside the Swale provide ideal breeding and feeding conditions for wild-fowl and waders. The RSPB's Elmley Marshes Reserve covers more than 3,300 acres, and is reached down a 2 mile track leading off the A249, a mile beyond the Kingsferry Bridge. As many as 10,000 wigeon, 4,000 teal and 1,800 white-fronted geese winter there, and breeding birds include redshanks, lapwings and shovelers.

Cars can be parked at Kings Hill Farm, about a mile from the hides which overlook the flooded lagoons and mud-flats. The reserve is open three days a week throughout the year.

(7) **SITTINGBOURNE**
The muddy Milton Creek winds its way into Sittingbourne, which was once a busy

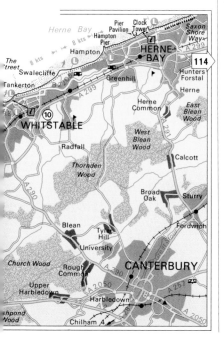

SITTINGBOURNE BARGES *At the Dolphin Yard Sailing Barge Museum the old Thames work-horses, the spritsail barges, lie at rest with sails neatly furled and black-tarred hulls high and dry.*

harbour town. Beside the creek, among warehouses, factories and reed-filled inlets, is the Dolphin Yard Sailing Barge Museum, which recalls the great days of the noble spritsail sailing barges that traded on the Thames and around the south-east coast of England.

The museum is housed in an old barge maintenance yard, and the buildings and relics on show include a spacious sail loft, a forge and a steam chest which was used to make timber pliable. There are also exhibits on the local brick and cement industries whose raw materials the barges once carried. The museum is open only on Sundays and Bank Holidays in summer, but visitors can often watch barges being repaired and restored in Dolphin Yard.

(8) **FAVERSHAM**
One of the prettiest towns in the whole of Kent, Faversham is well-loved and looked after by the people who live there. It has a neat white-painted Guildhall, with market stalls below its ground-floor arches; streets of fine Georgian and Tudor houses; two breweries in the main street; and a spacious creek that brings the river sights and smells within a stone's throw of the town centre. The church has an extraordinary steeple of pierced and carved stone, which is Faversham's most distinctive landmark.

Faversham was already a flourishing town in Saxon times, and an abbey was founded there by King Stephen in 1147. In later years it became an important centre for gun-powder-making, manufacturing much of the powder used in the Napoleonic and Crimean Wars; the restored Chart Gun-powder Mills are open at certain times.

North of Faversham, a lane leads from Oare to the south side of Harty Ferry, a disused ferry across the Swale. Boats can be launched from the old ferry slipway, which is a continuation of the lane. The Saxon Shore Way runs westwards along the river wall to Conyer and onwards to Sittingbourne.

(9) **GRAVENEY MARSHES**
Three miles of sea-wall and foreshore from Faversham Creek round to the Sportsman Inn, a mile north of Graveney village, make up the South Swale Local Nature Reserve, run by the Kent Trust for Nature Conservation. In winter, the mud-flats attract large numbers of waders and wildfowl, including Brent geese, and the grassland beside the sea-wall is rich in flowering plants. The sea-wall walk is part of the Saxon Shore Way.

(10) **WHITSTABLE**
The Romans knew Whitstable for its oysters, and though the industry went into eclipse as the result of pollution and the storms of January 1953 it is now flourishing again. The harbour area contains the largest oyster hatchery in Europe. A dignified brick building proclaims itself the Royal Native Oyster Stores, 'by Appointment to HM King George V, also to HM the late Queen Victoria'; this is in use each year during the Oyster Festival.

There is still more than a touch of the seafaring past about Whitstable, especially in the rows of weather-boarded fishermen's cottages, and the rickety black-tarred boat sheds overlooking the sea. Below the sea-wall the shingle is banked against the wooden groynes by a strong tidal current. Just east of the harbour the Sports and Water-ski Club has a powerboat channel marked by orange buoys, which swimmers are warned to avoid.

The quiet resort area of Tankerton lies east of the old town, separated from it by a tree-covered hill, with a ship's mast and a pair of cannon marking its highest point. Below Tankerton's seafront houses, a wide grass bank slopes down to the shingle beach.

From Tankerton beach, a long finger of shingle, known as The Street, juts out into the sea. At low tide it is uncovered for more than half a mile or more, and is a favourite place for collecting shells. Unpredictable currents make swimming dangerous near it.

LOCAL INFORMATION

Tourist information Whitstable 275482.

HM Coastguard Frinton-on-Sea 5518 for information, 999 in emergency (ask for coastguard).

Weather Medway 8091.

Local radio BBC Radio Kent, 290 m, 1035 kHz, 96.7 MHz; IBA Invicta Sound, 242 m, 1242 kHz, 103.8 MHz.

PLACES TO SEE INLAND

Boughton Monchelsea Place, 14 miles SW of Sittingbourne. Elizabethan manor. Weekends and Wed. afternoons in summer.

Chilham Castle Gardens, 8 miles S of Whitstable, off A252. Most afternoons in summer.

Fleur de Lis Heritage Centre, Faversham. Displays illustrating 1,000 years of history, in 15th-century inn. Weekdays.

Leeds Castle, 11 miles SW of Sittingbourne. Medieval. Daily in summer.

Maison Dieu, Ospringe, near Faversham. Roman artefacts. Weekends in summer.

Stoneacre (NT), Otham, 10 miles SW of Sittingbourne, off A20. 15th-century manor house. Some afternoons in summer.

Strongholds that watch over the busy Thames Estuary

At Gravesend the Thames is still a recognisable river, rather than the wide estuary it becomes a few miles further downstream. Gravesend and Tilbury face each other across a few hundred yards of water, while the twin Victorian forts of Coalhouse and Shornmead recall the strategic importance of the Thames little more than a century ago. East of the Isle of Grain, the Thames is joined by the Medway – smaller in size but just as full of history.

① EAST TILBURY
A road through East Tilbury ends by the river at Coalhouse Fort, a massive stone stronghold built in the 1860s to guard the lower reaches of the Thames. The gunports pierced in its curved front look out on to a peaceful little riverside park. There is a good walk westwards past the power station to Tilbury Fort, with wide views of Gravesend Reach.

② TILBURY
The road from East Tilbury to Tilbury is hardly more than a country lane – a rustic survival amid the industry of Thameside. It passes by West Tilbury, which looks out over the marshes and the river and is the probable site of the camp where Elizabeth I reviewed her troops in August 1588 before the onslaught of the Spanish Armada.

Tilbury itself is at river level. Its giant container port is largely hidden behind a high wall, with only the tops of the cranes visible from the road. The docks were opened in the 1880s, but have been greatly expanded in recent years and now handle timber, grain and general cargo. A passenger ferry runs every half-hour across the river to Gravesend.

Just downstream is Tilbury Fort, a long, low fortification built in 1682 to defend the Thames against the Dutch and French. Its brick walls are surrounded on the inland side by a moat, while on the river side it has an unusual entrance resembling a triumphal arch. It is open daily, and offers fine views across the Thames to Gravesend.

③ GRAVESEND
For centuries Gravesend has been a centre of activity on the Thames. As early as the 14th century Gravesend's ferrymen had the monopoly of waterborne passenger traffic to London (the 'Long Ferry'), and across to Tilbury (the 'Short Ferry') which still runs every half-hour. Gravesend is the headquarters of the Port of London Authority's Thames Navigation Service, which is housed in a modern building with radar scanners rotating on the roof. Below it is the pretty little Royal Terrace Pier, from which the PLA's two pilot boats put out to guide ships navigating from Gravesend to the Tilbury docks and the docks further upstream.

The best place from which to watch the busy shipping on the Thames is Gordon Promenade – a wide esplanade, with gardens behind, giving superb views of the Essex bank of the Thames. Just inland is a canal basin, full of small boats, which was once the Gravesend terminal of the Thames and Medway Canal linking the two rivers. The promenade is named after General Gordon, who as a Royal Engineers officer in the 1860s supervised the building of Coalhouse Fort and Shornmead Fort.

Gravesend's other famous character was the Red Indian Princess Pocahontas, whose bronze statue stands in St George's churchyard. A romantic and tragic figure, she saved the life of Captain John Smith, one of the early Virginia colonists, and married another settler, John Rolfe, who brought her back to England in 1616. The following year she died of fever as she set out on her return voyage to America, and was buried in the chancel of St George's.

Gravesend is the northern end of the Saxon Shore Way, a long-distance walking route which follows the coast for 140 miles to Rye in Sussex.

④ SHORNMEAD FORT
When they were built in the 1860s, the twin forts of Shornmead and Coalhouse would have provided murderous crossfire over the river, and even in decay they are still darkly impressive. Shornmead, today more ruined than Coalhouse, can be reached on foot along the river-wall from Gravesend. Cars can approach it down a side road from the A226 just north of Shorne as far as a locked level-crossing gate, after which there is a half-mile walk to the fort across a rifle-range, closed to the public when red flags are flying.

⑤ CLIFFE
West of Cliffe, worked-out quarries and gravel workings stretch for more than a mile to the river. As its name suggests, the village itself is on higher ground; its sturdy 13th-century church is built of alternate bands of stone and squared flints, and inside has considerable remains of medieval wall painting.

⑥ COOLING
By the road is the frowning battlemented gatehouse of Cooling Castle, built in the 1380s and decorated on one of the turrets with a large copper replica of a legal document and seal. In the early 1400s the castle was owned by Sir John Oldcastle, who is supposed to have been the model for Shakespeare's convivial knight Sir John Falstaff. Oldcastle, however, was a successful soldier, and as a follower of the church reformer John Wycliffe was tried as a heretic and burned at the stake in 1417. The castle is not open to the public.

⑦ NORTHWARD HILL NATURE RESERVE
This reserve, run by the RSPB, is hard to find; it is north of High Halstow village, and is reached from a housing estate up a path marked 'BP Oil Kent Refinery'. The reserve has Britain's largest heronry, with 220 pairs recorded in 1981; however, there are no herons to be seen from August to January. Other birds on the reserve include nightingales, whitethroats and blackcaps; and the rare white letter hairstreak butterfly can sometimes be seen. The ground gets very muddy after rain, so it is wise to wear thick footwear when visiting the reserve.

⑧ ISLE OF GRAIN
The name of the peninsula – almost, but not quite, separated from the mainland by the narrow Yantlet Creek – derives from the Old

Figurehead of the *Arethusa* at Upper Upnor

NORMAN CATHEDRAL *Though heavily restored, much of Rochester Cathedral dates from between 1179 and 1240. It stands on the site of a Saxon church which was destroyed by the Vikings.*

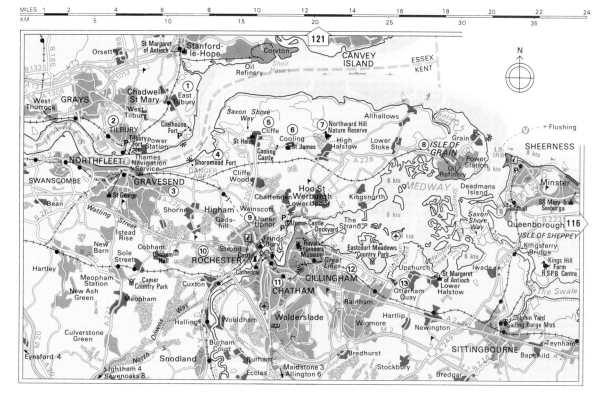

English *greon*, meaning 'sand' or 'gravel'.

The village of Grain has a small esplanade giving a distant view of Essex across the Thames, and a nearer one of Sheerness across the Medway. Port Victoria Road in the village recalls the days when a jetty was built on Grain from which Queen Victoria embarked on the royal yacht.

⑨ UPPER UPNOR

Jutting into the muddy waters of the Medway is the wedge-shaped bastion of Upnor Castle, built early in Elizabeth I's reign to guard the approaches to the naval dockyard at Chatham. The unobtrusive doorway to the castle is at the foot of Upper Upnor's steep little High Street; cars should be left in the car park beyond the village at the top of the hill. The castle has been excellently restored, with a ferocious frieze of sharp wooden stakes round the battlements, and exhibits inside showing the evolution of the Medway defensive system.

This system failed dismally the only time it was put to the test. In 1667 the Dutch admiral De Ruyter attacked and burned the fortress at Sheerness; he then sailed up the Medway, defied the guns of Upnor and attacked the British fleet anchored off Chatham, burning several ships and towing off the flagship.

Lower Upnor, a little way downstream, is a small sailing centre, with fine views across the river to Chatham. Until 1974 the sail-training ship *Arethusa* was moored off Upnor; but she has now been superseded by the land-based Arethusa Venture Centre, which runs environmental and adventure courses for young people. A new 70 ft ketch, completed in 1982 and also named *Arethusa*, carries on the sail-training tradition.

⑩ ROCHESTER

Charles Dickens called Rochester 'Dullborough' and 'Cloisterham'; and made it the background for many scenes in *Great Expectations* and *Pickwick Papers*. Mr Pickwick stayed at the Royal Victoria and Bull Hotel; Mr Jingle explored the castle and the cathedral; while the novelist himself spent the last 12 years of his life at Gadshill, 2 miles north-west of Rochester. A Charles Dickens Centre in Rochester, housed in a 16th-century mansion, has relics of the novelist

BISHOP'S CASTLE *Rochester Castle was started by Bishop Gundulph, who also built the White Tower in the Tower of London.*

and tableaux modelled on scenes from his books.

The story of Rochester goes back 2,000 years or more before Dickens. When the Romans came, there was already a British stronghold guarding the Medway crossing. The Romans had a camp there, and built a bridge to carry Watling Street, now the A2, across the river. The first bishop was appointed in AD 604, and soon after the Normans arrived they built the cathedral and the castle, which stand side by side overlooking the river.

The cathedral is on a small scale, but is architecturally fascinating and full of monuments, including one to Dickens, and has a magnificent Norman crypt. The spectacular castle keep, which is open daily, towers to over 100 ft, and gives magnificent views from its battlements. Among Rochester's many other historic buildings are the 16th-century almshouses of Watt's Charity, the 17th-century Guildhall Museum, and the Restoration House where Charles II is said to have stayed overnight on his journey to London at the time of his restoration to the throne in 1660.

⑪ CHATHAM

Chatham has been a naval dockyard since 1547, when Henry VIII first maintained a storehouse in 'Jillyngham Water'. Down the

centuries the great names of maritime history – Drake, Hawkins, Nelson and many others – have sailed from Chatham; and it is only with the recent closure of the dockyards that this long tradition has at last ended.

A commanding hill, known as the Great Lines, rises behind the town. The hill gets its name from the 18th-century earthworks which once defended it, and from its summit there are panoramic views of the Medway. Fort Amherst, a Napoleonic fortification on the Great Lines, is being restored. Dickens spent some years of his childhood at Chatham, where his father worked in the Navy Pay Office. Dockyard tours start from Main Gate.

⑫ GILLINGHAM

A sprawling residential town, Gillingham has a small shingle beach at The Strand, and an excellent, wide stone slipway in the Dock, reached down Pier Approach Road.

⑬ OTTERHAM QUAY

Seemingly miles from anywhere, Otterham stands at the end of a little creek, where ancient wooden pilings and boat hulls decay quietly into the mud.

LOCAL INFORMATION

Tourist information (Rochester) Medway 43666.

HM Coastguard Frinton-on-Sea 5518 for information, 999 in emergency (ask for coastguard).

Weather Medway 8091.

Local radio BBC Radio Kent, 290 m, 1035 kHz, 96.7 MHz; BBC Radio London, 206 m, 1458 kHz, 94.9 MHz; IBA Essex Radio, 210/220 m, 1431/1359 kHz, 95.3/96.4 MHz; IBA Invicta Sound, 242 m, 1242 kHz, 103.8 MHz.

PLACES TO SEE INLAND

Allington Castle, 7 miles S of Chatham, off A20. 13th century. Afternoons daily.

Cobham Hall, 4 miles W of Rochester. Elizabethan mansion. Some afternoons in summer.

Ightham Mote (NT), 15 miles SW of Gravesend. Medieval moated house. Some afternoons.

Knole (NT), near Sevenoaks, 16 miles SW of Gravesend, off A225. Medieval and Jacobean mansion. Most days in summer.

Lullingstone Roman Villa, near Eynsford, 10 miles SW of Gravesend, off A225. Daily.

Maidstone, 8 miles S of Chatham. Museum and art gallery, weekdays; Tyrwhitt-Drake Museum of Carriages, weekdays, Sun. afternoons in summer.

Playground for Londoners
and winter home for wildfowl

Away from the modern urban sprawl of Southend and the vast oil refinery of Coryton, this coast is full of reminders of its mysterious past as the haunt of smugglers, who would steal up the creeks between the mud-flats and land their cargoes at the local ale-houses. It is not far from the holiday bustle of Southend to the quiet banks of the Roach; though defence requirements mean that the whole of Foulness is closed to the public.

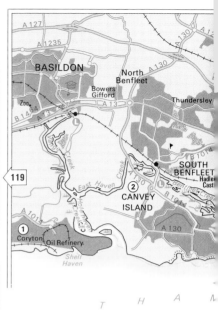

① CORYTON
The huge Shell oil refinery, one of the largest in England, sprawls for more than 3 miles along the north side of the Thames. Shell has been there since 1912; but industry arrived 40 years earlier when the brothers Cory – after whom Coryton is named – built a small refinery on the banks of the river. Now the storage tanks and tall chimneys of the processing plants form a major Thameside landmark, and the largest supertankers berth alongside the jetties. One of the inlets, Shell Haven, has nothing to do with the oil company: it already bore the name on charts of the Thames appearing in Henry VIII's time.

② CANVEY ISLAND
A massive new concrete sea-wall, with gaps that can be closed by steel floodgates, defends Canvey against the sea. Most of the island lies below high-water level; and though flood walls and drainage works have been constructed since the 17th century, their impotence against the full force of the sea was shown on the night of January 31, 1953, when the waters swept across the island, drowning 58 people.

Most of Canvey is now covered in bungalows and holiday chalets, built behind the high sea-wall. The top of the wall has wide views across the Thames Estuary shipping lanes, to the Isle of Grain on the Kent side of the river. Below the wall, a beach of muddy sand and shingle is safe for swimming within 2 hours of high water. Volunteer lifeguards patrol the beach on Sundays in summer.

③ TWO TREE ISLAND
The lonely expanse of windswept grass and saltings at Two Tree Island is reached down a road beside Leigh-on-Sea station. The road ends at a long concrete ramp leading into the Hadleigh Ray, and thence into the Thames Estuary. Boats can be launched at most states

WINTER VISITOR *The dark-breasted Brent goose is a common visitor to the Two Tree Island Nature Reserve between November and April.*

of the tide; a fee is payable at the harbour master's hut. The island is the site of a national nature reserve, providing an excellent place for watching wildfowl during the winter.

On the steep slope above the island is Hadleigh Castle, built for Edward III in the 1360s and strategically sited to guard the Thames Estuary against French retaliation after the king's successes in France. It was constructed on the site of an earlier castle built by Hubert de Burgh, Earl of Kent, in the 1230s. The castle is open daily.

④ LEIGH-ON-SEA
A narrow High Street of fishermen's cottages is cut off on the landward side by the railway, and the barrier has helped Leigh keep much of its old-world character. The street has several stalls selling jellied eels, and cockles are collected on Maplin Sands and brought in every day by cockle boat.

Leigh has a small timber yard, a boat-builders, and a sailing club. At the east end of the High Street, beyond Bell Wharf, is a small sandy beach, with a slipway down on to it. The only access by road is across the railway bridge, and in summer parking becomes difficult. There is a small car park below the bridge, at the entrance to Leigh; an alternative is to leave the car north of the railway and walk to Leigh across the footbridge.

There is a continuous seafront walk of 7 miles from Leigh to Shoeburyness.

⑤ SOUTHEND-ON-SEA
Southend is far more than a large seaside resort: it is a major residential and working town in its own right, with towering offices and an impressive civic centre set well back from the seafront. It was already becoming popular as a resort at the beginning of the 19th century, in Jane Austen's time, and grew rapidly during Victorian times, spreading westwards to Westcliff-on-Sea and Leigh, and eastwards to Thorpe Bay and Shoeburyness. The famous pier, the longest in the world at 1⅓ miles when it was built in

1889, was cut in two by a ship in 1986: but communication with the end of the pier has been restored. It is popular with walkers and anglers, who can use a miniature railway connecting the land with the shops, cafe and pub at the seaward end.

As well as its seaside attractions, Southend prides itself on its 1,100 acres of parks and gardens. These range from the seafront slope, covered with trees and shrubs, below the Royal Terrace where Nelson stayed, to Priory Park 1½ miles inland, a superb open space surrounding Prittlewell Priory.

The oldest building in Southend, Prittlewell Priory was founded by Robert of Essex in 1110. It is now a museum with exhibits dealing with local natural history, the history of the priory, and radio and television. Near the entrance is the 'Crow Stone' – a stone obelisk which once stood on Southend beach to mark the eastern limit of the City of London's control over Thames river traffic. Its successor now stands on the beach at Chalkwell. Prittlewell was one of the oldest villages in Essex, and Southend takes its name from the fishermen's cottages that stood at the village's southern end.

The beach is a mixture of sand and shingle, becoming muddy towards low-water mark. Swimming is generally safe, but bathers should take care when the tide is on the ebb, as there is then a strong undertow down river. At low tide the sea goes out for more than a mile, and it is advisable to look at a tide table before walking far from the esplanade. Two patrol boats operate every day in summer, and volunteer lifeguards patrol on summer Sundays and Bank Holidays.

Fishermen can get plenty of sport from the pier at Southend, where flounders, bass, eels and mullet are caught, or from one of the charter boats which take anglers out into the Thames Estuary for cod of up to 30 lb and tope of up to 40 lb. Each August two sailing-barge matches are held on the river between Southend and Greenwich in which 20 or more of the magnificent brown-sailed Thames barges take part. These vessels, built around the turn of the century, make a splendid sight as they glide majestically through the water. A link with a more distant era is given by a half-size replica of Sir Francis Drake's *Golden Hinde* in the boating pool by the pier.

HADLEIGH CASTLE *Two round towers, 36 ft in diameter, are the best-preserved parts of Edward III's fortification.*

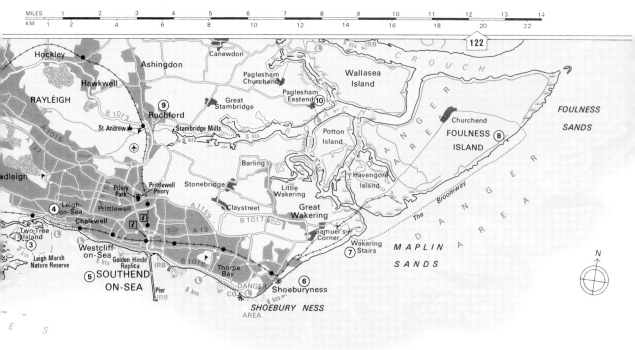

MINI MARINA

PLAYGROUND BY THE SEA *Most of Southend's seafront is dedicated to fun and frivolity, and children are catered for in Peter Pan's Playground below the Western Esplanade.*

⑥ SHOEBURYNESS

At the eastern end of Southend, beyond Thorpe Bay, spiked railings extending into the sea mark the boundaries of the Ministry of Defence artillery range, which takes up the whole tip of Shoebury's 'ness', or promontory. The railings enclose about 1½ miles of beach. An artillery barracks was first set up there in 1858, to test Armstrong guns against ironclad warships.

Round the Ness from Southend is the popular East Beach, mainly sand, shingle and low tide mud-flats sandwiched between the Ness and Wakering Stairs. Volunteer lifeguards patrol on Sundays and Bank Holidays in summer. Rampart Terrace, which runs behind the beach, gives magnificent views of the river and its shipping.

⑦ WAKERING STAIRS

A mile east of the straggling village of Great Wakering, public access ends abruptly at Samuel's Corner, where the Ministry of Defence takes over. The Ministry's Proof and Experimental Establishment covers the whole of Foulness and Potton islands, as the endless barbed-wire fences make clear.

However, when red flags are not flying and firing is not in progress, it is possible to drive to Wakering Stairs, and from there walk out on to the vast expanses of Maplin Sands. A short way offshore a track called The Broomway is uncovered at low tide; it gets its name from the wooden 'brooms' or poles which used to mark the route. The track runs parallel to the shore for about 5 miles, ending at Foulness Island.

⑧ FOULNESS ISLAND

The name means 'promontory of birds', and the fact that Foulness Island is now closed to the public because of Ministry of Defence activities means that geese and other wildfowl flourish there relatively undisturbed. Up to 10,000 Brent geese winter on the Maplin and Foulness Sands which cover some 35 square miles. When Maplin Sands were proposed as the site of London's third airport, the hazard posed by birds to aircraft landing and taking off was advanced as a major objection to the proposal.

⑨ ROCHFORD

This pretty little market town, still largely Georgian, stands at the first road crossing of the River Roach. The church of St Andrew is 15th century, and near by is the 16th-century Rochford Hall with Georgian additions. It was lived in for a while by Anne Boleyn. Though the Roach largely dries out at low tide, coasters still unload grain at Stambridge Mills a short way downstream.

⑩ PAGLESHAM EASTEND

As remote as anywhere in Essex, this hamlet, reached down a maze of dog-leg roads, gives the only proper access to the Roach – and then only by is a rough road, which starts from the pub. It is, however, a popular sailing centre, with a slipway closed by a strong wooden floodgate; permission to use it must be obtained from the boat-builders next to the gate. There is also a small oyster-processing plant which cleans oysters dredged from beds in the mud of the Roach.

From the river-wall, the tower blocks of Southend are visible more than 5 miles away. There are good walks upstream to Rochford, and downstream along Paglesham Pool to Wallasea Island.

Yachts on the long creeks where Saxon once clashed with Dane

Two rivers running deep inland, the Crouch and the Blackwater, provided invasion routes for marauding Danes in the centuries before the Norman Conquest. Today they provide sheltered waters for yachts and ochre-sailed Thames barges. Out on the lonely coast, near Bradwell-on-Sea, the 7th century and the 20th century confront each other in the forms of an ancient Christian shrine and a modern nuclear power station.

① CANEWDON
The village church has a tall 15th-century tower which dominates the surrounding landscape. Beacon Hill, on which it stands, is said to have been the Danes' command post before the Battle of Ashingdon. There in 1016 the Danish King Canute defeated the English Edmund Ironside.

② SOUTH FAMBRIDGE
Fresh lobsters can be bought at the lobster 'ponds' near the river. Upstream the river wall is breached after a mile, but downstream a walker can follow the Crouch for 5 miles.

③ SOUTH WOODHAM FERRERS
Named after a Norman knight called de Ferrers, who came over with William the Conqueror, Woodham Ferrers was until the 18th century the centre of the local saltmaking industry. Expansion began in the 1890s, when London commuters were tempted by the offer of buying 'quite a comfortable little cot' for only – £100. In recent years South Woodham Ferrers has expanded into a full-scale New Town, with an elegant town centre opened in 1981. Modelled on a traditional Essex town, it is brick-paved and completely pedestrianised, and has as its focus a white weather-boarded clock tower.

Between the town and the River Crouch lies Marsh Farm Country Park, occupying 320 acres of low-lying reclaimed marshland. Visitors can tour a commercially run farm which specialises in cattle, sheep and pigs, and shows how a modern farm works. There are traditional Essex farm buildings. Two picnic areas have been laid out, and there are more than 3 miles of riverside walks. At the eastern end of the park is a nature conservation zone, where migrant birds such as Brent geese can be seen in winter.

④ NORTH FAMBRIDGE
Old cottages look towards the Crouch, across an expanse of mud and tussocky grass, which is under water at high tide. Here in 1897 floods broke down the sea-wall, and the land has never been reclaimed. The rotting remains of timber stakes upstream from the access road show where the wall once stood. There is a good walk downstream along the sea-wall to Burnham-on-Crouch, 6 miles away, and beyond. The Ferry Boat Inn near the river wall dates from the 15th-century and is said to be haunted by an old ferryman.

⑤ CREEKSEA
The name derives from the Anglo-Saxon for 'landing-place at the creek', and the boating tradition is still carried on here by the local yacht club. Like Bosham in Sussex, Creeksea is said to be the place where King Canute tried to turn back the tide. The short section of road along the river gives good views, but parking is not allowed.

⑥ BURNHAM-ON-CROUCH
Once a centre of the oyster, cockle and whelk trade, Burnham has become the goal of thousands of yachtsmen, the 'Cowes of the east coast'. The elegant Georgian High Street, which runs parallel to the river, has an octagonal clock tower built in Victorian times. The equally elegant quayside is too narrow for cars, and so walkers can enjoy the views of river and boats in comfort.

Two of the biggest buildings are the headquarters of the Royal Corinthian Yacht Club (at Burnham since 1894) and the Royal Burnham Yacht Club. Burnham Week, one of the great events in the yachtsman's year, is held at the end of August, and there is an annual carnival at the end of September.

⑦ DENGIE FLAT
This expanse of saltings and mud-flats gets its name from the remote village of Dengie, which also gives its name to the whole peninsula between the Crouch and the Blackwater. The tide retreats up to 2 miles from the sea-wall, and the resulting stretch of muddy tussocks provides ideal feeding grounds for waders in spring and autumn, and for Brent geese, teal, shelducks and many other species in winter.

The Flat is classified as a Site of Special Scientific Interest, but is not open to the public. At its northern end is Bradwell Shell Bank, consisting of 30 acres of sand and shingle, combined with a spit of compressed and broken cockleshells. Part of an Essex Naturalists' Trust reserve, it is frequented by shore birds. There is no public access to the reserve, but a path leads near to it round the sea-wall.

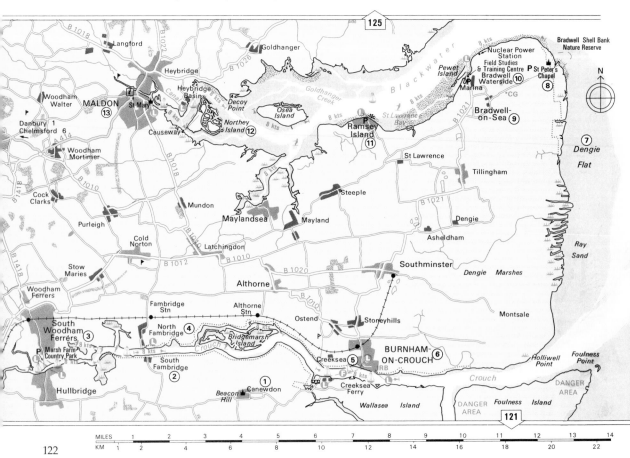

MALDON MOORINGS *Like elderly ladies at an old-time ball, Maldon's sailing barges wait for the moment when they will take the floor again and relive the past in the annual sailing-barge races.*

⑧ ST PETER'S CHAPEL

No cars are allowed as far as this lonely chapel, and the last half mile from Bradwell-on-Sea has to be covered on foot. Its full name is St Peter's-on-the-Wall, and it stands defiantly on a bank exposed to the fury of the North Sea storms. It was built about AD 654 by St Cedd, who came from Northumbria as a missionary to the East Anglians, and is thus one of the oldest places of worship in England.

St Cedd chose as his site the main gateway of the Roman fortress of Othona, which had been abandoned when the Romans left Britain in 410, and used Roman stone and bricks in its construction. Originally it had at its east end a rounded apse now marked out on the grass by stones. The chapel is still used by the non-denominational Othona Community.

There are good walks from the chapel along the sea-wall in both directions.

St Peter's Chapel

⑨ BRADWELL-ON-SEA

The name is misleading, as the village is today 1½ miles from the sea. Bradwell nuclear power station, on the coast, has occasional open days. The dates of these are advertised locally, and tickets are available from area electricity board showrooms.

⑩ BRADWELL WATERSIDE

Old houses line the road to Bradwell Creek, a narrow, sheltered stretch of water between Pewet Island and the mainland. Modern developments include a marina, and the Bradwell Field Studies and Sailing Centre, run by the Essex County Council for young people.

⑪ RAMSEY ISLAND

Away on the eastern skyline loom the twin grey blocks of Bradwell nuclear power station, which dominates this stretch of the Blackwater. At the end of the road is a holiday and residential village, looking towards Bradwell across St Lawrence Bay, which at low tide becomes a vast expanse of muddy shingle.

⑫ NORTHEY ISLAND

Reached by a causeway, covered at high tide, along a private road (marked South House Farm), Northey is primarily a bird reserve owned by the National Trust and administered by the Essex Naturalists' Trust. It can be visited only by permission in writing obtained in advance from the Warden at Northey Cottage, Northey Island, Maldon. The island is a small triangle of 260 acres, surrounded by muddy creeks, and was occupied by Stone Age man, whose flint scrapers have been found there.

In 991 a force of marauding Danes camped on the island, opposed by the East Anglian Saxons under their leader, Byrhtnoth, on the mainland. The Danes crossed the causeway and defeated the Saxons, whose downfall is told in the Old English epic poem *The Battle of Maldon*. The fighting is said to have lasted for 14 days, until all the Saxons were killed.

⑬ MALDON

This fine old town, built commandingly on a ridge above the Blackwater, has a name that goes back to Saxon times. Although a dozen miles from the sea, it has a nautical atmosphere and strong seafaring traditions. Two Maldon ships fought at the siege of Calais in 1348. The seagoing part of Maldon lies a little way downstream, by the Norman St Mary's Church. Here, carefully restored 19th-century Thames sailing barges can often be seen at their moorings, and the riverside promenade, overlooking a beach of muddy shingle, offers delightful views of the town. In the 19th century Maldon produced a type of barge all its own. Known as 'stackies', they were shallow and broad, and carried complete corn-stacks up the narrow inland creeks.

Sailing-barge races, called 'matches', are held during July, August and September, and cruises are available from March to October.

ELEGANCE IN WOOD *These Burnham-on-Crouch cottages are typical of many in Essex, where weather-boarding began in the 18th century.*

123

Oysters from the River Colne near Britain's oldest town

Since Roman times the River Colne has brought trade and prosperity to Colchester. The creeks and saltings of the nearby coast are thronged with water-loving birds, and oysters flourish on the spawning beds. Boat-building has thrived along the river since Elizabethan times, and each September the great days of sail are recalled when surviving fishing smacks and sailing barges compete in a race along the coast.

① HEYBRIDGE BASIN

During the 18th-century heyday of the canal trade the Chelmer and Blackwater Canal, which starts at Heybridge Basin, carried coal and goods traffic inland to Chelmsford. The moorings above the lock are crowded with sailing boats, from dinghies to a tall two-masted Baltic trader. An 11 mile towpath walk leads to Chelmsford.

② TOLLESBURY

This large village with a fine medieval church lies very much off the beaten track. From the centre of the village, Woodrolfe Lane leads down to a marina, backed by a row of two and three-storey wooden boat-houses, some of them now restored. The road is under water at high tide.

③ MERSEA ISLAND

Joined to the mainland by The Strood – a causeway liable to flooding at high tide – the island is a little world on its own, with lanes winding across open, gently undulating countryside.

East Mersea is the rural end of the island, where saltings lead to mud-flats backed by sand and shingle. The public is warned to beware of unexploded missiles from the nearby firing ranges. There are walks along the sea-wall in both directions. A 35 acre country park at Cudmore Grove, down Broman's Lane, has a large car park, picnic area and beach. There are dangerous currents off the end of the island.

West Mersea is the main resort and boating area, with boat-building yards and a public slipway. Oysters, known as 'West

Mersea Natives', can be bought and eaten at stalls on the foreshore, beside the old oyster storage pools, some of which are still in use. There is a small museum of local history and boat-making techniques. Volunteer inshore lifeboatmen patrol the beach at West Mersea.

RIVER DELICACY *The common British oyster,* Ostrea edulis, *thrives in the River Colne and the creeks around Mersea Island.*

④ ABBERTON RESERVOIR

More wildfowl are said to frequent Abberton than any other reservoir in the British Isles. There is a good view of the reservoir, which is 4 miles long and 2 miles wide at its widest point, from the road which crosses it at its western end.

⑤ FINGRINGHOE

This isolated village is notable for its fine church. Ferry Road leads down to the riverside, which gives excellent views across

to Wivenhoe. The marshes to the south are used as a firing range by the Colchester garrison and are closed to the public.

The headquarters of the Essex Naturalists' Trust is at Fingringhoe Wick, on the banks of the Colne, reached down South Green Lane. An information centre explains the topography and wildlife of the area, and a central watchtower gives wide-ranging views over the surrounding nature reserve. This consists of 125 acres of worked-out gravel pits, together with heathland, reed-beds, sandy beach and salt-marsh. More than 200 species of birds have been observed there, including huge wintering flocks of Brent geese. In spring and early summer the air is full of the song of breeding nightingales.

The reserve is open every day except Monday; there are three separate way-marked nature trails, for the general public, for the disabled, and for members of the Trust.

⑥ ROWHEDGE

This village, with an attractive river frontage overlooking the muddy upper reaches of the Colne estuary, is a good place from which to watch the cargo boats going to and from The Hythe at Colchester. Rowhedge was noted for its yachtsmen in the early years of this century, when ocean racing first became popular.

⑦ COLCHESTER

The oldest-recorded town and the first major Roman settlement in Britain, Colchester grew from a Roman fortress established in AD 43. It replaced the nearby British capital of Camulodunum, from which the pre-Roman kings ruled south-eastern England. Long stretches of the massive Roman town wall survive, and the Norman castle stands on the site of a temple dedicated to the Emperor Claudius. Inside the walls, the main streets still follow the Roman plan. In AD 60-61 the town was sacked by Boudicca (Boadicea), Queen of the Iceni, who led an unsuccessful revolt against the Romans. When the Romans left Britain the Saxons occupied the town and gave it its modern name, which means 'the Roman fortress on the River Colne'.

The castle keep, now the main museum, was built soon after the Norman Conquest, and was the largest ever built in Europe. It resembles the White Tower of London but is half as large again. During the Middle Ages Colchester became a prosperous town, with an important port (The Hythe, still used today) and a flourishing cloth industry. Since Napoleonic times it has been a garrison town. The Natural History Museum, in a converted church, displays plants and flowers of the nearby coast.

With a ruined priory and an estimated 250 buildings built before 1714, Colchester well repays exploration on foot. Town trails include 'The Siege of Colchester 1648', taking in the sites connected with the siege of the town by Roundheads during the Civil War. It takes in Siege House, a 15th-century house in East Street whose timbers are still riddled with bullet holes.

Colchester is noted for its oysters, which have been cultivated in the lower reaches of the Colne since Roman times. In September the oyster season is declared open by the mayor, who sails downstream and dredges the first oysters, drinking the Queen's health in gin accompanied by gingerbread. The Colchester Oyster Feast is held in October each year. The feast was first officially recorded in the reign of Charles II, but it had been held for centuries previously on the first day of St Deny's Fair, a great local annual event. Oysters were eaten not because they were a luxury item, but

TOLLESBURY BOATHOUSES *Tucked away in a creek off the Blackwater estuary, these old sail lofts date back to the turn of the century, when Tollesbury had a fishing fleet of more than 100 sailing smacks.*

RICH LEGACIES FROM ROMAN DAYS

In and around Colchester the earth has given up its treasures, and displayed today in the Castle Museum these cast a vivid light upon the period of the Roman occupation of Britain. A bronze boar, found in a Celtic burial mound of about AD 10, was to Celtic warriors a symbol of fearless fighting qualities – qualities which they emulated in vain when the Romans invaded. Some British tribes became allies of Rome, and a silver medallion of AD 16 found in the same grave bears the head of Emperor Augustus, suggesting that the king buried there was a trusted ally of Rome. The Romans introduced their gods into Britain, and some Britons accepted and worshipped them. A bronze statue of Mercury, fleet-footed messenger of the gods, was found near the site of a Romano-Celtic temple.

A silver medallion, excavated at Lexden, which may have belonged to Addedomarus, king of the Trinovantes tribe who lived in the area of Colchester

This boar came from a burial mound at Lexden

Mercury in bronze, a fine statue found at Gosbecks, near Colchester

Cinque Ports outside Kent and Sussex. The town's officials still swear allegiance to the Mayor of Sandwich in a ceremony held on the first Monday after St Andrew's Day (November 30).

Brightlingsea stands on its own 'island', surrounded by water on three sides, and can only be reached by a single road. The magnificent parish church, at the entrance to the town some 2 miles from the sea, has more than 200 memorial tiles commemorating local men who died at sea.

The town is the headquarters of the Smack Preservation Society, devoted to preserving the fine old Essex fishing boats. Each September there is a race for smacks and large sailing barges from Brightlingsea to Clacton and back; most of the boats were built at the beginning of the century.

The foreshore is muddy sand scattered with shingle. Strong and unpredictable currents can make bathing dangerous.

LOCAL INFORMATION

Tourist information Colchester 46379/712222.

HM Coastguard Frinton-on-Sea 5518 for information, 999 in emergency (ask for coastguard).

Weather Colchester 8091.

Local radio BBC Radio Kent, 290 m, 1035 kHz, 96.7 MHz; IBA Essex Radio, 210/220 m, 1431/1359 kHz, 95.3/96.4 MHz.

PLACES TO SEE INLAND

East Anglian Railway Museum, Chappel Station, 7 miles NW of Colchester. Weekends, steam days first Sun. in month in summer.

Gainsborough's House, Sudbury, 15 miles NW of Colchester. Birthplace of the artist Thomas Gainsborough. Paintings on show. Most days.

Layer Marney Tower, 6 miles SW of Colchester. Tudor house and gardens. Some afternoons in summer.

Paycocke's House (NT), Coggeshall, 9 miles W of Colchester. Tudor merchant's house. Some afternoons in summer.

---

because they could be taken from the river free of charge.

There is a rose show and carnival in July, and a tattoo in August every even-date year.

⑧ WIVENHOE
Beyond the railway, a steep and narrow street of old houses leads down to the little quayside, which can hardly have changed in 200 years. Shipbuilding at Wivenhoe began in Elizabethan times. During the Second World War wooden minesweepers were made there, and the shipyard is still busy. The parish church has superb memorial brasses to Sir George Beaumont and Elizabeth de Vere. In East Street is Garrison House, said to be named after Cromwell's troops who stayed there; it is decorated with some of the finest pargeting, or external plasterwork, in Essex.

In the 1750s there was an unsuccessful attempt to turn Wivenhoe into a spa, served by a regular boat service from London. Another unusual event in Wivenhoe's history occurred on April 22, 1884, when the town was shaken by an earthquake which damaged more than 200 buildings.

Just north of the town is Wivenhoe Park, the setting since the 1960s for the tower blocks of Essex University.

⑨ ALRESFORD CREEK
A narrow lane from Alresford village leads down to a creek of the River Colne, where herons spear for fish in the mud. This was once the site of a ford, and small boats can be

launched at high tide. The creek can be followed inland for almost 2 miles, to the road which runs from Brightlingsea to Thorrington.

⑩ BRIGHTLINGSEA
As the possessor of the finest boat-launching ramp for miles around, Brightlingsea is a centre for boats of every description. Fishing and boat-building have been staple industries for centuries, and the town was once famous for its oysters. In the Middle Ages Brightlingsea was an important port and the only 'limb', or associate member, of the

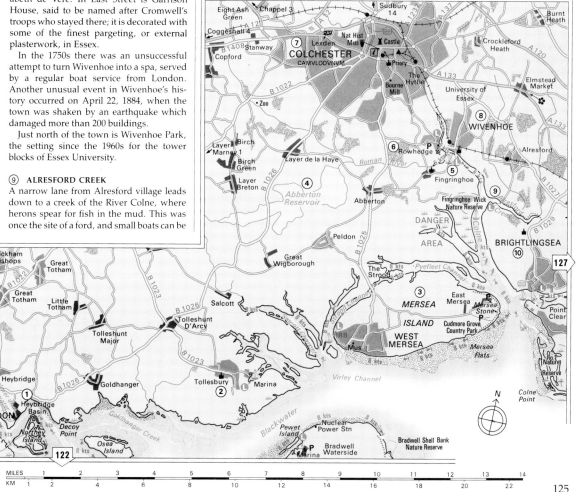

Long sandy beaches that sweep northwards to the Naze

From the chalet parks of Point Clear to the dockyard activity of Parkeston Quay, this stretch has something for everybody. At its centre, the fun-of-the-fair resort of Clacton contrasts with genteel Frinton close by. Away from the hustle and bustle of roundabouts and cranes a serene world of salt creeks, marshes and islands lies behind the Naze, where the Walton Backwaters are the haunt of vast numbers of water-birds.

ALL THE FUN OF THE PIER *Clacton's broad pier, built in 1871 and much extended since, has space for more seaside entertainments than most piers. They include an ice rink and an 'Ocean World'.*

① POINT CLEAR
This small peninsula at the mouth of the River Colne is covered by the caravans, chalets, bungalows and shops of a holiday village, beyond which an open stretch of shingle gives a good view of Brightlingsea across Flag Creek. The beach is sand and shingle, with mud at low tide. Small ships sailing to and from Wivenhoe on the Colne pass close to the shore.

② COLNE POINT
Some 400 acres of saltings and shingle are run as a nature reserve by the Essex Naturalists' Trust, and only members are allowed on the reserve. Brent geese, sanderlings, curlews, redshanks and little terns can be seen there. A public footpath runs along the sea-wall.

③ ST OSYTH
The gatehouse of St Osyth's Priory is the architectural glory of the area. Built in the 1480s in a richly ornamented design of flint and freestone, it leads into the grounds of the priory, whose later history is reflected in successive stages of Tudor and Georgian building. Most of the medieval abbey buildings have disappeared, including the church and cloister, but the 13th-century chapel of St Osyth still survives. Outside the priory, peacocks stalk about the lawns and deer browse in the park. The house and grounds are open in summer.

The village has a well-preserved centre with old weather-boarded houses. The original St Osyth was a 7th-century abbess, daughter of the king of the East Angles, who was murdered by marauding Danes in 653.

The road to Point Clear crosses St Osyth Creek, which has been dammed to form a lake wide and deep enough to allow water-skiing and windsurfing.

St Osyth's Priory gatehouse

④ SEAWICK AND JAYWICK
Both these small resorts have safe, sandy beaches, though the massive sea-wall is a reminder of the size of the waves that can lash this exposed stretch of coast. The coastal strip is covered by acres of caravans, chalets and bungalows, cut off from the hinterland by the network of channels and ditches that drain St Osyth Marsh. There are seaside amusements at Jaywick.

⑤ CLACTON-ON-SEA
After Southend, Clacton is the brightest resort on the Essex coast. As recently as 1860 it consisted only of the inland villages of Great and Little Clacton, and three Martello towers on the coast; one of these towers is now the coastguard station, with a children's zoo in the dry moat. The town grew rapidly at the end of the 19th century, and is now the 'capital' of the Tendring Peninsula – so called after the village of that name – which lies between the Stour to the north and the Colne to the south.

Behind the long sandy beach is a traffic-free promenade, backed by sloping gardens leading steeply up to the broad Marine Parade. The lively pier has a wide range of entertainments that give it a perpetual fairground atmosphere.

North-east of Clacton is the quieter, largely residential resort of Holland-on-Sea, beyond which there is a path along the sea-wall to Frinton.

Clacton has two theatres. Fishing trips can be arranged, and pleasure flights operate from Clacton Airfield.

⑥ FRINTON-ON-SEA
Developed as a resort in the 1890s by Sir Richard Cooker, Frinton still retains the gentility of those days, and is the only resort of any size in Britain without a pub. Its red-brick houses are built along broad, tree-lined avenues, leading to a sweeping expanse of grass called The Greensward. Below this, a fine sandy beach runs the whole length of the town. The main access for motorists is over the level crossing, as the railway seals off the landward side of the town.

⑦ WALTON-ON-THE NAZE
Walton is a family resort, with an excellent beach, sandy and safe, but almost completely covered at high tide. The town developed as a resort from about 1830; in its early days it was renowned for its sea holly, whose candied roots were sold for their supposed aphrodisiac qualities.

The pier, open in summer, is at nearly half a mile the second longest in England after Southend's. Walton's first pier was built in 1875 as a jetty for the paddle-steamers plying from London, but at low tide it did not reach the sea. It was rebuilt to its present length in the 1880s after the original pier was destroyed in a violent storm. Today privately owned, it offers a giant wheel, side-shows, and fishing for brill, cod, dab, haddock, hake, whiting and sole.

The Naze – the word is the same as Nose or Ness – is a wide area of grass and gorse north of the town, crowned by a tall octagonal brick tower built in 1720 as a navigational aid. Below the Naze, 40 ft sandstone cliffs drop to the shore; they are rich in fossils dating from the Ice Age. A 1¼ mile nature trail at The Naze gives the opportunity of seeing migrating birds in spring and autumn, and butterflies such as the Essex skipper and painted lady in summer. There are good views to Harwich and Felixstowe, and a 1½ mile walk along the sea-wall to Frinton.

⑧ KIRBY LE SOKEN QUAY
The quay is reached down Quay Lane from the village of Kirby le Soken. A footpath along the sea-wall gives good views over Walton Backwaters. The village takes its name from Norman times when it paid 'socage', or rent, to St Paul's in London.

⑨ BEAUMONT QUAY
Reached down a lane leading to Quay Farm (opposite Golden Lane), this quay, now lonely and derelict, is built of squared blocks of stone from Old London Bridge, built around 1200 and demolished in 1831. There are wide views across the marshes of Walton Backwaters, a solitary wilderness of tidal

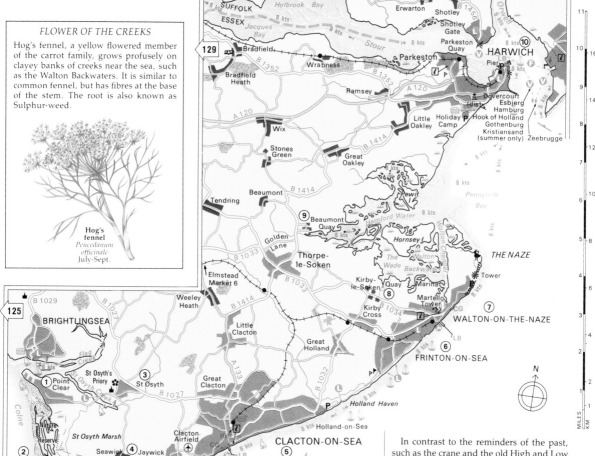

saltings and reed-fringed islands, the haunt of geese, sandpipers, terns and other water-birds. The parish is called Beaumont-cum-Moze, *moze* being Old English for 'marsh'.

⑩ HARWICH

Most of the great seafarers of the past have come to Harwich before setting out on their voyages, among them Raleigh, Drake, Frobisher and Nelson. In 1340 it was the assembly point for Edward III's fleet which defeated the French at Sluys, in the first major sea battle of the Hundred Years' War. The *Mayflower*, in which the Pilgrim Fathers set out from Plymouth in 1620, was an east-coast trading vessel which sailed from Harwich some time earlier and was chartered in the Thames for her American journey. Her master, Christopher Jones, lived in King's Head Street.

Another famous figure connected with Harwich was the diarist Samuel Pepys, commemorated by a plaque on the Town Hall. Pepys was Secretary of the Admiralty and MP for Harwich in Charles II's time, and the Merry Monarch himself took the first pleasure cruise from Harwich. Those days are recalled by the unique 17th-century treadmill crane, which stands on The Green just south of the harbour. Worked by manpower, it was designed to handle ammunition and stores.

In contrast to the reminders of the past, such as the crane and the old High and Low lighthouses, today's Harwich is a paradise for the ship-spotter. Fishing boats, Trinity House vessels including lightships, the modern Harwich lifeboat and ferries leaving from Parkeston can all be seen. A passenger ferry runs regularly across to Felixstowe from the Halfpenny Pier – so called because when it was opened the toll was a halfpenny – and in summer there are evening cruises on the Stour and Orwell.

The quayside at Harwich is the best place from which to see the big ships leaving Parkeston, itself so crowded with lorries that sight-seeing there is discouraged. From Parkeston, regular freight and passenger services go to the Hook of Holland, Esbjerg in Denmark, Gothenburg in Sweden, and Hamburg in Germany. Parkeston gets its name from Mr Parkes, the first chairman of the Great Eastern Railway in Victorian times, who built Parkeston Quay as a terminal for the packet-boat service to Holland.

Beyond Harwich Green is the resort area of Dovercourt, which has a sandy beach backed by a sea-wall. On the beach are low wooden groynes – walls built to check the drift of sand – and a pair of disused lighthouses on stilts. Built in 1863, they were replaced by buoys in 1917.

Launching facilities are available at Harwich Sailing Club (on the east side of the old town). There are two town trails, both less than a mile in length.

QUIET BACKWATERS *Kirby le Soken Quay overlooks the Walton Backwaters, a tranquil wilderness of reedy islands lying like the scattered pieces of a jigsaw puzzle behind The Naze.*

Stour valley scenes that made Constable a painter

The tidal waters of the Orwell and Stour brought wealth to the Suffolk-Essex border region in the Middle Ages, when Ipswich grew rich from the cloth trade. Both rivers are still busy waterways, with large ships loading and unloading at Ipswich and Mistley, and pleasure craft crowding the waters in summer. The spaciousness of the landscape has inspired paintings by many artists, from John Constable to Sir Alfred Munnings.

EAST BERGHOLT *Willy Lott's Cottage is as charming now as it was 200 years ago when John Constable made it the subject of his painting, now in the Christchurch Mansion Museum, Ipswich.*

① RAMSEY

This village on the way to Harwich has an attractive main street. Its landmark is a superb post-mill, built in 1842 and restored in the 1970s. Post-mills, once common in Suffolk, were so called because the body revolved on a central post and could be turned so that the sails faced the prevailing wind. The Ramsey mill is the only one of its type in Essex and can be visited by written arrangement with the owner at The Windmill House, Ramsey.

② WRABNESS

Beach huts down a lane leading from Wrabness mark one of the few sandy stretches on the Stour. Wrabness church has a detached belfry by the church gate. The single bell is housed in a wooden cage now overgrown with ivy. From Wrabness Point there is a fine view across the river to the Royal Hospital School.

③ MISTLEY

A tree-lined road called The Walls runs for half a mile westward along the river from Mistley to Manningtree, giving spectacular views of mute swans, part of a population of some 400 that live there. Mistley is now a flourishing port, trading in timber, grain and soya flour, with a quay taking boats up to 2,500 tons. It also has a Victorian-built malthouse still in operation, giving the air a malty smell.

Mistley's chief curiosity consists of a pair of identical church towers in the middle of a graveyard – the remains of a church built in the 1770s by Robert Adam. The church was part of an unsuccessful plan to turn Mistley into a spa, undertaken by Richard Rigby, a politician who made a fortune as paymaster-general of the forces. Another surviving part of the scheme is the stone swan fountain in the centre of Mistley.

④ MANNINGTREE

Once a busy port, this little Georgian town has now lost its trade to Mistley, a short way downstream. At the end of July Manningtree holds a regatta for the local punts – flat-bottomed boats with pointed bows, often home-made and originally fitted with wide-bore 'punt guns' for shooting wild-fowl. In the 17th century Manningtree was the headquarters of Matthew Hopkins, who terrorised East Anglia in his role of 'Witch Finder General'. With poetic justice, in 1647 he was himself accused of witchcraft, bound and thrown into the water – the usual test for witches. When he floated he was presumed guilty, and hanged.

⑤ EAST BERGHOLT

The birthplace in 1776 of John Constable is one of the most attractive villages in the area. Constable's father was the miller of Flatford Mill, a watermill 1 mile south of the village, now owned by the National Trust and run as a residential field studies centre. The beautiful brick mill and nearby white Willy Lott's Cottage are still as Constable painted them.

As a boy, Constable spent many hours on the banks of the Stour and became enchanted with the riverside scenery – scenes that, as he later wrote, 'made me a painter'. In 1799 he became a student at the Royal Academy in London, but returned to the Stour many times to make sketches for landscape paintings. The subjects he chose, such as Flatford Mill, Dedham Mill and stretches of the willow-lined river, make up the heart of 'Constable Country'. The house where the painter was born stood near the parish church, but only an outbuilding remains, now converted to a private cottage.

East Bergholt church has a timber-built bell cage, free-standing in the churchyard. Constable's parents and his friend Willy Lott are buried in the churchyard. John Constable himself is buried in the churchyard of St John's Church, Hampstead, London.

Stour Gardens, at the home of the late Randolph Churchill, are open daily.

⑥ ROYAL HOSPITAL SCHOOL

The school, moved from Greenwich in 1933, has an enormous tower, topped by a white stone pinnacle, that is a landmark for miles on both sides of the Stour. Greenwich Hospital was founded in 1694 for disabled and retired seamen of the Royal Navy; a school for their sons was founded in 1712, and the Holbrook school is its descendant. Preference is still given to the sons of seamen, including lifeboatmen.

South of the school is the isolated Stutton church, from which a path leads round Holbrook Bay to Shotley Gate. A landmark on the winding road that leads east from Holbrook to Shotley is the brick Tudor gatehouse of Erwarton Hall, built about 1550.

⑦ SHOTLEY GATE

At the end of the promontory that separates the Orwell and the Stour are the rows of buildings and towering fully rigged ship's mast that until 1977 made up HMS *Ganges*, a naval training base named after the training warship that formed the original base. It has now taken on a new lease of life as the Eurosports Village, a residential sports complex opened in 1981, providing training facilities for footballers, swimmers and gymnasts.

There is a good view across to the shipping of Harwich and Parkeston from the end of the road by Shotley pier.

⑧ PIN MILL

Reached down a lane from Chelmondiston village, Pin Mill is a famous riverside beauty spot. In summer the Orwell is crowded with pleasure boats of all sizes, from dinghies to red-sailed Thames sailing barges. At high spring tides, sailors can moor close to the walls of the Butt and Oyster Inn and order drinks without stepping ashore. The name Pin Mill has been explained in various ways;

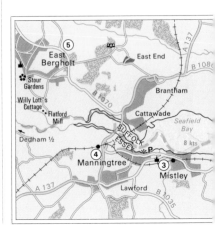

WORKHORSE OF THE THAMES

With their enormous red sails and broad, flat-bottomed hulls the Thames sailing barges were a familiar sight in Victorian times as they plied between London and the East Anglian ports. They carried grain, bricks and hay to the capital, returning with horse manure to fertilise farmland.

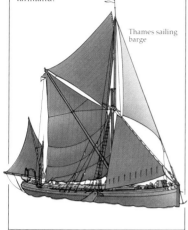
Thames sailing barge

one theory is that it derives from the wooden pegs or 'pins' that were made there and used in boat-building. The Pin Mill Barge Match is held there each July.

The National Trust owns the 17 acre Cliff Plantation, on the river bank between Pin Mill and Old Wharf, 1 mile to the east. Access is on foot only.

⑨ WOOLVERSTONE MARINA

A private road through parkland leads to the marina and sailing centre at Cat House where there are launching and casual-berth facilities. The name Cat House is said to date back to the 18th century, when the Orwell was a smugglers' river: a stuffed white cat, placed at night in a lighted window, was the signal that the coast was clear. The Royal Harwich Yacht Club has its premises at Woolverstone.

A path along the foreshore leads downstream to Pin Mill and upstream to Freston Tower. This is a lookout tower probably built about 1550, rising from trees beside the B1456.

⑩ IPSWICH

The county town of Suffolk, with a population of 123,000, Ipswich has been a port since the days of the Romans. In Anglo-Saxon times it was England's largest port, and throughout the Middle Ages it prospered with the growth of the wool trade. In 1404 it was made a 'staple port' – one of the ports from which wool could be legally exported – and also traded in skins, leather and fish. Cardinal Wolsey was born in Ipswich about 1475, and a few of the town's fine half-timbered buildings still survive from the Tudor period, notably the Ancient House, with superb pargeting, or moulded external plasterwork.

For centuries Ipswich was a centre of shipbuilding, with yards extending from the present dock area as far as Nacton. The town's official seal, dating from 1200, is the earliest known depiction of a ship with a

CONFECTION IN PLASTER *The plasterwork on the Ancient House in Ipswich, built in 1567, includes the coat of arms of Charles II.*

modern rudder instead of the traditional steering oar. As Ipswich is a dozen miles from the open sea, the port has been at constant risk from silting. By 1800 the harbour was almost choked, and it took almost half a century of dredging and dock-building before trade recovered. This period saw the building of the fine porticoed Old Custom House, opened in 1845, which is now the headquarters of the Ipswich Port Authority.

The dock area, stretching for more than a mile along both banks of the Orwell, handles timber, grain, general cargo and raw materials. A short way downstream, the immense Orwell Bridge links the A12 with the A45, and carries heavy lorries to Felixstowe harbour.

There are two museums: Ipswich Museum and Christchurch Mansion, a 16th-century house which has paintings by Constable and Gainsborough. There is a theatre, and a 1 mile town trail.

⑪ NACTON

A track on the east side of Orwell Park School leads down to the foreshore, an expanse of tidal flats with wide views and the bubbling sound of curlews calling. In the 18th century Orwell Park was the home of Admiral Sir Edward Vernon (1684-1757), whose nickname of 'Old Grog', given him because of his suit of coarse grogram cloth, was applied to the 'grog' introduced by him to the navy – a daily ration of rum mixed with water. By the house is a domed 19th-century observatory, and a medieval church lies on the other side of the lane.

⑫ SUFFOLK YACHT HARBOUR

This large marina, on the foreshore below the pretty village of Levington, has both launching and casual-berth facilities. Downstream are the lonely saltings of Trimley Marshes, across which a coastal footpath leads to Felixstowe.

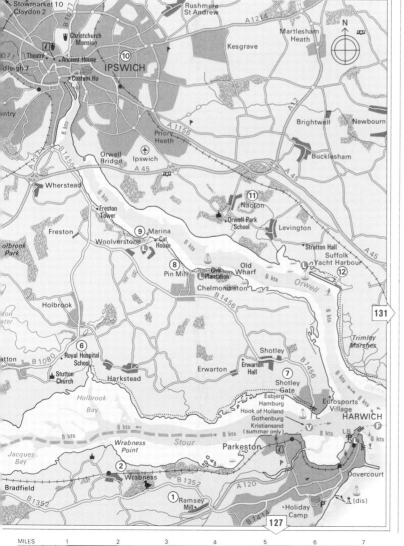

MILES 1 2 3 4 5 6 7
KM 1 2 4 6 8 10

Shingle beaches from Felixstowe to an island bird reserve

The River Deben, winding downstream between marshes and low wooded hills, reaches the sea between Felixstowe Ferry and Bawdsey Quay. There it forms the one major break in the long banks of red shingle that line the shore north of Landguard Point. The delights of this coast are quiet rather than spectacular, ranging from the sedate holiday pleasures of Felixstowe to the bird-haunted wilderness of Havergate Island.

TIDAL POWER *Woodbridge's tide mill, powered by the tide's ebb and flow, could work only for 2 hours either side of low water.*

① FELIXSTOWE

There are two distinct aspects to Felixstowe. One is the family seaside resort, consisting largely of gabled houses built around 1900, with the coming of the railway; the other is the busy container port which has expanded in recent years to become one of the largest in Europe.

Seaside Felixstowe is strung out round a gently curving bay, above a beach consisting of banks of red shingle, with patches of sand at low tide. The town prides itself on the beauty of its seafront gardens, especially the Spa Gardens, north of the pier. The Victorian atmosphere is heightened by the rows of bathing huts along the promenade. The Spa Pavilion provides theatrical entertainments, and there is fishing to be had from the pier and the beach.

At the south end of the town a road leads to Landguard Fort. The first fort was built on Landguard Point in the 1540s, to guard the eastern entrance to Harwich Harbour. The present fort dates mainly from 1718. The chapel above the gateway was the scene of a notorious scandal in 1763, when the acting governor of the fort held a dance in the chapel, and used the altar as a bar.

Just beyond the fort is a small public viewing area, with parking space for about a dozen cars, where ships from the port pass so near that the observer can almost reach out and touch them.

Swimming is safe, except at Landguard Point where there are dangerous currents. There are also hazards 1 mile north of the pier, where remains of an old pier are covered at high tide, and 2 miles north, where the remains of an old fort lie 75 yds from the low-water mark. Felixstowe is the southern end of the Suffolk Coast Path, which runs north for 50 miles to Lowestoft.

Day trips round Harwich and the Stour estuary run from Felixstowe docks, and there are cross-Channel day trips to Zeebrugge in Belgium. There is a ferry for foot passengers to Harwich.

② FELIXSTOWE FERRY

This small village is clustered round a Martello tower – one of three on the coast between the Deben and Orwell rivers. It is reached by road or on foot across the wide spaces of the Felixstowe golf course. The ferry, for foot passengers only, across the mouth of the River Deben to Bawdsey Quay runs at weekends in summer. Swimming is hazardous, as the tide at the river mouth can run at 4-5 knots.

③ WALDRINGFIELD

Twisting by-roads lead from Felixstowe through Kirton and Newbourn to this attractive little village on the River Deben. The waterfront is muddy shingle, with a small sandy beach, firm enough for launching boats. Waldringfield is a busy sailing centre, with ships' chandlers and boatyards on the narrow lane that runs along the foreshore. It is also a favourite place for the birdwatcher, with teals, wigeons, shelducks and turnstones to be seen.

Lovers of solitude can find it in riverside walks upstream and downstream, though breaks in the river wall limit them to 1 mile or so in both directions.

Parking at the waterfront is very restricted, but there is a large car park behind the Maybush Inn just up the hill.

④ WOODBRIDGE

Woodbridge must come high on anyone's list of the most picturesque small towns in East Anglia. From its central market place, dominated by the Dutch-gabled Shire Hall and the magnificent parish church of St Mary's, steep streets of old houses lead down to the level of the River Deben. The town's name is said to derive from the Anglo-Saxon *Woden Burh*, meaning 'Woden's town', and it was already an important place in Saxon times.

The quayside, reached by way of the level-crossing, is an attractive jumble of boatyards and chandleries, with yachts of all shapes and sizes lying at anchor, or stranded on the mud at low tide. Its chief landmark is the superb, white weather-boarded Tide Mill, built in the 1790s and now restored to working condition and open to the public as a museum; it is open daily from mid-July to mid-September, and at weekends during the remainder of the summer.

The first mill on the site was built about 1170, and its last successor remained in operation until 1957. As the tide rose, the pressure of the water opened the sluice gates and filled a 7½ acre pond behind the mill. When the tide turned, the first outflow of water closed the gates, leaving the pond full. When the tide had fallen far enough, the miller opened the sluice gates and released the water to drive the mill wheel.

Woodbridge's best-known resident was the 19th-century poet Edward FitzGerald, who translated *The Rubá'iyát* of Omar Khayyám from Persian into English. He died in 1883, and is buried in the lonely church-yard at Boulge. The rose tree above his grave was grown from a hip brought from Omar's grave in Iran.

South of the town is Kyson Hill, 4 acres of which belong to the National Trust. From the southern slopes of the hill there are panoramic views across the river. A footpath leads down to the Deben's muddy foreshore and then follows the river bank to Wood-bridge quay.

⑤ SUTTON HEATH

Much of the original heathland of the plateau east of the Deben has vanished before the needs of modern farming and forestry. Sutton Heath is a valuable reminder of what this whole tract of countryside was like a century ago. There are two car parks and picnic sites, backed by gorse, conifers and bracken, while a nature trail takes about an hour to walk.

⑥ RAMSHOLT QUAY

Ramsholt's pretty little boating haven, consisting of a waterfront pub, a disused ferry quay, and a shingle foreshore leading down to mud, is reached down Dock Road. Parking by the foreshore is limited, and the last 300 yds down to the quay is a private road, but there is a large car park at the top of the hill, giving glorious views towards the Deben estuary.

Ramsholt's lonely church of All Saints, which has a battered Norman round tower, can be reached by a half-mile walk along a footpath from the quay. Near by is a small sandy beach known as The Rocks.

⑦ BAWDSEY QUAY

Although the tip of the quay is Ministry of Defence property, leading to an RAF station, the public are allowed on to it and cars can park there. There is a passenger ferry across to Felixstowe Ferry. North of the quay is a

---

A SAXON KING'S TREASURE

At Sutton Hoo, across the River Deben from Woodbridge, lies a sandy heath where in 1939 the buried treasure of a Saxon king was found beneath a grave mound. A priceless hoard of jewellery, coins and regalia had been placed in a sea-going ship and buried in a great oval pit. The owner of the hoard may have been King Raedwald, King of East Anglia from about AD 610 to 625. But no trace of a body was found in the ship, so the burial may have been intended as a cenotaph rather than as a tomb. The treasures are now in the British Museum.

A fiercesome bronze and iron helmet is part of the Sutton Hoo treasure.

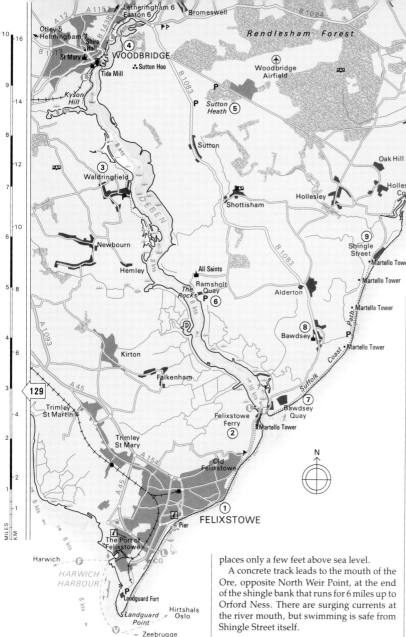

bird sanctuary. The water levels in the bare, muddy lagoons are artificially maintained to provide the correct depth of water for Britain's oldest and largest breeding colony of avocets, which returned there to nest in 1947, after being absent from Britain for 100 years. Gulls, terns, shelducks and redshanks are also present.

The island can be reached only by boat from Orford Quay. All tours are escorted by the warden; permits and visiting dates must be sought in advance from the Permit Secretary, 30 Mundays Lane, Orford, Woodbridge.

LOCAL INFORMATION

Tourist information Felixstowe 282122/282126.

HM Coastguard Frinton-on-Sea 5518 for information, 999 in emergency (ask for coastguard).

Weather Ipswich 8091.

Local radio IBA Radio Orwell, 257 m, 1170 kHz, 97.1 MHz.

PLACES TO SEE INLAND

Easton Farm Park, 8 miles N of Woodbridge. Working Victorian farm. Sun.-Fri. in summer.

Helmingham Hall, 8 miles N of Woodbridge, on B1077. Gardens and park. Sun. afternoons in summer.

Letheringham Watermill, 8 miles N of Woodbridge, off B1078. 18th-century mill. Some afternoons in summer.

Otley Hall, 6 miles NW of Woodbridge. 15th-century house. Occasional afternoons in summer.

---

places only a few feet above sea level.

A concrete track leads to the mouth of the Ore, opposite North Weir Point, at the end of the shingle bank that runs for 6 miles up to Orford Ness. There are surging currents at the river mouth, but swimming is safe from Shingle Street itself.

⑩ HAVERGATE ISLAND
This boomerang-shaped island of 300 acres, lying in the long channel that runs downstream from Orford to the sea, is an RSPB

small shingle beach, but bathing is dangerous. There is good fishing from the shingle beach south of the quay.

⑧ BAWDSEY
The road to Bawdsey village from Bawdsey Quay passes the radar 'ears' and sinister, dart-like missiles of RAF Bawdsey. It was there that radar was developed before the Second World War, and the modern dish aerials are the successors to the system that played an important part during the Battle of Britain.

The beach, reached down East Lane opposite the church, consists of steep banks of dark red shingle, held in place by frequent breakwaters, and backed by a large Second World War strongpoint, with limited car parking behind. The foreshore to the north is guarded by a row of Martello towers, reminders that this spot has long been a likely landing point for a would-be invader.

⑨ SHINGLE STREET
As its name suggests, Shingle Street, reached down a twisting road from Hollesley, is little more than a row of cottages built above a boat-studded stretch of shingle, which the sea has pushed up into a high bank. Hollows in the shingle enclose shallow lagoons left by the high tides. Behind the beach are peaceful water-meadows, in

SHINGLE STRAND *The beach that gives Shingle Street its name is vast, lonely and desolate, yet there is a compelling appeal in the row of white cottages, the sea-mirrored sky and the curving foreshore.*

A house in the clouds and a town lost beneath the waves

Down the centuries this long stretch of coast has been at the mercy of wind and tide, which can change the seashore overnight. Orford was once a prosperous seaport; at Aldeburgh, houses stood where there is now only shingle; and at Dunwich the most prosperous town of Norman Suffolk is now under the sea. Today Aldeburgh attracts music-lovers, while Minsmere offers one of the country's finest sites for birdwatching.

① DUNWICH

A solitary gravestone near the edge of a shallow cliff, with rabbits nibbling the turf and sand martins wheeling overhead, marks the death of old Dunwich. The stone is the last survivor of All Saints' Church, which collapsed into the sea about 1920, following Saxon, Norman and medieval Dunwich into the waves, carried away by the relentless erosion of wind and tide. It is said that at times the submerged church bells can be heard, ringing out a warning of an approaching storm.

In Saxon times Dunwich was a flourishing port on the River Blyth, with its own bishop and grammar school. Norman Dunwich was even more prosperous, with three churches, several chapels, and as many as 5,000 inhabitants. Erosion was kept at bay by the simple expedient of piling brushwood, weighted with stones, on the shingle – done each autumn, this was quite enough to give protection for the following winter. But in January 1326, in the course of a single night's storm, 1 million tons of sand and shingle were banked across the harbour mouth, cutting it off from the sea and diverting the River Blyth northwards. This effectively killed the town's trade. Merchants and citizens moved away, and Dunwich was abandoned to the elements. Year after year the sea took its toll; whole streets and buildings tumbled from the cliffs, and by 1677 the waves had reached the market place.

Apart from the gravestone, old Dunwich is recalled by the remains of the leper chapel beside the Victorian parish church, and by the archways of a medieval friary, which can be seen beside the road. There is an excellent little museum on the town's history.

② DUNWICH HEATH

This 214 acre expanse of sandy heathland, owned by the National Trust, stands on a crumbling cliff 2 miles south of the 'lost city' of Dunwich. Open all the year, it has a shop and information centre, and a large car park by the old coastguard cottages at the top of the cliffs. A waymarked walk leads round the edge of the heath, and gives a good idea of the varied terrain contained within such a small area. To the south, Sizewell nuclear power station can be seen across the wetlands of Minsmere.

③ WESTLETON

About 2½ miles inland from the crumbling cliffs of Dunwich lies Westleton, a village as English as the archers who once practised on its green; as tranquil as its village pond and as old world as its thatched-roof church.

St Peter's Church has stood on a rise near the green since 1340, an unprepossessing building with none of the grandeur of the great Suffolk churches built by wealthy wool merchants in the 17th century. Prosperity, it seems, passed Westleton by, and it is none the worse for it.

To the north-east of the village is Westleton Heath, one of the last surviving examples of Suffolk heathland where sheep once grazed. It encloses a nature reserve and is a splendid area for walking.

④ MINSMERE RESERVE

A 1,500 acre expanse at the mouth of the Minsmere river is administered by the RSPB as a bird reserve. Its mixed habitat, consisting of reedbeds, artificial lagoons and islands, together with heath and woodland, shelters the greatest variety of breeding birds of any reserve in the country. More than 100 species of birds that breed there include nightjars, woodcocks, nightingales, marsh harriers, bitterns and avocets; and there are many migrant species.

Shore birds can be watched from a large public hide reached along the shore from the National Trust car park on Dunwich Heath and open at all times. To visit the main reserve, permits must be obtained from the reception centre in the reserve; visiting dates can be obtained from the RSPB.

⑤ LEISTON ABBEY

The magnificent ruins of the abbey stand on the west side of the B1122, 1 mile north of Leiston. A footpath leads to the abbey from the outskirts of Leiston, but it is very overgrown. Founded at nearby Minsmere in 1183, the abbey was rebuilt on its present site in 1363. The brick and flint remains are substantial, and include a good deal of the transepts, presbytery and lady chapel. The Georgian house inside the ruins is used as a religious retreat.

Much of Leiston village was built by Richard Garrett, the 19th-century railway pioneer whose firm built the Garrett locomotive.

⑥ SIZEWELL

The first of two nuclear power stations planned for the site was built in the early 1960s and first produced power in 1966. Its vast grey bulk, supplying a network of enormous pylons, dominates the shore for miles. Producing enough electricity to power a city the size of Bristol, it stands on a 245 acre site and uses 27 million gallons of seawater per hour to cool the reactors. The warmed water, which returns to the sea through two large structures resembling oil-rigs offshore, attracts fish to the area, and the beach is popular with fishermen. A Nuclear Exhibition and Information Centre is open on weekdays.

Sizewell village consists of a few cottages, with boats on the shingle. In the 18th century it was a notorious smuggling village, where a record 8,000 gallons of gin were once landed in one night. Its beacon light was last used in 1918, as a navigation aid to British warships which took their bearings from it before bombarding Zeebrugge, in Belgium.

BIRDWATCHING AT MINSMERE

For almost 100 years avocets failed to breed in Britain, but they returned to the east coast in the 1940s when most of it was closed to the public because of the war. Now they breed regularly at the RSPB's Minsmere Reserve, which is also the home of the rare marsh harrier and some 100 other breeding species.

Avocet
Recurvirostra avosetta

Marsh harrier
Circus aeruginosus

HIGH WATER *The House in the Clouds at Thorpeness is really a water-tower – one of the many local buildings that are not what they seem – and the windmill once pumped water to it.*

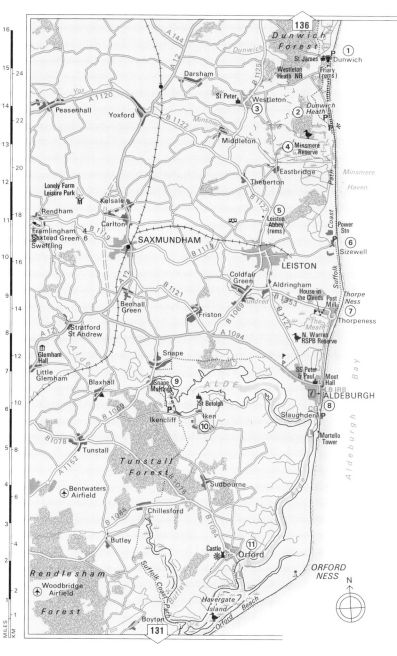

136

131

since 1948 it has won world-wide fame for its annual Music Festival in June.

Old Aldeburgh lives on in its half-timbered Moot Hall, built about 1512. The local council still holds its meetings upstairs, and the building is open to the public in summer, when old maps and other documents are on view. The Moot Hall is now almost on the shingle, but in the 16th century there were three roads, since washed away, between it and the sea.

The poet George Crabbe was born in Aldeburgh in 1754. His best-known poem, *The Borough*, describes the harsh life of the Suffolk coastal folk of his day; and Benjamin Britten used Crabbe's pen-portrait of the savage and tormented fisherman Peter Grimes as the basis for his first and best-known opera. At the time of his death in 1976, Britten had been directing the festival for almost 30 years. Aldeburgh's church of St Peter and St Paul has a memorial window to him by John Piper, and a memorial bust of Crabbe is on the wall near by.

South of the town is a massive sea-wall, wide enough for cars to drive along and park. Boats can be launched at Slaughden Quay into the River Alde. From there the river flows for 10 miles parallel to the sea. The Martello tower south of Slaughden is the northernmost of the chain built against Napoleon in the 1800s. A short way south of the tower the shingle is Ministry of Defence property, and there is no public access.

Swimming is safe, and there is fishing from the shore for plaice, sole, flounder, bass and cod.

MUSIC CENTRE *Every musical entertainment from ballet to jazz is performed at Snape Maltings, home of the Aldeburgh Festival.*

⑦ THORPENESS

This unique holiday village was laid out before the First World War by Glencairn Stuart Ogilvie, a dramatist and author. It was planned around a specially dug 65 acre lake, only 3 ft deep, called The Meare. The houses, built mainly of heavily disguised concrete, are in many different styles, including Tudor, Elizabethan, and traditional 18th-century East Anglian tarred weather-board.

The two most unusual buildings face each other, up a track called Uplands Road. They are The House in the Clouds, originally a water-tower, and a fully restored post mill. The mill, built in 1803, was moved to Thorpeness in the 1920s, and is now a coastal information centre.

Small boats can be hired on The Meare. Swimming from the shingle beach is safe, except 1 mile to the north, at Thorpe Ness, where large holes are formed in the shingle by strong winds and tides.

⑧ ALDEBURGH

A long main street of Georgian houses and older cottages, a wide strip of shingle, small huts selling fresh fish, and a smartly painted lifeboat on the beach – these are the first impressions given by the delightful little town of Aldeburgh. It has probably been settled since Saxon times (the name may mean 'old fort', *Aldburh* in Anglo-Saxon). In the Middle Ages and later it was a prosperous port and fishing centre, it became a seaside resort in the early 19th century, and

STANDING BY *The Aldeburgh lifeboat is a beach-launched vessel of the Rother class, one of the smallest of the modern long-range RNLI boats.*

⑨ SNAPE MALTINGS

These magnificent red-brick Victorian buildings, built to process barley, stand at the navigable limit of the River Alde. Though several of them still carry out a workaday role as stores for barley and offices for grain merchants, the Maltings are famous throughout the musical world for their concert hall, which was converted by the organisers of the Aldeburgh Festival in 1967, burned down in 1969, and restored the following year.

The Maltings complex now includes a teashop, an art gallery, a craft centre, and the Britten-Pears School for Advanced Musical Studies, named after the composer Benjamin Britten and the singer Peter Pears, who were largely responsible for establishing the Aldeburgh Festival in 1948. The mown grass between the Maltings and the estuary provides a fine setting for two sculptures by Henry Moore and Barbara Hepworth.

Visitors can walk out on to the marshes, but the paths are covered at high tide.

ALDEBURGH: A TOWN HOLDING THE SEA AT BAY

A sea-wall and rows of breakwaters hold back the sea that has shaped Aldeburgh and its history. Water laps the shingle where 300 years ago stood streets of houses – the homes of men who sailed with Drake in Pelican *and* Greyhound, *built in local yards. But the sea ended shipbuilding when the River Alde silted up, leaving Aldeburgh with only its charm to nurse and cherish.*

⑩ IKEN

Once an important fishing village, renowned for its herring, salmon and sea trout, Iken is now a scattered hamlet built on high ground above the marshes of the Alde. St Botolph's Church, reached down a narrow cul-de-sac, is a sad place, as its thatched roof was burned down in 1968 and has never been restored.

At Ikencliff, 1 mile west of the church,

there is a large picnic site with fine views across the reeds and mud-flats of the Alde. A footpath (impassable at high tide) leads to Snape Maltings. Birds to be seen include shelducks, redshanks and herons.

⑪ ORFORD

Today Orford is little more than an attractive village of mellow houses round a small square, with a road leading down to a quay.

That Orford was a more important community in earlier times is shown by the scale of its magnificent castle keep, built in 1165 by Henry II to control the prosperous and independent-spirited East Anglians. In those days the spit of shingle that now stretches 6 miles south-west from Orford Ness ended near the quay, but the gradual growth of the spit cut Orford off from the open sea, and the town's prosperity declined. In 1722, Daniel Defoe wrote that Orford 'is now decayed. The sea daily throws up more land, so it is a seaport no longer'.

North of the town the river is called the Alde, while south it becomes the Ore. Boats

can be launched from the foreshore, but permission is needed to use the slipway. A notice on the quay warns that bathing is dangerous.

The 90 ft castle keep, unusually constructed with three turrets, is open daily, and gives magnificent views from its battlements. Towards the sea, the most prominent landmark is the red-and-white lighthouse on Orford Ness, with various Ministry of Defence structures on the foreshore. Birdwatchers bound for Havergate Island take a boat from Orford.

A good hour's walk starts downstream along the river-wall, then returns inland to the castle.

SYMBOL OF POWER *Orford Castle was built by Henry II in the 12th century to regain royal power in East Anglia.*

LOCAL INFORMATION

Tourist information Felixstowe 282122/282126, Aldeburgh 3637 (summer).

HM Coastguard Frinton-on-Sea 5518, Great Yarmouth 51338 for information, 999 in emergency (ask for coastguard).

Weather Ipswich 8091.

PLACES TO SEE INLAND

Framlingham Castle, 14 miles NW of Aldeburgh. 12th-century. Daily.

Glemham Hall, 8 miles W of Aldeburgh. Elizabethan house. Some afternoons in summer.

Saxtead Green Windmill, 2 miles NW of Framlingham. 18th century. Daily in summer.

135

Ports ancient and modern at England's eastern tip

The golden weather-vane of St Margaret's Church, high above Britain's easternmost town of Lowestoft, is the first object in Britain to catch the light of the morning sun. Its beaches make Lowestoft a bustling seaside resort, while to the south the old-world charm of Southwold offers a different type of seaside holiday. Oulton Broad, the southernmost of the Broads, makes a delightful introduction to the entire network of inland waterways.

SHINING LANDMARK *Southwold lighthouse soars above Georgian houses and cottages, its white walls and golden weather-vane making it a landmark by day as well as by night.*

① LOWESTOFT

A popular seaside resort and a busy port, Lowestoft is split in half by the narrow strip of water called Lake Lothing. The two halves are linked only by a bascule bridge, whose two halves are raised to admit large merchantmen into the heart of the town.

The town's prosperity began in the mid-1800s, with the exploitation of the Dogger Bank and other North Sea fishing grounds. The main catch was herring, which were cured in the town and sent to London, the Midlands, and as far afield as Australia. By 1900 the old sailing luggers had been largely superseded by steam-powered drifters, so called because their large nets were allowed to drift with the tide while catching the herring. The height of the herring boom came just before the First World War, when more than 700 drifters worked from Lowestoft.

Overfishing in recent years has led to a decline in the herring, and today 60-70 per cent of the catch is plaice, 20 per cent is cod, and the remainder consists of dab, dogfish, brill and other fish. The fishing fleet today consists of fewer than 50 motor trawlers.

The trawler basin and commercial docks are north of the bridge, as are the old town (badly damaged by bombs during the Second World War), the lighthouse, and the splendid little Maritime Museum, full of relics of the golden age of the herring fishery. This part of the town has a unique series of parallel lanes, running steeply from the High Street down to foreshore level, known as 'Scores', perhaps because they were 'scoured' or cut out between the buildings. Lowestoft Ness has the distinction of being Britain's easternmost point.

South of the bridge and the harbour is the resort half of the town, largely laid out in the 19th century by Sir Samuel Morton Peto, the builder whose firm built Nelson's Column and the Houses of Parliament in London. His connection with Lowestoft began in the 1840s, when he built a railway so that fish could be delivered fresh from the market to Manchester.

The sandy South Beach, patrolled by lifeguards in summer, lies south of the South Pier of the harbour. Swimming is safe, except near the harbour entrance. Windsurfing is forbidden inside the harbour. There are amusement arcades and fishing on the South Pier and Claremont Pier, and a summer theatre. Guided walking tours of the fishing harbour start from the Tourist Information Centre on the Esplanade. North Beach, below Gunton Cliffs, is another favourite place for swimming.

Lowestoft marks the northern end of the Suffolk Coast Path, which runs south for 50 miles to Felixstowe.

② OULTON BROAD

Powerboats racing on this attractive stretch of water on a fine summer's evening present an unforgettable sight as they throw up clouds of spray against the setting sun. This inland water, fed by the River Waveney, is a popular centre for sailing and fishing, too. It is connected to Lowestoft by a lock and a lake, Lake Lothing. There is limited parking at the Boulevard, just south of the Broad, which leads into the Nicholas Everitt Park, a good place for watching the boats or for

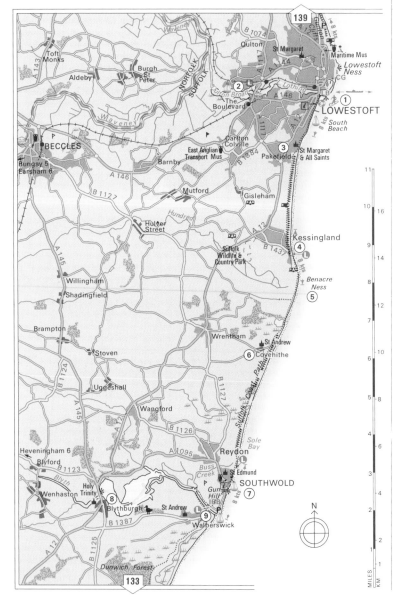

taking a stroll. The Boulevard is also the starting point for trips on the River Waveney, and boats can be hired there.

③ PAKEFIELD
A southern extension of Lowestoft, Pakefield has a sandy, shingle-scattered beach, below low grassy banks. The church of St Margaret and All Saints dates from the 14th century and was two churches in one until 1748, with two parishes and two rectors. It suffered badly from bomb damage in the Second World War, but has since been rebuilt.

④ KESSINGLAND
The beach consists of a wide shingle bank, covered in boats, with amusements behind. On the outskirts of the village, just off the A12, is the entrance to the Suffolk Wildlife and Country Park. Open daily in summer, it contains a wide variety of animals and birds in natural surroundings, including wallabies, timber wolves, sacred ibis and black swans.

⑤ BENACRE NESS
This shingle headland can be reached only on foot by a 1½ mile walk down a road that is closed to cars. It is the second most easterly point in England, after Lowestoft Ness. Swimming can be dangerous, as fast currents sweep round the point.

⑥ COVEHITHE
Lonely and dramatically sited, Covehithe's ruined church of St Andrew's is remarkable for its small thatched church built in 1672 inside the windowless and roofless nave. The original church, built in the 15th century, became too large for the parishioners to maintain, so they built the smaller church using the materials from the old.

The road ends at a gate a short way beyond the church. There is no public access to the beach beyond this point because of the dangerous state of the cliffs; however, a footpath starting just opposite the church leads under trees then across open heathland to low cliffs with a distant view of the roofs of Southwold to the south. The sand-and-shingle beach stretches in either direction as far as the eye can see, and a reedy lagoon among sand-dunes behind the beach teems with birdlife.

In 1672 a fleet led by the Dutch admiral de Ruyter confronted the combined French and English fleets off Covehithe, at the Battle of Sole Bay. The Dutch withdrew only after a bitter fight.

⑦ SOUTHWOLD
A strong malty smell pervades the air of Southwold, for this elegant little town is the home of Adnams' brewery, whose drays, loaded with barrels and pulled by pairs of magnificent percheron horses, are frequently seen in the streets. Southwold's redbrick and flint cottages and colour-washed houses are built round seven 'Greens' – open spaces which came into being after a great fire in 1659, and mark the sites of houses that were destroyed and never rebuilt. Domesday Book records that Southwold was a prosperous fishing port in the 11th century.

At its southern end, the town rises to the grassy slopes of Gun Hill, so called from the six cannons that stand there, pointing out to sea. The first guns were given to the town in the 1630s by Charles I, to protect Southwold ships against the 'Dunkirkers' – privateers operating from Dunkirk. The existing guns were given by George II in 1745 after the townspeople had complained that 'this place is in a very dangerous condition for want of Guns and Ammunition being naked and exposed to the insults of the Common Enemys'. They are 18-pounders, and at the time they were sent to Southwold were already about 150 years old. They were hidden away during the two world wars.

Southwold's sandy beach, lined with beach huts and protected by groynes, is safe for swimming except round the harbour entrance, half a mile south of Gun Hill. The seaward end of the pier, once popular among fishermen, was destroyed in a storm in 1979, but has been restored. There is an amusement arcade at the shore end.

Southwold is built virtually on an island, as on its north side it is cut off from the hinterland by Buss Creek, named after the herring 'busses', or fishing boats that once used the waterway, and on the south by the last mile or so of the River Blyth, lined with boatyards and huts selling fresh fish.

Southwold's museum in Victoria Street contains relics connected with local history. The parish church of St Edmund is one of the finest in Suffolk, with a glorious painted screen of about 1500 that escaped the attentions of both Henry VIII and Oliver Cromwell. It also has 'Southwold Jack', the 15th-century oak figure of a man-at-arms, carrying a sword and a battle-axe. When a cord is pulled the axe strikes a bell, to signal the start of services and the entry of the bride at a wedding.

⑧ BLYTHBURGH
The size and splendour of the church of the Holy Trinity at Blythburgh has earned it the nickname of the 'Cathedral of the Marshes'. When the church was built in the 15th century, Blythburgh was an important town, with a bustling quayside by the River Blyth, thronged with merchants made rich by the Suffolk wool trade. But ships grew in size, the Blyth silted up, and Blythburgh shrank to the size of the small village it is today.

In Cromwell's time the church was desecrated. His men used the great winged angels of the ceiling for target practice, and screwed tethering rings for their horses into the pillars. Unusual features of the church are the little priest's chamber above the south porch and, south of the altar, a 'Jack-o'-the-Clock'. This painted wooden figure holds a hatchet, which strikes against a bell when a string connected to it is pulled. At the same time his head turns.

North of the village, a layby on the A12 gives wide views over the estuary. After floods during the 1920s the Blyth engulfed the water-meadows on either side.

⑨ WALBERSWICK
The B1387 comes to an end past the village green of Walberswick, once a flourishing port at the mouth of the River Blyth. Just across the river lie the boatyards of Southwold; to reach them by road involves a journey of 8 miles.

Walberswick is popular with small-boat sailors. The river foreshore is muddy, with strong currents; but the beach, reached down an unmade road, is sandy and safe for swimming. The tall church of St Andrew outside the village is partly in ruins but the present church has been built inside the crumbling walls. A nature reserve is signposted on the north side of the road west of Walberswick.

LOCAL INFORMATION

Tourist information Lowestoft 65989, Southwold 722366 (summer).

HM Coastguard Great Yarmouth 851338 for information, 999 in emergency (ask for coastguard).

Weather Lowestoft 8091.

PLACES TO SEE INLAND

Beccles and District Museum, Beccles. Agricultural and industrial history. Some afternoons in summer, Sun. afternoons only in winter.

Bungay Castle, 14 miles W of Lowestoft. Norman remains. Daily.

East Anglian Transport Museum, Carlton Colville, 3 miles SW of Lowestoft. Weekends in summer, most afternoons in Aug.

Heveningham Hall Gardens, 14 miles SW of Southwold, on B1117. Daily in Aug.

Otter Trust, Earsham, near Bungay, 14 miles W of Lowestoft. Daily in summer.

Blythburgh's Jack-o'-the-Clock

SPLENDOUR IN THE MARSHES *Blythburgh church has the majesty of a cathedral, with its buttresses, long nave and Gothic windows. Inside, the quaint 'Jack-o'-the-Clock' stands poised to strike his bell.*

A fair on the beach, and forts built by the Romans and Normans

This stretch of coast spans almost 2,000 years of history, from the remains of Caister's Roman town to the booming port of Great Yarmouth, once a major fishing centre and now one of the main bases for the North Sea oil industry. Except for Great Yarmouth itself and its quieter neighbour Gorleston-on-Sea, the coast with its long sandy beaches is largely given over to seaside holidaymaking, with lines of caravans, chalet villages and holiday camps.

① HEMSBY

The road from the village leads down past amusement arcades to a wide sandy beach, with limited parking behind the dunes. Swimming is safe.

Newport Beach, a little way to the south, can be reached only by a footpath leading off the road which runs east out of Hemsby. Parking at the end of the road is extremely limited.

② CALIFORNIA

Named after the pub that stands at the top of a steep track leading down to the beach, California consists mainly of holiday villages and caravan parks. The beach is sandy, scattered with shingle, and is backed by low cliffs which are liable to falls.

③ CAISTER-ON-SEA

The name comes from the Latin *castra*, meaning a 'camp' or 'fortress', and the substantial remains of a Roman town can be seen on the north side of the road leading westwards out of the town towards Filby. Caister was founded in the 2nd century AD and was one of the chief towns of the Iceni, the East Anglian people ruled earlier by Queen Boudicca. The remains of Caister's 3rd-century Roman defences include part of the town wall and buildings of the main street, and a section of wide cobbled road, with a drain down the middle.

Caister's wide sandy beach, with dunes behind, is reached down Beach Road, where there is a large car park. Bathing is generally safe, but the beach shelves steeply in places, and there are signs warning the unwary against strong tides and deep water.

Caister Castle, down a by-road 2 miles west of the village, is a magnificent ruin. It was built in the 1430s by Sir John Fastolf (1378-1459), who commanded the English archers at Agincourt in 1415, and whose name was almost certainly the basis for Shakespeare's Falstaff. However, the original Fastolf, unlike Shakespeare's fat knight, was certainly not a coward.

Caister Castle has the added bonus of a motor museum, whose exhibits include a steam-powered car made in 1904, and a car used in the film *Chitty-Chitty-Bang-Bang*.

④ GREAT YARMOUTH

Yarmouth has achieved a peaceful coexistence between its spacious seafront, which runs for nearly 4 miles from the North Beach down to the South Beach, and its busy commercial harbour, which stretches for more than 2 miles along the River Yare, almost parallel to the seashore.

The town takes its name from the Yare, which after meandering across low-lying meadows east of Norwich, widens out into the expanse of Breydon Water, and then turns sharply south, creating the peninsula on which Yarmouth is built. The old town and port grew up along the east bank of the Yare, turning its back on the sea, then spread along the west bank into an area confusingly called Southtown. There are two bridges across the river, though there is a foot-passenger ferry further down the river below Southtown.

By the time of Domesday Book in 1086 Yarmouth merited a mention, and it grew steadily throughout the Middle Ages as a harbour and shipbuilding centre. A good deal of the town wall still survives. Between the wall and the river the houses were squeezed together into 145 narrow lanes known as 'Rows', one of them only 30 in. wide. A few of them can still be seen. Another relic of those early times is the splendid 13th-century Tolhouse, one of the oldest municipal buildings in England, with sinister dungeons below ground level.

During the Middle Ages and after, Yarmouth grew rich from the herring industry, coming into conflict first with the Cinque Ports of the south coast, which claimed control over all North Sea fishing rights, and later with the Dutch, who were far more serious rivals. Yarmouth's Free Herring Fair, held every autumn, was one of the greatest of the medieval trade fairs. The heyday of the herring trade came just before the First World War when over 1,100 drifters fished out of Yarmouth; but subsequent overfishing led to a decline, and the last Yarmouth drifter was sold in 1963. Yarmouth was saved from stagnation by the discovery of North Sea oil, when the town became the first base for oil and gas exploration.

The resort side of Yarmouth has all the fun of the fair, with a giant roller-coaster, amusement arcades, two piers, and a Marina Leisure Centre Complex, which has an indoor swimming pool and every kind of sporting facility. The Maritime Museum for East Anglia on Marine Parade was built as a home for shipwrecked sailors in 1861, and now contains exhibits covering all aspects of maritime history, including the herring fisheries, lifesaving and shipbuilding. Behind the South Beach is the Norfolk Pillar – the figure of Britannia on a 144 ft column, built in honour of Nelson in 1819. It can be climbed, in July and August only, by those willing to scale 217 steps. Nelson landed at Yarmouth after his victories at the Battles of the Nile (1798) and Copenhagen (1801), and there is a fine portrait of him in the Town Hall.

The main swimming beach, patrolled in summer by lifeguards, is between the two piers. Swimming is safe, except near the piers and the jetty between them, and off the

FANTASY WORLD *Great Yarmouth's giant funfair comes to life at night, with rides in the sky and rockets to the moon amid the dizzy swirl of lights and blaring music.*

MAGNIFICENT RUIN *Caister Castle was the first brick-built castle in England. Its 90 ft tower and much of the wall have survived.*

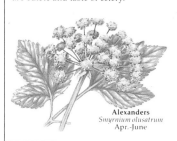
sand-dunes of North Denes, where currents sweep close inshore. There is fishing from the piers and jetty. A street market is held on Wednesdays and Saturdays, and on Fridays in summer. Museums include the Anna Sewell House, birthplace of the author of *Black Beauty*, on Church Plain; and the Elizabethan House Museum, a fine house built in 1596, on South Quay. Boat trips on the river and Broads start from Haven Bridge.

⑤ GORLESTON-ON-SEA
Yarmouth merges imperceptibly into Gorleston about halfway along the harbour. Though officially part of Great Yarmouth, it is quieter in character, and centres on the South Pier, which forms the southern arm of the harbour entrance and has amusements and a large open-air swimming pool. From the pier, there are attractive views of the colour-washed houses and disused lighthouse of old Gorleston, and southwards along the coast towards Lowestoft. Fishermen from the pier catch dab, sole, cod, whiting, bass, and the occasional poison-spined weever.

Swimming is safe, except between the breakwater guarding the South Pier and the model yacht pond. The sandy beach is protected by frequent groynes. Behind it is an esplanade, backed by a steep bank leading up to a wide expanse of grass, with neat seafront houses along the upper esplanade.

⑥ BURGH CASTLE
Three massive flint walls, banded with narrow layers of brick, survive from this mighty fortress, the Roman Gariannonum. It was one of the Forts of the Saxon Shore, built during the 3rd century at a time when the coasts of Britain were under remorseless attack from Saxon marauders sailing across the North Sea. Though it is now stranded more than 3 miles inland, it would at the time it was built have commanded access by water to the heart of East Anglia, and it seems likely that a fleet of warships was based there.

In the 7th century an early Christian community was founded inside the walls, and in Norman times a motte, or mound, was heaped up in one corner, probably with a timber-built stronghold on top. Now the inside of the fort is covered in summer by a waving crop of barley, and there are spacious views from the unwalled west side across the upper reaches of Breydon Water.

⑦ FRITTON LAKE
This beautiful lake, about 2 miles long, forms the main part of a country park just south of the A143. The lake is believed to have been formed by medieval peat-cutting and became noted for its duck decoys – long, tunnel-shaped nets along which wild duck were lured before being killed. Decoy nets have not been used since 1960.

Boats can be hired from the jetty below the main building complex, and visitors can see a wide variety of wildfowl.

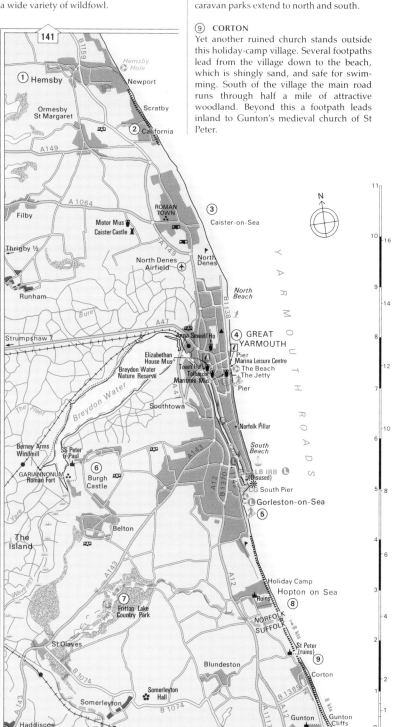

⑧ HOPTON ON SEA
Past Hopton's ruined church, on the south side of the village, Beach Road ends at a concrete ramp leading down to a sandy beach, with limited parking. Notices warn that the low cliffs are crumbling and are dangerous to walk over. Holiday camps and caravan parks extend to north and south.

⑨ CORTON
Yet another ruined church stands outside this holiday-camp village. Several footpaths lead from the village down to the beach, which is shingly sand, and safe for swimming. South of the village the main road runs through half a mile of attractive woodland. Beyond this a footpath leads inland to Gunton's medieval church of St Peter.

LOCAL INFORMATION

Tourist information Great Yarmouth 844313, 842195 (summer).

HM Coastguard Great Yarmouth 851338 for information, 999 in emergency (ask for coastguard).

Weather Norwich 8091.

Local radio BBC Radio Norfolk, 351/344 m, 855/873 kHz, 95.1 MHz.

PLACES TO SEE INLAND

Berney Arms Windmill, near SW corner of Breydon Water. 19th-century mill and windmill exhibition. Daily in summer.

Hales Hall, 12 miles SW of Great Yarmouth, via B1136. Medieval manor. Some afternoons in summer.

Somerleyton Hall, 3 miles W of Corton. Victorian mansion and garden with maze. Most afternoons in summer.

Strumpshaw Fen RSPB Reserve, 12 miles W of Great Yarmouth. Most days.

Thrigby Hall Wildlife Gardens, 5 miles NW of Great Yarmouth, off A1064. Daily.

Giant dunes and low cliffs on a curving coast of sand

With nothing but low, crumbling cliffs and high-piled sand-dunes to hold back the winter fury of the North Sea, this is one of the most vulnerable stretches of the East Anglian coast. Notices request visitors to keep off the dunes, which are planted with marram grass to stabilise them. Windmills, built originally for drainage, and the lofty towers of medieval churches are the principal landmarks in a flat landscape.

① MUNDESLEY
Mundesley (pronounced 'Munsley'), is a small resort which still has plenty of space between the buildings. The old High Street runs inland, at right-angles to the coast road, and a little way along is Cowper House, a white-painted Georgian house where the poet William Cowper (1731-1800) stayed, both during his boyhood and towards the end of his life. He is said to have been inspired to write the hymn *God Moves in a Mysterious Way* by the sight of a storm breaking over Happisburgh, 5 miles down the coast.

A ramp by the coastguard lookout station leads down to the promenade. The wide sandy beach is good for swimming, and small boats can be launched from the sand in settled conditions.

Just south of Mundesley is Stow Mill, a fine tower mill complete with sails. Some machinery is installed, and there is an exhibition of milling pictures and documents.

② PASTON
The village is famous in literary history as the home of the Paston family, whose 'Paston Letters' give a vivid account of life in Norfolk during the troubled times of the Wars of the Roses. A later Paston, Sir William, built the magnificent long thatched barn, dated 1581, which stands beside the road. St Margaret's Church has a number of Paston monuments, and the remains of 14th-century wall paintings.

③ BACTON
Between Paston and Bacton the road runs through acres of gasholders, pipes, control wheels and other gadgetry, all protected by formidable fences. This is the Bacton Natural Gas Terminal, which receives gas through pipelines from the offshore wells.

At the south end of Bacton, on the inland side of the main road, stands the ruined medieval gateway of Bromholm Priory, now a farm. Founded in 1113, Bromholm was famous in the Middle Ages for its possession of a piece of the True Cross, which was said to have the power to cure leprosy and bring the dead back to life. In Chaucer's *Reeve's Tale* the miller's wife calls for help on the 'hooly croys of Bromeholm'. More than a century later Mother Shipton, the South Wales prophetess, prophesied that 'Bacton Abbey shall be a farm' – a forecast that proved correct.

The beach is sand, protected by groynes and a sloping concrete sea-wall.

④ WALCOTT AND OSTEND
West of Walcott the road runs for a few hundred yards along the sea-wall, with steps down to the sandy beach. A launching ramp at Walcott Gap is usable only in settled weather.

Walcott runs into the village of Ostend, which has holiday camps, caravan sites, and another 'gap' through to the sandy beach. South of Walcott is its huge isolated church of All Saints, the main landmark of the flat countryside round about.

⑤ HAPPISBURGH
Traditionally the name of this old village is pronounced Hazeborough, but today's villagers are so often asked about 'Happy's burg' that they are beginning to call it that themselves. However, the dangerous sands, which run parallel with the coast for 9 miles, about 7 miles offshore, are still called Hazeborough Sands.

For centuries the bodies of shipwrecked sailors have been buried in Happisburgh churchyard. The large green mound north of the church is said to be the mass grave of 119

members of the crew of HMS *Invincible*, wrecked on the sands in 1801 when on her way to join Nelson's fleet at Copenhagen. The church has a 110 ft tower, perhaps built to serve as a beacon for sailors. Inside the church is a superb 15th-century font, carved with angelic musicians, the four Evangelists, and wild men carrying clubs on their shoulders. On the other side of the village is a lighthouse built in 1791 and strikingly banded in red and white.

The beach is quite separate from the village, with a car park above it. A concrete ramp leads down past the inshore rescue boat hut to a sandy beach, where deep pools may form as the tide comes in. Boats can be launched in settled weather.

⑥ ECCLES ON SEA
From Whimpwell Green, a lane leads to Cart Gap and the beach. Cart Gap has the only proper car park between Happisburgh and Sea Palling. The beach is superb, with gently sloping sand protected by zigzag wooden groynes. There is a ramp suitable for small boats, which should be taken out only in settled conditions.

Eccles on Sea is a straggling collection of beach chalets and holiday houses, on either side of an unmade road behind the dunes. The beach can be reached across the dunes at

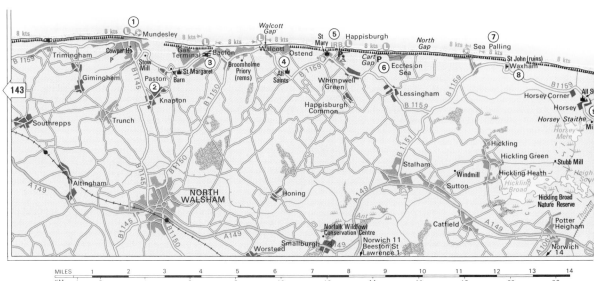

WAXHAM DUNES *Behind a beach of golden sands, tough marram grass knits together the wind-blown dunes to form a natural sea-wall, the only protection against the North Sea on this exposed coast.*

either end of the road, but elsewhere the dunes have been planted with marram grass, and walking on them is forbidden. North Gap, at the south end of Eccles Beach, can be reached by a minor road from Lessingham village.

⑦ SEA PALLING

A lane from the village leads to a concrete ramp over the dunes to the wide, sandy beach; boats can be manhandled on to it and launched at any state of the tide. Swimming is good, but the dunes have been wired off to protect the marram grass. A bronze plaque beside the concrete ramp records the completion in 1959 of 8 miles of sea defences from Happisburgh to Winterton, made necessary after the dunes had been breached during the tidal surges of January 1953.

⑧ WAXHAM

At Waxham the dunes take on the stature of small hills, and trees are beginning to colonise them – an indication of how vegetation can take hold on the dunes if it is left undisturbed.

Cars may be parked in the lane beside the disused church. At the end of the lane a steep sandy track leads over the dunes to the beach where the sand is soft and deep. By the side of the derelict church is a Tudor wall complete with corner turrets and gatehouse.

⑨ HORSEY

The beach can be reached in two places, down rough lanes followed by tracks across the dunes: from Horsey Corner, and from a lane in the village signposted 'by-road'. Presumably it was along these lanes that smugglers took their contraband to Horsey, where it was loaded on to wherries and taken inland by boat to Norwich. Horsey village is hardly more than a hamlet, with a few houses and the little thatched church of All Saints hidden beneath the trees.

Horsey Mere, just west of the village, is a pretty, 120 acre stretch of water, owned by the National Trust. An offshoot of the Norfolk Broads, it is crowded in summer with small boats which can moor at Horsey staithe, below the fine tower windmill built in 1912 as a drainage mill to pump off surplus water. In 1943 the mill was struck by lightning, and it is being gradually restored. There are wide-ranging views from the gallery at the top, towards the sand-dunes and the sea, and inland across the Broads, dotted with the sails of boats.

The mere is a breeding ground for wildfowl and marsh birds. Nelson is said to have learned to sail there, though it is some 40 miles from Burnham Thorpe, where his father was rector. According to legend, the Romans used to sink the bodies of dead children in the mere, and once a year at midnight it turns into a garden in which all the children can be seen playing together.

⑩ WEST SOMERTON

From this attractive little village, which is almost 2 miles from the sea, footpaths lead inland to Martham Broad and the quiet water-meadows of the River Thurne. The church of St Mary the Virgin is up a steep lane east of the village; it has a round Norman tower with an octagonal belfry on top, and the remains of 14th-century wall painting in the nave.

In the churchyard is the massive sarcophagus, standing on lion's paws, of Robert Hales, the 'Norfolk Giant'. Born in West Somerton in 1820, the son of a local farmer, he grew to 7 ft 8 in. tall, and weighed more than 32 stone. As a young man he toured the country with his sister Mary, who was also over 7 ft tall, and went as far afield as the United States. In the 1850s Hales became licensee of a London pub, was presented to Queen Victoria and was generally popular and successful. He died at Great Yarmouth in 1863.

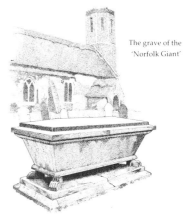

The grave of the 'Norfolk Giant'

⑪ WINTERTON-ON-SEA

The entrance to the village is dominated by the enormous tower of Winterton church, 132 ft high. Inside is a reminder of the destructive power of the North Sea – the 'Fishermen's corner', a memorial to all those lost at sea. Almost everything there has been to sea: the cross is made of ships' timbers, and the items kept there include ropes, an anchor and a ship's lamp. Fragments from wrecks on the Hazeborough Sands are often washed up on the shore at Winterton. When Daniel Defoe went there in about 1725 he wrote that half of the houses in the village were built of timber from wrecks.

The sea road leads directly down to a wide, sandy beach, where boats can be launched at any state of the tide. To look at, Winterton beach appears like any other on this coast, but prominent notices warn of the danger of drowning between two markers of the beach, and state that children should always be accompanied by an adult while bathing. There are volunteer lifeguards on Sundays in summer. To the north of the beach are high, grassy sand-dunes, part of which is a National Nature Reserve.

Overlooking the beach is a hotel consisting of separate round houses with thatched roofs, modelled on South African rondavels.

LOCAL INFORMATION
Tourist information Great Yarmouth 844313/732669.
HM Coastguard Great Yarmouth 851338 for information, 999 in emergency (ask for coastguard).
Weather Norwich 8091.
Local radio BBC Radio Norfolk, 351/344 m, 855/873 kHz, 95.1 MHz.
PLACES TO SEE INLAND
Beeston Hall, 8 miles SW of Sea Palling, via B1151. 18th-century house. Some afternoons in summer.
Hickling Broad National Nature Reserve, 2½ miles W of Horsey. Most days, Apr.-Oct., admission by permit only.
Norfolk Wildfowl Conservation Centre, near Smallburgh, 6 miles W of Sea Palling. Daily Apr.-Oct.
Norwich. Norman cathedral; Bridewell Museum of Local Industries, weekdays; Castle Museum and Art Gallery, daily; Colman's Mustard Museum, most days; Royal Norfolk Regiment Museum, most days; Sainsbury Centre for Visual Arts, University of East Anglia, most afternoons; St Peter Hungate Church Museum, weekdays; Strangers' Hall, museum of domestic life, weekdays.
Sutton Windmill, 3 miles W of Sea Palling. Daily in summer.

Marshes and salt creeks that line a shore snatched from the sea

Heading eastwards, shingle banks and salt-marshes give way to low cliffs, and then to the twin resorts of Sheringham and Cromer, with their fine beaches. A clifftop path takes the walker eastwards as far as Overstrand. But this coast is treacherous as well as alluring, and for 150 years the sailors who live here have risked their own lives to save others, venturing out in lifeboats to rescue the victims of North Sea storms.

① MORSTON

A lane leads down from the village to a tidal creek, which runs almost dry at low tide. In 1973 the National Trust bought 540 acres of Morston Marshes, together with Morston Quay – an extensive foreshore of hard sand, from which local boatmen by arrangement ferry visitors across to the bird sanctuary on Blakeney Point, with longer trips to see the seals basking on the sandbanks off the Point. Boats can be launched from the foreshore.

② BLAKENEY

A spick-and-span, popular sailing village, Blakeney lies at the end of a channel which almost dries up at low tide. The original village, called Snitterley, was long ago swallowed up by the sea. The High Street runs steeply down to the harbour; many of the houses have walls made of rounded flints, and brightly coloured doors and window frames.

The vast and impressive church of St Nicholas is on the main road, south of the village. At the east end it has an unusual second tower, which is far smaller than the main west tower and was probably built as a beacon for shipping. In the disastrous floods of 1953, Blakeney suffered along with the rest of the coast: a house on the corner of the High Street has a plaque marking the flood height, which is a good 6 ft above ground level.

Boats can be launched from the wide, hard foreshore, where there is a concrete slipway, plenty of parking space, and a sailing club. There is a good walk from the harbour, along the sea embankment to Blakeney Eye, and back to Cley next the Sea.

③ CLEY NEXT THE SEA

Cley was a busy fishing port in the Middle Ages, but the sea retreated, and there is now half a mile of marshland between it and open water. The village is built on a dogleg bend, and the main road traffic squeezing through hardly allows room for pedestrians to walk, let alone space to park a car. Its chief landmark is a noble 18th-century tower windmill, built right on the edge of the marsh, and looking across the River Glaven, which flows sluggishly northwards and then turns sharp west, blocked from the sea by the shingle barrier of Cley Eye.

Between the A149 road and the sea are the Cley and Salthouse Marshes, where the Norfolk Naturalists' Trust runs about 650 acres as a nature reserve. Cley Marshes, bought in 1926, was the first property acquired by the Trust. Just east of Cley, on the main road, the NNT has a visitors' information centre. Breeding species on the reserve include bearded tits, bitterns and common terns, while shore larks, snow buntings and many wildfowl can be seen in winter.

At Cley Eye there is a small car park below the shingle bank, which falls steeply down to the sea. The shingle continues to shelve steeply under the water, making bathing hazardous. From Cley Eye the shingle runs like a clean-cut sloping wall westwards to Blakeney Point.

④ BLAKENEY POINT

A nature reserve since 1912 and now owned by the National Trust, Blakeney Point marks the end of a long shingle beach running 9 miles westwards from Sheringham. On the landward side, the shingle gives way to dunes, mud-flats and salt-marshes, where the sea drains away at low tide, leaving a narrow channel to Blakeney harbour.

Blakeney Point can be reached by boat from Blakeney or Morston, or by a hard walk of 4 miles or so along the shingle from Cley Eye. It is a paradise for botanists and birdwatchers. Typical plants are thrift, sea lavender and samphire, while common terns, little terns and Sandwich terns nest between May and July.

⑤ SALTHOUSE

Just east of the village pond, where swans sail with their cygnets, a lane leads to a shingle bank with limited parking. There is a notice warning visitors of the danger of unexploded mines. Roadside notices in Salthouse advertise local crabs, cockles, shrimps, whelks and samphire.

MILL ON THE MARSH *Cley next the Sea's windmill, and the cottages clustered at its foot, stand on the remains of a quay at the edge of marshland. The mill is a guesthouse.*

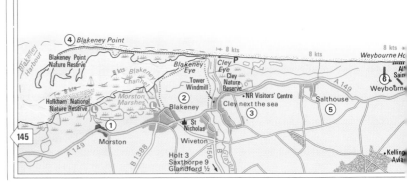

The Henry Blogg Memorial, Cromer

⑥ WEYBOURNE

Half a mile north of Weybourne village is Weybourne Hope, a shingle beach which slopes so steeply that invading ships could come close inshore – hence the old rhyme:

'He who would old England win
Must at Waborne Hoop begin.'

In 1588 it was considered of enough strategic importance to be garrisoned against the Spanish fleet. There is good fishing on the beach: flounder and bass can be caught there in summer, whiting and cod in winter. Above the shingle are low cliffs which are private property, with no access to the west.

Weybourne station, 1 mile south of the village, is now the western terminus of the North Norfolk Railway, formed by enthusiasts in 1960. The line, once part of the Midland and Great Northern Railway, runs for 3 miles to Sheringham. During the summer there are several trains a day in each direction.

⑦ SHERINGHAM

This busy little resort is centred on a bustling High Street, which has a neat clock tower at one end and the seafront at the other. The railway arrived in 1887, and squares of holidaymakers' houses soon sprang up round the old fishing village, some of whose cottages survive at the seaward end of the High Street. Sheringham still has a small fleet of fishing boats, which go out after lobsters and crabs. When not at sea, they are drawn up on the beach alongside the old lifeboat shed. The modern lifeboat is kept at the western end of the promenade.

The beach consists of gently sloping sand, protected by groynes, below shingle. Swimming is excellent, and lifeguards are on duty every day in summer. There are two slipways, but access is restricted and parking near the front is difficult.

THE TRAIN NOW LEAVING *Steam-hauled trains run between Sheringham and Weybourne on the North Norfolk Railway during summer.*

The station is now the eastern terminus and headquarters of the North Norfolk Railway, which runs to Weybourne. It has a fine display of steam locomotives, vintage carriages, and other railway relics.

At Upper Sheringham, a mile inland, Sheringham Hall is set in a fine park, with a spectacular display of rhododendrons in early summer. The park is open to the public on certain days.

⑧ WEST RUNTON

The beach, in one of the few gaps along this coast, is reached down Water Lane. It is sandy with pebbly patches, and is generally safe for swimming, though swimmers should watch out for offshore rocks just below the surface.

South of the A149 a road leads up to the so-called 'Roman Camp' on Beacon Hill, at 329 ft the highest point in Norfolk. The National Trust owns 71 acres of the hilltop, which is heavily planted with trees; gaps between them give views of the sea. There is space for parking.

At West Runton is the North Norfolk Heavy Horse and Pony Centre, a collection of horses large and small, from the massive Shire to the tiny Shetland. The centre is open daily in summer; the horses are shown at work, and can be driven or ridden.

Outside West Runton, on the Sheringham road, a track beside a caravan park and over a level crossing leads to the fine church of Beeston Regis, standing isolated on a clifftop in the middle of a field. It has a magnificent 15th-century choir screen, painted with figures of the Apostles.

⑨ EAST RUNTON

A steep ramp leads through East Runton Gap to the beach, which is sand below shingle, with safe swimming. At the foot of the ramp there are usually two or three crab boats, hauled up from the sea by tractors. Small boats can be launched in settled conditions, near high water.

⑩ CROMER

At the end of the 18th century, smart houses began to be built for summer visitors around the cottages of the old fishing port of Cromer. Its importance is shown by the size and magnificence of its church of St Peter and St Paul, which has a Perpendicular tower, 160 ft high and the tallest in Norfolk. Cromer originally stood some way inland, but the town of Shipden was gradually destroyed by the sea during the Middle Ages, and Cromer took its place.

Nowadays it is best known for two things – the quality of the crabs caught by its crab boats, which are usually drawn up on shore, and the brave deeds of its lifeboatmen, who during the Second World War saved 450 lives. The most famous lifeboatman of all, Henry Blogg, coxswain from 1909 to 1947, is commemorated by a bronze bust, which gazes out to sea from North Lodge Park, not far from the old lifeboat house, now a lifeboat museum. The museum is at the foot of a steep road called The Gangway, which is paved with granite blocks arranged with their corners sticking up, to give a grip to horses' hooves pulling cargo up from the beach. The modern lifeboat is housed above a slipway at the end of the pier. Behind the church, several cottages have been restored to create a museum that gives a picture of sailors' homes a century ago.

The beach is sand, scattered with shingle, with shallow pools left exposed at low tide. Swimming is safe, and there are lifeguards in summer. Boats can be launched from The Gangway, but access is steep and difficult. There is a small zoo, and the Pavilion Theatre has a summer season.

East of the town the ground rises steeply, with the lighthouse at the highest point. Built in 1833, it is 58 ft high and its light has a range of 23 miles. It is open to visitors on weekday afternoons, and is reached either on foot from Cromer along the cliffs, or by the entrance to the Royal Cromer Golf Club.

⑪ OVERSTRAND

The beach at Overstrand is good sand, with some shingle, and is protected by groynes. The village is large and mainly modern, with access to the beach from a car park above a 100 ft cliff, either by steps or a steep track with a hairpin bend halfway down. There is a clifftop walk of 2 miles to Cromer. Because of the dangerous state of the cliffs east of Overstrand, there is no access to the sea as far as Mundesley, 5 miles along the coast.

LOCAL INFORMATION

Tourist information Cromer 512497 (summer), Sheringham 824329 (summer).

HM Coastguard Great Yarmouth 851338 for information, 999 in emergency (ask for coastguard).

Weather Norwich 8091.

Local radio BBC Radio Norfolk, 351/344 m, 855/873 kHz, 95.1 MHz.

PLACES TO SEE INLAND

Blickling Hall (NT), 10 miles S of Cromer, via B1354. Jacobean house. Most days in summer.

Felbrigg Hall (NT), 3 miles S of Cromer, off A149. 17th-century house. Most afternoons in summer.

Holt Woodlands Country Park, 6 miles S of Blakeney, off B1149, via A148.

Kelling Park Aviaries, 2 miles SW of Weybourne. Daily.

Mannington Hall Gardens, near Saxthorpe, 12 miles SE of Blakeney on B1149, via A148. 15th-century manor house. Gardens some afternoons in summer; house by appointment.

Glandford Shell Museum, 2 miles SE of Blakeney. Weekdays.

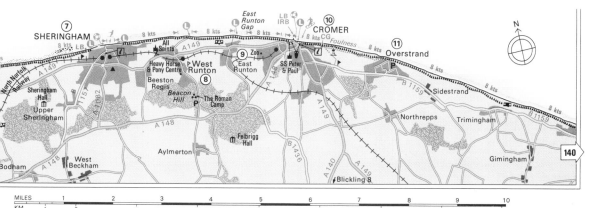

Layer-cake cliffs and shining creeks where bird life thrives

Between the striped cliffs of Hunstanton and the broad expanse of Stiffkey Marshes, where cockle-gatherers collect their evening meal, is a coast of flint-walled villages, cut off from the sea by dunes and salt-marshes which are constantly being reshaped as new land is won from the sea. The birds and plants that thrive on the marshes and creeks are protected by an almost continuous line of coastal nature reserves.

STRIPED CLIFFS *Erosion by the sea has revealed the distinct layers in Hunstanton's cliffs, with red chalk sandwiched between white chalk and carr stone, a type of brown sandstone.*

① HUNSTANTON

This quiet little Victorian resort has two unique features: it is the only seaside town in East Anglia which faces west, and it has about three-quarters of a mile of strange striped cliffs, 60 ft high. Below the cliffs the stone has fallen away in great boulders, and beyond is a splendid sandy beach, where at low tide wave-eroded rocks are exposed, full of little rock pools.

The resort grew up at the end of the 19th century, after the railway reached Hunstanton in 1862. The local landowners were the Le Strange family, who were largely responsible for the town's development; there are still notices on the beach claiming the Le Stranges' right to all oysters and mussels taken off the foreshore. As hereditary Lord High Admirals of The Wash, the Le Stranges could claim possession over anything on the beach, or in the sea as far as a man could ride his horse into it at low tide and then throw his spear.

On top of the cliffs are the remains of St Edmund's Chapel, where Edmund, King of the East Angles, is said to have landed in AD 850. A few yards away is a sturdy white-painted lighthouse, no longer in use.

All that is left of the pier is the main building, now an amusement centre; the seaward section beyond the promenade has disappeared. There are two ramps from the promenade to the beach; one, for sailing boats, is just north of the pier; the other, for powerboats, is at the southern end of the promenade. There are powerboat and sailing clubs, and water-ski championships are held. South of the pier the beach is protected by groynes, covered at high tide and marked by baskets on tall poles.

There is fishing from the beach for tope, dab and flounder. Boat trips go to Seal Island, a sandbank in The Wash where seals bask at low tide.

Half a mile to the north is Old Hunstanton, a village with red-roofed cottages of fishing days, an attractive church and Old Hunstanton Hall, a moated mansion dating back to Tudor times. There is a quiet beach,

reached down Sea Lane and across the dunes, or from the clifftop car park off Lighthouse Lane. A hut beside the track houses the inshore rescue boat; the public are sometimes admitted to see the collection of historic photographs and lifeboat relics.

② HOLME NEXT THE SEA

Holme is a pretty village at the end of the Peddars Way, a trackway which may date back to pre-Roman times and can be traced inland for 50 miles, through Castle Acre as far as Knettishall in Suffolk, near Thetford. It is now a long-distance footpath.

The beach, dunes leading to sand, can only be reached across Hunstanton's championship golf links, where notices beside the path warn walkers of the danger from flying golf balls. There is a car park just before the links.

A bumpy 1 mile track runs from the beach road to the Holme Dunes Nature Reserve, administered by the Norfolk Naturalists' Trust. It consists of about 500 acres of sand-dune and salt-marsh, rich in plant and animal life. Plants that grow there include sea bindweed, sea lavender, bee and pyramidal orchids, and sea buckthorn, which flourishes on the dunes. A 1½ mile nature trail starts from the car park.

Adjoining the nature reserve is the Holme Bird Observatory, administered by the Norfolk Ornithologists' Association. This includes a ringing laboratory and a number of hides. Among the 279 species that have been seen at Holme are 21 species of warblers, wrynecks, hoopoes, ospreys, sooty shearwaters, and the rare collared flycatcher and red-rumped swallow. Entomologists have recorded 363 species of moths on the reserve.

Joint permits for the bird observatory (open daily) and the nature reserve (open most days) are available from either warden.

③ TITCHWELL MARSH

A track a quarter of a mile west of Titchwell village leads to the car park and information centre of the RSPB's Titchwell Marsh Reserve, which comprises shingle beach, a reed bed and a marsh. In the 1780s sea-walls were built and the land was reclaimed for agriculture; but the defences were smashed in the tidal surge of January 1953, and the land has reverted to its original state.

Species that can be seen include ringed plovers, bearded reedlings and little terns in summer; Brent geese, waders and shore larks in winter; and many migrants in spring and autumn.

The reserve is open daily; the information centre is open on most days in summer.

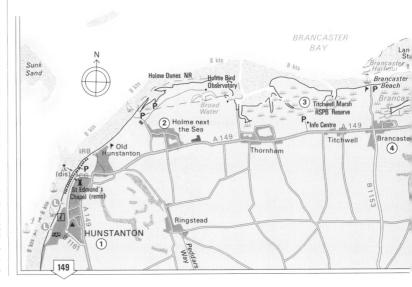

4 BRANCASTER

Nothing remains of the Roman fortress of Branodunum, built about AD 300 as one of the Forts of the Saxon Shore to defend the coast against marauders from across the North Sea. However, the name lives on – *Branoduni castra*, the fort of Branodunum, which has been contracted down the centuries to Brancaster.

From the neat village centre, a road runs north for more than 1 mile to Brancaster beach car park behind the dunes. A wooden ramp, suitable for manhandling small boats, leads over the dunes to a wide beach backed by a massive concrete sea-wall. The dunes are planted with marram grass, and protected by coils of barbed wire. Swimmers are warned of 'swift and very dangerous' incoming tides; visitors must leave the Wreck sands when the tide begins to flood, as the sands are quickly cut off and later completely covered.

This stretch of coast is administered by the National Trust.

5 BRANCASTER STAITHE

The Romans are said to have started gathering shellfish here, and the industry continues on a very small scale. Nowadays the small harbour is virtually landlocked; at low tide the tide runs out, leaving only a narrow channel between mud banks. Boats can be launched from the hard foreshore within 3 hours of high water, and there is room for parking. The harbourmaster's permission must be obtained for the use of powerboats.

Small boats take visitors across to Scolt Head Island at certain times, dependent on the tide.

6 SCOLT HEAD ISLAND

The National Nature Reserve on Scolt Head Island, at the entrance to Brancaster harbour, is owned jointly by the National Trust and the Norfolk Naturalists' Trust, and managed by the Nature Conservancy. A nature reserve since 1923, it is best known for its nesting colonies of common and Sandwich terns, which breed on a 4 acre ternery near the landing place for boats crossing from Brancaster Staithe and Overy Staithe.

A three-quarter-mile nature trail begins near the landing place. It is dangerous to walk across to the island at low tide, and visitors should not do so unless they have local knowledge. During the terns' breeding season of May, June and July the ternery cannot be entered and dogs are not allowed on the island; at other times of year entry is unrestricted.

ROUND TOWER *Burnham Deepdale's Norman church was built of flint, which was easier to form into a circular shape than a square one.*

7 BURNHAM DEEPDALE

Linked to Brancaster Staithe by continuous buildings, Burnham Deepdale is one of the villages known as the 'Seven Burnhams' (the others are Burnham Norton, Overy, Sutton, Thorpe, Ulph and Westgate). Its trim little parish church was probably built soon after the Conquest. Inside is one of the church treasures of North Norfolk – a medieval 'Seasonal Font', cut from a single block of stone and carved with 12 figures each carrying out a task suitable for the month of the year, such as pruning in April, threshing in September and so on.

Burnham Thorpe, 2 miles inland, is famous as Nelson's birthplace. The old rectory where he was born in 1758 was pulled down in 1802; but All Saints' Church, isolated from the village, has the font where he was christened, a crucifix made of wood from the *Victory*, and a bust of Nelson in the chancel.

8 BURNHAM OVERY STAITHE

There are extensive views across the saltings to Scolt Head Island from this delightful little sailing village. Boats can be launched from a wide slope of hard sand between 2 hours before and 3 hours after high water. At low tide the sea goes far out, and there are tracks out on the marshes; one of them, called the 'Cockle Path', has been restored and leads all the way to Scolt Head. There are boat trips to Scolt Head Island. A plaque on a house by the harbour reads 'Richard Woodget, master of the *Cutty Sark*, lived here 1899-1926', and it would be hard to imagine a

better place for the home of a windjammer's captain. The village has an annual regatta, and there are facilities for windsurfing and boat hire; the bar at the harbour entrance can be dangerous to small craft.

On the A149 just west of the village is a superb restored tower mill which has been converted to a private house and is not open to the public.

9 HOLKHAM GAP

Except for the harbour channel leading down to Wells-next-the-Sea, the whole 12 miles of coast between Overy Staithe and Blakeney forms the Holkham National Nature Reserve. Managed by the Nature Conservancy Council in co-operation with the Holkham Estate, it is the largest coastal nature reserve in England, covering almost 10,000 acres of unspoiled dunes, beaches and salt-marshes.

Holkham Gap is reached down the half-mile Lady Ann's Drive, opposite the main gate of Holkham Hall; there is a car park on the grass verge beside the road. A gate leads into the nature reserve, past pine trees first planted during the second half of the 19th century to stabilise the shifting dunes. The dunes are crossed by a board track, which gives access to the Gap – a half-moon sweep of firm sand with good and safe swimming, though care must be taken, as the tide comes in very fast.

RAKING IN THE 'BLUES'

As the tide retreats from Stiffkey Marshes a small army of cockle-gatherers strides out with rakes and buckets to collect the local delicacy – the prized cockles known as 'Stewkey blues'. The pronunciation 'Stewkey' for Stiffkey has died out, but is still used to describe the cockles.

The tide yields its latest harvest at Stiffkey.

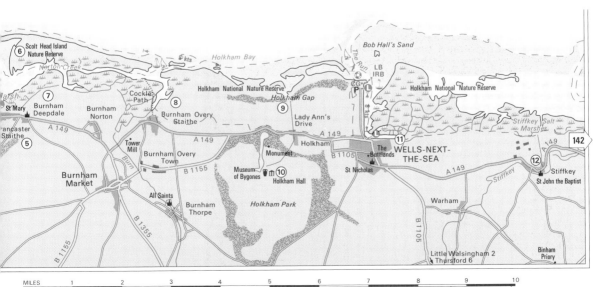

FRONTIERS LOST AND WON IN THE TIMELESS BATTLE WITH THE SEA

All around the coast of Britain, relentless tides and fast-flowing currents are constantly gnawing at the land, and nowhere are the shores more vulnerable to the attack than along England's east coast. Mud, sand, clay and shingle are driven by the sea into long desolate strips, and from time to time the tides repossess the land that man has fought to gain over the centuries. The battle against the sea is never ending. It is a struggle that has left villages beneath the waves and ports a mile from the sea in the constant redrawing of battle lines.

On some parts of the Suffolk coast, partial victory to the sea has been conceded; from Kessingland in the north to Felixstowe in the south, the advancing waves have gained a quarter of a mile in four centuries. Surviving Aldeburgh is today no more than three streets wide behind its sea-wall, but even so it has fared better than its former neighbour, Slaughden, which is now beneath the sea. Aldeburgh was once at the mouth of the River Alde, but now the river is turned southwards by a massive shingle bank. For 10 miles the river runs parallel to the shore, changing its name to the Ore on the way and finally breaking through the shingle at Orford Haven.

By contrast, on stretches of the north Norfolk coast, from Hunstanton to Cromer, cattle graze on meadows reclaimed from the sea and protected by massive walls of sand and shingle. Beyond the wall the mud creeks and sand spits are at the mercy of the currents. Long spits of sand at Scolt Head and Blakeney Point are constantly changing direction, like wisps of hair caught in a breeze. At high tide the sea sweeps across the salt flats and then retreats, marbling the sands with silvery veins. But man's grip on the land he has won is tenuous, and from time to time the forces of wind and water combine to break through the barrier. In 1953 a storm surge in the North Sea burst through the sea-wall like a battering ram, and for almost three months the reclaimed land was flooded.

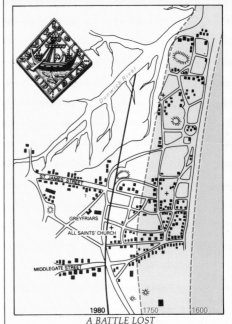

A BATTLE LOST

In the space of seven centuries the sea has reduced Dunwich from being a prosperous medieval town to becoming an almost deserted village that keeps a watchful eye on the skies. After the storms in the 14th century that destroyed the port the citizens lost heart, and by Elizabethan times, as this map shows, the sea had engulfed much of the town and was advancing unchecked. By the middle of the 18th century most of the town had gone, including its market place, and early in the 20th century All Saints' Church tumbled over the cliff edge. At very low tides flint rubble from the church may still be seen among the pebbles on the shore.

HOW GROYNES PROTECT THE BEACH

Direction of waves

TAMING THE WAVES *The build up or erosion of sand and shingle is caused by a dual action of the waves. When a wave breaks on the seashore it sends pebbles and sand towards the land; then as the wave retreats, the backwash or undertow claws them back again. But the power of the wave's two actions is seldom equal, so that sometimes more sand and shingle is built up than is sucked back, and vice versa.*

Where waves are driven ashore obliquely they carry material along the coast and form drifts and spits, which is what has happened at Spurn Head. This movement is arrested by the use of timber groynes or breakwaters. Shingle is swept away from one side of the groyne but trapped by the next groyne, so preventing it from being swept by the waves clear of the beach altogether.

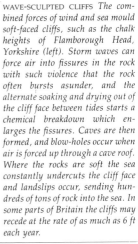

WAVE-SCULPTED CLIFFS *The combined forces of wind and sea mould soft-faced cliffs, such as the chalk heights of Flamborough Head, Yorkshire (left). Storm waves can force air into fissures in the rock with such violence that the rock often bursts asunder, and the alternate soaking and drying out of the cliff face between tides starts a chemical breakdown which enlarges the fissures. Caves are then formed, and blow-holes occur when air is forced up through a cave roof. Where the rocks are soft the sea constantly undercuts the cliff face and landslips occur, sending hundreds of tons of rock into the sea. In some parts of Britain the cliffs may recede at the rate of as much as 6 ft each year.*

Wooden groynes on a shingle beach

HUMBER SAND SPIT *The sand-and-shingle peninsula of Spurn Head (right), which curves across the mouth of the Humber, is formed from deposits washed from the crumbling cliffs of Holderness a few miles to the north. About every 250 years the sea breaks through the spit and the whole process starts again, with each new spit growing slightly west of its predecessor. The earliest record of Spurn dates from about AD 670, when a small monastery was established there. Since then there have been four spits; the present spit started to grow after the latest breakthrough by the sea in 1608. It is still growing, and erosion has been checked by groynes erected in the 1860s.*

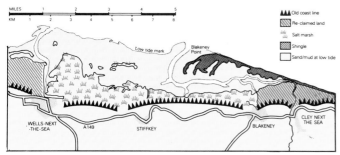

A BATTLE WON *On the north Norfolk coast the first strip of land to be reclaimed from the sea was Overy Marshes, bought from Charles I in 1639 by a man named John Parker. He built a sea-wall and then drained the marshes east of it. Parker's example was followed by others, and in particular by the Coke family at Holkham. Thomas Coke (1697-1759) re-claimed more salt-marsh from the sea, and his great nephew Thomas William Coke (1754-1842) did much to develop the new land for agriculture. The work was continued by his son, who built a sea-wall at Wells-next-the-Sea. As a result of the Coke family's successes, two ports found themselves high and dry; both Wells and Cley next the Sea are now a mile from open water. At Wells, a channel through the sea-wall leads to a quay where coastal vessels trade. But at Cley sheep graze today where boats once rode at anchor, and the 18th-century Custom House is the sole reminder that this was once a port.*

Thomas William Coke, England's foremost 18th-century agriculturist, became known as 'Coke of Norfolk'.

⑩ HOLKHAM HALL

This vast Palladian mansion, designed by William Kent for Thomas Coke, Earl of Leicester, was begun in the 1730s and took more than 30 years to complete. It is magnificently furnished and decorated, and contains paintings by Raphael, Rubens, Van Dyck, Reynolds and other masters.

A later Coke, the famous 'Coke of Norfolk', changed the face of English farming during the first half of the 19th century. Known as 'the first farmer in England', he changed over from rye-growing to wheat-growing, and experimented with improved livestock breeds. Across the park from the house is the monument put up to Coke by his tenants in 1845, three years after his death. More than 100 ft high, it has a carved wheatsheaf on top, and a Devon ox, Southdown sheep, a plough and a seed drill at the corners of the base.

There is a pottery shop with a working pottery attached, a garden centre and a museum of bygones. The house and grounds are open during certain afternoons during the summer.

⑪ WELLS-NEXT-THE-SEA

There are really three parts to Wells, though it is hardly larger than a village – the quayside, the old streets behind it, and the beach area a mile away to the north. The quay is a bustling jumble of cafes, amusement arcades and ships' chandlers, with a harbourmaster's office and a few fishing boats to give a nautical flavour. Quayside stalls sell local mussels, dressed crabs, cockles and samphire. The narrow High Street winds downhill to the large parish church of St Nicholas. Near by is the attractive tree-shaded green called The Buttlands, a grassy rectangle surrounded by dignified Georgian houses.

Access to the beach is either by road, on foot along the sea-wall, or by miniature railway. The main beach faces north and is sandy, but swimmers should avoid the spit of land on which the lifeboat house is built. The safe and dangerous areas are marked on a large plan at the entrance to the beach. Next to the car park is a large boating lagoon, for canoes and dinghies, known as Abraham's Bosom. There is a tide time indicator in the car park, and a beach lookout sounds a klaxon as the tide begins to turn, warning visitors on Bob Hall's Sand to return to the main beach or face being cut off by the tide.

The village has a water-ski club, and a sailing club with its own slipway.

⑫ STIFFKEY

A track opposite the church leads from this straggling village down to Stiffkey Marshes, owned by the National Trust. In July the marshes are coloured with the delicate purple flowers of sea lavender, a plant which is far less noticeable than the land variety, and scentless.

'TWIXT LAND AND SEA *At Blakeney the sea-wall is a thin green line running out from the town to the shore and dividing reclaimed marshland from salt-marshes and mud-flats. A winding creek provides a haven for small craft.*

147

Georgian towns and fertile farmland around The Wash

The great U-shape of The Wash cuts into northern Norfolk and Lincolnshire, and is bounded by marshland in the west and shingle and sand beaches in the east. The flat farmland around The Wash, which now grows potatoes, onions, cabbages and cauliflowers, has been gradually won back from the sea, as successive generations have built dykes and embankments to drain the marsh and keep the sea from flooding back in.

PERFUMED GARDENS *Lavender scents the air and paints the landscape in the fields around Heacham during July and August, when the crop is picked and its essence distilled.*

① FREISTON SHORE
This little hamlet, popular with bird-watchers, is sheltered behind a sea-wall 2 miles from Freiston village. It is possible to walk northwards along the sea-wall as far as Skegness; in the other direction the walk turns inland towards Boston. It can be dangerous to walk on the marshes beyond the sea-wall when the tide is coming in.

② FISHTOFT
In the middle of Fishtoft village a road sign with the unusual directions 'SCALP' and 'CUT END' points to the Pilgrim Fathers' memorial, on the bank of The Haven. The memorial marks the point on what was then Scotia Creek from which 13 Puritans, the earliest Pilgrim Fathers, tried to set sail for America in 1607. They were betrayed by the captain of their ship and brought back to Boston, to face trial and imprisonment for attempting to emigrate illegally.

PILGRIMS' PILLAR *Fishtoft's memorial to the Pilgrim Fathers was erected in 1957, 350 years after their first attempt to sail to America.*

③ BOSTON
The combination of some of the most productive agricultural land in England with a flourishing seaport gives Boston a unique flavour. Much of the town centre consists of red-brick Georgian buildings, and one of the main shopping streets is closed to traffic. The town's chief landmark is the mighty 'Stump', the tower of the parish church of St Botolph's with an octagonal lantern tower which once served as a beacon for navigators on The Wash. The Stump is 272 ft high, and the view from the top is spectacular – on a clear day it is possible to see Lincoln Cathedral, nearly 30 miles away.

The town grew up around a monastery founded in AD 654 by St Botolph, and its name is said to be a contraction of 'Botolph's Town', or 'Botolph's Stone' (the stone from which he first preached). During Norman times the town grew rapidly and was granted a charter by King John in 1204. By the end of the 13th century it was the most important port in England, but it declined in the 15th century because of floods and the silting up of the River Witham. Trade revived in the 18th century, with the opening of the Grand Sluice in 1766 and the deepening of the river. In 1882 the docks were constructed, and a straight channel was cut through to The Wash. Boston is now a modern port, trading in timber, fertilisers, fruit, potatoes and steel. It is also a shell-fishing centre, with fishing smacks unloading at quays in the middle of the town.

Boston's connections with America began in 1607, when the earliest Pilgrim Fathers tried to set sail from Scotia Creek, a short way downstream from the town. Arrested and brought back in open boats, they became a 'spectacle and a wonder to the

multitude', according to an old account. The cells in which they were imprisoned are on view in the medieval Guildhall, now the Borough Museum, open on weekdays. In 1608 they fled to Holland, and later formed part of the group that sailed from Southampton on board the *Mayflower* in 1620. Ten years later, in 1630, a further group set sail from Boston, and founded the city of Boston, Massachusetts.

Fydell House, next to the Guildhall, is a superb 18th-century house, and the Maud Foster Windmill is a five-sailed mill named after a wealthy Elizabethan landowner.

There is a market on Wednesdays and Saturdays, and an annual fair in May.

④ FRAMPTON MARSH
A dead-end lane, parallel with the south bank of The Haven, leads to a field path and then to the sea bank, with rich farmland behind and wild marsh stretching to the sea in front. There are good walks along the embankment in both directions, but the actual marshes are best avoided.

⑤ GEDNEY DROVE END
North of the A17 between Fosdyke Bridge and Sutton Bridge is a large half-moon of farmland, consisting mainly of reclaimed marsh. Narrow lanes lead through the vegetable fields to the sea embankment, which is well maintained and can be walked along.

The peace of this lonely region is shattered at intervals by RAF aircraft roaring low overhead, as the coast between Fleet Haven and the mouth of the Nene is a bombing range. Red flags are flown when training is in progress.

⑥ SUTTON BRIDGE
The embankment along which the main road runs was made in the first half of the 19th century, and the land behind it was drained. Robert Stephenson built the first bridge over the River Nene in 1850; the present swing bridge dates from the late 19th century. Sutton Bridge was a port that never grew, as docks built there in 1881 collapsed only a month after opening, and the scheme was never revived.

Sutton Bridge's 9-hole golf course is said to be on the site where King John lost his baggage train when this part of the land was still marshland. The king was on his way north after putting his seal to Magna Carta, and took refuge in Swineshead Abbey, 5 miles west of Boston.

⑦ TERRINGTON ST CLEMENT
The magnificent church of St Clement's, sometimes called the 'Cathedral of the Fens', dominates the village. It is kept locked, but the key is obtainable at the shop next door and at the vicarage. It was originally planned with a central tower, but because of the Black Death in the 14th century this was never built. The present Perpendicular 15th-century tower is completely detached from the body of the church.

⑧ KING'S LYNN
The Georgian age lives on in much of King's Lynn, in a sequence of elegant façades throughout the old centre of the town. But King's Lynn, or 'Lynn' as it is often called, is far more ancient than the 18th century. Built on the eastern bank of the Great Ouse, it was already a harbour at the time of the Domesday Book, when it was known as Lena or Lun. In 1204 King John granted it a charter, and by 1347 it was prosperous enough to contribute 19 ships to the English fleet, at a time when London sent 24. In the Middle Ages it was known as Bishop's Lynn (Lynn Episcopi); in 1537 the name was

changed to King's Lynn (Lynn Regis) by a charter of Henry VIII.

The parish church of St Margaret's was originally built about 1100, and is a mixture of building styles, including a Georgian 'Gothic' nave built in the 1740s, after a storm brought the old spire crashing down across the medieval nave. The Town Hall, opposite St Margaret's, was originally the Guildhall of the Holy Trinity, built in 1421. The town's treasures are displayed in the Regalia Rooms in the medieval undercroft.

St George's Guildhall, in King Street, was begun in 1406 and is the largest ancient guildhall in England to have survived intact. It belongs to the National Trust and serves as the headquarters of Lynn's annual summer festival. The theatre in the upper part of the Guildhall carries on an old theatrical tradition, and Shakespeare himself is said to have performed there. Both the Town Hall and Guildhall are built of flint in a striking black-and-white chequer design.

The town has a covered swimming pool, and a yacht club.

⑨ CASTLE RISING

Now just a hamlet dominated by the ruins of a Norman fortress, Castle Rising was once a rival to King's Lynn. It lost its trade, however, when the Babingley River silted up and boats became too large to use the narrow channel that remained.

The castle was built about 1150 by William de Albini, and the lower two stages of his keep survive, decorated with fine and precise carving on the outer walls. It is said to be haunted by the ghost of Queen Isabella, nicknamed the 'she-wolf of France', who was banished to Castle Rising by Edward III for her part in the murder of her husband, Edward II.

⑩ SANDRINGHAM

The house and grounds of the Queen's Norfolk home are open on most days from Easter until the end of September, except for the last week in July and the first in August. The grounds provide a glorious setting for the house, built in mock-Jacobean style by Edward VII in 1870 when he was Prince of Wales.

West of the A149 is Sandringham Warren, where great clumps of rhododendrons brush the road, and there are paths and open spaces for walks and picnics. At Wolferton, across the Warren, the Edwardian station where the royal family left the train and climbed into their carriages was purchased by a private owner when the line closed in 1969, and has been turned into a railway museum.

⑪ SNETTISHAM BEACH

The beach, 2 miles west of Snettisham village, consists largely of chalets and trailer parks, around a series of disused shingle pits. The road ends at a large car park behind the embankment, below which a bank of shingle and sand leads down to a wide expanse of sand at low tide.

The RSPB has a bird sanctuary with four hides on either side of the southernmost shingle pit. Among the many species to be seen there are common terns in summer, and waders and wildfowl in winter.

⑫ HEACHAM

This large seaside village has two beaches, and good walks in both directions along the sea-wall. It is the centre of Norfolk's lavender-growing industry, and in midsummer the fields glow with every shade of mauve and purple. Caley Mill, a watermill until 1923, has a lavender distillery which can be visited.

SYMBOL OF WEALTH *King's Lynn's Custom House was built in 1683 as a merchant exchange, with open ground-floor arcades.*

Long sandy beaches and dunes where wildlife thrives

The Lincolnshire coast is as flat as a table-top, and the land is so low-lying that a driver on the coast road from Saltfleet to Wrangle never catches a glimpse of the sea. But clamber up on the sand-dunes or the sea-walls, and a vast panorama of sand, sea and sky opens up. Resorts line the sands, but south of Skegness walkers can join the sea bank near Friskney and follow it for 15 miles to Boston, with only the singing of larks for company.

① THEDDLETHORPE ST HELEN

Unrestrained by man-made sea banks, the shoreline between Saltfleet Haven and Mablethorpe North End is constantly changing. As the sea deposits more sand, the wind whips it into extensive ridges of dunes, which become more stable as plant colonies grow. These 5 miles of natural coastline are a National Nature Reserve, with many rare plants growing on the dunes, salt-flats and freshwater marshland. Nesting birds include reed buntings and sedge warblers, and hen harriers spend the winter there.

A footpath through the reserve starts at the car park beside the pumping station on the A1031 just south of Saltfleet, and runs south for 4 miles, as far as Crook Bank. Part of the nature reserve is adjacent to Ministry of Defence land, and there are marked danger areas.

② MABLETHORPE

Tennyson chose Mablethorpe as a place to find peace and quiet on the day that his first book of poems was published in 1827. He came with his brother and they sat among deserted dunes, declaiming the verses to the empty sands. Today these same magnificent sands attract up to 50,000 visitors on a fine summer's day, and a modern Tennyson would need to walk far along the dunes to the north of the town to escape the noise of the amusement arcades on the promenade.

The first parish of Mablethorpe with its church of St Peter was swallowed by the sea in the Middle Ages, and the only trace of the original shoreline is a white strip, sometimes visible beyond the breakers at very low tides. Bathing is good, and lifeguards patrol the shore. The RAF use a firing range between Mablethorpe and Theddlethorpe St Helen, and it is not safe to walk along the dunes beyond North End when red flags are flown.

As well as the usual seaside amusements, Mablethorpe has a small zoo at North End, open daily in summer, where injured seals and sea-birds are nursed back to health. There is a motor museum in Victoria Road.

③ SUTTON ON SEA

Quieter and more sedate than neighbouring Mablethorpe, Sutton has residential streets set back behind concrete defensive sea-walls that were reinforced after disastrous floods in 1953. Pleasure gardens line the promenade, and an 18-hole golf course follows the shore to the south. There are firm sands and bathing is good, except near the groynes where depressions form.

④ HUTTOFT BANK

The car terrace at Huttoft Bank is one of the few places on the Lincolnshire coast where cars can park on top of the sea-wall, facing the sea. There is shingle on the foreshore with sand beyond, stabilised by groynes.

Swimming is good, but at nearby Anderby Creek there are treacherous mudbanks where the creek meets the sea.

⑤ CHAPEL ST LEONARDS

The village of brick villas, interspersed with chalets and caravan parks, hugs the shore behind a concrete sea-wall. Chapel Point is a small promontory on an almost perfectly straight coastline, and the new coastguard tower overlooks 4 miles of straight beaches in each direction. Bathing is good. Volunteer lifeguards patrol the beach at weekends and Bank Holidays in summer.

⑥ INGOLDMELLS

In 1936 Billy Butlin chose the sandy shore of Ingoldmells for the site of his first holiday camp. Day tickets admit visitors to the camp, with its indoor swimming pool. Volunteer lifeguards patrol the beach at weekends and bank holidays in summer.

Caravan and chalet parks fill the rest of Ingoldmells. Pleasure flights can be taken from the aerodrome west of the village.

⑦ SKEGNESS

Broad tree-lined avenues with grass verges, and front lawns running to large Victorian houses, give Skegness the atmosphere of an airy garden town. The generous scale of the buildings dates from the mid-19th century, when the local squire, Lord Scarborough, drew up one of Britain's first overall town plans to transform a little fishing village into a seaside holiday town.

The coming of the railway in 1875 confirmed Skegness as one of the principal seaside resorts for Midlands holidaymakers. It remains so today, and although many family houses have been split into holiday flatlets, and the pride of Victorian Skegness – its pier built in 1881 – was demolished after storm damage in 1978, the town behind the promenade retains an air of Victorian gentility and comfort.

Formal gardens along the seafront are stocked annually with 60,000 flowers. The seafront attractions include funfairs, lidos, boating lakes and a marine zoo. There are

---

THE TOAD THAT RUNS

The warm sands and shallow pools of Theddlethorpe Dunes are one of the last homes of the natterjack toad, an increasingly rare species as dunes are afforested and heaths ploughed. It is distinguished from the common toad by its small size, the yellow line down its back and the way it runs rather than hops.

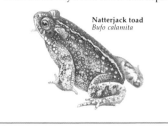

Natterjack toad
Bufo calamita

RIDERS BY THE SEA *Funfairs are among the attractions for young visitors to Skegness, latest in a flood of holidaymakers that started more than a century ago. Illuminations continue until October.*

SKEGNESS SKIPPER *Since 1908, Skegness's jolly fisherman has skipped across this classic of poster art created by John Hassall.*

6 miles of firm sandy beach with good bathing, and the beach is still growing as the sea recedes. Visitors can escape the crowds by walking south along the sands, past Seacroft golf course and on to the spacious dunes of Gibraltar Point.

Church Farm Museum has an evocative Victorian interior, down to the last detail of hat and cape hanging by the door. Farm machinery and rural craft workshops occupy the barns, and a timber-framed thatched cottage from a nearby village has been restored in the grounds.

⑧ GIBRALTAR POINT

A small promontory at the tip of the gently curving arc of coast that borders The Wash, Gibraltar Point is the centre of a 1,000 acre nature reserve. There is a visitor centre, and a network of footpaths leads through the dunes and salt-marshes. One of the rarest of Britain's breeding sea-birds, the little tern, nests on the Spit, together with several pairs of ringed plovers. In the autumn, huge flocks of wading birds – oystercatchers, dunlins and knots – roost there after feeding at low tide on the mud-flats of The Wash.

Volunteers man the bird observatory on the reserve where some 7,000 passage migrants are trapped, ringed and then released every year. Expert and amateur alike can use the hide beside the freshwater mere, where wildfowl, herons and kingfishers can be watched at close quarters.

There is a small harbour where the Steeping River enters the sea.

⑨ WAINFLEET ALL SAINTS

The Romans built a settlement called Vaiona just north of the present market town, and extracted salt from the tidal marshes. The marshes have since been drained and the huge flat fields, crossed by a network of dykes, are prime farming land.

Wainfleet has one notable medieval building, Magdalen College School founded in 1484 by William of Waynflete, Bishop of Winchester, to prepare students for his other foundation, Magdalen College, Oxford.

⑩ FRISKNEY

A large but scattered farming parish, Friskney has an impressive church, All Saints, with an original 14th-century beamed roof and wall paintings of 1320. A rare feature is the Georgian 'hudd', a wooden canopy like a sentry box in which the priest stood when conducting funerals by the graveside in bad weather.

The fertile farmland around Friskney has been reclaimed from marshland by dykes and sea banks. Friskney Sea Lane, which crosses the A52 beside the Barley Mow Inn, leads to a public footpath along the innermost of three sea banks. This first bank dates from 1810, the second from 1948 and the

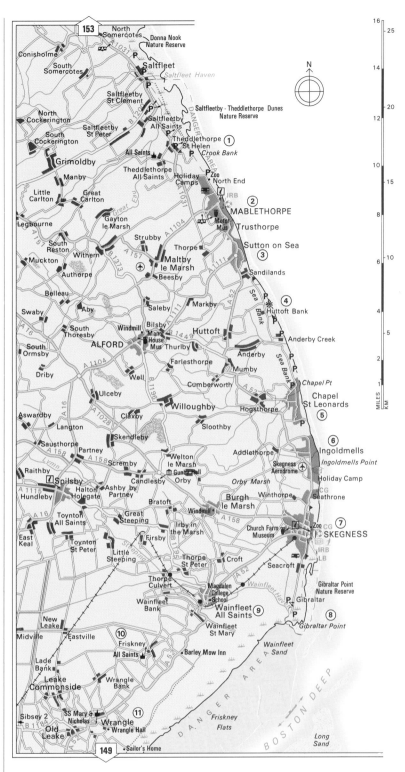

third from 1977 – showing how progressively more land has been reclaimed from the sea.

The footpath follows the coast past Wrangle and on as far as Boston, but walkers should not stray from the track as there is an RAF bombing range on Friskney Flats.

⑪ WRANGLE

The church of St Mary and St Nicholas has medieval stained glass and good brasses; when the church is locked the key can be obtained from the verger across the green. To reach the sea-bank footpath, take the road past the church to Wrangle Hall, turn right, then first left and follow the narrow road until it ends at a house called Sailor's Home. This is a wild spot, with marshy grazing land bordering the mud-flats of The Wash, over which the tide goes out 2 miles.

LOCAL INFORMATION

Tourist information Skegness 4821/5441 (summer).

HM Coastguard (North of Anderley Creek) Patrington 50351; (South of Anderley Creek) Great Yarmouth 851338 for information, 999 in emergency (ask for coastguard).

Weather Lincoln 8091.

Local radio BBC Radio Lincolnshire, 219 m, 1368 kHz, 94.9 MHz.

PLACES TO SEE INLAND

Alford, SW of Mablethorpe. Windmill, Bank Hols; Manor House Museum, most summer days.

Burgh le Marsh Windmill, 5 miles W of Skegness. Tower mill in working order. Daily in summer.

Gunby Hall (NT), 7 miles W of Skegness. 18th-century house. Certain afternoons in summer.

Sibsey Trader Mill, 5 miles W of Wrangle. Last six-sail, six-storey mill in country. Daily in summer.

Trawlers and trippers on the Humber's southern shore

Along the southern shore of the Humber estuary, areas of mud-flats alternate with intense industrial development. It is an inhospitable shoreline, but inland there are many unspoiled villages on the edge of the Lincolnshire Wolds. At Cleethorpes the holiday coast begins, with immense solitudes of sands. The sand-flats, dangerous at low tide, extend to Saltfleet and beyond, and the small villages are fringed with holiday development.

FISHY BUSINESS *Fresh from the sea, the previous night's catch of skate is laid out in Grimsby fish market, ready to be auctioned.*

① BARTON-UPON-HUMBER

In 1725 Daniel Defoe described Barton as 'a struggling mean town noted for nothing but an ill-favoured ferry'. Today it is noted as the place where the A15 becomes airborne over the Humber Bridge, substantially shortening the journey time across the river, which in Defoe's day took 4 hours.

In spite of the marvel of technology on its doorstep, and a sizeable influx of sightseers, Barton has kept its character as a handsome old market town. There are tree-lined streets of red-brick Georgian houses, and only a short step away from the large parish church of St Mary is a little gem of a church, St Peter's. This is being restored, and is one of the best-preserved Saxon churches in the country. The tower has characteristic rounded stone arcades, and the original Saxon nave is the little chapel to the west of the tower.

South of the town a fine Georgian house, Baysgarth Park, contains a small museum of local history; its wooded grounds are a public leisure area, with a swimming pool.

For a close-up view of the elegantly curving lines of the Humber Bridge, go to Barton Waterside, where there is a car park and information centre. A footpath straddles the riverside embankment that passes beneath the bridge. The path skirts a series of lakes which were once claypits from which 'Humber warp' clay was dug for brick and tile-making. In this lonely watery landscape the silence is broken only by the intermittent tolling of a bell-buoy out on the estuary.

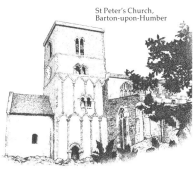

St Peter's Church, Barton-upon-Humber

② BARROW UPON HUMBER

Once a port, Barrow has the air of a forgotten town that is quietly letting the 20th century pass by. As a result it is quite unspoiled. A street of fine 18th-century houses bends round to the knoll on which stands the church. The narrow road down to Barrow Haven passes a mound where a castle once stood. Further on, over the level crossing, a small muddy creek is home to a few local boats. The mud-flats along the shore are noted for snipe, known locally as humming birds because of the vibrant noise made by their tail feathers.

③ NEW HOLLAND

A long street of grey houses leads to a desolate riverside scene. The decayed wooden pier is the one from which the Hull ferry used to depart before the Humber Bridge was built. A vandalised railway terminus adds to the bleakness, but there are good views upstream to the Humber Bridge, and across the river to the bustling docks of Hull.

④ GOXHILL HAVEN

A long road across flat pastureland ends at the tip of the promontory that reaches out into the river towards Hull. No boats can moor on the estuary's muddy banks, and only a single small farm crouches by the water.

The village of Goxhill, 2½ miles inland, has an attractive avenue of trees, and at the south end a moated farm house beside a ruined 14th-century priory; they are not open to the public.

A mile away, at Thornton, is the partly ruined Thornton Abbey, dissolved and demolished by Henry VIII. It is open daily.

⑤ IMMINGHAM

It was from Immingham that the Pilgrim Fathers set sail in 1608, bound for Holland on the first stage of the voyage which finally, in 1620, took them to America. But the muddy creek where they climbed aboard has disappeared under the concrete and steel of the huge docks and industrial complex, and the memorial to the voyagers has been moved from the bank of the Humber to a site in the town beside the church.

Immingham is expanding as one of the nation's most important ports for the shipping of oil, chemicals, fertilisers and iron ore. The four deep-water jetties can handle ships drawing up to 34 ft in draught at all states of the tide. The docks are closed to the public, but ship-spotters and lovers of industrial landscapes can join the footpath along the embankment that starts on either side of the docks' outer piers.

In the town, opposite the Bluestone Inn, is a small museum, once a chapel, which is devoted to local history.

⑥ GRIMSBY

Fish are the main business of Grimsby, and have been ever since a Danish fisherman named Grim landed there 1,000 years ago and began selling fish to the locals. The docks are lined with small seine-net trawlers, brightly painted and hung with small sails, fish baskets and fluorescent orange marker-buoys. A few dents and patches of rust are the marks of the buffeting these little boats receive in the North Sea.

Around the perimeter of the dock is the long covered arcade of the fish market. Every night during the week the fish –

mostly flatfish, scallops and cod – are unloaded from the incoming vessels and laid out along the market for the morning's auction at 7.30. The salesman moves rapidly along the rows of fish boxes, conducting the auction in a jargon that is impossible for an outsider to follow. White-coated merchants perch on boxes and indicate their bids with a wink, a nod or a twitch of the finger. Free permits to visit the fish docks and market during daylight hours are available at the Docks Office; gumboots are advisable.

The nationwide contraction in the fishing industry has hit Grimsby as other ports, and the fleet's decline has left empty moorings along the quayside. But gradually the older, larger trawlers are being replaced by more economical seine-net vessels which fish in relatively shallow waters.

Apart from fish, Grimsby is an important commercial dock, and has a near-monopoly of trade in Danish dairy products and bacon. There is a yacht marina in Alexandra Dock, but berths are not available for visiting yachts. Grimsby docks are tidal, and the dock gates are open for only 3½ hours either side of high tide.

The buildings of Grimsby docks are stolidly Victorian, and are presided over by a magnificent folly, the 309 ft high finger of the Dock Tower. The folly was modelled on a medieval tower of the Palazzo Publico in the Italian city of Siena, and is a landmark for miles out to sea.

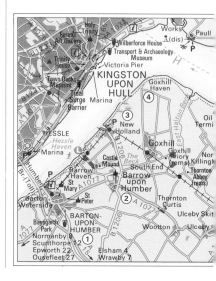

⑦ CLEETHORPES

Trippers arriving at Cleethorpes by train can step straight out of the station on to the promenade. Walkways extend almost a mile along the seafront – past a fairground, a stubby little pier and a new leisure centre with swimming pool – down to the pleasure gardens with boating lakes at the south end of the town. All the way along the promenade the gardens are bright with flowers in summer, some of them arranged in patterns that spell out names or mottoes.

The sea goes out almost a mile over the sands, but at low tide the beaches at Cleethorpes and south as far as Saltfleet can be very hazardous. Because the sea has so far to travel, it rushes in very fast, quickly filling the dips and valleys in the sand, so that large areas of the lower beach become islands of sand, surrounded by water. Swimming is safe at high tide, when the sea is only waist deep 70 yds out.

From the seafront there is a clear view across to the opposite bank of the Humber, and to Bull Sand Fort and Haile Sand Fort which straddle the estuary. Submarines patrolled between the forts in the Second World War to guard the Humber. At night the string of illuminations along the promenade is mirrored by the lights of shipping making its way past the flashing light of Spurn Head.

Away from the seafront, Cleethorpes has a short but delightful High Street. At Old Clee, hidden among the suburbs, 1 mile inland, stands a Norman church.

RUINED ABBEY *The gateway still stands at Thornton Abbey, a monastery torn down by Henry VIII.*

The seafront is taken up by a large holiday complex called the Fitties. Regiments of fixed caravans and chalets line the numbered streets, and there are restaurants and shops. Beyond the man-made sea bank the tide goes out more than a mile, and as at Cleethorpes unwary bathers run a risk of being cut off by the incoming flow. Volunteer lifeguards patrol the beach at weekends in summer.

⑧ TETNEY

Pleasant trees shade bungalows in the village, but towards the sea the view is dominated by rows of huge oil tanks, filled from tankers that discharge into a pipeline out at sea. The nearby canal, once used by barges coming up from the sea to Louth, is no longer navigable. Footpaths along the embankment on either side of the canal lead from Tetney Lock to the sea-wall which skirts the sand-flats and salt-marshes of Tetney Marshes – a bird reserve, with a breeding colony of little terns.

⑨ HORSE SHOE POINT

Just south of the hamlet of North Cotes, Sheepmarsh Lane cuts across flat fields, reclaimed from marshland by a network of dykes. There is a car park beside the sea bank. Horse Shoe Point is no more than a spit of land above high-water mark. A tiny stream meanders across the shore, and at low tide there are almost 2 miles of sand-

PORT WITH A DUAL ROLE *Container ships load and unload at Grimsby, best known for its trawler fleet but at the same time one of Britain's busiest cargo-handling ports.*

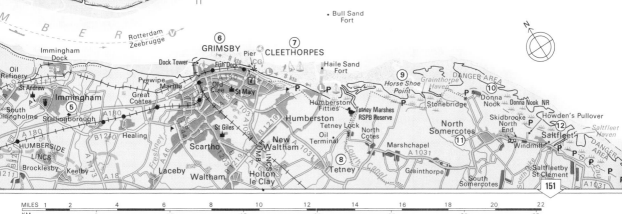

153

flats, deserted apart from the occasional cockle-digger striding barefoot across the flats with his fork and pail.

Care should be taken when walking across the flats, as the stream fills up rapidly as the tide begins to flood.

⑩ **DONNA NOOK**

A road, Marsh Lane, leads out of North Somercotes and across 2 miles of flat reclaimed farmland to the car park for Donna Nook at Stonebridge. Donna Nook takes its name from a ship once wrecked on its desolate shore. When the tide is out, the sea almost disappears from view beyond the flats and banks of muddy sand. Around the edge of the shore where the sea does not reach, a wispy cloak of vegetation has colonised the low dunes, but there is hardly a bush or tree in sight.

The vast sprawl of dunes and sand-flats between Grainthorpe Haven and Saltfleet includes a county trust nature reserve. Some 250 species of birds have been recorded there, including many rare passage migrants using Britain as a stopping-off point on the long journey between their breeding and wintering grounds. Both common and grey seals breed far out on the flats.

Part of the dunes is an RAF bombing range, and when this is in use danger areas are marked with red flags and with red lights on beacons and buoys. Otherwise, if visibility is good, it is safe to walk out on the sands as the tide ebbs – but be sure to turn back before the tide turns.

⑪ **NORTH SOMERCOTES**

A scattered farming community, North Somercotes has a few old brick cottages with an infill of modern bungalows. South-east of the village, sheltered within a wood, is a holiday park that uses a small lake for boating and fishing. There is access to the shore at Howden's Pullover, which is reached by a gravel track at Skidbrooke North End. The sand-flats here are part of Donna Nook nature reserve.

⑫ **SALTFLEET**

A small and sleepy village of red-brick cottages, overlooked by a derelict windmill, Saltfleet has one of the few natural harbours along the Lincolnshire coast. Saltfleet haven is the estuary of the Great Eau, and although narrow and muddy along its straight half-mile, it has moorings for small vessels. Boats can be launched for 2 hours on either side of high tide.

A rough track alongside the Haven leads to the seashore – a vast expanse of wind-swept dunes and flats of sand and mud.

LOCAL INFORMATION

Tourist information Barton-upon-Humber 57637, Cleethorpes 697472.

HM Coastguard Patrington 50351 for information, 999 in emergency (ask for coastguard).

Weather Grimsby 8091.

Local radio BBC Radio Lincolnshire, 219 m, 1368 kHz, 94.9 MHz; BBC Radio Humberside, 202 m, 1485 kHz, 96.9 MHz.

PLACES TO SEE INLAND

Blacktoft Sands Reserve (RSPB), Ousefleet, 30 miles W of Barton-upon-Humber, via A18 and A161.

Elsham Hall Country Park, 7 miles S of Barton-upon-Humber. Daily.

Normanby Hall, 9 miles W of Barton-upon-Humber, via B1430. Most days.

The Old Rectory, Epworth, 25 miles SW of Barton-upon-Humber, via A18 and A161. Birthplace of John and Charles Wesley. Daily in summer.

Scunthorpe Borough Museum and Art Gallery, 15 miles SW of Barton-upon-Humber. Daily.

Wrawby Windmill, 9 miles S of Barton-upon-Humber, via A18. Working post-mill. Certain days.

BOATS THAT REAP THE HARVEST OF THE NORTH SEA

Fishermen are among the few hunters still left in our society. Over the years the seas round our coast have brought modest fortunes to a few – but for the great majority the sea has meant long hours of desperately hard and often dangerous work for little reward.

Generations of fishermen have exploited the rich resources of the North Sea. Whitby cobles were fishing for crabs and lobsters when Captain Cook began his career at this Yorkshire port in 1746. Towns like Great Yarmouth and Lowestoft thrived for more than 300 years on the herring trade. The large trawler fleets of the Humber ports of Hull and Grimsby fished the Dogger Bank for cod, haddock and plaice.

Today's fisherman, although he lives more comfortably on his trawler and has the latest in electronic aids to help him track the fish, still has to spend hours on an exposed deck sorting the catch and mending torn nets. It is not a 9 to 5 job: once on the fishing grounds the trawl is 'shot' and 'hauled' continuously, and between hauls fish are sorted, gutted, washed, packed and covered in ice to keep them fresh.

Up in the wheelhouse the skipper is in command, and it is his task to find the fish and to make big catches. He may own his boat or work for a company. His second-in-command is the mate, and a North Sea trawler may have a further six or eight hands, including engineers and a cook. Weather is the fisherman's worst enemy, so when the weather is fine the crew of a fishing boat work without respite.

PORTS AND PREY *In days gone by, trawlers from Britain's east coast worked fishing grounds as far away as Iceland, the Labrador coast and well into the Arctic Circle. Today, the extension of territorial limits – to 200 miles in the case of Iceland – has deprived our fishermen of many distant water grounds, and many of the larger trawlers have been laid up, scrapped or converted to oil-rig support vessels. Most British fleets now work fishing grounds in the North Sea alongside German, Dutch, Belgian and French boats. To try to prevent overfishing, there are regulations restricting the size at which fish can be landed, and enforcing the use of larger mesh nets. But overfishing of cod, haddock and herring has already led to declining catches of these most important prizes of the North Sea.*

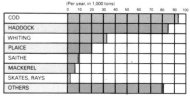

THE MAJOR PORTS

(Fish landed per year, in 1,000 tons)

	0	10	20	30	40	50	60	70	80	90	100
PETERHEAD											
ABERDEEN											
GRIMSBY											
FRASERBURGH											
LOWESTOFT											
HULL											
NORTH SHIELDS											
EYEMOUTH											
PITTENWEEM											
BRIDLINGTON											
SCARBOROUGH											
WICK											

PRINCIPAL FISH CAUGHT IN THE NORTH SEA

(Per year, in 1,000 tons)

	0	10	20	30	40	50	60	70	80	90	100
COD											
HADDOCK											
WHITING											
PLAICE											
SAITHE											
MACKEREL											
SKATES, RAYS											
OTHERS											

HOW TO RECOGNISE EAST COAST FISHING VESSELS

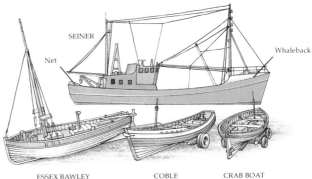

SEINER
Net
Whaleback

ESSEX BAWLEY   COBLE   CRAB BOAT

INSHORE BOATS *At 75 ft long, the seiner is among the largest of the vessels designed primarily for inshore fishing. Seiners can be recognised by the clear space behind the deckhouse, which allows room for the seine net to be hauled in over the stern. The 'whaleback' at the bow shelters the fishermen. The Essex bawley, used for shrimp, oyster and cockle fishing, is more often seen motorised for use as a private pleasure craft. The coble of the Northumbrian and North Yorkshire coast is a descendant of Viking longships, while crab boats of the Norfolk coast are designed for beach launching.*

SORTING THE CATCH *The crew of a Grimsby side trawler sort the catch – haddock, whiting, sole and plaice – after a 'haul'. The nets are cast, or 'shot', every 3 hours and the boat stays at sea for 5 to 12 days. This type of vessel operates anywhere in the North Sea, and has electronic navigation and echo-sounding equipment enabling it to locate and follow shoals of fish.*

HOW FISH ARE CAUGHT

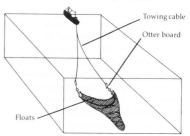

TRAWLING *Most deep-water fish such as cod, plaice and haddock are caught by trawling. The trawl is a conical net, the mouth of which is held open by two otter boards which are pushed outwards by the water resistance. Inshore shellfish such as oysters and mussels are caught by a dredge dragged across the sea-bed*

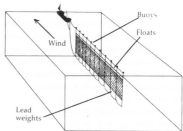

DRIFTING *One method of catching herring employs a net designed so that when the fish swim into it they become caught by their gills. The net hangs just below the surface in line with the vessel, which 'drifts' with the wind, towing the net behind it. Drifters operate at night, when the fish feed near the surface.*

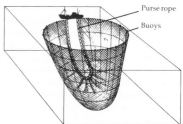

SEINING *The purse-seine net is used to catch shoals of fish such as herring or mackerel near the surface. The net is cast round the fish in a wide arc; then a rope along the bottom is pulled in like a draw-string, and the filled 'purse' is hauled in. Another form of seining uses a conical net to catch fish on or close to the sea bottom.*

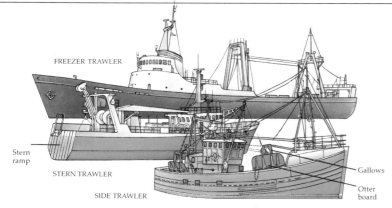

OCEAN-GOING BOATS *The freezer trawlers, usually more than 200 ft long, freeze and process their catch within hours of hauling it aboard. They can stay at sea for more than 3 months. Like the freezer trawler, the stern trawler is easily recognised by the wide ramp at the stern, up which the trawl is hauled. The catch is then sorted, gutted and boxed under cover on the lower deck. Side trawlers tow their trawls by cables passing through gantries, called gallows, on one side or both sides of the vessel. Otter boards are attached to the towing cables to hold the trawl open.*

WHERE THEY COME FROM

The letters painted on the bows of every fishing boat indicate where the vessel was first registered; but fishing boats are often seen far away from their home ports.

ENGLAND	
BH Blyth	SSS South Shields
BK Berwick-upon-Tweed	WI Wisbech
BN Boston	WS Wells
CK Colchester	WY Whitby
CL Carlisle	YH Yarmouth
F Faversham	
GY Grimsby	SCOTLAND
H Hull	A Aberdeen
HH Harwich	AH Arbroath
HL Hartlepool	DE Dundee
IH Ipswich	FR Fraserburgh
LN King's Lynn	GN Granton
LO London	INS Inverness
LT Lowestoft	K Kirkwall
MH Middlesbrough	KY Kirkcaldy
NE Newcastle	LH Leith
RR Rochester	LK Lerwick
SD Sunderland	ME Montrose
SH Scarborough	PD Peterhead
SN North Shields	PEH Perth
	WK Wick

From busy port to lonely headland north of the Humber

The ancient city of Kingston upon Hull is still a centre of seafaring although it stands some 22 miles up the River Humber from the open sea. East of Hull lie the flat fields of Holderness, punctuated by the towers and spires of old village churches. The fields come to an abrupt end to the east, where low earth cliffs drop to the sea along the edge of a straight stretch of sandy coast, which terminates to the south in the narrow appendix of Spurn Head.

① HUMBER BRIDGE

Opened in 1981, after nine years in the building, the Humber Bridge has the longest single span of any bridge in the world. At 1,542 yds, its main span is 122 yds longer than that of the Verrazano Narrows Bridge in New York. It has twin towers 533 ft high from which are suspended two main cables, each 27 in. across and containing 14,948 separate wire filaments. The total length of wire in the cables is 44,000 miles – more than 1½ times the circumference of the Earth.

The statistics are impressive, but there is no measure for the awesome beauty of the structure towering above the flat landscape of Humberside. The bridge is beautiful because it is unadorned functional, and its elegantly curving lines are born of engineering and aerodynamic necessity. There is a toll for motor vehicles crossing the bridge, but pedestrians and cyclists cross free.

② HESSLE

Although it is almost swallowed up within the suburbs of Hull, Hessle is still a village at heart, with a pleasant central square and good Georgian houses. Anchored off the foreshore is the paddle-steamer *Lincoln Castle*, which used to ferry cars and passengers across the Humber between Hull and New Holland. Now it has a new lease of life as a floating restaurant, with fine views of the Humber Bridge which brought its ferrying career to an end.

③ KINGSTON UPON HULL

When Edward I gave the first Charter to the port on the River Hull in 1299, the town took the name of Kingston (King's Town) upon Hull. Officially the town has retained its full name, but it is usually shortened to Hull. The River Hull was one of the town's watery boundaries, the Humber was another, and in 1321 a defensive moat was dug that joined the two rivers, thus fortifying the town on its own island. These fortifications are still in evidence, because sections of the moat were widened to create Hull's enclosed docks in the 18th and 19th centuries. The area between these docks and the River Hull is still known as the Old Town.

A stroll around Hull's Old Town is rewarding, with intriguing juxtapositions of old and new. The area still retains its medieval street pattern, and some of the buildings date back to the 18th century and earlier. In High Street is Wilberforce House, birthplace in 1759 of William Wilberforce who campaigned vigorously for the abolition of slavery in the British Empire. His statue stands on a tall column overlooking Queen's Gardens, and his birthplace is a museum to his memory. It contains some of the grim relics of the slave trade, such as whips, chains and leg-irons.

The River Hull itself, where the port's prosperity began, is still a busy harbour for river barges and small coasters. At the mouth of the river a huge tidal surge barrier has been built, with concrete towers supporting a steel gate like a guillotine, which can be dropped to prevent the city from being flooded.

The first of the enclosed docks, built in 1778, was filled in and is now a large open space, Queen's Gardens. The Humber Dock, also on the site of part of the original moat, is being converted to a yachting marina. The former Docks Authority office in Queen Victoria Square now houses a maritime museum, known as the Town Docks Museum. At the heart of the Old Town is Holy Trinity Church, England's largest parish church and, dating from the 14th century, the earliest major building of brick.

On the Boulevard stands a statue of George Smith, skipper of the trawler *Crane* which was involved in a bizarre incident in 1904 that became known as the 'Russian Outrage'. Russia was at war with Japan, and in the early hours of October 22 the Russian fleet opened fire on Hull trawlers fishing on Dogger Bank, mistaking them for Japanese torpedo boats. George Smith was killed instantly and his trawler sunk; three others were badly damaged.

The modern docks, which line 7 miles of Humber waterfront, include a North Sea ferry terminal for crossings to Rotterdam and Zeebrugge. The docks are not open to visitors, but a good point from which to watch the shipping is Victoria Pier, where the Humber ferry used to berth before the Humber Bridge was opened. This has been restored as an open space and decked-out with flowers, and there are band concerts in the summer.

④ HEDON

At first sight no more than a quiet and attractive little market town, Hedon has a few intriguing relics of a short but glorious past in the 12th century when it was a major port, important enough to send two MPs to Parliament. A muddy stream, Hedon Haven, is all that remains of the port, but a sunken grassy lane beside the stream is a silted-up canal, probably dug in the 12th century for mooring ships.

Once the town had three churches, but only one still stands. This is St Augustine's, a large and impressive 13th-century building with a fine tower. The grid-like pattern of streets, and street names such as Souttergate and Fletchergate, point to Hedon's medieval origins, but most of the town was destroyed by a fire in 1656. By then it had already been eclipsed by Hull.

SCRIMSHAW: THE SAILORS' ART

Seamen of the 19th-century whaling ships amused themselves in their off-duty hours by carving intricate designs on whales' teeth or walrus tusks. They used the blade of a jack-knife, and highlighted the design by rubbing lampblack or indian ink into the incised lines. Sometimes a sail needle was used to scratch particularly delicate patterns or portraits. Ships and whaling scenes were the most popular subjects of these carvings, which came to be known as scrimshaw and are now highly prized by collectors.

Scrimshaw carvings in the Town Docks Museum, Kingston upon Hull

A GIANT'S STRIDE *The suspension bridge opened by the Queen in 1981 spanned the Humber, created a new east coast road route and won Britain a world record for the length of its central span.*

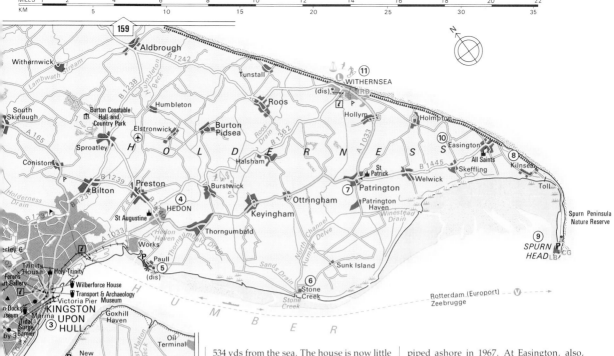

⑤ PAULL

Beside the road to Paull vast oil tankers, moored off the BP chemicals plant, loom incongruously above cornfields. A row of houses line the river front, with a car park beside the little redundant lighthouse, dated 1836. From the sea-wall there are good views back to Hull, and across to Immingham, with shipping making its way up the Humber to the two ports.

⑥ STONE CREEK

There is little stone at Stone Creek – only mud bordering the Humber estuary and, inland, flat hedgeless farmland stretching for miles all round with a few isolated dwellings. The little muddy creek is occupied by a few boats of the local sailing club, but sailing is hazardous because of strong tidal currents in the estuary. A stone wall protects the farmland from flooding, and at nearby Sunk Island, 12 square miles of land have been reclaimed from silt by dykes and banks.

⑦ PATRINGTON

A church of breathtaking beauty puts Patrington on the map for all lovers of the Decorated period of English Gothic architecture. The church of St Patrick is structured like a cathedral, with a central tower and spire, and transepts on either side. The entire church was built between the late 13th and the mid-14th centuries, and among its glories are some 200 carved stone faces – human, animal and grotesque – that peer down from the columns and the roof.

⑧ KILNSEA

A scattered community straddling the narrowing promontory that ends at Spurn Head, Kilnsea has two shores, a sandy one exposed to the North Sea, and a muddy but-sheltered shore within the Humber estuary. The majority of dwellings are on the Humber side.

One house, now a shop, has a plaque that states that it was built in 1847 and was then 534 yds from the sea. The house is now little more than 200 yds from the sea, which is a measure of the erosion that has taken place.

⑨ SPURN HEAD

A narrow spit of sand and shingle, the peninsula curves 3½ miles into the Humber estuary like a hook at the end of the arm of Holderness. Spurn has no rocky base. It has been built up over the centuries by the accumulation of sand from the eroding shores to the north, and by silt deposited by the Humber. Spurn itself is subject to erosion, and occasionally the narrow spit has been breached by the sea, only to be built up again a little further to the west.

In places only 50 yds wide, the peninsula is bordered by a sandy beach on the seaward side, and by flats of muddy sand on the Humber side, with sparse duneland vegetation where the sea does not reach. The area from Kilnsea to the tip of Spurn Head is a nature reserve, belonging to the Yorkshire Naturalists' Trust, and there is a charge for drivers using the road to the Head.

There is a car park near the lighthouse, from which the tip of the Head is only a few hundred yards walk along the shore. It is a wild and windswept spot, melancholy with the sound of oystercatchers and the drone of warning buoys out to sea. The shipping lanes into the Humber are narrow and difficult, and all ships entering and leaving the estuary are accompanied by pilots. Their boats can be seen speeding out from the jetty on Spurn Head. Moored off the jetty is the Humber lifeboat, one of only three in the country manned by a full-time crew.

Spurn is an important site for observing bird migrations, since it acts as a narrow funnel through which vast numbers of birds pass in spring and autumn on their journeys along the east coast.

⑩ EASINGTON

A few of the houses in this attractive little farming village are built of sea cobbles – large stones of various colours collected from the beach. The thatched red-brick barn behind the church dates from the 14th or 15th century. Coastal erosion is eating into the low cliffs that border the sandy beach, but the sea has not yet disposed of some ugly wartime concrete pillboxes. Bathers should beware of strong currents at right-angles to the beach.

To the north of the village is the gas terminal where the first North Sea gas was piped ashore in 1967. At Easington, also, pioneer work has been done in pumping gas back under the sea for storage when demand is low.

⑪ WITHERNSEA

The builders of the handsome lighthouse of 1894 at Withernsea may have been allowing for coastal erosion when they set it back several hundred yards from the sea, in the midst of residential streets. The seafront is remarkable only for a castellated gateway that leads nowhere but faces the beach like a yellow-brick sandcastle. The gateway was once part of a pier built in 1875 but long-since vanished.

Withernsea declined as a resort when it lost its railway in 1964. Nevertheless it has a good sand-and-shingle beach with safe swimming. On summer Sundays there is a general market.

LOCAL INFORMATION

Tourist information (Humber Bridge) Hull 640852, Hull 223344.

HM Coastguard Patrington 50351 for information, 999 in emergency (ask for coastguard).

Weather Grimsby 8091.

Local radio BBC Radio Humberside, 202 m, 1485 kHz, 96.9 MHz. IBA Viking Radio 258 m, 1161 kHz, 102.7 MHz.

PLACES TO SEE INLAND

Beverley, 8 miles N of Hull, off A1079. Minster, 13th-15th centuries; Art Gallery and Museum, weekdays.

Burton Constable Hall and Country Park, 8 miles NE of Hull. Elizabethan. Weekends and Bank Holidays in summer, most days in August.

Skidby Windmill, 3 miles NW of Hull, off A164. 19th-century working mill. Most days in summer.

Cliffs at Flamborough Head above a lively seaside town

At the foot of the white cliffs near Bempton and Flamborough, the sea has carved out little bays, decorated with dripping caves and pillars of chalk rock. South of Bridlington Bay, however, quite another kind of coast begins. Unrelieved by a single nook or promontory, the sands of Holderness stretch southwards for mile after mile, backed by low, crumbling cliffs of red mud and flat farmland, where the sea eats relentlessly into the land.

① BEMPTON CLIFFS

From April to mid-July the cliffs at Bempton pulsate with vast numbers of sea-birds, which nest on shelves and in crevices in the chalk. From the RSPB bird reserve car park a footpath leads to fenced viewing terraces. Below them the cliffs drop vertically for as much as 400 ft, every ledge crowded with mewing, screaming, cackling or cawing birds.

Some 33 species of birds breed there, including kittiwakes, guillemots, razorbills, puffins and gannets. In autumn, when most of the birds have flown back to the open sea, a few late gannets still perform their spectacular aerobatics, plummeting into the sea from 100 ft up in pursuit of mackerel.

CLIFF BIRD *Among the birds which nest on the cliffs are razorbills, named after the sharp upper mandible with which they grip their fish prey.*

② THORNWICK BAY

From the car park at North Landing an easy footpath skirts the cliffs to the west and down to this pretty cove. There is a beach of chalk shingle and large caves to explore at low tide. It is possible to walk round the rocks to other bays, but timing is important to avoid being cut off by the tide.

③ NORTH LANDING

Flamborough's North Landing is a picture postcard of a cove. Sheltered by an arcade of white cliffs, the little bay has a narrow strip of sand, and light reflected from the chalky sea-bed turns the water a luminous turquoise.

Fishing cobles are drawn up on a broad, steeply sloping ramp below the lifeboat station. The cobles are launched from the beach, and fishing excursions and short pleasure trips round the coast are available in them. This is the best way to see the spectacular rock formations, where the sea has chiselled out caves in the face of the cliffs. The cave mouths are framed by pillars and arches of chalk that rise out of the waves like the columns of a vast cathedral.

④ FLAMBOROUGH HEAD

This plateau of rolling turf is 150 ft up on the cliffs and surrounded on three sides by the sea. There are good footpaths around the cliffs, flat enough and wide enough to take a wheelchair. For the agile there is a footpath down the side of the cliffs to Selwicks (pronounced Silex) Bay; there are steep steps

at the foot of the path. From this chalky cove it is possible to walk below the headland and explore the lunar landscape of white chalk stacks and boulders and glittering rock pools.

⑤ SOUTH LANDING

Flamborough fishermen used to keep one coble at South Landing and another at North Landing so that one of them could be launched whichever way the wind was blowing. However, this is not a place for inexperienced sailors, for there are treacherous currents around Flamborough Head, particularly when the tide is on the turn.

The beach at South Landing consists of rough shingle and boulders of chalk, unsuitable for bathing, but popular among sunbathers who bask against the heat-reflecting cliffs. From the car park, footpaths lead to superb clifftop walks, east to Flamborough Head and west to Danes' Dyke and Sewerby.

⑥ DANES' DYKE

A deep ravine runs 2½ miles across the Flamborough peninsula from north to south. Largely man-made, it served as a fortification to isolate Flamborough Head and to defend it from the mainland. Despite its name, however, the ditch was dug long before the Danes occupied this coast in the 9th century. Flint arrowheads found on the site suggest a date before the Iron Age, making the dyke at least 2,000 years old.

The southern section of the dyke, between Bridlington Road and the sea, is laid out as a nature trail. A delightful path makes a circuit of 1¼ miles along the edge of the densely wooded dyke, dipping down occasionally into the ravine.

⑦ SEWERBY

The white cliffs of the Flamborough peninsula roll gently to an end at Sewerby, and the sands of Bridlington begin.

Sewerby is a tiny village with a few streets of terraced houses, a pub, a church, and a Georgian mansion, Sewerby Hall, set in 50 acres of parkland. The Hall houses a small museum and art gallery, and a collection of trophies and mementoes of the Yorkshire aviator Amy Johnson.

⑧ BRIDLINGTON

Two towns in one, with two distinct centres a mile apart, make up Bridlington. The livelier of the two has grown up around the seafront, where safe sandy beaches stretch a

LIGHT FANTASTIC *Flamborough Head's chalk cliffs may crumble, but its 85 ft high lighthouse has defied winds and weather since 1806. Its present beam has a range of 29 miles.*

SEASIDE GARDENS *The stately buildings that line Bridlington's Royal Crescent look across ornamental gardens towards the North Beach.*

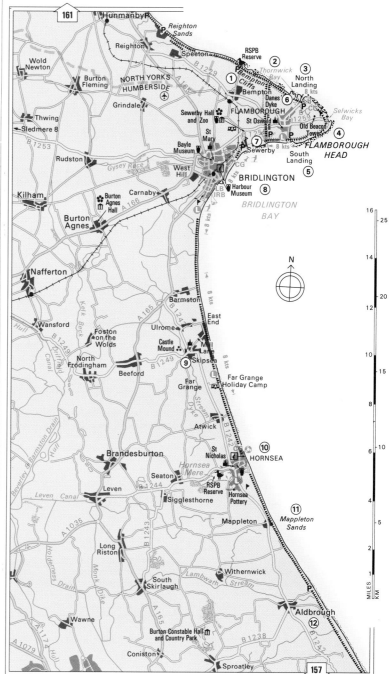

mile on either side of the busy tidal harbour. Pedestrian walkways encircle the stone walls of the harbour, a good vantage point from which to watch the fishing trawlers returning each evening to unload their catch at the quayside.

For the sea angler there are fishing trips in large cobles, and there is excellent fishing in the bay for codling and plaice, with good cod and haddock in winter. On the north side of the harbour is a museum of harbour history, with displays of sea-fishing methods, which is open daily in summer. Facing the harbour is the sleek prow-shaped building of the Royal Yorkshire Yacht Club.

A mile inland, just off the Scarborough Road and almost submerged in the suburbs of modern Bridlington, stands the priory church of St Mary, the focus of the old town centre. The 13th-century church contains intriguing carvings of mice running up the woodwork. The Bayle Museum of local antiquities is housed in the 14th-century gatehouse of the priory; there is limited opening, in summer only. Near by, the High Street has become a quiet backwater, with well-preserved 18th-century houses and shopfronts.

Bridlington has a regatta in mid-August and a sea-angling week in September.

⑨ SKIPSEA
The rapidly eroding clifftop of Skipsea is reached by Mill Lane, and there are steps down to the beach from East End, east of Ulrome. There are also steps to the beach from the track leading from the Far Grange holiday camp, 1½ miles south of Skipsea, and trailer-borne boats can be launched from there. A huge mound near Skipsea church is all that remains of a castle built by William the Conqueror's lieutenant, Drogo de Bevere.

⑩ HORNSEA
Along Hornsea's promenade the most popular entertainment is the bowling green. Inland, and separated from the seafront by an attractive park, the centre has kept its character as an old market town. In the main street, called Newbegin, is a farmhouse, dating back to the 16th century, which houses the North Holderness Museum of Village Life, open daily in summer. This has reconstructed Victorian rooms, collections of farm gear and railway relics and even, at the touch of a button, the recorded reminiscences of a local sage.

At 2 miles long, Hornsea Mere is Yorkshire's largest freshwater lake, and it is less than 1 mile from the sea. The eastern end of

the mere has been developed for recreation: there are sailing and rowing boats for hire, and fishing licences are available for coarse fish, including large pike. Visitors can bring their own boats, but if under 12 ft they must be 'Mirror' class.

Hornsea Mere is also a bird sanctuary, important as a breeding site for some 600 pairs of reed warblers and as a wintering place for thousands of wildfowl. The best viewing points are on the public footpath along the south side.

South of the town, the Hornsea Pottery has a leisure park and provides a wide range of entertainments for visitors who come primarily to see quality pottery in the making.

⑪ MAPPLETON SANDS
There is only a turning place where the beach road suddenly stops on the steadily eroding cliffs. There is no fixed path down to the sands, merely a track of hard-packed mud. Usage has made this track safe, but avoid climbing down the unstable mud cliffs elsewhere.

⑫ ALDBROUGH
The sleepy farming village is set back from the coast, which is just as well since the sea bites off about 16 ft of mud cliff every year. The road to the sea comes to an abrupt end with huge cracks in the tarmac, and drops at a drunken angle over the cliff. The wooden steps down to the beach are rebuilt every year. Above, a few shacks still perch on the clifftop.

LOCAL INFORMATION

Tourist information Bridlington 673474/679626; Hornsea 2919 (summer).

HM Coastguard Patrington 50351 for information, 999 in emergency (ask for coastguard).

Weather Grimsby 8091.

Local radio BBC Radio Humberside, 202 m, 1485 kHz, 96.9 MHz.

PLACES TO SEE INLAND

Burton Agnes Hall, 6 miles SW of Bridlington. Elizabethan house. Most afternoons in summer.

Sledmere House, 16 miles W of Bridlington. Georgian House. Most afternoons in summer.

Broad bays along the coast where sea-bathing started

The North York Moors National Park borders the sea as far south as Cloughton, and its grass and heather reach out into a craggy headland at Ravenscar. This is a walker's coast, with magnificent vistas of rugged cliff scenery; but the same cliffs block access to the shore along most of its length. Beyond the broad sandy bays of Scarborough, the cliffs, whose red clay is rich in fossils, end at last in the sandy crescent of Filey Bay.

① ROBIN HOOD'S BAY

Lined with flat rocks, and skirted by red cliffs, Robin Hood's Bay shares its name with the pretty fishing village that nestles in the bay's north cheek. Known locally as 'Bay Town', the village's connections with the outlaw are dubious, but one legend is that Robin Hood came to Whitby to help the abbot to repel Danish invaders.

Tiny fishermen's cottages with russet-tiled roofs snuggle along the steep twisting street that leads down to the shore. Little cobbled alleyways and terraces evoke images of smuggling, which flourished in the area in the 18th century. A tunnel through which King's Beck discharges into the sea was used by smugglers, and there are other tunnels branching from it. It was said that a smuggled bale of silk could pass from one end of the village to the other without appearing above the ground. Some of the old houses have interconnecting doors disguised as cupboards through which the smugglers could escape from the Revenue men.

Erosion caused several cottages to tumble into the sea before a 40 ft high sea-wall was completed in 1975 to protect the village. The beach is not suitable for bathing, because of its sharp and slippery rocks, but it is popular with fossil-hunters. On the rocks to the north of the village there is a danger of being cut off by the tide.

② BOGGLE HOLE

A little stream called Mill Beck has chiselled a gap in the cliffs of Robin Hood's Bay, and this valley is one of the few ways down to the shore. The old mill from which the beck takes its name is now a youth hostel. From the car park, which has space for only a dozen cars, there is a quarter-mile walk down a metalled track to a sheltered cove of shingle and rock. At low tide it is easy to walk across the rocks to Stoupe Beck Sands.

③ STOUPE BECK SANDS

The beach where Stoupe Beck meets the sea is the best stretch of sand along the otherwise rocky edge of Robin Hood's Bay. Motorists can reach it by following a narrow and precipitous road signposted 'cul de sac' from the crossroads beside the ruined windmill near Ravenscar. There are breathtaking views over the bay from the road, which ends at a small car park beside Stoupe Bank Farm. A paved track, sometimes slippery, leads through a steep wooded valley down to the beach.

④ RAVENSCAR

The broad sweep of Robin Hood's Bay stops short at the rugged headland of Old Peak at Ravenscar. Perched at the summit of the peak, 600 ft above the sea, is a large house, now a hotel, called Raven Hall, built in 1774 on the site of a Roman signal station. The hotel's gardens, golf course and open-air swimming pool are open to non-residents for a charge.

Around 1900 plans were made to build a resort at Ravenscar. A few houses were built, but the development company went bankrupt and Ravenscar remains a wild and deserted place, with good walks through National Trust land on the cliffs.

⑤ HAYBURN WYKE

A steep track through a delightful wooded glen leads down to the rocky shore, where a waterfall tumbles on to the beach. The scrub woodland beside the stream is a nature reserve, a rich habitat for damp-loving plants and beetles. Cars can be parked near Hayburn Wyke Hotel by arrangement with the proprietor.

⑥ CLOUGHTON WYKE

A sheltered and secluded bay, with a rocky shore, Cloughton Wyke can be reached along a farm road, but drivers should respect the country code and close the gates. The name comes from the medieval English *wic*, meaning 'dairy farm'. The road ends at a small car park above the cliffs, and a short grassy track leads down to the little bay. In calm weather swimming from the rocks is possible but uncomfortable.

⑦ CROOK NESS

The sea at Crook Ness can be reached from Burniston by Rocks Lane, which passes under a bridge of the disused Whitby – Scarborough railway line. Fork right at the coastguard cottages to a small car park; from there a narrow concrete path runs through a gap in the cliffs to the shore of flat rocks and boulders. There is a good view towards Scarborough's Castle Cliff.

⑧ SCARBOROUGH

The battlements of a medieval castle jut grim and grey above the crag which divides Scarborough's twin bays. The town rises steeply behind the sands, and elegant white terraces of hotels line the clifftops. The hillsides are landscaped with parks and public gardens. The port, at the foot of Castle Cliff, has an inner harbour for cargo and fishing vessels and an outer harbour for private pleasure craft; both are tidal.

Both North Bay and South Bay have safe swimming areas, and South Bay's foreshore vibrates with amusements as far as The Spa. Here the stately buildings set a more sedate

OUTLAWS' BAY The legendary Robin Hood is said to have visited the bay named after him, and in the 18th century smugglers found it isolated enough to carry on the tradition of lawlessness.

tone, which continues along the manicured walks of South Cliff Gardens. South Bay is dominated by the gargantuan Grand Hotel, with 365 bedrooms, 52 chimneys, 12 floors and 4 turrets representing the days, weeks, months and seasons of the year. The Grand, which was the biggest brick building in

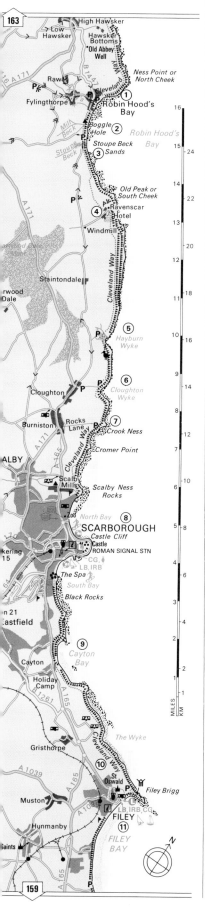

SCARBOROUGH FAIR *Fishing vessels crowd the harbour, streets and houses climb the slopes of a wooded cliff, and a Norman castle adds stately charm to the fair face of Scarborough's old town.*

Europe when it was put up in 1867, is now a Butlin's Holiday Centre.

The Romans built a signal station on the castle headland, and the foundations are still visible. But it was the Vikings who gave Scarborough its name, which means 'stronghold of Skarthi'. In 1620 a local resident named Elizabeth Farrer discovered springs of discoloured and sour-tasting water bubbling from a rock. Healing properties were claimed for the waters, and the town developed as a spa. In 1660 Dr Wittie of Scarborough became an advocate of sea-bathing. It soon became fashionable for men and women to leap naked into the sea, and thus Scarborough was born as a seaside resort, probably the first in Britain.

Among the unusual entertainments that Scarborough provides for summer visitors are the naval battles at Peasholm Park, when manned scale-models of ships re-enact naval skirmishes on a lake in the park. The resort is noted for its theatres, and has an art gallery and museums of natural history, local history and archaeology.

Donkey rides on the sands at Scarborough

⑨ **CAYTON BAY**
A path from the holiday camp at the top of the cliffs descends to the sandy beach. There are sandbanks on which the unwary can be trapped by the rising tide, and bathing is safest at high water. It is dangerous to cross the rocks at the southern extremity of the bay, and it is impossible to reach Filey along the beach at any state of the tide.

⑩ **CLEVELAND WAY**
In 1969 the Cleveland Way became the second long-distance footpath to be opened in England and Wales. Starting on the cliffs to the north of Filey, the path, which is clearly marked with an acorn symbol, weaves around the coast northwards as far as Saltburn-by-the-Sea where it turns inland and crosses the Cleveland Hills to Helmsley, a total distance of 93 miles. In the coastal section the path breaks at Scarborough and Whitby, but elsewhere it follows the cliffs, occasionally dipping down to shore-level. From the path walkers have spectacular views of a coastline that is largely denied to motorists.

Strong boots and protective clothing are vital for anyone attempting the path. The east coast is notorious for sudden changes in weather, and along the cliffs land-slips can be a hazard after rain. Good points to join the Cleveland Way are Church Cliff, Filey; Scalby Mills, Scarborough; Cloughton Wyke; Hayburn Wyke; Ravenscar; Boggle Hole; and Robin Hood's Bay.

⑪ **FILEY**
The handsome Victorian terraces of Filey are set back from the sea, with a steep tree-lined incline down to the promenade. A 6 mile sweep of sand, framed by red-clay cliffs and sheltered to the north by the natural stone breakwater of Filey Brigg, earns Filey its reputation as a family resort.

At the north end of the promenade brightly painted cobles are hauled up a ramp by tractors; there are good catches of crabs and lobsters off the coast in summer, cod and haddock in winter, and fishing trips with the coble fishermen can be arranged.

Filey Brigg is a finger of rocks that points a mile out to sea. At low tide in calm weather it is safe to explore the rock pools, and there is excellent fishing for codling and mackerel from the rocks. A nature trail along the Brigg starts at the foot of the cliff below Filey Country Park. Avoid the Brigg in rough weather; heavy seas can crash over the rocks, making them as perilous for walkers and anglers as they have been down the centuries for ships.

Filey's parish church of St Oswald has good Norman pillars and doorways and an unusual 13th-century effigy of a 'boy bishop'. The Folk Museum in Queen Street, housed in a farmhouse dating from 1696, is open daily except Saturdays in summer.

LOCAL INFORMATION

Tourist information Scarborough 72261/73333; Filey, Scarborough 512204 (summer).

HM Coastguard North Shields 572691 for information, 999 in emergency (ask for coastguard).

Weather Middlesbrough 8091.

Local radio BBC Radio York, 450 m, 666 kHz, 97.2 MHz; Radio Humberside, 202 m, 1485 KHz, 96.9 MHz.

PLACES TO SEE INLAND

Castle Howard, near Malton, 23 miles W of Scarborough, off A64. 18th-century mansion. Daily in summer.

Malton Museum, 19 miles SW of Scarborough. Romano-British artefacts. Daily in summer, some days in winter.

Pickering, 17 miles W of Scarborough. Beck Isle Museum of Rural Life, daily in summer; medieval castle remains, daily; North Yorkshire Moors Railway, daily in summer.

Clifftop walks above a chain of old fishing harbours

Red-grey crags climb to high cliffs at Boulby, then slope down to a rocky shoreline. Walkers can follow the Cleveland Way right along the coast, over cliffs and along the foreshore. The cliffs are breached by valleys that shelter fishing villages such as Staithes and Runswick, while on the broader valley of the River Esk lies the ancient port of Whitby. There, Captain Cook's statue overlooks a scene that has changed little since his day.

COVE OF INDUSTRY *In the 18th century, alum boats had to negotiate a narrow channel cut through the rocks of Hummersea Scar to load up with the valuable chemical mined near by.*

① SKINNINGROVE
The village of Skinningrove lies beside a stream at the foot of a valley, where gaunt cliffs rise from a sandy bay. Skinningrove was built to house the men who worked the iron mines at the head of the valley. Though the mines have closed, steel works have taken their place and the stream is permanently stained with the rusty colour of iron ore waste. Though Skinningrove is hardly a holiday centre, the sandy beach on each side of the quay and the spectacular cliff scenery would be the envy of many resorts.

② HUMMERSEA SCAR
Cut into the flat rocks of Hummersea Scar is a man-made channel that once formed a harbour in this inhospitable spot. The harbour, and the scars of mine workings on the cliffside, are relics of Britain's first chemical industry, the mining and purification of alum, that took place along the north Yorkshire coast between 1600 and 1870. Alum, a blueish stone, was used extensively in dyeing wool, tanning leather and sizing paper. In the days of James I, alum was a Royal monopoly, but this ended with the death of Charles I. The industry ceased when a way was found of making alum from coal shales treated with sulphuric acid.

To see the old mines, take the steep road up the hillside east of Skinningrove and, on the level ground above the village, turn left to Hummersea Farm, where cars may be parked with the farmer's permission. A track leads up to the headland, past a cottage, and the alum mines are near the highest point on the cliffs.

③ BOULBY
At their highest point, Boulby cliffs stand 666 ft above the sea, making them the highest cliffs on England's east coast. As such they are something of a disappointment, for they lack the drama of cliffs like Bempton in Humberside or Beachy Head in East Sussex that descend vertically to the shore. Boulby cliffs drop in stages; but from the summit footpath the effect is still exhilarating and the view magnificent. At the eastern end of the hillside a large potash mine disfigures an otherwise wild stretch of countryside.

④ STAITHES
Little houses cluster on the steep sides of a gorge that opens out like a funnel into the harbour at Staithes, which remains much as James Cook would have known it in 1744. As a lad of 16, Cook was apprentice to William Sanderson, a haberdasher at Staithes, but after 18 months the man who was to become one of the world's greatest explorers followed the example of many villagers and went to sea – as a servant aboard a Whitby ship.

The harbour is smaller than in Cook's day, but a fleet of fishing cobles is anchored in the shelter of the stream at the western end. From the harbour climb steep narrow alleys with quaint names such as Gun Gutter and Dog Loup, which is little over 18 in. wide.

The sandy bed of the harbour is revealed at low tide, creating a pleasant beach which is protected from the waves by the harbour piers. The only car park is at the top of the hill near the entrance to the village.

⑤ PORT MULGRAVE
The road ends at a row of houses perched on a high clifftop, and several hundred feet below is the dilapidated harbour of Port Mulgrave. It is a long steep climb down the cliff path to the harbour, where a few small fishing boats are moored.

At first it seems strange that anyone should build a harbour in such an inaccessible place. A tunnel near the foot of the cliff provides the explanation, for it leads a mile inland to the old ironstone mines at Dalehouse, south of Staithes. Until the mine closed in the 1920s, the iron ore was carried through the tunnel by a narrow-gauge railway and tipped into the holds of coasters in Port Mulgrave for shipment to the furnaces at Jarrow.

⑥ RUNSWICK BAY
A crescent of sand stretches south-east from the village of Runswick, which consists of a collection of cottages set apparently at random at the foot of the cliffs. Narrow alleyways weave between the cottages, revealing pretty gardens separated by stone walls. In 1682 an earlier village of Runswick slipped into the sea.

A long row of fishing boats is parked above the shore, with a tractor to haul them down the ramp. There is a sailing club at the southern end of the bay, and light dinghies can be launched from the sands.

CAPTAIN COOK COUNTRY

The explorer James Cook was born in 1728 in the village of Marton, 2 miles south of Middlesbrough. The cottage where he was born is no longer there, but the site is marked by a granite vase in Stewart Park and near by is a Birthplace Museum. At Great Ayton, where Cook went to school, part of the schoolhouse is now a Cook museum.

It was while working at Staithes that Cook first felt the urge to go to sea, but it is with Whitby that he is most closely associated. He was apprenticed to a Whitby shipowner, John Walker, and the house in which he lodged at this time – in Grape Lane – still stands; it is due to open as another Cook museum. All the ships used by Cook were built at the Fishburn shipyard in Whitby. A life-size statue of the explorer was erected on Whitby's West Cliff in 1912.

Captain Cook and his ship *Endeavour*

⑦ KETTLENESS

This isolated community of red-brick houses on the clifftop still has several relics of the now disused coastal railway line. The red-brick Victorian station stands incongruously in a field. A footpath follows the railway track from Staithes until it plunges into a long tunnel to the east of the hamlet; at this point walkers should stay on the surface and follow the Cleveland Way along the cliffs. At Overdale Wyke, 1 mile north of Sandsend, this footpath passes the remains of large alum workings in the cliff face. These mines opened in 1615 and were worked until 1867.

⑧ SANDSEND

Stretching from the west pier of Whitby harbour, 2½ miles of uninterrupted sands come to an end at Sandsend. There only a narrow pavement separates the road from the sea-wall, and at high spring tides the waves break violently against the wall, sending arches of spray over the road. Colourful boulders are scattered on the shore at the foot of the car park, north-west of the village, and diligent searchers occasionally find pieces of Whitby jet among them. Volunteer lifeguards patrol on Sundays in summer. Great care must be taken not to be cut off by the tide.

Near by, the stream of Mickleby Beck meets the sea, its valley lined by honey-coloured stone houses with pretty cottage gardens. There is a second stream, East Row Beck, a few hundred yards to the east, and

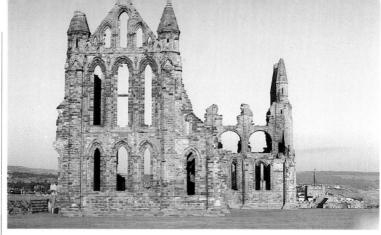

VICTIM OF HISTORY *Danes, Vikings and Henry VIII all had a hand in the destruction of Whitby Abbey, and in 1914 it was shelled during a German warship attack on the coastguard station.*

near by is the yard of one of the few remaining coble builders in the north-east. A footpath beside each stream leads into the beautiful Mulgrave Woods, whose owner allows walkers to roam the paths on Saturdays, Sundays and Wednesdays, except in May. The romantic ruins of Mulgrave Castle, 1½ miles into the woods, are girdled with ivy and overgrown with trees. Among the tumbled stones is the curious relic of a medieval stone lavatory seat.

⑨ WHITBY

Endowed with an incomparable setting on the steep banks of the estuary of the River Esk, Whitby is a jewel among towns, its harbour and streets of ancient buildings imbued with a rich history, yet bustling with modern life. The jagged ruins of Whitby Abbey surmount the East Cliff and provide an impressive landmark for miles along the coast. On the opposite clifftop, to the west, the statue of Captain Cook surveys the harbour, which was the birthplace of three ships, *Endeavour, Resolution* and *Adventure,*

WHITBY DELICACY *Herrings smoked over an oak fire produce the distinctive colour and flavour of the familiar kipper.*

that carried him around the world on his three great voyages of exploration. The two sides of the town are linked by a swing bridge. Built in 1909 it has a 70 ft centre span.

Just below the Cook monument is an arch made from the jawbone of a whale – a reminder of Whitby's history as a whaling port. Between 1753 and 1833 some 2,761 whales were brought back to Whitby, and their blubber was boiled on the quayside to make oil. As early as 1825 the streets of Whitby were lit by a gas made from whale oil. Whitby's most famous whaling captain was William Scoresby, the inventor of the 'crows nest', who accounted for 533 whales in his career.

Scoresby's journals are among the varied items on display in Whitby Museum, which is set among the floral gardens of Pannett Park. Mementoes of Captain Cook and his journeys jostle with flint arrowheads, Roman inscriptions, fossils found on the Whitby shore, stuffed birds, oriental antiquities and even the wizened hand of a murderer; severed at the wrist after his execution, this was used as a charm by burglars and it was believed to have the power of sending victims into a deep slumber. Whitby Museum also has examples of jewellery intricately carved from the jet found on the local shore.

Whitby jet is fossilised wood which has been subjected to chemical action in stagnant water and then flattened by enormous pressure. It was used in the manufacture of ornaments in the Bronze Age and by the Romans, and in medieval times was considered a potent charm against witchcraft. In Victorian times jet-working flourished in Whitby, after Queen Victoria introduced jet jewellery into court circles as a mark of

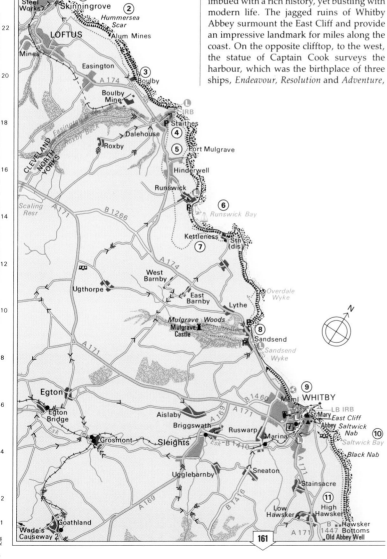

A VILLAGE SHELTERED FROM THE STORMY BLAST

Bluff headlands protect Staithes like a hand cupped around a flame, bringing a backwater stillness to the creek where brightly painted cobles lie at rest and, beyond the bridge, the greystone lifeboat station stands at the head of its ramp. Between the jumble of tall houses and snug cottages runs a web of alleys, some little more than 18 in. wide.

mourning for Prince Albert. It declined, however, after 1870 with the introduction of 'French jet' – black glass – and the import of jet from Spain, where children wore jet beads to ward off the evil eye.

Whitby has another connection with the occult: the author Bram Stoker set scenes of his novel *Dracula* on the 199 steps that lead up through the old town to the graveyard and church of St Mary on the East Cliff beside the abbey. This church has a unique wooden interior, crafted by 18th-century shipbuilders, with box pews, galleries and a towering three-storey pulpit.

The holiday activities of Whitby include bathing from safe sandy beaches, sailing from the marina in the harbour, sea and river fishing, or merely enjoying the taste of fresh fish at the restaurants by the quayside. There is a Lifeboat Museum in Pier Road which contains the last rowing lifeboat in the country. An angling festival is held in July and a three-day regatta in August.

⑩ SALTWICK BAY
Cradled between the rocky promontories of Saltwick Nab and Black Nab is the small

stretch of sand in Saltwick Bay. Steps lead down to the beach from the cliffside, the vast hollows of which are the remains of alum workings. Good fossils, including ammonites, are sometimes found on the shore, but fossil hunters should beware of being cut off by the tide when exploring the rocks at the edges of the bay.

Above the bay is the Whitby High Light and fog signal station. The light is 240 ft above sea level and has a range of 22 miles. The foghorn, known locally as 'The Hawsker Bull', can be heard 10 miles away.

⑪ HIGH HAWSKER
The moorland village is notable for its handsome stone-built farms. On the road from High Hawsker to Robin Hood's Bay a curious brick structure with a stone roof encloses an ancient spring. A notice in local dialect recalls that this was the well used by the Abbess St Hilda and the nuns of Whitby Abbey:

'Lang centuries aback,
This wor t'awd Abba well,
St Hilda, veiled i'black,
Supped frey it, an no lack.'

LOCAL INFORMATION

Tourist information Whitby 602674.

HM Coastguard North Shields 572691 for information, 999 in emergency (ask for coastguard).

Weather Middlesbrough 8091.

Local radio BBC Radio Cleveland, 194 m, 1548 kHz, 96.6 MHz.

PLACE TO SEE INLAND

Wade's Causeway, 3 miles SW of Goathland. Roman road.

Sandy havens between the ports of the Wear and the Tees

From Tyneside through Wearside and south to the Tees, Britain's coast is industrial, and though there are occasional seaside havens it is difficult to ignore the chimneys on the horizon and the coal dust darkening the sand. Durham's coastal mines extend 4½ miles out to sea; on the surface their waste is scattered over a long stretch of coast. South of the Tees high cliffs begin at Saltburn, where the Cleveland Hills meet the coast.

① WHITBURN

The old stone-built houses of Whitburn are set along spacious tree-lined streets, and there is a village pond. The sandy bay to the south is safe for swimming. To the north, a clifftop path leads round the coast for 3 miles to South Shields, but at Souter Point there are army firing ranges and the path is closed when red flags are flown. The path passes Whitburn Colliery – now defunct but used as a National Coal Board engineering works – and the brightly painted lighthouse at Lizard Point, which is open by appointment most weekday afternoons.

② SUNDERLAND

There has been a port at the mouth of the Wear for 1,000 years, and Sunderland remains a major ship-building centre, second only to the Clyde. The public are not allowed in the shipyards, but the parapet of the Wearmouth Bridge gives a good view of ships being fitted out on the Wear riverside. The bridge, with an arch of red and white steel girders, replaces a famous iron bridge of 1796 which decorated numerous 19th-century Sunderland lustre-ware jugs. A fine collection of these can be seen at the museum and art gallery in Borough Road.

Across the bridge at Monkwearmouth is a railway museum, and one of Northumbria's oldest churches, St Peter's. The museum, which is open daily, is housed in a grandiose building of 1848 which was Monkwearmouth Station until it closed in 1967. The booking office, with Edwardian fittings and a collection of model locomotives, inspires nostalgia for the age of steam. St Peter's Church, founded in AD 674 on a marshy promontory overlooking the sea, is today an island of calm amid a sea of high-rise flats and roaring traffic. The church, which was sister church to the Venerable Bede's church at Jarrow, has a Saxon wall and tower, and an information centre in the modern chapter house has vivid displays of the site's history.

Continuous with Monkwearmouth on the seaward side are the merged resorts of Roker and Seaburn. A sandy bay stretches southwards from Parson's Rocks to Roker pier, which is the northern arm of Sunderland's harbour. A spacious grassy sward faces the sea, and there are funfairs and amusements.

③ SEAHAM

Coal from mines around Seaham is taken by lorry to a plateau above Seaham harbour and tipped down chutes into the holds of ships 40 ft below. The harbour was founded by Lord Londonderry in 1828 as an outlet for his coal mines, and it is still privately run.

On a hill to the north of the town stands the white mansion of Seaham Hall, where in 1815 the poet Lord Byron married Anne Isabella Milbank, the niece of Lady Melbourne; the marriage lasted only a year. On the clifftop near by is a large car park, with steps down to a sandy beach. At Ryhope, 1½ miles further north, a Victorian pumping station has been made into an industrial museum where two large beam engines can be seen in operation on Bank Holidays.

④ CASTLE EDEN DENE

The beautiful wooded ravine of Castle Eden Dene is a welcome feature on the coast south of Seaham, which is for the most part a desolate mining area, with cliffs of crumbling coal slag from the coastal mines of Dawdon, Easington and Horden. This lovely valley runs south of Peterlee to meet the coal-polluted coast near Horden. It is a nature reserve, and the woods contain roe deer and a varied population of plants and birds. From the main coast road south of Horden footpaths follow the stream down to the coal-dusted shore, or inland up the valley for more than 3 miles. At Blackhall Rocks, 1½ miles to the south-east, there is a smaller nature reserve on the cliffs where plants defy the industrial pollution around them.

⑤ HARTLEPOOL

On a rocky limestone headland facing south to the sandy beach of Hartlepool Bay, the old town of Hartlepool retains glimpses of its interesting past. Crusader knights used the port on their way to the Holy Land, and there is still a stretch of medieval town wall, with an archway leading to a beach.

St Hilda's is a magnificent Early English church, built between 1189 and 1239 by the family of Robert Bruce on the site of a monastery founded by St Aidan. A row of Georgian houses faces the sea and near by there is a pier with a light beacon, from which fishing is good.

Among the docks complex are a fishing port that holds an early morning fish auction and two sailing clubs. Hartlepool Maritime Museum, in Northgate, illustrates the port's historic industries of shipbuilding, marine engineering, shipping and fishing. The museum contains ship models, boatbuilders' tools, a reconstructed fisherman's cottage and a ship's bridge among its nautical exhibits; it is open daily, except Sundays.

⑥ SEATON CAREW

A few seaside amusements and a fine stretch of sand at the peaceful resort of Seaton Carew are sandwiched between the industrial complex of Seal Sands and urban Hartlepool. Along the edge of the golf course on the dunes to the south, a track runs to North Gare Breakwater.

From the breakwater a broad sweep of sand stretches to the south, but this is unsafe for bathing and it is dangerous even to go to the water's edge because of shifting sands. It is a wild and lonely spot, and good for viewing the passage of shipping in and out of the Tees.

⑦ SEAL SANDS

Seals keep well clear of Seal Sands, where hardly a grain of sand remains exposed – the whole expanse of land projecting into the mouth of the Tees has been reclaimed to create a vast industrial complex. The area is traversed by pylons, wires and undulating pipelines, and is populated with oil tanks and gantries, cooling towers and chemical storage globes, behind security fences. To the south, at Port Clarence, the Transporter Bridge ferries cars to Middlesbrough in a cradle suspended over the river.

⑧ SOUTH GARE BREAKWATER

Like the still centre of a whirlpool, South Gare is a place of peace and wild solitude at the tip of a huge industrial area. Oil tankers and cargo ships pass on their way into the Tees estuary, factories belch smoke all around, but the desolate dunes of South Gare are a haven for many shore birds.

Towards the tip of the promontory is a harbour for fishing vessels, and near it, in a dell among the dunes, there is a collection of green-painted fishermen's huts. A yacht club, the South Gare lifeboat station and the Tees coastguard tower complete the scene.

⑨ REDCAR

Parked on the pavement of the promenade at Redcar is a long row of assorted fishing vessels. Tractors are at hand to haul the boats on trailers down a ramp into the sea.

SUNDERLAND LUSTRE-WARE

The Sunderland Pottery operated from about 1807 to 1865, and was noted for its lustre-ware – fine pottery given an iridescent glaze by painting it with a metallic film. Local scenes were transfer-printed on to the pottery, the original cast-iron Wearmouth Bridge being a favourite subject, sometimes accompanied by a piece of verse.

A lustre-ware 'bridge' jug of about 1820

The soaring arch of Wearmouth Bridge, dwarfing its railway counterpart, was built in 1927-9. On its parapet is a medallion showing the cast-iron bridge constructed in 1796 which it replaced.

Racehorses exercising on the sands at Redcar

The beach is sandy, with rocky reefs offshore on which the waves break. Notices warn against eating polluted shellfish from the foreshore.

Redcar is a popular resort with seaside amusements along the front, and the added attraction of a race course. The centrepiece of

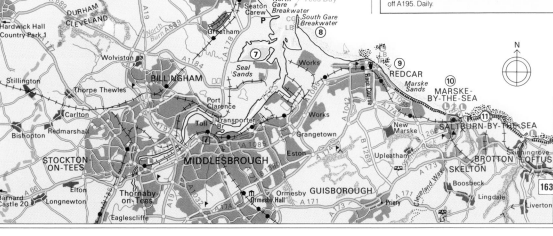

ANGLERS' PARADISE *Saltburn pier was once thronged with day trippers arriving by paddle-steamer; now the boats have gone and the only landings made on the landing stage are anglers' catches.*

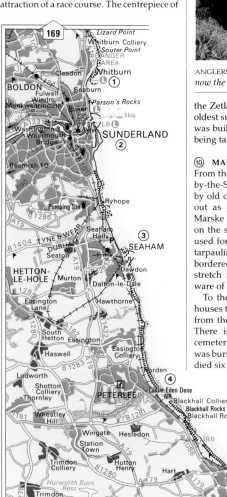

the Zetland Museum on the seafront is the oldest surviving lifeboat in the world, which was built in 1800 and saved 500 lives before being taken out of service in 1887.

⑩ MARSKE-BY-THE-SEA

From the attractive village centre of Marske-by-the-Sea, the narrow High Street, flanked by old cottages, leads through a valley laid out as gardens to a parking area beside Marske Sands. Fishing boats are drawn up on the sands, and numerous small tractors used for launching them gather rust under tarpaulins. To the north-west, fine sands bordered by low grass-topped sandy cliffs stretch for 2 miles. Swimmers should beware of strong tidal currrents.

To the south-east, rows of recently built houses turn their backs to the sea, separated from the sands by a grassy no-man's-land. There is access to the shore beside the cemetery in which Captain Cook's father was buried in 1779, unaware that his son had died six weeks earlier.

⑪ SALTBURN-BY-THE-SEA

A town on a promontory with a winding road dropping down through a valley to a pier and a fishing haven, Saltburn is a quiet resort that retains an air of faded Victorian grandeur. Fishing boats are drawn up on the shingle near the Ship Inn, behind which a steep track climbs the cliff – the beginning, for walkers travelling south, of the coastal section of the Cleveland Way. Less-serious walkers can enjoy a stroll through the wooded valley of Skelton Beck, which opens into an amusement park just before it reaches the sea.

LOCAL INFORMATION

Tourist information Hartlepool 66522; Middlesbrough 245432 (extension 3580).

HM Coastguard North Shields 572691 for information, 999 in emergency (ask for coastguard).

Weather Middlesbrough 8091.

Local radio BBC Radio Cleveland, 194 m, 1548 kHz, 96.6 MHz; IBA Radio Tees, 257 m, 1170 kHz, 95.0 MHz.

PLACES TO SEE INLAND

Bowes Museum, Barnard Castle, 29 miles W of Middlesbrough, on A67. European art. Daily.

Guisborough Priory, E of Guisborough. Augustinian priory remains. Daily.

Hardwick Hall Country Park, W of Sedgefield, off A177.

North of England Open Air Museum, Beamish, 13 miles W of Sunderland, via A693. Daily, except Mon. in winter.

Ormesby Hall (NT), 3 miles SE of Middlesbrough. 18th-century house. Some afternoons in summer.

Washington Old Hall (NT), 6 miles W of Sunderland, A195. George Washington's ancestral home. Most afternoons in summer.

Wildfowl Trust, Washington, 6 miles W of Sunderland, off A195. Daily.

White sands and cliffs north and south of historic Tynemouth

Coal has been a major influence on the coast north of the Tyne. Harbours were built for coal shipping at Amble and Blyth, and an early coal harbour of 1660 can be seen at Seaton Sluice. Between the ports the coast remains largely unspoiled, with lovely stretches of white sands and dunes that are often deserted. The people of Tyneside can travel to the seaside by Metro, and to the south, at Marsden Bay, there is a lift down the cliffs to the beach.

① AMBLE

At one time the harbour at Amble was bustling with ships loading coal from local mines. As many as 80 mine shafts were in operation in the mile between Amble and Hauxley, but they are all closed now, and Amble is adjusting to a quieter routine as a fishing and manufacturing town. There is a coble boat-builder's yard beside the River Coquet, and sailing boats moor in the estuary. The shore is sand, shingle and rock.

Although the Coquet estuary is known as Warkworth Harbour, Warkworth itself is 1 mile away, its castle prominent on the skyline. Coquet Island, 1 mile off Amble, has only a lighthouse, but it once had a monk's cell which was the refuge of the 12th-century ascetic, Henry the Hermit. He is said to have been directed in a vision to become a hermit, thus escaping a marriage that his parents were trying to impose upon him.

② DRURIDGE BAY

There is enough sand on Druridge Bay to satisfy the most imperial of sandcastle builders – 5 miles of it, backed by extensive dunes. The road, running along the dunes near Cresswell, makes the southern end of the bay easily accessible. It may be crowded in the summer, but those requiring a mile or two of sand to themselves only have to walk north from the National Trust car park at Druridge, where kestrels hover above the dunes and flocks of lapwings gather. Inland to the north of the bay scars of open-cast mines have been filled in, and there are now fields on land that recently yielded coal.

③ LYNEMOUTH

The skyline of chimneys, pylons and mining machinery and the constant thumping and whirring of industry keep visitors away from the Lynemouth shoreline. The beach is black with coal dust washed by the sea from the waste tips along the shore. The workings of the Lynemouth and Ellington collieries go several miles under the sea, and many people still collect waste coal from the beach.

Just south of Lynemouth, a hamlet called Woodhorn is a small oasis in the industrial desert. There is a windmill, and St Mary's Church has been converted into a museum, with Saxon and medieval tombstones.

④ NEWBIGGIN-BY-THE-SEA

Where the church stands on the headland at the north of Newbiggin Bay there is a macabre stretch of coast where the sea has cut into the graveyard, and fragments of human bones are powdered into a rough white sand among the rocks. Near by, a breakwater of large boulders protects the sandy bay, which is safe for swimming. In the Middle Ages Newbiggin was a large grain port, but it is a haven now only for a few leisure boats and a fleet of fishing cobles which are launched off the sands.

'BLOOD' ON THE CLIFFTOP

In summer, large clusters of bloody crane's-bill splash limestone cliffs and lime-rich dunes with patches of purplish-crimson, pink or, more rarely, white flowers. In autumn the rounded, deeply divided leaves turn a deep shade of blood-red; this and the beak-like fruits explain the plant's name.

Bloody crane's-bill
Geranium sanguineum
July-Aug.

Ashington, 2 miles inland on the River Wansbeck, is a mining town. Its Riverside Park is an imaginative leisure development that includes a 2 mile walk along the river banks to the sea. North of the town a colliery spoil heap has been transformed into a public country park, with a 40 acre lake used for sailing and windsurfing.

⑤ BLYTH

A beach of sand and shingle, speckled with coal dust, extends from North Blyth 2 miles north to the estuary of the River Wansbeck. Rocks shelter the northern pier of Blyth's harbour, which extends the line of the coast for almost another mile before allowing the River Blyth to meet the sea. The largely modern town of Blyth is 100 yds away across the harbour, but 5 miles by road.

Blyth's main harbour is busy with ships loading coal and unloading timber. In the South Harbour are fishing and sailing boats, cruisers, and the headquarters of the Royal Northumberland Yacht Club, housed in a redundant wooden lightship. South of the harbour a sandy beach, safe for swimming, stretches 2 miles to Seaton Sluice, where rocks begin again. Volunteer lifeguards patrol Blyth beach in summer.

⑥ SEATON SLUICE

The large dressed stones that line the tiny harbour at the mouth of the river recall Seaton's industrial past. A narrow canal, now silted up, cuts through the rock to make a second way to the sea. The stones have been in place since 1660, when Sir Ralph Delaval had the harbour built for the export of coal and salt. Even then the silting up of the harbour caused problems, and a novel solution was found in a sluice gate, which gave the village its name but no longer exists. At low tide the river water was held

back by the sluice gate. Horse-drawn ploughs were used to disturb the silt-bed of the harbour. Then the water was released from the sluice to wash the silt away.

The imposing dark stone mansion of Seaton Delaval Hall, 1 mile inland, was designed by Sir John Vanbrugh in 1718-19. The house, open by appointment only, was built for the Delaval family, one of whom ensured his election to Parliament by firing golden guineas into the crowd from a cannon. Volunteer lifeguards operate at Seaton Sluice beach in summer.

⑦ WHITLEY BAY

The sleek trains of the Tyneside Metro from Newcastle put passengers down within a few yards of the sea at the resort of Whitley Bay and neighbouring Cullercoats and Tynemouth. Hotels and guest houses line the seafront, and pleasant flower gardens decorate the grassy slopes between the road and the beach. Whitley Sands are safe for bathing, but visitors tempted to potter around the rocks at the southern end of the beach should take care not to get cut off by the tide.

The north end of the beach is also rocky, and at low tide it is possible to walk across a causeway to St Mary's Island, where there is a pretty group of houses and a lighthouse. Volunteer lifeguards operate on the beach at summer weekends.

Cullercoats was a fishing village that has become absorbed into the sprawling resort, but the stone walls of the little harbour survive, and shelter a sandy bay.

⑧ TYNEMOUTH

From the crescent of tall white-fronted houses and hotels set back from the road along the seafront, the eye is drawn to the mellow stone walls of the ruined Tynemouth Priory above the river mouth. Built as a Norman church in 1090, on the site of an Anglo-Saxon monastery, the priory was much altered in later centuries, particularly when the site was fortified and a Gate Tower built at the time of Richard II. Curiously eroded gravestones are gathered round the ruins, and from the clifftop lawns of the priory there are fine views down to the busy shipping in the Tyne.

Just below the priory is the little bay of Prior's Haven where sailing boats are drawn up on the sand and shingle, sheltered by Tynemouth's North Pier. On the hill above Prior's Haven is the timber watch house of the Tynemouth Volunteer Life Brigade, set up in 1864. The watch house contains a little museum with evocative mementoes of

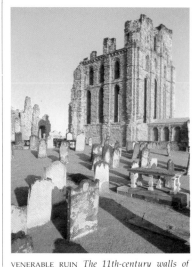

VENERABLE RUIN *The 11th-century walls of Tynemouth Priory were built by Benedictines, on the site of a 7th-century monastery.*

wrecks and rescues off the coast near by. Beyond the watch house a statue of Admiral Collingwood, Nelson's contemporary, stands aloof on his column facing the river. North of the priory is a little bay of sand girdled with rocks, beyond that Tynemouth's principal beach, Long Sands, stretches to Cullercoats.

The centre of Tynemouth, behind the seafront, has some fine 18th-century houses.

⑨ NORTH SHIELDS

Houses and pigeon lofts hang precariously on the hill that slopes sharply down from North Shields to the Tyne waterfront. Small fishing trawlers line the quayside, and they are serviced by a row of ships chandlers and provision merchants across the road.

The best time to see North Shields is in the early morning, when there is a fish market and the place bustles with buyers perching on fish boxes as the auctioneers move between them.

MARSDEN ROCK *Offshore from the crumbling limestone cliffs facing Marsden Bay, the buffeting winds and pounding seas have sculpted a huge triumphal arch, 139 ft high and 230 ft long.*

⑩ JARROW

Beside the dank inlet of the Tyne, overlooked by oil storage tanks and dwarfed by pylons, stands a blackened and modest-looking church with the shattered walls of a monastery beside it. St Paul's Church was one of the cradles of English literature and history, for it was there that the Venerable Bede wrote his *Ecclesiastical History of the English People*, a few years after the monastery was dedicated in AD 685. The dedication stone can still be seen, mounted in the stonework of the chancel arch. The Bede Monastery Museum at Jarrow Hall, across the green from the church, contains further relics of the Anglo-Saxon period.

⑪ SOUTH SHIELDS

The Romans built their fort of Arbeia on a hill commanding the southern bank of the Tyne, where South Shields now stands. Arbeia was a storage depot for grain for the Roman army in the north, and the foundations of several granaries can still be seen, together with a museum displaying objects of Roman army life.

From the hilltop a wooded park slopes down towards the south pier, which projects almost a mile into the sea. It is a pleasant walk to the end of the pier, but not one to be undertaken in stormy weather. The sandy beach north of the pier is safe for swimming, but bathing in Tyne water, albeit diluted by the sea, is not to everybody's taste. South of the pier a long sandy beach faces the open sea, and volunteer lifeguards patrol in summer. Currents make swimming dangerous at the northern end.

⑫ MARSDEN BAY

A grassy border lines the crumbling limestone cliffs south of South Shields. It is dangerous to go near the edge of these cliffs, which continue around the sandy arc of Marsden Bay. The bay is dominated by the spectacularly eroded arch of Marsden Rock, surmounted by a roost of sea-birds that breed on it. From the car park, a steep flight of steps leads to the beach. There is also a lift, taking visitors to a pub called the Grotto built into caves at the foot of the cliffs. The Grotto was built in 1782 by a miner who lived in the caves with his family.

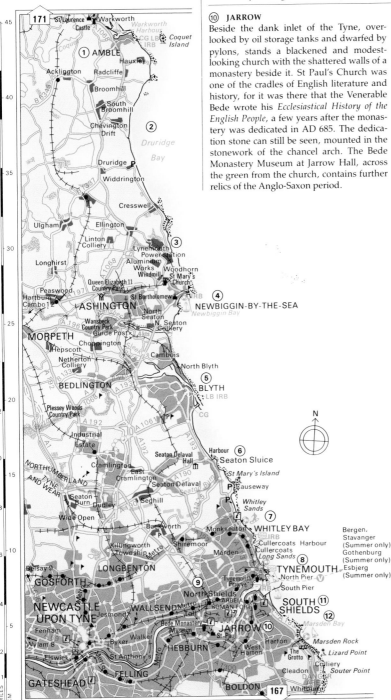

LOCAL INFORMATION

Tourist information Newcastle upon Tyne 817744; Whitley Bay 2524494 (summer).

HM Coastguard North Shields 572691 for information, 999 in emergency (ask for coastguard).

Weather Newcastle 8091.

Local radio BBC Radio Newcastle, 206 m, 1458 kHz, 95.4 MHz; IBA Metro Radio, 261 m, 1152 kHz, 97.0 MHz.

PLACES TO SEE INLAND

Bolam Lake Country Park, near Belsay, 13 miles NW of Newcastle.

George Stephenson's Cottage (NT), Wylam, 8 miles W of Newcastle, off A69. Birthplace of the inventor. Most afternoons in summer.

Meldon Park, Hartburn, 7 miles W of Morpeth on B6343. 19th-century house. Afternoons May-June.

Plessey Woods Country Park, near Bedlington.

Wallington (NT), Cambo, 12 miles W of Morpeth, via B6343. 17th-century house and gardens. Some afternoons throughout the year.

Wansbeck Country Park, Ashington.

A brooding castle on a rock above long, empty beaches

From the River Coquet to the Scottish border, the activities of man have even enhanced the natural beauty of this coastline of alternating sand and rock. Reefs have been extended to make little fishing harbours at Seahouses and Craster; rolling dunes have been tamed to make golf courses at Embleton and Alnmouth; and the natural fortifications of rock and river are emphasised by Dunstanburgh Castle and medieval Warkworth.

① FARNE ISLANDS

A scattering of rocky outcrops, between 1½ and 4½ miles from the mainland, the Farne Islands have been a retreat for hermit monks and the graveyard of countless shipwrecked sailors. They are also the nesting site of many species of sea-birds, and one of the principal breeding grounds of the grey seal.

There are up to 28 islands, but at high tide almost half of them are submerged. The islands form a nature reserve owned by the National Trust, and landing is allowed daily on Farne Island, or Inner Farne, and Staple Island in summer. Boat trips to the islands run in calm weather from Seahouses harbour. From a small boat at sea the islands look threatening, with towering cliffs of curious columnar structure rising to 80 ft above the waves. In places the sea has eroded the rock to form dramatic pillars and stacks.

Farne Island is, at 16 acres, the largest island of the group. It is particularly associated with St Cuthbert, who in AD 664 became Prior of Lindisfarne, now Holy Island, one of the earliest centres of Christianity in England. In 676 Cuthbert retired to Inner Farne and built himself a solitary cell of stone and turf. A tower built in 1500 by Thomas Castell, Prior of Durham, may stand on the original site of Cuthbert's cell.

Cuthbert lived alone on Inner Farne until 684, and after two years as Bishop of Lindisfarne returned to die there in 687. His body was removed to Durham during the Viking invasions. A 14th-century chapel dedicated to the saint stands near Prior Castell's tower. A nature trail starting at the chapel passes the island's automatically operated lighthouse, and gives an opportunity to observe the island's varied plant and bird life.

The lighthouse at Longstone island is well known for its association with Grace Darling. The lighthouse is still manned; the lighthousemen spend 56 days at a time on the island, where their only companions are the grey seals and a multitude of sea-birds, including puffins, kittiwakes and eiders.

② SEAHOUSES

The coast south of Bamburgh is sandy, bordered with dunes, with occasional spits of rock that become more concentrated around the little harbour of Seahouses. This is a working harbour, with a fleet of fishing cobles and a few larger vessels, and piles of fish boxes, crab pots and ropes on the quayside.

Trips to the Farne Islands, which take about an hour to reach, can be booked from booths at the quayside. The harbour is overlooked by terraces of dour grey houses, and in the main street a few amusement arcades provide a rather grating contrast in an otherwise unassuming little village.

③ BEADNELL

A string of holiday villas lines the coast road into Beadnell, continuing to the point where the road ends near Beadnell Sailing Club. Around the corner is one of the great surprises of the Northumberland coast. A fortress-like structure stands beside the sea, with round towers built of honey-coloured stone. These are 18th-century lime-kilns, perfectly preserved and now owned by the National Trust.

Opposite the kilns is a tiny harbour in which are moored a little family of fishing cobles, painted a uniform white and blue. The fishermen store their crab pots between the arches of the kilns.

From the harbour the dune-backed sands of Beadnell Bay sweep westwards and then southwards for 2 miles before sand gives way to rock at Snook Point. The beach is popular in summer, but it is easy to escape the crowds by following the track along the dunes into the National Trust land of Newton Links at the southern end of the bay.

SYMBOL OF POWER *Dunstanburgh Castle was a stronghold of John of Gaunt, the powerful baron who virtually ruled England as uncle to the boy king Richard II in the 14th century.*

④ LOW NEWTON-BY-THE-SEA

A sheltered courtyard of low-built fishermen's cottages with a pub amongst them faces the sandy beach of Low Newton. Waves break on a reef of rock offshore, which protects the beach from rough seas. The car park is a few hundred yards up the hill from the beach.

⑤ EMBLETON BAY

From the very limited parking space beside the road at Dunstan Steads, a path across the golf course leads to the inviting sands of Embleton Bay. Large boulders of rock begin at the southern end of the bay, a prelude to the promontory of basalt rock on which stand the ruins of Dunstanburgh Castle.

⑥ DUNSTANBURGH CASTLE

The nearest places to leave a car are 1 mile away, at Craster to the south or Dunstan Steads to the north, and the only way to reach the ruins of Dunstanburgh Castle is on foot. Once there was also a sea approach, because a harbour was made in the hard dolerite rock when Thomas, Earl of Lancaster ordered the building of the castle in 1313. But the harbour is earthed up now and there are no signs of it under the soft turf fields crossed on the path from Craster.

For the length of the walk the castle is

ON THE ROCKS *Clumsy and awkward ashore, the grey seals on the Farne Islands become sleek and graceful in the water.*

FAIRWAYS BY THE SEA *Remote and secluded, Embleton Bay offers sand and solitude to the walker and invigorating sport to the golfers on the links among the dunes.*

visible, a brooding presence of stone on its tapering ledge of rock above the sea. Fragments of the huge gatehouse project upwards like broken bones, seeming to defy gravity. This great gatehouse, its twin towers and walls several feet thick, was converted into the castle keep by John of Gaunt in 1380. The castle is open daily, and it is still possible to climb the stairs into one of the towers which gives a panoramic view over the 11 acres of castle site and down the steep incline of the castle rock to the rolling fields beyond.

The ragged profile of the ruined walls is evidence of the sieges that buffeted Dunstanburgh Castle during the Wars of the Roses. Neglect in the subsequent centuries made the castle a romantic ruin, immortalised in water-colours by the artist J. M. W. Turner.

⑦ CRASTER

Famous for its kippers, which are smoked in sheds above the little harbour, Craster is a quiet and unspoiled fishing village. Its houses are built of hard stone and look as though they have grown out of the dark rock on which they stand. The exceptionally hard whinstone used to be quarried behind the village, loaded on to barges and taken to London to be used for kerbstones.

The harbour is now used by leisure boats and by the few cobles that go out for lobsters and crabs. Herrings for kippering are in short supply; they are no longer caught from Craster, but are brought to the village for smoking from West Scotland.

National Trust land borders the sea from Craster to Low Newton, and a 3 mile section of coastal footpath begins at the wicket gate to the north of Craster village. The path follows the boulder-strewn bay leading up to Dunstanburgh Castle, skirts the western side of the castle and passes along the edge of the golf course among the dunes of Embleton Bay. Near its end the path passes Newton Pool, a nature reserve where blackheaded gulls breed in summer.

⑧ HOWICK

The coast south of Craster is rugged, with flat rock on the shore, dotted with rockpools. North-east of the little hamlet of Howick the road follows the coast for a short distance, alongside the coastal path between Craster and Boulmer. This is a good point to join the path, then to walk southwards along the low cliff edge. At Rumbling Kern heavy seas sometimes set up a resonance in a gully, like air in an organ pipe.

At Howick Haven there is a patch of sand

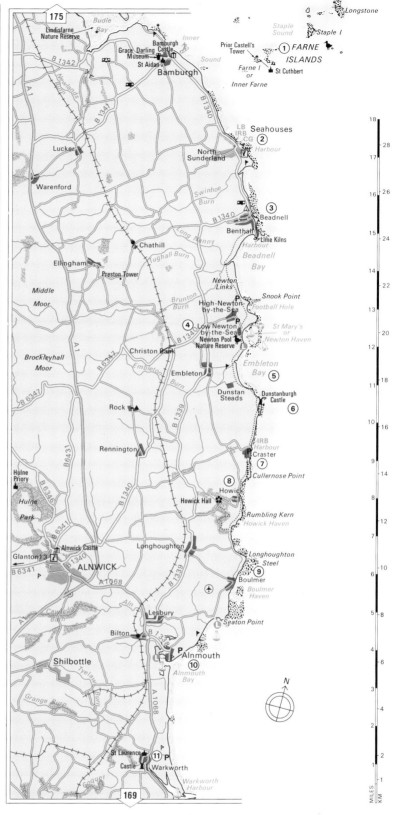

among the rock, and a few hundred yards to the south a little stream runs down to the beach. An idyllic footpath follows the wooded valley of this stream inland to the grounds of Howick Hall, a mile from the sea. The gardens are open daily in summer, and are at their best in spring and early summer, when a wealth of daffodils and tulips and more than 600 rhododendrons create a riot of colour.

⑨ BOULMER

The rocky shore with patches of sand continues south of Howick, but at Boulmer there is a sizeable sandy beach, safe for

bathing because it is sheltered by a reef of rock offshore. A gap in the offshore rocks makes Boulmer a natural harbour, and the hamlet is a fishing community, with a number of fishing cobles moored off the beach. A row of fishermen's cottages lines the shore just above high-water mark.

⑩ ALNMOUTH

Golfers and sailing enthusiasts are well provided for at Alnmouth. There are two golf courses, end to end along the grassy links lining the north shore of the village, and the sheltered estuary of the River Aln is a yachting haven. The village, once an

171

important port before the river changed course and the harbour silted up, has several houses of solid Victorian grandeur, and the collection of red roofs and stone walls on a headland makes an attractive group from across the river.

The shore, reached across grassy links, is sandy, but bathing is not safe near the mouth of the river because of dangerous currents. South of the river is a 3 mile stretch of sand, bordered by dunes, reached by tracks off the A1068 coast road.

WARKWORTH CASTLE *Harry Hotspur, who conspired to put Henry IV on the throne but then rebelled against him, was born at Warkworth.*

⑪ **WARKWORTH**
Just over a mile before it reaches the sea, the meandering River Coquet forms a horseshoe loop that almost encloses the ancient town of Warkworth. In the Middle Ages the river served as a natural moat, fortifying the town and protecting the castle that surmounts the hill to the south. The castle, which Shakespeare's Henry IV called a 'worm-eaten hold of ragged stone', is an impressive ruin.

A street of handsome stone houses leads down to the Norman church of St Laurence. There is an interesting survival from medieval times in the long strips of land, called stints, that are still cultivated by the townspeople; they can be seen from the footpath that runs behind the houses between the Sun Hotel and the bridge. The medieval bridge is remarkable for its fortified tower, one of very few in England. This narrow stone bridge, with its steep cobbled humpback, served the town from 1379 until 1965, when an unsightly new bridge was built beside it.

Across the bridge north of the town, a turning marked 'To the Beach and Cemetery' leads to a car park among the dunes, and a long beach of sand with safe swimming. There is a golf course on the dunes, which extend south to the edge of Warkworth Harbour, a natural basin in the Coquet estuary which boats can reach from the Amble side.

LOCAL INFORMATION

Tourist information Newcastle-upon-Tyne 817744.

HM Coastguard North Shields 572691 for information, 999 in emergency (ask for coastguard).

Weather Newcastle 8091.

Local radio BBC Radio Newcastle, 206 m, 1458 kHz, 96.3 MHz; IBA Metro Radio, 261 m, 1152 kHz, 97.0 MHz.

PLACES TO SEE INLAND

Alnwick Castle. 12th-century castle. Most afternoons in summer.

Glanton Bird Sanctuary, 13 miles W of Alnwick, via A697. Afternoons in summer.

Hulne Priory, 2 miles NW of Alnwick. 13th-century monastery. Daily.

Preston Tower, near Ellingham. 9 miles N of Alnwick, off A1. 14th-century pele tower. Daily in summer.

RESCUE AT SEA: THE BOATS AND MEN WHO ANSWER DANGER'S CALL

A ship in distress in a North Sea gale . . . an oil tanker ripped open by savage rocks off the Cornish coast . . . a yacht dismasted in the English Channel . . . a small boy adrift on his inflatable raft . . . whatever the weather or the hour, incidents such as these set into motion the oldest lifesaving service in the world – the Royal National Lifeboat Institution. It was formed in 1824 by Sir William Hillary, a member of the crew of the Douglas, Isle of Man, lifeboat. Hillary's proposal for a national lifeboat service ended the system whereby lifeboats were operated and paid for by local funds – though even today the RNLI is supported entirely by public subscriptions.

Where the first lifeboat operated from and who designed the first purpose-built boat are subjects of controversy. For many years, Bamburgh in Northumberland was thought to have had the first lifeboat in the world, dating from 1786. Records in Liverpool dated 1777, however, refer to a boat 'kept in Formby in readiness to fetch any shipwrecked persons from the banks'. It is unlikely that the Formby boat was specially designed for the task, however, and even Bamburgh's boat was no more than a coble, converted by a coachbuilder named Lionel Lukin. In 1789 the members of a club in North Shields offered a prize for the design of a lifeboat. It was won by a man named William Wouldhave, and the boat was built by a local man, Henry Greathead. Appropriately called the *Original*, the boat went into service at North Shields in 1790 and served for some 40 years. It has a strong claim, therefore, to be considered the first purpose-built lifeboat.

Since its foundation the RNLI has rescued more than 100,000 people from death at sea, and many of these rescues have been accompanied by deeds of great personal heroism on the part of the lifeboat crews. Even as radar and other navigational aids have lessened the chance of large vessels coming to grief, so the growing popularity of sailing and other water sports has increased the demand on the RNLI's services. From its headquarters at Poole the RNLI today operates a fleet of more than 250 lifeboats, based at some 200 different stations. Between them they respond to more than 3,000 calls every year.

A ROLL OF HONOUR
The name best known for courage in a rescue at sea is that of Grace Darling. She was the daughter of the Longstone lighthousekeeper, on Farne Island, and in 1838 during a violent storm she and her father rowed a coble out to the stricken steamer *Forfarshire* and rescued nine men. The exploit was immortalised in a painting by C. J. Staniland (above). Their boat was not a lifeboat, nor was it part of the lifeboat service, but the RNLI awarded William and Grace Darling their silver medal, and 100 years later established a Grace Darling museum at Bamburgh. The RNLI's Gold Medal (left) is the lifeboatman's 'VC', and is awarded for 'outstanding courage, skill and initiative'. Henry Blogg, coxswain of the Cromer lifeboat from 1909 to 1947, received it three times.

QUEST FOR SAFETY *The earliest lifeboats were said to be unsinkable, but many capsized with the loss of their crews. Self-righting boats were introduced in the 1850s, but later lost favour because of their instability. A century was to pass before the design of a lifeboat which combined self-righting capability with stability. In 1854 Captain John Ross Ward invented a cork lifejacket. Its value was proved seven years later when the Whitby lifeboat capsized with the loss of all its crew except for Henry Freeman (below), the only man wearing Ward's jacket. Kapok was later used, before today's buoyancy jackets.*

GALLEYS OF MERCY *Buoyancy and power have always been the prime factors in lifeboat design, and in the early days power depended on oars and the fitness of the crew. Oared lifeboats, known as 'pulling boats', such as this craft at Courtown in Ireland, were used for more than 100 years, and some were still in service at the beginning of this century. Great strength was needed to row a lifeboat through heavy seas, and often the crew were too exhausted to carry out rescue work when they arrived at a wreck.*

SAIL POWER *Sailing lifeboats went into service towards the end of the 19th century, though many 'pulling' boats used both oars and sail. Sailing lifeboats such as this one leaving Penzance harbour in 1900 generally proved more manageable in heavy seas whipped up by gales. The last sailing lifeboat in service was the* William Cantrell Ashley, *stationed at New Quay in west Wales until 1948.*

RESCUE FLEET *Different launching conditions round Britain's coasts call for different types of lifeboat. Five of the latest designs are named after rivers. The most powerful is the Arun class, which has a speed of 18 knots and a range of 117 miles. Inflatable lifeboats for inshore use are powered by an outboard motor which gives them a speed of more than 25 knots.*

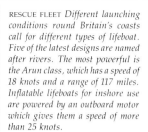

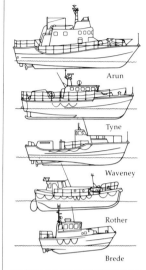

Arun

Tyne

Waveney

Rother

Brede

Inflatable lifeboat

INTO THE SURF *Where there is no harbour, lifeboats have to be launched from the beach or down a slipway. Before the use of tractors, crews had to manhandle their boats across the beach – often helped by local townspeople, as in the case of this Whitby 'pulling boat'.*

SPLASHDOWN *Launchings from slipways are often spectacular, as at Padstow, in Cornwall, where the Oakley class lifeboat hits the water in a welter of spray. Times of practice launchings, which the public can watch, are displayed at some lifeboat houses with slipways.*

Castles to guard the border and an island home of monks

Vast stretches of sand line the northern end of the Northumberland coast, towards the Scottish border. Some of the best beaches can be reached only on foot across the dunes. Echoes of Border battles linger, and the conspicuous silhouettes of Lindisfarne and Bamburgh Castles are reminders of Northumbria's warlike heritage. Holy Island, for centuries a focus of English Christianity, is today a refuge for countless birds.

① MARSHALL MEADOWS BAY
An unmarked turning off the A1 leads to Marshall Meadows Bay, the northernmost beach in England that can be reached by car. Drivers can park beside the lane, with the farmer's permission. There are caravans parked on a 180 ft clifftop, and access to the rocky beach is at the southern end of the site where a rough and precipitous path, slippery in wet weather, cuts down the side of the ravine.

② BERWICK-UPON-TWEED
The tranquillity of Berwick's setting on a peninsula between the sea and the River Tweed is at odds with the town's fierce and unsettled history. The mellow stone walls that encircle the town on its hill were erected by the Elizabethan military engineers to defend the town from attack. In the Middle Ages, Berwick passed like a shuttlecock between English and Scottish rule. Today it is still an English town, though Scottish in character, situated north of the natural border of the Tweed.

Berwick seems almost to turn its back to the sea and face instead the River Tweed, which has served as a natural moat in the past, and which now provides a port at Tweedmouth for Berwick's small fishing fleet and a few commercial vessels. The Tweed is one of Britain's premier salmon rivers, and during the netting season, which lasts from February 15 to September 14, Berwick's licensed salmon fishermen may be seen dropping their nets in an arc from a boat, before hauling them in from the shore. Good places from which to see the fishing are the stone pier that shelters the north side of the river mouth, and the south end of Spittal beach.

Within Berwick three distinctive bridges span the Tweed. The earliest, lowest, and nearest to the sea is the Jacobean Bridge, built between 1611 and 1635 in warm pink stone, with 15 arches that increase in size towards the town. Furthest upstream, its tall arches towering 125 ft above the river, is the greystone Royal Border Bridge built for the railway in 1847 by Robert Stephenson. Between the two, with four long arches of less-elegant concrete, is the Royal Tweed Bridge built in 1925-8 to carry the A1.

To the east of the town, between the ramparts and the sea, is an open expanse of grass called Magdalene Fields, with golf links at its northern end. The shore is predominantly rocky, but just north of the pier there is a sandy beach, sheltered from the strong tidal currents by a reef of rock offshore. It is safe to bathe inshore between the rocks and the beach.

③ SPITTAL
With its sandy beach, and an unobtrusive promenade, Spittal is a miniature resort just across the river from Berwick. Swimming is safe to the south, but at the northern end of the beach there are strong tidal currents at the river mouth, and unstable sand banks upon which the unwary may be cut off by the tide.

In season, fishermen net salmon off the beach, which terminates to the south with rocks. On the grassy banks above the rocks a coastal path leads for 1½ miles to Seahouse; on the way it passes Huds Head, where a discoloured stream trickling down the cliff is a remnant of the drainage system from the disused coal mines of Scremerston.

④ COCKLAWBURN BEACH
A seaward turning off the A1 at Scremerston leads across farmland, over a level crossing and along the edge of a sandy bay, with outcrops of rocks at its limits. Several rough areas beside the road are available for parking, and it is an easy scramble down the dunes on to Cocklawburn beach. Swimming is safe on an incoming tide, but there may be a dangerous undertow when the tide is going out.

An area of dunes to the south of the beach has been designated a nature reserve. Near the shore are the remains of 18th-century lime-kilns, and lime-loving plants grow on the nearby spoil heaps. The dunes are carpeted with cowslips in spring.

⑤ CHESWICK
Two large houses, a farm or two and a row of farmworkers' cottages make up Cheswick village. A road that crosses the railway line leads to dunes on the edge of vast and empty wastes of sand that stretch at low tide for 4 miles across to Holy Island.

It is inadvisable to walk to the island, as there is a danger of being cut off by the tide, and the added hazard of unexploded bombs. Treacherous currents make the beach unsafe for swimming, but lovers of solitude can enjoy miles of wild and open space.

⑥ BEAL
A cluster of farm buildings surmounts the hill overlooking Holy Island, and the road to the island rolls gently down to the shore, where it becomes a causeway, impassable for 2 hours before and for 3½ hours after each high tide. It is dangerous to cross while water still covers the causeway, and essential to take notice of the tide tables that are prominently displayed.

The car park beside the causeway at Beal is also a good base for walkers and bird-watchers, who have a choice of footpaths going north or south along the shore, following a line of concrete wartime defences, and skirting the sands of Lindisfarne National Nature Reserve.

⑦ HOLY ISLAND
For up to 11 out of every 24 hours, the sea cuts Holy Island, or Lindisfarne, off from the mainland. Bus timetables, postal deliveries and the lives of the 200 inhabitants and many visitors are controlled by the tides, the times of which are clearly displayed at the edge of the causeway. When the tide is out, Holy Island becomes the tip of a wide peninsula of sand, the feeding grounds,

CASTLE ON A CRAG *Impregnable as an eagle's eyrie, Lindisfarne Castle never had to fire a shot in anger. It was built in 1550 to defend Holy Island against Scottish raids.*

particularly in winter, of a vast population of wildfowl and wading birds.

The haunting whistle of the curlew must have accompanied the monk Aidan from Iona, when he first crossed the sands one low tide in the year 634 to found a monastery at Lindisfarne, at the request of King Oswald of Northumbria. Aidan's monastery was destroyed by the Danes in the 9th century, but a manuscript written and illuminated there in the 7th century has survived – the Lindisfarne Gospels, a masterpiece of English Celtic art, now one of the treasures of the British Museum.

Lindisfarne became a holy island for a second time when, in 1093, building began on a priory that was to be a branch of the monastery at Durham. The ruins of the Norman priory church, in red weathered sandstone, still stand today.

The little village of Holy Island is tight-knit, the houses huddled together and looking inward to small squares and narrow streets. The jetty is still used by a handful of fishermen who go out for crabs and lobsters, but the decline of the herring fleet is evident in the hulks of the old herring boats, cut in half, upturned and used as storage huts, that lie like great black beetles along the shore.

Beyond the harbour, perched on a steep cone of rock, is the romantic outline of Lindisfarne Castle. It was no more than a ruined 16th-century fort when recreated by the architect Edwin Lutyens in 1902. It is now owned by the National Trust and is open on most days in summer. East of the castle are the remains of lime-kilns, and broad acres of rabbit-grazed turf slope down to the rocky shore. The north side of the island has a wide strip of dunes, and there are fine sandy beaches, unsafe for bathing because of strong tidal currents.

⑧ ROSS BACK SANDS

The effort of walking almost a mile across the rolling grassy dunes of Ross Links is repaid by a splendid sandy beach, which stretches for 3 miles and is deserted on many days of the year. The beach, which is safe for swimming, looks north to the fairy-tale castle of Lindisfarne, and south-east to the looming presence of Bamburgh Castle.

⑨ BUDLE BAY

Almost cut off from the sea by a ridge of sand, Budle Bay is a large inlet of weed-covered flats of muddy sand, which are completely exposed at low tide. The flats are a feeding ground for large numbers of wildfowl and wading birds, which can be watched from the grassy banks beside the

road to the south. It can be dangerous to walk far out on the flats, as the sea comes rushing into the bay as the tide rises, and sections of the flats become cut off.

⑩ BAMBURGH

An outcrop of rock rises 150 ft above the sandy bay of Bamburgh, and the upward sweep of rock continues into the pink stone walls and battlements of one of England's most majestic castles. Bamburgh Castle covers 8 acres, and towers above the little village of Bamburgh and the rolling dunes on either side.

First fortified by the early Kings of Northumbria, Bamburgh became the capital under King Oswald, but was later pillaged

The Grace Darling Memorial
in Bamburgh churchyard

by the Danes. The oldest surviving feature of the castle is a well, 150 ft deep, that may date from the 8th century; it was dug for half its length through solid basalt, and the remainder through softer sandstone. The 12th-century castle keep retains its original walls, which are up to 11 ft thick, but much of the castle was over-lavishly rebuilt for the first Lord Armstrong between 1894-1905. The castle is open daily in summer.

Bamburgh village has a row of pretty 18th-century cottages round a little green, and a fine Early English church dedicated to St Aidan, who died outside an earlier church on the site. In the churchyard is a memorial to Bamburgh's own heroine, Grace Darling.

LOCAL INFORMATION

Tourist information Newcastle upon Tyne 817744.

HM Coastguard North Shields 572691 for information, 999 in emergency (ask for coastguard).

Weather Newcastle 8091.

Local radio BBC Radio Newcastle, 206 m, 1458 kHz; 96.3 MHz; IBA Metro Radio, 261 m, 1152 kHz, 97.0 MHz.

PLACES TO SEE INLAND

Heatherslaw Mill, Ford, 10 miles SW of Berwick on B6354. 19th-century watermill. Daily in summer.

Lady Waterford Hall, Ford, 10 miles SW of Berwick. 19th-century murals by Lady Waterford. Daily.

Norham Castle, 8 miles W of Berwick, via B6470. Border castle. Daily.

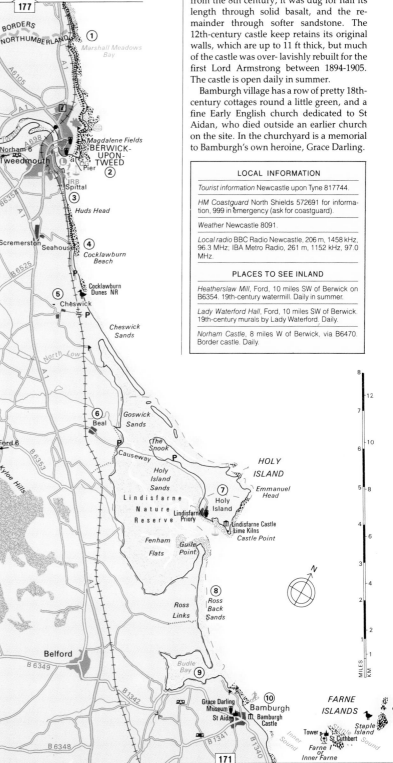

Scottish fishing ports in the shelter of craggy headlands

Where Scotland's east coast nears the English border, the countryside is of a startling prettiness. This was battle-torn ground in the centuries-long strife between the two nations, which is recalled today only in the ballads and in the tumbled castles that gaze empty-eyed over fields and villages. Towering cliffs shelter small fishing ports whose monuments to drowned crews are a reminder that war with the sea, at least, is eternal.

① BARNS NESS

The village of East Barns is covered with a fine film of white dust from the vast Blue Circle works that supplies most of Scotland's cement. The company, however, together with the local council, has presented some 2½ miles of coastline to the public, the whole comprising one of the most exciting and interesting reserves in this part of the country. The main theme is a geology trail that points out the features, and the fossils, of the various local limestones which supply the raw material for the cement works.

Long before the birth of the cement works, the limestone was quarried, broken and burned for use as a fertiliser, as a bleaching agent, and as a flux in iron foundries. The old Catcraig lime-kilns have been restored and are now a feature of the walk. Seaweed-scented, its short turf yellowed with bird's-foot-trefoil, the walk runs by a shore pitted with rock pools in which a myriad small sea creatures have established themselves.

Larger fish – codling, mackerel, wrasse, dab, plaice and flounder – may be caught off the rocks. Barns Ness, too, is a marvellous birdwatching centre; gannets from Bass Rock make their dizzying plunges offshore, and many migrant species are attracted by the beam of the lighthouse. White Sands bay, almost enclosed by rocky arms, is the ideal place for an early morning swim.

② INNERWICK

Deep Devon-like lanes and streams whose banks are rich with elder, dog-rose, wild sweet pea and ragged robin surround a village which has long made a prosperous living from the good red soil of the area. Its church is 18th-century Gothic and the manse elegant Georgian, while Temple Mains Farm is a group of early 16th-century buildings separated by narrow passages floored with stone setts and cobbles. The most modern feature is a tall stone chimney that once carried off the smoke from the steam threshing machine.

A pleasant walk leads south-eastwards from the village to its castle. Trees grow over the walls and through the empty windows, but the tumbled, venerable stones are of the same rosy-red colour as the houses in the village. For centuries the castle was a major stronghold of the Stewarts until it was besieged and destroyed during the English invasion of 1547.

③ COVE

Like a number of places in the area, Cove could pass for Cornish – except that it yet remains to be 'discovered'. The tiny village is largely separate from its harbour, which is packed into the foot of the cliffs and reached only by a steep track carved out of the rocks.

Occupations, past and present, also have a Cornish flavour; there are usually a couple of fishing boats riding on the serene waters of the little harbour, and for many years the smugglers of Cove were notorious along this coast. Their store-rooms were the caves that riddle the surrounding cliffs.

④ PEASE BAY

This lovely cove, with its red cliffs and tawny sands, lies at the foot of the steep Pease Dean. From the top of the approach road the place has a deserted, undiscovered air; this is dissipated as the visitor rounds the last curve to discover a large, neat caravan site.

About 1½ miles to the north-west is a gorge, cut through by the little Dunglass Burn. Trees and ferns grow almost horizontally from the precipitous sides, and the air is full of the scent of wild garlic. Three bridges soar over the valley, one of which, built in

EYEMOUTH HARBOUR *With only scavenging sea-birds for company, trawlers wait under gathering cloud, a dark reminder that storms blow up quickly on this part of the coast.*

1786, is nearly 130 ft high and was said, when it was built, to be the highest bridge in the world. A glance over the balustrade is still an awesome experience.

Near by is the attractive village of Cockburnspath, which local people call Co'path. The church is partly 14th century, and the ancient Mercat Cross is decorated with the emblems of the thistle and the rose, carved to celebrate the marriage between Princess Margaret, daughter of Henry VI, to James IV of Scotland in 1502.

VIEW FROM THE BRIDGE *Seen from one of its three bridges, the deep gorge of Pease Dean is softened by cascades of greenery.*

⑤ COLDINGHAM

The priory at Coldingham is one of the glories of this part of Scotland. It was restored in 1098, upon the ruins of an older building, by Edgar, King of Scots, in honour of St Cuthbert, under whose banner Edgar had been victorious against a usurper. In the following centuries it suffered the usual misfortunes of any large building on this major invasion route from England – sacked in 1216, burned in 1544, partially blown up by Cromwell in the course of a skirmish in 1645. But it survives as a parish church and one of the oldest places of continuous worship in the country, its solid, rose-red shape softened by crumbling outer arches and walls.

There are excellent sands and safe bathing in Coldingham Bay. Some 2 miles to the north-west there are monster brown trout in

CLIFFS ABOVE ST ABBS *Rising sheer from a rocky arm are tall pillars of red sandstone, carved by wind and sea. Freshly washed by a summer shower, they bask in the soft rays of a setting sun.*

Coldingham Loch, and the hummocks that run almost from the loch to the waterfall tumbling over the cliffs to the sea are the remains of an Iron Age settlement.

⑥ ST ABB'S HEAD

From the car park outside St Abbs village, a track climbs up over steep turf; sheep and black cattle share the fields. At the top of the cliff, kittiwakes mew like a thousand cats, but this is only the overture to the great and endless symphony of the 50,000 sea-birds that nest on the head – guillemots, razorbills, shags, fulmars, puffins and herring gulls, all flying about the dark, volcanic crags in a perpetual tumult. Dizzyingly far below the sea, like green-black marble veined with white, heaves and soughs between the stack and the cliffs.

The St Abb's Wildlife Reserve, owned by the National Trust for Scotland and managed in conjunction with the Scottish Wildlife Trust, extends over 192 acres, and many creatures other than sea-birds live there. Land birds such as wheatears, meadow pipits, skylarks and stonechats nest on the headland, and in spring and autumn thousands of migrants rest there. Several species of butterfly also occur on St Abb's Head, and there is a profusion of wild flowers. The clear and unpolluted sea about the cliffs is included in the reserve, and the marine animals and plants that live in them attract underwater photographers and explorers. Diving is allowed from the harbour at St Abbs, subject to certain restrictions. Permission to dive from Pettico Wick, on the north side of St Abb's Head, must be sought from the Ranger.

St Abbs village, tucked away at the foot of the cliffs, takes its name – as does the headland – from a convent that was built on the crags in the 7th century. The ruin on Nunnery Point, however, is not that of the convent, but of a medieval hall. All that can be seen of the religious settlement is a few bumps and depressions on Kirk Hill.

⑦ EYEMOUTH

A rigidly planned housing estate and a vast caravan site mask the approach to this old fishing port; but the town centre, with its winding, narrow streets, its busy fish market and harbour crowded with brightly painted fishing boats looks much as it must have done a century ago.

On October 14, 1881, Eyemouth suffered its cruellest day, when a gale blew up out of a clear sky and sank 23 of its boats and drowned 129 of its men. The story is told in an excellent museum opened on the cente-

nary of the disaster; what makes the tale particularly poignant is that the names of the boats involved – *Forget me not, Good Intent, Guiding Star* and so on – are so much like those of the boats in the harbour now.

The museum also shows the history of east-coast fishing in general, and tells of the lives of the fisher lasses who, between May and November each year, used to 'Travel the Herring' – follow the fleets from Eyemouth to Yarmouth and the Shetlands, cleaning and barrelling the fish. The museum is, in addition, the beginning of the Tourist Board's Fishing Heritage Trail that runs up to Lerwick in Shetland.

Eyemouth boats no longer catch herring, but fish for white fish instead. All the same, the highlight in the town calendar is still the

week-long Herring Queen Festival held in July, when the flag-bedecked fishing fleet escorts the newly elected Queen from St Abbs to Eyemouth.

Other attractions in the old town include Gunsgreen House, a Georgian mansion whose secret passages were admirably suited to its role as a smuggling gang's headquarters. The beach is a mixture of rock and sand and, because of breakers, bathing is not always safe. However, St Abbs and Eyemouth Voluntary Marine Nature Reserve offers a wide range of sub-aqua activities, and there is a 6 mile walk along the clifftop to St Abb's Head.

⑧ BURNMOUTH

This unprettified, toughly attractive collection of fishermen's cottages crouches at the bottom of a very steep hill. Yard-thick tarred sea-walls with worn steps leading up make a pleasant place to sit and contemplate the quiet waters of the harbour with its tiny inshore fishing boats and piles of lobster pots and nets on the one hand, and the harsh rocky beach on the other.

Out of the holiday season, Burnmouth is a lonely place. Like Eyemouth, it was hit by the disaster of 1881 in which a total of 188 local fishermen lost their lives; perhaps because it was so much smaller than Eyemouth, it took longer to recover. It is very much a Border village; fair-haired, bright-eyed children play round the harbour, using among themselves dialect words that echo those in the Border ballads. But to visitors they are unfailingly warm of manner, and highly informative about their coast and countryside.

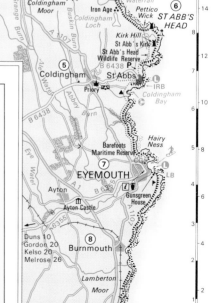

LOCAL INFORMATION

Tourist information Eyemouth 50678 (summer).

HM Coastguard Crail 50666 for information, 999 in emergency (ask for coastguard).

Weather Glasgow Weather Centre (041) 248 3451.

PLACES TO SEE INLAND

Abbotsford House, Melrose, 30 miles SW of Eyemouth, via A6105, A68 and B6361. Home of Sir Walter Scott. Daily in summer.

Ayton Castle, 2 miles SW of Eyemouth. 19th century. Some afternoons in summer.

Floors Castle, Kelso, 24 miles SW of Eyemouth, via B6437 and B6461. Built by William Adam in 1721. Most days in summer.

Jim Clark Memorial Trophy Room, Duns, 14 miles SW of Eyemouth, via A6105. Dedicated to the former World Champion racing driver. Daily in summer.

Manderston House, 2 miles E of Duns, via A6105. Edwardian mansion. Some afternoons in summer.

Mellerstain, Gordon, 24 miles SW of Eyemouth, via A6105 and A6089. 18th-century Adam house. Most afternoons in summer.

Sea-fringed golf courses and an island bird haven

Battles and witchcraft, great houses and romantic castles, bird sanctuaries and boat trips, old fishing ports and lovely villages – there is something to delight everyone on this stretch of coast. But its central theme is golf, which in this part of Scotland is played by everyone from near-toddlers to ancients. The links run for miles along the shore, their turf perfectly maintained by the sea air and by expert mowing.

① LONGNIDDRY

For 500 years Longniddry was a mining village, until in the 1920s the coal ran out; today it is almost Edinburgh commuter country. There are golf links and a rocky shore leading down to the flat Gosford Sands. But the area's best-known feature is something that most people never see – Gosford House, a seat of the Earl of Wemyss.

The house, designed by Robert Adam towards the end of the 18th century, and its park, lie behind a red wall that runs seemingly for miles along the shore road. Within the walls, trees lean inland, away from the wind. There are a number of gateways, one of them three storeys high.

Off the inland road behind the estate is the picturesque ruin of the 16th-century Redhouse Castle.

② ABERLADY BAY

The country around Aberlady Bay is wonderfully rich; old trees, heavy boughed, arch over the road or divide sprawling, heavy-cropping fields of cereals or potatoes. By contrast, the bay itself is a flat, windy expanse of salt-marsh, low dunes and creeks. Children should not be allowed to wander alone, and bathing is unsafe. The local mussels and winkles should not be eaten.

The lovingly composed Myreton Motor Museum, south-east of Luffness Mains, includes not only vintage cars, but motor cycles, old aeroplane engines and military vehicles. It is open daily.

MEDIEVAL CASTLE Dirleton Castle, partly 13th century, has been ruined both by time and by Cromwell's soldiers 300 years ago.

③ GULLANE

As horse training areas may be judged by the impeccability of their white rails, so the best golf courses may be recognised by the suavity of their turf. There is no more perfect turf in the world than that of the links around Gullane, occupied by club after club and by mile after mile of fiendishly contrived bunkers.

The holy of holies is Muirfield, founded by the Honourable Company of Edinburgh Golfers in 1891, and still considered by many to be the finest championship course of all. Visitors, on certain conditions, are welcome at all the courses around Gullane, while for those who do not care for the game, there are miles of coastal footpaths, with the wind, sea-birds and wild flowers for company.

Gullane village's preoccupation is made clear in pub and bar names like 'Golf Addicts', 'The 19th Hole' and 'The Golf Bag', but there are other attractions too. The handsome but roofless St Andrew's Church – whose last vicar was dismissed by James VI for smoking – dates from the 12th century; and the sands in Gullane Bay provide probably the best and safest bathing on this stretch of coast.

Golfing at Muirfield

④ DIRLETON

Nature and history have allied at Dirleton to provide a tourist's delight. Three sides of the great wide green are lined by cottages and houses of the 17th, 18th and 19th centuries, all built of the same rosy stone. So too is the venerable church, part of which dates from the 12th century. It is a beautiful building, nobly carved on the outside, but as plainly furnished as a classroom within.

The fourth side of the green is bounded by the massive bailey wall of the castle, which today encloses delightful gardens with a perfection of herbaceous borders and a bowling green that was laid out in the 17th century, its boundaries still defined by its original yews. This idyllic scene makes the castle itself even more dramatic – a gold-grey mass of stone that looks as though it had grown from the crag on which it stands. It dates partly from the 13th century, and was dismantled by Cromwellian troops in 1650.

Over some classic golf links, a well laid out nature trail leads to broad sands, where bathers are protected by the bulk of the island of Fidra, topped by a lighthouse.

⑤ NORTH BERWICK

Everywhere the visitor goes in the Firth of Forth, the 613 ft volcanic pyramid of North Berwick Law goes with him in views near or distant. From the summit, reached by a fairly tough climb, the odd shapes visible from below resolve themselves into a look-out post of the Napoleonic Wars, another constructed during the Second World War, and an arch made from the jawbones of a whale. There is an indicator that points out the enormous range of landmarks visible from this relatively lofty point; the trees clothing the side of the Law – a Scottish word for a hill – were planted in 1707 to celebrate the Union of Parliaments.

The lively and ancient burgh of North Berwick is gathered mostly about its harbour, which offers safe mooring to yachts, though space is limited; further anchorage is available outside. On either side of the harbour there are fine beaches, but bathing is dangerous if the sea is running even moderately high; the open-air, heated swimming pool near by is open from May to the end of August. Boat trips to the island of Fidra and to Bass Rock are available from the harbour.

By the harbour wall a forlorn little stone building is all that remains of the old kirk of St Andrews, and all that remains too of a scandal that in 1591 shook Scotland to its foundations. A year earlier, a local coven of witches had sought the death of James VI (later James I of England) by sorcery. The attempt was unsuccessful, but at the subsequent trial it was revealed that 200 witches had met in the kirk where they were addressed by the Devil in the form of a black goat. It is thought now that the 'Devil' might

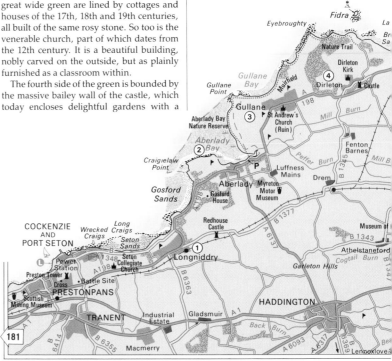

LONELY WATCH *Lighthouse keepers are the only human inhabitants of Bass Rock; the lighthouse was built in 1902. A round-the-island trip from North Berwick goes close inshore.*

John Muir

A PROPHET'S BELATED HONOUR

John Muir, born in Dunbar in 1838, was a tireless campaigner for the conservation of the countryside, yet it was in the USA that he became known as the father of the National Parks movement, and his work was not recognised in the country of his birth until 60 years after his death. Muir emigrated in 1849, and it was due to his writings that America's first national park, Yosemite, was established in 1890. Today more than 20 places in America bear his name; in Scotland the John Muir Country Park was opened in 1976.

well have been the heavily disguised Earl of Bothwell, heir-apparent to the throne. The earl escaped, but many of the women were condemned to the stake.

⑥ BASS ROCK
This is another one of those ancient volcanic cores – Edinburgh Castle Rock and North Berwick Law are among the others – that occur up and down the coast; the Bass, however, is particularly impressive, in that it rises a sheer 350 ft straight from the sea. It is best known nowadays as a sanctuary for sea-birds – gannets, fulmars, cormorants, razor-bills, puffins and many others, including an occasional wandering albatross – but in its long history, it was also a sanctuary for men. St Baldred, a disciple of St Kentigern, sought refuge there, and from 1691 to 1694 a Jacobite garrison held it for James II against the forces of William III.

⑦ TANTALLON CASTLE
One of the most evocative sights on this part of the coast is the rose-red Tantallon Castle, a ruin now, but still conveying a sense of immense power as it rides on its 100 ft promontory above the sea. Built mostly in the 14th century, it was a Douglas strong-hold through much of its history. In 1651, a

two-day battering by Cromwell's siege guns collapsed one of the walls into the moat, so creating a bridge. The Ironsides stormed across and took the castle.

The Tantallon headland offers the best mainland view of Bass Rock, towering from the sea about 1½ miles out.

⑧ JOHN MUIR COUNTRY PARK
The 8 mile stretch of sand and salt-marsh that includes Belhaven Bay, Tyne Mouth and Ravensheugh Sands is included in a country park named after the Victorian con-servationist John Muir. The area is a sanctuary for all kinds of sea-birds, waders and wildfowl, and visitors are offered a golf course, riding trails, a nature trail, barbecue areas and fishing. Bathing is not recommended.

The park is bordered to the north by the gardens and estate of Tyninghame House, which has been famed for its woodlands ever since the 6th Earl of Haddington created beech plantations there in 1707. By the 1940s, the trees had reached their full and magnificent maturity, when they were sacrificed to the war effort. Re-planting began in 1945.

Inland from the house is the pretty estate village of Tyninghame, its cottages smartly uniformed in rose-red stone and pantiles, while about 1½ miles to the north is Whitekirk, whose kirk, despite the name, is rose-red too. Dating from the 15th century, it is accounted one of the finest of small Gothic churches in Scotland, though it has had a somewhat chequered history. Cromwell is said to have stabled his horses in the building; the Covenanter Richard Blackad-der preached his last sermon there before being imprisoned on Bass Rock; and in 1914 it suffered the unusual fate of being set on fire by suffragettes. The church was gutted,

but magnificently restored by public sub-scription three years later.

⑨ DUNBAR
Standing on one of the classic English invasion routes into Scotland, Dunbar's history has been a tumultuous one. Two major battles were fought there, both disastrous to the Scots. In the first, which took place in 1292 at Spott, about 2 miles to the south, the Scots army under John Bailiol was soundly defeated by the forces of Edward I. The second battle, in 1650, was one of Cromwell's major victories. The Army of the Covenant abandoned its secure position on Doon Hill and rushed down to meet the battle-hardened Ironsides; 'the Lord hath delivered them into our hands', said Cromwell. The engagement was brief and bloody and, for the time being, fatal to the cause of Charles II.

Dunbar has a real, working fishing har-bour with piles of red nets and lobster pots and a deep-sea lifeboat; there is a lifeboat museum near by. In the background stand the tattered, dark-red remains of Dunbar Castle, to which the Earl of Bothwell brought Mary, Queen of Scots in 1567, after the murder of Darnley. Among other places of interest are Lauderdale House, designed by Robert Adam; the Old Cromwell Harbour, partly paid for by the Lord Protector; and 126 High Street, the birthplace of John Muir, now a museum.

Though there are sandy beaches, bathing is hazardous in Dunbar. However, there is a sailing club in Victoria Harbour.

LOCAL INFORMATION

Tourist Information, North Berwick 2197; Dunbar 63353.

HM Coastguard, Crail 50666 for information, 999 in emergency (ask for coastguard).

Weather, Edinburgh (031) 246 8091.

Local radio, IBA Radio Forth, 194 m, 1548 kHz, 96.8 MHz.

PLACES TO SEE INLAND

Hailes Castle, near East Linton. Medieval remains. Daily.

Lennoxlove, 2 miles S of Haddington, off B6369. 17th-century mansion. Some afternoons in summer.

Museum of Flight, near Athelstaneford, 4½ miles S of North Berwick. Daily July and August.

Preston Mill, (NTS), near East Linton. 16th-century watermill. Daily.

Traprain Law, near East Linton. Iron Age hill-fort. Daily.

MILES 1 2 3 4 5 6 7 8 9 10
KM 2 4 6 8 10 12 14 16

Yachts, beaches and fishing boats below Edinburgh's castle crag

Since its back is turned so resolutely upon the sea, it is easy to forget that Edinburgh – now that Leith has been included in the city – is a major port with a long coastline. The best way to appreciate the variety of this coast is to climb to the high, windy battlements of Edinburgh Castle and see the whole panorama of the Firth of Forth's southern shore, stretching from pretty Cramond to the witch-haunted hill of North Berwick Law.

The statue of Greyfriars Bobby in Candlemaker Row

① CRAMOND

With its white cottages and unexpected stone steps and alleys leading down to a snug little yacht anchorage in the River Almond, Cramond seems to have much more in common with Devon and Cornwall than with the busy dockland that begins at the eastern end of its fine golf links. Most of the village belongs to the 17th century, but its origins are far older, since it is built across a harbour and principal supply depot for the Romans' Antonine Wall.

In his campaigns against the North Britons at the beginning of the 3rd century AD, the Emperor Severus supplemented the defences with a powerful fort; much of its foundations, meticulously labelled, can be seen in a field behind the church. This is built mainly of stones quarried by the legions, and the site has been a place of Christian worship since the 6th century. A Roman bath-house was uncovered in 1975, and nine skeletons from medieval times were found crammed into the Roman drains.

From the shore a causeway, passable at low tide, runs out to the uninhabited Cramond Island, round which cormorants bob like black periscopes. Far beyond them is the island bird sanctuary of Inchmickery. The tides are dangerous at Cramond – and the mussels on the shore are not safe to eat.

A ferry runs across the River Almond to the start of a path that runs past Dalmeny House to Queensferry. At the eastern end of the path is Eagle Rock, so called because it bears a much-worn figure representing either an Imperial Eagle or Mercury, god of travellers, carved by some legionary to welcome the galleys ashore.

From the east side of Cramond harbour, the shore path continues for some 2 miles to Granton Point, running almost all the way between the fine, undulating golf links and the Drum Sands. About half a mile inland is Lauriston Castle, whose turreted tower house dates from 1590. The castle is open daily in summer, except Fridays, and on weekend afternoons in winter.

② GRANTON

Warehouses, storage tanks, gasholders, dockside debris and a lighthouse rising straight from the street – Granton is hardly picturesque. But the harbour is a fine one, and the headquarters of several yacht clubs, including the Royal Forth and the Forth Corinthian.

A little to the west of the harbour is the lovely 17th-century mansion of Caroline Park, originally called Granton House but renamed in honour of Queen Caroline in 1740. An inscription on the front reveals that it was built by Sir George McKenzie, Viscount Tarbat, a chief minister of Scotland. Now almost overwhelmed by industry, it is used as offices.

③ EDINBURGH

'Athens of the North' its citizens are fond of calling it – and if both its climate and its history are over-savage to merit such a description, there is no doubt that Edinburgh is one of the most handsome cities in the western world. And though no elected body has sat in its Parliament House since 1707, there is no doubt either that it is a capital city.

In fact, Edinburgh is two cities: the medieval town crammed along the ridge between the Castle and Holyroodhouse, and the elegant New Town of Georgian streets, squares and crescents whose building, to the plans of a 23-year-old architect, James Craig, began with the draining of the insanitary Nor' Loch in 1767. Its site is now occupied by Princes Street Gardens, and to gain an impression of the city it is only necessary to stand thereabouts – on the Waverley Bridge, say – and look up and around. Upon the surrounding hills, and therefore seemingly piled one upon another, are buildings representing every form of European architecture: the Grecian of the art galleries and the odd structures on Calton Hill, the Gothic crown on the High Kirk of St Giles, the severe Scots medieval of the Castle and the 'high lands', or tenements, of the Royal Mile, with here and there a touch of French chateau thrown in for good measure.

High on its volcanic rock, the Castle contains and guards the little chapel of St Margaret, Malcolm Canmore's queen who brought the Roman faith to Scotland in 1069; the Honours of Scotland, which are the country's Crown Jewels; the standards car-

ried at the Battle of Culloden in 1746; the splendid State apartments and the little panelled room where Mary, Queen of Scots gave birth to the prince who would become James I of the United Kingdom; and the sombre War Memorial.

The Royal Mile, comprising four successive streets running down from the Castle, is one of the most extraordinary streets in the world. Most of its buildings are 'lands', which must be among the earliest purpose-built blocks of flats in Britain. In them has lived almost everyone who has had to do with Edinburgh's history, from John Knox and Sir Walter Scott to princes and philosophers, poets and courtesans, thieves and murderers, and a hundred generations of ordinary Edinburgh folk. Its windows have witnessed the burning of witches, the parade of villains and heroes to the gallows in the Grassmarket, and the patience of Greyfriars Bobby, the terrier that for 14 years watched over its master's grave in the Greyfriars cemetery. At the foot of the Royal

WHITE HORSE CLOSE *In the 17th century, travellers to London boarded their coach at the White Horse Inn, now a private dwelling.*

LAIRD OF THE HALLS

Harry Lauder, Scotland's best-known music-hall entertainer, was born in Portobello in 1870, and from time to time the town presents a Sir Harry Lauder Festival which is attended by Scots from all over the world. Lauder, who was known in America as 'The Kilted Laird of Vaudeville', died in 1950 and is buried in Hamilton, near Glasgow.

Two guises of Harry Lauder

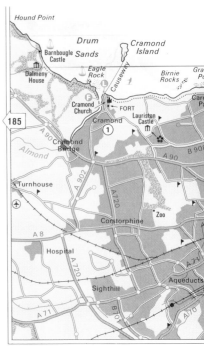

EDINBURGH EVENTIDE *Dusk brings a special air of romance to Princes Street, softening the stark outlines of Castle Rock and drawing a wispy veil across the pinnacled Sir Walter Scott Memorial.*

Mile stand the Abbey Kirk and the chateau-like royal Palace of Holyroodhouse built by James IV in the 15th century.

There is much to see in Edinburgh – the National Gallery and the Portrait Gallery, the Museum of Antiquities and the Royal Botanic Gardens, the view from Arthur's Seat that embraces the entire Firth of Forth. But if time is short, try at least to see the two buildings that comprise the National Trust for Scotland's exhibition 'A Tale of Two Towns', which shows Edinburgh's dual character to perfection. They are Gladstone's Land, built in 1617, in the Royal Mile, and No 7, Charlotte Square, designed by Robert Adam in 1791. Both houses have been decorated and furnished to show how they would have looked in the days of their first occupants.

Best of all is to see Edinburgh in Festival time, in August, when the city plays host to the world and offers a magnificent array of concerts, theatre, ballet, opera and a military tattoo.

④ LEITH AND NEWHAVEN

Leith has been Edinburgh's port for centuries, and despite the traditional rivalry between the two, it was finally absorbed into the city in 1920. A tough, seafaring town built where the Water of Leith enters the Forth, it did – and still does – considerable trade with the Low Countries and other parts of Europe, which is why the handsome old houses among the forests of cranes and grain elevators are more reminiscent of Bruges or Antwerp than of a British port.

Though it now runs into the port of Leith, Newhaven was always a fishing harbour rather than a port and was founded about 1500 by James IV. George IV held its fishwives to be the handsomest women he had ever seen, and it was they who wandered the streets of Edinburgh with their baskets of 'Caller (fresh) herrin'. The last fishwife retired in 1977, and the harbour is used partly by yachts. There is some shellfishing, and the town still has a reputation for seafood.

⑤ PORTOBELLO

The resort's very un-Scottish name was given to it by its founder, a sailor named George Hamilton who had fought with Admiral Vernon at Puerto Bello, Panama, in 1739. For two centuries, 'Porty' has been Edinburgh's playground, its citizens attracted by its bracing air, its long sweep of sand and its seaside festivities. Georgians and Victorians built houses there, and if nowadays, with its battered amusement park and closed and shuttered swimming baths, the place looks a little defeated, the long red esplanade still offers a fine walk and views. Light craft may be launched over the wide, if not too clean, sands.

⑥ MUSSELBURGH

In 1332 the citizens of Musselburgh cared for the dying Earl of Moray, Regent of Scotland. After his death the new Regent, the Earl of Mar, offered to compensate the townsfolk but they declined, whereupon he praised them for their honesty – and ever since, Musselburgh has been known as 'The Honest Town'. It was an important seaport in Roman times, and is still a busy, thriving

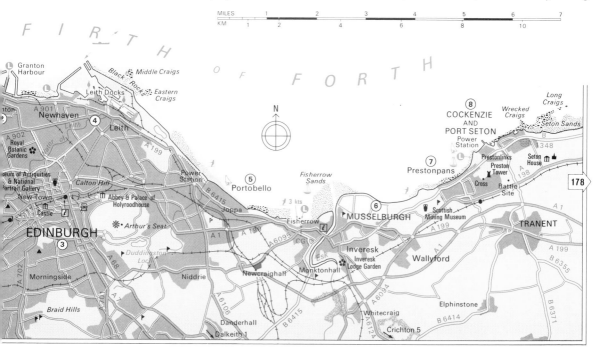

A BROAD FIRTH CROSSED BY TWO GREAT BRIDGES

The graceful rail and road bridges that link Edinburgh with the rugged Highlands symbolise the engineering skills of two successive centuries. The bridges are approached across a patchwork of farms and fields on the Forth's southern shore. The rambling Pentland Hills that edge the city's western outskirts give a hint of the wilder Border country that lies beyond.

little burgh with a tolbooth built of stones taken from the ancient Chapel of Loretto in 1590. The fine golf links are even more venerable, since they were played upon by James IV in 1504; the club dates from 1774, when the members offered a creel and shawl to the best player among the local fishwives. A racecourse has shared the links since 1816.

Adjoining Musselburgh to the south is the village of Inveresk, with its perfect 17th and 18th-century villas; they follow in a tradition established by the Romans, who had a civilian settlement there. Pinkie House in Musselburgh, once a seat of the Abbots of Dunfermline, is now part of Loretto School, a public school for boys.

(7) **PRESTONPANS**
The name means 'priests' pans', from the monks who established salt pans in the area in the 12th century; but the place is best remembered as the scene of Prince Charles

Edward Stuart's only significant victory in the Jacobite Uprising of 1745. Today the monument to the battle is backed by a huge power station.

Nevertheless, there are some fine old buildings in Prestonpans. The mercat cross is reputed to be the best in the country, and Preston Tower is a grim medieval fortification with a huge dovecot beside; Hamilton House and Northfield are graceful lairds' houses of the early 17th century.

Prestongrange, to the west of the town, where coal was mined for more than 700 years, is now the site of the excellent Scottish Mining Museum. Exhibits include a Cornish beam engine installed in 1874 and an old colliery locomotive.

⑧ COCKENZIE AND PORT SETON

Cockenzie is a little old Forth fishing village attached to a very large power station, built near Lothian's coalfields. However, some good stone cottages and fishing boats undergoing repairs on the stocks help to retain the flavour of yesteryear. In fact, the harbour of Port Seton, which is part of Cockenzie, is still an important fishing port, and though visiting yachts are welcome, their owners should take care not to moor in the fishermen's berths. A few moorings are also available at Cockenzie. Seton has an indoor swimming pond – not a pool – and miles of sands pinned down by ribs of reefs with dramatic names such as the Long Crags and the Wrecked Crags.

A little inland is Seton House, built about 1790 on the site of the old Seton Palace, of which some slight ruins remain. Just over the wall is the early 15th-century Collegiate Church, a good-looking building of red and grey stone with buttressed walls, tracery windows and a stumpy tower, standing among sweeping curves of shaven grass.

Because of the Reformation, various English invasions and sackings, and the loyalty of the Seton family to the Stuart cause, the church was never finished. Now it is empty, apart from bats fluttering about the vaulted ceiling, some stones commemorating recent burials and the effigies of a knight and his lady; probably he was the 3rd Lord Seton, killed at Flodden in 1513.

LOCAL INFORMATION

Tourist information Edinburgh (031) 226 6591; Musselburgh (031) 665 6597 (summer).

HM Coastguard Crail 50666 for information, 999 in emergency (ask for coastguard).

Weather Edinburgh (031) 246 8091.

Local radio IBA Radio Forth, 194 m, 1548 kHz, 96.8 MHz.

PLACES TO SEE INLAND

Crichton Castle, 9 miles SE of Musselburgh, via A68 and B6367. Daily in summer, weekends in winter.

Dalkeith Park, 7 miles SE of Edinburgh. Daily in summer.

Inveresk Lodge Garden (NTS), 6 miles E of Edinburgh. Some days.

Fine houses beside the Forth and an abbey on an island

Oil has replaced coal as the industrial theme of this part of the Forth, but the effects of both have been surprisingly local – so much so that within a mile or two of refinery or former coal mine it is easy to forget their existence. There are great houses, set in parks as gracious as any in Britain, and long green walks along the shore. Sailing and boating are magnificent, and admirably catered for in centres such as the Port Edgar Marina, near Queensferry.

① GRANGEMOUTH
For a place that is one of the great oil refineries of Europe, mid-town Grangemouth shows very little evidence of its industrial importance, consisting as it does of low, square-cut, stone houses around which rhododendrons bloom well into late June. Then, along the A904 Bo'ness road, the reek catches the throat, and ahead of you a thousand chimneys spout steam and a forest of cranes and flare-stacks blow banners of flame.

In the midst of it all, the BP Information Centre in Powdrake Road has mounted a small exhibition to acknowledge the debt that the oil industry owes to James 'Paraffin' Young. He was a self-taught Scots chemist who, in the 1850s, became the first man to produce and make commercial use of mineral oil products – paraffin wax, and fuel for domestic lighting.

② BO'NESS
The great pit-head wheels of the Kinneil colliery, while they still turned, drifted a layer of grime over most of Borrowstounness, as it is correctly (though never) called. Coal was part of Bo'ness life for a long time, but even a century ago the place was better known as a seaport and a base for whalers. One of the hills is still called Tidings Hill, for it was from there that wives and sweethearts used to watch for a first glimpse of the whaling ships returning from year-long voyages to Greenland.

The steam age began in Bo'ness, in a cottage by Kinneil House where, in the early 1770s, James Watt built his first full-scale steam pumping engine. It was not entirely successful, but the cylinder of a later, long-used Watt engine stands near by. Kinneil House itself is for the most part a 16th-century shell, where kestrels nest, but it has

been re-roofed and it is hoped one day to restore it to its former grandeur. Demolition was under way in 1936 when 16th and 17th-century wall and ceiling paintings were discovered beneath the plaster. This saved the house, and the rooms containing the paintings are restored and on view.

On The Foreshore at Bo'ness there is a steam railway, which has been restored by the Scottish Railway Preservation Society. The society's steam-engines operate at weekends in summer.

③ BLACKNESS
The story goes that during one of the many periods of English domination, the Scots asked the English king for permission to build a castle to defend the then-important port of Blackness. This was refused, and it was suggested that they should build a ship instead. The Scots then set about building a castle in the shape of a ship, and from certain angles the still-massive fortification does look like a medieval warship. It has been a royal castle and prison since the 15th century, and Covenanters were incarcerated there during the Civil Wars.

Blackness is no more than a village now. It has a boat club with a slipway, and there is a pleasant footpath that runs along the seaward edge of deep green Wester Shore Wood to Hopetoun House.

④ THE BINNS
The little fairy-tale castle was built by the Dalyell family in the early 17th century, and has been their home ever since. Most remarkable of a long race of distinguished soldiers and sailors was General Tam Dalyell who commanded an army for the king during the Civil War, and later reorganised the Russian forces for the Tsar. When Charles I was executed, he vowed never to cut his hair or beard until the monarchy was restored; and a portrait in the house proves that he kept his word.

After the Restoration in 1660, Dalyell commanded Charles II's forces in Scotland against the Covenanters, whom he suppressed with such severity that the name of 'Bluidy Tam' or 'The Bluidy Muscovite' became feared throughout the land. The Binns contains many relics and mementoes of Tam, of his family, and of the regiment he founded, the Royal Scots Greys. The house is open to the public in summer, and there is a woodland walk to Tower Viewpoint.

⑤ HOPETOUN HOUSE
Looking out across a gracious sweep of parkland is one of the loveliest houses in all Scotland. Hopetoun, the home of the Marquess of Linlithgow, dates from the early 18th century, and is mostly the work of William Adam and his sons, who were also responsible for the decoration of the main rooms. Much of the furniture stands where

it did when the house was completed, and there is a fine collection of paintings, including works by the school of Rubens, Canaletto, and Annibali Carracci. A museum reflects life in the house down the years, and an exhibition in the stables tells the story of 'Horse and Man in Lowland Scotland'.

A nature trail wanders through woodlands and the park where there are peacocks, deer and sheep. All kinds of special events – antique fairs, concerts, vintage vehicle rallies – take place in the house or grounds, which are open in summer.

⑥ QUEENSFERRY
In *Kidnapped*, Robert Louis Stevenson has David Balfour describe Queensferry as 'a fairly-built burgh, of good stone, many-slated' – a reasonable assessment of the handsome old town today. Stevenson began the novel in the Hawes Inn, now arched over by the awesome girders of the Forth Rail Bridge. For centuries Hawes Pier in front of the inn was the place where north-bound passengers caught the ferry across the Forth. Since 1964, the ferry's role has been usurped by the Road Bridge, and now the pier is an inshore rescue boat station, a base for Forth cruises, a dinghy harbour and a place to launch powerboats. The grey Forth races between the shore and Inch Garvie island – which, with its old forts, looks like an old-fashioned dreadnought.

Busy Queensferry town – often called South Queensferry to distinguish it from North Queensferry on the opposite bank of the Forth – is well worth exploring. There is an old tolbooth on which a notice of 1817 records the burghers' gratitude to Lord Rosebery for providing them with a water supply and a green on which to lay their

TRAVELLERS' REST *Many authors, including Sir Walter Scott, stayed at the Hawes Inn while waiting for the ferry across the Forth.*

ARISTOCRATS OF A STATELY PARK
In the grounds of Hopetoun House roams a flock of the rare black Hebridean sheep. These aristocratic animals are sometimes called St Kilda sheep because they originate from the St Kilda islands in the Outer Hebrides. The ram is a particularly magnificent creature, with four horns framing a handsome head.

Hebridean ram

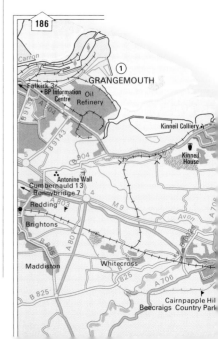

A KING'S THANKSGIVING *Built by a shipwrecked king, the Augustinian abbey on Inchcolm is one of the best-preserved examples of early medieval architecture in Scotland.*

Dalmeny village is a peaceful place – a wide green ranged about by single-storey stone cottages. The square-towered St Cuthbert's is probably the finest Norman parish church in Scotland. Its simple furnishings emphasise the wealth of carvings of all kinds of subjects, including a whole menagerie of animals, real and mythological. Lord Rosebery, the Prime Minister, is buried in the church with other members of his family, and there is a stained-glass window presented by Polish officers who served in the area during the Second World War.

⑨ **BARNBOUGLE CASTLE**

Perhaps the best way to see the castle is to make it a halfway goal on the 4 mile shore walk that runs from Queensferry round Hound Point to Cramond. The path runs between woods and parkland on one hand and, on the other, the wide Drum Sands which are frequented by thousands of sea-birds. There is a noble view of Dalmeny House, and the walk continues to the Cramond ferry across the River Almond.

Before the Roseberys came to the 13th-century Barnbougle Castle, it was owned by the Mowbrays, one of whom, Sir Roger de Mowbray, was killed in the Crusades, and his favourite hound with him. It is said that the animal's spirit returned to Hound Point, from which its howls can still be heard on stormy nights, and when the death of a Laird of Barnbougle is imminent. The castle was restored and used as a study by the 5th Lord Rosebery when he retired from public life. It is not open to the public.

cloth for bleaching. Plewlands (NTS), a town house of 1647, has been converted into flats. Festivities at the August Ferry Fair are led by the Burry Man, who is covered from head to foot with burrs and collects money for charity. It is thought that long ago his role was that of scapegoat, to ward off ill-fortune from the fishermen.

A little to the west of the town is the vast Port Edgar Marina, which has facilities for hauling out, berthing, boat sales and hiring, and slipways. A large number of watersport courses are also available.

⑦ INCHCOLM

The half-mile-long island can be seen from any part of the Firth of Forth, but is most easily visited by boat from Hawes Pier in Queensferry during the summer. The round trip takes just over 2 hours, including an hour ashore.

In 1123 the island was the home of a hermit who saved Alexander I from shipwreck and plied him with his own meagre rations of shellfish and milk. The king was so grateful that he built an Augustinian abbey there, and the island, like Iona, came to be regarded as holy, and as a desirable burial place for the rich and influential. Safeguarded by its island setting, the abbey is in an excellent state of preservation.

Sea-birds abound, and there are glimpses of grey seals in the surrounding waters.

⑧ DALMENY

In 1814 the 4th Earl of Rosebery finally tired of the draughts and damp in the castle of Barnbougle that his ancestors had occupied for the past 200 years, and engaged William Wilkins to build him a new home a little further east and a shade inland. The result was Dalmeny House, a mixture of Tudor and Gothic styles that served as the model for many other 19th-century Scottish houses.

The splendour of the interior is largely due to the 5th Earl, the great Lord Rosebery, who as a young man had three ambitions: to breed a Derby winner, to marry the world's richest woman, and to become Prime Minister. He achieved all three objectives. He succeeded Gladstone as Liberal Premier in 1894, bred three Derby winners, and married Hannah, only daughter of Baron Meyer de Rothschild. It was through this union that some of the greatest treasures of Mentmore, the Rothschild house in Buckinghamshire, eventually came to Dalmeny. There they mingle with the Roseberys' own collections in an unrivalled display of fine furniture and works of art. Of particular interest are the Goya tapestries on the staircase and the collection of relics and mementoes of Napoleon. The view from the windows is delightful, leading the eye over a sweep of park and trim golf links to the Forth. Dalmeny House is open to the public on most weekdays in summer.

LOCAL INFORMATION

Tourist information Falkirk 24911, Linlithgow 4600 (summer).

HM Coastguard Crail 50666 for information, 999 in emergency (ask for coastguard).

Weather Edinburgh (031) 246 8091.

Local radio IBA Radio Forth, 194 m, 1548 kHz, 96.8 MHz.

PLACES TO SEE INLAND

Beecraigs Country Park, 3 miles S of Linlithgow.

Cairnpapple Hill, 4 miles S of Linlithgow. Prehistoric burial cairns.

Falkirk Museum, 3 miles SW of Grangemouth. Weekdays.

Linlithgow Palace. 15th-century palace, birthplace of Mary, Queen of Scots. Daily.

Palacerigg Country Park, Cumbernauld, 13 miles W of Grangemouth, off A80.

Rough Castle, Bonnybridge, 7 miles W of Grangemouth, off B816. Roman fort on Antonine Wall. Daily.

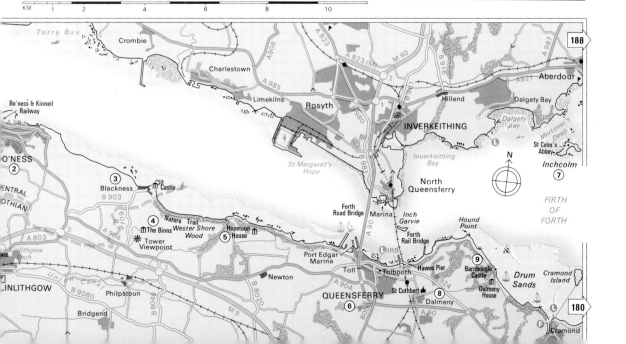

Scotland's historic heart on the Forth's northern shore

Inventors and saints, nuclear submarines and ancient kings, tycoons and hermits – all play a part in the country of contrasts that lies between the giant Forth Bridges and the more modest one at Kincardine. Dunfermline contains the grave of Robert Bruce and the glorious park donated by Andrew Carnegie; the coast is shared between the oil industry, the Royal Navy, and ancient burghs and harbours of great charm and character.

① KINCARDINE

This is where the Forth industrial belt begins in earnest, its gateway marked by vast power stations and coal mines. It was the presence of coal, coupled with that of the tidal waters of the river, that determined that the power stations should be built there. The largest of them, Longannet, is built upon land gained from the Forth by pouring in cinders from the Kincardine station.

An older Kincardine is still evident in the 17th-century Mercat Cross and houses – though they are almost overwhelmed by high-rise flats. The Kincardine Bridge, opened in 1936, was until the completion of the Queensferry Bridge in 1964 the only road bridge across the Forth between Stirling and the sea. However, the new bridge does not seem to have stolen too much of the older one's traffic; not the least of Kincardine's attractions is that it is toll-free.

② CULROSS

Though its outlook across oily mud-flats to a generating station is hardly prepossessing, the little Royal Burgh itself looks like a set for an historical film, and is often used as such. Many of the buildings, dating from the 17th century and earlier, have been restored by the National Trust for Scotland, and the Electricity Board has concealed its sub-station within an old town house. Once Culross was a well-known port, trading with the Low Countries; its ships brought back the red pantiles that cover the town's roofs, and some architectural ideas too, to judge from the Dutch flavour of many of the houses.

As early as 1575, Culross coal was being mined at 240 ft, thanks to the ingenious

methods of ventilation and drainage devised by the laird, Sir George Bruce. He it was who built 'The Palace', actually a unique example of a Jacobean merchant's house. It is open to the public all the year round, as is the 17th-century Town House, and The Study, so called from the small, quiet room at the top of its tower, with its fine painted ceiling. All through the burgh there are odd, unexpected delights, such as the House with the Evil Eye (so called because of its oddly positioned windows) and the old shops and cottages bearing the insignia and inscriptions of the trades that were once practised in them.

The Cistercians founded Culross Abbey in 1217, and became the first Scottish coalminers not long after. Part of the Abbey is now the parish church. Just outside the town there are the remains of a 16th-century chapel, traditionally built upon the site of the birthplace of St Kentigern who, better known by his nickname of Mungo (Latin-Welsh for 'dear friend'), became the patron saint of Glasgow.

At the western end of Culross, Dunimarle Castle houses a collection of paintings, glass, books and Empire furniture, some of which belonged to Napoleon.

③ CHARLESTOWN

Behind its neat little harbour and its foreshore of stones and oily mud, Charlestown has an odd air of Englishness. It has a village green, rare in Scotland, and about it are ranged the neat, low, white houses, some slate-roofed, some pantiled and all with considerable charm.

The name of the village reflects its origin,

being largely the creation of Charles, 5th Earl of Elgin. Having limestone and coal on his estate and the salt Forth at his doorstep, the earl cannily exploited them in salt pans and lime-kilns. Then, between 1756 and 1758, he established this model village. Little sign remains of the industries, but the village still thrives, as an attractive dormitory for Rosyth and other nearby towns.

④ DUNFERMLINE

Though a modern, busy, commercial town, Dunfermline has a medieval appearance, an effect created by the steep jumble of roofs, rising above streets that are nearly as steep, all reaching up to the tower and spire of the abbey. This, and the ruins of the palace and monastery near by, is the heart of the town, and in a sense, the heart of Scotland. For 600 years, it was the country's capital; seven kings – including Charles I of England – were born there, and the abbey is Scotland's royal sepulchre.

The most famous of the kings buried in Dunfermline Abbey is Robert Bruce, whose name is written in letters of stone at the top of the tower. His burial place was forgotten for many years until his skeleton was discovered during rebuilding work in the early 19th century. It was identified by its cloth-of-gold shroud and by the fact that the breastbone had been severed. On his deathbed in 1329, Bruce willed that his heart should be removed and taken by his friend, Lord James Douglas, to the Holy Land. Douglas was killed fighting the Saracens in Spain, and Bruce's heart was eventually returned to Scotland, where it was buried in Melrose Abbey; his grave in Dunfermline Abbey is marked by a plaque.

The abbey is a magnificent building – dark and quiet, its roof supported on massive Norman pillars. It was the inspiration of the English Princess Margaret who married the Scottish King Malcolm Canmore in 1070, and who was instrumental in ousting the old Celtic church from Scotland and replacing it with that of Rome.

Royalty apart, Dunfermline's most famous son is Andrew Carnegie, who was born in a cottage – still preserved – in Moodie Street in 1835, and emigrated to the USA where he made a vast fortune in the steel industry. He established some 3,000 libraries

Statue of Andrew Carnegie in Pittencrieff Park

COBBLED STREETS OF YESTERDAY *Culross is a town that time has passed by, a survivor from the 17th century with narrow streets of red-roofed houses converging on the Mercat Cross.*

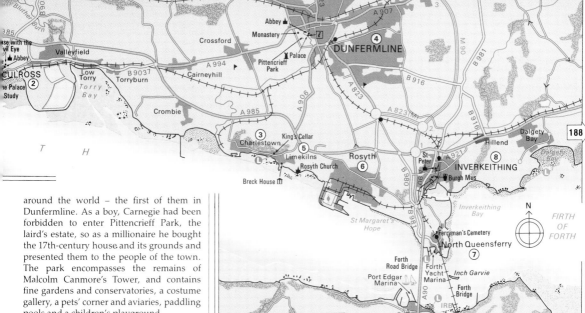

around the world – the first of them in Dunfermline. As a boy, Carnegie had been forbidden to enter Pittencrieff Park, the laird's estate, so as a millionaire he bought the 17th-century house and its grounds and presented them to the people of the town. The park encompasses the remains of Malcolm Canmore's Tower, and contains fine gardens and conservatories, a costume gallery, a pets' corner and aviaries, paddling pools and a children's playground.

⑤ LIMEKILNS

There is little sign now of the kilns that gave the place its name. The village consists mainly of a single row of stone houses – many built by retired mariners – situated between a steep, hanging wood and a rocky shore from which two drystone piers reach out to form a snug yacht harbour.

The oldest building is the 14th-century King's Cellar in which monks and then kings kept their wines. Since then it has been school, library, chapel, ballroom and an air-raid shelter; now it houses a Masonic Lodge. Breck House in Red Row is thought to be the place that Robert Louis Stevenson had in mind when, in *Kidnapped*, he described how David Balfour and Alan Breck waited at an inn in Limekilns for a boat to take them across the Forth.

⑥ ROSYTH

Correctly, this is HMS *Cochrane*, one of the greatest of British naval bases, Though it provides a great deal of employment locally, there is not much to see: neat squares of married quarters on the landward side and miles of wire fencing on the other. Occasionally a submarine or a ship of the Fisheries Protection Squadron may be glimpsed slipping out to sea, and now and again the Royal Navy unlocks its gates to the public at an Open Day.

Rosyth churchyard actually lies within the neighbouring parish of Limekilns. The church ceased to be used for worship about 1630, but burials continued for many years after. Stones in the Strangers' Ground record the names of foreign seamen who died of accident or disease and were buried there, and there is an early 19th-century vault in which corpses were kept for three months to prevent them from being stolen for dissection in the medical schools of Edinburgh.

⑦ NORTH QUEENSFERRY

This is the place where the Forth bridges – part of the scene all along the shores of the Firth – assume their true size, shape and colour. Each bridge complements the other, the Rail Bridge an intricate criss-crossing of girders, and the Road Bridge a soaring span of 8,244 ft supported by two slim towers that reach 512 ft above the water. The Rail Bridge, looking remarkably young for its 90-odd years of service, consists of two main spans each 1,710 ft long and resting on an island, Inch Garvie, while the overall length of the bridge is nearly 1¾ miles; the topmost girders stand 361 ft high.

FORGING A LINK *Work on the Forth Bridge had been in progress for three years when this picture of the huge cantilevers nearing completion was taken in 1888. The bridge was opened in 1890.*

North Queensferry stands in the shadow of the Rail Bridge, overhung by the girders whose red-oxide coating is being constantly renewed; it takes three years to paint the bridge, and when the job is completed, the painters go back to the beginning and start again. Trains booming overhead do not seem to disturb the always-busy Forth Yacht Marina by the Road Bridge.

The queen referred to in the town's name is Margaret who, in the 11th century, used to cross the Forth at this point when journeying betweeen Edinburgh and Dunfermline, and granted perpetual ferrying rights to the local people in consequence.

⑧ INVERKEITHING

The nucleus of Inverkeithing – its old, grey Royal Burgh – is ringed at a distance by housing estates, and the two are divided by steep, mown hillsides. The town's chief activity is shipbreaking, as is evident from the bright, rust-coloured water in the harbour. But much still remains of the days when Inverkeithing was an important market: the painted Mercat Cross, for example, that was set up in 1393, the Toll Booth, and some 17th-century town houses.

The tower of St Peter's Church dates from the 13th century and is said to be built on the spot where St Erat began converting the

local pagans in 744. The font, which is carved with the arms of Robert III's Queen Annabella and dates from the late 14th century, was discovered beneath the tower in 1806. Apparently it had been buried there for safety at the Reformation, and when unearthed was found to contain human bones. These are assumed to be those of St Erat, relics that had also to be concealed from the reformers.

LOCAL INFORMATION

Tourist information Dunfermline 720999 (summer).

HM Coastguard Crail 50666 for information, 999 in emergency (ask for coastguard).

Weather Dundee 8091.

Local radio IBA Radio Forth, 194 m, 1548 kHz, 96.8 MHz.

PLACES TO SEE INLAND

Castle Campbell, Dollar, 9 miles N of Kincardine, off A91, via B913. 15th-century ruins. Most days.

Doune, 21 miles NW of Kincardine, on A84, via A907. Medieval castle ruins, most days in summer; Motor Museum, daily in summer.

Menstrie Castle, 9 miles NW of Kincardine, on A91, via A907. Nova Scotia exhibition (NTS). Some afternoons in summer.

Scotland's Safari Park, Blair Drummond, 19 miles NW of Kincardine, on A84, via A907. Daily in summer.

A 'Lang Toun' of great men and an old port re-created

On this stretch of the Fife coast, busy, thriving Kirkcaldy contrasts oddly with quiet little burghs which have seen their ancient occupations – seaport, fishing, coal-mining – taken away, and have set themselves instead to entertain the visitor. They have much to offer; pretty streets of old houses, tales of famous men, fishing and sailing, and safe bathing – though some of the beaches are stained with the coal dust of the coastal mines.

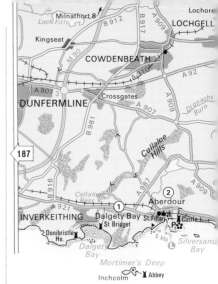

① DALGETY BAY
Most of the village consists of neat modern houses surrounded by expertly tended gardens. The outlook comprises a vast panorama of the Forth, with its bridges, bulk carriers riding at anchor, and, on the far side, the landmarks of Edinburgh in perfect silhouette. Perhaps the best place to see the view is from St Bridget's Kirkyard, full of massive, romantically tumbled tombstones. The ruined church, which dates from 1244, is maintained as a National Monument. From it a footpath leads down through a wood to a sandy cove.

Among the new houses and gardens stands the shell of Donibristle House. Close by, in 1592, the 'Bonnie Earl of Moray' was murdered by the Earl of Huntly, a deed immortalised in a ballad long familiar to Scottish schoolchildren.

② ABERDOUR
The castle, dating from the 14th century and once a Douglas stronghold, is now a ruin cared for by the Department of the Environment. Together with its giant stone dovecot, it stands in the midst of an exquisite formal garden of sieved earth, superbly spaced mature plants and velvety grass. Unusually in a Scottish castle, the gardens seem to have had their beginnings as long ago as the mid-16th century.

Just over the wall is St Fillan's Church. The interior is very quiet, with great round pillars and a little blue jewel of a window glowing through the Norman arch.

The bay, appropriately called Silversands, is a favourite resort of Edinburgh people on summer weekends. There is a fine little

CASTLE WELL *A well 52 ft deep in the east courtyard supplied water for Aberdour Castle, which fell into ruin around 1700.*

harbour that offers water-skiing, sailing and moorings on both sides of a central quay, and looks out upon the island of Inchcolm with its ruined abbey.

③ BURNTISLAND
The harbour appears again and again in Scotland's story, from the time that Agricola landed his legions there in the 1st century AD, to the mustering of convoys in the Second World War. Now the docks are mostly derelict, and Burntisland has dedicated itself instead to entertaining the holidaymaker. There is a wide sandy beach, backed by a promenade; there are summer regattas, and Highland Games are held in mid-July.

The spirit of the old port shines through, however. The parish church, with its attractive octagonal tower looking out upon the Forth, was the first post-Reformation church to be built in Scotland. It was there, in the presence of James VI (later James I of England), that the Authorised Version of the Bible was first suggested by the Assembly of the Church of Scotland. There are some fine 17th-century town houses in Somerville Street and Square – once called Quality Street because the 'quality' lived there.

④ KINGHORN
A Royal Burgh since the 12th century, Kinghorn is now an attractive seaside resort whose Lowland virtues are solidly expressed in the grey sandstone of its buildings. There are good golf links, and magnificent sands at Pettycur Bay.

Along the road to Burntisland a monument marks the spot where Alexander III, one of Scotland's wisest kings, was killed in 1286 when his horse stumbled in the dark and threw him over the cliff. Parking by the monument is not easy, but the place offers a grand prospect of the Forth, from the bridges on the right to Inchkeith island, with its battlemented lighthouse, 3 miles out, though it looks much closer.

⑤ KIRKCALDY
The 'Lang Toun', so nicknamed because at one time it was little more than a mile-long street stretching down the Firth of Forth, is now the largest town in Fife. Its prosperity stems mostly from linoleum, but its most striking export has perhaps been great men. Adam Smith, the 18th-century economist and author of *The Wealth of Nations*, was born there; so too were Robert and James Adam, who had such a profound effect upon Georgian architecture, and Michael Scott, medieval wizard and court astrologer to the Holy Roman Emperor. Thomas Carlyle was a local schoolmaster from 1816 to 1819, before achieving eminence as a historian. All are commemorated in the town by statues, plaques and the names of streets and public buildings.

There are some fine old houses in Kirkcaldy, notably the 17th-century Sailor's Walk, now occupied by HM Customs. The town also has an ice-rink, a first-class theatre in the Adam Smith Centre, an art gallery and an industrial museum. The burgh's wide sands are charcoal-grey with coal dust, and its docks covered with cut timber and the rusting debris of shipbreakers. But there is an excellent indoor swimming pool off the mile-long Esplanade, which in spring is the setting for the Links Market, one of the largest and oldest annual fairs in Britain.

The octagonal Ravenscraig Castle, built in 1460 and one of the first attempts to build a fortification that would withstand artillery, is surrounded by the lovely Ravenscraig Park. The park contains an elaborate children's playground and a nature trail that, in embracing woodland, cliff and seashore, presents a comprehensive picture of the geology and natural history of the Firth of Forth.

⑥ DYSART
In the 1960s Kirkcaldy Town Council and the National Trust for Scotland combined to rescue some derelict 16th and 17th-century houses in Dysart. The result was a perfect re-creation of the old port, in which gaps between the ancient buildings – their walls and stepped gables white-plastered now below their red pantiles – were filled with new houses built in the same idiom.

St Serf's church tower, stoutly built as a refuge from pirates, leans over little streets with enchanting names like Saut Girnal Wynd, Pan Ha' and Hie Gat.

The Tolbooth, with its grim, barred windows, was a powder magazine during the Civil War. It had its roof lifted off when a drunken Cromwellian trooper wandered in with a lighted torch, but it has been restored since. Near by, in Rectory Lane, the John McDouall Stuart Museum commemorates the Dysart man who made the first south-to-north crossing of Australia in 1861-2.

⑦ EAST WEMYSS
By the cemetery at the north-eastern end of the village there stands the still mostly solid red block of Macduff's Castle, maintaining watch over a shattered pepperpot of a dovecot. Tradition associates the castle with the character of Macduff in Shakespeare's *Macbeth*, and indeed it may well have been the clifftop stronghold of the Macduff thanes of Fife.

A walk along the rocky shore below the castle reveals about a dozen caves whose walls bear inscriptions indicating human occupation from the Bronze Age to the medieval period. The Court Cave, so called

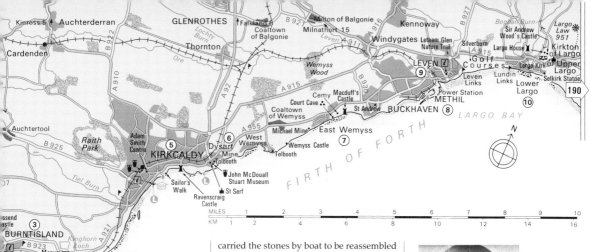

carried the stones by boat to be reassembled in their own town. There the Church of St Andrew stands still, with a church hall converted into a theatre.

because James V supposedly received some gypsies there, contains a rough Viking representation of Thor with his hammer, and a number of earlier Pictish carvings. The Doocot Cave has rows of deep, squared niches that may have contained funerary urns but are more likely to have been the nesting-boxes of a medieval dovecot. Notices warn that some caves are subject to rock falls and should not be entered.

Formerly shuttered and empty cottages in both East Wemyss and West Wemyss, witnesses to the closure of the Michael coal mine in 1967, are being restored.

⑧ BUCKHAVEN AND METHIL
Railyards, gasholders and the paraphernalia of heavy industry are the visitor's first impressions of the two towns that were united as a single burgh in 1891. But no place that has to do with ships and the sea can be dull, and the harbour is busy with the comings and goings of handsome little coasters from Hamburg, Copenhagen and ports of Spain. Near by, in the shipyards, there may stand a gigantic section of oil-rig, like a dinosaur skeleton.

Like so many Firth of Forth towns, Buckhaven and Methil grew out of fishing and coal – hard trades that brought the inhabitants periods of prosperity and troughs of depression. During one of the upswings, the fishermen of Buckhaven bought themselves a lovely little Gothic pre-Reformation church that had stood in North Street, St Andrews, for four centuries or so. They had it taken apart stone by stone and

⑨ LEVEN
The breezy golf courses of Leven and Lundin Links curve for some 2 miles round the eastern curve of Largo Bay, joining the little resort of Leven with Lower Largo. Fringing the links is a broad beach, part sand and part pebble, that to the east presents a panorama of the opening Firth all the way to Bass Rock.

For centuries, until shifting sands blocked its harbour, Leven was a port, and the sea-gate for Falkland Palace, a favourite residence of the Scottish Court, some 10 miles to the north-west. Later it became a coal port. Stolid, step-gabled buildings recall those times, but nowadays the town's chief interest is to attract the holidaymaker by offering golf on two 18th-century courses, safe bathing, a children's pool and playground, mackerel fishing and freshwater fishing in nearby streams. At The Centre, star-studded summer spectaculars, children's weeks and ceilidhs follow each other through the summer. By contrast, there are quiet walks in Letham Glen, which has a nature trail, and at Silverburn.

⑩ LOWER LARGO
A statuette of Largo's most famous son, goatskin clad, gazes from a niche on the site of the cottage in which he was born in 1676. He was Alexander Selkirk, whose adventures as a castaway were the inspiration for Daniel Defoe's novel *Robinson Crusoe*.

Lower Largo, where Selkirk was born, is a one-time fishing hamlet whose sandy, rocky beach looks out across the waters of the Forth to the distant Lammermuir hills.

The statue of Alexander Selkirk at Lower Largo, erected in 1885

Upper Largo, or Kirkton of Largo, is rather grander, with stone cottages draped with climbing roses. The spire of the 16th-century parish church is said to be unique in Scotland in being supported only by the chancel roof. Selkirk's parents are interred there, and so is Scotland's greatest admiral, Sir Andrew Wood, who, in his flagship the *Yellow Caravel*, led the Scots to victory against an English fleet in the Forth in 1489. When he retired, he dug a canal from his castle – of which a single tower remains – to the church, so that he might be rowed to the service by his old shipmates each Sabbath morning. In the churchyard is an early Christian Pictish stone carved with curious designs, including what appears to be a hunting scene with horsemen and hounds.

Standing high above both villages is the 952 ft volcanic mound of Largo Law, a splendid point from which to view the entire Firth. The ruin at its foot is that of Largo House, 18th-century home of the Durham family, lairds of Largo for nearly two centuries. Though its windows now gape empty, its fine lines still bear witness to the brilliance of its architect, Robert Adam.

VINTAGE PORT *The old port of Dysart lives again, looking very much as it did in the 17th century except for the modern boats in the harbour and the cars parked by the green.*

LOCAL INFORMATION
Tourist information Burntisland 872667; Leven 29464; Kirkcaldy 267775 (summer).
HM Coastguard Crail 50666 for information, 999 in emergency (ask for coastguard).
Weather Dundee 8091.
Local radio IBA Radio Forth, 194 m, 1548 kHz, 96.8 MHz.

PLACES TO SEE INLAND
Burleigh Castle, Milnathort, 18 miles W of Leven. 16th-century tower-house. Daily; key from farm.
Falkland Palace (NTS), 11 miles N of Kirkcaldy. 16th century. Daily in summer.
Loch Leven, by Kinross, 12 miles NW of Kirkcaldy. 15th-century island fortress; daily in summer; Loch Leven National Nature Reserve, daily; Vane Farm Nature Centre (RSPB), south side of Loch Leven, most days in summer and autumn, weekends in winter.
Lochore Meadows Country Park, 8 miles W of Kirkcaldy, via B920. Daily.

City of Scotland's patron saint and home of its ancient game

Long before it became the acknowledged home of golf, St Andrews was renowned as a seat of learning, and the area about it as a place of the saints. These were men like St Monan and St Fillan – whose chapel-cave can still be seen at Pittenweem – something of whose gentle, indomitable spirit seems to have been passed to the fisherfolk who built the little towns and harbours and worked the chilly waters of the North Sea.

① ST ANDREWS

Tradition has it that in AD 347, some three centuries after he was crucified on his X-shaped cross, the bones of St Andrew the Apostle were brought from Greece to this spot on the windy shores of Fife. St Rule, who was carrying them, was shipwrecked on the coast and there, somehow, the bones remained. Over and about them were raised a cathedral, a castle, several churches – including one named after St Rule, with a 108 ft tower – a university and one of the loveliest of Scottish cities. St Andrew became the patron saint of Scotland, and his cross the symbol.

St Andrews, with its three main streets, its colleges and red-gowned students, and its old houses with outside staircases, is essentially a medieval city, though it was savagely mauled in religious wars, and its cathedral used as a quarry by the townsfolk. Strife is woven into the city's history, as the monument to the Protestant martyrs burned to death overlooking the West Sands bears witness. So does the infamous Bottle Dungeon in the castle, considered escape-proof until one prisoner got away by exchanging clothes with his daughter.

Such passions have now been largely sublimated in the zeal for golf, for which St Andrews is famed the world over. Streets, hotels, bars and shops are all named after various aspects of the game, and four golf courses are open to all comers on a 'first come, first off' basis. The only exception is the Old Course, with its fiendish natural hazards such as Hell Bunker and Swilcan Burn, on which, from April to October, starting times are determined by ballot.

For those to whom golf will always remain a mystery, St Andrews offers many other diversions, including sailing, fishing and vast flat beaches on which oystercatchers and sanderlings strut at the water's edge.

② FIFE NESS

North of Crail the derelict huts and hangers and overgrown runways of a disused airfield appear much more doleful and haunted than the ancient tower at the airfield's end. This is all that remains of Balcomie Castle, where Mary of Guise, mother-to-be of Mary, Queen of Scots, spent her first few days in Scotland; a large farm has been built around it, and it is not open to the public.

Beyond the castle green, golf links sweep down through rich farmland to Fife Ness whose rocks, together with those of North Carr offshore, have claimed many ships down the centuries. On Fife Ness there was a Danish settlement and a later village, abandoned now, though the remains of its salt-pans can be seen. Along the beach path from the end of the links King Constantine's Cave, named after a Scottish king murdered there by Danes in 874.

Cambo, to the north, has an exhibition of 'The Living Land', centred upon an 18th-century farm and showing its life and work, past and present. It features rare breeds of farm animals, a pets' corner and an adventure playground; there are rock pools to explore and fossils to be sought.

③ CRAIL

At the bottom of a steep lane is a deep little harbour, the walls built in three giant steps of uncemented red boulders, each step or shelf piled with neat stacks of lobster-pots. The visitor can buy fresh crabs, lobsters and sea urchins, or simply sit on the wall and look out over the red-gold beach strewn with boulders tumbled from the cliffs.

Crail is a pretty little burgh, built mostly of the same red stone as the harbour, and with paler red-pantiled roofs. Many of the old fishermen's houses are of two storeys, with an outside staircase or forestair; the ground floor was used as a workshop and for net storage, while the family lived above. The large Tolbooth with its gilded salmon

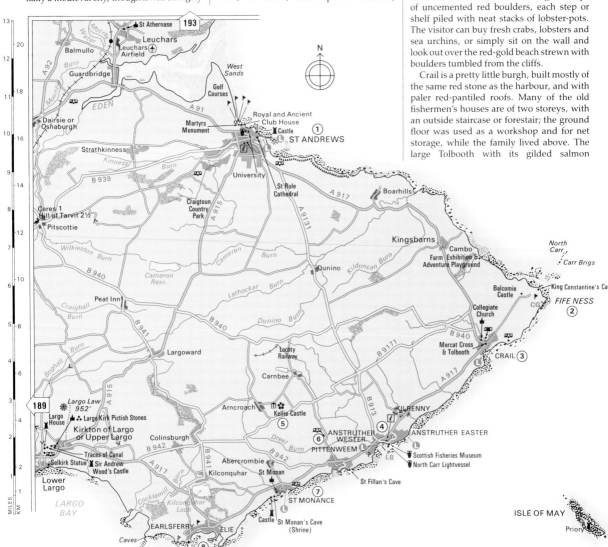

ST ANDREWS CASTLE *When the castle on its clifftop had outlived its usefulness in the 16th century many of its stones were removed for building material, but some 13th-century parts remain.*

THE ROYAL AND ANCIENT

The origins of golf, Scotland's great contribution to the world of sport, are obscure; but similar games were played on the Continent in medieval times, and the word golf may come from the Dutch *kolf*, meaning 'club'. All the Stuart monarchs played golf, and James I introduced it to England. In 1754 the first written rules for golf were drawn up by the Society of St Andrews Golfers, which in 1834 became the Royal and Ancient Golf Club. In 1897 the 'Royal and Ancient' became recognised as the controlling authority of the game.

The Royal and Ancient Golf Club at St Andrews is the supreme authority in golfing matters the world over.

weather-vane reflects the town's 17th-century prosperity that wilted under a savage attack of plague, never quite to return. The church dates partly from the 12th century, and contains an early Pictish cross. A museum in Marketgate, open daily in summer, outlines the history and heritage of Crail and the surrounding area.

④ ANSTRUTHER (Easter and Wester)

Until the Second World War, 'Anster', as it is known locally, was a fishing port, but nowadays its chief attraction for visitors is the Scottish Fisheries Museum. It is housed in a gathering of old town and ecclesiastical buildings, one of which dates back to the 16th century, and embraces the entire history of the fisheries and fisherfolk.

Inside the harbour is the North Carr lightvessel, removed from its station on Carr Brigs off Fife Ness in 1976, and now a maritime museum. Close by is the herring drifter *Reaper*, with her giant masts; she was launched in 1900.

The towering cliffs of the Isle of May loom offshore, surmounted by lighthouses like candles on a cake. It has a ruined priory built over the grave of St Adrian, murdered by the Danes in 870, and the island is a reserve for coastal and migratory birds.

⑤ KELLIE CASTLE

Dating back in part to the 13th century, Kellie Castle stands in the middle of rich, black-earth countryside rolling out to low, olive-green hills. Its record of owners reflects the ups and downs of Scottish history. The Earls of Kellie, for example, lost the castle, regained it, and lost it again down the centuries due to their adherence to the Stuart cause. Its state of preservation is largely due to the Lorimers, a talented family of architects and sculptors who, since 1875, have devoted themselves to restoring the old house, which now belongs to the National Trust for Scotland. The plasterwork, paintings and furniture are superb, and the walled garden, also restored, is a gracious place to saunter in.

⑥ PITTENWEEM

The crow-stepped gables of this toughly handsome Fife fishing port rise steeply above a great double harbour. The rough stone harbour walls – 10 ft across and more – are festooned with orange and green nets being repaired and spliced by fishermen. In the late afternoon the boats manoeuvre up to the fish market where visitors can buy codlings, flatfish, crabs and lobsters straight from the holds.

Pittenweem has its own saint, St Fillan, a 7th-century missionary. He must have been a man of some fortitude, for he used a cave as his chapel, and lived there too, sleeping on a stone shelf and drinking icy water from a little spring. Much later, Augustinians built a priory on the hill above the shrine and drove a flight of steps into it through the rock; later still, the cave was used as a smugglers' den and as a store-room.

In 1933, the Rector cleared the cave of centuries of debris and had it re-dedicated to St Fillan, whose spring, stone couch and chapel carved by water out of the rock can still be seen. It is cold and still in the cave, yet it conveys a very real sense of the serenity and power of the early church in Scotland. Pittenweem means 'the place of the cave'.

⑦ ST MONANCE

The busy, workaday harbour of St Monance and its climbing, curving streets of stone, red-pantiled houses are the very essence of old Fife. However, the burgh's principal business is not fishing or tourism, but boat-building and repairing, and on the slipways at the end of the little harbour there are usually a couple of fishing boats stripped down to their skeletons.

St Monance is named after St Monan, the slight remains of whose cave or shrine are visible near the church. This was built by David II in about 1370, in thanksgiving for being cured of an arrow wound at the shrine. The lovely, massively walled building is dark pink stone without and high, white and airy within. It contains a number of objects linked to the history of the town, including a model of a 100-gun man-o'-war donated by a local naval officer out of the prize money he had gained during the Napoleonic Wars, and a memorial to 37 St Monance fishermen who lost their lives in a storm in 1875.

⑧ ELIE AND EARLSFERRY

The old fishing port of Elie, and Earlsferry, a market town 'old past the memory of man' – according to James VI – have long been united into a single burgh devoted to entertaining the visitor with red-gold beaches, bowls and two magnificent golf courses. The largest building is the battlemented and towered Golf Hotel, but for the most part the burgh consists of low, crow-stepped stone houses, some washed white or pink, looking out to Bass Rock and North Berwick Law, with bulk carriers riding at anchor in the foreground.

An embracing view of the gentle town and its natural harbour is obtained from Chapel Ness, where there are slight remains of a chapel built in 1093 by the Earl of Fife to serve pilgrims to St Andrews. A little to the west is Kincraig Point, one of the volcanic plugs that abound in the area; one of the caves beneath it is said to have sheltered MacDuff from the wrath of Macbeth.

LOCAL INFORMATION

Tourist information Anstruther 310628; St Andrews 72021.

HM Coastguard Crail 50666 for information, 999 in emergency (ask for coastguard).

Weather Dundee 8091.

Local radio IBA Radio Tay, 258 m, 1161 kHz, 95.8 MHz.

PLACES TO SEE INLAND

Craigtoun Country Park, 2 miles SW of St Andrews. Daily.

Fife Folk Museum, Ceres, 7 miles W of St Andrews. Domestic and agricultural equipment. Most afternoons in summer.

Hill of Tarvit (NTS), 9 miles W of St Andrews. 17th-century mansion. Most afternoons in summer, gardens daily all year.

Lochty Railway, 6 miles S of St Andrews, off A915. Restored steam railway. Sun. afternoons in summer.

CRAIL HARBOUR *Crow-stepped gables, a peculiarly Scottish architectural feature, add a distinctive touch to Crail's harbourside.*

Towns beside the Firth of Tay that ring in Scottish history

The country about the Tay is certainly not of the Highlands, but it is not quite Lowland either. Even though the Carse of Gowrie is a gentle and fertile plain, it is backed by the dark swell of the Sidlaw Hills. So it is a fitting setting for the beginnings of Scottish nationhood – for abbeys and palaces, for struggles for political and religious freedom, for kings and heroes and for tales of high courage and desperate treasons.

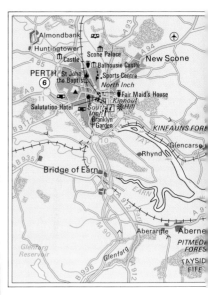

① LEUCHARS

Anywhere in the village the thunder of the jets taking off from RAF Leuchars comes up through the soles of the feet and rattles the teeth, and aircrew in bright overalls move purposefully about their business.

Serene above it all stands the church of St Athernase, one of the loveliest Norman parish churches in Scotland. It was built by a Crusader, Saier de Quinci, at the beginning of the 13th century, and much of the exterior, the arcades, arches and great rounded apse remain as the masons left them 700 years ago; indeed the marks of their axes on the stone can still be seen. The interior is carved with grotesque heads and Crusaders' crosses, but is otherwise very plain; among the few monuments is a charming one to 'ane lantern brycht', Sir William Bruce, who fought at Flodden and died in 1584, having built the nearby manor of Earlshall. The manor still stands.

St Athernase Church, Leuchars

② TAYPORT

Once the ferry port for Dundee, Tayport declined with the opening of the Tay Bridge, but it is still a pleasant, busy place with a harbour for yachts and small coasters. Offshore is a beacon light called The Pile, and beyond, on the other side of the Tay, is Broughty Ferry, with its great, solid block of a castle. Tayport's church of Ferry-Port-en-Craig is chiefly famed for its 17th-century tower, which has a distinct list to one side.

To the south-east lie the dark miles of Tentsmuir Forest, part of which is a nature reserve. The Forestry Commission has driven rides through the conifers, and established a parking and picnic place on the coast beyond the forest. Morton Lochs, just south of Tayport, are an important stopping-off point for migratory birds.

③ NEWPORT-ON-TAY

Regency and Victorian stone houses, ornamental and plain, recall the days when Newport was a harbour and ferry port for Dundee, where many businessmen built their villas. The town is still a popular residential area, and the villas are lovingly preserved. There are marvellous views of the delicately slim road bridge, completed in 1966, which put the 800-year-old Newport ferry out of business.

Wormit, 2 miles west, is the southern end of the even more majestic railway bridge, built in 1887. The piles breaking the surface all the way across are all that is left of an earlier bridge: whose central span fell into the river during a violent storm in December 1879, taking with it an engine, six coaches and 75 passengers and crew. A court of inquiry found that the bridge had been badly designed, badly constructed and badly maintained, and laid the blame upon its engineer, Sir Thomas Bouch. But what happened at the exact moment of disaster will never be known.

④ BALMERINO ABBEY

Beautifully situated on a hilltop, the fragile remains of the abbey look over the pale-streaked pewter of the Tay to the farmlands of the Carse of Gowrie and the backdrop of the Sidlaw Hills. The abbey was founded in 1299 as a daughter house of Melrose Abbey by Alexander III and his mother Queen Ermyngarde, who was buried there; it was brutally sacked by an English raiding party under Sir Thomas Wyndham in 1547, repaired, then sacked again at the Reformation.

The attractive grounds contain a venerable Spanish chestnut whose writhing boughs are supported on props. It is said that the tree was planted by Queen Ermyngarde at the abbey's founding in 1299, but borings into the trunk suggest that it is no more than 425 years old.

⑤ NEWBURGH

The town named by Edward III in 1266 rises up craggy Ormiston Hill and looks down on the head of the Firth of Tay, and to mud-flats that bear such names as Carthagena, Peesweep and Sure as Death. These are important bird sanctuaries, while MacDuff's Cross, an ancient monument south of the town, was, in the Middle Ages, a sanctuary for murderers. An assassin could expiate his crime by touching the cross, washing himself nine times in nearby Nine Wells and offering as recompense nine cows, which had to be tied to the cross.

The royal burgh grew up around Lindores Abbey, whose substantial red ruins may be seen at the eastern outskirts. Endowed by kings, it contains several royal graves, and was the headquarters in Scotland of the Inquisition; trials for heresy held there frequently concluded with the accused being sentenced to the stake.

The country about Newburgh is soothing and serene, with steep green straths sweeping up to apparently sculpted crags and gracious woods.

⑥ PERTH

Much of what the world knows about Scotland seems to have taken place in and around Perth, and the characters and events

that the city and its surroundings knew are like a pageant of the nation's story. Macbeth, Robert Bruce, Mary of Guise, John Knox, Charles II, Montrose, Cromwell, Prince Charles Edward and the Fair Maid are all players in the pageant, which includes seven sieges, the theft of the Stone of Scone, the clan battle on the North Inch, the murder of James I, the Ruthven Raid and the Gowrie Conspiracy.

When a French knight stormed Perth's walls at Robert Bruce's side, he thought the place 'a mean hamlet', but that was a long time ago, and nowadays the inhabitants tend to refer to it as 'The Fair City'. Its setting by the two road bridges over the swift-flowing Tay is certainly fair, but the city itself, laid out on a grid plan that might follow that of a Roman encampment, is better described as an attractive jumble of periods and styles. There is not much left of medieval Perth – only the old town water-mill, presented by Robert Bruce and now a hotel, and the church of St John the Baptist. It was there in 1559 that John Knox preached his sermon on idolatry, so sparking off a wave of church-wrecking that engulfed the nation; the first casualty was the interior of St John's. Montrose used the building as an arsenal, and Prince Charles Edward, who was staying in Room 20 at the Salutation Hotel, attended a service in the church in 1745.

PLACE OF KINGS *More than 40 kings have been crowned at Scone, including Robert Bruce in 1306 and his son, David II, in 1329.*

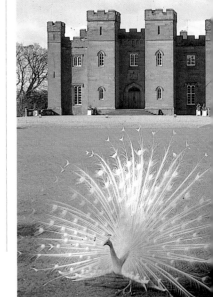

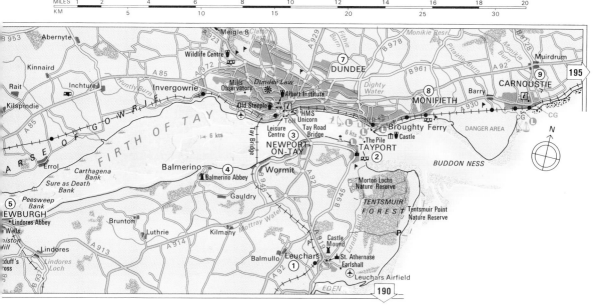

The house of Catherine Glover – the Fair Maid of Perth – looks ancient, but has been much restored and is now a craft shop. A characteristic feature of old Perth is the vennels – Salt Vennel, Meal Vennel, Baker's Vennel and so on – the little streets that run between the main thoroughfares and add a touch of Scots medieval to the largely Georgian and Victorian scene. The word comes from the French *venelle*, 'alley', and occurs only in one other Scottish town, Dumfries.

Perth's green places include the walk up Kinnoull Hill to its folly tower and views over symmetrical crags and steep-piled hanging woods to a rich, smiling landscape, and the walk to the North and South Inches, the riverside meadows that border Perth itself. The North Inch has one of the finest sports centres in the country.

Scone Palace, 5 miles north of Perth, is the home of the Earl of Mansfield and a joy to visit; so too are its magnificently landscaped grounds. The mound near the house is Moot Hill, the heart of the Kingdom of the Picts, and later the place where Scottish kings were crowned, seated upon the Stone of Scone, or Stone of Destiny, said to be the stone on which Jacob rested his head at Bethel. The stone was taken to London by Edward I in 1296 and is now incorporated in the Coronation Chair in Westminster Abbey.

(7) DUNDEE

Jute, jam and journalism are Dundee's traditional exports; marmalade and comics are still doing well, but jute is no longer what it was. But this bright, busy city has always prided itself on its versatility, and now it makes many other products as well. With its broad streets, shopping precincts and fine modern buildings, it hardly looks like one of the oldest royal burghs in Scotland, but so it is, with more than its share of battles, and of great men, too. George Wishart, the religious reformer, Admiral Duncan, the victor of Camperdown, and John Graham of Claverhouse, Viscount Dundee, were all natives of the city.

All Dundee and much of the country around it can be seen from the top of Dundee Law, the great plug of volcanic rock – and ancient hill-fort – that rises in the midst of the city. From there it seems that the 35 acres of docks are out of proportion to the city's size, but they were built in the days when the name of Dundee was synonymous with whaling and with steam whalers, several of which became famous as polar research ships. Scott's *Discovery* and Shackleton's *Terra Nova* were both built in Dundee. The

HILLTOP FOLLY *Kinnoull Tower, built on a rocky knoll above the Tay valley, is a 19th-century folly – the whim of the Earl of Kinnoull who had been impressed by the castles of the Rhine in Germany.*

old ship that lives permanently in the docks is not a whaler, but HMS *Unicorn*, a frigate. Launched in 1820, she is the oldest British-built warship still afloat, and now serves as a museum of the Royal Navy.

The Albert Institute is Dundee's principal museum and art gallery, and the Mills Observatory in Balgay Park is the only public astronomical observatory in Britain. There is a small museum of the city in the 16th-century Old Steeple; it was there in 1651 that the burghers of Dundee made their last stand against the troops of General Monk, who had besieged the city for six weeks.

Dundee also has a fine swimming and leisure centre, and, at Camperdown Park, a golf course, wildlife centre and nature trail. Broughty Ferry, an eastern suburb of Dundee, has a busy harbour with a slipway; sea-fishing trips can be arranged, and fishing from the pier is permitted. Broughty Castle was a military establishment and a coastal strongpoint from 1547 to 1945. It was held by an English garrison against a combined force of Scots and French, and was later stormed by Cromwell.

(8) MONIFIETH

This straggling village offers few points of access to the sea. But it has a caravan site just behind the shore, which consists of dunes knitted together by marram grass. Erosion has made the coast path dangerous. There is an attractive golf course whose roughs look impenetrable.

(9) CARNOUSTIE

The rather bland little town guards some of golf's greatest treasures – the Championship, Burnside and Buddon Links of the Carnoustie Golf Club, whose wide and serene acres have given joy and despair to the game's greatest personalities for almost a century and a half.

The Yachting Club welcomes new members and has a useful dinghy park.

LOCAL INFORMATION

Tourist information St Andrews 72021; Perth 22900; Dundee 27723; Carnoustie 52258.

HM Coastguard Crail 50666 for information, 999 in emergency (ask for coastguard).

Weather Dundee 8091.

Local radio IBA Radio Tay, 258 m, 1161 kHz, 95.8 MHz.

PLACES TO SEE INLAND

Branklyn Garden (NTS), Perth. Rare plants from all over the world. Daily in summer.

Huntingtower Castle, 3 miles NW of Perth. 15th-century mansion. Daily.

Meigle Museum, 13 miles NW of Dundee. Celtic Christian carved stones. Daily except Sun.

Beaches below sandstone cliffs and 'smokies' for the table

The beaches at St Cyrus, Montrose and Lunan Bay are among the best on Scotland's east coast. Elsewhere the waves have cut small coves from the sheer sandstone walls, and secluded crescents of rock and shingle await the adventurous explorer at the foot of narrow, ill-defined tracks. Coastal paths range from quiet lowland walks to tough clifftop trails, and nature reserves protect miles of marshlands, dunes and cliffs, all alive with sea-birds.

MONTROSE BAY *Below the headland of Milton Ness, grassy cliffs slope down to a rock-studded strand that stretches for 6 miles, broken only by the mouth of the North Esk River.*

① FOWLSHEUGH BIRD RESERVE
From Crawton – a largely abandoned village from whose shores fingers of dark lava reach out to sea – a path leads into the RSPB's Fowlsheugh Bird Reserve, one of the country's greatest sea-bird colonies. It consists of 2 miles of vertiginous cliffs – *heugh* means 'cliff' in the local dialect. The path is not well marked, and there are no barriers. Visitors may find the sight, the sound and in particular the smell of the thousands of birds almost overwhelming. In the breeding season, from March to July, there may be up to 30,000 pairs of guillemots and another 30,000 pairs of kittiwakes. There are also razorbills, herring gulls, fulmars, shags, puffins and eiders.

② CATTERLINE
Lines of cottages along the clifftop face the sea above a bay that is a tangle of crags and rocks. The picturesque setting has made the village popular with artists. A road leads steeply down to the bay, where there is a concrete pier. A scramble over the pudding-stone rocks to the north leads to Trelong Bay, an isolated spot where fulmars, kittiwakes, herring gulls and puffins wheel over grass-covered cliffs. A path leads along the clifftop for 1½ miles to Crawton.

③ INVERBERVIE
The small town of 'Bervie', as it is known locally, has grown in recent years as the result of recent influxes of commuters from Aberdeen. It has no harbour, but a seafood factory and jute mill employ local labour.

Inverbervie has a long history. It was granted a charter in 1341 by David II when he and his wife, Johanna, made a forced landing there on their return from nine years of exile in France. His ship was driven ashore in a storm after escaping from the English fleet. A rock known as 'King's Step' is said to mark the exact spot of his landing.

④ GOURDON
An amphitheatre of steep grassy cliffs encloses the village. There is a spinning-mill, and a dozen fishing vessels work from the harbour, in which there is sand at low tide. Boats can be hired for angling.

⑤ JOHNSHAVEN
This bustling lobster-fishing port has a two-basin harbour, a lobster processing plant and numerous holiday homes. For walkers, a major attraction is a 4 mile coastal path that runs north to Inverbervie along the track of the former Montrose to Inverbervie railway.

⑥ MILTON OF MATHERS
Ruined cottages stand side by side with the chalets of a new holiday village. The beach, which is mostly of pebble and rock, is good for swimming only between the rocks, but the slopes behind the village are fine for walking. The woods are cut through by two streams. The northern stream, which tumbles down a 40 ft waterfall, is known as Den Finella after a 10th-century queen who, according to legend, murdered her husband, King Kenneth, and then threw herself from the top of the waterfall.

⑦ ST CYRUS NATURE RESERVE
More than 300 varieties of wild flowers, including clustered bellflower and wild liquorice, have been recorded in the national nature reserve which occupies 3 miles of coastline from the mouth of the North Esk to the headland of Milton Ness. From an open, marshy expanse by the river mouth, the reserve narrows northwards as the inland hills approach nearer to the sea, becoming lava cliffs beyond St Cyrus.

The reserve can be entered at several points. At the bend in the side road leading from the A92 via Nether Warburton, where cars can park, a boardwalk leads away from a line of cottages for a few hundred yards over salt-marshes to the dunes. The main entry point is St Cyrus itself; from the car park a paved path leads along the clifftop, with fine views southwards across the bay.

⑧ MONTROSE
For holidaymakers, the Links of Montrose that lead north for 4 miles from the town offer immense sandy beaches backed by dunes. The beach is supervised by beach wardens during July and August. Behind the dunes lie two 18-hole golf courses. Bathing is safe, except near the mouths of the North Esk and South Esk.

Montrose's situation at the mouth of the South Esk has made it a thriving port, and new docks have been built to service the North Sea oil industry. Scurdie Ness lighthouse, accessible by a single-track road, is closed, but due to re-open in 1988.

Inland, the shallow Montrose Basin, which drains completely at low tide to form a mud plain of some 3 square miles, a nature reserve which attracts thousands of wild-fowl including, in winter, pink-footed Arctic geese.

⑨ FISHTOWN OF USAN
Two lines of ruined cottages flank an old lookout tower that once housed a lifeboat. The beach is shingle, with huge expanses of low-tide rock cut by an inlet used as a mooring for local boats.

⑩ BODDIN POINT
On this low-lying point, visitors can park to admire a fine view across the bay. Cod and lobster are still caught offshore, but some of the fishing cottages by the shore are abandoned. Low tide reveals seaweed-covered rocks and shingle on which agates can be found. The fortress-like structure on the tip of the point is a lime-kiln once used to prepare fertiliser for the surrounding farm land.

A quarter of a mile along a coastal path is Elephant Rock, a red-sandstone stack in which the sea has carved 'legs' and a 'trunk'.

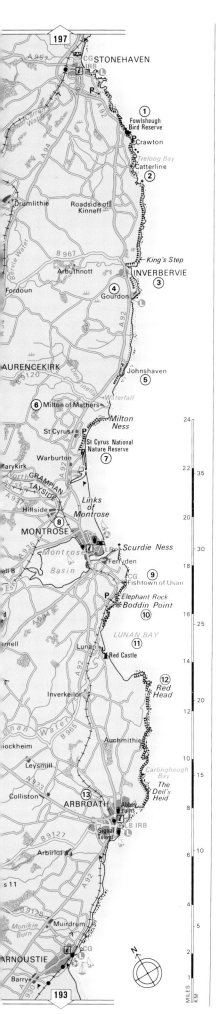

⑪ LUNAN BAY

The shady sweep of the bay, punctuated here and there by salmon nets set out on posts to dry, is cut in two by the serpentine Lunan Water and dominated by the nearby hilltop ruin of Red Castle. The castle, once owned by Robert Bruce, was in good repair until 1770 but is now starkly open to the sky. Its walls, built of the soft local sandstone from Red Head, are badly eroded. The shore, easily accessible from both Red Castle and Lunan, is safe for bathing except in the river mouth.

⑫ RED HEAD

The head can be reached only by a bumpy 1½ mile drive along an unpaved road, and partly for that reason it is one of the most glorious and unspoiled spots on Scotland's east coast. The 265 ft sandstone headland provides a superb view up and down the coast. Below the cliff edge, where the rock has collapsed, active visitors can scramble down a little-used path to the shore and walk for a mile in each direction over the shingle and the sandstone rocks that have fallen from the cliffs above.

⑬ ARBROATH

Handwritten signs throughout Arbroath advertise the locally made 'smokies' for which the fishing town is noted. To make them, freshly caught, cleaned and salted haddocks are smoked over a hardwood chip fire – and visitors are soon aware of the rich smell of smouldering wood drifting from the buildings near the harbour.

The town is dominated by the well-preserved ruins of its abbey, which was founded in the late 12th century by William, King of the Scots. William was an admirer of Thomas Becket, and as a tribute to Becket after his murder in Canterbury in 1170 he based his design for Arbroath Abbey on the towering Gothic style of Canterbury Cathedral. The abbey has a central place in the history of Scottish nationalism: in 1320, when Robert Bruce was trying to unify Scotland against the English, the Scottish nobles gathered at the abbey to sign the Declaration of Arbroath, asserting Scotland's independence.

The abbey was dissolved in 1608 and fell into decay; but its underlying significance to Scots was emphasised as recently as 1951 when the Stone of Scone, taken from

Westminster Abbey, was eventually found on the high altar at Arbroath. Today trim lawns replace the ancient floors, between the roofless red-sandstone walls. A museum recalls the abbey's history, and visitors can buy copies of the Declaration of Arbroath.

Overlooking the harbour, busy with fishing vessels, is the Signal Tower, another museum that recalls the burgh's history. The tower was built in the early 19th century to communicate with a lighthouse, the Bell Rock, which stands 11 miles offshore, warning ships to keep clear of the notorious Inchcape Reef. This reef, which claimed countless ships before the lighthouse was built, is the subject of Robert Southey's poem *The Inchcape Rock*, which tells of the feud between Arbroath's abbot and a wrecker named Ralph the Rover.

To the east the town has a broad esplanade with acres of grass and ample parking. From its northern end, a paved path designed as a nature trail leads along the clifftops. The path follows the cliffs – a superb, convoluted wall of red sandstone – for 3 miles through vegetation that combines coastal and inland species. Sea plantain and scurvy grass grow alongside red campion and wood vetch.

Halfway along the trail is a rock-stack known variously as The Deil's Heid, the Pint Stoup and The Poll – one of many oddly shaped rocks that puncture the shore. At the trail's northernmost point, in Carlingheugh Bay, is a cave that leads clear through a rocky point to the neighbouring bay; before venturing through the cave visitors should check the state of the tide to avoid the risk of being cut off.

LOCAL INFORMATION

Tourist information Arbroath 72609, 76680; Montrose 72000.

HM Coastguard Crail 50666 for information, 999 in emergency (ask for coastguard).

Weather Aberdeen 8091.

Local radio IBA Radio Tay, Dundee area, 258 m, 1161 kHz, 95.8 MHz.

PLACES TO SEE INLAND

Angus Folk Museum (NTS), Glamis, 16 miles W of Arbroath, via A94. Daily in summer.

Edzell Castle and Gardens, 10 miles NW of Montrose, via B966. 16th century. Daily.

Glamis Castle, 16 miles W of Arbroath, via A94. 17th century. Most afternoons in summer.

HARBOUR TRADE *Fishing vessels and the lifeboat are the main users of Arbroath harbour, which dates from 1795 and once exported grain, salt and paving stones.*

Sea-girt castle on a crag near Aberdeen, the 'granite city'

North of Aberdeen, glowing sands carried from the Cairngorms by the River Dee have been spread along the coast to form a 10 mile swathe of beaches and dunes. To the south, by contrast, ancient cliffs are cut by little bays almost totally devoid of sand. Tiny villages, robbed of their former fishing industries by Aberdeen, have been revitalised by commuters from the same city, a centre of the North Sea oil industry.

① BALMEDIE

One of Britain's most extensive sandy beaches stretches from the River Ythan for 10 miles southwards in a scarcely perceptible curve down to the River Don on Aberdeen's northern boundary. The sands are so huge that they are never crowded. Swimming is safe all along the beach, and a section near Balmedie is marked with flags and patrolled by lifeguards.

The beach is backed by extensive dunes. The sand is fine and easily blown by the wind, and the younger dunes nearer the sea shift constantly. At one point just north of the car park at Balmedie a section of young dunes has been blasted inland by the wind, drowning older established dunes and forming a miniature Sahara Desert. Older dunes further inland are anchored by coarse grasses such as marram and lyme, while further inland still the dunes have a permanent covering of herbs, grasses and flowers. Visitors are requested not to disturb the patches where new grass has been planted. A dozen burns cross the sands, where some 60 species of plants and 50 common bird species have been recorded. Shells, too, are plentiful on the beach.

There are few roads to the beach. The major access point is at Balmedie itself, where car parks and boardwalks (which are suitable for wheelchairs) lead over the dunes to the beach. There are occasional conducted walks through the area, advertised locally and starting from the car park at 2 p.m. Another access point is Blackdog, a little-used spot just south of a rifle-range, where red flags are raised when firing is in progress. An unpaved road ends at a tip, from which a path leads to the deserted beach.

② ABERDEEN

North Sea oil gave Aberdeen the greatest boom in its history. When oil prospers, the city's docks teem with vessels serving the needs of the industry, and helicopters thump back and forth between Dyce Airport and the rigs. Bustle is no new feature of Aberdeen's life, however, for the city has long been a major seaside resort and one of Britain's largest fishing ports. The fish market comes to life at 4 a.m., with sales starting at 7.30 a.m. Merchant vessels handling cargoes from potash to granite use Aberdeen harbour; quayside roads and two bridges provide vantage points for watching the busy scene at the mouth of the Dee.

Union Street, a mile of shops, offices, banks and restaurants built in the 19th century, gives Aberdeen a fine centrepiece. Much of the city is built of granite blasted from the immense Rubislaw quarry 2 miles west of the city centre. Flecks of mica make the silver-grey granite glitter in the sunlight, providing a good framework for the glorious displays of roses and tulips that light up the roadsides for eight or nine months of the year. The city has several times won the Britain in Bloom competition.

Modern Aberdeen contrasts with the little enclave of Footdee, pronounced 'Fittie' locally, that guards the northern shore of the harbour entrance. The huddle of little grey buildings was designed as a model village in the early 19th century, with the help of the fishermen themselves.

Northwards from Footdee runs the esplanade, an extensive shoreline recreational area. The long beach, divided by groynes, is backed by an open area with a fairground, playground and golf course. At the northern end of the esplanade, the River Don swings under the Bridge of Don. The river, with its sandy banks, is a popular place for fishing for flounders, eels and mackerel; but swimming in the fast current is not advisable.

Aberdeen's other attractions include 3,000 acres of park, including Hazlehead, where there are a golf course, maze and zoo. Among the museums, art galleries and concert halls are Aberdeen University's Museum of Anthropology, and Provost Skene's House, which re-creates everyday life in former centuries. South of the Dee stands the Girdle Ness lighthouse, designed by Robert Stevenson, grandfather of the author R. L. Stevenson.

③ ALTENS HAVEN

South of Nigg Bay, a footpath that can also be used as a cycle track follows a switchback course for 2 miles above a string of cliffs and rocky coves. The isolated Altens Haven is reached by scrambling down a steep track from an abandoned fisherman's house, or bothy. The clifftop footpath continues southwards, but stops short of Cove Bay.

④ COVE BAY

The road descends from the village to a picturesque harbour tucked into the lee of cliffs. Boats are pulled up on the shingle shore. A good-sized quay, with salmon nets drying on poles, makes the harbour doubly secure against high seas.

⑤ FINDON

The local pronunciation of this tiny village gave its name to Finnan Haddies, a lightly smoked haddock. In the 19th century, the Factory Act forbade the traditional method of smoking haddocks over open cottage fires, and the village almost died when the smokehouses of Aberdeen took over the industry. The village is now a commuter area for Aberdeen.

Access to the shore from the village is not easy. A road leads down to a fish-farming research station, but there is no parking. Walkers may follow a path through the station to two rocky coves and on round the cliffs to Portlethen.

⑥ PORTLETHEN VILLAGE

A steep road leads down to a small cove hemmed in by cliffs. Portlethen was once a

JOURNEY'S END *Stuck fast on Balmedie beach, this coastal vessel is one of several that have ventured close to the shore and have paid the penalty on the shifting, unremitting sands.*

DUNNOTTAR CASTLE *This spectacular maze of walls, courtyards and towers stands 160 ft above the sea on a flat-topped rock that forms a natural citadel, severed from the mainland cliffs.*

busy fishing village where boats were launched from the shingle beach, but the local fishermen were unable to compete with the large trawler fleets of Aberdeen and Peterhead and the village is now the hub of a new community for people working in Aberdeen.

⑦ DOWNIES

A road from the tiny hamlet of Downies comes to a dead end near the clifftop, with parking space for two cars. A superb short walk leads on to hillocks that give fine views over the rock-girt Cammachmore Bay. A steep rough track leads down to the cove.

⑧ NEWTONHILL

A steep road leads down to a good-sized bay, with three fisherman's bothies, where the Burn of Elsick gushes into the sea over a shingle foreshore.

A breakwater built when the village was a busy fishing port has been removed, and its stones set on the hillside above.

⑨ MUCHALLS

From the charming, white-painted village, which dates mainly from the 19th century, a road leads downhill under the railway to a dramatic foreshore: a scattering of bays and grass-covered pinnacles linked by a path. There is a fine view northwards along the coast which has spectacular rock formations, including stacks and deep caverns.

Muchalls Castle, set back from the village up an unpaved road signposted from the A92, is a fine example of Scottish architecture of the 17th century. It is noted for the plasterwork in the Great Hall which bears the coat-of-arms of the Burnett family. A tunnel once led from the castle to a smugglers' cove known as Gin Shore; it was blocked in the 19th century. The castle is open on occasional days in summer.

⑩ SKATIE SHORE

At the point where the A92 turns inland, close to the railway, a turning east down a small track leads to a golf course, which is bisected by a ravine. The ravine opens on to two pebbly coves, hidden by grassy cliffs from the golf course above.

A path leads on beside the golf course for 2 miles to Stonehaven, with glorious views over the rolling clifftop scenery and Stonehaven Bay.

⑪ STONEHAVEN

The northern end of Stonehaven is devoted to entertaining the holidaymaker, with a caravan site, amusement park, swimming pool and fine open beach. To the south is the Old Town, with its ancient and picturesque two-basin harbour. The Old Town retains the bustle, charm and intimacy of an old-fashioned fishing village, with boats packing a quayside crowded with lobster-pots and fishing gear.

The oldest building in the Old Town is the 16th-century Tolbooth, now a museum containing relics of local archaeology and history. The Tolbooth was the scene of a celebrated local incident in 1748 when three Episcopal clergymen were accused of breaking laws established after the English victory at Culloden, according to which Scottish

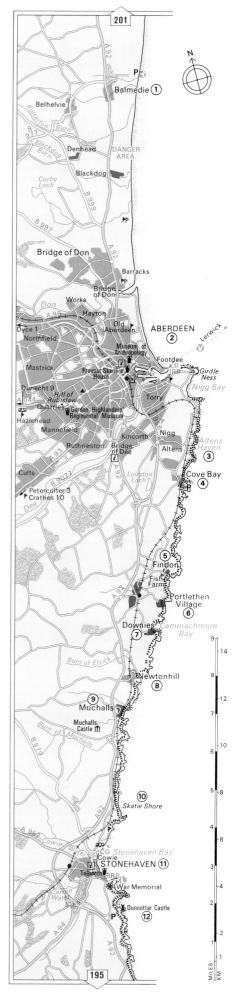

ministers were not allowed to hold services for more than five people. When the ministers were imprisoned in the Tolbooth, mothers smuggled new-born babies up to the prison window so that they could be baptised through it.

A walk along the promenade to the north leads to the village of Cowie, with its own small harbour. An earlier village on the site, said to have been created a Royal Burgh by David I, was destroyed by fire in 1645 on the orders of the Duke of Montrose, a Royalist supporter during the Civil War.

On the hill above Stonehaven to the south stands a war memorial which offers one of the best views in the area – an all-round panorama of Stonehaven, the adjoining coast and the hills inland. The war memorial, accessible by footpath from the A92, is a circle of pillars and pediments – but it is unfinished, symbolic of the unfinished lives it commemorates.

⑫ DUNNOTTAR CASTLE

The rock on which Dunnottar Castle stands was fortified from the 5th century, when it was a base for one of the earliest missionaries, St Ninian. The present castle was built up from a 14th-century structure, and played a role in Scottish history on several occasions. In 1645 the 7th Earl Marischal of Scotland, a Covenanter, retreated to the castle on the approach of a Royalist army led by the Duke of Montrose. The earl refused to parley with Montrose, who wreaked terrible revenge by burning all the earl's lands.

Another dramatic incident in the castle's history occurred in 1651 when Cromwell's Roundheads were besieging the castle to wrest from it the Scottish Crown Jewels, which had been put there for safe keeping. The regalia, however, were secretly lowered over the walls to a fishwife, who smuggled them in a basket past the surrounding Roundheads to Kinneff Church, 6 miles to the south.

In 1685, during Monmouth's rebellion, 122 men and 45 women were taken prisoner in the castle and herded into a gloomy cellar only 15 ft by 51 ft, known as the Whigs Vault. There they remained for several months, and many died. The vault survives largely unchanged, a dank and sinister place with algae on its semi-circular roof.

The castle fell into decay in the 18th century, but has been partially restored this century and now forms a dramatic tourist attraction. There is a spectacular approach from the mainland down the cliff and across the beach before rising again to the castle. A spine of stone once connected the castle rock to the mainland, but this was cut through by the castle's defenders for added protection. Inside, the store-rooms, kitchens, armouries and central keep, all clearly labelled, reveal that the castle was more like a fortified village than a single building.

LOCAL INFORMATION

Tourist information Aberdeen 632727; Stonehaven 62806 (summer).

HM Coastguard Aberdeen 592275 for information, 999 in emergency (ask for coastguard).

Weather Aberdeen 8091.

Local radio IBA North Sound, 290 m, 1035 kHz, 96.9 MHz.

PLACES TO SEE INLAND

Crathes Castle and Gardens (NTS), 15 miles W of Aberdeen. 16th-century baronial castle, with gardens. Daily in summer, gardens all year.

Castle Fraser (NTS), near Dunecht, 16 miles W of Aberdeen, off A944. 16th-17th century. Afternoons in summer.

Drum Castle (NTS), near Peterculter, 10 miles W of Aberdeen. 13th-17th century mansion. Afternoons in summer.

OIL 'ISLANDS' THAT CREATED A BOOM ON THE SCOTTISH COAST

Far out in the North Sea, giant man-made islands tower above the waves on iron legs, and from their decks men probe the sea-bed for the most precious commodity of the modern industrial age – oil. In less than a decade the green waters that were once only the lonely province of deep-sea trawlers became home to a new industry that brought new prosperity to north-east Scotland. Ports along the coast, hit by the declining fishing industry, were now supply depots for the oil rigs, with Aberdeen the 'capital' of this vast enterprise and the exploration headquarters of many firms. A large part of Aberdeen's harbour was adapted to meet the needs of the supply and service vessels that shuttle to and fro between the mainland and the rigs, making thousands of trips a year, and the air lanes out of Aberdeen Airport are the busiest in Britain after Heathrow.

Since 1971, when oil was first discovered under the North Sea, more than 20 oil platforms have gone 'on stream', pumping oil by pipeline to the mainland or directly into tankers; and the search for oil goes on, with numerous drilling platforms sinking new wells. Out in some of the most treacherous waters in the world, platforms may have to withstand winds of 120 mph and the pounding of 100 ft waves. To build them, fabrication yards were established at sites such as Nigg Bay on the Cromarty Firth, Ardersier on the Moray Firth, Methil on the Firth of Forth and Loch Kishorn on the west coast, where there is space and deep enough water to float and manoeuvre the massive structures.

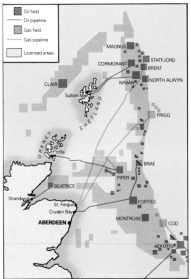

WHERE THEY ARE *From a point east of Edinburgh northwards to beyond the Shetlands the oil fields are strung out across the North Sea, following the strata of sedimentary rock below the sea-bed that holds the crude oil like a giant sponge. Each field consists of a platform or a group of platforms, equipped to drill and produce oil and in some cases natural gas. Some platforms pump the oil direct to another platform where it is stored. From there it may be fed to floating mooring points to be loaded into tankers, or it may be pumped to terminals ashore.*

At Sullom Voe in the Shetlands oil is received from Brent, one of the largest fields, where liquid gas (LPG) is separated from the oil and both products are loaded into tankers at the terminal's jetties. Natural gas is pumped from Brent direct to a gas terminal at St Fergus.

CONCRETE ICEBERG *One of the Brent field platforms is towed to its site off the Shetlands from the Norwegian fiord where it was built. The platform when set in position on the sea-bed, with its massive superstructure complete, stands in 460 ft of water and is 824 ft tall from top to bottom – the height of a 75-storey office block. The three concrete legs are surrounded at their base by cells which give the platform buoyancy while it is being towed. The cells are used as storage tanks for the crude oil when the platform is seated on the sea-bed. The legs are hollow; two of them carry drills and pipes while the other contains pump platforms and the distribution pipes which feed the oil to the storage tanks.*

THE DRILLERS *One drill floor worker steadies the drill pipe as it is withdrawn from the sea-bed to have the drilling bit changed, while another stands by with the power tongs used to unscrew the pipe section by section.*

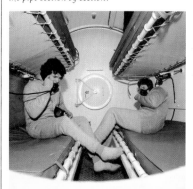

THE DIVERS *For up to 21 days at a time, teams of divers live in chambers pressurised to match the depth of the sea-bed which may be as much as 550 ft. At the end of their shift they spend up to a day in a decompression chamber.*

NERVE CENTRE *In the clinical calm of the computer room a control panel constantly measures and monitors production rates, temperatures and flow rates. The computer can also pinpoint leaks in the pipeline.*

PACKAGED FOR EFFICIENCY *The steel superstructure of an oil-production platform such as the huge Brent D Platform is made up of separate modules which fit together like a child's building toy. Power generators, oil processing and pumping units and control rooms are sandwiched beneath the main deck, which has an area of some 3,500 square yards. Above the deck is a three-storey accommodation unit for up to 200 men, a helicopter landing pad, the flare tower to burn off excess gas and the drilling derrick. As many as 40 drillings (left) may radiate from one main drillhead and descend as deep as 2 miles through water and rock. Some of the wells are used to inject water or gas back into the porous rock to force out the oil. Each platform may produce more than 100,000 barrels of oil per day: a barrel is equivalent to 36 gallons. On fields with more than one platform (below) the separate platforms are linked by pipelines before the oil is pumped to the mainland.*

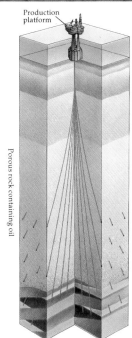

Production platform

Porous rock containing oil

Wells drilled at angles into oil 'reservoir'

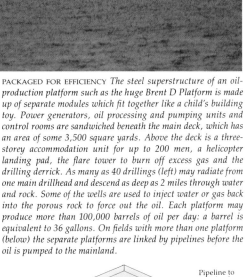

Pipeline to mainland

A 'field' of linked platforms

AIR LINK *Helicopters play a vital part in communications between the platforms and the mainland, operating a shuttle service that takes crews back and forth at the rate of thousands of men each month.*

A peaceful world of pink granite cottages and giant dunes

The oil industry has brought new wealth to this corner of the Buchan coast, without spoiling its essential character. There are fishing villages and old castles to visit, and shores where the walker can find solitude and peace broken only by the cries of millions of sea-birds. South of Peterhead there are miles of spectacular cliffs, carved into countless caves and ravines into which the waves thunder far below the grassy clifftops.

① ST COMBS

The narrow streets and compact cottages of St Combs continue into the adjoining village of Charlestown, while to north and south are clean, sandy beaches. St Combs derives its name from St Columba, and the ruins of the old parish church dedicated to him are to be seen in the graveyard overlooking the sea.

The neat rows of cottages were built in the late 18th century, but the fishermen they housed now sail from Fraserburgh, with its deeper harbour, leaving only a few small craft in St Combs.

② LOCH OF STRATHBEG

The loch, covering 550 acres, is an important breeding area for a wide range of terns, waterfowl and other birds. It is administered by the Royal Society for the Protection of Birds, and admission is by permit only, obtainable from the warden in advance.

③ RATTRAY HEAD

The headland is one of the few points accessible by car on the long strip of sandy shore that dominates this coast. Only the crumbling ruins of St Mary's Chapel mark the site of a once-flourishing community. The salting up of the harbour by the shifting dunes ended its brief existence. A castle built by the Comyn Earls of Buchan also stood on the headland, but there is nothing left of it now.

The narrow road to Rattray Head leaves the A952 half a mile east of Crimond, and twists its way to the dunes. A wide path through the dunes leads to the beach, within sight of the Rattray Head lighthouse which guards the shelving shore. Bathers should be cautious of the fast tide which rounds the head during a north-east wind.

From Rattray Head it is possible to walk along the shore to either St Combs, 5 miles to the north-west, or Inverugie, 6 miles to the south.

④ ST FERGUS

Now dominated by the great bulk of gas and oil terminals, this small village has a long history, being named after an 8th-century bishop. It provides a convenient access point to the long stretch of sandy beach that runs north from Peterhead. At the southern end of the village, take the lane signposted to Scotstown for about a mile. There is space to park there, and after crossing the dunes, the lover of solitude can walk for miles in either direction along a shore line frequented by a variety of wading birds but rarely disturbed by human beings. Visitors tempted to bathe should be wary of the strong tides.

South of St Fergus are the remains of Inverugie Castle, once the home of the Kieth family. To reach the ruins, follow the A952 for 2 miles then turn right, following the sign to Inverugie, and past the hill where the earlier Norman castle stood. The castle stands close to the road, opposite a garden centre.

⑤ PETERHEAD

Once Scotland's most important whaling port, Peterhead still maintains its strong links with the sea, both as a fishing port and as a base for the oil industry. Some 400 fishing boats operate from its harbour, and the offshore supply vessels for the oil rigs add to the activity of the harbour area.

Peterhead's huge harbour is known locally as the 'National Harbour of Refuge'; it was begun in 1886 but completed only in 1958, with the aid of prisoners from Peterhead Prison. In the north corner of the main harbour is the entrance to the smaller, inner harbour. This is a scene of almost continuous activity, and is particularly busy when the fish sales take place from 8.30 a.m. daily.

The town is clustered around the harbour and built almost entirely of pink granite quarried at nearby Boddam. In front of the severely elegant façade of the Town House is a statue of Field-Marshal James Kieth, who lived at Inverugie Castle and was one of the favourite generals of Frederick the Great. The statue was given to the town by the King of Prussia, William I. Of greater antiquity is the ruin of the pre-Reformation church of St Peter, standing among gravestones on South Road. Near by are the Kirkburn Mills, where wools and woollen cloth are produced.

The Arbuthnot Museum in St Peter Street has a display of local history, with particular relevance to the whaling industry. The community centre in Queen Street offers a wide range of recreational activities, including an indoor swimming pool. Peterhead Bay is suitable for sailing, while the River Ugie, at the northern end of the town, offers fishing for brown trout and sea trout. Beyond the Ugie estuary Craigewan beach stretches north for almost 2 miles.

SANDS OF FORVIE *Some 2,000 pairs of eider ducks are among the birds that breed on the Sands of Forvie in spring and early summer.*

OFFSHORE PERIL *A line of white water off the sand-dunes of Rattray Head marks the notorious Rattray Briggs, a reef where many ships were wrecked before the lighthouse was built in 1893.*

6 BODDAM

This granite fishing village, built above a harbour with massive cement walls, is dominated by a lighthouse that – like several in the area – was built by Robert Stevenson, grandfather of the author R. L. Stevenson. The lighthouse, dating from 1827, stands on Buchan Ness, and is linked to the mainland by a bridge. It is open most afternoons.

7 BULLERS OF BUCHAN

This tiny village huddles above a steep-walled bay. The main attraction for visitors is a second inlet that is surrounded by a gallery of rock with a narrow, grassy path leading along it. The path follows a knife-edge 100 ft above the waves, and is not a place for the nervous or for small children. At one point in the rock wall below, the sea has battered a hole and high seas turn the inlet into a 'monstrous cauldron', as Boswell described it after visiting the spot with Dr Johnson. His phrase recalls the origin of the word 'bullers', which is probably derived from 'boil'.

A footpath leads round to a second and larger bay, North Haven, which has a rocky shore with steep grass-covered banks.

8 CRUDEN BAY

The town of Cruden Bay, and its harbour, Port Erroll, are the centre of a fast-growing holiday area, with sandy beaches, dunes and a golf course.

Behind Port Erroll, overlooking the sea, is the stark and spectacular ruin of Slains Castle, which was built by the Earl of Erroll after the destruction of his previous castle, Old Slains Castle, at Mains of Slains, 5 miles to the south-west. The castle was greatly extended in the 17th century and was the centre of a tourist boom in Edwardian times, when the railway reached Cruden Bay. After the First World War, profits declined, and in 1925 the great house was partially demolished.

The fenced-off ruins, standing gauntly above equally gaunt cliffs, are the stuff of horror movies. Indeed, they may well have inspired the setting of the novel *Dracula*, whose author Bram Stoker used to holiday at Port Erroll.

9 WHINNYFOLD

A dozen cottages in four rows stand near the edge of an almost sheer grassy cliff, down which a track zigzags to a rock-and-shingle beach. A footpath leads 2 miles to Cruden Bay. A North Sea oil pipeline comes ashore near by; the pipe itself is deeply buried, but inland from Whinnyfold can be seen the grey installations where the oil is received.

10 OLD SLAINS CASTLE

The gaunt ruined tower of the Earl of Erroll's first castle stands at the end of an unpaved road, guarding nothing more today than its little headland, three houses and a gravelly beach. James VI personally supervised the destruction of the castle in 1594 after discovering that the earl was involved in a plot to land Spanish troops on the Aberdeenshire coast.

11 COLLIESTON

Neat grey cottages and grassy slopes overlooking a harbour with a broad encircling wall form a delightful little backwater. Collieston once flourished on fishing and smuggling, the contraband being hidden in the many caves that pierce the coast.

St Catharine's Dub, a rocky cove north of the village, takes its name from the Spanish galleon *Santa Caterina* which was wrecked there in 1594. There is a large car park. A footpath south of the village leads to the Sands of Forvie.

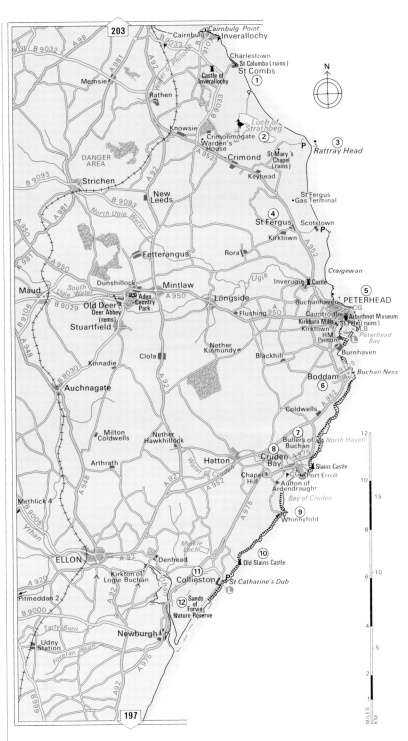

12 SANDS OF FORVIE

The Sands of Forvie National Nature Reserve is one of the largest dune systems in Britain. Some of the dunes are nearly 200 ft high and have an almost Saharan grandeur. They shift with the wind, and over the last 2,000 years have overwhelmed both Iron Age and medieval settlements. The reserve also includes the estuary of the River Ythan, which provides a source of food for huge flocks of wading birds and wintering wildfowl.

A section of the reserve is closed to visitors for part of the year, for shelduck nest in the dunes and terns breed in the estuary. Boardwalks are provided for easier walking. From a hide, visitors can watch the four species of tern that breed there: common terns, Arctic terns, little terns and Sandwich terns. The Sands also contain the largest population of breeding eiders in Britain, numbering some 2,000 pairs, and shelduck are also common.

LOCAL INFORMATION

Tourist information Ellon 20730 (summer only).

HM Coastguard Peterhead 4278 for information, 999 in emergency (ask for coastguard).

Weather Aberdeen 8091.

Local radio BBC Radio Aberdeen (Meldrum), 93.1 MHz. IBA Northsound Radio, 290 m, 1035 kHz, 96.9 MHz.

PLACES TO SEE INLAND

Aden Country Park, 10 miles W of Peterhead.

Deer Abbey, Old Deer, 10 miles W of Peterhead. Cistercian abbey remains.

Haddo House (NTS), 15 miles W of Cruden Bay, near Methlick. Georgian house and gardens. Afternoons in summer.

Pitmedden (NTS), 10 miles W of Collieston. Garden and museum of 17th-century farming life. Garden all year; museum daily in summer.

Tolquhon Castle, Pitmedden, 11 miles W of Collieston. 15th-16th-century ruined mansion. Weekdays and Sun. afternoons.

A stately Georgian town at a break in Banff's rugged shore

Precipitous cliffs and shelving, sandy beaches punctuate this section of the Moray Firth coastline, which is renowned for its dramatic scenery and brilliant sunsets. Villages and towns range from the Georgian formality of Banff to the tiny fishing hamlets of Gamrie Bay and the busy fishing port of Fraserburgh; between them narrow lanes and rough footpaths lead to secluded coves, castle ruins, sea-bird colonies and vast subterranean caves.

BETWEEN CLIFFS AND SEA *Like neighbouring Gardenstown, the tiny village of Crovie is perched on the edge of Gamrie Bay with grassy cliffs soaring to 350 ft behind the greystone cottages.*

① CULLEN

A mile of sandy beach and a challenging 'split-level' golf course are among the attractions of this bustling resort town. Cullen is built on two levels, divided by the graceful arches of a disused 19th-century railway viaduct. The broad main street and square of the upper village were constructed in 1823 by the Earl of Seafield and Findlater, who moved the town from its old site half a mile away to give his own house greater privacy. Within the grounds of the 17th-century Cullen House is the Auld Kirk – 14th century or earlier – which is still in use.

Seatown, the lower village, is a cluster of fishermen's cottages hugging the harbour. A short walk up Castle Hill behind Seatown yields a view of the distant mountains of Caithness and Sutherland. West of the harbour, the road ends at a burn, and a foot bridge leads to the golf club and the craggy rock formations of the 'Three Kings'. The best swimming is found between these natural sculptures and the massive hump of Boar's Craig.

A 45 minute walk westwards along the beach or golf links leads to caves along the headland and up the hill to Portknockie.

② FINDLATER CASTLE

The impressive ruins of this 15th-century Ogilvie stronghold, which was inhabited until about 1600, girdle a 150 ft cliff. To reach the castle by road, turn north off the A98 down an unmarked road at a crossroads 2 miles south-east of Cullen. Follow this road for nearly 1 mile, then turn north on to a track and park at the Barnyards of Findlater.

Just past a conical dovecot on the left, the track drops steeply down to the castle. A quarter of a mile to the west is the isolated crescent of Sunnyside Beach, one of the finest on the Moray Firth.

③ PORTSOY

Once a busy port and fishing village, this attractive resort is now primarily a haven for pleasure craft and holiday-makers. Its restored 17th and 18th-century harbour warehouses have received a number of conservation awards. A workshop sells souvenirs made from the red and green 'Portsoy marble', found in the surrounding cliffs.

An easy 2 mile coastal walk leads west to Sandend Bay which hosts the annual canoe surfing championships in October. To the east of the harbour, a 2 mile walk following the coastal path leads to the ruined 16th-century Boyne Castle – an Ogilvie stronghold set high above the Burn of Boyne. The castle can be reached by car from the B9139, by a path next to the burn.

④ WHITEHILLS

This small fishing village is built around a thriving harbour. The colourfully painted boats bring in cod, haddock, sole, plaice and whiting, which are sold fresh every weekday. The harbour road leads east past a children's playground to the edge of Boyndie Bay, and a stony track for walkers continues on to Banff – about 2 miles away. The chalybeate spring just off the track was once part of a fashionable 19th-century circuit for visitors 'taking the waters' around Banff.

⑤ BANFF

A town of architectural surprises, Banff has Greek columns, crow-stepped gables, Venetian windows and delicate steeples. Its many fine Georgian buildings were erected when Banff was a fashionable wintering resort. They include Duff House, a fine baroque mansion on the edge of the town, built between 1725 and 1740 by Lord Braco.

From Duff House, a 2 mile walk leads inland through the woods beside the River Deveron to the Bridge of Alvah, which crosses the river 40 ft above an impressive gorge. The path can be followed on past the Mains of Montcoffer, then by turning north over a wooded hill to join the main road near Banff Bridge, a circular walk of 4½ miles.

The seven-arched bridge which spans the estuary of the River Deveron was designed by John Smeaton, the architect of the third Eddystone lighthouse. Swimmers should stay clear of the river mouth, where there are dangerous undercurrents and shifting sands.

Originally a Hanseatic trading town of the 12th century, and later an important fishing port, Banff lost the use of its harbour when it silted up in the 19th century. The tidal harbour is now being dredged, and has grown as a sailing centre. A museum of local history displays silver, armour, and relics of James Ferguson, an 18th-century Banff astronomer.

GRACIOUS LIVING *Duff House in Banff, one of Britain's finest Georgian baroque houses, was designed by William Adam.*

⑥ MACDUFF

The busy fishing harbour is the focal point of this resort town, which is divided from Banff by the estuary of the River Deveron. Colourful salmon nets and lobster creels dry at the harbour's edge, and there is a boatyard on the western side. The Hill of Doune, reached by a path up the grassy slope from

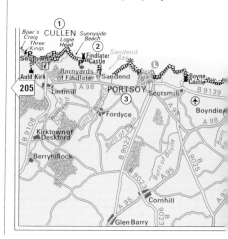

the east end of Banff Bridge, provides a fine view of Banff and the Deveron estuary.

A mile to the east, at Tarlair, are four man-made outdoor swimming and paddling pools sheltered by a ring of cliffs. A heather-clad path up the hill on the east side of the pools leads on to the fairways of the Royal Tarlair Golf Course.

⑦ GARDENSTOWN
Apparently challenging the laws of gravity, the houses of this active fishing village cling to a hillside that drops down to Gamrie Bay. The harbour, at the foot of the village, is protected from all but due north winds.

Castle Hill of Findon overlooks the village and yields a good view of the surrounding cliffs. To the west are the ruins of the church of St John the Evangelist, built in 1513 but commemorating a victory over the invading Danes in 1004. The twin village of Crovie is a 10 minute walk from the harbour's east end, along a railed cliff path.

⑧ TROUP HEAD
Rising to 368 ft above the ocean, the sheer cliff face of this headland is the refuge of thousands of sea-birds. The roar of the ocean is pierced by a riot of bird sound: the kittiwake calling its name, the laugh of gulls and the croaking call of shags and cor-morants. The headland is a 10 minute walk from Northfield Farm; park by the lower sheep pens.

⑨ PENNAN
This charming one-street village has a permanent population of about 25 that swells to more than 100 in summer. The steep road down to the stone cottages has hairpin turns; there is limited parking at the harbour.

West of Pennan the road plunges down to Cullykhan Bay, where waves pound into huge clefts and caves in the surrounding cliffs.

East of Pennan, sheer cliffs of red sand-stone march down to the glen of Aberdour, providing nesting sites for colonies of sea-birds and pitted with caves and tunnels accessible at low tide. A 3 mile footpath leads from Pennan to New Aberdour.

⑩ NEW ABERDOUR
This compact, self-contained community lies about a mile from the sea, its single street lined with fishermen's cottages and a few shops. A steep and twisting road leads to a pebble beach at the mouth of the Dour valley. The beach is surrounded by grassy banks, where wild flowers abound in spring and summer, and by red-sandstone cliffs, which are pierced at the eastern end by impressive caves. A path rising above the caves leads over a small headland to another sheltered sandy beach, enclosed between

two rocky points. The unwary can easily be cut off by the tide.

Between New Aberdour and the beach is the ruin of Old Aberdour church, one of the oldest in the north of Scotland and the centre of the original village. Dedicated to St Drostan, the church was founded by St Columba, and contains several interesting gravestones.

⑪ ROSEHEARTY
Surrounding a quiet and peaceful harbour, Rosehearty is one of the oldest sea-ports in Scotland. Its origins go back to the time of the Viking raids, and for many years it played a major part in the fishing industry. Although commercial fishing has now moved to Fraserburgh, Rosehearty's sandy harbour is still much used by inshore fishermen. An open-air, seawater swim-ming pool and a peaceful golf course are within easy reach of the town centre, and there is a small museum, open in summer, with a display of fishing gear and relics connected with local history.

Half a mile south of the town, along the road past the Mason's Arms, are the ruins of the Castle of Pitsligo. The castle was originally owned by the Frasers of Pilorth, and was the home of Lord Pitsligo who was a fugitive in the area after the failure of the 1745 Jacobite Uprising.

⑫ SANDHAVEN
This once-thriving fishing village, and the adjoining village of Pittulie, are now quiet, sleepy communities. Sandhaven's sea-walls were severely battered by storms in 1953, but they still provide protection for a few inshore fishing boats.

The rocky shoreline makes a good place for watching birds and seals and is easily accessible from points along the road to Fraserburgh. At the eastern end of the village stands a meal mill which stopped working in 1981 after 200 years of continu-ous use.

⑬ FRASERBURGH
Now one of the busiest fishing ports in the north-east, Fraserburgh stands facing the North Sea and the Moray Firth at the end of Kinnairds Head. The Head is rocky, but Fraserburgh Bay to the east has more than 2 miles of dune-backed sands.

Alexander Fraser built a castle on Kin-nairds Head in 1570, and in 1786 it was converted into a lighthouse, one of the oldest in Scotland. Close by, at the head of a steep cove, is the so-called Wine Tower. The purpose of this enigmatic building, which has no stairs between its three floors, is unknown.

In the harbour area the lifeboat shed is open at certain times in summer except Sunday, and fish are sold daily on weekdays

NIPPY CATCH *Boxes of crabs are unloaded ready for the morning fish market at Fraserburgh, still one of Scotland's busiest fishing ports.*

in the fish market at 7.30 a.m. Fishing trips can be arranged from the harbour, which is also used by pleasure craft.

⑭ CAIRNBULG
The lack of a harbour ended the prosperity of Cairnbulg and its neighbouring fishing community of Inverallochy, huddled to-gether in the shelter of Cairnbulg Point. They are now tranquil villages, a cluster of fishermen's cottages, their gable ends de-fiantly facing the sea to offer less resistance to winter gales. The narrow streets are chaotic and twisty. The beach around the Point is rocky, cut here and there by narrow clefts which serve as havens for colourful small craft.

LOCAL INFORMATION

Tourist information Fraserburgh 28315 (summer); Banff 2789, 2419 (summer).

HM Coastguard Peterhead 4278 for information. 999 in emergency (ask for coastguard).

Weather Aberdeen 8091.

Local radio BBC Radio Aberdeen (Meldrum). 93.1 MHz. IBA Moray Firth Radio, 271 m, 1107 kHz. 95.9 MHz.

PLACES TO SEE INLAND

Eden Castle, 5½ miles S of Banff. 17th-century ruins.

Dundarg Castle, 5 miles W of Fraserburgh. Ancient ruins of Comyn stronghold, destroyed after siege in 1334 but re-fortified in 16th century. Daily.

Memsie Burial Cairn, 3 miles SW of Fraserburgh. Bronze Age burial of about 1500 BC.

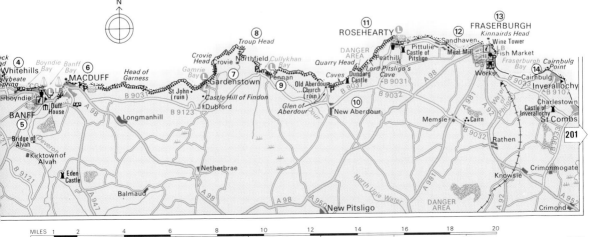

Fishing villages where the Spey flows into the Moray Firth

Steep cliffs and sandy beaches line the fertile southern shore of the Moray Firth, known as the 'Granary of the North'. This is a countryside of small fishing villages and quiet inland farms. The hills and forests provide miles of good walking, while the cliffs and the foreshore offer caves to explore as well as excellent birdwatching. In fine weather there are good views across the Firth towards the Black Isle and the mountains inland.

DUFFUS CASTLE *A wooden tower once crowned the Norman mound where the ruined stone keep of 1305 now stands. The castle was held by the ancestors of the Moray family.*

① DUFFUS

Planned and built in the 19th century, like many of the villages along this coast, Duffus is a quiet picturesque village set on a slope above level farmland. The surrounding area was once part of the vast Loch of Spynie, now drained to insignificant size. The old village, built on an island in the loch, was centred around the church of St Peter, now a ruin.

Duffus Castle, 2 miles south-east, rises massively above a Norman mound and dominates the flat country about it. The present structure, which is open daily, dates from the 14th century and was built by Sir Reginald Le Chan on the site of an earlier wooden castle. Although part of the keep has subsided, the castle is one of the most interesting in Moray, as well as one of the oldest.

The ruin is reached by turning east off the B9012, on to a narrow road signposted to Duffus Castle. Beyond the castle the road leads the visitor past RAF Lossiemouth, and the frequent sight and sound of fighter aircraft remind the visitor of the difference that 500 years has made to military strategy.

② LOSSIEMOUTH

This busy fishing town came into existence as the port for the inland town of Elgin, after the older port of Spynie silted up. The river's former estuary was at Covesea, 3 miles to the west. Branderburgh was founded on the rocky headland above in 1830, and the two communities are now joined.

Lossiemouth is a thriving fishing port that also has two excellent sandy beaches. The east beach has conditions suitable for surfing, while the west beach offers safe bathing and facilities for landing small craft, for which there is a small charge. Quiet streets

invite the visitor to wander at leisure among the neat houses and cottages. Anglers are well catered for, with fishing available both on the beach and along a length of the river, and there are two 18-hole golf courses.

Inland, off the road to Elgin, are the ruins of the 15th-century Palace of Spynie, home of the Bishops of Moray. The ruins, visible from the road, are not safe, but are in the process of being strengthened.

THE NOBLE SALMON

At Kingston the River Spey flows into the sea, and to fishermen the Spey means salmon. One of the most prized of all fish, salmon spend most of their lives in the North Atlantic but return over thousands of miles to the river of their birth to spawn. It is thought that some form of inbuilt 'compass' may enable them to steer by the earth's magnetic field or even by the stars. In coastal waters each fish can 'smell' its own river.

Salmon can leap a waterfall 11 ft high

The Spynie Canal, built to drain the former Loch of Spynie to create the fertile farmlands between Lossiemouth and Elgin, can be seen at the point where the A941 and B9013 cross it.

③ KINGSTON AND GARMOUTH

There is no longer any sign of the once flourishing boat-building industry that was carried on in these two small villages on the western bank of the Spey. Logs were floated downstream from the Rothiemurchus and Glenmore pine forests to be transformed into ships that sailed all over the world. Kingston is named after Kingston-upon-Hull because the timber merchants who started the logging came from there. It was not until the introduction of ships built of iron and steel that the industry declined.

Today the villages, with their narrow winding streets, are peaceful havens from a busy world. On the wall of Brae House in Garmouth a plaque commemorates the signing in the village of the Solemn League and Covenant by Charles II in 1650.

The coast abounds in bird life, and there is a good walk along the sand-and-shingle beach and across a footbridge to Lossiemouth, some 7 miles to the west.

④ SPEY BAY

A cluster of cottages at the mouth of the River Spey is all that remains to show that this village was once an important centre of the salmon-fishing industry. Although some salmon fishing continues, it is on a far smaller scale than in the past. On the edge of the river mouth is a restored ice house, in which salmon were stored before being sold. The building contains a permanent exhibition of various aspects of the salmon industry.

Spey Bay is the northern starting point of the 30 mile Speyside Way, which follows the eastern bank of the River Spey southwards along a series of fishermen's paths to Fochabers, and then onwards for a total of 30 miles to Ballindalloch. It is planned eventually to extend the path as far as Glenmore Lodge, near Aviemore. The footpath is well maintained and clearly marked, in one place following part of an old railway line. A series of leaflets describing the walk in four stages can be obtained from Elgin Tourist Information Centre.

For those preferring a shorter haul, there is a 2½ mile walk from Spey Bay along a shingly shore to Portgordon, or an even shorter walk over the disused viaduct to Garmouth, on the western bank of the river. The car park for this walk is about half a mile from the village, accessible over a rough track.

⑤ FOCHABERS

Lying beside an important crossing of the River Spey, Fochabers was built in the 18th century to a gridiron pattern, and has a wealth of elegant buildings. They include the Bellie Parish Church and the ornately decorated Milne's High School, built in the 19th century to rival nearby Gordon Castle.

There are a number of good walks around Fochabers. From the bridge over the Spey, a path runs alongside the river to the south, through pleasant woodland, before joining the Speyside Way. About a mile east of the village, off the A98, are the Winding Walks, a selection of well-made paths through Whiteash Hill Wood. A viewpoint at the top of the hill commands panoramic views of Fochabers, lower Speyside and the countryside east of Elgin.

The woods at Aultderg, to the south, are reached by taking East Street out of Fochabers and following the road for 1½ miles to a car park. From there a path runs along the

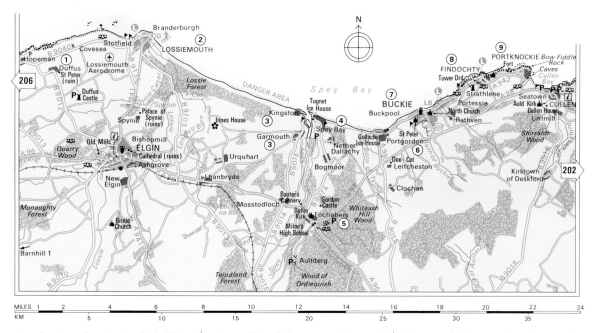

MILES	1	2		4		6		8		10		12		14		16		18		20		22		24
KM			5			10			15			20			25			30			35			

top of a steep slope, to the Earth Pillars, eroded stacks of red sandstone standing on the banks of the Spey.

West of the village a large food-processing factory offers guided tours to the public, and there is a fascinating reconstruction of the company's first shop opened in the 19th century.

⑥ PORTGORDON

The 18th-century village of Portgordon clusters about its tiny harbour. Rows of cottages form what used to be a centre of the net-and-line salmon-fishing industry, but the harbour is now only used by pleasure craft. A relic of the salmon-fishing industry can be seen along the foreshore towards Buckpool in the shape of the restored 19th-century Gollachy Ice House, where salmon were stored before being sold. To the west a 2½ mile walk along the foreshore takes the visitor to Spey Bay. Inland, at Leitcheston, stands a four-compartment dovecot, all that remains of a castle of which there is now no trace. The dovecot is clearly visible from the A98, a quarter of a mile east of its junction with the A990.

⑦ BUCKIE

Stretching for 2½ miles along the coast, from Buckpool in the west to Portessie in the east, Buckie displays a variety of different architectural styles. These range from the small cottages of the fishing community around Cluny harbour to the splendour of the Roman Catholic Church of St Peter, built in 1857, at the western end of West Church Street and the crowned tower of the North Church, built in 1879, in Cluny Square. Near this church is the town's First World War memorial, 21 ft high and one of the finest in Scotland.

Cluny harbour is still very much a fishing port. The main fish market is on Thursdays and Fridays, but fish are sold on other days whenever sufficient are landed. The older and smaller harbour of Buckpool has been filled in and made into gardens. Relics of Buckie's fishing past can be seen at the Museum in Cluny Place.

⑧ FINDOCHTY

Cottages painted in bright colours make Findochty one of the most cheerful-looking villages on the Moray coast. The paint was originally intended to weatherproof the houses against winter storms, but this form of decoration has now become both a tradition and a challenge.

The village skyline is dominated by its church, while the lower part of the village surrounds a sheltered sandy cove, from which a footpath runs eastwards to Portknockie. The western part of Findochty is centred on the harbour, long deserted by its fishing fleet but offering a safe haven for pleasure craft. An easy path starting near the war memorial runs westwards along the shoreline for 1 mile, following an old smugglers' route past hidden coves and caves to Strathlene, where there is an 18-hole golf course.

About half a mile inland, the ruined castle of the Ords family is clearly visible from the main coast road. The Ords played a significant part in the village's development, and Thomas Ord had workmen's cottages built there in 1716.

⑨ PORTKNOCKIE

Perched on top of steep cliffs above a rocky shore, this quiet fishing village has a long and varied history dating from the Iron Age. The harbour, sheltered by a rocky promontory with its 7th-century Pictish fort, is no longer used by fishermen, but is an excellent haven for small craft. Around the harbour the older cottages cluster in colourful disarray, while the newer cottages lie higher up the cliffs.

The cliffs that form the predominant feature of the village provide plenty of scope for exploration. Eastwards a path runs from the lower end of Admiralty Street along the clifftop and down to the rocky foreshore, where there are three caves; the largest of them, the Preacher's Cave, was used as a church during the religious revival of the early 19th century. A short walk further east leads on to the sandy beach at Cullen.

To the west, a 1½ mile path takes the visitor along the top of spectacular cliffs to Findochty, with superb views across the Moray Firth to the Black Isle.

BOW FIDDLE ROCK *This rock formation, its natural arch suggesting a violinist's bow, lies east of Portknockie harbour and can be seen from the clifftop walk east of the village.*

LOCAL INFORMATION

Tourist information Elgin 2666.

HM Coastguard Peterhead 4278 for information, 999 in emergency (ask for coastguard).

Weather Aberdeen 8091.

Local Radio BBC Highland, 94 Mhz; IBA Moray Firth, 271 m, 1107 kHz, 95.9 MHz.

PLACES TO SEE INLAND

Elgin, 6 miles S of Lossiemouth. Cathedral, 13th and 15th-century remains; Museum, antiquities, costumes, weekdays in summer. Old Mills, working mill, most days in summer.

Birnie Church, 3 miles S of Elgin, off A941. 12th century.

Innes House, near Elgin. Gardens most days in summer.

Pluscarden Abbey, Barnhill, 6 miles SW of Elgin, off B9010. 13th-century monastery. Daily.

A serene coast of sandy bays and quiet forests

From the sheltered sands of Nairn, the coast sweeps east in a series of graceful bays to the rocky headland of Burghead. Along this coastline yachtsmen enjoy fine sailing, while the many forests that make this one of the most thickly wooded coasts in Britain are a delight for walkers and birdwatchers. The beaches are sandy and deserted, bathing is safe, and the whole area is rich in history and relics of a turbulent past.

① NAIRN

A quietly prosperous town on the sheltered sandy shore of the Moray Firth, Nairn is rich in historical associations and modern attractions, as well as being a focal point for this stretch of coast.

The town's history goes back to the 12th century, when Alexander I granted it a royal charter. In 1746 the Duke of Cumberland spent his 25th birthday in a house in the High Street, now marked with an inscription, before going on to defeat Prince Charles Edward at Culloden. Nairn was once the home of a vigorous fishing industry, and though this has now declined the old fishing district, the Fishertown, a place of tightly packed cottages preserves its identity.

The past is admirably recreated at the Fishertown Museum in Laing Hall, King Street. The present is represented by the yard at Ardersier, on the eastern side of the spit towards Fort George, which makes rigs for the North Sea oil industry. Nairn's harbour is now used solely by pleasure craft, and has a free slipway. Visiting boats are welcome. To east and west are sandy beaches with safe bathing.

The town has ornamental gardens just off the High Street, and there are attractive walks along both sides of the River Nairn. Golfers are well provided for, with two 18-hole golf courses, both of which welcome visiting players. Seven miles of the River Nairn are available for anglers, and Highland Games are held in the town on the first Saturday after August 12 every year.

② AULDEARN

There is little to show that this quiet village was the scene of a major battle during the Civil War; but it was there, in 1645, that the Royalist Marquis of Montrose routed a much

larger force of Covenanters led by General Sir John Urry. A fine view of the battlefield may be seen from a small hill on the outskirts of the village, where a chart shows the positions held by the two sides. The hill is the motte, or mound, of a 12th-century castle. On it also stands a 17th-century dovecot, in the care of the National Trust for Scotland, and there are superb views of the Moray Firth and the Black Isle.

South-west of the village, off the B9101, is the empty shell of 13th-century Rait Castle, scene of a double act of treachery in 1424. It was the home of the Comyn family, who invited the MacIntoshes to a banquet with the intention of slaughtering them, but were massacred by their guests instead. The castle has been a ruin ever since.

WINTER STOCK *The dovecot at Auldearn, with its 546 nest holes, supplied food for the local laird's table during the winter.*

③ BRODIE CASTLE

Rising in the midst of beautifully landscaped grounds, Brodie Castle has for hundreds of years been the home of the Brodie family, one of the oldest untitled landed families in

Britain. Now administered by the National Trust for Scotland, the castle contains a fine collection of 18th and 19th-century furniture and paintings, and still retains the atmosphere of a family home. The castle was built originally in the 15th century as a tower, but later additions mean that three centuries of architecture can now be seen side by side.

Around the castle the grounds still retain a hint of the formal landscape garden that was laid out in the 18th century, mingled with schemes from later years. At the end of the east drive stands the Rodney Stone, a well-preserved Pictish monument found originally in the nearby churchyard at Dyke. The stone was set up in its present position to commemorate the victory of Admiral Rodney over the French at Dominica in 1782, during the American War of Independence.

④ CULBIN FOREST

The vast forest that today stretches for some 9 miles along the Moray coast from Nairn to the western edge of Findhorn Bay was once an area of sand-dunes so desolate as to be called the 'Scottish Sahara'. The dunes built up during a series of storms in the 17th century, finally burying the village of Culbin which stood at the heart of what had earlier still been rich farmland.

The forest, quiet and undisturbed, has

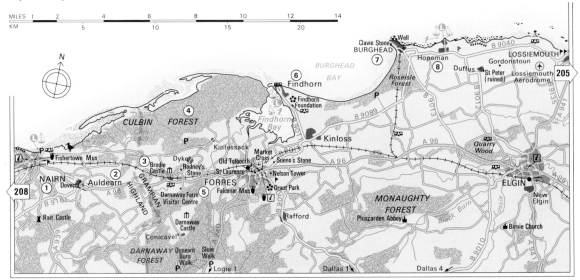

SEA, SAND AND SOLITUDE *From Findhorn, a 7 mile stretch of sand and dunes curves eastwards in a broad arc to Burghead on its stubby headland. From the beach, paths lead into the dense Roseisle Forest.*

A BIRD OF THE PINES

The male capercaillie may be seen and heard in Culbin Forest, showing off its tail feathers and uttering its gurgling mating call. The turkey-sized bird became extinct in Britain in 1783, but was re-introduced from Sweden in 1837. Its name may derive from the Gaelic – *capullcoille* – 'horse of the woods'.

The aggressive male, emerging from the pine trees, may threaten deer and sheep

a rich variety of wildlife, from roe deer to badgers and crested tits to capercaillie – the largest of British game birds, resembling a small turkey. The easiest approach to the forest is along the road from Kintessack, south of the forest, which is signposted from the A96. The Forestry Commission has laid out picnic areas, and there is extensive walking through the forest and down to the foreshore, where the various stages in the reclamation of the dunes can be seen.

⑤ FORRES

This ancient burgh, nestling among hills beside a major crossing of the River Findhorn, is the prosperous hub of a number of scattered communities. Busy streets alternate with quiet closes, showing the architecture of many ages. In the High Street are the Old Tolbooth, dating from the early 19th century, a 15th-century market cross, restored in the 19th century, and the 19th-century St Laurence's Church. In Tolbooth Street stands the Falconer Museum, with an interesting local history collection.

Dominating the skyline is the 70 ft Nelson Tower, built on a wooded hill in Grant Park.

A steep climb takes the visitor along well-made paths to the monument, which was built in 1806 to commemorate Nelson's victory at Trafalgar. From the top are wide views of the Moray Firth and the surrounding countryside. The key can be obtained from the Tourist Information Centre in Tolbooth Street.

Forres is a good centre for walks in the well-wooded countryside round about. Two particularly attractive walks are to the south-west of the town. The Dunearn Burn Walk in Darnaway Forest, starting 1¼ miles south of Conicavel, is signposted from the A96, 3 miles west of Forres. The Sluie Walk, signposted from the A940, 4 miles south of Forres, leads through open country and woodlands to the River Findhorn. Details of these and other walks are available at the Tourist Information Centre.

Also in Darnaway Forest is the Darnaway Farm Visitor Centre, where there are exhibits relating to the history of the Moray estate. Guided walks take in Darnaway Castle, where there is a fine hammer-beam roof and a contemporary painting of the murder, in 1591, of James, second Earl of Moray. The Visitor Centre is open at Easter and in the summer months.

An ancient pillar, the 23 ft high Sueno Stone, stands to the east of the town. The origins of this monument are unknown, but it is thought to commemorate a long-forgotten battle, as it is decorated with carvings depicting warriors and headless corpses. The stone is on the B9011 to Findhorn. The nearby Witches Stone marks the spot where, in the 17th century persecutions, women accused of witchcraft were put to death.

Six miles south-east of Forres is the village of Dallas, which has a link with the city of the same name in Texas. The connection arose through the American politician George Mifflin Dallas, who became vice president of the United States in 1844 and gave his name to Dallas, Texas, in 1845. He was a descendant of the Scottish landowner William de Ripley, who obtained the Scottish village of Dallas and the surrounding lands from the Crown in 1279. At about the same time he received a knighthood, becoming Sir William of Dallas. The village is on the River Lossie, and Dallas means 'watery valley'.

⑥ FINDHORN

The dunes surrounding Findhorn are a reminder of the village's unhappy past. The first settlement of Findhorn was buried beneath the sand during fierce storms in the 17th century. The second village was destroyed by floods in 1701, and the present village is the third to bear the name.

The modern settlement, which was an important port, is now the chief centre for sailing on this coast. There is racing throughout the summer, including several major competitions, and a variety of sailing courses are available.

The large tidal Findhorn Bay offers excellent birdwatching, and though bathing is not recommended in the bay, the north beach offers 5 miles of sands stretching eastwards towards Burghead.

A mile south of Findhorn is the home of the Findhorn Foundation, an international spiritual community founded in 1962 whose members have reclaimed the sand-dunes to grow vegetables. They make pottery, candles and other products, and a craft shop on the site sells a wide range of items made by the community. Courses based on the community's philosophy are run for non-members, and there are guided tours daily in summer.

⑦ BURGHEAD

The rocky bulk of a promontory jutting defiantly into the Moray Firth protects Burghead's harbour and once made it the foremost grain shipping port in Moray. This trade has gone, and the granaries that line the harbour have been adapted to other uses, but the harbour still serves as a base for fishing and pleasure craft, as well as for vessels carrying timber.

The site of an Iron Age fort at the end of the promontory is now occupied by the old coastguard station, but still visible is the Burghead Well, a chamber cut into the rock and thought to have served as an early Christian baptistry. Near by is the Clavie Stone, the scene of a traditional festival held every year on January 11, the old New Year's Eve. At the ceremony, which may be Norse in origin, the Clavie, a blazing tar barrel, is broken up after being carried round the village in procession.

To the west the Forestry Commission's Roseisle Forest has an attractive picnic site, with walks down to the sandy beach which stretches west to Findhorn.

⑧ HOPEMAN

The fishing village of Hopeman, set in a natural hollow among the cliffs, is now a centre for water sports. It was built in the 19th century and has the neat, sturdy appearance typical of many Scottish fishing villages. The small sheltered harbour is used by pleasure and fishing craft, while the village itself lies on a gentle slope away from the sea. The harbour was used by the Duke of Edinburgh and Prince Charles when they were pupils at nearby Gordonstoun.

There are sandy beaches both east and west of the harbour, and the village has a golf course. Fishing can be arranged, and water sports equipment may be hired.

LOCAL INFORMATION
Tourist information Forres 72938 (summer); Nairn 52753 (summer).
HM Coastguard Peterhead 4278.
Weather Aberdeen 8091.
Local radio BBC Radio Highland, 94 MHz; IBA Moray Firth, 271 m, 1107 kHz, 95.9 MHz.

PLACE TO SEE INLAND
Randolph's Leap, 1 mile SW of Logie, on B9007. Gorge on Findhorn river.

A battlefield where the Highlands sweep down to the firths

Sand-and-shingle beaches lining the Moray and Beauly Firths are backed by the hills and mountains of the Scottish Highlands. Wild birds abound on the foreshore, and there are cliffs pierced by caves steeped in legends. At the mouth of the River Ness stands Inverness, the 'Capital of the Highlands', and the road from Inverness to the east crosses Culloden Moor, the site of the last battle fought on British soil.

① FORTROSE

The streets that shelter below the steep surrounding hills are narrow and neat. Though the harbour at Fortrose is no longer used by the fishing fleets it has become a busy sailing haven and the base of the Chanonry sailing club, which welcomes visiting yachtsmen. There is safe bathing from a narrow beach east of the harbour. Fortrose's ruined cathedral was destroyed, it is said, by Cromwell, who wanted the stone for his new castle at Inverness.

The Moray Firth passes through its narrowest gap around Chanonry Point, a long finger stretching out into the Firth. At the tip of the Point stands a stone commemorating the death of Kenneth Mackenzie, the so called Brahan Seer who is believed to have lived in the 16th or 17th century; his name is derived from Brahan Castle, near Dingwall, a stronghold of the Seaforth family. Mackenzie's gift of 'second sight' brought about his death. He told the Countess of Seaforth that her husband was philandering with the ladies of Paris, which so irritated her that she had the seer tipped into a barrel of burning tar on Chanonry Point. Before he died, the seer foretold the extinction of the Seaforths, which actually took place in the early 19th century.

A good view of the whole of Fortrose and Chanonry Point can be obtained from the Hill of Fortrose, which can be reached by taking a rough, steep track starting just past the church, at the east end of the town.

② AVOCH

This thriving fishing village, whose inhabitants claim descent from Spaniards wrecked on this shore after the defeat of the Armada, is the only community on the Black Isle which still retains its fleet. Fishermen's cottages cluster about the small harbour, their gable ends facing the sea, so that fishing boats could be drawn up between them in rough weather.

There is an easy walk along farm lanes south of Avoch, on the north side of Munlochy Bay. Park at the southern end of the village and follow the lane for half a mile away from the sea. Then take the lane on the left, and follow it back to the starting point. The route gives splendid views of the bay and the mountains around it.

③ MUNLOCHY

Set on high ground at the end of the mud-flats of Munlochy Bay, this quiet farming community has had a long, and at times turbulent, history. Nearby Drumderfit Hill was in 1400 the scene of a bloody battle in which a large party of MacDonalds were slaughtered by the men of Inverness, which they were besieging.

The mouth of Munlochy Bay, which is renowned for its wintering wildfowl, is guarded by two hills. On the southern side stands Craigiehowe, where there is a herd of wild goats and a cave where, according to legend, a band of warriors known as the Fiann lie in magical slumber awaiting the horn call of their leader, the heroic Fionn mac Cumhaill, or Finn Mac Cool, to arouse them. The cave is accessible from the shore at Kilmuir.

④ NORTH KESSOCK

A line of small cottages lies stretched along the Beauly Firth's mud-and-shingle shore. Overshadowed by Ord Hill, North Kessock guards the entrance to the Beauly Firth and affords excellent views of the Kessock Bridge; this has now replaced the ferry which for centuries carried people across the Firth.

The Firth offers good fishing for sea trout, as well as a variety of bird life along the foreshore. There is a good walk from the eastern end of the village through forest on the slopes of Ord Hill, from where there are superb views of the Firth. An Iron Age fort caps the hill.

⑤ MUIR OF ORD

Its position at an important meeting point of roads makes Muir of Ord the gateway to the Black Isle. With heavy traffic now diverted to the Kessock Bridge near the mouth of Beauly Firth, the streets of Muir of Ord are quiet and the village, built of red sandstone, has an air of repose that it lacked for many years.

At one time the village was an important market centre, with drovers bringing cattle from all directions to be sold.

⑥ BEAULY

Set at the mouth of the valley of the River Beauly, this quiet, prosperous town serves as a focal point for the scattered farms around it and as a dormitory town for Inverness. The river meanders past the town to the Firth, where vast mud-flats are the home of a variety of waders and wildfowl.

The main street is dominated by the war memorial and the ruins of 13th-century Beauly Priory, which contains a fine monument to Sir Kenneth Mackenzie dating from the 16th century.

There is an attractive walk through the Reelig Glen, 3 miles south-east of Beauly. Leave the main road south of Kirkhill along a lane signposted to Moniack Castle and Clunes, then turn along an unmarked lane, leading to a car park just before the bridge.

⑦ CRAIG PHADRIG

Rising to 556 ft above the Beauly Firth and Inverness, Craig Phadrig provides varied walks through open woodland to the remains of an Iron Age vitrified fort on the hilltop. This fort is said to have been the stronghold of King Brude, a ruler of the Picts, and it commands wide views of the Moray and Beauly Firths, and of the mountains to the west.

To find the hill, cross the Caledonian Canal on the A82, then turn north towards Leachkin. After about a mile, take the turning on the left signposted to Craig Phadrig Hospital, and then after a further quarter of a mile turn right towards Upper Leachkin and Blackpark. The car park, with a map of the woods, is 100 yds further on.

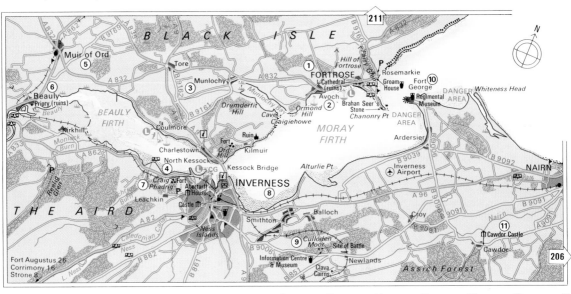

BONNY BANKS *Brushed with autumnal tints and framed by misty mountain peaks, Beauly Firth lives up to the Norman name – beau lieu – a 'beautiful place'.*

PRINCE'S SAVIOUR *A statue of Flora Mac-Donald, who aided Prince Charles Edward's escape in 1746, stands at Inverness Castle.*

⑧ INVERNESS

Straddling the Caledonian Canal and the River Ness at the eastern end of the Great Glen, Inverness has come to be known as the 'Capital of the Highlands'. Its dominating feature is its castle, built in the 19th century on the site of earlier buildings. Today the castle serves as a court house and as administrative offices for the council. In 1921 Inverness was the scene of the first cabinet meeting held outside London, when ministers met in the Town House because Lloyd George, the Prime Minister, was on holiday in northern Scotland.

The oldest building in Inverness, Abertarff House in Church Street, built in 1592, is owned by the National Trust for Scotland. The museum in Castle Wynd contains relics of the 1745 Uprising. There are displays on archaeology and local and natural history, and an exhibition on the life of the clans. The steeple that stands at the junction of Church Street and Bridge Street is all that remains of the ancient Tolbooth.

It is to the River Ness that the town owes its earliest development, and there are pleasant walks along the banks – especially to the Ness Islands, where a series of bridges carries the visitor from one island to the next along a maze of wooded paths.

The Caledonian Canal that links the Moray Firth to Loch Ness and the west coast has become a centre for pleasure craft. There are boats for hire, and cruises on the loch.

⑨ CULLODEN MOOR

Open farmland and dark forest cover the site of the last battle fought on British soil, and the clash of steel, the thunder of guns and the cries of fighting men have given way to bird-song and the sound of an occasional car. But the 19th-century cairn and the gravestones marking the burial places of the clans recall the bloody engagement of 1746, when the Duke of Cumberland's army defeated that of Prince Charles Edward and finally dissipated Stuart hopes of the throne.

The National Trust for Scotland owns the site and has established an Information Centre, an audio-visual exhibition and a museum in the old Leanach farmhouse that witnessed some of the most desperate moments of the fight. A waymarked trail takes in landmarks of the battle, but the scene in 1746 is difficult to envisage, since the area was then mostly open moor.

Just over a mile to the south-east lie graves of more ancient times. The Clava Cairns date from the late Stone Age and are surrounded by rings of standing stones. The site is reached by proceeding east from Culloden for a few hundred yards, then turning south on a signposted route.

⑩ FORT GEORGE

Built after the defeat of the 1745 Uprising, Fort George is one of the finest 18th-century artillery fortresses in Europe. The visitor, entering by two tunnels through the ramparts and over a wooden bridge, is immediately struck by the power of the defences; every approach is covered by at least two cannon-lined walls, and often more.

Within the ramparts are the elegant Georgian barracks and the Regimental Museum of the Queen's Own Highlanders. Other parts of the building are also open to the public. The guardhouse near the principal entrance has a permanent exhibition of plans of the fort, and from the ramparts there are fine views of the Black Isle and the Moray Firth.

⑪ CAWDOR CASTLE

Standing strong and defiant amid woods of beech and oak, the ancient castle of Cawdor has been the home of the Thanes, later the Earls, of Cawdor for many centuries. The dominating 14th-century keep was added to in the 17th century to change what had been a powerful fortress into a comfortable, but still defensible, home. The castle is still occupied by the sixth earl, which gives a lived-in air to the many elegant rooms.

The mellow stone from which the house is built combines with the calm atmosphere created by the surrounding trees to give the castle a pleasant and friendly air. The rooms contain a superb collection of family portraits, as well as tapestries and some excellent furniture. Around the castle are three separate gardens in varied styles.

Mortar and shells of 1850 at Fort George

LOCAL INFORMATION

Tourist information (North Kessock) Kessock 73505; (Inverness) Inverness 234353.

HM Coastguard Peterhead 4278 for information, 999 in emergency (ask for coastguard).

Weather Glasgow Weather Centre (041) 248 3451.

Local radio BBC Radio Highland, 94 MHz; IBA Moray Firth Radio, 271 m, 1107 kHz, 95.9 MHz.

PLACES TO SEE INLAND

Corrimony, 20 miles SW of Inverness, via A831. Neolithic cairn and standing stones. Daily.

Fort Augustus, 32 miles SW of Inverness. 19th-century abbey, guided tours daily in summer; Great Glen Exhibition, history of Great Glen, daily in summer.

Loch Ness Monster Exhibition, Drumnadrochit, near Strone, 14 miles SW of Inverness. Daily.

Urquhart Castle, near Strone, 14 miles SW of Inverness. 14th century. Daily.

A long haven for ships sheltered by the Black Isle

The Cromarty Firth, entered through a narrow gap between the North Sutor and the Sutors of Cromarty, is one of the largest natural harbours in Europe. To the Vikings it was Sykkersand, or 'Safe Sand', and the Tain peninsula north of the Firth has many Viking associations. To the south lies the Black Isle, actually a peninsula whose mild climate leaves its earth dark and bare when the surrounding country is white with snow.

① INVERGORDON

Built around a fine deep-water anchorage which was used by the Home Fleet of Royal Navy in both World Wars, the small town of Invergordon has a long history as the landing point for a ferry to the Black Isle. A castle was built there in the 13th century, but the town's main development came in the 18th century, when the castle and estate were bought by Sir William Gordon of Embo. He drew up plans for the town and changed its name from Inverbeakie. The ferry to the Black Isle has long stopped running, but fuel storage tanks remain as a reminder of the town's days as a naval and seaplane base which ended in 1956.

Behind the town is an aluminium smelter, built in the hope of bringing jobs to the area but closed in 1981. Inland, quiet lanes lead through magnificent country, while the foreshore abounds in bird life, especially at the Sands of Nigg, which is a nature reserve. In winter great flocks of waterfowl make the sands a paradise for birdwatchers.

② ALNESS

The village sits astride the River Averon, which flows into the Firth at Alness Point. A narrow lane through woodlands follows the river from the village to its mouth, where there are mud-flats and shingle.

For a while, it seemed as though Alness would develop as a dormitory for Invergordon, but expansion ceased with the closing of the aluminium smelter, and the village has regained much of its former quiet. The countryside inland is one of woods, glens and lochs.

③ EVANTON

By-passed by the new A9, Evanton is a small village of neat houses sheltering under massive hills. On the top of Cnoc Fyrish is an unusual monument erected in 1782 by General Sir Hector Munro, who gained distinction at the Relief of Negapatam, in India, in 1781. The monument, a replica of an Indian gate, was built to provide work during a time of unemployment.

The most spectacular landmark in the area is the Black Rock Gorge, a chasm 200 ft deep and only 10 ft wide in places, with the River Glass thundering through it. The gorge can be reached by taking the lane signposted to Glen Glass at the northern end of the village, and following it for about a mile. A muddy track leads off to the left to a small wooden bridge that spans the gorge. This bridge is not for the faint-hearted; between the narrow slats the river can be seen foaming and tossing some 70 ft below. From the bridge the gorge extends ·for 1 mile westwards.

A series of paths and lanes from Evanton lead down to the muddy foreshore, an excellent place to watch sea-birds and waders.

④ DINGWALL

Houses of pink stone line the narrow streets of Dingwall, the administrative centre of Ross and Cromarty. The town has a long history, having been originally a Viking settlement, and is now a bustling market town, where cattle sales are frequently held.

The Town House dates in part from the 18th century, and is attached to a much older

SECRETS OF THE SANDSTONE

Hugh Miller of Cromarty was a stonemason whose interest in geology began while he was working in quarries on Black Isle. He discovered many fossils which were new to science, and a winged fish found in Old Red Sandstone was given the name of *Pterichthyodes milleri*.

Hugh Miller, and the cottage at Cromarty which contains many of his geological specimens

tower; it contains a museum. Next to it is Dingwall's oldest building, dating from 1650 and once used as the school house. The town is dominated by a tall tower on Mitchell Hill erected in memory of General Sir Hector MacDonald (1853–1903), the great Victorian soldier who began his career in the ranks of the Gordon Highlanders. From the top of the hill there are wide views of the Firth and of the hills around the Victorian spa village of Strathpeffer. Dingwall's harbour is now derelict, but the muddy foreshore offers excellent birdwatching at the estuary of the Conon. There is also fishing for sea trout.

A few miles inland is the tiny village of Fodderty. Beside the gate of its former parish church lie two massive stones said to have been thrown there from the summit of Knockfarrel by Finn mac Cool, or Fionn mac Cumhaill, hero of ancient Celtic legends. Finn mac Cool's men are said to lie in an entranced sleep in a cave at Munlochy, 6 miles south-west of Rosemarkie.

⑤ CONON BRIDGE AND MARYBURGH

Although at one time separate communities, the expansion of Maryburgh has blurred the boundary between these two villages at the head of the Cromarty Firth. The bridge from which Conon Bridge takes its name was built

HARBOUR OF SAFETY *Dingwall lies among low hills deep in Cromarty Firth, a natural harbour which ancient map-makers called* Portus Salutis *– 'The Harbour of Safety'.*

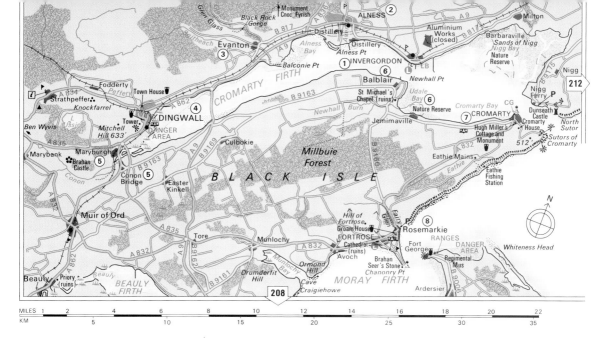

by Thomas Telford in 1809, but there is little left of his original structure. There are pleasant walks upstream along the river on its southern bank and, when there is no firing on the ranges, northwards around the point to Dingwall.

Nearby Brahan Castle, now a ruin, was the home of the Seaforth family, whose extinction was predicted by the Brahan Seer before his death at the hands of Lady Seaforth. He stated that the last earl would see all his sons die before him, and this indeed happened, many years later. The castle's gardens, open on certain days in midsummer, include a beautiful shrubbery, while around it there are pleasant drives along quiet lanes through attractive countryside.

⑥ UDALE BAY AND BALBLAIR

At low tide sand-flats stretch across the western end of Udale Bay in an unbroken layer, dotted with flocks of waders and wildfowl of all kinds. The village of Balblair is a small cluster of cottages on Newhall Point, and was at one time the departure point for the ferry across the Firth to Invergordon, now superseded by the new bridge 8 miles upstream.

Near the shore is the roofless ruin of St Michael's Chapel, where the tombs of many important families of the parish are to be found, the most ancient being those of the Holms of Ferryton which are 400 years old. There is a pleasant circular 2 mile walk along the lane from the chapel, northwards along the shore to Newhall Point, and then back through the village to the chapel.

⑦ CROMARTY

Set at the mouth of the Cromarty Firth, in the lee of the massive bulk of the Sutors of Cromarty, the town of Cromarty is impressive by any standards. The fine natural harbour of Cromarty Firth was used during both World Wars as an anchorage for the Royal Navy, and the gun emplacements that guarded the narrow entrance between the Sutors can still be seen. The present settlement is the second on the site, the previous village having been swept into the sea. Most of the houses are small fishermen's cottages, but here and there are buildings of considerable architectural merit.

One of Cromarty's most famous sons is Hugh Miller, the 19th-century antiquarian folklorist and amateur geologist, whose work upon the fossils of the Old Red Sandstone was considered revolutionary at the time. The cottage in which he was born

FAIRY GLEN *Silver birch trees stand tall and slender by a trickling stream, nodding ferns beckon and a leafy path invites the walker into a natural wonderland inland from Rosemarkie.*

still stands in Church Street, and is in the hands of the National Trust for Scotland: it is the only thatched cottage in Cromarty. A monument on the hill above the town is dedicated to Miller's memory.

Some of the fossil beds that Miller visited are still to be seen, those on the shore at Eathie being the most accessible. Take the A832 from Cromarty, and after about a mile take the lane signposted to Eathie. After another 1½ miles this lane brings the visitor to Eathie Mains, where permission should be sought from the farmer to park in his yard rather than blocking field gates or passing places. A path runs across the field to the clifftop, where it descends steeply to the foreshore. The fossil beds lie south-east of the farm building.

A path north-eastwards along the coast leads after half a mile to the point where the river Eathie reaches the sea by a wild gorge, full of fallen trees and undergrowth, where Hugh Miller records that he saw fairies.

Another worthwhile walk from Cromarty leads along a road for about a mile up to the Sutors of Cromarty, from where there are spectacular views. The road leads past Cromarty House, which is approached by a curious tunnel – built, it is said, so that the owner need not be reminded of the existence of servants.

It is also possible to follow the foreshore from the eastern end of Cromarty round the base of the Sutors. Visitors should not attempt to climb the cliffs as the rocks are unstable.

⑧ ROSEMARKIE

Bounded on one side by the sea, and on the other by a great sandstone cliff, Rosemarkie's red sandstone houses shelter in delightful confusion. The red sand of the beach further helps to give the village an appearance of warmth, and the sheltered coves make it particularly attractive to children. Groam House is a small museum of local interest, with a fine Pictish stone outside it.

Inland is the Fairy Glen, a delightful valley which follows the burn as far as two impressive waterfalls; the visitor can walk behind them on a natural ledge. The footpath to the glen, made famous by local geologist Hugh Miller, starts on the road to Cromarty, by the bridge, a few hundred yards north of the village. There is a car park close by.

LOCAL INFORMATION

Tourist information Strathpeffer 21415 (summer); (North Kessock) Kessock 73505.

HM Coastguard Peterhead 4278 for information, 999 in emergency (ask for coastguard).

Weather Glasgow Weather Centre (041) 248 3451.

Local radio BBC Radio Highland, 94 MHz; IBA Moray Firth Radio, 271 m, 1107 kHz, 95.9 MHz.

PLACES TO SEE INLAND

Ben Wyvis, 10 miles NW of Dingwall, east of A835. Views from 3,433 ft summit.

Strathpeffer. Spa town. Highland Games on the Sat. before Aug. 12.

211

Mirror-bright waters in the bays between two firths

Forests of birch among dramatic hills provide a back-drop for the ancient settlements which owe their existence to the Vikings who settled on this coast. Inland there are drives along wild glens amid spectacular Highland scenery. Large tracts of almost totally uninhabited land are the result of the Highland Clearances in the 19th century. The sea cliffs and inland glens and forests are the homes of a wide variety of birds and plants.

① DORNOCH

Built almost entirely of mellow local stone, the town of Dornoch is centred around its cathedral and the last remaining tower of a castle, built by the Bishops of Caithness, which is now a hotel.

The cathedral was begun in 1224, but except for the central tower it was destroyed by fire in 1570. It was partially restored in the 17th century, and largely rebuilt in the 19th century. The interior stonework, plastered over during restoration, has since been revealed once more.

The streets in the town centre, wide and well planted with trees, have an atmosphere of quiet elegance. At the western side of the cathedral stand the weather-worn remains of the Mercat Cross. There are two golf courses, one to the north and one to the south of the town. A stone on the southern edge of the town marks the spot where in 1722 one of the last witches in Scotland was burned, for having turned her daughter into a pony and taken her to the Devil to be shod.

② SPINNINGDALE

The hamlet of Spinningdale lies at the head of a shallow bay below impressive hills. By the shore stand the ruins of the old mill that gave the village its name. In 1790 a local philanthropist built a cotton mill in the valley, hoping to bring prosperity to the area. However, fire gutted the mill 18 years

later, and all that now remains is its gaunt shell. Bathing is unsafe off Spinningdale because of currents.

The road westwards to Bonar Bridge runs beside Dornoch Firth through groves of oak and birch, past the steeply mounded hill of Dun Creich, which is capped by the remains of an ancient fort. To the east the road turns slightly inland, the hills giving way to more gentle scenery. The tall Ospis Stone beside the road is, like the nearby village of Ospisdale, named after a Norse chieftain.

Skibo Castle, just off the main road 1 mile further east, was built by the millionaire philanthropist Andrew Carnegie in 1898. It is not open to the public.

③ BONAR BRIDGE

The neat houses and cottages of Bonar Bridge form a focal point for the scattered farming and crofting community between the mountains and Dornoch Firth. The bridge that gives the village its name was built to Thomas Telford's design in 1812, and spans the strait where the Kyle of Sutherland and Dornoch Firth meet. The bridge was damaged by floods in 1892, but soon restored.

The main road to the north-west leads after 1 mile to a car park at the starting point of walks in Balblair Forest. Five miles further on is the start of the Falls of Shin Forest Walk, deep in the Achany Glen.

④ ARDGAY

As Dornoch Firth narrows it becomes more like an inland loch, its calm waters reflecting the hills around it. Sheltered beneath the hills at the head of the firth is the village of Ardgay, on a shore thick with birches and larches. The Eitag Stone in the village marks the site of an annual cattle market held there throughout the 19th century.

From Ardgay, a narrow lane leads inland for some 4 miles, through magnificent scenery, to Culrain in the Kyle of Sutherland. A number of forest walks are clearly signposted. The modern Carbisdale Castle, built for the Duchess of Sutherland, is now a youth hostel.

⑤ EDDERTON

The village of Edderton clusters on the narrow shelf between the mountains and the Dornoch Firth. North of the church a 10 ft Pictish stone, its carving weatherbeaten, commemorates a bloody battle fought near

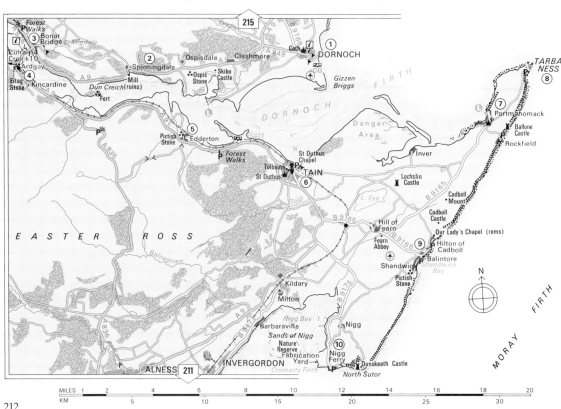

HARVEST OF LAND AND SEA *Beyond the golden fields of harvest time at Nigg Ferry rise the rigs and cranes that reaped a new harvest from the riches of North Sea oil.*

by against the Vikings. Bronze Age burial chambers and other relics of the district's early inhabitants dot the slopes inland.

A car park 2 miles east of Edderton is the starting point for walks in the Redburn Forest. These lead the visitor through miles of Forestry Commission plantations, the haunt of a variety of creatures, including the elusive wildcat.

⑥ TAIN

The tower of the 17th-century Tolbooth stands high above the skyline of the peaceful town of Tain, and is a stark reminder of the days when the town acted as an administrative centre for the Highland Clearances. It is set on high ground above the River Tain, and its history goes back to Viking times; Tain is a corruption of the Viking word *thing*, meaning 'council'.

Throughout the Middle Ages Tain was a major place of pilgrimage through its association with St Duthus, who was born there in about AD 1000 and established a chapel, now a ruin, just outside the town. In 1065 Duthus died in Ireland and his remains were brought back to Tain, where the magnificent new St Duthus Church was built in 1360. James IV often made the pilgrimage – the road west of the A9 is still known as the King's Causeway – and it was from the sanctuary there that Robert Bruce's wife was dragged into captivity in England. A small museum houses an interesting local history collection.

Tain's varied architectural styles range from the Tolbooth to the Victorian Gothic of the Town Hall. Outside the Tolbooth is a restored Market Cross, while halfway along the High Street is a rose garden.

⑦ PORTMAHOMACK

The peaceful lobster-fishing village of Portmahomack lies in a semi-circle on a low hill facing a quiet harbour overlooking Dornoch Firth. The harbour is used by inshore fishermen, whose gaily painted boats add to the beauty of the setting as they shelter in the lee of the single breakwater. Pleasure craft also use the harbour.

The curious Reformation church, behind the village, has a unique and intact domed tower. South of the harbour is a sandy beach sheltered from North Sea winds and ideal for children. Above the beach is a Victorian

Iron Fountain, erected in 1887 to commemorate the introduction of 'Gravitational Water' to the village.

⑧ TARBAT NESS

The long, low, windswept promontory sweeping towards Tarbat Ness, its highest point no more than 150 ft above sea level, guards the entry to Dornoch Firth. It is dominated by its tall white lighthouse, which keeps shipping clear of a dangerous sand-bar called the Gizzen Briggs, a name derived from the Norse.

From the lighthouse a coastal footpath leads south-west for 3 miles, along low cliffs haunted by sea-birds, to Rockfield. This hamlet comprises little more than a jetty and some score of sturdy cottages tucked well under the cliffs; it can also be reached by a lane from Portmahomack which drops steeply down to the coast.

On the cliffs just north of Rockfield are the gaunt ruins of Ballone Castle, built for the Earl of Ross, later owned by the Mackenzies, but abandoned in the 19th century.

⑨ BALINTORE

The cottages of the former fishing community of Balintore are centred on its small harbour and along the rocky foreshore to the north. The massive north wall of the harbour protects the village from the fury of winter

gales, while to the south a sandy beach stretches into Shandwick Bay. From the sand, the coastline rises towards the high cliffs which stretch towards North Sutor.

Fearn Abbey, 2 miles inland, was founded in the 12th century. The roof of this greystone building collapsed in 1742 during a service, killing 42 people – a disaster foretold by the Brahan Seer, a 16th-century Highlands prophet whose powers were said to have come from a magic stone left for him by fairies. Although the roof of the nave has been restored, the north and south chapels remain open to the skies.

Hilton of Cadboll, 1 mile to the north-east, is an attractive former fishing village, with the remains of an ancient chapel. Near by are the ruins of Cadboll Castle. Cadboll Mount, 1½ miles further north, is said to have been built by the Laird of Cadboll so that he could look down on his neighbour, MacLeod of Geanies, with whom he was having a feud.

⑩ NIGG FERRY

Sheltered by the red-sandstone cliffs of North Sutor, the tiny village of Nigg Ferry at the narrow mouth of Cromarty Firth is dominated by the giant cranes of a construction yard for North Sea oilfield platforms. Oil tankers pass the deserted quay which was once the starting point of the ferry to Cromarty, used in the Middle Ages by countless pilgrims making for the shrine of St Duthus in Tain.

From Nigg Ferry an attractive walk leads for about half a mile along the sandy beach to the base of North Sutor. A steep lane leads to the summit, from which there are fine views of Cromarty Firth.

High on North Sutor stand the remains of Dunskeath Castle – 'Fort of Dread' in Gaelic – built in the 12th century to protect the passage into the firth. The wide Sands of Nigg form a nature reserve, noted for a wide range of ducks, geese and wading birds.

STONE OF SORROW *Near the village of Shandwick stands a Pictish stone, the 'Clach a' Charridh', marking the spot where all unbaptised infants who died in the parish were buried.*

Valleys to the coast from Sutherland's high wilderness

Towering cliffs rising to the 750 ft Ord of Caithness are a feature of this stretch of coast. They are punctuated by sheltered, deserted coves, with a few harbours near which neat Victorian villages cluster. For the most part, however, it is a wild and desolate shore, with many castles and brochs witnessing its warlike past. The cliffs ring to the cries of sea-birds while inland are quiet glens rich in prehistoric remains.

BERRIEDALE WATER *Down from Knockfin Heights rushes a ribbon of blue water, snaking across the carpet of autumn-brown ferns on its way to the sea at Berriedale.*

① WHALIGOE
The tiny village of Whaligoe is notable for an unusual relic of the herring fishing industry that flourished in the 19th century. This is a flight of 365 steps cut into the steep cliffs and plunging to the sheltered cove below. The womenfolk of the village climbed these Whaligoe Steps with fully laden baskets of fish on the first part of their journey to carry the catch to Wick, 7 miles north.

The steps are slippery when wet, and great care should be taken when making the descent.

② LYBSTER
A single broad street runs down a gentle slope towards the sea at Lybster, which is still an active fishing community. Lybster's harbour, situated a quarter of a mile from the village, is set amid steep cliffs facing Lybster Bay and dominated by its lighthouse. The ancient quays are a base for crab and lobster fishermen whose boats dance on the gentle swell.

③ LATHERONWHEEL
From a quiet single street of cottages a steep and sharply twisting lane leads down to Latheronwheel's small but attractive harbour. High cliffs add to the protection offered by the breakwater, and a rocky stack stands defiantly against the sea at the mouth of the tiny bay. The Burn of Latheronwheel, brown with peat brought down from the hills, meets the sea beside the breakwater.

Latheron, 1 mile north-east at a meeting place of roads, acts as a centre for the thinly scattered community. Just north of the village are two fine standing stones set up by a forgotten people who settled in this area in the Bronze Age.

④ DUNBEATH
The village of Dunbeath, set around the harbour, is sheltered beneath rocky cliffs, and was at one time an important centre of the herring fishing industry. A few boats still operate from Dunbeath, but most have moved to Wick.

Laidhay Caithness Croft, just north of the village, is an early 18th-century croft complex, including a stable, house and byre, fully restored to its original appearance and furnished in the style of the time. It is open daily in summer.

Dunbeath Castle, built in the 15th century, stands high on the cliffs just south of the village. One of the many strongholds of the Earls of Caithness, it was enlarged in the 19th century. It is still inhabited, and can be clearly seen from the road and the harbour, but is not open to the public.

Another castle built by the Earls of Caithness dominates the small cluster of houses at Berriedale, 5 miles south of Dunbeath. The hill slopes inland from the village are rich in brochs, cairns and other relics of prehistoric settlements.

⑤ ORD OF CAITHNESS
The coast road twists to climb the steep Ord of Caithness, a vast natural bastion of rock and heather 750 ft above sea level. From the summit, which marks the old county boundary between Sutherland and Caithness, the views of the coast in all directions are superb.

It is said to be unlucky for a Sinclair to cross the Ord on a Monday wearing green. This superstition arose in 1513 when William, Earl of Caithness, led a local force of 300 to fight for James IV at the Battle of Flodden. The soldiers were clad in green tartan, and only one survived the battle in which 10,000 Scotsmen died.

⑥ HELMSDALE
The fishing village lies at the mouth of the River Helmsdale, claimed by some to be the best salmon river in Scotland. A small harbour is used by pleasure craft and a small fleet of fishing boats, while the village itself

---

THE HIGHLAND BROCHS

The stone towers, or brochs, whose remains are found in many parts of the Highlands, were built by Iron Age tribes between 100 BC and AD 100 to defend their families against enemies. The towers were circular, tapering upwards to a height of 30 ft or more. Inside was a living space about 30 ft across, where timber buildings surrounded a central hearth. The walls were hollow, and between the two shells were galleries and a staircase rising to the top of the walls.

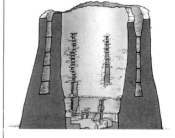

An artist's reconstruction of a typical broch

lies above the harbour, on the northern bank of the river. Its streets are lined with neat cottages and houses, surrounded by the rocky slopes of mountains.

The climate on this stretch of coast is unexpectedly mild, and palm trees grow at Portgower, 2 miles south-west. Though the foreshore around Helmsdale is rocky, there is a sandy beach 2 miles south-west of Portgower, reached by a footpath north of Lothmore.

Helmsdale is the starting point for a long drive north-west along the Strath of Kildonan, through some of the most glorious scenery in Sutherland. The main road is little more than a lane as it twists and climbs alongside the River Helmsdale, then past Loch an Ruathair into Strath Halladale. The route passes through open moorland and birchwoods, while all the time the mountains provide a spectacular back-drop. There are few houses or people in the Straths, and little traffic on the road which emerges, after 30 miles, on the north coast near Melvich, west of Dounreay.

WATER'S END *At Berriedale, Langwell Water and Berriedale Water become one, and are spanned by a quaint suspension footbridge before looping around a rocky foreshore to the sea.*

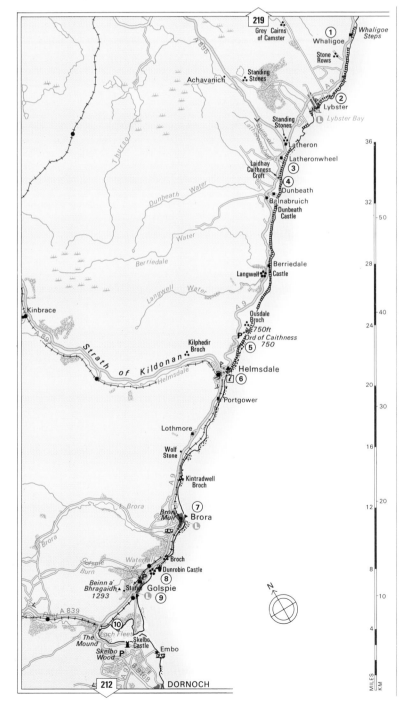

⑦ **BRORA**

Centred around a small square, the village of Brora stands astride the mouth of the River Brora. Behind the village is the Brora Muir, one of the few sizeable level stretches of land in the district, dotted with many crofts and small farms.

Two Iron Age brochs, or fortified towers, stand on the coast near Brora. Kintradwell Broch, 3 miles north of the village, is the better preserved. It measures 31 ft across within its double walls, and two headless skeletons were found there during excavations in 1880. The second broch is visible from the road 3 miles south of Brora, near the railway bridge.

There is good fishing for salmon and trout in the area, an 18-hole golf course, and a wealth of impressive scenery along the shores of Loch Brora, which reaches to within 3 miles of the village.

Beside the road 5 miles north of Brora stands the Wolf Stone, erected to commemorate the shooting of the last wild wolf in Scotland in about 1700.

⑧ **DUNROBIN CASTLE**

One of Scotland's oldest inhabited houses, Dunrobin Castle has been the home of the Earls, later the Dukes of Sutherland, since the 13th century. Set firmly on a natural terrace above the sea amidst beautiful

DUCAL DOMAIN *Dunrobin Castle, seat of the Dukes of Sutherland, was rebuilt in Victorian baronial style by Sir Charles Barry.*

215

gardens, the original castle was built in about 1225, possibly on the site of an earlier broch, and the massive keep dates from about this time. Modifications made around 1840 by Sir Charles Barry, architect of the Houses of Parliament, and restored by Sir Robert Lorimer after a fire in 1915, give the castle its present fairy-tale pinnacles and turrets. Lorimer also designed the library, dining-rooms and drawing-rooms in 1921.

The gardens are open to the public in summer, and there is a small museum of local history in the summerhouse. The castle, which is open daily in summer, is reached by a turning off the main coast road just over 1 mile north-east of Golspie.

⑨ **GOLSPIE**
The narrow coastal strip on which the village of Golspie stands seems almost overwhelmed by the mountains looming behind it. The mountain directly behind the village is 1,293 ft Beinn a' Bhragaidh; and on its summit, clearly visible for miles around, stands a massive statue by the English sculptor Sir Francis Chantrey of the First Duke of Sutherland, the man whose clearances of people from the area in favour of sheep has left a lasting mark on the Highlands and on folk memory. A memorial to an earlier member of the Sutherland family is the fine Sutherland Loft of 1737, in the 17th-century church at the northern end of the main street. A relic of the 3rd Duke is the private railway station, near Dunrobin Castle. At one time the duke also had his own private carriages and locomotive.

Golspie is a good base for walks and drives inland. A track leads in 2½ miles to the summit of Beinn a' Bhragaidh, from which there are fine views over Loch Fleet and Dornoch Firth. A car park off the main road just north of Golspie is the starting point for a nature trail alongside the Golspie Burn; it leads after 1 mile to a waterfall, beyond which the burn can be followed for another 3 miles.

There is good fishing off Golspie, for a variety of species.

⑩ **LOCH FLEET**
The waters of Loch Fleet are sheltered and calm, the natural breakwaters at the eastern end leaving only a narrow passage to the sea. A ferry used to cross this passage until 1815, when it was replaced by a causeway, built by Thomas Telford in the area known as The Mound, at the head of the loch.

Guarding the entrance to the loch, on the southern shore, are the crumbling ruins of the 14th-century Skelbo Castle, now the haunt of jackdaws but not open to the public. In the nearby Skelbo Wood the Forestry Commission has laid out several forest trails; they start from a car park reached by a lane turning east from the A9 just under a mile north of its junction with the B9168 from Dornoch.

LOCAL INFORMATION

Tourist information Helmsdale 640 (summer).

HM Coastguard Peterhead 4278, Kirkwall 3268 for information; 999 in emergency (ask for the coastguard).

Weather Glasgow Weather Centre (041) 248 3451.

Local radio BBC Radio Highland, 94 MHz; IBA Moray Firth Radio, 271 m, 1107 kHz, 95.9 MHz.

OTHER PLACES TO SEE

Achavanich Standing Stones, 6 miles NW of Lybster.

Grey Cairns of Camster, 6 miles N of Lybster. Two Stone Age chambered cairns.

Kilphedir Broch, Helmsdale.

Langwell, Berriedale. Gardens. Two Sun. afternoons in Aug. only.

Ousdale Broch, Helmsdale.

CROFTING: A WAY OF LIFE THAT MEANS TOIL ON LAND AND SEA

Crofting, or small farming, is one of the few means of making a living from the land in the Highlands and Islands. It is not a lucrative living; the soil is poor, and of the 18,000 or so registered crofters, most make more than half their income by spending part of the year with the fishing fleet, the merchant service or the oil rigs, and by catering for holiday-makers. But the raising of a few lambs and calves for later fattening in the Lowlands does give the crofter a stake in the land. However hard the life, it rescues him from the spectre that his forebears dreaded: exile to the big cities or overseas.

Crofting began with the breakdown of the clan system, deliberately fostered by the Government in the years following the Jacobite Uprising of 1745. Until then, clan territory and all the creatures upon it were common property, and the chiefs were no more than nominal landlords. An Act of Parliament, however, made them landlords in the English sense, and turned their people into a property-less peasantry. With game barred to them, and lacking the means to buy livestock, the only livelihood open to them was subsistence fishing and farming. The staple crop was the potato, but in the 1840s the crop was devastated by blight and the people were rendered destitute. To the morality of the day, eviction and enforced emigration – the infamous Clearances – seemed the only solution, for the land could not support the people.

For the crofters that remained, life was as harsh as ever, and the threat of dispossession for failing to pay the rent constant. But after a series of protests their plight was recognised, and in 1886 the Crofters' Act was passed, followed later by the founding of the Crofters' Commission. Today, crofters have security of tenure, government grants and the right to buy their crofts. Their contribution to British agriculture is not large, but it has helped to ensure that the Highlands and Islands are not peopled only by memories and legends.

PAST AND PRESENT *The ruined croft house by Loch Obe on the island of Barra tells a pitiful and silent story, for Barra was one of the islands worst hit by the Clearances. In 1857 the majority of the island's crofters were evicted by Colonel John Gordon. In South Uist, too, almost 2,000 crofters were driven from their homes. But today there are still many scattered crofts on the island, like the one below, perched beside Loch Bee.*

THE TOILERS *Crofters and their wives have always worked side by side on the land. In this photograph taken in Skye in 1885 the men use foot ploughs, called 'caschroms', to dig the rows for planting potatoes while the women spread seaweed from the shore as fertiliser. Potatoes were a staple food both for the crofting family and for their livestock during winter. Peat was cut as fuel for winter fires; the back-breaking task of carrying the cut peat back to the house was also performed by the womenfolk, using huge wicker baskets, called 'kishies', held by a rope or strap across the shoulders.*

INSIDE A CROFT *At Boddam, on South Voe, Shetland, a restored croft house gives a glimpse of a crofter's home life in the 19th century.*

THE HIGHLAND CLEARANCES, WHEN SHEEP WERE WORTH MORE THAN MEN

Towards the end of the 18th century, Scottish landowners made the discovery that there was more profit in sheep than in men. Prices for wool and mutton were high, whereas the crofters, struggling to scratch a living from the soil, were barely able to pay their rents. The failure of the potato crop in the 1840s aggravated the situation. Some chiefs and landlords beggared themselves to aid their tenants, but a large number did not. Instead they initiated the most callous stage of the Highland Clearances, when landowners, often with ruthless disregard for the suffering caused, carried out large-scale evictions of the crofters and their families to make room for sheep. All over the Highlands and Islands people were driven from their homes, which were then put to the torch, while in Westminster an uncaring Government stood idly by. Many roofless crofts scattered through the area still bear witness to the extent of the Clearances. In some areas crofters were resettled on poor land near the coast, but thousands more left their homeland crowded into leaky emigrant ships.

Cheviot sheep, able to survive the hard Highland winters, replaced the evicted crofters and were tended by shepherds brought in from the Lowlands.

A monument to the First Duke of Sutherland, by the sculptor Sir Francis Chantrey, stands on a mountain top near Golspie. Known as 'The Leviathan of Wealth', the Duke evicted some 15,000 tenants between 1810 and 1820, often with violence, and grassed their fields to raise sheep.

Thomas Faed's painting The Last of the Clan *depicts the misery of enforced emigration.*

Cliffs above the racing tides beyond John o'Groats

Memories of the early Viking settlers live on in the un-Scottish place-names of small, isolated communities in this northernmost corner of Scotland. Roads along the north coast pass through acres of fertile cornfields and low-lying expanses of windswept grassland speckled with grazing cattle. By contrast, waves have lashed the red-sandstone cliffs around Duncansby Head into lofty sea stacks and arches.

① SCRABSTER

Like many other ports in Caithness, Scrabster started as a centre for exporting flagstones in the 19th century. It has changed very much since then. Ferry services now run daily from Scrabster to Stromness in the Orkneys. Scrabster also offers anchorage to trawlers and sailing boats. There is a sailing club and the opportunity for fishing off Scrabster rocks. For those who can stomach the incessant Atlantic swell, boats may be arranged for sea-angling expeditions, in search of cod, pollack, coalfish, conger eel, skate and halibut.

Past the lifeboat station, which is sometimes open to visitors, a walk along a private motor road leads to a small lighthouse. From there a track leads up over high grassy cliffs to Holborn Head and its spectacular sea-sculptured cliffs.

② THURSO

The population of Thurso, the northernmost town on the British mainland, has more than trebled since the opening in the 1950s of the nuclear power station at Dounreay. Modern housing estates have sprung up along the eastern bank of the River Thurso, but the character of the western bank has changed little.

A clutch of restored fishermen's cottages stands above the harbour, and behind them there are tidy rows of houses which date from the early 19th century, when Thurso first became a centre for exporting flagstones. This part of the town was planned on a rectangular grid pattern by Sir John Sinclair, a local landowner, whose statue

A craftsman rolls and shapes the molten glass.

dominates Sir John Square.

The harbour is overlooked to the east by the gaunt ruined outline of Thurso Castle, a 17th-century castle which was substantially rebuilt in 1872; it is not open to the public. Beyond the castle is Harold's Tower, built over the grave of Earl Harold who ruled part of Caithness, Orkney and Shetland in the 12th century.

Places to visit in Thurso include the Thurso Folk Museum and the ruins of the old church of St Peter, which dates from the

13th century. Thurso also has the only indoor heated swimming pool on the north coast.

③ CASTLETOWN

It used to be said that when a man from Caithness was in Edinburgh or Glasgow he trod the stones of his native county. For in the 19th century, Castletown exported paving-stones to towns in Britain and to corners of the Empire as far-flung as Calcutta, Melbourne and Auckland. Even today the fields in some parts of Caithness are bordered with great slabs of flagstone rather than with walls.

The heart of Castletown is a neat village of squat stone cottages, built on a grid pattern. It was founded in the early 19th century when the local quarries began large-scale production of flagstones. The quarries at Castlehill are now filled-in, but most of the quarrymen's cottages have been renovated for visitors. The sleepy little harbour from which the stones were shipped is now used for salmon-netting, and by pleasure craft.

The road which leads from Castletown towards Dunnet Bay passes through woodlands planted by James Traill, who founded the quarries in 1824. The sands of Dunnet Bay sweep northwards for more than 2 miles, and are backed by tall, grass-topped dunes and a forest.

④ DUNNET HEAD

From the little village of Dunnet, the road snakes over a lonely moorland wilderness past lochs and streams towards the most northerly point on the British mainland. Although its lighthouse is perched on cliffs more than 300 ft above the sea, stones thrown up by the winter waters of the Pentland Firth have been known to smash against the windows.

On a clear day the views from the lighthouse are magnificent – from Cape Wrath in the west and Duncansby Head in the east to Orkney and the Old Man of Hoy in the north. But it is the panorama from the viewpoint above the lighthouse which really gives the impression that Caithness is at the edge of the world. From this point it is possible to watch changes in the weather for miles inland. While beams of sun spotlight certain patches of golden cornfield, other areas of ground are wreathed in palls of glowering cloud.

⑤ BROUGH

A steep track leads down from the village of Brough to a rocky bay whose shingly beach is sticky with seaweed. The stone pier which juts out into the sea is overlooked by the Little Clett – a tall, grass-topped sea stack white with sea-birds. The pier was built early last century to take supplies by sea to the lighthouse at Dunnet Head and other isolated lighthouses, but helicopters and larger vessels have robbed it of its former role.

⑥ HAM

From the harbour at Ham, corn and oatmeal used to be shipped to ports in Scotland, England and Europe. Today the watermill which ground the corn stands derelict above the beach; and the pier, which is constructed from flagstones stacked side by side, is little used.

At low tide, the ledges of layered rock projecting into the sea are dotted with hundreds of little pools. From the western arm of the cove there are superb views of the cliffs of Dunnet Head.

At Scarfskerry, 2 miles east, a ribbon of squat cottages has sprung up at a point where a narrow inlet in the rocks forms a

DUNCANSBY HEAD *Chiselled to fine points by wind and waves, the Duncansby Stacks thrust from a turbulent sea. In the red-sandstone cliffs the sea has punched a hole known as Thirle Door.*

WICK HARBOUR *In its heyday as a fishing port, Wick harbour had a herring fleet of more than 1,000 vessels. Fishermen still use the harbour, and there is a large fish market.*

natural harbour. The village's seafaring tradition is kept alive today by a boat-builder who crafts clinker-built fishing boats and cruisers from larch and oak.

⑦ HARROW

The harbour at Harrow was built in the 19th century for exporting flagstones from the nearby quarries. Beside the road to the harbour stand a flagstone-cutting factory dated 1871 and the overgrown track of a light railway line. Today, however, the harbour is used by lobster-fishing boats.

The nearby Castle of Mey, set amid one of the few areas of woodland along this stretch of coast, has been a summer residence of Queen Elizabeth, the Queen Mother, since 1952. It was built as one of the strongholds of the Sinclairs, Earls of Sutherland, and has been restored from its near-ruinous condition by the Queen Mother. The gardens are open on certain days in summer.

⑧ JOHN O' GROATS

Often regarded as the northernmost point in mainland Britain, John o' Groats can in fact only claim to be the most northerly village, for Dunnet Head extends nearly 2 miles nearer the Arctic Circle. The settlement is named after a Dutchman, Jan de Groot, who was commissioned by James IV in 1496 to start a ferry service to Orkney, which the king had just won from Norway and brought under Scottish rule. A grassy mound and flagstaff mark the site of de Groot's house.

The cottages, shops and hotels that form John o' Groats are dotted over a wide area, but its focal point is a harbour from which a ferry crosses Orkney during the summer months. On a clear day the view across the Pentland Firth to the distant islands lining the horizon is breathtaking.

⑨ DUNCANSBY HEAD

The headland, the north-east tip of mainland Britain, is capped by a lighthouse marking the entrance to the treacherous Pentland Firth, through which tides rip at up to 12 mph.

From the lighthouse car park a short walk leads down to the southern side of the head and to a good view of the chasms, arches and castle-like stacks which the pounding waves have carved from the red-sandstone cliffs.

⑩ KEISS

Built on a gentle slope above a small harbour, Keiss is an important crab-fishing community. An old warehouse and icehouse recall former times, when herring was the main catch, and a few bright boats add colour to the scene. To the north-east the 16th-century Keiss Castle is perched on top of low cliffs, with the newer 18th-century castle behind it.

To the south of Keiss stretch 3 miles of sands facing Sinclair's Bay, the largest stretch of sands on the Caithness coast. It is backed by dunes which are crossed by footpaths leading from the main road.

⑪ WICK

The ancient town of Wick has a busy past – but unlike many towns along the east coast from which industry has ebbed over the centuries, Wick still remains a bustling commercial centre. It was an early Viking anchorage and settlement – its name, like that of the Vikings themselves, comes from the Norse word *vik*, meaning 'creek'. The 12th-century castle of Old Wick, whose ruinous keep stands guard at the top of steep cliffs just south of the town, is one of the oldest castles in Scotland. It is still three storeys high, and its walls are 7 ft thick. The castle can be reached by a signposted turning off the main road, or by a coastal walk of about 2 miles along Wick's South Head.

Wick's stone-built houses and shops follow the medieval street plan, although the buildings themselves are largely 18th-century. Wick's history is displayed in the Wick Heritage Centre near the harbour.

A lighthouse and the ruins of two spectacular clifftop fortresses stand at Noss Head, 3 miles north-east of Wick. Castle Girnigoe, which dates from the 15th century, and Castle Sinclair, built two centuries later, were both seats of the Sinclairs, Earls of Caithness.

Along the coast 1½ miles further west can be seen the five-storey Ackergill Tower, which after passing through the hands of the Keiths, the Earls of Caithness and the Campbells, in 1699 reached the Dunbars, who lived there until 1986. Footpaths lead down to small rocky caves.

Castle Girnigoe (left) and Castle Sinclair

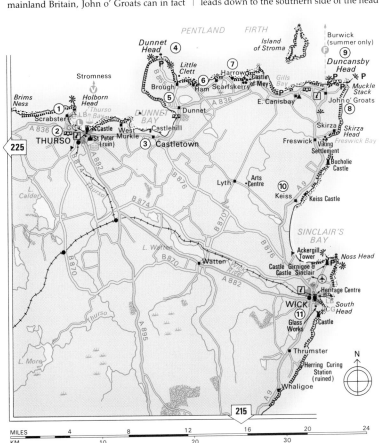

219

Island homes of early man around a historic harbour

There are some 70 islands in Orkney, of which 18 are now inhabited – a mere shadow of former ages. Archaeological evidence tells of continuous occupation for 6,000 years, from Stone Age peoples to Picts and Celtic priest-kings who made treaties with the Romans, to Viking and Stewart overlords and to Italian prisoners in the Second World War. There are antiquities to explore, excellent fishing, and teeming bird life among the awesome cliffs.

ACT OF FAITH *Italian prisoners of war working on the Churchill Barriers built this chapel from two Nissen huts, using scrap materials.*

① HOY

With its wild hills of heather and bog and its soaring cliffs wearing eternal clouds of sea-birds, Hoy forms most of the south-western shore of Scapa Flow, one of the finest natural harbours in the world and a vital naval anchorage during both World Wars. It was from Scapa Flow that the Grand Fleet sailed to the Battle of Jutland in May 1916, and it was in the same harbour that HMS *Vanguard* blew up in 1917. The German High Seas Fleet scuttled itself in Scapa Flow in 1919; seven of the original 74 ships sunk still lie below the surface, and thousands of divers visit Scapa Flow each year to seek them.

In 1939 HMS *Royal Oak* was torpedoed in Scapa Flow by the submarine U47, which made a daring attack through Holm Sound. The sound was later sealed by the Churchill Barriers, and some of the *Royal Oak's* 800 dead are buried, beside those from other battles, in the Naval cemetery near the deserted and decaying dockyard of Lyness. The remainder still lie within the ship's hull, an officially designated war cemetery.

A far more ancient grave in the island is the Dwarfie Stane, a monument unique in Britain, since its two chambers were hewn out of solid rock, probably in about 1900 BC. Legend, and Sir Walter Scott, suggest it is the home of Trolld, the malevolent dwarf of the Norse Sagas.

The island's best-known feature is the sheer 450 ft stack, the Old Man of Hoy, first climbed in 1966. Near by is St John's Head which, at 1,040 ft, is the highest perpendicular sea-cliff in Britain. The Martello towers guarding Longhope sound were built to cover an assembly point of Baltic convoys during the Napoleonic Wars.

Almost a mile offshore is the island of Flotta, almost totally flat as its name suggests, and still bearing the fortifications of two World Wars. It also bears an oil terminal, with enormous tankers in attendance.

Because of its myriad wild flowers, some of them rare alpines, and its bird life, Hoy is designated an area of special scientific interest.

② MAINLAND

Considering that for much of human history Orkney was considered to lie at the very edge of the world, it is astonishing that the islands have been continuously occupied much longer than a good deal of Scotland. Perhaps their remoteness offered safety, while added attractions were their fertility and their lochs filled with fish.

Mainland, the largest of the islands, cannot have greatly changed since the Stone Age villagers abandoned their settlement at Skara Brae some 4,500 years ago, when a great sandstorm buried their homes. Stone was, and still is, the principal building material on virtually treeless Orkney, and

not only the houses, but stone beds, cupboards and hearths survive to give a vivid picture of life in that distant era.

A little to the south-east are the lochs of Stenness and Harray, noted now for their wild brown trout but once of much greater significance. At the southern end of the Loch of Stenness is the Unstan chambered tomb, whose construction is as cunning as that of the pyramids. On the southern shore of the Loch of Harray are two magnificently sited and precisely spaced stone circles, the Ring of Brogar and the smaller Standing Stones of Stenness. Near by is Maeshowe, a 4,000-year-old tomb which is one of the finest pieces of prehistoric engineering in Western Europe. Scribblings left by 12th-century Viking raiders on its walls complain that someone has forestalled the writers and removed a great treasure.

All over the island are the mounds of prehistory, and ruins such as that of Broch of Gurness, a fort occupied in turn over a millennium by Picts and Vikings, or the remains on the Brough of Birsay that link the Norsemen with the coming of Christianity.

There are fine beaches and splendid walks, such as the one on Marwick Head, whose cliffs are a breeding ground for kittiwakes, guillemots and razorbills. On the top is a weatherworn monument to Lord Kitchener, who was drowned near by when HMS *Hampshire* was sunk by a German mine in 1916. Another cliff adventure is a visit to The Gloup, a fearful chasm in Deerness that can be visited by boat through a tunnel from the sea. On a sunny day, the water in the tunnel lights up to an iridescent green.

The island's capital, and Orkney's, is Kirkwall, centred upon a busy harbour in which there is a constant coming and going of lobster boats, coasting 'puffers' and ferries. The houses are handsome and steep gabled, and there are some old, narrow streets where cars and pedestrians compete for right of way. Kirkwall's most impressive building is the Cathedral of St Magnus, built in 1137 as a monument to the Norse Jarl of Orkney and saint murdered 20 years earlier. His skeleton was rediscovered in the building at the beginning of this century; there

THE HIGH ISLAND *The Vikings gave Hoy its name – the 'high island' – a land of majestic sandstone cliffs towering to more than 1,000 ft, with a wispy halo of sea mist for a crown.*

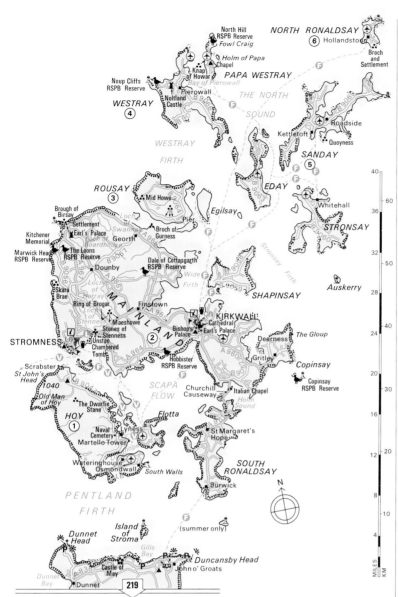

subjugation of Orkney. Some years ago, a large Viking cemetery was discovered beneath the sand-dunes.

A little to the west of Pierowall is Noltland Castle, built by Gilbert Balfour in 1560. He was implicated in the murder of Lord Darnley, husband of Mary, Queen of Scots in 1567, and finished his career on the gallows nine years later, hanged for treason. His castle, though ruinous, is still grimly handsome. There are several sandy beaches on Westray, and trout fishing may be arranged in the lochs.

The smaller island of Papa Westray gets its name from the 'Papae' or Celtic priests who used to live on the island; among its other claims to fame is the briefest scheduled airline service in the world – 2 minutes by Loganair from Westray. The oldest standing houses in Orkney, and perhaps in north-western Europe, are the pair at Knap of Howar. They were inhabited by people who kept livestock, grew crops, hunted deer and collected shellfish from the shore some 5,500 years ago.

⑤ SANDAY

For such a northerly island, Sanday has a remarkably southern appearance, with miles of shining beaches embracing like a halo the isthmuses of which it is largely composed. The chilly sea does not deter the thousands of wading birds that have made the sands their home.

Most of the island is cultivated, growing root crops and oats, but the plough has spared at least one major antiquity, the chambered tomb of Quoyness. The drystone walls of the main chamber are composed of huge, flat boulders built to a height of 12 ft; human remains discovered in the chamber and inside cells indicate that the tomb was in use around 2900 BC.

The island is so low-lying in mist or haze that many old-time mariners simply failed to see it until they drove the bows of their vessels into its shores, so providing a welcome addition to the islanders' economy. Sanday's income is derived from more conventional sources now, including holiday-makers. Kettletoft, where the ferry comes in, is a pleasant place to stay.

⑥ NORTH RONALDSAY

The northernmost island of Orkney, North Ronaldsay consists of some 4 square miles of flat, fertile land, completely surrounded by a wall built just above high-water mark. The wall was built to exclude the sheep that must, for lack of other grazing, feed upon seaweed.

There are several prehistoric monuments, including a broch or fort at the island's southern tip, and no doubt many more have now disappeared under the plough. The candy-striped lighthouse dates from 1789 and is one of the highest land lights in Britain.

was an axe cut in the skull, which accords with the manner of his death as described in the old sagas.

Kirkwall also has two palaces, the 12th-century Bishop's Palace and the Earl's Palace, built by one of the Stewart Earls in 1600. The Public Library, founded in 1683, is the oldest in Scotland.

Stromness, Mainland's other principal town, is also a port and consists mainly of a single, long, narrow street, many of whose seaward houses have little jetties of their own. There is a good museum devoted principally to seamen and whalers, and an art centre containing an internationally renowned collection of modern works.

From the south-east end of Mainland, the causeway over the Churchill Barriers connects it with several other islands.

③ ROUSAY

The island is mostly high moorland dotted with pewter-coloured lochans, and over all bright skies filled with birds' cries. Stone Age cairns and chambered tombs are everywhere. The most impressive of these is Mid Howe, now protected by a modern building yet still maintaining its air of ancient solemnity. The remains of 25 people were found in the 100 ft long burial chamber when it was excavated; carbon dating indicated that they had been placed there around 3000 BC. A Norse cemetery, a Viking ship burial and a Stone Age village have also been uncovered.

There are large sea-bird colonies on the cliffs, and peregrines and hen harriers on the moors. Fishermen may seek permission to pursue the brown trout in the lochs or go sea-angling or skin-diving at the hotel by the pier. Or, more simply, visitors may buy crabs, scallops or lobsters from the processors near by.

④ WESTRAY

Some 10 miles long by 3 miles across, much of it good farmland, Westray is one of the largest and most populous of the islands. The principal village is Pierowall, tucked at the back of its attractive bay and natural harbour that in 1136 attracted Jarl Rognvald and his longships at the beginning of the

ARCTIC TERN *Britain's largest colony of these summer visitors with their long tail streamers is in the bird reserve on Papa Westray.*

LOCAL INFORMATION

Tourist information Kirkwall 2856; Stromness 850716 (limited opening in winter).

HM Coastguard Kirkwall 3268 for information; 999 in emergency (ask for coastguard).

Weather Kirkwall 3802.

Local radio BBC Radio Orkney, 93.7 MHz.

HOW TO GET THERE

By air. British Airways: daily services to Kirkwall from Glasgow, Inverness and Aberdeen, with connections from London, Birmingham and Manchester; Kirkwall (0856) 3359. Loganair: daily services from Edinburgh, Inverness and Wick, with connection from Glasgow; Kirkwall 3457.
By sea. P&O: car ferry from Scrabster to Stromness; daily; Stromness 850655. Thomas and Bews: passenger ferry John O'Groats to South Ronaldsay daily in summer; Barrock 619 in winter, John o'Groats 353 in summer.

Sea-birds and seals on Shetland's fiord-cut islands

Shetland lies 110 miles north-east of Scotland's north coast, and the islands' traditions are more Norse than Scottish. Less than 100 miles further north-east lie some of the biggest North Sea oil fields, and their exploitation has brought changes to parts of the islands. Elsewhere, however, they retain their wild appeal. They are windswept, treeless and peat-covered, and the sea lochs that cut deeply into them are the domain of sea-birds.

JARLSHOF *A circular Iron Age dwelling, or 'wheel-house', with seven roofed bays is overlooked by the 17th-century Laird's House.*

① LERWICK

Shetland's capital, and the islands' only town, was a Dutch settlement in the 17th century. It became a thriving fishing port after Fort Charlotte was founded in 1653 to exploit the military potential of Bressay Sound. The oil boom of the 1970s brought dramatic growth. In that decade, there was a ten-fold increase in harbour traffic, and a 40-fold increase in revenues. The many new houses – stern and grey as the older ones are – reflect that growth, and today Lerwick holds a third of Shetland's total population of 22,000. However, the old town along the front is intact, and there are still no traffic lights or parking meters.

A mile from the centre, in the Loch of Clickimin, are the remains of a broch dating from the 4th to 2nd centuries BC. The Shetland County Museum in Lerwick contains replicas of Celtic silver treasures found in 1958 on St Ninian's Isle, Norse remains and relics of maritime history. At Veensgarth, 3 miles north-west, there is a museum devoted to domestic life, agriculture and fishing.

The Tourist Centre issues permits for inland fishing, and most lochs are well stocked with brown trout. Boats for sea-angling can also be hired.

Lerwick's main annual celebration is the fire festival of 'Up-Helly-Aa'. Held on the last Tuesday of January, the festival is an 18th-century adaptation of a Norse feast, Uphalliday, marking the end of Yule and the long winter nights. A replica of a 30 ft Viking galley is hauled through the streets by 'guizers' – men disguised with masks – and ceremonially burned as a prelude to a night of revelry.

② ISLE OF NOSS

The island, a national nature reserve, is one of Europe's greatest sea-bird colonies, with an estimated 70-80,000 birds. It was once farmed, but there are no permanent inhabitants now. In the course of a walk around the

island, taking 2-3 hours, visitors can see eider ducks, Arctic terns and great skuas, or 'bonxies' as they are known locally. Ledges of sandstone provide nesting sites for gannets, kittiwakes and guillemots. The walk includes the 600 ft Noup of Noss cliff, with views that range from Fair Isle to Unst.

③ MOUSA

This small uninhabited island, which can be reached only by specially hired boat from Sandwick, has on its west coast the most complete example of an Iron Age broch in existence today. The tower rises 43 ft on walls that are at the base 12 ft thick and hollow. Inside this fireproof protection, a clan of Picts built a 'wheelhouse' of thatched wooden rooms set in a circle.

④ SUMBURGH

The village is dominated by a new airport, its two radar domes poised like giant golfballs on nearby hills. Until North Sea oil was found in 1971 the airport had a single runway, and a man was employed to drive sheep off it so that planes could land. Now there are two modern runways and a new terminal to serve the regular flights from Aberdeen, London, Birmingham, Manchester, Glasgow and Edinburgh, and the helicopters that fly back and forth from the oil platforms.

Just south of the airport lies Jarlshof, one of the country's most remarkable archaeological sites. Nestling around trim, grassy hillocks are the remains of 3,000 years of settlement, from the Stone Age through the Bronze and Iron Ages to Viking times. Iron Age remains include those of a broch, one of the 500 circular drystone defensive towers built by tribes all over northern Britain

between about 400 BC and AD 200. There is a small museum on the site.

Round nearby Sumburgh Head, sea-birds by the thousand roost, and seals clamber on and off the rocks below. To the west lies the sandy Bay of Quendale, and beyond towers a 900 ft hill, Fitful Head. A steep, rough road climbs to the radar dome at the summit. From the top, North Sea fogs permitting, there is a magnificent view over Mainland's cliffs, inlets and rolling inland hills.

At Boddam, 4 miles north of Sumburgh on the A970, a mid 19th-century croft house has been restored to its original state and furnished in the style of the time.

⑤ ST NINIAN'S ISLE

Despite its name, St Ninian's – named after a 6th-century Irish missionary – is not an island. It is linked to Mainland by a narrow isthmus formed by two beaches of pure sand back to back. On the hillside facing Mainland are the remains of a 12th-century chapel. There, in 1958, archaeologists found a treasure of 27 Celtic silver pieces which had been buried around AD 800, presumably to keep them from marauding Vikings. The St Ninian's Treasure is now in the National Museum of Antiquities in Edinburgh.

SULLOM VOE *In this winding fiord the waters of the North Sea thrust deep into the isle of Mainland, cutting it almost in two and coming within 120 yds of the Atlantic Ocean.*

SHETLAND'S TOUGH LITTLE PONY

Measuring only 42 in. high at the shoulder when fully grown, the Shetland pony was once in great demand for work in coal mines and on Scottish crofts. Now it is sold the world over as a pet, and is often the first mount ridden by pupils at riding schools.

Shetland pony

⑥ EAST AND WEST BURRA

The road to these islands leads south from Scalloway over a narrow causeway and provides dramatic views of Clift Hills on Mainland. Hamnavoe, a small fishing village, is the islands' principal community.

To the west, 24 miles away, lies Foula, its dominating 1,373 ft mountain, The Sneug, clearly visible in good weather. Its cliffs are spectacular, rising sheer to 1,220 ft at a point called the Kame. Often called Britain's loneliest inhabited island, Foula has about 40 inhabitants who may be cut off by gales for a month at a time. In good weather, a mail-boat runs from Walls, on Mainland, but the island has no harbour and the boat must be lifted clear of the water at each visit.

⑦ SCALLOWAY

The settlement which was once the capital of Shetland is named after a Norse *skali*, or hall, now long vanished. But the town is still dominated by a latter-day *skali* – the towering, gaunt ruin of a castle built in 1600 by Earl Patrick Stewart, who forcibly replaced Norse law by Scottish feudal law. The key to the castle is available from a cottage opposite the entrance.

Close to the castle, and surrounded by the houses of the 1,000-strong community, is the harbour, busy with fishing vessels and alive with seagulls. During the Second World War, Scalloway was the main base for Norwegian patriots who smuggled saboteurs in and refugees out of their homeland, an operation known as 'the Shetland Bus'.

⑧ ESHA NESS

This headland is one of Shetland's many startling clifftop viewpoints, and one of the few accessible by car. The road leads up to a lighthouse and car park over a high, barren, peat plain strewn with lava boulders. Fulmars soar over the ragged cliffs, and puffins burrow in the soil.

An inlet a few yards to the north, Calder's Geo, is a collapsed cave where Atlantic breakers smash in over rock that once formed the cave's roof. There are fine walks over the springy turf. Ronas Hill, 5 miles to the north-east, is Mainland's highest point, at 1,475 ft.

⑨ SULLOM VOE

This deep, ice-scoured fiord – or 'voe' in the Shetland dialect – is the terminal for the two oil pipelines from the East Shetlands Basin, and is the largest oil terminal in Europe. The lines, emerging from the ocean 2 miles away across a peninsula, deliver a stream of oil to huge, grey tanks, ready for transfer to tankers in the voe. A flare, visible for miles, burns off excess gas.

At the head of the voe, where the road leads northwards, is a neck of land known as Mavis Grind – from the Norse *maev eiths grind*, 'the gate of the narrow isthmus'.

⑩ YELL

The second largest island in Shetland, 17 miles long, is a place of rolling peat hills speckled with lochs and surrounded by cliffs. West Sandwick, however, has a fine sandy beach and 3 miles north is Whale Firth, a voe with shingle beaches, steep grassy slopes, rugged cliffs and several caves. Frequent car ferries link Mainland to Yell, and Yell to Fetlar and Unst.

⑪ UNST

Britain's northernmost island lacks Shetland's usual thick carpet of peat, but is instead a place of screes and stony outcrops. Of all the islands, it has the densest population of Shetland ponies. In the south-east stand the austere rocks of Muness, Britain's northernmost castle.

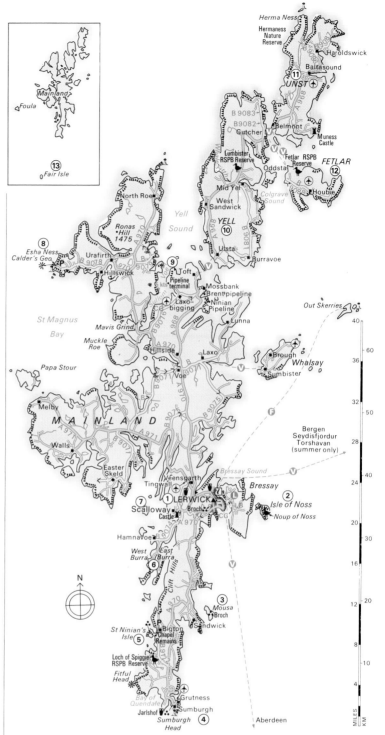

At the island's northern tip is the Herma-ness National Nature Reserve. The cliff ledges are crowded with guillemots and razorbills, while above wheel kittiwakes, fulmars and other sea-birds.

⑫ FETLAR

The island is well known to ornithologists, particularly for its Arctic skuas and storm petrels. In 1967 a pair of snowy owls began to breed there, an event that caused 1,700 acres of Fetlar to be declared a bird reserve. In 1975 the only male vanished, but a few female birds can still occasionally be seen. Otters, common seals and grey seals abound.

⑬ FAIR ISLE

Fair Isle, 25 miles south-west of Sumburgh, is visited twice a week by air from Lerwick and by boat from Grutness, on Mainland. Its 70 inhabitants are still noted for their knitting, the intricate patterns of which were supposedly introduced by Spanish survivors of the Armada.

Fair Isle belongs to the National Trust for Scotland and is noted for its bird life, including numerous migrants.

LOCAL INFORMATION

Tourist information Lerwick 3434.

HM Coastguard Lerwick 2976 for information, 999 in emergency (ask for coastguard).

Weather Sullom Voe 242069.

Local radio BBC Radio Shetland, 92.7 MHz.

HOW TO GET THERE

By sea. P & O Ferries: car and passenger services from Aberdeen to Lerwick, Mon. Wed. and Fri.; Aberdeen 572615.

By air. British Airways: flights to Sumburgh from London, Birmingham, Manchester, Glasgow, Edinburgh, Aberdeen and Inverness; for information and reservations contact local BA office. Loganair: scheduled flights from Edinburgh to Tingwall (Lerwick), and inter-island flights; Gott 246.

A lonely coast of plunging cliffs and secluded bays

Scotland's Far North is one of the most sparsely inhabited areas of Britain. Most of its settlements are little more than hamlets of greystone that are slowly giving up the struggle to make a living from an infertile land. Instead, they now provide good centres for visitors interested in fishing or wildlife, or are attracted simply by the wild beauty of a coast where the cliffs break regularly to plunge into wide, white sandy bays.

① BALNAKEIL

The broad sands of Balnakeil Bay sweep away over the dunes towards Faraid Head. In spring the cliffs on the eastern side of the headland are the home of nesting puffins.

At the southern end of the bay stands a ruined church, dating from 1619. A tomb decorated by a skull and crossbones is built into a niche in the south wall. It commemorates Donald MacLeod, a notorious local highwayman, who is believed to have committed at least 18 murders. Fearing that his many enemies would desecrate his grave after he had died, MacLeod is said to have paid £1,000 for this privileged last resting place.

Balnakeil Craft Village lies half a mile inland from the church, its workshops set amongst the unprepossessing barracks of an obsolete 'early warning' station. There are several independently owned and operated businesses in the village, run by craftsmen from all over the world. During the summer visitors may watch the craftsmen at work; they include jewellers, bookbinders and weavers.

② DURNESS

The small crofting and sheep-farming centre of Durness stands on grassy limestone bluffs. To the south-east, as far as Loch Eriboll, the cliffs plunge into a series of safe, sandy bays, backed by rich pastures.

One of the most impressive features of this coast is the Smoo Cave – a name derived from the Norse word *smjuga*, meaning a 'narrow cleft' or 'creek'. The main chamber, a cathedral-like cavern 200 ft long and 110 ft wide, is easily accessible from the road. It echoes the drips of the Allt Smoo, a burn which flows off the moors inland and drops 80 ft down an open vertical shaft into a deep pool in a second chamber. A third chamber extends a further 120 ft. The second and third chambers can be reached only by experienced potholers.

Durness holds a Highland Gathering at the end of July.

③ LOCH ERIBOLL

The still, narrow waters of Loch Eriboll bite 10 miles into one of the least inhabited areas of the northern coast. The loch, sheltered by steep hills, is in places 350 ft deep, making it one of the deepest lochs on the west coast.

During the Second World War the loch was used for assembling North Atlantic convoys, whose crews came to know it as Loch 'Orrible'. This is unfair, for when the sun shines it picks out the creases of the pink cliffs on the loch's eastern shore in a breathtaking play of light and shade. In fact the name Eriboll derives from Norse words meaning 'home on a gravelly beach'.

The island in the middle was used as target-practice for bombers about to destroy the German battleship *Tirpitz* in a similarly

shaped Norwegian fiord in 1944. Finally, at the end of the war, German U-boats surrendered to the British Navy in Loch Eriboll.

Only a sprinkling of cottages line the shores of the loch, for this is Sutherland – an area where sheep outnumber people by more than 20 to 1.

Hidden by the bracken, just off the road on the loch's western side, lies a souterrain. This dark underground chamber, which is reached by a flight of steps, was probably used for storing food during the Iron Age.

At the head of the loch, Craig na Faoilinn rises to 934 ft. To the west are the peaks of Cranstackie and Beinn Spionnaidh, both more than 2,000 ft high and providing spectacular mountain scenery.

④ TALMINE

A group of small crofting communities centred on Talmine was set up as a result of the 19th-century Highland Clearances, when crofters were evicted from their lands to make room for sheep. Some of the most notorious evictions took place in 1814 and 1819 in the glens of Strathnaver. They were supervised by the new leaseholder Patrick Sellar, already a hated figure in the Highlands for his evictions on behalf of the Sutherland Estates. The evicted crofters were resettled along the coast where they quarried flagstones and learned how to fish. For a century and a half they eked a living from their crofts. But the land has finally proved too inhospitable, and former crofters' cottages now being renovated for holidaymakers.

Along this stretch of coast there is a series of white sandy beaches which are safe for bathing. At low tide, it is possible to walk across a narrow causeway of sand to the grassy mounds of the Rabbit Islands; but it would be wise to consult a local resident before attempting the crossing.

FLOWER OF THE NORTH

Found only in Sutherland, Caithness and Orkney, the tiny Scottish primrose grows abundantly in damp, windswept pastures near the sea. It is smaller than a common primrose, growing only to 2-3 in. (5-7.5 cm.) high, and has a cluster of purple or pink flowers on a single stalk.

Scottish primrose
Primula scotica
June - Sept.

---

⑤ TONGUE

As the road from Durness approaches Tongue, it passes over an expanse of bleak moorland which is dominated, to the south, by the solitary mass of Ben Hope and the shapely granite peaks of Ben Loyal. The lush, wooded land on the east bank of the Kyle of Tongue comes as a pleasant surprise.

The village of Tongue is set back from the shore. It is a good centre for hill-walking; for fishing in Loch Loyal, 4 miles to the south; for bathing at the sandy beach of Coldbackie; and for exploring an area that is steeped in several thousand years of history.

From the village a footpath leads across a burn to Castle Varrich, which is perched on a neighbouring hillock. The ruined castle is reputed to have been a Viking look-out, but the buildings which remain suggest that it was a 14th-century stronghold. The white-washed church of St Andrew, with stepped gables that are typical of the area, dates from 1680. Inside, the boxed wooden gallery at the back was once used by the family of the chief of the Mackay clan.

Tongue House, set amidst wooded parkland north of the village, was rebuilt in 1678 on the site of an earlier house burned down during the Civil War. Originally the home of the chiefs of Mackay, Tongue House is now part of the Sutherland estates; its grounds are open to the public only occasionally.

The 17th-century Church of St Andrew at Tongue

⑥ SKERRAY

Bright-red letterboxes in the middle of nowhere stand out against the grey and purple of the moors beside the road which leads to a collection of small crofts based on Skerray.

From the pier at Skerray it is possible to hire boats for sea-angling or for visits to the two uninhabited islands which lie off the shore. Neave Island, the site of the earliest Christian settlement in the area, is so close that when St Cormaic, a follower of St Columba, preached there it is said that he could be heard by people congregated on the mainland.

Eilean nan Ròn, 'seal island', which contains several striking natural arches of red sandstone, was abandoned by its inhabitants only in 1938.

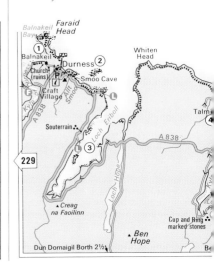

MOORLANDS BY THE SEA *Deep in the throat of the Kyle of Tongue, open moors sweep down to ragged cliffs, and to the water's edge on the sandy beach of Coldbackie.*

⑦ BETTYHILL

In the early 19th century Bettyhill would have looked more like a refugee camp than the crofting centre and resort it is today. For during the Highland Clearances, many of the tenants who were evicted from the inland estates were resettled in Bettyhill. The village which grew up as a result owes its name to Elizabeth, Countess of Sutherland, the wife of the Duke of Sutherland who was responsible for many of the evictions.

Bettyhill clambers untidily up a slope overlooking the sands of Torrisdale Bay, the estuary of the River Naver and the dunes of the Invernaver Nature Reserve. To the north lies the sandy beach at Farr Bay, where semi-precious stones can sometimes be found.

Anglers fish for salmon in the River Naver and for trout in Loch Naver, 15 miles inland. An 18th-century church half a mile east of the village now houses the small Strathnaver Museum, while the Farr Stone – a fine example of early Christian Celtic art – stands outside in the churchyard. Beside the minor road which leads south to Skelpick, groups of stones mark the remains of an Iron Age broch, a Neolithic chambered cairn and a ruined Clearance village.

⑧ STRATHY

On the eastern bank of the River Strathy as it flows through this scattered hamlet, a lane passes turfs of peat piled high outside greystone cottages. Several of the outbuildings are thatched, rather than slated – a rare sight in the Highlands these days. Past a lonely graveyard, the lane peters out; but the sandy beach of Strathy Bay is only a few hundred yards away across the dunes.

At Baligill, 1 mile east, a steep track leads over the grassy clifftops to a thin finger of rock, perched high above creeks that echo to the hissing and sucking of the waves. A few stones are all that remain of an Iron Age fort.

North of Strathy a road leads for 3 miles along a cliff-girt peninsula to Strathy Point, where the seas have carved caves and a natural arch in the rocks around a lighthouse opened in 1958. During gales, waves of spray have smashed against the reinforced glass at the top of the tower, 135 ft above sea level. The lighthouse can be visited most afternoons; on a clear day it affords views ranging from Cape Wrath to Dunnet Head and Orkney. Gannets and skuas nest on the cliffs, and puffins and storm petrels are often seen.

DOUNREAY'S SPHERE *The world's first fast reactor produced electricity for 18 years before being superseded by a giant new reactor.*

⑨ MELVICH BAY

The surf creams calmly over orange sands towards the grassy dunes of Melvich beach, which is reached by footpath from Melvich village. The Halladale River cuts through the dunes to reach the sea.

Bighouse, a greystone mansion, stands on the opposite side of Strath Halladale; it was originally the ancestral home of one of the families of the Clan Mackay. Melvich has pony-trekking.

Portskerra, on the western side of the bay, is a fishing hamlet created at the time of the Clearances. Waves foam over the rocky shore, and fishing boats have to be pulled up on to the steep grassy cliffs.

⑩ SANDSIDE BAY

Although the tides billow into Sandside Bay, the little harbour on the shore at Fresgoe is as calm as a pond. Its mirror surface is only occasionally disturbed by spray from the waves which crash against the jetty. The harbour mouth provides a window into another world. For framed between its stone walls, lobster-pots and anchors is a clear view towards the steel sphere of the Dounreay Fast Reactor.

Reay, the village at the head of the bay, has a whitewashed parish church of 1740, when the village was rebuilt after being buried by sand-dunes. The pulpit faces the 'laird's loft' – a raised gallery where the laird and his

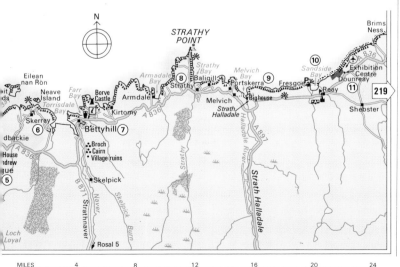

BARE ROCKS AND WARRENS AT THE TIP OF THE TONGUE

A trawler passes the Rabbit Islands, which lie just outside the Kyle of Tongue. There are three islands, named after the suitability of their sandy soil for rabbits. They were once known as Eilean na Gaeil, 'The Island of Strangers', because Norsemen landed there, and in 1745 a French sloop bringing gold to Prince Charles Edward went aground on one of the islands.

family worshipped. In the 17th century the name of 'Reay country' was given to large tracts of mountain and deer forest in Sutherland which belonged to Mackay of Farr, chief of the Clan Mackay who took the title of Lord Reay.

⑪ **DOUNREAY**

For miles around, the flat coastal areas of Caithness are dominated by the steel sphere of Dounreay's experimental nuclear power station. The sphere, which belongs to the Dounreay Fast Reactor, has a diameter

of 135 ft – 3 ft more than the dome of St Paul's Cathedral.

It was the first fast reactor in the world to produce electricity for public use, but it closed in 1977 and it is now dwarfed – in technology as well as size – by the massive block of the Prototype Fast Reactor which began operating at Dounreay in 1974.

The main function of Dounreay is to develop the technology of fast reactors. A fast reactor can extract energy from uranium fuel about 50 times more effectively than a

conventional nuclear power station; as a result, 1 ton of uranium can be used to generate as much power as some 2 million tons of coal. Dounreay also supplies electricity to the national grid through the rows of pylons which radiate from Dounreay and march away inland across the moors.

From May to September, an exhibition centre near the site explains the work of the station and organises tours. The Tourist Information Office in Thurso can also arrange tours.

Sands and cliffs that stretch to Scotland's far North-west

The far north-west coast of Scotland is riven with bays and sea lochs which bite deep into the hills, making the coastal roads long and winding. But the care needed to negotiate them is well rewarded, for they lead to bustling fishing ports; to large nature reserves; and to quiet coves where boats may be hired for angling or for trips to small islands. Mountain walks should not be attempted without first informing the local police station.

TURNING POINT *At Cape Wrath the Vikings turned south to the Hebrides. Wrath derives from the Norse* hvraf *, 'a turning point'.*

① CAPE WRATH

The north-western tip of mainland Britain, Cape Wrath is a red-rock headland rising sheer from the sea for 360 ft, and topped by a lighthouse 70 ft tall. Inland lies one of the largest expanses of uninhabited land in Britain – the 100 square miles of peat-bog, heather, scrub and rock known as The Parbh.

The only link between Cape Wrath and the outside world is a narrow track which runs from the lighthouse to a ferry across the Kyle of Durness. In summer a minibus, which runs sporadically and by arrangement with the ferry operator, carries passengers from the ferry to the lighthouse.

South-east of the Cape, the highest cliffs on the British mainland culminate in Cléit Dhubh – the 'Black Cliff' – which rises 850 ft sheer from the sea. This coast is pounded in winter by mountainous seas which sweep in from the Arctic – and on occasions in summer by the guns of Royal Navy warships which use the area as an artillery range.

South from Cape Wrath, more cliffs, broken here and there by rocky coves, run for 8 miles to Sandwood Bay.

② SANDWOOD BAY

Pale pink sand shelves gently up from the sea to huge dunes held in place by marram grass. More than a mile from end to end and a quarter of a mile from sea to dunes, the beach at Sandwood Bay is one of the finest in Britain, and except for sea-birds and the occasional walker it is completely deserted. The chill waters do not encourage bathing, which is in any case hazardous because of strong currents.

The only access to the bay is by a rough track from the tiny settlement of Blairmore, 4 miles to the south. The first 2½ miles of the track are passable by cars – with care. The final 1½ miles to the bay are along a deeply rutted path marked by cairns.

③ KINLOCHBERVIE

At first sight Kinlochbervie appears little busier than the other secluded settlements which straggle along the shores of Loch Inchard. It is, however, the most important fishing port in the far north-west of the Highlands. Down by its double harbour – either side of a narrow isthmus between Loch Inchard and Loch Clash – fishing boats from the east coast of Scotland land catches of white fish which are then transported to Aberdeen, Grimsby, Hull and the Continent.

To the north lies a series of tiny villages, overlooking wide, south-facing sweeps of deserted sand, which are good for bathing. The road passes Blairmore – the starting point of the track to Sandwood Bay – and ends by the crofts at Sheigra, 10 miles south of Cape Wrath.

④ SCOURIE

Lying in a sheltered hollow scooped out of the rocks on either side of a bay, Scourie is a good base for hill-walking and birdwatching, and for fishing for brown trout in the many lochs inland. To the north lie Tarbet, from which it is possible to visit Handa Island, and Fanagmore, from where there are boat trips to view the seal colonies of Loch Laxford.

Several families used to inhabit Handa. They lived on potatoes, fish and birds' eggs and had their own queen – the oldest widow on the island. The potato famine of 1848 forced them to emigrate to America, however. Since 1962 the island has been a bird reserve, where vast colonies of sea-birds, including guillemots, kittiwakes, razorbills and fulmars, nest on the ledges of the red-sandstone cliffs.

⑤ KYLESKU

Between Kylestrome on the north bank and Unapool on the south, Loch a' Chàirn Bhàin divides into Lochs Glencoul and Glendhu, which then probe deep inland. From the junction of the three sea lochs there are spectacular views of the surrounding mountains – in particular of Quinag and Glas Bheinn. A bridge across the junction has replaced the car ferry which long saved motorists a 100 mile detour.

South-east of the Kylesku bridge, but difficult to reach on foot, are the Eas a Chùal Aluinn waterfalls, the highest in Britain. Their vertical drop of some 650 ft makes them four times as high as Niagara. The falls can be reached on foot by a steep and rugged 3 mile track starting from the A894, 2½ miles south of Unapool. Alternatively a boat up Loch Glencoul into Loch Beag gives the visitor a close look at the falls; ask at the Kylesku Hotel.

⑥ STOER

A series of crofting and fishing hamlets lines the coast either side of Stoer. Salmon nets are hung out to dry beside cottages on sandy coves; while a mile inland the neatness of the drystone walls and the greenness of the pastures convey an air of relative prosperity.

But it is the beaches and the wildlife which attract most visitors to Stoer. There are safe, white sands at Achmelvich Bay and the Bay of Clachtoll, and pink sands at Clashnessie. Falcons and fulmars, seals and whales are all to be seen in the area.

The road along the peninsula ends at Stoer lighthouse. Built on top of a sandstone cliff, the lighthouse looks across The Minch towards Lewis. A walk continues to the Point of Stoer along cliffs that teem with nesting birds. On the way it passes the Old Man of Stoer, a finger of rock surrounded by a ring of seething breakers.

⑦ ARDVRECK CASTLE

The ruined tower of Ardvreck Castle pokes up from a grassy point on the bare shores of Loch Assynt. It was built in 1597 as the home of the MacLeods of Assynt. In 1650 the Marquis of Montrose, while a fugitive, took

ANCIENT ROCKS *Thrust up when the Earth was new, then carved by Ice Age glaciers, Beinn Mor Coigach soars to 2,265 ft in the Coigach hills, whose rocks are among the oldest in the world.*

refuge in the castle but was betrayed into captivity and subsequent execution by his host, Neil MacLeod.

The road to Lochinver skirts the shores of the loch, on which a scattering of tiny islands bristle with withered pines, and passes the slopes of Quinag to the north. Approaching Lochinver, the road follows the course of the River Inver which wriggles its way, between banks of rowan and birch, into the village.

⑧ LOCHINVER

When fishing boats from the east coast of Scotland land their catches of white fish at Lochinver, the port is transformed into a bustling market. For the rest of the week, during the summer months, a holiday atmosphere prevails among the stone cottages which run along the village's pebble shore.

Lochinver is the chief village of Assynt – a rocky moonscape cratered with hundreds of hill lochs and lochans. There are facilities for sea-angling and water-skiing, and a string of safe, sandy beaches to the north-west.

⑨ INVERPOLLY NATIONAL NATURE RESERVE

Great Britain's second largest nature reserve, after the Cairngorms, comprises 26,827 acres of almost uninhabited wilderness. It includes the sandstone peaks of Cùl Mor, Cùl Beag and Stac Pollaidh; Loch Sionascaig; and an expanse of undulating moorland which stretches to the sea at Enard Bay.

The best introduction to the reserve is the nature trail which begins from the information centre at Knockan. This introduces the visitor to some of the plants and animals that are to be found in the reserve's wide range of habitats – lochs, streams, bogs, scree, barren mountain tops and a scattering of birch, hazel and rowan woodlands.

A geological trail explains the local rock formation, which is only found in the north-west of Scotland. At the base is Lewisian gneiss, between 1,400 and 2,800 million years old – the oldest British rock. Above it lies red Torridonian sandstone. The type of rock on top varies, but it includes the white quartzite that builds the summits of many of the hills in the area.

The boundaries of the reserve can be toured by road, and there are tracks into the reserve at various points along the road.

⑩ ENARD BAY

At Achnahaird a large sandy bay bites deep into flat and windy moorland around the shores of Enard Bay. As the road from Achiltibuie to Lochinver crosses the River Polly, however, the scenery changes from sandstone moorland to outcrops of gneiss – a hard and crystalline rock which is usually covered in coarse grass. Flanking the Inverpolly nature reserve, the road rises and falls, twisting and turning along glens that lead beside rushing burns to the sea.

At Inverkirkaig the road crosses the wooded valley of the River Kirkaig and enters Sutherland – the 'South Land' of the Vikings. From the village, a path leads up the river, where salmon can often be seen leaping, and it is possible to walk past the Falls of Kirkaig to the summit ridge of Suilven.

⑪ ACHILTIBUIE

Although they are often known as crofting 'townships', the small settlements overlooking the Summer Isles consist only of strings of scattered cottages. From Achiltibuie, the largest of these, it is possible to take boat trips around the islands.

The road from Ullapool to Achiltibuie skirts the southern boundaries of the Inver-

polly nature reserve. To the north rises the jagged crest of Stac Pollaidh, while to the south, across a chain of gleaming lochs, stretch the hills of Coigach. Much of Coigach is owned by the Royal Society for Nature Conservation and managed jointly by the society and the Scottish Wildlife Trust. The local wildlife includes golden eagles, pine martens, otters and red deer.

Although the road leading south from Achiltibuie peters out at Culnacraig, a track leads along the cliffs for another 6 miles to Strath Kanaird.

LOCAL INFORMATION

Tourist information Lochinver 330 (summer).

HM Coastguard Stornoway 2013 for information, 999 in emergency (ask for coastguard).

Weather Glasgow Weather Centre (041) 248 3451.

SPEEDY HUNTER *The pine marten uses its speed and agility to catch small prey such as rabbits and squirrels.*

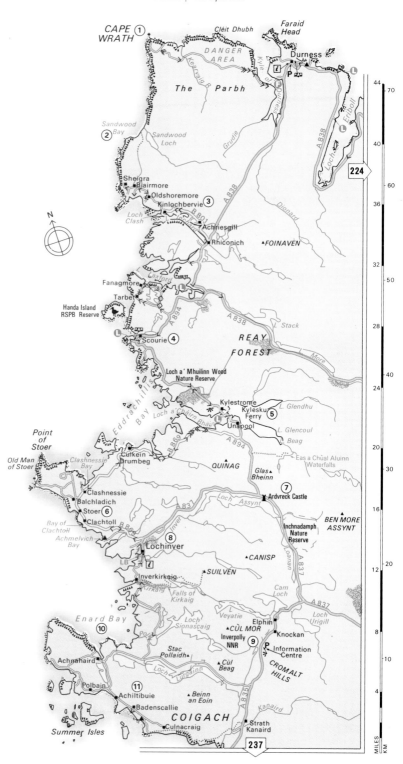

White sands and ancient stones in the Outer Hebrides

Lewis and Harris form a single island that, together with the Uists, Benbecula and Barra, provides a 150 mile long storm-break for the Inner Hebrides and the Western Highlands. Though some 25,000 people live on Lewis and Harris, the island nevertheless contains huge areas of emptiness. What is not peat-bog and water is mostly rock. The seas are cold, but the white sands are wonderful to walk upon and the antiquities are spectacular.

① STORNOWAY

The metropolis of the Western Isles and the only town of burgh size in the Hebrides, Stornoway is not particularly beautiful, but poised as it is between the sea and the bleak and boggy hinterland, it has a gallantry to be admired.

The town, sitting at the end of its fine natural harbour, is a seaport, a fishing port, a market and a centre of the Harris-tweed industry. The mock-Tudor Lews Castle at the west end of the town is a technical college, but it is also a monument to forlorn hopes. It was built in the 1840s by Sir James Matheson, a merchant who had amassed a fortune in the Far East; he also imported vast amounts of soil from the Scottish mainland in which to plant the splendid woods that surround the house. Sir James and his wife spent a fortune on land improvement, building schools and starting new industries, but the islanders were reluctant to abandon the old ways and the scheme sank into oblivion.

In 1918 Lord Leverhulme bought the estate, and all of Lewis and Harris with it. His dream was to turn Stornoway into the greatest fishing port and fish-processing plant in Europe, but after spending £750,000 he too met the island's indifference. A dispute over claims to land by returning ex-servicemen, supported by the Government, was the last straw. Sadly, Leverhulme presented the Stornoway estate to its inhabitants and went to Harris, where Leverburgh was named after him.

At the beginning of the Eye Peninsula,

TWEED FROM THE ISLES

Weavers working in their own homes make the Harris tweed that is famous the world over for its quality. The cloth is identified by the symbol of an orb. Weaving takes place not only in Harris, but in Lewis and other islands of the Outer Hebrides. The work is always done by hand using traditional methods.

A Harris weaver works at a traditional loom.

generally called Point and almost a suburb of Stornoway, there is a much more ancient monument in the derelict 14th-century St Columba's Church and the graveyard of Ui. Nineteen MacLeod chieftains are buried there, and the effigy of one of them, said to be Roderick MacLeod, the 7th MacLeod of Lewis, lies in the church, his features now rather weather-beaten.

② BUTT OF LEWIS

The shiver experienced at the Butt of Lewis is not entirely due to the gales that blow much of the time; the Butt of Lewis is the northernmost point of the Outer Hebrides, truly a Land's End. To the north, 46 miles away, is the tiny island nature reserve of North Rona, and beyond that the Faeroes; due west lie northern Newfoundland and the entrance to Hudson's Bay.

A little below the point are the village of Eoropie and the restored Teampull Mholuidh, or St Moluag's Chapel. Moluag, a companion of St Columba, established a church there in the 6th century, but the present building dates from 600 years later, the period of the Norse occupation. Until the Reformation it was a place of pilgrimage and was especially noted for the cure of lunatics. But despite its fame, the building fell into decay until it was restored by the Episcopal Church in 1912. The 7th-century cross on the altar came from North Rona, and the Celtic cross by the door is a monument to the men of Lewis who fell in the First World War.

③ ARNOL

A glimpse into the old – and not so old – way of life in the Outer Hebrides is afforded by the folk museum in this small township on the west coast of Lewis. It is a *tigh dubh* – 'black house' – which has stone walls 6 ft thick and a roof of thatch tied down by ropes weighted with stones; this type of house had no chimney, and the smoke from the peat fire in the centre of the floor stained everything a rich black. Such houses are rare in the Inner Isles and on the mainland.

However, on the western shores of Lewis, exposed to the full weight of the winter gales, 'black houses' had many advantages. Cunningly sited, and with never a crack to admit a draught, they lay warm and snug beneath the west wind. The one at Arnol, with its straw-filled box beds and crofters' furniture, was still a working household 60 years ago.

④ DOUNE CARLOWAY

Standing stolid on a crag above the village is the Iron Age dun or fort that gave the place its name. Though it was built some 1,700 years ago, its walls still rise in places to a height of 30 ft, with quite enough remaining to give an excellent idea of the strength and brilliance of the construction of such places. It consists of a central courtyard, some 25 ft across, surrounded by double walls between which are galleries, chambers and stairs.

The views from the dun are astonishing. To the east and south-east there is the old crust of Lewis, worn by ice and time into a thousand holes filled with dark water, and to the south-west the shattered archipelago of East and West Loch Roag. The largest island is Great Bernera, which is reached by a road that goes by the Grimersta river, said by many to be the finest salmon river in Scotland, and thence by a bridge that runs over an arm of Loch Roag and thus, technically, over the Atlantic.

There are a few villages and a lobster fishery on Great Bernera, but mostly it is a picturesque waste of rock and water where it really is possible to see golden eagles. There is a lovely beach at Bosta, though the waters are chill.

⑤ CALLANISH

One of the great sights of Lewis – and, indeed, of Britain – is the stone circle at Callanish, which rivals even that of Stonehenge in its inscrutability and the majesty of its setting. The dozens of stones and the chambered cairn in their midst were quarried locally and raised into their present position some 4,000 years ago, but for what

WEST LOCH ROAG *Numerous islands are scattered in the loch and its neighbour, East Loch Roag, which penetrate deep into the rugged western coast of the Isle of Lewis.*

ENIGMATIC STONES *Theories abound as to the purpose of the Callanish stones. It has been suggested that the circle may have been a king's mausoleum, an observatory – or a UFO beacon.*

purpose is likely to remain forever an enigma. The stones, which are planted roughly in the shape of a Celtic cross, seem to align with other circles and standing stones in the area, but it is possible to read almost any meaning into them.

⑥ TARBERT

Harris's capital and principal port consists of a single row of houses and shops leaned over by bleak, boulder-strewn hills. However, it has a hotel, a motel and an information centre, and the shops are cheery, selling everything from Harris tweed and sweaters to lamb chops and cheese.

Tarbert is also the heart of Harris's road system – one narrow road and a number of others narrower still – that for the most part hugs the coast, since the inland terrain is so fretted by lochans that it seems as though Harris cannot make up its mind whether to be land or archipelago. One of the narrowest roads runs round the inlets and sea lochs of South Harris's eastern coast, mostly a wasteland of rock and water. Here and there, however, there are crofting settlements worked by people whose ancestors were driven from the more fertile west coast to make way for sheep.

Because they had no other means of making a living, they built small fields, or 'lazybeds', of peat, rotted seaweed and shell-sand upon the naked rock, and planted oats and potatoes in them. All the work was done by hand. Lazybeds occur in many other places in the Highlands and Islands, but nowhere have they been created from less promising beginnings than on Harris.

⑦ SEILEBOST

The hamlet on the shore of Tràigh Lusken-tyre in South Harris is shielded on the seaward side by deep sand-dunes populated by rabbits, sea-birds and waders. A marvellous place to picnic in, the dunes are also a fine introduction to the machair, that soil formation unique to the western coasts of the Hebrides. It consists of wind-blown shell-sand on which marram grass has taken root to make a pasture where cattle graze. If enriched with seaweed, it can be turned into an arable soil 12 in. deep; but for visitors and generations of Gaelic bards, the chief joy of the machair is in early summer when it is covered with shoals of bright flowers.

⑧ LEVERBURGH

Some 2 miles north-west of Rodel, reached by a road that overlooks a confetti of islands, is Leverburgh, a township that started out as Obbe but was renamed by Lord Leverhulme in 1923 when he attempted to turn it into a major fishing port.

Despite some initial success, the dream slowly crumbled after Lord Leverhulme's death, and though it still incorporates some of the best housing in the island, Leverburgh has a somewhat forlorn air. A ferry runs through the lovely scatter of islets and reefs to North Uist on weekdays in summer and three times a week in winter.

⑨ RODEL

The handsome little port at the very tip of South Harris is further blessed with what is still, despite two major patchings and restorations, the finest example of ecclesiastical architecture in the Hebrides. The cruciform St Clement's Church, constructed of Mull sandstone, was built at the beginning of the 16th century by the MacLeods of Dunvegan, and contains three MacLeod monuments. The finest of them, carved in local black gneiss and dating from 1528, depicts Alastair Crotach, 8th Chief of Dunvegan, as a knight in armour.

It was the custom to inter the standard-bearers of the Dunvegan MacLeods in a tomb in the chancel. The body of the dead standard-bearer was laid in a stone coffin floored with an iron grating, the bones of his predecessor being sifted through into the recess below.

⑩ SCALPAY

The busy little island of East Loch Tarbert is the home port for a dozen or more fishing boats whose crews supplement their incomes by growing crops upon the small fertile lazybeds. The island is served by a vehicle ferry from Kyles Scalpay on Harris.

LOCAL INFORMATION

Tourist information Stornoway 3088; (Tarbert) Harris 2011 (summer).

HM Coastguard Stornoway 2013/4 for information, 999 in emergency (ask for coastguard).

Weather Stornoway 2282.

Local radio BBC Radio Highland and Radio Nan Eilean (Gaelic), 92.9/93.5 MHz.

HOW TO GET THERE

By sea. Caledonian MacBrayne Ltd: car ferries Ullapool to Stornoway, Mon.-Sat.; Uig (Skye) to Tarbert, Mon.-Sat.; Lochmaddy (North Uist) to Tarbert, most days in summer, certain days in winter; Gourock 33755.

By air. British Airways: Glasgow to Stornoway, Mon.-Sat.; Inverness to Stornoway, Mon.-Sat. (041) 887 1111.

231

A fretwork of lochs and bays
in the 'long island' of the Hebrides

North Uist, Benbecula and South Uist have been linked by bridges and causeways to form a single 'long island'. Each, however, has an individual flavour, evolved out of differing terrains and separate histories. What they, and outlying Barra, have in common is a rocky east coast, cut by long sea lochs, and a western coast of shell-sand backed by grasslands, bright with wild flowers and of a beauty vividly expressed by the islands' musicians.

① NORTH UIST

Lochmaddy, the island's port and capital, stands on a sea loch of the same name which winds among a myriad islets so jumbled up with headlands and promontories that it is difficult to tell where North Uist begins. On the eastern side of the island there is at least as much water, salt and fresh, as land, and fishermen grow misty-eyed at the recollection of the salmon, brown trout and sea trout that reside in it.

Ancient forts, ruins and standing stones are everywhere in the island, suggesting

WINTER FUEL *Blocks of peat stand drying for the crofters' fires on North Uist. Peat is a fuel readily available on this treeless island.*

that the prehistoric population was greater than the present one. Three miles north-west of Lochmaddy, on the slopes of Blashaval, is the group of stones called Na Fir Bhreige – 'The False Men' – variously said to be wife-deserters turned to stone or the grave markers of spies who were buried alive. Beyond is the sandy peninsula of Machair Leathann, with evidence of continuous occupation from the Bronze Age to the 19th century.

Near Carinish, in the south-west, are the still impressive remains of Teampull na Trionad, Trinity Temple, a 13th-century monastery and college in which the sons of many western chiefs were educated. It was founded by Beatrice, daughter of Somerled of the Isles. Roofless crofts recall the Highland Clearances which, though not so horrendous as those in South Uist, were bad enough. However, the northern men fought back, and there are records of bloody battles between crofters and imported constabulary in the 1850s.

One of North Uist's greatest attractions is the Balranald Nature Reserve, a wilderness of dunes, marsh and lagoons that provides a home for a wide variety of ducks, geese, swans and waders. The wading birds include the red-necked phalarope, which nests only occasionally in the British Isles. Access to the reserve is limited, and permission should be sought from the warden.

② BENBECULA

As befits a buffer state, Benbecula is not Protestant like North Uist, nor Catholic like South Uist, but a mixture of the two; it seems to be an amicable arrangement. It is separated from its neighbours by stretches of shell-sand and quicksand, and joined to them by causeways that carry the A865. This road runs through all three islands and takes in a fourth, Grimsay, which specialises in dispatching live lobsters by air to the markets of the south.

Benbecula means 'mountain of the fords', no doubt a reference to the days before the causeways, while the 'mountain' must be the 408 ft Rueval, the only bump of any size on the island. Despite its modest height, Rueval presents splendid views of Benbecula, the Uists and more distant members of the Outer Hebrides. On the southern slope of the hill there is a cave in which Prince Charles Edward hid while waiting for Flora MacDonald to bring him clothing suitable to his role as her maid for his journey 'over the sea to Skye' on June 28, 1746.

Benbecula makes its living from crofting, lobster fishing and HM Forces; the army has a rocket base there (and a firing range on South Uist), while the RAF shares some of the airport facilities with Loganair and British Airways. There is still enough island left for visitors. The freshwater loch fishing is as good as that in the Uists and there are some lovely beaches, notably at Culla, with its creamy sand. Bathing there, though safe, is chilly, since the water is the open Atlantic.

③ SOUTH UIST

Like Benbecula, South Uist has a strong Royal Artillery presence: a rocket range whose missiles are tracked at St Kilda, 55 miles off, as they pursue their course out into the Atlantic. As in Benbecula, the army is on excellent terms with its hosts.

The range only slightly mars the 20 mile long, white-sand beach that forms the island's west coast. Behind it are the grasslands of the machair, grazed by cattle and sheep, and behind that again, freshwater lochs, full of trout. Loch Druidibeg, one of the few British breeding grounds of the greylag goose, is a national nature

FERRY AND FORTRESS *The Oban Ferry calls at Castlebay on the island of Barra, where at high tide the grim walls of Kiessimul Castle on its islet seem to rise straight from the water. The castle was restored in the 1930s by Robert Lister MacNeil, 45th Chief of the MacNeil Clan.*

WEATHER PROOF *Ropes weighted by stones hold down the heather thatch of this cottage on North Uist. It is typical of the primitive but snug homes in the Hebrides.*

reserve; it can only be visited with the warden's permission. A little to the north is the 30 ft high statue of Our Lady of the Isles, by Hew Lorimer, erected in 1957; the granite Madonna and Child gaze over the rocket range to the sea. To the south, by Mingary, Jacobite enthusiasts may seek out the birthplace of Flora MacDonald, but it is only a tumble of stones now.

The east coast is mountainous and barren, slashed deep by sea lochs, one of which, Loch Eynort, nearly bisects the island. South · of it is Loch Boisdale, a mass of islands, promontories and reefs, among which is Lochboisdale township, the port of South Uist.

Settlement has always been in the west and south, and it was in these areas in 1850 that some of the most brutal of the Highland Clearances took place. It was not until 1918 that a group of Hebridean ex-servicemen invaded the island and began farming it again. The government then confirmed them in their claims.

④ ERISKAY

Many people who are not quite sure where Friskay is, nevertheless know its name from *An Eriskay Love Lilt,* one of the first Hebridean songs collected by Marjory Kennedy Fraser at the beginning of this century. In its lyrics and music are all the wistfulness and joy of the western islands and seas. Further fame came to the island in 1941, when the SS *Politician,* bound for New York with 243,000 bottles of whisky on board, foundered between Eriskay and South Uist. The shallow sea allowed much of the

bonanza to be salvaged; local lore says that it was given a rapturous welcome not only by the population but by the livestock too, and it was even used to light fires. The incident was used by Sir Compton Mackenzie as the basis for his novel *Whisky Galore,* though when the book was filmed Barra was chosen as the setting.

It was on Eriskay, too, that Prince Charles Edward first set foot on Scottish soil, on his way from France to the Scottish mainland full of high hopes in the summer of 1745. The pink sea-convolvulus *Calystegia soldanella* which grows in the Hebrides only by the beach where he landed, and on Vatersay, is said to have been first planted there by the prince.

With its neat, painted houses and white beaches, Eriskay is as lovely as its music, and its colours as soft and pure as its Gaelic verse, for which it has been famed for centuries. Fishing, crofting and going to sea with the Merchant Navy are the chief occupations of the islanders, but they are also developing a market for their sweaters, which are knitted in a traditional and individual pattern.

⑤ BARRA

Like most of the Outer Hebrides, Barra has a wild and rocky east coast, and an interior deserted apart from some ancient forts and standing stones to suggest that the climate was once kindlier. Those who come to Barra by air may see the full glory of the western mountains and islands unfold before they land on an airstrip that is covered by the tide twice daily.

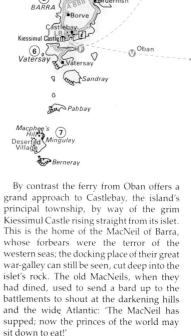

By contrast the ferry from Oban offers a grand approach to Castlebay, the island's principal township, by way of the grim Kiessimul Castle rising straight from its islet. This is the home of the MacNeil of Barra, whose forbears were the terror of the western seas; the docking place of their great war-galley can still be seen, cut deep into the islet's rock. The old MacNeils, when they had dined, used to send a bard up to the battlements to shout at the darkening hills and the wide Atlantic: 'The MacNeil has supped; now the princes of the world may sit down to eat!'

Though avoiding direct participation in the Uprising of 1745, and despite the benefit of some savage Clearances, the family became bankrupt early in the 19th century, and it was not until 1937 that a MacNeil returned from America to buy back 12,000 acres of his ancestors' island and restore the long derelict castle to its former glory. It is open to the public on certain days in summer.

A narrow road encircles most of the

LOCATION SCOTLAND: A STARRING ROLE FOR SCENERY ON THE SILVER SCREEN

David Niven as Bonnie Prince Charlie

I t is little wonder that film directors have chosen the west coast of Scotland and its islands as the setting for scores of productions. For the land has a history more colourful and violent than any scriptwriter could imagine; there are the works of Scottish novelists such as Sir Walter Scott, Robert Louis Stevenson and Sir Compton Mackenzie to draw upon for dramatic story-lines; and the scenery is of a magnificence that no set designer could hope to imitate.

Films with Scottish backgrounds were already popular in the 1930s. It was not until after the Second World War, however, that a spate of films made almost entirely on location received world-wide acclaim. *I Know Where I'm Going*, made in 1945, set the pace, its title perhaps portentous for the British film industry which followed up with *The Brothers*, made in 1947, *Bonnie Prince Charlie* (1948) and *Whisky Galore* (1949). Several film versions of Stevenson's *Kidnapped* include one made mainly on Mull in 1971. In the realm of fact, *Ring of Bright Water* (1969) told the true story of the writer Gavin Maxwell and his pet otter.

Such films as these were about Scotland and Scottish people. But film makers have also seized on Scotland's unforgettable scenery for episodes in other stories. The coast around Crinan was the backdrop for the exciting sea-chase in the James Bond film *From Russia with Love*, while Alistair Maclean's novel *When Eight Bells Toll* was filmed largely in northern Argyll. And in recent years television, too, has begun to exploit the strong visual appeal of Scottish backgrounds.

FILMING THE '45 *Claymores flash in the sun, battle-cries reverberate among the hills and the skirl of the bagpipes echoes across the still waters of Loch Shiel as the standard of Prince Charles Edward Stuart is raised at the start of his ill-fated Uprising of 1745. Sir Alexander Korda recreated the scene in its original location at Glenfinnan for his epic* Bonnie Prince Charlie, *one of the big international spectaculars which Korda made after the Second World War to challenge the supremacy of Hollywood in world markets. The film, released in 1948, starred David Niven as the debonair Prince. The film did not achieve the success Korda had hoped for. Reviews were harsh – but critics praised the splendour of the Scottish locations.*

ISLANDERS WITH A SECRET *In 1941 a boat carrying 243,000 bottles of whisky was wrecked in the Sound of Eriskay. Compton Mackenzie used the incident as the basis for his novel* Whisky Galore, *describing the islanders' efforts to prevent the precious elixir from falling into official hands. The film director Alexander MacKendrick turned the novel into one of the most popular of the Ealing comedies, using the nearby island of Barra for much of the filming.*

ISLAND ROMANCE *A solitary girl waits on a quayside on the island of Mull for a boat to take her to Kiloran, the Hebridean island home of the wealthy Sir Robert Bellinger whom she is contracted to marry. Wendy Hiller played the part of Joan Webster in the film of* I Know Where I'm Going, *a piece of romantic escapism whose successful ingredients included wild Hebridean scenery, a trained hawk and the dangerous whirlpool of Corryvreckan, off Jura. Joan's wait on the quay was in vain. A storm rose, preventing her fiancé from sending a boat. Instead she found true love with a young and handsome laird of Mull.*

TALL SHIPS *Stately sailing vessels of an earlier age return to the waters of Loch Linnhe for the filming of Walt Disney's 1960 version of* Kidnapped. *It starred Peter Finch as Alan Breck Stewart and James MacArthur as David Balfour. The film unit was based at Oban, and filmed at Ballachulish, Glen Nevis, Ardgour and other locations amid the wild Argyll scenery. Robert Louis Stevenson's novel has been a favourite of film makers since 1938, when the earliest version featured the child star Freddie Bartholomew as David Balfour. In a 1971 re-make Michael Caine appeared as Alan Breck.*

GUARDIAN OF THE BEACH *Sand-dunes near Mallaig are the setting for the confrontation between the oil tycoon Felix Happer, played by Burt Lancaster, and the beachcomber Ben (Fulton Mackay) in the 1983 comedy* Local Hero, *produced by Bill Forsyth. Other scenes were filmed in Pennan, Banff. The story concerns Happer's attempt to buy up a Scottish village as an oil refinery site; though most of the villagers are eager to sell, Happer's plan is thwarted by Ben's refusal to sell the land on which his shack stands.*

island, taking in its heavenly scenery and most of its villages. Their living comes from crofting, fishing, the manufacture of knit-wear and perfumes, and from exporting shell grit for outdoor paints.

Some of the minor roads are also worth exploring, especially the one that runs over the dunes and past the airstrip to Cille-bharra, where there are two roofless chapels and the church of St Barr. This is the cemetery of the MacNeils and there too, in this lovely place that looks west to the dazzling sands of Tràigh Eais and north-east to Uist, is the grave of the author Sir Compton Mackenzie, who lived on Barra.

⑥ VATERSAY

The island is shaped like an hour-glass, with a narrow waist of sand-dunes joining the hilly northern and southern sections. Most of the 100-odd inhabitants live in the south, in a casual collection of cottages round which cattle and sheep graze. The little township, whose name is the same as that of the island, does not contain the school, which for some reason is in the northern peninsula; perhaps it was placed there to ensure that no child of Vatersay village or from any of the scattered crofts had to walk further than another.

Early this century the remote island achieved national fame when landless men from Barra, desperate for a livelihood, invaded it. They put their trust in an ancient custom by which anyone who built a dwelling-place and had a fire burning in its hearth within a single day was entitled to the land on which it stood. But the owner, Lady Gordon Cathcart, who had visited her estate once in half a century, soon disillusioned them. In 1908 ten of the 'Vatersay Raiders' were given two months' imprisonment in Edinburgh, but such was the national outcry that their sentences were quashed, and in 1909 the Congested Districts Board purchased Vatersay and divided it among the squatters.

⑦ MINGULAY

One of the best of the Hebridean boat songs or sea-shanties is *Homeward Bound for Mingulay*, but it is a museum piece now, for the island has been deserted for half a century. Its tale is a common one in the Western Isles; long ago, it had benevolent MacNeil landlords and the people made a living by crofting and harvesting sea-birds' eggs from the sheer 750 ft cliffs of the western shore. But there was insufficient workable land for the population, and many left their homes to seek a living elsewhere.

By the 1930s there were only two people on Mingulay, and now all that remains of human occupation are some empty crofts by the eastern shore. Ornithologists visit the island in the breeding season to study the auks and kittiwakes that crowd in thousands on the cliffs and the three great stacks.

LOCAL INFORMATION

Tourist information Lochmaddy 321 (summer); Lochboisdale 286 (summer); Castlebay 336 (summer).

HM Coastguard Stornoway 2013/4 for information, 999 in emergency (ask for coastguard).

Weather Stornoway 2282.

Local radio BBC Radio Highland and Radio Nan Eilean (Gaelic), 92.9/93.5 MHz.

HOW TO GET THERE

By sea. Caledonian MacBrayne Ltd: car ferry services to Lochmaddy from Uig, Isle of Skye, Mon.-Sat.; and to Lochboisdale and Castlebay from Oban, Mon.-Sat. in summer; Gourock 33755.

By air. Loganair Ltd: flights to Barra from Glasgow, Mon.-Sat., (041) 889 3181. British Airways: flights to Benbecula from Glasgow, Mon.-Sat.; (041) 887 1111.

Long sea lochs with red sands and blooms all the year

Although the coast of Wester Ross is on the same latitude as Siberia and Hudson Bay, the North Atlantic Drift softens the blast of the prevailing winds. Subtropical plants and exotic trees flourish in gardens near the sea. The red-sandstone hills shelter sandy coves which are generally safe for bathing. Villages which once made their living from the sea are now small tourist resorts and good bases for fishing, hill-walking and touring.

① ULLAPOOL

The string of whitewashed stone cottages that stretch either side of the pier at Ullapool shine out across Loch Broom, the longest sea loch in the North-west Highlands. Behind them lies the immaculate grid-pattern of village streets which bears witness to the fact that Ullapool was a strictly planned settlement.

In 1788 the British Fisheries Society founded a fishing station at Ullapool to take advantage of the herring fishing industry which had flourished in Loch Broom since the 16th century. Less than 100 years later the area had been overfished and the herring shoals had vanished. Many of the houses originally built by the society have survived, however; these include the fishermen's cottages along Shore Street, the Arch Inn and the old herring-curing factory which now houses a tiny museum.

Despite the collapse of the herring industry, however, Ullapool has flourished. Its attractions now include sea-angling for whiting and skate, and game fishing for salmon and trout in the Ullapool River and the nearby lochs.

Boat trips visit the Summer Isles; a ferry crosses Loch Broom to Allt na h-Airbhe; and the Ullapool-Stornoway ferry service links the port to Lewis in the Outer Hebrides.

② LITTLE LOCH BROOM

Rocky crags and steel-grey streams tumble down towards the loch's southern shore from the heights of An Teallach – the 'forge'. The mountain is so called after the curls of smoke-like mist which permanently wreathe its summit ridge.

Near the village of Dundonnell, the Dundonnell River flows into the loch through low-lying woodlands. The single-track road along the eastern bank of the river leads through green pastures and thickets of beech, lime and chestnut before traversing barren hillsides yet again. After about 4 miles, at the point where the road turns sharply west towards Badrallach, a footpath leads north-eastwards for 1 mile from the road to the inn at Allt na h-Airbhe from where, during the summer, a ferry runs four times daily across Loch Broom to Ullapool.

③ GRUINARD BAY

Viewed at its best from Gruinard Hill, the shore of Gruinard Bay is indented with pink sandy coves formed of red sandstone. These make it one of the most beautiful bays on the west coast.

The small road along the western shore passes the remains of a ruined chapel, on a site where St Columba is said to have founded a church. Further along the road to Mellon Udrigle, a track on the left leads over the purple windswept moors of the peninsula to Slaggan, where the ruins of a deserted village perch above a bay of curving golden sand.

Access to Gruinard Island is prohibited. During the Second World War the island was used for experiments in germ warfare. Anthrax was introduced, killing the sheep on the island. Scientists make annual inspections, but the land is still contaminated.

④ LOCH EWE

The best views of the loch and the low-lying Isle of Ewe are obtained from the main road between Aultbea and Poolewe, and from the smaller road along the loch's western shore, which runs through scattered crofting communities out to Cove. Along this shore are several small bays which are safe for bathing. Their pink sands tone with the turquoise of the sea, the russet of the bracken and the emerald of the foreshore grass to give the landscape an exotic colouring.

At a viewpoint just north of Cove stand concrete pillboxes and gun emplacements – the forlorn remains of a wartime defensive site. During the Second World War, North Atlantic convoys assembled in the sheltered waters of Loch Ewe, and an anti-submarine boom was stretched across its mouth. Even today there is a naval presence on the loch. Across the water at Mellon Charles there is a Royal Navy depot, and in the hillside behind Aultbea a NATO oil fuel depot.

The loch contains haddock, coalfish, cod and pollack, and boats for sea-angling may be hired in Aultbea.

PARADISE WON *The exotic Inverewe Gardens live on as a tribute to Osgood MacKenzie, who turned a wilderness into a paradise.*

⑤ INVEREWE GARDENS

Loch Ewe lies on almost the same line of latitude as Leningrad and Labrador; and yet Inverewe Gardens on its shore are a riot of subtropical colour. The transformation of a barren peninsula of red sandstone into a green oasis of fertility was the vision of one man – Osgood MacKenzie.

MacKenzie, a Scottish laird, acquired the peninsula in 1862. The only soil was acid black peat, and the only vegetation it

ULLAPOOL *The 18th-century engineer Thomas Telford approved the plans for this fishing village, which still retains the neat and tidy look given to it by its orderly minded creators.*

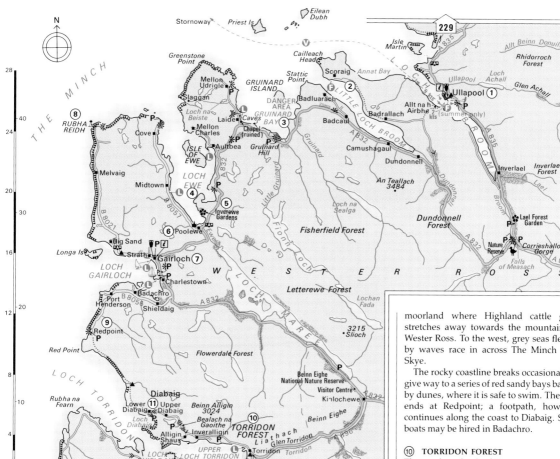

supported was some stunted heather and a single dwarf willow 3 ft high. MacKenzie realised, however, that the North Atlantic Drift, which gives the coasts of Ireland and Scotland their mild, humid weather, might encourage plants to grow. So he started to plant trees as shelter-belts against the strong prevailing winds, and to replace the stony soil with creels of the blue clay that was washed up on the shore. Over the next 60 years he created and improved his wild, woodland gardens.

Today, Inverewe Gardens are owned by the National Trust for Scotland. Paths meander through 64 acres of Monterey pines and magnolia, rhododendrons and hydrangea, eucalyptus and exotic shrubs from all over the world. No matter what time of year it is, some plant will be in bloom.

⑥ POOLEWE

The cluster of stone houses which forms Poolewe stands on a narrow neck of land between Loch Maree and Loch Ewe, and is divided by the waters of the River Ewe which bound through the village. In summer Poolewe relies heavily on tourism, for it is an excellent place from which to visit Inverewe Gardens and to tour Loch Ewe. There are boats for hire; pleasant walks to the wooded banks of Loch Maree; and fishing in the nearby rivers and lochs.

⑦ GAIRLOCH

Twenty years ago Gairloch and the nearby port of Charlestown made their living from the sea. These days, however, fishing fleets have to travel further for large hauls. As a result, the wooded inlet which harbours the pier at Charlestown is less busy than it used to be, and the village's main income comes from the tourist industry.

Gairloch has some of the finest scenery in

the West Highlands. It stands at the head of Loch Gairloch, with the sheltered bays at Shieldaig and Badachro to the south, the sandy beaches around Rubha Reidh to the north and magnificent views westward across The Minch to Skye.

The village has a quarter-mile curve of safe and sandy beach, where windsurfing and sailing are popular. Visitors can hire boats for sea-angling or acquire permits to fish for brown trout, sea trout and salmon.

⑧ RUBHA REIDH

The peninsula ending in the headland of Rubha Reidh – or Ru 'Re as it is abbreviated locally – projects north of Gairloch into The Minch. From the lighthouse at the tip of the promontory there are fine views of the Hebrides.

A single-track road passes the sandy beach at Strath and the sweep of dune-fringed beach at Big Sand, before winding across moorland speckled with sprigs of purple heather. Many of the stone cottages along the 9 miles to Melvaig are in ruins – a sad sign that it is now very difficult to make a living out of crofting. Nevertheless, the swathes cut into the moors to extract peat for fuel are proof that the local communities still follow their traditional way of life.

From Melvaig the road to the lighthouse is closed to private cars; but it is possible to walk the last 3 miles, along cliffs indented with coves and caves.

⑨ REDPOINT

The first stretch of the road to Redpoint meanders gently between banks of birch and oak trees along the southern bank of Loch Gairloch. It passes Badachro – a small village at the head of a bay sheltered by a string of outlying islands. Then the character of the landscape changes. To the east, low-lying

moorland where Highland cattle graze stretches away towards the mountains of Wester Ross. To the west, grey seas flecked by waves race in across The Minch from Skye.

The rocky coastline breaks occasionally to give way to a series of red sandy bays backed by dunes, where it is safe to swim. The road ends at Redpoint; a footpath, however, continues along the coast to Diabaig. Small boats may be hired in Badachro.

⑩ TORRIDON FOREST

The northern bank of Upper Loch Torridon is bounded by ranges of red-sandstone mountains, whose quartzite caps sometimes catch the sun and flash a brilliant white. They include Beinn Eighe and Liathach whose series of peaks rise to more than 3,000 ft. Torridon – an area of some 16,000 acres – is owned by the National Trust for Scotland. The Trust's visitor centre offers introductions to the walks in the area and to the wildlife, which ranges from Britain's largest land mammal, the red deer, to its smallest, the pygmy shrew.

⑪ DIABAIG

A single-track road snakes 9 miles along the northern bank of Upper Loch Torridon to Diabaig. To the north rises Beinn Alligin, while to the south the boulder-strewn slopes descend to the green pastures of crofting villages. The road climbs through the Bealach na Gaoithe – the Pass of the Winds – past streams which pour into peaty lochs, until suddenly a view of the sea opens out to the west.

At the bottom of a steep descent stand the whitewashed cottages of Lower Diabaig. The village has its own loch – a bay sheltered by grey cliffs which plunge into the water. Small boats for exploring the lochs may be hired in the village.

LOCAL INFORMATION

Tourist information Gairloch 2130; Ullapool 2135 (summer).

HM Coastguard Stornoway 2013/4 for information, 999 in emergency (ask for coastguard).

Weather Glasgow Weather Centre (041) 248 3451.

Local radio BBC Radio Highland and Radio Nan Eilean (Gaelic), 92.9/93.5 MHz.

PLACES TO SEE INLAND

Beinn Eighe National Nature Reserve (NCC). Daily.

Corrieshalloch Gorge National Nature Reserve (NTS and NCC). Daily.

Lael Forest Garden, 7 miles S of Ullapool. Daily.

Mountain grandeur behind the rugged shores north of Knoydart

For those who like scenery on the grand scale, this is the place. True, there are the steep-massed conifers planted by the Forestry Commission, a few pretty villages like Applecross and Plockton, some prehistoric forts and medieval castles. But all these are yesterday's work when compared with the barren 750-million-year-old mountains that have nothing to do with the human race and will probably long survive it.

① SHIELDAIG

Loch Shieldaig, off Loch Torridon, was famous for herrings even in the days of the Norse overlords, and herrings too – until they went away – were the chief business of the little whitewashed, slate-roofed village by the shore. Shieldaig was founded by the Admiralty in 1800, when, at the height of the Napoleonic Wars, Britain was chronically short of trained seamen. It was intended as a 'nursery' for the Royal Navy, and tax remissions and boat-building grants were offered to fishing families who went to live there. With the coming of peace, official interest waned, grants slipped into abeyance and the fisherfolk were left to their own devices.

The roads from Shieldaig present the Highlands at their wildest and most magnificent. The view from the A896 running east along Upper Loch Torridon and looking north to the fantastically worn ridges of Beinn Alligin, Beinn Dearg and Liathach is especially humbling. Their reddish sandstone is 750 million years old, about the oldest rock on the face of the planet. To the west are the younger but scarcely less-dramatic ranges of the Applecross peninsula.

② APPLECROSS

In 672 St Maelrubha built a monastery on the quiet bay at the foot of the great hills and declared it a sanctuary for all fugitives. Nothing of his foundation remains save the fragments of a stone cross preserved in the parish kirk which may well be parts of his own monument. But something of the sense of sanctuary can still be felt beside the row of cottages on the shore that forms the present village. This is due not so much to St Maelrubha as to the sheer remoteness of the place which, until the building of the coast road from Shieldaig in the early 1970s, was one of the most inaccessible parishes in mainland Britain.

The old road to Applecross is now called the Applecross Scenic Route, but is better known as Bealach na Bà – the Pass of the Cattle. From the side of Loch Kishorn this old drovers' road shoots up in a series of dizzying hairpins to 2,053 ft, skirting a couple of dreadful precipices on the way. At the top it traverses a flattened moonscape of shattered rock before swooping down to Applecross.

③ PLOCKTON

Apart from the tremendous backdrop of the Applecross Forest, there is something Mediterranean about Plockton. Tucked away in an inlet off Loch Carron and surrounded by jewels of islets and promontories, the village consists of a line of houses along the shore, their bright gardens filled with roses – and with palm trees, too, for Plockton falls under the benign influence of the North Atlantic Drift. All summer long, yachts and dinghies flurry the waters of Plockton's bay. It is a pretty place, as a number of artists have discovered.

Lochcarron village, at the landward end of Loch Carron, is also an attractive string of white-painted houses and hotel along the shore, but like most of the loch, its greatest concern is with the builders of the oil-rig platforms whose products brought much-needed work to the region.

④ KYLE OF LOCHALSH

The bustling little township with its provision stores, souvenir shops, abusive seagulls and general feeling of coming and going has all the air of a busy fishing port. It is the home of the British Underwater Testing and Evaluation Centre, and a ferry point for Skye.

Since it is a place of transit, not many people linger in the village, which is a pity, for it is an excellent place from which to explore the 6,400 acre Balmacara estate, belonging to the National Trust for Scotland, that runs over the peninsula to embrace Plockton and the southern shore of Loch Carron. No Highland wilderness this, but a gentle place of woodland walks, quiet lochans and streams.

⑤ EILEAN DONAN CASTLE

No scene in Scotland has been more photographed, yet familiarity does not dim its wonder – the castle on its islet, the blaze of gold down Loch Alsh, the great hills, and the dimming light in Loch Duich and Loch Long: a glimpse of true majesty.

The original castle was built by Alexander II in 1230, and a century later its walls were festooned with 50 heads by the Earl of Moray. This first building was bombarded into ruin by a pair of frigates of the Royal Navy in 1719, when it was held by a Spanish garrison for the Old Pretender, son of the deposed James II. Eilean Donan remained a ruin until 1912, when Colonel MacRae, a descendant of its hereditary constables, began to restore it. The building is open to the public daily in summer and contains MacRae portraits and furniture.

Another noble sight, not far from Eilean

SEA-GIRT STRONGHOLD *Set on a rocky island at the meeting place of three lochs, the former Jacobite fortress of Eilean Donan Castle is today joined to the mainland by a causeway.*

CASTLE OF INDUSTRY *On Loch Kishorn oil-rig platforms built for the North Sea oilfields take the place of the granite towers and battlements that rise above many a Scottish loch.*

Donan, are the famed Falls of Glomach, at the head of Loch Long, but they are by no means easy to reach. The best route, perhaps, is to take the road up the west side of Loch Long to Killilan House, where permission must be sought before proceeding further – deerstalking may be in progress. Five bumpy miles beyond the house there is a little bridge, and from there a rough, wet path that climbs 800 ft in 1½ miles beside the Allt a' Ghlomaich leads to the Falls. They are tremendous. The burn throws itself down a full 750 ft, though about half-way it hits a buttress then continues down in two white tresses.

⑥ BEALACH RATAGAIN

The Bealach Ratagain, or Mam Ratagan Pass, is one of the major strategic routes through the western Highlands, which is why the British government confirmed it with a road at the beginning of the 18th century. The military road, and the modern one that closely follows it, come up in a series of breathtaking zigzags from Shiel Bridge to the head of the pass at 1,116 ft.

For a view, the visitor has to wait until he reaches the Forestry Commission's viewpoint just above the treeline. Far, far below are the toy shapes of Invershiel village, Shiel Bridge and the tiny Loch Shiel, while to the north lies the whole glorious expanse of Loch Duich. But what immediately commands the attention is the group of great billowing hills, known as the Five Sisters of Kintail, to the south-east.

⑦ GLENELG

Sealed from the world by the wild hills of Glenshiel Forest, Glenelg's only means of access from the landward side is the road that comes over the Mam Ratagan Pass and follows the Glenmore River to the sea. It was by this road that Dr Johnson and Mr Boswell came in 1773 to take the ferry that since time immemorial has run across the narrows of Kyle Rhea to Skye. It runs still, but only in summer.

Bernera Barracks, just outside Glenelg, echoed with the stamp of drilling troops in the 18th century, for the government kept a garrison there from 1722 to 1790. Now it is a desolate shell, with trees sprouting from the gaping windows.

Along Gleann Beag, south of Glenelg, are the remains of a pair of Pictish brochs – Dun Telve and Dun Trodden – said to be the best preserved of their kind in the country.

⑧ LOCH HOURN

A road of sorts, rough and steep, runs round the coast to the north shore of Loch Hourn and another comes out of Glen Garry and follows Loch Quoich to Kinloch Hourn at the landward end. That is about the total extent of the world's impingement upon Loch Hourn, the most remote and most spectacular of the western sea lochs. At its eastern end it narrows abruptly and becomes a dog-leg that thrusts its way through mountains that tower 2,000 ft and more on either hand.

The peninsula to the south is Knoydart – walker's country, for not even the 18th-century London government put a road through it.

⑨ LOCH NEVIS

The only way of getting about in the neighbourhood of Loch Nevis is by boat or by putting one foot before the other. There are no roads at all, even to Inverie, the village on the northern shore, whose only obvious means of access to the outside world is by ferry to Mallaig. But with the great peaks withdrawn to the north and east and only the much lower hills of North Morar to the south, it is an open, happy place, quite unlike dark Loch Hourn, and does not feel nearly so remote.

Anyone with stout boots and a taste for long walks can work out all kinds of escape routes. Best of all, perhaps, is to cross over from Tarbet on the southern shore to Loch Morar, along whose side a path leads, after 8 miles, to Morar and eventually to Mallaig.

LOCAL INFORMATION

Tourist information Gairloch 2130; Kyle of Lochalsh 4276 (summer).

HM Coastguard Oban 63720/63729 for information, 999 in emergency (ask for coastguard).

Weather Glasgow (041) 248 3451.

Local radio BBC Radio Highland and Radio Nan Eilean (Gaelic), 92.9/93.5 MHz.

PLACES TO SEE INLAND

Lochalsh Woodland Garden (NTS), Balmacara estate, near Kyle of Lochalsh. Daily.

Strome Castle (NTS), north bank of Loch Carron. Medieval ruins. Daily.

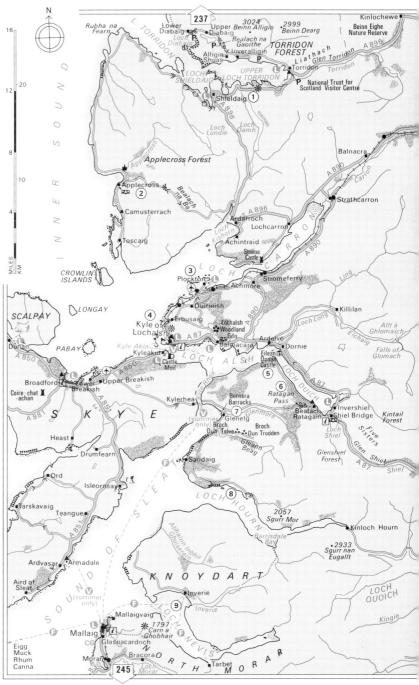

Isle of Clouds, with a Fairy Flag that protects an ancient clan

From the sea, Skye's cloud-cap can be seen long before its dark mountains climb over the horizon; so the Norsemen called it Skuyo, 'Isle of Clouds'. Composed mostly of mountain and moor, Skye is a gathering of peninsulas. Tourism apart, crofting – small farming – is still the main occupation, though the Clearances hit the island hard and its present population of 7,500 is a third of what it was in the middle of the last century.

SKYLINE AT SKYE *The stumpy-walled Castle Moil at Kyleakin was never more than a miniature keep even when it was built in the 13th century, but it still dominates the tiny harbour.*

① KYLEAKIN

The harbour of the little fishing and ferry port is watched over by the jagged-tooth ruin of Castle Moil, a stronghold of the MacKinnons. The castle's chatelaine long ago – so the story goes – was a fierce Norwegian princess who bore the unlikely name of Saucy Mary; she ran a chain across the narrow Kyle Akin strait to sink any ship that did not pay a toll. The strait is probably named after the Norwegian King Haakon who brought his fleet through the narrows to subsequent annihilation at the Battle of Largs in 1263.

To the south is the even narrower strait of Kyle Rhea, where, despite a fearsome tiderip, Skye cattle were once swum across to Glenelg on the mainland.

② BROADFORD

A crofting village, and a scattering of houses, shops and a bank lie beneath the light-filled clouds rolling down the slopes of the Red Hills. The tiny, flat-topped Isle of Pabay lies out in the bay, and beyond are the seemingly unreal silhouettes of the mighty Applecross mountains on the mainland, dull black, or dappled and raised up by a shaft of sunlight.

The liqueur Drambuie was first brewed at the Broadford Hotel, following a secret recipe entrusted to the landlord by Prince Charles Edward.

③ LUIB

Crofting, or subsistence farming, is the principal occupation on Skye, and the croft, a low, single-storey house built of large, squared boulders and roofed with rushes weighted down with stones, its most usual kind of building. The many roofless, abandoned crofts are probably the result of the land clearances of the last century.

At Luib, a croft has been turned into a folk museum showing the tools, appurtenances and ways of a crofter's life a century ago. The walls and ceiling are lined with planks, plates wink on the dresser, and with peat burning in the range the effect is cosy.

④ LOCH SLIGACHAN

The scenery on the road north from Loch Ainort represents Skye at its most majestic. The few houses at the foot of Leathad Chrithinn are turned to toys by the tremendous flanks of the hills; the summits, as often as not, are hidden in near-liquid cloud. The hills are immensely old, worn round and smooth, and scarred with ancient gullies; nothing grows on them but tough grass and heather, and with the seasons, their dress changes from olive-green to purple to old-gold.

The countryside is wild and magnificent, if lonely. But the people of Skye are not to be intimidated; at Sconser, on the shore of Loch Sligachan and at the base of the 2,500 ft Glamaig, they have established a defiant nine-hole golf course. Despite such apparent nonchalance, the hills must be treated with respect; no one should walk among them without heavy boots and waterproof clothing, nor without an experienced guide.

In the hotel at the head of the loch,

MacDonald of Clanranald met the Skye chiefs in an unsuccessful attempt at persuading them to rise for Prince Charles Edward. Later it became a favourite centre for early mountaineers in the Cuillins. A viewpoint beside the hotel looks over to those frowning battlements, though seeing them is another matter; not for nothing is Skye's alternative name Eilean a' Cheo, 'the Isle of Mist'.

⑤ PORTREE

A mighty headland, Vriskaig Point, guards Skye's capital, which consists mainly of neat white houses and small hotels grouped about the harbour or climbing the slope above. The name Portree – Port-an-Righ – means 'king's port', and refers to a visit by James V in 1540 when he arrived with a fleet of 12 ships to persuade unruly chieftains of Skye that it was time to swear allegiance. Skye's oldest building, built in Portree between 1720 and 1745, now houses the Tourist Information Office.

Most of Skye's roads link at Portree, making it a natural touring centre as well as a resort in its own right. Highland games are held there in the summer.

Six miles to the north, reached by a road through a rolling desert of heather where every rock spouts water, is a great ridge called The Storr. In front of it stands a 150 ft high rock pillar, the Old Man of Storr.

⑥ KILMUIR

There are many ancient ruins and monuments on Skye, from standing stones to roofless crofts, but the shell of Monkstadt has a special place in the island's story. It was there, in June 1746, that the 24-year-old Flora MacDonald brought the defeated and fugitive Prince Charles Edward, after landing at what is now Prince Charles's Point, just below the house.

A cluster of crofts near the cemetery have been restored and refurbished as the Skye Cottage Museum to show the life of a crofting community 100 years and more ago. The picture that emerges is one of astonishing self-reliance; almost everything was made, grown or contrived by the community.

⑦ UIG

The little ferry port for the Outer Isles is of no great architectural merit; the only building that really catches the eye is a tower of vaguely medieval aspect that was built in the 19th century by a Captain Fraser and is known as Captain Fraser's Folly. But the setting is breathtaking – a great amphitheatre ending in two tremendous headlands that contains the green shore, the port and horseshoe of the natural harbour. Thus protected, green grass and even a few trees manage to grow within the shelter of the bowl, in marked contrast to the windswept heathery wilderness all about.

The road hairpins so high above Uig that to look down upon it is to see it miniaturised, as though from the air: a tiny pier, with fishing boats and puffers – Highland coasters – leaning amicably against it and, further out, the neat, red-funnelled ferry trailing its white wake to Tarbert on Lewis.

From Uig, a single-track road runs northeast for 6 miles across the Trotternish peninsula to pretty Staffin Bay, taking in some swooping hills on the way. At its highest point it passes the Quiraing, one of the most astonishing rock formations in Britain, a fearsome jumble of pinnacles and peaks thrown up in some geological cataclysm of the distant past. There is something uncanny about the Quiraing, especially in the evening when wreaths of mist begin to drift about its battlements.

Legend says that the Fairy Flag, in Dunvegan Castle, will save the MacLeod clan if waved at moments of great danger. It is said to have been given by the fairy wife of an early chief, but may have been the flag of Harald Haardrada of Norway who was defeated by King Harold of England in 1066. The Fairy Flag is made of Mediterranean silk, and Harald's flag came originally from Constantinople.

The Fairy Flag was defended by 12 swordsmen when taken into battle.

⑧ DUNVEGAN

The square-towered castle on the crag is seven centuries old, and the oldest house in Britain to have been continuously occupied by the same family since its building. True to their motto of 'Hold Fast', 20 generations of MacLeod chieftains have lived there, administering their lands and holding their people together with remarkable tenacity. There were never any Clearances in MacLeod country, and having lost 700 clansmen fighting for Charles II at the Battle of Worcester in 1651 later chiefs were reluctant to respond to subsequent calls from the Stuarts. Thus the clan was spared the ravages that followed the Uprising of 1745.

There are many MacLeod treasures in the castle, including the 12th-century chief's drinking horn that holds the equivalent of two bottles of claret which he drained at a draught, and the clan's famous Fairy Flag.

The curious, flat-topped mountains to the south-west are known as MacLeod's Tables, and it is said that a long-ago chieftain held a banquet on one of them, illuminated by torches carried by a hundred brawny clansmen, to impress a Lowlander with the boundlessness of Highland hospitality. Another glimpse of the chieftains' life-style may be obtained by visiting Borreraig, on the opposite shore of Loch Dunvegan. This was the home of the MacCrimmons, hereditary pipers to the MacLeods. There is a monument to them there, and a Piping Centre.

At Colbost, 3 miles up the loch shore from Borreraig, there is a folk museum based upon a croft of a much earlier period than the ones at Kilmuir. The peat fire is not in a range with a chimney, but in the centre of the floor. The smoke, in theory, escaped through a hole in the ceiling; it is little wonder that these older crofts are called Black Houses.

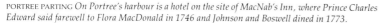

PORTREE PARTING *On Portree's harbour is a hotel on the site of MacNab's Inn, where Prince Charles Edward said farewell to Flora MacDonald in 1746 and Johnson and Boswell dined in 1773.*

⑨ TRUMPAN

High up on the western coast of the lonely Waternish peninsula, at Trumpan, there is a ruined church whose state is due not to the ravages of time but to an unpleasant incident in the endless feud between the Mac-Donalds and the MacLeods. On a Sunday morning in 1578, a party of MacDonalds, raiding from Uist, discovered a congregation of MacLeods at worship in the church. They fired the church, cutting down anyone who tried to escape. The only survivor was an old woman who ran over the moors to Dunvegan to raise the alarm.

The Fairy Flag was unfurled – the only certain occasion on which it was displayed in battle – and armed MacLeods appeared as if by magic, racing for Trumpan. The outnumbered MacDonalds ran for their galleys, but they were beached on a falling tide, and the raiders were butchered to a man. The dead were buried by toppling a wall upon them.

⑩ ELGOL

For those who do not wish to climb the Cuillins this little hamlet on the southern peninsula of Straithaird offers best of all views of the faintly terrible mountains, whose mighty bastions fill the sky to the north-west. See them especially in the long gloaming of a summer evening, when the vast, black shapes seem to grow up the daffodil sky, then turn to see Soay, Rhum, Canna and Eigg adrift on a golden sea.

⑪ ARMADALE

Ferry passengers from Mallaig disembark at Armadale, where part of a 19th-century castle has been restored to house a Museum of the Isles and an audio-visual display

241

STILL WATERS BENEATH RED GRANITE HILLS

Majestic as a jewelled crown, formidable as a castle's ramparts, Leac nan Fionn in north Skye rises to craggy, flat-topped bluffs, casting dark shadows on the polished-glass waters of Loch Langaig. Less jagged in outline than the Cuillins to the south, the pink granite hills tower a mile or so north of the Quiraing and west of the A855 near Flodigarry.

which tell the history of the mighty Clan Donald. By the roadside, a former stable block now serves as a visitor reception centre, with restaurant and craft shop. There are numerous nature trails through the gardens and the surrounding farmland and shoreline.

The fertile peninsula of Sleat on which Armadale Castle stands is often called the 'Garden of Skye' because of its luxuriant coastal vegetation. A road from Ardvasar leads to the Aird of Sleat, from which a 2 mile walk leads to the Point of Sleat, Skye's southernmost point.

⑫ **RAASAY**

The 13 mile long island is a far-away sort of place, its only contact with the outside world being the ferry to Sconser on Skye. Most of the 150-odd islanders are crofters, living in or about the village of Inverarish. They remain through love for the island, dependence upon one another, and the unifying influence of the strict Protestant denomination to which most of them belong.

Unlike MacLeod of Dunvegan, MacLeod of Raasay actively supported the Jacobite cause in 1745 and sent 100 men from Raasay

and neighbouring Rona to join the Prince. The government responded by burning every house on the islands, slaughtering every domestic beast and destroying all the boats. Recovery was slow, and a century later 100 families were evicted to make way for sheep and game.

Protected by the bulk of Skye, Raasay is much more gentle and lush than the larger island – but there is not a great deal to do. There is an ancient chapel, and the ruins of Brochel Castle, a MacLeod stronghold. But best of all might be to climb the 1,456 ft hill of Dùn Caan, and from its flat summit look out to the mountains of Applecross, to all the islands, and to the great clouds rolling in from the Atlantic. Then, as James Boswell did on the hill in 1773, the watcher might dance a reel from the sheer joy of living.

LOCAL INFORMATION	HOW TO GET THERE
Tourist information Portree 2137, Broadford 361 (summer).	*Skye. By sea.* Caledonian MacBrayne: car ferry Kyle of Lochalsh to Kyleakin, daily; Mallaig to Armadale, Mon. to Sat. in summer (passengers only in winter); Gourock 33755. M.A. Mackenzie: car ferry Glenelg to Kylerhea, Mon. to Sat. in summer. Glenelg 224. *By air.* Loganair Ltd: Glasgow to Broadford most days; Glasgow (041) 889 3181.
HM Coastguard Oban 63720/63729 for information, 999 in emergency (ask for coastguard).	
Weather Glasgow (041) 248 3451.	
Local radio BBC Radio Highland and Radio Nan Eilean (Gaelic), 92.9/93.5/93.9 MHz.	*Raasay.* Caledonian MacBrayne: car ferry Sconser to East Suisnish, Mon. to Sat. Gourock 33755.

Lochs and green hills at the end of the Road to the Isles

With the Islands beckoning to the west, this part of the Highlands offers new adventures, an invitation that is underlined at the busy little ports and by the westward-bound wakes of the ferries. Inland there are lochsides and hills that vary from the grand and desolate to the pretty and intimate. Every castle, ruin and white-sanded bay has its heroic legend, while over all there drifts the sad but gallant shade of Prince Charles Edward.

① MALLAIG

The Road to the Isles – 'By Ailort and by Morar to the sea' – comes to a triumphant end among the rattle of winches and the shouting of gulls at this busy fishing and ferry port. The harbour, surrounded by white-painted stone houses, a hotel or two and the terminus of the West Highland railway line, is a place of constant bustle. Lobsters, prawns and fish by the ton, it seems, are hauled out of the fishing boats; these are skirted by the big, red-funnelled ferries from Armadale in Skye, and by the little ones from Inverie on Loch Nevis and other places.

Providing weather, boots and inclination are in trim, it is an excellent idea to scale the rocky Carn á Ghobhair – a track goes most of the way from Glasnacardoch, 1 mile south of Mallaig. From its 1,797 ft summit, there is a panorama unrivalled in the Highlands. To the east are Lochs Morar and Nevis and the wilderness of Knoydart; and to the west, Rhum and the Cuillin Hills of Skye.

② MORAR

The hilly village of Morar looks out over its beach of pure-white quartzite sand to pale green seas and the grand silhouettes of Rhum and Eigg. The narrow neck of land on which it stands is all that divides the 11 mile long Loch Morar from the sea, and even this is cut by the half-mile-long Morar River. The thunderous weir on the river is all that remains of some once-famous falls; they were tamed to meet the requirements of a hydro-electric scheme, whose power station is discreetly built into a cliffside.

A narrow road runs along the northern shore of the loch to Bracora, which consists of little more than seven crofters' houses and a telephone box; beyond this point the road soon turns into a footpath. It is a pleasant track, by fast-falling streams from the hills of North Morar, and with herons and buzzards for company.

The waters of Loch Morar conceal the deepest abyss in Britain, a fearsome chasm of 1,017 ft. The loch may also conceal a monster named Morag, a relative of the better-known creature in Loch Ness. However, she does not flaunt herself to tourists and is said only to appear when the death of a MacDonald of Clanranald is imminent.

③ ARISAIG

The village of Arisaig on Loch nan Ceall looks over a shattered jigsaw of islets and skerries to Rhum, Eigg and the Cuillins of Skye. It is at Arisaig that the Road to the Isles turns north along the coast towards Mallaig, and this final stretch across the peninsula of Arisaig is celebrated with a gentleness and joyfulness not often associated with Highland scenery. The air is frequently balmy – a benefit conferred by the North Atlantic Drift

– the woods of birch, rowan and oak are mossy and deep, wild flowers grow in profusion and there are birds everywhere. Arisaig is not the only place on the western mainland from which to watch and be overwhelmed by the sunset over the islands – but it is certainly one of the best.

Prince Charles's Cairn at Loch nan Uamh

④ LOCH NAN UAMH

To followers of the romance of *Prionnsa Tearlach*, or Bonnie Prince Charlie, there are few more significant places than this sea loch, where the adventure began and ended. With a few companions, Charles Edward landed on the shores of the loch on July 25, 1745, and thence, on September 20, 1746, he departed, with a larger number of companions and a price of £30,000 on his head.

Though lonely, the loch is a green and happy place, surrounded by woods of birch, larch and oak, trailing streamers of lichen, and full of islets and promontories, where seals pop their heads out of the calm water. Nevertheless, most of the memories seem to cling to the final days of the prince's wanderings; to the cave by the shore below Arisaig House, for instance, where tradition has it that he and his followers lived for a

week or more. At the head of Loch nan Uamh, a cairn marks the place where the fugitives embarked in the early hours of that September morning, and sailed to exile in France.

⑤ GLENFINNAN

Just as Loch nan Uamh witnessed the beginning and the end of the 1745 Uprising, so Glenfinnan saw its moment of greatest optimism. It was also its point of no return, for there, on the afternoon of August 19, 1745, the clans gathered to witness the raising of the Royal Standard and to declare themselves for the prince and the Stuart cause.

A stone tower topped by a kilted figure now marks the spot; the statue is not of the prince, as is often supposed, but of a bearded warrior representing all the clansmen who gave so much in the Stuart cause. Visitors can climb to the top of the statue by an inner staircase for a good view of the surrounding countryside.

⑥ MOIDART

The lovely but fairly impenetrable tract of country known as Moidart that lies between Loch Ailort and Loch Shiel was once Clanranald territory, but now there are few inhabitants apart from river and loch anglers in their seasons, and deer stalkers in theirs. However, an adventurous road skirts its northern and western shores.

At the tiny hamlet of Glenuig, on its sandy cove, the road sweeps southwards and inland to emerge again at Loch Moidart, which at low tide consists mostly of sand-flats. In a meadow near Kinlochmoidart a group of seven beech trees commemorates the 'Seven Men of Moidart', the sum total of the army that Prince Charles Edward brought with him from France. At the south-western end of the loch, on an islet usually linked to the mainland, stands the 14th-century Castle Tioram. Though apparently intact, the castle is, in fact, a shell, having been fired by its owner, Clanranald, during the Uprising of 1715 to prevent it from falling into the hands of the Campbells.

Those who find the Stuarts and their doings overwhelming may find it restful to sit on a hillock and look westwards over the ragged islands to the sea, and to a view that was heartbreakingly beautiful before kings were dreamed of.

⑦ ARDNAMURCHAN

Each of the peninsulas down the jagged coast of the North-West Highlands has a flavour of its own. Ardnamurchan is a good deal gentler than most, and in addition it is

HIGHLAND HERO *On top of the stone tower at Glenfinnan a lone warrior gazes towards the hills from which, in 1745, 1,500 Highlanders came swinging into the glen to support Prince Charles Edward.*

RAIL ROAD TO THE ISLES *The West Highland line skirts Loch Eilt on its 164 mile journey from Glasgow to Mallaig through some of the most spectacular scenery in Britain.*

the westernmost place in mainland Britain. Point of Ardnamurchan – the 'Point of the Great Ocean' – juts some 23 miles further into the Atlantic than Land's End, and the view from its lighthouse embraces Mull, Coll and all the Inner Hebrides, and far out, on a clear day, the distant shapes of Barra and South Uist.

The road enters Ardnamurchan at Salen, then runs west along Loch Sunart to Glenborrodale. The turreted and battle-mented Glenborrodale Castle was built at the turn of the century on the site of a much earlier stronghold and is now a hotel.

From there, the road runs inland to skirt Ben Hiant, the Holy Mountain, whose jagged ramparts of volcanic rock can be seen for miles around. Further west is the village of Kilchoan and, near by, the shell of the 13th-century Mingary Castle. On the north shore there are white sands and good fishing, especially at Sanna Bay just north of Point of Ardnamurchan, and at Achateny Beach and Kilmory Sands, which are also excellent places for seekers after rare sea-shells.

⑧ STRONTIAN

From the demure village by Loch Sunart side, a nature trail climbs through oak and conifers – many hung with duck-egg green lichen – to the wild hills above that pour roaring spates down to the Strontian River. Just below the trail, a steep, bumpy road forks to the west to a place described on the map as Scotstown. It consists mainly of shattered, roofless cottages, while above them lie the old mine workings that made the name of Strontian famous the world over.

Between 1722 and 1904, silver, lead, zinc and other minerals were extracted from the mines. The minerals included one called strontianite from which, in 1808, a metallic element named strontium was isolated; this burns with a bright crimson glow, and was for many years used in the manufacture of fireworks and flares. The name is best known, however, from strontium 90, an isotope of the same metal that occurs as a by-product of nuclear fission.

Today the mines lie open to the sky, a sinister grouping of chasms, craters and shafts braced by ancient timbers, while far below there is the sound of water falling. Round about there is glorious moorland scrambling among the heather, white water and grey rocky outcrops. Take care to keep away from the workings, however.

⑨ LOCHALINE

The sea lochs Sunart and Linnhe and the Sound of Mull together almost turn the lonely moorland miles of Morvern into an island. The only road of any size runs from the head of Loch Sunart, across Morvern to the shores of Loch Aline and hence to Drimnin which looks across to Tobermory bay.

Lochaline village at the mouth of the loch was a pretty place once, but in 1940 it was discovered that its sand is almost pure silica, and some 60,000 tons of it are removed each year for the manufacture of optical glass. However, the church has a 15th-century Celtic cross, and the nearby ruined church of Keil has a medieval gravestone depicting a man wearing what looks very much like a kilt; if he is, it is the earliest known portrayal of that garment.

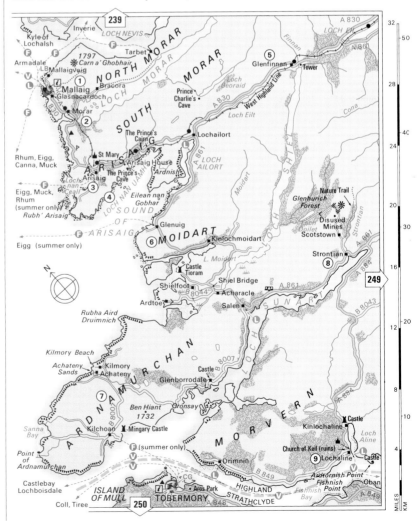

Solitude on the peaks and shores of the Inner Hebrides

Like the islands of Greece, the Inner Hebrides have similar legends of blood and heroes, similar memories of poverty, famine and exile, the same kind of songs about the sea, and love, and war. Above all, they share a beauty that can entrap the heart. But lovely though all the Inner Hebrides are, each island is an individual; mountainous and forbidding or open and welcoming; deserted and achingly lonely or busy, bustling and progressive.

Sea eagle
Haliaetus albicilla

① CANNA

Having suffered dreadfully in the Clearances – in the 1840s, two-thirds of the population was shipped wholesale to Canada – fate has made amends to Canna in the last century and given it two enlightened and benevolent landlords. The last of these, Dr John Lorne Campbell, has over the past 40-odd years turned the 5 mile long island into a single farming estate that concentrates upon early potatoes, pedigree Highland cattle and Cheviot sheep. He presented the entire island to the National Trust for Scotland in 1981.

The population, estate workers, crofters and lobster fishermen, still amounts to only about a score, a shadow of what it once was. Before the Clearances, there was even a township on Canna; it was called A'Chill, and its pathetic remains – a Celtic cross, a curious pink standing stone, a burial ground and the shadows of vegetable plots – may be seen not far from the pier.

The island has one of the finest deep-water harbours in the Hebrides, making it a popular place with yachtsmen in the summer, despite its curious navigational hazards; the basalt rocks of the cliffs are so magnetic that they distort compass bearings 3 miles away.

Apart from yachtsmen, the principal visitors to Canna are naturalists and day-trippers; there is no accommodation on the island, though campers are welcome if permission is asked from the National Trust for Scotland in advance. Day trips from Arisaig allow visitors 4 hours ashore.

② RHUM

In 1826 almost the entire population of Rhum was shipped to Newfoundland, and since then the island's 40-odd square miles have remained virtually uninhabited, apart from red deer and the people who went to shoot them. Not that much of the island was habitable anyway, since a large proportion of it rises steeply from the sea to volcanic peaks of 2,300 ft and more. However, in 1957 it was acquired by the Nature Conservancy Council as a nature reserve and outdoor laboratory for long-term experiments, to study for instance the restoration of vegetation after over-exploitation by grazing and burning.

Accommodation is very limited on Rhum, and permission must be sought from the Nature Conservancy Council for an overnight stay. But even a day trip from Arisaig is well worth while, since it affords time to explore at least one of the two signposted nature trails which begin at Kinloch on Loch Scresort, at the point where the ferry comes in. Eider ducks and gulls nest among the ruins of the old village of Port nan Caranean, there are Manx shearwaters seemingly by the million and golden eagles are by no means rare. Red deer are every·here, and

GRAND MANOR *Rhum's Kinloch Castle, now an hotel, was built in 1902. This room is kept as a museum of the Edwardian period.*

common seals may be seen on the rocks. Look out for the little Rhum ponies bred on the island to carry deer carcasses down from the hills.

③ EIGG

By the standards of Small Islands Parish, which also includes Canna, Rhum and Muck, Eigg is positively teeming. It has a population of about 80, guest houses, self-catering cottages, a tea-room and a craft shop, and even a mini-bus service connecting the two villages of Galmisdale, where the boat comes in, and Cleadale to the north.

Eigg in earlier years suffered the usual vicissitudes of clan wars, famine and Clearances, including the transportation of its young men to the West Indies after the 1745 Uprising. During the last century, however, the island has been generally fortunate in its landlords, who have tried to make the island a viable place for their tenants to live in.

From the mainland side, the towering lava cliffs of the sphinx-shaped ridge of An Sgurr gives Eigg a forbidding appearance, but it improves on closer acquaintance. By judicious use of time and the mini-bus, it is possible to explore many of the island's attractions, even in the 4 hours allowed by the ferries from Arisaig and Glenuig.

The Singing Sands at Camas Sgiotaig are quartzite and squeak when walked upon or even emit a long, continuous moan if the wind is in the right direction. There are some good, if more conventional, beaches at various points around the coast, and fine walks for naturalists and geologists among the cliffs of An Sgurr. Bicycles, mopeds, ponies and dinghies may be hired by the energetic.

JAGGED SKYLINE *The peaks of Rhum, seen from the 'Singing Sands' on the neighbouring island of Eigg, were thrust up from the earth's crust by volcanic action some 60 million years ago.*

An insight into the darker side of Hebridean history is afforded at MacDonalds' Cave, which lies about half a mile south-west of the pier at Galmisdale. In this, in 1577, 395 MacDonalds, hiding from a raiding party sent by MacLeod of Skye, were suffocated. The Macleods lit brushwood fires at the narrow entrance and let the smoke blow in. Close by is Cathedral Cave, which Catholics used as a church in the days when their faith was proscribed. Their altar still stands in the cave.

④ MUCK

The island's name comes from *Muc*, which means, variously, a heap, a pig or perhaps a sea-pig, or porpoise. None of the meanings seems appropriate to the pretty, fertile, low-lying island, whose 1,500 acres of pasture and arable land are now worked as a single farm, supporting a couple of dozen people. Muck's fertility is due to its friable basalt foundation, sweetened with shell-sand; and its cheerful climate to the North Atlantic Drift and the protection given by its higher and bigger neighbours.

During the Napoleonic Wars, its inhabitants made a good living by burning seaweed to make potash, an ingredient of gunpowder. After the wars, the landlord, Maclean of Coll, determined to turn the island into sheep pasture. He evicted most of the crofters and despatched them to Nova Scotia, where many of their descendants still speak Gaelic.

It cannot be said that Muck is a lively place, but it is certainly suitable for a restful holiday. The summer meadows are bright with wild flowers, there are several safe, sandy beaches and often, in the long summer evenings, there are ceilidhs – Highland dancing and singing. Accommodation is in a guest house and holiday cottages.

⑤ COLL

The eastern seaboard of the 12 mile long island looks inhospitably craggy as the ferry approaches it. But once the steamer penetrates Loch Eatharna to the pier at Arinagour the interior is seen to consist of gentle, heathery moorland, dotted with slaty-dark lochans. Much of the west coast is bright shell-sand, blown into dunes of 100 ft and more, whose slopes are knitted by grass into a machair on which cattle graze.

Coll's history is the not unusual Hebridean one of Pict, Viking, Lords of the Isles, Macleans and evictions. Both the Lords of the Isles and the Macleans of Coll at different times occupied the magnificent 15th-century Breachacha Castle, which stands at the head of the sea loch of the same name. However, in 1750 the Macleans, no doubt tiring of the chill of the old place, built a more modest castle near by; Dr Johnson, who stayed in it 20 years later, described it, rather loftily, as a 'tradesman's box'. The medieval building, having been ruinous for many years, has now been restored and is the headquarters of an educational trust. The stream that flows into the loch is called Struthan nan Ceann, 'the stream of the heads', in memory of a fearful defeat inflicted by the Macleans of Coll upon those of Duart in 1593. According to a report of the time, ducks swam in Duart blood and the stream was choked by Duart heads.

A number of prosperous farms concentrate mainly upon cattle and sheep. For visitors there are sandy and secluded coves and bays galore, and the bright township of Arinagour, gay with flowers and containing shops, a craft centre and a tea-room. There is accommodation in the Coll Hotel and in a number of self-catering cottages and caravans.

SWEET COLL *Perhaps it was Hogh Bay, with its long sand-dunes, on Coll's west coast, that a Gaelic poet had in mind when he called the island 'Fair gem of the ocean, sweet Coll of my song'.*

⑥ TIREE

Apart from three bumps at one end, Tiree is so low-lying that it looks like a pencil stroke upon the horizon. Closer inspection reveals pale sand and, since in spring and early summer the sun is so often shining, something of the air of a tropical isle. However, there are no palm trees or, indeed, trees of any kind; the 120 knot gales that come off the Atlantic in winter make their growth impossible. It is said in the Hebrides that Tiree people may be recognised by their stance, which is always 10 degrees off the vertical. But indoors at least they can stand upright, for their low, snugly thatched crofts have white-painted walls 6 ft thick.

The island's name means 'Land of Corn', and to this day, the fertility of the machair – grassland overlying shell-sand – helps to support a population of about 1,000, one-fifth of what it was 150 years ago. By local standards, Tiree is still a bustling place with several villages. There is Scarinish, just around the corner from deep-sanded Gott Bay where the Oban ferry comes in, and pretty Balemartine on Hynish Bay. It takes in Hynish, where there is a derelict collection of houses, a pier and a signalling station used when Alan Stevenson, uncle of the novelist Robert Louis Stevenson, built the far-out Skerryvore lighthouse in the 1840s.

Most attractive, perhaps, is Balephuil, which lies behind its lovely bay flanked by Ben Hynish and the steep headland of Ceann a' Mhara with its two prehistoric forts. From there, the view lies over the deep-rolling Atlantic to Skerryvore, whose 150 ft high light has defied the western storms for a century and more.

For early summer visitors to Tiree, the chief attractions are the hours of sunshine – it has the national record in May – its miles of empty, perfect beaches, and its carpeting of wild flowers.

LOCAL INFORMATION

Tourist information Oban 63122/63551; Fort William 3781.

HM Coastguard Oban 63720; Greenock 29988 for information, 999 in emergency (ask for coastguard).

Weather Glasgow Weather Centre (041) 248 3451.

HOW TO GET THERE

By sea. Caledonian MacBrayne Ltd: ferry from Mallaig to Rhum, Eigg, Muck and Canna, Mon., Wed. and Sat. in summer; Mon. and Wed. in winter. Car ferry from Oban to Coll and Tiree, Mon., Wed., Fri. and Sat. in summer; Tues., Thurs. and Sat. in winter; Gourock 33755.
Murdo Grant, Arisaig Marine Ltd: Arisaig to Eigg, Muck and Rhum. Most days in summer; Arisaig 224/678.

By air. Loganair Ltd: weekday service from Glasgow to Tiree; (041) 889 3181.

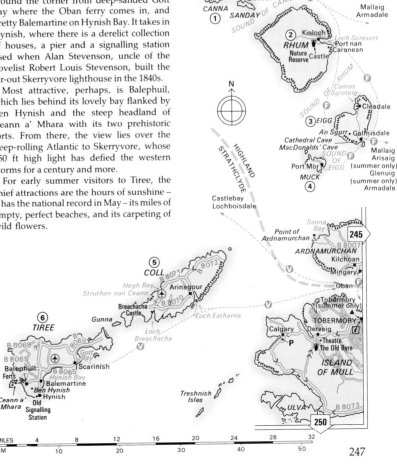

Wild hills that tower over the long road round Loch Linnhe

In most of Britain people have been content to let the memories of ancient battles fade beneath modern fields and suburban development. But no changes have come to this landscape, whose stern and dramatic beauty is particularly suited to the tales of battle, murder and sudden death with which it is liberally sprinkled. For the traveller among these wild and sombre hills, names like Glen Coe and Appin take on a deeper significance.

ISLAND CASTLE *Castle Stalker, in Loch Laich, was once given away by its Stewart owner in exchange for a Campbell galley.*

① INVERSANDA

The road from Strontian on Loch Sunart runs 8 miles through towering Glen Tarbert and emerges on Loch Linnhe at the tiny hamlet of Inversanda; it then bears north to Corran. There is some magnificent scenery in and around the glen, and some good climbing too, especially on the 2,903 ft Garbh Bheinn, beloved of cragsmen, to the north; but it is not for unaccompanied novices. The 2,800 ft Creach Bhienn to the south is easier and offers splendid views, but for visitors without the right equipment and muscle-training, it is better admired from the road.

② GLEN COE

With its high black peaks and naked, sunless rocks eternally spouting water, Glen Coe is an appropriate setting for the most infamous murder story in Scottish history. The victims were some 40 members of the MacDonald clan, who had failed to swear allegiance to William III and to forswear the Jacobite cause by the time appointed by the Government.

On February 1, 1692, a company of Argyll militia arrived in the glen, under the command of Captain Robert Campbell of Glenlyon. Campbell told Maclan, chief of the Glen Coe MacDonalds, that his barracks were overcrowded, and asked if he and his troops might be billeted upon the Mac-Donalds. After enjoying 12 days' hospitality, the troops turned on their unsuspecting hosts and butchered them. It is possible, however, that some of the soldiers were not overzealous in carrying out their duty; they were, after all, Highland men themselves. Most tragic were the women and children who fled to the high corries and died, within hours, among the ice and snow. Something of their anguish seems to cling to the place still.

The National Trust for Scotland runs a Visitor Centre 1½ miles south of Glencoe village.

③ SOUTH BALLACHULISH

By the end of the bridge at South Ballachulish, and looking down the whole lovely length of Loch Leven, there is a monument to James Stewart, or James of the Glen, who was hanged on that spot in November 1752. As everyone who knows Robert Louis Stevenson's *Kidnapped* and *Catriona* is aware, he was hanged for a murder he had no part in.

The victim was Colin Campbell of Glenure, Government Factor for the forfeited Cameron and Stewart estates in the neighbourhood. On a May afternoon in 1752, as he was riding homewards, someone shot him. The place is marked by a cairn in the woods, about a mile south-west of the Ballachulish narrows, and just south of the present road.

Whoever the assassin was, it was not James Stewart, who was seen working in his fields at the time. Nevertheless, he was charged as an accessory before a predominantly Campbell jury and sentenced to death. After his execution, the corpse was suspended until it rotted, then the bones were wired together and re-hung. Finally, they were laid to rest at Keil churchyard by Loch Linnhe. The real murderer was never discovered.

④ PORTNACROISH

A stone in the churchyard records a bloody battle fought between the Stewarts and the MacDougalls in 1468. But a better-known monument is Castle Stalker, which stands on a grassy knoll in the midst of seaweed-strewn sand-flats near by. Its Gaelic name is *Caisted an Stalcaire*, 'Castle of the Hunter', for in the mid-16th century it was a hunting lodge of James V. Ownership of the castle alternated down the centuries between Stewarts and Campbells. It is now in private hands and rarely open to the public. Nevertheless, its tall, rectangular shape set against the majestic gloom of the peaks of Appin makes a memorable spectacle.

⑤ LISMORE

The short route to the island is by pretty Port Appin, a harmonious collection of low stone cottages, an old black-and-white hotel and a lighthouse near the pier. Cars, however, must travel from Oban.

Geographically, the 10 mile long island is one of the Inner Hebrides, but it is so wrapped about and leaned over by land that it is sometimes difficult to remember that it is an island at all. Certainly there is no finer viewpoint in western Scotland. Stop anywhere on the single-track road, and all about there are islands and mountains rolling away into the blue distance – Mull, Jura, Ben Cruachan, Ben Nevis, all of wild Lochaber, Lorn and Appin.

Lismore is a calm, green and gentle place, eminently suited to its role as one of the earliest Christian sites in the country. St Moluaig arrived there in about 560, at the same time that Columba was working in Iona, and after founding a number of

NOBLE CROWN *The mock Colosseum above Oban's bustling harbour adds a whimsical touch to the town, and a platform on the seaward side gives breathtaking views westwards to Mull.*

religious communities in different parts of Scotland, died and was buried in the churchyard at Lismore in 592. The parish church of Kilmoluaig is the choir of a cathedral built and dedicated to him in the 13th century. The remainder of the building was destroyed at the Reformation, but Moluaig's staff still survives in Inveraray Castle.

⑥ LOCH CRERAN

The Sea Life Centre which has been established about halfway along the southern shore of the loch is one of the most exciting and original concepts of its kind in the world. In its waters there live some 2,000 specimens of Atlantic sea-creatures – eels, dogfish, salmon, cod, sole, bass, wrasse, mullet and dozens of others including such curiosities as angler-fish, pipe fish and blennies. But the ingenuity of the place lies in its lighting and reproduction of habitats, so that looking into the tanks – through which new water from the loch constantly flows – is like gazing into the twilight world of the undersea.

The show-stealers are the young seals, who can be seen on the surface outside the building, or underwater within. They grin through the glass at the audience, then show off in a display of sub-aqua acrobatics.

The Centre is owned by a fish-farming company, and there are displays of fish-farming techniques. Some products, such as salmon and lobster, are eaten in the restaurant. Near by, the Forestry Commission laid out some delightful, if steep, walks, and near the mouth of Loch Creran can be seen the 17th-century Barcaldin Castle.

⑦ CONNEL

Beneath the unlovely but practical bridge that carries the road to Fort William are the famous Falls of Lora which, if not exactly falls, are nevertheless extremely impressive rapids. At ebb-tide, the weight of Loch Etive's water is forced through the Connel narrows and across a submerged ledge. There its dark smoothness is abruptly converted into great kicks and swirls of white, pouring under the bridge down towards Loch Linnhe.

⑧ DUNSTAFFNAGE CASTLE

The 10 ft thick outer walls are now almost indistinguishable from the black crag on which they were raised in the 13th century. The castle is on or near the site of the capital of Dalriada, the original Kingdom of the Scots, where the Stone of Destiny was kept until its transfer to Scone in AD 843.

In the 14th century a branch of the Campbells became hereditary constables of Dunstaffnage Castle, and their descendants have been known as the Captains of Dunstaffnage ever since. A large number of them are buried in the roofless chapel that lies half concealed in a nearby wood. In 1746 Flora MacDonald was imprisoned in the castle for ten days on her way to the Tower of London.

⑨ OBAN

There is a touch of the eccentric in Oban's undoubted charm. Its curiosities include a blue and white railway station, whose architectural style is somewhere between Scots baronial, Tudor and the Wild West; the unfinished shell of the salt-water spa that never was; and McCaig's Tower, a granite building resembling the Colosseum of Ancient Rome, which is floodlit by night. John McCaig, a banker and art critic, built the Tower between 1890 and 1900, partly as a monument and partly to give work to local masons. It was to have been a museum and art gallery, but it was never finished.

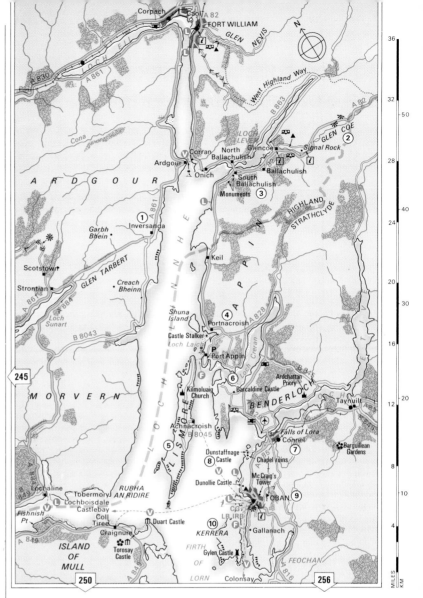

Throwing the hammer, a traditional event at the Oban Highland Games

Oban, essentially a creation of the railway and steamer, looks inland for tourists and outwards to the Isles, and serves both very well. There are shoals of hotels along the front, Highland games and ceilidhs, shinty (a devastating ancestor of hockey), an annual regatta and excellent facilities for yachtsmen, water-skiers and divers. By the piers and among the fishing boats there is a constant coming and going of big ferries for the Inner and Outer Hebrides, smaller ferries serving tiny ports up lochs and inlets, and puffers, the once ubiquitous coasters of the Scottish mainland and islands.

An older Oban is apparent in the creeper-clad ruin of Dunollie Castle, nobly sited on a crag at the northern end of the bay. The present structure was a MacDougall stronghold dating mostly from the 15th century, but there has been a stronghold on the crag for much longer.

⑩ KERRERA

Considering how close it is to bustling Oban, the island is surprisingly wild and lonely; sad, too, with the memory of vanished farms in its tumbled walls. Reached by a ferry 2 miles south of Oban, it provides good, rough walking, and glorious views of Mull and the islands of the Firth of Lorn.

The ruined Gylen Castle, majestically brooding on its crag over the waters of Lorn, was a MacDougall fortress which, during the Civil War, was stormed and burned by a force of Covenanters. One of the Covenanting officers, a Campbell, took from the shambles the famous Brooch of Lorn, a MacDougall heirloom that had reputedly belonged to Robert Bruce. For nearly 200 years, the MacDougalls believed that the jewel had been destroyed in the fire; then in 1825 it was returned to them by a descendant of the Campbell officer.

LOCAL INFORMATION

Tourist information Fort William 3781; Ballachulish 296 (summer); Oban 63122/63551.

HM Coastguard Oban 63720/63729 for information, 999 in emergency (ask for coastguard).

Weather Glasgow (041) 248 3451.

PLACES TO SEE INLAND

Ardchattan Priory, 12 miles NE of Oban, on N side of Loch Etive. Ruined 13th-century priory and gardens. Gardens daily in summer.

Barguillean Gardens, 14 miles E of Oban, via Taynuilt. Daily in summer.

A legend of a lost galleon and a burial place of kings

Roofless crofts are the monuments to the people who, in the 19th century, were driven from their homes to take their names and brave spirits to the New World. Yet the Island of Mull is a smiling and happy place, whose mood is that of its upland meadows, bright with wild flowers and waterfalls and the gaily painted houses of Tobermory. There are reminders of ancient cataclysms in the gigantic lava terraces and basalt columns of Staffa.

① CRAIGNURE

The voyage from Oban to Craignure on Mull takes 45 minutes and presents an ever-changing vista of mountains, sea and islands. Craignure itself is an attractive collection of houses, shops, a tea-room and an inn jammed between a wooded cliff and the pier. On the quayside, a few vehicles and passengers are generally waiting.

About a mile south of Craignure, by road or woodland path, is Torosay Castle, a handsome Victorian mansion in the Scots baronial style. It contains good furniture and pictures, and photographic displays of life at the turn of the century. The terraced gardens and the statue walk are glorious, with views of the Appin coast from Ben Cruachan to Ben Nevis. The house is open during the summer, and the gardens all year round.

② SALEN

A collection of snug stone cottages, a ruinous pier, a general store and a post office make Salen the first place of any size encountered by the visitor to Mull. It was the creation in about 1800 of Major-General Lachlan MacQuarie, a native of Ulva – a smaller island off Mull's west coast – who later became Governor of New South Wales.

On a headland above a sandy bay to the north of Salen are the picturesque, but extremely battered, remains of Aros Castle, one of the chain of great fortifications built by the Lords of the Isles through the Inner Hebrides and western mainland, and last occupied in 1608.

③ TOBERMORY

The capital of Mull takes its name from the ancient, and long-vanished, Tobar Mhoire (the chapel of the Well of Mary). The present town, however, dates from no later than the 1780s, when the British Society for Encouraging Fisheries decided to found a port upon its wonderful natural harbour.

It is a pretty place of bright, colour-washed houses and hotels; and of shops that sell chandlery and diving gear, or fishing tackle, guns and paperbacks, or sweet-scented new bread. Also among Tobermory's temptations are a good anchorage, ferries to Coll and Tiree, golf and pony-trekking, Highland games and crafts, and woodland walks by rhododendrons and waterfalls in Aros Park.

Tobermory's best-known feature is its galleon, a straggler from the Spanish Armada, that lies about 300 yds off the pier. Legend has always said that it is the *Florencia* or *San Francisco*, the vessel carrying the fleet's pay chests, blown up by accident or design while anchored in the bay. Recent research, however, suggests that the *San Francisco* and *Florencia* were two ships, and that there is no seabed treasure. The *San Francisco* returned to Spain; and the *Florencia* (also called the *San Juan Bautista*), which went down at Tobermory in 1588, was a warship and troop-carrier. Without doubt it was powerful enough to lend Maclean of Duart an officer, 100 men and two guns – probably in exchange for supplies – for his successful attack on Mingary Castle in Ardnamurchan.

④ DERVAIG

The road from Tobermory is steep and single-tracked, and seems to go through a hundred hairpin bends as it skirts drops into slaty lochans or leaps over tiny stone bridges with ridges to catch the wheels of the unwary. Stop beside one of the little trout-filled lochs and drink in the peace of the wide straths and old-gold hills scattered with ruined shielings, and something comes to mind of the pain of the Clearances victims who were forced to leave so enchanting a place.

Dervaig village was built by Maclean of Coll in 1799, and consists mostly of single-storey stone houses, though some have squeezed a first floor with dormer windows out of the roof. Their design could not be simpler, but they are given individuality and prettiness by whitewash and brightly painted windows and doors.

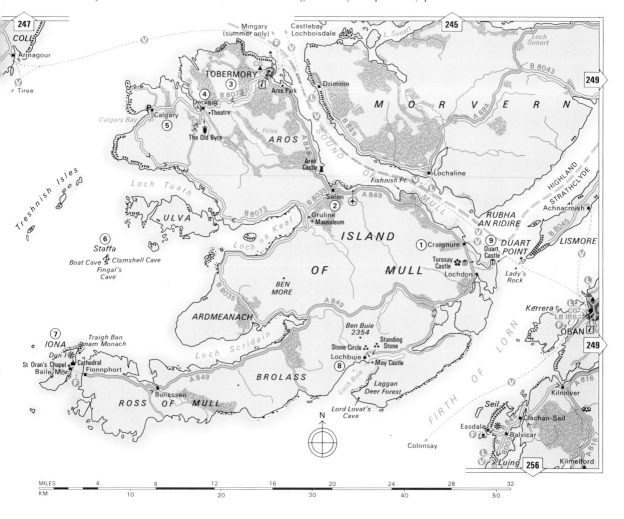

CROFTING ON MULL *In the shadow of cloud-capped Ben Buie a crofter's house stands amid neatly fenced fields, contrasting with the roofless reminders of the Clearances elsewhere on the island.*

Half a mile along the Salen road is the Mull Little Theatre which, with its seating capacity of 40, is probably the smallest professional theatre in Britain. The Old Byre is a crofting museum that presents an audio-visual account of the Clearances, with recordings of local people telling stories and singing songs handed down from their forbears.

⑤ CALGARY

The village is small indeed, but it stands on the loveliest bay in Mull. The peace of its white sands and grassy plain behind becomes a little less than infinite in summer, as the holiday crowds flock in, but it is beautiful nonetheless.

The views from the roads leading to and from the bay are as grand as any in the Hebrides, embracing Coll and the Treshnish Isles to the west, and Skye and Ardnamurchan to the north.

⑥ STAFFA

This extraordinary island is named from the Norse for stave, a fairly good description of the symmetrical basalt columns of which the place is largely composed. Despite its ancient name, it did not come to the world's attention until the 1770s, when it was glimpsed by Sir Joseph Banks on an expedition to Iceland. Its lonely grandeur precisely suited the mood of the Romantic movement, and in the first half of the 19th century it was visited by Tennyson, Wordsworth, Queen Victoria and many other famous people including, of course, Mendelssohn, who gained inspiration to write his *Hebrides Overture* from his visit to Fingal's Cave. This enormous cavern, 66 ft high and 76 yds deep, is named after the Irish-Scots hero Fionn mac Cumhaill, who is also credited with building the Giant's Causeway in Ulster.

Getting to Staffa is not easy. There are motor-boat trips from Iona that will land passengers for a brief visit if the weather is good, but the most comfortable way to see the island is to take the 'Sacred Isle' steamer cruise from Oban to Iona. Passengers on this cruise are not landed at Staffa, however.

⑦ IONA

St Columba called it 'Iona of my heart', but long before he chose it as the site for his monastery, it must have been regarded as a place set apart, for the Druids built a temple there. This feeling of separateness, of enchantment, has persisted to this day.

Some of this is no doubt due to the fact that it takes a deliberate and conscious effort to get there. Iona is not on the way to anywhere else, and to reach the island it is necessary to travel right across Mull to Fionnphort for the passenger ferry, or to make the long sea journey from Oban. But almost any effort is worth while, since quite apart from its associations it is of a loveliness that lifts the spirits just to behold.

Of Columba's monastery, built probably of wattle and daub in 563, nothing remains; after the saint's death it was sacked several times by the Vikings, and its community massacred; some of them on the beach still known as Traigh Ban nam Monach, 'the White Stand of the Monks'. But throughout the Dark Ages, somehow the community persisted, devoted to the memory of its founder; and because it was such a holy place, 60 kings were buried there. They came from Ireland, Norway and Scotland, and included Shakespeare's Macbeth and his victim, Duncan.

The oldest building still standing is St Oran's Chapel, built by Queen Margaret in 1080, while near by is the 15th-century cathedral, restored in the early 1900s; facing it is the beautifully carved St Martin's Cross, 17 ft high and more than 1,000 years old.

It requires weeks to explore Iona properly, but to sum up the island's character climb the 328 ft hill of Dun I and look over the island, with its fringe of machair – dazzling white shell-sand backed by grass – to all of the Hebrides.

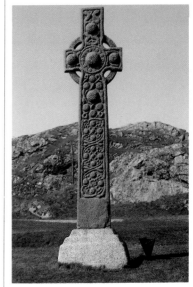

CARVED CROSS *Ornamental designs cover the east face of St Martin's Cross, outside the West Door of Iona Cathedral.*

⑧ LOCHBUIE

A number of standing stones and stone circles around the village on the fertile plain at the head of Loch Buie attest that people have lived thereabouts for a very long time. But the most famous relic in the area, Moy Castle, is rather younger. Dating from the

---

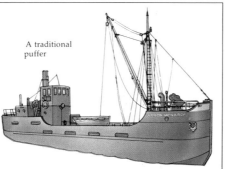

WORKHORSE OF THE ISLES

Scotland's 'puffers', the tough little work-boats that ply along the west coast and among the islands, grounding on the seaweed-strewn beaches to unload, are as much a part of Scottish tradition as white heather and haggis. They were immortalised in Neil Munroe's 'Para Handy' stories, which were made into a television series. A few of the traditional steam-powered puffers still survive, many privately owned, but the modern vessels are diesel-powered, with sleeker lines.

A traditional puffer

THE TREASURED CHARM OF A TREASURE-HUNT TOWN

Stories that doubloons by the thousand, priceless gems and gold and silver plate lie in a sunken galleon at the bottom of Tobermory's bay have made Mull's principal town famous. But though a vessel is there, little of note has been recovered and it is unlikely that any treasure exists within her rotting timbers. Tobermory's real treasure is her smart waterfront set below wooded hills.

14th century, it is the former stronghold of the MacLaines of Lochbuie, an offshoot of the Macleans of Duart. It is a grim fortress containing a well of crystal-clear water that never runs dry, and a dungeon in which the prisoner was forced to sit in darkness on a boulder with 9 ft of water around him.

Because of its crumbling condition the building is not open to the public, and since it stands in private property permission should be sought at the lodge before visiting it. Should a headless horseman be glimpsed in the estate, this is Ewen a'Chinn Bhig (Ewen of the Little Head), a chief of the Lochbuie MacLaines who was beheaded in a clan battle some centuries ago, and now

is said to ride furiously round the castle whenever the death of a descendant is imminent.

There are some fine coastal walks around the loch, which is leaned over by the massive 2,354 ft Ben Buie, and there are many caves to explore. Particularly impressive is Lord Lovat's Cave on the southern tip of the Laggan peninsula – 150 ft high, and running 300 ft back into the cliffs.

⑨ DUART CASTLE
Of all the fortresses in the islands, none is more expressive of the power and majesty of

the medieval chieftains than Duart. Its massive walls rose from the *dubh aird* ('dark headland'), in the 13th century, when the Macleans ousted the MacDonalds from their supremacy as Lords of the Isles. During the next 300 years, the Macleans of Duart added to the castle until it encompassed more than 100 rooms; then, through their adherence to the Jacobite cause, they lost their ascendancy to the Campbells, and were dispossessed.

For a time, Duart was occupied by government troops, but it gradually fell into ruin and it was not until 1912 that Sir Donald

Fitzroy Maclean, the chief of that time, was able to restore the castle to its former grandeur, and to its position as Duthus, or rallying place, of the Clan Maclean. The present chief, 27th of the line, is Lord Maclean of Duart, who was for many years leader of the Scouting Movement in the Commonwealth.

The castle, open in the summer, contains collections of family and Scottish relics and a Scouting exhibition. A tableau in the dungeon shows the figures of two Spanish officers said to have been imprisoned in the castle when the galleon *Florencia* sought

shelter in the bay. The views from the building, and especially from the Sea Room, are breathtaking.

LOCAL INFORMATION
Tourist information Tobermory 2182 (summer).
HM Coastguard Oban 63720 for information, 999 in emergency (ask for coastguard).
Weather Glasgow (041) 248 34521.
How to get there. Caledonian MacBrayne Ltd: car ferry Oban to Craignure and Tobermory (passengers only), sailings every day except Sunday, in winter. Gourock 33755.

Isles of moors and lochs, and whisky with the tang of peat

Much of Jura is a boggy desert, while Islay, where the Lords of the Isles harboured their war-galleys, sparkles with white farms and the pagoda-like vents of distillery drying rooms. Colonsay, under the influence of the North Atlantic Drift, has subtropical gardens and evidence that people have lived there since the Stone Age. Oronsay is holy ground, a calm and lovely island that in the Middle Ages was a place of pilgrimage and sanctuary.

COLONSAY HOUSE *The 18th-century mansion is surrounded by woodland gardens, open to the public, where visitors can wander among mimosa, eucalyptus, palm trees and rare rhododendrons.*

① COLONSAY AND ORONSAY

The two islands become one island for 3 hours at each low tide when they are linked by a sandy beach to form a single entity, not counting the dozen or so islets and fretted skerries around the southern and western end. Together, Colonsay and Oronsay are no more than 10 miles long, yet they have quite different characters.

Colonsay seems to have been occupied since time's beginning. Flint tools and other Stone Age remains have been found, there are about a score of Pictish forts and half a dozen sets of standing stones, while beneath the sands of lovely Kiloran Bay was discovered, a century ago, the remains of a Viking warlord, together with his ship and his horse. The MacPhies held the island in historic times. Almost alone among the Hebrides it suffered no forced evictions during the Highland Clearances; therefore it lacks that sad, haunted quality that possesses so many of the others.

The family of the island's present owner, Lord Strathcona, has during four generations improved the amenities of the place, and created subtropical gardens around Colonsay House. The house was built in 1722 from the stones of Kiloran Abbey; no trace remains today of the abbey, which is said to have been founded by St Columba.

The nearby Kiloran Bay is one of the island's finest beaches. A long headland protects it from the full force of the Atlantic and makes bathing safe, though strong westerly winds can provide rollers for surfing. A natural rock pool is deep enough for diving, and the beach is backed by sand-dunes. Caves in the cliffs at either end of the bay contain evidence of human occupation stretching back 6,000 years.

Oronsay belongs to the days of the saints. It is said that St Columba landed there on his way to Iona from Ireland in the middle of the 6th century. There was a monastery there in the 6th century, and the present priory dates from the 13th century. Within the still substantial ruins there is a beautiful Celtic cross and a high altar, in which are placed the human bones that occasionally come to the surface in the ancient burial ground. The graveyard, with its stone slabs bearing the carved portraits of warriors and priests, is almost certainly overcrowded, since until the Reformation Oronsay was considered to be the holiest ground in Scotland after Iona. The nearby farm buildings are built of stone quarried from the priory.

In the middle of The Strand, the sandy stretch between the two islands, there used to be a cross; any fugitive from Colonsay passing it was held to be within the jurisdiction of the priory and could, in theory, claim sanctuary from his enemies for a year and a day.

Colonsay and Oronsay enjoy almost as much sunshine as Tiree, the record-holder for Scotland, and a much lower rainfall than that of the mainland. Walking is rugged rather than difficult; there are antiquities to explore, white, empty beaches, and seal colonies on the islets and skerries. Wild goats flourish at Balnahard and on Oronsay – long-horned, black-fleeced creatures said to be descended from goats that swam ashore from ships of the Spanish Armada wrecked off the shores in 1588. Rabbits abound, for there are no foxes, stoats or weasels, but danger lurks in the air where high-flying golden eagles soar in readiness to swoop down on silent wings.

There is an 18-hole golf course, and dinghies can be hired from the Colonsay Yacht Club at the hotel; accommodation is at the hotel, or in self-catering cottages or flats at Colonsay House.

② JURA

Most of Jura's 94,000 acres consist of a wilderness of rock, moor and peat-bog, inhabited only by deer and their hunters; its deer must have been famous even in the days of the Vikings, for its name comes from the Norse *Dyr Oe*, 'Deer Island'. Those who hear the Call of the Wild should resist it; the interior, one of the largest uninhabited areas in Britain, can be dangerous for inexperienced walkers, and is especially so from mid-August to February, when the deer-stalkers are active.

All of this is in astonishing contrast with the island's green and fertile south-eastern tip, where fuchsias, rhododendrons and even palm trees grow. There live most of Jura's population of some 200, and there too

ISLAND WILDERNESS *Jura is one of the wildest of the Hebridean islands. Beyond the deep-sea inlet of Loch Tarbert, open moorlands and peat-bogs climb towards the northern peaks.*

is the island's capital, Craighouse, which contains the island's only shop, hotel, cafe, garage and distillery. There are some more scattered houses further up the east coast, but not many; one of them, at Barnhill, far to the north, was occupied for a time by George Orwell, who wrote some of his best-known novels there, including *Animal Farm* and *1984*.

The island's best-known landmarks are the three conical mountains, about 2,500 ft high, known as the Paps of Jura. They can be seen from the mainland, and from all over the Hebrides, blued with distance, faintly mysterious and generally wearing a fine veil of cloud over their summits.

Another famous, or infamous, feature is the Gulf of Corryvreckan, which lies between Jura and near-uninhabited Scarba. A 10 knot tide race channelled into the narrow gulf becomes a seething maelstrom of broken white water and whirlpools whose roar can be heard miles away. It has claimed many vessels down the centuries, and who shall live and who shall drown is said to be determined by the Cailleach, the witch who controls the race.

The only access to Jura is by the 5 minute ferry from Port Askaig on Islay to the pier at Feolin Ferry. Accommodation on the island is limited.

③ ISLAY

While so many of the Inner Hebrides seem to be slipping away into a gentle Celtic reverie, Islay, the southernmost of them, is positively vibrant. It has a population of 4,000 and each year it presents to the Exchequer the equivalent of £7,000 for each man, woman and child on the island.

The reason for these riches is *uisgebaugh*, 'the water of life' – whisky, which Islay produces in large quantities from several distilleries. And the reason for the distilleries is Islay's streams and Islay's peat. Much of the island's 235 square miles consists of peat, and every year each of the distilleries burns 800 tons of it, hand-cut from black trenches, to dry the malt. And since the Atlantic mists have been soaking into the turf for thousands of years, it is not

NO HIDING PLACE *Bowmore's church, on Islay, was built circular in shape so that the Devil would find no corners in which to hide.*

surprising that the smoke imparts a special flavour to Islay whisky; slightly harsh and dry, with a far-off hint of the sea.

There are also more than 500 farms on Islay, and away from the boggy lowlands there is a wide variety of scenery, from the wild cliffs of the Mull of Oa – where there is a monument to the American servicemen who died when the troopships *Tuscania* and *Otranto* sank near by in 1918 – to the incredible blueness of Loch Gorm in Kilchoman. Or there is the contrast between the Rhinns of Islay with its ancient stone circles and breakers slow-marching in from the Atlantic, and the sonorous peace of Laggan Bay, which offers 5 uninterrupted miles of shell-sand and is called, appropriately, The Big Strand. At its northern end the River Laggan flows to the sea – a river with a good autumn run of salmon and sea trout.

The chief ways to Islay (pronounced I'la) are by air, when aircraft from Glasgow expertly skim the spine of Kintyre and open up views of the entire Hebrides, or by ferry from Kennacraig to Port Ellen and Port

Askaig. This is a charming village on Kilnaughton Bay where there is safe bathing and sailing; some of the most famous Islay distilleries are near by, and occasionally offer guided tours. Some 7 miles to the north-east is the ruined Kildalton chapel with its beautiful 8th-century Celtic cross. When this blew down 100 years ago, the skeletons of a man and a woman were discovered beneath it; the man at least had been horribly tortured to death.

Bowmore, however, is the administrative centre of the island. At the head of the wide main street is a perfectly round church built in 1767; a plaque on its tower records that it was built by 'Daniel Campbell, Lord of this Island'. The distillery, which dates from 1779, has a museum. Among several other townships on Islay is Port Charlotte, compact and neat, which contains a comprehensive folk museum and a creamery where Islay cheese – rather like a strong Cheddar – is made.

Despite its busyness, Islay is still unspoiled. Even the whisky is nothing new; the island was famous for it in the Middle Ages when the MacDonald Lords of the Isles ruled their empire from there.

An island fringe, and lochs that cut deep into Knapdale

South of Oban, the coast of Scotland looks as though it had dropped from a great height and shattered into a thousand islands, islets, promontories and sea lochs. The islands furthest out are called, with simple poetry, the Isles of the Sea, the Garvellachs. The nearest ones are known, more prosaically, as the Slate Islands; the quarries on them, abandoned now, were worked for hundreds of years, and have twice roofed Iona Cathedral.

① CLACHAN BRIDGE

Seil Sound, which separates Seil island from the mainland, is so narrow that it is spanned at Clachan by a bridge designed by Thomas Telford in 1792. Geographically the sound is part of the Atlantic Ocean, so the bridge is known locally as 'the bridge over the Atlantic'. The hump-backed stone bridge arches between grassy banks little more than 50 yds apart and hardly warrants such a grandiose title.

On the west coast of Seil, at the village of Easdale, there is a viewing point – a wonderful place, if the weather is right, from which to contemplate the southern part of the Firth of Lorn and the islands.

② LUING

South of Seil island, Luing island is another former slate-quarrying area. Between the islands the tides run fast and furious and wait for no man, and the visitor is better off searching the rocky beaches for semi-precious stones than risking bathing in the treacherous currents. There are safer beaches at the southern end of the island.

③ ARDFERN

Sheltered by the Craignish peninsula, the village of Ardfern runs along the northern shore of Loch Craignish with its scattering of islands that offer many secluded moorings. Gently sloping shingle beaches are safe for swimming and boating.

④ CRINAN

In a little inlet off the Sound of Jura, and tucked under low, wooded cliffs, is Crinan, the north-western terminus of the Crinan Canal. There is not much of it, but what there is, is attractive – a complex of neat locks, quays and basins surrounded by lawns, a hotel outside which people in short yellow wellingtons and orange anoraks watch the yachts coming through the canal with varying expressions of envy or amusement, and a few stone houses.

But Crinan's chief joy and entertainment is the endless parade of boats through the locks. There are tough little fishing boats, festooned with nets or lobster-pots; sleek yachts and a dinghy that is a family's pride; beginners trying to look like old salts, and local children throwing ropes round bollards with contemptuous ease; and the occasional 80 ft giant with brilliant brass, a gleam of perfect table linen through the porthole and a bar in the cockpit.

Across the loch is Duntrune Castle, one of the oldest inhabited houses in Scotland. It used to be a Campbell stronghold, and some years ago a skeleton was discovered beneath the floorboards. It was said to be that of an imprisoned MacDonald piper who, during the Civil Wars of the 17th century, played a wild pibroch from the walls to warn his fellow-clansmen of an impending trap.

⑤ TAYVALLICH

Tucked into Loch a' Bhealaich, an inlet among the shattered, heavily wooded collection of promontories and bays that compose the upper end of Loch Sween, is the splendid natural harbour of Tayvallich. The village that grew about its shores was once important in the herring and lobster fisheries, but now it concentrates mainly upon the energetic holidaymaker, offering fine walks into Knapdale, safe bathing from its pebbly shores and comfortable sailing and fishing in the loch. Less than a mile to the west is Carsaig Bay, which has a viewpoint looking over to the wild, olive-dun hills of Jura.

⑥ KILMORY

The Point of Knap is an unexpectedly gentle jut of land that separates the heavily wooded Loch Sween from the wilder Loch Caolisport. The Point consists mostly of crofting pastures, and the only settlement of any size is the pleasant stone-built village of Kilmory, which looks out over the Sound of Jura to the three conical mountains known as the Paps of Jura. The ruined church contains a magnificent collection of Celtic grave slabs portraying warriors, chiefs and hunters; outside stands the 12 ft high 'MacMillan's Cross', whose intricate, medieval carving has been compared to the finest of the monuments on Iona.

Some 3 miles to the north up the coast are the bleak remains of the 12th-century Castle Sween. Its ruined condition is largely the

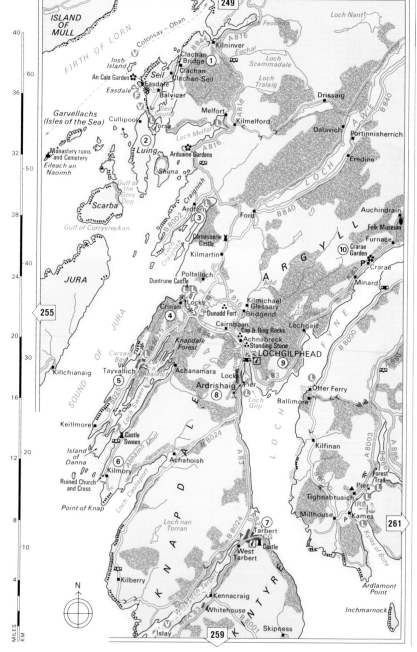

SHORT CUT *Boating enthusiasts use the Crinan Canal to reach the sea from Loch Fyne, preferring even the arduous task of negotiating 15 locks to the long haul around the Mull of Kintyre.*

handiwork of Colkitto MacDonald, the stormy Scots-Irish lieutenant of the Marquis of Montrose who, in the Civil War, raised the Highland clans on behalf of Charles I.

EFFIGIES IN STONE *Celtic grave slabs, remarkable for their detailed carvings, are housed in the ruined church at Kilmory.*

⑦ TARBERT

In this busy, bustling port and resort, the masts of fishing boats and yachts jostle against a background of cafes and, in summer, the occasional harbourside fairground. Once Tarbert was the chief port of the Loch Fyne herring industry, and though this has declined, the Fish Quay is still busy every morning as the boats come in to unload their catches of prawns, clams and fish. The village takes fish seriously, and holds seafood festivals that present the harvests of all the west-coast fishing grounds, cooked, smoked or preserved in a dozen delicious ways.

The last relic of the days of sail is a square raised platform in the middle of the harbour known as the 'The Beilding'. A capstan used to be mounted on it and cables run out to haul sailing boats into their berths. But the only sails to be seen now are those of dozens of yachts, whose owners use Tarbert as a base from which to explore Loch Fyne and the waters around Kintyre. They are well serviced by a boatyard and by the excellent harbour facilities.

The ivy-coloured remains of the 15th-century keep on the hill above the harbour is the latest of several castles on the site, most of which were built as a defence against the Vikings. Kintyre was in fact for many years a Norse province. It gained this status as the result of an agreement between King Magnus Barefoot and the Scottish King Edgar

that King Magnus should hold any land that his longship could circumnavigate. In 1098 King Magnus had himself dragged in his longship across the isthmus of Tarbert – and so claimed Kintyre for the Norse. Norse rule ended in 1263 when Alexander III annihilated the Viking fleet at the Battle of Largs.

A mile across the isthmus are the headwaters of West Loch Tarbert, whose valley, bordered by dark, hanging woods, leads out to the Sound of Jura. At the north-eastern end of the loch there is a pier, with neat piles of lobster pots and net floats, and a dozen or so sturdy fishing boats. Thus the fishermen of Tarbert have the waters of both Loch Fyne and the Atlantic as their province.

⑧ ARDRISHAIG

The grey village with its handsome harbour and little lighthouse stands at the southern end of the Crinan Canal, and was largely created by it. Started in 1794 by John Rennie, the canal runs for 9 miles across the northern end of Knapdale, linking Loch Fyne with the Sound of Jura and the open Atlantic, so cutting out the 120 mile voyage round Kintyre.

From the beginning, the canal was much used not only by the herring fleets and the coasters but by the people of the West Highlands, who found the water route an easier way to get to Glasgow and the south than the wearisome journey by road or rail. Many of them came by paddle-steamer, the magnificent 300 ft *Columba*, pride of the David MacBrayne fleet. In the summer season she thrashed her way up from Glasgow at 19 knots, carrying up to 2,000 passengers in her luxurious saloon and cabins, and offering services that included bookstalls, a hairdresser's saloon, and a post office.

Today the fisheries and the passenger trade have both declined, and in the basin hewn from solid rock yachts and dinghies outnumber the fishing boats. Now and then a little 'puffer' – one of the ubiquitous breed of Highland coasters – comes through as a reminder of greater days.

⑨ LOCHGILPHEAD

A pleasant half moon of Victorian and later stone houses stands on a slope of near-parkland at the top of Loch Gilp – an inlet off Loch Fyne. The Crinan Canal runs just outside the small town, and contributed to its 19th-century growth. It looks a pleasant

place to live in, and there are some good, old-fashioned shops.

People have found the area attractive for a very long time, as is apparent from the large number of prehistoric monuments in the district. A mile to the north, at Achnabreck, there is a large standing stone just over the wall of the modern cemetery, and a little beyond there are rocks carved with enigmatic Bronze Age 'cup and ring' markings – hollows surrounded by rings. No one knows the significance of these symbols, but they are frequently found at ancient burial and sacred sites in Scotland and the north of England.

⑩ CRARAE GARDEN

With the wild, dark hills of Argyll behind and the wide, restless waters of Loch Fyne in front, Crarae, some 12 miles south-west of Inveraray, hardly seems the most encouraging place to establish a collection of rare trees and shrubs. Yet the climate is kind and the rainfall high, and there, in 1912, Sir Archibald and Lady Campbell of Succoth began planting specimen trees round their house. The range was extended by their son and grandson, and today Crarae, with its rare mixture of wild Highland glen and exotic trees and shrubs, is one of the most delightful gardens in Argyll.

The pivot of the garden is the steep little burn that falls into Loch Fyne. Around the burn have been planted 20 species of eucalyptus, magnolias, and many other trees collected from as far away as Chile, New Zealand and the Himalayas. Visitors can follow an inner trail, or a more extended tour that involves some moorland scrambling. Plants and trees are offered for sale. Crarae is open daily and visitors with a taste for a spectacular display of rhododendrons should try to time their visit for late May or early June.

LOCAL INFORMATION

Tourist information Tarbert 429 (summer). Lochgilphead 2344 (summer).

HM Coastguard Oban 63720/63729 (north of Crinan Canal); Greenock 29988 (south of Crinan Canal) for information; dial 999 in emergency (ask for coastguard).

Weather Glasgow (041) 248 3451.

PLACES TO SEE INLAND

An Cala Garden. Easdale, Seil island. Flowering shrubs, roses and rock gardens. Mon. and Thurs. afternoons in summer.

Arduaine Gardens. 14 miles S of Clachan Bridge. Most days in summer.

Carnasserie Castle. 2 miles N of Kilmartin. Late 16th-century remains of a towerhouse and courtyard. Daily.

Dunadd Fort. 4 miles S of Kilmartin. Hill-fort. Daily.

SORTING THE CATCH *Tarbert fishermen head for home with their catch, with the ever-hungry seagulls in their wake.*

Beaches and valleys in Kintyre and peaks and plains in Arran

Were it not for a tiny isthmus, Kintyre would be the innermost of the Hebrides, and indeed it possesses much of the remoteness and individuality of an island. And of a tropical island at that, with its long, rarely trodden beaches and secret valleys filled with ferns and great trees. Arran, a true island, is quite different – a gentle southern plain, and to the north wild mountains that are treated with respect even by Himalayan climbers.

① GIGHA ISLAND

The name *Gigha* means 'God's Island' in Gaelic. It is a serene and temperate place, scattered with the duns, or forts, and standing stones of prehistoric peoples, and there is a tiny, ruined chapel dedicated to St Cattan. A little to the south of the hamlet of Ardminish is Achamore House Estate, belonging to the National Trust for Scotland, whose 50 acre gardens are a glory of magnolias, fuchsias, camellias, azaleas and other flowering trees and plants.

Most of Gigha is easily explored on foot, and Ardminish is only half an hour on the passenger ferry from Tayinloan on the mainland.

② RONACHAN BAY

Six miles north of Tayinloan on the A83 along the west coast of Kintyre, look out for the car park overlooking Ronachan Bay. From there, among the bracken and wild flowers, there are wonderful views across the Sound of Jura to the Inner Hebrides; and keen inspection of the reefs offshore reveals grey seals, the largest of British wild mammals.

③ MACHRIHANISH

There are few beaches on this coast of Kintyre, but the one at Machrihanish makes up for it – 3½ miles of sand the colour of pale corn, running north to Westport, with pale green surf racing in from Islay, Jura and the coast of north Antrim. It is a tempting shore, but one better suited to beach-walking than to bathing or surfing, for the undertow is dangerous.

At the Machrihanish end there is a breezy golf course, much favoured by those who like the game with scenery. Not so attractive are the low shapes of the buildings of the airfield, which is part NATO and part staging-post for the gallant little Trilander aeroplanes that hop between Glasgow and the Highlands and Islands.

④ SOUTHEND

The little resort with its sandy beaches and golf links is almost at the southern extremity of Kintyre; Ireland is no more than 15 miles away. Tradition has it that St Columba first set foot on Scottish soil there, in about AD 560, and a ruined chapel at Keil Point, 1 mile to the west, is dedicated to him. Behind the churchyard is St Columba's Well, whose waters are considered holy.

The caves below Keil Point contain a slab that may have been an altar, but most remarkable are the prints of two right feet incised into the rock of the knoll at the churchyard's western end. These are known as 'St Columba's Footsteps', but may be as much as 3,000 years old, and are probably an example of the 'Fealty Foot', in which chiefs of long ago used to stand to promise protection and allegiance to the tribe.

⑤ CAMPBELTOWN

The site may once have been the capital of the ancient Celtic kingdom of Dalriada, but the present town and its name belong to the early 1600s, when Archibald Campbell, Earl of Argyll, was given a licence to develop the lands in Kintyre formerly belonging to Clan Donald. With its old stone buildings about the harbour dwarfed by the high, bare hills behind, there is something grim about Campbeltown; and there is something wistful about the little group of fishing boats tied up in a harbour designed to accommodate many times their number. A century ago, the burgh was important in the whaling, coal, distilling and herring-fishing trades, but the first two have vanished, and the others are diminished.

But Campbeltown is recovering swiftly, and is making a name for itself as a sailing and holiday resort. Island Davaar at the mouth of the loch makes for sheltered moorings, and there is good sea-fishing. A museum presents a thoughtful portrait of the burgh's past.

⑥ CARRADALE

The little natural harbour on the east coast of Kintyre is snug even when it is blowing half a gale in the Kilbrannan Sound outside. There is a small fleet of fishing boats, a few houses and a combined grocery shop and tea-room; most of the village is on the hill behind. Perhaps the chief attraction for visitors is the selection of forest walks on the Forestry Commission's 16,000 acre estate. Beginning at the little Forest Centre, the walks radiate outwards to offer views of Arran – dominated by the 2,345 ft bulk of Beinn Bharrain – and shore walks to Carradale and its point, where there is a

vitrified fort dating back to 1500 BC.

Almost buried in the trees and shrubs at the seaward edge of Saddell Forest, 4 miles south of Carradale, are the melancholy remains of Saddell Abbey, which in the early Middle Ages rivalled Iona in ecclesiastical importance. All that remains are a few crumbling arches, but their setting is glorious, and at the entrance there is a shelter protecting a dozen tombstones carved in Argyll between 1300 and 1560. They portray warriors in pointed helmets and armour, a priest with his chalice and a Cistercian monk. The background to the figures consists of a tangle of weapons, foliage, deer hunts and war-galleys.

⑦ SKIPNESS

The village by the curving, sandy beach is tiny, and made to seem all the more so by comparison with the massive red castle. Dating in part from the 13th century, this lacks a roof but is otherwise well preserved. It was never involved in a major battle, and was a Campbell stronghold until it was abandoned around 1700.

⑧ LOCHRANZA

The hills of north Arran sweep superbly down to Glen Chalmadale and the little sea loch at its foot. There is a scattering of stone cottages about the harbour and pier, where the ferry arrives from Claonaig on the mainland. The ruined, twin-towered castle overhanging the loch dates mainly from the 17th century, but an earlier one on the same site is believed to be where Robert Bruce stayed when he first came from Ireland in 1306 to make his bid for the Scottish throne.

The beach is wide and pebbly, but bathing

HIGH-SPEED HUNTER

At speeds up to 180 mph the peregrine falcon dives on other birds and kills its prey with a single blow of its talons, then swoops down to retrieve its meal from the ground. The birds pair for life, and breed on inland crags and sea cliffs on Kintyre and the Island of Arran.

Peregrine falcon
Falco peregrinus
15-19 in (38-48 cm).

LAST OF THE FEW *Fishing boats in Campbeltown harbour huddle together as if seeking the protecting companionship of the few remaining vessels in a fleet that once numbered more than 600.*

ICE SPECTACULAR *Across Kilbrannan Sound from Skipness rises the glistening massif of the Arran mountains, thrusting ten of the island's peaks to more than 2,000 ft in an area of 12 square miles.*

vivors of that breed of little cargo steamers that wander the Highlands and Islands, and were immortalised by Neil Munro in his *Para Handy* tales.

Many visitors are drawn to Brodick to attempt the ascent of the 2,866 ft Goat Fell, whose sombre bulk leans over the village. It and neighbouring peaks are under the protection of the National Trust for Scotland. So too is Brodick Castle, a stark fortification that for centuries was a seat of the Dukes of Hamilton. It was enlarged in 1844 and contains a priceless collection of furniture, porcelain and paintings. The gardens include rare rhododendrons, semi-tropical plants and a walled garden.

Brodick has diving and sea-angling centres with boats and tackle for hire.

LOCAL INFORMATION

Tourist information Campbeltown 52056; (Arran) Brodick 2140/2401.

HM Coastguard Greenock 29988 for information, 999 in emergency (ask for coastguard).

Weather Glasgow (041) 248 3451.

PLACES TO SEE INLAND

Auchagallon Bronze Age Monument, 5 miles N of Blackwaterfoot. Daily.

Heritage Museum, Brodick. 19th-century Arran cottage and blacksmith's shop. Most days in summer.

HOW TO GET TO THE ISLANDS

Arran. Car ferry Ardrossan to Brodick, daily; Claonig to Lochranza (Arran) in summer.
Gigha. Caledonian MacBrayne Ltd: ferry from Tayinloan, daily; Gourock 33755.

is safe and the underwater scenery spectacular, it is particularly attractive when the open sea is too rough for diving. Cod, conger and haddock may be fished from the shore or from a boat.

⑨ BLACKWATERFOOT

It is often said that Arran is Scotland in miniature – having wild mountains to the north and a quiet fertile plain to the south. Blackwaterfoot is very much a Lowland hamlet, and the fact that people have made a living thereabouts for a very long time is apparent from the large number of standing stones, forts and burial chambers of the Iron and Bronze Ages, and traces of even earlier occupation. Most evocative of these misty eras are the 15 standing stones grouped about the graves of long-forgotten Bronze Age chieftains some 4 miles to the north.

On the coast 2 miles north of Blackwaterfoot is King's Cave, one of a number of Scottish caverns believed to have been inhabited by Robert Bruce before he gained the throne; but the king referred to may be Fingal, the legendary Celtic hero.

Blackwaterfoot offers safe bathing from sandy beaches, good fishing, pony trekking, a golf course and indoor swimming pool.

⑩ LAMLASH

Arran's largest village and its serene, shingle-edged bay are protected by the 1,000 ft high sentinel of Holy Island. The island's holiness is derived from St Molaise, or Laserian, who accepted 30 diseases all at once in place of purgatory, and died in AD 639. The cave in which he lived has Runic inscriptions and is situated on the bay side of the island, which can be visited by boat with permission.

Lamlash Bay offers good dinghy sailing and superb fishing for flatfish, conger,

haddock, ray and skate, while underwater enthusiasts can visit the *Derwent* brig, wrecked off Holy Island in 1880. There is a golf course with views out to the island.

⑪ BRODICK

Situated on a sandy bay that is outstanding even on this lovely coast, Brodick is generally regarded as the capital of Arran. It is certainly the island's main port; into its harbour come the ferries from Ardrossan, and even the occasional 'puffer', last sur-

259

Forested hills above the lochs of Cowal and lowland Bute

For centuries the Cowal peninsula, between Loch Fyne and Loch Long, was dominated by Clan Campbell. Its dominance was frequently challenged, which accounts for the number of ruined fortifications and for the dark tales of murder and treachery that lie behind the sunny visages of the little resorts. Piers clad in barnacles and weeds rise out of the glass-clear water on which yachts heel to the wind, their sails white as gulls' wings.

A POET'S LOVE *The statue of Mary Campbell gazes from Dunoon across the Firth of Clyde. Mary inspired some of Robert Burns's finest lyrics, including* Highland Lassie *and* To Mary in Heaven.

① AUCHINDRAIN

To say that Auchindrain is a museum is to do it less than justice; rather, it is a time capsule that affords a glimpse into the life of the most basic of communities – the communal-tenancy farm. The site may well have been occupied from prehistory, but the little stone cottages and sheds that can be seen today are mostly about 200 years old. For the greater part of its history, the farm of Auchindrain would have supported about ten families who grew potatoes as their chief crop, grazed a few cows and pigs, shared the labour and lived only a little above subsistence level.

Auchindrain was typical of thousands of Highland communities that were swept away in the Clearances of the 1830s and 1840s to make way for sheep. But

PRIMITIVE SURVIVOR *This stone-and-thatch crofter's cottage at Auchindrain Farm Museum survived the Highland Clearances.*

Auchindrain was not swept away; it continued in the same manner until 1935 when it was taken over by a single tenant, and now it is being restored to its state of a century ago to show what ingenuity Highlanders are capable of in the face of adversity. There are home-made dyes and soaps, good home-made furniture, and a loom made of driftwood in 1760 and still in working order. There is also the community's still, discovered a few years ago, to show that its life was not entirely bleak.

After a visit to Auchindrain, the visitor sees the hundreds of roofless crofts scattered through the Highlands with a more understanding eye.

② INVERARAY

Some 6 miles from the head of Loch Fyne, down its western shore, stands the blue-grey, Scots-baronial Inveraray Castle, surrounded at a respectful distance by the perfect little Georgian Royal Burgh of Inveraray itself. The grouping is the headquarters of the Clan Campbell, one of the most powerful of all the clans throughout the long, turbulent history of the Highlands, and the castle is the seat of its chieftains, the Dukes of Argyll, who for centuries were monarchs of this part of Scotland in all but name.

Town and castle, both built at about the time of the 1745 Jacobite Uprising, when the Campbells fought for the Government, reflect their power. The castle's interior is glorious; the Drawing Room hung with Beauvais tapestries, the State Dining Room bright with delicately painted panels, the Armoury with its array of 1,300 swords and firearms, the Gainsboroughs, Raeburns and Landseers, and the furniture, make it one of the most exciting houses in Britain to visit. The grounds, too, are immensely attractive, with garden and woodland walks, and there is a splendid view of the whole glen from the watchtower on top of the 800 ft Dunchuach. Far to the north-west rises the 3,700 ft bulk of Ben Cruachan, whose name is the Campbell war-cry.

There has been a village on the site of the present burgh since the days of legend, but no trace of it remains. Georgian Inveraray looks across a wide swathe of turf to its war memorial on the edge of the loch. It is approached from the north-east over a pretty, hump-backed bridge, and its buildings, with the exception of the great bell tower on the Episcopalian church, form a harmonious whole. The ancient cross in the Main Street is said to come from Iona.

③ TIGHNABRUAICH

The village's name means 'The House on the Hill', and its cottages are not ranged along the shore, but scattered up a hillside of woods and gardens. Tighnabruaich makes few concessions to the seeker after general seaside amusements, and concentrates wholeheartedly upon sailing. The Kyles of Bute Sailing Club has its headquarters there; it welcomes visitors and organises a visitors' racing series in summer. At the northern end of the village, a long wooden pier runs out to greet the steamers.

About a mile to the north, a viewpoint presents a panorama of airy splendour down the entire Kyles of Bute. Beyond that again, along the A8003, there is a forest trail from which may be seen blue hares and deer, heron and wild geese.

④ DUNOON

The town has been a holiday resort since 1779, when a family named Reid hired a boat and set forth to spend the summer in the wild Gaelic village of Dunoon. With the coming of the paddle-steamers, Glasgow's merchant princes began building their summer retreats there, and a little later, humbler folk came to enjoy the esplanade, the gardens and the tea shops. Thus it was that Dunoon, and places like Morag's Fairy Glen, with its little waterfalls, to the south, entered Glasgow's folklore. Today the town offers every conceivable amusement, entertainment and shop to the visitor.

Once Dunoon had a castle, but it was burned in 1685, some 20 years after a horrendous massacre in which the Clan Campbell slew hundreds of Lamont prisoners on Castle Hill. The castle is no more than a tumble of stones now, but the hill is a fine viewpoint. At its foot is a bronze statue to Robert Burns's 'Highland Mary' – Mary Campbell, who was born in Dunoon, and was a nursemaid in Ayr when the poet met and fell in love with her in 1780.

There is some notable sea-fishing at Dunoon, especially from the rocks known as The Gantocks, some 600 yds off the end of the pier, where the wreck of a Swedish ore carrier provides a home for – so it is said – cod of up to 46 lb, and giant angler-fish.

⑤ HUNTER'S QUAY

Though more or less a suburb of Dunoon, tiny Hunter's Quay has a personality all its own. Named after the Hunter family who cannily bought large stretches of the Cowal coast in the early steamship days, and built the first Dunoon pier, it consists of little more than a few handsome Victorian houses, a pretty little post office and the terminus of the Gourock Ferry. But it has long been famous in the annals of yachting,

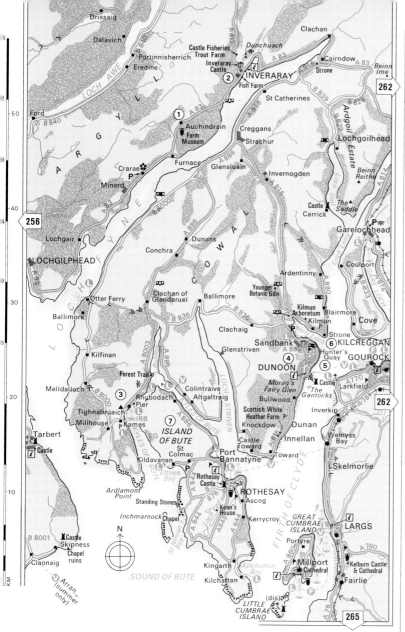

ship in the loch, from which clangings echo across the water. Sandbank, a pleasant village on the southern shore, is world-famous for ocean racing yachts and smaller sailing vessels. Britain's beautiful but unsuccessful challengers for the America's Cup, *Sceptre* and *Sovereign*, were built there.

⑦ ISLAND OF BUTE

Visitors may reach the Island of Bute all the year round by way of the Colintraive-Rhubodach Ferry, or by the big car ferry from Wemyss Bay. But whichever route they choose, it will bear them swiftly to Rothesay, the largest, and perhaps the best loved, of all the Clyde resorts. The buildings backing the long, broad esplanade and the little curving, sandy beach are mostly gracious 19th century, and this too is the era to which the pier and harbour complex largely belongs.

The old Winter Garden, known to generations of top music hall acts, is closed now; but it wears its shabbiness with an air, and the gardens and putting greens surrounding it are as immaculate as ever. There are bus tours, pony trekking, boat trips, and fishing charters. Bicycles can be hired. Evening concerts and ceilidhs are presented at the Pavilion.

At the back of the town are the massive red-sandstone remains of Rothesay Castle, much of which dates back to the 13th century. Near the castle is a museum that tells the story of Bute from prehistory to paddle-steamer, and includes an excellent section on the island's natural history.

With the mountains of Arran to the south, and those of Argyll to the north, Bute is a lowland island in a Highland setting. Loch Fad, running south from Rothesay's boundaries, is placid and shallow, with rich, steep woods on one side and rising pasture on the other. The actor Edmund Kean lived at Woodend on the northern shore, and though the house is private its gates bear the portraits of actors and dramatists. Much of the island consists of low hills, rounded like those of Dorset, patterned and divided by hedgerows and stone walls, and there are quiet beaches everywhere – such as Kilchattan Bay, to the south, and St Ninian's Bay, with its standing stones and ruined chapel, to the west.

The wide, empty curve of Ettrick Bay, 2 miles north of St Ninian's Bay, is so quiet that the voices of children playing at the water's edge 400 yds away come clearly across the sands. Opposite, on the eastern shore, is Port Bannatyne, a village no more than three streets deep that rises up from the coast road. It runs almost down to Rothesay, yet has a character all its own – part Highland village, part sailing centre, with a boat-builder's yard and chandlery. There are seldom fewer than 20 yachts and dinghies moored offshore.

---

and provides a fine anchorage where the Sandbank Sailing School moors its dinghies and offers boats for hire to experienced sailors.

⑥ HOLY LOCH

The story goes that the name is derived from a shipment of earth despatched from the Holy Land as a foundation for Glasgow Cathedral; but the vessel carrying it sank in the loch before it could make delivery. Holy or not, this inlet off the Clyde is certainly majestic – deeply cut into the Argyll hills

whose steep northern slopes have been clothed in varying shades of pale and dark green by the Forestry Commission. These woods, that climb from the loch shore to almost 1,000 ft, are part of the Kilmun Arboretum, a magnificent collection of trees from all over the world, including cypresses, Sitka spruce, eucalyptus, hemlock, cedars and a large number of pines and firs. A number of walks of varying lengths have been laid out through the arboretum.

The green hills make an oddly serene backdrop to the US Polaris submarine depot

---

CASTLE OF KINGS *Among the many Scottish monarchs who used Rothesay Castle as a holiday retreat was Robert III. He made his eldest son Duke of Rothesay, a title held today by the Prince of Wales.*

Ports and resorts where the Highlands meet the Clyde

Ships and sailors dominate this part of the Clyde. There are ghosts of Viking longships in Loch Long. The *Cutty Sark* was built in the shadow of Dumbarton Castle crag. And *Comet*, one of the earliest steamships, came from Port Glasgow. Tall black submarines slip in and out of Faslane and Holy Loch, and the shipyards of Greenock, sadly not so busy as they were, are a reminder of what the world's merchant fleets owe to Clyde-built ships.

① ARROCHAR

The village is a pleasant collection of white stone hotels and guest houses, a neat church and a general store that also sells fishing tackle – all gathered about the head of Loch Long. But Arrochar's main preoccupation is with rock climbing and hill-walking among the irresistible mountains crowded on every hand – Beinn Ime, 3,318 ft; Beinn Narnain, 3,038 ft; and Ben Arthur, better known as 'The Cobbler', 2,891 ft.

From Tarbet pier, on Loch Lomond, a little over a mile away to the east, there are cruises that take in all the sights of the loch from its 'Bonnie banks' and golden eagles to Rob Roy's cave. It was the closeness of Loch Long and Loch Lomond that tempted the Vikings into a brilliant foray in 1263, when King

Haakon of Norway led a fleet against Scotland. Part of the fleet was diverted up Loch Long, and when the ships reached its head, the crews dragged them across land into the fresh waters of Loch Lomond, enabling them to raid deep into Scotland. But despite the cunning ploy, it was the Scots who were eventually victorious, when Haakon's armada was annihilated at the Battle of Largs.

② LOCH LONG

The road from Garelochhead to Arrochar climbs high on the eastern side of Loch Long, and looks out over the wide sheet of water that is the parting of the ways, the place where Loch Goil begins its wander into the hills to the north-west. On the steep promontory that divides the lochs, the dark, pine-clad slopes of Ardgartan Forest lead the eye up to the spectacular wilderness of the Ardgoil Estate, the peaks of Beinn Reithe and The Saddle and, west of Loch Goil, a majestic grey ridge dominated by Sgurr a' Choinnich, lifting its shoulders to more than 2,000 ft. Near at hand, on the eastern shore, the scene is gentle, with oaks and birches, and beneath them, wild flowers, tall grass and bracken sweeping down to the salty waters of the loch.

The Royal Navy has a torpedo range in Loch Long, but there is still plenty of room for fishermen. Cod, dabs, flounders, plaice, congers, rays and mackerel are among the species that may be tempted by bait obtainable in Garelochhead, and boats may be hired in several places on the shores of Loch Long.

③ GARELOCHHEAD

The Royal Navy dockyard at Faslane Port to the south extends its fencing almost to the village, but Garelochhead seems to have settled down fairly happily with its neighbours. The beach, where Gare Loch comes to an end among the hills, is rocky and not too attractive, but gardens run to the shore, and

the village – white, slate-roofed cottages, antique shops and a tea-room or two – is charmingly set upon tree-clad slopes that reach up to the wild, bare hills behind. Hills rear high all round; the whole panorama is best seen from a picnic place and viewpoint about a mile north of Garelochhead on the road to Arrochar.

There is sailing and windsurfing at the loch's end, and a useful, if weed-covered, slipway.

④ HELENSBURGH

The plan of this largely Victorian resort was laid out in 1776 by Sir James Colquhoun, who named the town after his wife. The beach is too rocky to encourage bathing, but sailing is the true passion in Helensburgh, and boats of all shapes and sizes are catered for at the sailing club or at the marina at Rhu, 2 miles up Gare Loch. The obelisk on the front is a monument to Henry Bell, designer of the *Comet*, Europe's first commercially successful steamship, whose flywheel stands in Hermitage Park. Bell's wife managed what is now the Queen's Hotel while her husband worked at his ship designs. He died in 1830, and is buried in the churchyard at Rhu.

Boat trips to Holy Loch and up Gare Loch start from the pier. In the old, regular paddle-steamer days, Helensburgh's port was Craigendoran, slightly to the south, but its pier is derelict now, and falling into ruin.

⑤ DUMBARTON

Created on an unstormable crag of volcanic basalt above the lowest fordable point of the Clyde, Dumbarton has a longer recorded

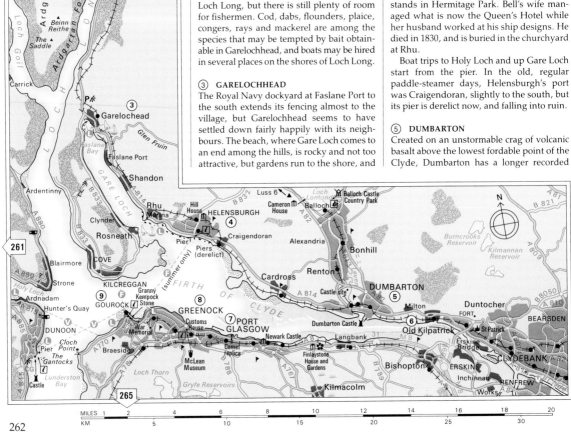

CLYDESIDE RESORT *Gourock owes much of its development to the paddle-steamers that once brought trippers from Glasgow. Their place is taken today by the car ferries that bustle across the Firth.*

history than any other stronghold in Britain. In the 6th century it was the capital of the Kingdom of Strathclyde that ran from Loch Lomond to Lancashire. The successive castles that were built on the rock that reaches 240 ft above the meeting of the Clyde and Leven were never far from the heart of Scottish history.

Besieged in innumerable wars, Dumbarton also had a role in the tragic affairs of Mary, Queen of Scots. She stayed there for a few months at the age of five before being sent to France. Much later, after Mary's flight into England in 1568, the garrison held out on her behalf until 1571. Little of the castle that Mary knew remains, since most of the present fortifications date from the 18th century. The view from the top of the rock is airy and breathtaking.

Distilling is Dumbarton's chief industry now, but it was once equally famous for its glass and shipbuilding. The windjammer *Cutty Sark* was launched there in 1869, and named after the swiftest of the witches, distinguished by her short shirt or 'cutty sark', in Burns' ballad *Tam o' Shanter.*

Robert Bruce, having commanded Sir James Douglas to carry his heart to the Holy Land, died near Dumbarton, in a castle

whose site is a matter of considerable controversy. The most favoured spot seems to be by Dalmoak Farm, just south of the A82, on the west bank of the River Leven.

⑥ OLD KILPATRICK

Though the present church dates only from 1812, the parish is of immense age. The first known church on the site was built about AD 800. Tradition has it that St Patrick was born in the village, as a holy well dedicated to him, and the name of the place, bear witness. The western end of the Roman Antonine Wall, built about AD 143, lies under the Shell oil terminal by the shore; though there is nothing to be seen at that point, the base of a rampart and a few stones of an Antonine fort stand in Duntocher Park, 2 miles to the east.

Floating high over the line of the wall, and over Old Kilpatrick, is the Erskine Bridge, the westernmost bridge over the Clyde. Its narrow ribbon of road soars 180 ft above countryside and river, borne on seemingly delicate towers that carry 30,000 tons of concrete and steel and are designed to withstand winds of up to 130 mph.

⑦ PORT GLASGOW

The town, which grew out of the old village of Newark, was intended to serve as Glasgow's port, as its name implies. But the Clyde was deepened to take big ships into Glasgow, and Port Glasgow turned to shipbuilding. Among the coppices of cranes stands Newark Castle, a turreted mansion built by the Maxwells in the 16th century.

The centre of the town consists of tall red closes – tenements – gathered about the worn but elegant Municipal Hall. In pride of place is a replica of the *Comet*, the steamship designed by Henry Bell of Helensburgh. The original was launched in Port Glasgow in 1812, and worked between Glasgow and Greenock until she was wrecked in 1820. The replica was built in the same yard in 1962.

⑧ GREENOCK

In the 17th century, Greenock shipped herring to France and the Baltic; hence the town's motto 'Let herring swim that trade maintain'. During the next two centuries, Greenock added shipbuilding and industry to its dock facilities. A few graceful old buildings, such as the early 19th-century Customs House, emerge through the tower-

ing cranes and derricks. Such buildings are not plentiful, however, for Greenock suffered badly in a savage two-night blitz in March, 1941.

James Watt, the discoverer of steam power, was born in Greenock in 1736. There is a statue of him, and a dock, a lecture hall and a scientific library are named after him. The McLean Museum contains a number of Watt relics, and has an adjoining art gallery.

The Clyde roadstead off Greenock, known as Tail of the Bank, was one of the most important assembly points for Atlantic convoys during the Second World War.

⑨ GOUROCK

Red-stone houses that climb steeply up the hills from the water ring this pleasant busy Clydeside town. On Lyle Hill, between Gourock and Greenock, there is a monument in the combined forms of an anchor and Cross of Lorraine; it commemorates the Free French sailors who died in the Battle of the Atlantic in the Second World War. By Castle Mansions is a monument of a very different kind – a prehistoric monolith that young couples used to embrace to ensure that their marriage would be blessed with children. In 1662 a number of women were condemned and burned for attempting to throw the Granny Kempock stone into the sea as part of a spell that was intended to sink ships by witchcraft.

The town looks out across the Clyde to the hills that on a calm evening look as unreal as a stage set, an effect heightened by the twinkling lights of Kilcreggan below. It is a quietly pretty place, with many attractions for the visitor, including moorings, bowls and an outdoor swimming pool.

VIVAT VICTORIA *Gourock gained a permanent memento of Queen Victoria's Diamond Jubilee in this fountain constructed in 1897.*

CLYDE LANDMARK *The Cloch lighthouse, built in 1797, stands on the Firth's south bank across the river from Dunoon.*

A playground coast for Glasgow along the Firth of Clyde

The Firth of Clyde has long been Glasgow's playground, and its little towns hold a special place in the citizens' hearts. Though the traditional glories of piers and hydropathics may have faded a little, the resorts today provide some of the best facilities in Britain for water sports. The combination of wild hills and gentler countryside in the surrounding scenery is another part of the magic that first enticed Glaswegians 'doon the watter'.

LAST OF A LINE *The* Waverley *is Britain's only surviving seagoing paddle-steamer, and still carries holidaymakers to the Clyde resorts during the summer months.*

① INVERKIP

In the 17th century, this little seaside village leaned over by wooded hills was a notorious centre of witchcraft, and in the 18th century it was a den of smugglers. Now it is remarkable chiefly for its huge power station, and for the Kip Marina, one of the largest yacht havens in Scotland, which boats can enter and leave at any state of the tide.

Near by, pleasant Lunderston Bay with its picnic site is dominated to the north by Cloch Point and a sturdy white lighthouse built in 1797.

② WEMYSS BAY

To generations of Glaswegians, Wemyss Bay was the gateway to 'doon the watter' – the resorts of the Clyde – and to this day the very name evokes memories of childhood holidays in many a western Scottish breast. Wemyss Bay is one of the main passenger ports on the Clyde, the place from which the famous paddle-steamers sailed – *Duchess of Hamilton, Caledonia, Marchioness of Lorne, Queen Mary II, Glen Sannox* and the rest – their rakish funnels pouring banners of smoke, their paddles churning the water to sparkling white and pale green as their helmsmen took them smoothly to and from the pierheads.

Sadly, the paddle-steamers are all gone now, except one, the *Waverley*. But their spirit is kept very much alive by the lovely Edwardian station and pier which, with their fresh paint, glass roofs and banks of flowers, resemble a conservatory; there is even a greenhouse beside the ticket office. Then, down the glass-covered tunnel con-necting the two, where the water glints beneath the floorboards, the magnificently carved crests of the old steamers are lined up, their heraldic colours of scarlet, gold and azure gleaming as freshly as ever. Beside them, there are photographs of the ships in their heyday – racing from Dunoon perhaps, or in dull wartime grey on their way to lift troops off the beaches at Dunkirk.

③ SKELMORLIE

This cheerful little resort has a red, rocky beach – but the rocks are flat, and therefore good for sunbathing and picnicking. The outstanding building is a large, turreted, red-sandstone structure, about the size of an abbey, that stands among woods at the top of the cliffs. It was one of the leading Clyde 'hydropathics', to which middle-class Glaswegians repaired for austere holidays that involved a large number of seawater baths. From the 1860s to the 1930s these early 'health farms' played an important role in the social life of Glasgow.

④ LARGS

The town's long esplanade above its stony beach offers boat trips, fishing trips, shell-fish stalls, amusement arcades and all the fun of the fair. A monument known locally as 'The Pencil' commemorates the Battle of Largs and recalls the stormy day in 1263 when a Viking fleet commanded by King Haakon of Norway was driven ashore and bloodily defeated by the Scottish western levies under Alexander III.

Sheltered by the Cumbraes, Largs has some of the best sailing in Britain, with frequent regattas from the end of May to the middle of September. Just inland is the Inverclyde National Sports Training Centre. Its primary function is to run courses for coaches and physical training instruc-tors, and to train promising athletes to international standard.

⑤ THE CUMBRAE ISLANDS

Whatever the maps say about Great and Little, the islands are known along the Clyde as Big and Wee Cumbrae. The smaller island, with its 18th-century lighthouse and ruined castle, is visited only by yachtsmen, fishermen and divers. Big Cumbrae, however, is some 5 square miles in extent, a lovely patchwork of wide fields embracing Millport, a perfect little holiday resort, and the smallest cathedral – the Cathedral of the Isles – in Scotland. There is an 18-hole golf course, the sands are good and the bathing safe; even the great basking sharks that frequently cruise round the islands are harmless.

The Cumbraes are reached by ferry from Largs.

⑥ FAIRLIE

The little village is overshadowed by giants of modern industry. They include Hunt-erston Nuclear Power Station and a huge iron-ore complex with a conveyor belt a mile or so long that carries ore from the jetty to the dump. They are linked by a rocky beach off which dinghies are moored.

A little way inland is the Kelburn Country Centre, which incorporates a glen through which the little Kel Burn falls 700 ft from the moors to the sea in a series of waterfalls. The gardens are magnificent, containing rhodo-dendrons, azaleas and other shrubs and plants that provide a continuous display of colour from January to June. The centre also has a museum, a weaver's workshop, a pets' corner, walks with splendid views over the Clyde, pony treks, guided nature walks and an adventure course.

In the harbour at Fairlie there is an old-established boatyard, and it was there in the 1890s that Glasgow's hero, Sir Thomas ('Tommy') Lipton, built his famous ocean-racing yachts *Shamrock I* and *Shamrock II*. Born in a Glasgow tenement, Lipton made a fortune in the grocery business, then spent a great deal of it on trying unsuccessfully to win the America's Cup yachting trophy for Britain.

⑦ WEST KILBRIDE AND SEAMILL

The two villages are linked by modern housing, among which stand the sad, boarded-up remains of Law Castle, a 15th-century tower house. At the bottom of the hill, in Seamill, some of the houses are Victorian Scottish baronial, with red-sand-stone turrets looking down steep gardens to the golf links. Below the coast road are the red-gold, boulder-strewn sands of Ardneil Bay.

The north end of the bay is protected by Farland Head, on which stands the little sea-washed hamlet of Portencross, with its ruined 15th-century castle. Just to the east of the castle is a vitrified fort, one of those Iron Age curiosities that occur throughout Scot-land. Was the stone of their walls melted by accident or design? One theory is that the forts were built of alternate layers of timber and stone to give them resilience under catapult attack, and that when the buildings were fired – during a siege or deliberately by the occupants – the heat produced by the burning timber caused the stones to fuse together.

⑧ ARDROSSAN

The town is a deliberate piece of town planning by the Earl of Eglinton in 1805, as is still evident in the many good, square stone houses around the great sandy sweep of South Bay. Offshore is the hump of Horse Isle, a nature reserve.

Ardrossan is deeply interested in tourism – hence its indoor bowling club and nearby golf driving range, and its good moorings. But it also possesses a large oil depot, and its harbour is an important passenger and cargo terminus.

⑨ SALTCOATS

One of Glasgow's favourite weekend escapes, Saltcoats is a busy, bustling, cheery seaside resort with plenty of amusements and cafes, and an indoor swimming pool. The handsome wall about the rocky harbour was erected in 1686, and the harbour contains a number of fossilised trees, visible at low tide. There is good fishing around Saltcoats, both from the rocks and from boats.

⑩ IRVINE

Once the main port of Glasgow, before the River Clyde was deepened in the 18th century, Irvine is today lively in its pursuit of leisure, both indoor and outdoor. Near the old Tide Signal Station is the Magnum Leisure Centre, which offers indoor swimming, bowls, a curling rink, squash, a rifle-range and a fitness salon. The surrounding Irvine Beach Park offers boating and all kinds of water sports, sea and river angling, sand yachting and safe bathing along miles of open beaches. The West of Scotland Maritime Museum, in Irvine's eastern harbour, traces shipbuilding history from the driftwood craft of the Isles to the steamships of the Clyde.

⑪ TROON

This small, pretty town is notable for its towered and turreted red-sandstone Victorian houses that look upon the sea to one side and upon five golf courses to the other. The most famous belongs to the Royal Troon Golf Club, a frequent host to the British Open Championship and other international contests.

The marina, a large harbour with a forest of dinghy masts, offers berths, chandlery, saunas, squash and a windsurfing school; near by there are opportunities for tennis, bowling and sea-angling. Divided by the rocky promontory that gives the town its name (*trwyn* being Old Welsh for 'nose') are the wide sands of North Bay, or Barassie Bay, and South Bay, that provide safe bathing.

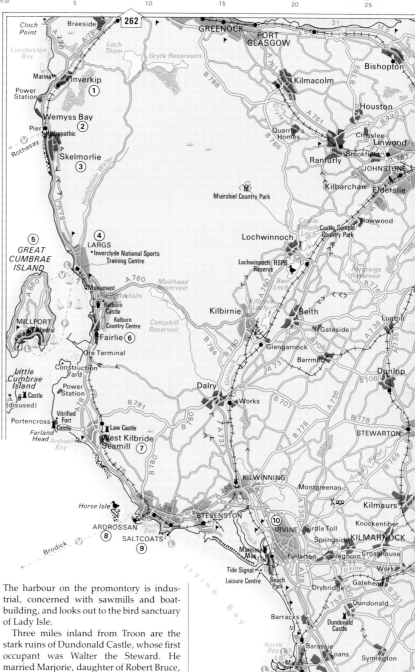

The harbour on the promontory is industrial, concerned with sawmills and boatbuilding, and looks out to the bird sanctuary of Lady Isle.

Three miles inland from Troon are the stark ruins of Dundonald Castle, whose first occupant was Walter the Steward. He married Marjorie, daughter of Robert Bruce, giving rise to the Scottish Stuart dynasty.

⑫ PRESTWICK

Busy as it is, Prestwick's international airport impinges very little upon Prestwick itself, which is one of the oldest burghs in Scotland. Its most ancient building is the ruined church of St Nicholas, which probably dates from the 12th century, while its Mercat Cross cannot be more than a century younger.

On the shore side of the Ayr Road is Bruce's Well, whose waters are said to have brought relief to Robert Bruce, who suffered from a disease resembling leprosy. The ruins beside it are those of the chapel of a leper hospital founded by the king.

Prestwick is a neat, bright town with good shops, and a promenade running round the gentle curve of Ayr Bay. The tawny sands of the bay provide safe bathing, and sailing and windsurfing are popular. The thyme-scented golf links that run down to the beach are those on which the first Open Championship was played in 1860, and club members have included the Duke of Windsor and President Eisenhower. There is an excellent indoor bowling stadium.

LOCAL INFORMATION

Tourist information Gourock 31126; Largs 673765; Troon 315131.

HM Coastguard Greenock 29988 for information, 999 in emergency (ask for coastguard).

Weather Glasgow (041) 247 8091.

Local radio IBA West Sound, 290 m, 1035 kHz, 96.2 MHz.

PLACES TO SEE INLAND

Kilmarnock, 6 miles E of Irvine. Dean Castle and Country Park, castle afternoons in summer, park daily; Dick Institute Museum, weekdays; Burns Museum, Kay Park, on application.

Lochwinnoch RSPB Reserve and Nature Centre. 10 miles E of Largs. Most days.

265

Seaside resorts and golf courses along the coast south of Ayr

Sandy beaches and a mild climate combine to make Ayr, and the towns and villages that surround it, the main resort area of Scotland's west coast. The area also has a strong literary and historical legacy: Robert Burns was born near Ayr in 1759, and ruined strongholds dating from the 13th to 17th centuries recall strife between warring factions in earlier days. A series of golf courses offers magnificent views westwards to Arran.

① AYR

Long stone quays that run out towards the sea are a reminder that Ayr was once the chief port of western Scotland. Today, it is Scotland's principal west-coast resort, with 2½ miles of safe, sandy beaches and a variety of seaside amusements. Early in the morning the beach is a favourite exercise ground for racehorses.

A swimming-pool complex close to the beach includes a sauna, Turkish baths and a fully equipped gymnasium. Sea-anglers catch flounders, dabs, dogfish, cod and mullet on the Newton shore. Boats may be hired at Ayr Bay, and there are sailing and sub-aqua clubs around the busy working harbour.

The River Ayr cuts through the centre of the town, where it is crossed by two bridges close together – the Twa Brigs. The Auld Brig dates from the 13th century and was the scene of a battle between the Kennedys of Cassillis and the rival Kennedys of Bargany in 1601. The bridge is very narrow, as Robert Burns observed in his poem *The Brigs of Ayr*, calling it a 'poor, narrow footpath of a street'. The Auld Brig was restored in 1910 and is now used by pedestrians. Its close neighbour, New Bridge, was built in 1788 and rebuilt in 1878.

At the southern end of New Bridge the 126 ft high steeple of the Town Buildings dominates the town. Built in 1828, its upper part consists of an octagonal turret with tall, narrow windows.

Benefactions from wealthy residents have given Ayr a number of public parks. Craigie Park has scenic riverside walks, Belleisle Park includes a walled garden, an aviary, a deer park and two of Ayr's three golf courses, while Rozelle Park has a pond with swans, wooded walks, nature trails and an art gallery. A three-day flower show, the largest in western Scotland, is held in Ayr in August. On Tuesdays and Thursdays Ayr

Robert Burns

A POET'S BIRTHPLACE

Ayr's most notable link with the past is with Scotland's national poet, Robert Burns, who was born in the village of Alloway, now part of Ayr, in 1759. Burns' Cottage birthplace, the Burns Monument Gardens and the ruin of Alloway Kirk are all open to the public. The Land O'Burns Centre houses a permanent exhibition of the poet's life and times. In Ayr itself is the Tam O'Shanter Museum, a former ale house in which Burns and his friends once met. And it is still possible to stroll across the Auld Brig O'Doon, where the witches' chase in the most famous of all Scottish ballads, *Tam O'Shanter*, came to its exciting close.

becomes a bustling market town, when farmers from round about arrive to sell their cattle.

② HEADS OF AYR

Beyond Doonfoot, where the sands of Ayr Bay end, a shoreline walk past the ruins of Greenan Castle, a 16th-century stronghold of the Kennedy family, leads after 2 miles to the Heads of Ayr, a line of cliffs topped with grazing land stretching outwards into the sea. Above the walk is a holiday camp.

Inland, a narrow and twisting road climbs over a shoulder of Brown Carrick Hill, past picnic areas with fine views over Arran, Ailsa Craig, Kintyre and the whole sweep of the Firth of Clyde.

③ DUNURE

Whitewashed stone houses line a small but active harbour at the foot of the cliffs, and the rocky coastline round about is ideal for sub-aqua exploration. The harbour was once a base for smugglers who brought 'Arran water' from the illicit whisky stills on the Island of Arran, some 20 miles offshore. It is now used by yachtsmen and sea-anglers.

South of the harbour the bay shelves steeply, and young swimmers risk finding themselves quickly out of their depth. The bay is dominated by the forbidding ruins of Dunure Castle, where the lay abbot of Crossraguel was roasted alive in 1570 to force him to hand over the rich abbey lands to the 4th Earl of Cassillis, head of one branch of the Kennedy family.

④ CULZEAN CASTLE

The architectural masterpiece of Culzean Castle was designed by Robert Adam and completed for the 10th Earl of Cassillis in 1790. Its splendid clifftop site is now owned by the National Trust for Scotland and open to the public in summer. Among its finest features are Adam's imaginative oval staircase, and the round drawing room with its views over the Firth of Clyde. The top flat in the castle was given to President Eisenhower in recognition of his wartime achievements, and there is a display devoted to his life.

Culzean Castle was built around an ancient tower belonging to the Kennedy family, who are associated with many of the ancient strongholds on this stretch of coast. The family split in the 16th century into two warring factions, the Kennedys of Culzean, or Cassillis, and the Kennedys of Bargany. After long feuds the Cassillis branch of the family emerged triumphant.

Many of Adam's plans for Culzean are on show in what was originally the Home Farm. Built of local sandstone, it was restored in 1971-3 to serve as the visitor centre for Culzean Country Park. The formal features of the park include a fountain court with an orangery, a walled garden and an aviary. But the network of informal walks is one of the major attractions of Culzean.

A clifftop walk starting on the west side of the castle runs along the top of the lava cliffs before dipping steeply down to a tiny bathing beach at Port Carrick. From there it is possible to walk back along the shoreline below the cliffs for about a mile to Segganwell Gorge, which is deeply cut out of the softer sandstone east of the castle. Agates, chalcedony and other forms of quartz may be found along the shore. There are weathered natural arches and entrances to a network of interconnected caves.

⑤ MAIDENS

Named after treacherous offshore rocks, this village nevertheless offers safe bathing on the sand-and-shingle beach north of the harbour. Maidens was once little more than a line of fishermen's cottages and fish-curing sheds along the shore. In the 1950s the local villagers used rubble from abandoned wartime RAF buildings to provide Maidens with a new harbour wall, and shortly after that the present harbour was built. It is now used only for fishing and recreational sailing.

Burns's *Tam O'Shanter* was based on the real-life Douglas Graham, occasional smuggler and tenant of Shanter Farm, which stood on the hillside above the caravan sites which surround modern Maidens. *Tam O'Shanter* was the name of Graham's boat.

⑥ TURNBERRY

Fine silver sands stretching for 1½ miles are protected from the east wind by grassy dunes. Access to the beach is by a pathway past the fourth tee on the Ailsa golf course – the tee is called Woe-be-Tide.

Culzean Castle,
Robert Adam's Gothic masterpiece

UNFRIENDLY RELATIONS *Gannets crowding together on Ailsa Craig regard each other with a wary eye. They are aggressive at nesting time, and will attack if another bird approaches.*

The Ailsa course is one of two famous settings for golf at Turnberry. It is notable for its fearsome shoreline holes and views across the Firth to Ailsa Craig. The neighbouring Arran course, downhill from the white-walled and red-tiled Turnberry Hotel, is equally spectacular.

At Castle Port, north of the golf courses, lies Turnberry Castle, once the home of the Countess of Carrick, mother of Robert Bruce who is said to have been born there. Turnberry lighthouse stands in the middle of the castle ruins.

Souter Johnnie's House, 3 miles to the north-east, was the thatched cottage home of John Davidson, a village cobbler, or souter, at the end of the 18th century who was immortalised in Burns's poem *Tam O'Shanter*. The cottage contains contemporary tools of the cobbler's craft, and items associated with Burns.

⑦ GIRVAN

Flanked by gardens and pathways, a sheltered and colourful harbour at the mouth of the winding Water of Girvan is the base of a fishing fleet. On the north side is a yard which specialises in building traditional wooden fishing boats. There is good swimming from the sands, which stretch for more than a mile to the south.

Girvan sailing club operates from the harbour, and boats may also be hired by sea-anglers. Cod, haddock, herring and mackerel are caught regularly, and record weights of whiting and wrasse have been caught. Fishing on the Girvan yields trout and occasional salmon.

The imposing 15th-century Penkill Castle, where Dante Gabriel Rossetti wrote poetry, lies 4 miles east.

⑧ AILSA CRAIG

Reached only by boat from Girvan, 10 miles to the east, Ailsa Craig is the most impressive landmark in the Firth of Clyde. This huge granite island, 1,114 ft high and 2 miles in circumference, is the core of an ancient volcano. Most of the island is rimmed by spectacular cliffs, and off the exposed south-west corner is the rock of Little Ailsa, made up of hundreds of basalt pillars.

Ailsa Craig granite used to be quarried for curling stones, but since the quarries closed the island has become one of Scotland's greatest gannetries. More than 10,000 pairs breed there every summer, and there are colonies of razorbills, guillemots and kittiwakes. In the past, tenants of the island used to pay their rents in gannet feathers.

A lighthouse was built on Foreland Point in 1868. Boats land there, and the pathway to the summit passes the ruins of a long-abandoned castle.

⑨ LENDALFOOT

Overlooking a small shingle beach with rocky outcrops, Lendalfoot is a hamlet of whitewashed houses where the Water of Lendal pushes out from its steep-sided valley into the sea. Beyond a row of holiday chalets to the south is a picnic area just above the shoreline rocks.

On the hills above Lendalfoot is the ruin of Carleton Castle. Sir John Cathcart of Carleton was the villain of a fictional ballad telling how he married seven rich heiresses in turn and threw them all to their deaths over the cliffs of Games Loup, south-west of the castle. However, Sir John's eighth bride was more spirited, and threw him over instead.

⑩ BALLANTRAE

As its Gaelic name *Baile-an-Traigh* makes clear, this is a 'village on the shore'. Throughout the 18th century it was the headquarters of a highly organised smuggling ring. The village stands back from a sand-and-shingle beach which continues for 1½ miles to the north, beyond a harbour.

At the south end of the village stands the ruin of Ardstinchar Castle, built like Greenan Castle by the Kennedy family. It overlooks the River Stinchar's meandering outflow of tidal creeks and lagoons, administered as a nature reserve by the Scottish Wildlife Trust. The reserve is a breeding site for terns, and nesting areas should be avoided in late spring and early summer.

⑪ FINNARTS BAY

At the seaward end of Glen App, a side road and a rough track lead to a picnic area overlooking the entrance to Loch Ryan. Remains of wartime gun-sites are half-hidden among the scrub, and an abandoned observation post stands lonely guard on the clifftop north of the bay.

A fish farm at the mouth of the Water of App sells direct to the public. To the north, an exhilarating 6 mile walk goes high over Finnarts Hill and along the coastline northwards to Ballantrae.

LOCAL INFORMATION

Tourist information Ayr 284196; Girvan 2056/7.

HM Coastguard Greenock 29988 for information, 999 in emergency (ask for coastguard).

Weather Glasgow (041) 248 3451.

Local radio IBA West Sound, 290 m, 1035 kHz, 96.2/97.1 MHz.

PLACES TO SEE INLAND

Crossraguel Abbey, 5 miles E of Maidens. Remains of 13th-century monastery. Daily except Friday.

Loch Doon Castle, 28 miles E of Girvan. 14th-century remains. Daily.

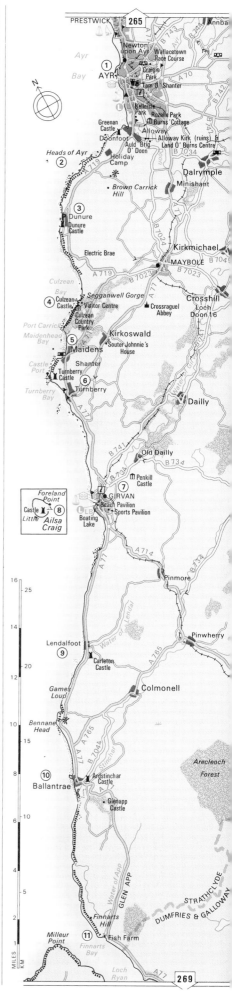

Harbours and exotic gardens of the Rhins peninsula

Much of the Rhins peninsula, stretching down to the dramatic headland of the Mull of Galloway, is rocky and wild; but oases of calm and colour offer rich rewards to the visitor. There is good sailing on the sheltered inlet of Loch Ryan – though swimming there is not recommended – while the influence of the warm North Atlantic Drift allows a variety of exotic plants to flourish in acres of carefully tended gardens.

① CAIRNRYAN

In the 18th century, ships sailing from the Clyde to the West Indies often sheltered inside Loch Ryan when overtaken by storms, close to a village known as 'the Cairn'. During the Second World War this quiet lochside settlement, by then called Cairnryan, became one of the main landing points for supplies from the United States.

The wartime harbour is now largely derelict, and though the village houses are bright and colourful, an extensive shipbreakers' yard on the outskirts gives the area a semi-industrial atmosphere.

Shore fishing from Cairnryan has produced several record catches, notably a 54 lb tope. Sea-anglers fishing from boats, however, have to avoid the two car-ferry routes, one from Cairnryan and one from Stranraer, which pass out through the mouth of the loch to Larne in Northern Ireland.

Lochryan House, east of the harbour, was built in 1701 in the Dutch style of architecture, which is unusual in Scotland. The house is not open to the public.

② STRANRAER

Curving round the head of Loch Ryan, Stranraer is the railhead for the main ferry and freight service to Larne. Cruises to Larne in summer are linked with bus tours to the Giant's Causeway and the Mountains of Mourne.

The railway pier forms the east side of Stranraer's natural harbour sheltered by the Rhins of Galloway. On the west side is the fishing quay, beyond which an area of reclaimed land known as Clayhole Bank includes a swimming and boating lake as well as a beach where low tide reveals extensive sands. Boats can be hired, and there are sailing and sub-aqua clubs.

The old Castle of St John dates back to 1510, while the house called North West Castle, overlooking the railway pier, was built by Sir John Ross, the Arctic explorer who spent much of his life in search of the North-west Passage; his house is now a hotel. Stranraer Show is held in July, and there is a pipe-band contest on the first Saturday in June.

Castle Kennedy Gardens, 2½ miles east, contain the ivy-clad ruins of Castle Kennedy, which dates from the 15th century and was burned down in 1716. It was then the home of the 2nd Earl of Stair, a field marshal who used the troops under his command to create mounds and terraces in a garden notable also for its splendid displays of magnolias, azaleas, rhododendrons and other flowering shrubs.

Also within Castle Kennedy Gardens is Lochinch Castle, which was built in 1867 to replace Castle Kennedy and is the home of the present Earl and Countess of Stair. It is surrounded by its own more formal Victorian gardens.

③ THE WIG

In the two world wars, this inlet of Loch Ryan was a base for sea-planes and flying boats. A launching ramp built for the flying boats is today used by Wig Bay Sailing Club, the main sailing centre on Loch Ryan.

The north side of the bay, an area of shingle known as Wig Sands, ends in a curving spit of land called the Scar. All this area, which is rich in bird life, is reached by an unmade side road starting beyond the sailing club. Terns nest there in early summer, and hundreds of eider duck assemble off the Scar. In autumn and winter the tidal margins provide food for dunlins and redshanks, and oystercatchers are raucously present at every season.

④ CORSEWALL POINT

Deep-cut rock fissures which bring the waves battering upwards into plumes of spray form the invigorating surroundings of Corsewall lighthouse. Designed by the grandfather of the novelist R. L. Stevenson, the lighthouse was opened in 1816 at the north-western tip of a windswept, well farmed but almost treeless peninsula. Today it operates automatically.

Although jagged and dangerous from the sea, the coastline here is not high and there is good scrambling among its lichen-covered rocks. Lady Bay, on the east side of the peninsula, is a stretch of sandy shore sheltered from the prevailing south-westerly winds and looking across to the hills above Finnarts Bay.

LEADING LIGHT *Corsewall lighthouse was built by Robert Stevenson, father of the Scottish lighthouse system.*

⑤ PORTPATRICK

Set around a cliff-girt inlet on a forbidding and enclosed coast, Portpatrick is one of the brightest villages on the Rhins peninsula, with ranks of colour-washed houses, villas and hotels spreading upwards from a secure harbour. For hundreds of years this was the Scottish end of a short sea crossing from Donaghadee in Northern Ireland. But the waves eventually destroyed the Victorian piers, and in 1862 the Irish packet-boat service was transferred to Stranraer.

There is a tiny stretch of sandy beach in the outer harbour, which is also a base for sailing and water-skiing. Two golf courses are laid out above the northern cliffs. Pathways run up the cliffs, then down again to bays along the coast, where there is good shore fishing. Boats may also be hired for sea-angling. From the southern cliffs, another pathway leads to the high ruin of the 15th-century Dunskey Castle.

⑥ LOGAN BOTANIC GARDEN

In this windy south-western corner of Scotland it is astonishing to find a garden packed with exotic trees and flowering

IRELAND'S GRETNA GREEN *When Portpatrick was the Scottish terminal for the Irish ferry, runaway couples travelled the 21 miles across the water to be married in the port's 17th-century church.*

QUITE CONTRARY *In Logan Botanic Gardens exotic plants grow in a mild climate amid an otherwise wild and rocky landscape.*

shrubs from South America, Australia, China, Australia and New Zealand. But the warm air brought by the North Atlantic Drift, as well as walled enclosures sheltered by banks of native trees, allowed the Victorian lairds of Logan to create a local mini-climate. Plants which in most of Britain need to be cultivated in glasshouses flourish out of doors at Logan.

Some of the most striking sights are the avenues of cabbage palms and Chusan palms, the water garden, the Australasian tree ferns and, in the middle of the lawn, a vivid scarlet Patagonian fire tree. Since 1969 the garden has been associated with the Royal Botanic Garden in Edinburgh, and is open to the public every day in summer.

Ardwell House, 2 miles north, has a more traditional Scottish garden. Open in summer, it has a fine display of spring flowers, shrubs and rock plants, and there are pondside walks with views over Luce Bay.

⑦ PORT LOGAN

A sea-wall carrying the road flanks a long, curving shingle beach. Low tide reveals stretches of firm sand, but strong winds can make bathing hazardous. There is good sea and shore fishing around Port Logan Bay, although the 19th-century harbour which gave this village of whitewashed houses its name has long since been abandoned.

On the north side of the bay is the curious Logan Fishpond, a tidal pond excavated from rocks behind the shore in 1800 to catch fresh fish for the kitchens of Logan House. But the fish soon came to be treated as family pets rather than as food for the table. The pond is still stocked with tame cod, which come to be fed by hand. It is open to the public most days in summer.

⑧ MULL OF GALLOWAY

The southernmost tip of Scotland, guarding the entrance to the Solway Firth, is a wild peninsula ringed by precipitous cliffs of multi-coloured rock. A narrow but well-surfaced road winds up from the isthmus between West and East Tarbet bays to the lighthouse set up in 1830, which can be visited. The view from the tower extends to Ireland, the Isle of Man, the Lake District and even the tips of some Inner Hebridean peaks.

The Mull of Galloway's cliffs, now an RSPB reserve, are a riot of sea-birds in summer. Rock ledges at all levels are crammed with nests, and there is a constant bustle as adult birds fly to and from the offshore feeding grounds. Gannets are sometimes seen as they cruise by from their own colony on the deserted rock stacks known as the Scares in the mouth of Luce Bay.

On this headland, according to legend, the two last Picts, a father and son, turned to face the Scots who had driven their race into the far south-western corner of their country. Rather than betray the secret of the Pictish drink known as heather ale, the old man let the Scots hurl his son over the cliffs, then leapt over after him.

⑨ DRUMMORE

Scotland's southernmost village runs uphill from a row of whitewashed cottages overlooking a sandy beach at the edge of Luce Bay. It has a harbour which, like many of those on the Solway, dries out at low tide.

Once a centre of smuggling, Drummore is now the main sea-angling centre on the west side of Luce Bay. Skate, bass and porbeagle shark are found, and the biggest tope ever caught in Scotland, weighing 62 lb, was hauled aboard a boat out of Drummore. Boats may be hired locally, but fishermen using their own craft must beware of the strong tides south of Drummore and around the Mull.

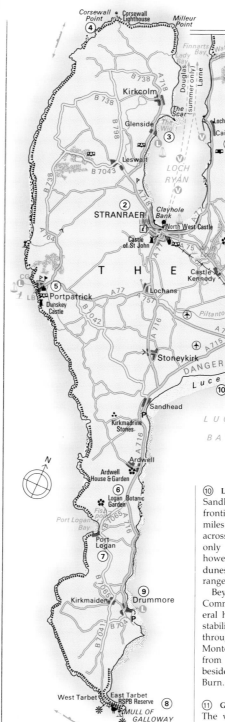

⑩ LUCE SANDS

Sandhead, with a parking and picnic area fronting the beach, is at the western end of miles of uninterrupted sands which stretch across the head of Luce Bay. The public can only reach 2 miles beyond the village, however, because the remainder of the dunes and beaches are part of a bombing range.

Beyond the prohibited area, the Forestry Commission's Bareagle Forest includes several hundred acres of conifers planted to stabilise the shifting dunes. A forest walk through Sitka spruce and Corsican and Monterey pine leads to a picnic area 2 miles from the public road at Ringdoo Point, beside the tidal outflow of the Piltanton Burn.

⑪ GLENLUCE

The village is set back from the narrow opening of the glen which gives it its name. To the west are the shoreline links of the Wigtownshire County Golf Club, looking across the water to Bareagle Forest at Ringdoo Point.

The village grew after the founding in 1190 of the Cistercian Abbey at Glenluce. The abbey ruins, which include a Chapter House added in the 15th century, occupy a peaceful site 1½ miles north-west, among farmlands by the windings of the Water of Luce. They are open to the public.

LOCAL INFORMATION

Tourist information Stranraer 2595.

HM Coastguard Ramsey 813255 for information, 999 in emergency (ask for coastguard).

Weather Glasgow Weather Centre (041) 248 3451.

Local radio BBC Radio Solway 92.5 MHz.

PLACE TO SEE INLAND

Kirkmadrine Stones, 9 miles S of Stranraer. Early Christian monuments. Daily.

A saint's retreat on a coast of estuaries and rocky coves

With its sheltered harbours, wide marshy estuaries and rocky coves, this coastline was once a haven for smugglers. The town at the head of each estuary once supported a large fishing fleet, but since the decline of fishing these towns have become centres for farming and for tourism. The religious conflicts of the 17th century brought the notorious 'Killing Times' to the area; but today quiet elegance is its keynote.

SAINT'S RETREAT *The cave in the cliff where St Ninian spent many hours in prayer is now a place of Christian pilgrimage.*

① AUCHENMALG BAY

At the northern end of this sandy bay is the beautiful hamlet of Auchenmalg. Catches of flatfish, bass and mullet can be taken from the shore, and boats can be hired for good offshore sea-angling for dogfish, tope, rays and conger. A much longer beach extends to the south, from the roadside parking area at Craignarget's bay.

On the Mull of Sinniness, just to the west of Auchenmalg Bay, a private house still retains the name of Sinniness Barracks. The barracks were built in the 1820s for a company of 50 revenue men, sent to stamp out the Solway smuggling trade.

The 18th-century harbour at Stair Haven, 2 miles north of Auchenmalg Bay, is all but derelict. Lobster fishermen still sail out of Stair Haven's bay, and a picnic site has been laid out above the rocky shore.

② PORT WILLIAM

Built along a pebble beach at the foot of low hills, this bright village is a holiday and sailing centre, and a base for shark fishing in Luce Bay. Skate and rays are also caught – boats can be hired – and good catches of cod and bass have been made from the shore. The curving harbour is left dry at low tide.

The coast road along the rocky shore to the north leads, after 5 miles, to the remains of the 10th-century Chapel Finian, built near a landing place used by Irish pilgrims on the way to St Ninian's Kirk at Whithorn.

③ MONREITH

The long sandy bay below the village of Monreith curves round to the Point of Lag, one of the most attractive miniature landscapes on the Solway coast. The point separates the safe sandy beaches of Front Bay and Back Bay, and a sheltered picnic area is reached by a road behind Back Bay dunes. The St Medan golf course occupies the middle hills.

Looking down on Front Bay is the ruin of Kirkmaiden church; the wind-sculptured trees that tower above it show the force of the prevailing south-westerly winds.

④ ST NINIAN'S CAVE

The first Christian missionary to Scotland, preceding St Columba by some 150 years, was St Ninian, who founded a church at Whithorn in about AD 397 after returning from a pilgrimage to Rome. A cave among the shoreline cliffs which was his place of retreat is reached from a car park at Kidsdale, by a pathway down the wooded Physgill Glen. Christian crosses have been carved into the rock of the cave. An annual church service is held there, but although the cave may be approached, it is sometimes closed to visitors.

⑤ ISLE OF WHITHORN

Originally the port for the inland burgh of Whithorn, the village of Isle of Whithorn continues to be a busy though unspoiled sailing resort in summer. The safe harbour is the base of Wigtown Bay Sailing Club, and there is a coastguard station. Boats may be hired for sea-angling, and the rocky inlets are good for shore fishing. At low water there is a foreshore of mud and shingle.

A causeway links the village to the grassy peninsula of what was once a genuine 'Isle' and is now a public park. On it stands the ruin of a 13th-century chapel traditionally associated with St Ninian.

Before the causeway was built, the shallow tidal channel between island and mainland was once the scene of a masterstroke of sailing. A smuggler pursued by a revenue cutter raced his ship into the channel at high tide. To the amazement of the customs men he escaped through an apparent dead end. Later, at low tide, the gouge-marks of his keel could be traced in the sand.

⑥ GARLIESTON

Above the sand and shingle on the west side of Garlieston Bay is a trim village of colour-washed houses. The main street behind the sea-wall forms two shallow crescents, allowing just enough space for one of Scotland's narrowest bowling greens. Small boats use the sheltered harbour, and boats can be hired for sea-angling for mackerel, cod and flatfish.

Behind the village to the south is the Georgian mansion of Galloway House, designed by John Douglas and Lord Garlies in 1740. Its walled gardens, containing rhododendrons and fine trees, are open daily.

⑦ WIGTOWN

Saltings, marshland and an extensive area of tidal sands cover the estuary at the head of Wigtown Bay. The harbour, long disused, has been renovated, with parking and picnic areas beside the winding tidal channel of the River Bladnoch.

The salt-marshes of Wigtown Bay are a wintering place for greylag geese. However, the bay has a more sombre side to its history: in 1685 two women Covenanters aged 18 and 65 were tied to stakes and drowned by the rising tide because they refused to change their religious allegiance. A memorial stone, reached by a pathway, marks the traditional site of their martyrdom.

With a distillery on one side of the river and a creamery on the other, Wigtown is centred on a wide and airy square. Colourful gardens and a bowling green occupy the centre, and at one side of the square are the handsome County Buildings of 1863, housing a tiny museum where relics of the ancient burgh are displayed.

⑧ CREETOWN

Set on the marshy estuary of the River Cree, Creetown is an 18th-century 'planned' village that became a thriving 19th-century port, whose main export was granite. The harbour is now used only by private craft, but the centre of the village still bears witness to this bygone age: a clock-tower, built to mark Queen Victoria's Diamond Jubilee in 1897, is made of the same sturdy granite used in the construction of the Thames Embankment and the Mersey Docks in Liverpool.

In the old school on the Rusko road, high up in the village, is the Gem Rock Museum. Its collection of rose quartz, amethyst, jasper, cornelian and other gems from around the world, open daily, is one of the finest in the country.

The ruined 15th-century Carsluith Castle stands back from the roadside 3½ miles south of Creetown. A side road up the wooded glen of the Kirkdale Burn, where deer are sometimes seen among the plantations, leads to the Neolithic tombs of Cairn Holy, built around 4,000 years ago.

TRIBUTE TO AN AUTHOR

On a headland above Monreith a bronze otter has been set up in memory of Gavin Maxwell, the naturalist and author of *Ring of Bright Water* which told the story of the author's pet otters. Maxwell spent his childhood at House of Elrig, near Port William, when his family owned the Monreith estate. Later he moved to Sandaig about 9 miles south of Kyle of Lochalsh, to a house he called Camusfearna, where he kept his otters and wrote about them.

The bronze otter above Monreith churchyard.

ON THE BANKS OF THE DEE *Low water at Kirkcudbright and the gently flowing River Dee have inspired many artists whose works are displayed in the white-painted Harbour Art Gallery.*

⑨ GATEHOUSE OF FLEET

The Water of Fleet divides this elegant 18th-century town in two. Gatehouse owes its present form to James Murray of Cally, the landowner who in 1790 began to develop it as a cotton manufacturing centre. A brewery, tannery, soap factory and brickworks were also established, and the channel of the Water of Fleet was dredged to create a harbour beside the town. Industry flourished for 70 years, leaving Gatehouse a happy hunting-ground for industrial archaeologists.

At the Murray Arms Hotel in the town centre in 1793, Robert Burns wrote *Robert Bruce's March to Bannockburn*, which begins 'Scots, wha hae wi' Wallace bled'. The grounds of Cally House Hotel, south of the town, now belong to the Forestry Commission, which has waymarked several forest walks.

The writer Thomas Carlyle once told Queen Victoria that he believed the coast road between Gatehouse and Creetown to be the finest in her kingdom. On a striking hilltop site above the A75 main road 1 mile south-west of Gatehouse stands the 15th-century Cardoness Castle, one of the best-preserved castles of its period in Scotland

and notable for its elaborate fireplaces.

The water at the sandy mouth of the Skyre Burn, beyond Cardoness, looks tempting, but bathers must take care, for high tides hide the deep channel. There are safer beaches among the rocky outcrops of Mossyard Bay.

⑩ SANDGREEN

A series of sandy bays separated by grassy headlands stretches southwards down the coast opposite the Islands of Fleet. Sandgreen is the most popular of these bays, while from Carrick's bay it is possible at low tide to walk across to the biggest of the islands, Ardwall.

For almost 50 years Ardwall was inhabited by a family called Higgins, who kept open house for smugglers. The island was honeycombed with hiding places, and trains of packhorses used to move to and from it at night, loaded with contraband.

⑪ KIRKCUDBRIGHT

Its long years as county town have given Kirkcudbright some elegant buildings. The 16th-century McLellan's Castle, in the town centre, is partially restored and open to the

public, while the Georgian Broughton House in the High Street was bequeathed to the town by its last private owner, the artist Edward Hornel, several of whose paintings are on show there. Painters, weavers, sculptors and potters have created an artists' colony at Kirkcudbright, and some of their work is exhibited in a gallery beside the harbour. The town's name, pronounced 'Kirkcoobrie', probably derives from St Cuthbert who converted much of southern Scotland to Christianity.

The water level of the harbour drops spectacularly at low tide, and can be controlled at other times according to the outflow from Tongland Electricity Power Station, a hydro-electric scheme 2 miles up-river which can be visited by arrangement.

Sailing is possible at suitable tides, but the coast around Kirkcudbright is too rugged for easy small-boat or dinghy fishing. Sea-angling excursions usually go to the open coast, about 3 miles away, where excellent catches of tope are taken. The lifeboat station is outside the town on the east shore of a bay called 'Manxman's Lake', a legacy of its smuggling connections with the Isle of Man. There is a picnic area by the sands near Gull Craig, on the western side of Kirkcudbright Bay.

A large stretch of farmland between the Kirkcudbright-Dundrennan road and the sea was taken over for tank testing in 1942, and the area is still a military zone. Roads through it may be closed when exercises are in progress, and the rumble of gunfire is often heard in the town.

LOCAL INFORMATION

Tourist information Gatehouse of Fleet 212 (summer); Kirkcudbright 30494 (summer); Newton Stewart 2431 (summer).

HM Coastguard Ramsey 813255 for information, 999 in emergency (ask for coastguard).

Weather Glasgow (041) 248 3451.

Local radio BBC Radio Solway, 92.5 MHz.

PLACES TO SEE INLAND

Drumtroddan Stones, 2 miles NE of Port William. Bronze Age cup and ring markings. Daily.

Galloway Forest Park, Forestry Commission land covering 240 square miles.

Stones of Torhouse, 3 miles W of Wigtown. A circle of 19 Bronze Age standing stones. Daily.

MILES	4	8	12	16	20	24	28	32	36
KM	10	20	30	40	50				

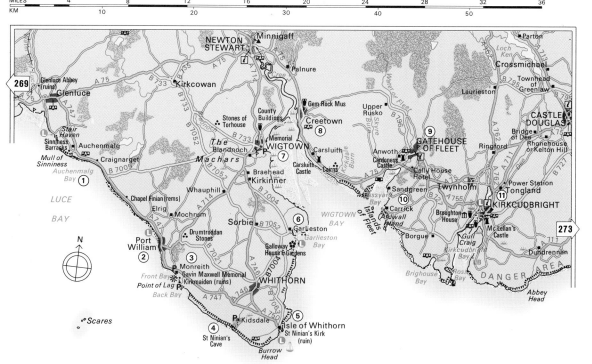

Sands and yachting harbours along the shore of the Solway Firth

Narrow inlets along the shore of the Solway Firth where smugglers once landed contraband wines and tobacco now provide sheltered anchorages for yachtsmen and fishermen. Eastwards from Port o'Warren stretch miles of sands, but the Solway's fast-flowing tides require caution on the part of bathers, anglers and walkers. The salt-marshes east of the Nith are the haven of countless sea-birds, on one of Britain's most remarkable bird reserves.

KIPPFORD *Wooded hills shelter this quiet resort at the head of Rough Firth and give it a mild climate in which palm trees can grow. The sandy bay is a haven for small boats.*

① DUNDRENNAN ABBEY

A 13th-century chapter house and some Norman stonework beside the Abbey Burn are the remains of a Cistercian Abbey founded in 1142. The ruins are open daily, and there are many fine sculptures, including a larger-than-life-size group depicting a murdered abbot and his assassin.

It was at Dundrennan Abbey that Mary, Queen of Scots is believed to have spent her last night on Scottish soil, on May 5, 1568, after being forced to abdicate in favour of her infant son James VI. The next day she sailed from the little inlet now known as Port Mary, 1 mile to the south, and crossed the Solway Firth in an open boat to seek refuge in England. However, on Queen Elizabeth's orders she was imprisoned – a fate that was to culminate in her execution 19 years later.

② AUCHENCAIRN BAY

Clustered behind the pebble beaches of Auchencairn Bay are the whitewashed cottages and farms of Auchencairn village, an old smuggling centre. The bay dries out at low water, leaving acres of sand and exposed pebbles.

Balcary House, now a hotel with a fine outlook over the bay to Hestan Island, was built in the 18th century by one of the most successful smuggling concerns as a head-quarters and secret store for its contraband wines and tobacco.

At Balcary Fishery, salmon are caught, in stake-nets set out across the sands. Bass are also caught and boat trips operate from Balcary Bay. The invigorating walk to Balcary Point gives an opportunity to observe the sea-birds which gather around it.

Orchardton Tower, 2½ miles north of Auchencairn village, dates from the 15th century. A narrow spiral staircase rising inside its double walls leads to a circular parapet wall.

③ PALNACKIE

A tiny, silted-up harbour which dries out at low tide gives Palnackie a maritime atmosphere, even though it is 1 mile upstream from the estuary of Urr Water. Several of the houses in the village were built with two storeys to provide lodgings for sailors on the trading sloops that used to ply along this coast.

The estuary offers good fishing for flat-fish, and every year on a Saturday in late July or early August Palnackie is host to the World Flounder-Tramping Championships. The contest is held on the mud-flats off the peninsula of Glen Isle; competitors must use only their bare feet and a three-pronged spear, and prizes are awarded for the heaviest and lightest catches.

④ KIPPFORD

The main channel of Urr Water passes close to the village of Kippford, and its safe high-tide anchorage is the base of the Solway Yacht Club. Kippford is also an attractive small resort, with a pebble beach overlooked by stone houses built on a hillside. When the tide goes out across Rough Firth, wide mud-flats are exposed. It is then possible to walk out along a shingle spit known as the Rack to Rough Island, a bird sanctuary maintained by the National Trust for Scotland where waders, scaups, shelduck and mergansers can be seen.

The National Trust also maintains the high-level Jubilee Path which joins Kippford to the neighbouring resort of Rockcliffe, 1 mile south-east. There are magnificent views from the path over bays and headlands to the distant mountains of Galloway. The path also passes close to the hilltop Mote of Mark, a vitrified fort inhabited by a Celtic community from around the 6th century AD. Brooches, pottery and glass produced by Celtic craftsmen have been found there.

Rockcliffe developed as a seaside resort in Victorian times. It has a sandy beach, sheltered by Rough Island and broken up by ribs of rock. Beyond Rockcliffe the coastal path continues southwards for 1 mile to Castlehill Point, then turns east to run for a further 3 miles above Port o'Warren Bay and Portling Bay to Sandyhills.

⑤ SOUTHERNESS

A disused lighthouse stands sentinel on the headland of Southerness, facing across the Solway Firth to Cumbria. The wide sands around it have given rise to a holiday hamlet just inland from the lighthouse, with cottages, chalets and a caravan site, and there is a golf course to the west.

The lighthouse was built in 1748 to guide schooners sailing out of Dumfries bound for the American colonies. Another link with the New World is commemorated in the name of the nearby hotel, the Paul Jones. The boy who was born John Paul in 1747, the son of a gardener on the nearby Arbigland Estate, was to become famous as Paul Jones, a hero of the American navy.

The cottage in which John Paul was born and the Arbigland gardens, spread round a quiet bay, where he and his father worked, are open to the public on certain days every week in summer. They are reached by a turning off the road to Powillimount Farm; beyond Powillimount, the road ends at another sandy beach.

AMERICA'S MAN OF WAR

John Paul Jones, the son of a Kirkbean gardener, became an American naval hero in 1778 when he sailed into the harbour at Whitehaven, on the Cumbrian coast, captured a small fort and attempted to burn three British ships. The raid, during the American War of Independence, was followed a year later by a victory over British ships in the Baltic. Jones was decorated on his return to America, where he came to be regarded as the American navy's first commander.

Jones shoots a mutinous sailor

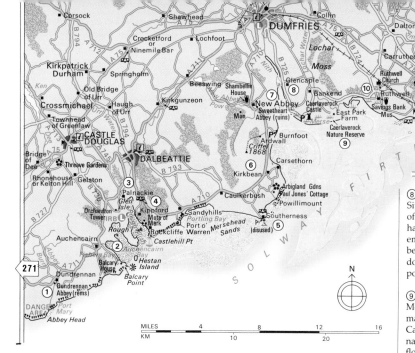

Westwards from Southerness are the Mersehead Sands, the most extensive on the Solway coast, stretching for 6 miles to Port o'Warren. They are safe near the shore, but walkers venturing further out must take extreme care, since the tide sweeps in at faster than walking pace and the channels, shallow at low tide, soon become deep rushing rivers.

Southerness was originally Salters' Ness – the name given to the headland in the 12th century when the sands around it were an important centre for salt-panning.

⑥ KIRKBEAN

The well-kept village with its bright gardens spreads out from an unusual domed parish church. In front of the church is a sundial, built in 1826, showing the time not only at Kirkbean, but also at places such as Madras, Calcutta and Gibraltar, where local men took up careers in Victorian times. Inside the church is a baptismal font presented in 1945 by officers and men of the United States Navy to honour Paul Jones, who was baptised there, as the navy's 'First Commander'.

A minor road from Kirkbean leads to the coastal village of Carsethorn, which looks eastwards across the estuary of the Nith. Many of its houses were built for coast-guards in the middle of the 19th century, but they are all now in private hands. Stake-nets for salmon are set out across the tidal sands.

⑦ NEW ABBEY

The greystone village of New Abbey is set among woods on the banks of the New Abbey Pow and is dominated by the soft red-sandstone ruins of the romantic Sweetheart Abbey.

The abbey was founded in 1273 by Devor-gilla, the widow of John Balliol, whose heart she built into the abbey walls. Balliol owned large estates in Scotland, England and France, and endowed the students' hostel at Oxford which eventually became Balliol College.

Set into the wall of a nearby cottage is a stone carving said to commemorate three women who crewed the boat that brought sandstone blocks for the abbey from a quarry on the opposite side of the estuary of the Nith. South-west of the village, near West Glen, is a 60 ft high monument to local men who fell at Waterloo.

Shambellie House, a Victorian mansion set among pinewoods just north of New Abbey, houses a museum of costume which is open on most days in summer. At Burnfoot, 2 miles south-east, there is a parking area close to the sands. Bathers must be careful of the fast-flowing tides sweeping in from the Solway Firth.

The 1,868 ft granite summit of Criffel looms over the village to the south. The best approach to the summit is from Ardwall, reached by a track turning off the main road 2 miles south of New Abbey, from where a path runs uphill beside a stream.

⑧ GLENCAPLE

Situated on the east bank of the tidal channel of the Nith, Glencaple was once a satellite harbour for the port of Dumfries, handling emigrant ships and coastal vessels. Now, because of the tides, not much sailing is done there, but Glencaple is popular with powerboat enthusiasts and windsurfers.

⑨ CAERLAVEROCK NATURE RESERVE

More than 13,000 acres of merse, or salt-marsh and foreshore, comprise the Caerlaverock National Nature Reserve. Barnacle geese from Spitzbergen and large flocks of pink-footed geese and greylag geese feeding on the saltings in autumn and winter are among the species which make Caerlaverock one of the most notable bird sanctuaries in Britain.

A car park on the road south from Glencaple gives access to the western end of the Merse, though walking is hazardous because of deep channels among the saltings, and occasional quicksands.

The Wildfowl Trust controls a refuge area at East Park Farm, with carefully sited hides and observation towers; it is open to the public from September to May.

Overlooking the Merse from a wooded mound are the striking red-sandstone ruins of Caerlaverock Castle. Built towards the end of the 13th century, the castle was besieged many times during the border wars between Scotland and England, and finally reduced to ruins in 1640.

⑩ RUTHWELL

The secluded village of Ruthwell lies east of the mouth of Lochar Water, at the foot of hills that rise gently to the north.

In the parish church, a specially designed apse houses the Ruthwell Cross, one of the most impressive examples of 7th-century stone carving in Europe. It is inscribed with verses from the oldest-known English poem, *The Dream of the Rood*. After years of neglect, the cross was rediscovered by the parish minister, Dr Henry Duncan, a man of immense energy and wide-ranging interests. In 1810 he founded the world's first savings bank, and a cottage alongside the original bank is now the Duncan Savings Bank Museum.

⑪ POWFOOT

This village at the mouth of the little Pow Water was created towards the end of the 18th century as a sea-bathing resort. Set above a sandy beach, with grassy parking areas, it provides a fine view across the Solway to the Lake District hills.

The resort is noted for its golf course, where several open tournaments are held, and the beach is used by sand yachts. Swimmers should not venture far out into the fast-moving tides and shifting channels.

Kinmount Gardens, 2 miles north of Powfoot, contain a variety of flowers and shrubs. A flock of Canada geese are among the resident wildfowl, and the many laid-out walks include two that circle the lakes in front of Kinmount House. The gardens are open daily in summer.

CAERLAVEROCK CASTLE *Built in the shape of a triangular shield, with a tower at each corner, the red-sandstone castle commanded a strategic landing point on the Solway Firth.*

FISHING NORWEGIAN STYLE IN THE RIVER NITH

From February to September, fishermen can be seen fishing in the Nith with haaf-nets – the word haaf comes from the Norwegian for 'heave'. This form of fishing requires good balance and strong muscles. The fishermen wade out into the channel with nets fixed to a long wooden spar; when a salmon or sea trout swims into a net the fisherman flicks the net over the spar to trap the fish.

⑫ **ANNAN**

This Victorian red-stone town stands on the eastern bank of the River Annan and is the 'capital' of the Annandale and Eskdale District. The river is popular with anglers, who fish for salmon, sea trout and brown trout, and there are pleasant walks along both banks to Brydekirk. On the coast, commercial fishing is done by haaf-nets and stake-nets. Sailing can be hazardous.

An overgrown embankment 1 mile east of the mouth of the River Annan once led on to a railway bridge across the Solway Firth to the Cumbrian shore. It was dismantled in 1935.

⑬ **GRETNA**

The borderlands south of Gretna are mostly made up of marshland and mud-flats flanking the estuaries of the Sark and Esk rivers. Overlooking the estuary of Kirtle Water is the 7 ft high Lochmaben Stone, which probably formed part of a prehistoric stone circle.

Gretna's history goes back to Roman times, but during the 14th-century border wars between the Scots and the English the town was completely destroyed.

The Old Blacksmith's Shop in the village of Gretna Green, just to the north, is noted

for its long tradition of anvil weddings. An English law of 1754 prevented young lovers from marrying without parental consent. The law did not apply in Scotland, however, where all the couple had to do was to declare in front of witnesses that they wished to be man and wife; and so Gretna Green, the first settlement across the border, established a trade in runaway marriages. The last 'anvil priest', Mr Richard Rennison, conducted more than 5,000 weddings between 1905 and 1940, when anvil weddings were made illegal by Act of Parliament. One of the old marriage registers is on display in the hotel.

LOCAL INFORMATION

Tourist information Kirkcudbright 30494 (summer); Gretna 37834 (summer).

HM Coastguard Ramsey 813255 for information, 999 in emergency (ask for coastguard).

Weather Glasgow Weather Centre (041) 248 3451.

Local radio BBC Radio Cumbria, 397 m, 756 kHz, 95.6 MHz; BBC Radio Solway, 92.5 MHz.

PLACES TO SEE INLAND

Thomas Carlyle's Birthplace (NTS), Ecclefechan, 6 miles N of Annan. Contains collection of relics and letters. Weekdays in summer.

Dumfries. Burns' House Museum, Burns Street, house where Robert Burns died in 1796, daily, except Sun. and Mon. in winter; Dumfries Museum, with 1836 Camera Obscura, Windmill Tower, summer. Old Bridge House Museum, 17th-century house and furnishing, daily in summer.

Rammerscales, 10 miles NW of Annan. Georgian house and grounds; Jacobite relics and links with Flora MacDonald. Some afternoons in summer.

Threave Gardens (NTS), near Castle Douglas. Daffodils; flowering trees; rock, woodland and heather gardens. Daily.

A flat, green coast where Hadrian's Wall reached the sea

The Cumbrian shore that faces westwards and northwards across the broad waters of the Solway Firth offers more to the walker than to the bather. Muddy sands and treacherous tides make this a generally uninviting coast for swimming or any other water sports. The views, however, are superb, and the seclusion and lack of commercialisation give the area a timeless quality which busier, more popular places have lost.

① ALLONBY

Allonby Bay faces north-west towards the open sea rather than towards the Scottish shore, so conditions here are safer for bathing than they become further east. Allonby itself is an unassuming but attractive village of cottages which straggles along the Silloth to Maryport coast road. The town became popular as a holiday resort about 200 years ago, after a darker and more violent history as a centre for landing smuggled whisky from the opposite coast of the Solway.

Christ Church, at the southern end of the town, contains a memorial to Joseph Huddart, born in Allonby in 1741 and a surveyor who added to 18th-century knowledge of the coasts and harbours of the Far East. Huddart became wealthy through an invention which grew out of a disaster he witnessed when a cable snapped at sea; he devised a method of rope-making which ensured that the stresses were divided evenly between the fibres. He set up as a ropemaker in London, and was buried at St Martin-in-the-Fields.

② BECKFOOT

The coast between Allonby and Silloth is one long bank of shingle, with muddy sand and a scattering of rocks below the high-water mark. The tide goes out more than a mile at low water, leaving vast areas of sand and rock pools, but care must be taken when the tide turns.

Near by are the fragments of a Roman fort, part of the coastal defences intended to prevent the Picts to the north from making a landing behind the line of the Hadrian's Wall defences.

③ SILLOTH

Established in the last century as a harbour for coastal shipping, Silloth soon became popular as a holiday resort with the arrival of the railway in 1856. Its name, though, is much older. The Cistercian monks of Holme Cultram Abbey, a few miles south-east, established a salt-making trade and grew grain on the fertile Cumbrian fields. The harvested grain was kept in granaries called 'laths' on the site where Silloth later grew up, and the town took its name from the 'sea laths' belonging to the abbey.

Silloth's cobbled streets show a Victorian order and precision in their planning, and the small harbour from time to time still sees ships, bringing grain for the large flour mill and conducting a thriving trade in local cattle. The sand-and-shingle beach has a few patches of mud, but bathing is generally safe except when the tide is on the ebb, when the strong currents flowing from the Solway Firth make conditions dangerous.

The holiday attractions of Silloth are set around a large open space called The Green,

with 40 acres of lawns, flower beds and rose gardens. The promenade and harbour offer splendid views of the Scottish mountains, especially towards evening and in clear weather.

④ SKINBURNESS

It is difficult to imagine that this tiny village, dominated today by a large hotel, was the spot chosen by Edward I as a base from which to attack his turbulent enemies in Scotland. In 1303, however, a flood swept away most of the settlement and the villagers moved to Newton (or 'Newtown') Arlosh, founded on a safer site further inland.

Today the sea to the east and south has retreated, leaving a wild tract of salt-marsh on which sheep and cattle graze. Nearby Grune Point gives a wide view of the estuary and of the waders and wildfowl which live along its borders.

⑤ ABBEYTOWN

A Cistercian abbey founded in 1150 gave this little farming village its name. The monks grew grain, raised large flocks of sheep and established a thriving trade in salt from the estuary marshes. The abbey was closed by Henry VIII in 1538, but part of the nave survived to become St Mary's Parish Church.

Parts of the original foundations still visible outside the church show how big the abbey must have been in its heyday. The magnificent Tudor doorway, built by Abbot Robert Chamber in 1507, still survives; the abbot's crest, a bear on a chain ('chained bear', or 'Chamber'), survives, on his memorial in the porch. A tomb in the porch is that of the Lord of Annandale, father of Robert Bruce.

⑥ NEWTON ARLOSH

This little village was founded by the monks of Holme Cultram after the disaster of the flooding of Skinburness in 1303. Newton is safe enough from the sea, but in the 17th century this exposed corner of England's border country was subject to perils of another kind from raiders coming across the Solway Firth to plunder and rob.

⑦ HERDHILL SCAR

A small headland projecting out into the Solway Firth from the Cumbrian coast is all that remains of the embankment and approach to a railway viaduct which once ran for more than a mile across the firth to the Scottish shore. The viaduct was opened during the railway building boom of 1869 to provide a direct link between the iron-ore mines of Cumbria and the smelting furnaces of Lanarkshire, by-passing the main line through Carlisle and Gretna.

The viaduct never carried heavy traffic, and was vulnerable to wind and weather. In the winter of 1875, water penetrated into the hollow centres of the bridge pillars and froze, expanding and cracking the supports. Six years later drifting ice floes were blown against the bridge supports, tearing open gaps in two places.

Amazingly, the viaduct was repaired, and trains continued running across it until the 1920s; the viaduct was not demolished until 1935. Until then the mile-long route across the estuary was a popular walk in good weather, especially among thirsty Scots wanting to enjoy a drink at an English pub on a Sunday evening.

⑧ BOWNESS-ON-SOLWAY

On the flat coastal meadows of the Solway at

DISTANT HILLS *Across the Solway Firth from Silloth the Scottish hills are seen at their best when dressed in diaphanous evening mists and the setting sun turns the water to shimmering gold.*

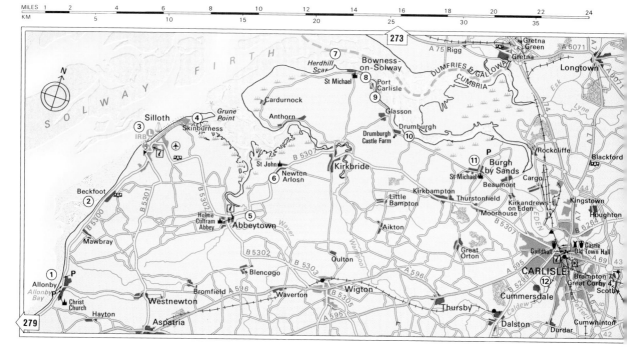

Bowness, the switchback course of Hadrian's Wall reached its western limit. The Roman wall at this point was only a turf rampart, so that few signs of it remain.

One link with a later episode in Bowness's violent past has, however, survived. Stealing church bells was a popular activity among the raiders who crossed the Firth in the 17th century, and one party of Scots who stole the bells of St Michael's Church managed to get halfway back across the estuary before they were overtaken and had to abandon them. The bells now in the church porch at Bowness were seized from villages on the other side of the Solway in retaliation. The narrow, winding streets of Bowness today slumber in rural peace.

⑨ PORT CARLISLE

A lonely little village, comprising little more than two terraces of cottages flanking a late Georgian house, are a memorial to a commercial venture ruined by the unpredictability of nature. Port Carlisle, as its name implies, was established in 1819 to provide a harbour for coastal shipping, with a fast and efficient link by canal to markets in Carlisle and beyond. But in the 1860s the tidal currents changed and the harbour silted up. Today the visitor has to search carefully for signs of the old harbour and the remains of the canal, while the traces of the railway which replaced it as a link with Carlisle are also fast disappearing.

⑩ DRUMBURGH

The small village marks the site of the next Roman fort to Bowness eastwards along Hadrian's Wall. The fort itself has gone, but the road through the village still twists around the line of its outer walls, and to the east of the village the low sea-wall follows the line of the original turf rampart.

Nearby Drumburgh Castle farm was built on the ruins of an old fortified tower-house established by Thomas, Lord Dacre early in the 16th century. The end wall, built of Roman stones from the fort, has an outside staircase leading to an upper doorway with a heavily studded door at first-floor level.

⑪ BURGH BY SANDS

The village of stone, brick and whitewashed cottages is built over the site of a Roman fort. St Michael's Church is built with stones from the Roman defences, and stands in the middle of the site. It, too, had a defensive role to play, as a refuge from Scottish raiders, and

RAIDERS' COAST *The salt-marshes at Bowness-on-Solway face the narrowest point of the Solway Firth. In the 17th century, English and Scottish raiders kept up a steady feud across the firth.*

the 14th-century tower has no outside doorway. The only entrance is through a heavily bolted iron gate from the nave, while the tower windows are small slits. Edward I died on nearby Burgh Marshes in 1307 while campaigning against the Scots, and his body was brought to lie in state in St Michael's Church.

The road leading west from Burgh by Sands follows the line of the old Roman vallum, the southern ditch of Hadrian's Wall. The high bank on its inland side carried the railway line to Port Carlisle. The wall itself ran on the seaward side, but now there is nothing to prevent high tides flooding across the road.

⑫ CARLISLE

Founded by the Romans as a base for the Hadrian's Wall defences, Carlisle became a vital strongpoint in the centuries of border wars in later years. The castle, with its huge keep dating back to 1092, was the focal point of the defences, but the town was also defended by a ring of ramparts, a stretch of which survives close to the castle on the northern side of the town.

Carlisle's Museum and Art Gallery, which is housed in a 17th-century house just

off Castle Street, has a large collection of objects from Roman Carlisle, and is also a national study centre for the whole Hadrian's Wall defensive system. The Museum of the Border Regiment is housed in the castle's Queen Mary Tower.

In the centre of the city is the timber-framed Guildhall, built in 1407 as a private house. Near by is the Old Town Hall, facing the steps of the Market Cross from which, in August every year, the opening of the 600-year-old Carlisle Great Fair is proclaimed.

277

Beaches between the ports that grew in Cumbria's industrial past

The coastline from Allonby Bay southwards along the western edge of Cumbria is bordered by low dunes and grassland, interrupted by three industrial areas which developed in the 18th century when miners exploited the coastal coalfields. Cliffs surround the massive bulk of St Bees Head, and south of the headland stretch 17 miles of quiet beaches, the only major landmarks being the cooling towers of Calder Hall Nuclear Power Station.

① MARYPORT

The Romans built their fort of Alauna at Maryport to prevent seaborne raiders from the north outflanking the defences of Hadrian's Wall. Unlike many Roman forts in this part of England, Alauna can still be identified, sections of its ramparts being visible at the northern end of the town.

Maryport owes its name to Mary, the wife of a local landowner, Humphrey Senhouse, who built the docks and harbour in the 18th century to serve the local coal trade. One of the two docks, the Elizabeth Dock, was named after the Senhouses' elder daughter. The later Senhouse Dock was used for loading ships with cargoes of iron rails, made in Cumbria for railways all over the world. At one time a million tons of cargo left these quays every year.

The town, with its gridiron pattern of streets and terraces of 18th and 19th-century houses, still has an air of elegance, especially in the old cobbled market square. The Maritime Museum on the edge of the harbour contains many reminders of the days when the port was bustling with trade. Over the years the silting up of the harbour has caused business to dwindle to the point where it is now only a refuge for sailing yachts and small fishing craft.

② WORKINGTON

Coal used to be shipped from collieries around Workington to the markets of southern England. The deep-water port is still used to ship railway lines, made in the local steel works, and coal, though on a much smaller scale than before. Workington has several parks, and the hills inland offer good touring and walking country.

The Helena Thompson Museum, on the road to Cockermouth, conjures up Workington's vanished past. There are a local history gallery, displays of costume, furniture, glass and pottery, and a Victorian period room interior.

On a hill overlooking the River Derwent stands the derelict Workington Hall, noted for its association with Mary, Queen of Scots. It was at Workington Hall that Mary arrived on May 17, 1568, after crossing the Solway in an open boat with 30 fellow-refugees from the Battle of Langside. She stayed a night at the Hall, as Sir Henry Curwen's guest, before riding to Carlisle and 19 years' imprisonment before her execution.

③ WHITEHAVEN

In 1566 Whitehaven consisted of six fishermen's cottages and possessed a single 9 ton vessel, the *Bee*. Early in the next century the small fishing community, and the estate of St Bees of which it formed part, was acquired by the Lowther family, who developed Whitehaven as a port for shipbuilding and the export of Cumbrian coal. They laid out the town to a regular gridiron pattern, making it the first deliberately planned town in England since the Middle Ages.

By 1730 Whitehaven was one of the major ports in Britain; its population reached 9,000 by 1760 and was to double again by 1860. An indication of the port's importance in the 18th century is the fact that John Paul Jones, the Scots-born American naval commander, mounted an attack on it in 1778, during the American War of Independence. He knew the port well, having served as an apprentice seaman there before going to America. Although he captured a small fort defending the harbour, his attempt to set fire to the merchant fleet was a failure.

Though the coal and iron trade which founded the town's prosperity have dwindled sharply in later years, the town's Haig colliery, which runs under the sea, still supplies local blast furnaces, and the harbour still handles cargo. Whitehaven has also built up a successful holiday trade; it has a wealth of Georgian and Victorian buildings, and its history is outlined in the museum and art gallery in the civic hall.

At the South Beach recreation area stand two of the mines which led the Lowthers to build the town. They are Duke Pit, sunk in 1747, its buildings looking like a ruined medieval castle, and the Wellington Pit of 1840, an even more elaborate fantasy in a similar style.

④ ST BEES

The village of St Bees lies in a valley to the south of St Bees Head, where the Pow Beck has cut its way through to the sea. St Bee, or St Bega, is said to have been an Irish princess of the 7th century who took a childhood vow to devote herself to God and established a nunnery at this spot. A nunnery established about AD 650 by the Benedictines was later destroyed by the Vikings and refounded by the Normans in 1120.

The parish church of St Mary and St Bega is the much-restored church of the original nunnery, but the neighbouring buildings belong to a school founded by Archbishop Grindal in 1583.

A road leads past a hotel to a car park almost at the water's edge, close to St Bees Head. From there footpaths lead to the top of the headland, and to the lighthouse at North Head. These are the only cliffs on the coast of Cumbria, and in clear weather give a splendid view of the Isle of Man.

⑤ EGREMONT

This small town with a broad main street of colour-washed stone houses straddles the coast road and is dominated by the ruins of its Norman castle, set on a hill overlooking a bend of the River Ehen at the southern end of the main street. It was built in 1130 by William de Meschines, and part of the hall and outer wall survive.

Egremont is famous for its annual Crab Fair – so-called because when the fair was founded in 1267 crab apples were given away to visitors. The parade of the Apple Cart still takes place during the fair.

⑥ SELLAFIELD

The site of the controversial nuclear fuel reprocessing plant, formerly known as Windscale, also includes Calder Hall, which in 1956 became the first nuclear power station in Britain to generate electricity on a commercial scale. The four cooling towers of the Calder Hall reactors, which are still generating electricity, can be seen from the coast road. An exhibition centre is open daily, and there are organised tours.

Two miles away stand the ruins of Calder Abbey, founded in the 12th century by monks from Furness Abbey but raided by

BYGONE PORT *The tide of trade has ebbed for Maryport, leaving empty berths on North Quay and an almost deserted harbour where ships from all over the world once gathered to load cargo.*

MARYPORT'S MUTINEER

Fletcher Christian, first officer of HMS *Bounty* and leader of the mutiny against Captain Bligh, was born near Maryport in 1764. Incensed by Bligh's harsh treatment of the crew, Christian set him adrift in a boat in the Pacific with a few loyal officers. They reached Timor, 4,000 miles away, while the mutineers landed on Pitcairn Island. Christian Street in Maryport is named after the mutiny leader.

The Bounty *mutineers turn Captain Bligh adrift.*

the Scots soon afterwards. The monks fled to set up another community at Byland in Yorkshire, but Calder Abbey was refounded and soon became a Cistercian house in 1148.

⑦ RAVENGLASS

Three rivers, the Esk, the Mite and the Irt, converge at Ravenglass, and this dominating position must have been one reason why the Romans built a coastal fort there, at the spot they called Glannaventa. The fort's bath-house still stands, its 12 ft high walls making it the best-preserved Roman building in the north of England.

The curving estuary, its inner stretches sheltered from onshore winds by sandspits, made an ideal anchorage for fishing boats, and for generations the village of Ravenglass made its living from the sea.

Today Ravenglass makes a peaceful, unspoiled refuge, but bathing is dangerous. The meeting of the waters from three rivers, the curving estuary channels and the sweep of the incoming and outgoing tides create swirling currents and tide-rips fast enough to sweep any unwary bather out of his depth in seconds.

The Ravenglass and Eskdale Railway

Ravenglass is the terminus of the Ravenglass and Eskdale Railway, a steam railway that carries passengers for 7 miles up the lovely and unspoiled valley of Eskdale. The railway, the first narrow-gauge railway in England and known locally as 'T'laal Ratty' (The Old Ratty), was built in 1875 to carry iron ore from the Eskdale Valley down to the main Furness Railway along the coast. A railway museum at Ravenglass records the history of the line and the area.

⑧ MUNCASTER CASTLE

A fine collection of antique furniture, tapestries and portraits is housed in this castle on a hilltop, 1 mile east of Ravenglass. The house dates from about 1200, but was rebuilt

and extended in the 1860s. During the Wars of the Roses, shepherds found Henry VI wandering the nearby fells after the Battle of Hexham and took him to Muncaster Castle. The room in which the king was hidden is still called King Henry's Room, and the bowl he presented to his hosts on leaving nine days later still remains in the castle. The oak panelling in the billiard room is said to have been taken from HMS *Témeraire*, one of Nelson's fleet at Trafalgar.

Muncaster Castle is surrounded by gardens, laid out originally in the 17th century and renowned for hydrangeas, azaleas and rhododendrons. The house and gardens are open most afternoons in summer.

Muncaster Mill, 1 mile to the north where the road crosses the River Mite, is an old watermill, recently restored to working order, which grinds and sells wholemeal flour.

⑨ ESKMEALS

This long sandy beach south of Ravenglass is closed to the public when firing is taking place at the Ministry of Defence experimental establishment tucked away among the dunes. The beach is often littered with spent shells washed up by the tide.

These risks apart, this stretch of coast is utterly unspoiled, with wide sea views and, in the opposite direction, an impressive landscape of high fells and moorland.

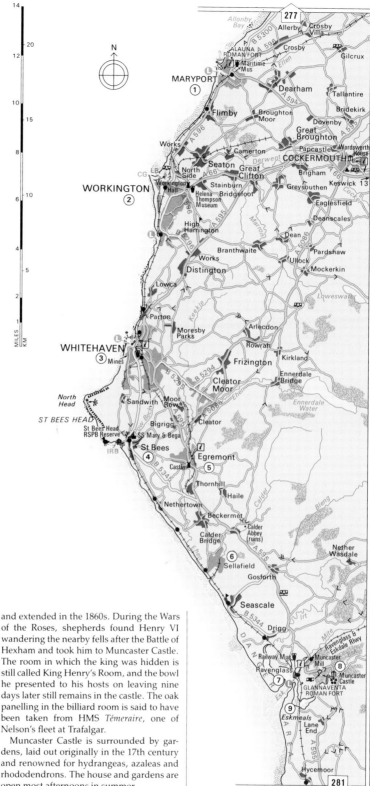

LOCAL INFORMATION

Tourist information Maryport 3738; Whitehaven 5678; Ravenglass 278 (summer).

HM Coastguard Liverpool (051) 931 3341.

Weather Windermere 5151.

Local radio BBC Radio Furness, 358 m, 837 kHz, 96.1 MHz; BBC Radio Cumbria, 397 m, 756 kHz, 95.6 MHz. (Whitehaven area 206 m, 1458 kHz) BBC Radio Solway, 92.5 MHz.

PLACES TO SEE INLAND

Castlerigg Stone Circle, near Keswick, 13 miles E of Cockermouth. Prehistoric circle.

Wordsworth House (NT), Cockermouth. Birthplace of the poet. Most days in summer.

Long sands that sweep outwards from the Duddon's broad estuary

Cumbria's southernmost coastline is usually by-passed by holidaymakers bound for the Lake District. However, this wild and unspoiled region of long sandy beaches, spattered with outcrops of rocks and split by river estuaries which run far inland towards the lakes and fells, has its own particular charm. Not always easy to reach by road, the shoreline retains a natural grandeur interrupted only by the shipyards of Barrow-in-Furness.

HAVERIGG HEIGHTS *Dunes almost 70 ft high in places sweep round Haverigg Point, with tenacious marram grass binding the soft sand. The broad foreshore is more than a mile wide at low tide.*

① ANNASIDE
Because it is some 2 miles from the nearest main road, the long stretch of rock-strewn sand centred on Annaside does not attract the crowds, making the effort of reaching it well worth while on a good sunny day.

To reach the shore, leave the main coast road and go through Bootle village. Turn left down a lane which leaves the road after about half a mile and follow it under the railway. The lane winds for just over a mile to a small private bridge over the River Annas, from where footpaths lead to the shore – a 4 mile strip of land sandwiched between the Lakeland hills and the sea, where hundreds of shallow rock pools form at low tide. A walk northwards along the shore leads to the tiny Selker Bay, where the Annas flows to the sea.

② GUTTERBY SPA
The difficulty involved in reaching this stretch of wild, open beach often leaves it deserted even on the hottest summer day. The approach track, narrow and badly surfaced, turns off the Whitehaven to Broughton in Furness coast road and winds for more than a mile down to the beach. The journey is amply rewarded by the emptiness of the beach and the splendour of the view, with the mountains inland dominated by the 1,970 ft Black Combe.

The beach of sand and shingle is backed by high cliffs – but nowhere is there any sign of the mineral spring which it was once hoped would turn Gutterby into a spa resort.

③ SILECROFT
Easier to reach than most neighbouring beaches, Silecroft's sand-and-shingle beach is a busy spot in the summer, and it is overlooked by a caravan and camping site. The beach is reached by a turning off the main coast road to Millom, which crosses the railway line and passes through the village of Silecroft, then runs down almost to the water's edge.

④ HAVERIGG
The 12 mile long sweep of beach which stretches from the estuary of the River Esk at Ravenglass to the estuary of the River Duddon ends at Haverigg in a long expanse of low-tide sand, backed by broad sand-dunes. On one side of the little village is a modern open prison, on the other the remains of old ironstone mines and quarries, some of which have been flooded to create the Hodbarrow Hollow lake.

The beach is ideal for picnics and sunbathing, and swimming is safe enough close to the shore when the tide is rising. Further out in the estuary, strong currents have scoured deep channels, making conditions treacherous. Footpaths along the edge of the dunes give views across the estuary to Barrow and the coast of the Isle of Walney.

⑤ DUDDON SANDS
From Broughton in Furness the River Duddon widens out into a broad estuary extending southwards to the sea. At low tide the vast expanse of water dries out to a stretch of sand 2 miles across at its widest point. In the upper reaches of the estuary footpaths link villages on opposite banks, at low tide, but visitors should not use them without local advice as the sands are treacherous and the rising tide rapidly floods the area. The mudflats are the home of huge numbers of wading birds.

⑥ MILLOM
An unassuming little town on the western side of the Duddon estuary, Millom grew up around its 14th-century castle and the adjacent 12th-century church of the Holy Trinity, which is notable for its fine windows. Both the castle and church are situated near a bend in the road leading to Duddon Bridge, a mile or so north of the present town centre.

In later years, the local mining industry made Millom prosperous. During the late 19th century, when most of Millom was built, its iron mines had 11 working shafts, making them the largest and busiest in Britain. The last of the workings closed only in 1968. Among the exhibits at Millom's folk museum are a reconstruction of a miner's cottage and a replica of one of the working levels of the old Hodbarrow Iron Mine, at nearby Haverigg.

⑦ DALTON-IN-FURNESS
Two roads down the Furness peninsula – one from Duddon Bridge and the other from Ulverston – meet at Dalton-in-Furness. The whole area is honeycombed with old iron-ore quarries and mine workings. The splendour of St Mary's Church, with its large nave and imposing west tower, bears witness to the past prosperity of the village. This was the birthplace in 1734 of the portrait painter George Romney, who died in 1802 and was buried in the churchyard.

Nearby Dalton Castle is owned by the National Trust, and there is a small museum on the site. On the edge of the Duddon estuary, 3 miles west of Dalton, are the sand-dunes of Sandscale Haws, where miles of open sands are exposed at low tide. Bathing is safe only at high water, when the incoming sea holds back the dangerously fast river currents.

⑧ BARROW-IN-FURNESS
The town of Barrow originally grew up around Furness Abbey, established by the Cistercians in 1127. The ruins which stand on the north side of the town still give a vivid impression of an abbey which was second only to Fountains Abbey in Yorkshire in its wealth and importance. The monks smelted iron on the nearby Isle of Walney and had their own fleet of trading ships.

By the time the monastery fell into ruin, the town of Barrow had grown up to the south of the abbey, and the iron ore which the monks had used became the fuel for a new prosperity. The first local furnaces were built during the 18th century, and by the end of the century high-grade local ore was being shipped out from the harbour to feed steelworks all over England. By 1870, Barrow's own steelworks were the biggest in the world.

The town which grew up around the steelworks and shipyards was carefully planned, with wide, tree-lined streets and blocks of flats for the workers. Later, at the beginning of the present century, a planned suburb called Vickerstown was built on the Isle of Walney in the 'garden city' style. There is a good view of the docks from the road which leads to Walney.

BARROW DOCKS *Since 1852 the docks have supplied ships for the Royal Navy, from ironclads to the modern HMS* Invincible, *and from Britain's first submarine to the nuclear submarines of today.*

⑨ ISLE OF WALNEY

This 12 mile long strip of land, curved at either end, provides the shelter from the open sea which makes Barrow such a splendid natural harbour. On its inland side is a wide expanse of water, dotted with rocks and islands, and moorings for yachts and other pleasure craft. Beyond are visible the dockside cranes and fitting-out sheds of the Barrow shipyards.

On the seaward side of Walney is a straight beach more than 10 miles long, dotted with 'scars', or clumps of rock among the sand. The island is only a quarter of a mile across in places and, apart from the built-up area opposite Barrow, consists mainly of dune and grassland. During particularly violent storms in the past years, mountainous seas have washed right across the island. At the southern end is a large nature reserve with herring gulls and black-backed gulls.

⑩ PIEL ISLAND

Standing in the gap between the mainland and the southern end of the Isle of Walney, Piel Island was ideally placed for the defence of Barrow Harbour. A castle was first built there in the 12th century, but 100 years later the monks of Furness Abbey set up a fortress and a warehouse for the goods traded from the abbey, such as food, wine and wool. The ruins of the warehouse can still be seen. In 1486 Lambert Simnel, impersonating the imprisoned Earl of Warwick, landed at Piel Island in an attempt to seize the crown from the new king, Henry VII. He was later defeated and captured at Stoke, and was given a job as a servant in the royal household.

The island can be reached at weekends by boat from Roa Island, or at very low tides by walking across the sands from the Isle of Walney.

INVASION CASTLE *The last foreign invasion of England began at Piel in 1486, by Irish and Flemish supporters of Lambert Simnel.*

LOCAL INFORMATION

Tourist information Barrow-in-Furness 25795/21250; Millom 2555 (summer).

HM Coastguard Liverpool (051) 931 3341.

Weather Windermere 5151.

Local radio BBC Radio Furness, 358 m, 837 kHz, 96.1 MHz.

PLACES TO SEE INLAND

Coniston, 22 miles N of Barrow-in-Furness. Brantwood, home of John Ruskin, daily in summer; Ruskin Museum, daily in summer.

Graythwaite Hall, near Newby Bridge, 19 miles NE of Barrow-in-Furness. Gardens. Daily in spring.

Hawkshead Courthouse (NT), 25 miles NE of Barrow-in-Furness. Key from NT Information Centre.

Lake District National Park Visitor Centre, Brockhole, Windermere, 27 miles NE of Barrow-in-Furness, on A591 via A592. Daily in summer.

Stagshaw (NT), near Ambleside, 30 miles NE of Barrow-in-Furness. Gardens. Spring and autumn.

From gleaming sands to swirling waters in Morecambe Bay

Morecambe Bay is a vast bite out of England's north-western coast, more than 150 square miles of water which dry out at low tide to leave a vast expanse of golden sands. However, local inhabitants know the treacherous tides well enough not to venture far out over these sands on foot. Visitors tempted to explore them need to exercise extreme care because of the speed with which the waters race back with the incoming tide.

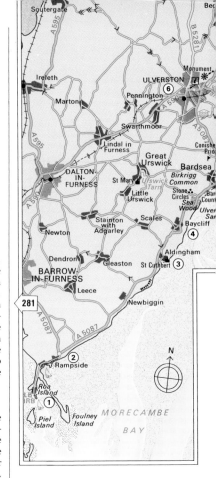

① ROA ISLAND
Despite its name, Roa Island is very firmly part of the mainland, linked to it by a half-mile causeway which carries the road from Rampside. Another spit leads more than 1 mile to the south-east to Foulney Island, which is the home of large nesting colonies of terns during the spring and summer. The shelter provided by the causeway has led to Roa Island's development as a yachting centre.

② RAMPSIDE
A single main street runs along the edge of a muddy shingle beach, which at low water extends 2 miles out to sea. Deep pools and gullies have been scoured out by the fast currents which funnel out of this corner of Morecambe Bay, and bathing is safe only at high water. The late-17th-century Rampside Hall has a row of prominent diagonally set chimneys, known locally as the Twelve Apostles.

③ ALDINGHAM
Over the centuries, Aldingham has lost more and more of its houses to the advancing sea. The parish church of St Cuthbert, which dates back to the 12th century, and the headstones in its little churchyard today stand just above high-water mark. Behind them are the narrow curving lanes of the more enduring part of the village which was built on the hill overlooking the sea.

④ BAYCLIFF
The village of Baycliff has no need to fear the sea, being set at the summit of the low banks which border the west side of Morecambe Bay. Half a mile to the north the attractive public woodlands of Sea Wood lie across the main coast road. Birkrigg Common, 1½ miles north-west of Baycliff, is notable for its prehistoric stone circles.

In the nearby village of Great Urswick, on the edge of Urswick Tarn, the 13th-century church of St Mary contains crosses made by the Angles and Vikings as well as stained-glass windows brought from Furness Abbey.

⑤ BARDSEA COUNTRY PARK
The coast road by-passes Bardsea, to run closer to the sea beside the Bardsea Country Park, which has car park and picnic spaces, marked footpaths and information boards right on the edge of Morecambe Bay. The view across to Morecambe and Heysham is dominated by the bulk of the nuclear reactor at Heysham Power Station.

Conishead Priory, north of Bardsea, was founded in the 12th century by a Norman nobleman, Gamel de Pennington, who chose the site because it was easily reached from the sea. The present house dates from the Gothic revival of the 1820s and has splendid wood panelling and elaborate plaster

ceilings. The cost bankrupted the owner, who had to sell the house, unaware that the iron-ore veins under the estate were rich enough to have paid all his debts and more.

The priory's present owners, the Tibetan Mahayana Buddhist Monks, are carefully restoring the building, which is open to the public on some days in summer and has a craft shop and cafe. Set among trees in the fine gardens are the original lake, grotto and hermitage established by Gamel de Pennington.

⑥ ULVERSTON
A Saxon landowner named Ulph gave the town of Ulverston its name. After the Norman Conquest it became the property of the monks of Furness Abbey, and a favourite target for raiders from Scotland under Robert Bruce, who burned the town twice, in 1316 and 1322. Ulverston suffered again in the Civil War, being fought over by both sides. By the 18th century, however, it had become a prosperous port and an important stopping place for the mail coach from Lancaster and the south, which in those days saved hours of pounding over rough roads by taking a short cut across the sands of Morecambe Bay.

The cobbled streets of the old town, centred on its busy market square, became such a centre for trade that it was known as 'the London of Furness'; but the same sands which assisted one kind of communication were to inhibit another, when shifting sandbanks silted up the harbour. To avoid this bottleneck the 2 mile long Ulverston Canal was built in 1795, to link the town with the sea at Canal Foot. The canal gave Ulverston another century as a busy port and ship-building centre, but fell into decline with the coming of the railway and was sealed off at its seaward end in the 1940s.

Today the tranquil waters of Ulverston Canal, and especially the area around the lock where the canal joined the sea, are favourite spots for fishermen and walkers enjoying the view across the estuary. The town has a market each Thursday, and for four days in May or early June and again in mid-November every year the Whit and Michaelmas fairs are held at the Gill, near the centre of the town.

On Hoad Hill, north-east of the town, a monument in the form of a lighthouse commemorates Sir John Barrow, geographer, explorer and Secretary to the Admiralty, who was born in Ulverston in 1764. The view from the hill is well worth the climb to the 435 ft summit.

⑦ GREENODD
Because of its position near the confluence of the River Crake and River Leven, Greenodd harbour was for many years an important outlet for the local iron ore and Cumberland slate. When the Furness Railway line was built along the coast through Grange-over-Sands and Ulverston, a branch line was laid through Greenodd to the shores of Windermere 5 miles to the north-east. Much of this line has now vanished, but a 3½ mile section

HOLKER HALL *The South Front dates from Elizabethan times. In the 19th-century New Wing is a screen embroidered by Mary, Queen of Scots in 1570 when she was confined at Chatsworth.*

The screen embroidered by Mary, Queen of Scots

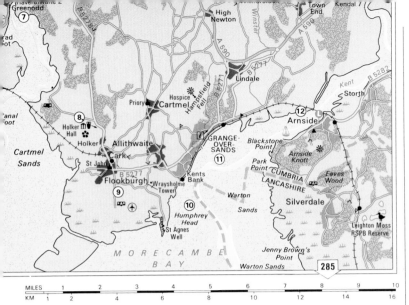

SHADES OF GOLD *Low tide at Arnside, and below the railway viaduct the waters of the River Kent unveil a canvas of glistening sands and patchwork tints, spread like shades on an artist's palette.*

Leven, rise to 172 ft, giving wide views over the sands to the Lancashire coast to the south. At the foot of the cliffs is St Agnes Well, whose waters were supposed to cure a variety of ailments including gout, ague and worms. The well brought a steady stream of pilgrims during the Middle Ages and, later, traders who sold phials of the water in the markets of Morecambe.

Near by the 14th-century Wraysholme Tower, an old fortified farmhouse, was once the home of John Harrington, who was said to have killed on Humphrey Head the last wolf seen in England.

⑪ GRANGE-OVER-SANDS

All the amenities of a modern holiday resort are found at Grange in the surroundings of a genteel Victorian watering place. The town takes its name from the grange, or granary, once built there by the Augustinian monks of Cartmel Priory which stood 1½ miles inland. Grange grew in the 16th and 17th centuries on the thriving coastal trade in coal, and its modern role as a holiday resort was assured when it was joined to the main Furness Railway line in 1857.

Grange's position, facing south-east and therefore sheltered from westerly winds, makes it a gardener's paradise, and its ornamental gardens are renowned. Bathing is best confined to the public swimming pool, because of currents off the beach and the rapid approach of the incoming tide. Hampsfield Fell, behind the town, is crowned by the Hospice, a shelter for travellers built by Thomas Remmington, Vicar of Cartmel between 1835 and 1854. An indicator on the 700 ft hilltop identifies the peaks which make up the spectacular view.

The fine church at the village of Cartmel belonged to the Augustinian priory built there in 1188, and was spared when the priory itself was destroyed after the Dissolution. Its stalls and screen are among the finest examples of 17th-century carving in England. The nave has an old wooden door, called Cromwell's Door, scarred by bullets said to have been fired by Parliamentary cavalry who stabled their horses in the church during the Civil War.

⑫ ARNSIDE

This pretty little fishing village was once an important boat-building centre, and is now increasingly popular as a holiday resort and sailing centre. It is also an ideal base for the walker and ornithologist. The mud-flats provide a home for almost every sea-bird known in Britain, while Arnside Knott is criss-crossed by footpaths and bridle paths.

Close to the pier is the railway viaduct which carries the line from Carnforth to Barrow, a short cut across the Kent estuary.

---

of it is still used by the Lakeside and Haverthwaite Steam Railway. Steam locomotives carry passengers from Haverthwaite, 2½ miles north-east of Greenodd, through a succession of tunnels and rock cuttings alongside the Leven, to connect with steamer sailings from Lakeside steamer pier on Windermere.

There is a large car park in the old goods yard of Haverthwaite station, beside the Ulverston to Newby Bridge main road.

⑧ HOLKER HALL

This fine mansion was built in Tudor times by the Cavendish family, but additions were made in succeeding centuries and the house is a splendid jumble of styles. The Victorian part of the house is open to the public, and so are 22 acres of formal and woodland gardens, which include a deer park.

Other attractions in the grounds of Holker Hall include spectacular displays of azaleas and rhododendrons in the spring, the annual Lakeland Rose Show in July, and events

which range from hot-air balloon races to rallies for old cars and horse-team driving. There is also a Lakeland Industries Museum, a Countryside Museum, a Lakeland Motor Museum, a baby animal farm and a craft museum.

⑨ FLOOKBURGH

A thriving fishing fleet operates from Flookburgh, and its catches of flukes (the local name for flounders) gave the village its name. It is also an important centre for the local shrimping industry.

Flookburgh was originally granted a borough charter in the reign of Edward I, and the original charter can be seen in the parish church, which has a weathervane in the form of a fluke, or flatfish, crowning its massive west tower.

⑩ HUMPHREY HEAD

Most of the Morecambe Bay coast is low-lying, but the cliffs at Humphrey Head, between the estuaries of the Rivers Kent and

Playgrounds of the north, and a county town with a busy past

The northern end of Lancashire's coast, looking out across Morecambe Bay, still has much of the wild beauty of nearby Lakeland, while to the south a line of bustling popular resorts begins at Morecambe. An earlier and different type of prosperity is recalled by the elegant Georgian houses lining the narrow streets of the older parts of Lancaster, built when the town was one of the busiest ports in the whole of Britain.

① SILVERDALE

The village of Silverdale, once on the River Kent, was left high and dry in the 1920s when the river changed its course to reach the sea further westwards. The deep-water channel of the Kent is now 4 miles away, and it is hard to imagine that steamers once called at Silverdale with holidaymakers cruising from Morecambe.

The winding lanes round Silverdale give occasional glimpses of the sea, and the village is an excellent centre for walking. Paths lead through Eaves Wood, owned by the National Trust, and around Park Point and White Creek to Arnside.

The Victorian novelist Mrs Gaskell lived in Silverdale at the house called Lindeth Tower and Charlotte Brontë, as a young girl, stayed with friends in the village.

② JENNY BROWN'S POINT

A track from Silverdale leads down to the edge of the foreshore at Jenny Brown's Point, named after an old lady who lived on the shore in the 18th century. This was once a centre for copper smelting, but the only remains of the industry to be seen today is an old stone chimney stack.

The springy, close-textured grass is much in demand for garden lawns and bowling greens. There were plans during the last century to enclose large areas of the salt-marsh between Park Point, near Arnside, and Bolton-le-Sands to reclaim the land, in the manner of the polders which the Dutch have reclaimed from the Zuider Zee. A length of the old wall out on the mud-flats is the only remaining evidence of the £84,000 spent before the scheme was abandoned.

The bird reserve at nearby Leighton Moss is a northern outpost for bitterns and bearded reedlings, which breed mainly in East Anglia.

③ CARNFORTH

The town was once a busy industrial town with a steelworks which processed the

NOBLE CREST *Railway company crests were once as impressive as those of any noble family, as this crest at Carnforth's Steamtown shows.*

Cumbrian iron ore. This closed in 1931, but Carnforth remained important as a railway junction; the Furness Railway line diverges at Carnforth from the main London to Glasgow railway line to run along the Cumbrian coast to Carlisle, giving fine views of the coast and Morecambe Bay.

At Steamtown, signposted from the town centre, steam-engines are housed in Carnforth's old steam-engine shed. They are on view daily, and are used for regular main-line excursions.

④ BOLTON-LE-SANDS

This residential village overlooks the southern end of salt-marshes which attract wading birds and waterfowl on their early autumn migrations to the Continent. Behind the houses, on the inland side of Bolton-le-Sands, runs the Lancaster Canal, which originally connected Lancaster with Kendal on the edge of the Lake District.

⑤ HEST BANK

This residential suburb 4 miles north of Lancaster lies at the start of an ancient low-tide route across the open sands of Morecambe Bay to Kents Bank, near Grange-over-Sands. At one time the route ran all the way to Bardsea, near Ulverston. When it is safe, there are organised walks along the 11 mile route to Kents Bank, under the control of an experienced guide – an essential precaution in an area where the incoming tide can advance with terrifying speed and little warning. The walk should not be attempted without a guide. For bookings contact Mr C. Robinson, Guides Farm, Cart Lane, Grange-over-Sands (tel. 2165).

⑥ MORECAMBE

A 4 mile long promenade along the edge of Morecambe Bay is Morecambe's priceless asset as a holiday resort. The curving promenade gives a panoramic view across the width of the bay, from Piel Island to the heart of the Lakeland hills. Marine Road is lined with a cheerful bustle of hotels, guest houses, shops and seaside amusements.

Morecambe developed in Victorian times from three small fishing villages, as a resort for holidaymakers from the northern mill towns. Fishing boats still bob in the bay, providing a colourful spectacle as well as supplying whitebait, codling and shrimps, the local delicacy.

The Leisure Park has an outdoor heated swimming pool, paddling pools and sun-bathing terraces. The Superdome is a venue for indoor sports during the day and a variety of entertainments in the evening. Near by, on the old Stone Jetty, is Marineland, where trained dolphins perform daily in summer. There is an International Folk Lore Fiesta in August.

⑦ HEYSHAM

Modern Heysham is centred on the freight harbour from which ferries also carry cars and day trippers to the Isle of Man. The huge square block of Heysham's nuclear power station can be seen from as far away as Barrow, on the opposite side of Morecambe Bay.

Old Heysham, to the north, is a village of twisting narrow streets dating back to the 7th century. On the cliff above the village is the ruined chapel of St Patrick, only 28 ft long by 9 ft across, the sole surviving example of a Saxon single-cell chapel in England, having no partitions or porches. A few yards away are several ancient graves cut into the rock, shaped for the head and body with a socket to hold a wooden cross. When these graves were made, perhaps 1,200 years ago, they would have been covered by stone slabs.

LANCASHIRE LUNG *Morecambe grew with the industrial north, providing fresh air and fun for workers from the mill towns. Its promenade blazes with coloured lights in autumn.*

GRAVEYARD IN STONE *Their only roof the sky, these graves carved from the solid rock near the ruined St Patrick's Chapel above Heysham may date back to the 8th or 9th century.*

St Peter's Church, set among the trees on the headland overlooking the bay, has a Saxon west doorway and west window, and an early Norman chancel arch with mouldings representing ropes – perhaps because St Peter was a fisherman. The bellcote was added in the 17th century and the north aisle as late as 1864. Inside the church is a ridged or 'hog back' stone carved with a figure of a bear biting into each end, and Viking figures along the sides.

⑧ SUNDERLAND

This tiny hamlet stands on the western side of the River Lune, where the river broadens into Morecambe Bay. The only road into Sunderland is flooded at high tide, when the houses can be reached only by following a footpath which skirts the high-water mark. Yet 200 years ago this was the site of a commercial harbour, the base for ships sailing to and from the West Indies.

⑨ LANCASTER

In the middle of the 18th century, Lancaster was a busy port, trading with the West Indies and shipping more cargoes than any port in the country except London, Bristol and Liverpool. But its history goes back much further: the Romans built a fort on the hill overlooking a bend in the River Lune, and the Norman military engineers followed their example centuries later, when they founded a castle of their own, which still stands. The view from its tallest tower embraces a huge sweep of the coast and, on a clear day, extends as far as the mountains of the Isle of Man.

The castle has been a courthouse and prison for centuries. It contains Hadrian's Tower and the Witches' Tower where prisoners languished while awaiting trial and execution; they included the ten Lancashire witches convicted and hanged in 1612. On show are grim relics such as the clamp and iron used to fasten a criminal's arm while the initial 'M' (for 'malefactor') was burned into his hand; this was last used as recently as 1811.

The Georgian Old Town Hall houses the Lancaster City Museum and the museum of the King's Own Royal (Lancaster) Regiment, and the Judges' Lodgings on Castle Hill contain a Museum of Childhood which gives a fascinating glimpse of what it was like to grow up in old Lancashire. In the Market Square, Charles II was proclaimed king in 1651. A period cottage, 15 Castle Hill, gives a glimpse of the lifestyle of a modest household of the early 19th century.

St George's Quay is the centre of the old river port. Its tall, gabled, 18th-century warehouses have doors at top-floor level allowing goods to be raised and lowered with block-and-tackle. Near by is the Old Custom House, but although small craft are still able to moor there, the old port died because of the silting up of the navigable channel. Later trade was carried by the Lancaster Canal, which ran northwards to Kendal on the edge of the Lake District, and southwards to a new outlet nearer the sea at Glasson.

In Williamson Park, on the eastern side of the town, is the high-domed Ashton Memorial, built in 1909 by Lord Ashton in memory of his wife.

⑩ GLASSON

The Lancaster Canal meets the sea at Glasson's docks, whose cheerful bustle makes a happy contrast with the commercial decay of many other harbours on this coast. The harbour was built in 1783, and its docks were among the earliest in England to have lock-gates which could keep the water level constant as the tide outside rose and fell.

The original West Indies trade through Lancaster died early in the last century. Glasson is now an important boating centre, while its nearness to the M6 has revived the coastal trade, and small trading vessels are now using the dock again.

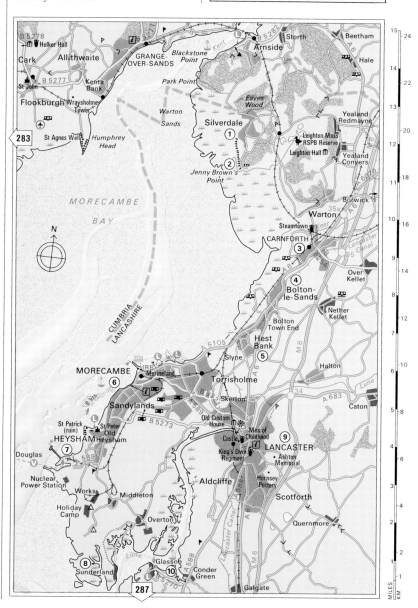

The Fylde peninsula, holiday mecca of the north-west

Between the estuaries of the Lune and the Ribble lies the broad, flat peninsula of the Fylde. Its sandy beaches are lined with holiday resorts, and its fertile farmland supports small but prosperous villages. Blackpool has elevated mass seaside entertainment to the level of a major industry. Its season has been carefully prolonged by the world-famous illuminations along the seafront, and by the fostering of the conference trade.

HEADING FOR THE SEA *Ostrich-feather hats and bowlers were the headgear for the day for a walk along Blackpool's North Pier in 1912, when the popularity of seaside piers was at its height.*

① THURNHAM HALL

The house, set in its park on the eastern side of the coast road between Lancaster and Preesall, dates from the 13th century. Because of the danger of raids from the sea the original building was a pele tower – a fortified house built as a single keep to defend its inhabitants against raids from across the border. A Tudor mansion was added in the 16th century, and more alterations and additions followed in later centuries.

The house fell into decay, but it has now been carefully restored. It has a fine Elizabethan hall, a Jacobean staircase and a priests' hide-out. A Gothic-style chapel houses a permanent exhibition based on a replica of the Holy Shroud of Turin.

Thurnham Hall was not open to the public in 1986, but there were plans to turn it into an hotel.

② COCKERSAND ABBEY

Some scattered ruins on the top of a headland projecting into the Lune estuary are all that remain of what was once one of the wealthiest religious houses in the north-west. The abbey was built in 1190, and its buildings covered at their greatest extent more than an acre. The surviving fragments of walls show the outline of the cloisters and of the chapter house which, built in 1230, was used 600 years later as the burial chapel for the Dalton family, who owned the abbey land.

Close to the chapter house is a stretch of beach with a small lighthouse and the walls of a fish-trap, built by the monks of Cockersand Abbey to catch salmon from the river estuary as the tide fell. Over the centuries, stone and other materials have been taken from the abbey ruins and incorporated in other buildings. Crook Farm, 2 miles north, has several windows and doorways which apparently came from the abbey.

In the nearby village of Cockerham, the church of St Michael has a 17th-century tower, but the rest of the church was built in 1910. The churchyard has many old gravestones, including that of a vicar who, at the time of the Great Plague, buried 11 of his parishioners in a single month before dying of the plague himself.

To the south-west of Cockerham lie Cockerham Marsh and Pilling Marsh. It is not safe to walk across the marshes, but a footpath from the ruins of Cockersand Abbey skirts the eastern edge of Cockerham Marsh before joining the main road. From the path there are views of the channels leading to the sea and the Lune estuary, and of the sea-birds which nest there.

③ KNOTT END-ON-SEA

A wide sandy beach, with stretches of softer mud, has made Knott End-on-Sea a popular resort. For the energetic, there are long walks along a footpath above the foreshore to Pilling, 2½ miles east, and upriver to Hambleton, 4 miles south. The foreshore walk is particularly attractive on a sunny evening at low tide, when the beach gleams like a sheet of gold.

④ SHARD BRIDGE

Drivers travelling from Lancaster and the North to Fleetwood and the northern end of the Blackpool beaches have to pay a toll to cross the Wyre between Hambleton and Thornton by this privately owned bridge, which marks the upstream limit for sailing boats on the Wyre. There is another toll bridge 4 miles upstream at Cartford Bridge, reached after a detour along winding lanes; the first free bridge is at St Michael's on Wyre, 2 miles further upstream.

⑤ THORNTON

Marsh Mill, built in 1794, stands 110 ft high beside one of the main roads through the town. The mill has not ground corn since the 1920s, but it is being restored to working order. On Sunday afternoons in summer visitors can see the four sets of giant millstones, 6 ft across, and the simple but solid engineering which produced hoists, shafts, gearwheels and drums from such woods as oak, apple, pine, beech, hornbeam and hawthorn.

At Stanah, at the north-eastern edge of Thornton, there is a large picnic area on the banks of the Wyre, with a slipway for dinghies and powerboats.

⑥ FLEETWOOD

The port established in 1836 became famous for its deep-water trawlers, which fished the distant waters of Iceland and the Arctic,

LYTHAM *High on the seafront, Lytham's windmill was well placed to catch the prevailing wind. Near by, the old lifeboat house is a reminder that the sea is also a force to be reckoned with.*

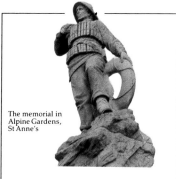

The memorial in
Alpine Gardens,
St Anne's

LIFEBOAT TRAGEDY RECALLED

The worst lifeboat disaster in British lifeboat history is recalled by a memorial in St Anne's. It occurred in 1886, when the St Anne's lifeboat answered a distress call from the German barque *Mexico*. In trying to reach the ship the lifeboat and her 13 man crew were lost, together with all but two of the 16 man crew of the Southport lifeboat, which had turned out for the same emergency. The double tragedy led to an improvement in lifeboat design.

before the 'cod wars' with Iceland dealt the industry a mortal blow. Nowadays, Fleetwood is increasingly busy with roll-on, roll-off container ships working in and out of the riverside docks, and plying to Northern Ireland and the Irish Republic.

The seaward face of the town is a popular resort, with a long promenade stretching as far south as Cleveleys, a swimming pool, a boating lake, and a regular service to Blackpool on one of Britain's few remaining tram networks. The broad, sandy beach provides swimmers with safe bathing away from the strong currents at the mouth of the River Wyre.

The Marine Hall, set in gardens on the seafront, offers a range of entertainments, and a model yacht lake said to be the largest in Europe. Fleetwood pier, built in 1910, serves mainly as a landing jetty, but there are amusements at the shore end. A model railway runs a service from the main car park to the Beach Road picnic site.

⑦ CLEVELEYS

Less bustling than its close neighbour Blackpool, Cleveleys is the northernmost point of 15 miles of intensively developed coastline. Like Blackpool it offers a sandy beach, where lifeguards patrol daily in summer. There are ample car parks, picnic sites, gardens and amusement centres, a miniature railway and a boating lake.

The neighbouring town of Thornton is notable for its 70 ft high Marsh Mill, a brick tower windmill built in 1794 and in use until 1922. It has been renovated in recent years and has its four sails, its fan-tail and four sets of millstones 6 ft in diameter. The mill is open to the public at certain times in the summer.

⑧ BLACKPOOL

Brash and cheerful, Blackpool stretches in a long, multi-coloured ribbon by the sea, punctuated by three piers and dominated by the steel finger of the Tower. Yet like many other British holiday resorts, Blackpool began as a small and undistinguished fishing village. In 1840 the seafront consisted of a single row of houses; but with the coming of the railway in 1846, the opening of Central Station and the North Pier in 1863 and the Winter Gardens in 1876, the town's future was established. The number of visitors increased from 3 million at the beginning of the present century to more than 8 million during the 1960s. Today it is estimated that around 6 million different people visit Blackpool each year; but because

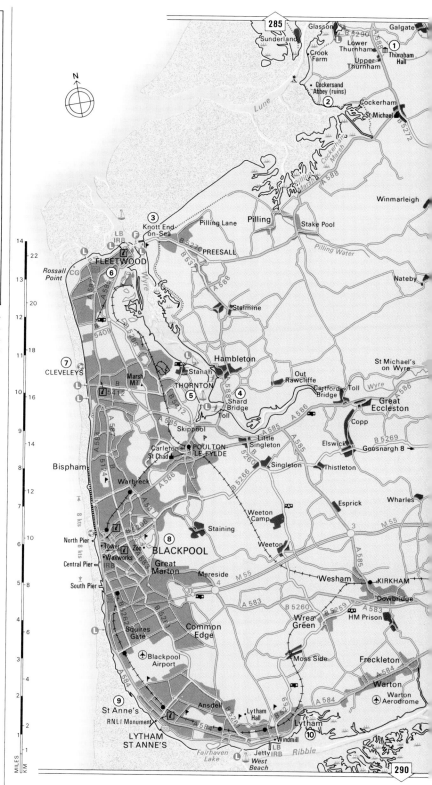

many people return time and time again, the total is about 16 million a year.

Present-day Blackpool is probably best known for its Tower, a landmark which can be seen from Cumbria in the north to the hills of North Wales to the south-west. Built in 1894, it was for many years the highest building in Britain; the 518 ft ascent gives a breathtaking view of Blackpool and the surrounding coast, and the Tower also houses a circus, a ballroom, an aquarium and an Educational Heritage Exhibition, as well as bars and restaurants.

Below the Tower is the stretch known as the Golden Mile – in fact more like a quarter of a mile in length. Freak-shows and fortune-tellers have been replaced by amusement centres, discos, bars, restau-

rants and a waxworks. Each of the three piers has its own theatre, providing live entertainment during the season. The 40 acre Pleasure Beach amusement park offers rides such as the first 360 degree 'loop the loop' roller-coaster in Britain, and tram services run the length of the 7 mile promenade and on into Fleetwood, turning inland to avoid breaks in the promenade. It is possible to walk the whole length of the seafront between Fleetwood in the north and Squires Gate in the south. During the autumn evenings, from September to late October, the whole front is ablaze with more than 375,000 bulbs, laser beams, animated displays and tableaux.

Other attractions include a Zoo Park, ice and roller-skating rinks, a boating lake, a

BLACKPOOL, THE SEASIDE TOWN WHERE FUN AND FRIVOLITY ARE BIG BUSINESS

Other resorts may be sunnier and more sophisticated than Blackpool, but Blackpool fears them not. Benidorm and Torremolinos have their anthill-like hotels and Spanish waiters serving cocktails beside oddly shaped swimming pools; Blackpool's boarding-house landladies have answered the challenge with a minuscule cocktail bar in the corner where the aspidistra used to stand, and paella on the menu once a week. And if some hotels have managed to squeeze a swimming pool into the back garden, the simple claim of '2 minutes from sea' is still attraction enough for most visitors.

Blackpool is an English tradition, and while its rivals have shaken off the braces-and-knotted-handkerchief image they have lost something of the informality that Britain's largest holiday resort still offers. It has kept abreast of the times with its discos, hot-dog stands and juke-boxes; but if the Victorians who created the place in the late 19th century could return they would still find Punch and Judy shows, seafront trams and horse-drawn carriages, splendid Gothic hotels and slender, iron-legged piers.

From its beginnings Blackpool has been the playground of the North. By the 1780s, well-to-do families from Manchester were arriving for the 'bathing season', and it was not long before day-trippers followed them; most came by cart, but some even walked 40 miles for a breath of sea air on Sunday. When the railway reached Blackpool in 1846 it brought the seaside within easy reach of millions of people in the fast-growing textile towns. From then on it was the Lancashire cotton workers who shaped Blackpool's character, making demands for fun that the town was quick to meet. Today, Blackpool is still the North's most popular resort, and millions return year after year. And more and more southerners are forsaking their traditional resorts, at least for a year, to sample the delights of this unashamedly vulgar curiosity somewhere north of Watford.

LANCASHIRE LANDMARK *For almost 100 years Blackpool Tower has been a landmark on the Lancashire coast, and a symbol of the Victorian determination to keep the town abreast of the times. Paris had its Eiffel Tower and Blackpool was not to be outdone, even though its tower is only half the height of its rival. It is the town's best-loved institution, most majestic in the autumn when it dominates the famous seafront illuminations.*

PLEASURES OF THE SEASIDE *For the young, a successful day by the sea depends on paraphernalia such as buckets and spades, moulds to make a giant sandcastle and windmills to spin in the breeze. Adults need nothing more than a deckchair on the beach, where sun is much more important than solitude. And after watching a confectioner deftly putting the lettering into a stick of Blackpool rock, what better souvenir could there be to take back to the folks at home?*

HIGH ENDEAVOUR *The Tower Circus opened its doors on Whit Monday 1894, and while many circuses throughout the world have long since struck their tents for the last time, Blackpool's high-wire artistes, stilt-walkers, jugglers and acrobats still draw crowds.*

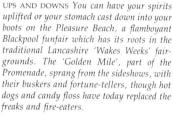

UPS AND DOWNS *You can have your spirits uplifted or your stomach cast down into your boots on the Pleasure Beach, a flamboyant Blackpool funfair which has its roots in the traditional Lancashire 'Wakes Weeks' fairgrounds. The 'Golden Mile', part of the Promenade, sprang from the sideshows, with their buskers and fortune-tellers, though hot dogs and candy floss have today replaced the freaks and fire-eaters.*

IN THE MANNER GRAND *The Tower Ballroom was built in the style of the Paris Opera, and its elaborate plasterwork, painted ceiling and sumptuous gilding set new standards for places of entertainment when it was opened in 1899.*

model village and golf courses. On the beach there are donkey rides, boat trips and Punch and Judy shows.

⑨ ST ANNE'S

The smaller scale and more peaceful seaside resort of St Anne's, the western part of the twin resorts of Lytham St Anne's, offers a quiet alternative to the brasher delights of Blackpool. The pier dates from 1885, but the pier entrance was built this century – a quaint, mock-Tudor building with gables and imitation timber framing. Solid red-brick Victorian and Edwardian villas and genteel private hotels face a broad stretch of sandy beach, which has become renowned as a centre for the fast and spectacular sport of sand-yacht racing. Beginners can take lessons before trying their hand at this exhilarating sport.

There is safe bathing for those favouring more traditional seaside recreation, and an open-air heated swimming pool. The Promenade Gardens overlook a boating pool, and there is a miniature railway.

In the centre of the town, close to the shopping centre, Ashton Gardens has tree-lined walks, wide lawns and a watercourse with rock pools and waterfalls.

⑩ LYTHAM

Lying at the eastern end of Lytham St Anne's, where the coast meets the estuary of the Ribble, Lytham is a town almost surrounded by golf courses. They include the Royal Lytham and St Anne's, used for major international tournaments, the Fairhaven and the Green Drive.

At the western end of the seafront is Fairhaven Lake, a large body of water used for yachting, motor-boating, rowing and canoeing. There are bowling greens and tennis courts near by.

At the eastern end of the seafront a large windmill stands on the wide expanse of Lytham Green, facing the Ribble. In 1929 a freak gust of wind set the sails spinning the wrong way, wrecking the machinery and putting a stop to the mill's working life.

Lowther Gardens, off West Beach, has flower beds, bowling greens, tennis courts and a putting green. There is an indoor swimming pool.

At the end of a long avenue is the late-Georgian mansion of Lytham Hall, built on the site of a farming cell belonging to the Abbey of Durham which passed to the Clifton family after the Dissolution of the Monasteries. The gateway of 1850 was built at the northern end of the town's cheerful market square, the centre of a thriving community before it found a new prosperity as a seaside resort.

The beach becomes muddier at the eastern end of the town, towards the Ribble estuary, where strong currents and fast-flowing tides make swimming and walking across the sands less safe than it is further west.

Grassy sand-dunes where sea-birds and swimmers throng

The marshes and saltings on the southern side of the Ribble estuary are the home of countless sea-birds and a regular stopping-off place for flocks of migrants. Further to the south, away from the mud-flats, quicksands and fierce currents of the river, the coast becomes sandier and safer for boating and swimming, and the holiday resorts of Southport and Formby reach almost to the northern fringes of the port of Liverpool.

① FRECKLETON

A large straggling village on the road which runs along the north bank of the River Ribble, Freckleton has a small brick church built in 1837 which has box pews and a lovely Jacobean pulpit which came from Kirkham church. The pulpit's eight sides are embellished with miniature, minutely detailed faces and the inscription: 'Cry aloud, spare not: lift up thy voice like a trumpet'.

On the marshland near the edge of the River Ribble a force of Roundheads under the command of Colonel Booth defeated the Royalists in the Battle of Preston in 1648, taking 1,000 prisoners.

② PRESTON

Over the centuries, Preston has had an importance far beyond its size. It was once a prosperous inland port, and though in recent years its trade has declined, part of the old port area is now being redeveloped. It was also an important railway junction, and its position midway between London and the cities of Scotland led to the building of hotels where weary passengers could rest before completing the second half of the journey.

Richard Arkwright, born in Preston in 1732, was the inventor of the spinning frame, an innovation which helped to make the town a centre for cotton-spinning for 150 years. It is still a busy industrial town with a modern shopping centre near the main street, Fishergate, whose modern shop fronts have been built on to Georgian, Victorian and Edwardian premises.

The treasures of the Harris Museum and Art Gallery in the Market Square include 19th-century water-colours by British artists, Georgian drinking glasses and costumes, pottery, toys and games from the 18th century to more recent times, Bronze Age burial urns and coins from a Viking treasure hoard found buried near a ford across the Ribble. The museum is an imposing building in the Classical style, built in 1893 with money left to the town by E. R. Harris, a local man.

Preston was the second oldest borough in England and has been represented in Parliament since the 13th century. It was given the right to hold a Merchant Guild, a form of regular market for merchants, under the charter of Henry II in 1179, and the Guild has been celebrated every 20 years since 1542, with only one break during the Second World War. The Fulwood Barracks, at the northern end of the city, is the home depot of the Queen's Lancashire Regiment and also houses the Regimental Museum with uniforms, medals and weapons dating back to the regiment's beginnings in the 18th century.

Hoghton Tower, 6 miles east on the road to Blackburn, is a 16th-century fortified manor house with a walled garden, an old English rose garden and a collection of dolls and dolls' houses. It is at Hoghton Tower that James I is supposed to have bestowed a knighthood on a joint of beef, to produce the cut known as 'sirloin'.

③ SOUTHPORT

From the point where the mud-flats and saltings of the Ribble estuary give way to the open Lancashire coast, a long stretch of flat, firm sand stretches as far as industrial Merseyside. On this wide beach is the resort of Southport, which despite a wide variety of modern holiday attractions still preserves much of the style and atmosphere of a Victorian or Edwardian watering-place. Its

ELEGANT PORTAL *An ornate canopy of glass and wrought iron has embellished a Southport shopping arcade since Victorian times.*

FORMBY DUNES *Driven sands, fashioned into ridges and soft contours by the changing winds, lie in the valleys of older dunes that tower above the solitary walker on Formby beach.*

HOW DUNES ARE FORMED

Dunes start to form when hardy plants such as sea rocket germinate on the strand-line. These check the movement of sand blown towards the land and allow the growth of marram grass, which forms a network of roots and also grows upwards, so trapping more moving sand. A new series of dunes often forms to seaward of the original dunes, protecting them and allowing other plants such as sea spurge to fill the gaps between the marram grass and complete the consolidation of the sand.

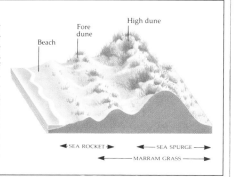

Beach
Fore dune
High dune

◄─SEA ROCKET─► ◄── SEA SPURGE ──►
◄─────── MARRAM GRASS ───────►

popularity goes back to the late 18th century, when William Sutton, an innkeeper in the village of Churchtown, used driftwood from the beach to build the first bathing house, in which people could change into the right clothes for a sedate paddle in the shallows.

The main street of the town, the elegant tree-lined boulevard of Lord Street, was built during the 1820s, and tablets honouring William Sutton can still be seen in the wall bordering the gardens at the junction of Lord Street and Duke Street. The promenade was added in 1835, and expansion has continued ever since. Now more than 300,000 visitors every year are attracted to Southport's sandy beach and its acres of sand-dunes.

Other attractions of Southport include the Pleasureland amusement park, a zoo, a model village, a Marine Lake covering 86 acres and a pier three-quarters of a mile long, served by its own miniature railway. The shopping centre of the town around Lord Street, where many of the shops are set under the cover of elegant verandas, has been designated a Conservation Area for the quality of its Victorian architecture. Steamport Transport Museum, in Derby Road, houses a collection of preserved railway engines and vintage road vehicles.

④ AINSDALE

So firm are the sands at Ainsdale beach that motorists often use them as a road along which to drive to neighbouring Southport. They have to observe a 10 mph speed limit, which is broken only when official motor races are held on the sands, or when light aircraft take off from them.

Behind the beach, a wilderness of dunes stretches all the way to Hightown to the

south and Southport to the north. A road curves through the dunes, following the line of an old railway, and the Royal Birkdale championship golf course lies to the east of the road. More than 1,700 acres of the dunes are nature reserves, with varied plant life as well as colonies of the rare natterjack toads and sand lizards.

The national nature reserve has 6 miles of marked paths, including the Fisherman's Path which leads to the shore from the car park near Freshfield Station. Visitors must keep to these routes, as the dune vegetation is fragile. A special nature trail is available to booked school parties in early summer.

Along the 4 miles between Ainsdale and Southport swimmers should stay in the areas marked by red and white flags. These are patrolled by lifeguards, some of whom operate from amphibious vehicles.

⑤ FORMBY

More than a mile of high sand-dunes separate the town of Formby from its beach. Two lanes lead to beachside car parks from which there are splendid walks with views of the ships entering and leaving the Mersey, backed by the distant mountains of North Wales.

Bathing from the sandy beach is only safe close inshore, because of strong currents further out at sea and the speed with which the incoming tide can cut off whole areas of beach with little or no warning. To the south, near the point where the little river Alt flows into the sea by Hightown, the dunes are used as firing ranges. Volunteer lifeguards patrol from Formby Point south to the Alt.

Formby began as a fishing and farming community, and had a lifeboat station as early as 1804; the station was closed in the

1920s when it was replaced by lifeboats further along the coast. Ironically, while many communities along this coast have lost their connections with the sea because harbours and estuaries have silted up, Formby has had problems persuading the sea to keep its distance. On the south-western side of the town, in the district known as Raven Meols, the sea has been steadily encroaching on the land for more than 700 years. In 1730 the 12th-century Formby Chapel had to be abandoned and a new church built inland, where the present town was established at a safe distance from the sea.

The building of the railway from Southport to Liverpool caused the town to expand quickly during the last century as a commuter town serving Liverpool, and few relics of the older Formby survive today. One exception is the church of St Luke, built on the site of a Norman chapel; it contains a Norman font with carving worn smooth by the sharpening of tools over the centuries, and a gravestone from York Minster which once covered the tomb of Richard Formby, of Formby Hall. Formby was armour-bearer to two kings, Henry IV and Henry V, in the early 15th century and stood 7 ft tall, earning himself the name of Richard the Giant.

In the churchyard is a cross which once stood on the village green. The hollows in the base of the cross are said to have once held vinegar, used to purify coins passing in and out of the village during times of plague.

Holiday towns and quiet glens on the Isle of Man's eastern shore

The Isle of Man is a self-governing part of the British Isles whose Tynwald is the oldest Parliamentary assembly in the world, having met regularly for more than 1,000 years. Only 32 miles long by 13 miles wide at its widest point, the island has cliffs and narrow glens plunging down to the sea on its eastern, western and southern sides. At the northern end it is flat and low-lying, behind a long sweep of beach backed by sand-dunes.

① BLUE POINT

A narrow turning off the coast road swings down the face of an ancient earthwork in a double hairpin to reach a small car park behind the dunes. The flat beach stretches for 12 miles south-west to just north of Peel and, to the north-east, for 5 miles past Rue Point to the island's northernmost tip, the Point of Ayre.

② POINT OF AYRE

The 4 mile stretch of coast between Rue Point and Point of Ayre is called The Ayres, from an old Norse word meaning a bank of sand or gravel. A road from the village of Bride leads after 3 miles to the lighthouse on the point, from which there is a wide view of sea and low-lying land round three-quarters of the horizon and, behind, to the frowning bulk of the mountains in the island's interior. The picnic site is a fine vantage point from which to watch the ferryboats passing between Douglas and Ardrossan in Scotland and Belfast in Northern Ireland.

Two miles west of the point, a turning off the coast road runs north to a car park near the sea, where a visitor centre and picnic site mark the start of the Ayres Nature Trail. The trail, arranged by the Manx Nature Conservation Trust, illustrates the geology and natural history of this wild and lonely part of the island.

③ RAMSEY

Set in the centre of the long sweep of Ramsey Bay, the town marks the transition between

---

CAT WITHOUT A TAIL

A cross between a cat and a hare was once thought to be the origin of the tailless Manx cat; but it is now known that the lack of a tail is due to a genetic mutation, deliberately preserved by human selection. The cat is unique to the Isle of Man, where it enjoys official protection. A cattery in Nobles Park, Douglas, maintains the breed.

The completely tailless Manx cat is also called a 'rumpy'.

---

the low-lying coast to the north and the cliffs which line the eastern margin of the island. The harbour formed where the Sulby River reaches the sea is packed with yachts and pleasure craft.

Ramsey is sheltered from the prevailing south-westerlies and has a mild climate – palm trees grow on the seafront – while two sandy beaches, one on either side of the river mouth, offer safe bathing. There is also good fishing from the pier, from the beach or from boats which ply from the harbour; catches include cod, pollack, flatfish, conger, dog-fish and mackerel.

The Mooragh Park covers 40 acres, which includes a children's playground and a 12 acre boating lake, where sailing boats are hired out and lessons given. The Albert Tower on the hill behind the town is named after the Prince Consort, and was built to commemorate the visit of Victoria and Albert to the town in 1847. The trams of the Manx Electric Railway run from Ramsey all the way to Douglas, through Laxey and Onchan.

④ MAUGHOLD HEAD

The pretty little village of Maughold is set back from the clifftops of Maughold Head. There is limited parking space near the entrance to the churchyard, from which a path leads to the top of the headland and the lighthouse. There are good views of the cliffs and coves of the island's eastern coast.

⑤ PORT MOOAR

A steep plunge down a narrow lane which leaves the main road half a mile south-west of Maughold leads to this deep, funnel-shaped cove in the cliffs, where the waves roll up a beach of smooth, sparkling pebbles. Cars can be parked on a broad grassy bank just above the beach, while the high ground behind it shelters the cove from all but south-easterly winds.

⑥ PORT CORNAA

This tiny but beautiful cove is not easy to find. Driving south along the Ramsey-Douglas road, look out for a pub on the right-hand side of the road about 4 miles south of Ramsey. On the other side of the road, a narrow lane descends steeply across a level-crossing, then loops back on itself before turning seawards through a deep tree-lined glen down to a pebbly beach flanked by cliffs. There is limited parking on the shingle bank which overlooks the beach.

⑦ DHOON GLEN

One of the most spectacular glens on the Isle of Man, Dhoon Glen is formed by a fast-running stream which cuts its way down through the cliffs to fall into the sea at Dhoon Bay. The path down to the shore crosses the fern-clad glen by a series of rustic bridges, passing two steep waterfalls, each of which drops 60 ft or more. For those who find the

---

GROUDLE GLEN *A picturesque cove, Port Groudle, lies at the mouth of Groudle Glen, where the rushing Ballacottier river tumbles through a fern-clad and wooded valley to the sea.*

STAR TURN *Laxey's water-wheel, the largest of its kind in the world, bears the three-legged symbol of the Manx coat of arms.*

climb back too steep, there is a less attractive but easier return path on the south side of the glen.

⑧ LAXEY

The compact little town has a working woollen mill and a tiny harbour, packed with yachts, which dries out at low tide. The short broad promenade overlooks a sand-and-pebble beach, with safe bathing away from the harbour mouth.

One of the Isle of Man's best-known sights is the huge Wheel of Laxey – a mighty water-wheel, also known as the 'Lady Isabella', which stands in a narrow river valley at the top end of the town. The wheel was constructed in 1854 to pump water out of the lead-mine workings under Snaefell, the island's highest mountain, and was named after the wife of the Lieutenant Governor who administered the island at the time. It has a diameter of 72 ft 6 in. and a circumference of 217 ft, and when running at top speed it turns through a complete revolution in 30 seconds.

On the opposite side of the valley from the wheel the Snaefell Mountain Railway runs in a long spiral up to the island's highest point, 2,036 ft above sea level. The half-hour journey ends at a spectacular viewpoint, but there is no access by road.

⑨ GROUDLE GLEN

Trains on the Manx Electric Railway stop at Groudle Glen, one of the island's best-known glens. Paths with bridges descend a narrow valley through groves of beech, larch and pine and past rocky cliffs and rushing rapids to a small stony beach.

⑩ ONCHAN

The small town of Onchan spreads around the rocky mass of Onchan Head at the northern end of the long sweep of Douglas Bay. Near by is the Summerland leisure centre, rebuilt after a disastrous fire in 1973. There is also an outdoor sports stadium. There are regular services to Douglas by horse-drawn trams, and the electric trams of the Manx Electric Railway pass through Onchan on their route between Douglas and Ramsey.

⑪ DOUGLAS

The island's capital and largest town spreads along the 2 mile curve of Douglas Bay, which forms a fine natural harbour. Ferries from England, Scotland and Ireland tie up at the docks at the southern end of the town, under the shelter of Douglas Head. The busy promenade overlooks a beach with sand exposed at low water. Among the unusual attractions of Douglas are its horse-drawn trams which in summer run the length of the promenade. The service began in 1876, and uses about 50 horses.

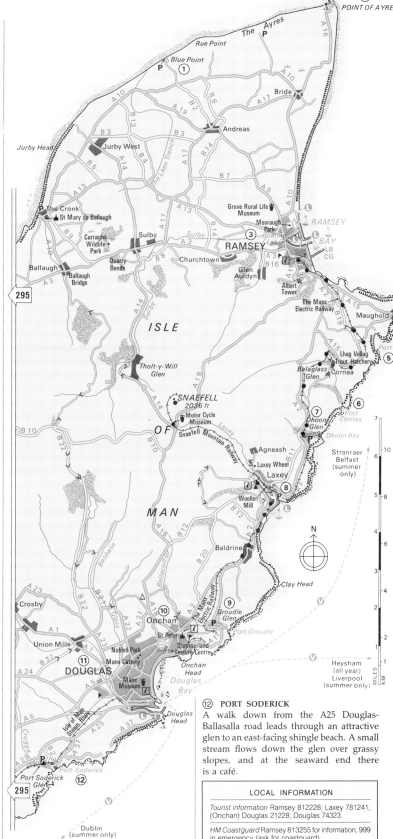

Near the harbour is the terminus of the Isle of Man Steam Railway, a 3 ft gauge steam-hauled line which runs to Port Erin on the island's south-west coast in summer. The railway was opened in 1874 and originally had branches from Douglas to Peel and from Peel to Ramsey.

The Manx Museum in Douglas has a wide collection covering all aspects of island life. In Nobles Park on the northern side of the town are the grandstands which mark the start and finish of the Tourist Trophy motor-cycle race course.

⑫ PORT SODERICK

A walk down from the A25 Douglas-Ballasalla road leads through an attractive glen to an east-facing shingle beach. A small stream flows down the glen over grassy slopes, and at the seaward end there is a café.

LOCAL INFORMATION

Tourist information Ramsey 812228; Laxey 781241; (Onchan) Douglas 21228; Douglas 74323.

HM Coastguard Ramsey 813255 for information, 999 in emergency (ask for coastguard).

Weather Castletown 823313.

Local radio Manx Radio, 219 m, 1367 kHz, 96.9/89.0 MHz.

PLACE TO SEE INLAND

Sulby Glen, 1 mile S of Sulby. Wooded glen.

HOW TO GET THERE

By sea. Isle of Man Steam Packet Company Ltd: car ferry Heysham-Douglas daily, except Sun. in winter; Liverpool, Belfast, Dublin, Stranraer to Douglas weekly in summer; Douglas 23344 or Heysham 53802.

By air. Airlines operate regular flights from London, Manchester, Liverpool, Glasgow and other cities.

The ancient Manx capital, and a town with a Viking past

The southern and western coasts of the Isle of Man are lined for most of their length with cliffs, broken here and there by glens cut into the rock by fast-flowing streams, and by small fishing harbours, rocky coves and sandy beaches. Exposed to the Atlantic weather, this side of the island is wilder than the eastern half. Towns such as Peel and Castletown still show signs of their Viking past, and from the mountain slopes there are views to Ireland.

CASTLETOWN SENTINEL *The medieval Castle Rushen stands on the site of an original Viking stronghold, overlooking the mouth of the Silver Burn and defending Castletown Bay.*

① BALLAUGH

Ballaugh Bridge is a favourite viewpoint for spectators on the northern part of the Tourist Trophy motor-cycle course. A turning north from the crossroads in the centre of Ballaugh leads, after 1½ miles, to a hamlet called The Cronk, which is notable for its old Church of St Mary de Ballaugh, which dates back to before the 13th century. From The Cronk a winding lane leads to a small car park beside an RAF radar site, on the edge of miles of sandy beach and lonely dunes.

At the Curraghs Wildlife Park, about a mile east, visitors can see the Manx tailless cats and the loghtan, or four-horned Manx sheep.

② GLEN MOOAR

A narrow lane off the coast road, nearly a mile south-west of Kirk Michael, leads to a small car park in Glen Mooar above the waterfall of *Spooyt Vane* – 'White Spout' in Manx. Above the west bank of the stream are the remains of a Christian chapel dating back some 1,000 years, with a hermit's cell called in Manx *Cabbal Pheric*, or 'Patrick's Chapel'.

③ PEEL

Even by Manx standards Peel is spectacular – an old fishing harbour, with narrow, winding streets is dominated by the vast fortress of Peel Castle on St Patrick's Isle. The so-called 'isle' is linked to the mainland and forms an arm protecting the harbour from the west. The castle stands on the site of a much older fortification which was captured by the Vikings in AD 798. Its main walls date back to the 14th century; within are a massive Round Tower and the ruins of the 13th-century St German's Cathedral.

On the eastern side of the harbour the town's promenade overlooks a sandy beach with safe swimming. There is good fishing for mackerel at the entrance to the harbour, or for mullet, skate, pollack, conger eel or flatfish from the breakwater beyond the castle.

Tynwald Hill at St John's, 3 miles south-east, was the meeting place of Tynwald, the ancient Viking Parliament of the Isle of Man. Tynwald still meets there early in July each year, to hear details of the year's new Acts read in Manx and English by the island's two Deemsters, or High Court Judges.

④ GLEN MAYE

The coast road running south from Peel leads into the steep, narrow valley of Glen Maye. In front of the Waterfall Hotel there is a large car park, from which a path leads down the glen and past a magnificent waterfall and a fast-flowing stream. A lane from the hotel runs parallel to the glen and

leads to a small park near to the point where the stream reaches a pebbly beach through steep, overhanging cliffs. The meeting place of the path and the lane is the starting point of another footpath which runs for 3 miles over Contrary Head, with marvellous views all the way.

⑤ NIARBYL BAY

A minor road leaves the main coast road at the village of Dalby and reaches the sea at a small parking area by a group of small cottages. The tiny, sheltered bay is guarded by a threatening promontory of rocks which projects out to sea and gives the bay its name, *niarbyl* being Manx for 'tail'. A footpath climbs round the cliff-face to the south, eventually reaching a lane at the top of the slope; this lane rejoins the main road 3 miles further south, near the summit of Cronk ny Arrey Laa.

⑥ FLESHWICK BAY

The turning to Fleshwick Bay, signposted from the main road, ends on a grassy slope overlooking a shingle beach amid clusters of rocks. The bay faces northwards towards the cliffs which line the coast all the way to Peel.

⑦ PORT ERIN

Sheltered by the high cliffs of two headlands, the small resort of Port Erin has gardens, tennis courts, seaside amusements and car and photographic museums. It is also the western terminus of the sole surviving line of the Isle of Man Steam Railway, which runs along the southern coast of the island to Douglas. The journey takes about an hour in each direction.

Exhibits at Port Erin's Railway Museum include the first engine to enter service on the line, the *Sutherland* of 1873, and the last, the *Mannin* of 1926. Carriages, signals, tickets and photographs are also on display.

A footpath round Bradda Head gives a panoramic view of Port Erin, while further round the headland there are magnificent views out to sea from Milner's Tower, and the area near the coastguard lookout. The path skirts the edge of Bradda Hill to the north, and eventually rejoins the road to Fleshwick Bay.

⑧ CALF OF MAN

The road from Port St Mary reaches the south-western tip of the Isle of Man at a car park on a grassy slope overlooking the treacherous, rock-strewn passage of Calf Sound. To the left is the massive cliff of Spanish Head; a footpath leads to its summit, from which there are fine sea

---

THRILLS ON TWO WHEELS

Early in June, 38 miles of Isle of Man roads are closed to ordinary traffic for the annual Tourist Trophy motor-cycle races. The gruelling course, which starts and finishes at Douglas, includes such testing hazards as the hump-backed Ballaugh Bridge, a sharp hairpin bend at Ramsey, and the twisting road over Snaefell.

Man and machine – one streamlined shape

views. Straight ahead are the islets of Kitterland, and behind them the now uninhabited island of the Calf of Man. This is owned by the Manx National Trust, and is a nature reserve for large colonies of guillemots, razorbills, kittiwakes and puffins. There are also smaller groups of hooded crows and choughs.

Boat trips can be made to the Calf of Man from Port Erin or Port St Mary when the weather is settled. In storms, these waters can be treacherous: the white stone cross on the edge of the cliffs commemorates the bravery of local lifeboatmen in the rescue of the crew of the French schooner *Jeanne St Charles* in 1858.

⑨ CREGNEISH

The little hamlet of Cregneish, midway between Port St Mary and the Calf Sound, forms an open-air folk museum of the old Manx way of life. From the car park on the north side of the main road, visitors walk into the village to a group of old thatched cottages which include a smithy, a weaving shed and a turner's workshop with an old treadle lathe. Harry Kelly's Cottage is a crofter's home built more than 150 years ago. Demonstrations of wool spinning and smithying are given regularly during the summer.

⑩ PORT ST MARY

Standing back-to-back with Port Erin, Port St Mary faces south-east from the shelter of the gap between the twin headlands of Kallow Point and Gansey Point. Once a fishing village, it is now a popular centre with yachtsmen, because of the good deep-water moorings close inshore, and with trailer-boat owners because of the easy launching facilities and sheltered waters. Two beaches of firm, dry sand offer safe swimming: Chapel Bay at the northern end of Port St Mary Bay, next to Gansey Point, and the wider sweep of Bay ny Carrickey, on the other side of the headland.

CREGNEISH COTTAGES *At a folk museum, homes of crofters and fishermen have been restored to show life in the 19th century.*

Paths lead westwards to the spectacular cliff scenery of Spanish Head and the Chasms, and eastwards to Black Rocks. There is good sea-fishing from boats off The Carrick and Langness, where a 16 lb brill caught with rod and line in 1950 established a new British national record.

⑪ CASTLETOWN

The narrow winding streets of Castletown seem to huddle for protection round the medieval fortress of Castle Rushen. Castletown was the capital of the island until 1874, and a building now occupied by the Castletown Commissioners was used for meetings of the House of Keys, the elected lower house of Tynwald, the Isle of Man Parliament.

On the edge of Castletown's picturesque inner harbour is the Manx Nautical Museum, where ships and models recall the time when much of the island's life depended on seaborne trade. Exhibits include the armed yacht *Peggy*, last in a line of clippers made in the Isle of Man in the 17th and 18th centuries.

⑫ DERBY HAVEN

This deep, curving bay faces eastwards, separated from the larger Castletown Bay by the rocky headland of Langness. Two viewpoints show the island's coastal scenery at its best: one is by the Dreswick Point lighthouse, and the other is at the north-eastern end of the headland, by the old fort on St Michael's Island.

At Hango Hill, on the road to Castletown, the ruins of an old summerhouse stand on top of a mound facing the sea. The mound became an execution site during the Civil War, when the leader of the local rebels who sympathised with the Parliamentary cause was shot there on the orders of the Stanleys, the Royalist owners of the island.

The name of Derby Haven is associated with the classic horse race. In 1627 the Earl of Derby, who then owned the island, organised a horse race along the greensward on the western side of the bay, in an attempt to encourage local horse breeders. The race was called 'The Derby', but it was a later Lord Derby whose name was given to the race run at Epsom for the first time in 1780.

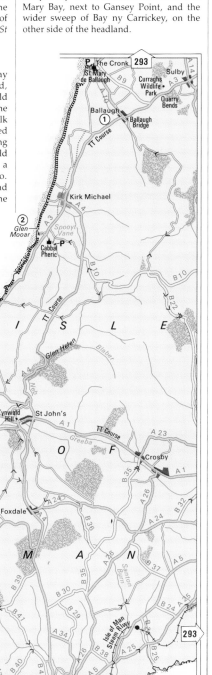

LOCAL INFORMATION

Tourist information Castletown 823518/822041; Port St Mary 832101; Port Erin 832298; Peel 842341.

HM Coastguard Ramsey 813255 for information, 999 in emergency (ask for coastguard).

Weather Castletown 823313.

Local radio Manx Radio, 219 m, 1367 kHz, 96.9/89.0 MHz.

PLACES TO SEE INLAND

Glen Helen, 4 miles E of Peel. Woodland valley. Daily.

Rushen Abbey, Ballasalla, 2 miles NE of Castletown. 12th-century remains, gardens, museum of archaeology. Daily in summer.

Liverpool, where the past survives in today's bustling port

Liverpool is still one of our busiest ports, shipping more cargo than at any time in its history. However, the shift of the main dock system downriver to new centres such as the Seaforth container-port complex means that many of the older docks are now quiet, and so more of the rich maritime history of the city can be appreciated. Several gaps in the miles of wharves and warehouses provide vantage points for watching river traffic.

Liverpool's liver bird carrying the 'laver' seaweed in its beak

① CROSBY

The original Crosby was the hamlet of Little Crosby, 1½ miles inland, which has changed little over the years; the Georgian Crosby Hall stands beside the old smithy and a group of 17th-century cottages. The name of the village comes from two Norse words meaning 'the place of the crosses' and one of these survives – a wayside cross used to mark a resting place beside an old 'church way', along which coffins were carried to the burial grounds.

Modern Crosby, which retains a sense of period charm, began in the district called Waterloo, at the edge of the sea. It was there that wealthy Liverpool merchants, anxious to escape the bustle of the city for the peace and fresh air of 'the seaside, built their houses. The area still has a strong Regency flavour, with terraces and crescents of late Georgian houses, wrought-iron balconies and verandas. Later settlers expanded Crosby inland, to make it a Victorian suburb of Liverpool.

The deep Crosby Channel runs parallel to the shore and less than a mile from the beach, and the district called Waterloo makes an ideal viewpoint for watching the busy river traffic. The sandy beach is safe for bathing, but small-boat sailors need to beware of the busy shipping lanes. The beachside Marina is a large enclosed stretch of water where beginners can learn to sail in safe surroundings. Other attractions include a model boating lake, a children's playground, a heated indoor swimming pool, and bowling and putting greens.

② SEAFORTH

During the 1970s Seaforth became the focus for the changes which totally altered the pattern of the Liverpool docks system as it had grown up in the last century. Seaforth Container Dock Terminal now handles the most modern cargo ships, including bulk-carriers of up to 75,000 tons each.

The road leading south into Liverpool provides a panorama of the older ways of cargo handling as it skirts the edge of the original dock system all the way into the city.

③ BOOTLE

If Seaforth presents a picture of the modern shipping trade, Bootle provides an immediate contrast. This is the Mersey of the past, with a long line of docks stretching along the river, protected by a massive granite wall like the battlements of a medieval fortress, an impression reinforced by the round gate pillars and the frowning bulk of the massive warehouses within. These were built between 1824 and 1860, and many of them are still in use. Gaps in the 18 ft high wall give glimpses of lock gates, swing bridges and merchant ships from ports all over the world loading and unloading.

Some of the dock basins have been taken over by ship-breakers, and the rusting, disembowelled skeletons of vessels being cut up for scrap point their ribs to the sky. Against this background, it is difficult to imagine that Bootle (the name comes from an old English word meaning 'dwelling house') was once a fashionable seaside resort like Crosby, until its new commercial role took over in the 1860s.

④ LIVERPOOL

When Chester was a thriving port, Liverpool was a small fishing village, but from the early 18th century, when the silting up of the Dee cut off Chester's trading lifeline, Liverpool began to grow into one of the biggest and most prosperous ports in the world. By 1880 lines of docks stretched for 7 miles along the banks of the Mersey, and 40 per cent of the world's trade was carried in Liverpool ships. Today much of this vast industrial system has fallen into disuse, with the shift to bulk-carriers and containerisation, and for the first time it is possible to take a closer look at this part of Britain's maritime history.

Liverpool Maritime Museum, opened in the old Liverpool Pilotage Headquarters beside the Pier Head, is the nucleus of a major preservation scheme for the old dock area. The museum houses a good collection of objects from the past, including the original builders' scale-model for the ill-fated *Titanic*, a Liverpool ship. There is a restored piermaster's house, and an exhibition recalling emigrants to the New World, including a reconstructed 'steerage' deck. Visitors can take in Albert Dock, built in the 1840s, and neighbouring Salthouse Dock, opened almost a century earlier.

A different viewpoint is obtained by approaching Liverpool from Birkenhead on the other side of the Mersey. The ferries unload at Pier Head, where disembarking passengers are faced by three massive buildings. To the left is the Royal Liver Insurance Company headquarters, crowned by the largest clock in Britain and by effigies of the mythical Liver Birds, which also appear on the city's crest. To the right are the Dock Board offices, and in the centre stands the Cunard Building.

Apart from regular ferry services across the river, there are frequent cruises up and down the Mersey. The wide, open area of the Pier Head is a good point from which to watch coasters, passenger boats, tankers and container ships making for the refineries of Stanlow and the entrance to the Manchester Ship Canal.

Inland from the waterfront, there are other reminders of Liverpool's maritime past. In an alley called Hackins Hey, off Dale Street, an inn called Ye Hole in Ye Wall was renowned in sailing-ship days, and the scene of at least one pitched battle between merchant seamen and the Royal Navy's press-gangs.

Liverpool became a city in 1880 and now has two cathedrals. The Anglican cathedral was originally intended to be larger than St Peter's in Rome, and even though the

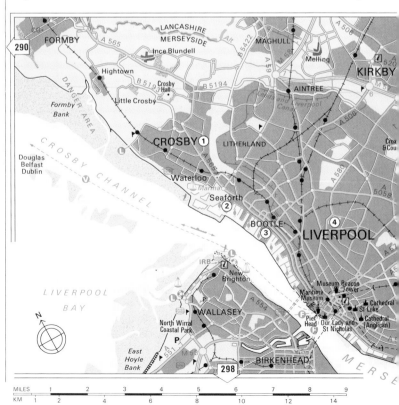

MODERN MERSEYSIDE *Giant container ships enter the vast Seaforth Container Dock Terminal through lock gates from the River Mersey, and huge cranes load and unload their cargoes.*

plans were later cut back, it still took 75 years to finish; it has the largest organ and the heaviest peal of bells in the world. At the other end of Hope Street stands the Roman Catholic cathedral, remarkable for its unusual circular design. Liverpool's original parish church of Our Lady and St Nicholas, close to the Pier Head and known as the 'Sailors' Church', was built in 1360. In 1810 the tower collapsed, and a replacement built the following year was the only part left standing after the air raids of 1941; the rest of the church was rebuilt after the war.

Liverpool has three major museums, a concert hall, three art galleries, and a planetarium.

⑤ OTTERSPOOL

What was once a riverside rubbish dump has been cleared, landscaped and transformed into a 3 mile long promenade with walks, car parks and a wide view across an open grassy slope to the Wirral shore beyond. Northwards from here to Liverpool's Pier Head, the old Southern Docks block public access to the riverbank.

⑥ SPEKE HALL

The Norris family built their magnificent half-timbered mansion 8 miles away from what was then the tiny fishing village of Liverpool. In 1490, when the house was begun, this involved a long and tiring journey over rough roads. The house was finished in 1612: its wings surround a central courtyard, and the entrance drive crosses

the old moat by a small stone bridge. It has a Tudor Great Hall, beautiful plasterwork and tapestries, and two ancient yew trees called Adam and Eve in the courtyard. Like many houses of its period, it has hiding places for priests escaping persecution, and it played its part in the Civil War.

ELIZABETHAN ARTISTRY *Speke Hall is a superb example of the South Lancashire and Cheshire style of 'black and white' timber-framed house.*

⑦ HALE HEAD

A by-road from the main Widnes to Liverpool road leads to the village of Hale. This was, in the 17th century, the home of the so-called 'Child of Hale', John Middleton, who was reputed to stand 9 ft 3 in. tall and was so

renowned a wrestler that local landowner Sir Gilbert Ireland sent him to London to fight the champion of James I. Middleton won, and retired to the village with a prize of £20; he was buried in the churchyard, and is commemorated on the sign of the village inn.

To the west of the church are the ruins of Hale Hall, which belonged to the Irelands. The southern façade was redesigned by John Nash, who built the Regent's Park terraces in London. A lane leads south from the village to the promontory of Hale Head and its disused lighthouse, overlooking a stretch of mud-flats and rock-strewn sand.

South of the headland the Mersey widens into its estuary, while upstream the view takes in the bowstring girder road bridge and stone railway viaduct which span the river between Widnes and Runcorn. Beyond the bridges, chemical works and refineries line the Manchester Ship Canal, and at night their distant lights form a spectacular horizon.

⑧ WIDNES

The Mersey narrows between Widnes and Runcorn, making this the first possible bridging point. Low land beside the river meant that considerable ingenuity in engineering was necessary to build bridges high enough to allow shipping to pass beneath. The London and North Western Railway carried its main line on a tall stone viaduct decorated by towers and battlements and approached by rows of arches. The original road bridge built at the beginning of the century was a transporter bridge, which carried traffic across on a gondola at ground level, slung from a deck supported between two tall towers. It was replaced in 1961 by an elegant bowstring girder bridge – at the time the third largest in the world.

Widnes has been a centre of the chemical industry since the first alkali works opened in 1847. The Victoria Promenade offers a breezy walk and a good view of the river bridges, unobstructed by the industry which lines the banks upstream.

⑨ RUNCORN

Separated from Widnes by the 300 yd wide River Mersey, Runcorn is another centre of canals and chemical plants. The old part of the town is almost encircled by a pair of canals, one built at the very beginning of the Canal Age – the Bridgewater Canal of the mid-18th century – and the other the Manchester Ship Canal, built a century and a half later to carry deep-sea ships all the way to Manchester Docks.

The road link from the bridge to the M56 gives a spectacular view of miles and miles of chemical works, which at night glitter with light on an extravagant scale. A mile to the north-east the ruins of Norton Priory stand in 7 acres of woodland gardens, with a museum and exhibition centre.

LOCAL INFORMATION

Tourist information Liverpool (051) 709 3631.

HM Coastguard Liverpool (051) 931 3341 for information, 999 in emergency (ask for coastguard).

Weather Liverpool (051) 246 8091.

Local radio BBC Radio Merseyside, 202 m, 1485 kHz, 95.8 MHz; Radio City IBA 194 m, 1548 kHz, 96.7 MHz.

PLACES TO SEE INLAND

Croxteth Hall and Country Park, 5 miles NE of Liverpool. Park, gardens and farm. Park daily; hall, farm and gardens daily in summer.

Prescot Museum of Clock and Watch-making, 8 miles E of Liverpool. Most days.

Pilkington Glass Museum, St Helens, 12 miles E of Liverpool. Daily.

Sandstone hills with a view of the Wirral's green fields

The Wirral peninsula, sandwiched between the estuaries of the Dee and the Mersey, is a green oasis separating the docks and factories of Liverpool and Birkenhead from the steel and chemical plants of the north-east coast of Wales. Seaside resorts such as New Brighton seem a world apart from the urban sprawl of Merseyside, while inland lie commuter villages whose rural peace is a complete contrast with the industrial areas around them.

① THURSTASTON
Thurstaston itself is little more than a tiny group of buildings just off the road from West Kirby to Heswell, centred on a church, a hall and several farms. But Thurstaston Hill, on the opposite side of the road, is a wilderness of sandstone rocks and sandy trails, ideal for children to wander in and for picnics. It is often used for orienteering events, and from its highest point offers fine views of the mountains of North Wales just across the estuary. On top of the hill is Thor's Stone, a 25 ft high pinnacle of red sandstone weathered into a rounded shape.

The road which leads through the village continues almost to the edge of the estuary, and its last stretch passes the site of the old railway station, now the centre for the Wirral Country Park. This is based on the route of the old branch railway line from Hooton, on the Chester to Rock Ferry line, to West Kirby. The route provides rare seclusion and glimpses of an amazing variety of bird, animal, plant and insect life. There are car parks and information centres at intervals, and one former station – Hadlow Road, on the outskirts of Willaston – has been restored as a reminder of what the line was like in the 1960s.

② WEST KIRBY
One of the problems with holiday resorts on the Dee estuary is that the sea recedes so far for so long. West Kirby solved the problem by trapping 32 acres of water in its own marine lake, where sailing dinghies, canoes, sailboards and rowing boats may be hired. Lessons are available, and with the necessary licence, obtainable at the Department of Leisure Services and Tourism in Hamilton Street, Birkenhead, visitors can use their own boats on the lake.

Walking on the sands can be dangerous, because of the speed of the returning tide. There is safer walking to be had in the Wirral Country Park, which follows the course of the abandoned West Kirby to Hooton railway line.

③ HILBRE ISLANDS
Hilbre Island and Little Hilbre Island are surrounded by a scattering of other rocks and islets, including Little Eye, on the fringe of the wide sandbank which stretches out from the Wirral shore at low water. This part of the estuary is a refuge for many different kinds of water birds – curlews, redshanks, ring-tailed plovers, knots, bar-tailed godwits, oystercatchers, dunlins and sander-

lings are all found here. Basking seals may occasionally be seen, and Hilbre Island is a nature reserve.

It is possible to visit the islands on foot: apply for a permit from the Department of Leisure Services and Tourism and follow the route shown on the map beside the lake entrance in Dee Lane. The walk takes 1 hour, and walkers should remember that the tide surrounds the islands 3 hours before high water until about 3 hours afterwards. There are no shops, toilets or even fresh drinking water on the islands, and little shelter against bad weather.

④ HOYLAKE
Best known as a golfing centre, Hoylake's name came from the Hoyle Lake, which was a broad, deep stretch of water sheltered from the open sea by sandbanks. When the Dee changed its course in the 18th century, with catastrophic effects on the harbours further up the estuary, the sand filled up the Hoyle Lake, creating the broad sandbank which stretches northwards from the promenade at low water, providing a beach more than 2 miles across.

Swimmers need to beware of sudden deep channels and pools in the otherwise flat sand, and bathing is dangerous near the harbour, where sailing boats tie up to moorings which dry out at low water. Volunteer lifeguards patrol the beach at weekends in summer, and daily during school holidays.

⑤ LEASOWE
Leasowe's lighthouse tower stands on flat ground behind a rampart of dunes and a sea-wall, but when it was built in the late 18th century this was a soft and treacherous area of shifting sand which was unable to support a structure tall enough to give ships warning of the dangerous banks and shoals offshore. In the end, it took a disaster to put matters right. It is said that in 1760 a ship loaded with cotton was stranded on the sands, and its cargo left to rot on what was then the beach. The tough cotton bales served to bind together the sand and the vegetation into a base solid enough to support a tower.

This whole area is now the North Wirral Coastal Park, in which shrubs and plants are being used to create picnic areas, and homes for wildlife. From Leasowe it is possible to walk along the coastal path as far as Hoylake promenade to the west, or, to the east, to the start of the New Brighton coastal defences and thence along the promenade wall as far as Wallasey. There is a sports centre.

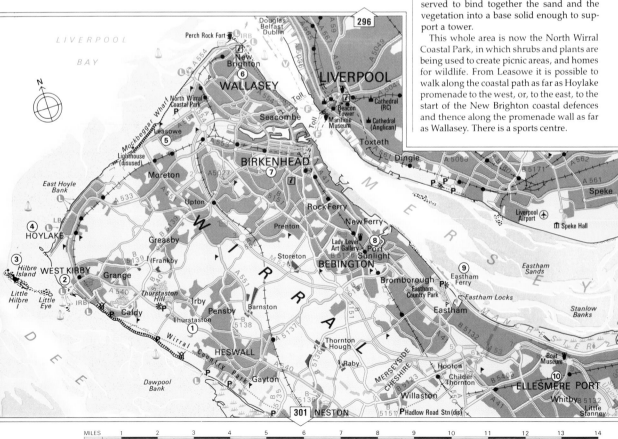

East of Helsby Hill the River Weaver winds lazily across a flat plain of patchwork fields, which contrast with the grey ribbon of a motorway and the distant towers and chimneys of industry.

LIFE ON THE NARROW BOATS

The brightly painted canal boats of the Ellesmere Port Boat Museum today lie at rest in buildings that were once part of the finest canal port in England. Thomas Telford, whose Ellesmere and Chester Canal formed part of the Shropshire Union Canal system, built the port in 1833 at the point where the canal met the River Mersey; it now joins the Manchester Ship Canal at the same point.

The port's main building was its Great Warehouse, shaped like a letter E with arches beneath so that the boats' cargoes could be hauled up directly to the first floor. The warehouse was burned down in 1970 but other buildings survived and were turned into a museum in 1976.

The museum contains a collection of more than 50 boats from the earliest type of canal craft to the Mersey flat boat *Mossdale*, built in the 1870s. There are also steam-driven pumping engines and a restored boatbuilders' workshop. On the canal, visitors can take a trip on a working narrow boat.

Narrow boats come ashore – and enter history.

The canal-boat painter says it with roses.

⑥ NEW BRIGHTON

New Brighton's fortunes have changed over the years. It grew to prosperity as a seaside resort because of the ferry connection from Liverpool, and in 1898 the New Brighton Tower was finished, the tallest structure in Britain and a prominent local landmark. During the First World War, however, it fell into neglect, and in 1921 it had to be demolished. Only the ground-level building was left as a theatre and ballroom, and this was destroyed by fire in April 1969.

Later, the pier which provided New Brighton's ferry-boat connection was closed and demolished. The sands were scoured away by changes in currents caused by the building of the container docks and terminal at Seaforth, on the opposite bank of the Mersey, leaving a rocky outcrop honey-combed with pools and slabs of slippery, weed-covered stone.

Bathing is dangerous along the foreshore, with sandbanks further out and strong offshore currents, and is recommended only in those areas marked with red and yellow

flags and under the care of the Beach Patrol. But the town still offers a wide range of seaside attractions from beauty contests to powerboat racing, with an outdoor swimming pool.

⑦ BIRKENHEAD

Birkenhead's once bustling docks traffic has declined in recent years, and a glance from any one of the three roads which cross through the dock area between Wallasey and Birkenhead will reveal more empty berths than full ones. But the town is still the focal point of a busy and prosperous Wirral, with attractions that include an indoor swimming pool, a theatre and several playgrounds and sports fields.

⑧ PORT SUNLIGHT

Naming it after the trademark of the soap which made him rich, Lord Leverhulme built this garden village for his workers in 1888, and created one of the most spectacular examples of enlightened town planning of his time. In the centre is the Lady Lever Art Gallery and, near the railway station, an information centre. In nearby Bebington is a sports centre with swimming pool, sauna and an artificial ski-slope.

⑨ EASTHAM FERRY

The first ferry between Eastham and Liverpool was Job's Ferry, run by a brotherhood of local monks, but regular ferry-boats plied between here and Liverpool, carrying passengers and freight from Chester and Shrewsbury, from the early 1800s until 1929. Since then, the commercial bustle has been replaced by an oasis of calm represented by the Eastham Country Park.

⑩ ELLESMERE PORT

Ellesmere Port came into being as the port where the original Ellesmere Canal reached the Mersey and eventually the sea, and it later became the hub of the whole Shropshire Union Canal system.

Thomas Telford built a magnificent set of warehouses and a complex of canal buildings for the port. Some of these buildings house Ellesmere Port Boat Museum, which is open daily, except Fridays in winter.

⑪ HELSBY

Helsby Hill, an outcrop of sandstone, rises steeply out of the flat lands bordering the Mersey, and offers wide views from its 462 ft summit of the refineries and chemical works along the river, and the greener country of the Wirral with, to the south, the Bickerton and Peckforton Hills. Near the summit is an Iron Age hill-fort, one of a chain of fortifications stretching right across Cheshire. There is limited parking alongside roads and lanes; the climb to the summit takes about 5 minutes, along well-marked paths.

LOCAL INFORMATION

Tourist information Birkenhead (051) 652 6106; New Brighton (051) 639 3929 (summer); West Kirby (051) 625 9441.

HM Coastguard Liverpool (051) 931 3341 for information, 999 in emergency (ask for coastguard).

Weather Liverpool (051) 246 8091.

Local radio BBC Radio Merseyside, 202 m, 1485 kHz, 95.8 MHz; IBA Radio City, 194 m, 1548 kHz, 96.7 MHz.

PLACES TO SEE INLAND

Chester, 7 miles S of Ellesmere Port. 14th-century cathedral, 18th-century castle and Cheshire Regiment Museum, medieval city walls, Grosvenor Museum of Roman antiquities, zoo and gardens, daily; King Charles Tower (Civil War displays), Water Tower (city history), daily in summer; Heritage Centre, St Michael's Church, daily.

Delamere Forest Trail, 6 miles SE of Helsby.

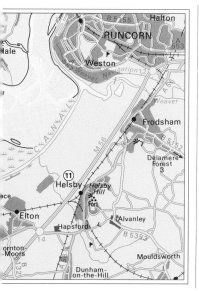

Holiday resorts on a sandy shore beyond the Dee estuary

Industrial Deeside offers little in the way of bathing beaches; even if there were no factories, the treacherous mudbanks and swirling currents of the Dee estuary would make swimming uninviting and dangerous. There are, however, ruined castles that tell of the turbulent past of this traditional invasion route between England and Wales, while Point of Ayr marks the eastern end of the busy holiday coast of North Wales.

① RHYL

Brash and breezy, Rhyl offers every kind of amusement and attraction, from bingo to windsurfing. The 3 miles of sand offer safe bathing, provided swimmers do not venture too close to the mouth of the Clwyd near the western end of the beach, especially when the tide is going out. Tidal currents scour deep channels parallel to the shore between sandbanks, so it is wise to stay close to the beach.

Foryd Harbour is the oldest part of the seafront, and provides moorings for yachts and fishing-trip boats. The town's pier has gone, and the old open-air swimming pool is now a fishing lake, stocked with sea trout; but there is an indoor heated swimming pool in the Sports Centre, and a surfing pool in the promenade Suncentre. Other attractions include a rink for roller-skating and skate-boarding, paddling and boating pools, the Butterfly Jungle and Ocean World, and a rooftop monorail in the Suncentre. Sailing dinghies, rowing boats, pedaloes and sail-boards can be hired on the Marine Lake, close to the harbour.

Rhyl's promenade runs all the way to Prestatyn where it joins up with a newer stretch of coast defences, providing a continuous walk of more than 5 miles along the shore.

② PRESTATYN

Prestatyn's beaches divide into three main areas. On Ffrith Beach to the west, near the boundary with Rhyl, steep dunes overlook the low stone sea-wall and the ranks of wooden groynes, or breakwaters, which stabilise the broad sweep of sand. A large amusement park includes a motor-boat pool, and tracks for go-karts and motor-cycles.

Central Beach has the Nova with its restaurant, bars and indoor heated swimming pool and sun lounge, and ballroom and summer shows. The public can use the pool, where swimming lessons for children are available. Further east, Barkby Beach is backed by large holiday-village complexes. Pontin's Prestatyn Sands village has its own indoor heated swimming pool.

There is a nature trail over hillsides to the south of the town, where the Offa's Dyke Path to South Wales begins. Energetic walkers who prefer to stay within arm's length of the sea can follow the sea-wall to its end by the slipway outside the Grand Hotel, and then continue along the shore all the way to the beginning of the Dee estuary, by the old lighthouse of Point of Ayr. There are bracing walks over the hills inland from the town, towards Gwaensygor and Trelawnyd.

③ TALACRE

Talacre is a place of holiday camps and caravan sites, but the shore itself is guarded by a range of steep and wild sand-dunes. At the eastern end, near the Point of Ayr lighthouse, there are open views across the broad Dee estuary to the Wirral and Hilbre Island, and further along the shore to the Point of Ayr colliery, whose workings run out under the estuary for almost a mile. This pit, one of two working mines left in the whole of North Wales, is the site of investigations into the making of oil from coal.

④ MOSTYN

As the silting-up of the Dee robbed places such as Chester and Parkgate of their shipping trade, Mostyn became the last harbour in the estuary that sea-going ships could reach. Now occasional coasters call at this tiny harbour, close to the site where the old iron works has been replaced by modern small factories and workshops.

A mile and a half to the south-east is the dock at Llannerch-y-môr, where a former cruise liner has been permanently moored as a shopping and amusement centre, called the Fun Ship. Near by is a craft centre.

⑤ HOLYWELL

This small town overlooking the Dee estuary was best known in the Middle Ages for St Winefride and her well. Legend says that Winefride was beheaded by a rejected suitor, but healed and brought back to life by her uncle, St Beuno, in the 7th century. A well which sprang up on the site was said to have miraculous healing powers, and pilgrims came from far and wide to visit the spot; they included Henry V in 1416. The chapel and crypt were built soon afterwards by the Countess of Derby. The well, one of the traditional Seven Wonders of Wales, is a quarter of a mile north of the town centre, on the road to Greenfield.

The narrow valley this road follows down to the coast was one of the earliest sites of the Industrial Revolution, but it is now largely green and overgrown. On a hill to the right of the junction of this road with the coast road are the ruins of Basingwerk Abbey,

KING'S LODGINGS *Basingwerk Abbey, now in ruins, was used as a base by Edward I during the building of Flint Castle in the 13th century.*

founded in the 12th century. By the 15th century, its guests stayed in such numbers that meals, accompanied by fine wines, were served in two sittings, but the monks themselves were only allowed to speak to one another in a special room.

The Grange Cavern Military Museum, housed in underground limestone quarry workings off the main road in Holywell, has a collection of more than 40 lorries, jeeps, motor-cycles and armoured cars. Near by is a heated indoor swimming pool and children's playground.

⑥ BAGILLT

This stretch of coast is difficult and dangerous for boating, with its strong currents and shifting sandbanks, and impossible for swimming, with its muddy foreshore. Walkers and bird-watchers, however, can enjoy the miles of mud-flats and saltings reached by crossing the bridge at the site of Bagillt's old railway station on the still-busy main line.

⑦ FLINT

Flint's castle has a unique place in history: the first of Edward I's chain of castles in North Wales, it was set on the edge of the sea so that it could be kept supplied by water, and the keep is detached from the rest of the fortifications and surrounded by its own defensive ditch. It was at Flint Castle that Shakespeare portrays Richard II as being trapped by the usurper Bolingbroke and

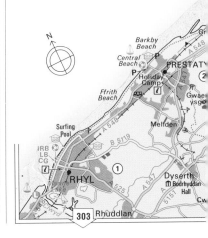

ANCIENT AND MODERN *Beyond Rhyl's harbour at the mouth of the River Clwyd stretches a holiday seafront where giant funfairs and a Suncentre rub shoulders with sedate Victorian hotels.*

Parkgate took over the packet trade with Ireland from Chester during the 18th century, and its promenade still has a fishing-village quality about it. The old harbour wall now overlooks acres of salt-marsh, covered by sea only at the highest tides, instead of the waters of the Dee. The marshes are feeding grounds for countless birds, and there are fine views across the estuary to the mountains of North Wales.

Nearby Neston, now a dormitory suburb for Merseyside, was the birthplace of Nelson's mistress, Lady Hamilton. The 19th-century parish church is notable for its stained-glass windows by Edward Burne-Jones.

⑪ HESWALL

Travellers who follow the A540 from Chester to West Kirby down the western edge of the Wirral will miss much of Heswall if they stay on the main road. The older part of the village lies at a lower level, closer to the estuary, with picturesquely winding streets, some inviting pubs and a craft centre.

Heswall has no promenade as such: instead several lanes lead down to the foreshore, each one ending in a car park from which the miles of saltings which edge the estuary can be explored. At the northern end are sewage works, but beyond lies an uninterrupted 4 mile walk along the foreshore to West Kirby. It follows the line of an old railway, now the Wirral Country Park.

---

forced to surrender as his prisoner though historians now believe the surrender took place in Conwy Castle. Today the dock and channel are silted up, and the castle is ruined and crowded in by the railway and later buildings. A market is held every Friday.

⑧ CONNAH'S QUAY

The advance of the sands along the Dee estuary, silting up port after port and shifting the centres of the coastal trade from Chester to the sea, can be measured by the rise and fall of each of the harbours along this section of coast. After Chester became unreachable by seagoing vessels, it was the turn of Connah's Quay, named after the 18th-century landlord of the local inn. But the sands blocked the harbour there too, and though it is just possible for shallow-draught boats to reach the jetty on high tides, the trade vanished long ago, first to Flint and then to Mostyn.

There is an indoor heated swimming pool in the Civic Centre, and the sports centre at the High School is open to the public outside school hours and during the holidays.

⑨ QUEENSFERRY

Queensferry marks the point at which the broad estuary of the Dee narrows down into the canalised section which was dredged in a vain attempt to keep the port of Chester open to shipping. There is a leisure centre with a large ice-skating rink, sports halls and a children's playground.

Near by are the ruins of Ewloe Castle, a Welsh fortress probably built by Prince Llywelyn the Last in the 13th century, and the Norman fortress of Hawarden, twice besieged during the Civil War. The nearby 18th-century Hawarden Castle was for 59 years the home of William Gladstone, Britain's long-serving Liberal Prime Minister during Victorian times.

LOCAL INFORMATION

Tourist information Birkenhead (051) 652 6106; Holywell 780144 (summer); Prestatyn 2484 (summer); Rhyl 31515 (55068 summer).

HM Coastguard Liverpool (051) 931 3341 (England); Holyhead 2051/3911 (Wales) for information, 999 in emergency (ask for coastguard).

Weather Liverpool (051) 246 8091/8093.

Local radio BBC Radio Clwyd, 457 m, 657 kHz, IBA Radio City, 194 m, 1548 kHz, 96.7 MHz; IBA Marcher Sound, 238 m, 1260 kHz, 95.4 MHz.

PLACES TO SEE INLAND

Bodrhyddan Hall, 4 miles SE of Rhyl. 17th-century manor and gardens. Some afternoons in summer.

Ness Gardens, 2 miles S of Neston. University of Liverpool Botanic Gardens. Daily.

Rhuddlan Castle, 3 miles S of Rhyl. Medieval remains. Daily.

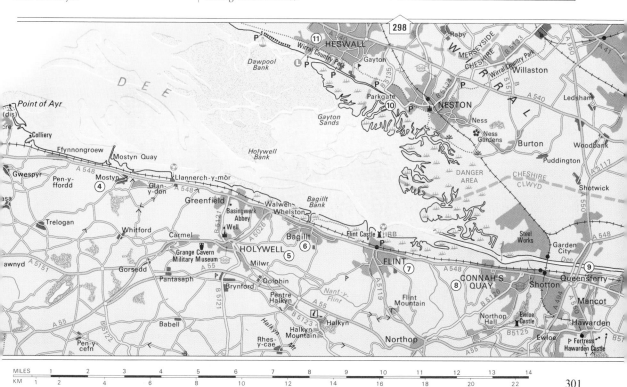

Castles, bays and beaches along the holiday coast of North Wales

This is one of Britain's most popular holiday coasts, studded with a chain of resorts ranging from quiet villages such as Penmaenmawr to the grander centres of Llandudno and Colwyn Bay. At Conwy, one of Edward I's great Welsh castles dominates the Conwy estuary. Inland the background varies from the rich flat meadows of the Vale of Clwyd to the towering peaks of Gwynedd, faced across Conwy Bay by the low broad back of Anglesey.

① LLANFAIRFECHAN

Before the building of the bridges over the Menai Strait, Llanfairfechan was the place from which intrepid travellers set out to cross the Strait. They faced a long and dangerous walk across the sweep of the Lavan Sands at low tide, until the deep channel brought them to a stop; their fate then depended on attracting the attention of the ferryman on the Beaumaris shore before rising waters made them retreat to safety.

Llanfairfechan offers safe bathing close inshore: but beware of the deep gullies scoured in the wide sweeping sand by tidal currents further out. Fishermen will find bass in these deeper channels.

The area is one for hill walking and pony-trekking, sailing and golf, bowls, tennis and minigolf. A walk along the embankment to the west of the main seafront on a fine summer's evening gives a splendid view of the sunset.

② PENMAENMAWR

A favourite holiday resort of Mr Gladstone, Penmaenmawr – the name means 'large stone head' – is squeezed between the mountains and the sea. The main coast road burrows through tunnels on either side of the town to find its way round the steep cliffs, and when Robert Stephenson built the railway line along this stretch of coast he had to protect it with avalanche shelters and a strong sea-wall. Even in prehistoric times, the tough local stone found a ready market; a historic trail leads visitors to a hilltop 1,200 ft above the town to the site of a Stone Age axe factory, whose stone tools have been found

as far apart as Wiltshire and Northern Ireland. Quarrying goes on here even today, and visitors can watch coasters being loaded at the nearby jetty. Bathing is safe, and water-skiing and sailing are popular.

③ CONWY

Probably the best-preserved medieval fortified town in Britain, Conwy's battlemented walls and narrow gateways constitute a major obstacle to holiday traffic threading its way along the North Wales coast. But the frowning bulk of Edward I's great castle, dominating the bridges across the Conwy estuary, makes an unforgettable composition.

Started in 1283, the castle was completed in 1292, as one of Edward's 'Iron Ring' of fortified places designed to keep the Welsh in subjection. Conwy's walls – up to 15 ft thick – and eight massive round towers were quickly needed, for the Welsh rose two years after it was finished and besieged King Edward in his own castle. In 1401 Welsh insurgents overran Conwy while its 75-strong garrison was at church. Held for Charles I during the Civil War, it was attacked and captured again in 1646.

There are three bridges: Telford's elegant suspension bridge, now used by pedestrians, Robert Stephenson's tubular railway bridge, and the graceful modern road bridge. Telford's bridge, opened in 1826, was designed to blend with the medieval turrets and walls of the castle, but the design of the railway bridge running alongside it was governed by practical factors. A suspension bridge would not have been rigid enough to carry railway tracks, so Stephenson used two rectangular iron tubes, each 424 ft long

and resting at one end on balls and rollers. The bridge was opened in 1848.

The enclosing walls have survived almost complete. So far it is possible to walk only a half mile of the ramparts, but they offer a fine view of the plan of the town's fortifications. Inside the walls are more than 200 buildings listed as being of special architectural interest. They include Aberconway House, which dates from around 1300, the Elizabethan Plas Mawr, Jacobean and Georgian houses and rows of early Victorian terraces. Down on the quayside is what is said to be the smallest house in Britain, measuring just 6 ft across and 10 ft 2 in. to the top of its upper storey.

Fishing trips and pleasure cruises up the river (which offer a spectacular view of the castle from water level) leave from the quayside, where boats land their catches of mackerel, plaice, whiting and the famous Conwy dabs. For bathing, strong currents make the estuary dangerous and it is better to make for Morfa Beach, 1½ miles north-west.

④ DEGANWY

Deganwy was originally called Dinas Conwy, which means 'fortress on the Conwy', and the hill above the village was fortified 600 years before Edward's castle was built on the opposite bank. It was fought over, destroyed (once by lightning) and rebuilt many times before falling into disuse, but even now it offers a splendid viewpoint of its later rival to the south.

As a holiday resort, Deganwy has the advantage of facing south-west, so that it tends to be sheltered, sunny and warm. There are good moorings for boats, fishing

---

TINY WINGS ON A HEADLAND

Along the cliffs of Great Ormes Head flits the dwarf grayling, a sub-species of the grayling that is found only in this part of North Wales. It is smaller than other graylings, with a wingspan up to 1½ in. (4 cm). It is also duller in colour and flies late in June, a little earlier than most English graylings.

Dwarf grayling
Hipparchia semele thyone   Wing underside

CONWY CURIOSITY *The tiny house on Conwy's quayside has only two rooms – cramped space for its last occupant, who was 6 ft 3 in. tall.*

307

MILES 1 2 3 4 5 6 7 8 9 10
KM 1 2 4 6 8 10 12 14 16

CONWY WATERFRONT *Fishing boats, fishermen and a quayside piled high with lobster-pots have a dramatic backcloth in the sombre grey walls of the most expensive of all Edward I's castles.*

trips and a shingle beach with stretches of sand at low tide. Bathing can be dangerous in the currents where the river reaches the sea, but is safer inshore.

⑤ GREAT ORMES HEAD

The larger of the two headlands which hold Llandudno's main curving beach between them like a pair of limestone bookends, the Great Orme's 679 ft summit is the easier to reach. Visitors can drive to the top from a branch of the toll road which runs right round its precipitous cliffs, or they can ride up in comfort by Britain's longest cable-car, which travels 5,320 ft, or by a funicular railway built in 1877. From the top, when conditions are clear, they have a splendid view of Snowdonia and even, on occasions, the hills of Cumbria and the Isle of Man.

On the sheltered eastern slopes of the Great Orme are the gardens of Haulfre and Happy Valley with splendid views over the town and the beach, while on the exposed northern face is the little church of St Tudno, after whom the town was named.

⑥ LLANDUDNO

One of the major holiday resorts of Wales, Llandudno owes its well-planned streets and wide promenade to Edward Mostyn and Owen Williams, who in the mid-19th century laid out a new town on former marshland below the Great Orme. Llandudno provides not one beach but two. On the side of the headland facing Conwy is West Shore, with a terraced sea-wall and a sand-and-shingle beach, backed by dunes. Bathing is safe at high water, but the sea recedes a long way at low tide, and venturing too far out on the sand could mean being cut off by the rising water. West Shore provides a children's playground and paddling pool and a putting green.

On the opposite side of the Great Orme is the North Shore, a 2 mile sweep of beach bordered by a promenade, with the pier at the western end and Little Ormes Head at the eastern end, where shingle begins to take over from the sand. Water-skiing, sailing and fishing trips are available from the jetty.

⑦ LITTLE ORMES HEAD

For those who find the Great Orme too crowded, commercialised and easy to ascend, Little Ormes Head offers the answer. Although only just over two-thirds the height of its larger neighbour, visitors must walk to reach the 464 ft summit, where they can enjoy the view in greater seclusion, over cliffs almost equally spectacular.

⑧ PENRHYN BAY

A long, sweeping, sand-and-shingle beach on the opposite side of the Little Orme from Llandudno proper, Penrhyn Bay offers interesting sand and rock pools with casting for mullet, plaice, flounders and, occasionally, bass, conger eels and rays, with prawns and mackerel in the offshore waters.

Lewis Carroll and some of his immortal characters – Alice, the turtle and the griffon

CREATOR OF A WONDERLAND

An association between Llandudno and the writer Lewis Carroll is commemorated by a statue on the town's West Shore, which depicts the White Rabbit from *Alice in Wonderland*. Lewis Carroll – the Rev. Charles Dodgson – was a friend of Henry Liddell, an Oxford dean, and records in his diary telling his stories to the dean's daughter Alice in a punt on the Isis. The Liddell family had a holiday home in Llandudno, and Lewis Carroll is believed to have stayed there as the guest of the Liddells and strolled on the sands with the real-life Alice.

⑨ RHOS-ON-SEA

Facing eastwards with a splendid view along the coast as far as Rhyl and the estuary of the Dee, Rhos-on-Sea marks the western end of the long Colwyn Bay sands. Close to the western end of the main promenade, where Rhos merges into Penrhyn Bay, is a tiny, stone-built chapel dedicated to St Trillo and once said to date from the 6th century, though in fact it was almost certainly built in the 16th century. The chapel, only 12 ft long and 6 ft wide, was associated with a nearby monastery, whose monks also built an ingenious fish trap out on the sands. The remains of the trap can just be seen at low tide: a set of roughly triangular stone walls, which formed an enclosure and caught unwary fish as the water level within them dropped with the ebbing tide.

Bathing is safe off a wide sandy beach, and there are sailing and water-skiing. A breakwater protecting the promenade opposite the Cayley Arms Hotel is accessible only at low water, and care should be taken to avoid being stranded by the rising tide.

⑩ COLWYN BAY

Colwyn Bay, together with its neighbours of Rhos-on-Sea and Old Colwyn, adds up to a sweep of 3 miles of sandy beach, with good, safe bathing, water-skiing, sailing and seaside amusements. The beach is bordered by a promenade and road, with two railway tracks: the main North Wales line of British Rail and a promenade miniature railway. In the centre is Colwyn Bay's pier, and overlooking the bay, at Eirias Park, are amusements including a heated indoor swimming pool, a leisure centre and a Dinosaur World.

Further up, on a hillside overlooking the town and the beach, is the Welsh Mountain Zoo, with varied animals, birds and reptiles.

⑪ LLANDDULAS

The village nestles beneath a new elevated section of the main coast road. Both the road and the main railway line have to squeeze into the narrow space between the hills and the sea, and still leave room for the limestone quarries from which the local

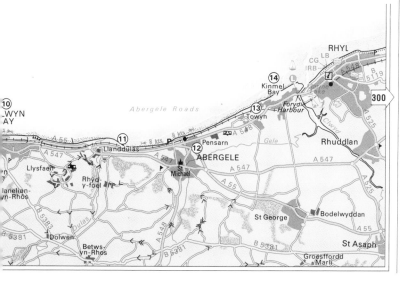

LLANDUDNO; A RESORT FASHIONED IN A GENTEEL AGE

From the towering crags of Great Ormes Head, Llandudno looks much as it did when frock-coated Victorian gentlemen escorted their wasp-waisted ladies along the broad promenade. The elegant, bow-windowed and balconied hotels are still there, lining a bay whose sandy beaches, spectacular views and glorious sunsets have attracted visitors for more than 100 years.

stone is shipped out in coasters which tie up at small jetties to the west. Station Road, from the centre of the village, turns back under the main road and winds down to a quiet, sandy beach.

In such tranquil surroundings, it is difficult to imagine Llanddulas as the scene of a terrible railway disaster in 1868, when a string of runaway wagons rolled down the hill from the quarry sidings, and the Irish Mail express ran into them. The wagons

were loaded with paraffin, the coaches of the express were lit by gas, and the passengers were locked into the compartments for safety; the result was that 33 people died, and were buried in St Michael's churchyard in nearby Abergele.

⑫ ABERGELE AND PENSARN
Abergele is a small market town 1 mile inland on the old coast road, with a livestock sale every Monday. Pensarn is the centre of a

7 mile stretch of beach, with shingle giving way to sand as the water recedes on the ebbing tide. It was at Pensarn that Captain Matthew Webb trained before becoming the first man to swim the English Channel in 1875. There are seaside amusements at the beach, and in Abergele there are sports facilities.

⑬ TOWYN
Finding the beach at Towyn depends on locating the gap in a long line of holiday camps and caravan parks where a road runs down to a level-crossing over the railway line. But there is good swimming off the sand-and-pebble foreshore, and there are seaside amusements near by.

⑭ KINMEL BAY

Situated at the easternmost end of the long coastal strip between Colwyn Bay and Rhyl, and separated from Rhyl only by the River Clwyd, Kinmel Bay has a popular sandy beach, backed by bungalows. There is good swimming along most of the beach. At the eastern end, however, the currents around the mouth of the Clwyd where it emerges from Foryd Harbour can be treacherous.

BEACH RIDERS *At Kinmel Bay, young riders on the beach enjoy one of the most enduring of seaside attractions.*

Across the Menai Strait to a fortress and priory on Anglesey

The turbulent waters of the Menai Strait and the wide sweep of Conwy Bay separate two very different landscapes: the low-lying hills and meadows of the isle of Anglesey, and the mighty mountains of the mainland of Wales. Old quarries and crumbling buildings bear witness to the industrial past, while brightly coloured sails and the white wakes of powerboats scarring the blue waters point to the tourist trade which has replaced it.

① RED WHARF BAY

When the tide recedes from this deep, curved bite into Anglesey's rugged coast, it leaves behind a vast expanse of sand, 2½ miles wide and 1½ miles across. The hamlet of Red Wharf Bay itself is at the western end of the cove. A row of cottages protected by a sea-wall marks all that is left of a once-prosperous shipbuilding settlement which made cargo vessels for the Anglesey copper-exporting trade.

There is a pleasant walk to the north, past the vast limestone bulk of Castellmawr ('Great Castle'), named after the ancient fort built on its summit, and round the headland. Southwards, too, walkers can follow the long, curving boundary between the sands and the low dunes inland. But the tide ebbs and flows quickly, and walkers who take a short cut across the often soft sands risk being cut off by the fast-rising waters. Swimmers need to beware of the strong out-going tide.

② PENTRELLWYN

The tiny hamlet stands above the more remote, eastern end of Red Wharf Bay, at the end of the road from the village of Llanddona. The beach can be reached down either of two, steep, narrow lanes which lead to opposite ends of a short, beachside track with a car park. Parking is prohibited on the beach and dunes.

③ PUFFIN ISLAND

The island, off the easternmost tip of Anglesey, owes its Welsh name of Ynys Seiriol to the saint who established a monastic settlement there 14 centuries ago; some of its ruins can still be seen. St Seiriol also had a chapel on the mainland, at Penmaenmawr, 5½ miles away across the waters of Conwy Bay, and was supposed to know a secret route across now-vanished sandbanks which connected the two places at low tide.

The island's English name comes from the colonies of puffins which breed here, survivors of much larger groups decimated over the centuries by rats, and by the local inhabitants, who once thought pickled puffin to be the tastiest of delicacies. Separated from Anglesey by a narrow channel, the island is private land; permission to land is obtainable from the Baron Hill Estate Office in Beaumaris.

④ PENMON

Penmon's ruined priory was the successor to a religious settlement founded in the 6th century by relatives of St Seiriol, who lived on nearby Puffin Island. The church was rebuilt in the 12th century, and some of the splendid Norman architecture still survives, while the other monastery buildings date from the 13th and 16th centuries. Among them are the ruins of a dormitory, the refectory, and the house of the prior.

MEDIEVAL LARDER *The dovecot at Penmon was built in about 1600 to hold 1,000 birds for the table of a local landowner, Sir Richard Bulkeley.*

A footpath leads to a hermit's cell and to a well said to have been used by St Seiriol for baptising pilgrims to Penmon. A toll road, which is free to pedestrians, leads to Black Point (Trwyn Du), with its old lifeboat station and castellated lighthouse; a mournfully tolling bell warns shipping away from the rocks which stud the channel between the point and nearby Puffin Island. There are spectacular views across the Strait to the mountains of Snowdonia, but the beaches are pebbly, with rock pools and strips of sand exposed at low tide, and the strong currents make bathing dangerous. There is limited parking.

⑤ BEAUMARIS

This elegant little town owes its name not to the Welsh, but to the Norman-French of Edward I, who built there the last castle in his chain of fortresses designed to control the turbulent Welsh. On the *beau marais*, or 'beautiful marsh', his engineers designed a magnificent fortress with concentric rings of defensive walls inside a deep moat, with a jetty which allowed the castle to be supplied from the sea. In the town is the Museum of Childhood, with collections of toys and games, which is open daily in summer.

The beach is mainly shingle, with stretches of sand exposed at low tide. Bathing is reasonably safe while the tide is coming in, but at other times strong currents make it dangerous. There is fishing from the pier for codling, whiting, pollack and bass.

⑥ MENAI BRIDGE

The town starts at the Anglesey end of Thomas Telford's magnificent suspension bridge, built in 1826 to carry his Holyhead Road over the swirling, treacherous waters of the Menai Strait. Fully rigged sailing ships could pass under the bridge's 100 ft high central span. The town is one of the centres of the Menai Strait regatta fortnight each August, and also host to the Ffair y Borth, one of the largest local fairs in Wales, which has been held each October for some 400 years.

For a spectacular view of the bridge – and the Strait – follow the promenade beneath the bridge along the Belgian Walk, built by refugees during the First World War. Near by is the handsome little 14th-century church of St Tysilio on Church Island, which can be reached by walking along a causeway exposed at low water. The Tegfryn Art Gallery shows work by local and national artists.

There is good sea-fishing from the shore or from hired boats for bass, conger eel, codling, pollack, flatfish and whiting.

⑦ LLANFAIRPWLLGWYNGYLL

Probably the only village in Britain to qualify as a tourist attraction on its name alone, Llanfair P.G. owes its tongue-twisting title to a decision taken in late Victorian times to blend the names of two neighbouring hamlets (in full: Llanfairpwllgwyngyllgogerychwyrndrobwll – 'The church of St Mary by the white hazel over the whirlpool' – and Llantysiliogogogoch, or 'The church of St Tysilio close to the red cave').

The magic still works: in 1973, in response to public demand, British Rail reopened the village's railway station, earlier closed as part of the Beeching cuts, and it still issues the largest platform tickets in Britain. There is a model railway exhibition, and there are links with an earlier form of travel in the old tollhouse, with its list of charges varying from fourpence for each horse pulling a carriage, to three-halfpence for a horse pulling a load of lime to be burned for fertiliser.

MOATED FORT *Edward I showed respect for his Welsh foes in the elaborate design of Beaumaris Castle. It was so powerful that it was never challenged, nor was the original plan completed.*

MEMORIAL TO A MASTER *Thomas Telford's 1,000 ft long Menai Suspension Bridge, built in 1826, is still in use today – a practical memorial to a master road and bridge builder.*

plant mentioned in the Bible which has been able to stand up to the Welsh climate; these range from the fig tree of the Garden of Eden to a Judas tree, named because it was said to be the tree from which the betrayer of Jesus hanged himself.

Another section of Bishop's Garden has trees and shrubs associated with the festivals and saints of the medieval church, such as the Glastonbury Thorn and the Royal Fern of St Matthias.

The Museum of Welsh Antiquities covers the development of North Wales from prehistoric times to the present day. Bangor also has an art gallery, a theatre and a heated indoor swimming pool.

⑩ PENRHYN CASTLE

This vast and elaborate 19th-century idea of what a medieval castle ought to look like was built by the architect Thomas Hopper for the Pennant family, and paid for by profits from the West Indies sugar trade and the wealth created by the family's slate quarries around Bethesda in North Wales.

Appropriately, the castle contains a slate Grand Staircase, a slate-floored Great Hall, a slate billiard table, several slate fireplaces and a slate bed. There is also a doll museum with more than 1,000 dolls, and a collection of industrial locomotives, some of them from the quarries which made the building of the castle possible.

⑧ PLAS NEWYDD

This splendid house was built by James Wyatt for the Paget family, later the Marquesses of Anglesey. The first Marquess was second-in-command to Wellington at the Battle of Waterloo, but was wounded by a French cannon-ball which shattered his right leg. The limb was amputated and replaced by an artificial substitute made of wood, leather and metal, which was known as the Anglesey Leg. The Marquess lived for another 39 years, joking that for all that time he was a man 'with one foot in the grave'. He is commemorated by a 100 ft column of Anglesey marble on the nearby hill of Craig-y-Dinas.

Those energetic enough to climb all 115 steps of the spiral staircase inside the column can find at the top the Marquess's statue and a stupendous view of Snowdonia and the Strait. The house is owned by the National Trust and has relics of the Marquess and of Waterloo, together with a collection of military uniforms, some beautiful gardens, and splendid views.

Near by is Britannia Bridge, built in 1850 by Robert Stephenson to carry two railway tracks, each one enclosed in an iron tube. In 1970 the tubes were damaged by fire and the bridge had to be closed. Eventually the tubes were removed and the bridge was reopened with the railway tracks supported on new arches between the original columns; above was added a new road deck to relieve the congestion on Telford's Menai Bridge.

⑨ BANGOR

The university and cathedral city on the Menai Strait dates back to the foundation of a cathedral by St Deiniol in AD 548, 81 years before the founding of Canterbury. Near the cathedral is the Gardd yr Esgob, or Bishop's Garden, notable for its collection of every

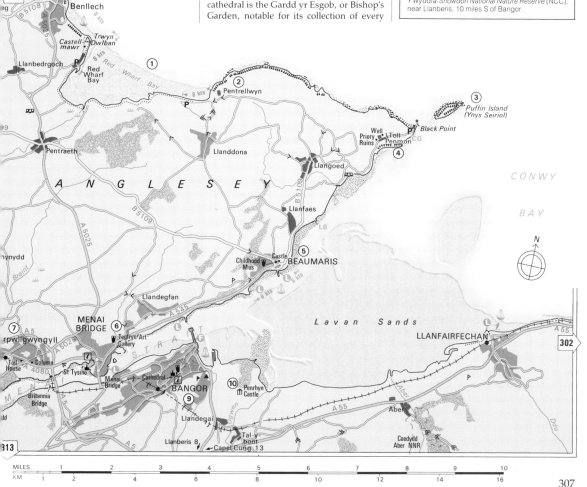

A maze of clifftop paths above sheltered Anglesey coves

Anglesey's northern and eastern coasts, notorious for their violent past of smuggling and shipwreck, offer shelter from the south-west winds that makes them ideal for summer-holiday resorts. There are many different coves and harbours, the more remote among them offering peace and seclusion. Above them, clifftop walks provide breathtaking views, and reminders of the peoples who lived on this coastline in earlier days.

LLIGWY BAY *The sea goes out almost half a mile at Traeth Lligwy, and gentle grassy cliffs shelter the firm low-tide sands from the prevailing westerly winds.*

① HEN BORTH

This tiny, remote cove with a sand-and-shingle beach is approached by a footpath from the right-angle bend in the minor road 150 yds back from the clifftop; there is limited parking on the verge. Because of its remoteness, it is often possible to find relative solitude at Hen Borth even on a sunny summer's day.

Mynachdy (Monks' House), half a mile to the west, is built on the site of an old monastery. Local legend says there is an underground passage from the monastery cellars underneath the house to a cave in the cliffs where the monks' treasure was hidden for safe keeping.

② WYLFA HEAD

Near the headland is one of the two nuclear power stations in North Wales (and the eighth built in Britain) – a 1,000 megawatt station providing electricity for North Wales and north-west England. The nuclear reactor needs 55 million gallons of seawater every hour to cool it. There is an exhibition and public observation tower on the edge of the site, and on weekdays throughout the year tours of the station start from the Information Centre. The headland is open to the public, and there is a waymarked cliff walk on the south-eastern side which starts from the power-station car park and takes about an hour to complete.

③ CEMAES BAY

Before Amlwch's harbour was built at the end of the 18th century, Cemaes Bay was the centre of the coastal trade in this part of Anglesey, and of the smuggling that went with it. Since then, the fishing trade has risen and then declined, to be replaced by tourism. Within the bay are no fewer than five beaches, three predominantly sandy and two with stretches of pebbles, but all providing safe bathing.

There are good cliff walks, too, westwards towards Wylfa Head and eastwards across cliffs owned by the National Trust, with superb scenery, to Llanbadrig. The clifftop church there is said to have been founded by St Patrick in gratitude for surviving a shipwreck on the Middle Mouse rocks just offshore.

④ PORTH WEN

This three-sided bay, a deep bite into Anglesey's northern cliffs, is more difficult to reach, and therefore more secluded, than most bays in the vicinity. Follow the farm road leading off the A5025 Cemaes to Amlwch road, and then the track down to the beach. The bay was not always so quiet, for the ruins on the western side of the cove are those of the once-flourishing Cemais Brick Works.

A clifftop path leads over the old hill-fort of Dinas Gynfor, perched on the northernmost headland of Wales, to the even smaller and lonelier cove of Porth Llanlleiana. The ruined buildings at the head are the remains of a china-clay industry once centred on Dinas Gynfor.

⑤ BULL BAY

Once a busy little shipbuilding port, and later a depot for the four-oared pilot boats which rowed out to guide incoming ships safely into harbour, Bull Bay has settled easily into a newer role as a holiday resort. The rocky beach offers plenty of pools left by the falling tide, and the cliffs contain sheltered coves and caves. Boats can be hired from the harbour. There are cliff walks with unrivalled sea views, fishing from the rocks for flatfish and codling, and an 18 hole golf course.

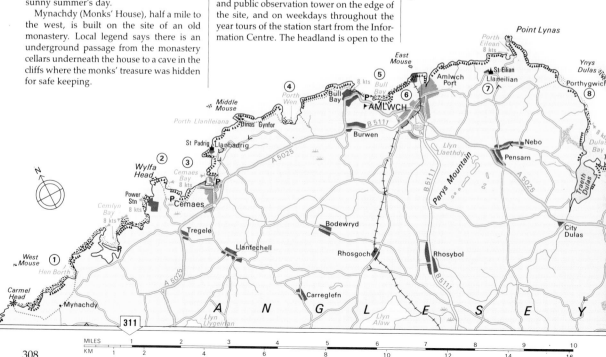

⑥ AMLWCH

At the beginning of the last century this was the busiest and most prosperous part of all Anglesey, with 1,500 men, women and even children toiling high on the lunar industrial landscape of nearby Parys Mountain to produce 80,000 tons of top-grade copper ore a year. So good was the copper that when the country ran short of small change at the end of the 18th century the Parys Mountain Copper Company minted its own coinage: 250 tons of pennies and 50 tons of halfpennies, each with the company's initials on one side and a Druid's head on the other.

The old port of Amlwch was built in 1793 to load the ships which took the ore all over the world, and the ruins of the warehouse, offices and smelting shops can still be seen on the quayside today. But by the end of the 19th century the boom was over, and falling prices, due to competition from American and African mines, caused the mines and the harbour to fall into disuse. Many ships were built at Amlwch, and the remains of the yards and slipways can still be seen.

Now the quays and the waters of the bay are busy again, with pleasure-boats and the traffic resulting from Shell's offshore marine terminal, from which supertankers can pipe their liquid cargo direct to Stanlow refinery in England. In the town is a sports and leisure centre with a heated indoor swimming pool.

Llyn Alaw, 4 miles to the south-east, is Anglesey's largest lake – 77 acres of water with fishing for trout and picnic areas on its banks.

A 'Druid' halfpenny from the mint at Amlwch

⑦ LLANEILIAN VILLAGE

The village is close to the cliffs of Point Lynas and to the pebbles, rock pools and firm sand which appear at low water in the little bay of Porth Eilian, lying below the road leading from the village to the Point Lynas lighthouse. The lighthouse, signal and telegraph station were established in 1835 by the trustees of Liverpool docks. Six-oared pilot boats used to be moored at the Point, and ships making for Merseyside still take on pilots here.

The village church is mainly 15th century, though the pepper-box tower dates from the 12th century and there was a church there for 700 years before that. Look out for the tongs, used for separating fighting dogs, the painted skeleton with the motto 'Colyn Angan yw Pechod' (The Sting of Death is Sin), and the chapel through the small doorway in the chancel. Inside the chapel is the wooden base of a panelled shrine with a missing panel. Traditionally anyone who can squeeze through and turn without touching the sides will have good luck.

⑧ PORTHYGWICHIAID

The shingle beach is one of several south of Point Lynas that can be reached only from the sea or by a 10-15 minute walk across fields. The footpaths leading to the shore start from narrow lanes where parking is difficult.

Ynas Dulas, about a mile offshore, is a rocky islet where many ships came to grief in the days of sail.

⑨ TRAETH LLIGWY

One of the wide, sandy beaches typical of the east-facing coast of Anglesey, Traeth Lligwy offers good swimming and plenty of space. To the south, a clifftop walk leads to Moelfre, while to the north a trek leads to a more secluded but equally sandy beach at Traeth yr Ora.

The lane from the southern end of Traeth Lligwy leading back to the main road passes two echoes of the remote past: the fortified village of Din Lligwy, dating back more than 1,600 years and one of the major native settlements of the Roman period, and the even older Lligwy burial chamber, a vast tomb which, when it was excavated in the early years of this century, was found to contain the bones of more than 30 people.

⑩ MOELFRE

The picturesque little village straggles along the edge of a rocky headland, which presents a dangerous obstacle to shipping in stormy weather. So Moelfre's lifeboat is justly famous, with almost 1,000 lives saved in 150 years. Its two most famous rescues occurred a century apart, to the very day.

On the night of October 25/26, 1859, a ferocious storm smashed 114 ships on to the rock-bound coast of Wales. One of them was the iron-hulled sailing ship *Royal Charter*, homeward bound from Australia to Liverpool with a cargo of wool, sheepskins and half a million pounds' worth of gold when she was driven on to an underwater ledge of rock just north of Moelfre. A sailor managed to swim to shore with a line, and the rescuers set up a breeches buoy on the cliffs; but before they could pluck the passengers to safety, the ship broke her back in the high seas. The sailors, the villagers and the lifeboat crew managed to save a dozen lives, while more than 400 men, women and children, many of them gold-miners and their families, were drowned.

Two-thirds of the *Royal Charter's* gold was later recovered. Two months after the tragedy Charles Dickens visited Moelfre and adapted the story of the wreck for a tale in *The Uncommercial Traveller*. There is a memorial to the victims in nearby Llanallgo Church, and another on the cliffs where the rescuers strove in vain.

On the 100th anniversary of the *Royal Charter* shipwreck, another local emergency had a happier ending, when eight crew members of the 650 ton coaster *Hindlea* were rescued by the Moelfre lifeboat, a feat which earned coxswain Richard Evans his second RNLI gold medal for gallantry.

Those who visit Moelfre in better weather can swim in safety from its pebbly beach. There are boats for hire, and the sheltered waters of the bay are popular among sailing and water-ski enthusiasts. There are splendid walks around the headland from the small car park at the end of the main street, with good views of the Anglesey coastline. Keen fishermen can try for mackerel from the rocks beyond the lifeboat station.

⑪ TRAETH BYCHAN

A small sheltered bay, flanked by rocks and banks of shingle, Traeth Bychan (small beach) is one of Anglesey's most popular places for small-boat sailing. The sailing club has a slipway, but there is a speed limit for powerboats in the bay. Swimming is safe close inshore, but beware of fast currents sweeping round the bay further out, especially when the tide is ebbing.

⑫ BENLLECH

A long stretch of beach is backed by cliffs which are studded with fossils – mainly corals, showing that this was once a subtropical sea-bed. Bathing is safe, as is boating in settled weather, for the island offers shelter from the prevailing south-west winds. Ramps lead down to the beach, and small boats can be manhandled across the sand. There are tennis and bowls in the village, and riding stables near by for exploring the area on horseback.

LOCAL INFORMATION

Tourist information Menai Bridge 712626.

HM Coastguard Holyhead 2051/3911 for information, 999 in emergency (ask for coastguard).

Weather Colwyn Bay 8091.

PLACE TO SEE INLAND

Llangefni, 9 miles SW of Moelfre. Open air market, Thurs; leisure centre, daily.

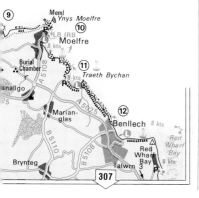

PROUD TRADITION *Moelfre lifeboat sits on its slipway, the latest in a line of vessels which have saved almost 1,000 lives from ships wrecked offshore during the last 150 years.*

An island lighthouse that marks the approach to Holyhead

The north-western coast of Anglesey is still surprisingly untouched by tourism. Tiny coves hidden below the cliffs and far from the nearest village are often difficult to find, and difficult to reach; but their remoteness ensures tranquillity even in the best weather and at the height of the holiday season. Holyhead Mountain looks down on one side to the port of Holyhead and on the other to the lighthouse set dramatically on South Stack.

① CARMEL HEAD

The headland was an important landfall in the days of sail. Anxious Liverpool shipowners could be reassured about the arrival of their vessels by semaphore messages passed from there, by way of Mynydd Eilian, Puffin Island, the Great Orme at Llandudno and Hilbre Island, off the Wirral, in just 5 minutes.

But the headland has its dangers too, three-quarters of a mile to the north-east lies the group of rocks called West Mouse, and 2 miles to the north-west are the Skerries, with their lonely lighthouse. This was built in 1841 to replace a fire in a brazier kept burning by a man and wife who lived out on the rocks to maintain this lonely duty. The lighthouse was once privately owned and ships paid a toll each time they passed.

There are boat trips to the islands in settled weather, and fishermen can try for skate, ray, tope, pollack and mackerel.

② CHURCH BAY

This beach, partly pebble and partly sand, can be approached by road as far as the car park at the top of the cliff. Small boats can be taken down the narrow, twisting track to the beach for launching. The bay offers safe swimming, against the dramatic backdrop of Holyhead Mountain across the water.

The bay owes its English name to the church which sits 200 yds from the top of the cliffs behind the bay. In Welsh, however, it is known as *Porth Swtan*, 'The Cove of the Swedes', suggesting that it was once a landing place for Viking raiders who plagued this coast in the Dark Ages.

③ PORTH TYWYN MAWR

A sweep of sand edged by dunes rather than cliffs, Porth Tywyn Mawr is also known as Sandy Beach, and is best approached along the track leading to Sandy Beach Farm from Llanfwrog. Parking is limited along the verge of the road, but the bay offers safe swimming and seclusion.

④ PORTH PENRHYN MAWR

This quiet shingle beach lies on the opposite side of Holyhead Harbour from the town of Holyhead. To reach it, take the minor road west from Llanfwrog, then instead of turning right for Sandy Beach Farm take the track straight ahead.

⑤ HOLYHEAD

Anglesey's largest town is called in Welsh Caergybi. 'Caer', or fortress, refers to the fort the Romans built here in the 3rd century AD, and 'gybi' is St Cybi, patron of the church which dates back 14 centuries, though most of the existing building is Tudor. There are links with the town's older past, too: the little church of Eglwys-y-Bedd (Church of the Grave) is supposed to contain the tomb of Seregri, leader of a band of Irish raiders who was killed in battle by the Welsh chieftain Caswallon Llawhir (Longhand) in the 5th century AD.

Holyhead's harbour was built a century ago. The massive breakwater, nearly 2 miles long and sheltering some 700 acres of water from the fury of storms from the north-west, took almost 30 years to build. A triumphal arch put up in 1821 commemorates the opening of Thomas Telford's road from London and the visit of George IV. The road was soon joined by the railway, and now the harbour sees a brisk trade in container traffic as well as passenger and car traffic to and from Dun Laoghaire and Dublin.

Salt Island, in the centre of the harbour, was named after an unsuccessful 18th-century experiment to produce salt from the sea. Between Salt Island and the breakwater, the shingly Newry Beach provides safe swimming close to the centre of the town.

⑥ HOLYHEAD MOUNTAIN

Despite its name, Holyhead Mountain is only 720 ft high, a mere stripling compared with the giants on the other side of the Menai Strait, but by far the highest land on Anglesey. Because of this, it offers splendid views in clear weather – as far as the Isle of Man and even the mountains of Ireland in the right conditions.

The mountain is also covered with evidence of centuries of man's occupation. Caer y Twr comprises the elaborate and massive defences of a 17 acre ancient hill-fort, while the Cytiau'r Gwyddelod (Irishmen's Huts) are the stone foundations of a village of circular huts which belonged to a group of skilled workers in wood and metal dating back some 1,700 years; the positioning of the massive stone slabs shows where the inhabitants placed their fires, their seats and their beds.

⑦ SOUTH STACK

South Stack is a tiny island off the north-western tip of Holy Island – itself an island off the north-western tip of Anglesey. It is joined to Holy Island by a small suspension bridge for pedestrians, at the foot of a steep flight of 350 steps down the cliffs, and is crowned by a 90 ft lighthouse, now automatically operated.

High on the cliffs to the south of the lighthouse is Ellin's Tower, built by the Stanleys of Alderley as a summerhouse, and now converted by the RSPB into a visitor centre for their clifftop bird sanctuary. From the sanctuary there are good views of guillemots and razorbills. A nature trail follows the cliff staircase, while further north the precipitous cliffs of Gogarth Bay, once popular for the hunting of gulls' eggs for the table, now offer a training ground for intrepid rock-climbers.

⑧ TREARDDUR BAY

A long, sandy beach with rocky outcrops offers good swimming. It is popular with skin-divers for the clearness of the water, and with surfers for the big rolling waves which sweep in when the wind is westerly. Sailing boats use the bay, too, while fishermen can expect tope and ray. At Towyn Lodge, on the south side of the bay, Thomas Telford stayed while supervising the building of the final stages of his London to Holyhead coaching road, the A5, in the early 1800s.

Porth Dafarch, 2 miles to the west, is another sandy bay that offers good swimming, and surfing when westerlies blow. It is popular among small-boat sailors and skin-divers.

⑨ RHOSCOLYN

A quarter of a mile from the village of Rhoscolyn, down a narrow, winding road, is

SEA-BIRD ISLAND *Choughs nest on South Stack, a rocky fist below cliffs towering 500 ft high. The lighthouse was built in 1808 by David Alexander, who also built Dartmoor Prison.*

HOLYHEAD FERRY *The first packet service to Ireland began in 1573, but Telford's road from London to Holyhead and the arrival of the London and North Western Railway gave it a new importance.*

hill-fort which stood on the headland overlooking the bay, and its English name of Cable Bay to the transatlantic cable which comes ashore here.

In calm weather, it is safe to swim off the rocks at the entrance to the cove at high tide, while more boisterous conditions bring in waves ideal for surfing. There is a car park next to the main road, and a path to Barclodiad y Gawres, an ancient burial chamber on the headland with elaborate Stone Age wall carvings.

a small picturesque, sandy bay called Borthwen or 'White Cove' with safe bathing, and a small car park. There are spectacular walks along the coastal cliffs to the west, to Rhoscolyn Head, the ancient sacred well of Ffynnon Gwenfaen, and on to the Bwa Du, or Black Arch. Fishermen can cast from the rocks for pollack and bass.

China clay was once quarried locally, and marble from nearby quarries was used in the building of Bristol, Peterborough and Worcester cathedrals.

⑩ RAF VALLEY
The airfield is an advanced training school for jet pilots and a base for part of No. 22 Squadron's search-and-rescue helicopters, which have saved numerous lives from sinking ships and sheer cliff-faces all round the North Wales coast. Inland emergencies are dealt with by the RAF Mountain Rescue Unit, which has its headquarters at Valley, and the seaborne arm of the Air Force is represented by rescue launches. Holyhead's coastguard cliff team are also involved in mountain rescue, covering the formidable cliff area of North and South Stack.

Visitors can watch the airfield at work from a viewing enclosure reached from near the railway bridge at Llanfair-yn-Neubwll. The road to Carnau leads to an even more spectacular view, from a parking area at the end of one of the runways. From there a footpath leads down to the shore at Cymyran.

The name Valley did not exist before 1822. It was created by Thomas Telford when, during the building of the A5 road, a cutting was made through a small hill. Excavations in the area during the Second World War disclosed by chance an Iron Age hoard of weapons which are now in the National Museum of Wales in Cardiff.

FLYING CLASSROOM *Two-seater Hawk trainers are used at RAF Valley, where pilots learn the skills of flying high-speed jet aircraft.*

⑪ RHOSNEIGR
Rhosneigr's neat, clean streets of whitewashed cottages give little evidence of its past. The village was once a shipbuilding centre for western Anglesey, while the Afon Crigyll, north of the village, was the haunt of the Wreckers of Crigyll, a gang so notorious

that a ballad was written to mark their trial at Beaumaris in 1741 and subsequent hanging.

Today the waters where the wreckers lured ships to their doom are crowded with sailing dinghies and fishing boats. The sandy beach, studded with rocky outcrops, offers good swimming and, when weather conditions are right, spectacular surfing. Riding stables offer a chance to explore the miles of gorse and sand-dunes of Tywyn Trewan Common on horseback. The name Rhosneigr is said to be derived from Rhos-y-Neidr ('Moor of the Adder').

⑫ PORTH TRECASTELL
A sheltered sandy cove between steep cliffs only a stone's throw from the A4080, Porth Trecastell owes its Welsh name to the ancient

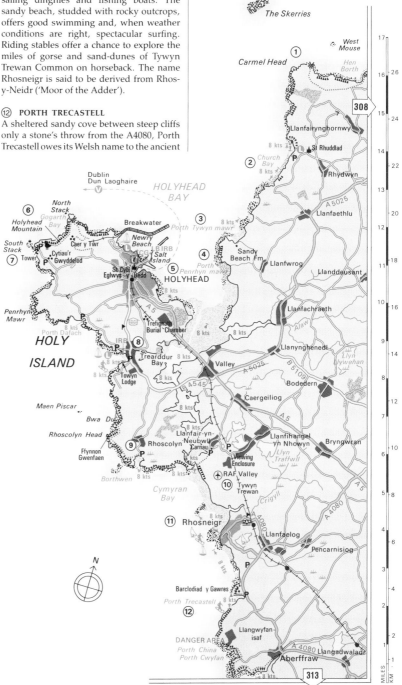

311

Dunes fringing a quiet land where Druids worshipped

At Anglesey's southern corner the land meets the sea in long beaches and ranks of dunes, with the towering mountains of Snowdonia on the mainland and the spine of the Lleyn Peninsula forming an impressive backdrop. Small villages dotted along the Menai Strait give fine views across to the stately walls and towers of Caernarfon Castle. Bathers should avoid the Menai Strait, because of its strong tide flow and undercurrent.

LLANDDWYN BAY *Sea, sand and solitude give enchantment to this southern corner of Anglesey, a lonely place where walkers can stroll for miles and bathers can swim from a gently shelving beach.*

① ST CWYFAN'S CHURCH
This little church, built 1,300 years ago and restored in 1893, has one of the most spectacular settings in Britain. Perched on a rock between two coves, Porth Cwyfan and Porth China, it can be reached by walking out along a causeway at low water. There is a road from Aberffraw, but cars cannot be driven right down to the coves. As an alternative, the 2 mile clifftop path from Aberffraw provides spectacular views all the way.

② ABERFFRAW
This picturesque little village became the capital of the Principality of North Wales in AD 870 under Rhoderic the Great, and remained so until Llywelyn the Last was defeated and killed by the forces of Edward I in the 13th century. No trace remains of the princes' castle, though a Norman-style arch in the church of St Bueno is said to have come from their palace. There is also an ancient packhorse bridge across the river next to the main road bridge. The beach, Traeth Mawr, is sandy and safe, and backed by miles of open dunes.

③ MALLTRAETH
Like many of the villages on the west coast of Anglesey, Malltraeth was sacked by Viking raiders in the Dark Ages. Another enemy, the sea, was kept at bay by Malltraeth Cob, an embankment built by the engineer Thomas Telford at the end of the 18th century to reclaim farmland. At one time,

Malltraeth was the centre of Anglesey's coal-mining industry, and its pits supplied the fuel for the copper mines at Parys Mountain, near Amlwch. It is possible to see the remains of one of the mines at Pentre Berw, 5 miles to the north-east, where the A5 crosses the edge of Malltraeth Marsh. The village also had a busy shipbuilding yard in the 18th and 19th centuries.

Downstream from Malltraeth, the north shore of the estuary is private land, but the opposite bank is now a national nature reserve, noted for waders such as red-shanks, greenshanks, lapwings and sand-pipers which use it as a staging post on their spring and late-summer migrations.

At the end of the estuary, the long sweep of Malltraeth Sands extends all the way to the rocky mass of Llanddwyn Island which, in spite of its name, is joined to the land by a causeway at all stages of the tide.

④ LLANDDWYN BAY
East of Llanddwyn Island, Llanddwyn Bay is bounded by a 4 mile stretch of sands, with spectacular views across to the mountains of Snowdonia, and backed by a vast stretch of dunes. The best way to reach the beach is to follow the road from Newborough through the Forestry Commission plantations and park in the picnic and parking areas at the end of the road, just a single row of dunes distant from the beach.

Llanddwyn Island is a nature reserve, but in earlier times was best known for the cross of St Dwynwen, who founded a convent

there after suffering a heartbreaking end to a love affair. She became the patron saint of Welsh lovers, and pilgrims flocked to the well she built on the north side of the island, and to the church built 1,000 years later on the site of her oratory. Beside the well is a rock which, according to legend, was split in two so that the dying St Dwynwen could use it as a seat from which to watch her last sunset.

More recently, Llanddwyn Island was important to seafarers: a stone tower built in 1800 provided a navigational mark, and a lighthouse was built in 1873 to replace it. Pilot boats were kept there, and the pilots' cottages are now used to display a traditional interior. Near by is the cannon which was once used to call out the Newborough lifeboat.

⑤ NEWBOROUGH WARREN
The Warren was named after its rabbit population; until the outbreak of myxomatosis in 1954, between 80,000 and 100,000 rabbits were caught there every year. At one time the area was rich agricultural land, but a series of violent storms in the Middle Ages blew so much sand ashore that the farmland was overwhelmed and turned into the biggest area of sand-dunes on the west coast of Britain. Elizabeth I introduced laws to encourage the planting of marram grass, which produced a local industry in mat, rope and basket making which survived until the 1930s.

Today, part of Newborough Warren is a national nature reserve, while another part is occupied by the Forestry Commission plantation of Newborough Forest. There are a series of trails across the wilderness. One of them is open to cars and starts from Newborough Village, passing through the forest to a car park a few yards from the foreshore of Llanddwyn Bay. The plantation consists mainly of Corsican pines and was begun in 1948 to prevent wind-blown sand blocking roads and covering crops.

⑥ TAL-Y-FOEL
At the end of a road leading from Dwyran to the edge of the Menai Strait, a group of cottages and a small sea-wall provide limited room for parking and an unexpected view of Caernarfon Castle on the mainland. For more than 400 years, from 1425 until 1849, a ferry ran from this point to the mainland.

For fishermen, the chances of bass and flatfish are good, and there are pleasant walks along the shore. Swimming is dangerous because of fierce currents.

⑦ MERMAID INN
An attractive little pub stands beside the remains of an old pier projecting into the Menai Strait. There is limited parking and a firm sandy strip of beach, though swimming is unsafe. Sea-fishing trips and fishing holidays are organised from the inn, and there are pleasant walks along the foreshore, with good views of the mainland mountains.

⑧ BRYNSIENCYN
East of the village, beside a bend in the lane which leads towards the Menai Strait and then swings back to rejoin the main road, is

Bodowyr burial chamber

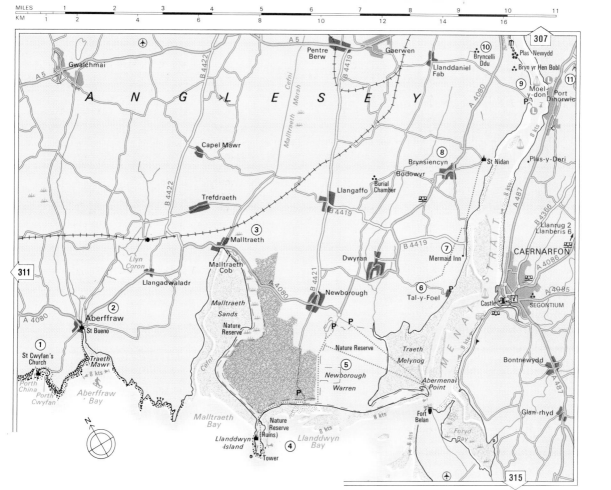

311

315

the ancient church of St Nidan, founded 1,300 years ago. Apart from an annual service the church is unused, but a stone in the rear porch traps water which is supposed to have healing properties.

Older still by some 3,000 years is the Stone Age Bodowyr burial chamber, to the north-west. Four stone uprights sunk securely into the ground form a framework which is crowned with a huge capstone, 8 ft by 6 ft. The builders dragged this capstone into place up a specially constructed earth slope. The entire chamber was originally buried under a vast earth mound.

⑨ MOEL-Y-DON

Another narrow road leading down to the edge of Menai Strait ends at the hamlet of Moel-y-don. There is parking in a field at the end of the road, with good views across the Strait to the mainland. The beach is muddy sand, with a strip of shingle at the high-water mark. At one time Moel-y-don was a thriving shipbuilding port, with a ferry across the Strait to Port Dinorwic; the timbers of one old ship still stand out of the mud at the harbour's edge.

⑩ BRYNCELLI DDU

Down a track to the east of the village of Llanddaniel Fab lies one of the best preserved Stone Age monuments in North Wales, a vast, chambered burial mound dating back some 4,000 years, crowned by a cairn which was originally 160 ft across. This was a centre of the Druids, whose religion was stamped out by the Roman invasion of Suetonius Paulinus, largely because it involved human sacrifice.

Another local monument, Bryn yr Hen Bobl, 'Hill of the Old People', on the other side of the A4080, was found to contain human skeletons, and many of the bones showed signs of cannibalism.

BURIAL MOUND *The Stone Age tomb at Bryncelli Ddu has a long entrance passage leading to a central chamber 10 ft long. In the chamber stands an upright stone, probably used in rituals.*

⑪ PORT DINORWIC

On the mainland side of the Menai Strait, Port Dinorwic was built as the outlet for the export trade from the great Dinorwic slate quarries in the mountains of Snowdonia. But the short-lived boom in the slate industry during the 19th century was only a brief episode in the story of a port whose history can be traced back to the 8th century, when Viking raiders used this part of the Strait as a secure anchorage.

Today, the old slate quays provide berths for pleasure craft within easy reach of the open sea beyond Abermenai Point. There are sailing schools, and sizeable yachts which can be chartered with or without skipper and crew, while fishing boats can take anglers within reach of bass and flounders.

At Plas-y-Deri, 1½ miles south-west along the shore of the Menai Strait, the National Outdoor Pursuits Centre, administered by the Sports Council for Wales, runs residential courses in sailing, sea and surf canoeing, climbing and mountain leadership.

LOCAL INFORMATION

Tourist information Menai Bridge 712626.

HM Coastguard Holyhead 2051/3911 for information, 999 in emergency (ask for coastguard).

Weather Colwyn Bay 8091.

PLACES TO SEE INLAND

Bryn Bras Castle, Llanrug. 4 miles S of Port Dinorwic. Early Victorian house. Most afternoons in summer, also mornings in Aug.

Llanberis, 7 miles SE of Port Dinorwic. Dolbadarn Castle, medieval castle remains, daily; Oriel Eryri, Welsh Environmental Museum, daily in summer; Padarn Country Park, lake and woodland walks, old slate quarry, daily; Llanberis Lake Railway and Snowdon Mountain Railway, daily in summer; Welsh Slate Museum, daily in summer.

Tranquil unspoiled bays near Caernarfon's mighty splendour

The coast of the Lleyn Peninsula which runs north-east to Caernarfon has a wild, remote feeling, with its secluded coves, ancient churches and tiny, slumbering villages as yet hardly touched by tourism. Prehistoric remains show that early men built fortresses in the area long before Edward I built Caernarfon Castle. In the Middle Ages, pilgrims passed this way when seeking to visit the tombs of the saints on remote Bardsey Island.

THE WELSH LANGUAGE

The Welsh are proud of their language, and understandably so since it is the oldest living language in mainland Britain, having been spoken for at least 1,400 years. It is a form of the language spoken throughout Britain before it was displaced by English. Many Welsh place-names are descriptive of their setting or physical features, and some common terms are listed below.

aber river mouth	*maen* stone
afon river	*maes* open field
bach small	*mawr* great
caer fort	*moel* bare hill
coch red	*morfa* marsh
croes cross or cross-road	*mynydd* mountain
	nant valley, brook
ddu black	*penrhyn* headland
dyffryn a valley	*porth* gateway, harbour or bay
ffordd way or road	
llan church	*traeth* beach
llyn lake	*ynys* island

① PORTH DINLLAEN

This beautiful little harbour, once the home of a small fleet of herring fishing boats, nestles among the rocks at the western end of the bay below Morfa Nefyn. Road access is restricted to the cars of residents and members of the local golf club; other visitors must leave their transport in Morfa Nefyn and walk down the private road leading to the village. At the end of the 1 mile walk they will find two tiny coves of silver sand, with beach huts for hire, and fishing from the shore. Bathing is good, except at the tip of the headland where there are strong currents.

So peaceful is Porth Dinllaen today that it is difficult to imagine that the village was nearly chosen instead of Holyhead as the road and railway terminal for the Irish ferries. In 1806 a company was formed to build a harbour, but two years later a Parliamentary bill to make Porth Dinllaen the packet port for Ireland failed to find support, and Holyhead was chosen instead. Rivalry flared again in 1837 with the arrival of the railways, and Holyhead gained the advantage with the building of the Chester and Holyhead railway. Porth Dinllaen formed its own railway company in 1844, but the line was never built and the village's hope of becoming a major port vanished.

② MORFA NEFYN

A long, curved sandy beach attracts bathers, and there is good swimming except at the western end of the bay where currents surge close to the rocks. Parking space is limited to the top of the cliffs, though boats can be launched from the ramp at the bottom of the narrow road down to the beach.

③ NEFYN

Nefyn was originally a fishing village, which in 1284 was chosen by Edward I as the site of a great tournament held to celebrate the downfall of Llywelyn the Last and the conquest of North Wales. In 1355 Nefyn became one of the ten royal boroughs in North Wales.

The long, crescent-shaped beach has firm sand with a strip of shingle behind, making it ideal for holidaymakers. Swimming is safe, and there are beach huts and chalets for hire. When the tide goes out there are rock pools, especially near the headland at the western end of the bay. There is limited parking space at the bottom of the road which cuts through the cliffs. Boat trips, fishing, sailing and pony trekking are available; and when the waves roll in from the north-west there is surfing in the bay.

④ PISTYLL

The church dedicated to St Beuno was a stopping place for pilgrims on the way to Bardsey Island, and possibly dates from the 6th or 7th century. It is beautifully sited in a grove of trees below the road. The stream which flows past the church leads to a long, mainly shingle beach.

⑤ YR EIFL

The name means 'The Fork', and describes the triple peaks of the mountains which straddle the road south of Trevor. In English this has become 'The Rivals', which suits the peaks just as well. The summit nearest to the coast is cut into a staircase of terraces by generations of granite quarrying on the seaward side, but the inland slopes, easily reached by footpath from a lane which leaves the road at the eastern end of Llithfaen, are crowned by the hut circles and ramparts of the hill-fort of Tre'r Ceiri (the Giants' Town). The massive stone walls, 15 ft thick in places, are built between natural rock barriers to encircle the remains of an Iron Age fort with some 150 stone-walled dwellings. The settlement was virtually impregnable, and flourished during most of the Roman occupation. In clear weather, there are awe-inspiring views across to Snowdonia and even the mountains of Ireland.

Hidden on the north-western side of the mountain is the valley of Nant Gwrtheyrn, named after the Celtic chieftain Vortigern, who fled there after losing his kingdom to the Saxons. At the seaward end of the valley, above the bay of Porth y Nant, a village built for workers in the nearby granite quarries but abandoned in 1959 has been restored as a centre for the teaching of Welsh and other Celtic languages. It can be reached by a steep path from the old quarry road north of Llithfaen.

⑥ TREVOR

Down a steep, winding lane from the village of Trevor is a small sand-and-shingle beach, on the edge of a harbour enclosed by a short breakwater and used until relatively recently for loading coasters with stone from the granite quarries on the slopes of Yr Eifl. Boats can be launched from a slipway.

Near by is the village of Llanaelhaearn, where local residents, alarmed at the pressures of rising unemployment and rural depopulation, have formed a crafts co-operative under the name of Antur Aelhaearn (Aelhaearn Adventure).

⑦ CLYNNOG-FAWR

This village of whitewashed cottages which straggles along the coast road has one of the best-known churches in Wales, founded by St Beuno in the 7th century, and a stopping place for pilgrims on the road to Bardsey

TOWERS OF STRENGTH *Queen's Tower and the three-turreted Eagle Tower are the most imposing of Caernarfon Castle's mighty fortifications overlooking the Menai Strait.*

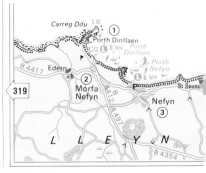

PORTH DINLLAEN *The sequestered charm of this sandy cove, with its neat cottages and waterfront inn, would cause no one to mourn the village's lost ambition to become a ferry port for Ireland.*

Island. St Beuno's Well is close to the roadside, and inside the church is St Beuno's chest, a wooden trunk which used to hold money paid by the owners of lambs or calves born with the mark of the saint upon them. The water from the well was believed to have curative powers, but sufferers taking the water had to complete the cure by spending the night on the saint's tomb.

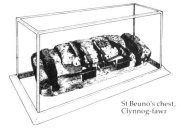

St Beuno's chest,
Clynnog-fawr

⑧ ABERDESACH

Aberdesach, like its close neighbour, Pontlyfni, has a pebble beach with a strip of sand exposed at low tide, close to the main road. Fishermen can catch bass from the beach in late summer and autumn. At Pontlyfni there is a self-catering holiday centre at West Point for rock-climbing, mountain walking, windsurfing and canoeing.

⑨ DINAS DINLLE

The holiday village is named after the hill-fort on the crest of a 100 ft hill, which dominates this otherwise flat stretch of coast. The fort was built long before the arrival of the Romans, and from its ramparts there is a clear view across to Anglesey and along the Lleyn Peninsula.

To the north is a 3 mile beach, a long sandy strip lined with a shingle rampart which protects the low-lying land from floods, and is itself backed with shops and bars. There is parking alongside the road, safe swimming and, if the right conditions are available, good surfing.

Off the coast, about 1 mile to the south, is Caer Arianrhod where on a map of 1573 a village was shown to exist. According to Welsh legend the village was the home of Arianrhod, one of the three most beautiful women in Britain. No traces of the village have been found, however, and all that is to be seen there now is a rock exposed only at low tide.

⑩ FORYD BAY

This wide, desolate bite out of the shore teems with bird life, mainly wildfowl and wading birds. There are patches of soft sand, mud and shingle, but bathing is dangerous because of quicksands in the bay and fast currents further out.

To the west of the bay, and reached by a road from Dinas Dinlle, is an old RAF station from which there are pleasure flights.

A bracing 2 mile walk north-eastwards along the foreshore leads to the end of the pedestrian lift bridge below the ramparts of Caernarfon Castle.

The splendid castle is one of the most powerful fortresses in the chain built by Edward I in the 13th century to keep the Welsh in subjection to the English Crown. The oldest part of the town itself shelters behind high walls that extend from the castle and enclose a maze of narrow streets lined with ancient houses, shops and inns.

Caernarfon was a fortified town long before Edward's time. Twthill is the site of a Celtic fortress dating from pre-Roman times, and the Roman legions built a fort at Caernarfon, which they called Segontium. The site, on Llanbeblig Road, still shows the remains of the commandant's house, the underground strongroom where the pay for the auxiliary troops who manned the fort was kept, and the regimental chapel where the eagle standard was lodged for safe keeping.

The Roman fort was built in AD 78, while Caernarfon Castle was finished 1,205 years later, having been 37 years in the building. The first ten years saw Edward spend the equivalent of £1¼ million in today's currency, but the resulting structure was well-nigh impregnable. It has only a single encircling wall, instead of the then-fashionable concentric rings of defences. But this wall was a warren of defensible passages; and the main or King's Gate was protected by a drawbridge and a succession of massive doors and portcullises, all covered by fire from many arrow loopholes.

The private apartments are unusually magnificent for a fortress – the Eagle Tower, which contained the lodgings of the castle's governor, dominates all around it. The reason is that the castle was designed not only as a strongpoint, but also as the centre of English government for North Wales.

It was at Caernarfon Castle in 1301 that Edward I proclaimed his eldest son Prince of Wales, a title that has been conferred on the male Heir Apparent ever since. In 1969 Prince Charles was invested with the title within the castle wall. An audio-visual display in the Eagle Tower tells the story of the castle, while the Queen's Tower, originally known as the Banner Tower, houses the museum of the Royal Welsh Fusiliers.

The castle still forms the centre for the life of the town. From the quay below the castle, there are boat trips up and down the Menai Strait, and on Castle Square in front of the battlements an open-air market is held every Saturday. In the square is a statue of David Lloyd George, the 'Welsh Wizard' who became one of Britain's most colourful prime ministers. Caernarfon also remembers Lloyd George in another capacity – as a Constable of the Castle and the town's MP for 56 years.

There is also an art gallery, an exhibition centre, a floating restaurant, and holiday centres for walking, rock-climbing, sailing, canoeing, riding and bird-watching. The fishing is excellent, especially for tope and bass, and there are bracing walks along the foreshore towards Foryd Bay and the open sea coast.

LOCAL INFORMATION

Tourist information Caernarfon 2232 (summer); Pwllheli 613000 (summer).

HM Coastguard Holyhead 2051/3911 for information, 999 in emergency (ask for coastguard).

Weather Colwyn Bay 8091.

PLACES TO SEE INLAND

Welsh Country Life Museum, Felin Faesog, Tai'r Ion, 2 miles E of Clynnog-fawr. Daily in summer.

Sygun and Nantmor Copper Mines, near Beddgelert, 10 miles SE of Caernarfon. Remains of disused mine buildings. Daily.

THE CASTLES OF WALES: FORTRESSES THAT RING AN INDOMITABLE LAND

Around the North Wales coast, from Aberystwyth to Ewloe, stand some of the finest medieval castles in the world. Some, like Ewloe, were the strongholds of the Welsh princes Llywelyn ap Iorwerth (Llywelyn the Great) and his grandson Llywelyn ap Gruffydd (Llywelyn the Last), but most are the so-called 'Edwardian' castles built by Edward I of England after his crushing defeat of the Welsh in 1282. With walls 15 ft thick, deep moats and fortified barbicans, Edward's castles are a tribute to the skill and ingenuity of their builders, but they are a tribute also to the fiercely independent Welsh they were intended to overawe. Only the strongest and most formidable castles were considered good enough to subdue the nation that had defied the Normans for more than 200 years.

Edward was a brilliant commander, and when he launched his armies into Wales in 1277 a series of swift victories brought Llywelyn the Last to his knees. A treaty agreed at Aberconwy stripped Llywelyn of most of his lands and left him Prince of Wales only in title. Five years later Llywelyn led a new revolt, but was killed in a skirmish near Builth. Determined to crush the threat of any further uprising, Edward built a chain of castles in Wales. Many of them were built on the coast so that they could be provisioned by sea, and each was situated and fortified in such a way that it could be held by a garrison of fewer than 100 men. No expense or effort was spared in building the castles, and their cost brought Edward to the verge of bankruptcy. But the fortresses served their purpose well, and never again was Edward's rule seriously threatened.

The castles of Wales saw action again during a new Welsh bid for independence, led by Owain Glyndwr, early in the 15th century. Glyndwr seized Harlech and made it the centre of his court for five years, before his rebellion was crushed. Conwy was also captured, but Caernarfon held out. The Wars of the Roses, 50 years later, saw Harlech as a Lancastrian stronghold, defended for eight years by the famed 'Men of Harlech'. During the Civil War, Aberystwyth and Beaumaris were among the castles held by the Royalists which surrendered to Cromwell's forces only when Charles I's cause was all but lost.

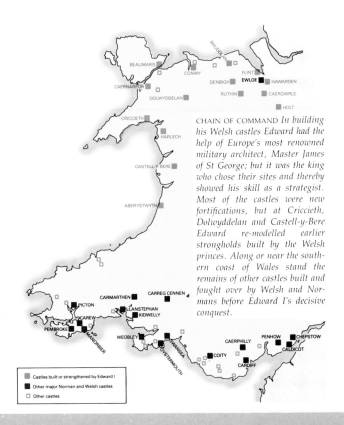

CHAIN OF COMMAND *In building his Welsh castles Edward had the help of Europe's most renowned military architect, Master James of St George; but it was the king who chose their sites and thereby showed his skill as a strategist. Most of the castles were new fortifications, but at Criccieth, Dolwyddelan and Castell-y-Bere Edward re-modelled earlier strongholds built by the Welsh princes. Along or near the southern coast of Wales stand the remains of other castles built and fought over by Welsh and Normans before Edward I's decisive conquest.*

■ Castles built or strengthened by Edward I
■ Other major Norman and Welsh castles
□ Other castles

KING AND ADVERSARY *When Edward I came to the throne in 1272 it was his ambition to unite Britain under his rule. He began by demanding loyalty from the Welsh leader Llywelyn ap Gruffydd, and when the proud prince refused, Edward launched his armies into Wales and quickly humbled the rebellious Welshman. But an uneasy peace ensued, and in 1282 Llywelyn, spurred on by his brother David, rose in revolt. The rebellion lasted eight months, and ended at Cilmery, near Builth, when Llywelyn was killed by an English trooper, Stephen Frankton, who ran him through with a lance, not knowing who his victim was. In doing so he dealt the cause of Welsh independence its death blow. Edward then proceeded to build a castle to dominate every area in which another uprising might occur.*

Edward I, king of England from 1272 to 1307.

Llywelyn the Last, defiant Prince of Wales, with fallen foes: a statue in Cardiff City Hall.

DEFENCE BY WALL AND WATER
New techniques in castle building made fortresses such as Beaumaris (above) virtually impregnable until the invention of the cannon in the 14th century. An aerial view of the well-preserved castle today shows its symmetrical design. Round towers gave archers an all-round view of the walls. The huge gatehouses to the inner ward were built out of alignment with the outer gateways; this meant that an enemy who breached one of the two outer gates would still have to cross the courtyard between the walls at an oblique angle, under intense archer fire, before he reached one of the main gatehouses. The inner ward was protected by six tall towers. The octagonal outer wall, with 16 drum towers at the corners, was ringed by a broad moat, now partially filled in.

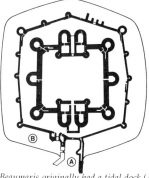

Beaumaris originally had a tidal dock (A) which enabled supply ships to sail right up to the moat (B) from the Menai Strait.

SURVIVOR OF A KING'S REVENGE *Caernarfon Castle had a Parliamentary garrison at the end of the Civil War, and on his restoration Charles II ordered it to be destroyed. But his order was disobeyed and the castle survived, to be extensively restored in Victorian times.*

Long beaches and sandy coves on the Lleyn Peninsula

The western part of the Lleyn Peninsula is one of the least-changed parts of Wales. The roads are twisting and narrow, edged with high banks and tall hedges, with gaps which suddenly reveal distant mountains, or the sheen of sunshine on blue water. Beautiful in fine weather, the seas below its rugged cliffs savage and dangerous when the gales blow, this is a world away from the more traditional holiday resorts of the North Wales coast.

TRAETH PENLLECH BAY *On this away-from-it-all beach, grassy cliffs tumble down to golden sands, and the clear, blue waters are good for bathing and underwater swimming.*

① RHÔS-Y-LLAN

Rhôs-y-llan is a tiny hamlet on a lane which leaves the coast road just north of Tudweiliog. From a car park beside the road, next to a farmhouse, a path leads towards the sea. Rounded, grassy hills slope down to the water, and there are several small coves where sandy strips of beach are dotted with low-tide rock pools.

② PORTH YSGADEN

Another in the succession of tiny, cliff-backed coves which stretch along the northern side of the Lleyn, Porth Ysgaden is not one beach but two, separated by a small headland and studded with rocks. The sand is still speckled with the grains of coal dust left from the days when coastal colliers landed their cargoes on these beaches for customers in the neighbouring villages.

When conditions are right, there are good waves for surfing along this stretch of coast. Swimming is safe, except near the headlands where there may be treacherous currents.

③ TRAETH PENLLECH

The lane which runs from Penllech Bach to Pen-y-graig crosses a stream at a right-angle bend at the bottom of a steep hill. From this point a path alongside the stream runs down a steep ravine to the mile-long sandy beach of Traeth Penllech.

The clear waters are popular with divers,

and there is a choice of other, even more secluded coves and beaches. A 10 minute walk over the headland to the north-east leads to Porth ychen, a tiny bay with rocks, shingle and sand at low water. Even closer in the opposite direction is Porth Colmon, where there are rock pools and safe, sheltered bathing.

④ PORTH IAGO

Porth Iago is a difficult beach to reach, and is best approached from one or other of the tracks leading from the coast road towards the clifftops. In each case, the last stretch involves a steepish climb down to the sands, which can be difficult in wet weather. But the bay offers good surfing, and diving from the rocks at the edge of the bay.

⑤ PORTHOR

The English name for this little cove is Whistling Sands, because the white sand actually whistles – or, more accurately, squeaks – when footsteps cause the fine grains to vibrate together. A steep track leads from a car park in a field at the top of the cliff to the long, sandy beach. At low tide there are rock pools to explore at the western end of the beach.

There is a small cafe where the track reaches the sand. Canoes and finned surfboards are not allowed on the beach between 10 a.m. and 6 p.m. in June, July and August.

⑥ MYNYDD MAWR

The long outstretched arm of the Lleyn Peninsula ends in the dramatically clenched fist of the 524 ft high Mynydd Mawr. The winding, single-track road reaches a parking area on the grassy slopes just after crossing a cattle-grid. From there, two paths diverge. One leads to a cairn on a nearby headland, with views southwards across cliffs and coves towards Bardsey Island out at sea. The other follows a gully between the hills down to the water's edge.

The road carries on up the mountain, to end in a paved car-parking area beside a coastguard lookout point at the summit. From there, a concrete footpath leads down to the foundations of an old wartime radar station. A rougher track continues to sea level, and to St Mary's Well, where the Bardsey pilgrims would drink before boarding the ship for the last stretch of their long journey.

⑦ BARDSEY ISLAND

The island faces the mainland across a 2 mile wide strip of water which, because of the strong tidal currents funnelling around the end of the long peninsula, almost always seethes with whirlpools and tide-rips. This remote mass of rock, dominated by a 548 ft high hill, was a tranquil refuge for Christians fleeing the chaos of mainland Britain after the Romans left.

A church was founded there as early as the 3rd century AD, and at one time three pilgrimages to Bardsey were reckoned equal to one pilgrimage to Rome in terms of religious credit. Many of the pilgrims stayed on the island, and because they were buried there it is often called the Isle of the Twenty Thousand Saints. The Welsh name is more prosaic, but just as accurate: Ynys Enlli, or the 'Isle of the Eddies'.

At the beginning of the century, Bardsey still supported a population of more than 100 farmers and fishermen and their families, who appointed a 'king' to settle disputes. This office continued until a few years after the First World War. According to legend, Bardsey was also the home of the wizard Merlin of the Arthurian legends. Now, however, its only inhabitants are the custodians of the lighthouse and the bird observatory. In settled weather boat trips round the island set out from Aberdaron, but landing on the island is not encouraged.

⑧ ABERDARON

This tiny fishing village, its whitewashed cottages nestling snugly in a fold of the rugged coastline, has been touched little by the passing centuries. The church was built at a safe distance from the sea 1,400 years ago, but the advancing waters have made it necessary for it to have its own sea-wall.

The building which now serves as a cafe

BIRD OF THE WESTERN SHORES

On the coasts of Wales, Ireland and the Isle of Man, colonies of choughs nest in caves, on ledges and in high cliff crevices. In flight they often perform aerobatics together, displaying their flight feathers like outspread fingers and diving, soaring and rolling in spectacular fashion.

Chough
Pyrrhocorax
pyrrhocorax

and gift shop at the other end of the village, Y Gegin Fawr, 'The Big Kitchen', dates from the 14th century. It was originally built as a resting-house.

The beach offers 1½ miles of sand, sheltered from all winds except from the south and south-west, and when these blow they can create ideal surfing conditions. At calmer times the bay is popular with divers, and boats can be launched from a ramp leading down to the beach beside the church and its sea-wall. There are boat trips from the village for offshore fishing and to cruise round Bardsey Island.

⑨ PORTH YSGO

This delightful little bay is reached by a walk of about 10 to 15 minutes from the un-classified road leading east from Aberdaron. The walk itself is a pleasant one, along a valley of ferns, gorse and foxgloves and following a stream that cascades down to the sea in a series of small waterfalls. The sand-and-shingle beach, sheltered by grassy cliffs, is covered at high tide.

⑩ PORTH NEIGWL

This long sweep of sand and cliffs bears the English name of Hell's Mouth, testimony to the threat it presented to sailing ships making their way to any of the ports of West Wales. Any ship unfortunate enough to be blown inshore by strong south-west gales risked being embayed – trapped within the long curving crescent of the bay by the onshore wind, and eventually driven on to the rocks.

Nowadays, when the south-west wind blows, the rollers sweep in to offer the strongest swimmers spectacular surfing conditions. When the weather is quieter, the sands offer seclusion and safe bathing, reached by a steep footpath, where care is needed in wet weather, leading down from the road between Llanengan and Rhydolion.

⑪ LLANENGAN

This little village has a twin-naved church which dates back 1,400 years and was founded by St Einion, King of Lleyn. A stone commemorating 'Melus the doctor, son of Martinus', carved in the 5th century AD, is the first mention of a doctor anywhere in Wales. There is also a beautifully carved rood screen, a solid oak coffer and sacred

VILLAGE PRIDE *Neat stone cottages and garden walls have earned Llangian near Llanengan, a 'Best kept Village in Wales' award.*

vessels which came originally from the abbey on Bardsey Island.

Just over a mile to the north is the beautiful and unspoiled little hamlet of Llangian.

⑫ ST TUDWAL'S ISLANDS

These two small islands to the south of the peninsula include another of Wales's sacred places, this one founded by a saint from Brittany who fled, like the pilgrims of Bardsey, to escape the religious persecution of the Dark Ages after the fall of the Roman Empire. The ruins of an 800-year-old chapel on the eastern island can still be seen from the boats which sail from Abersoch when the weather is good, but the islands are privately owned and landing is not allowed.

⑬ ABERSOCH

The one real intrusion of the modern world into the timeless charm of the Lleyn Penin-sula, Abersoch has been transformed over

the years from a quiet fishing village to a busy centre for powerboat enthusiasts. There are sailing boats, too, and two sandy beaches which face east, away from the prevailing wind, separated by a rocky headland and a small and muddy harbour.

The beach to the south is edged by chalets which climb in tiers up the side of the headland, while further south there are massive dunes, a car park and a golf course. Northwards, the sands run for 2 miles to the headland of Trwyn Llanbedrog. The swim-ming is safe and there is good fishing, mainly for bass.

⑭ LLANBEDROG

The village of Llanbedrog lies to the north of the main road from Abersoch to Pwllheli, but a lane leads down to a beach of sand and shingle, sheltered from the prevailing winds by the wooded headland of Trwyn Llan-bedrog. There is limited car parking and a ramp for launching boats; canoes, boats and pedal floats can be hired. Above the headland, the 400 ft peak of Mynydd Tirycwmwd can be reached by a path which gives fine views of the coastline towards Pwllheli.

LOCAL INFORMATION

Tourist information Pwllheli 613000 (summer).

HM Coastguard Holyhead 2051/3911 for informa-tion. 999 in emergency (ask for coastguard).

Weather Colwyn Bay 8091.

PLACES TO SEE INLAND

Carn Fadryn. 4 miles NW of Llanbedrog. Hilltop prehistoric fort. Daily.

Mynydd Rhiw. 3 miles E of Aberdaron. 1,000 ft hill with views of Lleyn Peninsula.

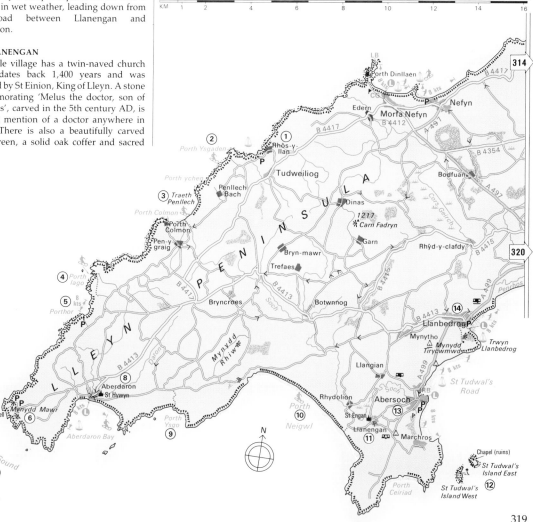

Castles and a campanile along a sheltered shore

The southern coast of the Lleyn Peninsula has the best of both worlds, climatically speaking. The long arm of the Lleyn shelters it from the worst of the prevailing weather from the west; it also traps the warm waters of the Gulf Stream to create a climatic zone entirely different from that of the bleak mountains which rear their lofty heads inland. There are sandy beaches and coves, and grey-walled castles guarding the shore.

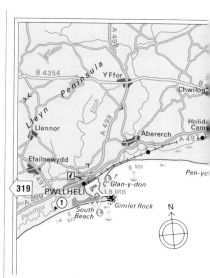

① PWLLHELI
The biggest and busiest town on the Lleyn, Pwllheli has been a port and market town for centuries. It was given its charter as a borough by the Black Prince in 1355, and a street market is still held each Wednesday in the Maes.. The inner harbour has silted up, but the outer harbour provides berths for a few fishing boats and increasing numbers of yachts and sailing dinghies.

The South Beach is a long strip of sand, backed by shingle, while the Glan-y-don beach, east of the harbour, has almost 4 miles of sand, with safe bathing, except near to the harbour mouth and the Gimlet Rock. The sands stretch eastwards to the sheltering headland of Pen-ychain, skirting the secluded village of Abererch which has cafes, shops and a car park.

② LLANYSTUMDWY
In this village of greystone houses astride the turbulent little River Dwyfor the Liberal politician and prime minister David Lloyd George grew up. His simple and dignified grave, marked by a great boulder inscribed 'DLG 1863-1945', is set on a slope overlooking the rapids just upstream from the bridge. A museum houses some of the gold and silver caskets, deeds of freedom and other honours and gifts he was given during his career. The stone cottage where he lived until 1890, marked with a plaque, stands beside the main Criccieth to Pwllheli road.

Just below the village, the River Dwyfach joins the Dwyfor to form a long estuary,

offering pleasant riverside walks, and there are pony-trekking stables near by for those who want to explore further afield. A walk of about a mile down to the estuary leads to an isolated beach with wide patches of sand and rock pools at low tide.

③ CRICCIETH
The Welsh began to build Criccieth Castle in 1230 and finished it, with a strong main tower and a high outer wall, in 1260. By 1282, however, Edward I had captured the fortress and incorporated it into his defensive scheme for his new Welsh dominions. Though in ruins, the castle still betrays evidence of its eventful past. The Engine Tower on the north side was built to site a siege engine, or catapult, with which to bombard attackers. The fortress was taken from the English by Owain Glyndwr during his rebellion in 1404, and the scorchmarks on the Leyburn Tower probably date from that siege, as do the splits, caused by intense heat, in the stones of the tower doorway.

The magnificent setting of Criccieth Castle, perched as it is on a towering headland, effectively divides the town into two: to the west is a short pebbly beach, with ranks of groynes and backed by terraces of white-painted hotels. To the east is a longer, curving sweep of sand, which offers sheltered bathing.

④ MORFA BYCHAN
The Welsh name of this village means 'Little Marsh', but the English name of Black Rock

TWENTIETH-CENTURY WIZARD
David Lloyd George, Liberal politician and Britain's prime minister from 1916 to 1922, was known as the 'Welsh Wizard' because of his spellbinding oratory. He retired from political life in 1944 and died a year later at Llanystumdwy, where his bronze bust stands outside a museum devoted to him.

Sands is more appropriate for the long sandy beach which it faces. There are caves among the rocks on the headland at the western end, and it is possible to dive from the rocks in good weather when the tide is high.

In the right conditions the bay provides good surfing waves, and there is ample parking on the beach, with a slipway for launching boats. Swimming is safe, except for strong currents at the south-east end of the beach, on the edge of the Glaslyn estuary.

⑤ BORTH-Y-GEST
A legend that upsets the history books is attached to this quiet village, for it is said that it was from here that Prince Madog, son of Owain Gwynned, set sail to discover America – more than 300 years before Christopher Columbus.

The village, on the bank of the Glaslyn just below Porthmadog, has a sand-and-pebble beach, with a slipway for boats and a path round the headland to another small cove further downstream. Bathing is safe close inshore, but there are fast currents further out. Trim cottages line the seafront, sheltered by the towering crags of Moel-y-gest, and there are splendid views across Traeth Bach to Harlech and the Rhinog mountains.

⑥ PORTHMADOG
This little harbour town was created early in the 19th century when the local MP, William Alexander Maddocks, built the 1 mile long embankment called the Cob across the Glaslyn estuary to reclaim 7,000 acres of land from the river's mud-flats. The town's prosperity was founded on the slate trade; the output from the quarries of Blaenau

HARLECH CASTLE *Where a creek once wound inland to the watergate of Edward I's castle, rolling dunes and the Royal St David's golf course now stretch like a gold and green apron.*

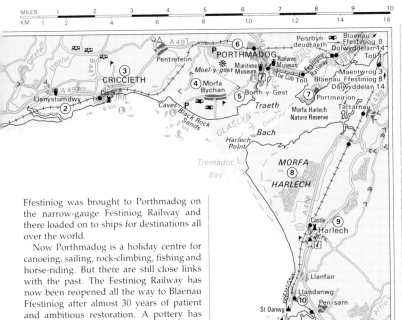

Ffestiniog was brought to Porthmadog on the narrow-gauge Festiniog Railway and there loaded on to ships for destinations all over the world.

Now Porthmadog is a holiday centre for canoeing, sailing, rock-climbing, fishing and horse-riding. But there are still close links with the past. The Festiniog Railway has now been reopened all the way to Blaenau Ffestiniog after almost 30 years of patient and ambitious restoration. A pottery has been established in the mill which used to grind the corn for the ships' biscuits in the days of sail, and a maritime museum is housed in an old ketch, the *Garlandstone*, which used to sail from the port and is now permanently berthed at Oakley No. 3 Wharf in the old harbour.

RAILWAY REVIVED *Painstakingly restored, the sturdy little engines of the Festiniog Railway operate on a line first opened in 1836.*

⑦ PORTMEIRION
In the 1920s the architect Clough Williams-Ellis became captivated by the Mediterranean fishing village of Portofino, which he discovered while touring Italy. He returned home determined to recreate his dream village in Britain, and the result is Portmeirion.

It was pure chance that decreed that Williams-Ellis should choose Portmeirion. For years he had searched in vain for a suitable site, and by 1925 he had almost given up when he was asked to find a buyer for a derelict piece of land in a sandy estuary between Porthmadog and Harlech. As soon as he saw it he knew that his search was over, and set about hacking down the jungle of tangled thickets. Out of this wilderness grew the king of follies, an extravaganza of Italianate buildings rubbing shoulders with architectural oddments acquired from all over Britain. Yet it was a folly with a purpose: in the architect's own words, 'a lighthearted "live" exhibition of architecture, decor and landscaping'.

In Battery Square a tall campanile contrasts oddly with shuttered, box-windowed and weather-boarded buildings below. The Gloriette, looking like a ducal palace, is a mere façade built of rescued oddments, and the 17th-century Town Hall was rebuilt stone by stone after being saved from demolition elsewhere. Among the other rescued buildings and adornments are a colonnade from Bristol, a brewery clock and a once-abandoned ballroom.

Distinguished visitors from all over the world have gazed with awe and wonderment at Williams-Ellis's creation, from royalty such as King Zog of Albania to writers such as Bernard Shaw and John Steinbeck. The playwright Noel Coward stayed there to write *Blithe Spirit*. The hotel where so many celebrities stayed in the 1930s was converted from a 19th-century house that stood on the site when Williams-Ellis acquired it. The main building was badly damaged by fire in 1981 but is being restored. It stands by the water's edge close to a sandy beach, backed by gardens of subtropical plants and trees which make a perfect setting for this extraordinary 'Mediterranean' village below the rugged heights of Snowdonia.

⑧ MORFA HARLECH
The rivers Glaslyn and Dwyryd meet to form a broad, sandy estuary, which reaches the sea by funnelling through the narrow gap between Morfa Bychan to the north and Harlech Point to the south. Behind Harlech Point is Morfa Harlech, a wide stretch of flat land reclaimed from the sea, now a nature reserve with colonies of wading birds. Entry is by permit only, from the Nature Conservancy Council's North Wales Regional Office at Plas Penrhos, Ffordd Penrhos, Bangor, Gwynedd LL57 2lQ.

The sands of Traeth Bach, along the northern edge of the Morfa, are unsafe for bathing, because of the strong currents and the danger of being cut off by the tide.

⑨ HARLECH
Another of Edward I's massive and threatening fortresses, built to hold down a turbulent Wales, Harlech's castle is perched dramatically on a rock bluff high over what was once a tidal creek, with a moat defending it from high ground to the south and east. It is unusual in its plan, in that its strongest part is its huge gatehouse, instead of the usual massive central keep.

The castle's commanding position enabled it to be held by a garrison of only 37 men during the rebellion of Madoc ap Llywelyn in 1294. The defenders were supplied by sea from Ireland, the supplies being brought up a staircase which still climbs the west side of the 200 ft castle rock today. In 1404, however, Owain Glyndwr captured the castle and made it the residence of his court until it was

retaken by the English five years later.

Harlech Castle played a prominent part in the Wars of the Roses, when it was held by the Lancastrians. Its seige, which ended in surrender, is commemorated in the song 'Men of Harlech'. The castle was in ruins by the time of the Tudors, only the Prison Tower being left intact and used as a debtors' prison.

⑩ LLANDANWG
Part of this old village, including the church of St Danwg, has been half-buried by the shifting sand-dunes on the edge of the estuary of the River Artro. The sandy beach, dotted with rocks, offers safe bathing, except on a falling tide when strong currents swirl around the submerged rocks. At nearby Llanbedr is a holiday centre for pony-trekking, hill-walking, orienteering and canoeing, while the old wharf at Pen-sarn is now the home of a water-sports centre.

⑪ SHELL ISLAND
Early last century the local landowner, the Earl of Winchelsea, diverted the River Artro to add reclaimed land to his estates. The old channel dried up, eventually becoming covered with tall dunes. Because of the peculiarities of the offshore currents, this peninsula, also called Mochras, is covered in shells of more than 200 different kinds.

LOCAL INFORMATION

Tourist information Pwllheli 613000 (summer); Porthmadog 2981 (summer); Harlech 780658 (summer).

HM Coastguard Holyhead 2051/3911 for information, 999 in emergency (ask for coastguard).

Weather Colwyn Bay 8091.

PLACES TO SEE INLAND

Blaenau Ffestiniog, 10 miles NE of Porthmadog. Gloddfa Ganol Mountain Tourist Centre, tours of old slate mine workings, daily in summer; Llechwedd Slate Caverns, daily in summer.

Coedydd Maentwrog National Nature Reserve, 7 miles NE of Porthmadog. Daily.

Dolwyddelan Castle, 14 miles NE of Porthmadog. 12th-century remains. Daily.

ITALY IN WALES *A green-domed Parthenon looks down on gardens and statues in Williams-Ellis's fantasy world of Portmeirion.*

321

Sandy beaches and hill tracks from Barmouth to the Dyfi

The coast between the estuaries of the Artro and Dyfi rivers is one long sandy shore, backed to landward by the craggy peaks of the Rhinog mountains and Cader Idris. The main coast road threads its way through a succession of neat, stone-built villages. Each has its own stretch of beach and its own connection to a network of mountain tracks and paths which makes this area particularly rewarding for the energetic walker.

① DYFFRYN ARDUDWY

The name means the 'Valley of Ardudwy', and applies to the area of coastline as well as to the village which straddles a winding section of the Harlech to Barmouth coast road. On the north-west side of the village is the stretch of dunes called Morfa Dyffryn, the central and northern part of which is a national nature reserve. Entry is by permit only, which can be obtained from the Nature Conservancy Council's North Wales Regional Office at Plas Penrhos, Ffordd Penrhos, Bangor, Gwynedd LL57 2LQ.

② LLANABER

The village lies between the hills and the sea, and fits tightly into a narrow gap already half filled by the main coast road and the BR line from Machynlleth to Pwllheli. The little parish church, hidden below road level, dates back to the early 13th century and is one of the best examples of the Early English style in this part of North Wales. The churchyard tombs are said to have been used for hiding contraband spirits during the heyday of smuggling along this coast in the 18th century.

③ BARMOUTH

There are three names for this little resort town at the mouth of the beautiful Mawddach estuary. Apart from the English one, there are two Welsh versions: Abermaw, a contraction of *Aber-mawddach* (the estuary of the Mawddach) and Y Bermo. Whatever its title, it offers the usual resort attractions with one or two special ones of its own, such as the art exhibition held in August and the arts festival held each September. Barmouth is also the starting point of the Three Peaks International Yacht Race held in June; competitors sail to Fort William, stopping on the way to run to the top of Snowdon, Scafell Pike and Ben Nevis.

Bathing is safe along the sandy beach which sweeps northwards along the coast, but at the southern end of the town, where the waters of the Mawddach meet the sea in swirling currents and eddies, conditions can be treacherous. Water-skiing and surfing are popular when the weather permits, and dabs and flounders can be caught in the estuary.

This is also first-class walking country, with a wide variety of routes to choose from. One is the climb up to Dinas Olan, which in 1895 became the first piece of land to be owned by the National Trust. A Panorama Walk skirts the edge of the estuary up to Cutiau, while a footpath along the wooden railway bridge offers the only pedestrian way across the river without a detour of several miles upstream.

④ DOLGELLAU

Dolgellau is a neat, stone-built market town on the banks of the River Wnion, a tributary of the Mawddach. The ancient stone bridge dates back to 1638, and has the unusual feature of a tannery built on to it. The countryside round about is still well known for the quality of the sheep and cattle it raises, and the street and livestock market each Friday is well attended by farmers and their families from all over Meirionnydd. The sober respectability of the town today is hard to reconcile with the days in the last century when it was the centre of a local gold rush. The hills round about were mined for gold by the Romans, and gold for the Royal Family's wedding rings is still mined here. The keen walker is almost spoiled for choice. Apart from the stiff climb up the network of paths leading to the summit of Cader Idris, 2 miles to the south, there are gentler strolls like the Precipice Walk which starts from near Llanfachreth and provides splendid views of the Mawddach estuary, or the Torrent Walk which follows the course of the Clywedog above the town.

⑤ PENMAENPOOL

The village is centred around a riverside hotel and a small wooden toll-bridge, whose planks rattle and rumble alarmingly under the car wheels, but which provides the nearest crossing of the Mawddach for road traffic heading south from Barmouth. The disused railway line from Ruabon and Llangollen to Barmouth now provides a walking route along the southern shore of the estuary, and the old Penmaenpool signal-box has been restored and converted into a Wildlife Information Centre.

⑥ ARTHOG

This little village on the road from Dolgellau to Fairbourne, along the southern bank of the Mawddach estuary, is a useful base for hill-walking, with routes into the foothills of Cader Idris, to the waterfalls below the hill of Llys Bradwen and to Llynnau Cregennen – the Lakes of Cregennen.

⑦ FAIRBOURNE

The Victorians' love of the seaside led to the establishing of a small resort at Fairbourne. Extended by more modern building, the village is set in the flat strip of coast between the hills and the dune-covered peninsula of Morfa Mawddach, which stretches out towards Barmouth like a pointing finger.

Fairbourne is the starting point of the smallest of the Welsh narrow-gauge railway lines. Originally a horse-drawn tramway laid to carry the materials used for building the village, it was equipped with steam locomotives to run on its 15 in. gauge tracks in 1916. Today services connecting with the ferry across the estuary to Barmouth are run during summer by four steam locomotives and two diesels.

Narrow-gauge locomotive on the Fairbourne Railway

⑧ LLWYNGWRIL

A mile-long beach of low-tide sand, backed by a strip of shingle, offers a wide panorama of the coast northwards to Barmouth and beyond to Harlech and the mountains of Snowdonia.

⑨ LLANEGRYN

This little village is best known for its church, which has a beautiful 16th-century carved rood screen, thought to have been taken there from Cymmer Abbey, near Dolgellau, after the Dissolution of the Monasteries. The grapes, berries, leaves and twining vines make an eloquent testimony to the carver's skill. Near by stood the old stately home of Peniarth, home of the Peniarth Manuscripts, the earliest-known documents written in the Welsh language, which were among the first acquisitions of the National Library of Wales at Aberystwyth. Further up the valley, at Craig-yr-Aderyn (Bird Rock), are colonies of cormorants and guillemots, and a couple of miles further on stand the melancholy ruins

PANORAMIC VIEW *Barmouth's Panorama Walk gives sweeping views of the mountains fringing the Mawddach estuary and the slender thread of the mile-long railway bridge which crosses it.*

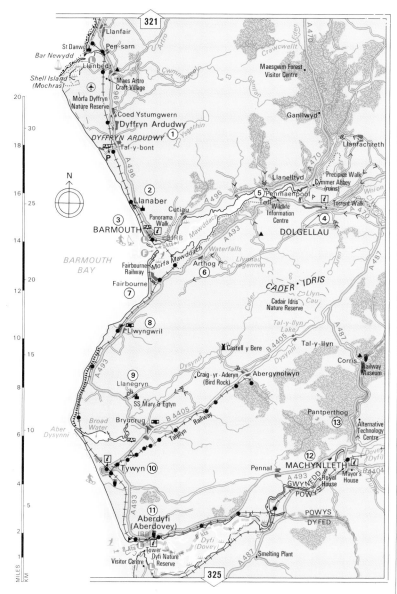

321

Map labels: Llanfair, St Danwg, Pen-sarn, Bar Newydd, Llanbedr, Shell Island (Mochras), Maes Artro Craft Village, Morfa Dyffryn Nature Reserve, Coed Ystumgwern, **Dyffryn Ardudwy** ①, DYFFRYN ARDUDWY, Tal-y-bont, Maesgwm Forest Visitor Centre, Ganllwyd, Llanfachreth, ② Llanaber, Cutiau, Panorama Walk, ③ **BARMOUTH**, BARMOUTH BAY, Llanelltyd, Precipice Walk, Cymmer Abbey (ruins), ⑤ Penmaenpool, Toll, Wildlife Information Centre, Torrent Walk, ④ **DOLGELLAU**, Fairbourne Railway, Morfa Mawddach, Waterfalls, Arthog, ⑥, Llynnau Cregennen, Fairbourne ⑦, CADER IDRIS, Llyn Cau, Cadair Idris Nature Reserve, ⑧ **Llwyngwril**, Castell y Bere, Tal-y-llyn Lake, Tal-y-llyn, Corris Railway Museum, ⑨ Llanegryn, Craig-yr-Aderyn (Bird Rock), Abergynolwyn, SS Mary & Egryn, Bryncrug, Pantperthog ⑬ Alternative Technology Centre, Broad Water, Talyllyn, Railway, Aber Dysynni, ⑫ **MACHYNLLETH**, Tywyn ⑩, Pennal, Royal House, Mayor's House, GWYNEDD, POWYS, DYFED, ⑪ **Aberdyfi (Aberdovey)**, Dyfi (Dovey), Tower, Dyfi Nature Reserve, Visitor Centre, Smelting Plant

325

CENTRE POINT *Like a rocket on its launching pad, Machynlleth's clock tower straddles the main street and dominates the town centre.*

Machynlleth's oldest building is probably Royal House, which dates from the 15th century. It is believed to have been the home of Owain Glyndwr. Dafydd Gam, who attempted to assassinate Glyndwr during his crowning as Prince of Wales, was imprisoned there in 1404. A stone building of about 1450 in Maengwyn Street is said to stand on the site of the building where Owain Glyndwr held the first Welsh Parliament, during his rebellion in 1404 against the English Crown. Further up the street is a timber-framed building of 1628 known as the Mayor's House, and at the centre is an imposing clock tower, presented to the town in 1873 by the local landowner, the Marquis of Londonderry.

A later marquis gave an even more lavish gift in 1949 – the 17th-century mansion of Plas Machynlleth, just outside the town on the road to Aberystwyth. The mansion now houses the council offices, and its grounds form a public park.

⑬ PANTPERTHOG

Situated among buildings which once belonged to one of the string of old quarries lining the Corris valley is the Centre for Alternative Technology. It was set up in 1974 to display and promote ways of reducing energy consumption. Among the projects demonstrated are a specially designed house which needs far less heating than the average dwelling, solar-heating panels, windmills and water generators.

There are also woodland and vegetable gardens, a working smallholding, a bookshop and a restaurant, a maze and an adventure playground. The centre is open daily, and also runs short courses.

---

of Castell y Bere, a Welsh fortress perched on a precipitous crag in a superb defensive position. Originally, it could only be approached across a timber bridge crossing the dry moat hacked out of the rock. Edward I captured it during his campaigns in Wales, but it was retaken during the rebellion of 1294, after which it fell into ruins.

⑩ TYWYN

The Welsh name means 'sand dune', highly appropriate for a resort set at the northern end of a sand-and-shingle beach, backed by ranks of dunes which stretch for almost 4 miles to the Dyfi estuary and the town of Aberdyfi, and broken only by a golf course and an old rifle-range.

The town is probably best known as the terminus of the Talyllyn Railway, a narrow-gauge line established in 1865 to run 7¼ miles up the valley to Abergynolwyn and the quarries at Nant Gwernol, but never reaching the place after which it was named. The line came under threat of closure in 1951 but it was taken over by a private preservation society, the first line in Britain to be run in this way, and survived to celebrate its centenary. The story is told in the Narrow-Gauge Railway Museum at Tywyn's Wharf station, which also has exhibits from other narrow-gauge lines in Britain and overseas.

⑪ ABERDYFI

Once proposed as a serious rival to Holyhead and Fishguard for the ferry trade to Ireland, Aberdyfi, or Aberdovey, is now a busy but attractive holiday resort at the mouth of the River Dyfi. It has a wide, sandy beach and bathing is safe except near the river mouth.

The local yacht club's sail marking of a black bell recalls the song *The Bells of Aberdovey* which first appeared in an 18th-century opera, but which harks back to the old Welsh legend of Cantre'r Gwaelod, a city said to lie beneath the waters of Cardigan Bay. It is said that the bells of the city can be heard ringing when trouble threatens.

There is a maritime museum housed in the old warehouses on the jetty – behind the bustling seafront are quiet streets and squares of houses built for the sea-captains engaged in trade with ports all over the world. Even now, names like 'The Old Custom House', next to the Britannia Inn, and 'Liverpool House' in The Square, are reminders of the town's prosperous and cosmopolitan past.

⑫ MACHYNLLETH

The town is built at the last crossing point of the Dyfi before the estuary widens into the open sea. It forms the focal point for the farming communities of this part of mid-Wales, and on Wednesdays the streets are crowded for the open-air market, held under a charter which dates back to the 13th century and also authorises a twice-yearly fair. On alternate weeks the market also deals in livestock.

LOCAL INFORMATION

Tourist information Harlech 780658 (summer); Barmouth 280787 (summer); Dolgellau 422888 (summer); Tywyn 710070 (summer); Aberdyfi 321 (summer); Machynlleth 2401.

HM Coastguard Dale 218/459 for information, 999 in emergency (ask for coastguard).

Weather Llanberis 870120.

PLACES TO SEE INLAND

Cadair Idris National Nature Reserve.

Cymmer Abbey, 9 miles E of Barmouth. Ruined 13th-century abbey. Daily.

Corris Railway Museum, 5 miles N of Machynlleth. Some afternoons in summer.

Maesgwm Forest Visitor Centre, 8 miles N of Dolgellau. Daily in summer.

Aberystwyth, resort among the cliffs that face Cardigan Bay

Southwards from the beautiful wooded estuary of the River Dyfi, the West Wales coastline turns from low-lying meadows to steeper, wilder cliffs and headlands, interrupted by gaps where rivers have cut valleys through the rock. Some beaches are small and secluded; others are larger and more easily reached. The Ystwyth and Rheidol rivers pour into the largest gap of all, on which stands the resort and university town of Aberystwyth.

① FURNACE

This village on the river Einion owes its name to a magnificent monument from West Wales's industrial past. At the bend in the centre of the village, the large stone building with a huge water-wheel at one side is a smelting plant dating back to the early 18th century. Iron ore was refined there, using charcoal made by burning local timber, and the water-wheel drove the furnace bellows. The ironworks is being restored.

Below the building the river cascades over moss-covered rocks as it rushes down from a ravine. A lane climbs steeply alongside the water into the ravine, and a waymarked path provides a delightful walk of about a mile through the woods.

② TALYBONT

The attractive village of Talybont was a centre of the wool trade in the 18th and 19th centuries, and still has links today with the traditional ways of weaving. There are tweed mills near by, at the bridge where the road crosses the river Leri at the southern end of the village.

In the centre of the village is a green on which two pubs stand side by side; one, finished in light stucco, is called the White Lion and the other, in the dark local stone, is called the Black Lion.

A signposted road from the village leads

after 7 miles to the Nant-y-môch reservoir and crosses the dam, which is 172 ft high and 1,150 ft long. The reservoir is part of the Rheidol hydro-electric scheme and covers 680 acres. Submerged beneath 1,150 million cu. ft of water are Nant-y-môch farm, a small chapel and a cemetery.

Water from Nant-y-môch flows 5 miles to drive the generator of Cwm Rheidol Power Station, between Aberystwyth and Devil's Bridge. The power station can be seen from the Vale of Rheidol Railway, or visited by road from Capel Bangor, 5 miles east of Aberystwyth. There are guided tours over the power station during the summer, and the cascades over the weir are floodlit on summer evenings. There is a 2½ mile nature trail around the water's edge.

③ YNYSLAS

The Welsh name means 'green-blue island', for though Ynyslas is now definitely part of the mainland, its northernmost part used to be cut off at high tide. The whole estuary up to the high-water mark, together with the adjoining Cors Fochno bog and the Ynyslas dunes, now forms the Dyfi National Nature Reserve. An information centre explains the local natural history, and visitors can follow a nature trail which shows how the dunes are formed and gives glimpses of the flowers, birds, butterflies and small animals

which live among them. Marram grass knits the loose sand with its tenacious roots, and sea spurge grows profusely. There are rabbits in the dunes, preyed on by polecats and weasels. Bathing is unsafe in the estuary because of dangerous currents.

On the sandbank between Ynyslas and Aberdyfi stands a curious tower framework. When the railway line was built from Machynlleth to Aberystwyth in 1864, a branch line was added to take passengers to the ferry across the Dyfi estuary. The tower was built as a refuge where passengers could wait for the ferry to cross from Aberdyfi to collect them. After the line to Pwllheli was built along the northern bank of the estuary the ferry fell into disuse and the railway tracks were removed, leaving only the tower framework.

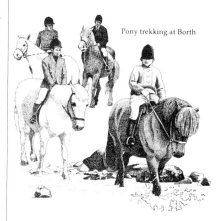

Pony trekking at Borth

④ BORTH

South of Ynyslas, empty dunes give way to the straggling main street and promenade of this busy holiday village. It straddles the narrow strip of dry land between the sea and the Cors Fochno swampland for 2 miles. The beach offers safe bathing away from the Dyfi estuary. There is a golf course, while anglers can cast from the beach for bass, and surfers can enjoy good sport when the wind blows from the west and the rollers sweep in from Cardigan Bay.

Cors Fochno is a desolate wilderness of semi-liquid peat, 20 ft deep, and though crossed by paths made by peat cutters it can be dangerous to enter.

RIVERMOUTH RESORT *Seen from Constitution Hill, the chateau-style old university college heads a dignified parade of buildings along the seafront at Aberystwyth.*

THE WELSH CALIFORNIA

Silver and lead have been mined along the Ystwyth and Rheidol valleys since the Middle Ages, and some local mines supplied silver for Charles I's mint at Aberystwyth Castle. One such 'Mine Royal' was at Cwmsymlog, 9 miles east of Aberystwyth, reached by a minor road off the A4159; remains of the village can still be seen, together with part of the winding house and an engine-house chimney.

At Llywernog, 11 miles east of Aberystwyth on the A44, the 6½ acre open-air Llywernog Silver Lead Mine Museum includes a rock-crusher house, a water-wheel pit and three working water-wheels. Visitors to this old mine can follow a Miners' Trail, and also go underground to see the Blue Pool, a floodlit cavern formed from a prospecting pit sunk about 1795. The main building on the site contains a mining exhibition, 'California of Wales'. The museum is open daily from Easter to October.

Old mining equipment is on display at Llywernog.

⑤ WALLOG

The beach at Wallog is separated from Borth by a stretch of cliffs. Its main attraction is its seclusion, as it can be reached only by following the narrow, twisting coast road from Borth to Clarach. Opposite a turning where a road leads to Llandre is a track which ends in a footpath leading down a small beach of sand and shingle, with a rushing stream flowing down from the hills.

A finger of shingle, Sarn Cynfelyn, points out from the beach and runs for several miles under the surface of the sea. It was probably left by a retreating glacier at the end of the Ice Age, but legend links it with the drowned city of Cantref-y-Gwaelod, said to lie beneath the waters of Cardigan Bay. The shingle bank, according to the legend, was one of the dykes protecting the low-lying city. A drunken watchman named Seithenyn failed to warn the citizens of an approaching storm, and the city was lost beneath the sea, and the watchman with it.

⑥ CLARACH BAY

The bay is formed by a stream which cuts its way down to the sea from the village of Clarach a mile to the east. A road follows the valley to a pleasant sand-and-shingle beach, where there is safe bathing except in the strong currents around the headlands to the north and south.

Chalets and caravan camps crowd the bay, but walkers can escape the throng by searching the rock pools for crabs and shrimps, or by following the cliff walks – northwards to Wallog and Borth or southwards over Constitution Hill to Aberystwyth.

⑦ ABERYSTWYTH

The principal seaside resort of West Wales, Aberystwyth lies at the centre of the long sweep of Cardigan Bay. As well as providing a wide range of seaside attractions, it is the home of the National Library of Wales and of one of the colleges that form the University of Wales. The library contains more than 3 million volumes, including the world's largest collection of books in the Welsh language or relating to Wales.

Aberystwyth's two beaches are divided by a headland on which stands the ruined gatehouse of Aberystwyth Castle. Begun in 1277 by Edward I, it was later captured and held by Owain Glyndwr. During the Civil War the castle was pounded by Cromwell's cannons and the rubble removed by local residents to build houses. The Victorian Gothic building near by was planned as a hotel but used for Aberystwyth's original university college; it still houses some college departments, but the main college campus is now on Penglais Hill, overlooking the town.

A museum of local history tells the story of the neighbourhood from the Stone Age to the present day. The Coliseum is a restored Victorian music hall; and there is a camera obscura on Constitution Hill.

The North Beach offers safe bathing. The South Beach, between the castle and the old harbour at the river mouth, has a steeper shingle bank which makes it suitable only for strong swimmers. There are fishing trips from the old harbour, which also provides a safe haven for pleasure craft.

There are splendid views along the coast from the top of Constitution Hill at the northern end of the seafront; the hill is reached by a stiff climb up a cliff path, or more easily by a cable railway.

Further up the valleys of the Ystwyth and the Rheidol are the old lead, copper and silver mines on which the prosperity of the whole area once depended. A narrow-gauge railway line built to carry ore from the Rheidol Valley for shipment from Aberystwyth survives today as the Vale of Rheidol Railway, British Rail's only steam-operated line. It starts from Aberystwyth Station and runs inland for 12 miles through magnificent scenery, rising to 680 ft near Devil's Bridge. There are daily services in summer.

⑧ MORFA BYCHAN

The name means 'small marsh', and this rocky little beach is one of the few breaks in the long, cliff-edged stretch of coast which stretches from Aberystwyth almost to Aberaeron. It is difficult to reach: follow the signs from the main road, then turn off down a narrow and winding lane which meanders close enough to the clifftop for a path to reach a steep ramp down the cliff face to the water's edge.

⑨ LLANRHYSTUD

This small village is on the main coast road from Aberystwyth to Aberaeron, where it crosses the River Wyre. There are two beaches, one on either side of the river, each with a stretch of shingle and sand at low water. The southern beach is the easiest to reach, by a road leading down to a car park. The beach on the northern side of the river can be reached only by walking down the lane from the church. A stream flows down the main street, and a green mound marks the site of a 12th-century castle.

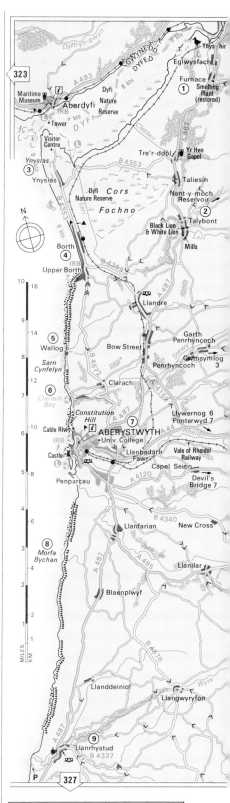

LOCAL INFORMATION

Tourist information Aberystwyth 612125/617911, ext. 264.

HM Coastguard Dale 218/459 for information, 999 in emergency (ask for coastguard).

Weather Cardiff 379020.

PLACES TO SEE INLAND

Bwlch Nant-yr-Arian Forest Visitor Centre, off A44, near Ponterwyd, 10 miles E of Aberystwyth. Daily in summer.

Devil's Bridge, 12 miles E of Aberystwyth, on A4120. Waterfalls and three bridges on Mynach and Rheidol rivers.

Yr Hen Gapel, Tre'r-ddôl, 8 miles N of Aberystwyth, on A487. Museum of 19th-century religious life in Wales. Weekdays in summer.

Quiet coves between the cliffs on a wild Welsh coast

The coast between Cardigan and Aberaeron, on the long sweeping curve of Cardigan Bay, is remote and secluded. The main coast road swings inland, and the sea can be reached only by following a lane to one of the villages or coves which nestle in gaps in the impressive cliffs. The wildness of this part of the Welsh coast is well suited to those looking for quiet pleasures such as picnicking, sunbathing or walking clifftop paths.

① GWBERT-ON-SEA
At the northern end of the village, facing west across the Teifi estuary, the dunes give way to the beginning of the rocky cliffs that stretch almost without interruption to New Quay. The beach is covered with shingle, though as the tide ebbs it uncovers a stretch of muddy sand. Bathing is safe close to the shore, but further out the river currents make conditions treacherous and the water is best avoided when the tide is on the ebb.

② CARDIGAN ISLAND
Like so many of the small islands off the Welsh coast, Cardigan Island is a nature reserve – owned, in this case, by the West Wales Naturalists' Trust. It is small – only 40 acres – and a mere quarter of a mile from the shore, but the rock-strewn approaches and steep cliffs all round the island make landing difficult. There is a flock of Soay sheep on the island, as well as nesting gulls and fulmars. Attempts are being made to establish a colony of Manx shearwaters, by introducing fledglings from Skomer Island.

③ TRAETH-Y-MWNT
This beautiful spot is well worth the drive along a narrow and tortuous lane off the main road. The drive ends with a spectacular view down into a small sandy cove, bounded at the northern end by a 250 ft high rocky headland which is National Trust property. Beside the car park in the clifftop meadows, at the top of the path leading down to the beach, is the 700-year-old church of the Holy Cross, its whitewashed walls standing out against the green slopes.

No trace is now left of the battle fought at this spot in 1155 when a party of Flemish raiders was defeated, a victory which until the 18th century was celebrated each year with a festival called the 'Bloody Sunday of Mwnt'. Human bones and rusting weapons are still occasionally turned up by the ploughs of local farmers.

④ ABERPORTH
A Government test centre for missiles, and its airfield and research establishment, are sited along the road which leaves the main coast road at Blaenannerch and leads to Aberporth. The village, clustered round its sheltered bay, has two beaches, separated by a small rocky headland, with good access to the water for boats.

Bathing is safe except when the wind is blowing from the north; it then causes currents to funnel around the bay, creating a strong and dangerous undertow which could trap unwary swimmers. Another hazard is from test firings of weapons from the missile base, but these are heralded by signal flags and a patrol boat; the target-area can be seen from the clifftops. Lifeguards patrol the beach during the holiday season.

⑤ TRESAITH
Compared with some of the beaches along this stretch of coastline, Tresaith is easy to reach, as the road leads almost to the water's edge. Parking is extremely limited, with space for only half a dozen cars or so, though there is more parking space at the top of the hill.

The beach is covered with wide, hard sand, below a strip of shingle, and the clear waters are popular with divers. When the tide is out, the beach of Penbryn, a mile to the east, is an easy walk along the sands.

⑥ TRAETH-PENBRYN
Penbryn beach can be reached by road down a track from the village of Penbryn. Boats can be taken down to the beach for launching, but there is no parking space, and cars have to be left a 10 minute walk away in a nearby farmyard and camping site.

The sand, the low dunes and the wooded valley tucked into a gap in the cliffs cut by a small stream make a tranquil place to while away a summer afternoon.

⑦ LLANGRANOG
Two roads from the main Cardigan to Aberaeron coast road, and a narrow, winding lane from the west lead to Llangranog. It is a pretty little village with pubs and restaurants, slipways and a sandy beach bounded by rocky headlands. If the sea is rough, bathing is inadvisable (especially near the rocks), but a walk along the clifftops to the headland of Ynys-Lochtyn, owned by the National Trust, a mile to the north will provide spectacular views of the breakers.

A 541 ft hill between the village and the

TRESAITH BEACH *At low tide, Tresaith's tiny cove becomes a broad apron of firm, glistening sand below the line of shingle, with seaweed-covered rocks washed by a spume-flecked surf.*

FEEDING THE LAND
In many coves along the Welsh coast, stone-built lime-kilns still stand on the shore. They are relics of the days in the 18th century when coasters called in with cargoes of limestone. This was then burned in the kilns to provide fertiliser for nearby farmlands which were acid through lack of underlying chalk.

Stone lime-kilns stand near a Welsh shore.

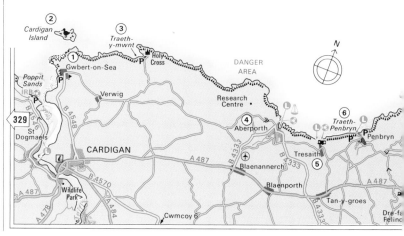

UNDER GREEN HILLS *Llangranog clings to the sides of a steep valley that cuts into the hills of the Ceredigion coast. A clifftop path leads to a pair of secluded coves.*

headland has the remains of a prehistoric fort, while a scramble down a narrow path leads to a pair of quiet, sandy coves on the north-eastern side of the headland.

⑧ CWMTUDU

This secluded beach can be reached only by driving for several miles along narrow, winding lanes. At the end of the journey there is a small car park overlooking a small shingle beach, approached by a steep path, and edged by cliffs with caves and rock pools. There are the remains of an old lime-kiln on the shore.

⑨ NEW QUAY

New Quay lives up to most people's idea of how a fishing village should look: narrow, hilly streets sloping down to a pretty little harbour, where the long stone quay points like a finger to a long crescent of sheltered sandy beach. The building of the quay after which the town was named in 1835 provided the only safe harbour along this whole stretch of coast, and a century ago there was a thriving shipbuilding and ship-repairing trade here. Look for the list of tolls on the

notice board on the quayside, which dates back to the time when there was also a busy coastal trade. It cost 6d to bring ashore a box of cigars, a shilling for a ton of gunpowder, two for a coffin and five for a marble tombstone.

Fishing boats still put out from New Quay, and anglers can cast for pollack from the rocks near New Quay Head, to the north of the village. If the flavour of the place is reminiscent of Dylan Thomas's *Under Milk Wood,* this is no coincidence: the poet lived there in the 1940s and after a stroll through the village wrote *Quite Early One Morning* in which can be seen the beginnings of *Under Milk Wood.*

⑩ ABERAERON

Ranks of beautiful Regency houses painted in contrasting pastel shades give the harbourside streets of Aberaeron a Mediterranean flavour, offset slightly by the gridiron regularity of the town plan. The port was the creation of a local landowner, the Reverend Alban Gwynne, who decided to establish a town at the mouth of the river Aeron early in the last century. It was centred on a large and

spacious harbour – the building materials had to be brought in by sea – and there was soon a busy shipbuilding industry here, using timber from local oak forests.

Later in the century better roads, and the railway from Aberystwyth down the coast to Carmarthen, with branches to coastal towns including Aberaeron and Cardigan, killed off much of the coastal trade, but the town lives on as a busy holiday resort. The harbour shelters yachts and small fishing boats. The nearby beaches, though they have little sand, are blessed with crystal-clear water and in settled weather conditions offer safe bathing. There is an aquarium beside the harbour.

⑪ ABERARTH

Once a prosperous port for coastal shipping, all that remains of Aberarth now is a tiny village alongside the Cardigan to Aberystwyth coast road, at the point where it crosses the little river Arth. On either side of the river, narrow lanes lead towards the shingle beach, backed by a sea-wall built of rock. Parking is difficult.

⑫ LLANSANTFFRAID AND LLANON

Llanon lies on the main coast road, from which a lane leads to its near neighbour of Llansantffraid, where the Peris stream flows to the sea. It is possible to drive down the lane as far as the handsome little parish church, with its stone tower and walls faced in purple slate, beside a bridge over the stream. But parking space is limited and the beach can be reached only on foot.

LOCAL INFORMATION

Tourist information Aberaeron 570602 (summer); Cardigan 613230 (summer).

HM Coastguard Dale 218/459 for information. 999 in emergency (ask for coastguard).

Weather Cardiff 397020.

PLACES TO SEE INLAND

Felin Geri Mill, Cwmcoy, 8 miles SE of Aberporth. 16th-century working watermill. Daily in summer.

Maesslyn Mill Museum, near Llandyssul, 14 miles S of New Quay. Working museum of wool cloth weaving. Weekdays in summer.

Museum of the Woollen Industry, Dre-fach Felindre, 14 miles S of Cardigan. Weekdays in summer.

Pumpsaint, 21 miles SE of Aberaeron. Roman gold mines. Daily in summer.

Strata Florida Abbey, near Pontrhydfendigaid. 24 miles E of Aberaeron via A485 and B4343.

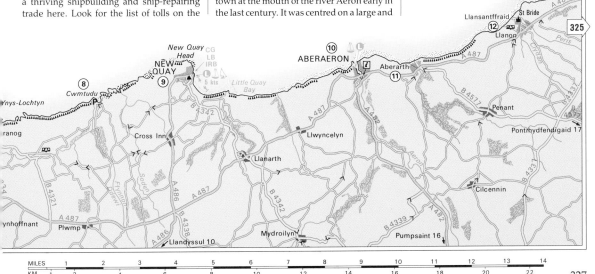

Shores where the last invaders of Britain met their match

The rocky promontory of Strumble Head is one of the nearest points in south-west Wales to the coast of Ireland, and the port of Fishguard on its fine natural harbour is a busy ferry terminal with its services to and from Rosslare. The rest of this part of the coast is dominated by long stretches of steep cliffs. The Pembrokeshire Coast Path gives energetic walkers a chance to enjoy the spectacular scenery from a high vantage point.

HARBOUR TOWN *Lower Fishguard and its old harbour town lie below steep, wooded slopes, with the distant 1,100 ft peak of Mynydd Carningli giving a hint of wilder country beyond.*

① STRUMBLE HEAD
The lighthouse for which Strumble Head is noted is built on an island linked to the mainland by a bridge. The headland is approached by a network of narrow but well signposted lanes, and there is car parking on the clifftop opposite the lighthouse. From this point there are splendid views of the coastal cliffs, and of the strong currents which swirl around the headland even in calm weather.

Strumble Head is also a landmark on one of the principal air routes across the Atlantic, and frequent vapour trails streak the sky overhead on a clear day.

② CARREGWASTAD POINT
This headland at the western end of a small, rockbound bay was the site of the last landing by a foreign army on the soil of mainland Britain. It occurred in 1797 during the Napoleonic Wars, and the event is commemorated by a small stone pillar.

The reality failed to live up to the French invaders' ambitious orders, which were to march north through Wales, living off the country, and finally to take and burn the port of Liverpool. A force of 1,400 men was put ashore, half of them soldiers, half prisoners released from jail on condition they joined the force, all under the command of an elderly Irish-American named Colonel Tate.

The original intention was to land in Ireland, where the force might have fared better. As things were, the men were landed in

this exposed part of Pembrokeshire in mid-February without any tents or protection, and before they could set off on their long march they were attacked by an equally mixed force of yeomanry and villagers. In two days their surrender was accepted, and the last invasion of Britain was over.

The countryside around Carregwastad Point can have changed little since the invasion. The headland itself can be reached only

on foot, either along the coastal footpath, or else from the little hamlet of Llanwnda or from Tre-Howel.

③ TRE-HOWEL
The handsome old farmhouse, at the end of a short drive off the lane from Strumble Head to Llanwnda, was seized by the French invaders of 1797 and used by Colonel Tate as his headquarters after the landing. From the farmhouse a footpath leads after about a mile to Carregwastad Point.

④ GOODWICK
Fishguard's near neighbour, on the western side of Fishguard Bay, was a creation of the Great Western Railway, originally planned as a terminal for transatlantic liners sailing to and from New York. A railway embankment was built along the foot of the cliffs to a purpose-built harbour, and the line was connected to the main rail network leading eventually to Paddington Station in London. But although the liner *Mauretania* called at Goodwick in 1906, the long-distance sea trade soon shifted to Southampton, and the port settled down to developing a steady if less ambitious trade with Ireland.

Above the railway line is the Fishguard Bay Hotel, built by the GWR to house its America-bound passengers. At the southern end of the harbour, the Fishguard road swings left past the low-lying land called Goodwick Sands, where in 1797 the French invasion force was drawn up to surrender to the British commander, Earl Cawdor, and his troops.

⑤ FISHGUARD
The main part of Fishguard is on top of a hill overlooking Fishguard Bay. It is centred on the Square, in which stands an old inn called the Royal Oak. Inside this inn, the table on which the French surrender of 1797 was signed can still be seen.

The lower part of Fishguard has a totally different character. Still recognisably an old fishing village, set around wharves and quays, it made an ideal location for filming Dylan Thomas's *Under Milk Wood* in the 1960s.

The river Gwaun, which gives the town its Welsh name of Abergwaun, 'Estuary of the Gwaun', flows to the sea through attractive countryside. This can be sampled at its best by taking the Narberth road to the village of Llanychaer Bridge, with its old watermill, or by following lanes leading to the old bridges at Pontfaen and Cilrhedyn.

⑥ DINAS HEAD
This massive lump of rock projects from the coastal cliffs to form a barrier between Fishguard Bay to the west and Newport Bay to the east. It can be reached by a path from the

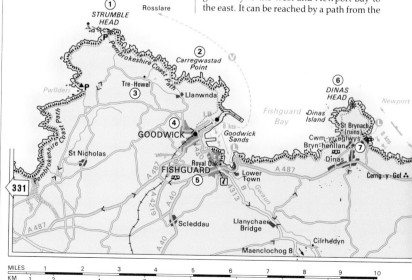

village of Bryn-henllan, itself approached down a lane from Dinas on the main Fishguard to Newport coast road. There are wide sea views from a nature trail around the headland which, despite its other name of Dinas Island, is in fact firmly joined to the mainland by a low-lying saddle of land.

⑦ CWM-YR-EGLWYS
At the eastern end of the neck of land which joins Dinas Head to the mainland is the village of Cwm-yr-eglwys, 'Valley of the Church' – once a port, but now a shadow of its old self. The great storm of 1859, which wrecked more than 100 ships off the coast of Wales in a single night, destroyed the church of St Brynach on the foreshore. Now all that survives is one crumbling wall and the old bell tower, a mute reminder of the power and fury of the sea.

The sand-and-shingle beach is studded here and there with rock pools. There is a car park almost on the beach, and boats can be launched from a ramp near by.

⑧ NEWPORT
The Normans founded Newport in 1195, when William de Turribus was driven out of nearby Nevern by the Welsh. Since then, his castle has been converted into a private house and riding school, and Newport has in turn flourished and then declined as a busy port. An old quay still survives, with several old warehouses, and there are sandy beaches on both sides of the Nyfer estuary, which is well stocked with sea trout and bass. Volunteer lifeguards patrol the beach at weekends in summer.

A mile to the south of the town, on the edge of the Presely Mountains, is Carningli Common, an open plain studded with ancient hut circles. It was from these mountains that 80 bluestone columns were quarried and then transported some 240 miles to Stonehenge in Wiltshire around 2000 BC. On the other side of the range, between Crymych and Maenclochog, is the stone circle of Gors-fawr, a smaller version of Stonehenge.

⑨ NEVERN
A tranquil village in the valley of the Nyfer, behind the higher coastal cliffs, Nevern centres on the ancient church of St Brynach. The churchyard is notable for its avenue of mighty yews. One of these, the 'Bleeding Yew', drips with sap which is blood-red in colour. Near by is the 11th-century carved Nevern Cross. According to local tradition, the cuckoo first sings on top of the cross on April 7, the feast day of St Brynach.

The castle of Nevern, built by the Normans, is now a grassy mound, but some of the later buildings have lasted longer – among them a 17th-century mansion called Trewern, and Llwyngwair Manor, which is now a hotel.

CELTIC CROSS *The Great Cross of St Brynach at Nevern stands 13 ft high. Its intricate carvings show a strong Irish influence.*

⑩ MOYLGROVE
This pretty, well-kept little village is hidden in the maze of narrow, winding lanes behind the coastal cliffs between Cardigan and Newport. It is useful as a base for exploring the coastal footpath along this particularly deserted stretch of coastline. The lanes themselves are attractive, and provide sheltered walking country, though they lack the open vistas of the clifftop paths. A lane from the village leads to Ceibwr Bay, a narrow gap in the cliffs where coasters used to land cargo, and where a little shingle beach is exposed at low tide.

⑪ POPPIT SANDS
Where the Teifi estuary meets the open waters of Cardigan Bay to the east of Cemaes Head, the broad beach of Poppit Sands faces across the estuary to Gwbert. There are rows of dunes behind the beach. There is plenty of car-parking space near by, and with access so easy the sands are often crowded. Bathing is safe at slack water, though the currents run stronger at mid-tide, and the deep-water channel further out should be avoided at all times.

⑫ ST DOGMAELS
The little town of St Dogmaels, which faces across the Teifi to Cardigan, grew up around an abbey which was established there by the Welsh, probably in the 7th century. The abbey was sacked by the Vikings and rebuilt by the Normans in the 12th century, before finally falling into ruin in Tudor times.

The village still has a fishing industry, based on salmon and sea trout and now centred mainly on the river. Boat trips also run out to sea and along the coast. In the other direction, inland along the Teifi, lies the Cardigan Wildlife Park, the home of a wide variety of birds and animals typical of this area of south-west Wales. St Dogmaels is the starting point for the Pembrokeshire Coast Path, which runs southward for 168 miles to the old county's southern border with Carmarthenshire near Amroth.

⑬ CARDIGAN
A market town and holiday resort, Cardigan's history goes back as far as 1136, when this crossing point near the mouth of the river Teifi was the scene of a Welsh victory over the Norman invaders. In later centuries the town became a major port, until the silting up of the estuary and the coming of the railways forced it to seek a new future as a base for fishing and touring holidays.

At the end of Cardigan's main street, the ruins of its castle stand on a wooded knoll overlooking the Teifi. Built in the time of Richard I, the castle changed hands many times in later years. It was for a time the seat of Rhys ap Gruffyd, effectively the ruler of South Wales, who held the first national eisteddfod there. The castle was destroyed by the Parliamentarians during the Civil War. The land on which the ruins stand is private; but tours are available.

LOCAL INFORMATION
Tourist information Cardigan 613230 (summer); Fishguard 873484 (summer).
HM Coastguard Dale 218/459 for information, 999 in emergency (ask for coastguard).
Weather Saundersfoot 812516.

PLACES TO SEE INLAND
Cerrig-y-gof, near Newport. Bronze Age burial chamber. Daily.
Cilgerran Castle, 3 miles S of Cardigan. 13th-century remains. Daily.
Newcastle Emlyn Castle, 11 miles SE of Cardigan. 13th-century remains. Daily.
Penrhos Cottage, near Maenclochog, 10 miles SE of Fishguard. 19th-century with walls of clay, straw and twigs. Most days in summer.
Pentre Ifan Burial Chamber, 4 miles SE of Newport. Daily.

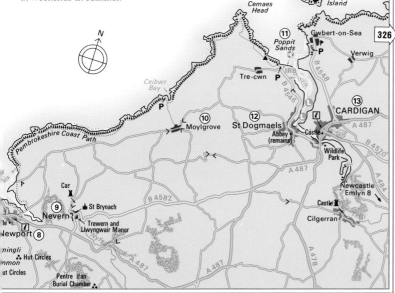

The smallest city, and a goal for medieval pilgrims

This part of Dyfed has much in common with Cornwall – greystone headlands thrusting into the turbulent ocean, lonely coves approached by winding lanes, and the traces of past industries in the form of mills and quarries active until earlier this century. In the 6th century Ramsey Island became a holy place and a destination for generations of pilgrims, while Wales's patron saint founded St David's, now the smallest cathedral city in Britain.

① PWLLDERI
This rock-and-pebble bay on the western side of Strumble Head is easier to see than to reach. The clifftop lane is bordered by a small car park, a youth hostel and a memorial to the local poet Dewi Emrys, who immortalised in the Pembrokeshire dialect the beauty of this lovely stretch of coastline. There are magnificent views of the completely unspoiled coast from the clifftop. Reaching the bay involves a long descent down a steep path, followed by a hard climb back to the road.

② TREVINE
Picturesque cottages, once the homes of numerous sea-captains, make up Trevine. A poet, William Crwys Williams, made the village well known to generations of Welsh schoolchildren when he wrote about the lonely little ruined mill overlooking the beach at Aberfelin to the west of the village. The poem begins:
  'Nid yw'r felin heno'n malu,
  Yn Nhrefing ym min y mor',
or in English:
  'The mill is not grinding corn tonight,
  In Trevine, on the edge of the sea'
and it predicts the changes which were to come to the countryside all too soon. Like many of the local corn mills, the Trevine mill was a centre for the local community until it closed in 1918. The old millstones still lie there, and below the mill, the stream which provided its power plunges into a pebble-and-sand cove sheltered from the open sea.

③ PORTHGAIN
A lane leads down to a narrow inlet, where a small and attractive village is centred around a picturesque pub but surrounded on every side by the ruins of industry that died some 50 years ago. The granite cliffs were quarried for their stone, which was crushed in the huge plant overlooking the quay. The plant closed in 1932. Coasters came inshore to reach the compact little harbour, protected by two breakwaters, and load the crushed stone; they were guided by cairns on the headland, which were painted white to stand out from the surroundings. There is also a ruined brickworks.

Today the harbour, with plenty of parking space, is a safe haven for pleasure craft, and the village is a good base for exploring the coastal footpath.

④ ABEREIDDY
Follow the lanes down from the main coast road between Cardigan and St David's to find this beach of dark grey sand made of fine particles of slate pounded by the sea. Abereiddy's past is hidden around the headland at the northern end of the bay. There are the ruins of a once busy quarry, and on the other side of the main headland is a hollowed-out harbour where the clear water is turned to a deep Mediterranean blue by the slate walls. The harbour provides an ideal anchorage for small boats, and is known locally as the Blue Lagoon. The clifftop path leads to Traethllyfn, a sandy bay sheltered by 150 ft walls of rock.

⑤ WHITESAND BAY
This wide expanse of sand, set into a curving bay to the south of St David's Head, is one of the finest surfing beaches on the Welsh coast. The lanes leading to it are well signposted from St David's, and there is a large car park. Lifeguards are on duty during the holiday season, and the beach is divided into different areas for bathing and surfing.

It was at Whitesand Bay that St Patrick was said to have had a vision of converting the whole of Ireland to Christianity, and from there that he sailed to turn his vision into a reality. A memorial tablet next to the car park marks the site of St Patrick's Chapel.

North of the beach the coves of Pwlleuog and Porthmelgan are secluded and sandy, but bathing is dangerous in the currents swirling around St David's Head.

⑥ RAMSEY ISLAND
The legends attached to this holy island date back to the 6th century, when a Breton saint named Justinian built a cell there. Craving solitude, he took an axe to the land bridge which at that time joined Ramsey to the mainland, leaving only the rocks now called the Bitches. According to the legend Justinian proved too stern a disciplinarian for his followers, who cut off his head.

Boat trips around the island, starting from Porthstinian daily in summer, give an impressive view of its precipitous cliffs, capped by groups of noisy sea-birds, and of the heads of bobbing seals in the waters at their foot. Landings can sometimes be arranged locally.

⑦ PORTHSTINIAN
The lovely but rockbound cove takes its name from St Justinian, the saint of Ramsey Island, and the spot where the saint was buried is marked by a ruined chapel at the top of the hill overlooking the lifeboat station. There are boat trips to Ramsey Island, and to the surrounding coves and inlets.

⑧ PORTH-CLAIS
The clear waters of this narrow little inlet attract fishermen, small-boat sailors and divers. The lime-kilns, now carefully restored, on its banks show that it was once an important port of call for coasters bringing limestone for burning to produce fertiliser for the local farmers. The old harbour wall probably dates back to the early Middle Ages, when this secluded spot was the port for St David's.

SOLVA CREEK *Small craft lie motionless on a glass-smooth inlet that once was busy with coasters. In the early 19th century, 30 vessels worked out of Solva, fetching limestone for the village's kilns.*

AWAITING DANGER'S HOUR *Porthstinian cove is a gentle haven on a calm day, but when storms rage along this violent coast the St David's lifeboat stationed there is often called into action.*

during a violent storm. His partner, Thomas Howell, lashed Griffiths's body to the gangway until help could arrive, so that he could prove Griffiths's death had been due to natural causes. Help took three months to arrive, by which time Howell was half mad. Since that time the minimum crew of a lighthouse has always been three keepers.

⑫ NEWGALE

The beach at Newgale, with its 2 miles of broad, safe sands, is not only ideal for surfing in the right weather, but must be one of the easiest beaches to reach on this stretch of coast, as the main road between St David's and Haverfordwest runs along the edge of the shingle bank behind the sands.

The sea retreats a long way at low tide, sometimes uncovering the stumps of a prehistoric drowned forest. At the northern end of the beach is the so-called Brandy Brook stream, said to divide the Welsh-speaking north of Wales from the English-speaking south.

⑨ ST DAVID'S

Judged by size alone, St David's hardly rates as more than a large village. Its cathedral, however, qualifies it as Britain's smallest city. It was founded by St David, the patron saint of Wales, in the 6th century. The cathedral dedicated to him dates from the late 11th century, and its secluded position in a fold of the hills helped it to survive the turbulent years which followed its building. The fine fan vaulting in the roof of the Holy Trinity Chapel forms a canopy of intricate patterns, and there are witty carvings on the choir-stall misericords. Building the cathedral proved to be a long and difficult task. The tower collapsed in 1220, and the foundations were badly shaken by an earthquake in 1248.

St David's became a centre for pilgrimage; in the Middle Ages, two visits to St David's earned the same merit as a single visit to Rome. A casket behind the altar contains bones found during restoration work in the last century and said to be those of St David and St Justinian. In the grounds of the cathedral stand the ruins of the Bishop's

Palace, built in 1340 by Bishop Gower and destroyed only two centuries later by a successor, Bishop Barlow.

⑩ CAERFAI

A lane leading southwards from St David's main street leads to a clifftop car park overlooking Caerfai Bay, which can be reached by a steep and winding path down the face of the cliffs. At the bottom is a safe, sandy beach, under stone cliffs tinted in contrasting patches of red, purple and green. The purple stone from Caerbwdi Bay, to the east, was used to build St David's Cathedral.

⑪ SOLVA

Steeply overhanging hills give Solva the appearance of a narrow Scandinavian fiord. Its seclusion at the head of a winding creek protected the village from the attention of passing pirates and raiders in earlier times, and today makes it a popular sailing and boating centre.

At one time the rocks along this treacherous coast claimed a high toll of shipping, and in 1770 it was decided to build a lighthouse on the Smalls, to the west of Skomer. It was the scene of a grim tragedy in 1802 when its keeper, Thomas Griffiths, died

St David's Cathedral

LOCAL INFORMATION

Tourist information St David's 720747 (summer).

HM Coastguard Dale 218/459 for information, 999 in emergency (ask for coastguard).

Weather Saundersfoot 812516.

PLACES TO SEE INLAND

Longhouse, Mathry. 2 miles E of Porthgain. Bronze Age burial chamber. Daily.

Promontory Fort, St David's Head. Iron Age fort. Daily.

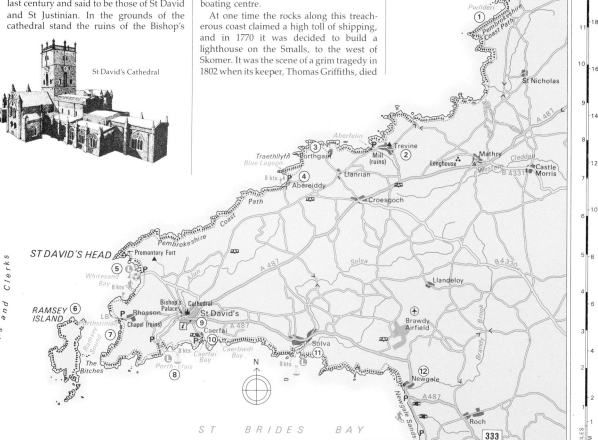

333

331

Beaches below the steep cliffs facing St Brides Bay

The broad promontory of St Ann's Head divides this part of the coast into two portions, the west-facing St Brides Bay, and the more sheltered waters of Milford Haven. This vast natural harbour was the centre of naval activity during the days of sail, and is now a port for supertankers; but industry has not destroyed the charm of this part of West Wales, where sea and land meet in a variety of creeks and headlands, inlets and harbours.

① NOLTON HAVEN

This pretty little village, spilling down a narrow cleft in the cliffs to a narrow cove with a small sandy beach overlooked by grassy slopes, is hard to reconcile with an industrial past. In fact it once had a quay where coasters loaded anthracite from a colliery further up the little valley – but only from April to October, as Lloyds refused to insure boats on such a wild stretch of coast in the winter months.

The lane heading inland up the valley on the northern side of the village follows the line of the old tramway, which carried loaded tubs of coal from the mine down to the ships. The house at the bend in the road, where the tramway line continues as a path past a caravan site, is called the Counting House; there the loaded trucks were counted and entered in the company's books.

Half a mile north of the village, the chimney and waste heaps of the cliffside coal mine of Trefrân, closed in 1905, still stand in a sheltered gully between the cliffs. They can be clearly seen from the footpath.

② DRUIDSTON HAVEN

The village, which takes its name from a 12th-century Norman called Drue, is a few hundred yards away from a mile-long beach of sand backed with shingle which is popular with surfers and swimmers alike. Parking is limited to the clifftop lanes. There are traces of coal seams and even old workings in the cliffs to the south of the beach.

③ BROAD HAVEN

As its name implies, Broad Haven has a wide beach of sand and rock pools. A shingle bank separates them from the road. Bathing is safe, except in the currents near the headland at the northern end of the beach, and boats can be launched from the foreshore.

④ LITTLE HAVEN

This small but attractive little harbour came into being in the 1850s as a port from which coal from local collieries was shipped to markets in other parts of Britain. The beach is sandy at low water, backed by a stretch of pebbles; there are rock pools at the southern end, near The Point. Boats can be launched from the beach, and there are good views along St Brides Bay. Where the road to Broad Haven to the north climbs over the intervening cliff, a path leads to The Settlands, a sandy cove among the cliffs.

⑤ ST BRIDES HAVEN

This remote cove, like the bay of which it is a part, is named after the 6th-century Irish saint, Brigid of Kildare. Facing the small cove of red-speckled sand is the ancient church of St Bride, whose churchyard includes early Christian tombs set into the cliffs. This was a good safe anchorage in the days of sail, and the ruined lime-kilns and the rusty iron mooring rings recall the coasters which once called there regularly.

Bathing is safe inshore, and there are many rock pools to explore. The large Georgian mansion to the west is Kensington House. Built in 1800 by Lord Kensington, who owned St Brides, it was used as a hospital for many years.

⑥ MARLOES

The village of Marloes is close to two beaches facing in almost opposite directions on either side of a headland. To the north is the cliff-backed cove of Musselwick Sands, approached by a path across the fields from the village. This secluded beach faces north and west. The cliffs are too steep and dangerous to climb, so visitors must be careful not to let the incoming tide cut them off from the only path in and out of the cove.

To the south of Marloes village is the south-west-facing surfing beach of Marloes Sands, accessible by footpath from the roadside car park. Above the western end of the beach is the swampy area of Marloes Mere, where the villagers collected leeches in the 18th century. These were sent to Harley Street, where doctors prized them for their blood-letting capabilities.

⑦ ST ANN'S HEAD

The high cliffs of St Ann's Head mark the approach to Milford Haven from the open sea. They make a splendid viewpoint from which shipping of all sizes, from small yachts to vast supertankers, can be seen slipping into and out of the haven. A lighthouse and coastguard station stand on the cliffs, and behind them is a row of early 19th-century cottages built for the keepers and their relief crews. Below the cliffs east of the headland is the little cove called Mill Bay in which Henry Tudor landed on August 7, 1485, on his way to defeat Richard III at Bosworth Field and start his own reign as Henry VII.

HOLY LIGHT *St Ann's lighthouse stands on the site of a chapel dedicated to St Ann and said to have been built by Henry VII.*

On the western side of the headland are Welshman's Bay and Frenchman's Bay, with spectacular cliffs which can be seen from the coastal footpath. Access is difficult, except at Mill Bay and Westdale Bay, and at the west-facing beach of Westdale swimmers must be careful of the strong undertow. At Great Castle Head, overlooking Westdale Bay, is a huge Iron Age hill-fort, with a double set of ramparts, on the crown of the headland. Walkers should take care, for the cliffs are of soft red sandstone, and the path is crumbling in places.

⑧ DALE

This village is ideal for boating holidays. It is protected from the prevailing south-westerly winds by the bulk of St Ann's Head, and its sheltered anchorage faces east into the waters of Milford Haven. Pastel-washed cottages make a soft contrast to the brightly coloured sails which dot the inlet. Dale is said to have the most hours of sunshine of any village in Wales, and the shingle-and-sand beach is far enough up the Dale Roads inlet to be remote from the currents of the tides funnelling in and out of the haven.

The narrow streets in the village have been organised into an effective one-way scheme which helps to reduce congestion, but parking is very limited. At the end of the headland at the southern side of the inlet is a 19th-century coastal defence fort, built in the days when Milford Haven was an important naval centre. This is now the Dale Fort Field Centre, where courses are run in subjects ranging from diving to ornithology.

This whole coast was once a paradise for smugglers, with so many quiet inlets and secluded houses where contraband could be stored. In Tudor times Dale was well known for the produce brought in by its resourceful seamen without payment of duty.

⑨ SKOMER AND SKOKHOLM ISLANDS

Skomer Island, some 720 acres in extent, was made a National Nature Reserve in 1959. From April to September, except on Mondays, when Skomer is closed, there is a boat service from Martin's Haven to the island. Manx shearwaters breed there in summer, nesting in clifftop burrows. There are fulmars and puffins, and the island is also the home of the unique Skomer vole.

The reserve is owned by the Nature Conservancy Council and run by the West

Cliff paths from Great Castle Head lead down to beaches on either side.

⑪ **SANDY HAVEN**

The village lies at the end of a narrow lane, west of the creek called Sandy Haven Pill. This beautiful anchorage, the setting for many paintings by Graham Sutherland, dries out at low water leaving a wide expanse of red sand; but the sands are more easily reached from the other side, following the lanes from Herbrandston, on the Milford Haven side of the inlet.

LOCAL INFORMATION

Tourist information Broad Haven 412 (summer); Haverfordwest 3110 (summer).

HM Coastguard Dale 218/459 for information, 999 in emergency (ask for coastguard).

Weather Saundersfoot 812516.

PLACES TO SEE INLAND

Scolton Manor Country Park Museum, 8 miles N of Haverfordwest. Georgian mansion and grounds. Grounds daily all year, except Mon.; museum daily in summer, except Mon.

SUNTRAP BEACH *Facing south-west and dotted with rocks that give shelter from wind and sun, Marloes Sands are ideal for swimming or sunbathing. Onshore winds provide good surfing.*

Wales Trust for Nature Conservation, as is the neighbouring island of Skokholm, where weekly accommodation is available. Details are available from the trust's office at 7 Market Street, Haverfordwest.

GOLDEN BLAZE OF SUMMER

On the west coast of Wales, in high summer and late autumn, the clifftops are ablaze with the yellow flowers of western gorse. Though gorse is common throughout Britain in spring, western gorse is a different species, with smaller flowers and shorter spines.

Western gorse
Ulex gallii
July-Sept.

⑩ **ST ISHMAEL'S**

The little village of St Ishmael's lies among the narrow lanes to the south of the road from Dale to Haverfordwest. It was once the site of a Norman castle, now marked by a circular mound at the side of the road leading into the village. From the centre of the village a footpath leads down to the little cove of Monk Haven, where low tide exposes a strip of sand below the pebble beach.

To the east are the headlands of Great Castle Head and Little Castle Head, so-called because both are crowned by ancient fortifications. The footpath to Great Castle Head, leading off the road out of St Ishmael's towards Sandy Haven, gives a good view of the two automatic lighthouses, built to guide tankers towards the refinery jetties in Milford Haven, and of the tankers

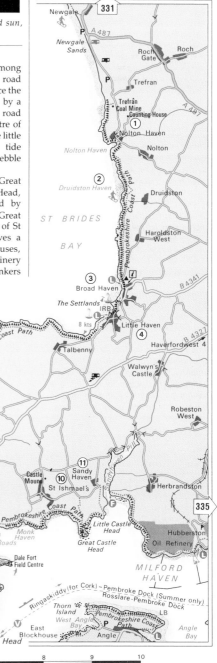

Industry and isolation on the deep estuary of Milford Haven

Milford Haven's spectacular harbour, with more than 70 miles of sheltered coastline fanning out from an entrance to the open sea only 1½ miles across, has seen almost every kind of vessel down the centuries. Coastal colliers and fishing trawlers, sailing warships and supertankers have found berths on its waters, and even the ranks of refineries which today line stretches of the shore fail to mar its unchanging beauty.

① MILFORD HAVEN

The neat gridiron of streets at the heart of Milford Haven shows that the town was deliberately planned. The land on which it stands was owned by Sir William Hamilton, husband of the Emma who became Nelson's mistress; Hamilton's nephew, Charles Greville, was the driving force behind the planning of the town.

The town's original trade was founded on whaling. A colony of Quakers from Nantucket in the USA had fled to Newfoundland to avoid the fighting of the War of Independence. There, however, they found themselves too isolated from the main market for their produce – sperm oil to light the streets of London – and they moved to Greville's new harbour at the beginning of the 19th century. Another boost for the new town was a contract to build ships for the Admiralty, then heavily involved in the war against the French.

Two blows then struck at Milford Haven's new-found prosperity. First, as a result of Greville increasing his prices, the Admiralty transferred its shipbuilding to a new site at Pembroke Dock in 1814. Later, the whale-oil market collapsed with the introduction of gas-lighting in the London streets. To save the situation, new docks were then built to form the basis of a fishing industry.

In recent years fishing, too, has declined, but Milford has now found a new lease of life as a base for one of the largest oil ports in the whole of Europe. It seems as if the fortunes of this little town, which as well as its harbour facilities has a wide range of seaside attractions for holidaymakers, are assured at last.

② NEYLAND

This little town has been blessed with three names in 200 years. Until 1859 it was known as Milford Haven, and when Milford itself adopted this name, it became known as New Milford. The present name dates from the beginning of this century. In Victorian times, its importance rivalled that of Milford itself, and with the coming of the railway in the 1860s it became the terminal for the packet service to Ireland.

Isambard Kingdom Brunel, who built the railway, knew what a good anchorage Neyland offered for ocean-going ships, and he established a special mooring there for the largest of his three steamships, the *Great Eastern*, a decision commemorated by the name of Great Eastern Terrace in the town.

To the eastern side of Llanstadwell Church, there is a shingle bank which provides shelter for small boats and a stretch of water with safe swimming.

③ HAZELBEACH

A line of sheltered rock and shingle coves, edged with grass, starts from the western end of Llanstadwell, itself a long and straggling village spread out along the foreshore and separated from Milford Haven by the Gulf Oil refinery.

There is an inn almost on the beach, and bathing is safe except around the point to the west of the inn, when the tide is falling.

④ LLANGWM

The name of this riverside village may be a corruption of the Flemish *Lang Heim*, 'a long way from home', for it was founded by Flemish refugees fleeing from religious persecution in Europe in the 16th century.

Tucked away at the head of a muddy creek, the villagers kept intruders away by stoning them. They earned their living by mining and by fishing for herrings and oysters, and their tough womenfolk walked 12 miles to markets at Tenby carrying baskets of fish on their heads.

⑤ HOOK

Hidden on the edge of a quiet reach of the Western Cleddau 4 miles below Haverfordwest, Hook still bears some marks of its industrial past. Visitors can see the old quay where coasters tied up to be loaded with coal from local pits. Some of these are bell-pits – little more than huge holes in the ground where, in the 17th and early 18th centuries, miners using picks and shovels hacked away at the seams just under the surface, working outwards from a central shaft. Hook Pit closed as late as 1949, and the remains of rail and tramway links which served the old industries can still be seen.

⑥ HAVERFORDWEST

Walking the steep streets of Haverfordwest today, beneath the bulk of its 12th-century castle, it is difficult to imagine that the town was a busy port for more than 200 years. This was the tidal limit of the Western Cleddau, and ships could just reach the quays below the New Bridge at high water. Now the river offers pleasant walks.

There are still links with the past. One of the town's pubs is called the Bristol Trader, and the town's mayor is still entitled to call himself Admiral of the Port of Haverfordwest. John Nash, the architect responsible for the Regent's Park terraces in London, also practised in his home county of Pembrokeshire; Foley House, in Goat Street,

---

AN ARTIST IN WALES

The artist Graham Sutherland (1903-80) is perhaps best known for his tapestry *Christ in Glory* in Coventry Cathedral and for his controversial portrait of Winston Churchill. However, the Pembrokeshire coastline was a constant source of inspiration to Sutherland, and many scenes he painted there are displayed in the Graham Sutherland Gallery at Picton Castle.

The contorted trees on the riverbanks influenced many of Sutherland's paintings.

LANDSCAPE IN OILS *An oil refinery fills the horizon above Neyland, but the town itself is peaceful and a slipway built for flying boats is now the domain of anglers.*

is a good example of his work, and there are other fine Georgian houses in the narrow streets and alleyways of the town. The castle now houses a museum.

⑦ PICTON CASTLE
The castle was built in the 12th century, and was taken and sacked by Owain Glyndwr in his rebellion of 1405. It is the home of the Philipps family, and its gardens are open to the public most days in summer.

Near by, the road drops down to the bank of the Eastern Cleddau, whose banks are lined with the twisted trees which appear in many paintings by Graham Sutherland, who was a frequent visitor to this part of the Pembrokeshire coast. The Graham Sutherland Gallery, opened in 1976 at the rear of Picton Castle, is open most days in summer.

At Picton Ferry, trams of coal from the local pits were carried by boat across to the opposite bank, to be dragged to Landshipping for loading on to coasters.

⑧ LANDSHIPPING QUAY
Another forgotten industrial centre, Landshipping Quay was once a busy little port where coastal colliers tied up to fill their holds with coal from local mines. It was a prosperous, but always dangerous, trade; at nearby Garden Pit, 45 men and boys died in an accident in 1845. Now the quays are derelict, almost hidden by the lovely riverside scenery.

⑨ LAWRENNY
Because of Milford Haven's fiord-like contours, a picturesque little hamlet like Lawrenny, though more than 12 miles from the sea, can still offer deep enough water close inshore to provide superb moorings for large, deep-draught yachts. A picnic site on the hillside above the church offers lovely views of the Carew and Cresswell rivers, tributaries of the Daugleddau.

⑩ CAREW
The name of Carew may be an adaptation of the Welsh word *caerau*, meaning 'fortresses', and if so it is appropriate enough, since Carew is best known for its Norman castle. It is a massive rectangular fortress with a tower at each corner, and was built by Sir Nicholas de Carew in the late 13th century. It later

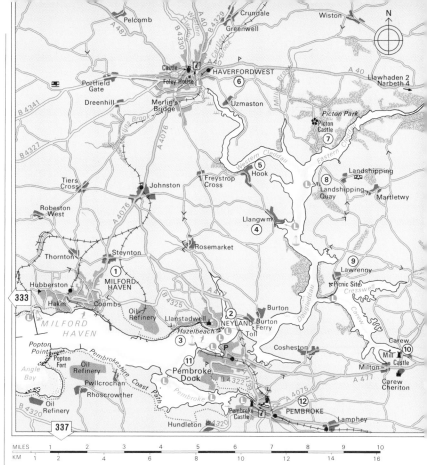

belonged to Sir Rhys ap Thomas, one of the followers of Henry Tudor, who became Henry VII after his victory at the Battle of Bosworth. A later owner, Sir John Perrot, Lord Deputy of Ireland under Elizabeth I, built the North Gallery, but before his work at the castle was finished he had fallen out of royal favour and was imprisoned in the Tower of London. The castle was besieged during the Civil War and left in ruins afterwards. The ruins are open to the public on most days in summer.

Near by is Carew mill, which relied on the rise and fall of the tides to work the machinery for grinding corn. The mill's existence was first recorded in 1541, but the present building dates from the early 19th century and remained in operation for about 100 years. It has been restored and is open to visitors daily in summer.

⑪ PEMBROKE DOCK
When Charles Greville put up his shipbuilding prices at Milford Haven, during the most critical phase of the Napoleonic Wars, the Admiralty called his commercial bluff by moving its operations to the little hamlet of Pater Church in 1814. There they built a new dockyard, and above it grew up the town of Pembroke Dock.

The wide, straight streets of Georgian houses are set out in a gridiron pattern, sloping down the hill towards the old dockyard where, over more than a century, more than 200 ships were built; they included all the Royal yachts except the earliest (Charles II's *Mary*) and the latest (today's *Britannia*). The biggest three-decker man-of-war ever built, the *Duke of Wellington*, left Pembroke Dock in 1852 to become the flagship of Admiral Napier in the Crimean War.

The dockyard closed in 1926, but during the Second World War it was a base for Sunderland flying boats protecting the Atlantic convoys, and as a result the little town came under heavy German bombing attack.

⑫ PEMBROKE
Pembroke's main street is a delightful jumble of styles and periods of building, dominated at the upper end by the castle, a massive fortress centred on its great circular keep, almost 80 ft high with walls 20 ft thick. This was the birthplace in 1457 of Henry Tudor, later Henry VII, but Pembroke itself dates back to a charter of 1090. It was defended by its own walls, some stretches of which still survive, and by the waters of two small rivers which provided it with natural moats on three sides.

A Museum of Gypsy Caravans, Romany Crafts and Lore is open daily in summer. A big fair is held in October.

Pembroke Castle

335

Holiday resorts and holy places on the Pembrokeshire Coast Path

The southern face of Dyfed's south-western peninsula is wilder and older than the shoreline that faces Milford Haven. It is characterised by extravagantly eroded cliffs that project defiantly into the restless sea. At the western end, natural seclusion is reinforced by Army security at the Castlemartin tank-training range, but on the sheltered eastern side lies a string of delightful little holiday resorts such as Tenby and Saundersfoot.

① ANGLE

The little village of Angle lies at the far end of the road leading from Pembroke to the western end of the peninsula. It slopes down to the edge of Angle Bay, an almost landlocked sweep of shingle and sand, overlooked on its southern and eastern sides by the tanks of the BP oil refinery. More secluded, though less sheltered from the prevailing westerly winds, is West Angle Bay, a smaller sandy beach facing the open sea.

Angle's position at the entrance to Milford Haven made it an important link in the harbour's defences. The old fort of East Blockhouse was built by the Tudors, but in Victorian times General Gordon (of Khartoum) helped to survey and plan a whole chain of defensive forts. One of these, on Thorn Island, is now a hotel while another, on Popton Point, which overlooks Angle Bay from the east, is now the headquarters of the refinery.

The village has a lifeboat station near by, and the harbour provides good deep-water mooring so close inshore that local sailors say they do not need to drop anchor until they can read the time from the clock in the hall of the Point House Inn.

② FRESHWATER WEST

A beautiful open sandy beach is edged by rocks and backed by ranks of dunes. Surfing is popular, but strong offshore currents and

---

SWEET SMELL OF SUCCESS

Gorse blooms and fragrant herbs grown on Caldey Island are used by Cistercian monks to make perfumed sachets which are sold to visitors. Natural essences are blended to make the well-known Caldey Abbey perfume. The thriving monastery farms most of the island's 600 acres, with dairy and sheep farming the main enterprises. Dairy produce from the Jersey herd is used and sold on the islands.

Monks gather gorse blooms on Caldey Island.

---

undertows make bathing dangerous. The wind-blown dunes cover Stone Age and Bronze Age sites.

Seaweed used to be collected on this shore for the making of laver bread, a South Wales delicacy. One of the huts in which the seaweed was dried out before being boiled still stands on the southern headland; it is the last survivor of more than a dozen such huts built 60 years ago.

③ CASTLEMARTIN RANGE

Almost 6,000 acres of the south-western corner of Pembrokeshire are cut off from public access by the Castlemartin ranges of the Royal Armoured Corps. But during periods when training is suspended lanes lead to a spectacular walk along the cliffs.

Castlemartin village was the base of the Castlemartin Yeomanry, who were rushed north to Fishguard to crush the French invasion of 1797. By doing so they earned the only battle honour to be awarded to a regiment for action on British soil. The village was also the home of the Castlemartin Black Cattle, a breed now merged in the

thriving Welsh Black herds. A link with this aspect of the village's past is the medieval cattle pound, one of only two in Britain, on the traffic roundabout in the middle of the hamlet.

④ ELEGUG STACKS

These massive pillars of limestone rising sheer from the sea owe their Welsh name to the colonies of guillemots (*heligog* in Welsh) which nest on them, along with razorbills, kittiwakes and fulmars. The Stacks, officially classified as bird sanctuaries, are only a few yards from the cliffs, and can be seen from a clifftop path which begins at the end of the lane leading southwards through the Army ranges from the main road near Warren. The path provides a superb vantage point for watching the birds crowding the ledges and overhangs.

Just west of the Elegug Stacks is the huge natural arch called the Green Bridge of

---

CHAPEL OF MYSTERY *Little is known about St Govan, whose tiny chapel stands on a rocky ledge. Some say he was King Arthur's knight, Sir Gawaine, who became a hermit after the king's death.*

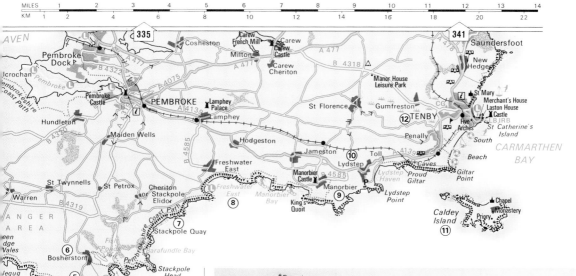

Wales. Eastwards the path stretches past spectacular cliff scenery, including the vast gash in the cliffs known as Huntsman's Leap, so called because it was once jumped by a local huntsman. It is said that when he looked back and saw the awfulness of the chasm over which his horse had leaped, 130 ft deep and 16 to 18 ft wide, he dropped dead from fright.

⑤ ST GOVAN'S CHAPEL
The clifftop walk from the Elegug Stacks meets the point where a lane from Bosherston winds down towards the sea. It reaches the cliffs at a spot where the little 13th-century chapel of St Govan stands tucked into a tiny crevice far below. The chapel is reached by a steep flight of steps which, according to tradition, never count the same going up as going down; there are, in fact, 52. The little bell-cote above the entrance is empty, but is said to have once held a silver bell which was stolen by pirates. The story goes that sea-nymphs rescued the bell and placed it on a nearby rock, which rings when struck. Just below the chapel is a well, now dry, also dedicated to St Govan; it was supposed to be beneficial for curing ailments of the eye.

⑥ BOSHERSTON
This village, on the road which leads down to St Govan's Chapel, is best known for its lily ponds – 80 acres of small, interconnecting fishponds, covered with water-lilies, and crossed by a network of footbridges. The ponds are a haunt for many varieties of birds, chiefly waders and waterfowl, during the winter. They also lay claim, along with several other stretches of water, to being the place where the dying King Arthur disposed of his sword Excalibur.

To the south-east of Bosherston is the fine, sandy beach of Broad Haven, edged by rocks and divided from the fishery ponds themselves by a narrow band of dunes. A road leads to a National Trust car park on the headland above Broad Haven beach, and the beach can also be reached by a steep path from the village.

⑦ STACKPOLE QUAY
A harbour built to serve a quarry where limestone was dug out of the cliffs is now a secluded spot where fossils are plentiful. To the south a clifftop path leads over the headland to Barafundle Bay, where a wide sweep of sand, backed by dunes, gives good bathing. To the east, the limestone cliffs give

'AGREEABLE' TENBY *In his* Tour through Great Britain *of 1724, Daniel Defoe described Tenby as 'the most agreeable town on all the south coast of Wales, except Pembroke'.*

way to the red sandstone that lines the coast eastwards to Tenby.

At Stackpole Head the sea has carved arches through the rocks, and on one side of the head caves have collapsed into blow-holes. At high tides in rough weather the sea bursts through the holes in spectacular fashion.

⑧ FRESHWATER EAST
A steep road giving fine views across the bay leads to a sandy beach, crossed by a stream and backed by extensive low sand-dunes.

⑨ MANORBIER
The splendid Norman castle at Manorbier was the birthplace in 1146 of the 12th-century writer Giraldus Cambrensis (Gerald of Wales), who in 1188 went on a tour of the country with Archbishop Baldwin to try to raise support for the Third Crusade, and left, in his chronicles, a detailed portrait of life in the Middle Ages.

The castle, which Gerald called 'the most delectable spot in all Wales', was so far off the beaten track that Manorbier suffered little in later wars. As a result, the ruins still give a vivid picture of the kind of community which was established by the Norman conquerors of this part of south-west Wales. Below the castle is a sandy bay, with scattered stretches of shingle.

To the south of Manorbier Bay is the King's Quoit, a burial chamber about 5,000 years old with a massive 15 ft capstone resting on the ground at one end and supported by two upright stones at the other.

⑩ LYDSTEP
The sandy bay of Lydstep Haven is privately owned, but pedestrians may reach it down a toll road from the main Tenby to Pembroke coast road. There is a fine view across to Caldey Island, and the caves of the rocky headland of Proud Giltar are worth exploring at low water. The opposite headland of Lydstep Point, at the southern end of the bay, is owned by the National Trust, and a nature trail runs round the top of the cliffs.

⑪ CALDEY ISLAND
Like many of the islands off the Welsh coast, Caldey became the home of a religious community, the Benedictines, in the 12th century. There is still a thriving monastery on Caldey, but today the monks are Cistercians, and they make chocolate, cream, yoghurt and perfume for sale to visitors. The watchtower, now the Chapel of Our Lady of Peace, the old priory and the churches are open to the public, but only male visitors are allowed to enter the monastery. There are splendid views of colonies of seals and sea-birds from the top of the hill which crowns the island. Tenby is the starting point for boats to Caldey Island; they run from Monday to Friday, from the middle of May to the end of September. The island is closed at all other times.

⑫ TENBY
Called in Welsh Dinbych-y-Pysgod ('Denbigh of the Fish'), to distinguish it from the Dinbych, or Denbigh, in North Wales, Tenby harbour must be one of the most

TOWERS OF BABEL WHERE SEA-BIRDS THRIVE

The Elegug Stacks, carved from the limestone cliffs by the relentless tides, are home for many sea-birds, and a hunting ground for others. Guillemots crowd the stack tops and upper ledges, their raucous cries echoing across the tiny cove. Razorbills and fulmars nest below, while black-backed gulls wheel ceaselessly on the look-out for unguarded chicks or eggs.

beautiful anywhere in Britain. Ranks of Georgian and Regency buildings overlook the harbour, but the origins of Tenby go back much earlier than its days as a prosperous and popular holiday resort. Its position at the end of a rocky headland pointing into Carmarthen Bay made it an ideal site for a castle in the 12th century. By the 14th century a town had grown up on the landward side of the castle, protected by its own massive walls.

The castle and walls were part of a plan to make Tenby impregnable, but any threat that existed seems to have been negligible as the walls took 50 years to complete. In 1644, however, the fire power of Cromwell's army proved too much for Tenby, which fell to the Parliamentarians after bombardment both by land and by ships lying off shore.

Though the remains of Tenby's castle are slight, the 14th-century town walls are the most complete in South Wales. The unique Five Arches are in fact the old South Gate of the town wall, miraculously surviving the onslaught of modern traffic. Later prosperity is shown by the splendid parish church of St Mary, dating from the 13th and 15th centuries and claimed to be the largest in Wales, and the beautiful 15th-century Tudor Merchant's House,

owned by the National Trust and open to the public.

In later years, the town fell into decline, but when foreign travel became impossible during the Napoleonic Wars, Tenby was developed as a watering place by Sir William Paxton. Laston House, beside the harbour, was built by Paxton in 1811 to accommodate seawater baths, and the building is inscribed with the message in Greek: 'The sea washes away the ills of man.'

Tenby was the birthplace of a little-known Tudor scientist who nevertheless made a major contribution to mathematics. His name was Robert Recorde, and he invented the sign of = for 'equals' and introduced algebra to Britain.

Tenby has four sandy beaches, South Beach being the largest, at 1½ miles. The beach south of the castle and headland gives a clear view of Caldey Island, and access at low tide to St Catherine's Island. The old fortress on the island was one of many which were hastily constructed along the coast by Lord Palmerston in the 1860s, and became known as 'Palmerston's Follies'. To the north of the headland, another sweep of sand looks eastwards into Carmarthen Bay.

Sandy beaches and a poet's home by the shores of Carmarthen Bay

The eastern half of Carmarthen Bay is lower and less spectacular than the cliff scenery to the west. But broad beaches, cut through by a series of wide river estuaries, offer seclusion and solitude away from the busier resorts. The traces of industry here are both obvious and recent, though large-scale developments like the Pembrey Country Park are turning yesterday's factories and airfields into leisure and tourist centres.

SANDS OF TIME *In 1924 Sir Malcolm Campbell set a new land-speed record of 146.16 mph at Pendine. As speeds rose, even Pendine's 6 miles of sands became too short for record attempts.*

① SAUNDERSFOOT
In the 19th century, Saundersfoot was established as a port for exporting high-quality anthracite coal mined from local pits at Kilgetty and Stepaside. The coal wagons were brought down the 2 ft gauge Saundersfoot railway to a purpose-built harbour, until the outbreak of the Second World War when the last of the mines closed. Now the broad quays and safe anchorage make Saundersfoot one of the finest yachting centres in Wales. The wide sands of Saundersfoot Bay, sheltered from the westerly winds, are popular for windsurfing and bathing.

② WISEMAN'S BRIDGE
This little seaside hamlet, where a stream flows down from the hillside on to a sand-and-shingle beach, is separated from Saundersfoot by a rocky hill, so that the narrow road has to wind inland between the two resorts. Walkers can take the direct route by following the coastal footpath, which runs through the hillside along the route of the old Saundersfoot Railway.

③ AMROTH
The village, once a mining community, has a sandy beach backed by a stony bank, with rock pools. At exceptionally low tides, the remains of tree stumps, deer antlers and fossilised acorns from a drowned prehistoric forest have been found in the sand.

Amroth is the eastern end of the Pembrokeshire Coast Path, which runs westwards and northwards for 168 miles to St Dogmaels, near Cardigan.

④ PENDINE SANDS
The 6 miles of firm, hard, flat sand which stretch along the foreshore from the little village of Pendine were, in the 1920s, Britain's equivalent of Daytona Beach or Bonneville Salt Flats – a natural site for land-speed record attempts. On Pendine Sands drivers such as Sir Malcolm Campbell and Parry Thomas pushed records higher and higher. For Parry Thomas, the quest for ever greater speed proved fatal, when the driving chains of his Leyland Special speed record car 'Babs' broke during a run on Pendine Sands, and killed him. The car was buried where it crashed in 1927 for almost half a century, until it was dug up in 1969 and taken to Capel Curig for restoration.

The sands are hard enough to provide a vast natural car park at Pendine village. To the east, a Ministry of Defence firing range begins 1 mile from the village, but the sands are open for much of their length when there is no firing.

⑤ LAUGHARNE
Laugharne, pronounced 'Larne', is known for the huge keep of its castle, built by the Welsh prince Rhys ap Gruffydd, and for its associations with the poet Dylan Thomas, who lived for many years in the Boat House, with its lovely views over the peaceful estuary of the Taf. The boathouse is now open to the public.

The town is a picturesque jumble of cottages and small houses set in winding streets. It was given a charter as long ago as 1307, and even now the Court Leet and Court Baron meet to discuss local issues on alternate Mondays in the Town Hall, presided over by a Portreeve and comprising a foreman and a jury of 20 men.

Dylan Thomas is the reason why most visitors come to Laugharne, although the poet himself was said to have caused a lot of ill-feeling in the town among people who thought they recognised themselves among the gallery of characters in his classic *Under Milk Wood*. In fact, most of Thomas's inspiration for the work probably dates back to the time when he lived in New Quay on the west coast, but Laugharne still fits the description of the fictional Llaregub very closely. The local Llaregub Players still occasionally perform *Under Milk Wood* and other works in the village.

The Boat House has been restored to the condition it was in when the poet knew it. Near by is the little hut where Thomas wrote many of his later poems, while his grave in the newer part of the local churchyard is another place of pilgrimage for admirers from all over the world. Dylan's spirit is probably most tangible in Brown's Hotel, where he used to drink with friends.

⑥ LLANSTEPHAN
This peaceful little village nestles near the shore on the land between the estuaries of the Taf and the Tywi rivers, protected by a 12th-century castle set between the village and the sea. The castle's massive original gateway was walled up in the 15th century and a new entrance opened up. Above the original gateway, it is possible to see the chute down which boiling water could be poured to drive off attackers trying to batter the gate down.

Upriver from the castle, a wide grassy area called The Green leads to the sandy foreshore. Bathing is safe when the tide is coming in, but dangerous at other times because of strong river currents. Half a mile west of the castle is St Anthony's Well, the

LAUGHARNE CASTLE *Most of the ruined castle dates from Tudor times, when the stronghold was converted to a mansion by Sir John Perrott, said to be an illegitimate son of Henry VIII.*

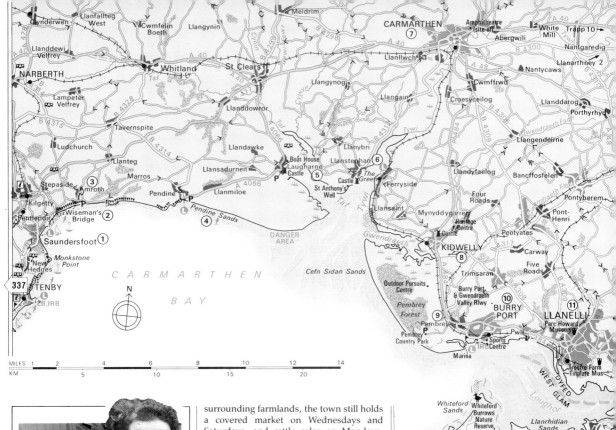

A POET AND HIS WORKSHOP

A wooden hut overlooking the River Taf has been restored to look exactly as it did when Dylan Thomas (1914-53) wrote many of his poems there. He described its view of the 'mussel pooled and heron priested shore' in his *Poem in October*. There, too, he wrote much of his play *Under Milk Wood*, which follows the waking hours of a Welsh fishing village and gives life to a gallery of local characters including Captain Cat, Polly Garter and Mrs Ogmore-Pritchard.

---

waters of which were once believed to have medicinal powers. The empty niche in the side of the well once contained an effigy of the saint.

⑦ CARMARTHEN

The Romans built the camp and fort of Moridunum at Carmarthen after their conquest of Britain: the site of their amphitheatre can still be seen beside the old Roman road to Llandeilo, now followed by the A40 out of the town. At the beginning of the 12th century the Welsh princes built a castle at Carmarthen, which fell to the Normans. Since then, the town's history has been less stormy, apart from incidents such as the burning at the stake of Robert Farrar, Bishop of St David's, during the reign of Queen Mary in 1555.

As an important market centre for the rich surrounding farmlands, the town still holds a covered market on Wednesdays and Saturdays, and cattle sales on Mondays, Wednesdays and Thursdays. Until the 1950s, Carmarthen was an important railway junction, with the main line from Cardiff to Pembrokeshire spawning branches to Llandeilo, Aberystwyth and Cardigan. These branches have since closed, but one has been partially re-opened as the privately owned and restored Gwili Railway, which runs from Bronwydd Arms, 2 miles north of the town on the road to Newcastle Emlyn, to Cwmwyslan at Bank Holidays and during summer weekends.

Carmarthen Museum, at Abergwili east of the town, has a collection of local finds including Roman relics.

⑧ KIDWELLY

Henry I gave Kidwelly its charter, and the town still has a tangibly medieval air, with its massive castle dominating the town across the 14th-century bridge over the Gwendraeth Fach. From the 18th century Kidwelly became an important industrial centre, and its manufacturing past is recalled in a Heritage Centre, on the site of a former tinplate works.

⑨ PEMBREY

Sands stretch for 6 miles between the estuaries of the Tywi and the Loughor, but for many years access was difficult because of the remains of a wartime ordnance factory. Now the derelict buildings have been cleared away and the area transformed into the 520 acre Pembrey Country Park. There are grasslands and woods, with picnic spots and nature trails, and unrestricted access to the beach where swimming is safe.

Near by, the old Pembrey airfield is being converted into an Outdoor Pursuits Centre for such activities as motor and motor-cycle racing and equestrian events, while the old silted-up harbour is to be a marina.

⑩ BURRY PORT

Before the Industrial Revolution, Burry Port was a small fishing harbour. But when the booming coal industry further up the Gwendraeth Valley needed an outlet to the sea, the Burry Port and Gwendraeth Valley Railway was built and the harbour became busy with colliers. By the end of the Second World War, however, the pits were worked out and the harbour closed down as a commercial port. In recent years it has gained a new role as a centre for yachtsmen sailing the sheltered waters of Carmarthen Bay. Swimming is unsafe because of the fast currents of the estuary of the Loughor.

As part of the Pembrey Country Park and other developments in the area, Burry Port's old power station may be converted into an indoor sports centre.

⑪ LLANELLI

Once a busy port, and a centre for the South Wales tinplate industry, Llanelli is still a trading centre, and its covered market caters for shoppers from all over West Wales. The Trostre Tinplate Works on the eastern side of the town maintains a private museum of the old days of the industry. Exhibits include working models, prints, clothes and examples of early tinplate products such as beer cans. The museum may be opened to certain visitors: permission must be obtained in advance from the Works Manager, telephone Llanelli 2260.

The Parc Howard Museum, on the north side of the town, is housed in an old tinplate master's house, and contains more relics of the tinplate industry, as well as exhibits from the days when Llanelli was also a centre for the now-dead South Wales pottery industry.

LOCAL INFORMATION

Tourist information Carmarthen 231557 (summer); (Kilgetty) Saundersfoot 813672/3 (summer).

HM Coastguard Dale 218/459; Swansea 66534/67761 for information, 999 in emergency (ask for coastguard).

Weather Saundersfoot 812516

PLACES TO SEE INLAND

Carreg Ceanen Castle, Trapp, 15 miles NE of Llanelli. 13th-century hilltop castle with underground passage to spring. Daily.

Dryslwyn Castle, Llanarthney, 8 miles E of Carmarthen. 12th-century castle of Welsh princes. By arrangement with Mr Williams, Dryslwyn Farm, Llanarthney.

Bays and cliffs of the Gower, playground of South Wales

Between the estuaries of the Loughor and the Tawe rivers the clenched rocky fist of the Gower peninsula stretches out into the Bristol Channel. It is a surprisingly secluded and remote offshoot from the South Wales coast. Narrow winding lanes lead to quiet bays and harbours, while spectacular cliffs towering 200 ft above the sea stretch eastwards to Mumbles Head, the southern limit of the curving sweep of Swansea Bay.

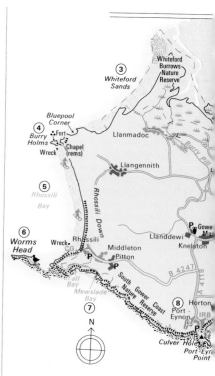

① PEN-CLAWDD

The waters of this stretch of the Loughor estuary are dangerous because of soft mud which can trap walkers and strong estuary currents which can sweep swimmers out to sea. But these hazards are braved regularly by the cockle fishermen of the river, working from centres such as Pen-clawdd. They go out at low tide on to the mud-flats with horse-drawn carts to rake cockles out of the mud, and bring them back to boil and sell.

Each fisherman has a licence which allows him to take a specified daily weight of cockles from the estuary. But the problem facing the cockle fishermen is that more and more cockles are being taken by the vast flocks of oystercatchers which nest in the area.

② WEOBLEY CASTLE

The castle was built in the early 14th century in an almost ideal defensive position high on the southern side of the Loughor estuary. Nevertheless, the castle was attacked, captured and partly destroyed during the rebellion of Owain Glyndwr in 1400. As more peaceful times arrived towards the end of the 15th century, the castle was rebuilt as a fortified manor house.

③ WHITEFORD SANDS

The north-western tip of Gower is edged by a strip of sand which can be reached by following a footpath from the village of Llanmadoc. The sands themselves are secluded, with plenty of pools, but swimming is unsafe because of strong offshore currents at the mouth of the estuary. Behind the beach and a line of dunes is the National Nature Reserve of Whiteford Burrows.

④ BURRY HOLMS

This small island off the northernmost tip of Rhossili Bay can be reached by a short walk across the sands, but only for 2 hours or so before and after low water. As befits such an easily defended spot, its top is crowned with an Iron Age fort. It later became associated with a religious hermit of the 6th century called St Cenydd, and the ruins of an ancient chapel can be seen.

On the mainland half a mile to the north-east, a bay called Bluepool Corner contains a rock pool where 400-year-old gold coins from a Spanish wreck have been found.

⑤ RHOSSILI BAY

The bay's long sweep of sand makes it one of the most spectacular beaches on the Welsh coast, especially when seen from the clifftop path to Worms Head. It faces almost due west, which makes it ideal for surfing when conditions are right, but made it a death-trap for storm-wracked shipping in bygone years. Even now, it is possible to see the ribs of two wrecks of the last century at opposite ends of the beach – the *City of Bristol* to the north and the *Helvetia* to the south.

The beach can be reached by a path from the clifftop village of Rhossili, where there is a small car park. Volunteer lifeguards patrol the northern end of the bay daily in summer. On the cliffs above the beach is Rhossili Down, also owned by the National Trust.

⑥ WORMS HEAD

The southern end of Rhossili Bay points towards the sharp-spined rock mass of Worms Head. The name, appropriately enough for the shape of the island, is derived from the Old English name for a sea serpent. A cliff path from Rhossili village leads down to a causeway, exposed at low tide, which leads out to Worms Head, where there is a National Nature Reserve. The walk needs care, for the path is close to the cliff edge and the tide can sweep in quickly; safe crossing times should be checked with the local coastguard station.

⑦ MEWSLADE BAY

Footpaths from Rhossili and Middleton lead after half a mile down to Mewslade Bay and its neighbour to the west, Fall Bay. There is no closer approach by road, and as a result the bays remain peaceful and undisturbed.

⑧ PORT-EYNON

This pretty little village has a sandy beach, backed by dunes, which offers safe bathing sheltered from westerly winds. The rock-bound headland of Port-Eynon Point, at the southern end of the bay, contains caves which were used as homes in prehistoric times, and there is a semicircular cove about 200 yds wide.

Beyond this cove is Culver Hole, a huge natural cleft in the cliff face which is sealed off by a huge wall, 60 ft high, with openings for door and windows. Its origin and purpose are unknown. Culver Hole can be reached along the beach at low tide from Port-Eynon, or by a clifftop path over the headland.

At Llanddewi, 2 miles north, is the Gower Farm Museum, where visitors can tour a restored farm and follow two farming trails.

⑨ OXWICH

The village is sheltered from the sea by the high dunes of Oxwich Burrows, which line more than 2 miles of sandy beaches facing Oxwich Bay. Water-lilies and bulrushes grow in the damp, low-lying land behind the dunes, which is part of a National Nature Reserve.

The old fortress of Penrice Castle, 1 mile north, was deserted in the early 16th century by the Mansel family for a less fortified but

WORMS HEAD VIEW *Three miles of golden sands backed by downs rising to 632 ft stretch northwards along Rhossili Bay from Worms Head to Burry Holms.*

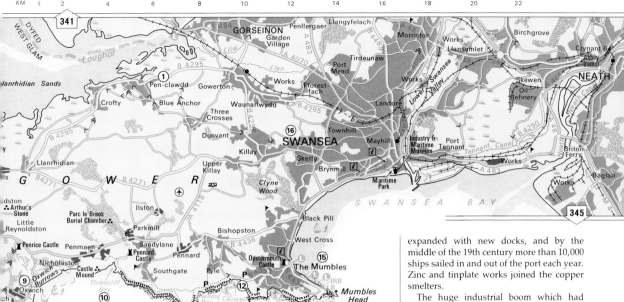

MILES
KM

GORSEINON

SWANSEA

SWANSEA BAY

345

NEATH

FLOWER OF GOWER

The hoary rock-rose grows on rocky, limestone turf on the steep south-facing cliffs of the Gower coast. It is distinguishable from the common rock-rose, with which it grows, by its smaller flowers and the white, hairy leaves which give it its name.

Hoary rock-rose *Helianthemum canum* May-July

more comfortable mansion in Oxwich itself. Called Oxwich Castle, the mansion is now being partially restored. It has an impressive gateway, emblazoned with the Mansel crest.

⑩ THREECLIFF BAY

A footpath from Penmaen leads for about half a mile down to Threecliff Bay, where a stream called Pennard Pill cuts its way across a broad sandy beach to the sea. The remains of an old castle mound on the western side of the valley are balanced by the ruins of the 13th-century Pennard Castle on the east.

The cliffs have suffered as much as the fortresses from the erosion of time; one effect is the impressive natural arch through the three triangular crags that give the bay its name.

⑪ PWLLDU BAY

The secluded beach of sand and shingle can only be reached by following the coastal footpath for 1½ miles from Southgate, or by taking a footpath from Pyle and following a steep track down to the bay.

The rocky promontory of Pwlldu Head shelters the bay on the west. To the east, a clifftop path passes Brandy Cove, once a haunt of smugglers, on the way to Caswell Bay.

⑫ CASWELL BAY

Facing south-west, the bay has an ideal beach for surfing as well as swimming. But bathers need to beware of a strong undertow when the tide is on the ebb; warning flags fly when conditions are dangerous. Lifeguards patrol the beach during the summer.

⑬ LANGLAND BAY

When the wind is southerly, Langland Bay can offer waves big enough to keep surfers happy, though all swimmers need to avoid the water when the tide is falling, because of the strong undertow; warning flags fly when conditions are treacherous. The sandy, rock-flanked beach is backed by ranks of clifftop houses and hotels.

⑭ LIMESLADE BAY

This bay and the neighbouring cove of Bracelet Bay on the southern side of Mumbles Head have small stretches of sand exposed at low tide. Swimming is safest when the tide is coming in.

⑮ THE MUMBLES

From the high headland of Mumbles Head, Swansea Bay can be seen sweeping northwards and eastwards for almost 8 miles to the estuary of the rivers Tawe and Neath. The Mumbles has a lighthouse and a lifeboat station, and was the terminus of one of Britain's earliest railways – a cross between a seaside tramway and a genuine railway which ran along the edge of the beach to Swansea from early in the last century until the mid-1950s.

Few traces of the railway remain, and where it ran there is now a pleasant promenade and, at the Mumbles end, a string of parking areas for sailing dinghies and small boats of all kinds. The wide expanse of sand, with scattered rocks, is lined by a strip of hotels, pubs, shops, amusement arcades and other seaside attractions which stretches all the way to the outer limits of Swansea.

⑯ SWANSEA

Before the Industrial Revolution, Swansea was a small harbour and fishing village at the point where the River Tawe flows into the sea – hence its Welsh name of Abertawe. But in the 18th century, the plentiful supply of cheap coal, together with deposits of copper ore, led to smelting works being built on the river above the town. The harbour was

expanded with new docks, and by the middle of the 19th century more than 10,000 ships sailed in and out of the port each year. Zinc and tinplate works joined the copper smelters.

The huge industrial boom which had begun two centuries earlier came to an end after the Second World War. Within less than a decade the Lower Swansea Valley had turned into an industrial moonscape of scarred tips and derelict factories. Over the last 20 years, however, an ambitious and determined restoration and reclamation plan has turned the valley back into productive use, with schools, houses, new factories and sports and leisure centres replacing the old desolation. The city has 700 acres of parkland, the largest market in Wales, an industrial and maritime museum which houses a working woollen mill, theatres and concert halls, golf courses and gardens, and sandy beaches with safe bathing.

LOCAL INFORMATION

Tourist information Swansea 468321; (Mumbles) Swansea 61302 (summer).

HM Coastguard Swansea 66534/67761 for information, 999 in emergency (ask for coastguard).

Weather Swansea 8091.

Local radio IBA Swansea Sound, 257 m, 1170 kHz, 95.1 MHz.

PLACES TO SEE INLAND

Arthur's Stone, Reynoldston, 11 miles W of Swansea. Bronze Age tomb. Daily.

Neath Abbey, 6 miles NE of Swansea. 13th-century remains. Daily.

Parc le Breos, 9 miles W of Swansea. Neolithic tomb. Daily.

Cefn Coed Coal and Steam Centre, Crynant, 13 miles NE of Swansea, via A4109. Open daily in summer.

OYSTERMOUTH CASTLE *The Normans controlled Gower from their castle built in the 12th century at the southern end of Swansea Bay.*

Steelworks and long sands on the shore of Swansea Bay

Along the eastern side of Swansea Bay runs a long strip of flat beaches, bordered by dunes 200 ft high in places. Industry and leisure share the coast, with steelworks beside surfing beaches, and old coal harbours cheek by jowl with modern caravan sites. Only at the far eastern end do the cliffs return – splintered and treacherous banks of limestone which nevertheless offer wonderful views across the Bristol Channel.

① ABERAVON AND PORT TALBOT

To the west of Port Talbot harbour, where iron-ore ships dock to serve the nearby steelworks, a wilderness of sand-dunes has been reclaimed and turned into a man-made beach of 2 miles of firm sand, backed by Wales's newest holiday resort of Aberavon. Facing south-west, the beach offers ideal surfing conditions in the right weather.

If the weather is bad, the Afan Lido, the largest leisure and entertainments centre in Wales, offers a solarium, an indoor heated freshwater swimming pool, a sauna bath, squash courts and an undercover stadium with seating for 400 spectators. Outside, the 2 mile promenade has ample car parking, and a large fairground with an amusement arcade.

Further up the Afan valley, 4 miles north-east of Port Talbot on the road to Cymmer, lies the Afan Argoed Country Park. The park has walks, nature trails and a Welsh Miners' Museum of Coal.

② MARGAM SANDS

Because they are more difficult to reach, Margam Sands are more secluded than Aberavon, but just as splendid. There is access from the M4, or from a lane which leaves the A48 Swansea to Bridgend road opposite the turning for Margam Abbey and Margam Country Park. After passing an old factory and a crematorium, continue on foot along the lane, crossing the railway line at a level crossing and eventually reaching the edge of a 3 mile stretch of sand, backed by dunes and overlooked by the blast furnaces of Port Talbot's steelworks.

Bathing is safe, and there are good surfing waves when the wind blows from the south-west. On the opposite side of the main road are the ruins of Margam Abbey, with the old Abbey Church and its Museum of Early Christian Memorial Stones. These lie within Margam Country Park, which also has an Iron Age fort and an 18th-century orangery. An unusual feature of the park is its maze, which covers an acre of land and is claimed to be the largest in the world.

③ KENFIG SANDS

Access to Kenfig Sands is difficult, as they can be reached only on foot, either from Margam Sands or, in the other direction, from Rest Bay and Porthcawl. From the inland side they can be reached by a footpath from the road which leads from Mawdlam to Nottage and Porthcawl. The only sign of habitation is Sker House, on top of the headland of Sker Point, at the southern end of the sands: this was used by R. D. Blackmore, author of *Lorna Doone*, as the setting of his romantic novel *The Maid of Sker*.

The town of Kenfig was a busy and thriving community 800 years ago, but by Tudor times it was in ruins, choked by a tide of advancing sand-dunes. Only the castle ruins are still visible, between the railway line and Kenfig village. It was almost 500 years after the town was buried before Parliament passed an Act formally dissolving the Corporation of Kenfig. The dunes now form the Kenfig Burrows Nature Reserve, where a visitor centre explains the plant and bird life of the area.

④ REST BAY

This wide, sandy bay lies between Sker Point and the town of Porthcawl. Bordered by large car parks and a cafeteria, it offers a mile of smooth sand, with sheltered rocky outcrops. Surfing conditions are ideal, but only in an onshore wind.

⑤ PORTHCAWL

Coal from the collieries in the inland valleys was once exported from Porthcawl harbour, but there is little trace of the workaday past in the present-day holiday resort. The dock was built in the 1860s, but the expansion of Barry as a major coal port 30 years later killed the trade at Porthcawl and forced the town to turn to the holiday trade for its prosperity.

The old dock has been filled in and part of it turned into a car park, but the outer harbour remains as an anchorage for pleasure craft. Near by is a miniature railway, and the vast Coney Beach amusement park is one of the largest and best equipped in the country. A long promenade runs along the seafront, and part of the promenade's lower tier has been roofed to create a series of sheltered suntraps. There is good swimming from the sandy, rock-fringed beaches of Sandy Bay and Trecco Bay east of the town, though swimmers should avoid the waters round the headlands.

⑥ MERTHYR MAWR

This little hamlet, with its thatched grey-stone cottages, must rank as one of the prettiest in Wales. It is reached by a narrow lane off the A48 between Cardiff and Port Talbot, which ends at the edge of the wide stretch of dunes known as Merthyr-mawr Warren. Beside the dunes is Candleston Castle, a 15th-century fortified manor house which was lived in until the 19th century, and is now open to the public.

A walk across the dunes to the south-west leads to the sandy beach of Traeth yr Afon, where there is safe bathing. Closer to the Ogmore estuary the currents are dangerous, and swimming is prohibited.

DUNRAVEN BAY *Tide-washed rocks and sands glisten in the sun while behind the beach the horizontal layers of rock rise like tiers in an amphitheatre.*

⑦ OGMORE-BY-SEA

The village faces Porthcawl across the estuary of the Ogmore River, and straggles along the clifftop road. Below the cliffs is a grassy area which serves as a beach car park, and beyond it, a stretch of sand on which marker flags show where it is safe to bathe, well clear of the fast-flowing estuary currents. Out to sea the vicious spines of the Tusker Rock are visible at low tide.

Ogmore Castle, 1½ miles upstream, guards a crossing of the Ogmore which is still marked by a set of stepping stones. Crossing-places like these were vital strategic routes for attackers, which is why the fortress was built there by William de Londres in the early 12th century.

⑧ SOUTHERNDOWN

Grey limestone cottages line the streets of this pleasant little village, set back from the cliffs above Dunraven Bay. A clifftop path from Southerndown leads to Ogmore-by-Sea. To the south, a road leads to the villages of Monknash and Marcross, from which lanes and paths wind on to more of the secluded bays along this wild stretch of coastline, such as Traeth Bach, Traeth Mawr and St Donat's Bay.

DRYSTONE CLIFFS *Alternate layers of limestone and shale give the cliffs at Southerndown their unusually regular pattern.*

⑨ DUNRAVEN BAY

The spectacular cliffs behind Dunraven Bay's flat and open sands are dangerous to walkers on the top of the cliffs and below them, because their crumbling limestone layers are prone to landslides. Visitors should keep clear of the most eroded areas of cliff, and confine their swimming to inshore waters at high tide, well clear of the strong currents near the headland of Trwyn y Witch at the southern end of the shallow bay.

According to a local legend, ships used to be lured to their doom at Dunraven Bay by a family of 17th-century wreckers who fixed lanterns to the horns of cattle grazing on the clifftops. The ships would come close inshore to look for the harbour entrance, and run aground on the rocks at the base of the cliffs, where the crews were murdered and their cargoes looted. The story is told that one gang leader gave up the lucrative trade after one of his followers showed him the severed hand of a sailor's corpse, bearing several rings. He recognised one of the rings as belonging to his only son, who had run away to sea several years before.

⑩ TRAETH MAWR

Traeth Mawr, or 'Large Beach' (its neighbour of Traeth Bach, 'Little Beach', lies just to the north), is a wide sandy beach backed by cliffs towering 200 ft high, and flanked by layers of rock so flat that they look like a man-made pavement. The cliffs are crumbling, and best avoided.

The only access to the beach is by a lane from Monknash, and a half-mile footpath which follows a gully cut down through the cliffs by a stream.

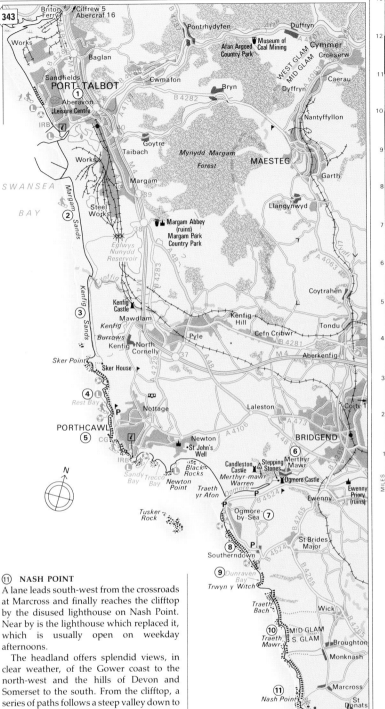

⑪ NASH POINT

A lane leads south-west from the crossroads at Marcross and finally reaches the clifftop by the disused lighthouse on Nash Point. Near by is the lighthouse which replaced it, which is usually open on weekday afternoons.

The headland offers splendid views, in clear weather, of the Gower coast to the north-west and the hills of Devon and Somerset to the south. From the clifftop, a series of paths follows a steep valley down to a tiny beach, with flat layers of rock and a small stretch of sand.

LIGHT POINT *The second Nash Point lighthouse was built in 1830. Its 144,000 candlepower light can be seen 20 miles away.*

Clean beaches west of Cardiff where coal was once king

Wild cliffs and lonely bays encircle Nash Point, only a few miles from the docks and harbours of Barry, Penarth and Cardiff. Early this century, this part of the South Wales seaboard was the centre of the world's busiest coal trade. Now the coal trade has dwindled almost to nothing; but the docks are still busy – with cleaner cargoes – and new coastal development in the area is devoted increasingly to the holiday trade.

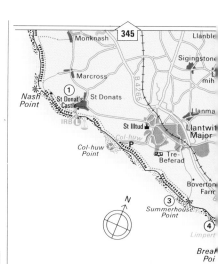

PENARTH PIER *A fire in 1931 and a ship collision in 1947 have brought about major changes to the pier built 100 years ago, but the pavilion is a striking example of pier architecture.*

① ST DONAT'S CASTLE
The castle looks like a film set, or a mock-Norman fantasy built by a Victorian industrialist. In fact it is a genuine 14th-century fortress, but it was bought earlier this century by the American newspaper millionaire William Randolph Hearst, who restored and modernised it, turning it into his own highly individual conception of what a castle should be like. Hearst had parts of other ancient buildings dismantled and brought to St Donat's to be rebuilt into the castle – among them a Tudor long gallery and the hall from a medieval monastery, complete with hammerbeam roof.

The castle is now the home of the United World College of the Atlantic, where students from all over the world follow a two year sixth-form course. It is occasionally open to visitors, and there is a theatre and arts centre in the grounds. A public footpath runs down beside a church to a small bay, bordered by rocks, with a low-tide beach of sand and shingle.

② LLANTWIT MAJOR
The Welsh name for this picturesque stone-built village of narrow, winding streets is Llanilltud Fawr, after a saint from Brittany named Illtyd who arrived in the 5th century and set up a monastery where St David and St Teilo were both said to have studied. The monastery has disappeared, but the parish church of St Illtyd has a stone font at least 1,000 years old and crosses dating back to the 8th century carved with the names of monks who taught there. Some fine painted frescoes have been revealed on the walls of the church.

The village lies on a stream called the Col-huw – and a road follows the brook down to the sea. A beach car park provides easy access to a stretch of sand and shingle, with rock pools. Walks lead up to the headlands on either side of the bay.

③ SUMMERHOUSE POINT
A lane from Llantwit Major leads past Tre-Beferad and Boverton Mill Farm to end almost at the top of the cliffs above this rocky headland. From the coastguard lookout there is a fine view across the Bristol Channel.

④ LIMPERT BAY
This stretch of coast is dominated by the huge chimneys and tall blocks of Aberthaw power station, built in the 1960s alongside the old silted-up harbour of Aberthaw. A lane from the village of Gileston leads after half a mile to Limpert Bay, which has rocks, shingle and a stretch of sand exposed at low tide. A footpath follows the coast eastwards to Leys Beach which, despite the nearby power station, is an attractive beach with sand, shingle and rock pools.

⑤ PORTHKERRY COUNTRY PARK
A long, gently curving beach, backed by rolling green countryside, makes up the park which is little more than a mile from the docks and town centre of Barry. There is a golf course, and there are fine views from the clifftops. The park is crossed by a viaduct built in the late 19th century to carry the Barry Railway's branch line to Bridgend.

⑥ BARRY
This is a town with two faces: the docks which once exported coal all over the world, and the gaudy arcades of a popular resort.

Barry was a creation of the boom in South Wales coal which began in the late 19th century. Barry Island was joined to the mainland by a causeway, and this provided the western shelter for a new set of docks and coal sidings which were planned to outstrip those of Cardiff to the east. A new railway line, the Barry Railway, was built, and by 1889, when the work was complete, the population of Barry had expanded from 87 to 13,000. The £2 million harbour enclosed 74 acres of water, and it was soon breaking all records in the export of coal.

But the boom was short-lived, for the bottom fell out of the export trade in the slump which followed the First World War. Now coal exports have dwindled to a trickle, and are handled by a single conveyor instead of ranks of coal hoists and miles of

ST DONAT'S CASTLE *Restored in 1925, the castle dates from Norman times. Its fine condition reflects its almost continuous occupation.*

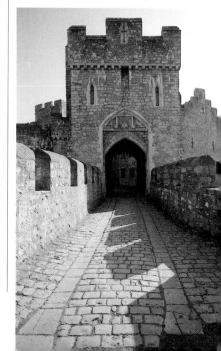

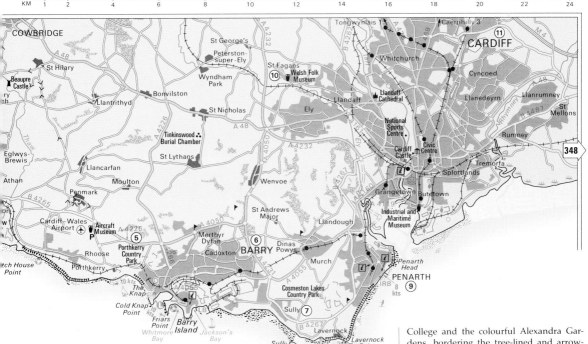

sidings. Many of British Rail's old steam engines were consigned to Barry's large scrapyard – and some have been rescued from oblivion by enthusiasts who have bought and restored them for operation on privately run railways all over Britain.

Barry's other face, as a brash and booming holiday resort, is as busy as ever. On the southern face of Barry Island is a large holiday camp, and there is a pleasure park and shopping centre. Part of the harbour is filled with yachts and pleasure craft.

There are three good beaches, patrolled by volunteer lifeguards at weekends in summer. Jackson's Bay, to the east of the holiday camp, faces south-east. Whitmore Bay is a long sweep of sands between the holiday camp and Friars Point. The shingle stretch of the Knap at the western end of the town, beyond Cold Knap Point, has a large car park, a boating lake and an open-air swimming pool.

⑦ SULLY
Geographically, Sully is a smaller edition of what Barry must have been like before its harbour was built, with a small offshore island nestling in the bay, accessible by a causeway at low tide. The beach is mainly pebbles, with a car park near by. Swimmers should keep clear of the currents which swirl in between the island and the mainland shore.

⑧ ST MARY'S WELL BAY
The beach at St Mary's Well Bay is wild and inaccessible, with patches of sand between rocks and pebbles, walled in by crumbling cliffs. It is reached by a steep path from the road to Lavernock Point. The path becomes very slippery in wet conditions. The bay is overlooked by Lavernock Point, where in 1897 the first wireless telegraph message, consisting of the three words 'Are you ready?', was successfully received from Marconi's transmitter on the island of Flat Holm in the Bristol Channel.

⑨ PENARTH
Like Barry, Penarth is another link in the once busy chain of South Wales coal ports which have now been turned into seaside resorts. The original dock is now partly filled

in, but yachts and pleasure boats use the outer basin, and pleasure trips leave from the pier to cruise in the Bristol Channel.

The beach is stone and shingle, below a promenade lined with pleasant gardens and other seaside attractions. Bracing walks along the clifftops and up to Penarth Head lead to splendid views across the Bristol Channel to the coast of Somerset.

⑩ ST FAGANS
The estate of St Fagans Castle, an Elizabethan mansion belonging to the Earls of Plymouth, is the home of the Welsh Folk Museum. Buildings from all over Wales have been rescued and carefully re-erected; they include a working woollen mill, a tannery, a tollhouse, a smithy and a chapel. There is a collection of farm wagons and machinery, and in the outbuildings there are demonstrations by resident craftsmen – among them a cooper, or barrel-maker, and a woodturner.

⑪ CARDIFF
The capital of Wales and a major city in its own right, Cardiff's fortunes were founded on coal, and it was at one time one of the busiest ports in the world. It was founded by the Romans, and the fortress of Cardiff Castle in the centre of the city is on the site of the original Roman fort. The Castle's Norman and medieval core was added to in the 19th century by the Marquis of Bute, in an extravagant mock-Gothic style.

Coal from the valleys to the north was the lifeblood of Cardiff's expansion – good steam coal that was exported all over the world to feed the furnaces of the Industrial Revolution. In 1839 the 2nd Marquis of Bute expanded the docks and linked them by rail to the pitheads and ironworks. The area to the east of the Taff became known as Tiger Bay, frequented by seamen from all parts of the world. Today, Tiger Bay is a modern city suburb with an up-to-date dock.

North of the castle, in Cathays Park, is the Civic Centre which was built from 1897 onwards on land presented to the city by the Marquis of Bute. It contains the handsome City Hall, Law Courts and the National Museum of Wales, which is noted for its fine collection of French impressionist paintings. Behind the museum are the University

College and the colourful Alexandra Gardens, bordering the tree-lined and arrow-straight King Edward VII Avenue. There are theatres and concert halls, parks and sports centres. In Roath Park there is a 1½ mile long boating lake, and the National Sports Centre has an artificial ski slope at Fair Water.

The Welsh Industrial and Maritime Museum, on the edge of the docks, has a specially designed hall housing massive exhibits such as a triple-expansion steam-engine, a beam engine and a turbo-alternator, used in ships, mines and power stations. Outside, on the edge of the old Bute West Dock Basin, the museum displays an early Bristol Channel tug, a turn-of-the-century sailing cutter which used to carry the Barry harbour pilot, dockside cranes, a narrow boat, and a steam locomotive and wagons.

LAND AND SEA *A saddle-tank locomotive and a lifeboat are among the exhibits at the Industrial and Maritime Museum in Cardiff.*

LOCAL INFORMATION

Tourist information Barry 747171 (summer); Penarth 706555 (summer); 706223 (winter); Cardiff 27281.

HM Coastguard Swansea 66534/67761 for information, 999 in emergency (ask for coastguard).

Weather Cardiff 8091.

Local radio IBA Cardiff Broadcasting, 221 m, 1359 kHz, 96.0 MHz.

PLACES TO SEE INLAND

Beaupre Castle, 3 miles NE of Llantwit Major. Elizabethan mansion remains. Daily.

Caerphilly Castle, 7 miles N of Cardiff. 13th-century fortress. Daily.

Castell Coch, Tongwynlais, 5 miles NW of Cardiff. Victorian folly, part medieval. Daily.

Tinkinswood, 5 miles NW of Barry. Neolithic burial chamber. Daily.

Marks of the Romans on the flat shoreline of Gwent

As the estuary of the Severn narrows towards the road bridge linking Wales with England, the coast sinks below river level, protected from regular flooding only by a long sea-wall. In most of the waterside villages, markers on church walls show how high the waters have reached in freak tidal conditions. Roman townships show that this fertile corner of Wales was settled 2,000 years ago, while elsewhere stand the industrial ruins of more recent times.

① PETERSTONE WENTLOOGE

Lying well off the main Cardiff to Newport road, this lonely little hamlet seems to cower behind the long, low rampart which protects it from the sea. The wall runs, with only minor interruptions, all the way to Newport and the estuary of the Usk. A carved stone on the church wall records that in 1606 the floods reached a height of almost 6 ft above ground level. After that catastrophe, the church was restored, retaining the 15th-century structure; it was subsequently restored on two other occasions, receiving a peal of six bells in 1722.

The flat, fertile meadows round about are criss-crossed with an elaborate network of drainage ditches and channels to carry rainwater through sluice gates to the sea.

② NEWPORT

In some ways, Newport seems to have weathered the changing economic and industrial fortunes of Britain with less resilience than Cardiff. Much of the once-thriving dock area is derelict, and warehouses have given way to vacant lots or small workshops along the river frontages which once welcomed cargo boats from all over the world.

There are castle ruins alongside the Usk, and the open space in front of the Westgate Hotel at the bottom of Stow Hill was, in November 1839, the scene of a pitched battle in which rioting Chartists were shot down by soldiers. Other links with the past include a restored stretch of the Monmouthshire and Brecon Canal at the Fourteen Locks Centre on Henllys Road.

One landmark of Newport which can be seen for miles around is the Transporter Bridge which carries cars on a moving platform across the River Usk. The unusual design of the bridge was made necessary by the low river banks and the need to clear the tall masts of ships; an arched bridge would have been too steep and more expensive to build. The bridge was built in 1906, and it is possible to climb the stairs to the towers and walk across the river on the upper deck, enjoying spectacular views of the city from 240 ft above the river. There are only two bridges of this type left in Britain, the other being at Middlesbrough.

On the south-western outskirts of the city is Tredegar Park, a late 17th-century house and park. The estate belonged to the Morgan family for more than 500 years and is now a country park.

③ CAERLEON

In Roman times, Caerleon was to South Wales what Chester was to the North – a legionary fortress which was the military base to hold down a turbulent area of the Empire's furthest conquests. The biggest difference, so far as today's visitors are concerned, is that while Chester grew into a modern city, and in doing so obliterated many traces of its ancient past, Caerleon has stayed much the same size as when the legionaries trod its streets.

The Welsh name is a shortened version of Caer-y-Leon, or 'Fort of the Legion', and the streets still follow the plan laid down by the Roman army engineers some 2,000 years ago. On the south-western side of the little town, tucked with sound tactical sense into an easily defended loop of the Usk, the original ramparts can still be seen. Inside the Roman wall are the foundations of the orderly lines of barrack blocks which housed the legionaries; outside it is the amphitheatre, which was used for gladiatorial contests, sporting events, arms drill and weapons practice.

In the centre of the town a museum built in the style of a Roman temple contains objects found during excavations of the Roman fortress.

④ GOLDCLIFF

Another of the small villages which hug the low-lying shore of the Severn estuary, Goldcliff, too, has had its share of catastrophe caused by the turbulent waters which are now held back by the stone sea-wall. In the flood year of 1606, the waters reached 2 ft 3 in. above the level of the chancel floor in the parish church. A brass plate records the toll of 22 people drowned and £5,000 worth of damage.

FISH TRAPS *At Goldcliff, large conical baskets are used to catch salmon swimming out into the Severn estuary from the Severn and Wye.*

⑤ CAERWENT

Even in an area which is rich in Roman remains, Caerwent is something out of the ordinary. Because Wales was a frontier zone in Roman times, most of the ruins and sites tend to be military in character – fortresses, small forts, military signal stations, temporary camps and the like. But this south-eastern corner of Wales must have been

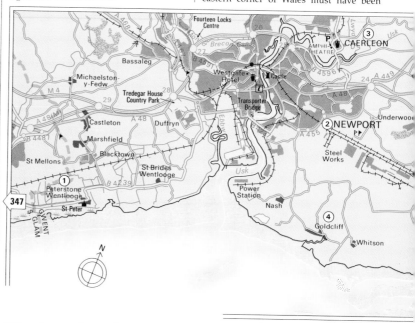

ROMAN ARENA *Gladiatorial contests took place in the Caerleon amphitheatre, which could seat the legionary fortress's entire garrison of 6,000.*

ACROSS THE USK *More than 70 years after it was built, Newport's Transporter Bridge is still an engineering wonder. The carriage can bear loads up to 120 tons and withstand winds of 110 mph.*

Avon bank of the Severn estuary. It is built along both sides of a railway track and is dominated by a huge pumping station. Beneath the village passes the 3½ mile long Severn railway tunnel.

The tunnel dates from the 1870s, when the Great Western Railway, desperate to win a bigger share of the rich coal export trade of South Wales, wanted to cut 60 miles off its route to London by building a direct line across the 2 mile wide estuary. A bridge was out of the question, so a tunnel was dug instead. Because the rock through which the tunnel was bored was honeycombed with watercourses, the railway company built a series of pumping stations, of which Sudbrook was the most important.

For almost a century the steam-engines, and their modern replacements, have pumped 60 million gallons of water out of the tunnel and back to the river every day, so that the trains can keep passing beneath.

⑦ BLACK ROCK

A lane down to the river bank from the road between Portskewett and Chepstow gives a clear view of the English shore and the Severn Bridge. There is a car park and a picnic area, and a walk along the foreshore.

⑧ CHEPSTOW

Of all the castles and minor fortresses built by the Norman invaders of Wales in the early Middle Ages, none has a more spectacular setting than that of Chepstow. The castle sprawls like a sleeping lion on a cliff overlooking a loop in the River Wye. Below, the river surges along the gorge it has cut through the high ground on its way to join the Severn. Chepstow Castle was built by a general named Strongbow, who went on to conquer much of Ireland for the Normans.

The town which huddles next to the castle still has much of its medieval character. Cramped streets twist up and down the hill beside the fortress, and much of the ancient town wall still stands, including the gate where tolls were levied on traders coming in for the town markets.

Chepstow is an ideal base for exploring the Wye Gorge, which winds past cliffs and wooded hillsides to Tintern Abbey and, eventually, to Monmouth.

⑨ BEACHLEY

Before the building of the Severn Bridge, a ferry from Beachley to Aust saved motorists a long detour upriver to Gloucester and back down the opposite bank. Where cars once queued to wait for space on the next crossing, it is now possible to sit and enjoy an unusual view of the Severn Bridge from below, as it leaps from bank to bank in a single graceful span.

more settled, for Caerwent is a splendid example of a civilian Roman town.

In the 2,000 years or so since its founding as Venta Silurum ('Venta of the Silures', a local tribe, to distinguish it from Venta Belgarum, 'Venta of the Belgae', the modern Winchester) Caerwent has scarcely outgrown its Roman boundaries. Seen across the flat fields where the course of the Newport to Chepstow main road diverges from the old Roman road, the Roman ramparts around the village are unmistakable – a high stone barrier, pierced by the foundations of gates. The roads through the village follow lines laid down by the Romans, and near the parish church is the site of a Roman temple.

⑥ SUDBROOK

The village of Sudbrook stands at the end of a cul-de-sac reaching down to a point where the Welsh shore swings out towards the

<table>
<tr><td colspan="2" align="center">**LOCAL INFORMATION**</td></tr>
<tr><td colspan="2">*Tourist information* Newport 842962, Chepstow 3772 (summer).</td></tr>
<tr><td colspan="2">*HM Coastguard* Swansea 66534/67761 for information, 999 in emergency (ask for coastguard).</td></tr>
<tr><td colspan="2">*Weather* Newport 8091.</td></tr>
<tr><td colspan="2">*Local radio* IBA Gwent Broadcasting 230 m, 1305 kHz, 104.0 MHz.</td></tr>
<tr><td colspan="2" align="center">**PLACES TO SEE INLAND**</td></tr>
<tr><td colspan="2">*Caldicot Castle Museum*, 5 miles SW of Chepstow. Local history, Norman castle remains, exhibitions. Daily in summer.</td></tr>
<tr><td colspan="2">*Gwent Rural Life Museum*, Usk, 10 miles NE of Newport. Agricultural, craft and domestic equipment. Some afternoons in summer.</td></tr>
<tr><td colspan="2">*Penhow Castle*, 7 miles E of Newport. Norman manor house. Most days in summer.</td></tr>
<tr><td colspan="2">*Raglan Castle*, 17 miles NE of Newport. 15th-century remains. Daily.</td></tr>
<tr><td colspan="2">*Tintern Abbey*, 5 miles N of Chepstow. Ruined 13th-century Cistercian abbey. Daily.</td></tr>
</table>

349

EXPLORING THE LIVING WORLD OF OUR SEASHORE

*How to recognise the plants and animals
of sandy shores and rock pools, shingle beaches
and estuaries*

Our varied coastline is the product of thousands of years of erosion by wind and waves. Beating and tearing at the original rocks – some hard, some soft – the elements have shaped them into sheltered bays or exposed headlands, sheer cliffs or shifting sand-dunes. Working on the fallen rocks, the same elements have slowly ground them down into particles of various sizes, producing the four clearly distinct types of foreshore that occur round our coastline.

A visitor to the seaside can recognise by a glance at the surface underfoot which of these types of coast he is on. In descending order of the size of their particles the four types are: rocky shores, shingle beaches, sandy shores, and muddy estuaries and salt-marshes.

Habitat paintings for 'fixed' species

Living organisms 'recognise' and are adapted to the different types of coastline, or 'habitats'. If they are rooted plants or immobile animals, it is possible to predict fairly accurately where particular species will be found on the shore. The identification section which follows commences with four double-page paintings showing you where to look for particular species on the four main types of coastline.

Beginners looking at shore-life for the first time may find it easiest to start by searching for and becoming familiar with the organisms illustrated in these habitat paintings. In the paintings showing a rocky shore, a sandy shore and an estuary, additional species which may occur – sometimes at 'zones' or levels higher up the shore – are shown in inset panels. In the painting of a shingle beach, the panel illustrates a variety of pebbles which the beachcomber may discover.

Spotter's charts for species that move

Many organisms, however – especially those of the open sea and the air – are not so rigidly fixed to any particular part of the shore. Though they may use one habitat rather than another in which to breed or feed, it would be misleading to regard them as being confined to that habitat.

For this reason the remaining pages in this section are devoted to identification charts of clearly defined groups of more mobile animals – fish and mammals, birds and butterflies, hard-bodied creatures and soft-bodied creatures.

Equipment for the keen observer

Many marine organisms lose their shape or colour if removed from the water. To appreciate their beauty to the full, and to assist identification, it is wise to use a rectangular white enamel dish in which any animals caught in a simple shrimping net can be watched and identified before they are returned to the sea. In addition, on the coast as anywhere else, the complete naturalist would also carry a lens with a magnification of ×10, a pair of lightweight binoculars and a single-lens reflex camera.

With this equipment, and the help of the following pages, you should soon become familiar with most of the common plants and animals of the seashore.

THE ROCKY SHORE: LIFE ON BOULDERS AND IN POOLS

Rocky shores range widely in character, from wave-battered boulder beaches on which few species can survive to quiet protected corners with crevices and rock pools where a thousand or more species of animals and seashore plants may occur. The number of species also depends on the types of rock and the steepness of their slopes. Horizontal soft rocks such as sandstone that weather to a smooth surface provide fewer footholds or sheltered fissures than inclined hard rocks such as limestone, shales and slates.

Species are found in distinct zones up the shore according to the extent to which the various zones are exposed between tides. On exposed coasts the zones occur higher because of the effect of salt spray created by breaking waves and carried in the wind.

Parts of this 'zonation' can be seen repeated in miniature at any part of the shore where vertical rocks surround a temporary pool. On the sheltered face, a broad band of brown channelled wrack at the top often gives way to a zone of spiral wrack, while the pool itself harbours a number of red seaweeds which on exposed shores are normally found much lower down.

These red seaweeds provide food and shelter for a multitude of animals. Some, such as periwinkles, live by grazing the seaweeds. Others, including barnacles and sponges, are suspension feeders which feed on particles floating in the sea around them, often creating a current of water to draw these particles inside their bodies. A pool left at low water will also contain predators such as sea anemones, crabs and several species of shoreline fish.

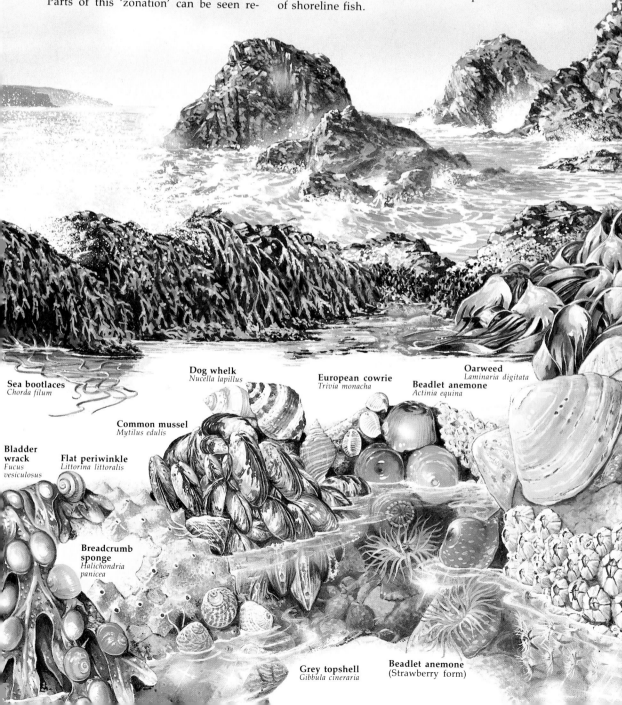

Sea bootlaces
Chorda filum

Dog whelk
Nucella lapillus

European cowrie
Trivia monacha

Oarweed
Laminaria digitata

Beadlet anemone
Actinia equina

Common mussel
Mytilus edulis

Bladder wrack
Fucus vesiculosus

Flat periwinkle
Littorina littoralis

Breadcrumb sponge
Halichondria panicea

Grey topshell
Gibbula cineraria

Beadlet anemone
(Strawberry form)

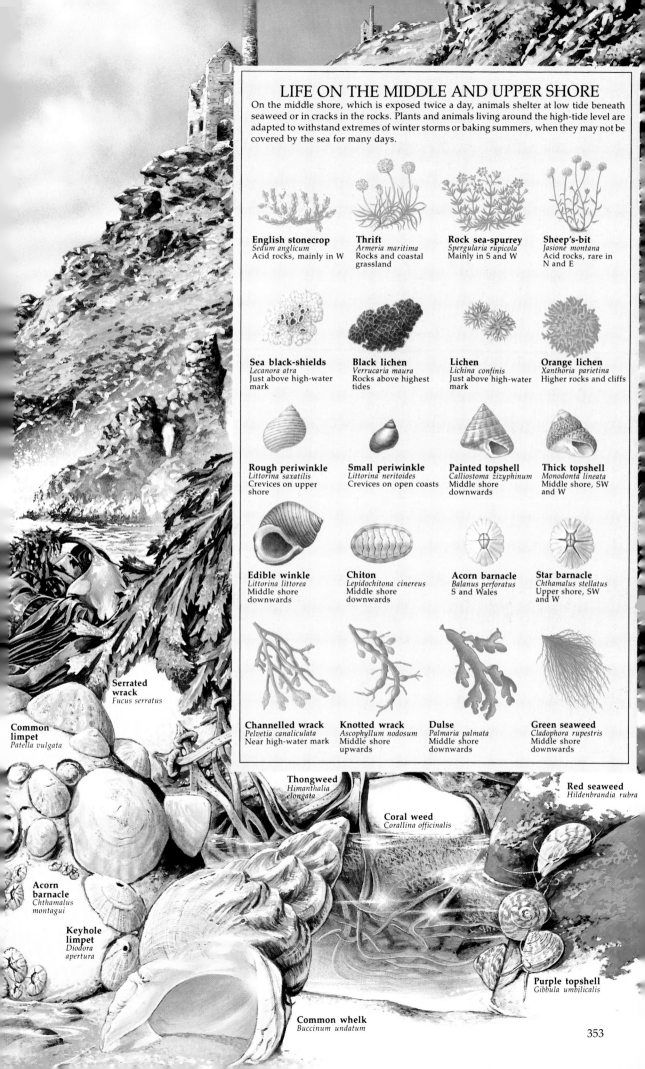

LIFE ON THE MIDDLE AND UPPER SHORE

On the middle shore, which is exposed twice a day, animals shelter at low tide beneath seaweed or in cracks in the rocks. Plants and animals living around the high-tide level are adapted to withstand extremes of winter storms or baking summers, when they may not be covered by the sea for many days.

English stonecrop
Sedum anglicum
Acid rocks, mainly in W

Thrift
Armeria maritima
Rocks and coastal grassland

Rock sea-spurrey
Spergularia rupicola
Mainly in S and W

Sheep's-bit
Jasione montana
Acid rocks, rare in N and E

Sea black-shields
Lecanora atra
Just above high-water mark

Black lichen
Verrucaria maura
Rocks above highest tides

Lichen
Lichina confinis
Just above high-water mark

Orange lichen
Xanthoria parietina
Higher rocks and cliffs

Rough periwinkle
Littorina saxatilis
Crevices on upper shore

Small periwinkle
Littorina neritoides
Crevices on open coasts

Painted topshell
Calliostoma zizyphinum
Middle shore downwards

Thick topshell
Monodonta lineata
Middle shore, SW and W

Edible winkle
Littorina littorea
Middle shore downwards

Chiton
Lepidochitona cinereus
Middle shore downwards

Acorn barnacle
Balanus perforatus
S and Wales

Star barnacle
Chthamalus stellatus
Upper shore, SW and W

Channelled wrack
Pelvetia canaliculata
Near high-water mark

Knotted wrack
Ascophyllum nodosum
Middle shore upwards

Dulse
Palmaria palmata
Middle shore downwards

Green seaweed
Cladophora rupestris
Middle shore downwards

Serrated wrack
Fucus serratus

Common limpet
Patella vulgata

Acorn barnacle
Chthamalus montagui

Keyhole limpet
Diodora apertura

Thongweed
Himanthalia elongata

Coral weed
Corallina officinalis

Red seaweed
Hildenbrandia rubra

Purple topshell
Gibbula umbilicalis

Common whelk
Buccinum undatum

SHINGLE BEACHES: WHERE LIFE CLINGS TO THE STONES

Shingle beaches fringe many miles of Britain's coast, especially in southern and eastern England. Formed by the interaction of waves and currents, they are constantly moving and changing their shape. They are composed of water-worn rounded stones of various sizes derived from hard rocks or from flints formerly embedded in the chalk.

The commonest type of shingle shore is one which fringes the coast and is found, for example, at the foot of chalk cliffs. However, where currents flowing along the shore meet the mouths of rivers, remarkable 'moving' spits are formed, such as those at Spurn Head on the north side of the Humber and at Orford Ness on the Suffolk coast.

Shingle spits built up across bays sometimes extend to the opposite side, thereby forming a bar and cutting off an area of water to form a brackish lagoon or, if fed by a stream, a freshwater lake. A good example is Slapton Ley in South Devon.

Fringing beaches made entirely of large stones and boulders are almost barren, but when the stones are smaller and mixed with sand or mud they can be rich in plant and animal life. On spits and bars such as Chesil Beach in Dorset, which largely encloses the tidal lagoon known as the Fleet, it is the sheltered and more stable land-facing sides which provide the principal habitats for a wide range of species.

Vegetation seldom covers a shingle shore completely. The bare areas between the clumps of plants are often the breeding sites of a number of ground-nesting birds, particularly ringed plovers and terns whose pebble-coloured eggs are hard to detect.

Rock samphire
Crithmum maritimum
South and west

Curled dock
Rumex crispus var. *trigranulatus*

Hornwrack
Leaf-like frond of colonial animal
Flustra foliacea

Cuttlefish bone
Remains of internal shell of *Sepia officinalis*

Mermaid's purse
Egg-case of dog-fish
Scyliorhinus canicula

Whelk egg mass
Egg capsules of common whelk
Buccinum undatum

PEBBLES OF OUR SHORES

Fragments of rock are broken by rivers and waves from mountains and cliffs and then pounded by ferocious seas until their rough corners become sand and the remains are rounded into pebbles. Often beautiful when wet but dull when dry, they can be brightened by a coat of clear varnish.

Basalt
W Scotland

Quartz
Widespread

Chalk
Mainly S and
E England

Granite
Cornwall, Wales,
E Scotland

Carnelian
Cornwall and
East Anglia

Jasper
Widespread

Flint
Mainly S
and E England

Limestone
Mainly W coasts

Serpentine
Lizard, Anglesey
and Ayr

Jet
Whitby, N Yorks

Amber
Lincolnshire
and Norfolk

Quartzite
S Devon
and Dorset

Shale
Mainly N and E coasts

Red sandstone
Widespread

Citrine
Cornwall and
East Anglia

Agate
Widespread

Red fescue
Festuca rubra

Bittersweet
Solanum dulcamara
var. *marinum*

Sea spleenwort
Asplenium marinum
Absent from east
and south-east

Sea-kale
Crambe maritima
Absent from
N Scotland

**Yellow
horned poppy**
Glaucium flavum
Rare or absent
north and east

Sea campion
Silene maritima

THE SANDY SHORE:
HIGH AND DRY
AS THE TIDE EBBS

The millions of tiny grains of sand which make up the typical sandy shore are the product of long centuries of erosion by weathering of the sandstone or other soft rocks forming the coastline. As the tide recedes the sand dries, then becomes loose and is blown up the beach. When it meets an obstacle, natural or man-made, the sand settles and begins to form mini-dunes.

The first obstacle may be the strand-line, at the high-water mark, where shells accumulate and flowering plants grow nearest to the sea. Here nutrients from the decay of seaweeds enrich the sands, and annual plants such as saltwort and various oraches grow.

These mini-dunes are invaded by perennial plants, particularly by grasses such as lyme grass and marram. These plants form an extensive system of roots and underground stems which bind and consolidate the sand. Within the shelter of the grasses, other pioneer species such as sea holly and sand-dune moss become established.

On exposed coasts it is not long before these primary dunes are destroyed by winter gales and stormy seas. On more sheltered shores, however, they become stabilised, often creating a series of ridges which attract such sand-loving species as viper's-bugloss and lady's bedstraw. The hollows between the ridges are called 'slacks'; they are frequently wet, supporting marshland plants and animals.

On the north-west Scottish islands, the great Atlantic rollers pound shells into fragments and these are incorporated into the lime-rich sands of the so-called machair, where wild flowers grow abundantly.

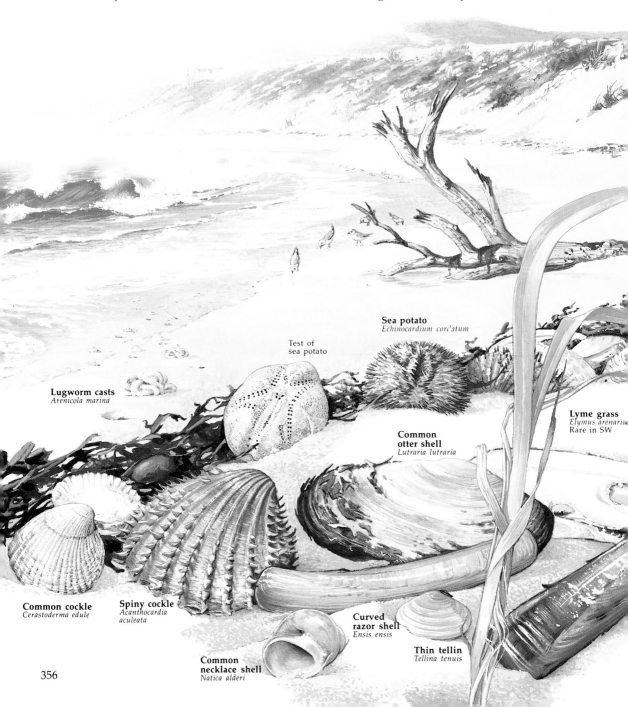

Sea potato
Echinocardium cordatum

Test of
sea potato

Lugworm casts
Arenicola marina

Lyme grass
Elymus arenaria
Rare in SW

Common
otter shell
Lutraria lutraria

Common cockle
Cerastoderma edule

Spiny cockle
*Acanthocardia
aculeata*

Curved
razor shell
Ensis ensis

Common
necklace shell
Natica alderi

Thin tellin
Tellina tenuis

PLANTS OF THE SAND-DUNES

Sand-dune plants have to be adapted to withstand long periods of drought and frequent high winds. Some have leaves modified to reduce water loss: they may be narrow, like the leaves of lady's bedstraw, succulent like those of saltwort, or covered in a thick layer of hairs as in viper's-bugloss. Other sand-dune species, such as sand couch and sea holly, have long roots enabling them to tap sources of water several feet below the surface. As the early colonisers of dunes become established and the plant cover spreads, the dunes gradually become fixed and many other flowering plants and shrubs can take root on them.

Sand-dune screw moss
Tortula ruraliformis

Yellow feather moss
Camptothecium lutescens

Dog lichen
Peltigera canina

Lichen
Cladonia furcata

Sea-buckthorn
Hippophae rhamnoides
Birds feed on orange berries

Spear-leaved orache
Atriplex hastata

Sea holly
Eryngium maritimum

Scarlet pimpernel
Anagallis arvensis

Viper's-bugloss
Echium vulgare

Lady's bedstraw
Galium verum

Henbane
Hyoscyamus niger

Hawkweed
Hieracium umbellatum

Sticky groundsel
Senecio viscosus

Marram
Ammophila arenaria
Planted to bind sand

Sand couch
Agropyron junceiforme

Sand sedge
Carex arenaria

Sea bindweed
Calystegia soldanella

Prickly saltwort
Salsola kali

Pod razor shell
Ensis siliqua

Banded carpet shell
Venerupia rhomboides

Large sunset shell
Gari depressa
Commonest in SW

Ship worm
Teredo navalis
Burrows in wood

Striped venus
Venus striatula

Tower shell
Turritella communis

Thick trough shell
Spisula solida

Warty venus
Venus verrucosa

Rayed trough shell
Mactra corallina

357

ESTUARY AND MARSH: WHERE THE TIDES INVADE THE LAND

The salt-marsh that develops in sheltered bays and estuaries forms a transitional zone between land and sea. It is an area where land organisms must be adapted to frequent immersion in salt water at high tide – and where marine organisms must tolerate long periods of exposure at low tide.

Relatively few higher plants can withstand the periodic inundation and the high salt content of the sediments around their roots. Those so adapted either have mechanisms for excreting salt from their leaves, such as sea-lavender, or else are succulents, such as glasswort, which can limit the concentration of salt to a level that does not damage their tissues.

The earliest colonists of salt-marshes are often glassworts and eel grass, though in very sheltered estuaries cord grasses are more likely. Once established, their stems slow down the movement of the water; this in turn encourages the deposition of fine particles from the sea, and generally raises the level of the land. As the land rises, so it is exposed for longer and longer periods between tides, and species which are less tolerant to immersion, such as annual seablite and sea aster, are able to invade.

Higher up the shore, salt-marsh is dominated by sea-lavender and, particularly in the south, by sea-purslane. At the top of the marsh, where the land is inundated only during high spring tides, there develops a grassy sward on which sea rush and salt-marsh grass can grow. Such areas are often banked and enclosed as grazing land.

Common sea-lavender
Limonium vulgare
Rare in Scotland

Common cord-grass
Spartina anglica

Sea-purslane
Halimione portulacoides
Rare in Scotland

Annual seablite
Suaeda maritima

Glasswort
Salicornia europaea

Eel grass
Zostera marina
Leaves lie flat
at low tide

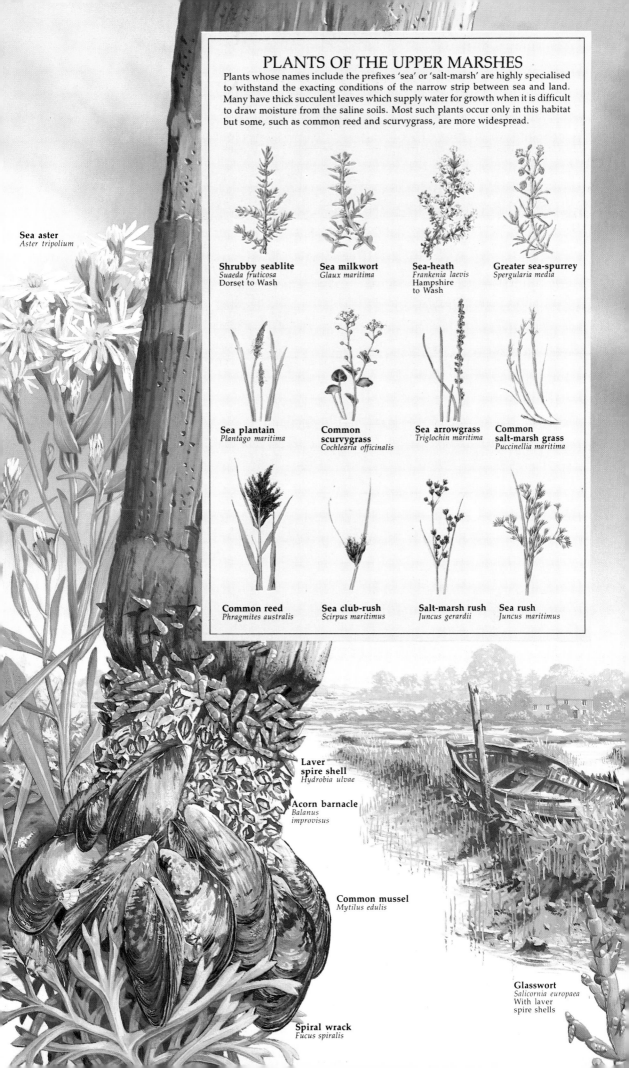

Sea aster
Aster tripolium

PLANTS OF THE UPPER MARSHES

Plants whose names include the prefixes 'sea' or 'salt-marsh' are highly specialised to withstand the exacting conditions of the narrow strip between sea and land. Many have thick succulent leaves which supply water for growth when it is difficult to draw moisture from the saline soils. Most such plants occur only in this habitat but some, such as common reed and scurvygrass, are more widespread.

Shrubby seablite
Suaeda fruticosa
Dorset to Wash

Sea milkwort
Glaux maritima

Sea-heath
Frankenia laevis
Hampshire
to Wash

Greater sea-spurrey
Spergularia media

Sea plantain
Plantago maritima

**Common
scurvygrass**
Cochlearia officinalis

Sea arrowgrass
Triglochin maritima

**Common
salt-marsh grass**
Puccinellia maritima

Common reed
Phragmites australis

Sea club-rush
Scirpus maritimus

Salt-marsh rush
Juncus gerardii

Sea rush
Juncus maritimus

Laver
spire shell
Hydrobia ulvae

Acorn barnacle
*Balanus
improvisus*

Common mussel
Mytilus edulis

Glasswort
Salicornia europaea
With laver
spire shells

Spiral wrack
Fucus spiralis

BIRDS OF THE SEA AND SHORE

Cliffs and open seas

Many cliffs and stacks on the west and north coasts of Britain support enormous colonies of nesting birds. In these inaccessible places, eggs and chicks are safe from predators such as man and his domestic animals.

Many of these species, such as fulmars, gannets and great skuas, are true sea-birds. They feed on marine organisms and spend their winters at sea, often thousands of miles from our shores. Others, however, such as shags, cormorants and many gulls, remain in their nesting area throughout the year.

Resident wildfowl such as mallards and pochards are joined in winter by huge flocks of migrants including Brent geese and pink-footed geese that fly in from their Arctic breeding grounds.

Jet-black head

Little gull *Larus minutus*
11 in. (28 cm)
Mostly winter visitor

Black-headed gull
Larus ridibundus
14-15 in. (36-38 cm)
Migrants join natives in winter

Brown head

White leading edge to wings

Rounded wings

Fulmar
Fulmarus glacialis
18 in. (45 cm)
Cliff sides, especially N and W

Black back

Thick neck

Heavy yellow bill, red spot

Grey wings

All-red bill

Translucent wing-patch

Great black-backed gull
Larus marinus
25-31 in. (64-79 cm)
Migrants join natives in winter

Slate grey above

Arctic tern
Sterna paradisaea
15 in. (38 cm)
Summer visitor, commonest in N isles

Orange-red bill, black tip

Common tern
Sterna hirundo
14 in. (36 cm)
Mainly summer visitor

White forehead

Little tern
Sterna albifrons
10 in. (25 cm)
Summer visitor, sand and shingle

Yellow bill, black tip

Lesser black-backed gull
Larus fuscus
21-22 in. (53-55 cm)
Mainly summer visitor

Black-and-white wingtips

Herring gull
Larus argentatus
22-26 in. (55-66 cm)
Commonest coastal gull

Black wingtips

Yellow bill, red spot

White cheeks

Puffin
Fratercula arctica
12 in. (30 cm)
Commonest in N and W

Black-and-white wingtips

Triangular brightly coloured bill

Yellow-green bill

Yellow bill, red spot

Common gull
Larus canus
16 in. (40 cm)
Only common in Scotland

Kittiwake *Rissa tridactyla*
16 in. (40 cm)
Steep cliffs, especially N and W

Long narrow wings

Immature

Gannet
Sula bassana
36 in. (90 cm)
Dense colonies on rocky islands or stacks in N and W

Black tips

Great skua
Stercorarius skua
23 in. (58 cm)
Mainly summer visitor

Pointed tail

Dark brown above

Slim pointed bill

White wing-patch

Razorbill
Alca torda
16 in. (40 cm)
Nests in cliff crevices

Black upper parts

Rusty brown underparts

Guillemot
Uria aalge
16 in. (40 cm)
Dense colonies on cliff ledges

Black guillemot
Cepphus grylle
13½ in. (34 cm)
N and W coasts of Scotland

Flat bill with white line

Shag
Phalacrocorax aristotelis
30 in. (76 cm)
Nests on rocky cliffs and islands

Short crest in breeding season

White cheeks

White patch on thighs

Cormorant
Phalacrocorax carbo
36 in. (90 cm)
Nests on cliff ledges

No white on forehead

Pink and black bill

White forehead

White-fronted goose
Anser albifrons
26-30 in. (66-76 cm)
Winter visitor

Black bars on belly

No black bars on belly

Orange legs

Greylag goose
Anser anser
30-35 in. (76-89 cm)
Breeds mainly in Scotland, some in E England

No white on forehead

Orange bill

No black bars on belly

Pink legs

Pink-footed goose
Anser brachyrhynchus
24-30 in. (60-76 cm)
Winter visitor from Iceland

Black head and neck

Small white neck-patch

White spot

Goldeneye
Bucephala clangula
18 in. (46 cm)
Mainly winter visitor, estuaries

Green head

Male

Maroon breast

Violet-blue wing-patch

Mallard
Anas platyrhynchos
23 in. (58 cm)
Estuaries and mud-flats in winter

Female

Brent goose
Branta bernicla
22-24 in. (56-60 cm)
Winter visitor to SE coasts

Red-breasted merganser
Mergus serrator
23 in. (58 cm)
Mainly on estuaries in winter

Shorter crest

Female

White throat and neck

Double crest

White collar

Male

Pochard
Aythya ferina
18 in. (45 cm)
Migrants join natives in winter

Female Dull brown

Red head

Black breast

Male

Male

White stripe on neck

Long tail

Pintail
Anas acuta
26 in. (66 cm)
Mainly winter visitor, estuaries

White wing-patch

Wigeon
Anas penelope
18 in. (46 cm)
Immigrants increase winter numbers

Pointed tail

Pale cheeks

Orange-yellow bill patch and knob

Female

Male

Common scoter
Melanitta nigra
19 in. (48 cm)
Mainly winter visitor

White forehead

Male

Blackish head and breast

Upturned bill

Red-throated diver
Gavia stellata
21-23 in. (53-58 cm)
Commonest in winter, breeds NW Scotland

Female

Blunt tail

Scaup
Aythya marila
19 in. (48 cm),
Winter visitor,
feeds on estuary molluscs

Red throat, in summer

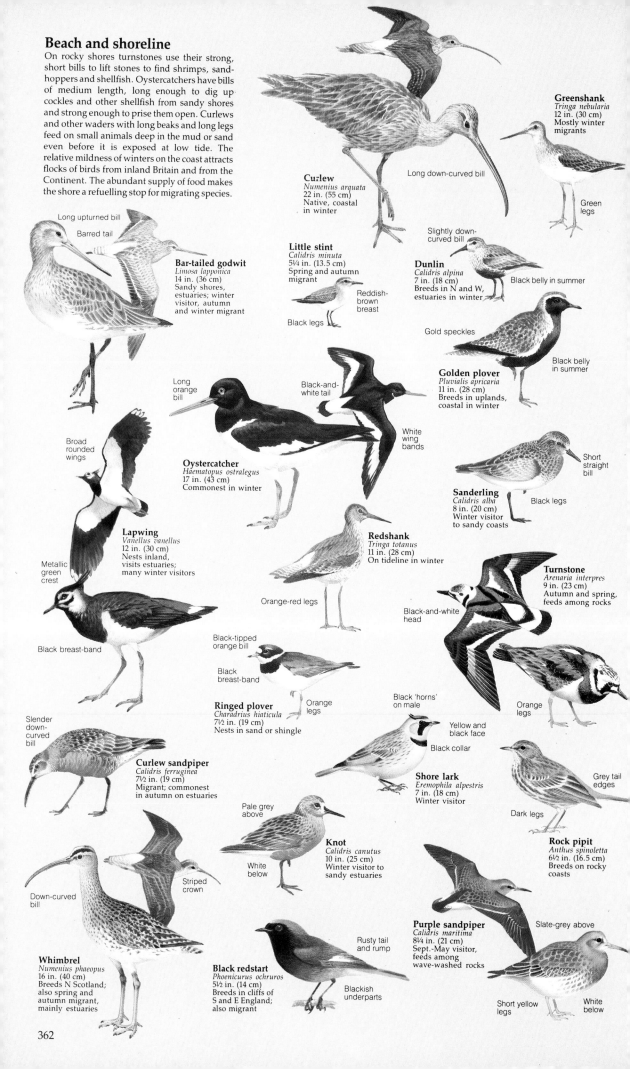

Beach and shoreline

On rocky shores turnstones use their strong, short bills to lift stones to find shrimps, sand-hoppers and shellfish. Oystercatchers have bills of medium length, long enough to dig up cockles and other shellfish from sandy shores and strong enough to prise them open. Curlews and other waders with long beaks and long legs feed on small animals deep in the mud or sand even before it is exposed at low tide. The relative mildness of winters on the coast attracts flocks of birds from inland Britain and from the Continent. The abundant supply of food makes the shore a refuelling stop for migrating species.

Curlew
Numenius arquata
22 in. (55 cm)
Native, coastal
in winter

Long down-curved bill

Greenshank
Tringa nebularia
12 in. (30 cm)
Mostly winter
migrants

Green legs

Long upturned bill

Barred tail

Bar-tailed godwit
Limosa lapponica
14 in. (36 cm)
Sandy shores,
estuaries; winter
visitor, autumn
and winter migrant

Little stint
Calidris minuta
5¼ in. (13.5 cm)
Spring and autumn
migrant

Reddish-brown breast

Black legs

Slightly down-curved bill

Dunlin
Calidris alpina
7 in. (18 cm)
Breeds in N and W,
estuaries in winter

Black belly in summer

Gold speckles

Golden plover
Pluvialis apricaria
11 in. (28 cm)
Breeds in uplands,
coastal in winter

Black belly in summer

Broad rounded wings

Black-and-white tail

White wing bands

Oystercatcher
Haematopus ostralegus
17 in. (43 cm)
Commonest in winter

Short straight bill

Sanderling
Calidris alba
8 in. (20 cm)
Winter visitor
to sandy coasts

Black legs

Lapwing
Vanellus vanellus
12 in. (30 cm)
Nests inland,
visits estuaries;
many winter visitors

Redshank
Tringa totanus
11 in. (28 cm)
On tideline in winter

Metallic green crest

Orange-red legs

Turnstone
Arenaria interpres
9 in. (23 cm)
Autumn and spring,
feeds among rocks

Black-and-white head

Black breast-band

Black-tipped orange bill

Black breast-band

Ringed plover
Charadrius hiaticula
7½ in. (19 cm)
Nests in sand or shingle

Orange legs

Orange legs

Slender down-curved bill

Black 'horns' on male

Yellow and black face

Black collar

Curlew sandpiper
Calidris ferruginea
7½ in. (19 cm)
Migrant; commonest
in autumn on estuaries

Shore lark
Eremophila alpestris
7 in. (18 cm)
Winter visitor

Grey tail edges

Dark legs

Pale grey above

White below

Knot
Calidris canutus
10 in. (25 cm)
Winter visitor to
sandy estuaries

Rock pipit
Anthus spinoletta
6½ in. (16.5 cm)
Breeds on rocky
coasts

Striped crown

Down-curved bill

Rusty tail and rump

Purple sandpiper
Calidris maritima
8¼ in. (21 cm)
Sept.-May visitor,
feeds among
wave-washed rocks

Slate-grey above

Whimbrel
Numenius phaeopus
16 in. (40 cm);
Breeds N Scotland;
also spring and
autumn migrant,
mainly estuaries

Black redstart
Phoenicurus ochruros
5½ in. (14 cm)
Breeds in cliffs of
S and E England;
also migrant

Blackish underparts

Short yellow legs

White below

BUTTERFLIES OF THE COAST

Clifftops and woods

Surroundings in which butterflies abound, such as mixed scrub, grassland and sunlit woodland clearings, are fast disappearing inland but are still to be found on Britain's coasts. Exposed clifftops, especially in the west, are covered in gorse and blackthorn, interspersed with drifts of kidney vetch and thrift. Sheltered valleys harbour woodland plants which provide leaves for caterpillars and nectar for mature insects.

In the woods occur species of fritillary – hard to identify, as they move fast and settle infrequently. Marbled whites and speckled woods are easier to pick out in flight. In open areas common blues are not easily mistaken, and are frequently seen with other small butterflies such as small coppers and small heaths. These are joined in midsummer by the medium-sized gatekeeper, feeding almost exclusively on brambles.

Dark-green fritillary
Argynnis aglaja
Meadows and woodland clearings, mostly S and W
July and Aug.

Yellowish-green on underside

Pearly margin on hind-wings

Small pearl-bordered fritillary
Boloria selene
Woodland clearings, S and W
May and Aug.

Small tortoiseshell
Aglais urticae
Open country, widespread
May – Oct.

White spot on fore-wings

Grey scales on veins

Lilac-blue upper side

Male
Silvery blue

Male

Chalk-hill blue
Lysandra coridon
Chalk or limestone grassland, S and E England
July and Aug.

Female
Brown

Green-veined white
Artogeia napi
Clifftops and meadows, widespread
June – Sept.

Common blue
Polyommatus icarus
Grassland, widespread
Apr. – Sept.

Peacock
Inachis io
Open country; England and Wales. July – Sept.

Large 'eye' on wings

Jagged shape

Male
Orange patch on fore-wings

Female
No orange patch

Orange tip
Anthocharis cardamines
Meadows and woods, England and Wales
Late Apr. – early June

Small heath
Coenonympha pamphilus
Open country, very common
May – Sept.

Grey border to wings

Comma
Polygonia c-album
Open country, Wales and S England. July and Aug.

Black apex to fore-wings

Brimstone
Gonepteryx rhamni
Open country, Wales and S England. Early spring and midsummer

Long dark line on fore-wings

Male
Lemon-yellow

Large white
Pieris brassicae
Widespread; some from Europe
Apr. and May, July and Aug.

Faint greyish marks on fore-wings

Small white
Artogeia rapae
Meadows; absent Shetland and W Isles. very common elsewhere
Mar. – Sept.

Black eye-spot, white centre

Small skipper
Thymelicus flavus
Widespread, S and central England and Wales
June – Aug.

Thick black marks on fore-wings

Black eye-spot

Gatekeeper
Pyronia tithonus
In brambles, England and Wales
July and Aug.

Large skipper
Ochlodes venatus
Chalk downs, England and Wales
June – Aug.

Female

Dark spots and border

Twin spots on hind-wings

Small copper
Lycaena phlaeas
Grassland, widespread except far N
Spring to autumn

Female
Orange markings

Male

Meadow brown
Maniola jurtina
Dry grassland, very common
June – Aug.

Clouded yellow
Colias croceus
Migrant from south
Apr. – Sept.

White spots

White spots on fore-wings

Painted lady
Cynthia cardui
Open country, immigrant, widespread
June – Sept.

Red admiral
Vanessa atalanta
Migrant from south and south-east
May – Oct.

Scarlet band

Eye-spots on fore-wings

Grayling
Hipparchia semele
Open heaths and dry hillsides, widespread
July – Sept.

FISH AND SEA MAMMALS

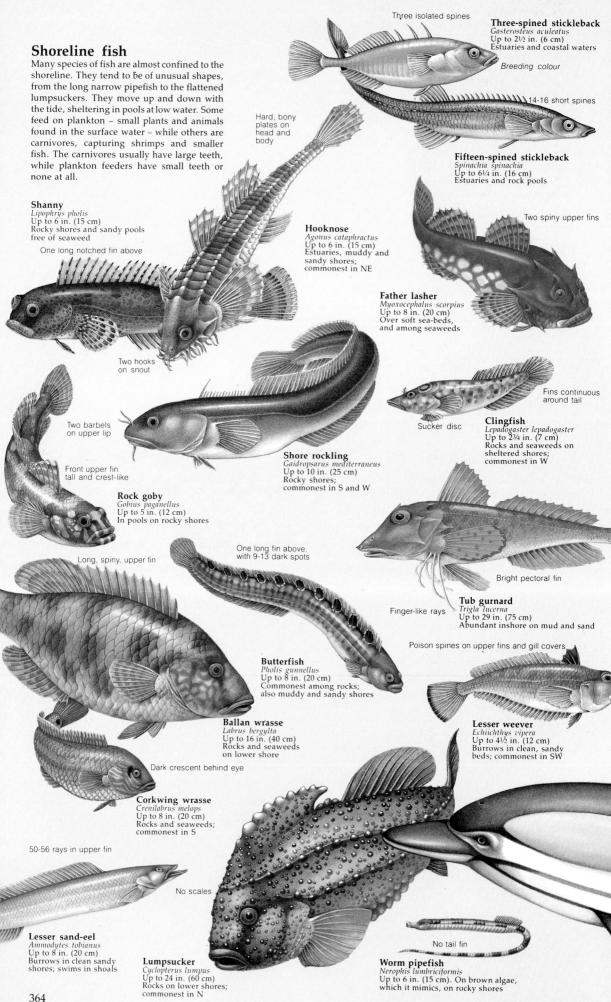

Shoreline fish

Many species of fish are almost confined to the shoreline. They tend to be of unusual shapes, from the long narrow pipefish to the flattened lumpsuckers. They move up and down with the tide, sheltering in pools at low water. Some feed on plankton – small plants and animals found in the surface water – while others are carnivores, capturing shrimps and smaller fish. The carnivores usually have large teeth, while plankton feeders have small teeth or none at all.

Three isolated spines

Three-spined stickleback
Gasterosteus aculeatus
Up to 2½ in. (6 cm)
Estuaries and coastal waters

Breeding colour

14-16 short spines

Fifteen-spined stickleback
Spinachia spinachia
Up to 6¼ in. (16 cm)
Estuaries and rock pools

Hard, bony plates on head and body

Two spiny upper fins

Shanny
Lipophrys pholis
Up to 6 in. (15 cm)
Rocky shores and sandy pools free of seaweed

One long notched fin above

Hooknose
Agonus cataphractus
Up to 6 in. (15 cm)
Estuaries, muddy and sandy shores; commonest in NE

Father lasher
Myoxocephalus scorpius
Up to 8 in. (20 cm)
Over soft sea-beds, and among seaweeds

Two hooks on snout

Fins continuous around tail

Sucker disc

Clingfish
Lepadogaster lepadogaster
Up to 2¾ in. (7 cm)
Rocks and seaweeds on sheltered shores; commonest in W

Two barbels on upper lip

Shore rockling
Gaidropsarus mediterraneus
Up to 10 in. (25 cm)
Rocky shores; commonest in S and W

Front upper fin tall and crest-like

Rock goby
Gobius paganellus
Up to 5 in. (12 cm)
In pools on rocky shores

One long fin above, with 9-13 dark spots

Long, spiny, upper fin

Bright pectoral fin

Finger-like rays

Tub gurnard
Trigla lucerna
Up to 29 in. (75 cm)
Abundant inshore on mud and sand

Poison spines on upper fins and gill covers

Butterfish
Pholis gunnellus
Up to 8 in. (20 cm)
Commonest among rocks; also muddy and sandy shores

Ballan wrasse
Labrus bergylta
Up to 16 in. (40 cm)
Rocks and seaweeds on lower shore

Lesser weever
Echiichthys vipera
Up to 4½ in. (12 cm)
Burrows in clean, sandy beds; commonest in SW

Dark crescent behind eye

Corkwing wrasse
Crenilabrus melops
Up to 8 in. (20 cm)
Rocks and seaweeds; commonest in S

50-56 rays in upper fin

No scales

No tail fin

Lesser sand-eel
Ammodytes tobianus
Up to 8 in. (20 cm)
Burrows in clean sandy shores; swims in shoals

Lumpsucker
Cyclopterus lumpus
Up to 24 in. (60 cm)
Rocks on lower shores; commonest in N

Worm pipefish
Nerophis lumbriciformis
Up to 6 in. (15 cm). On brown algae, which it mimics, on rocky shores

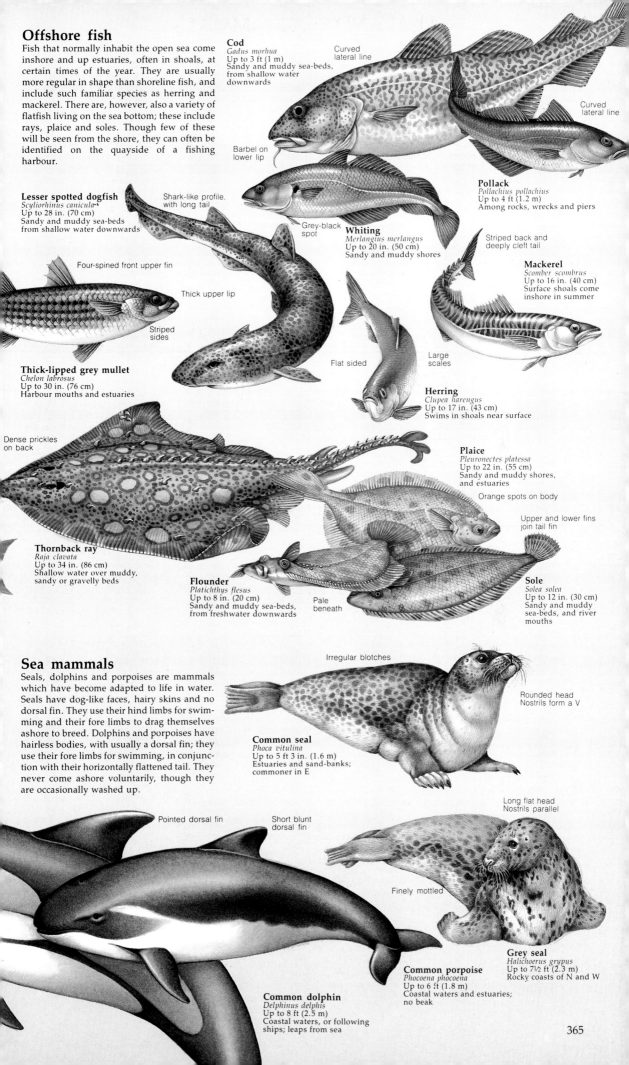

Offshore fish

Fish that normally inhabit the open sea come inshore and up estuaries, often in shoals, at certain times of the year. They are usually more regular in shape than shoreline fish, and include such familiar species as herring and mackerel. There are, however, also a variety of flatfish living on the sea bottom; these include rays, plaice and soles. Though few of these will be seen from the shore, they can often be identified on the quayside of a fishing harbour.

Cod
Gadus morhua
Up to 3 ft (1 m)
Sandy and muddy sea-beds, from shallow water downwards

Curved lateral line

Curved lateral line

Barbel on lower lip

Pollack
Pollachius pollachius
Up to 4 ft (1.2 m)
Among rocks, wrecks and piers

Shark-like profile, with long tail

Lesser spotted dogfish
Scyliorhinus canicula
Up to 28 in. (70 cm)
Sandy and muddy sea-beds from shallow water downwards

Grey-black spot

Whiting
Merlangius merlangus
Up to 20 in. (50 cm)
Sandy and muddy shores

Striped back and deeply cleft tail

Four-spined front upper fin

Mackerel
Scomber scombrus
Up to 16 in. (40 cm)
Surface shoals come inshore in summer

Thick upper lip

Striped sides

Thick-lipped grey mullet
Chelon labrosus
Up to 30 in. (76 cm)
Harbour mouths and estuaries

Flat sided

Large scales

Herring
Clupea harengus
Up to 17 in. (43 cm)
Swims in shoals near surface

Dense prickles on back

Plaice
Pleuronectes platessa
Up to 22 in. (55 cm)
Sandy and muddy shores, and estuaries

Orange spots on body

Upper and lower fins join tail fin

Thornback ray
Raja clavata
Up to 34 in. (86 cm)
Shallow water over muddy, sandy or gravelly beds

Flounder
Platichthys flesus
Up to 8 in. (20 cm)
Sandy and muddy sea-beds, from freshwater downwards

Pale beneath

Sole
Solea solea
Up to 12 in. (30 cm)
Sandy and muddy sea-beds, and river mouths

Sea mammals

Seals, dolphins and porpoises are mammals which have become adapted to life in water. Seals have dog-like faces, hairy skins and no dorsal fin. They use their hind limbs for swimming and their fore limbs to drag themselves ashore to breed. Dolphins and porpoises have hairless bodies, with usually a dorsal fin; they use their fore limbs for swimming, in conjunction with their horizontally flattened tail. They never come ashore voluntarily, though they are occasionally washed up.

Irregular blotches

Rounded head
Nostrils form a V

Common seal
Phoca vitulina
Up to 5 ft 3 in. (1.6 m)
Estuaries and sand-banks; commoner in E

Long flat head
Nostrils parallel

Pointed dorsal fin

Short blunt dorsal fin

Finely mottled

Grey seal
Halichoerus grypus
Up to 7½ ft (2.3 m)
Rocky coasts of N and W

Common dolphin
Delphinus delphis
Up to 8 ft (2.5 m)
Coastal waters, or following ships; leaps from sea

Common porpoise
Phocoena phocoena
Up to 6 ft (1.8 m)
Coastal waters and estuaries; no beak

HARD-BODIED CREATURES

Insects and insect-like animals

Only a few small insects live on the seashore. Centipedes and false scorpions may be found in rock crevices or among rotting debris on the shore line. Sea-spiders occur low down the shore amongst seaweed, often attached to sea anemones on which they feed. Slaters and sand-hoppers, resembling insects, are in fact crustaceans. Slaters are marine forms of woodlice, with bodies flattened from above. Sand-hoppers are compressed sideways and usually appear rather curled up.

Antennae two-thirds length of body

Sea-slater
Ligia oceanica
Up to 1 in. (2.5 cm)
Under stones and seaweed

Upper and lower antennae same length

Pill-bug
Gammarus locusta
Up to ¾ in. (2 cm)
Under stones on middle and lower shore

Bores holes into wood

Thick body and legs

Gribble
Limnoria lignorum
Up to ⅛ in. (3 mm)
Often in timber washed ashore

Long hair-like point

Sea-spider
Pycnogonum littorale
Body up to 1 in. (2.5 cm) long
Under stones on lower shore

Short upper antennae

Bristle-tail
Petrobius maritimus
Up to ½ in. (13 mm)
In rocks; jumps when exposed

Feelers on head

Legs on each segment

Centipede
Strigamia maritima
Up to 1½ in. (4 cm)
Rocks and crevices on upper shore

Sand-hopper
Orchestia gammarella
Up to ¾ in. (2 cm)
Among decaying seaweed in sand. Jumping animal

Pincers like scorpion's

False scorpion
Neobisium maritimum
Up to ¼ in. (6 mm)
Deep crevices on upper shore

Land snails

Tall plants growing on sand-dunes, particularly on dunes of the west coast which have a high calcium content in the sand, often carry large numbers of snails. Species with alternating bands of varied colours are prominent, but after death they become bleached white by the elements.

Broken, blotchy bands

Variable colour and banding

Dark brown lip

Grove snail
Cepaea nemoralis
Up to 1 in. (2.5 cm)
Absent from far N Scotland

Wrinkled snail
Candidula intersecta
Up to ½ in. (13 mm)
Common except in N Scotland

Pointed snail
Cochlicella acuta
Up to 1 in. (2.5 cm)
Absent from E coast

Barnacles

Though they look like molluscs, barnacles are more closely related to crabs. They fix themselves head downwards on rocks or wood. Their bodies are protected by a series of plates and their legs become adapted to catching food. The legs are feathery and continuously protrude and contract into the shell when immersed.

Lump attached to underside of shore crab

Parasitic barnacle
Sacculina carcini
Up to 1½ in. (4 cm)

Long stalk

Five white plates

Goose barnacle
Lepas anatifera
Up to 2 in. (5 cm) long
Attached to boats and driftwood

Prawns and shrimps

All these decapods have five pairs of 'walking' legs, the front pair of which are adapted for feeding. Prawns and shrimps have light, vertically flattened skeletons and can swim. The head and body are fused and shielded by a shell with a forward-pointing extension, called a rostrum, between the eyes; this is prominent and toothed in the prawns, but much reduced in the shrimps. There are two pairs of antennae.

Six to eight teeth

No teeth

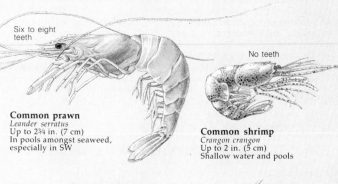

Common prawn
Leander serratus
Up to 2¾ in. (7 cm)
In pools amongst seaweed, especially in SW

Common shrimp
Crangon crangon
Up to 2 in. (5 cm)
Shallow water and pools

Seven to ten teeth

Norway lobster
Nephrops norvegicus
Up to 6 in. (15 cm) long
On mud and sand, lower shore downwards

Slender shape

Prawn
Leander squilla
Up to 2 in. (5 cm)
In pools, amongst seaweed

Often transparent

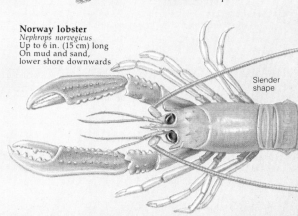

Chameleon shrimp
Praunus flexuosus
Up to 1 in. (2.5 cm)
Shallow water and pools, amongst eel-grass and seaweed

Crabs and lobsters

These creatures are called decapods because they have five pairs of legs; but the first pair are usually large, conspicuous pincers or end in a claw-like joint. They have broad shells and horizontally flattened skeletons but cannot swim; instead they walk on the shore or sea-bed. Lobsters have long antennae and a prominent 'fan' tail which they contract suddenly to dart backwards through the water. Crabs have shorter antennae, and no prominent tail.

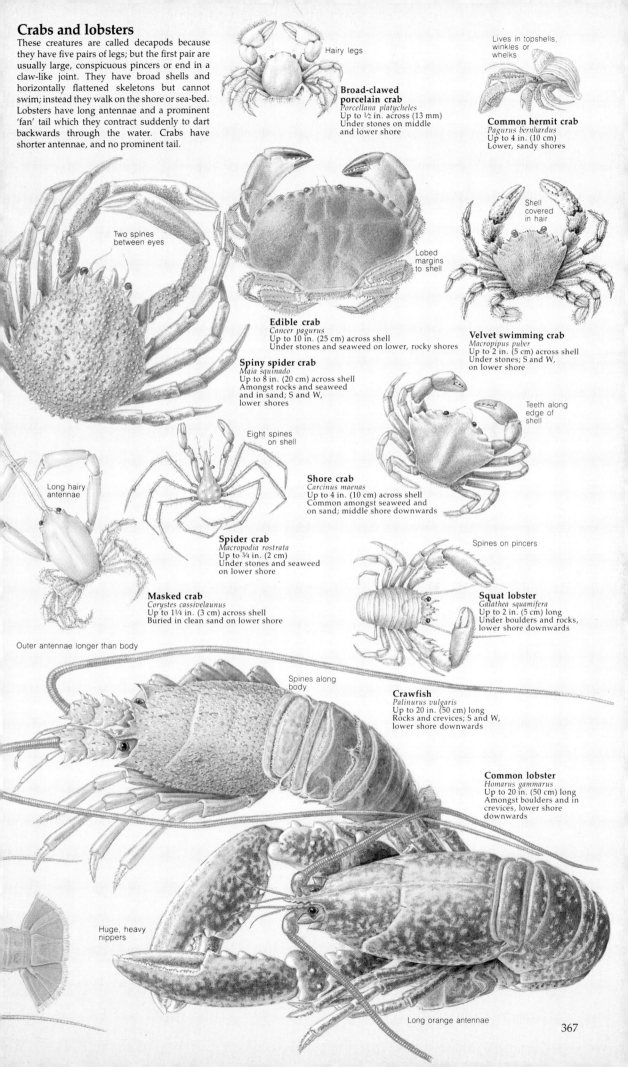

Hairy legs

Broad-clawed porcelain crab
Porcellana platycheles
Up to ½ in. across (13 mm)
Under stones on middle and lower shore

Lives in topshells, winkles or whelks

Common hermit crab
Pagurus bernhardus
Up to 4 in. (10 cm)
Lower, sandy shores

Two spines between eyes

Lobed margins to shell

Shell covered in hair

Edible crab
Cancer pagurus
Up to 10 in. (25 cm) across shell
Under stones and seaweed on lower, rocky shores

Velvet swimming crab
Macropipus puber
Up to 2 in. (5 cm) across shell
Under stones; S and W, on lower shore

Spiny spider crab
Maia squinado
Up to 8 in. (20 cm) across shell
Amongst rocks and seaweed and in sand; S and W, lower shores

Eight spines on shell

Teeth along edge of shell

Shore crab
Carcinus maenas
Up to 4 in. (10 cm) across shell
Common amongst seaweed and on sand; middle shore downwards

Long hairy antennae

Spider crab
Macropodia rostrata
Up to ¾ in. (2 cm)
Under stones and seaweed on lower shore

Spines on pincers

Masked crab
Corystes cassivelaunus
Up to 1¼ in. (3 cm) across shell
Buried in clean sand on lower shore

Squat lobster
Galathea squamifera
Up to 2 in. (5 cm) long
Under boulders and rocks, lower shore downwards

Outer antennae longer than body

Spines along body

Crawfish
Palinurus vulgaris
Up to 20 in. (50 cm) long
Rocks and crevices; S and W, lower shore downwards

Common lobster
Homarus gammarus
Up to 20 in. (50 cm) long
Amongst boulders and in crevices, lower shore downwards

Huge, heavy nippers

Long orange antennae

367

Worms

Four main groups of worms occur in the sea. Flatworms are small, leaf-shaped creatures which glide beneath rocks propelled by tiny hair-like cilia. Ribbon worms are round, and burrow in mud or sand. Bristle worms are also round, but their bodies are divided into bristly segments; they include many of the most commonly seen worms, including the fisherman's rag worms. Bristle worms that live in tubes of shell or stone are known as tube worms and include the lugworm.

Two tentacles on head

Wavy flatworm
Prostheceraeus vittatus
Up to 1¼ in. (3 cm)
Under stones or gravel
on lower shore

Head wider
than rest
of body

Red ribbon worm
Lineus ruber
Up to 6¼ in. (16 cm)
Under stones or gravel on
middle and lower shore

Four pairs of
tentacles

Green
triangular
paddles

Mat of hairs on
upper surface

Green leaf worm
Eulalia viridis
2-6 in. (5-15 cm)
Among rocks
on middle and
lower shore

Sea-mouse
Aphrodite aculeata
4-8 in. (10-20 cm)
On sandy lower shore or washed up

Red line
down back

Four antennae
and four tentacles

Yellow leaf-shaped
paddles

King rag worm
Nereis virens
Up to 16 in. (40 cm)
Burrows in sand;
mainly N and W
on lower shore

Rag worm
Nereis diversicolor
Up to 4½ in. (12 cm)
Burrows in sand or mud on
middle and lower shore

Paddle worm
Phyllodoce paretti
6-12 in. (15-30 cm)
Under stones on
lower shore

Scales with bristles

Thick body

Scale worm
Harmothoë impar
Up to 1 in. (2.5 cm)
Under stones and seaweed
on lower shore

Tube larger towards
trumpet-shaped mouth

Serpulid worm
Serpula vermicularis
2¾-4 in. (7-10 cm)
Attached to rocks and shells
on lower shore
and washed up

Spirorbid worm
Spirorbis spirorbis
Up to ⅛ in. (3 mm)
Attached to brown seaweeds
on middle and lower
shore

Cat-worm
Nephtys caeca
4-10 in. (10-25 cm)
Burrows in sand
on middle
and lower shore

Lugworm
Arenicola marina
4-8 in. (10-20 cm)
In sand on middle
and lower shore

Tubes in coils

Thread
at tail

Peacock worm
Sabella pavonina
4¼-10½ in. (11-26.5 cm)
In mud and sand on
lower shore

Tail lacks bristles or gills

Tube of
coarse sand
and shell

Colonies of tubes made
of large sand grains

Honeycomb worm
Sabellaria alveolata
Up to 1½ in. (4 cm)
Encrusts rocks and shells
on lower shore

Smooth tube
of fine mud

Sand mason
Lanice conchilega
6-12 in. (15-30 cm)
Sand, lower shore

Sea slugs and sea squirts

Sea slugs are molluscs which, like their land-living relatives, have lost their shells; the sea lemon is closely related. The sea cucumber and sea gherkin are sea urchins which lack conspicuous spines or a tough skeleton, the skeleton being embedded in the skin. The primitive-looking sea squirt is in fact an advanced animal, with tadpole-like larvae.

One pair of
tentacles

Star sea squirt
Botryllus schlosseri
Up to 6 in. (15 cm) across patches
on rocks, stones and seaweeds on
lower shore

Transparent,
with two
openings

Grouped like stars

Sea lemon
Archidoris pseudoargus
Up to 2¾ in. (7 cm)
On boulders on lower shore

Tube sea squirt
Ciona intestinalis
Up to 4½ in. (12 cm) high
Rocks, seaweeds and pier
on lower shore

Sea gherkin
Cucumaria elongata
Up to 6 in. (15 cm)
Amongst mud and
stones on lower shore

Warts on upper side

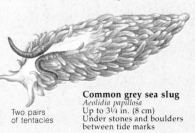

Two pairs
of tentacles

Common grey sea slug
Aeolidia papillosa
Up to 3¼ in. (8 cm)
Under stones and boulders
between tide marks

Five double rows
of tube-like feet

Sea cucumber
Holothuria forskali
Up to 8 in. (20 cm)
Amongst rock and seaweed;
S and W on lower shore

Starfish and sea urchins

The group of marine animals known as echinoderms, to which starfish and sea urchins belong, is remarkable for its unique form of radial body symmetry. The body may be globe-shaped, as in sea urchins, or it may be extended into five or more arms, as in starfish and brittle-stars. Seawater enters the animal through a mouth at the centre of its body. The changing pressure of the water controls the movement of double rows of tube-feet which enable the animal to move. The brittle skeletons, or tests, of dead sea urchins are often washed up.

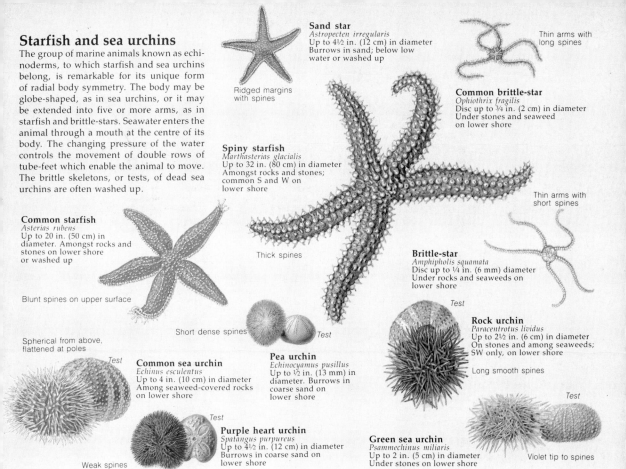

Sand star
Astropecten irregularis
Up to 4½ in. (12 cm) in diameter
Burrows in sand; below low
water or washed up

Ridged margins
with spines

Thin arms with
long spines

Common brittle-star
Ophiothrix fragilis
Disc up to ¾ in. (2 cm) in diameter
Under stones and seaweed
on lower shore

Spiny starfish
Marthasterias glacialis
Up to 32 in. (80 cm) in diameter
Amongst rocks and stones;
common S and W on
lower shore

Thin arms with
short spines

Common starfish
Asterias rubens
Up to 20 in. (50 cm) in
diameter. Amongst rocks and
stones on lower shore
or washed up

Thick spines

Brittle-star
Amphipholis squamata
Disc up to ¼ in. (6 mm) diameter
Under rocks and seaweeds on
lower shore

Blunt spines on upper surface

Short dense spines

Test

Rock urchin
Paracentrotus lividus
Up to 2½ in. (6 cm) in diameter
On stones and among seaweeds;
SW only, on lower shore

Test

Spherical from above,
flattened at poles

Test

Common sea urchin
Echinus esculentus
Up to 4 in. (10 cm) in diameter
Among seaweed-covered rocks
on lower shore

Pea urchin
Echinocyamus pusillus
Up to ½ in. (13 mm) in
diameter. Burrows in
coarse sand on
lower shore

Long smooth spines

Test

Purple heart urchin
Spatangus purpureus
Up to 4½ in. (12 cm) in diameter
Burrows in coarse sand on
lower shore

Green sea urchin
Psammechinus miliaris
Up to 2 in. (5 cm) in diameter
Under stones on lower shore

Violet tip to spines

Weak spines

Test

Squids and octopuses

The most obvious feature of the cephalopods, the group to which cuttlefish, squids and octopuses belong, is the four or five pairs of tentacles which are formed from the head and surround it. They are used for catching prey, which they reach by darting forward suddenly, ejecting a jet of water through a funnel formed from the modified foot. The eyes are as efficient as those of backboned animals.

Common octopus
Octopus vulgaris
Up to 40 in. (100 cm)
Pools amongst rocks;
southern coasts,
on lower shore

Arms with two rows of suckers

Common cuttlefish
Sepia officinalis
Up to 12 in. (30 cm)
Over sand, or in sheltered
bays or estuaries, on
lower shore

Broad oval shape

Common squid
Loligo forbesi
Up to 24 in. (60 cm)
Free swimming, rarely
close to shore

Long pen-like
shape

Jellyfish

Resembling free-floating sea anemones, jellyfish when immersed in water are umbrella-shaped, with a mouth at the centre underneath surrounded by long tentacles which trail behind the animal as it swims. These tentacles paralyse the prey with stinging cells on their surface, and then pass the food to the mouth. Portuguese man-o'-war float on the surface by a blue gas-filled bladder. Long trailing tentacles have dangerous stinging hairs.

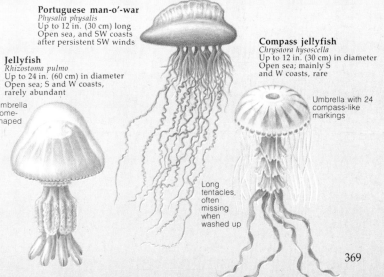

Portuguese man-o'-war
Physalia physalis
Up to 12 in. (30 cm) long
Open sea, and SW coasts
after persistent SW winds

Compass jellyfish
Chrysaora hysoscella
Up to 12 in. (30 cm) in diameter
Open sea; mainly S
and W coasts, rare

Jellyfish
Rhizostoma pulmo
Up to 24 in. (60 cm) in diameter
Open sea; S and W coasts,
rarely abundant

Umbrella
dome-
shaped

Umbrella with 24
compass-like
markings

Common jellyfish
Aurelia aurita
Up to 10 in. (25 cm) in diameter
Open sea; commonest species

Four frilly mouth
arms

Long
tentacles,
often
missing
when
washed up

369

THE SEASIDE IN SUMMER: HOW TO CHOOSE THE RIGHT TIME AND PLACE

Britain is noted for its fickle weather, which is caused by airstreams blowing over the country from different directions and over different terrain. For example, the hills near the west coast break up the moisture-laden west winds, which lose their moisture in the form of rain as they cross the country. Parts of the east coast therefore get drier weather – but they are chilled by east winds from the Continent. Weather conditions often change within a short distance, but these charts show the broad pattern of weather from April to September recorded over the years in ten main regions. Day-to-day forecasts can be obtained by telephoning the number listed in the Local Information panel for each area in the book.

NORTH-WEST SCOTLAND

With up to 50 in. of rain a year, this is the wettest part of Britain's coast. There are, however, local variations. Sunshine hours in southern parts of the Inner Hebrides average about 4 hours a day over the year; in some years Tiree, in the Inner Hebrides, has been Britain's sunniest spot during May. The climate is generally mild even in winter, when severe frosts and heavy snowfalls are rare. In sheltered areas exotic plants grow all year round. In exposed areas Atlantic storms are frequent, and gusts of 100 mph or more have been recorded at Tiree. Fogs occur on fewer than 10 days a year, and north-westerly airstreams from the polar region often produce a crystal-clear atmosphere.

	Av. daily sun	Av. hottest temp.	Av. rainfall
April	5.4 hrs	10°C (50°F)	2.7 in.
May	6.6 hrs	13°C (55°F)	2.3 in.
June	6.2 hrs	15°C (59°F)	2.7 in.
July	4.7 hrs	16°C (61°F)	3.2 in.
Aug.	4.8 hrs	16°C (61°F)	3.4 in.
Sept.	3.7 hrs	15°C (59°F)	4.6 in.

SOUTH-WEST SCOTLAND

The hills of Northern Ireland, Kintyre and Arran shelter this region from Atlantic storms and rain-bearing winds, giving it a climate that is generally drier, sunnier and less windy than other parts of the western coast of Scotland. In addition the coast is washed by warm ocean currents, and this combined with the mild climate has made it a popular area for holiday-makers. In June it shares with Fife the distinction of being one of the sunniest parts of Scotland's coast, with an average of around 6 hours of sunshine a day. Snow and fog are rare, and some areas are virtually frost-free. At Logan Gardens, on the Mull of Galloway, subtropical plants flourish outdoors.

	Av. daily sun	Av. hottest temp.	Av. rainfall
April	4.8 hrs	12°C (54°F)	2.5 in.
May	5.9 hrs	15°C (59°F)	2.9 in.
June	6 hrs	18°C (64°F)	2.5 in.
July	5 hrs	19°C (66°F)	3.2 in.
Aug.	4.7 hrs	19°C (66°F)	3.7 in.
Sept.	3.6 hrs	17°C (63°F)	4.3 in.

NORTH-WEST ENGLAND

This coast is sunnier than other parts of Britain at similar latitudes, especially during spring and early summer; there are nearly 7 hours of sunshine a day in May and June. It can be very hot on the Lancashire coast when winds blow from the south and south-east. Rainfalls are moderate, especially in the south and on the Isle of Man. Spring is the driest season and autumn the wettest, with more than twice as much rain in September as in April. The climate is usually bracing but winters are mild, with very few severe frosts or heavy snowfalls; any snow that does fall clears quickly. In areas sheltered from the prevailing winds and rain, exotic plants grow outdoors.

	Av. daily sun	Av. hottest temp.	Av. rainfall
April	5.6 hrs	12°C (54°F)	2.3 in.
May	6.8 hrs	15°C (59°F)	2.6 in.
June	7 hrs	18°C (64°F)	2.5 in.
July	5.8 hrs	18°C (64°F)	3 in.
Aug.	5.5 hrs	18°C (64°F)	3.7 in.
Sept.	4.3 hrs	16°C (61°F)	4.1 in.

WALES

In comparison with inland Wales, the coastline is relatively dry and sunny. In North Wales the rainfall of 30 in. a year at the coast compares with more than 100 in. in Snowdonia; and the coast has an annual average of more than 4 hours of sunshine a day. The exposed coasts of Dyfed and Gwynedd, however, have gales on some 30 days a year. Gusts of more than 100 mph have been recorded at St Ann's Head and Holyhead. Frost and snow are rare. The north coast has mild winters; Rhyl, Colwyn Bay and Llandudno have had temperatures of 17°C (63°F) in January – the highest recorded in Britain at this time of the year. On Anglesey, variations occur within a small area.

	Av. daily sun	Av. hottest temp.	Av. rainfall
April	6.2 hrs	12°C (54°F)	2 in.
May	7.1 hrs	14°C (57°F)	2.1 in.
June	7.7 hrs	17°C (63°F)	2.2 in.
July	6.5 hrs	18°C (64°F)	2.2 in.
Aug.	6.3 hrs	18°C (64°F)	2.7 in.
Sept.	4.8 hrs	17°C (63°F)	3.2 in.

SOUTH-WEST ENGLAND

England's south-west peninsula has one of the sunniest coasts in Britain, with Torbay, the Channel Islands and Scilly recording the highest sunshine records of all. June is the best month, with an average of 7½ hours a day. July and August may be warmer but are usually less bright. Onshore winds bring frequent sea fogs in summer and autumn. In winter there is less sea fog, and the south-west then has the highest sunshine totals and the mildest weather in the British Isles. Frost and snow are rare. Strong winds are frequent, and exposed areas experience some 30 days of gales a year. If the weather is poor in one place, better conditions can sometimes be found on the opposite coast.

	Av. daily sun	Av. hottest temp.	Av. rainfall
April	6.2 hrs	12°C (54°F)	2.4 in.
May	7.2 hrs	15°C (59°F)	2.8 in.
June	7.5 hrs	18°C (64°F)	2.3 in.
July	6.7 hrs	19°C (66°F)	2.9 in.
Aug.	6.3 hrs	19°C (66°F)	3.6 in.
Sept.	5 hrs	18°C (64°F)	3.7 in.

EASTERN SCOTLAND

High land to the west protects this coast from the rain-bearing westerly winds. Rainfall is particularly low in the areas bordering the Moray Firth and the Firth of Forth; one of Scotland's driest spots is Fidra in the Firth of Forth, with less than 21 in. of rain a year. June is the sunniest month, with more than 6 hours of sunshine a day from the Moray Firth southwards. Even so, summers are generally cool, and a chilling sea fog, or 'haar', often occurs when there is an onshore wind. Winters are cold, with frequent snow; Aberdeen has an average of more than 30 days of snow a year. Orkney and Shetland are cold and strong winds are frequent.

	Av. daily sun	Av. hottest temp.	Av. rainfall
April	4.8 hrs	9°C (48°F)	2.5 in.
May	5.3 hrs	11°C (52°F)	2.5 in.
June	5.4 hrs	14°C (57°F)	2.3 in.
July	4.6 hrs	16°C (61°F)	2.9 in.
Aug.	4 hrs	16°C (61°F)	3 in.
Sept.	3.6 hrs	14°C (57°F)	3.5 in.

NORTH-EAST ENGLAND

Spring arrives late, due to the influence of the cold North Sea, and even in May and June the weather is usually dull and cold. Hours of sunshine are the lowest of any part of the English and Welsh coasts, with an average of less than 4 hours a day over the year. Autumn is usually the finest season, with relatively dry, bright and bracing weather. Strong north winds and violent gales are frequent, and fog occurs on more than 40 days a year along the coasts of Durham and Northumberland. In late spring and early summer, onshore winds often bring in a chilling 'sea fret' or 'sea roke'. An offshore wind, however, often gives fine, dry weather. Winters are cold, with frequent snow.

	Av. daily sun	Av. hottest temp.	Av. rainfall
April	5.4 hrs	11°C (52°F)	1.5 in.
May	6.1 hrs	13°C (55°F)	1.8 in.
June	6.5 hrs	17°C (63°F)	1.8 in.
July	5.7 hrs	18°C (64°F)	2.2 in.
Aug.	5.3 hrs	18°C (64°F)	2.9 in.
Sept.	4.6 hrs	17°C (63°F)	2 in.

BATHER'S BRITAIN: WHERE THE SEA IS WARMEST

Britain lies in the path of the warm waters of the Gulf Stream, an equatorial current that starts in the Gulf of Mexico, flows northwards along the east coast of the United States and is deflected across the Atlantic by the cold waters of the Labrador current. When it reaches Britain's shores it is known as the North Atlantic Drift. In summer the seas around the coast are further warmed by the sun, the highest temperatures occurring in shallow waters such as the Thames Estuary and off the Lancashire coast. Because the sea is slow to warm up, maximum temperatures are not reached until August; but the sea is also slow to cool, so that in some areas the water remains warm through September. The hotter the summer, the warmer and longer-lasting the sea temperature.

Water surface temperatures in August:

12°C (54°F)	13°C (55°F)	14°C (57°F)	15°C (59°F)	16°C (61°F)	17°C (63°F)

EASTERN ENGLAND

Temperatures range widely between warm summers and cold winters, and snow occurs more frequently than on the southern and western coasts. Rainfall is light, and Shoeburyness in Essex is the driest spot on Britain's coast. Hours of sunshine are above the national average, with 7 hours a day in June and more than 5 hours a day in September. The east coast often has warm, dry periods in summer when the rest of the country is affected by the rain-bringing south-westerly winds. In spring, however, piercing easterly winds are common. Fog occurs on 20 to 25 days a year; onshore breezes bring a damp 'sea fret' which blots out the sun and cools the temperature rapidly.

	Av. daily sun	Av. hottest temp.	Av. rainfall
April	5.5 hrs	13°C (55°F)	1.5 in.
May	6.6 hrs	16°C (61°F)	1.7 in.
June	7 hrs	19°C (66°F)	1.6 in.
July	6.2 hrs	21°C (70°F)	2.2 in.
Aug.	6 hrs	21°C (70°F)	2.3 in.
Sept.	5 hrs	19°C (66°F)	2 in.

SOUTH-EAST ENGLAND

This region has the greatest extremes of climate on Britain's coast, with warmer summers and colder winters than the average, and because of its closeness to the European mainland it is affected by Continental weather conditions. Rainfall, however, is light, and one of the driest parts of Britain's coast occurs on the North Kent coast bordering the Thames estuary. Most of the area has plenty of sunshine, averaging nearly 5 hours a day and reaching a June peak of more than 8 hours. The sunniest spots are along the Sussex coast. Spring is the driest season and autumn the wettest. Fogs average 30 to 40 days a year, and Beachy Head is one of the foggiest spots on the entire coast.

	Av. daily sun	Av. hottest temp.	Av. rainfall
April	6.2 hrs	10°C (50°F)	1.6 in.
May	7.4 hrs	15°C (59°F)	1.7 in.
June	8.2 hrs	18°C (64°F)	1.3 in.
July	7.4 hrs	20°C (68°F)	2 in.
Aug.	6.8 hrs	20°C (68°F)	2.5 in.
Sept.	5.5 hrs	18°C (64°F)	2.4 in.

SOUTHERN ENGLAND

England's southern coast has the best combination of temperature and sunshine records in Britain. Summers are warm and sunny, with an average of more than 7½ hours of sunshine in the long days of June. Poole Harbour and the south-east corner of the Isle of Wight are among the sunniest spots on the coast. Rainfall is moderate, and occurs mostly in autumn. The mild winters allow subtropical plants to be grown in sheltered gardens, and snow is rare. The coast has its share of winter gales, and in summer there are occasional thunderstorms. The hills inland, however, protect the coast from northerly and easterly winds. Fogs occur round the Isle of Wight, but are seldom persistent.

	Av. daily sun	Av. hottest temp.	Av. rainfall
April	6.1 hrs	13°C (55°F)	1.9 in.
May	7.2 hrs	16°C (61°F)	2.2 in.
June	7.8 hrs	19°C (66°F)	1.9 in.
July	7.2 hrs	21°C (70°F)	2 in.
Aug.	6.5 hrs	20°C (68°F)	2.6 in.
Sept.	5 hrs	18°C (64°F)	3 in.

THE WEATHER AT SEA

For the purpose of forecasting weather at sea, the coast of Britain is divided into named areas which are used by the Meteorological Office in giving details of sea conditions, visibility and wind speeds. Reports or forecasts of gales or storms use a scale called the Beaufort Scale, which defines the wind force by a number. For example, force 4 refers to a moderate breeze of 13 to 18 mph, and force 6 means a strong breeze of 25 to 31 mph. Small boats may be unsafe in conditions of force 4 upwards, and should never put to sea above force 6. When winds of force 8 (39 to 46 mph) are expected within 6 hours, gale warnings are issued and black cones are hoisted at coastguard stations and on piers and harbours. Force 11 indicates a violent storm with winds up to 73 mph, the highest normally recorded in Britain.

SAFETY AT THE SEASIDE: SIMPLE RULES THAT WILL KEEP YOU OUT OF DANGER

The three main hazards facing a visitor to the coast are weather, tides and currents. Their dangers can be minimised by checking local weather forecasts regularly; by reading the local tide-tables; and by asking the lifeguards or the local coastguard station about special dangers such as treacherous currents or underwater rocks. Most sporting activities, such as sailing, surfing and water-skiing, have their own codes of conduct which explain how to avoid danger and what to do if in distress. Learn the rules appropriate to the form of recreation you enjoy, and obey them: prevention of accidents is better than cure.

EXPLORING THE SEASHORE

Scrambling across rocks and seeking out the shells, stones and tidal pools left by the tide is an absorbing pastime – and therein lies its danger. It is very easy to lose track of time and distance, with possibly disastrous results. Some tides turn very quickly and can sweep up hidden channels, cutting off the retreat of those who have ventured too far. This can mean several uncomfortable hours spent waiting for the tide to turn again; it could even result in drowning.

Make sure you know the times of the tides and other local conditions before setting out, and allow yourself plenty of time to get back before the tide turns. Remember that particularly high tides, called spring tides, occur just after the new moon and full moon; neap tides, which have the lowest range between high and low water, occur during the moon's first and last quarters. Wear footwear suitable for scrambling over slippery rocks, such as rope-soled shoes; otherwise you may fall, hurt yourself and become trapped.

- DO NOT *go exploring alone.*
- DO *wear sensible shoes.*
- DO *check the times of the tides.*

SWIMMING

Wait until one hour after a meal before swimming, and remember that when swimming in the sea your ability will be affected by waves, tides and the temperature of the water. Never swim out to sea; it is safer to swim parallel to the shore, staying within or close to your depth. If you cannot swim do not go into the sea above waist height. The best place to learn to swim is in a swimming pool, with expert tuition.

Swim with friends, not on your own. Hundreds of people are saved from drowning every year because they are seen in time. Lonely and unfrequented beaches may look inviting, but if you get into difficulties it is better to be near a beach where help is available. So swim from a beach patrolled by lifeguards if possible.

The first rule for a swimmer in distress is to keep calm, then either float or tread water with one arm raised above the head; this is the recognised distress signal.

Watch out for changes in the surface of the water which indicate danger. Large, steep-faced waves which collapse from their crest into shallow water are called 'dumpers' and can hurl swimmers to the bottom with great force. Areas of smooth water indicate the presence of strong currents; a fast-moving channel of water returning to the sea is called a rip current. Never try to swim against a current. Instead, swim across it diagonally using a slow, strong stroke.

If you get carried out to sea in heavy surf, swim towards the shore in the troughs of the waves. As soon as you can touch bottom, dig into it with hands and feet to anchor yourself against the undertow as the wave breaks, then swim shorewards with the next wave.

Be very cautious about using snorkel equipment unless you have been given professional advice on its use. And remember that air-beds and inflatable toys, though fun on the beach, can become deadly objects on the water, where currents and breezes can sweep them and their passengers far out to sea.

- DO NOT *swim when red flags are flying.*
- DO NOT *go swimming alone.*
- DO NOT *use air-beds on the water.*

FURTHER INFORMATION: Amateur Swimming Association, Harold Fern House, Derby Square, Loughborough, Leicestershire LE11 0AL. Tel. Loughborough 230431.

SURFING

Surfboard riding is for competent swimmers only and should never be attempted by anyone not fully aware of his or her abilities and limitations. Before you go surfing, find out from the lifeguards or other local authorities what regulations apply – restricted areas, for example – and check for tide movements, underwater obstacles and where rip currents may be running. Make sure you are insured against public liability in case you accidentally injure someone.

When buying or hiring a board, remember that a board which is too long will be difficult to control, while one that is too short will not support you properly. Ask an expert to advise you on the right board for your experience and body weight.

Some beaches have exclusive areas for surfing, indicated by black-and-white quarter flags. You must surf between these markers, and avoid swimming areas which may be indicated by red-and-yellow flags. When paddling out, manoeuvre around the surfing area to avoid incoming riders, and in crowded conditions watch out for fallen riders and loose boards. If you and your board part company, try to hold on to it – an ankle leash is an essential part of your equipment. If caught in a rip current never leave your surfboard. Paddle across the current until you move into an area of breaking waves which will propel you to shore.

- DO *use the right length board.*
- DO *leave the water before becoming tired.*
- DO *avoid swimming areas.*
- DO *insure yourself.*

FURTHER INFORMATION: British Surfing Association, Room G5, Burrows Chambers, East Burrow Road, Swansea SA1 1RF. Tel. Swansea 461476.

WATER-SKIING

Like most sports requiring a certain amount of skill, water-skiing requires expert training to ensure maximum safety and enjoyment. Even if you are a good swimmer, always wear a life-jacket; and before taking to the water, check your skis for loose wing nuts, loose binding, splinters and sharp metal.

Do not ski in water less than 3 ft deep, and once you are ski-borne watch the water ahead for obstacles such as rocks, banks, buoys, breakwaters and jetties. Do not ski within 200 yds of the shore or anywhere near swimmers or other water users.

Avoid falling forwards if possible. Instead, either sit down or fall sideways, curling yourself into a ball. Throw away the towing handle on falling and recover your skis as soon as possible to help keep afloat. Signal that all is well after a fall by holding up your hand or a ski. There should always be two people in the boat, one to drive and one to watch the skier. Understand and use the approved signals between skier and crew.

- DO *take lessons before attempting to ski.*
- DO *wear a life-jacket.*
- DO NOT *ski in water less than 3 ft deep.*
- DO *avoid other water users.*
- DO *have a competent driver and an observer in the boat.*

FURTHER INFORMATION: British Water Ski Federation, 390 City Road, London EC1V 2QA. Tel. (01) 833 2855.

FLAGS AND SIGNALS THAT WARN AND ADVISE

Danger: Do not enter the water here today.

Danger: Never swim at this point.

Surfing lane: Bathing is unwise.

Gale approaching from the south.

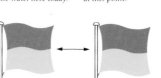

Zone supervised by lifeguards: Swim only between the two flags.

Divers below: Surfers and boat users beware.

Gale approaching from the north.

Red flags indicate that bathing is temporarily unsafe; they are usually accompanied by a warning notice fixed to the flag pole. Places where it is always dangerous to bathe are marked by notice boards coloured red with white lettering. Red-and-yellow flags indicate areas supervised by lifeguards. Black-and-white flags mark areas designated for surfing, and blue-and-white flags warn that scuba divers are operating in the area. Gale warning signals are hoisted on piers and jetties when winds of force 8 (39-46 mph) or above are expected.

BOARDSAILING (Windsurfing)

This rapidly growing sport has fewer restrictions than other forms of sailing, and there are few places where sailboards cannot or should not go. As in any other waterborne activity, however, consideration for others is important – so keep clear of bathing areas, busy harbours and anglers.

Wear suitable clothing, such as a wetsuit and light windproof jacket, and always wear a buoyancy aid which carries the anchor symbol of the Ship and Boat Builders' National Federation. Buoyancy aids are designed for active water sports; they do not serve the same function as a life-jacket, and should only be worn by reasonably good swimmers. Carry a flare, and a spare length of line.

Check tide times and the weather forecast. Do not sail in an offshore wind unless you are very experienced. If you find yourself far from the shore and cannot get back, undo the sail from the boom, roll and tie it to the mast. Remove or retract the daggerboard, place the rig on the sailboard and kneel or lie on top of it then paddle ashore. If you require assistance, raise one arm and wave it slowly from side to side.

- DO *keep clear of other water users.*
- DO *wear a buoyancy aid.*
- DO *acquaint yourself with emergency drill.*
- DO NOT *sail in an offshore wind.*

FURTHER INFORMATION: Royal Yachting Association, Victoria Way, Woking, Surrey GU21 1EQ. Tel. Woking 5022. UK Board Sailing Association Ltd, Masons Road, Stratford-upon-Avon. Tel. Stratford-upon-Avon 299574.

SMALL-BOAT SAILING

Lessons with a club or with a training establishment recognised by the Royal Yachting Association will give experience in emergency actions such as capsize drill and 'man overboard' drill, as well as the Rules of the Road Afloat. Small-boat sailors should also be able to swim at least 50 yds in light clothing and in a life-jacket.

Before setting sail, obtain a weather forecast and study local tide-tables. Ask people with local knowledge about rocks or wrecks. Check harbour bye-laws and restricted areas for swimmers, surfers or water-skiers. Ensure that all your equipment is in good order. Tell a responsible person where you are going and when you expect to be back. Don't forget to report your safe return.

If you are launching from the beach or from a slipway, an offshore wind will soon speed you on your way, but you may have difficulty in turning back. If you are not experienced in sailing into the wind it is better to launch in an onshore wind. Launching and landing in breakers and surf pose special problems, and expert advice is needed. It is inadvisable to sail in winds above force 4 on the Beaufort Scale, and you should never sail in winds of a strength above force 6.

If all your efforts to right the boat after a capsize fail, then stay with the boat. Do not attempt to swim for the shore, for it is invariably further away than it looks. Climb on to the boat if you can and wait for help. If you have to stay in the water your life-jacket will keep you afloat; avoid unnecessary movements, to conserve body heat.

- DO *check weather forecasts and tide-tables.*
- DO *observe harbour bye-laws.*
- DO *tell someone where you are going and when you expect to return.*

FURTHER INFORMATION: Royal Yachting Association, Victoria Way, Woking, Surrey GU21 1EQ. Tel. Woking 5022.

WHEN DANGER THREATENS: WHO WILL HELP YOU AND HOW TO HELP YOURSELF

Safety in the water starts on dry land. The best way to avoid accidents is to understand the hazards that water presents, and learn how to avoid them. Remember that the absence of a warning sign does not mean that there is no danger. On the great majority of beaches there are no warning signs – and no facilities for immediate rescue.

Many popular beaches are, however, supervised by lifeguards, and in addition HM Coastguard controls a network of permanently manned rescue centres. If you see anyone in difficulties, remember that a team effort is more effective than an individual rescue attempt. If you are in difficulties yourself, don't panic, but do your best to attract attention, and keep calm until help arrives.

Lifeguard services

Lifeguards may be professionals employed by local authorities, or volunteers provided by the Surf Life Saving Association of Great Britain or the Royal Life Saving Society. All lifeguards have life-saving equipment appropriate to the conditions on the particular section of beach they are supervising. Many of them also have inshore rescue boats and oxygen-powered resuscitation equipment. They are able to call out other rescue services if necessary.

In some resorts with long beaches or several beaches, lifeguards may supervise a single beach or part of a beach. Supervised areas are marked out with red-and-yellow flags. Do not bathe when red flags are flying, and at all times follow the advice of the lifeguards, who know the particular beach and its hazards and are there to help.

Royal National Lifeboat Institution

Since 1963 the RNLI has complemented its fleet of lifeboats with high-speed inflatable power boats designed specifically for going to the rescue of small boats close inshore. There are now about 120 of these inflatable lifeboats – previously called inshore rescue boats – in operation. They can be called quickly into service, not only to rescue sailing craft but also to go to the aid of people cut off by the tide or children adrift on air-beds and inflatable toys. For an account of the foundation and development of the RNLI, from its beginnings in 1824 to the present day, see pp. 172-3.

HM Coastguard

The Coastguard Service was created in 1922 to fight smuggling, but since 1925 it has had the very different role of saving life at sea. Its responsibility is to co-ordinate all civil maritime search-and-rescue operations for people and vessels in distress around the United Kingdom and its 6,000 miles of coastline. These operations range from countering major disasters offshore to recovering people stranded on cliffs or cut off by the tide.

The Coastguard Service has no rescue craft of its own, but operates an extensive network of permanently manned modern rescue centres. These are capable of calling upon the assistance of Royal Navy and Royal Air Force helicopters, RNLI lifeboats, ships at sea and, when required, police and fire services. HM Coastguard Rescue Companies do, however, retrieve people from stranded vessels or from cliffs.

In addition, each Coastguard Rescue Centre will give information on tides and local weather, sea and coastal conditions. This service is available to all members of the public, and the telephone numbers to ring for information are listed in the 'Local Information' panel for each section of coast in this book.

WHAT TO DO IN AN EMERGENCY

Behind a 'seaside holiday tragedy' headline in the newspapers all too often lies a story of ignorance, lack of caution or downright foolhardiness. To avoid accidents it is vital to have a realistic understanding of your own abilities in and on open water, and to seek advice before going in or on the water if you are not fully aware of local conditions.

Whether swimming, canoeing or even fishing, don't go alone; because if trouble occurs there could be no one on hand to help. If an emergency does occur, prompt action is needed, but the action must be taken decisively and without panic.

Helping yourself

If you fall into the water and cannot reach safety:
- *Keep calm and resist the temptation to struggle.*
- *Turn over and float on your back.*
- *Attract attention by waving one arm and shouting for help.*
- *When a lifeguard or rescuer arrives, remain calm and do not clutch hold of him.*

Helping others

If you see someone in difficulties, don't go into the water after him, however good a swimmer you are, if you can possibly avoid it. Other methods of rescue are usually safer for the rescuer and the victim.

Try first to find someone who will help you. One person can then seek expert assistance from a lifeguard, or by dialling 999 and asking for 'Coastguard'. While waiting for help, consider other methods of rescue:
- *Look for something to help pull the swimmer out – a stick, a piece of rope or an article of clothing.*
- *Lie flat to prevent yourself from being pulled in, and hold out the object for the victim to grab.*
- *Near shore, if conditions allow, several rescuers may link hands to make a human chain to reach the victim.*
- *If you cannot reach the person in distress, throw a floating object – a lifebuoy if available, a spare wheel, an upturned bucket – for him to hold on to.*
- *If a boat is available, row it to the victim stern first so that it does not capsize when he grabs it.*

FURTHER INFORMATION: Royal Life Saving Society, Mountbatten House, Studley, Warwickshire B80 7NN. Tel. Studley 3943. Royal Society for the Prevention of Accidents, Cannon House, The Priory Queensway, Birmingham B4 6BS. Tel. (021) 233 2461. Surf Life Saving Association of Great Britain, 4 Cathedral Yard, Exeter EX1 1HJ. Tel. Exeter 54364.

LAW AND THE COAST: WHERE YOU MAY GO, WHAT YOU MAY DO

Most of Britain's shores and coastal waters can be freely used by anyone for any normal form of recreation. There are some exceptions, however. Though the foreshore is nearly always open to the public, the beach above it may be privately owned and closed to the public. In certain areas even the foreshore may be closed for special reasons. And though beachcombing can be fun, removing objects from the beach may in some cases be against the law.

VISITING THE SEASHORE

Q *Where does the land end?*

A The land ends, according to the law, where the sea starts at low water on the lowest ebb of the tide. Land that can be privately owned usually ends at the average high-water line. The area in between is known as the foreshore. Most of Britain's foreshore belongs to the Crown, which hands it to local councils or port authorities to manage; and normally the public has the right to walk on it. Even a private landowner whose property runs down to the high-water line cannot keep the public off the foreshore.

Q *When is the foreshore private?*

A Some stretches of fore-shore are owned by government departments – for example, by the Ministry of Defence for use as a firing range. A government department is entitled to prohibit the public from going on to its beach and to prevent boats from landing there.

Other stretches of foreshore may be owned privately – as for example where quarrying takes place on or near the shore and piers run into the sea. Some stretches of foreshore have been leased for private use, mainly by holiday companies and the National Trust. An owner or tenant of such a private beach is generally entitled to exclude the public, or charge a fee for entrance. Such areas are usually clearly marked.

Q *What laws apply on the foreshore?*

A Most of the laws of our country remain in force as far as the outer edge of our territorial waters. These extend 3 nautical miles (3.4 land miles) from low-water level. They also include any estuary or bay less than 24 nautical miles (27.2 land miles) wide, and water between the mainland and islands.

Local authorities may, however, make their own bye-laws regulating the use of a beach for up to 1,000 metres out to sea from low-water level. For instance, swimming areas may be restricted, either for the swimmers' own safety or to safeguard a nature reserve; or a stretch of beach may be closed because of a rock fall.

Local councils will be able to tell you if any such laws apply in the areas under their control.

Q *How can I reach the shore?*

A Although the foreshore itself is open to the public, to get to it you must either use a public right of way – usually a public road or a footpath – or, if you cross private property, have the landowner's permission to do so.

If a public right of way exists, it can be used even if someone has tried to block it. If a footpath is blocked, you have a right to remove the obstacle.

English and Welsh local councils must keep 'definitive maps' showing all public paths in their areas. They are also required to erect signposts at every point where a public footpath leaves a road. Many of these paths on or near the coast are marked by a red dotted line on the maps in this book. If in doubt, or if you find a path blocked, check at the local council offices.

Often the land adjacent to the coast is publicly owned and open at all times, so that you can cross it freely to reach the shore. But if the land is private, the land-owner is entitled to charge you for crossing his land – or to refuse to let you cross. A person attempting to cross land without permission is trespassing and may be removed by force if he refuses to leave when asked to do so.

Anyone may land on the foreshore by boat, and may walk across it to and from his boat, even though public access from the landward side is impossible.

Q *Can I do what I like on the shore?*

A Traditionally, everyone is allowed to use the fore-shore for normal recreational purposes. No council or other authority will stop you from swimming, sunbathing, picnicking or building sandcastles on any beach in Britain, provided

---

THE RIGHTS ABOUT WRECKS

Members of the public have no rights to take property from wrecks. On the contrary, anyone finding a wreck or derelict property is required by law to hand it over or report it to the local Receiver of Wrecks, a senior Customs official. Anyone failing to do this may be fined up to £400 – and even have to recompense the true owner up to twice the value of the objects taken.

The term 'wreck' means not merely a shipwrecked vessel but also property found on or near the foreshore after the wreck of a ship or aircraft. Such property may be of one of three kinds:

● **FLOTSAM** *This is property which has floated off a shipwreck.*

● **JETSAM** *This is property that has been deliberately thrown off a vessel in distress to lighten the load.*

● **LIGAN** *This term covers items cast into the sea, but marked by buoys to locate them at a later date.*

In addition, there is a duty to report finding:

● **DERELICT** *This is property abandoned at sea by those in charge of it, without hope of recovering it or intention of returning to it.*

● **FISHING BOATS** *that have been wrecked, abandoned or stranded, or their nets, tackle or equipment.*

---

you have reached it by a legal route.

Increasingly, however, local authorities lay down bye-laws to control the public use of beaches. Such laws may prevent people from using noisy transistor radios, lighting fires, or playing certain games on parts of the foreshore.

Bye-laws may be used to divide the beach into sections, with different parts set aside for different purposes. For example, part of a beach may be set aside for nude bathing or sunbathing, while elsewhere on the same beach nude bathers might risk prosecution for indecency. Similarly, water-skiers or speedboats may be banned from using certain parts of a beach, and cars and camping may be banned.

Q *What if there is no beach?*

A In places where the land falls vertically into the sea – as with a steep cliff or a harbour wall – there may be no foreshore even at low tide. In such situations there are no general public rights of use, even for fishing from the harbour wall or a convenient rock.

Q *Where may I park the car?*

A There are only two situations in which you are legally permitted to park at any time. These are in an authorised car park, and on private land where you have the owner's permission. In practice you may, in addition, usually leave your car at the roadside in a place where there are no restrictions and where you are not obstructing the highway. But there is no legal right to do this, and you may be prosecuted if you leave your car there for a long period.

In all other situations, parking is an offence or a trespass.

BEACHCOMBING

Q *Can I take pebbles from the beach?*

A Anything forming part of the beach or in it is the property of whoever owns that section of beach. Above high water the owner may be a private landowner or a body such as the National Trust; below high-water line it is usually the Crown.

This applies even to rocks, pebbles, shells and sand. In practice nobody will stop you taking small numbers of shells or pebbles, or small quantities of sand or seaweed – but any abuse of this freedom can be stopped. In some areas the local residents have traditional rights to take objects from the beach, as for example coal from parts of the coast of Durham and seaweed from parts of the coast of South Wales. But these are not public rights.

HOW COASTAL WILDLIFE IS PROTECTED

Strict laws have been passed to protect wild birds, endangered animals and plants and their habitats, as well as to protect the natural beauty of the countryside. In some areas these laws may prevent the public visiting certain stretches of coast, or allow them to do so only at certain times and under certain conditions, as in the case of designated nature reserves. In some marine nature reserves special bye-laws prohibit fishing, skin-diving and pleasure boating.

Most wild birds and their eggs are protected, and it is an offence to kill or injure a bird, or to take or destroy its eggs or nest. The only sea-birds not protected are great and lesser black-backed gulls and herring gulls. A strict close season for wildfowl shooting extends from February 21 until August 31 each year, the main breeding season.

Some mammals, such as seals, dolphins, porpoises and whales, are protected, in the same way as burbot. Rare plants are protected, and it is illegal even to pick flowers from protected plants. These include sea knotgrass, sea lavender, some of the sandworts and several kinds of orchids. It is an offence intentionally to uproot any wild plant, including seaweed, without authority.

THE COUNTRY CODE

Anyone visiting the coast for recreation should know the rules incorporated in the Country Code. This is designed to safeguard the farmer's place of work, and to preserve the countryside for others to enjoy. The code says:

● GUARD AGAINST FIRE *Carelessness may cost thousands of pounds. Do not throw away glass, lighted matches or cigarettes.*

● FASTEN ALL GATES *A farm animal on a road may cause an accident; in a wrong field it may gorge itself to death.*

● KEEP DOGS UNDER CONTROL *The friendly household pet may prove a killer in the open countryside.*

● KEEP TO PUBLIC PATHS *Even grass is a valuable crop, and what looks like grass may be young wheat, oats or barley.*

● AVOID DAMAGING FENCES *Fences, hedges and walls are there for a purpose, and replacing them is expensive.*

● LEAVE NO LITTER *Take litter home after a picnic.*

● SAFEGUARD WATER SUPPLIES *Take care not to pollute country streams with rubbish or waste food.*

● PROTECT WILDLIFE *The countryside is a community of animals, plants and trees – all depending on each other for survival. Do not pick or root up flowers or break off branches.*

● GO CAREFULLY ON COUNTRY ROADS *A tractor or a flock of sheep, hidden by a corner, can cause an accident. When walking, keep in single file and face oncoming traffic.*

● RESPECT THE LIFE OF THE COUNTRYSIDE *Enjoy the countryside and respect its life and work. Do not harm animals, farm machinery or property.*

Lost or abandoned objects which have become buried in the sand also belong to the landowner. However, valuable objects such as gold, silver, plate or coins which have been deliberately hidden by their owner and never recovered are classified as Treasure Trove and belong to the Crown. Anybody making such a find should report it to the police. If after inquiry by a Coroner the Crown retains the property, the finder is likely to be rewarded.

Property found on the surface of a beach, rather than buried in it, belongs to the finder only if it has been genuinely lost and if, after proper enquiries have been made, the true owner cannot be found. If you find anything on the beach that appears to be of any value you should hand it to the local police. If the owner does not claim it within a few months, the police will return it to you.

Driftwood and normal debris washed up on the beach can be removed without fear of penalty. However, this does not apply in the case of a wreck or derelict property, which belongs to the Crown or to those granted special rights by the Crown.

FISHING

Q *Can I fish where I like?*

A Sea-fishing by rod and line is largely unrestricted in Britain, though local bye-laws may limit it in some places – for example, to protect a marine nature reserve or underwater installations or fish farming. There is no close season for sea-fishing, and no ban on night fishing. The only protected species of fish is the burbot.

No licence is necessary for anglers either on shore or in boats using rod and line or similar methods. You may need permission from the landowner before fishing from a jetty or harbour, but you are free to fish on or over the foreshore.

WATER SPORTS

Q *How are water sports controlled?*

A Sports such as surfing, windsurfing and water-skiing are subject to control by local councils. This may be enforced, for example, by banning access to the shore where there is no public right of way – for example, to power boats – as well as by bye-laws.

Anybody taking part in these sports should also be insured in case of accidents caused by them to others, as might happen if a swimmer were hit by a water-skier and injured. Personal injury and damage to property caused when taking part in these sports is excluded from normal householder's insurance policies.

Q *What are the rules about skin-diving?*

A The sea-bed out to the edge of the territorial sea belongs to the Crown, like the foreshore, and much the same rules apply to it. Diving may be prevented in nature reserves and fish farms. It may also be banned in historic wreck sites. Ask for local advice. Taking fish from nets belonging to others is theft.

SAILING AND BOATING

Q *Do I need a licence?*

A No licence is required to sail a boat round the shores of Britain, unless you use it commercially for fishing or for carrying passengers or cargo. Boats used for private recreation do not need licences for private use, nor do their helmsmen or drivers.

Q *Where may I take my boat?*

A Everyone has the right to sail where he wishes in tidal waters. This includes the tidal sections of estuaries and rivers, and the waters that cover the foreshore at high water.

There are few limits on this. Boats may be banned from military training areas, and boats used for recreation may be excluded from marine nature reserves. Power boats may be subject to speed limits within 1,000 metres of the shore, usually off busy beaches, and water-skiing may be limited to defined areas of water. Many of the areas where such limits apply are indicated on the maps in this book. Regulations are usually displayed by the waterside, or can be obtained from local council offices.

Q *Where may I launch, land and moor?*

A Boats may only be launched from land where there is a public slipway or other public access to the sea for boats. Otherwise the landowner's permission is needed. An owner, such as a harbour authority providing a public launchway, may charge for its use, if there is no public right to launch a boat there.

Once at sea, boats may be landed anywhere on the foreshore, except in banned areas, and launched again. Bye-laws sometimes limit how close power boats may approach to busy beaches.

Subject to the requirements of good navigation and safety, boats may anchor freely at sea, but in harbour local rules apply. Normally, permission is needed from the harbour-master, and a fee paid. Boats must obey the harbour-master's instructions while navigating in and near the port.

If an accident occurs through the negligence of anyone owning or using a boat, he will be liable for damages and compensation in the same way as someone responsible for a road accident. Boats and crews should therefore be adequately insured against accidents and liability to others.

You should also check the insurance position when hiring a boat. Is the owner insured against accidents occurring while you are using the vessel? If not, are you insured yourself? If not, the owner could hold you responsible for any accident.

ACCIDENTS AT SEA

Q *What happens when there is an accident at sea?*

A When accidents occur, anyone able to do so should inform the coastguard or police as soon as possible. To contact the coastguard in an emergency dial 999 and ask for coastguard. Any vessel able to do so has a duty to help to rescue any person or vessel in distress.

Air-sea rescuers and coastguards make no charges for their duties. But anyone voluntarily rescuing a person or property in real and appreciable danger is entitled to salvage reward. This can technically be claimed by anyone involved in a rescue, including those supplying advice or setting the rescue in motion. If the amount of reward is not agreed, it will be settled by a court, and may normally amount to up to half the value of property saved.

Lifeboat crews, being volunteers, are entitled to claim salvage, but rarely do so. If they do, the RNLI requires the crew to pay for the use of fuel and equipment on the rescue, and for any damage to the lifeboat, as well as forfeiting the small payments received for each trip.

WHERE TO FIND OUT MORE

TOURIST INFORMATION

A phone call to the Tourist Information Centres listed for each section of the coast will bring you leaflets and maps of the area, accommodation lists and programmes of forthcoming events. For further information contact the appropriate tourist board:

English Tourist Board,
Thames Tower, Blacks Road, London
W6 9EL.
Tel. (01) 846 9000.

Scottish Tourist Board,
23 Ravelston Terrace, Edinburgh EH4 3EU.
Tel. (031) 332 2433.

Wales Tourist Board,
3-6 Bridge Street, Cardiff CF1 2EE.
Tel. Cardiff 27281.

Cumbria Tourist Board,
Ashleigh, Holly Road, Windermere,
Cumbria LA23 2AQ.
Tel. Windermere 4444.

East Anglia Tourist Board,
Toppesfield Hall, Hadleigh,
Suffolk IP7 5DN.
Tel. Ipswich 822922.

East Midlands Tourist Board,
Exchequergate, Lincoln LN2 1PZ.
Tel. Lincoln 31521/3.

Isle of Man Tourist Board,
7-13 Victoria Street, Douglas, Isle of Man.
Tel. Douglas 74323.

Isle of Wight Tourist Office,
Quay Store, Town Quay, Newport,
Isle of Wight PO30 2EF.
Tel. Newport 524343.

Northumbria Tourist Board,
Antley Head, Durham DH1 5UX.
Tel. Durham 46905.

North-West Tourist Board,
The Last Drop Village, Bromley Cross,
Bolton, Lancashire BL7 9PZ.
Tel. Bolton 591511.

South-East England Tourist Board,
1 Warwick Park, Tunbridge Wells,
Kent TN2 5TA.
Tel. Tunbridge Wells 40766.

Southern Tourist Board,
Town Hall Centre, Leigh Road, Eastleigh,
Hampshire SO5 4DE.
Tel. Eastleigh 616027.

West Country Tourist Board,
Trinity Court, 37 Southernhay East,
Exeter, Devon EX1 1QS.
Tel. Exeter 76351.

Yorkshire and Humberside Tourist Board,
312 Tadcaster Road, York YO2 2HF.
Tel. York 707961.

States of Guernsey Tourist Board,
PO Box 23, White Rock, St Peter Port,
Guernsey C.I.
Tel. Guernsey 26611.

States of Jersey Tourist Board,
Weighbridge, St Helier, Jersey C.I.
Tel. Jersey 78000.

WILDLIFE AND NATURE CONSERVANCY

Several organisations will give information on wildlife, natural history and nature conservancy. They include:

British Trust for Ornithology,
Beech Grove, Tring, Hertfordshire
HP23 5NR. Tel. Tring 3461.

Council for the Protection of Rural England,
4 Hobart Place, London SW1W 0HY.
Tel. (01) 235 9481.

Council for the Protection of Rural Wales,
31 High Street, Welshpool, Powys
SY21 7JP. Tel. Welshpool 2525.

Nature Conservancy Council,
Northminster House, Northminster,
Peterborough PE1 1UA.
Tel. Peterborough 40345.

Royal Society for Nature Conservation,
The Green, Nettleham, Lincoln
LN2 2NR. Tel. Lincoln 752326.

Royal Society for the Protection of Birds,
The Lodge, Sandy, Bedfordshire
SG19 2DL. Tel. Sandy 80551.

Scottish Ornithologists' Club,
21 Regent Terrace, Edinburgh EH7 5BT.
Tel. (031) 556 6042.

Scottish Wildlife Trust,
25 Johnston Terrace, Edinburgh
EH1 2NH. Tel. (031) 226 4602.

SAILING AND BOATING

Whether you sail or drive a power boat you will need to know in advance about berthing facilities, slipways and repair or maintenance workshops. Full details from:

The National Yacht Harbour
Association Ltd,
Hardy House, Somerset Road, Ashford,
Kent TN24 8EW. Tel. Ashford 43837.

UNDERWATER SWIMMING

The British Sub-Aqua Club is the governing body for the sport of underwater swimming. It has 1,000 branches, where qualified divers are welcome. Details from:

The British Sub-Aqua Club,
16 Upper Woburn Place, London
WC1H 0QW. Tel. (01) 387 9302.

CLEAN BEACHES

A list of beaches which have been monitored and found to comply with the European Economic Community's directive on the quality of bathing water is published by:

The Coastal Anti-Pollution League Ltd,
Alverstoke, 94 Greenway Lane, Bath,
Avon BA2 4LN. Tel. Bath 317094.

ANGLING

Information about sea angling, such as the best places to fish and what can be caught, can be obtained from:

National Anglers' Council,
11 Cowgate, Peterborough PE1 1LZ.
Tel. Peterborough 54084.

National Federation of Sea Anglers,
26 Downsview Crescent, Uckfield,
East Sussex TN22 1UB. Tel. Uckfield 3589.

WALKING AND OUTDOOR COURSES

Two of Britain's long-distance paths, designated by the Countryside Commission, follow the coast for most of their length. The 515 mile South-West Peninsula Coast Path runs from Minehead in Somerset to Studland in Dorset, while the Pembrokeshire Coast Path follows the coast of south-west Wales for 168 miles from Amroth to St

Dogmaels. Three other long-distance paths have long coastal stretches. Particulars from:

The Countryside Commission,
John Dower House, Crescent Place,
Cheltenham, Gloucestershire GL50 3RA.
Tel. Cheltenham 21381.

The corresponding organisation for Scotland is:

The Countryside Commission for Scotland,
Battleby, Redgorton, Perth PH1 3EW.
Tel. Perth 27921.

Information about long-distance paths and other walks is also available from:

The Open Spaces Society,
25a Bell Street, Henley-on-Thames,
Oxfordshire RG9 2BA.
Tel. Henley-on-Thames 573535.

Numerous nature trails follow sections of the coast, and particulars of these can be obtained from the English Tourist Board, regional tourist boards or local tourist information centres. In addition, the Forestry Commission has marked trails in many of its woodlands. Particulars from:

Forestry Commission,
231 Corstorphine Road, Edinburgh
EH12 7AT. Tel. (031) 334 0303.

General information about walking can be obtained from:
The Ramblers' Association,
1/5 Wandsworth Road, London SW8 2XX.
Tel. (01) 582 6878.

Long-distance path walkers can obtain overnight accommodation at youth hostels. In England and Wales, contact:

The Youth Hostels Association,
Trevelyan House, St Albans, Herts
AL1 2DY. Tel. St Albans 55215.

In Scotland, contact:

The Scottish Youth Hostels Association,
7 Glebe Crescent, Stirling FK8 2JA.
Tel. Stirling 72821.

Practical conservation work at weekends and on working holidays is organised by:

British Trust for Conservation
Volunteers,
36 St Mary's Street, Wallingford,
Oxfordshire OX10 0EU.
Tel. Wallingford 39766.

Residential courses in outdoor subjects are run at nine centres, three of them on the coast, managed by:

Field Studies Council, Montford Bridge,
Shrewsbury SY4 1HW.
Tel. Shrewsbury 850674.

HISTORIC PLACES

Many historic houses, castles and other places of interest are owned or maintained by the National Trust or the National Trust for Scotland:

The National Trust,
36 Queen Anne's Gate, London
SW1H 9AS. Tel. (01) 222 9251.

The National Trust for Scotland,
5 Charlotte Square, Edinburgh EH2 4DU.
Tel. (031) 226 5922.

Details of historic ships that can be visited are obtainable from:

The Maritime Trust, 16 Ebury Street,
London SW1W 0LH. Tel. (01) 730 0096.

INDEX

Page numbers in **bold** type indicate a main entry, often accompanied by an illustration on the same page.
Page numbers in *italics* indicate other illustrations. Page numbers in roman type denote shorter text references.

ACKNOWLEDGMENTS

The great majority of the illustrations in this book were specially commissioned by Reader's Digest from the photographers and artists whose names appear on page 4.

Other illustrations were provided by the sources listed below.

The position of illustrations on each page is indicated by the letters after the page number:
T = top; B = bottom; L = left; C = centre; R = right.

10-11 City of Bristol Museum. **11** TR BBC Hulton Picture Library; CL Reece Winstone. **19** Roger Wilmshurst/Bruce Coleman Ltd. **20** Neville Fox-Davies. **22** Neville Fox-Davies. **23** John Vigurs. **24-25** Neville Fox-Davies. **27** Ronald Youlton. **29** H. Tempest. **34** John Vigurs. **37** T John Vigurs; CL Royal Institution of Cornwall; BL Royal Institution of Cornwall; BR Ann Ronan Picture Library. **40** L G. E. Gibson. **41** TL G. E. Gibson; R Pamla Toler. **42** TR Homer Sykes; BL Aerofilms Ltd. **54** 'The Departure of the Pilgrim Fathers from Plymouth, 1620', by B. F. Gribble, RBC, RSMA (1873-1962), on loan from Dr L. H. Hurrel to the City Museum and Art Gallery, Plymouth, and reproduced by kind permission. **56** BR *Tony Evans*. **57** Impact Photos/Alain le Garsmeur. **68** The Tate Gallery, London. **70** T Jane Burton/Bruce Coleman Ltd; B Jeff Foott/Bruce Coleman Ltd. **76** Impact Photos/Alain le Garsmeur. **77** Impact Photos/Alain le Garsmeur. **78** Stewart Galloway/Susan Griggs Agency Ltd. **79** Jarrold Colour Publications. **83** *Patrick Thurston*. **85** The National Motor Museum at Beaulieu. **87** T Beken of Cowes; C Department of the Environment. **88** Sealand Aerial Photography. **92** BL Michael Holford. **93** C. J. Smale/AQUILA. **95** Aerofilms Ltd. **96** Victoria and Albert Museum, Crown Copyright. **98-99** Beside the sea – Valentines of Dundee; Brighton belles – Mansell Collection; legacy in stone – *Peter Keen*; Punch & Judy – Mary Evans Picture Library; Dr Russell – Mary Evans Picture Library; Prince Regent – Mansell Collection; fantasy palace – Angelo Hornak; Daddy Long Legs – J. S. Gray; souvenir – e.t.archive; postcard – Donald McGill/Hutchinsons; Pier – Brighton Public Library. **101** TR N. A. Callow/Robert Harding Picture Library; BL Roger Scruton. **102-3** Roger Scruton. **107** Dennis Green/Bruce Coleman Ltd. **108** Roger Scruton. **109** L Barbara Heller Archive. **112** Skyphoto's Collection. **113** T R. Cowan Collection; BL R. Larn Collection; CR P. Powell Collection; BR (ship) Robin Jacques. **115** Adam Woolfitt/Susan Griggs Agency Ltd. **116** BBC Hulton Picture Library. **120** GeoScience Features. **125** L & C Patrick Thurston/Colchester & Essex Museum; R Mike Freeman/Colchester & Essex Museum. **126** Aerofilms Ltd. **130** BL Michael Holford. **146** BR Aerofilms Ltd. **147** T Courtesy of Viscount Coke – © Jarrold Colour Publications; B Aerofilms Ltd. **150** T *John Norris-Wood*; B Roger Scruton. **152** Roger Scruton. **155** Roger Scruton. **156** T both pictures, City of Kingston upon Hull Museums and Art Gallery. **158** Robert Gillmore/Bruce Coleman Ltd. **160** Roger Scruton. **162** BR The National Maritime Museum, London. **163** Roger Scruton. **164-5** Roger Scruton. **166** From the collection at Sunderland Museum & Art Gallery, reproduced by permission of Tyne & Wear County Council Museums. **170** Kim Taylor/Bruce Coleman Ltd. **172** TL Mary Evans Picture Library; BL Royal National Lifeboat Institution; BR Frank Meadow Sutcliffe Collection. **173** TL Royal National Lifeboat Institution; TC F. E. Gibson; CL Frank Meadow Sutcliffe Collection; CR John Watney; B Royal National Lifeboat Institution. **175** *Helen Cowcher*. **179** East Lothian District Council. **180** both Harry Lauder photographs from BBC Hulton Picture Library. **181** *Malcolm Aird*. **182-3** Johnstone Syer. **187** from 'The Forth Bridge in its Various Stages of Construction', by Philip Phillips. **192** Jarrold Colour Publications. **197** Creative Services/Aberdeen Journals. **198** 'A Shell Photograph'. **199** all 'Shell Photographs' except BR Colin Molyneux. **200** J. Swedberg/Ardea London. **204** Frank W. Lane/Bruce Coleman Ltd. **207** W. Curth/Ardea London. **216** T John Watney; B Jarrold Colour Publications. **217** TL Aberdeen University Library; TR copyright School of Scottish Studies, University of Edinburgh; CL City of Aberdeen Libraries Department; CR Highlands & Islands Development Board; B Glasgow Art Gallery and Museum. **218** T Caithness Glass Ltd. **220** T British Tourist Authority; B © Charles Walker/Fay Godwin's Photo File. **221** Gordon Langsbury/Bruce Coleman Ltd. **225** United Kingdom Atomic Energy Authority. **228** Martin Adelman. **229** Hans Reinhard/Bruce Coleman Ltd. **230** T Malcolm Aird; B John Watney. **231** Malcolm Aird. **232** T John Sims; B John Watney. **233** Patrick Thurston. **234** TL The Kobal Collection. **234-5** The Kobal Collection. **234** CL The Kobal Collection; CR Ronald Grant Archive; B Ronald Grant Archive. **235** © BBC Photo Library; B 'Local Hero', an Enigma Production for Goldcrest. **238** T Jon Wyand. **241** T *Eric Fraser*. **242-3** Martin Adelman. **245** Impact Photos/Alain le Garsmeur. **246** T Martin Adelman; B John Watney. **247** Martin Adelman. **248** T Jon Wyand. **252-3** Neville Fox-Davies. **254** T Neville Fox-Davies; B David Beatty/Susan Griggs Agency Ltd. **225** T White Horse Distillers; B K. M. Andrew. **260** Jon Wyand. **264** John M. Forgie. **266** Scottish Tourist Board. **267** Michael Gore/Nature Photographers. **269** *Penny Tweedie*. **272** B Mary Evans Picture Library. **278** T National Maritime Museum. **282** Hourds Marketing Ltd/Holker Hall. **283** Aerofilms Ltd. **284** Aerofilms Ltd. **286** Blackpool District Libraries. **288** Blackpool Tower, illuminated, Derek Widdicombe. **291** The National Trust. **292** Animal Photography Ltd. **294** B Gerry Cranham. **303** TR Gernsheim Collection, Humanities Research Center, University of Texas at Austin. **314** Neil Holmes. **317** TR Wales Tourist Board; TC Mansell Collection; TL Cardiff City Council; B Mary Evans Picture Library. **326** Tenby Museum. **334** T photograph, copyright by Gilbert Adams, FRPS. **336** Photo Precision Limited. **341** BBC Hulton Picture Library. **350** Nigel Bradley.

Illustrations shown in *italics* first appeared in
AA Illustrated Guide to Britain,
Book of the British Countryside and *AA Hand-Picked Tours in Britain* (Drive Publications);
Folklore, Myths and Legends of Britain, Nature Lover's Library and
Roman Britain (Reader's Digest).

The publishers express their thanks to the following people and organisations for their help in the preparation of this book:

John Bartholomew and Son Ltd; British Railways Board; British Surfing Association; British Water Ski Federation; Camborne School of Mines Geological Museum (Dr R. L. Atkinson); Richard Cavendish; Michele Clarke; Clyde Cruising Club; Countryside Commission; Countryside Commission for Scotland; Crofters Commission; Eric Edwards; Ross Finlay; Forestry Commission; Patrick Hickman Robertson; International Windsurfer Schools UK; The Maritime Trust; The National Trust; The National Trust for Scotland; Norfolk Ornithologists' Association; Northern Lighthouse Board; Ordnance Survey; Leigh Parker; Royal Life-Saving Society; Royal National Lifeboat Institution; Royal Society for the Prevention of Accidents (Tom Sanders); Royal Yachting Association; Scottish Wildlife Trust; Scottish Youth Hostels Association; Shell UK Ltd; Surf Life Saving Association of Great Britain; Trinity House, London; Stella M. Turk, MSc, FZS; UK Boardsailing Association; Youth Hostels Association (England and Wales).

The publishers also acknowledge their indebtedness to the following books which were consulted for reference:

Atlas of the Seas Around the British Isles (Ministry of Agriculture, Fisheries and Food); *Beside the Seaside* by James Walvin (Allan Lane); *Blue Guide to England* (Benn); *Boardsailing Access* (Royal Yachting Association); *British Isles Airfield Guide* (Merseyside Aviation Society); *Buildings of England* by Nikolaus Pevsner (Penguin); *The Cleveland Way* by Alan Falconer (Countryside Commission/HMSO); *Coastal Walks* by David Bellamy (Hamlyn); *Collins Handguide to the Sea Coast* by Denys Ovenden and John Barrett (Collins); *Companion Guide to Kent and Sussex* by Keith Spence (Collins); *Companion Guide to the West Highlands of Scotland* by W. H. Murray (Collins); *Cornwall Coast Path* by Edward C. Pyatt (Countryside Commission/HMSO); *The Country Life Book of the Natural History of the British Isles* (Country Life); *Country Parks Handbook* (Countryside Commission/HMSO); *A Concise History of Scotland* by Fitzroy Maclean (Thames & Hudson); *The Dorset Coast Path* by Brian Jackman (Countryside Commission/HMSO); *England by the Sea* by Elizabeth Gundrey (English Tourist Board/Severn House); *Getting Afloat* (Link House Publications); *Getting Around the Highlands and Islands* (Highlands and Islands Development Board); *Golf Course Guide to the British Isles* (The Daily Telegraph/Collins); *Goodwin Sands Shipwrecks* by Richard Larn (David and Charles); *The Hamlyn Guide to the Seashore and Shallow Seas of Britain and Europe* by A. C. Campbell (Hamlyn); *A Guide to the Mines of West Cornwall* by D. B. Baryon (D. Bradford Burton); *The Highland Clans* by Sir Iain Moncreiffe of that Ilk (Barrie & Rockliff); *The Highland Clearances* by John Prebble (Penguin); *Historic Houses, Castles and Gardens in Great Britain and Ireland* (ABC Historic Publications); *A History of Scotland* by Rosalind Mitchinson (Methuen); *The Islands of Western Scotland* by W. H. Murray (Eyre Methuen); *Key to the Fishes of Northern Europe* by Alwyne Wheeler (Warne); *Lifeboat: In Danger's Hour* by Patrick Howarth (Hamlyn); *Martello Towers* by Sheila Sutcliffe (David and Charles); *Municipal Yearbook* (Goddard & Smith); *Museums and Galleries in Great Britain and Ireland* (ABC Historic Publications); *The National Trust for Scotland Guide* ed Robin Prentice (Cape); *The National Trust Guide* (Cape); *'The Observer' Island Britain* ed Peter Crookston (Macdonald); *The Oxford Dictionary of Saints* by Denis Hugh Farmer (OUP); *The Pembrokeshire Coast Path* by John H. Barrett (Countryside Commission/HMSO); *Pooley's Flight Guide United Kingdom* (Robert Pooley); *The Prince in the Heather* by Eric Linklater (Hodder); *The Saxon Shore Way* (Kent Rights of Way Council); *The Shell Book of the Islands of Britain* by David Booth and David Perrott (Guideway/Windward); *The Shell Guide to Scotland* by Moray McLaren (Ebury Press); *Seaside Architecture* by Kenneth Lindley (Hugh Evelyn); *Seaside Piers* by Simon H. Adamson (Batsford); *Smuggling in Cornwall and Devon* by Lisa Newcombe (Jarrold); *The Somerset and North Devon Coast Path* by Clive Gunnell (Countryside Commission/HMSO); *The South Devon Coast Path* by Brian le Messurier (Countryside Commission/HMSO); *The South-West Peninsula Coastal Path* by Ken Ward and John H. N. Mason (Letts); *Visit an English Garden* (English Tourist Board); *The West Highland Way* (Countryside Commission for Scotland/HMSO).

Maps produced by the Cartographic Department of the Automobile Association

Typesetting, separations, paper, printing and binding by:

APEX COMPUTERSETTING, LONDON; FOTOLITHO DROMMEL BV, ZANDVOORT; MULLIS-MORGAN LTD, LONDON; C. TOWNSEND HOOK PAPER CO. LTD, SNODLAND; JARROLD AND SONS LTD, NORWICH.

01.001.4

HOW TO FIND THE RIGHT PAGE

ILLUSTRATED GUIDE TO BRITAIN'S COAST divides the coastline into 145 sections, each of which is indicated by a box on the key maps on these end-papers (showing Northern England and Scotland) or on the end-papers at the front of the book (showing Southern England and Wales).

The number in each box is the number of the page on which the description of each section of coastline begins. The numbering starts at the Severn Bridge, near Bristol, and the guide proceeds anti-clockwise round the entire coast of Britain and main offshore islands.

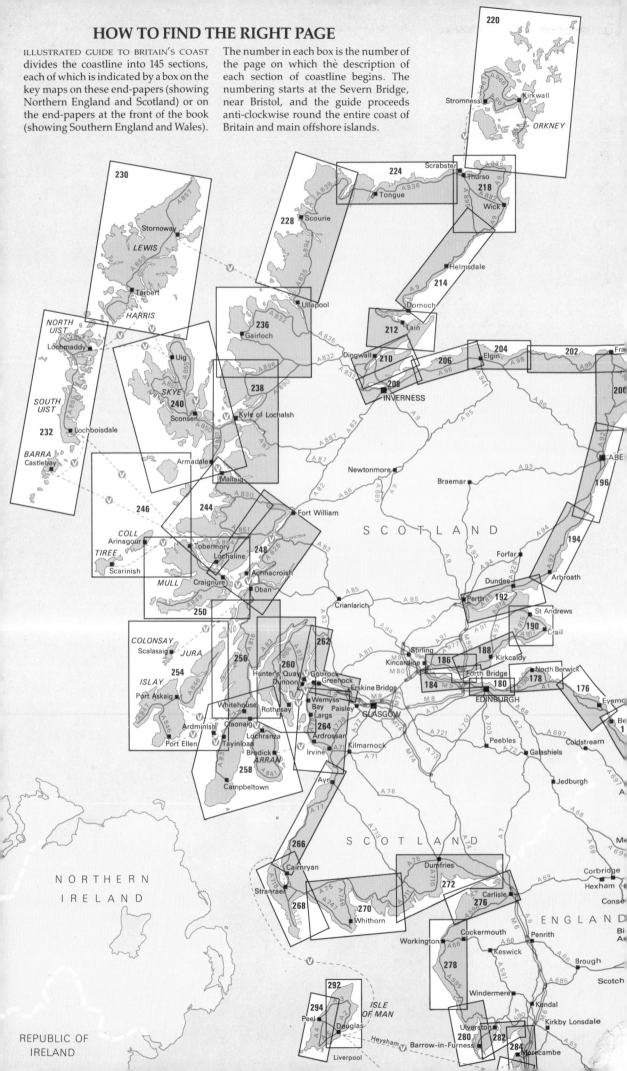